FEDERAL PRETRIAL PRACTICE

FEDERAL PRETRIAL PRACTICE

MYRNA S. RAEDER
Professor of Law
Southwestern University School of Law
Member of the Bars of
the State of California,
the District of Columbia,
and the State of New York

Wiley Law Publications
JOHN WILEY & SONS
New York • Chichester • Brisbane • Toronto • Singapore

Library of Congress Cataloging in Publication Data:

Raeder, Myrna S.
Federal pretrial practice.

Bibliography: p.
1. Pre-trial procedure—United States. I. Title.
KF8900.R28 1987 347.73'72 87-21030
ISBN 0-471-88065-5 347.30772

Printed in the United States of America

10 9 8 7 6 5 4 3 2 1

To Terry and Tommy,
who remind me daily that life
extends well beyond litigation practice.

FOREWORD

Lawyers who do not specialize in federal court practice often feel uneasy—even threatened—when undertaking an occasional federal case. Overburdened dockets and understaffed courts have combined to produce, in many federal courts, tense, highly pressurized environments. Such courts are not nurseries where novice lawyers may cut their teeth. The pace is brisk, and most federal judges expect counsel to be competent, well prepared, thorough, and careful. Judges as well as attorneys would prefer a more relaxed, less stressful workplace, but heavy caseloads make that impossible if the court's work is to be kept moving and if reasonably prompt justice is to remain available for all.

To further complicate matters, many of the procedures and practices one encounters in federal pretrial practice are not defined in sources readily accessible by traditional research. In many jurisdictions, they have evolved by local tradition and appear only in court hand-out documents. All too often, there are substantial variations in the way pretrial matters are handled from court to court and even among the judges of a single court.

For the seasoned federal court specialist earning his or her living in a particular federal court, the maze of local pretrial practices, once mastered, becomes at least tolerable, if not comfortable. But for the sometime federal practitioner seldom venturing beyond state courts, guiding a case through the rocky shoals of federal pretrial procedure can be an unnerving and difficult experience.

There has long been a need for a comprehensive yet concise and affordable treatise on federal pretrial practice for those who only occasionally get into federal court. In this book, Professor Myrna Raeder has met that need. Not every lawyer can have quick access to one of the well known multivolume works that cover this subject. But few can afford to be without this thorough one-volume treatise.

Although the author's present status in academia might lead one to expect a theoretical approach, the book is full of practical insights that evidence her real-life experience in federal practice. She not only notes and marks most of the pitfalls and danger spots, but she suggests means of avoiding them as well.

For one seeking an entry citation to begin researching a particular point of law, this book will be most helpful. The leading cases and other authorities are cited without overburdening the book with redundant footnotes. For the veteran federal practitioner, this is a fine review tool, well organized, thorough, and well written.

Denver, Colorado
July, 1987

JIM R. CARRIGAN
United States District Judge

PREFACE

This book is written primarily for diversity practitioners and novices to federal practice who usually do not have the luxury of reading multivolume treatises to answer their every question. Hopefully, it answers many of the questions about federal practice which I asked while practicing and which I have been asked over the years by other litigators as well as current and former students of my federal civil practice course. I have attempted to combine basic knowledge with strategy, in addition to alerting attorneys about common pretrial pitfalls. Moreover, the current managerial and sanctions orientation of many judges led me to devote what some might consider a disproportionate amount of the book to sanctions under Rules 11, 37, and 41.

My general goal was to create a one-volume work which could actually be used to simplify a lawyer's work by not only providing answers to easy questions and suggesting alternatives, but also by including enough citations to shortcut research. The difficulty with much of pretrial practice is that very few areas are directly governed by Supreme Court decisions. As a result, each circuit and even each judge may have widely differing views concerning specific questions. Therefore, although no one-volume work can completely reflect these disparities, my intention was to include enough references to case law and other authority so that readers can quickly determine the applicable answer in their own circuit. Because references could not be included for all circuits, the larger circuits are cited more often. If the reader finds that statements appear to be hedged, this reflects the reality of a federal system sorely lacking in uniformity. In fact, I have no doubt that some readers will consider that I ought to have qualified other statements which are not.

I would appreciate any comments which readers have about practices which vary in their circuit or local district, as well as any suggestions for increasing the usefulness of this book.

Los Angeles, California
August 1, 1987

MYRNA S. RAEDER

ACKNOWLEDGMENTS

I would like to thank my friends and colleagues at Southwestern University School of Law for their encouragement while I wrote this book. In particular, I appreciated the administrative support which Dean Leigh H. Taylor provided to me. Jeanne Nicolson and Sandra Montgomery were very helpful concerning word processing requests throughout the entire project, while I learned more about word processing than I ever desired to know. Special thanks for cite checking are extended to my research assistant Mark Weitz.

My husband, Terry Kelly, also deserves recognition for keeping me current on life as a litigator, as well as for understanding, as only a litigator can, about the long hours required for this extended endeavor. I also wish to thank Margaret Keogh, who has provided worry-free child care for my son during this entire period, so that I could devote my energies away from home to my work.

M.S.R.

SUMMARY CONTENTS

DETAILED CONTENTS

PART 1

FORUM SHOPPING

CHAPTER 1

DECIDING WHETHER TO LITIGATE IN FEDERAL COURT

§ 1.1 Introduction

Although the term is often used pejoratively, forum shopping is an inevitable part of every lawsuit. Experienced counsel should never file a case in the nearest state court or defend an action there without considering the availability of alternative forums, because the selection of the forum can effectively determine the outcome of the litigation in some actions. For example, the length of the appropriate statute of limitation, the extent of requirements needed for recovery of a products liability claim, the availability of punitive damages, or even the convenience of litigating in a particular forum may be critical in a given action. Forum shopping is not limited to plaintiffs, since a defendant often has the power to remove a state action to federal court.[1] A potential defendant also can opt to

[1] See **ch. 3**.

initiate a suit by filing for declaratory relief in federal court, if jurisdiction is otherwise appropriate.

In deciding which court to select, many factors must be weighed. The commonly held belief that plaintiffs should file in state court and defendants remove the action whenever possible may be inappropriate due to individual considerations peculiar to the case. Probably the most important precursor to successful forum shopping is a detailed analysis of the case, which should reveal the factors that are significant in the given action.

§ 1.2 Judges

Usually state court judges do not have the same level of qualifications as federal judges. This disparity in background is reinforced by the differences in practice resulting from both the limited jurisdiction of federal courts and the fact that federal judges handle an individual calendar with cases assigned to a judge upon filing. In several large state systems such as California and Illinois, where a master calendar system is used, a trial judge knows nothing about the case until it is assigned out as ready for trial. Thus, as a general rule, federal judges tend to preside over more sophisticated litigation and have a longer opportunity to acquaint themselves with the particular complexities of the action than state judges. Federal judges are also more likely to be active case managers, requiring demanding discovery schedules and encouraging early settlement discussions. Although in a given case these differences may favor the plaintiffs as well as the defendants, most defendants prefer federal court for complex matters unless the local state judges are well versed in handling protracted cases.

Large corporate defendants may also prefer federal court because of the fear that a state judge's ruling will favor the local party. Similarly, counsel who are not from the locality may also favor federal court to mitigate any hometown advantage the opponent may have. Conversely, most individual plaintiffs usually prefer state court, unless they are litigating controversial issues. Since federal judges are appointed for life, they are less likely to be concerned about taking an unpopular position than a state judge who must face reelection. On the other hand, if a party draws a particular federal judge who is either unfavorably disposed toward its legal claims or expects exacting adherence to individualized procedural rules, judicial disqualification is almost an impossibility. In contrast, some state systems allow each party to disqualify one judge. If counsel has filed a diversity action which is assigned to a federal judge who is hostile to such suits, it may be wise immediately to dismiss the action voluntarily and refile it in state court. However, this tactic will work only if the refiling is within the applicable statute of limitations and opposing counsel either cannot or is unlikely to remove the action back to the federal court, where it will be reassigned to the original judge.

§ 1.3 Jury

Jury panels may differ significantly between the local federal and state court. The average federal juror is more educated and more affluent. Federal juries are also drawn from a larger geographical area than the average state jury. In federal court, civil matters are determined by a unanimous jury, while some states do not require unanimity for civil verdicts. Defendants usually prefer this federal requirement, since it can bring about a retrial of cases which would result in adverse judgments in state court. Counsel should also ascertain the size of the jury permitted in each forum, since some districts, as well as state courts, impanel fewer than 12 jurors. Procedurally, it is easier to lose the right to a jury in federal court than in most states, because a federal jury demand must be made within 10 days of the last pleading in the case, while in many states the demand is not required until shortly before trial. The availability of a jury book, listing public information concerning each juror, may also differ.

The conduct of the voir dire is much more formal in federal than state court. A federal judge generally conducts the entire voir dire, and counsel's role is limited to submitting written questions which the judge may ask the jury panel. In most state courts, after the judge asks some preliminary questions, counsel are primarily responsible for the voir dire. In general, the tenor of any jury trial is apt to be less formal in state court. Depending on counsel's witnesses and jury style, this may be a significant factor in determining which forum to select. Folksy trials are rarely conducted in federal court. Indeed, the very size of the average federal courtroom inhibits informality.

§ 1.4 Procedural Considerations

Numerous procedural considerations affect the decision where to litigate. Counsel should consider differences between state and federal practice concerning motions, discovery, pretrial requirements, and evidence.

§ 1.5 —Federal and Local Rules

The Federal Rules of Civil Procedure and local rules applied in federal court are usually much more detailed and work intensive than most state rules. Extensive pretrial statements are more often required in federal than state court. Similarly, local rules concerning motion practice can be quite cumbersome in federal court. Therefore, litigating under the federal rules may be more costly than state practice due to the extensive pretrial requirements.

Doe pleadings permitted by some states are more likely to preserve a plaintiff's ability to file against presently unknown parties than the federal doctrine of relation back.[2] Moreover, the ability to obtain interlocutory review of pretrial orders is quite limited in federal court, unlike some state systems, where writs reviewing pretrial matters are frequently granted.

In general, an in-depth knowledge of the rules is a significant advantage in federal practice. Lawyers whose primary practice is in state court must be careful to follow appropriate procedures, since federal judges do not hesitate to sanction counsel who violate the federal or local rules.

§ 1.6 —Discovery

Discovery in federal court is often more liberal than in state court. However, some states are more permissive than federal courts concerning videotaping of depositions, telephone depositions, and depositions of experts. The ease of obtaining subpoenas in federal court is a factor which may be important when litigating a case in which witnesses are scattered, since states usually have detailed procedures which must be followed to obtain out-of-state discovery.

Interrogatory practice may also differ. Local rules in either state or federal court may limit the number of interrogatories which are permitted without leave of court. Moreover, in some states counsel may not be able to respond to an interrogatory requesting a compilation of data by allowing the adverse party to inspect business records.

§ 1.7 —Evidence

The Federal Rules of Evidence apply to diversity actions as well as federal actions. There may be times when the federal rules will be more favorable to counsel's position; in other cases, the state evidentiary code will be preferable. For example, the federal rules have several hearsay exceptions which are not available in many states.[3] The admission of subsequent remedial measures in a products liability action may differ between the local state and federal court.[4] If an important piece of evidence would be inadmissible in state court but admissible in federal court, this may be determinative in selecting the forum.[5]

---

[2] Fed. R. Civ. P. 15(c); see **ch. 8**.

[3] *E.g.*, Fed. R. Evid. 803(4), 803(24), 804(5).

[4] *See* Fed. R. Evid. 407.

[5] *See generally* Seidelson, *The Federal Rules of Evidence and the Discriminating Selection of Forum,* 23 Duquesne L. Rev. 559 (1985).

§ 1.8 —Coordination, Change of Venue, and Forum Non Conveniens

Federal court is usually a better choice for defendants in cases which involve multiple plaintiffs suing in different locations. Removal ensures that the cases can be either multidistricted to coordinate pretrial discovery or transferred for the convenience of the witnesses. It may even be possible to try the case as a nationwide class action.[6] In state court, cases can be coordinated within the jurisdiction, but they cannot be joined with out-of-state litigation concerning the same matter. Similarly, in an individual action, if counsel wishes to litigate the case in another state than the one where the action was filed for statute of limitations or other choice of law issues, federal court permits motions to transfer for the convenience of witnesses.[7] Federal forum non conveniens law permits a dismissal when a foreign court is the more convenient alternative.[8] Thus, practitioners have more flexibility in federal court when geographic considerations are significant.

§ 1.9 Registration of Judgment

If enforcement of judgment will likely be required in another state, federal court provides an easy method of registering federal judgments in any district court.[9] State laws on enforcing judgments vary and may require a separate civil action.

§ 1.10 Jurisdictional Considerations

Usually, it is important to ensure that all related claims of the parties can be litigated in one forum in order to avoid fragmenting the case. Therefore, both jurisdiction[10] and venue[11] must be proper in the forum. Since subject matter is limited in federal court, some potential parties and claims may have to be deleted in order to obtain federal jurisdiction. Similarly, a federal court may use its discretion to remand pendent claims or parties to state court. Cross-claims and counterclaims may also be more limited in federal court due to both pleading and jurisdictional requirements.[12] On the other hand, certain types of actions fall

---

[6] See **ch. 10**.

[7] See **ch. 6**.

[8] *Id.*

[9] 28 U.S.C. § 1963 (1982).

[10] See **ch. 2**.

[11] See **ch. 6**.

[12] See **ch. 7**.

within the exclusive jurisdiction of federal court. For example, bankruptcy actions must be brought in federal court and must follow rules specifically enacted for that category of cases. The availability of antitrust or R.I.C.O. actions as federal counterclaims should be considered by plaintiffs as well as by defendants who are contemplating removal.

Personal jurisdiction must also exist in the selected forum. Federal court is usually a better alternative when the existence of personal jurisdiction is an issue, since the court has the power to transfer the case to a district in another state where jurisdiction is proper without dismissing the action.[13]

If jurisdictional questions are significant, it makes sense to file in a state court where jurisdiction is certain. This avoids the expense and embarrassment of having the case dismissed. If statute of limitations problems will preclude refiling the action, a dismissal may also raise the possibility of a legal malpractice action.

§ 1.11 Substantive Law Questions

In diversity cases, *Erie Railroad v. Tompkins*[14] dictates that federal courts must apply the law of the state's highest court. This means that state court is the better forum when counsel is attempting to press innovative theories of state law,[15] since federal courts can only apply state law, not change it.[16] If the highest court has not spoken, the federal court must ascertain from all available data what the state law is and apply it.[17]

Choice of law issues may also be important in deciding where to litigate. The federal court in diversity cases generally applies the choice of law rules of the forum state, which may or may not make the substantive law of that state govern the action.[18] A state court may be more likely to choose its own substantive law than a federal court located within the state.[19] Issues such as the length of the appropriate statute of limitations, the availability of punitive damages, and restrictions on products liability theories or contributory negligence defenses will be key in determining which state or district court is best in a particular case.

---

[13] 28 U.S.C. § 1631 (1982); see **ch. 6.**

[14] 304 U.S. 64 (1938).

[15] Anderson v. Marathon Petroleum Co., 801 F.2d 936, 942 (7th Cir. 1986).

[16] Demars v. General Dynamics Corp., 779 F.2d 95, 101 (1st Cir. 1985).

[17] Francis v. INA Life Ins. Co., 809 F.2d 183, 185 (2d Cir. 1987); Kifer v. Liberty Mut. Ins. Co., 777 F.2d 1325, 1329–30 (8th Cir. 1985); McCoy v. Richards, 771 F.2d 1108, 1110 (7th Cir. 1985); Bailey v. V & O Press Co., 770 F.2d 601, 604 (6th Cir. 1985); *see* G.E. Credit Corp. v. Ger-Beck Mach. Co., 806 F.2d 1207, 1209 (3d Cir. 1986); Peoples Bank of Polk County v. Roberts, 779 F.2d 1544, 1546 (11th Cir. 1986).

[18] *See* Klaxon Co. v. Stentor Elec. Mfg. Co., 313 U.S. 487, 496–97 (1941).

[19] *See, e.g.*, Blakesley v. Wolford, 789 F.2d 236, 240–43 (3d Cir. 1986).

§ 1.12 Alternative Forums

Alternative forums should also be considered. Litigation may be necessary in an agency before review can be sought in court. Binding arbitration may be a desirable or required alternative or prerequisite to court proceedings.[20] Mediation or some other form of alternative dispute resolution may be appropriate in a given case. Even if a case is filed in court, a few states and federal districts require nonbinding arbitration of claims.[21]

Some specialized actions can be brought in a variety of forums. For example, federal tax matters can be brought in Tax Court, the Court of Claims, or the federal district court, each having different rules.

§ 1.13 Time to Trial

Often one of the most significant factors in selecting a forum is the time to trial. Although the backlog in some state courts is the equivalent of the local federal district court, usually it takes significantly less time to litigate a case in a federal court than in a state court when both are located in an urban center. In some states it may take as long as five years from filing to trial, while in many district courts, the average case is heard within two years.

§ 1.14 Conclusion

In a particular case one or many of the factors discussed in this chapter will sway counsel's decision about where to litigate. However, if federal court is the appropriate forum, lack of familiarity with federal practice should not deter counsel from filing there. Federal procedure may appear mystical to the uninitiated, but a state practitioner can and should be able to untangle the federal maze as the action unfolds. The remainder of this book points out many of the pitfalls where lawyers can go astray on the pretrial path.

---

[20] *See, e.g.*, Shearson/American Express, Inc. v. McMahon, ____ U.S. ____, 107 S. Ct. 2332, 55 U.S.L.W. 4757 (June 8, 1987) (civil RICO and 10(b) securities claims are arbitrable); Dean Witter Reynolds, Inc. v. Byrd, 470 U.S. 213, 217 (1985) (pendent claims based on securities violations are arbitrable); Lorber Indus. v. Los Angeles Printworks, 803 F.2d 523, 525 (9th Cir. 1986) (copyright claims are arbitrable); *see also* Note, *Appealability of District Court Orders Granting or Denying Stays of Arbitration Under 28 U.S.C. Section 1291(a),* 36 Case W. Res. L. Rev. 122 (1985).

[21] *See generally,* Levin & Golash, *Alternative Dispute Resolution in Federal District Courts,* 37 U. Fla. L. Rev. 29 (1985); Nejelski & Zeldin, *Court-Annexed Arbitration in the Federal Courts: The Philadelphia Story,* 42 Md. L. Rev. 787 (1983).

CHAPTER 2

MEETING FEDERAL JURISDICTIONAL REQUIREMENTS

§ 2.1 Introduction

One of the most basic problems facing practitioners evaluating the relative merits of litigating in a federal versus a state forum is whether jurisdiction exists in federal court and, if so, whether related claims not within federal jurisdiction can be heard there. Preliminary considerations such as the existence of a case or controversy and the applicability of abstention doctrines may affect the practical availability of a federal forum. The availability of pendent and ancillary jurisdiction to hear related claims may also be important if the goal is to avoid fragmentation of the action.

Jurisdiction is a multifaceted topic.[1] The jurisdictional investigation may be as easy as determining the citizenship of private parties or locating a relevant federal statute or as complex as locating the principal place of business of a foreign corporation or determining whether a state cause of action is completely preempted by federal law. Therefore, this chapter is designed to give a general overview of the major issues which arise in the jurisdictional inquiry and to indicate the sources which should be consulted for more intensive research.

---

[1] *See generally* R. Casad, Jurisdiction in Civil Actions (1983); 1 J. Moore et al., Moore's Federal Practice (2d ed. 1986) [hereinafter Moore's Federal Practice]; 13, 13A & 13B C. Wright, A. Miller, et al., Federal Practice and Procedure (2d ed. 1984) [hereinafter Federal Practice and Procedure].

JUSTICIABILITY

§ 2.2 Constitutional Requirements

Federal courts can consider only genuine cases or controversies.[2] The fundamental inquiry as to the justiciability of an issue is whether the conflicting contentions of the parties present a real, substantial controversy between parties having adverse legal interests and a definite and concrete dispute rather than a hypothetical or abstract question.[3] Justiciability encompasses standing, mootness, and ripeness[4] and is considered to be quasijurisdictional. In addition, courts will not decide political questions, primarily due to separation of powers.[5] Such dismissals do not preclude a later action on the same claim if the justiciability problem is overcome.[6]

Although these issues usually arise in cases challenging the constitutionality of legislation or other governmental activities, they can arise in other contexts. For example, several unsuccessful attempts have been made to assert that, in a declaratory relief action, an insurer does not have a case or controversy against the party allegedly injured by its insured.[7] Counsel must determine that the action is justiciable at the outset of litigation, since this issue can be raised by opposing counsel or the court[8] to defeat the claim at any stage of the proceeding, including appeal.[9]

§ 2.3 —Standing

As a threshold requirement, plaintiffs must establish that they have standing to sue.[10] Standing is required to assure the presentation of a legal question "in a

[2] U.S. Const. art. III; SEC v. Medical Comm. for Human Rights, 404 U.S. 403, 407 (1972).

[3] Babbitt v. United Farm Workers Nat'l Union, 442 U.S. 289, 298 (1979).

[4] *See generally* 13 Federal Practice and Procedure § 3529.

[5] *See* Baker v. Carr, 369 U.S. 186, 217 (1962); *see generally* 13A Federal Practice and Procedure §§ 3534–3534.3.

[6] McCarney v. Ford Motor Co., 657 F.2d 230, 233 (8th Cir. 1981); *see* 18 Federal Practice and Procedure § 4436 (1981); 1B Moore's Federal Practice ¶ 0.405[5].

[7] *See* Maryland Casualty Co. v. Pacific Coal & Oil Co., 312 U.S. 270, 272–73 (1941); Federal Kemper Ins. Co. v. Rauscher, 807 F.2d 345, 352–53 (3d Cir. 1986).

[8] *See, e.g.*, Kittitas Reclamaton Dist. v. Sunnyside Valley Irrigation Dist., 763 F.2d 1032, 1034 n.1 (9th Cir. 1985) (mootness).

[9] *E.g.*, Allstate Ins. Co. v. Wayne County, 760 F.2d 689, 691 (6th Cir. 1985) (standing).

[10] City of Los Angeles v. Lyons, 461 U.S. 95, 101 (1983); *see generally* 13A Federal Practice and Procedure §§ 3531–3531.15.

concrete factual context conducive to a realistic appreciation of the consequences of judicial action."[11] In order to demonstrate standing, a plaintiff must show the existence of an "injury in fact."[12] Courts have identified three components of this requirement:

1. There has been an actual or threatened injury
2. The injury can be fairly traced to the challenged action of the defendant, and
3. The injury is likely to be redressed by a favorable decision.[13]

The causation and redressability requirements are theoretically distinct but often overlap and are treated as if they were identical.[14]

In addition to this constitutional test, judicially created limitations have developed which include a general prohibition on raising another person's legal rights, a preference for the resolution of generalized grievances in the representative branches, and the requirement that a plaintiff's complaint fall within the zone of interest protected by the pertinent law.[15] When injunctive relief is sought, courts also require a credible threat of recurrent injury.[16]

Standing can be an issue in antitrust,[17] RICO,[18] and taxpayer[19] actions. In the antitrust context, the United States Supreme Court has noted that, unlike the

---

[11] Valley Forge Christian College v. Americans United for Separation of Church & State, Inc., 454 U.S. 464, 474 (1982).

[12] *Id.* at 473; *see* McKinney v. U.S. Dept of Treasury, 799 F.2d 1544, 1550 (Fed. Cir. 1986); *see generally* Note, *"More Than An Intuition, Less Than A Theory": Toward A Coherent Doctrine of Standing,* 86 Colum. L. Rev. 564 (1986).

[13] *See, e.g.,* Phillips Petroleum Co. v. Shutts, 472 U.S. 797, 804–05 (1985); Valley Forge Christian College v. Americans United for Separation of Church & State, Inc., 454 U.S. 464, 472 (1982); Allstate Ins. Co. v. Wayne County, 760 F.2d 689, 692 (6th Cir. 1985).

[14] *See* Mideast Systems, Inc. v. Hodel, 792 F.2d 1172, 1176 (D.C. Cir. 1986).

[15] Allen v. Wright, 468 U.S. 737, 750–52 (1984); Saladin v. City of Milledgeville, 812 F.2d 687, 690 (11th Cir. 1987); LaDuke v. Nelson, 762 F.2d 1318, 1323 (9th Cir. 1985).

[16] City of Los Angeles v. Lyons, 461 U.S. 95, 111 (1983).

[17] *See* Associated Gen. Contractors of Cal., Inc. v. California State Council of Carpenters, 459 U.S. 519, 536 (1983); Brunswick Corp. v. Pueblo Bowl-O-Mat, Inc., 429 U.S. 477, 487–88 (1977); Illinois Brick Co. v. Illinois, 431 U.S. 720 (1977); Exhibitors' Serv., Inc. v. American Multi-Cinema, 788 F.2d 574, 577–78 (9th Cir. 1986); Province v. Cleveland Press Pub. Co., 787 F.2d 1047, 1050–51 (6th Cir. 1986).

[18] *See* Sedima, S.P.R.L. v. Imrex Co., 473 U.S. 479 (1985); Terre Du Lac Ass'n, Inc. v. Terre Du Lac, Inc., 772 F.2d 467, 472–73 (8th Cir. 1985), *cert. denied,* _____ U.S. _____, 106 S. Ct. 1460 (1986). For a comprehensive discussion of RICO actions, see P. Batista, Civil RICO Practice Manual (1987).

[19] *See* Valley Forge Christian College v. Americans United For Separation of Church & State, Inc., 454 U.S. 464 (1982); Flast v. Cohen, 392 U.S. 83 (1968); Comment, *Taxpayers' Suits: Standing Barriers and Pecuniary Restraints,* 59 Temple L.Q. 951 (1986).

constitutional standing requirement which requires harm to a plaintiff, the court must make a further determination of whether the plaintiff is a proper party to bring a private antitrust action.[20]

Standing to assert third party rights is an unsettled area.[21] Associations have standing to redress a direct injury to the organization,[22] although at least one circuit requires that the organization must prove a drain on its resources caused by the injury.[23] In limited circumstances, an association can also seek redress of an injury to its members.[24] However, such standing generally requires a claim for injunctive or declaratory relief rather than damages.[25]

Because standing is independent from the merits of the action, it is proper for courts to make factual findings on disputed standing issues.[26] While such factual findings on jurisdictional issues are accepted on appeal unless clearly erroneous, legal conclusions are subject to de novo review.[27] Dismissal on the pleadings is usually considered inappropriate if standing may be satisfied by making the allegations of the complaint more definite.[28] However, the Supreme Court has refused to entertain an alternative standing theory on appeal which had no factual support in the record but was supported merely by references gleaned from briefs or appellate arguments.[29]

---

[20] Associated Gen. Contractors of Cal., Inc. v. California State Council of Carpenters, 459 U.S. 519, 535 n.31 (1983).

[21] *See* FAIC Sec. Inc. v. United States, 768 F.2d 352, 356–61 (D.C. Cir. 1985); Monaghan, *Third Party Standing,* 84 Colum. L. Rev. 277 (1984); *see also* Darring v. Kincheloe, 783 F.2d 874, 877 (9th Cir. 1986); Diamantis v. Milton Bradley Co., 772 F.2d 3, 4 (1st Cir. 1985).

[22] *See* Havens Realty Corp. v. Coleman, 455 U.S. 363, 379 (1982); Simon v. Eastern Kentucky Welfare Rights Org., 426 U.S. 26, 27 (1976).

[23] *See* Cleburne Living Center v. City of Cleburne, 726 F.2d 191, 203 (5th Cir. 1984), *aff'd in part on other grounds,* ____ U.S. ____, 105 S. Ct. 3249 (1985). *But see* Haitian Refugee Center v. Gracey, 809 F.2d 794, 799 n.2 (D.C. Cir. 1987).

[24] *See* International Union, UAW v. Brock, ____ U.S. ____, 106 S. Ct. 2523, 2528–29 (1986); Hunt v. Washington State Apple Advertising Comm'n, 432 U.S. 333, 342–43 (1977); Warth v. Seldin, 422 U.S. 490, 511, 515 (1975).

[25] Telecommmunications Research & Action Center v. Allnet Communication Servs, Inc., 806 F.2d 1093, 1095 (D.C. Cir. 1986).

[26] Bruce v. United States, 759 F.2d 755, 758 (9th Cir. 1985).

[27] *Id.*

[28] *See* Havens Realty Corp. v. Coleman, 455 U.S. 363, 377–78 (1982). *But see* Bender v. Williamsport Area School Dist., ____ U.S. ____, 106 S. Ct. 1326, 1335 (1986) (plaintiff required to apply for intervention if alleging individual rather than official status to support standing).

[29] Bender v. Williamsport Area School Dist., ____ U.S. ____, 106 S. Ct. 1326, 1333–35 (1986).

§ 2.4 —Mootness

Courts will not hear moot cases.[30] Generally, an action is mooted when the issues presented are no longer live or the parties lack a legally cognizable interest in the outcome.[31] Mootness rests on court-created jurisprudential grounds as well as on Article III jurisdictional requirements.[32] The issues related to mootness are similar to those which pertain to standing, but the standing inquiry looks to the nature of the injury to the recipient, while mootness turns on whether an injury still exists and can be properly recompensed by the relief requested.[33] The mere fact that a defendant lacks the means to satisfy any judgment rendered against it does not make a case moot.[34] Mootness is often an issue in declaratory judgment actions.[35]

An exception to the mootness doctrine is recognized in actions that are capable of repetition yet evade review.[36] This exception can occur when the duration of a challenged action is too short to be fully litigated prior to its termination and a reasonable expectation exists that the same complaining party would be subjected again to the same action.[37] Similarly, a defendant's voluntary cessation of a challenged practice does not moot a case, since the defendant would otherwise be free to return to its old ways.[38] A case can become moot, however, if there is no reasonable expectation that the violation will recur and interim events have completely and irrevocably eradicated the effects of the alleged violation.[39]

Partial relief in another proceeding does not moot an action seeking additional relief.[40] Usually, the availability of damages or other monetary relief avoids

---

30 *See generally* 13A Federal Practice and Procedure §§ 3533–3533.11.

31 Murphy v. Hunt, 455 U.S. 478, 481 (1982) (per curiam).

32 *See* Detroit, Toledo R.R. v. Consolidated Rail Corp., 767 F.2d 274, 278 (6th Cir. 1985); Kirby v. United States Gov't, 745 F.2d 204 (3d Cir. 1984).

33 International Union of Bricklayers v. Meese, 761 F.2d 798, 805 (D.C. Cir. 1985); *see* City of Los Angeles v. Lyons, 461 U.S. 95, 105 (1983).

34 Ratner v. Sioux Natural Gas Corp., 770 F.2d 512, 516–17 (5th Cir. 1985) (bankruptcy); *see* Firefighters Local Union No. 1784 v. Stotts, 467 U.S. 561, 569–70 (1984).

35 *See* Golden v. Zwickler, 394 U.S. 103, 108 (1969); Michigan State Chamber of Commerce v. Austin, 788 F.2d 1178, 1181–82 (6th Cir. 1986).

36 Weinstein v. Bradford, 423 U.S. 147, 149 (1975);

37 *Id.; see* Sample v. Johnson, 771 F.2d 1335, 1340–43 (9th Cir. 1985), *cert. denied,* ____ U.S. ____, 106 S. Ct. 1206 (1986) (discussing how to establish injury is likely to recur); *see generally* 13A Federal Practice and Procedure § 3533.8.

38 City of Mesquite v. Aladdin's Castle, Inc., 455 U.S. 283, 289, n.10 (1982); County of Los Angeles v. Davis, 440 U.S. 625, 631 (1979).

39 County of Los Angeles v. Davis, 440 U.S. 625, 631 (1979).

40 Wong v. Department of State, 789 F.2d 1380, 1384 (9th Cir. 1986); 13A Federal Practice and Procedure § 3533.2.

mootness questions which are presented by demands for injunctive and declaratory relief.[41]

§ 2.5 —Ripeness

A case must also be ripe before a federal court will hear the dispute.[42] Ripeness addresses the question of when it is appropriate for a court to consider the asserted claim.[43] It depends on the fitness of the issues for judicial decision and the hardship to the parties of withholding court consideration.[44] Ripeness can become an issue in reviewing action taken by an administrative agency, since the appropriateness of an issue for judicial review depends upon such factors as whether the agency action is final, whether the decision requires no additional factual developments, and whether further action is needed to clarify the agency's position.[45] When prudential considerations of comity to state institutions are involved in deciding whether a case is ripe, the ripeness analysis may overlap with the decision whether to invoke the abstention doctrine to refrain from exercising jurisdiction.[46]

LIMITATIONS ON JURISDICTION

§ 2.6 Abstention Doctrine and Other Limitations

In exceptional cases,[47] a federal court can decline to invoke its jurisdiction under the abstention doctrine. Abstention prohibits interference with pending state proceedings due to the proper relationship between the state and the federal judiciary.[48] Although most abstention questions arise in criminal cases, the

---

[41] Ellis v. Brotherhood of Ry. Airline & S.S. Clerks, 466 U.S. 435, 442 (1984).

[42] *See* Regional Rail Reorg. Act Cases, 419 U.S. 102, 138 (1974); Allstate Ins. Co. v. Wayne County, 760 F.2d 689, 696 (6th Cir. 1985); *see generally* 13A Federal Practice and Procedure §§ 3532–3532.6.

[43] Action Alliance of Senior Citizens v. Heckler, 789 F.2d 931, 940 (D.C. Cir. 1986).

[44] Abbott Laboratories v. Gardner, 387 U.S. 136, 149 (1967).

[45] Action Alliance of Senior Citizens v. Heckler, 789 F.2d 931, 940 (D.C. Cir. 1986).

[46] Crane v. Fauver, 762 F.2d 325, 328 (3d Cir. 1985). See § **2.6**. *See* 13A Federal Practice and Procedure § 3532.1, at 115.

[47] Hawaii Hous. Auth. v. Midkiff, 467 U.S. 229, 236 (1984).

[48] *See* Younger v. Harris, 401 U.S. 37 (1971); Railroad Comm'n of Tex. v. Pullman, 312 U.S. 496 (1941); *see generally* 1A Moore's Federal Practice pt. 2, ¶ 0.203; *see also* Shapiro, *Jurisdiction and Discretion,* 60 N.Y.U. L. Rev. 543 (1985).

issues can arise in a civil or regulatory context.[49] There are several types of abstention, each having its own rules.

Burford[50] abstention is appropriate when difficult questions of state law bearing on policy problems of substantial public importance transcend the result in the case at bar and when the exercise of federal review would be disruptive of state efforts to establish a coherent policy with respect to a matter of substantial public concern.[51]

Pullman[52] abstention exists when difficult and unsettled questions of state law must be resolved before a federal constitutional question can be decided.[53] However, a federal court need not abstain on *Pullman* grounds when a state statute is not fairly subject to an interpretation which will raise the federal constitutional question.[54]

Younger[55] abstention is invoked when an ongoing state judicial proceeding implicates important state interests and affords an opportunity to raise the federal constitutional challenge.[56] Typically, *Younger* abstention arises when the federal plaintiff is a defendant in ongoing or threatened state court proceedings and is seeking to enjoin continuation of the state action.[57] Bad faith or harassing prosecution if considered an exception to *Younger* abstention,[58] but the mere fact of multiple prosecutions does not constitute bad faith.[59] When *Younger* abstention is applied in civil cases, a state or one of its agencies usually is a party.[60] However, the Supreme Court required abstention in a dispute between private litigants in which a federal court had issued an injunction barring any action to enforce a state court's monetary judgment because of the defendant's failure to

[49] *See, e.g.*, Kentucky W. Va. Gas Co. v. Pennsylvania Util. Comm'n, 791 F.2d 1111 (3d Cir. 1986).

[50] Burford v. Sun Oil Co., 319 U.S. 315, 332–34 (1943).

[51] Colorado River Water Conservation Dist. v. United States, 424 U.S. 800, 814 (1976); *see* generally Davies, *Pullman and Burford Abstention: Clarifying the Roles of State and Federal Courts in Constitutional Cases,* 20 U.C. Davis L. Rev. 1 (1986).

[52] Railroad Comm'n of Tex. v. Pullman Co., 312 U.S. 496, 500–01 (1941).

[53] *See, e.g.*, Hawaii Hous. Auth. v. Midkiff, 467 U.S. 229, 236 (1984); *see* Bank of Am. Nat'l Trust & Sav. Ass'n. v. Summerland County Water Dist., 767 F.2d 544, 546 (9th Cir. 1985); *see generally* Note, *Pullman Abstention: Reconsidering the Boundaries,* 59 Temple L.Q. 1243 (1986).

[54] Hawaii Hous. Auth. v. Midkiff, 467 U.S. 229, 236 (1984).

[55] Younger v. Harris, 401 U.S. 37, 49 (1971).

[56] Middlesex County Ethics Comm. v. Garden State Bar Ass'n, 457 U.S. 423, 432 (1982).

[57] Monaghan v. Deakins, 798 F.2d 632, 636–37 (3d Cir. 1986) (citing cases).

[58] Huffman v. Pursue, Ltd., 420 U.S. 592, 611 (1975).

[59] *See* Collins v. County of Kendall, 807 F.2d 95, 99 (7th Cir. 1986) (instituting 30 criminal prosecutions over two-year period not bad faith).

[60] *See* Eitel v. Holland, 787 F.2d 995, 999–1000 (5th Cir. 1986) (discussing cases).

satisfy the state's appellate bond requirement.[61] The federal anti-injunction act,[62] which generally forbids federal courts from enjoining state court proceedings, is based on considerations similar to the *Younger* issues.

A court can also apply the *Colorado River*[63]/*Moses H. Cone*[64] doctrine, which permits it to dismiss or stay an action when exceptional circumstances such as the existence of parallel litigation justify this result on the basis of judicial economy. Several factors are considered, including the inconvenience of the federal forum, the desirability of avoiding piecemeal litigation, the order in which jurisdiction was obtained in the concurrent forums, whether state or federal law is controlling, the adequacy of the state court action to protect the federal plaintiff's right, the relative progress of the state and federal proceedings, the presence or absence of concurrent jurisdiction, the availability of removal, and the vexatious or contrived nature of the federal claim.[65] However, the mere fact that a state action raises substantially the same issues is not sufficient reason for a federal court to refuse to exercise its diversity jurisdiction.[66] Abstention appears to be available in declaratory judgments as well as other actions.[67] Considerations of full faith and credit as well as comity and federalism may also limit a federal court's decision to enjoin state litigation in civil actions.[68]

Abstention orders are reviewed for abuse of discretion.[69] Delay in moving for abstention is a factor weighing against abstention but is not determinative.[70] In a given case, the refusal to grant a stay can be an abuse of discretion.[71]

---

[61] *See, e.g.*, Pennzoil Co. v. Texaco, Inc., ____ U.S. ____, 107 S. Ct.1519, 55 U.S.L.W. 4457 (Apr. 6, 1987).

[62] 28 U.S.C. § 2283 (1982).

[63] Colorado River Water Conservation Dist. v. United States, 424 U.S. 800, 817–19 (1976); *see generally* Mullenix, *A Branch Too Far: Pruning the Abstention Doctrine,* 75 Geo. L.J. 99 (1986).

[64] Moses H. Cone Memorial Hosp. v. Mercury Constr. Corp., 460 U.S. 1, 15–16 (1983).

[65] Lumen Constr., Inc. v. Brant Constr. Co., 780 F.2d 691, 694–95 (7th Cir. 1986) (discussing precedent).

[66] *See* Bethlehem Contracting Co. v. Lehrer/McGovern, Inc., 800 F.2d 325, 327–28 (2d Cir. 1986).

[67] *See* Transamerica Occidental Life Ins. Co. v. Digregorio, 811 F.2d 1249, 1253–55 (9th Cir. 1987); Lumbermens Mut. Cas. Co. v. Connecticut Bank & Trust Co., 806 F.2d 411, 413 (2d Cir. 1986).

[68] *See, e.g,* Parsons Steel, Inc. v. First Alabama Bank, ____ U.S. ____, 106 S. Ct. 768 (1986); Kremer v. Chemical Constr. Corp., 456 U.S. 461 (1982); *see generally,* Luneburg, *The Opportunity to be Heard and the Doctrines of Preclusion: Federal Limits on State Law,* 31 Villanova L. Rev. 81 (1986).

[69] Law Enforcement Ins. Co. v. Corcoran, 807 F.2d 38, 40 (2d Cir. 1986); Mobil Oil Corp. v. City of Long Beach, 772 F.2d 534, 540–41 (9th Cir. 1985).

[70] Robinson v. State of New Jersey, 806 F.2d 442, 449 (3d Cir. 1986).

[71] *See* Microsoftware Computer Sys., Inc. v. Ontel Co., 686 F.2d 531, 538 (7th Cir. 1982); *see also* Note, *The Appealability of Federal Court Orders Denying Stays in Deference to Concurrent*

Another limitation on jurisdiction is the Eleventh Amendment, which has been interpreted as a grant of sovereign immunity to the states in federal court[72] barring federal actions against a state by citizens of another state as well as its own citizens.[73] Its applicability is determined by the essential nature and effect of the proceedings rather than merely by the names of the titular parties.[74] For example, when an action names only individual defendants but attempts to collect from a state for the actions of its employees, the Eleventh Amendment applies.[75]

Suits against state agencies are considered to be suits against the state.[76] However, the Eleventh Amendment does not bar actions against state officials or employees individually for their tortious conduct[77] as long as damages are executed solely against the official's personal assets.[78] Suits against state officials seeking injunctive relief from unconstitutional actions are also permitted.[79]

Factors analyzed by courts in determining whether an entity is entitled to Eleventh Amendment immunity include the following:

1. The powers and characteristics of the entity as created by state law
2. Whether state law views the agency as an arm of the state
3. The source of the entity's funding
4. The degree of local autonomy
5. Whether the entity is concerned primarily with local rather than statewide problems and
6. Whether it has the authority to sue and be sued in its own name and to hold property.[80]

State Court Proceedings, 59 Ind. L.J. 65 (1983). *But see* Mayacamas v. Gulfstream Aerospace Corp., 806 F.2d 928, 930 (9th Cir. 1986) (not permitting appeal of order denying stay pending resolution of parallel state proceeding).

[72] United States v. Union Gas Co., 792 F.2d 372 (3d Cir. 1986); *see* Pennhurst State School & Hosp. v. Halderman, 465 U.S. 89, 98–99 (1984).

[73] Hans v. Louisiana, 134 U.S. 1, 15 (1890); *see* Edelman v. Jordan, 415 U.S. 651, 663 (1974).

[74] Scheuer v. Rhodes, 416 U.S. 232, 237 (1974); *see* Fay v. South Colonie Cent. School Dist., 802 F.2d 21, 27 (2d Cir. 1986).

[75] Edelman v. Jordan, 415 U.S. 651, 668–69 (1974); *see* Pennhurst State School & Hosp. v. Halderman, 465 U.S. 89, 98–99 (1984).

[76] Pennhurst State School & Hosp. v. Halderman, 465 U.S. 89, 100 (1984).

[77] Great N. Life Ins. Co. v. Read, 322 U.S. 47, 50–51 (1944); Wilson v. Beebe, 770 F.2d 578, 587 (6th Cir. 1985).

[78] Kentucky v. Graham, 473 U.S. 159, 167–69 (1985); Brunken v. Lance, 807 F.2d 1325, 1329–30 (7th Cir. 1986).

[79] Pennhurst State School & Hosp. v. Halderman, 465 U.S. 89, 102–03 (1984); Edelman v. Jordan, 415 U.S. 651, 667–68 (1974).

[80] Clark v. Tarrant County, Tex., 798 F.2d 736, 744–45 (5th Cir. 1986).

The Eleventh Amendment can be explicitly waived,[81] but courts will scrutinize whether the state official had authority to waive sovereign immunity.[82] Therefore, even removal by a state official will not per se waive the state's Eleventh Amendment immunity.[83]

Claims under federal statutes do not override the Eleventh Amendment in the absence of a clear showing of congressional intent to the contrary.[84] For example, Title VII claims generally override the Eleventh Amendment,[85] but claims under 42 U.S.C. § 1983[86] do not. Appellate courts consider 42 U.S.C. § 1981 and 1985 as barred by the Eleventh Amendment.[87] The Sherman Act also does not limit a state's immunity.[88] Similarly to other jurisdictional bars, an appellate court can consider an Eleventh Amendment defense even if not raised below.[89]

Due to considerations of comity, federal courts have discretion to decline jurisdiction based on the domestic relations exception to diversity jurisdiction.[90] However, the federal court has jurisdiction if domestic relations issues are only tangentially implicated.[91] Recently, federal courts appear to be more willing to entertain suits involving domestic relations.[92] Several circuits view the Parental Kidnapping Prevention Act[93] as giving jurisdiction to the federal district court to determine which of two conflicting state custody decrees is valid.[94]

---

[81] *See* Florida Dept. of Health & Rehabilitative Servs. v. Florida Nursing Home Ass'n, 450 U.S. 147, 150 (1981).

[82] *See* Atascadero State Hosp. v. Scanlon, _____ U.S. _____, 105 S. Ct. 3142, 3146–47 (1985); Terrell v. United States, 783 F.2d 1562, 1565 (11th Cir. 1986).

[83] Silver v. Baggiano, 804 F.2d 1211, 1214 (11th Cir. 1986).

[84] Quern v. Jordan, 440 U.S. 332, 343–44 (1979).

[85] Fitzpatrick v. Bitzer, 427 U.S. 445, 456 (1976); Clark v. Tarrant County, Tex., 798 F.2d 736, 743 (5th Cir. 1986).

[86] Quern v. Jordan, 440 U.S. 332, 341 (1979).

[87] *See* Freeman v. Michigan Dept. of State, 808 F.2d 1174, 1178–79 (6th Cir. 1987); Rucker v. Higher Educ. Aids Bd., 669 F.2d 1179, 1184 (7th Cir. 1982).

[88] Charley's Taxi Radio Dispatch, Inc. v. SIDA of Hawaii, 810 F.2d 869, 874 (9th Cir. 1987); *see* Southern Motor Carriers Rate Conference, Inc. v. United States, 471 U.S. 48, 55–57 (1985).

[89] Gomez v. Illinois State Bd. of Educ., 811 F.2d 1030, 1036 (7th Cir. 1987); *see* Alabama v. Pugh, 438 U.S. 781, 782 & n.1 (1978).

[90] Goins v. Goins, 777 F.2d 1059, 1061 (5th Cir. 1985); Fern v. Turman, 736 F.2d 1367, 1370 (9th Cir. 1984), *cert. denied,* 469 U.S. 1210 (1985); Lloyd v. Loeffler, 694 F.2d 489, 492 (7th Cir. 1982); Sutter v. Pitts, 639 F.2d 842, 843 (1st Cir. 1981); *see generally* 13B Federal Practice and Procedure § 3609.

[91] Csibi v. Fustos, 670 F.2d 134, 137 (9th Cir. 1982); *see* Lynk v. LaPorte Super. Ct. No. 2, 789 F.2d 554, 558 (7th Cir. 1986).

[92] *See e.g.,* McIntyre v. McIntyre, 771 F.2d 1316, 1317–19 (9th Cir. 1985); Baron, *The Evolution of Domestic Relations Cases in Our Federal Courts,* 1985 S. Ill. U.L.J. 353.

[93] 28 U.S.C. § 1738A (1982).

[94] Hickey v. Baxter, 800 F.2d 430, 431 (4th Cir. 1986); McDougald v. Jensen, 786 F.2d 1465, 1474–75 (11th Cir. 1986); Heartfield v. Heartfield, 749 F.2d 1138, 1140–41 (5th Cir. 1985);

Although federal courts generally do not possesss jurisdiction over probate matters, they may entertain suits in favor of creditors, legatees, and heirs to establish claims once the will has been probated, as long as other jurisdictional requirements are met.[95]

§ 2.7 Subject Matter Jurisdiction

Federal courts have limited jurisdiction that is defined by statute.[96] The parties cannot confer subject matter jurisdiction on the court by consent, collusion, laches, waiver, or estoppel if it does not in fact exist.[97] However, it is well established that a court has jurisdiction to determine whether it has jurisdiction.[98] Since lack of jurisdiction can be raised at any time,[99] counsel must ascertain that federal jurisdiction exists before filing suit, because the opponent can wait until the statute of limitations has run before raising the issue.

The most common types of jurisdiction are based on the existence of a federal question[100] or on diversity.[101] Jurisdiction also exists in admiralty, bankruptcy, antitrust, patents, and copyright actions as well as in other specific cases to which Congress has extended jurisdiction.[102]

FEDERAL QUESTION JURISDICTION

§ 2.8 Federal Questions

In general, a case is not cognizable in federal court in the absence of diversity, unless it appears from the face of the complaint that the action depends on a

---

DiRuggiero v. Rodgers, 743 F.2d 1009, 1015 (3d Cir. 1984). *But see* Rogers v. Platt, 814 F.2d 683, 689–96 (D.C. Cir. 1987); Thompson v. Thompson, 798 F.2d 1547, 1550 (9th Cir. 1986) (denying jurisdicion), *cert. granted,* ____ U.S. ____, 107 S. Ct. 946 (1987).

95 Robertson v. Robertson, 803 F.2d 136, 138 (5th Cir. 1986).

96 28 U.S.C. § 1330 et seq. (1982).

97 Jackson v. Consolidated Rail Corp., 717 F.2d 1045, 1055 (7th Cir. 1983); *see also* Louisville & N. R.R. v. Mottley, 211 U.S. 149, 152 (1908); Fitzgerald v. Seaboard Sys. R.R., 760 F.2d 1249, 1251 (11th Cir. 1985); Rubin v. Buckman, 727 F.2d 71, 72 (3d Cir. 1984); Rauch v. Day & Night Mfg. Corp., 576 F.2d 697, 699–700 (6th Cir. 1978).

98 *See* Chicot County Drainage Dist. v. Baxter State Bank, 308 U.S. 371, 375–76 (1940); Gould v. Mutual Life Ins. Co. of N.Y., 790 F.2d 769, 774 (9th Cir. 1986); 13A Federal Practice and Procedure § 3536.

99 *See* Liberty Mut. Ins. Co. v. Wetzel, 424 U.S. 737, 740 (1976).

100 28 U.S.C. § 1331(a) (1982).

101 *Id.*

102 *See, e.g.,* 28 U.S.C. § 1330 *et seq.* (1982 & Supp. 1985).

federal question.[103] There is no longer any jurisdictional amount required in actions based upon a federal question.[104] Federal question jurisdiction extends to claims arising under the Constitution, laws, or treaties of the United States.[105] Unfortunately, the phrase *arising under* does not have a precise definition.[106] It is clear that a suit arises under the law that creates the cause of action.[107] Therefore, the vast majority of federal question jurisdiction cases are those in which federal law created the cause of action.[108] Claims founded upon federal common law as well as those of statutory origin fall within federal jurisdiction.[109]

A right or immunity created by the Constitution or laws of the United States must be an essential element of the plaintiff's cause of action.[110] Words used to describe the federal element in actions finding jurisdiction include *basic, necessary, pivotal, substantial, direct and essential,* and *paramount.*[111] Claims in which the federal element is described as *collateral, tangential, merely possible, attenuated,* or *incidental* deny federal jurisdiction.[112]

Suits brought upon a state statute do not arise under federal law merely because of the presence of a federal issue in a state-created cause of action.[113] For example, in a suit by Mississippi tax authorities against a bank for failing to pay its predecessor's tax liabilities, the mere fact that the state's authority to tax the bank stemmed from the federal constitution did not provide federal jurisdiction.[114]

Federal jurisdiction can extend to cases in which the vindication of a right under state law necessarily turns on some construction of federal law.[115]

---

103 Pan American Petroleum Corp. v. Superior Ct., 366 U.S. 656, 663 (1961); *see generally* 13B Federal Practice and Procedure §§ 3561–3567.2.

104 *See* 28 U.S.C. § 1331 (1982).

105 *Id.*

106 *See* Franchise Tax Bd. v. Construction Laborers Vacation Trust, 463 U.S. 1, 8 (1983); Hale, *The "Arising Under" Jurisdicion of the Federal Circuit: An Opportunity for Uniformity in Patent Law,* 14 Fla. St. U.L. Rev. 229 (1986).

107 Franchise Tax Bd. v. Construction Laborers Vacation Trust, 463 U.S. 1, 8–9 (1983) (quoting American Well Works Co. v. Layne & Bowler Co., 241 U.S. 257, 260 (1916) (Justice Holmes)).

108 Merrell Dow Pharmaceuticals Inc. v. Thompson, _____U.S._____ 106 S. Ct. 3229, 3232–33 (1986).

109 Illinois v. City of Milwaukee, 406 U.S. 91, 100 (1972).

110 Franchise Tax Bd. v. Construction Laborers Vacation Trust, 463 U.S. 1, 11–12 (1983) (quoting Gully v. First Nat'l Bank, 299 U.S. 109, 112 (1936)).

111 See discussion in Hunter v. United Van Lines, 746 F.2d 635, 646 (9th Cir.), *cert. denied,* _____U.S._____, 106 S. Ct. 180 (1985).

112 *Id.*

113 *See* Franchise Tax Bd. v. Construction Laborers Vacation Trust, 463 U.S. 1, 11–12 (1983).

114 *See* Gully v. First Nat'l Bank in Meridian, 299 U.S. 109, 111–12, 117 (1936).

115 Franchise Tax Bd. v. Construction Laborers Vacation Trust, 463 U.S. 1, 9 (1983); *see generally* Hirshman, *Whose Law Is it Anyway? A Reconsideration of Federal Question Jurisdicion Over Cases of Mixed State and Federal Law,* 60 Ind. L.J. 17 (1984).

However, if Congress has not permitted a private remedy for the violation of a federal cause of action, such as for misbranding a drug in violation of the Federal Food, Drug, and Cosmetic Act, no federal question jurisdiction is available for a state claim which is based upon violation of the federal statute.[116] Similarly, violation of an executive order concerning affirmative action has not been construed as providing a private right of action which would permit federal jurisdiction.[117]

§ 2.9 —The Well Pleaded Complaint and Artful Pleading

Whether a claim arises under federal law is determined by reference to the well pleaded complaint.[118] The well-pleaded complaint rule, which applies to cases brought in federal court as well as those removed there,[119] requires that the federal question be determined from the plaintiff's complaint, unaided by the answer or anything alleged in anticipation of avoiding defenses.[120] Thus, federal defenses to state law claims do not supply federal jurisdiction.[121] However, if a state cause of action is preempted by federal law, such as in the labor law area, a plaintiff's artful pleading does not defeat federal jurisdiction.[122] For example, an employer's suit against a union for violating the no-strike clause in its collective bargaining agreement did not prevent removal despite the employer's sole reliance on state contract law.[123]

Declaratory judgment and Rule 22 interpleader are procedures which enable a potential defendant to initiate an action, as long as federal jurisdiction would have existed if the opposing party had brought a coercive action against it.[124] However, those procedures do not extend federal jurisdiction to cases in which it

---

[116] Merrell Dow Pharmaceuticals Inc. v. Thompson, _____U.S._____, 106 S. Ct. 3229, 3232 (1986).

[117] *See* Utley v. Varian Assocs., Inc., 811 F.2d 1279, 1286 (9th Cir. 1987).

[118] Merrell Dow Pharmaceuticals Inc. v. Thompson, _____U.S._____, 106 S. Ct. 3229, 3232 (1986); *see generally* 13B Federal Practice and Procedure § 3566.

[119] See § **3.2**.

[120] Franchise Tax Bd. v. Construction Laborers Vacation Trust, 463 U.S. 1, 10 n.9, 15–16 (1983); *see* Phillips Petroleum Co. v. Texaco, Inc., 415 U.S. 125, 127–28 (1974).

[121] Phillips Petroleum Co. v. Texaco, Inc., 415 U.S. 125, 128 (1974).

[122] *See* Allis-Chalmers Corp. v. Lueck, 471 U.S. 202, 220 (1985); *see also* Metropolitan Life Ins. Co. v. Taylor, _____U.S._____, 107 S. Ct.1542, 55 U.S.L.W. 4468, 4469–70 (Apr. 7, 1987) (ERISA preemption under § 502(a)).

[123] *See* Avco Corp. v. Aero Lodge No. 735, 390 U.S. 557, 560 (1968); *see generally* Twitchell, *Characterizing Federal Claims: Preemption, Removal, and the Arising-Under Jurisdiction of the Federal Courts,* 54 Geo. Wash. L. Rev. 812 (1986).

[124] Bell & Beckwith v. IRS, 766 F.2d 910, 914 (6th Cir. 1985); Gelfgren v. Republic Nat'l Life Ins. Co., 680 F.2d 79, 81 (9th Cir. 1982).

does not otherwise exist.[125] It is questionable whether a claim of federal preemption can be used to assert jurisdiction when the plaintiff in a declaratory relief action has independent grounds for federal relief such as an injunction.[126]

§ 2.10 Doe Pleadings in Federal Actions

Doe pleading in a federal action does not defeat jurisdiction. However, it should be avoided unless necessary to protect the privacy of a party or when the identity of the defendant is currently unknown. Rule 10(a) requires that the complaint include the names of all parties. Therefore, approval appears necessary before a Doe can be pleaded, and the appropriateness of such a pleading is unsettled.[127] One court dismissed a Doe pleading on the ground that it was ineffective to commence the action.[128] Obviously, such a dismissal can have adverse statute of limitations consequences.

If a defendant's identity is unknown to the plaintiff at the time the suit is commenced, the court will usually give the plaintiff an opportunity to amend the complaint to name the particular defendant after allowing a reasonable period of time for discovery.[129] Some circuits consider a Doe dismissal proper only if the true identity of the defendant cannot be learned through discovery.[130] Other circuits view Doe pleadings in civil rights actions with disfavor.[131]

Plaintiffs may also bring Doe pleadings to preserve their privacy or to ensure that they will not be injured because of bringing the action.[132] Some courts permit anonymity only if the plaintiff is challenging constitutional, statutory, or regulatory validity of governmental activity.[133]

---

[125] *See* Skelly Oil Co. v. Phillips Petroleum Co., 339 U.S. 667, 671–72 (1950), Marathon Oil Co. v. United States, 807 F.2d 759, 763 (9th Cir. 1986), and Federal Kemper Ins. Co. v. Rauscher, 807 F.2d 345, 351 (3d Cir. 1986) (declaratory judgment); Bell & Beckwith v. IRS, 766 F.2d 910, 914 (6th Cir. 1985) (interpleader).

[126] *See* Middle South Energy v. Arkansas Pub. Serv. Comm'n, 772 F.2d 404, 410 & nn.14–16 (8th Cir. 1985) (upholding jurisdiction); Note, *Federal Jurisdiction over Declaratory Suits Challenging State Action,* 79 Colum. L. Rev. 983 (1979).

[127] *See generally* Note, *Anonymity in Civil Litigation: The "Doe" Plaintiff,* 57 Notre Dame Law. 580 (1982).

[128] Roe v. New York, 49 F.R.D. 279, 282 (S.D.N.Y. 1970).

[129] *E.g.,* Martinez v. Winner, 771 F.2d 424, 442 (10th Cir. 1985), *vacated on other grounds,* _____U.S._____, 106 S. Ct. 1787 (1986).

[130] Munz v. Parr, 758 F.2d 1254, 1257 (8th Cir. 1985); *see also* LeGrand v. Evan, 702 F.2d 415, 417 (2d Cir. 1983).

[131] *See, e.g.,* Strauss v. City of Chicago, 760 F.2d 765, 770 n.6 (7th Cir. 1985); Gillespie v. Civiletti, 629 F.2d 637, 642 (9th Cir. 1980).

[132] *See generally* Note, *Anonymity in Civil Litigation: The "Doe" Plaintiff,* 57 Notre Dame Law. 580 (1982).

[133] *E.g.,* Southern Methodist Univ. Ass'n v. Wynne & Jaffe, 599 F.2d 707, 712–13 (5th Cir. 1979).

Even in the most restrictive courts, plaintiffs have several options which may initially protect their identity.[134] A fictitious name can be used in the complaint, but verification must be given in the plaintiff's true name or in an attached document. After filing, a protective order can be sought to ensure confidentiality of the plaintiff's true name. Alternatively, the complaint can reveal the plaintiff's true name, and a protective order or leave to amend can be sought after filing.[135] If the statute of limitations is not a problem, the plaintiff should file under a pseudonym and argue the issue if the complaint is not initially dismissed. Some local rules appear to permit Doe pleading in federal cases.[136] Of course, the plaintiff will have to reveal his identity to the defendant, regardless of whether the public learns the party's true identity.[137]

DIVERSITY JURISDICTION

§ 2.11 Introduction

Diversity cases have two basic requirements: first, the plaintiffs' citizenship must be completely diverse from that of the defendants, and second, the amount in controversy must exceed $10,000.[138] Diversity jurisdiction is strictly construed.[139] Indeed, many federal judges do not hide their distaste for diversity cases[140] and delight in strictly applying federal and local court rules to discourage such filings. Similarly, counsel who litigate mainly in federal court can be relied upon to use their understanding of federal practice to bedevil practitioners who are unfamiliar with federal jurisdiction and practice. Therefore, a plaintiff must understand the requirements of diversity when determining where to bring the action. Even if a state venue is preferred, understanding diversity can ensure that the action remains in state court. In other words, counsel can include viable parties who destroy diversity, thereby eliminating the possibility of removal to federal court. Conversely, the defendant must understand diversity in order to determine if a state action can be removed to federal court, or if a declaratory

---

[134] *See generally* Note, *Anonymity in Civil Litigation: The "Doe" Plaintiff,* 57 Notre Dame Law. 580 (1982).

[135] *See* Roe v. New York, 49 F.R.D. 279, 281 (S.D.N.Y. 1970).

[136] *See, e.g.,* C.D. Cal. R. 3.7.2.2.

[137] *See, e.g.,* Doe v. Stegall, 653 F.2d 180, 182 (5th Cir. 1981).

[138] 28 U.S.C. § 1332 (1982); *See generally* 13B Federal Practice and Procedure §§ 3601–3630; 14 Federal Practice and Procedure §§ 3631–3642.

[139] Shamrock Oil & Gas Corp. v. Sheets, 313 U.S. 100, 108–09 (1941); Kantor v. Wellesley Galleries, Ltd., 704 F.2d 1088, 1092 (9th Cir. 1983).

[140] *See, e.g.,* Ebker v. Tan Jay Int'l Ltd., 739 F.2d 812, 813 (2d Cir. 1984) (Friendly, J.); Phillips, *Diversity Jurisdiction: Problems and A Possible Solution,* 14 Toledo L. Rev. 747, 749 n.6 (1983).

relief action is appropriate in federal court before suit has been initiated by the opposing party.

§ 2.12 Amount in Controversy

The rules concerning the amount in controversy are fairly simple.[141] The amount is determined at the time the action is filed.[142] The sum alleged by the plaintiff controls if the claim is made in good faith, and it "must appear to a legal certainty that the claim is really for less than the jursidictional amount to justify dismissal."[143] The Ninth Circuit interprets legal certainty to include cases in which a rule of law or limitation of damages would make it virtually impossible for a plaintiff to meet the amount in controversy requirement, going beyond the pleadings to determine the applicability of the law.[144] Similarly, if the factual allegations fail to demonstrate anything more than a trivial loss, the action will be dismissed. For example, when plaintiffs alleged merely that a stewardess brusquely refused to permit them to sit in a first-class seating section, the court properly dismissed the action.[145] On the other hand, dismissal was unwarranted in a personal injury action in which the specific damages were far less than $10,000, but the plaintiff alleged continuing pain and suffering, loss of consortium, and possible permanent injury.[146]

Multiple claims can be aggregated by a single plaintiff against a defendant in order to reach the jurisdictional amount as long as such claims can be properly joined under Rule 18.[147] Consumer class actions are rare in federal court because individual claims of plaintiffs cannot be joined to meet the jurisdictional amount.[148] The Supreme Court has also held that minority shareholders could not aggregate their damages in a class action involving recovery of a premium that majority shareholders received for their sale of stock.[149] However,

---

[141] *See generally* 1 Moore's Federal Practice ¶¶ 0.90–0.99 (2d ed. 1986); 14A Federal Practice and Procedure § 3702.

[142] Sellers v. O'Connell, 701 F.2d 575 (6th Cir. 1983); 14A Federal Practice and Procedure § 3702.

[143] St. Paul Mercury Indem. Co. v. Red Cab Co., 303 U.S. 283, 288 (1938); *see* Mt. Healthy School Dist. Bd. of Educ. v. Doyle, 429 U.S. 274, 276–77 (1977).

[144] Pachinger v. MGM Grand Hotel-Las Vegas, Inc., 802 F.2d 362, 364 (9th Cir. 1986). *But see* Zacharia v. Harbor Island Spa, Inc., 684 F.2d 199, 202 (2d Cir. 1982). *See generally* 14A Federal Practice and Procedure § 3702.

[145] Diefenthal v. CAB, 681 F.2d 1039, 1052–53 (5th Cir. 1982).

[146] Martin v. Gibson, 723 F.2d 989, 991–92 (D.C. Cir. 1983).

[147] Hunter v. United Van Lines, 746 F.2d 635, 650 n.9 (9th Cir. 1984), *cert. denied*, ____ U.S. ____, 106 S. Ct. 180 (1985); *see* Snyder v. Harris, 394 U.S. 332 (1969); *see generally* 14A Moore's Federal Practice ¶ 0.97; Federal Practice and Procedure § 3704.

[148] Zahn v. International Paper Co., 414 U.S. 291, 301 (1973).

[149] Snyder v. Harris, 394 U.S. 332, 338 (1969).

minority shareholders have been permitted to aggregate their damages based on a common and undivided claim of wrongful depletion of corporate assets.[150] Interest, costs, and attorney's fees are excluded from determination of the jurisdictional amount[151] except when they are elements of damages.[152]

It is fundamental that the existence of subject matter jurisdiction is determined by looking to the complaint or removal petition at the time it was filed.[153] Thus, an amendment to reduce the prayer to an amount under the jursidictional requirement does not divest the court of its subject matter jurisdiction.[154] The existence of a valid defense also does not deprive the court of jurisdiction.[155]

The jurisdictional determination is made on the basis of the allegations and is not a decision on the merits.[156] The party asserting jurisdiction bears the burden of supporting the jurisdictional elements if challenged[157] and can amend the pleadings or submit affidavits so the court can determine whether the jurisdictional amount is satisfied.[158] In appropriate cases, discovery can be used to amplify the meaning of the allegations.[159]

§ 2.13 Complete Diversity

The general rule is that 28 U.S.C. § 1332 requires that complete diversity exist between all plaintiffs on the one hand and all defendants on the other.[160] When applied to multiple parties, this requirement means that all plaintiffs must be diverse from all defendants. In other words, plaintiffs or defendants can be citizens of the same state as long as no opposing party is a citizen of that state. Citizenship requires an individual's physical presence in the state coupled with an intention to remain there indefinitely.[161]

---

[150] Eagle v. AT&T, 769 F.2d 541, 546–47 (9th Cir. 1985), *cert. denied,* _____U.S._____, 106 S. Ct. 1465 (1986).

[151] 28 U.S.C. § 1332(b) (1982).

[152] Brown v. Webster, 156 U.S. 328 (1895); *see* 1 Moore's Federal Practice ¶ 0.99.

[153] Boelens v. Redman Homes, Inc., 759 F.2d 504, 507 (5th Cir. 1985).

[154] St. Paul Mercury Indem. Co. v. Red Cab Co., 303 U.S. 283, 292 (1938).

[155] *Id.* at 289; *see generally* 14 Federal Practice and Procedure § 3702.

[156] Zacharia v. Harbor Island Spa Inc., 684 F.2d 199, 202 (2d Cir. 1982). For Fed. R. Civ. P. 12(b)(1) procedures, see §§ **14.8–14.16**.

[157] St. Paul Mercury Indem. Co. v. Red Cab Co., 303 U.S. 283, 287 n.10 (1938).

[158] Diefenthal v. CAB, 681 F.2d 1039, 1052 (5th Cir. 1982); 14A Federal Practice and Procedure § 3702.

[159] Zacharia v. Harbor Island Spa Inc., 684 F.2d 199, 202 (2d Cir. 1982); see § **14.16**.

[160] Strawbridge v. Curtiss, 7 U.S. (3 Cranch) 267 (1806); Owen Equip. & Erection Co. v. Kroger, 437 U.S. 365, 373–74 (1978).

[161] Blakemore v. Missouri Pac. R.R., 789 F.2d 616, 618 (8th Cir. 1986).

A United States citizen with no United States domicile cannot sue in diversity,[162] nor can a stateless person who has no nationality.[163] Moreover, diversity does not exist if only aliens are on both sides of the litigation.[164] Diversity also does not permit a citizen to sue a foreign government or agency in federal court, although a foreign state can be a plaintiff.[165] If the foreign state action upon which the claim is based is commercial activity, jurisdiction may be appropriate under 28 U.S.C. § 1330(a).[166] Suits between a state and citizens of another state are not cognizable in diversity, although this rule does not apply when the state is a nominal party.[167] Statutory interpleader actions require only minimal diversity between any two adverse claimants rather than complete diversity.[168] This contrasts with interpleader under Rule 22, which requires complete diversity to be established.[169]

In determining the existence of complete diversity, the court can align a party according to its actual interest in the litigation rather than by the fact that it is designated as a plaintiff or defendant. Diversity is determined by the citizenship of the parties at the time of the filing of the complaint, not when the cause of action arose.[170] For these purposes citizenship of an individual is the equivalent of domicile.[171] Jurisdiction cannot be created retroactively by substituting a diverse claimant for a nondiverse party.[172]

§ 2.14 Determining Domicile

A person's domicile is the location where he has established a fixed habitation or abode and intends to remain permanently or indefinitely.[173] Domicile is

---

[162] Rubin v. Buckman, 727 F.2d 71, 73 (3d Cir. 1984).

[163] Kantor v. Wellesley Galleries, Ltd., 704 F.2d 1088, 1092 (9th Cir. 1983).

[164] Giannakos v. M/V Bravo Trader, 762 F.2d 1295, 1298 (5th Cir. 1985); Corporacion Venezolana de Fomento v. Vintero Sales Corp., 629 F.2d 786, 790 (2d Cir. 1980), *cert. denied,* 449 U.S. 1080 (1981).

[165] 28 U.S.C. § 1332(a)(4) (1982); Riedel v. Bancam, S.A., 792 F.2d 587, 590 (6th Cir. 1986).

[166] *See* Riedel v. Bancam, S.A., 792 F.2d 587, 591 (6th Cir. 1986); Callejo v. Bancomer, S.A., 764 F.2d 1101, 1107 (5th Cir. 1985).

[167] District of Columbia v. Transamerica Ins. Co., 797 F.2d 1041, 1047 (D.C. Cir. 1986); 13B Federal Practice and Procedure §§ 3602, 3605.

[168] 28 U.S.C. § 1335 (1982).

[169] See § **9.6**.

[170] Smith v. Sperling, 354 U.S. 91, 93 n.1 (1957); Mann v. City of Tucson, Dep't of Police, 782 F.2d 790, 794 (9th Cir. 1986); Prakash v. American Univ., 727 F.2d 1174, 1179 n.28 (D.C. Cir. 1984); *see generally* 13B Federal Practice and Procedure § 3608.

[171] Valedon Martinez v. Hosp. Presbiteriano de la Comunidad, Inc., 806 F.2d 1128, 1132 (1st Cir. 1986).

[172] Aetna Casualty & Sur. Co. v. Hillman, 796 F.2d 770, 776 (5th Cir. 1986); Field v. Volkswagenwerk AG, 626 F.2d 293, 304–05 (3d Cir. 1980).

[173] Lew v. Moss, 797 F.2d 747, 750 (9th Cir. 1986); 1 Moore's Federal Practice ¶ 0.74[3.–3].

determined at the time the lawsuit is filed by reference to a variety of factors, including current residence, voting registration, location of personal and real property, location of brokerage and bank accounts, location of spouse and family, membership in organizations, place of employment or business, driver's license and automobile registration, and payment of taxes.[174] Courts view domicile objectively, giving little weight to statements of intent which conflict with facts.[175] The party asserting diversity has the burden of showing that the parties' domiciles are diverse.[176]

There is a presumption affecting the burden of production that an old domicile is not lost until a new one is acquired.[177] Acquiring a new domicile requires both physical presence at the new location and an intention to remain there indefinitely.[178] For example, when a plaintiff had clearly moved to Miami to join her sister, the fact that she later returned to Puerto Rico to obtain free medical treatment from her father and enrolled in college there did not change her domicile, in light of her intention to reside in Florida and her continuing contacts there.[179] Since domicile is a mixed question of law and fact but primarily factual, the district court's determination is usually reviewed under the clearly erroneous standard.[180]

§ 2.15 Subsequent Events

If diversity exists at the commencement of the action, it is not lost by subsequent events affecting the original parties to the action.[181] Therefore, intervention of a nondiverse party will not destroy diversity unless the intervenor was an indispensable party when the complaint was filed.[182] The requirement of diversity applies fully to parties who must be joined under Rule 19.[183] If addition or joinder of an indispensable party destroys diversity, the case must be dismissed for lack of jurisdiction. On the other hand, if a nondiverse party is not

---

[174] Lew v. Moss, 797 F.2d 747, 750 (9th Cir. 1986) (citing 13B Federal Practice and Procedure § 3612, at 529–31).

[175] Lew v. Moss, 797 F.2d 747, 750 (9th Cir. 1986); Freeman v. Northwest Acceptance Corp., 754 F.2d 553, 556 (5th Cir. 1985).

[176] Lew v. Moss, 797 F.2d 747, 749 (9th Cir. 1986); 13B Federal Practice and Procedure § 3611, at 522–23; *see* McNutt v. General Motors Acceptance Corp., 298 U.S. 178, 189 (1936); **§ 14.8.**

[177] Lew v. Moss, 797 F.2d 747, 750–51 (9th Cir. 1986).

[178] *Id.;* 13B Federal Practice and Procedure § 3613, at 544–45.

[179] *See* Valedon Martinez v. Hosp. Presbiteriano, 806 F.2d 1128, 1131–32 (1st Cir. 1986).

[180] *See id.* at 1132; Lew v. Moss, 797 F.2d 747, 750 (9th Cir. 1986); 13B Federal Practice and Procedure § 3612, at 540–41.

[181] Aetna Casualty & Sur. Co. v. Hillman, 796 F.2d 770, 776 (5th Cir. 1986); Keishian v. Buckley, 752 F.2d 1513, 1515 (11th Cir. 1984).

[182] American Nat'l Bank & Trust Co. v. Bailey, 750 F.2d 577, 582 (7th Cir. 1984), *cert. denied,* 471 U.S. 1100 (1985).

[183] Freeman v. Northwest Acceptance Corp., 754 F.2d 553, 555 (5th Cir. 1985).

indispensable, the plaintiff can bring a motion under Rule 21 to drop that party from the action on such terms as are just in order to retain diversity jurisdiction.[184] Similarly, leave to amend to dismiss nondiverse parties may be requested.[185] Although such amendments are discretionary,[186] some circuits require the amendment to be granted unless it appears that the nondiverse defendant cannot be dropped from the action without prejudice to the remaining defendants.[187] Similarly, when diversity will exist if nondiverse parties are dropped, the bare fact that a state court forum exists in which all parties can be sued in one action does not by itself make it appropriate to dismiss the federal action.[188] In contrast, if a plaintiff moves to add a nondiverse party who is not indispensable in order to defeat removal, many courts will not permit the amendment.[189]

§ 2.16 Independent Basis for Jurisdiction When Diversity Is Absent

The presence of nondiverse parties does not destroy diversity jurisdiction over others when an independent basis of federal jurisdiction, such as the Jones Act,[190] exists over the nondiverse parties.[191] Similarly, ancillary or pendent jurisdiction is sufficient to support jurisdiction of related claims which are not otherwise diverse.[192] Therefore, a Rule 13(g) cross-claim does not require an independent basis of federal jurisdiction.[193] Nor can a defendant defeat the plaintiff's right to a federal forum by impleading a resident of the plaintiff's state under a Rule 14(a) third party complaint.[194] Even severance of the federal question claims upon which jurisdiction is based does not destroy jurisdiction over nondiverse claims, because the trial court retains discretion whether to exercise jurisdiction over pendent state claims.[195]

---

[184] Fritz v. American Home Shield Corp., 751 F.2d 1152, 1154 (11th Cir. 1985); 7 Federal Practice and Procedure § 1685.

[185] Fed. R. Civ. P. 15(a).

[186] Zenith Radio Corp. v. Hazeltine Research, Inc., 401 U.S. 321, 330 (1971).

[187] *See, e.g.*, Samaha v. Presbyterian Hosp., 757 F.2d 529, 531 (2d Cir. 1985).

[188] *Id.*

[189] *See, e.g.*, Provident Bank & Trust Co. v. Patterson, 390 U.S. 102 (1968).

[190] 46 U.S.C. § 688 (1982).

[191] *See* Romero v. International Terminal Operating Co., 358 U.S. 354, 359 (1959).

[192] See §§ **2.25–2.30**.

[193] American Nat'l Bank & Trust Co. v. Bailey, 750 F.2d 577, 581 (7th Cir. 1984).

[194] Fidelity & Deposit Co. v. City of Sheboygan Falls, 713 F.2d 1261, 1266 (7th Cir. 1983); 6 Federal Practice and Procedure § 1444, at 223–25 (1971).

[195] Brown v. Mine Safety Appliances Co., 753 F.2d 393, 395 (5th Cir. 1985); *see* United Mine Workers of Am. v. Gibbs, 383 U.S. 715, 726 (1966).

§ 2.17 Collusive Joinder

Diversity cannot be obtained if a party has been improperly or collusively joined, by assignment or otherwise, in order to invoke the jurisdiction of the court.[196] The status of administrators has posed a problem for courts in determining whether diversity was collusively obtained,[197] since an out-of-state administrator can provide diversity jurisdiction for an otherwise nondiverse real party in interest.

Both a *motive-function test*[198] and a *substantial stakes test*[199] have been used to assess whether joinder is collusive. The motive approach considers whether the out-of-state administrator has any duty or function beyond creating diversity as only one of the factors in its decision.[200] Therefore, if an out-of-state heir is appointed as the representative of the estate, that individual's beneficial interest in the outcome of the litigation is sufficient to withstand an attack on diversity. The substantial stakes test rests solely on whether the administrator has a substantial stake in the outcome of the suit, regardless of the absence of evidence that the motive for the appointment is to manufacture diversity.[201] In other words, personal preference, kinship, and business experience do not elevate a representative above the level of a nominal party. The Tenth Circuit appears to take an intermediate approach, looking to motive only if the administrator has no substantial stake.[202] In addition to these tests, the American Law Institute has proposed that diversity be measured by the decedent's citizenship.[203]

---

[196] 28 U.S.C. § 1359 (1982); *see* Kramer v. Caribbean Mills, Inc., 394 U.S. 823, 828–29 (1969) (legal assignment considered collusive for purposes of diversity when made to create jurisdiction); *see generally* 3A Moore's Federal Practice ¶ 17.05[3]; 14 Federal Practice and Procedure §§ 3637–3642.

[197] *Compare* Wilsey v. Eddingfield, 780 F.2d 614, 616–17 (7th Cir. 1985), *cert. denied,* _____U.S. _____, 106 S. Ct. 1660 (1986) (real parties determine diversity, even if administrator has stake in outcome) *with* Hackney v. Newman Memorial Hosp., Inc., 621 F.2d 1069, 1071 (10th Cir. 1980) (diversity decided by citizenship of representative who is more than nominal party); *see* Pallazola v. Rucker, 797 F.2d 1116, 1119–27 (1st Cir. 1986) (thoroughly reviewing state of law and declining to choose any particular test); *see generally* Mullenix, *Creative Manipulation of Federal Jurisdicion: Is There Diversity After Death,* 70 Cornell L. Rev. 1011 (1985).

[198] McSparran v. Weist, 402 F.2d 867, 873 (3d Cir. 1968) (en banc), *cert. denied,* 395 U.S. 903 (1969); *see also* Bianca v. Parke-Davis Pharmaceutical Div., 723 F.2d 392, 398 (5th Cir. 1984); Gross v. Hougland, 712 F.2d 1034, 1039 n.10 (6th Cir. 1983), *cert denied,* 465 U.S. 1025 (1984); O'Brien v. Avco Corp., 425 F.2d 1030 (2d Cir. 1969).

[199] Bishop v. Hendricks, 495 F.2d 289, 297 (4th Cir.), *cert. denied,* 419 U.S. 1056 (1976); *see also* Betar v. DeHavilland Aircraft of Canada, Ltd., 603 F.2d 30, 35–36 (7th Cir. 1979), *cert. denied,* 444 U.S. 1098 (1980).

[200] Bianca v. Parke-Davis Pharmaceutical Div., 723 F.2d 392, 398 (5th Cir. 1984).

[201] Bishop v. Hendricks, 495 F.2d 289, 297 (4th Cir.), *cert. denied,* 419 U.S. 1056 (1976).

[202] Martinez v. United States Olympic Comm., 802 F.2d 1275, 1279 (10th Cir. 1986).

[203] American Law Institute, Study of the Division of Jurisdiction Between State and Federal Courts § 1301(b)(4), at 11 (1969).

§ 2.18 Effect of Does on Diversity

In diversity cases, the complaint must positively demonstrate the basis of jurisdiction.[204] Therefore, Doe pleading is unacceptable in diversity cases because the Doe may be a nondiverse party. Some local court rules prohibit filing Doe pleadings. Similarly, Does prevent removal unless they are considered nominal parties or are fraudulently joined. This can become a major issue in removal, since the case will be remanded to the state court if diversity does not exist. The various approaches to the presence of Does in a removal action are discussed in detail in § **3.11**.[205]

§ 2.19 Citizenship Questions

A common mistake in pleadings is the allegation of residency rather than citizenship. Such an allegation does not satisfy diversity.[206] If the diversity of the parties is unclear from the pleadings for any reason, courts will often issue show cause orders as to the propriety of their jurisdiction. However, it is often the appellate court, rather than the parties or the district judge, that raises the issue. If diversity is lacking, a case will be dismissed even though it has been tried to conclusion.[207] Usually, if it is likely that diversity exists, most appellate courts will remand the action to determine whether diversity jurisdiction is appropriate[208] or permit affidavits to supply the missing information.[209]

§ 2.20 —Corporate Citizenship

Another issue which frequently arises is the citizenship of a corporation. For purposes of diversity, a corporation is considered a citizen of the state where it is incorporated as well as the state where it has its principal place of business.[210]

---

[204] Thomas v. Board of Trustees, 195 U.S. 207, 210 (1904); Illinois Cent. Gulf R.R. v. Pargas, Inc., 706 F.2d 633, 636 (5th Cir. 1983).

[205] *See generally* Comment, *Doe Defendants and Other State Relation Back Doctrines in Federal Diversity Cases,* 35 Stanford L. Rev. 297, 304–06 (1983); Note, *John Doe, Where Are You: The Effects of Fictitious Defendants on Removal Jurisdiction in Diversity Cases,* 34 Ala. L. Rev. 99 (1983).

[206] Strain v. Harrelson Rubber Co., 742 F.2d 888, 889 (5th Cir. 1984).

[207] *See* Kanzelberger v. Kanzelberger, 782 F.2d 774, 779 (7th Cir. 1986)

[208] Strain v. Harrelson Rubber Co., 742 F.2d 888, 889 (5th Cir. 1984).

[209] *See* 28 U.S.C. § 1653 (1982); Stockman v. LaCroix, 790 F.2d 584, 587 (7th Cir. 1986).

[210] 28 U.S.C. § 1322(c) (1982); *see generally* 13B Federal Practice and Procedure §§ 3623–3630.

This dual citizenship makes it more likely that complete diversity does not exist. Both places must be stated in the complaint to support diversity jurisdiction.[211] Professional corporations appear to be treated as corporations rather than partnerships in determining diversity.[212]

Often, a corporation's principal place of business is not obvious. Several tests have been developed to determine the principal place of business,[213] the most often cited being the *nerve center* approach,[214] which focuses on the location of the executive and administrative functions of the corporation, and the *place of operations* approach,[215] which emphasizes the corporation's production or service activities. An *alterego* analysis may also be employed if the corporation is a mere conduit used by the principal for its own business purposes.[216] However, the alterego approach is irrelevant for determining the place of incorporation.[217] Although the alterego doctrine is used to defeat diversity, it cannot be used to extend such jurisdiction.[218]

Determining the citizenship of an alien corporation is equally troublesome, especially when its principal place of business is located in the United States. Courts are not consistent in making this determination. Some circuits apply 28 U.S.C. § 1332(c), which deems a corporation a citizen of the state of its incorporation and the state where it has its principal place of business,[219] while others do not.[220] If alien corporations are on both sides of a diversity action, this does not by itself defeat diversity under 28 U.S.C. § 1332(a)(3) as long as a

---

211 Illinois Cent. Gulf R.R. v. Pargas, Inc., 706 F.2d 633, 636 (5th Cir. 1983); *see* District of Columbia v. Transamerica Ins. Co., 797 F.2d 1041, 1043–44 (D.C. Cir. 1986).

212 Cote v. Wadel, 796 F.2d 981, 983 (7th Cir. 1986); Saxe, Bacon & Bolan, P.C. v. Martindale-Hubbell, Inc., 710 F.2d 87, 89 (2d Cir. 1983).

213 Co-Efficient Energy Sys. v. CSL Indus., Inc., 812 F.2d 556, 558 (9th Cir. 1987); *see generally* 1 Moore's Federal Practice ¶ .077 [3.-1]–[3.-4]; 13B Federal Practice and Procedure § 3625.

214 *See, e.g.*, Wisconsin Knife Works v. National Metal Crafters, 781 F.2d 1280, 1282 (7th Cir. 1986); Scot Typewriter Co. v. Underwood Corp., 170 F. Supp. 862, 864–65 (S.D.N.Y. 1959).

215 *See, e.g.*, Murray v. Commercial Union Ins. Co., 782 F.2d 432, 434 (3d Cir. 1986); Inland Rubber Corp. v. Triple A Tire Serv., Inc., 220 F. Supp. 490, 496 (S.D.N.Y. 1963).

216 *See* Panalpina Welttransport GMBH v. Geosource, Inc., 764 F.2d 352, 354 (5th Cir. 1985); Fritz v. American Home Shield Corp., 751 F.2d 1152, 1153 (11th Cir. 1985).

217 Fritz v. American Home Shield Corp., 751 F.2d 1152, 1154 (11th Cir. 1985).

218 Panalpina Welttransport GMBH v. Geosource, Inc., 764 F.2d 352, 354 (5th Cir. 1985).

219 *E.g.*, Chick Kam Choo v. Exxon Corp., 764 F.2d 1148, 1152 (5th Cir. 1985) (suit by individual alien against alien corporation with principal place of business in U.S. cannot be maintained); Jerguson v. Blue Dot Inv., Inc., 659 F.2d 31 (5th Cir. 1981) (alien corporation with principal place of business in a particular state is not subject to suit in federal court by citizen of same state).

220 Chemical Transp. Corp. v. Metropolitan Petroleum Corp., 246 F. Supp. 563, 567 (S.D.N.Y. 1964); *see generally* 13B Federal Practice and Procedure § 3628; Note, *Alien Corporations and Federal Diversity Jurisdiction,* 84 Colum. L. Rev. 177 (1984); Note, *Diversity Jurisdiction and Alien Corporations: The Application of Section 1332(c),* 59 Ind. L.J. 659 (1984); *Comment, Diversity Jurisdiction: The Dilemma of Dual Citizenship and Alien Corporations,* 77 Nw. U.L.Rev 565 (1982).

controversy exists between diverse citizens and the aliens are additional parties.[221]

A plaintiff suing a corporation must be extremely careful when deciding whether diversity is appropriate, since the court can raise that question sua sponte even if opposing counsel does not object.[222] Therefore, if the principal place of business is not stated, an appellate court can dismiss the complaint or remand to the district court for clarification,[223] although amendments in the trial and appellate courts of defective jurisdictional allegations are authorized.[224] Similarly, opposing counsel can wait until after the statute of limitations has run before challenging diversity. This will prevent refiling in all states which lack saving statutes to permit late filings for cases dismissed on jurisdictional grounds.

§ 2.21 —Unincorporated Entities

Care must also be taken in determining the citizenship of unincorporated associations, particularly limited partnerships, for purposes of diversity. Partnerships and other unincorporated associations rarely fall within diversity jurisdiction, because the citizenship of each member is considered.[225] However, despite an old Supreme Court case which considered the citizenship of individual limited partners,[226] the circuits disagree on their treatment for purposes of diversity.[227] A few circuits look only to the citizenship of the general partners,[228] while other circuits also consider the citizenship of limited partners.[229]

---

[221] Transure, Inc. v. Marsh & McLennan, Inc., 766 F.2d 1297, 1298–99 (9th Cir. 1985); Goar v. Compania Peruana de Vapores, 688 F.2d 417, 420 n.6 (5th Cir. 1982); 13B Federal Practice and Procedure § 3604. *But see* Note, *Federal Jurisdiction Over Suits Between Diverse United States Citizens with Aliens Joined to Both Sides of the Controversy under 28 U.S.C. § 1332(a)(3),* 38 Rutgers L. Rev 71 (1985).

[222] *See, e.g.,* Fitzgerald v. Seaboard Sys. R.R., 760 F.2d 1249, 1250–51 (11th Cir. 1985).

[223] Jason's Food Inc. v. Peter Eckrich & Sons, Inc., 768 F.2d 189, 190–91 (7th Cir. 1985).

[224] 28 U.S.C. § 1653 (1982); *see* District of Columbia v. Transamerica Ins. Co:, 797 F.2d 1041, 1043 (D.C. Cir. 1986); see **§ 14.10**.

[225] *See* Navarro Sav. & Loan Ass'n v. Lee, 446 U.S. 458, 461 (1980); City of Clinton v. Moffitt, 812 F.2d 341, 342 (7th Cir. 1987).

[226] Great S. Fire Proof Hotel Co. v. Jones, 177 U.S. 449, 456 (1900).

[227] *See generally* Note, *Including Limited Partners in the Diversity Jurisdiction Analysis,* 54 Fordham L. Rev. 607 (1986); Note, *Diversity of Citizenship and the Limited Partnership: A "Real Party" Rule as Federal Common Law,* 71 Iowa L. Rev. 235 (1985); Note, *Who are the Real Parties in Interest for Purposes of Determining Diversity Jurisdiction for Limited Partnerships,* 61 Wash. U.L.Q. 1051 (1984).

[228] Mesa Operating Ltd. Partnership v. Louisiana Intrastate Gas Corp., 797 F.2d 238, 240–42 (5th Cir. 1986); Colonial Realty Corp. v. Bache Co., 358 F.2d 178, 183 (2d Cir.), *cert. denied,* 385 U.S. 817 (1966).

[229] New York State Teachers Retirement Sys. v. Kalkus, 764 F.2d 1015, 1019 (4th Cir. 1985); Elston Inv., Ltd. v. David Altman Leasing Corp., 731 F.2d 436, 438–39 (7th Cir. 1984); Carlsberg Resources Corp. v. Cambria Sav. & Loan Ass'n, 554 F.2d 1254, 1259 (3d Cir. 1977).

The Supreme Court has held that a business trust's amenability to diversity is determined by the citizenship of the trustees without regard to the citizenship of the beneficial shareholders.[230] This same principle probably applies to receivers.[231] On the other hand, the citizenship of a labor union is determined by that of each of its constituent members.[232]

§ 2.22 Other Limitations on Diversity

Other limitations in meeting diversity requirements include the following.

1. In class actions, diversity is determined by the citizenship of the class representatives.[233]
2. In derivative actions brought by shareholders,[234] diversity is determined by treating the corporation as aligned with the defendants when the shareholders are antagonistic to the corporation's interests.[235]
3. Some congressional statutes limit the federal court's jurisdiction to hear otherwise appropriate cases, although a state legislature cannot divest a federal court of its subject matter jurisdiction.[236] For example, 28 U.S.C. § 1332(c) provides that, in direct actions against any insurer to which the insured is not joined, the insurer is deemed to be a citizen of the same state as the insured as well as of any state in which it has been incorporated or has its principal place of business. However, this does not destroy diversity if the suit is based not on the primary liability covered by the policy, but on the insurer's failure to settle within policy limits or in good faith.[237] This provision also has not been applied to suits against sureties.[238]
4. Limitations on federal jurisdiction when the Federal Deposit Insurance Corporation acts as a receiver of a bank[239] have been applied to eliminate jurisdiction based upon diversity.[240]

---

[230] Navarro Sav. Ass'n v. Lee, 446 U.S. 458, 465–66 (1980).

[231] F.D.I.C. v. Elefant, 790 F.2d 661, 665 (7th Cir. 1986); Gross v. Hougland, 712 F.2d 1034, 1038 n.6 (6th Cir. 1983), *cert. denied,* 465 U.S. 1025 (1984).

[232] United Steelworkers v. R.H. Bouligny, Inc., 382 U.S. 145 (1965).

[233] Snyder v. Harris, 394 U.S. 332, 339–40 (1969); *see* § **10.4–10.5**.

[234] *See* Fed. R. Civ. P. 23.1; § **10.18**.

[235] *See* Swanson v. Traer, 354 U.S. 114, 116 (1957).

[236] Webb v. Tom Brown, Inc., 807 F.2d 783, 784 (9th Cir. 1987).

[237] John Cooper Produce v. Paxton Nat'l Ins. Co., 774 F.2d 433, 435 (11th Cir. 1985); Beckham v. Safeco Ins. Co., 691 F.2d 898, 901–02 (9th Cir. 1982); Velez v. Crown Life Ins. Co., 599 F.2d 471, 473 (1st Cir. 1979).

[238] *See* District of Columbia v. Transamerica Ins. Co., 797 F.2d 1041, 1049 (D.C. Cir. 1986); Burgoyne v. Frank B. Hall & Co. of Hawaii, Inc., 781 F.2d 1418, 1420 (9th Cir. 1986).

[239] 12 U.S.C. § 1819 Fourth (1982).

[240] FDIC v. Elefant, 790 F.2d 661, 666 (7th Cir. 1986); FDIC v. Sumner Financial Corp., 602 F.2d 670, 677–80 (5th Cir. 1979).

5. Federal courts cannot hear actions concerning state public utility rates.[241]
6. Federal jurisdiction cannot be invoked in diversity cases involving Indian matters which are subject to tribal remedies until those remedies have been exhausted, at which time only the assertion of jurisdiction by the tribal court can be challenged, not that court's decision.[242]
7. Workman's Compensation cases are specifically nonremovable to federal court.[243]

However, not all jurisdictional references in statutes defeat diversity. For example, in a case involving a statute which stated that certain claims were to be brought in District of Columbia courts, both removal and original federal jurisdiction were still permitted.[244] Similarly, if diversity exists, the automatic stay provision in the bankruptcy law[245] does not authorize the district court to dismiss the civil action but only to await resolution of the bankruptcy court proceeding.[246]

§ 2.23 Substantive Considerations in Diversity Cases

Whenever a diversity case is filed, the *Erie*[247] doctrine requires that the appropriate state law be applied. Therefore, the state statute of limitations governs the action.[248] Similarly, state tolling rules which are an integral part of the statute of limitations are generally applied absent a direct conflict between a state and federal rule or countervailing federal considerations.[249]

Even if the plaintiffs claim diversity and have a judgment entered against them, they can raise lack of jurisdiction.[250] Although the court can allow discovery to determine if the plaintiffs' allegations controverting diversity are true,[251] an absence of diversity will cause the case to be dismissed. However, when a district court implicitly rejected a plaintiff's jurisdictional argument, the

---

[241] 28 U.S.C. § 1342 (1982); *see* Miller v. New York State Pub. Serv. Comm'n, 807 F.2d 28, 31 (2d Cir. 1986) (jurisdictional bar includes claims for compensatory damages as well as injunctive relief).

[242] Iowa Mut. Ins. Co. v. La Plante, _____ U.S. _____, 107 S. Ct. 971, 977–78 (1987).

[243] 28 U.S.C. § 1445(c) (1982).

[244] District of Columbia v. Transamerica Ins. Co., 797 F.2d 1041, 1046–47 (D.C. Cir. 1986).

[245] 11 U.S.C. § 362 (Supp. III 1985).

[246] Griffin v. Sandy Howard Prod., 800 F.2d 612 (6th Cir. 1986).

[247] Erie R.R. v. Tompkins, 304 U.S. 64, 79–80 (1938).

[248] Guaranty Trust Co. v. York, 326 U.S. 99, 109–12 (1945).

[249] Walker v. Armco Steel Corp., 446 U.S. 740, 751 (1980); *See* Cook v. G.D. Searle & Co., 759 F.2d 800, 802–03 (10th Cir. 1985).

[250] Rubin v. Buckman, 727 F.2d 71, 73 (3d Cir. 1984).

[251] *Id.*; see § **14.16**.

Second Circuit refused to permit a plaintiff on appeal to argue a theory which would have destroyed diversity, thereby escaping an unfavorable judgment.[252]

OTHER TYPES OF JURISDICTION

§ 2.24 Admiralty Jurisdiction

The federal courts have admiralty jurisdiction if a tort occurred on or over navigable waters and bore a significant relationship to traditional maritime activity.[253] An allegation of navigational error is key to finding admiralty jurisdiction when dealing with small pleasure crafts.[254] Product liability claims are cognizable under general maritime law, but no recovery is permitted for purely economic loss.[255] Most circuits do not extend jurisdiction to damage claims by land-based ship repair or construction workers for employment-related asbestos-induced disease.[256] However, even if maritime jurisdiction is not present, the court can decide the action if it has diversity jurisdiction.[257]

§ 2.25 Ancillary and Pendent Jurisdiction Generally

Ancillary and pendent jurisdiction enable the court to hear claims which do not satisfy federal jurisdictional requirements but are closely related to actions properly pending before the federal court. Their purpose is to avoid piecemeal litigation.[258] Ancillary jurisdiction typically involves claims by a defending

---

[252] Musico v. Champion Credit Corp., 764 F.2d 102, 108–10 (2d Cir. 1985).

[253] Executive Jet Aviation, Inc. v. City of Cleveland, 409 U.S. 249, 268 (1972); *see also* Foremost Ins. Co. v. Richardson, 457 U.S. 668, 674 (1982); Solano v. Beilby, 761 F.2d 1369, 1371 (9th Cir. 1985).

[254] Hogan v. Overman, 767 F.2d 1093, 1094 (4th Cir. 1985); *see* Medina v. Perez, 733 F.2d 170, 171 (1st Cir. 1984), *cert. denied,* 469 U.S. 1106 (1985).

[255] East River S.S. Corp. v. Transamerica Delaval Inc., _____U.S._____, 106 S. Ct. 2295, 2302–04 (1986).

[256] Drake v. Raymark Indus., 772 F.2d 1007, 1015–16 (1st Cir. 1985); *cert. denied,* _____U.S. _____, 106 S. Ct. 1994 (1986); Oman v. Johns-Mansville Corp., 764 F.2d 224, 227 (4th Cir.) (en banc), *cert. denied,* _____U.S._____, 106 S. Ct. 351 (1985); Harville v. Johns-Mansville Prods. Corp., 731 F.2d 775, 781 (11th Cir. 1984); Lowe v. Ingalls Shipbuilding, 723 F.2d 1173, 1187 (5th Cir. 1984); Keene Corp. v. United States, 700 F.2d 836, 844–45 (2d Cir.), *cert. denied,* 464 U.S. 864 (1983); Owen-Illinois, Inc. v. United States Dist. Ct., 698 F.2d 967, 970–71 (9th Cir. 1983).

[257] *See, e.g.,* May v. Transworld Drilling Co., 786 F.2d 1261, 1264 (5th Cir. 1986).

[258] *See generally* Teruya, *Ancillary and Pendent Jurisdiction of Federal Courts,* 31 Fed. Bar News & J. 154 (June 1984); Matasar, *A Pendent and Ancillary Jurisdiction Primer: The Scope and Limits of Supplemental Jurisdicion,* 17 U.C. Davis L. Rev. 103 (1983).

party hauled into court against its will, or by a nonparty whose rights might be irretrievably lost unless they can be asserted in the federal action.[259] Pendent jurisdiction usually applies when a plaintiff seeks to join a related state claim to its federal claim against the defendant.[260] Pendent party jurisdiction permits the related state claim to be brought against a nonparty to the federal claim.[261]

The Supreme Court has noted that these doctrines are "two species of the same generic problem."[262] Confusion between them have resulted in some courts' viewing the issue raised as problems of supplemental or incidental jurisdiction without otherwise labelling them.[263] Although the standards applied to ancillary and pendent jurisdiction are similar, the Supreme Court has not merged the two concepts.[264] Courts use a three-prong test, determining whether constitutional power exists to hear the claim, whether Congress has expressly or by implication negated the Court's exercise of jurisdiction, and whether the Court should exercise its power to hear the claim.[265] As a practical matter, some circuits are looking at the particular claim and its relationship to the jurisdictional tests proposed by the Supreme Court rather than the characterization of the claim as either ancillary or pendent.

§ 2.26 Ancillary Jurisdiction

The test for ancillary jurisdiction is whether the nonfederal claim arises from the same transaction or occurrence as the federal claim. Most courts interpret this to mean a logical relationship between the underlying claim and the claim

---

[259] Owen Equip. & Erection Co. v. Kroger, 437 U.S. 365, 376 (1978).

[260] *Id.* at 370.

[261] *See* Aldinger v. Howard, 427 U.S. 1, 18 (1976).

[262] Owen Equip. & Erection Co. v. Kroger, 437 U.S. 365, 370 (1978).

[263] *See* County of Oakland v. City of Berkeley, 742 F.2d 289, 296 (6th Cir. 1984); Birmingham Fire Ins. v. Winegardner & Hammons, 714 F.2d 548, 550 n.3 (5th Cir. 1983); Matasar, *A Pendent and Ancillary Jurisdicion Primer: The Scope and Limits of Supplemental Jurisdiction,* 17 U.C. Davis L. Rev. 103 (1983); Note, *A Closer Look at Pendent and Ancillary Jurisdiction: Toward a Theory of Incidental Jurisdiction,* 95 Harv. L. Rev. 1935 (1982).

[264] *See, e.g.,* Owen Equip. & Erection Co. v. Kroger, 437 U.S. 365, 370–74 (1978); Aldinger v. Howard, 427 U.S. 1, 14–15 (1976); United Mine Workers of Am. v. Gibbs, 383 U.S. 715, 725–26 (1966); *see generally* Miller, *Ancillary and Pendent Jurisdicion,* 26 S. Tex. L.J. 1 (1985); Note, *Developing A Unified Approach to Pendent and Ancillary Jurisdiction: A Merger Made in Heaven,* 11 Vt. L. Rev. 505 (1986).

[265] *See* Jones v. Intermountain Power Project, 794 F.2d 546, 551 (10th Cir. 1986); Ambromovage v. United Mine Workers of Am., 726 F.2d 972, 976 (3d Cir. 1984); *see also* United States v. City of Twin Falls, 806 F.2d 862, 867–68 (9th Cir. 1986); *see generally* Note, *Developing A Unified Approach to Pendent and Ancillary Jurisdiction: A Merger Made in Heaven,* 11 Vt. L. Rev. 505 (1986).

joined.[266] Most joinders permitted by the federal rules of civil procedure are considered as falling within the court's ancillary jurisdiction.[267] For example, nonfederal claims can be considered if they are compulsory counterclaims under Rule 13(a)[268] or cross-claims under Rule 13(g).[269] Ancillary jurisdiction is also available to impleaded third party defendants under Rule 14(a),[270] interpleaded parties under Rule 22[271] and intervenors as of right under Rule 24(a).[272] Ancillary jurisdiction has even been exercised over claims involving attorney-client fee disputes.[273] It is unclear whether the court has any discretion to refuse to accept jurisdiction over a claim falling within its ancillary jurisdiction.[274]

On the other hand, permissive counterclaims alleging affirmative relief[275] and permissive joinder of parties under Rule 20 do not fit within ancillary jurisdiction, because they are not required for a fair evaluation of the action. Absent indispensable parties under Rule 19 and permissive intervenors under Rule 24(b)[276] also do not fall within ancillary jurisdiction. In addition, the Supreme Court has limited ancillary jurisdiction over nondiverse parties in diversity actions.[277] Not only must the nondiverse claim arise from the same core of operative facts as does the diverse claim, but it must also bear a logical relationship to that claim.[278] In addition, a plaintiff in a diversity action cannot assert a claim against a third party defendant when there is no independent basis for federal jurisdiction.[279]

---

[266] Matasar, *A Pendent and Ancillary Jurisdiction Primer: The Scope and Limits of Supplemental Jurisdiction,* 17 U.C. Davis L. Rev. 103, 149 (1983).

[267] *Id.* at 144; *see* Owen Equip. & Erection Co. v. Kroger, 437 U.S. 365, 375 & n.18 (1978); *see generally* 3A Moore's Federal Practice ¶ 22.15; 13 Federal Practice and Procedure § 3523.

[268] *E.g.,* Finkle v. Gulf & W. Mfg. Co., 744 F.2d 1015, 1018 (3d Cir. 1984); Crouse-Hinds Co. v. Internorth, Inc., 634 F.2d 690, 699–700 (2d Cir. 1980).

[269] *E.g.,* American Nat'l Bank & Trust Co. v. Bailey, 750 F.2d 577, 581 (7th Cir. 1984), *cert. denied,* 471 U.S. 1100 (1985); *see* Allstate Ins. Co. v. James, 779 F.2d 1536, 1539 (11th Cir. 1986).

[270] Finkle v. Gulf & W. Mfg. Co., 744 F.2d 1015, 1018 (3d Cir. 1984) and cases cited therein (third party impleader).

[271] *See* Eagerton v. Valuations, Inc., 698 F.2d 1115, 1119 n.8 (11th Cir. 1983).

[272] Curtis v. Sears, Roebuck & Co., 754 F.2d 781, 784 (8th Cir. 1985) (intervenor).

[273] *See* Novinger v. E.I. DuPont de Nemours & Co., 809 F.2d 212, 217–18 (3d Cir. 1987) (surveying case law).

[274] *See* Matasar, *A Pendent and Ancillary Jurisdiction Primer: The Scope and Limits of Supplemental Jurisdicion,* 17 U.C. Davis L. Rev. 103, 184 (1983); Miller, *Ancillary and Pendent Jurisdiction,* 26 S. Tex. L.J. 1, 7 (1985).

[275] Federman v. Empire Fire & Marine Ins. Co., 597 F.2d 798, 812 (2d Cir. 1979); *see* EEOC v. Nevada Resort Ass'n, 792 F.2d 882, 886 (9th Cir. 1986).

[276] *See generally* 13 Federal Practice and Procedure § 3523.

[277] *See* Owen Equip. & Erection Co. v. Kroger, 437 U.S. 365, 377 (1978).

[278] *Id.* at 376.

[279] *Id.* at 370; *see also* Travelers Ins. Co. v. First Nat'l Bank, 675 F.2d 633, 638–40 (5th Cir. 1982).

§ 2.27 Dismissal of Ancillary Claims

Some circuits apply the criteria set forth in *United Mine Workers of America v. Gibbs*[280] to permit the court to exercise discretion whether to retain jurisdiction over ancillary claims after dismissal of the underlying action.[281] These courts focus on judicial economy, fairness (particularly as to statute of limitations questions), convenience to litigants, and novelty or difficulty of state law issues.[282] The Supreme Court has long permitted a compulsory counterclaim arising out of an antitrust claim to be retained in federal court after the antitrust action is dismissed for failure to state a claim.[283] Similarly, courts have discretion to retain ancillary jurisdiction of a compulsory counterclaim or a claim brought by virtue of an intervention of right after the principal claim has settled.[284] Some dispute exists as to whether a court has jurisdiction over ancillary claims when the main action is dismissed for lack of subject matter jurisdiction.[285]

§ 2.28 Pendent Jurisdiction

Pendent jurisdiction exists when both a state claim and a substantial federal claim derive from a common nucleus of operative fact and are such that the plaintiff would ordinarily be expected to try them all in one judicial proceeding.[286] It is unclear whether the common nucleus of operative fact approach is more limited than the transaction or occurrence test for ancillary jurisdiction.[287] As a practical matter, most courts seem to require only a minimal factual overlap for pendent jurisdiction.[288] Both constitutional and statutory constraints exist when determining whether the federal court has jurisdiction over an ancillary

---

[280] 383 U.S. 715, 726 (1966).

[281] *See, e.g.*, United States v. Zima, 766 F.2d 1153, 1158 (7th Cir. 1985). *See also* United States v. City of Twin Falls, 806 F.2d 862, 868 (9th Cir. 1986); Stamford Bd. of Educ. v. Stamford Educ. Ass'n, 697 F.2d 70, 72 (2d Cir. 1982).

[282] United States v. Zima, 766 F.2d 1153, 1158–59 (7th Cir. 1985); *see* United Mine Workers of Am. v. Gibbs, 383 U.S. 715, 726 (1966).

[283] Moore v. New York Cotton Exch., 270 U.S. 593, 608–09 (1926).

[284] Curtis v. Sears, Roebuck & Co., 754 F.2d 781, 784 (8th Cir. 1985); *see* Cenco Inc. v. Seidman & Seidman, 686 F.2d 449, 452 (7th Cir. 1982) (Rule 13(g) cross-claim can be heard if main claim not dismissed before trial).

[285] *See* Waste Sys., Inc. v. Clean Air Water Corp., 683 F.2d 927, 930 (5th Cir. 1982) and cases cited therein.

[286] United Mine Workers of Am. v. Gibbs, 383 U.S. 715, 725 (1966).

[287] Matasar, *A Pendent and Ancillary Jurisdiction Primer: The Scope and Limits of Supplemental Jurisdiction,* 17 U.C. Davis L. Rev. 103, 129–34 (1983).

[288] *Id.* at 130–34.

claim or should retain a pendent claim.[289] However, a state cannot limit the pendent jurisdiction of the federal court by a state statute limiting the claimant's remedies.[290]

After the court determines it has power to adjudicate a pendent claim, it must engage in a second inquiry to determine whether to exercise its power.[291] Factors weighing against the assumption of jurisdiction include the possibility of jury confusion,[292] the existence of novel and difficult questions of state law,[293] whether the state issues substantially predominate, the convenience of the litigants, and general considerations of judicial economy and comity.[294] Although it has been considered unusual for a court to decline to exercise pendent jurisdiction when it exists,[295] some district courts have dismissed pendent claims prior to disposition of the claim providing federal jurisdiction.[296] In fact, a number of circuits reject pendent jurisdiction of related state claims if the only substantive federal claim arises under Title VII.[297]

§ 2.29 Dismissal of Pendent Claims

If the district court dismisses the plaintiff's federal claim before trial, the Supreme Court indicated in *United Mine Workers of America v. Gibbs* that the state claims should also be dismissed.[298] However, in *Rosado v. Wyman,* [299] the Supreme Court held that a district judge has the power to decide a pendent claim which arises out of the same facts as the dismissed federal action.[300] Some circuits are generally hostile to the retention of pendent claims.[301] Nevertheless,

[289] *See* Aldinger v. Howard, 427 U.S. 1, 18 (1976); Owen Equip. & Erection Co. v. Kroger, 437 U.S. 365, 372 (1978).

[290] Thompkins v. Stuttgart School Dist. No. 22, 787 F.2d 439, 441 (8th Cir. 1986).

[291] United Mine Workers of Am. v. Gibbs, 383 U.S. 715, 726 (1966); Dimond v. District of Columbia, 792 F.2d 179, 188 (D.C. Cir. 1986).

[292] Moor v. County of Alameda, 411 U.S. 693, 716–17 (1973); United Mine Workers of Am. v. Gibbs, 383 U.S. 715, 726 (1966).

[293] *See* Hagans v. Lavine, 415 U.S. 528, 548 (1973).

[294] United Mine Workers of Am. v. Gibbs, 383 U.S. 715, 726 (1966); Dimond v. District of Columbia, 792 F.2d 179, 188 (D.C. Cir. 1986).

[295] Phillips v. Smalley Maintenance Servs., Inc., 711 F.2d 1524, 1531 (11th Cir. 1983).

[296] *See* 13B Federal Practice and Procedure, § 3567.1.

[297] Bouchet v. National Urban League, Inc., 730 F.2d 799, 805 (D.C. Cir. 1984).*But see* Jones v. Intermountain Power Project, 794 F.2d 546, 553 (10th Cir. 1986).

[298] 383 U.S. 715, 726 (1966); *see also* Koke v. Stifel, Nicolaus & Co., 620 F.2d 1340, 1346–47 (8th Cir. 1980) (summary judgment on federal claim); *see generally* 3A Moore's Federal Practice § 18.07[1–3].

[299] 397 U.S. 397 (1970).

[300] *Id.* at 404–05; *see* Christy v. Cambron, 710 F.2d 669, 672 n.2 (10th Cir. 1983).

[301] *See, e.g.,* Durham v. Kelly, 810 F.2d 1500, 1506 (9th Cir. 1987); LaPorte Constr. Co. v. Bayshore Nat'l Bank, 805 F.2d 1254, 1257 (5th Cir. 1986); Province v. Cleveland Press Pub. Co., 787 F.2d 1047, 1055 (6th Cir. 1986).

if the statute of limitations has run on the pendent claim, jurisdiction usually is retained.[302]

If the federal action has been dismissed at the time when the plaintiff seeks leave to add a pendent claim by amendment, jurisdiction over the additional action is not appropriate.[303] Similarly, if subject matter jurisdiction over the original federal claim was lacking, the pendent state claims must be dismissed without prejudice.[304] Courts also dismiss pendent claims if the main action was dismissed under the abstention doctrine.[305] The district court's dismissal of pendent claims is judged on an abuse of discretion standard.[306]

§ 2.30 Pendent Party Jurisdiction

Pendent jurisdiction to add new parties over whom there is no independent basis of federal jurisdiction is more limited than pendent jurisdiction to add claims between parties with respect to whom federal jurisdiction exists.[307] The Supreme Court has held that a state claim could not be the basis for joining a party over whom no independent federal jurisdiction existed simply because it derived from the common nucleus of facts pertaining to a federal claim.[308] Similarly, pendent party jurisdiction has been rejected for identical claims.[309] Pendent party jurisdiction is also unavailable in class actions to aggregate damages,[310] which results in the dismissal of class members who have insufficient damages.[311] The circuits vary in their approach toward pendent party jurisdiction; several circuits reject the doctrine.[312] Even within a circuit, differences may

---

[302] *See* United Beverage Co. v. Indiana Alcoholic Beverage Comm'n, 760 F.2d 155, 160 (7th Cir. 1985); *cf.* Prater v. United Mine Workers of Am., 793 F.2d 1201, 1208 (11th Cir. 1986) (abuse to dismiss pendent party claim when statute of limitations had expired). *But see* Ottensmeyer v. Chesapeake & Potomac Tel. Co., 756 F.2d 986, 994 n.14 (4th Cir. 1985) (discretion of trial judge).

[303] Baer v. R & F Coal Co., 782 F.2d 600, 603 (6th Cir. 1986).

[304] Dunton v. County of Suffolk, 729 F.2d 903, 910–11 (2d Cir. 1984).

[305] *See* Hefner v. Alexander, 779 F.2d 277, 281–82 (5th Cir. 1985).

[306] *Id.;* L.A. Draper & Son v. Wheelabrator-Frye, Inc., 735 F.2d 414, 420 (11th Cir. 1984).

[307] *See e.g.*, Aldinger v. Howard, 427 U.S. 1, 18 (1976).

[308] *Id.* at 9. (Insofar as *Aldinger* denied pendent jurisdiction of a state claim against a county it has been overruled. *See Owen Equip. & Erection Co. v. Kroger,* 437 U.S. 365, 373 n.12 (1978)).

[309] Sarnoff v. American Home Prods. Corp., 798 F.2d 1075, 1079 (7th Cir. 1986); *see* Zahn v. International Paper Co., 414 U.S. 291, 292 (1973).

[310] *See* Snyder v. Harris, 394 U.S. 332, 339–40 (1969).

[311] *See* Zahn v. International Paper Co., 414 U.S. 291, 292 (1973).

[312] *Compare* Carpenters S. Cal. Admin. v. D & L Camp Constr., 738 F.2d 999, 1000 (9th Cir. 1984) *and* Hixon v. Sherwin-Williams Co., 671 F.2d 1005, 1008–09 (7th Cir. 1982) (refusal to allow additional parties under pendent jurisdiction) *with* Lykins v. Pointer Inc., 725 F.2d 645, 647–49 (11th Cir. 1984) (permitted pendent party jurisdiction in 28 U.S.C. § 1346(b) action) *and* Weinberger v. Kendrick, 698 F.2d 61, 76–77 (2d Cir. 1982), *cert. denied,* 464 U.S. 818 (1983)

emerge, such as the rejection of pendent party jurisdiction in diversity cases and its acceptance in federal question litigation.[313]

SANCTIONS

§ 2.31 Sanctions for Improper Assertions of Jurisdiction

Rule 11, which requires counsel to certify after reasonable inquiry that the pleadings are well grounded in fact and law,[314] applies to jurisdictional allegations. Sanctions have been imposed when it appears that an attempt has been made to create jurisdiction where it does not exist or that no good faith effort was made to determine if federal jurisdiction was proper.[315] Therefore, when jurisdiction is questionable, counsel must not only consider possible statute of limitations consequences of a wrong guess but must also recognize that the adverse party can be awarded attorneys' fees if the complaint violates Rule 11.

CHECKLIST

§ 2.32 Jurisdiction Checklist

Justiciability

1. Is there a substantial controversy?

2. Do the parties have adverse legal interests?

3. Is there a concrete (rather than hypothetical) dispute?

4. Does plaintiff have standing to sue?

- **a.** Can plaintiff prove an injury in fact?
  - **(1)** Was there an actual or threatened injury?
  - **(2)** Was the injury caused by the challenged action of the defendant?
  - **(3)** Can the injury be redressed by a favorable decision?

(permitted pendent party jurisdiction in consolidated state and federal class action); *see generally* Note, *Unravelling the Pendent Party Controversy: A Revisionist Approach to Pendent and Ancillary Jurisdiction,* 64 B.U.L. Rev. 895 (1985).

313 *See* Graf v. Elgin, Joliet & E. Ry., 790 F.2d 1341, 1342 (7th Cir. 1986).

314 See **ch. 28**.

315 Fitzgerald v. Seaboard Sys. R.R., 760 F.2d 1249, 1251 (11th Cir. 1985); *see* Rubin v. Buckman, 727 F.2d 71, 73 (3d Cir. 1984).

   b. If injunctive relief is sought, is there a credible threat of recurrent injury?
   c. Can standing be shown by association or third party?

5. Is the action moot?
   a. Are the issues still live?
   b. Do the parties still have a legal interest in the outcome?
   c. Can the injury be recompensed by the relief requested?
   d. Is it likely that the injury will recur?

6. Is the time ripe for consideration of the claim by the court?
   a. Would withholding consideration cause hardship to the parties?
   b. Have administrative procedures been followed and remedies exhausted?

7. Does the dispute involve a political question which concerns different branches of government?

Abstention Issues

1. Does the case involve difficult state law questions of public policy, or would federal review interfere with state policy (*Burford* abstention)?

2. Are there unsettled state law questions which must be resolved before the federal question can be decided (*Pullman* abstention)?

3. Is there an ongoing state judicial proceeding in which the federal question might be raised (*Younger* abstention)?

4. Do exceptional circumstances (e.g., parallel litigation) justify abstention on the basis of judicial economy (*Colorado River/Moses H. Cone* abstention)?
   a. Is the federal forum inconvenient?
   b. Should piecemeal litigation be avoided?
   c. Is state law controlling?
   d. Does the state action adequately protect the federal plaintiff's right?
   e. How are the state and federal actions progressing relative to one another?
   f. Is there concurrent jurisdiction?
   g. Is removal available?
   h. Is the federal claim vexatious or contrived?

Eleventh Amendment Limitations

1. Is the essential nature of the proceeding an action against a state by its own citizens or the citizens of another state?

2. Is the entity being sued entitled to immunity?
   a. How will the court view the entity's powers and characteristics?
   b. Does state law view it as an arm of the state?
   c. What is its source of funding?
   d. Is it locally autonomous?
   e. Is it primarily concerned with local or statewide problems?
   f. Can it sue and be sued in its own name, and can it hold property?
3. Do any claims under federal statutes (such as Title VII) override Eleventh Amendment immunity?

Comity

1. Is it likely that the federal court will decline jurisdiction due to considerations of comity?
   a. Is this a domestic relations issue?
   b. Is this a probate matter?

Subject Matter

1. Has jurisdiction been conferred in the specific area by statute (e.g., admiralty or bankruptcy)?

Federal Questions

1. Does the claim arise under U.S. Constitution, statues, common law, treaties, or federal common law?
2. If the claim arises under a state statute, can the federal element in the claim be described as *basic, necessary, pivotal, substantial, direct and essential,* or *paramount*?
3. Can the federal question be determined from the plaintiff's complaint alone (well-pleaded complaint rule)?
4. If not, is the state cause of action preempted by federal law (artful pleading)?

Diversity

1. Does the amount in controversy exceed $10,000?
2. Is the citizenship of all plaintiffs diverse from that of any defendant?
   a. Is a nondiverse party omitted from the complaint?
   b. Are the parties aligned according to their real interests?

   - **c.** Determine the effect of alien as party.
   - **d.** Determine the effect of Does as parties (e.g., if sham, they will not defeat diversity).
   - **e.** If federal government is a defendant, has it waived its sovereign immunity?
3. What is each party's domicile at the time of the suit, as determined by:
   - **a.** Current residence
   - **b.** Voting registration
   - **c.** Location of real and personal property
   - **d.** Location of brokerage and bank accounts
   - **e.** Location of spouse and family
   - **f.** Place of employment or business
   - **g.** Driver's license and auto registration
   - **h.** Jurisdiction where taxes are paid
   - **i.** Intent to remain?
4. If an out-of-state administrator is a party, does that individual's presence meet one of the following tests (to avoid collusive joinder):
   - **a.** Motive-function: Does the administrator have any duty or function beyond creating diversity?
   - **b.** Substantial stakes: Does the administrator have a substantial stake in the outcome?
5. If a corporation is a party,
   - **a.** Where is it incorporated?
   - **b.** Where is its principal place of business?
     - **(1)** Determine applicable test, e.g., nerve center.
     - **(2)** State both locations in complaint.
6. What is the citizenship of each member of a limited partnership or unincorporated association? (Check your circuit's treatment of which members are considered.)
7. Are there any other limitations in meeting diversity (e.g., class actions, derivative actions, state public utility rates)?
8. What are the applicable state statute of limitations and tolling rules?

Ancillary and Pendent Jurisdiction

1. Does the nonfederal claim arise from the same transaction or occurrence as the federal claim? I.e., is there a logical relationship between the two claims (ancillary jurisdiction)?
2. Are both state and federal claims derived from a common nucleus of operative fact (pendent jurisdiction)?

3. Is it likely that federal claim will be terminated before trial, resulting in dismissal of pendent claims?

Complaint

1. Allege statute or other ground supporting jurisdiction.
2. In diversity cases, allege:
   a. Citizenship, not residence.
   b. Corporation's place of incorporation and principal place of business.
   c. Amount in controversy.
3. Request amendment to correct technical pleading deficiency.

Rule 11

1. After reasonable inquiry, can the attorney certify that the pleadings are well grounded in law and fact?

Timing

1. Lack of jurisdiction can be raised at any time.
2. Party opposing jurisdiction can delay raising issue until statute of limitations has run.

CHAPTER 3

REMOVING THE ACTION FROM STATE COURT

§ 3.1 Removal Jurisdiction and Procedures

Removal jurisdiction offers a defendant the benefits of a federal forum when the plaintiff has chosen a state or District of Columbia court.[1] Usually, the defendant makes a tactical decision to remove based on an assessment of the advantages and disadvantages of being in federal rather than state court.[2] Often, the main consideration in removal is the transfer of the entire action to a more convenient location,[3] for example, to the city in which defense counsel practices. Because the underlying rationale of removal in diversity cases is to protect defendants from local prejudice, only defendants who are not citizens of the state in which the action is brought can remove an action.[4] Therefore, removal is improper whenever any defendant is local.[5] Federal questions are removable without regard to citizenship.[6]

§ 3.2 Federal Questions: The Well Pleaded Complaint and Artful Pleading

Removal jurisdiction is determined by reference to the well pleaded complaint rule, which prohibits removal from being predicated on a federal defense[7] or a counterclaim.[8] In essence, the federal question must be obvious from the nature of the plaintiff's claim. Therefore, an action cannot be removed even if both parties admit that the defense of federal preemption is the only question truly at

---

[1] 28 U.S.C. §§ 1441, 1451 (1982).

[2] See **ch. 1**.

[3] 28 U.S.C. § 1404(a); *see, e.g.,* Abels v. State Farm Fire & Casualty Co., 707 F.2d 26 (3d Cir. 1985) (case removed in California, transferred to Pennsylvania, ordered remanded to original state court); *see generally* 1A J. Moore *et al.* Moore's Federal Practice, ¶ 0.157[10.-2] (2d ed. 1987) [hereinafter Moore's Federal Practice]; **ch. 6**.

[4] 28 U.S.C. § 1441(b) (1982).

[5] McKay v. Boyd Constr. Co., 769 F.2d 1084, 1087 (5th Cir. 1985); Percherski v. General Motors Corp., 636 F.2d 1156, 1160 (8th Cir. 1981); *see generally* 14A C. Wright, A. Miller, *et al.,* Federal Practice and Procedure § 3723 (2d ed. 1985) [hereinafter Federal Practice and Procedure].

[6] 28 U.S.C. § 1441(b) (1982).

[7] Merrell Dow Pharmaceuticals Inc. v. Thompson, ____ U.S. ____, 106 S. Ct. 3229, 3232 (1986); Franchise Tax Bd. v. Construction Laborer's Vacation Trust, 463 U.S. 1, 9–10 (1983); *see generally* Comment, *Federal Preemption, Removal Jurisdiction and the Well-Pleaded Complaint Rule,* 51 U. Chi. L. Rev. 634 (1984).

[8] Takeda v. Northwestern Nat'l Life Ins. Co., 765 F.2d 815, 822 (9th Cir. 1985); La Chemise Lacoste v. Alligator Co., 506 F.2d 339, 343–45 (3d Cir. 1974), *cert. denied,* 421 U.S. 937 (1975); *see generally* 1A Moore's Federal Practice ¶ 0.160[3].

issue in the case.[9] Similarly, if a claim would arise only as a defense to a state-created action, the federal court does not have jurisdiction if the claim is brought as a declaratory judgment.[10]

In exceptional circumstances, a federal court will not permit a plaintiff's artful pleading to disguise the real nature of the claim.[11] In other words, a federal claim artfully pleaded in terms of state law is still removable.[12] Therefore, if a federal cause of action completely preempts a state cause of action, as in many labor law questions, any complaint that comes within the scope of the federal cause of action will be removable even if the plaintiff cites only state law.[13] For example, the Supreme Court rejected a plaintiff's claim that his suit was founded upon a breach of contract and recharacterized the complaint as being preempted by § 301(a) of the Labor Management Relations Act[14] because the plaintiff actually sought to enjoin a labor strike which allegedly violated a collective bargaining agreement.[15] Similarly, an action brought in tort which omitted a union as a defendant and made no reference to federal labor law was held removable when the employer was being sued for wrongful discharge in violation of a collective bargaining agreement.[16] However, even some labor law issues are not within the scope of preemption.[17] Banking law is also not considered exclusively federal, thereby prohibiting removal of an action based solely on state law.[18] In contrast, the Supreme Court has held that a former employee could

---

[9] Franchise Tax Bd. v. Construction Laborer's Vacation Trust, 463 U.S. 1, 12 (1983); *see generally* Collins, *The Unhappy History of Federal Question Removal,* 71 Iowa L. Rev. 717 (1986).

[10] Franchise Tax Bd. v. Construction Laborer's Vacation Trust, 463 U.S. 1, 10 (1983) (state declaratory judgment action); Skelly Oil v. Phillips Petroleum Co., 339 U.S. 667, 671–72 (1950) (federal declaratory judgment action); *see generally* 10A Federal Practice and Procedure § 2767.

[11] Federated Dep't Stores, Inc. v. Moitie, 452 U.S. 394, 397 (1981); Hunter v. United Van Lines, 746 F.2d 635, 640–44 (9th Cir. 1984), *cert. denied,* ____ U.S. ____, 106 S. Ct. 180 (1985); Eitmann v. New Orleans Pub. Serv., Inc., 730 F.2d 359, 365–66 (5th Cir.), *cert. denied,* 419 U.S. 1018 (1984); *see generally* 14A Federal Practice and Procedure § 3722.

[12] 14A Federal Practice and Procedure § 3722, at 266–79.

[13] *See* Franchise Tax Bd. v. Construction Laborer's Vacation Trust, 463 U.S. 1, 22 (1983); Note, *Removal Doctrine Reaffirmed: Franchise Tax Board v. Construction Laborers Vacations Trust,* 70 Cornell L. Rev. 557 (1985).

[14] 29 U.S.C. § 185(a) (1982).

[15] Avco Corp. v. Aero Lodge No. 735, 390 U.S. 557, 558–59 (1968); *see generally* Twitchell, *Characterizing Federal Claims: Preemption, Removal and the Arising-Under Jurisdiction of the Federal Courts,* 54 Geo. Wash. L. Rev. 812 (1986).

[16] *See* Johnson v. Hussmann Corp., 805 F.2d 795, 797 (8th Cir. 1986).

[17] *See* Williams v. Caterpillar Tractor Co., 786 F.2d 928, 935–37 (9th Cir. 1986).

[18] United Jersey Banks v. Parell, 783 F.2d 360, 368–69 (3d Cir. 1986), *cert. denied,* ____ U.S. ____, 106 S. Ct. 2892 (1986).

not preclude removal based on § 502(a) of ERISA by simply alleging state claims for breach of contract and wrongful termination of disability benefits, since such claims were displaced by ERISA.[19]

One approach to determining if a state law claim is completely preempted is a two-step inquiry[20] which first looks to whether federal law provides the plaintiff with a remedy for the state cause of action and, if so, decides if the state's law has been preempted.[21]

§ 3.3 Jurisdictional Requirements

Removal statutes are strictly construed,[22] with all doubts resolved against removal.[23] Federal jurisdiction must exist in order to remove a case,[24] and the burden of establishing such jurisdiction rests with the party seeking removal.[25] Therefore, either diversity jurisdiction, including an amount in controversy exceeding $10,000, or a federal question must be present at the time the action is removed to federal court.[26] Some circuits require the district court to verify the existence of subject matter jurisdiction when a case is removed on the basis of diversity[27] and review the district court's determination de novo.[28] Removal petitions have been reviewed to clarify whether the action is within federal jurisdiction,[29] particularly to determine if the complaint has been artfully

---

[19] Metropolitan Life Ins. Co. v. Taylor, ____ U.S. ____, 107 S. Ct. 1542, 55 U.S.L.W. 4468, 4470 (Apr. 7, 1987).

[20] Williams v. Caterpillar Tractor Co., 786 F.2d 928, 932–33 (9th Cir. 1986).

[21] Sorosky v. Burroughs Corp., 798 F.2d 1274, 1277 (9th Cir. 1986).

[22] Shamrock Oil & Gas Corp. v. Sheets, 313 U.S. 100, 108–09 (1941).

[23] Abels v. State Farm Fire & Casualty Co., 770 F.2d 26, 29 (3d Cir. 1985); Fajen v. Foundation Reserve Ins. Co., 683 F.2d 331, 333 (10th Cir. 1982); 14 Federal Practice and Procedure § 2642, at 149.

[24] Merrell Dow Pharmaceuticals Inc. v. Thompson, ____ U.S. ____, 106 S. Ct. 3229, 3232 (1986).

[25] Steel Valley Auth. v. Union Switch & Signal Div., 809 F.2d 1006, 1010 (3d Cir. 1987); Wilson v. Republic Iron & Steel Co., 257 U.S. 92, 97 (1921); Miller v. Grgurich, 763 F.2d 372, 373 (9th Cir. 1985).

[26] Pullman Co. v. Jenkins, 305 U.S. 534, 537 (1939); Miller v. Grgurich, 763 F.2d 372, 373 (9th Cir. 1985); 14A Federal Practice and Procedure § 3723, at 311; see **ch. 2**.

[27] *See, e.g.,* Allen v. Ferguson, 791 F.2d 611, 615 (7th Cir. 1986).

[28] Takeda v. Northwestern Nat'l Life Ins. Co., 765 F.2d 815, 818 (9th Cir. 1985).

[29] *See, e.g.,* Comment, *Intimations of Federal Removal Jurisdiction in Labor Cases: The Pleading Nexus,* 1981 Duke L.J. 743; 14 Federal Practice and Procedure, § 3733, at 533 (1985); *cf.* Charles D. Bonanno Linen Serv., Inc. v. McCarthy, 708 F.2d 1, 3–4 (1st Cir.), *cert. denied,* 464 U.S. 936 (1983) (discussing case law permitting outside materials, but presuming adequacy of allegation).

pleaded.[30] Similarly, even if the defendant's citizenship does not appear in the complaint, diversity can be established by reference to the information supplied in the petition.[31]

The removal statute has been amended to permit a federal court to hear a claim even though no jurisdiction existed in the state court prior to removal.[32] This means that, if a case falling within the federal court's exclusive jurisdiction is improperly brought in state court, it can be removed, although jurisdiction was originally absent in state court. Removal under 28 U.S.C. § 1441 is improper if a state agency is the defendant, since the Eleventh Amendment bars the exercise of federal jurisdiction unless the state has authorized suit in federal court.[33]

Some post-removal events can have an effect on jurisdiction.[34] For example, the addition of a nondiverse party defendant after removal has been held to defeat federal jurisdiction and require a remand,[35] although leave to amend to add nondiverse parties will usually be denied.[36] Similarly, the omission of an indispensable party which would destroy diversity defeats removal, even though diversity existed at the time the petition was filed.[37] If complete diversity does not exist, several circuits consider removal improper even if the plaintiff attempts to dismiss the nondiverse party, unless the district court finds that the complaint did not state a cause of action against that party.[38]

If removal is based on a federal question, the court acquires jurisdiction over pendent state law claims regardless of whether the federal claim is later dismissed.[39] However, once the federal defendant upon whom removal was premised is dismissed, the district court has discretion to retain the action,[40] although at least one circuit views the exercise of such jurisdiction as improper.[41]

---

[30] Williams v. Caterpillar Tractor Co., 786 F.2d 928, 931 n.1 (9th Cir. 1986).

[31] Schroeder v. Trans World Airlines, Inc., 702 F.2d 189, 191 (9th Cir. 1983).

[32] Pub. L. No. 99–336, § 3(a), 100 Stat. 637 (effective June 19, 1986), to be codified at 28 U.S.C. § 1441(e).

[33] McKay v. Boyd Constr. Co., 769 F.2d 1084, 1086 (5th Cir. 1985); *see* Pennhurst State School & Hosp. v. Halderman, 465 U.S. 89, 99 n.9 (1984).

[34] *See* IMFC Professional v. Latin Am. Home Health, 676 F.2d 152, 156–58 (5th Cir. 1982).

[35] Desert Empire Bank v. Insurance Co. of N. Am., 623 F.2d 1371, 1374 (9th Cir. 1980).

[36] *See* 14A Federal Practice and Procedure § 3739.

[37] Takeda v. Northwestern Nat'l Life Ins. Co., 765 F.2d 815, 819 (9th Cir. 1985); *see* Steel Valley Auth. v. Union Switch & Signal Div., 809 F.2d 1006, 1010–11 (3d Cir. 1987).

[38] McKay v. Boyd Constr. Co., 769 F.2d 1084, 1087 (5th Cir. 1985); Coker v. Amoco Oil Co., 709 F.2d 1433, 1440 (11th Cir. 1983).

[39] Salveson v. Western States Bankcard Ass'n, 731 F.2d 1423, 1430 (9th Cir. 1984); *see* Rosado v. Wyman, 397 U.S. 397, 405 (1970); see §§ **2.28–2.29**.

[40] Bushman v. Seiler, 755 F.2d 653, 654 (8th Cir. 1985); Falls Riverway Realty, Inc. v. City of Niagara Falls, 732 F.2d 38, 42 (2d Cir. 1984); *see* United Mine Workers of Am. v. Gibbs, 383 U.S. 715, 725–28 (1966); *see generally* 1A Moore's Federal Practice ¶ 0.154[1]; 14A Federal Practice and Procedure § 3739.

[41] *See, e.g.*, Wren v. Sletten Constr. Co., 654 F.2d 529, 536 (9th Cir. 1982).

§ 3.4 Independent Claims

The entire action can be removed when a separate and independent claim which would be removable, if sued upon alone, is joined with nonremovable claims or causes of action.[42] The district court has discretion whether to determine all issues or remand matters not within its original jurisdiction.[43] The utility of this provision has been questioned,[44] and it is construed narrowly to reduce the number of cases removable from state to federal court.[45]

Generally, diversity cases cannot be removed pursuant to this provision, since claims arising from a single wrong to the plaintiff are not separate and independent.[46] Most courts agree that third party claims cannot be removed under this provision.[47] Some litigants have argued that a federal claim, such as RICO, which is joined with state fraud claims against the same defendant cannot be removed because it is subject to the § 1441(c) requirement that removal is proper only if the claims are separate and independent.[48]

§ 3.5 Removal by the United States

Removal is also available to any officer of the United States or any agency thereof.[49] 28 U.S.C. § 1442(a)(1) grants an independent jurisdictional ground to cases involving federal officers which a district court would not otherwise have the power to hear.[50] Courts have interpreted this section broadly to allow federal agencies to remove when sued in state court.[51] The right of removal is considered absolute for conduct performed under color of federal office.[52]

---

[42] 28 U.S.C. § 1441(c) (1982); *see generally* 1A Moore's Federal Practice ¶ 0.163.

[43] *Id.*

[44] Thomas v. Shelton, 740 F.2d 478, 483 (7th Cir. 1984).

[45] McKay v. Boyd Constr. Co., 769 F.2d 1084, 1087 (5th Cir. 1985).

[46] Gardner & Florence Call Cowles Found. v. Empire, Inc., 754 F.2d 478, 481 (2d Cir. 1985); *see* American Fire & Casualty Co. v. Finn, 341 U.S. 6, 13–14 (1951); *see generally* 14A Federal Practice and Procedure § 3724.

[47] Comment, *Third Party Removal of an Entire Case: Who Can Remove, Who Cannot,* 41 Wash. & Lee L. Rev. 1533, 1540 (1984); Comment, *Third-Party Removal under Section 1441(c),* 52 Fordham L. Rev. 133, 134 (1983); *see generally* 1A Moore's Federal Practice ¶ 0.167[10]; 14A Federal Practice and Procedure § 3724. *Compare* Thomas v. Shelton, 740 F.2d 478, 488 (7th Cir. 1984) (denying third party removals) *with* Carl Heck Eng'rs v. Lafourche Parish Police Jury, 622 F.2d 133, 135–36 (5th Cir. 1980) (permitting third party removal).

[48] *See* Smith, *Removal and Remand: Unraveling the Mysteries,* 8 CEB Civ. Litig. Rep. 277, 281–83 (Dec. 1986). *But see* Thomas v. Shelton, 740 F.2d 478, 483 (7th Cir. 1984).

[49] 28 U.S.C. § 1442(a) (1) (1982).

[50] Loftin v. Rush, 767 F.2d 800, 904 (11th Cir. 1985); 1A Moore's Federal Practice § 0.164[1].

[51] District of Columbia v. Merit Sys. Protection Bd., 762 F.2d 129, 131 n.2 (D.C. Cir. 1985).

[52] Arizona v. Manypenny, 451 U.S. 232, 242 (1981).

Therefore, the fact that the federal officials are sued in their individual capacities and their acts are alleged to have been maliciously motivated does not defeat removal.[53]

This section also covers all cases in which federal officers can raise a colorable defense arising out of their duty to enforce federal law.[54] For example, a contempt action against a federal official for failure to comply with a state court order is removable.[55] However, several circuits do not extend such jurisdiction to garnishment cases in which the government is merely a stakeholder and not a real party in interest.[56]

§ 3.6 Removal in Civil Rights Actions

Civil rights actions can be removed by a defendant who is denied or cannot enforce in state court a right under any law providing for equal civil rights.[57] A defendant can also remove a civil case concerning any act under color of authority derived from any law providing for equal rights, or for refusing to do any act on the ground that it would be inconsistent with such law. The statute's seemingly expansive jurisdictional grant has been narrowly construed by the Supreme Court.[58]

§ 3.7 Venue

The only venue which is relevant to removal jurisdiction is the district or division where the state action is pending.[59] Therefore, a case can be removed to a district in which venue would not have been proper if the matter had originally been brought in federal court. Previously, if proper venue in the state court was a state jurisdictional requirement, actions having improper venue could not be properly

---

[53] Willingham v. Morgan, 395 U.S. 402, 409 (1969); Palermo v. Rorex, 806 F.2d 1266, 1269–70 (5th Cir. 1987).

[54] Willingham v. Morgan, 395 U.S. 402, 406–07 (1969).

[55] Swett v. Schenk, 792 F.2d 1447, 1450 (9th Cir. 1986).

[56] *See* Franchise Tax Bd. v. U.S. Postal Serv., 467 U.S. 512, 520 n.19 (1984); Murray v. Murray, 621 F.2d 103, 107 (5th Cir. 1980); *cf.* Loftin v. Rush, 767 F.2d 800, 804 (11th Cir. 1985) (removal proper when United States was considered a debtor). *But see* Nationwide Investors v. Miller, 793 F.2d 1044 (9th Cir. 1986) (generally permitting government to remove garnishments).

[57] 28 U.S.C. § 1443(1) (1982); *see generally* 1A Moore's Federal Practice ¶ 0.165 (1986); 14A Federal Practice and Procedure § 3728.

[58] *See, e.g.*, Georgia v. Rachel, 384 U.S. 780, 789–90 (1966); City of Greenwood v. Peacock, 384 U.S. 808, 818, 828 (1966); *see generally* Dittman, *Removal In Civil Rights Cases Under 28 U.S.C. Section 1443(2),* 31 Loyola L. Rev. 855 (1986).

[59] 28 U.S.C. § 1441(a) (1982).

removed.[60] However, the change to 28 U.S.C. § 1441(e) permitting removal even if jurisdiction is lacking in state court may have completely eliminated improper venue as a bar to removal.

§ 3.8 Prohibitions on Removal

Removal of certain actions, including those arising under the Federal Employers' Liability Act, the Jones Act, and state workmen's compensation laws, are prohibited by statute.[61] However, authority supports the removal of such actions under 28 U.S.C. § 1441(c) if a separate removable claim exists.[62] Since prohibitions on removal must be explicit, a statute providing that suits brought under the Fair Labor Standard Act can be maintained in any federal or state court[63] was interpreted as not prohibiting removal.[64]

§ 3.9 Preventing Removal

The plaintiff can prohibit removal in several ways.[65] For example, the presence of Does or a nondiverse party generally defeats diversity. Similarly, joining a defendant who is domiciled in the state defeats removal based on diversity as long as it is not a nominal party. Courts will disregard a nondiverse defendant only if there is absolutely no possibility or arguably reasonable basis that it will be liable to the plaintiff in state court.[66] Another way to defeat removal is to assert a state claim without joining a federal action. However, if the federal claim is not raised, it may be precluded by res judicata in later proceedings.[67] Once an action is removed, the plaintiff can voluntarily dismiss in federal court, but this tactic works only if the new complaint (1) is within the statute of limitations and (2) can be tailored to avoid removal. Prevention of removal can be important to a plaintiff, since once a case is removed, the court can remand only in limited circumstances.

---

[60] Transure, Inc. v. Marsh & McLennan, Inc., 766 F.2d 1297, 1300–01 (9th Cir. 1985).

[61] 28 U.S.C. § 1445 (1982).

[62] Gonsalves v. Amoco Shipping Co., 733 F.2d 1020, 1023 (2d Cir. 1984); *see* 14A Federal Practice and Procedure § 3724 (1985); 1A Moore's Federal Practice ¶¶ 0.163[4.-4], 0.167[2].

[63] 29 U.S.C. § 216(b) (1982).

[64] Cosme Nieves v. Deshler, 786 F.2d 445, 451 (1st Cir. 1986).

[65] *See, e.g.*, Gully v. First Nat'l Bank, 299 U.S. 109, 112, 116 (1936); Garibaldi v. Lucky Food Stores, Inc., 726 F.2d 1367, 1370 (9th Cir. 1984), *cert. denied,* 471 U.S. 1099 (1985); *see generally* 1A Moore's Federal Practice ¶ 0.160[3-3] at 232; 14A Federal Practice and Procedure § 3722, at 266–68.

[66] Robinson v. National Cash Register Co., 808 F.2d 1119, 1123 (5th Cir. 1987).

[67] Williams v. Caterpillar Tractor Co., 786 F.2d 928, 935 (9th Cir. 1986).

§ 3.10 The Voluntary-Involuntary Rule

If a state action includes nondiverse parties, it cannot be removed until they have been dismissed[68] or otherwise eliminated from the action. The voluntary-involuntary rule[69] has long been used to evaluate the propriety of a removal which is based upon the dismissal of a nondiverse party. The rule permits removal if dismissal of the nondiverse party results from the plaintiff's voluntary action. Conversely, if dismissal is involuntary, removal is improper. In other words, if the nondiverse defendant is dismissed by the state court, this is considered involuntary and defeats removal.[70] The fact that a nondiverse defendant is not served does not make the action removable.[71]

Voluntary actions supporting removal include a settlement concerning the nondiverse party,[72] amending the complaint to exclude the fictitious defendants, striking them from the complaint, or discontinuing the action against them.[73] Even a closing argument to the jury abandoning the plaintiff's claims against nondiverse parties has triggered removal.[74]

§ 3.11 Effect of Does on Preventing Removal

Whether the presence of a Doe defendant will defeat removal is difficult to answer simply. Even within a circuit, the effect of Does on diversity is often unclear,[75] although ordinarily their presence defeats diversity.[76] Various approaches exist to determine whether the presence of fictitious defendants defeats

---

[68] American Car & Foundry Co. v. Kettlehake, 236 U.S. 311, 316 (1915).

[69] Powers v. Chesapeake & Ohio Ry., 169 U.S. 92, 99–101 (1898); *In re* Iowa Mfg. Co. of Cedar Rapids, 747 F.2d 462, 464 (8th Cir. 1984); Self v. General Motors Corp., 588 F.2d 655, 658 n.4 (9th Cir. 1978).

[70] *See* Self v. General Motors Corp., 588 F.2d 655, 658–60 (9th Cir. 1978).

[71] Clarence E. Morris, Inc. v. Vitek, 412 F.2d 1174, 1176 (9th Cir. 1969).

[72] Chohlis v. Cessna Aircraft Co., 760 F.2d 901, 903 n.2 (8th Cir. 1983).

[73] Coker v. Amoco Oil Co., 709 F.2d 1433, 1440 (11th Cir. 1983).

[74] Heniford v. American Motors Sales Corp., 471 F. Supp. 328 (D.S.C. 1979), *appeal dismissed,* 622 F.2d 584 (4th Cir. 1980); *cf.* Preaseau v. Prudential Ins. Co. of Am., 591 F.2d 74 (9th Cir. 1979) (Doe claims abandoned at trial). *But see* Davis v. Veslan Enters., 765 F.2d 494, 498–500 (5th Cir. 1985).

[75] *See, e.g.,* Othman v. Globe Indem. Co., 759 F.2d 1458, 1462 n.7 (9th Cir. 1985); *compare* CTS Printex, Inc. v. American Motorists Ins. Co., 639 F. Supp. 1272, 1275 (N.D. Cal. 1986) (interpreting Lindley v. General Elec. Co., 780 F.2d 797 (9th Cir. 1986) as rendering previous Ninth Circuit case law irrelevant, and holding that any Doe allegation conforming to California Doe pleadings rules defeats removal) *with* McCabe v. General Foods Corp., 811 F.2d 1336, 1339 (9th Cir. 1987) (disregarding 100 boilerplate Does).

[76] Bryant v. Ford Motor Co., 794 F.2d 450, 452 (9th Cir. 1986).

removal in diversity cases.[77] Nominal parties are ignored in evaluating removal petitions, but the mere fact that a defendant is fictitious does not determine its status.[78] Indeed, a fictitious defendant is not the same as a fictitiously named defendant.[79] Fictitious defendants are not identified; fictitiously named defendants are identified but incorrectly named.

Some courts disregard Does as a sham unless the complaint sufficiently identifies them and their relationship to the allegations in the complaint.[80] The clearest case for disregarding Does is when the complaint merely includes them in the caption, without any charging allegations.[81] Complaints containing only very general, catch-all allegations against Does have fared no better.[82] Therefore, to avoid removal, a plaintiff must describe the Doe in more than boilerplate language and include the Doe's specific connection to the claim, rather than merely alleging the Doe's liability. Stating that the Does were employees and agents who were responsible for specifically enumerated acts has been considered sufficient to defeat diversity in the absence of fraudulent joinder.[83]

Even if a Doe is adequately described, if the uncontradicted evidence indicates that complete diversity exists, the Doe will be ignored.[84] Usually the decision does not require any evidentiary hearing.[85] However, the Ninth Circuit has considered affidavits by the defendant concerning the citizenship of Does when no controverting proof was submitted.[86] Even when the plaintiff alleged that a Doe defendant lived in the plaintiff's home state, some evidence was required to prove that the Doe actually existed and that his domicile defeated diversity.[87]

Another major consideration in disregarding a Doe for diversity purposes is whether the Doe has been fraudulently joined by the plaintiff to defeat federal

---

[77] *See generally* Note, *John Doe, Where Are You: The Effects of Fictitious Defendants on Removal Jurisdiction in Diversity Cases,* 34 Ala. L. Rev. 99 (1983).

[78] *Id.* at 102; Abels v. State Farm Fire & Casualty Co., 770 F.2d 26, 29 & n.3 (3d Cir. 1985); *see also* 13B Federal Practice and Procedure § 3606.

[79] *See* Comment, *Doe Defendants and Other State Relation Back Doctrines in Federal Diversity Cases,* 35 Stanford L. Rev. 297, 319 (1983).

[80] Pelleport Investors, Inc. v. Budco Quality Theatres, Inc., 741 F.2d 273, 279 (9th Cir. 1984); *see* Abels v. State Farm Fire & Casualty Co., 770 F.2d 26, 29 (3d Cir. 1985); Coker v. Amoco Oil Co., 709 F.2d 1433, 1439 (11th Cir. 1983).

[81] Abels v. State Farm Fire & Casualty Co., 770 F.2d 26, 30 (3d Cir. 1985); *see* Chism v. National Heritage Life Ins. Co., 637 F.2d 1328, 1330 (9th Cir. 1981).

[82] Abels v. State Farm Fire & Casualty Co., 770 F.2d 26, 30 (3d Cir. 1985); *see* Lopez v. General Motors Corp., 697 F.2d 1328, 1331 (9th Cir. 1983).

[83] Abels v. State Farm Fire & Casualty Co., 770 F.2d 26, 32 (3d Cir. 1985).

[84] Pelleport Investors, Inc. v. Budco Quality Theatres, Inc., 741 F.2d 273, 279 (9th Cir. 1984).

[85] Green v. Amerada Hess Corp., 707 F.2d 201, 205 (5th Cir. 1983), *cert. denied,* 464 U.S. 1039 (1984).

[86] West Am. Corp. v. Vaughn-Bassett Furniture Co., 765 F.2d 932, 936 (9th Cir. 1985); Pelleport Investors, Inc. v. Budco Quality Theatres, Inc., 741 F.2d 273, 279 (9th Cir. 1984).

[87] West Am. Corp. v. Vaughan-Bassett Furniture Co., 765 F.2d 932, 936–37 (9th Cir. 1985).

jurisdiction.[88] Joinder is considered fraudulent when there is no reasonable basis in fact or colorable ground supporting the claim or no good faith intention to prosecute the action against the defendant.[89] However, even when the basis of the claim is suspect, an appellate court can remand the action considering it premature to declare that no basis in fact exists for the Doe allegations.[90] Failure to identify the Does through discovery or to substitute named defendants are factors indicating fraudulent joinder.[91] Courts vary about the relevance of lack of service upon a Doe defendant in evaluating the propriety of removal.[92] Whether the defendant is no longer in business or has declared bankruptcy is also relevant.[93]

§ 3.12 Removal Procedures

It is important to understand how removal is effectuated, since technical errors can affect whether a case must be remanded as well as whether any intervening action by the state court is proper.

§ 3.13 —Timing

The defendant must act quickly to remove the case.[94] Removal must be accomplished within 30 days after receipt of the initial pleading or service of a summons if the pleading has been filed but is not required to be served.[95] If the initial pleading is not removable, the petition must be filed within 30 days after receipt of the paper from which it can first be ascertained that the case is removable.[96]

---

[88] *See e.g.,* Abels v. State Fire & Casualty Co., 770 F.2d 26, 32 (3d Cir. 1985); West Am. Corp. v. Vaughan-Bassett Furniture Co., 765 F.2d 932, 936 (9th Cir. 1985); Polyplastics, Inc. v. Transconex, Inc., 713 F.2d 875, 877 (1st Cir. 1983); Coker v. Amoco Oil Co., 709 F.2d 1433, 1440 (11th Cir. 1983); Green v. Amerada Hess Corp., 707 F.2d 201, 205 (5th Cir. 1983), *cert. denied,* 464 U.S. 1039 (1984); *see generally* 14 Federal Practice and Procedure § 3642.

[89] Abels v. State Farm Fire & Casualty Co., 770 F.2d 26, 32 (3d Cir. 1985).

[90] *See id.* at 33.

[91] *Id.*

[92] *Compare* Lopez v. General Motors Corp., 697 F.2d 1328, 1331 (9th Cir. 1983) (removal proper) *with* Coker v. Amoco Oil Co., 709 F.2d 1433, 1440 (11th Cir. 1983) *and* Pecherski v. General Motors Corp., 636 F.2d 1156, 1159–60 (8th Cir. 1981) (removal improper).

[93] Fousekis & Brelsford, *Removal,* 11 Litigation 39, 41 (Summer 1985).

[94] *See generally* J. Wagstaffe, W. Schwarzer, W. Tashima, & B. Gray, Commencing and Removing Actions to Federal Court (1984) [hereinafter Commencing and Removing Actions to Federal Court].

[95] 28 U.S.C. § 1446(b) (1982).

[96] *Id.*

§ 3.14 —Effect of Does on Timing

The presence of Does in the complaint also affects the timing of removal. Since the defendant has only 30 days to remove the action after that option becomes available,[97] arguably the presence of a sham or nominal Doe does not enlarge the time in which to remove the action.[98] However, in the absence of proof that the allegations against the fictitious defendants are fraudulent, the complaint does not become removable until the plaintiff takes some affirmative action indicating that it will not pursue such claims.[99] In a questionable case, counsel should consider an immediate removal, because a remand will ensure that no timing issue could be raised if the Doe is later dismissed.[100] However, such tactics may be considered as violating Rule 11's requirement that the petition is factually and legally warranted.[101] Once removed, if the plaintiff delays in seeking a remand or participates in the proceedings in the district court, it may be deemed as waiving the 30-day limitations period, since that provision is not considered to affect the jurisdiction of the court.[102]

§ 3.15 —Effectuating Removal

To effectuate the removal,[103] a verified petition must be filed which contains a short and plain statement of the facts which support removal, together with a copy of all process, pleadings, and orders served.[104] Verification on information and belief by the defendant's attorney is sufficient, although verification based on knowledge of the defendant is preferable.[105] When there are multiple defendants in a diversity action, the signature of all defendants' attorneys satisfies the requirement.[106] A bond must accompany any petition not brought on behalf of the United States, which is sufficient to pay all costs and disbursements

---

[97] 28 U.S.C. § 1446(b) (1982).

[98] Note, *John Doe, Where Are You: The Effects of Fictitious Defendants on Removal Jurisdiction in Diversity Cases,* 34 Ala. L. Rev. 99, 118–24 (1983).

[99] Coker v. Amoco Oil Co., 709 F.2d 1433, 1439 (11th Cir. 1983); *see also* Preaseau v. Prudential Ins. Co. of Am., 591 F.2d 74, 79 (9th Cir. 1979).

[100] *See* Abels v. State Farm Fire & Casualty Co., 770 F.2d 26, 33 (3d Cir. 1985) (remanding case with suggestion that removal may later become appropriate).

[101] See **ch. 28**.

[102] Leninger v. Leninger, 705 F.2d 727, 729 (5th Cir. 1983); Fontenot v. Global Marine, Inc., 703 F.2d 867, 870 (5th Cir. 1983).

[103] *See generally* 1A Moore's Federal Practice ¶ 0.168.

[104] 28 U.S.C. § 1446(a) (1982).

[105] Jones v. Newton, 775 F.2d 1316, 1317 (5th Cir. 1985).

[106] Murray v. Commercial Union Ins. Co., 782 F.2d 432, 434 (3d Cir. 1986); Alexander v. Cox, 348 F.2d 894, 896 (5th Cir. 1965).

incurred by reason of removal if it is determined that the case was not removable or was improperly removed.[107] The amount of the bond and surety requirements will often be found in local court rules. If not, the clerk's office can usually supply this information. Usually a $500 bond is sufficient.

The defendant must give written notice to all adverse parties and file a copy of the petition with the state court clerk promptly after filing the petition.[108] The notice to the clerk effects the removal and divests the state court of jurisdiction.[109] Local federal court rules may add additional requirements.[110] Removal has been considered proper even though the petitioner did not file all the necessary papers with the district court, since such a procedural failure does not defeat federal jurisdiction.[111] However, removal is not effective until notice is given to the state court.[112] Problems arise due to this hiatus in the removal process whereby the state court retains jurisdiction of a removed matter until notified of the removal,[113] and the federal court has concurrent jurisdiction.[114] Therefore, counsel should ensure that notice is immediately given to the state court. Such notice can be actual or constructive.[115] For example, notice of the removal to opposing counsel has been considered notice to the state court in absence of proof that opposing counsel failed in their duty as officers of the court to advise the state court of the removal when seeking a state default judgment.[116]

Any state order which has been issued is not conclusive on the district court but is binding until set aside.[117] Often the defendant removes the action before provisional relief is granted by the state court, since some state courts are perceived as more likely to grant temporary restraining orders[118] than their federal counterparts. Since removal can technically be accomplished within one day, even if advance notice has been given that the plaintiff will request a temporary restraining order or a decision is pending, once the case is removed in the interim and the state court has been notified of the removal, it is without jurisdiction to act. Any state-ordered provisional relief automatically expires at

---

[107] 28 U.S.C. § 1446(d) (1982).

[108] 28 U.S.C. § 1446(e) (1982).

[109] *Id.*

[110] *See, e.g.*, Commencing and Removing Actions to Federal Court at 171 (California rules).

[111] Dukes v. South Carolina Ins. Co., 770 F.2d 545, 547 (5th Cir. 1985); *see* Usatorres v. Marina Mercante Nicaraguenses, S.A., 768 F.2d 1285, 1286 (11th Cir. 1985); 14A Federal Practice and Procedure § 3737.

[112] Stephens v. Portal Boat Co., 781 F.2d 481, 482 n.1 (5th Cir. 1986); 14A Federal Practice and Procedure § 3737.

[113] Murray v. Ford Motor Co., 770 F.2d 461, 465 (5th Cir. 1985); *see* 1A Moore's Federal Practice ¶ 0.168[3.8-3].

[114] *See* Dukes v. South Carolina Ins. Co., 770 F.2d 545, 547 (5th Cir. 1985).

[115] *Id.*

[116] *Id.*

[117] 28 U.S.C. § 1450 (1982).

[118] See § **11.2**.

the timing provided by federal rather than state law.[119] Therefore, a temporary restraining order issued for more than 10 days is limited by that time frame upon removal.[120]

All defendants must join in the removal of diversity actions under U.S.C. § 1441(a).[121] This can be accomplished by joining in the petition for removal or by filing a separate concurrence in the removal. Subsequently served defendants cannot remove the action if the original defendants did not seek or effect a timely removal.[122] However, in a given case, the plaintiff may decide voluntarily to dismiss a newly added defendant who indicates its willingness to test this restriction in federal court after removal. Any consents which are necessary should be included with the removal petition, although a party who is served need not be joined.[123] One problem which may occur is that a later served defendant can demand a remand to state court if it does not want to litigate in a federal forum. Consent of other defendants is not necessary for removal under § 1441(c) as long as the claim against the removing defendant is separate and independent from the other claims in the suit.[124]

§ 3.16 Remand

Remand is required if it appears that an action was removed improvidently and without jurisdiction.[125] Therefore, remand is considered appropriate only if no subject matter jurisdiction existed at the time removal was granted.[126] In other words, the federal court has no discretion to remand for reasons not authorized by the controlling statute.[127] For example, if a plaintiff attempts to amend the complaint to delete the federal claim, the district court has jurisdiction to hear the remaining action.[128] However, the court also has discretion to dismiss the state claims. Dismissal of the state claims is without prejudice; however, a court

---

[119] Granny Goose Foods, Inc. v. Brotherhood of Teamsters & Auto Truck Drivers, 415 U.S. 423, 427 (1974).

[120] *Id.* at 439–40; *see* Fed. R. Civ. P. 65(b).

[121] Brown v. Demco, Inc., 792 F.2d 478, 481 (5th Cir. 1986); Bernstein v. Lind-Waldock & Co., 738 F.2d 179, 183 (7th Cir. 1984); Fontenot v. Global Marine, Inc., 703 F.2d 867, 870 n.3 (5th Cir. 1983); 14A Federal Practice and Procedure § 3731.

[122] Brown v. Demco, Inc., 792 F.2d 478, 481 (5th Cir. 1986); 1A Moore's Federal Practice ¶ 0.168[3.5–5], at 586–87; *see also* 14A Federal Practice and Procedure § 3732, at 531–32 (criticizing rule).

[123] Salveson v. Western States Bankcard Ass'n, 731 F.2d 1423, 1429 (9th Cir. 1984).

[124] Bernstein v. Lind-Waldock & Co., 738 F.2d 179, 183 (7th Cir. 1984); 1A Moore's Federal Practice ¶ 0.168[3.-2-2].

[125] 28 U.S.C. § 1447(c).

[126] Thermtron Prod., Inc. v. Hermansdorfer, 423 U.S. 336, 341 (1976).

[127] *Id.* at 345.

[128] See §§ **2.29** & **3.3**.

can dismiss the federal claim with prejudice to ensure that the plaintiff does not refile the federal claim in the state court.[129]

The circuits are split on the issue of whether all discretionary, nonstatutory grounds for remand have been eliminated.[130] This issue often arises concerning whether pendent claims can be remanded rather than dismissed once the federal claim which was the basis for removal has been eliminated. Similarly, a few circuits consider remand rather than dismissal appropriate for cases which are removed by a federal officer under 28 U.S.C. § 1442(a)(1) after the federal defendant is dismissed.[131]

The issue of remand for lack of subject matter jurisdiction can be raised at any time, since that is not a waivable defect.[132] If a case is remanded, the district court can order the payment of just costs[133] and, in appropriate cases, impose Rule 11 sanctions.[134]

§ 3.17 Waiver of Defects in Removal Procedure

If the plaintiff believes removal is improper, a motion to remand the case to state court should be filed as soon as possible, because nonjurisdictional defects in removal procedure are waived if the party does not object or if a motion to remand is not timely made.[135] An example of a waivable defect is the presence of a local defendant in a case in which complete diversity exists.[136] For example, the presence of a California defendant in an action brought by a New York plaintiff would defeat removal from a California state court if a timely objection were raised. However, since the parties are diverse, this defect is subject to waiver. On the other hand, the specific statutory bar to removal[137] of a Jones Act claim, or a claim against a railroad brought under the Federal Employer's Liability Act (FELA)[138] was not considered a waivable defect.[139]

---

[129] Austwick v. Board of Educ., 555 F. Supp. 840, 843 (N.D. Ill. 1983).

[130] *See In re* Romulus Community Schools, 729 F.2d 431, 436–39 (6th Cir. 1984) (extensive discussion).

[131] *E.g.*, Williams v. City of Atlanta, 794 F.2d 624, 628 (11th Cir. 1986).

[132] Murray v. Commercial Union Ins. Co., 782 F.2d 432, 433 (3d Cir. 1986); *see* Liberty Mut. Ins. Co. v. Wetzel, 424 U.S. 737, 740 (1976).

[133] *Id.*

[134] See § **3.23**.

[135] *See, e.g.*, Loftin v. Rush, 767 F.2d 800, 805 (11th Cir. 1985); Harris v. Edward Hyman Co., 664 F.2d 943, 944–45 (5th Cir. 1981).

[136] McKay v. Boyd Constr. Co., 769 F.2d 1084, 1087 (5th Cir. 1985); Woodward v. D.H. Overmyer Co., 428 F.2d 880, 882 (2d Cir. 1970), *cert. denied,* 400 U.S. 993 (1971); 1A Moore's Federal Practice ¶ 0.157[3.-4].

[137] 28 U.S.C. § 1445(a) (1982).

[138] 45 U.S.C. §§ 51–60 (1982).

[139] *See* Lirette v. N.L. Sperry Sun, Inc., 810 F.2d 533, 534 (5th Cir. 1987).

The Supreme Court has considered a remand motion untimely when delay was unreasonable and the plaintiff had participated in the action in federal court.[140] Similarly, a knowing failure to object to removal has been held to waive any objection to procedural defects in the removal process.[141] Even if the timeliness of the removal is not waived by the plaintiff, an appellate court can disregard a technical removal defense to an adverse judgment on the rationale that it has power to review an untimely petition.[142] Whether an oral remand hearing is required or permitted usually is determined by local practice.[143]

§ 3.18 Dismissals Compared with Remands

A dismissal is not the functional equivalent of a remand, since there are crucial distinctions for purposes of statute of limitations, priority upon the action's return to state court, and appellate review of the order.[144] The mere fact that a claim is barred by the statute of limitations if dismissed does not give the court power to remand the claim in the absence of statutory authority.[145] Of course, a court has discretion to retain pendent jurisdiction over a state claim, even if the federal claim has been dismissed, in order to avoid a statute of limitations bar.[146] Conversely, a court will dismiss a case, rather than remand, if the state court would be required to dismiss it upon remand.[147]

§ 3.19 Review of Remand Orders

Orders remanding cases to state court under 28 U.S.C. § 1447(c) are not reviewable,[148] except for designated civil rights actions,[149] unless the remand is issued on grounds not authorized by the statute.[150] Therefore, the court of appeals is without jurisdiction to review a remand order based on lack of

---

[140] Grubbs v. General Elec. Corp., 405 U.S. 699, 702 (1972); *see* Meadows v. Bicrodyne Corp., 785 F.2d 670, 672 (9th Cir. 1986) (citing case law).

[141] Dukes v. South Carolina Ins. Co., 770 F.2d 545, 548 (5th Cir. 1985).

[142] Loftin v. Rush, 767 F.2d 800, 805 (11th Cir. 1985).

[143] *E.g., see* Jones v. Newton, 775 F.2d 1316, 1318 (5th Cir. 1985) (not required in Fifth Circuit).

[144] Cook v. Weber, 698 F.2d 907, 908 (7th Cir. 1983).

[145] *Id.*

[146] *Id.; see* General Inv. Co. v. Lake Shore Ry., 260 U.S. 261, 288–89 (1922); § **2.29**.

[147] Jones v. Newton, 775 F.2d 1316, 1318–19 (5th Cir. 1985).

[148] 28 U.S.C. § 1447(d) (1982); *see* Nasuti v. Scannell, 792 F.2d 264, 267–68 (1st Cir. 1986) (extensive citations).

[149] 28 U.S.C. § 1443 (1982); Whitaker v. Carney, 778 F.2d 216, 219 (5th Cir. 1985), *cert. denied*, _____ U.S. _____, 107 S. Ct. 64 (1986).

[150] Thermtron Prod., Inc. v. Hermansdorfer, 423 U.S. 336, 346 (1976).

complete diversity.[151] In addition, an order remanding a case to state court cannot be appealed, even though erroneous.[152] Similarly, if the court later decides the order was erroneous, it cannot be vacated.[153] There is some question whether appellate review of a remand order is proper when the order is based solely on a matter of substantive law.[154] Mere failure to cite § 1447(c) or mention its buzzwords does not per se give the court license to review a remand order.[155] For example, appealing from the dismissal of an action for declaratory and injunctive relief was viewed as a collateral attack on the remand of an earlier related action, thereby defeating appeal.[156] Generally dismissals, even without prejudice, are final orders subject to appellate review when they end the litigation.[157] Thus, an order dismissing a party which results in a remand to state court is reviewable,[158] although the remand order is not.

Remand orders not based on statutory grounds have been reviewed by mandamus[159] or as collateral orders.[160] It has been suggested that both a notice of appeal and petition for writ of mandate should be filed to best assure reviewability.[161] Examples of nonstatutory grounds for remand which have been reviewed include remands based on the condition of the court's docket,[162] the defendant's waiver of the right to remove the action,[163] the substantive effect of a forum selection clause,[164] and the fact that the federal court has more restrictive relief available than does the state court.[165]

---

[151] Gravitt v. Southwestern Bell Tel. Co., 430 U.S. 723 (1977) (per curiam).

[152] *See, e.g., id.* at 723–24 (per curiam); New Orleans Pub. Serv., Inc. v. Majoue, 802 F.2d 166, 167 (5th Cir. 1986).

[153] *See, e.g.,* Browning v. Navarro, 743 F.2d 1069, 1078 (5th Cir. 1984); Pelleport Investors, Inc. v. Budco Quality Theatres, Inc., 741 F.2d 273, 279 n.3 (9th Cir. 1984).

[154] *See* Glasser v. Amalgamated Workers Union Local 88, 806 F.2d 1539, 1540 (11th Cir. 1986); Clorox Co. v. United States Dist. Ct., 779 F.2d 517, 520–21 (9th Cir. 1985).

[155] Loftin v. Rush, 767 F.2d 800, 802 (11th Cir. 1985); *In re* Weaver, 610 F.2d 335, 337 (5th Cir. 1980).

[156] New Orleans Pub. Serv., Inc. v. Majoue, 802 F.2d 166, 167–68 (5th Cir. 1986).

[157] *See, e.g.,* Cook v. Weber, 698 F.2d 907, 910 (7th Cir. 1983).

[158] Allen v. Ferguson, 791 F.2d 611, 613 (7th Cir. 1986) (extensive citations); *see* 1A Moore's Federal Practice ¶ 0.169[2.-2]. *But see* Encoder Communications, Inc. v. Telegen, Inc., 654 F.2d 198, 203 (2d Cir. 1981).

[159] Thermatron Prod., Inc. v. Hermansdorfer, 423 U.S. 336, 351–53 (1970); Loftin v. Rush, 767 F.2d 800, 802 n.3 (11th Cir. 1985).

[160] National City Bank v. Coopers & Lybrand, 802 F.2d 990, 992 n.2 (8th Cir. 1986); Pelleport Investors, Inc. v. Budco Quality Theatres, Inc., 741 F.2d 273, 277–78 (9th Cir. 1984).

[161] Fousekis & Brelsford, *Removal,* 11 Litigation 39, 40 (Summer 1985); *cf.* Clorox Co. v. United States Dist. Ct., 779 F.2d 517, 520 (9th Cir. 1985) (fairness required mandamus to be considered as appeal).

[162] Thermatron Prod., Inc. v. Hermansdorfer, 423 U.S. 336, 351–53 (1970).

[163] Clorox Co. v. United States Dist. Ct., 779 F.2d 517, 520 (9th Cir. 1985).

[164] Pelleport Investors, Inc. v. Budco Quality Theatres, Inc., 741 F.2d 273, 276–77 (9th Cir. 1984).

[165] Sheet Metal Workers Int'l Ass'n v. Seay, 693 F.2d 1000, 1005–06 (10th Cir. 1982).

If a court denies a remand, that order by itself is not appealable.[166] Nor can it be reviewed as a collateral order, because it is reviewable on appeal from a final judgment.[167] However, if a claim is removed to a bankruptcy court, mandamus has been used to review whether the action was properly removed, but not whether the bankruptcy court had proper jurisdiction.[168] Many courts will review a removal order as part of an interlocutory appeal of an anti-suit order, prohibiting another court from proceeding with the case.[169] Similarly, a denial of remand may be reviewable in conjunction with an interlocutory order reviewing the granting or denial of an injunction.[170]

§ 3.20 Jurisdictional Attacks on Actions Improperly Removed

If after removal a case is tried on the merits without objection and the federal court enters judgment, the issue on appeal is not whether the case was properly removed, but whether the district court would have had original jurisdiction if it had been filed in that court in the posture it had at the time of entry of final judgment.[171] Essentially, the rule requires that the party contesting jurisdiction attempt to obtain interlocutory review of the remand order, which is unlikely to be granted, or risk that subject matter will exist at final judgment and the issue of improper removal will be deemed waived.[172] This rule has been extended to cases in which final judgment is by summary judgment.[173] Thus, a district or appellate court can dismiss a Doe who is not indispensable to cure the jurisdictional defect.[174]

---

[166] Chicago, Rock Island & Pac. R.R. v. Stude, 346 U.S. 574, 578 (1954); Polyplastics, Inc. v. Transconex, Inc., 713 F.2d 875, 877 n.2 (1st Cir. 1983).

[167] Rohrer, Hibler & Replogle, Inc. v. Perkins, 728 F.2d 860, 862 (7th Cir. 1984).

[168] *In re* National Developers, Inc., 803 F.2d 616, 619–20 (11th Cir. 1986); Browning v. Navarro, 743 F.2d 1069, 1076 n.21 (5th Cir. 1984).

[169] See extensive discussion in Polyplastics, Inc. v. Transconex, Inc., 713 F.2d 875, 878–80 (1st Cir. 1983), which rejects this position; *see generally* 14A Federal Practice and Procedure § 3740; Note, *Polyplastics, Inc. v. Transconex, Inc.: Antisuit Orders as Interlocutory Injunctions Under 28 U.S.C. § 1292(a)(1),* 80 Nw. U. L. Rev. 1066 (1986).

[170] Takeda v. Northwestern Nat'l Life Ins. Co., 765 F.2d 815, 818 (9th Cir. 1985); James v. Bellotti, 733 F.2d 989, 992 (1st Cir. 1984); Beech-Nut, Inc. v. Warner Lambert Co., 480 F.2d 801, 803 (2d Cir. 1973); 1A Moore's Federal Practice ¶ 0.169[2.-3], at 706–07. *But see* La Chemise Lacoste v. Alligator Co., 506 F.2d 339, 341 (3d Cir. 1974) (per curiam), *cert. denied,* 421 U.S. 937 (1975).

[171] Grubbs v. General Elec. Credit Corp., 405 U.S. 699, 702 (1972).

[172] Gould v. Mutual Life Ins. Co. of N.Y., 790 F.2d 769, 774 (9th Cir. 1986). *But see* Gonsalves v. Amoco Shipping Co., 733 F.2d 1020, 1026 n.6 (2d Cir. 1984).

[173] Gould v. Mutual Life Ins. Co. of N.Y., 790 F.2d 769, 773 (9th Cir. 1986).

[174] Othman v. Globe Indem. Co., 759 F.2d 1458, 1463 (9th Cir. 1985).

§ 3.21 Post-Removal Procedures

The federal district court can issue all necessary orders and process to bring the parties before it[175] and can issue process to complete any defective or unperfected process served before removal.[176] The federal rules apply to all service after removal.[177] One open question is how Rule 4's requirement that service be made within 120 days after filing the complaint is measured in a removal action. It has been suggested that the timing should run from the filing of the petition, since in some jurisdictions the complaint may be on file well beyond that time before removal.[178]

If the defendant has not answered the complaint prior to removal, Rule 81(c) requires a response within 20 days after receiving a copy of the initial pleading or being served with a summons of an initial pleading which has been filed, or within five days after the filing of the petition for removal, whichever period is longer. When a case is removed, the federal court takes it as though everything done in the state court had in fact been done in federal court.[179] Therefore, it is not necessary to replead a case once it has been removed.[180] Although failure to include a copy of a motion filed in state court with the removal petition does not waive state defenses,[181] a safer procedure is to either file a copy of the motion with the petition or refile the motion in federal court.[182] After removal, motions challenging subject matter jurisdiction are heard prior to other motions.[183]

§ 3.22 Right to Jury Trial in Removed Cases

One problem that frequently arises for state court practitioners is how to preserve the right to a jury trial after the action is removed. Rule 81(c) provides that, if at the time of removal all necessary pleadings have been served, a jury demand must be served by the petitioner within 10 days after the removal petition is filed and by other parties within 10 days after service of the notice of filing the petition. The Seventh Circuit has held that merely checking the box on the civil cover sheet indicating that a jury is demanded does not preserve the right to a

---

175 28 U.S.C. § 1447(a) (1982).

176 28 U.S.C. § 1448 (1982).

177 Allen v. Ferguson, 791 F.2d 611, 615 (7th Cir. 1986).

178 Commencing and Removing Actions to Federal Court at 183.

179 Murray v. Ford Motor Co., 770 F.2d 461, 464 (5th Cir. 1985).

180 Fed. R. Civ. P. 81(c).

181 Usatorerres v. Marina Mercante Nicaraguenses, S.A., 768 F.2d 1285, 1286 (11th Cir. 1985).

182 *See* Fed. R. Civ. P. 81(b).

183 *See* Allen v. Ferguson, 791 F.2d 611, 615–16 (7th Cir. 1986).

jury trial.[184] Local rules may also exist which govern the exact format of the jury demand.[185]

A defendant who desires a jury trial should include the demand in the removal petition, unless local rules require otherwise. If this procedure is followed, the petition must be served on the other parties,[186] whereas the removal can be effected by giving written notice to adverse parties without actually serving them.[187] In any event, simple courtesy dictates that a copy of the petition should be promptly forwarded to all parties. Of course, the decision to demand a jury trial should be carefully analyzed, since a demand cannot be withdrawn without the consent of all of the parties.[188]

If a demand is made in accordance with state law prior to removal, no further action is necessary.[189] If state law does not require an express demand to be made, no demand is necessary after removal unless the court directs the parties to do so on its own motion or at the request of any party.[190] However, federal courts are inconsistent in their treatment of the timeliness of demands when state law requires a demand without specifying the exact time that it is due.[191] If a demand is untimely, the court has discretion to relieve the party from its waiver,[192] but many federal judges are usually unsympathetic to plaintiffs whose only excuse is that they are unfamiliar with the federal rules.[193]

§ 3.23 Sanctions for Improper Removal

If the removal is improper, Rule 11 sanctions must be imposed if the court finds the removal was not legally or factually warranted. District court judges may be reluctant to award such sanctions, but appellate courts do remand cases for imposition of sanctions when required by Rule 11.[194] Although bad faith is not a prerequisite to a Rule 11 violation, sanctions were awarded when a removal was in bad faith to delay entry of a state judgment.[195] Both the amount of lost interest

---

[184] *See, e.g.,* Wall v. National R.R. Passenger Corp., 718 F.2d 906 (9th Cir. 1983).

[185] *See, e.g.,* Commencing and Removing Actions to Federal Court at 171 (California rules).

[186] *See* Fed. R. Civ. P. 38(b).

[187] 28 U.S.C. § 1446(e) (1982).

[188] Fed. R. Civ. P. 38(d).

[189] Fed. R. Civ. P. 81(c).

[190] *Id.*

[191] *Compare* Noonan v. Cunard S.S. Co., 375 F.2d 69, 70 (2d Cir. 1967) (demand untimely) *with* Cascone v. Ortho Pharmaceutical Corp., 702 F.2d 389, 392 (2d Cir. 1983) (permitted late jury demand).

[192] Fed. R. Civ. P. 39(b).

[193] *See* Chandler Supply Co. v. G.A.F. Corp., 650 F.2d 983, 987 (9th Cir. 1980).

[194] See **ch. 28**.

[195] *See* Davis v. Veslan Enters., 765 F.2d 494, 497–500 (5th Cir. 1985).

because of the delay in entering the state judgment and attorney's fees were assessed.[196] Sanctions have also been imposed when the grounds for removal had no legal support.[197] Rule 11 sanctions can be invoked against a plaintiff who has been removed to federal court only for proceedings following removal, not for the original complaint.[198] When removal effectively bifurcated what should have been a single action, thereby increasing the costs of the litigation, a defendant was not permitted to recover Rule 11 sanctions against the plaintiff.[199] In addition to Rule 11 sanctions, the bond usually will be fortified if the case is remanded.[200]

§ 3.24 Removal Checklist

Presence of Federal Jurisdiction

1. Does complaint demonstrate federal question or diversity jurisdiction?
   a. In diversity action, is any defendant local?
   b. In federal question action, is artfully pleaded state claim preempted by federal law?
2. Is an independent claim combined with otherwise nonremovable claims?
3. Is the United States or officer or agency of the United States the removing defendant?
4. Determine limitations on removal if claim alleges a violation of civil rights.
5. Do other statutory restrictions bar removal (*e.g.*, worker's compensation claims)?

Timing

1. Petition must be filed within 30 days of receipt of pleading or paper which demonstrates a removable event.
   a. Timing is not enlarged by sham Does.

---

[196] *Id.*

[197] Hewitt v. City of Stanton, 798 F.2d 1230, 1232–33 (9th Cir. 1986); Pravic v. U.S. Indus.— Clearing, 109 F.R.D. 620, 622–24 (E.D. Mich. 1986).

[198] Brown v. Capitol Air, Inc., 797 F.2d 106, 108 (2d Cir. 1986); *see, e.g.*, McCabe v. General Foods Corp., 811 F.2d 1336, 1340–41 (9th Cir. 1987) (upholding Rule 11 sanctions for responses to interrogatories and amended complaint in removed action).

[199] Brown v. Capitol Air, Inc., 797 F.2d 106, 108 (2d Cir. 1986).

[200] 28 U.S.C. § 1447(c) (1982).

2. After removal, state provisional relief expires according to timing of federal rules (*e.g.*, 10 days for injunctive relief).

Removal Procedures

1. Allege requisite jurisdictional basis if not in complaint.
   a. In diversity action, allege amount and citizenship, including dual citizenship of corporation.
      (1) Explain reasons why Does are sham.
   b. In federal question action, allege statutory or other grounds supporting jurisdiction, including why complaint is artfully pleaded.
2. Has consent of other defendants been obtained for § 1441(a) removal?
3. Has petition been verified?
4. Has jury trial demand been included, if not previously requested?
5. Have state pleadings and orders been included?
6. Has bond been obtained (check with clerk or local rules for amount)?
7. Has written notice of removal been given to adverse parties?
8. Has actual or constructive notice of removal been given to the state court?

Obtaining a Jury Trial

1. Has a previous state demand been made if state law requires one?
   a. If a jury has not been waived, the petitioner has 10 days to make demand after filing petition, and other parties have 10 days after being notified of petition.
2. Has the federal district judge ordered that a demand be made, if state law did not require it?

Ways to Defeat Removal

1. In a diversity action, have Does been alleged who are not sham or boilerplate?
2. Do not voluntarily abandon claims in state court against nondiverse parties or Does.
3. Is it feasible to amend the complaint to add a nondiverse party or to reduce damages below $10,000?
4. Is a remand motion appropriate?
   a. Timeliness is required for a motion alleging a technical defect.

Obtaining Review of Remand Rulings

1. If the order grants a remand:
   a. Appeal if a civil rights action
   b. In other cases, if remand is based on nonstatutory grounds, attempt review via mandamus or collateral order doctrine
   c. If action has been dismissed, appeal from dismissal order
   d. Request review in connection with appeal from order concerning injunctive relief.
2. If the order denies remand:
   a. Mandamus is unlikely to be granted
   b. Request review in connection with appeal of order concerning injunctive relief or anti-suit order.

Rule 11

1. After reasonable inquiry, can the attorney certify that the removal petition or the motion to remand is well grounded in law and fact and not imposed for an improper reason?

CHAPTER 4

ESTABLISHING PERSONAL JURISDICTION OVER THE DEFENDANT

§ 4.1 Introduction

One of the most contested issues in any lawsuit involving out-of-state defendants is the existence of either general or specific personal jurisdiction. Plaintiffs suing such defendants often prefer to litigate in federal court, because judges can transfer venue to a district in another state having jurisdiction over the defendant despite the absence of personal jurisdiction in the state where the action was brought.[1] Moreover, if personal jurisdiction is appropriate in the original

[1] 28 U.S.C. § 1631 (1982); Goldlawr, Inc. v. Heiman, 369 U.S. 463, 465–66 (1962).

district, a change of venue for the convenience of witnesses can result in the application of the original jurisdiction's favorable substantive law in a district where the plaintiff resides.[2]

From the defendant's perspective, if personal jurisdiction is found lacking, the suit may be effectively ended. First, even if the action is transferred without personal jurisdiction, the statute of limitations in the appropriate district may have run prior to the institution of litigation. In addition, it may be prohibitively expensive as well as procedurally undesirable for the plaintiff to sue a foreign defendant in its own country. Therefore, plaintiffs must understand the requirements of personal jurisdiction to ensure the best choice of law, while defendants must be alert to this issue to ensure that a viable means of ending the litigation or making it less attractive is not inadvertently waived.

§ 4.2 General Jurisdiction

General jurisdiction permits a state to exercise personal jurisdiction over a defendant in a suit not arising out of or related to the defendant's contacts with the forum, based on the systematic and continuous activities of the defendant in the forum.[3] However, mere purchases, even if they occur at regular intervals, are not enough to warrant general in personam jurisdiction over a nonresident corporation.[4] If the defendant's activities are not sufficiently pervasive to support general jurisdiction, the nature and quality of the forum-related activities must be evaluated in relation to the specific cause of action.[5]

§ 4.3 Specific Jurisdiction

Specific jurisdiction can be exercised in the absence of general jurisdiction only if the defendant has purposefully directed its activities at residents of the forum[6] and the litigation results from alleged injuries that arise out of or relate to those activities.[7]

Most personal jurisdiction attacks focus on specific jurisdiction. The constitutional touchstone for such personal jurisdiction is whether the defendant

---

[2] 28 U.S.C. § 1404(a) (1982); Van Dusen v. Barrack, 376 U.S. 612, 639 (1964).

[3] Helicopteros Nacionales de Colombia, S.A. v. Hall, 466 U.S. 408, 414 n.9 (1984); Perkins v. Benguet Consolidated Mining Co., 342 U.S. 437, 445–47 (1952); *see generally* Brilmayer, *How Contacts Count: Due Process Limitations on State Court Jurisdiction,* 1980 Sup. Ct. Rev. 77.

[4] Helicopteros Nacionales de Colombia, S.A. v. Hall, 466 U.S. 408, 417 (1984); *see* Holt Oil & Gas Corp. v. Harvey, 801 F.2d 773, 779 (5th Cir. 1986).

[5] Olsen By Sheldon v. Government of Mexico, 729 F.2d 641, 648 (9th Cir.), *cert. denied,* 469 U.S. 917 (1984).

[6] Keeton v. Hustler Magazine, Inc., 465 U.S. 770, 774 (1984).

[7] Helicopteros Nacionales de Colombia, S.A. v. Hall, 466 U.S. 408, 414 n.8 (1984).

purposefully established minimum contacts in the forum state.[8] The due process clause protects an individual's liberty interest in not being subject to the binding judgments of a forum with which he has established no meaningful contacts, ties, or relations.[9] Traditional concepts of fair play and justice require that individuals have fair warning that a particular activity will result in jurisdiction's being proper.[10] Thus, the due process clause allows potential defendants to structure their primary conduct with some minimum assurance as to where they will be liable to suit.[11]

§ 4.4 Determining Minimum Contacts

In judging minimum contacts, a court focuses on the "relationship among the defendant, the forum and the litigation."[12] The foreseeability of causing injury which is necessary to uphold jurisdiction is that the defendants' conduct and connection with the forum are such that they should reasonably anticipate being haled into court there.[13] Only if the defendant deliberately engaged in significant activities within the state or created continuing obligations within the state is personal jurisdiction proper.[14] Random, fortuitous, or attenuated contacts or the unilateral activity of another party or third person do not satisfy the requirements of contact with the forum.[15] Due to the nature of the inquiry concerning minimum contacts, personal jurisdiction must be decided on a case-by-case basis.[16]

The Supreme Court reiterated and clarified personal jurisdiction standards in *Burger King v. Rudzewicz.*[17] *Burger King* permitted a national franchisor to sue a

---

[8] Burger King Corp. v. Rudzewicz, 471 U.S. 462, 474 (1985) (citing International Shoe Co. v. Washington, 326 U.S. 310, 316 (1945)); *see generally* Brilmayer, *How Contacts Count: Due Process Limitations on State Court Jurisdiction,* 1980 Sup. Ct. Rev. 77; Knudson, *Keeton, Calder, Helicopteros and Burger King—International Shoe's Most Recent Progeny,* 39 U. Miami L. Rev. 809 (1985); Stein, *Styles of Argument and Interstate Federalism in the Law of Personal Jurisdiction,* 65 Tex. L. Rev. 689 (1987).

[9] Burger King Corp. v. Rudzewicz, 471 U.S. 462, 471–72 (1985) (citing International Shoe Co. v. Washington, 326 U.S. 310, 319 (1945)).

[10] 471 U.S. at 472; Shaffer v. Heitner, 433 U.S. 186, 218 (1977) (Stevens, J., concurring in judgment).

[11] Burger King Corp. v. Rudzewicz, 471 U.S. 462, 472 (1985) (citing World-Wide Volkswagen Corp. v. Woodson, 444 U.S. 286, 297 (1980))

[12] Helicopteros Nacionales de Colombia, S.A. v. Hall, 466 U.S. 408, 414 (1984) (quoting Shaffer v. Heitner, 433 U.S. 186, 204 (1977)).

[13] Burger King Corp. v. Rudzewicz, 471 U.S. 462, 474 (1985) (quoting World-Wide Volkswagen Corp. v. Woodson, 444 U.S. 286, 295 (1980)).

[14] 471 U.S. at 476.

[15] *Id.* at 475.

[16] *Id.* at 485–86.

[17] 471 U.S. 462 (1985).

Michigan franchisee in Florida, where the franchisor's headquarters were situated. The franchisee's contract was judged as providing a substantial connection to Florida by obligating the defendant to a 20-year relationship with the Miami-based franchisor. The choice of law provision in the contract reinforced the defendant's affiliation with the forum asserting jurisdiction, although it would have been insufficient standing alone to confer jurisdiction.[18]

The Court noted that a contract with an out-of-state party cannot alone establish sufficient minimum contacts in the other party's home forum, since the unilateral activity of the plaintiff cannot satisfy the requirement that the nonresident defendant have contact with the forum state.[19] In other words, *Burger King* reaffirmed that a single act can confer jurisdiction only if it creates a substantial connection with the forum.[20] Therefore, even after *Burger King,* the mere fact that a contract is made in the forum is insufficient by itself to confer jurisdiction.[21] However, defendants should be aware that the plaintiff's residence can enhance the defendant's contacts due to the defendant's relationship with the plaintiff.[22] For example, the plaintiff's residence may be the focus of the activities of the defendant out of which the suit arises.[23]

§ 4.5 Effect of Communications and Shipments

The defendant need not be physicially present in a state to establish minimum contacts.[24] Whether mailed communications confer jurisdiction is not always clear. As the Fifth Circuit has noted, the quality of the contacts as demonstrating purposeful availment, not their number or status, is at issue.[25] Therefore, generalized reference to interstate contacts via telephone and mail was not sufficient alone to confer jurisdiction.[26] Similarly, two telephone calls and one mailing into the state does not satisfy a long arm statute's requirement that the defendant transact business or contract to supply goods or services in the state.[27] Solicitation of an insurance modification by mail has been considered sufficient

---

[18] *Id.* at 482.

[19] *Id.* at 478; *see* Hanson v. Denckla, 357 U.S. 235, 253 (1958).

[20] Burger King Corp. v. Rudzewicz, 471 U.S. 462, 475 n.18 (1985).

[21] *See* Sea Lift, Inc. v. Refinadora Costarricense, 792 F.2d 989, 993–94 (11th Cir. 1986); Bond Leather Co. v. Q.T. Shoe Mfg. Co., 764 F.2d 928, 935 (1st Cir. 1985).

[22] Keeton v. Hustler Magazine, Inc., 465 U.S. 770, 780 (1984).

[23] *Id.*

[24] Burger King Corp. v. Rudzewicz, 471 U.S. 462, 476 (1985).

[25] Stuart v. Spademan, 772 F.2d 1185, 1194 (5th Cir. 1985).

[26] *See* Nicholas v. Buchanan, 806 F.2d 305, 307 (1st Cir. 1986).

[27] *See* Fiedler v. First City Nat'l Bank, 807 F.2d 315, 317 (2d Cir. 1986); *see also* Caldwell v. Palmetto State Sav. Bank, 811 F.2d 916, 918 (5th Cir. 1987) (one letter not enough).

to permit exercise of jurisdiction;[28] mailing of a contract acceptance,[29] a school admission application,[30] or checks[31] has not. Advertisements which focus on a national market can convert an otherwise insignificant percentage of sales into a proper basis to assert jurisdiction.[32] Required delivery in the forum has also supported limited jurisdiction.[33]

Personal jurisdiction over a corporation is proper if the corporation delivers its products into the stream of commerce with the expectation that they will be purchased by consumers in the forum state who are subsequently injured.[34] Because modern transportation and communications have made it much less burdensome for parties to defend themselves in a state where they engage in economic activity, it is not considered unfair to hold defendants accountable when they have purposefully directed their activities toward the forum residents.[35] Therefore, it is usually easier to satisfy due process over a nonresident seller who ships goods into the forum than over a nonresident buyer.[36]

Some courts consider the relevant scope of the foreseeable market to be generally broader with respect to manufacturers and primary distributors of products at the start of a distribution system who thereby serve and derive economic benefit from a wider market.[37] However, several circuits have rejected jurisdiction when the defendant merely knew the ultimate destination of a product on the basis that the sale did not initiate a stream of commerce but merely an "isolated splash."[38] The Supreme Court recently divided over this issue without resolution in *Asahi Metal Industrial Co. v. Superior Court*.[39] In that case, four justices favored a requirement of additional conduct directed to the forum besides the mere act of placing the product into the stream. Four justices disagreed, and one justice did not reach the issue.[40]

---

[28] August v. HBA Life Ins. Co., 734 F.2d 168, 173 (4th Cir. 1984).

[29] Lakeside Bridge & Steel Co. v. Mountain State Const. Co., 597 F.2d 596, 604 (7th Cir. 1979), *cert. denied,* 445 U.S. 907 (1980).

[30] Gehling v. St. George's School of Medicine, Ltd., 773 F.2d 539, 544 (3d Cir. 1985).

[31] Sea Lift, Inc. v. Refinadora Costarricense, 792 F.2d 989, 994 (11th Cir. 1986); Stuart v. Spademan, 772 F.2d 1185, 1194 (5th Cir. 1985).

[32] *See, e.g.,* Vault Corp. v. Quaid Software Ltd., 775 F.2d 638, 640 (5th Cir. 1985).

[33] *See* Decker Coal Co. v. Commonwealth Edison Co., 805 F.2d 834, 840 (9th Cir. 1986).

[34] World-Wide Volkswagen Corp. v. Woodson, 444 U.S. 286, 297–98 (1980).

[35] Burger King Corp. v. Rudzewicz, 471 U.S. 462, 474–75 (1985).

[36] Precision Constr. Co. v. J.A. Slattery Co., 765 F.2d 114, 118 (8th Cir. 1985); *see* Giotis v. Apollo of the Ozarks, Inc., 800 F.2d 660, 667 (7th Cir. 1986); Borg-Warner Acceptance Corp. v. Lovett & Tharpe, Inc., 786 F.2d 1055, 1058–59 (11th Cir. 1986) (extensive citations).

[37] Montalbano v. Easco Hand Tools, 766 F.2d 737, 743 (2d Cir. 1985); Nelson by Carson v. Park Indus., Inc., 717 F.2d 1120, 1125 (7th Cir. 1983), *cert. denied,* 465 U.S. 1024 (1984).

[38] Dalmau Rodriquez v. Hughes Aircraft Co., 781 F.2d 9, 15 (1st Cir. 1986); *see* Burger King Corp. v. Rudzewicz, 471 U.S. 462, 475 n.18 (1985); Brand v. Menlove Dodge, 796 F.2d 1070, 1074–75 (9th Cir. 1986); Chung v. Nana Dev. Corp., 783 F.2d 1124, 1126 (4th Cir.), *cert. denied,* ____ U.S. ____, 107 S. Ct. 431 (1986).

[39] ____ U.S. ____, 107 S. Ct. 1026 (1987).

[40] *Id.*

§ 4.6 Effect of Corporate Status

When personal jurisdiction depends on a contract, post-execution contacts can be factored into the due process analysis.[41] Similarly, the pre-incorporation acts of a promoter have been considered in conjunction with post-incorporation acts in assessing a corporation's amenability to personal jurisdiction.[42] On the other hand, the mere existence of a parent-subsidiary relationship is insufficient to establish personal jurisdiction over a defendant.[43] The fiduciary shield doctrine holds that an individual's transaction of business within the state solely as a corporate officer does not create personal jurisdiction over the individual, even though there is jurisdiction over the corporation.[44] In other words, due process does not allow the directors of a national corporation to be sued by its shareholders anywhere the corporation happens to be present.[45] However, the Supreme Court has indicated that the defendants' status as employees does not insulate them from jurisdiction if their individual contacts are sufficient to warrant jurisdiction.[46] Moreover, the fiduciary shield doctrine does not apply if the corporate entity is disregarded because the individual or subsidiary is the alterego of the corporation or its parent[47] or if active participation of the parent results in some fraudulent consequence.[48] Conversely, if the corporation is considered the alterego of the individual, courts attribute the corporation's contacts with the forum to the individual.[49]

---

[41] *See* Cutco Indus., Inc. v. Naughton, 806 F.2d 361, 367 (2d Cir. 1986); Borg-Warner Acceptance Corp. v. Lovett & Tharpe, Inc., 786 F.2d 1055, 1058–59 (11th Cir. 1986).

[42] Rees v. Mosaic Tech., Inc., 742 F.2d 765, 769 (3d Cir. 1984).

[43] Transure, Inc. v. Marsh & McLennan, Inc., 766 F.2d 1297, 1299 (9th Cir. 1985); *see* Keeton v. Hustler Magazine, Inc., 465 U.S. 770, 781 n.13 (1984); Cannon Mfg. Co. v. Cudahy Packing Co., 267 U.S. 333, 336 (1925); Miller v. Honda Motor Co., Ltd., 779 F.2d 769, 771–72 (1st Cir. 1985); *see generally* Brilmayer & Paisley, *Personal Jurisdiction and Substantive Legal Relations: Corporations, Conspiracies, and Agency,* 74 Cal. L. Rev. 1 (1986); Note, *Jurisdiction Over Alien Corporations Based on the Activities of Their Subsidiaries in the Forum: Whither the Doctrine of Corporate Separateness*?, 9 Fordham Int'l L.J. 540 (1986).

[44] Ten Mile Indus. Park v. Western Plains Serv. Corp., 810 F.2d 1518, 1527 (10th Cir. 1987); Cutco Indus., Inc. v. Naughton, 806 F.2d 361, 367 (2d Cir. 1986); Stuart v. Spademan, 772 F.2d 1185, 1197 (5th Cir. 1985); *see generally* Note, *Personal Jurisdiction and the Corporate Employee: Minimum Contacts Meet the Fiduciary Shield,* 28 Stan. L. Rev. 813 (1986).

[45] Young v. Colgate-Palmolive Co., 790 F.2d 567, 572 (7th Cir. 1986); *see* Shaffer v. Heitner, 433 U.S. 186, 203 (1977).

[46] Calder v. Jones, 465 U.S. 783, 790 (1984); Keeton v. Hustler Magazine, Inc., 465 U.S. 770, 781 n.13 (1984).

[47] Stuart v. Spademan, 772 F.2d 1185, 1197 (5th Cir. 1985).

[48] *See* Miller v. Honda Motor Co., Ltd., 779 F.2d 769 , 772 (1st Cir. 1985); Marine Midland Bank, N.A. v. Miller, 664 F.2d 889, 904 (2d Cir. 1981).

[49] Stuart v. Spademan, 772 F.2d 1185, 1197 (5th Cir. 1985) (extensive citations).

§ 4.7 Effects Test for Intentional Torts

The Court has utilized an effects test for intentional torts permitting jurisdiction in a libel action in the jurisdiction where the libel was focused.[50] However, merely asserting that the defendant has committed an intentional tort in a state where the defendant has no contacts does not confer jurisdiction but is assessed as part of the analysis of the defendant's contacts with the forum.[51] Whether these effects, alone or in combination, are sufficient to support jurisdiction turns on the facts of the particular case.[52] For example, filing legal papers in a state pursuant to litigation located elsewhere was not sufficient to permit an assertion of personal jurisdiction over an attorney.[53]

§ 4.8 Reasonableness

Once minimum contacts are shown, they are considered in light of other factors to determine whether the assertion of personal jurisdiction comports with "fair play and substantial justice."[54] Such factors as the burden on the defendant, the forum state's interest in adjudicating the dispute, the plaintiff's interest in obtaining convenient and effective relief, the interstate judicial system's interest in obtaining the most efficient resolution of controversies, and the shared interest of the several states in furthering fundamental substantive social policies can be evaluated and may serve to establish the reasonableness of jurisdiction upon a lesser showing of minimum contacts than would otherwise be required.[55] On the other hand, if minimum contacts are found, a defendant must present a compelling case that jurisdiction is unreasonable.[56] This is extremely difficult, since choice of law rules and change of venue are available.[57] However, jurisdictional rules may not be employed to make litigation so gravely difficult and inconvenient that a party is unfairly at a severe disadvantage in defending the action.[58] The Supreme Court has found jurisdiction to be unreasonable in circumstances closely resembling a forum non conveniens dismissal.[59]

---

[50] Calder v. Young, 465 U.S. 783, 789 (1984).

[51] Wallace v. Herron, 778 F.2d 391, 394–95 (7th Cir. 1985), *cert. denied*, ____ U.S. ____, 106 S. Ct. 1642 (1986).

[52] *Id.*

[53] *Id.*

[54] Burger King Corp. v. Rudzewicz, 471 U.S. 462, 476 (1985) (quoting International Shoe Co. v. Washington, 326 U.S. 310, 320 (1945)).

[55] *Id.* (quoting World-Wide Volkswagen Corp. v. Woodson, 444 U.S. 286, 292 (1980)).

[56] *Id.* at 477.

[57] *Id.*

[58] *Id.* at 478.

[59] *See* Asahi Metal Indus. Co. v. Superior Ct., ____ U.S. ____, 107 S. Ct. 1026, 1034–35 (1987); *see also* Fields v. Sedgwick Associated Risks, Ltd., 796 F.2d 299, 302–03 (9th Cir.

§ 4.9 Quasi in Rem and Transient Jurisdiction

International Shoe and its progeny apparently control quasi in rem jurisdiction as well as personal jurisdiction.[60] The mere presence of property owned by a nonresident defendant in the forum state is insufficient to support quasi in rem jurisdiction over a claim unrelated to the property.[61] Similarly, personal service on an agent of an unincorporated association[62] or corporation[63] in the forum is insufficient to support personal jurisdiction without a minimum contacts inquiry.

§ 4.10 Specific Jurisdictional Problems

Several important personal jurisdictional issues have been resolved by the Supreme Court. It is now settled that the personal jurisdiction inquiry in a libel case is the same as that used in other cases.[64] Therefore, no greater contacts are necessary for a finding of personal jurisdiction in First Amendment cases. As a result, plaintiffs can sue in any jurisdiction where the media defendant has contacts rather than in the defendant's home state or the place where the major effect of the article occurred. Moreover, the effects test which affirms jurisdiction for libel intentionally focused on the plaintiff's home state[65] appears to loosen the jurisdictional requirements for nonresident publishers and authors.[66] However, the exact wording of the long-arm statute must be consulted to determine if mailing of libelous materials into the state is sufficient to confer jurisdiction.[67]

The court has also clarified the personal jurisdiction requirements concerning multistate class actions.[68] Nonresident plaintiffs do not need to possess the minimum contacts with the forum which are necessary for jurisdiction over

---

1986); *see generally,* Stewart, *Forum Non Conveniens: A Doctrine in Search of a Role,* 74 Cal. L. Rev. 1259 (1986) (arguing forum non conveniens has outlived its usefulness in light of appropriate personal jurisdiction analysis).

[60] International Shoe Co. v. Washington, 326 U.S. 310 (1945). *See* Shaffer v. Heitner, 433 U.S. 186, 212 (1977).

[61] Shaffer v. Heitner, 433 U.S. 186, 212 (1977).

[62] Nehemiah v. Athletics Congress of U.S.A., 765 F.2d 42, 47 (3d Cir. 1985).

[63] Amusement Equip., Inc. v. Mordilt, 779 F.2d 264, 267 (5th Cir. 1985).

[64] Keeton v. Hustler Magazine, Inc., 465 U.S. 770, 780 n.12 (1984); Calder v. Jones, 465 U.S. 783, 790–91 (1984).

[65] Calder v. Jones, 465 U.S. 783, 789 (1984).

[66] *See generally* Note, *Personal Jurisdiction Over Nonresident Publishers and Authors: What Contacts are Needed After Keeton v. Hustler Magazine, Inc., and Calder v. Jones,* 34 Cath. U. L. Rev. 1125 (1985).

[67] *See* Moncrief v. Lexington Herald-Leader Co., 807 F.2d 217, 221 (D.C. Cir. 1986) (rejecting jurisdiction based on interpretation of D.C. long-arm statute).

[68] See § **10.5**.

nonresident defendants, as long as the class action procedures satisfy due process. However, the forum cannot apply its own law to such plaintiffs.[69] Although a national class action can be maintained in one forum, this decision limits its desirability, since plaintiffs will have to be divided into categories depending on choice of law questions. Indeed, the entire purpose for suing in a particular forum is often to obtain the benefits of the forum's state law. Of course, class actions based on diversity jurisdiction are available in federal court only to plaintiffs whose individual injuries exceed $10,000.[70]

§ 4.11 Analysis of Due Process by the Circuits

The circuits have adopted varying approaches to analyzing personal jurisdiction issues, but the factors considered are basically identical. The Ninth Circuit probably has established the most elaborate framework with its three-pronged approach to analyzing limited jurisdiction. The court focused first on whether the nonresident defendant has done some act or consummated some transaction within the forum or performed some act by which it purposefully availed itself of the privilege of conducting activities in the forum. Second, it determines whether the claim arises out of or results from the defendant's forum-related activities. Finally, if both these prongs are met, the exercise of jurisdiction must still be reasonable.[71] Variations of this test are used in other circuits.[72]

Thus, if exercise of the jurisdiction is unreasonable even though the first two prongs are met, personal jurisdiction will be found lacking.[73] The following seven factors are considered in determining reasonableness: (1) the extent of purposeful interjection, (2) burden of defense, (3) conflict with the sovereignity of the nonresident's forum, (4) interest of the forum state, (5) most efficient forum to resolve the dispute, (6) most convenient and effective relief for the plaintiff, and (7) the existence of an alternative forum.[74] It should be noted that the Ninth Circuit considers that *Burger King* has relaxed its three-prong test for personal jurisdiction because of three factors: (1) a foreign act having effect in the forum can show purposeful availment; (2) a lesser showing of minimum contacts is required if dictated by considerations of reasonableness; and (3) a presumption of reasonableness exists upon a showing of purposeful availment, which can only be overcome by presenting a compelling case that jurisdiction would be unreasonable.[75] Therefore, even if purposeful availment is absent,

---

[69] Phillips Petroleum Co. v. Shutts, 472 U.S. 797, 822–23 (1985).

[70] Zahn v. International Paper Co., 414 U.S. 291, 301 (1973); Synder v. Harris, 394 U.S. 332, 338 (1969).

[71] Data Disc., Inc. v. Systems Technology Assocs., Inc., 557 F.2d 1280, 1287 (9th Cir. 1977).

[72] *See, e.g.,* Dollar Sav. Bank v. First Sec. Bank of Utah, 746 F.2d 208, 213 (3d Cir. 1984) (two-step process considering identical factors).

[73] Pacific Atl. Trading Co. v. M/V Main Express, 758 F.2d 1325, 1331 (9th Cir. 1985).

[74] Insurance Co. of N. Am. (I.N.A.) v. Marina Salina Cruz, 649 F.2d 1266, 1270 (9th Cir. 1981).

[75] Haisten v. Grass Valley Medical Reimbursement, 784 F.2d 1392, 1397 (9th Cir. 1986).

sufficient contacts may exist which allow the exercise of personal jurisdiction if considerations of reasonableness dictate.[76]

The Eighth Circuit refers to a minimum contacts test which considers: (1) the nature and quality of the contacts with the forum state; (2) the quantity of contacts with the forum state; (3) the relation of the cause of action to the contacts; (4) the interest of the forum state in providing a forum for its residents; and (5) the convenience of the parties.[77] Factors four and five are considered secondary to the analysis.[78]

The Fifth Circuit utilizes a two-pronged test requiring that the nonresident have minimum contacts with the forum state and that subjecting the nonresident to jurisdiction be consistent with traditional notions of fair play and substantial justice.[79] When an out-of-state act causes effects within the forum, three factors are considered in evaluating purposeful availment: (1) the existence and degree of purposefulness with which the effect in that forum was created; (2) whether the defendant has other substantial contacts with the forum unrelated to the suit, and (3) the substantiality of the effect itself.[80] In evaluating the contacts a nonresident has with the forum, the basic approach is to consider the totality of the circumstances.[81]

Reasonableness or fairness is integral to whichever analysis the circuit uses.[82] The general factors mentioned in determining reasonableness are usually focused on whether the forum state has any special interest in exercising jurisdiction, and whether the convenience of the parties favors litigating in another state.[83]

§ 4.12 *Erie* Considerations

In diversity cases, personal jurisdiction is determined by reference to the law of the jurisdiction in which the federal court sits.[84] A two-part test is followed when determining questions of personal jurisdiction. The court must determine first if

---

[76] Brand v. Menlove Dodge, 796 F.2d 1070, 1074 (9th Cir. 1986).

[77] Institutional Food Marketing Assocs. v. Golden State Strawberries, Inc., 747 F.2d 448, 455 (8th Cir. 1984); *see* Piper Acceptance Corp. v. Roudybush, 748 F.2d 471, 473 (8th Cir. 1984).

[78] Precision Constr. Co. v. J.A. Slattery Co., 765 F.2d 114, 118 (8th Cir. 1985).

[79] Thompson v. Chrysler Motors Corp., 755 F.2d 1162, 1169 (5th Cir. 1985).

[80] Waffenschmidt v. MacKay, 763 F.2d 711, 723 (5th Cir. 1985), *cert. denied,* ___ U.S. ___, 106 S. Ct. 794 (1985).

[81] *See* Cutco Indus., Inc. v. Naughton, 806 F.2d 361, 365 (2d Cir. 1986); Stuart v. Spademan, 772 F.2d 1185, 1192 (5th Cir. 1985); Olsen by Sheldon v. Government of Mexico, 729 F.2d 641, 649 (9th Cir.), *cert. denied,* 469 U.S. 917 (1984).

[82] *See, e.g.,* Thompson v. Chrysler Motors Corp., 755 F.2d 1162, 1173 (5th Cir. 1985).

[83] *Id.* at 1173–74; *see* Piper Acceptance Corp. v. Roudybush, 748 F.2d 471, 473 (8th Cir. 1984).

[84] Fed. R. Civ. P. 4 (e); Hoffritz for Cutlery, Inc. v. Amajac, Ltd., 763 F.2d 55, 57 (2d Cir. 1985); Thompson v. Chrysler Motors Corp., 755 F.2d 1162, 1166 (5th Cir. 1985); *see* Erie R.R. v. Tompkins, 304 U.S. 64 (1938) (requiring state substantive law to be applied in diversity cases).

statutory authority exists for the exercise of jurisdiction under the laws of the state and second if the exercise of jurisdiction complies with federal constitutional standards of due process.[85] Although the reach of the state long-arm statute is a question of state law and federal courts are required to accept the interpretation given the statute by the state Supreme Court, the extent to which the reach of the long-arm statute is limited by due process is a question of federal law.[86] If the long-arm statute confers jurisdiction coextensive with federal due process, the court follows the federal due process approach,[87] although it can consider state cases as persuasive.[88] Many states currently permit jurisdiction to the extent permitted by the Constitution; others limit assertions of jurisdiction to persons or entities transacting or doing business in the state for actions arising from such transactions.[89]

§ 4.13 Admiralty Cases

Controversy exists about how due process is evaluated in admiralty cases. Although the due process clause of the Fifth Amendment determines whether the court has personal jurisdiction over the defendant in admiralty,[90] some courts require a Fourteenth Amendment minimum contacts analysis, because service in admiralty is made pursuant to state long-arm statutes.[91] Other courts reject the view that federal jurisdiction is limited by a state's power, because due process requires only sufficient contacts within the United States as a whole when jurisdiction is national in scope.[92]

---

[85] Giotis v. Apollo of the Ozarks, Inc., 800 F.2d 660, 664–65 (7th Cir. 1986); Jenkins v. Whittaker Corp., 785 F.2d 720, 723 (9th Cir.), *cert. denied,* ____ U.S. ____, 107 S. Ct. 324 (1986); Blue Ridge Bank v. Veribanc, Inc., 755 F.2d 371, 373 (4th Cir. 1985); Thompson v. Chrysler Motors Corp., 755 F.2d 1162, 1166 (5th Cir. 1985).

[86] Scullin Steel v. National Ry. Utilization Corp., 676 F.2d 309, 311 (8th Cir. 1982); Lakeside Bridge & Steel Co. v. Mountain State Constr. Co., 597 F.2d 596, 599 (7th Cir. 1979), *cert. denied,* 445 U.S. 907 (1980); *see generally* 2 J. Moore *et al.,* Moore's Federal Practice ¶ 4.41-1[4.-2] (2d Cir. 1986).

[87] *See, e.g.,* Paccar Int'l, Inc. v. Commercial Bank of Kuwait, 757 F.2d 1058, 1063 (9th Cir. 1985).

[88] *E.g.,* Data Disc, Inc. v. Systems Technology Assocs. Inc., 557 F.2d 1280, 1287 n.3 (9th Cir. 1977).

[89] *See, e.g.,* Young v. Colgate-Palmolive Co., 790 F.2d 567, 569 (7th Cir. 1986) (Illinois law); Gray v. O'Brien, 777 F.2d 864, 867 (1st Cir. 1985) (Massachusetts law); Farnham v. Bristow Helicopters, Inc., 776 F.2d 535, 537–38 (5th Cir. 1985) (Louisiana law); *see also* Rann v. McInnis, 789 F.2d 374, 376–77 (6th Cir. 1986) (narrowly applying Michigan law).

[90] Pacific Atl. Trading Co. v. M/V Main Express, 758 F.2d 1325, 1327 (9th Cir. 1985); Handley v. Indiana & Mich. Elec. Co., 732 F.2d 1265, 1271 (6th Cir. 1984); DeJames v. Magnificence Carriers, Inc., 654 F.2d 280, 283 (3d Cir.), *cert. denied,* 454 U.S. 1085 (1981).

[91] Pacific Atl. Trading Co. v. M/V Main Express, 758 F.2d 1325, 1327 (9th Cir. 1985); DeJames v. Magnificence Carriers, Inc., 654 F.2d 280, 284 (3d Cir.), *cert. denied,* 454 U.S. 1085 (1981) (both applying state long-arm statutes).

[92] Trans-Asiatic Oil Ltd. S.A. v. Apex Oil Co., 743 F.2d 956, 959 (1st Cir. 1984); F.T.C. v. Jim Walter Corp., 651 F.2d 251, 256 (5th Cir. 1981); *see* Handley v. Indiana & Mich. Elec. Co., 732 F.2d 1265, 1272 (6th Cir. 1984).

§ 4.14 Federal Question Cases

Similarly, there is some question if a state long-arm statute limits personal jurisdiction in a federal question action. In federal cases, the Fifth Amendment applies and imposes a general fairness test including minimum contacts.[93] However, the issue arises whether the minimum contacts must exist with the particular district or state where the defendant was sued or merely with the United States. When nationwide service is authorized, courts usually require minimum contacts with the United States rather than any particular district.[94] Most circuits have held that, if the federal statute is silent as to the service of process in a federal question case, the state long-arm statute must be applied.[95] A few courts permit jurisdiction over a foreign corporation to be founded on the corporation's contacts with the United States as a whole as opposed to its contacts with the forum state. This is referred to as national contacts or aggregrate contacts theory.[96]

The RICO statute,[97] which provides for nationwide service of process when "the ends of justice" require it, has been interpreted as requiring (1) that personal jurisdiction exist over at least one of the participants in an alleged multidistrict conspiracy; and (2) that no other district exist in which a court has personal jurisdiction over all of the alleged coconspirators.[98] Similarly, there is no independent federal civil coconspirator theory of personal jurisdiction.[99] There is some question whether pendent personal jurisdiction may be asserted over state claims if personal jurisdiction over the federal claim is dependent on a

---

[93] Max Daetwyler Corp. v. Meyer, 762 F.2d 290, 293 (3d Cir.), *cert. denied,* ____ U.S. ____, 106 S. Ct. 383 (1985).

[94] *See, e.g.,* Securities Investors Protection Corp. v. Vigman, 764 F.2d 1309, 1316–17 (9th Cir. 1985) (S.E.C. action); Johnson Creative Arts, Inc. v. Wool Masters, 743 F.2d 947, 950 (1st Cir. 1984); F.T.C. v. Jim Walter Corp., 651 F.2d 251, 256 (5th Cir. 1981); Mariash v. Morrill, 496 F.2d 1138, 1143 (2d Cir. 1974).

[95] *See* Point Landing, Inc. v. Omni Capital Int'l, Ltd., 795 F.2d 415, 426–27 (5th Cir. 1986) (en banc), *cert. granted,* ____ U.S. ____, 107 S. Ct. 946 (1987) (Commodity Exchange Act); Max Daetwyler Corp. v. Meyer, 762 F.2d 290, 297 (3d Cir. 1985), *cert. denied,* ____ U.S. ____, 106 S. Ct. 383 (1985) (patent infringement case); Wells Fargo Co. v. Wells Fargo Express Co., 556 F.2d 406, 418 (9th Cir. 1977) (Lanham Act).

[96] Chrysler Corp. v. Fedders Corp., 643 F.2d 1229, 1237–38 (6th Cir.), *cert. denied,* 454 U.S. 893 (1981); *see generally* Born, *Reflections on Judicial Jurisdiction in International Cases,* 17 Ga. J. Int'l & Comp. L. 1 (1987); Lilly, *Jurisdiction Over Domestic and Alien Defendants,* 69 Va. L. Rev. 85, 127–45 (1983); Note, *National Contacts as a Basis for In Person Jurisdiction Over Aliens in Federal Question Cases,* 70 Cal. L. Rev. 686 (1982); Note, *Alien Corporations and Aggregate Contacts: A Genuinely Federal Jurisdictional Standard,* 95 Harv. L. Rev. 470 (1981).

[97] 18 U.S.C. § 1965(b) (1982).

[98] Butcher's Union Local No. 498 v. SDC Inv. Inc., 788 F.2d 535, 539 (9th Cir. 1986); *see* Caldwell v. Palmetto State Sav. Bank, 811 F.2d 916, 918 (5th Cir. 1987) (defendant must be conducting business in forum).

[99] Davis v. A & J Elecs., 792 F.2d 74, 75–76 (7th Cir. 1986).

statute authorizing nationwide service.[100] For example, if the defendant is served pursuant to RICO, can state fraud charges be heard if the defendant has insufficient contacts with the forum to satisfy minimum contacts?

§ 4.15 Conclusion

In structuring business dealings, the potential for being haled into a distant, inconvenient forum should always be considered. However, it is clear that as long as many states are authorizing jurisdiction to the extent permitted by the Constitution, nationwide marketing can be considered the same as nationwide jurisdiction.[101] Generally, only single sales have escaped the reach of minimum contacts. Therefore, as a practical matter, most personal jurisdiction motions should be served concurrently with alternative motions for change of venue for the convenience of the witnesses or for dismissal on forum non conveniens grounds.[102] Although these two motions are not waived if brought at another time, the judge may be more disposed to granting an alternative motion when considering the jurisdictional issue than later when it may appear to be simply a strategic ploy. On the other hand, the personal jurisdiction motion should request dismissal rather than transfer to a district where jurisdiction is proper, since the plaintiff rather than the defendant should suggest this alternative. In fact, some courts grant dismissals rather than transfers on the theory that counsel has a basic obligation to understand jurisdictional requirements. The procedural considerations concerning personal jurisdiction motions are considered in depth in §§ **14.17–14.30**.

§ 4.16 Personal Jurisdiction Checklist

General Jurisdiction

1. Have there been continuous or substantial activities in the forum?
   a. If so, the litigation can concern acts unrelated to the forum.

---

[100] *See generally* Note, *Personal Jurisdiction and the Joinder of Claims in the Federal Courts,* 64 Tex. L. Rev. 1463 (1986).

[101] *See* Hirsch v. Blue Cross, Blue Shield of Kansas City, 800 F.2d 1474, 1479 (9th Cir. 1986) (insurer knew that insuree employed people nationwide); Eli Lilly & Co. v. Home Ins. Co., 794 F.2d 710, 720–21 (D.C. Cir. 1986) (national insurer aware nationwide manufacturer could be haled into any court).

[102] See **ch. 6**.

Specific Jurisdiction

1. Does the litigation arise from activities in the forum?
2. Is due process satisfied?
   a. Does defendant have minimum contacts with forum?
      (1) Has the defendant purposefully availed itself of the benefits of the forum?
      (2) Was the harm to the plaintiff in the forum foreseeable?
      (3) Is the act an intentional tort which has "effects" in the forum?
      (4) Is defendant's placing of goods into the stream of commerce sufficient to assert jurisdiction?
      (5) Has defendant appealed to nationwide market?
      (6) Separate individual from corporate contacts.
      (7) Disregard unilateral acts of plaintiff, unless they enhance defendant's contacts to forum.
      (8) Contract with a forum resident by itself is not sufficient to assert jurisdiction.
      (9) Choice of law provision by itself is not sufficient to assert jurisdiction.
   b. Is the assertion of jurisdiction reasonable?
      (1) What is the burden on the defendant?
      (2) What is the forum's interest in litigating the dispute?
      (3) Would asserting jurisdiction result in an efficient resolution of the conflict?
      (4) Does assertion of jurisdiction further substantive social policies?
3. If the forum is reasonable, a lesser showing of minimum contacts may suffice.
4. If minimum contacts are present, less reasonableness is required.

Diversity Jurisdiction Two-Part Test

1. Are requirements of the forum state's long-arm statute met?
2. If long-arm jurisdiction is met, does assertion of jurisdiction satisfy federal due process standards?

Admiralty and Federal Question Litigation

1. Does the relevant circuit or statute apply the forum state's long-arm statute, or is jurisdiction appropriate if defendant has minimum contacts with United States?

Possible Alternative Motions

1. Rule 12(b)(2) motion to dismiss for lack of personal jurisdiction (see §§ **14.17–14.30**)
   a. Motion due within 20 days (Rule 12 timing)
2. Rule 12(b)(3) motion to dismiss for improper venue (see §§ **14.31–14.37**)
   a. Motion due within 20 days (Rule 12 timing)
3. § 1406(a) motion to transfer for improper venue (see § **6.9**)
   a. Motion due within 20 days (Rule 12 timing)
4. Motion to dismiss for forum non conveniens (see §§ **6.15–6.21**)
   a. No timing limitation, but often brought with Rule 12(b)(2) motion
5. § 1631 motion to transfer to cure want of jurisdiction (see § **6.9**)
   a. No timing limitation, but often brought in response to Rule 12(b)(2) motion
6. § 1404(a) motion to transfer for convenience of witnesses (see §§ **6.7–6.8**)
   a. No timing limitation, but often brought with Rule 12(b)(2) motion
7. All of the above motions should be supported by affidavits where feasible.

CHAPTER 5

SERVING THE DEFENDANT

§ 5.1 Service of Process

Rule 4, which controls the mechanisms for service of process, is considered a flexible rule to be liberally construed as long as a party receives sufficient notice of the complaint.[1] However, the 1983 changes to Rule 4 have created several pitfalls for unwary practitioners. It is important to understand the requirements of service, because ineffective service of process results in inability to obtain personal jurisdiction over the defendant[2] and not being able to enter a default judgment.[3]

---

[1] United Food & Commercial Workers Union v. Alpha Beta Co., 736 F.2d 1371, 1382 (9th Cir. 1984); F.T.C. v. Compagnie de Saint-Gobain-Pont-A-Mousson, 636 F.2d 1300, 1312 (D.C. Cir. 1980); *see generally* 2 J. Moore *et al.*, Moore's Federal Practice ¶ 4.02 (2d ed. 1986) [hereinafter Moore's Federal Practice].

[2] *See, e.g.*, Delta S.S. Lines, Inc. v. Albano, 768 F.2d 728, 730 (5th Cir. 1985).

[3] Feist v. Jefferson County Comm'rs Court, 778 F.2d 250, 252 (5th Cir. 1985); Zeviar v. Local No. 2747, Airline Employees, 733 F.2d 556, 558 n.3 (8th Cir. 1984).

Service must be distinguished from personal jurisdiction, since the fact that a defendant is properly served pursuant to Rule 4 does not guarantee that the court had personal jurisdiction over the defendant. For example, service may be technically correct, yet personal jurisdiction may be deficient because of the absence of minimum contacts. Conversely, personal jurisdiction may exist in the jurisdiction if the defendant was properly served but the actual service was defective.

§ 5.2 Geographical Limits of Effective Service

Federal courts do not have nationwide personal jurisdiction or service of process unless specifically authorized.[4] With minor exceptions, in all other instances a federal court's territorial limit of effective service is the state in which it sits.[5] Therefore, the usual manner of obtaining service in other states is pursuant to the law of the state in which the federal district court is located.[6] Thus, the state's long-arm statute always governs in diversity cases and also is controlling in most federal actions. It should be noted that Rule 4(f) permits service on a third party defendant within a 100-mile bulge area. Courts differ as to whether such jurisdiction is determined by contacts with the forum or the bulge area,[7] but service appears to be permitted under this rule even though it would not be appropriate pursuant to state law.[8]

§ 5.3 Methods Used in Effective Service

Rule 4 provides a fairly complex scheme by which a party can obtain service. The basic ways of effectuating service within the United States are pursuant to the law of the state in which the district court sits,[9] by mail,[10] or through personal service.[11] Regardless of the method of service used, the summons and complaint must be served together.[12]

---

[4] Fed. R. Civ. P. 4(e), (f); *see, e.g.*, Securities Investors Protection Act, 15 U.S.C. § 78aa (1982); Securities Investors Protection Corp. v. Vigman, 764 F.2d 1309, 1314 (9th Cir. 1985) and cases cited therein.

[5] Fed. R. Civ. 4(f).

[6] Fed. R. Civ. 4(e).

[7] *See generally* Walker, *The 1983 Amendments to Federal Rule of Civil Procedure 4—Process, Jurisdiction and Erie Principles Revisited,* 19 Wake Forest L. Rev. 957, 979 (1983).

[8] Quinones v. Pennsylvania Gen. Ins. Co., 804 F.2d 1167, 1177 (10th Cir. 1986); Sprow v. Hartford Ins. Co., 594 F.2d 412, 417 (5th Cir. 1979).

[9] Fed. R. Civ. P. 4(c)(2)(C)(i).

[10] Fed. R. Civ. P. 4(c)(2)(C)(ii).

[11] Fed. R. Civ. P. 4(d).

[12] *Id.*

§ 5.4 Substantive Considerations Concerning Process

When process is served according to state law, federal law determines whether the method of service is constitutional, and state law governs the method of service and its interpretation.[13] Due process dictates that defendants be given notice which is reasonably calculated, under all the circumstances, to apprise them of the existence of the action and to afford them an opportunity to present objections.[14] Therefore, counsel must be careful whenever posting is employed, since the constitutionality of this method depends upon whether in the circumstances of the case the notice is reasonably calculated to inform those served.[15] Similarly, service in a foreign country pursuant to Rule 4(i), which permits the plaintiff to use the law of the state forum, may be scrutinized for exactitude when service is made by publication.[16]

The requirements of state law are extremely important in diversity cases since the federal court applies the state's statute of limitations[17] and follows state rules concerning when the action commences.[18] Thus, when the act of service is an integral part of the state statute of limitations, a federal court requires service before the statute is tolled.[19] In other words, in those states, the statute of limitations is not tolled until the defendant has been served.[20] Therefore, Rule 3's provision that the filing of an action commences the suit is ineffective in diversity cases when the state provides that the summons must be served within the statutory period. As a result, counsel cannot rely on Rule 3 in diversity cases without reviewing the state's commencement statute or rule to determine if it requires service in addition to filing. If this is so, and the end of the statutory period is imminent, it is necessary to determine if the state's commencement law is procedural or substantive, an issue that is not always self-evident and which may require interpretation of several state statutes.[21] If the state statute governs

---

[13] FDIC v. Schaffer, 731 F.2d 1134, 1136 (4th Cir. 1984); 4 C. Wright & A. Miller, Federal Practice and Procedure § 1075 (1969) [hereinafter Federal Practice and Procedure].

[14] Mullane v. Central Hanover Bank & Trust Co., 339 U.S. 306, 314 (1950).

[15] Greene v. Lindsay, 456 U.S. 444, 449–50 (1982); *see* Greenbaum, *The Postman Never Rings Twice: The Constitutionality of Service of Process by Posting after Greene v. Lindsey,* 33 Am. U. L. Rev. 601 (1984).

[16] *See, e.g.*, Senior Loiza Corp. v. Vento Dev. Corp., 760 F.2d 20, 24–25 (1st Cir. 1985) (affidavit or verified complaint necessary unless judicial notice provides substantiation); *see also* Ristau, *Service of Process in Foreign Countries Under the Hague Service Convention,* 8 CEB Civ. Litigation Rep. 85 (1986).

[17] Guaranty Trust Co. v. York, 326 U.S. 99, 109–12 (1945).

[18] Walker v. Armco Steel Co., 446 U.S. 740, 751–52 (1980); *see generally,* Note, *Commencement Rules and Tolling Statutes of Limitations in Federal Court,* 66 Cornell L. Rev. 842 (1981).

[19] Walker v. Armco Steel Co., 446 U.S. 740, 751–52 (1980); Blaha v. A.H. Robbins & Co., 708 F.2d 238, 239 (6th Cir. 1983).

[20] *See, e.g.,* Rosa v. Cantrell, 705 F.2d 1208, 1211 (10th Cir. 1982), *cert. denied,* 464 U.S. 821 (1983) (discussing N.Y. Civ. Prac. L. & R. 203b).

[21] *See* Cambridge Mut. Fire Ins. Co. v. City of Claxton, 720 F.2d 1230, 1233 (11th Cir. 1983); Calhoun v. Ford, 625 F.2d 576 (5th Cir. 1980).

and service is untimely, any state provision which excuses late service if the plaintiff was diligent in attempting to serve the defendant is interpreted according to state law,[22] although the method of service is still dictated by the appropriate federal rules.[23]

Even if the state law also provides for commencement by filing, service within the statute of limitations period may became key if a mistake has been made in naming the defendant, since Rule 15(c) provides for an amendment to relate back to filing of the original complaint only if the party received notice within the limitations period. In other words, a complaint timely filed just before the limitations period expires but served beyond the statutory period does not permit a later filed amendment adding or modifying parties to relate back to the original complaint.[24] Therefore, it is always safer to serve the defendants within the appropriate limitations period.

§ 5.5 Commencement in Federal Actions

Rule 3's provision for commencement upon filing also does not control when service is made pursuant to a federal statute that provides otherwise. For example, the Federal Torts Claims Act[25] has been interpreted by several circuits to require commencement by service of process,[26] since notice within the statutory period is required.[27] In a federal action when the court borrows a state statute of limitations, it appears that the federal commencement rule applies.[28] Therefore, in a hybrid claim alleging breach of fair representation by a union, service was timely when made within 120 days of filing, even though that period fell outside the six-month statute of limitations for such actions.[29]

§ 5.6 Personal Service

Rule 4(d) provides that personal service can be made on an individual, other than an infant or incompetent, by delivering a copy of the summons and complaint personally to the defendant, or by leaving copies at the defendant's dwelling or

---

22 *See* Cambridge Mut. Fire Ins. Co. v. City of Claxton, 720 F.2d 1230, 1233 (11th Cir. 1983).

23 Hanna v. Plumer, 380 U.S. 460, 463–64 (1965).

24 Schiavone v. Fortune, ____ U.S. ____, 106 S. Ct. 2379, 2384–85 (1986).

25 28 U.S.C. § 2401(b) (1982).

26 Stewart v. United States, 655 F.2d 741, 742 (7th Cir. 1981); Carr v. Veterans Admin., 522 F.2d 1355, 1357–58 (5th Cir. 1975); Evans v. Veteran's Admin., 391 F.2d 261, 262 (2d Cir. 1968), *cert. denied,* 393 U.S. 1040 (1969).

27 *See* Hughes v. United States, 701 F.2d 56, 58 (7th Cir. 1982).

28 West v. Conrail, ____ U.S. ____, ____ S. Ct. ____, 55 U.S.L.W. 4466, 4467 (Apr. 7, 1987).

29 *Id.*

usual place of abode with some person of suitable age and discretion residing there, or by delivering a copy of the summons and complaint to an agent authorized by appointment or by law to receive such service. The 1983 amendment to Rule 4 virtually eliminated service of summons by marshals, since any nonparty over 18 can properly serve a summons.[30] Service by a marshal is generally restricted to court-ordered service unless service is made on behalf of the United States or its officers or agencies.[31]

§ 5.7 Serving Entities

Under Rule 4(d)(3), a party may personally serve an officer, a manager, or a general agent of a corporation. Federal, not state, standards define who such agents are.[32] Rule 4(d)(3) is a procedural method for acquiring but not conferring jurisdiction.[33] It provides a federal alternative to any state method of obtaining process upon a domestic or foreign corporation.[34] However, care must be taken in utilizing this rule to serve unincorporated associations in diversity cases.[35] Such associations cannot be served under a common name pursuant to this rule unless state law so provides.[36] Merely adding the representative of an unincorporated association to the heading of a complaint does not provide a basis for service if the individual is not included in any allegations in the complaint.[37]

§ 5.8 Serving the United States

Rule 4(d) sets out the requirements for service on the United States and its officers or agencies. Rule 4(d)(4) specifies that service upon the United States is completed by delivering a copy of the summons and complaint to the United States attorney, an assistant United States attorney, or an employee designated by the United States attorney for the district in which the action is brought. In addition, a copy of the summons and complaint must be sent by registered or certified mail to the attorney general of the United States, and in actions attacking the validity of an order of an officer or agency not made a party, the

---

[30] Fed. R. Civ. P. 4(c)(2)(A).

[31] *See* Fed. R. Civ. P. 4(c)(2)(B).

[32] Jim Fox Enters. Inc. v. Air France, 705 F.2d 738, 741 n.8 (5th Cir. 1983); *see* 4 Federal Practice and Procedure § 1103.

[33] Arrowsmith v. United Press Int'l, 320 F.2d 219, 223–31 (2d Cir. 1963), *cited with approval in* Jim Fox Enters. Inc. v. Air France, 705 F.2d 738, 741 (5th Cir. 1983).

[34] *Id.*

[35] *See* Oyler v. National Guard Ass'n of United States, 743 F.2d 545, 550 (7th Cir. 1984).

[36] *Id.*

[37] *Id.* at 551.

officer or agency must also be served by registered or certified mail. Rule 4(d)(5) authorizes service upon an officer or agency of the United States by serving the United States in addition to serving the officer or agency by registered or certified mail. Agencies which are corporations can be served as ordinary corporations pursuant to Rule 4(d)(3).

Courts are usually unforgiving about errors in serving the United States[38] and often discuss the mandatory nature of the procedures.[39] As the Ninth Circuit noted, failure to read the Rules of Civil Procedure is not good cause to excuse improper service upon the United States.[40]

Some failures in service have been forgiven. For example, failure to personally serve the United States attorney did not result in dismissal when (1) the party not personally served received actual notice; (2) the defendant suffered no prejudice from the defect in service; (3) there was justifiable excuse for the failure to serve properly; and (4) the plaintiff would have been severely prejudiced if the complaint had been dismissed.[41]

Appealing from a dismissal may not always be the wisest decision. As the Eighth Circuit observed in a case involving improper service, counsel might be better served by refiling the complaint and making certain that it is properly served rather than contesting a dismissal if the statute of limitations is likely to run in the interim.[42]

§ 5.9 Service by Mail

Changes made to Rule 4 in 1983 concerning first class mail have spurred litigation.[43] Service by mail is now appropriate under federal procedure and also if the law of the state forum authorizes it. Federal procedure pursuant to Rule 4(c)(2)(C)(ii) sets forth a complicated scheme which requires that personal service be made if the plaintiff does not receive an acknowledgment of service within 20 days of mailing, even if the defendant has received actual notice.[44] To serve a defendant by first class mail, the plaintiff must send the summons,

---

[38] C & L Farms, Inc. v. Federal Crop Ins. Corp., 771 F.2d 407, 408 (8th Cir. 1985).

[39] *See* Sanchez-Mariana v. Ellingwood, 691 F.2d 592, 594 (1st Cir. 1982).

[40] Whale v. United States, 792 F.2d 951, 953 (9th Cir. 1986); Reynolds v. United States, 782 F.2d 837, 838 (9th Cir. 1986).

[41] Borzeka v. Heckler, 739 F.2d 444, 446–48 (9th Cir. 1984).

[42] C & L Farms, Inc. v. Federal Crop Ins. Corp., 771 F.2d 407, 409 (8th Cir. 1985).

[43] *See generally* Siegel, *Practice Commentary on Amendments to Federal Rule 4,* 96 F.R.D. 88 (1983); Walker, *The 1983 Amendments to Federal Rule of Civil Procedure 4—Process, Jurisdiction and Erie Principles Revisited,* 19 Wake Forest L. Rev. 957 (1983); Note, *Rule 4: Service by Mail May Cost You More Than A Stamp,* 61 Ind. L.J. 217 (1986); Note, *Service of Process by First-Class Mail under Rule 4 of the Federal Rules of Civil Procedure,* 15 Rutgers L.J. 993, 1012 (1984).

[44] *See* Armco, Inc. v. Penrod-Stauffer Bldg. Sys., 733 F.2d 1087, 1089 (4th Cir. 1984).

complaint, two copies of the notice and acknowledgment, and a return envelope to the defendant.[45] Courts may overlook minor discrepancies, such as the omission of the return envelope or a slightly different wording of the form than that recommended.[46] However, complete failure to indicate that acknowledgment is necessary warranted dismissal when copies of the notice or acknowledgment specifically prescribed by the rule and a stamped self-addressed envelope were not included.[47]

If the plaintiff waits to serve the defendant by mail until the statute of limitations has almost run, personal service required by the defendant's failure to acknowledge service may occur after the limitations period. The timeliness of such service can be an issue in jurisdictions requiring service to commence an action. The Second Circuit has upheld such service, viewing service as complete upon mailing;[48] other circuits appear to consider mail service as completed only upon acknowledgment or, failing that, when the defendant is personally served.[49] Moreover, one circuit has held that if the defendant does not acknowledge service by mail under Rule 4(c)(2)(C)(ii), the plaintiff must employ personal service pursuant to that rule and cannot convert the service into a method otherwise authorized under state law.[50] Therefore, even though state service rules authorize ordinary or certified mailing, the plaintiff may not be able to choose that method once federal service by mail has been attempted.

Rule 4(c)(2)(D) provides that the plaintiff can recover the cost of personal service for an unacknowledged service by mail. However, this is small consolation if the statute of limitations bars the action before personal service can be effectuated. Although it can be argued that a defense counsel should not be able to frustrate service by failing to acknowledge it if this results in the action's being untimely, if counsel does nothing to mislead the plaintiff, Rule 4 permits this option subject only to paying the cost of personal service.[51]

It has been suggested that if service is made by mail, a return receipt should be requested or certified mail should be used rather than first class mail, as called for in the rule.[52] Although the Second Circuit has considered certified mailing as

---

[45] Fed. R. Civ. P. 4(c)(2)(C)(ii).

[46] *See* Fed. R. Civ. P. App. of Forms, Form 18-A.

[47] Norlock v. City of Garland, 768 F.2d 654, 656 (5th Cir. 1985).

[48] Morse v. Elmira Country Club, 752 F.2d 35, 37–38 (2d Cir. 1984).

[49] *See, e.g.*, Stranahan Gear Co. v. N.L. Indus., Inc., 800 F.2d 53, 56–57 (3d Cir. 1986); Norlock v. City of Garland, 768 F.2d 654, 657 (5th Cir. 1985); Armco, Inc. v. Penrod-Stauffer Bldg. Sys., Inc., 733 F.2d 1087, 1089 (4th Cir. 1984).

[50] Armco, Inc. v. Penrod-Stauffer Bldg. Sys., 733 F.2d 1087, 1089 (4th Cir. 1984). *But see* Humana, Inc. v. Jacobson, 804 F.2d 1390, 1393 (5th Cir. 1986). *See generally* Vairo, *Amended Rule 4 of Civil Procedure and Its Effects on Process Serving,* Nat'l L.J. 32 (Dec. 17, 1984); Comment, *Civil Procedure-Service of Summons and Complaint under State Law Subsequent to Attempted Service under Rule 4(c)(2)(C)(ii),* 14 Memphis St. U. L. Rev. 565 (1984).

[51] Stranahan Gear Co. v. NL Indus., Inc., 800 F.2d 53, 57 (3d Cir. 1986).

[52] *Id.*

unnecessary, and not invalidating service,[53] it can be argued that such mailing is not authorized by the rule. The Fifth Circuit has held that certified mail delivery alone without any acknowledgment device was not the equivalent of service under Rule 4(c)(2)(C)(ii).[54] Similarly, the defendant's signing of a certified mail receipt but not the acknowledgment has not been considered sufficient service.[55]

If the state mailing provision is less ambiguous than the federal provision, state law should be employed. When using state mailing procedures counsel must be careful to follow the state procedures exactly; otherwise, the court may decide that federal procedures were used which require return and acknowledgment by the defendant.[56]

§ 5.10 Timing for Answering Complaint When Service Is by Mail

Questions also exist as to the running of the 20-day period to answer the complaint if service is made by mail,[57] since Rule 4 is silent on when service is complete for purposes of answering a complaint. It is equally plausible to argue that service is completed on receipt or that it is completed upon acknowledgment by the defendant. If acknowledgment is the key date, a defendant can wait until the end of the 20-day period to acknowledge receipt, in effect giving the defendant almost 40 days to answer a complaint,[58] or can entirely withhold acknowledgment, which makes the answer due 20 days after personal service. On the other hand, if a court views service as complete on receipt, the defendant can be technically in default well before 20 days after returning the acknowledgment,[59] although the court would likely vacate any such default judgment.

§ 5.11 120-Day Service Period

Probably the greatest pitfall for the state practitioner is found in Rule 4(j), which requires plaintiffs to serve process within 120 days following the filing of the

---

[53] Morse v. Elmira Country Club, 752 F.2d 35, 36 n.2 (2d Cir. 1984).

[54] Delta S.S. Lines, Inc. v. Albano, 768 F.2d 728, 730 (5th Cir. 1985).

[55] United States v. Gluklick, 801 F.2d 834, 835–37 (6th Cir. 1986).

[56] *See, e.g.*, Delta S.S. Lines, Inc. v. Albano, 768 F.2d 728, 730 (5th Cir. 1985).

[57] *See, e.g.*, J. Wagstaffe, W. Schwarzer, W. Tashima, & B. Gray, Commencing and Removing Actions to Federal Court 312–15 (1984); Note, *Rule 4: Service by Mail May Cost You More Than a Stamp,* 61 Ind. L. J. 217, 235–36 (1986).

[58] Note, *Service of Process by First-Class Mail under Rule 4 of the Federal Rules of Civil Procedure,* 15 Rutgers L.J. 993, 1021 (1984).

[59] *Cf.* Morse v. Elmira Country Club, 752 F.2d 35, 37–38 (2d Cir. 1984) (no tack-on period for service, but statute of limitations tolled with mailing, even though no acknowledgment sent).

complaint. This provision differs significantly from service requirements in many state systems, which permit as much as several years for service to be completed.[60] Rule 4(j) provides that if counsel does not serve the defendant within 120 days and no showing of good cause exists, the complaint must be dismissed. The only exception is when the defense of insufficient service has been waived by such conduct as failure to timely assert it, stipulating to a settlement, or agreeing to accept service.[61]

Rule 4(j) determines the time only for completing service, not for tolling the statute of limitations. Therefore, the 120-day period does not tack on to the applicable statute of limitations. In jurisdictions where the statute is tolled on filing the complaint, counsel has 120 days to complete service after filing, which may include time after the statute has run. If proper service is not made within the 120 days, the case cannot be refiled after it is dismissed.[62] In states where the statute of limitations is not tolled until service,[63] the service must fall within the statute of limitations period to be timely, regardless of the fact that Rule 4 appears to provide 120 days for service.[64]

Although the 120-day service period does not apply to service in a foreign country pursuant to Rule 4(i), it has been applied to service of foreign defendants under other provisions of Rule 4.[65] The 120 days for service provided by Rule 4(j) has actually resulted in giving plaintiffs additional time in cases filed under § 10(b) of the National Labor Relations Act[66] and § 301 of the Labor Management Relations Act.[67] For example, the Supreme Court has held that § 301 complaints need not be served within the six-month limitations period as long as service is effected within the 120 days authorized by Rule 4(j).[68] Courts are split as to whether the requirement that admiralty suits be served "forthwith" means that service within 120 days provided by Rule 4(j) can ever be deemed untimely.[69]

---

[60] *E.g.*, Cal. Civ. Proc. Code § 583.210 (West Supp. 1987).

[61] United States v. Gluklick, 801 F.2d 834, 837 (6th Cir. 1986); *cf.* Insurance Corp. of Ireland, Ltd. v. Compagnie des Bauxites de Guinee, 456 U.S. 694, 703–04 (1982) (waiver of personal jurisdiction).

[62] *See* 2 Moore's Federal Practice ¶ 4.46, at 4-574.

[63] *E.g.*, N.Y Civ. Prac. L. & R. 304 (McKinney 1972).

[64] *See* Norlock v. City of Garland, 768 F.2d 654, 658 (5th Cir. 1985); Morse v. Elmira Country Club, 752 F.2d 35, 39–40, 42 (2d Cir. 1984); *see generally* 2 Moore's Federal Practice ¶ 4.46; Siegel, *Practice Commentary on Amendments to Federal Rule 4,* 96 F.R.D. 88, 106 (1983).

[65] Montalbano v. Easco Hand Tools, 766 F.2d 737, 740 (2d Cir. 1985).

[66] 29 U.S.C. § 160(b) (1982).

[67] 29 U.S.C. § 185 (1982).

[68] West v. Conrail, ____ U.S. ____, ____ S. Ct. ____, 55 U.S.L.W. 4466, 4467 (Apr. 6, 1987).

[69] *Compare* Jones & Laughlin Steel v. Mon River Towing, Inc., 772 F.2d 62, 65–66 (3d Cir. 1985) (4(j) controls) *with* Amella v. United States, 732 F.2d 711, 713 (9th Cir. 1984) (service must be forthwith).

§ 5.12 Rule 4(j) Dismissals

Counsel must be extremely careful about Rule 4 timing. Since Rule 4(j) dismissals are reviewed under an abuse of discretion standard,[70] appellate courts do not substitute their judgment for that of the trial court. For example, a Rule 4(j) dismissal has been affirmed even though no hearing was held in the district court, no opportunity was given to the plaintiff to serve process after the motion was noticed, and the Fifth Circuit recognized that the dismissal might result in the case being time barred.[71] Moreover, Rule 4(j) provides that a court can raise the lack of timely service on its own initiative if it gives notice to the plaintiff. Thus, counsel cannot rely on the failure of the opposing party to move for dismissal pursuant to Rule 4(j). The trial court usually warns the plaintiff in advance that it will dismiss for failure to serve a defendant, but disregard of a warning, although relevant, is not a prerequisite for a dismissal.[72] Therefore, Rule 4 should be viewed as virtually requiring the attorney to ensure that service is properly perfected by mail or through a private process server. In addition, once the plaintiff is aware that service is being contested, it may be prudent to attempt to serve or complete service properly, since the court can view the failure to do so as evidence of lack of good cause if it finds that the original service was improper.[73]

To avoid dismissal, if counsel is experiencing difficulty with service before expiration of the 120-day period, a Rule 6(b)(1) motion should be filed in an effort to extend the time for service.[74] If the 120-day period has expired, an extension can be granted only if the plaintiff shows good cause for failure to serve the defendant.[75] It is unclear whether good cause is the same as excusable neglect, which permits untimely extensions under Rule 6(b)(2) or requires due diligence.[76]

Evasion of service likely provides good case. Reliance of an incarcerated pro se in forma pauperis plaintiff upon service by United States marshals has also provided good cause.[77] However, other appropriate excuses are unclear. At a

---

70 United States *ex rel.* DeLoss v. Kenner Gen. Contractors, Inc., 764 F.2d 707, 709 (9th Cir. 1985); Edwards v. Edwards, 754 F.2d 298, 299 (8th Cir. 1985).

71 Norlock v. City of Garland, 768 F.2d 654, 657 (5th Cir. 1985).

72 United States *ex rel.* DeLoss v. Kenner Gen. Contractors, Inc., 764 F.2d 707, 710 (9th Cir. 1985).

73 *See* Norlock v. City of Garland, 768 F.2d 654, 657 (5th Cir. 1985).

74 United States *ex rel.* DeLoss v. Kenner Gen. Contractors, Inc., 764 F.2d 707, 711 (9th Cir. 1985).

75 *Id.*

76 *See* Winters v. Teledyne Movible Offshore, Inc., 776 F.2d 1304, 1306 (5th Cir. 1985) (good cause requires at least as much as excusable neglect); *see generally* 4 Federal Practice and Procedure §§ 1137–1138; Note, *Service of Process by First-Class Mail under Rule 4 of the Federal Rules of Civil Procedure,* 15 Rutgers L.J. 993, 1012 (1984).

77 *See* Romandette v. Weetabix Co., 807 F.2d 309, 311 (2d Cir. 1986).

minimum, all steps undertaken regarding service should be documented. Good cause was not found when the plaintiff alleged that he desired to amend his complaint before effectuating service, since a complaint can be amended after service.[78] The standard excuse that counsel inadvertently neglected to calendar the 120-day limit also does not provide good cause.[79] Equally unavailing was the strategic excuse for nonservice that a better settlement in the state compensation action was likely before the defendant developed his federal defense through discovery.[80] Several circuits have held that the fact that the dismissal results in time barring the claim is not a consideration in determining whether attorney neglect is considered good cause.[81]

§ 5.13 Conclusion

Plaintiffs should always attempt to serve defendants well within the statute of limitations; otherwise, the federal rules concerning process may act as a barrier to their claims. When actions are filed near the deadlines, careful adherence to the rules and an understanding of the interrelationship between federal and state law are required to ensure that service is proper. Conversely, the defendant must decide what posture it wishes to take concerning service, since defects in service are subject to waiver.

§ 5.14 Process Checklist

Provisions for Service

1. Does federal statute provide for national service?
2. If not, is service outside forum provided by state long-arm statute?
3. Is service to be made on a third party defendant who can be served within 100-mile bulge area?
4. Is service to be effected in a foreign country?
   a. Check alternatives provided by Rule 4(i)(1).

---

[78] Wei v. Hawaii, 763 F.2d 370, 372 (9th Cir. 1985).

[79] *Id.*

[80] Redding v. Essex Crane Rental Corp. of Ala., 752 F.2d 1077, 1078 (5th Cir. 1985).

[81] *Id.;* Winters v. Teledyne Movible Offshore, Inc., 776 F.2d 1304, 1307 (5th Cir. 1985).

Commencement of Action

1. Federal question litigation is commenced by filing the complaint, unless the relevant statute requires that service must be within specified time.
2. Diversity litigation is commenced by filing the complaint, unless the relevant state statute requires service in order to toll the statute of limitations.

Timely Service

1. Generally, has service been made within 120 days after filing complaint?
2. If state requires service to toll limitations period, has service been made before the expiration of that period, as well as within 120 days after filing (i.e., no tack-on period permitted for timely complaint for relation back purposes)?
3. If service was not timely, is a dismissal appropriate?
   a. Was good cause shown for failure to serve?
   b. Was an extension granted prior to the expiration of 120 days?
   c. Was the issue waived by acceptance of late service or failure to timely raise issue?
4. **Warning:** A dismissal for lack of timely service may prevent refiling due if new complaint is barred by the statute of limitations.

Return of Service

1. Has the return been made promptly within time for response?
2. Untimely return does not affect the validity of service.

Who Serves Complaint

1. Is the person a private process server?
2. Is the person a nonparty over the age of 18?
3. Has a court order been issued permitting a marshal to serve a complaint for a party other than the United States?

Who Can Be Served

1. Was the defendant the person served?
2. Was the person served of suitable age residing at defendant's dwelling or usual abode?

3. Was the corporate defendant's officer, manager, or agent served?
4. Was the unincorporated entity served under common name if permitted by state law?
5. Did service on the United States include service on the U.S. attorney, assistant U.S. attorney, or designated employee, plus a copy sent by registered or certified mail to the attorney general, and if relevant the agency being challenged?

Federal Service by Mail

1. Was first class mail used?
2. Were two copies of the acknowledgment and notice sent?
3. Was a return envelope enclosed?
4. Was the acknowledgment executed under oath or affirmation and sent within 20 days of mailing?
   a. If not, was personal service effected?
   b. Does circuit permit alternative state service by mail?
5. **Warning:** Use state mailing provisions if feasible when nearing end of limitations period.

Possible Motions Concerning Process

1. Rule 12(b)(4) motion to dismiss for insufficiency of process (see §§ **14.38, 14.39**)
   a. Motion due within 20 days (Rule 12 timing)
2. Rule 12(b)(5) motion to dismiss for insufficiency of service of process (see §§ **14.38, 14.39**)
   a. Motion due within 20 days (Rule 12 timing)
3. Rule 12(b)(2) motion to dismiss for lack of personal jurisdiction (see §§ **14.17–14.30**)
   a. Motion due within 20 days (Rule 12 timing)
4. Rule 4(j) motion to dismiss for failure to serve defendant within 120 days of filing (see §§ **5.11, 5.12**)
   a. No timing limitation, but can be waived

CHAPTER 6

CHOOSING THE MOST APPROPRIATE VENUE

§ 6.1 Venue Overview

Although jurisdiction and venue are often confused, there is a fundamental difference between them. Jurisdiction concerns the court's power to consider the suit on the merits, while venue merely concerns the place where the suit should be heard for the convenience of the litigants.[1] Thus, venue is not a jurisdictional prerequisite and does not affect a court's authority to adjudicate.[2] The only time venue is considered a jurisdictional element is upon removal when the federal court's derivative jurisdiction is defective, because improper venue is a state jurisdictional element.[3] However, the removal statute now permits federal jurisdiction, when appropriate, even if the state does not have jurisdiction.[4] Therefore, it is doubtful that venue can ever be a jurisdictional bar. Venue problems are often intertwined with questions of personal jurisdiction, but the two must be separated for purposes of Rule 12 motions.[5]

§ 6.2 Venue Provisions

The basic venue requirements are found in 28 U.S.C. §§ 1391–1407, although venue provisions can be found in a variety of other statutes.[6] The venue provision used in diversity cases is found in 28 U.S.C. § 1391(a), which provides that venue is proper in the judicial district in which all plaintiffs or all defendants reside or in which the claim arose.[7] Most other venue provisions do not permit venue to be established by the plaintiff's residence. Therefore, in an action based on a federal question, the plaintiff's residence cannot be relied upon as the basis for venue.[8]

If venue is based upon the plaintiffs' residence, all plaintiffs must reside in the same judicial district, not just the same state. On the other hand, if venue is based on defendants' residence, when defendants reside in different districts of the same state, venue is proper in any of such districts.[9] Since an individual's residence is his domicile, a person can be a resident of only one district.[10] In class actions, only the residences of the named representatives are considered.[11]

---

[1] *See* Leroy v. Great W. United Corp., 443 U.S. 173, 180 (1978); Panhandle E. Pipe Line Co. v. Federal Power Comm'n, 324 U.S. 635, 639 (1945).

[2] Harris Corp. v. National Iranian Radio & Television, 691 F.2d 1344, 1349 (11th Cir. 1982); *see* Neirbo Co. v. Bethlehem Shipbuilding Corp., 308 U.S. 165, 167–68 (1939).

[3] Transure, Inc. v. Marsh & McLennan, Inc., 766 F.2d 1297, 1300–01 (9th Cir. 1985).

[4] Pub. L. No. 99-336, § 3(a), 100 Stat. 637 (1986), to be codified at 28 U.S.C. § 1441(e).

[5] See **ch. 14**.

[6] *See generally* 15 C. Wright, A. Miller, *et al.*, Federal Practice and Procedure §§ 3810–25 (2d ed. 1986) [hereinafter Federal Practice and Procedure].

[7] 28 U.S.C. § 1391(a) (1982).

[8] 28 U.S.C. § 1391(b) (1982).

[9] 28 U.S.C. § 1392 (1982).

[10] See 1 J. Moore, *et al.* Moore's Federal Practice ¶ 0.142[5.-1-2] (2d ed. 1986) [hereinafter Moore's Federal Practice]; *see* 15 Federal Practice and Procedure § 3805 (criticizing minority position that residence and domicile are not identical).

[11] 15 Federal Practice and Procedure, § 3807, at 78.

Section 1391 applies to transitory actions and does not govern local actions which affect property.[12] Local actions must be brought where the property is found.[13]

§ 6.3 Corporate Residence

A defendant's corporate residence is the place where it is incorporated[14] and where it is licensed to do business or is doing business.[15] This broadened concept of residence does not apply to corporate plaintiffs, whose residence is limited to the place of incorporation.[16] Determining where a corporation is doing business has generated significant litigation in connection with personal jurisdiction and venue issues.[17] Commentators argue that the determination of doing business should be the same under the venue statute as for whether a corporation is amenable to service of process—that is, whether minimum contacts exist with the forum.[18] Several circuits, however, do not equate these concepts.[19] Instead, they view doing business for venue purposes as engaging in transactions in the district to such an extent and of such a nature that the state in which the district is located could require the foreign corporation to qualify to do business there.[20] In other words, if the state could require the foreign corporation to comply with its licensing scheme, venue is proper.[21] The venue of an unincorporated association also includes the place where it is doing business.[22] Residence of an unincorporated association focuses on the association or partnership entity rather than the residence of its individual members.[23]

---

[12] 1 Moore's Federal Practice ¶ 0.142[2.-1].

[13] *Id.*

[14] 28 U.S.C. § 1391(c) (1982); *see generally* 1 Moore's Federal Practice ¶ 0.142[5.1-3].

[15] 28 U.S.C. § 1391(c) (1982); *see generally* 15 Federal Practice and Procedure § 3811; *see also* 28 U.S.C. § 1400(b) (1982) (patent venue statute).

[16] *See* Rueben H. Donnelley Corp. v. FTC, 580 F.2d 264, 269 (7th Cir. 1978); 1 Moore's Federal Practice ¶ 0.142[5.-1-3], at 1414–16; 15 Federal Practice and Procedure § 3811, at 106–08.

[17] *See* 1 Moore's Federal Practice ¶ 0.142[5.-1-3], at 1409; Stern, *Federal Venue Demystified,* 7 C.E.B. Civ. Litigation Rep. 93, 95 (1986).

[18] 1 Moore's Federal Practice ¶ 0.142[5.-1-3], at 1411; Federal Practice and Procedure § 3811, at 117–18.

[19] *See* Eli Lilly & Co. v. Home Ins. Co., 794 F.2d 710, 721 (D.C. Cir. 1986); Johnson Creative Arts, Inc. v. Wool Masters, 743 F.2d 947, 954 (1st Cir. 1984).

[20] Eli Lilly & Co. v. Home Ins. Co., 794 F.2d 710, 721 (D.C. Cir. 1986).

[21] *Id* at 721–22.

[22] Denver R. G. & W. R.R. v. Brotherhood of R.R. Trainmen, 387 U.S. 556, 562 (1967).

[23] *See id.* at 559–60; Decker Coal Co. v. Commonwealth Edison Co., 805 F.2d 834, 841 (9th Cir. 1986).

§ 6.4 Determining Where the Claim Arose

Another common venue question is determining where the claim arose. *Leroy v. Great Western United Corp.,*[24] is the leading case examining this issue. Since venue provisions protect the defendant against the risk that a plaintiff will select an unfair or inconvenient place of trial,[25] *Leroy* concluded that there will usually be only one district in which the claim arose[26] and that this is determined by federal law.[27] In the unusual cases in which it is not clear where the claim arose, venue is determined by the availability of witnesses, accessibility of other relevant evidence, and the convenience of the defendant.[28] Courts have articulated different standards for determining where the claim arose, including significant contacts,[29] place of injury, and convenience of the parties,[30] but it is unclear whether these tests survive *Leroy.*[31]

Several circuits consider that a claim for breach of contract arises at the place of performance rather than at the place of repudiation.[32] In actions to enforce judgments, the claim arises in the state where the judgment was obtained, not the state in which the underlying claim arose.[33] Venue to confirm an arbitration award is proper in a district other than the district where the award was granted, as long as the court has subject matter jurisdiction over the action.[34] A district court sitting in bankruptcy can enter an order fixing the venue for trial of personal injury cases in the district court in which the bankruptcy case is pending or in which the claim arose.[35] However, the district court has discretion to abstain from exercising its bankruptcy jurisdiction.[36]

---

[24] 443 U.S. 173 (1978).

[25] *Id.* at 184.

[26] *Id.* at 185.

[27] *Id.* at 183 n.15.

[28] *Id.*

[29] *See, e.g.,* Data Disc, Inc. v. Systems Technology Assoc's, Inc., 557 F.2d 1280, 1289 (9th Cir. 1977).

[30] *See* Rosenfeld v. S.F.C. Corp., 702 F.2d 282, 284 (1st Cir. 1983).

[31] *See* Noxell Corp. v. Firehouse No. 1 Bar-B-Que Restaurant, 760 F.2d 312, 317 n.8 (D.C. Cir. 1985); 15 Federal Practice and Procedure § 3806.

[32] Decker Coal Co. v. Commonwealth Edison Co., 805 F.2d 834, 842 (9th Cir. 1986); American Carpet Mills v. Gunny Corp., 649 F.2d 1056, 1059 (5th Cir. 1981).

[33] Water West, Inc. v. Entek Corp., 788 F.2d 627, 629 (9th Cir. 1986).

[34] Smiga v. Dean Witter Reynolds, Inc., 766 F.2d 698, 706 (2d Cir. 1985), *cert. denied,* ____ U.S. ____, 106 S. Ct. 1381 (1986).

[35] 28 U.S.C. § 157(b)(5) (Supp. III 1985); A.H. Robins Co. v. Piccinin, 788 F.2d 994, 1010 (4th Cir.), *cert. denied,* ____ U.S., ____ 107 S. Ct. 251 (1986).

[36] A.H. Robins Co. v. Piccinin, 788 F.2d 994, 1010–1016 (4th Cir.), *cert. denied,*____ U.S. ____, 107 S. Ct. 251 (1986); Taggart, *The New Bankruptcy Court System,* 59 Am. Bankr. L.J. 231, 253 (1985).

§ 6.5 Venue of Coconspirators

A coconspirators venue theory has been adopted by several circuits in deciding venue in multidefendant litigation alleging violations of the federal securities statutes.[37] Generally, venue in securities cases is restricted to the district where any act or transaction constituting the violation occurred, or where the defendant is found, is an inhabitant, or transacts business.[38] Under the coconspirators theory, as long as venue is established for any of the defendants in the forum district, it is proper for all defendants, even in the absence of any contact by some of the defendants with the forum.[39] However, this theory of venue has been rejected by the Supreme Court in antitrust cases.[40]

§ 6.6 Dismissals and Transfers for Venue Reasons

Understanding the requirements of the individual transfer statutes, their relationship to dismissal motions, and their choice of law consequences can be critical in developing an overall strategy in a case which presents a variety of potential forums. The ability of federal courts to transfer actions out of state is probably one of their greatest advantages to diversity practitioners who would otherwise be limited by a state court's jurisdictional boundaries.

Venue motions are brought by defendants for one of three reasons:

1. To terminate the litigation because the dismissal results in time barring of the claim
2. To transfer the case for reasons of convenience, which also may result in the tactical advantage of making litigation more difficult for the plaintiff, and
3. To transfer the case for improper venue, which may play a significant role in the outcome of the litigation because the choice of law of the transferee court will apply.

Plaintiffs usually bring venue motions for two reasons:

---

[37] Securities Investors Protection Corp. v. Vigman, 764 F.2d 1309, 1317 (9th Cir. 1985); Hilgeman v. National Ins. Co. of America, 547 F.2d 298 (5th Cir. 1977); Wyndham Assocs. v. Blintiff, 398 F.2d 614 (2d Cir.), *cert. denied,* 393 U.S. 977 (1968).

[38] 15 U.S.C. § 78aa (1982).

[39] Securities Investor Protection Corp. v. Vigman, 764 F.2d 1309, 1317 (9th Cir. 1985); *see* 15 Federal Practice and Procedure § 3824.

[40] Bankers Life & Casualty Co. v. Holland, 346 U.S. 379, 384 (1953).

1. If venue is proper, the plaintiff can obtain the transferor's favorable law in a location which is convenient for its parties and witnesses; or
2. If venue is improper, a transfer to a proper district preserves the action.

Courts rarely dismiss an action outright for improper venue under Rule 12(b)(3)[41] or 28 U.S.C. § 1406 because of the existence of transfer provisions in 28 U.S.C. §§ 1404(a) and 1406(a), whose purpose is to permit transfers instead of dismissals.[42] However, defense counsel should always request an outright dismissal for improper venue rather than a § 1406(a) transfer, since district courts sometimes do dismiss actions when the plaintiff's venue choice is considered unreasonable, because a transfer is warranted only in the interest of justice.[43] Similarly, although most § 1404(a) motions requesting a venue change for reasons of convenience are brought by defendants, such motions should be considered by plaintiffs who desire the choice of law of the original forum and the convenient location of the transferee court.[44] In addition, either party can bring a motion under 28 U.S.C. § 1407 to obtain coordinated or consolidated pretrial proceedings in multidistrict litigation. Motions pursuant to §§ 1404(a) and 1406(a) can result in transfer only to a district in which venue is proper, while a § 1407 motion can transfer a case to any district. However, litigation transferred pursuant to § 1407 for pretrial purposes can be tried only in a jurisdiction having proper venue.[45]

§ 6.7 Section 1404(a) Transfers

Section 1404(a) provides that a district court can transfer any civil action for the convenience of parties and witnesses, in the interest of justice, to a district where it might have been brought. The § 1404(a) transfer is completely discretionary and based on factual considerations concerning convenience of witnesses, access to proof, and judicial economy.[46] Since § 1404(a) rather than forum non conveniens applies to domestic actions,[47] a dismissal for lack of convenience is not authorized when an alternative United States forum exists.[48]

---

[41] See §§ **14.31–14.37**.

[42] Van Dusen v. Barrack, 376 U.S. 612, 634 (1964).

[43] *See* Noxell Corp. v. Firehouse No. 1 Bar-B-Que Restaurant, 760 F.2d 312, 317 (D.C. Cir. 1985); Dubin v. United States, 380 F.2d 813, 816 n.5 (5th Cir. 1967).

[44] *See, e.g.*, Gonzalez v. Volvo of Am., 734 F.2d 1221, 1223–24 (7th Cir. 1984).

[45] *See* 28 U.S.C. 1407(a) (1982).

[46] See Van Dusen v. Barrack, 376 U.S. 612, 643 (1964).

[47] Piper Aircraft Co. v. Reyno, 454 U.S. 235, 253 (1981); see § **6.15**.

[48] Norwood v. Kirkpatrick, 349 U.S. 29, 32 (1955); Kontoulas v. A.H. Robins Co., 745 F.2d 312, 314–15 (4th Cir. 1984).

Courts often look to forum non conveniens considerations in deciding a § 1404(a) transfer motion.[49] The degree of deference due the plaintiff's choice of forum has ranged from primary consideration to little weight.[50] Since the defendant has the burden of showing the desirability of any transfer it requests, it is not sufficient that the defendant prefers another forum,[51] and a forum selection clause does not bar a § 1404(a) change.[52] The mere fact that related litigation is pending in another district is not dispositive if other factors mitigate against transfer.[53] However, the economy of trying multidistrict litigation in one district by a judge who is familiar with the pretrial proceedings can outweigh the plaintiffs' convenience in a given case.[54] The court can consider financial burdens in weighing the factors[55] but otherwise disregards counsel's convenience.[56] Convenience of witnesses is generally more important than convenience of parties.[57] Docket conditions have been accorded varying weight.[58]

A limitation on § 1404(a) motions is that any transfer must be to a district in which venue is proper.[59] The Supreme Court has held that a § 1404(a) transfer is precluded over a plaintiff's objections to a district in which venue is improper.[60] This restriction has been narrowly construed, so that a transfer is considered proper if the defendants to whom venue is lacking have settled and venue is proper for the remaining defendants.[61] Section 1404(a) has also been interpreted to require that the defendant must be amenable to process in the transferee court.[62]

---

[49] *See* Decker Coal Co. v. Commonwealth Edison Co., 805 F.2d 834, 843 (9th Cir. 1986); see **§ 6.16**.

[50] 15 Federal Practice and Procedure § 3848.

[51] *Id.* § 3849.

[52] *Id.* § 3847.

[53] *See* Codex Corp. v. Milgo Elec. Corp., 553 F.2d 735, 739 (1st Cir. 1977); 15 Federal Practice and Procedure § 3854, at 452.

[54] *See In re* Fine Paper Antitrust Litig., 685 F.2d 810, 819–20 (3d Cir. 1982).

[55] 15 Federal Practice and Procedure § 3849.

[56] *Id.* § 3850.

[57] *See id.* § 3851.

[58] *Id.* § 3854.

[59] Hoffman v. Blaski, 363 U.S. 335, 343–44 (1960).

[60] *Id.* at 343.

[61] *In re* Fine Paper Antitrust Litig., 685 F.2d 810, 819–20 (3d Cir. 1982).

[62] 1 Moore's Federal Practice ¶ 0.145[6.-1]; 15 Federal Practice and Procedure § 3845.

§ 6.8 Section 1404(a) Procedures

The moving party bears the burden on a motion to transfer.[63] Although authority exists that a § 1404(a) transfer can be raised sua sponte by the court,[64] at least one circuit reserves such transfers for exceptional circumstances.[65] The transfer can be requested at any time.[66] Transfer decisions are reviewed on an abuse of discretion standard.[67] A district court to which an action has been transferred has the power to reject a transfer and order the case returned to the original district under § 1404(a).[68] In a § 1404(a) transfer, the law of the transferor court applies,[69] unless the suit has been brought in an improper forum.[70]

§ 6.9 Section 1406(a) Motions

Section 1406(a) provides that the district court shall dismiss or, in the interest of justice, transfer a case having improper venue to any district in which it could have been brought. Section 1406(a) motions are governed by Rule 12 timing and must be brought quite early in the action to avoid waiver.[71] In a § 1406(a) transfer, the choice of law of the transferee court applies in order to prevent a plaintiff from suing in a forum lacking personal jurisdiction or venue merely to capture that forum's law, which would not otherwise be available.[72] However, the

---

[63] Murphy v. Allen County Claims & Adjustments, Inc., 550 F. Supp. 128, 133 (S.D. Ohio 1982).

[64] *In re* Scott, 709 F.2d 717, 721 (D.C. Cir. 1983); Lead Indus. Ass'n v. Occupational Safety & Health Admin., 610 F.2d 70, 79 n. 17 (2d Cir. 1979); I-T-E Circuit Breaker Co. v. Becker, 343 F.2d 361, 363 (8th Cir. 1965).

[65] *In re* Scott, 709 F.2d 717, 721 (D.C. Cir. 1983).

[66] 1 Moore's Federal Practice ¶ 0.145[4.-3] (2d ed. 1986); 15 Federal Practice and Procedure § 3844.

[67] Decker Coal Co. v. Commonwealth Edison Co., 805 F.2d 834, 842 (9th Cir. 1986); Arkla Exploration Co. v. Texas Oil & Gas Corp., 734 F.2d 347, 353 (8th Cir. 1984).

[68] *See* Savidge v. Fincannon, 768 F.2d 639, 640 (5th Cir. 1985), *modified on other grounds,* 784 F.2d 186, 187 (5th Cir. 1986).

[69] Van Dusen v. Barrack, 376 U.S. 612, 639 (1964); *see generally* 15 Federal Practice and Procedure § 3846; *see generally* Steinman, *Law of the Case: A Judicial Puzzle in Consolidated and Transferred Cases and in Multidistrict Litigation*, 135 U. Pa. L. Rev. 595 (1987).

[70] Manley v. Engram, 755 F.2d 1463, 1470 (11th Cir. 1985); Gonzalez v. Volvo of Am. Corp., 734 F.2d 1221, 1224 (7th Cir. 1984); Ellis v. Great Sw. Corp., 646 F.2d 1099, 1108 (5th Cir. 1981); *see* 1 Moore's Federal Practice ¶ 0.145[4.-5] (re statute of limitations problems).

[71] 1 Moore's Federal Practice ¶ 0.146[1].

[72] Manley v. Engram, 755 F.2d 1463, 1470 (11th Cir. 1985); Ellis v. Great Sw. Corp., 646 F.2d 1099, 1108 (5th Cir. 1981).

mere fact that a forum's choice of law is being applied does not guarantee that the court will decide the action by reference to its own law, since the forum's resolution of the conflicts of law question may dictate that it apply the substantive law of another jurisdiction.[73]

Although § 1406(a) refers to improper venue, it has been applied even when an obstacle exists in the original court. For example, the Supreme Court upheld a § 1406(a) transfer when venue was proper in the transferor court but personal jurisdiction over the defendant was lacking there.[74] Indeed, there is some confusion whether a transfer is equally appropriate under §§ 1404(a) and § 1406(a) when both personal jurisdiction and venue are absent in the original court,[75] an issue which can arise if the motion refers only to § 1404(a). Regardless of which statute governs the transfer, courts apply the transferee's law if the original forum was improper.[76] Plaintiffs should move to cure defects in personal jurisdiction under 28 U.S.C. § 1631, which was enacted specifically to permit transfers where the original district lacks jurisdiction and provides that the transferred action retains its original filing date.

§ 6.10 Reviewing Transfer Orders

Decisions of a transferor court are not reviewed by the transferee court.[77] Moreover, the transferee court will not retransfer the case except under the most compelling and unusual circumstances or if the transfer order is manifestly erroneous. On the other hand, if unanticipated post-transfer events frustrate the original purpose for a transfer, the court can retransfer the case.[78] Since a mere tactical error on the part of the party who made the original transfer request does not support a retransfer,[79] counsel must analyze the various choice of law questions and convenience issues before moving to transfer.

There is no immediate appeal from an order granting or denying a change of venue from one district court to another, and it is unlikely that this issue will be

---

[73] *See* Acme Circus Operating Co. v. Kuperstock, 711 F.2d 1538, 1540 (11th Cir. 1983).

[74] Goldlawr, Inc. v. Heiman, 369 U.S. 463, 466–67 (1962); *see* Sinclair v. Kleindienst, 711 F.2d 291, 294 (D.C. Cir. 1983); Dubin v. United States, 380 F.2d 813, 816 (5th Cir. 1967).

[75] *See, e.g.*, Liaw Su Teng v. Skaarup Shipping Corp., 743 F.2d 1140, 1145 & n.7 (5th Cir. 1984); 1 Moore's Federal Practice ¶ 0.145[4.-5]; 15 Federal Practice and Procedure § 3827.

[76] *See* Nelson v. International Paint Co., 716 F.2d 640, 643 (9th Cir. 1983) and cases cited therein.

[77] *In re* Cragar Indus., Inc., 706 F.2d 503, 505 (5th Cir. 1983); Starnes v. McGuire, 512 F.2d 918, 924 (D.C. Cir. 1974) (en banc).

[78] *In re* Cragar Indus., Inc., 706 F.2d 503, 505 (5th Cir. 1983); *see* 15 Federal Practice and Procedure § 3846.

[79] *In re* Cragar Indus., Inc., 706 F.2d 503, 505 (5th Cir. 1983).

ground for reversal after trial.[80] A split exists as to the availability of review under the collateral order doctrine for transfers to the Claims Court.[81]

Courts are hostile toward granting interlocutory review of district court decisions under the All Writs Act,[82] since § 1404(a) transfers are based upon the trial court's discretion.[83] Similarly, § 1406(a) orders are rarely reviewed.[84] Factors considered in whether to issue a writ include whether the district court failed to construe and apply the statute correctly, whether the relevant factors incident to a motion to transfer were considered, whether there was a clear abuse of discretion,[85] and whether the judge lacked power to order a transfer, or considered improper factors or followed incorrect procedures.[86] A district court's refusal to consider the issue of transfer under § 1404(a) has warranted mandamus to require that the motion be heard.[87]

One problematic issue is whether the transfer can be reviewed in the appellate circuit to which the case has been transferred. A few circuits have held that they lack jurisdiction to review the decision of a district court located in another circuit.[88] Therefore, counsel must bring a mandamus action before the case is actually transferred, or the transfer will be unreviewable, since the court transferring the action loses jurisdiction once the file is given to the transferee court.[89] Usually, a stay should be requested immediately in the transferor court to avoid this result.[90] Local rules should always be consulted, since they may provide for an automatic stay.[91]

---

[80] 15 Federal Practice and Procedure § 3855.

[81] *Compare* Gower v. Lehman, 799 F.2d 925, 927 (4th Cir. 1986) *and* Goble v. Marsh, 684 F.2d 12, 14–15 (D.C. Cir. 1982) (permitting review) *with* Raines v. Block, 798 F.2d 377, 379 (10th Cir. 1986) (denying review).

[82] 28 U.S.C. § 1651 (1982).

[83] *See In re* Cragar Indus., Inc., 706 F.2d 503, 504 (5th Cir. 1983); *see generally* 15 Federal Practice and Procedure § 3855.

[84] 15 Federal Practice and Procedure § 3827.

[85] *In re* Cragar Indus., Inc., 706 F.2d 503, 504 (5th Cir. 1983).

[86] *In re* Scott, 709 F.2d 717, 719 (D.C. Cir. 1983).

[87] Hustler Magazine v. United States Dist. Court, 790 F.2d 69, 70–71 (10th Cir. 1986).

[88] Roofing & Sheet Metal Servs., Inc. v. La Quinta Motor Inns, Inc., 689 F.2d 982, 985–86 (11th Cir. 1982); Vinnell v. Sloan, 636 F.2d 65, 67 (4th Cir. 1980); Illinois Tool Works, Inc. v. Sweetheart Plastics, Inc., 436 F.2d 1180, 1188 (7th Cir. 1971); *cf. In re* Corrugated Container Anti-trust Litig., 620 F.2d 1086, 1090 (5th Cir. 1980) (contempt order). *But see* American Fidelity Fire Ins. Co. v. United States Dist. Court, 538 F.2d 1371, 1377 n.4 (9th Cir. 1976); Magnetic Eng'g & Mfg. Co. v. Dings, 178 F.2d 866, 867–69 (2d Cir. 1950).

[89] Starnes v. McGuire, 512 F.2d 918, 924 (D.C. Cir. 1974).

[90] *See generally* Recent Decisions, *Review of Intercircuit Transfer Order Under Section 1404(a),* 35 Ala. L. Rev. 167 (1984).

[91] *See, e.g.,* N.D. Cal. R. 205(4).

§ 6.11 Multidistrict Litigation

In complex litigation having multiple plaintiffs and defendants who have sued in different districts, counsel should consider the applicability of 28 U.S.C. § 1407, which provides for coordination or consolidated pretrial proceedings of civil actions involving one or more common questions of fact. Typical multidistrict cases include private antitrust actions, mass disaster cases such as air crashes, patent and trademark suits, certain product liability actions and cases alleging violations of securities law. Such actions can be transferred to any district, regardless of whether an action could have been brought there.[92]

§ 6.12 Requirements for Transfer

The multidistrict panel can initiate the transfer procedure even without a request from counsel,[93] although notice and a hearing must be afforded regardless of who initiates the process.[94] Transfer is permitted for the convenience of parties and witnesses and to promote the just and efficient conduct of such actions.[95] The party moving for a transfer has the burden of demonstrating its appropriateness.[96] Tagalong actions which involve common questions of fact with actions previously transferred can also be transferred for consolidation.[97] The panel has established its own rules of procedure tailored to multidistrict litigants.[98]

§ 6.13 Review of Orders

No appeal or review is authorized for an order denying a motion to coordinate proceedings, and an order granting a transfer can be reviewed only by mandamus.[99] The review of any order of the district court in a transferred cause, made before transfer, is within the jurisdiction of the court of appeals of the

---

[92] 28 U.S.C. 1407(a) (1982); 15 Federal Practice and Procedure § 3863.

[93] 28 U.S.C. § 1407(c)(i) (1982).

[94] 28 U.S.C. § 1407(c) (1982); *see generally* D. Herr, Multidistrict Litigation 39–68 (1986).

[95] 28 U.S.C. § 1407(a) (1982); *see generally* D. Herr, Multidistrict Litigation 69–132 (1986); 15 Federal Practice and Procedure § 3863.

[96] *In re* Buffalo Valley Gas Auth. Litig., 429 F. Supp. 1029, 1032 (J.P.M.L. 1977).

[97] *See* D. Herr, Multidistrict Litigation 175–89; 15 Federal Practice and Procedure § 3865.

[98] Reprinted in 15 Federal Practice and Procedure § 3865.

[99] 28 U.S.C. § 1407(e) (1982); *see generally* D. Herr, Multidistrict Litigation 233–38 (1986).

circuit to which the cause has been transferred.[100] Review of orders subsequent to transfer also goes to the transferor district.[101] However, if the judge holds a deponent in contempt over the telephone, the appeal goes to the jurisdiction where the deposition is being taken on the theory that the judge is acting as a judge of that court for purposes of supervising the deposition.[102]

§ 6.14 Coordinated Proceedings

Once a case has been transferred, it may become subject to the procedures suggested by the second edition of the Manual for Complex Litigation,[103] which encourages the judge actively to supervise counsel to ensure efficient pretrial procedures. Lead and liason counsel or coordinating committees are common in such cases, significantly limiting the role of individual counsel in formulating strategy and implementing discovery. Once the case has been transferred, the transferor court loses jurisdiction to act until the case is remanded.[104] Although previous orders are binding, the transferee judge can modify or rescind them.[105] On the other hand, when the case is remanded, the original court is bound by all previous orders.[106] However, if the subsequent order of the original court does not conflict with the transferee judge's discovery program, it will be upheld.[107]

Since consolidation is authorized only for purposes of pretrial activities, each action must be remanded to the original district for trial.[108] In practice, relatively few cases have been unconditionally remanded because of settlements, disposition by summary judgment, and tactics designed to have the transferee judge hear the action.[109] For example, multidistrict judges have been assigned to

---

[100] Astarte Shipping v. Allied Steel & Export Serv., 767 F.2d 86, 87 (5th Cir. 1985); *see* Magnetic Eng'g & Mfg. Co. v. Dings, 178 F.2d 866, 870 (2d Cir. 1950); *see generally* Steinman, *Law of the Case: A Judicial Puzzle in Consolidated and Transferred Cases and in Multidistrict Litigation,* 135 U. Pa. L. Rev. 595 (1987).

[101] *In re* Corrugated Container Anti-trust Litig., 662 F.2d 875, 880 (D.C. Cir. 1981).

[102] *Id.* at 880–81.

[103] Manual for Complex Litigation (Second) (1985), *reprinted* in 2 Moore's Federal Practice pt. 2; *see generally* D. Herr, Multidistrict Litigation 202–10; 15 Federal Practice and Procedure § 3868.

[104] Glasstech, Inc. v. AB Kyro Oy, 769 F.2d 1574, 1576 (Fed. Cir. 1985); Astarte Shipping v. Allied Steel & Export Serv., 767 F.2d 86, 87 (5th Cir. 1985).

[105] Astarte Shipping v. Allied Steel & Export Serv., 767 F.2d 86, 87 (5th Cir. 1986); *In re* Multi-Piece Rim Prods. Liability Litig., 653 F.2d 671, 676–78 (D.C. Cir. 1981).

[106] D. Herr, Multidistrict Litigation 194.

[107] *In re* Multi-Piece Rim Prods. Liability Litig., 653 F.2d 671, 677 (D.C. Cir. 1981).

[108] 28 U.S.C. § 1407(a) (1982).

[109] *See generally* D. Herr, Multidistrict Litigation 211–16; 15 Federal Practice and Procedure § 3866.

sit as the trial judge, parties have consented to the transferee judge, and actions have been remanded subject to the requirement that they be bound by the outcome of test cases regarding common factual issues. Moreover, § 1404(a) transfers have been granted to the district where the pretrial activities are being coordinated when jurisdiction and venue over the remaining parties to the action are proper there.[110]

§ 6.15 Forum Non Conveniens

The doctrine of forum non conveniens allows a court with jurisdiction over the parties and subject matter to dismiss the action because of considerations based primarily on convenience.[111] State court practitioners often confuse motions to transfer venue for convenience of witnesses with forum non conveniens motions. In state courts, where jurisdiction is limited by territorial boundaries, a forum non conveniens motion can be brought to dismiss an action that should be litigated in another state as well as in a foreign country. In federal court, jurisdiction exists to transfer actions between district courts in different states.[112] Therefore, forum non conveniens issues arise only when the alternative forum is outside the jurisdiction of the United States[113] or on rare occasions when a state court is the alternative forum. The usual forum non conveniens case includes either plaintiffs or defendants who are domiciled in a foreign country or United States citizens who are litigating a dispute centered elsewhere.

From the defendant's perspective, a forum non conveniens dismissal can result in termination of the litigation or an advantageous settlement because of the difficulties the plaintiff may face in litigation outside the United States. On the other hand, the continuation of such cases in the United States may also be unfair when the incident in dispute is located elsewhere. As the Fifth Circuit noted, "[a]s a moth is drawn to light, so is a litigant drawn to the United States."[114] Therefore, courts usually try to balance both parties' interests in continued litigation in federal court, even placing conditions on a defendant as to the conduct of foreign litigation when granting forum non conveniens dismissals.

---

[110] *See, e.g., In re* Fine Paper Antitrust Litig., 685 F.2d 810, 819–20 (3d Cir. 1982).

[111] *See* Piper Aircraft Co. v. Reyno, 454 U.S. 235, 249 (1981); *see generally* 15 Federal Practice and Procedure § 3828; Stein, *Forum Non Conveniens and the Redundancy of Court-Access Doctrine,* 133 U. Pa. L. Rev. 781 (1985); Note, *Foreign Plaintiffs and Forum Non Conveniens: Going Beyond Reyno,* 64 Texas L. Rev. 193 (1985); Note, *Forum Non Conveniens and the Extraterritorial Application of United States Antitrust Law,* 94 Yale L.J. 1693 (1985).

[112] 28 U.S.C. §§ 1404, 1406 (1982).

[113] *See* Kontoulas v. A.H. Robins Co., 745 F.2d 312, 314–15 (4th Cir. 1984).

[114] Liaw Su Teng v. Skaarup Shipping Corp., 743 F.2d 1140, 1146 (5th Cir. 1984).

§ 6.16 Criteria for Deciding Forum Non Conveniens Motions

In determining whether to dismiss the action, the district court first must consider whether an adequate alternative forum exists where the defendant is amenable to process[115] and then must weigh the private and public interest factors originally outlined in *Gulf Oil Corp. v. Gilbert.*[116] The defendant's agreement to submit to the jurisdiction of the alternative foreign forum satisfies the two-forum requirement, even if the defendant could not be sued there absent the agreement.[117] *Gilbert* listed the following private interest factors which affect the convenience of the litigants:

1. The relative ease of access to sources of proof
2. The availability of compulsory process for attendance of unwilling witnesses
3. The cost of obtaining attendance of willing witnesses
4. The possibility of viewing the premises, if appropriate; and
5. All other practical factors that make trial of a case easy, expeditious, and inexpensive.[118]

Gilbert also identified the following public interest factors which affect the convenience of the forum:

1. The administrative difficulties flowing from court congestion
2. The local interest in having localized controversies decided at home
3. The interest in having the trial of a diversity case in a forum that is at home with the law that must govern the action
4. The avoidance of unnecessary problems in conflicts of law, or in the application of foreign law; and
5. The unfairness of burdening citizens in an unrelated forum with jury duty.[119]

---

[115] Piper Aircraft Corp. v. Reyno, 454 U.S. 235, 254 n.22 (1981); Gulf Oil Corp. v. Gilbert, 330 U.S. 501, 506–07 (1947); De Melo v. Lederle Laboratories, 801 F.2d 1058, 1061 (8th Cir. 1986); TrampOil & Marine Ltd. v. M/V Mermaid I, 743 F.2d 48, 50 (1st Cir. 1984); *see* Note, *Forum Non Conveniens in the Absence of an Alternate Forum,* 86 Colum. L. Rev. 1000 (1986).

[116] 330 U.S. 501 (1947).

[117] Veba-Chemie A.G. v. M/V Getafix, 711 F.2d 1243, 1245 (5th Cir. 1983); Macedo v. Boeing Co., 693 F.2d 683, 687 (7th Cir. 1982).

[118] 330 U.S. at 508.

[119] *Id.* at 509.

Even when all the parties are foreign, not only the number of United States contacts but also their significance is important in determining the comparative efficacy and efficiency of trying a case in the United States.[120] At least one circuit does not require the district court to weigh the public factors, unless it determines that the balance of the private interests are in equipoise or near equipoise.[121] In other words, if the private interests favor the plaintiff, its forum choice will not be disturbed.

Reliance on the *Gilbert* standard was reaffirmed in *Piper Aircraft Co. v. Reyno.*[122] *Piper* held that the fact that the applicable substantive law in the alternative forum is less favorable to the plaintiffs than that of the present forum ordinarily should not be given conclusive or even substantial weight in the forum non conveniens inquiry.[123] Only if the remedy provided by the alternative forum is so clearly inadequate or unsatisfactory that it is no remedy at all will the court give that factor substantial weight in determining whether to grant a dismissal.[124] Moreover, if the case will be resolved by foreign law, it should ordinarily be dismissed in favor of a foreign tribunal.[125] Traditionally, the plaintiff's choice of forum was rarely disturbed unless the balance strongly favored the defendant.[126] However, *Piper* recognized that even a citizen's forum choice should not be given dispositive weight and that a foreign plaintiff's choice of forum should be given less deference than that accorded a citizen.[127]

§ 6.17 Conditional Dismissals

Courts are sensitive to the fact that a forum non conveniens dismissal may in effect end the litigation. Therefore, conditional dismissals are quite common, and some courts require the trial judge to ensure that the plaintiffs can file their suit in the alternative forum without undue inconvenience or prejudice.[128]

---

[120] La Seguridad v. Transytur Line, 707 F.2d 1304, 1309 (11th Cir. 1983); Manu Int'l, S.A. v. Avon Prods., Inc., 641 F.2d 62, 65 (2d Cir. 1981).

[121] *See* Friends for All Children v. Lockheed Aircraft Corp., 717 F.2d 602, 606–09 (D.C. Cir. 1983).

[122] 454 U.S. 235 (1981).

[123] *Id.* at 249–55.

[124] *Id.* at 254.

[125] *Id.* at 263.

[126] Gulf Oil Corp. v. Gilbert, 330 U.S. at 509.

[127] 454 U.S. at 256.

[128] La Seguridad v. Transytur Line, 707 F.2d 1304, 1307 (11th Cir. 1983); Pain v. United Technologies Corp., 637 F.2d 775, 784–85 (D.C. Cir. 1980), *cert. denied,* 454 U.S. 1128 (1981).

Problems obtaining personal jurisdiction or evidence in the alternative jurisdiction can be eliminated by conditioning the dismissal on the defendant's agreement voluntarily to submit to jurisdiction and provide the relevant records.[129] However, when multiple defendants exist, the dismissal must be conditioned on the agreement of all defendants to service.[130] Similarly, a condition that only the defendant be subjected to American discovery rules in the foreign country was reversed.[131]

The defendant may be required to waive any statute of limitations defense that did not exist prior to the institution of the pending actions[132] and to agree to submit to the judgment of the foreign court.[133] Some orders are quite detailed and include timing requirements for filing.[134] If a plaintiff incurs difficulty in filing suit within the specified period, a motion to stay judgment or a Rule 60(b) motion alleging excusable neglect should be filed to avoid the possibility that the conditional dismissal will become final before any alternative suit has been commenced.[135]

§ 6.18 Admiralty Cases

Several circuits consider whether American or foreign law governs the plaintiff's action as preliminary to any forum non conveniens analysis in maritime matters brought under the Jones Act.[136] If United States law applies, the court will entertain the suit, but if foreign law applies, the court can dismiss the action if there is another, more convenient forum.[137] The refusal of a court to dismiss

---

[129] *See* Piper Aircraft Co. v. Reyno, 454 U.S. 235, 257 n.25 (1981); *see* also Note, *Forum Non Conveniens,* 17 Creighton L. Rev. 1407, 1417 (1984).

[130] Watson v. Merrell Dow Pharmaceuticals, Inc., 769 F.2d 354, 357 (6th Cir. 1985); 15 Federal Practice and Procedure § 3828.

[131] *In re* Union Carbide Corp. Gas Plant Disaster, 809 F.2d 195, 205–06 (2d Cir. 1987).

[132] *See, e.g.,* Dowling v. Richardson-Merrell, Inc., 727 F.2d 608, 611 (6th Cir. 1984).

[133] *See, e.g.,* Watson v. Merrell Dow Pharmaceuticals, Inc., 769 F.2d 354, 356 (6th Cir. 1985).

[134] *See, e.g.,* Cuevas v. Reading & Bates Corp., 770 F.2d 1371, 1375–76 & n.8 (5th Cir. 1985).

[135] *See* Newball v. Offshore Logistics Int'l, 803 F.2d 821, 826–27 (5th Cir. 1986).

[136] *See, e.g.,* Pereira v. Utah Transport, Inc. 764 F.2d 686, 688 (9th Cir. 1985), *cert. denied,* ___ U.S. ___, 106 S. Ct. 1253 (1986); Needham v. Phillips Petroleum Co. of Norway, 719 F.2d 1481, 1483 (10th Cir. 1983); Szumlicz v. Norwegian American Line, Inc., 698 F.2d 1192, 1195 (11th Cir. 1983); Fisher v. Agios Nicolaos V, 628 F.2d 308, 315 (5th Cir. 1980), *cert. denied,* 454 U.S. 816 (1981); *see generally* Edelman, *Forum Non Conveniens: Its Application in Admiralty Law,* 15 J. Mar. L. & Com. 517 (1984). *But see* Cruz v. Maritime Co. of Philippines, 702 F.2d 47, 48 (2d Cir. 1983).

[137] Cuevas v. Reading & Bates Corp., 770 F.2d 1371, 1377–78 (5th Cir. 1985).

on forum non conveniens grounds when American law applies has not been extended to other types of maritime cases.[138]

§ 6.19 Alternative United States Forum

On occasion, the alternative forum consists of one or more federal or state courts as well as a foreign court. Courts are not consistent in their approach to such cases. Although most courts dismiss if the most convenient forum is an alternative foreign court, there is some precedent for transferring to another federal court rather than dismissing.[139] When the only alternative forum is another federal court, forum non conveniens has been displaced by the § 1404(a) transfer for convenience purposes.[140]

§ 6.20 Procedural Considerations

The defendant has the burden of making a showing sufficient to justify the district court's refusal to retain jurisdiction.[141] There is no time limit on when the motion can be brought,[142] but, practically speaking, it is raised quite early.

In support of its motion, a defendant must provide enough information to enable the district court to balance the parties' interests, but is not required to submit detailed affidavits identifying witnesses who would be called in the alternative forum and their testimony.[143] However, if it is feasible, affidavits describing the particular difficulties of holding a trial in the United States should be presented. It appears that federal rather than state forum non conveniens law is applicable in diversity cases, although this issue is not free from doubt.[144]

---

[138] *See* Ali v. Offshore Co., 753 F.2d 1327, 1333 n.14 (5th Cir. 1985); La Seguridad v. Transytur Line, 707 F.2d 1304, 1310 n.10 (11th Cir. 1983).

[139] *See* Macedo v. Boeing Co., 693 F.2d 683, 690 (7th Cir. 1982); *see generally* Note, *Forum Non Conveniens,* 17 Creighton L. Rev. 1407, 1426–27 (1984).

[140] Miskow v. Boeing Co., 664 F.2d 205, 207 (9th Cir. 1981); *see* Piper Aircraft Co. v. Reyno, 454 U.S. 235, 253–54 (1981).

[141] La Seguridad v. Transytur Line, 707 F.2d 1304, 1309 (11th Cir. 1983); Philippine Packing Corp. v. Maritime Co., 519 F.2d 811, 812 (9th Cir. 1975).

[142] 15 Federal Practice and Procedure § 3828.

[143] Piper Aircraft Co. v. Reyno, 454 U.S. 235, 238 & n.25 (1981).

[144] *Compare* Sibaja v. Dow Chem. Co., 757 F.2d 1215, 1219 (11th Cir.), *cert. denied,* ____ U.S. ____, 106 S. Ct. 347 (1985) *and* 15 Federal Practice and Procedure § 3828 (federal law applies) *with* Piper v. Reyno, 454 U.S. 235, 248 n.13 (1981) (not reaching issue since federal and state law was identical); Miskow v. Boeing Co., 664 F.2d 205, 207 n.2 (9th Cir. 1981) (not reaching issue, but indicating it was inclined to follow state law); Stein, *Forum Non Conveniens*

Counsel should request that the district court judge make factual findings or articulate the reasons underlying a dismissal, since the appellate court has the power to remand for further elucidation when review would be substantially hindered without such information.[145]

§ 6.21 Reviewing Forum Non Conveniens Dismissals

Forum non conveniens dismissals have been considered final and appealable by right.[146] This principle appears to apply even if the dismissal is conditioned on the acceptance of conditions such as consenting to jurisdiction and waiving limitations defenses which, if not met, allow the plaintiff to reassert jurisdiction in federal court.[147] However, to ensure appealability, the conditional order should be drafted to be presently effective, containing conditions subsequent rather than conditions precedent to the dismissal itself.[148] Although denial of a forum non conveniens motion is not appealable, at least one circuit has permitted review under the collateral order rule, although this appears to be a minority position.[149] A denial of a motion to dismiss challenging the district court's extension of the time in which the plaintiff could initiate the foreign suit also was reviewed under the collateral order doctrine.[150] In another case, the Fifth Circuit requested the district court to certify its order pursuant to 28 U.S.C. § 1292(b), which permits interlocutory appeals in limited circumstances.[151]

The forum non conveniens decision is within the court's discretion and is reversed only if a clear abuse of discretion is shown.[152] Some circuits view their role as solely to determine whether the action of the district court was so

---

and the Redundancy of Court-Access Doctrine 133 U. Pa. L. Rev. 781, 820–21 (1985), *and* Note, *Foreign Plaintiffs and Forum Non Conveniens: Going Beyond Reyno,* 64 Tex. L. Rev. 193, 212–14 (1985) (both arguing state law should apply).

[145] *See* DeShane v. Deere & Co., 726 F.2d 443, 446 (8th Cir. 1984); Nebenzahl v. Credit Suisse, 705 F.2d 1139, 1140 (9th Cir. 1983).

[146] Koke v. Phillips Petroleum Co., 730 F.2d 211, 214–15 (5th Cir. 1984); *see* 15 Federal Practice and Procedure § 3914.

[147] Sigalas v. Lido Maritime, Inc., 776 F.2d 1512, 1516 (11th Cir. 1985); Koke v. Phillips Petroleum Co., 730 F.2d 211, 214–15 (5th Cir. 1984).

[148] Cuevas v. Reading & Bates Corp., 770 F.2d 1371, 1376 (5th Cir. 1985).

[149] Hodson v. A.H. Robins Co., 715 F.2d 142, 145 n.2 (4th Cir. 1983). *But see* Rosenstein v. Merrell Dow Pharmaceuticals, Inc., 769 F.2d 352, 353–54 (6th Cir. 1985); Coastal Steel v. Tilghman Wheelabrator Ltd., 709 F.2d 190 (3d Cir.), *cert. denied,* 464 U.S. 938 (1983); Nalls v. Rolls-Royce Ltd., 702 F.2d 255 (D.C. Cir.), *cert. denied,* 461 U.S. 970 (1983).

[150] Newball v. Offshore Logistics Int'l, 803 F.2d 821, 824–25 (5th Cir. 1986).

[151] *See In re* McClelland Eng'rs, Inc., 742 F.2d 837, 837–38 (5th Cir. 1984).

[152] Piper Aircraft Co. v. Reyno, 454 U.S. 235, 257 (1981).

unreasonable or so arbitrary as to be beyond the range of discretion[153] or whether the district court failed to balance the relevant factors.[154] As a practical matter, it appears that the extent of review depends on the disposition in the district court, with courts scrutinizing dismissals more carefully than decisions exercising jurisdiction.[155]

§ 6.22 Selection of Forum Checklist

Venue Alternatives in Diversity Actions

1. Do all plaintiffs reside in judicial district?
2. Do all defendants reside in district?
3. Did claim arise in district?

Venue Alternatives in Federal Question Actions

1. Do all defendants reside in district?
2. Did claim arise in district?

Determining Corporate Venue

1. If a corporation is a defendant:
   a. Where was it incorporated?
   b. Where was it licensed to do business or is doing business?
2. If a corporation is a plaintiff, where was it incorporated?

§ 1404(a) Transfers

1. Is the change for the convenience of parties?
2. Is the change for the convenience of witnesses?
3. Is the transfer to a district in which venue is proper?
4. Has moving party met its burden of showing transfer is in the interest of justice?

---

[153] Kontoulas v. A.H. Robins Co., 745 F.2d 312, 314 (4th Cir. 1984).

[154] *See, e.g.*, La Seguridad v. Transytur Line, 707 F.2d 1304, 1308 (11th Cir. 1983).

[155] *See, e.g.*, Irish Nat'l Ins. Co., Ltd. v. Aer Lingus Teoranta, 739 F.2d 90, 92 (2d Cir. 1984).

5. Upon transfer, the choice of law of transferor court applies, unless the original suit was brought in an improper forum.

§ 1406(a) Transfers

1. Is venue of suit improper?
2. Is there any other procedural obstacle blocking suit in forum?
3. Is transfer to a district having venue?
4. Is the motion brought within 20 days of service (Rule 12 timing)?
5. Upon transfer, the choice of law of transferee court applies.

Interlocutory Appellate Review of Transfer Orders

1. Is mandamus likely to be granted?
2. Has a stay been obtained to block the transfer?

§ 1407 Multidistricting

1. Will multidistricting promote justice?
2. Is multidistricting for the convenience of parties?
3. Is multidistricting for the convenience of witnesses?
4. How many separate actions are involved?
5. Are the actions located in different districts?
6. Are the issues complex?
7. Is this a tagalong action with common factual questions to multi-districted case?
8. Procedure can be initiated by notice and hearing before multidistrict panel.
9. Case can be transferred to any venue for pretrial purposes, but can be tried only in district having proper venue.
10. No interlocutory review of panel decisions other than by mandamus is permitted.

Forum Non Conveniens Dismissal Motions

1. Are one or more parties foreign?
2. Did the cause of action occur outside the United States?
3. Is there an alternative forum outside the United States in which the case can be tried?

4. Do the following private factors make the chosen forum in the United States unreasonable?
   a. What is the ease of access to sources of proof?
   b. Does compulsory process reach likely witnesses?
   c. What is the cost of attendance for willing witnesses?
   d. Is a view of the premises feasible, if appropriate?
   e. What other practical problems exist?
5. Do the following public factors make the chosen forum in the United States unreasonable?
   a. What administrative difficulties exist?
   b. Is there any local interest in deciding the controversy?
   c. Does the case involve conflicts of law problems?
   d. Will the forum's own law be applied?
   e. Is it unfair to burden a local jury with the case?
6. Has a conditional dismissal been requested to ensure the feasibility of the alternative forum?
7. A dismissal can be appealed, but mandamus is the only review for denial of a forum non conveniens motion.

Alternative Motions to Change Forum

1. Rule 12(b)(3) motion to dismiss for improper venue (see §§ **14.31–14.37**)
   a. Motion due within 20 days (Rule 12 timing)
2. § 1406(a) motion to transfer for improper venue
   a. Motion due within 20 days (Rule 12 timing)
3. Rule 12(b)(2) motion to dismiss for lack of personal jurisdiction (see §§ **14.17–14.29**)
   a. Motion due within 20 days (Rule 12 timing)
4. § 1631 motion to transfer to cure want of jurisdiction
   a. No timing limitations
5. § 1404(a) motion to transfer for convenience of parties or witnesses
   a. No timing limitations, but often brought with Rule 12(b)(2) motion
6. Motion to transfer pretrial proceedings in multidistrict litigation
   a. No timing limitation
7. Motion to dismiss for forum non conveniens
   a. No timing limitation, but often brought with Rule 12(b)(2) motion.
8. All of the above motions should be supported by affidavits when feasible.

PART II

COMMENCING THE ACTION

CHAPTER 7

FEDERAL PLEADING

§ 7.1 Pleadings

Although pleadings in federal court generally do not look much different than pleadings in state court, counsel should be aware of the current federal philosophy concerning pleadings to avoid potential problems. If counsel is in doubt as to the contents of a federal pleading, the Appendix of Forms to the Federal Rules of Civil Procedure contains models of complaints which are sufficient under the Rules,[1] and Bender's Federal Practice Forms is a multivolume work which includes examples of many types of pleadings as well as motions.

---

[1] *See* Fed. R. Civ. P. 84; American Nurses' Ass'n v. Illinois, 783 F.2d 716, 723 (7th Cir. 1986).

§ 7.2 Notice Pleading

Unlike the requirements in some jurisdictions that ultimate facts be pleaded, Rule 8(a)(2) requires only a short and plain statement of the claim showing that the pleader is entitled to relief. Many attorneys do plead facts in order to educate the judge concerning the nature and probable merits of the case or to set the stage for an advantageous settlement by a show of strength.[2] Factual pleading may also be desirable if it is possible that a later amendment will be sought, since this enhances the likelihood that the new claim will relate back for statute of limitations purposes.[3] Pleading facts does not by itself result in a dismissal, since an action cannot be dismissed for failure to state a claim unless the plaintiff can prove no set of facts in support of its claim that would entitle it to relief.[4] However, a detailed complaint may invite dismissal when it includes factual allegations which, if true, demonstrate that no legal right was invaded.[5] As a practical matter, even if a complaint is insufficient, most courts will grant an amendment if any likelihood exists that the deficiency can be corrected.[6] As a result, the possibility that a plaintiff's action will be dismissed for technical pleading errors is minimal. On the other hand, if the plaintiff persists in violating Rule 8, the district court is justified in dismissing the complaint with prejudice.[7] Similarly, when a first complaint consisted of 38 unnumbered pages which were repetitous and confusing and the amended complaint contained 98 pages, a dismissal with prejudice was affirmed.[8]

§ 7.3 When Specificity Is Required

Some concern has been voiced that courts are in fact requiring more specificity in pleadings, regardless of whether the complaint technically falls within Rule 9(b), which requires particularity for certain matters such as fraud and special damages.[9] For example, every circuit has articulated some necessity for

---

[2] American Nurses' Ass'n v. Illinois, 783 F.2d 716, 723–24 (7th Cir. 1986).

[3] See §§ **8.11–8.16.**

[4] Conley v. Gibson, 355 U.S. 41, 45–46 (1957); see § **14.42**.

[5] American Nurses' Ass'n v. Illinois, 783 F.2d 716, 724 (7th Cir. 1986); Kaiser Aluminum & Chem. Sales, Inc. v. Avondale Shipyards, Inc., 677 F.2d 1045, 1050 (5th Cir. 1982), *cert. denied*, 459 U.S. 1105 (1983); 5 C. Wright & A. Miller, Federal Practice and Procedure § 1357 (1969) [hereinafter Federal Practice and Procedure].

[6] *E.g.*, Schreiber Distrib. v. Serv-Well Furniture Co., 806 F.2d 1393, 1401 (9th Cir. 1986); see **ch. 8**.

[7] Michaelis v. Nebraska State Bar Ass'n, 717 F.2d 437, 439 (8th Cir. 1983).

[8] *Id.*

[9] *See generally,* Marcus, *The Revival of Fact Pleading under the Federal Rules of Civil Procedure,* 86 Colum. L. Rev. 433 (1986); Saveri & Saveri, *Pleading Fraudulent Concealment in an Antitrust Price Fixing Case: Rule 9(b) v. Rule 8,* 17 U.S.F. L. Rev. 631 (1983).

specificity in civil rights actions.[10] The Supreme Court has required factual pleadings concerning questions of standing.[11] Some circuits require specificity regarding actions against public officials[12] and in RICO claims.[13] Conspiracy actions have also been subjected to requirements of particularity by some courts.[14]

When Rule 9 applies, as in securities fraud cases, counsel must be extremely careful to plead sufficient detail, since some circuits scrutinize such complaints with an eye toward dismissal.[15] Mere allegations of fraud, corruption, or conspiracy, averments to conditions of mind, or referrals to plans and schemes may be considered too conclusionary to satisfy the particularity requirement.[16] Even if a fraud action is based on diversity, Rule 9(b) requires the specification of the time, place, and content of the alleged false representation, although not the circumstances from which fradulent intent could be inferred.[17] Although a complaint can be dismissed under Rule 9(b), it may be more efficient also to request consideration under Rule 12(b)(6) for failure to state a claim.[18]

Complaints dismissed pursuant to Rule 9(b) are invariably dismissed with leave to amend.[19] Indeed, the Second Circuit considers it an abuse of discretion to refuse leave to amend when the complaint has not previously been amended.[20]

---

[10] Morrison v. City of Baton Rouge, 761 F.2d 242, 244 (5th Cir. 1985) (quoting Hobson v. Wilson, 737 F.2d 1, 30 (D.C. Cir. 1984), *cert. denied,* 470 U.S. 1084 (1985)); *see* Barr v. Abrams, 810 F.2d 358, 363 (2d Cir. 1987). *But see* Bergquist v. County of Cochise, 806 F.2d 1364, 1367 (9th Cir. 1986); *see generally,* Wingate, *A Special Pleading Rule for Civil Rights Complaints: A Step Forward or a Step Back?,* 49 Mo. L. Rev. 677 (1984).

[11] Warth v. Seldin, 422 U.S. 490, 508–09 (1975).

[12] *See* Smith v. Nixon, 807 F.2d 197, 200 (D.C. Cir. 1986).

[13] 18 U.S.C. §§ 1961–1968 (1982 & Supp. III 1985); *see, e.g.,* Schreiber Distrib. v. Serv-Well Furniture Co., 806 F.2d 1393, 1400–01 (9th Cir. 1986); Haroco v. American Nat'l Bank & Trust Co., 747 F.2d 384, 405 (7th Cir. 1984), *aff'd,* ____ U.S. ____, 105 S. Ct. 3291 (1985); Moss v. Morgan Stanley Inc., 719 F.2d 5, 19 (2d Cir. 1983), *cert. denied,* 465 U.S. 1025 (1984). For RICO elements, see Sedima, S.P.R.L. v. Imrex Co., 473 U.S. 479 (1985) and Haroco v. American Nat'l Bank & Trust Co., *aff'd,* ____ U.S. ____, 105 S. Ct. 3291 (1985).

[14] *See* Hayduk v. Lanna, 775 F.2d 441, 443 (1st Cir. 1985), *cert. denied,* ____ U.S. ____, 106 S. Ct. 1790 (1986); Segal v. Gordon, 467 F.2d 602, 607 (2d Cir. 1972).

[15] *See, e.g.,* Connecticut Nat'l Bank v. Fluor Corp., 808 F.2d 957, 962–63 (2d Cir. 1987); Semegen v. Weidner, 780 F.2d 727, 731 (9th Cir. 1985); *see generally* Sovern, *Reconsidering Federal Civil Rule 9(b): Do We Need Particularized Pleading Requirements in Fraud Cases?,* 104 F.R.D. 143 (1985); Note, *Pleading Securities Fraud Claims With Particularity Under Rule 9(b),* 97 Harv. L. Rev. 1432 (1984).

[16] Hayduk v. Lanna, 775 F.2d 441, 444 (1st Cir. 1985), *cert. denied,* ____ U.S. ____, 106 S. Ct. 1790 (1986); Segal v. Gordon, 467 F.2d 602, 697–08 (2d Cir. 1972).

[17] Hayduk v. Lanna, 775 F.2d 441, 443–44 (1st Cir. 1985), *cert. denied,* ____ U.S. ____, 106 S. Ct. 1790 (1986).

[18] *See, e.g.,* Luce v. Edelstein, 802 F.2d 49, 55 (2d Cir. 1986).

[19] 2A J. Moore *et al.,* Moore's Federal Practice ¶ 9.03 (2d ed. 1986) [hereinafter Moore's Federal Practice].

[20] Luce v. Edelstein, 802 F.2d 49, 56–57 (2d Cir. 1986).

§ 7.4 Common Pleading Problems

A common error which should be avoided is forgetting to state in the complaint the grounds for federal jurisdiction. For example, citizenship must be alleged in diversity cases,[21] as well as the jurisdictional amount.[22] In the case of a corporation, both the state of incorporation and principal place of business must be pleaded.[23] The absence of jurisdictional allegations can be challenged at any time. Although a procedural failure can be corrected, if a substantive jurisdictional bar exists, counsel may find that the appropriate statute of limitations has run when the complaint is later filed in a state court.[24]

§ 7.5 Procedural Considerations

Alternative and hypothetical pleading are permitted under the Federal Rules but are subject to the requirements of Rule 11.[25] Each claim is made in a numbered paragraph, which should be limited to a statement of a single set of circumstances.[26] Separate counts should be stated when the claims are founded upon different transactions, and separate legal theories should be indicated. Similarly, defenses other than denials should be separately stated to facilitate their presentation.[27] Statements may be adopted by reference in pleadings or motions, but their source should be fully disclosed.[28] Counsel should carefully consider the advisability of attaching exhibits to the pleadings, since such attachments can be reviewed in any motion challenging the sufficiency of the complaint without converting the motion into one for summary judgment.[29]

Normally, factual assertions in pleadings and pretrial orders are considered to be judicial admissions conclusively binding on the party who made them.[30] Therefore, counsel must carefully draft the pleading to avoid inadvertent admissions which cannot be contradicted. If counsel's theory of the case changes after pleading or defendants are dropped or dismissed from the action, statements in the pleadings which originally were favorable or neutral may be transformed into admissions. Therefore, counsel should always reread the pleadings after discovery to see if a motion is necessary to amend them. An amended pleading which supersedes the original pleading will result in the

---

[21] See §§ **2.13–2.14**.

[22] See § **2.12**.

[23] See § **2.20**.

[24] See §§ **2.23** and **5.4**.

[25] Fed. R. Civ. P. 8(e)(2); 2A Moore's Federal Practice ¶¶ 8.31–8.33; see §§ **28.2–28.6**.

[26] Fed. R. Civ. P. 10(b).

[27] *See id.*

[28] See § **14.47**.

[29] See § **15.25**.

[30] White v. Arco/Polymers, Inc., 720 F.2d 1391, 1396 (5th Cir. 1983).

former admission being considered only as an evidentiary admission which can be contradicted.[31] Opposing counsel must also be careful not to treat a judicial admission as merely evidentiary, or the court can consider the issue waived and permit the admission to be contradicted.[32]

Pleadings do not require verification unless required by rule or statute.[33] However, they must be signed by an attorney or pro se litigant. The signature is treated as an objective certification that the pleading or motion has been read and is warranted by existing law or a good faith argument for the extension, modification, or reversal of existing law and that it is not interposed for any improper purpose, such as to harass or cause unnecessary delay or needless increase in the cost of litigation.[34] If a pleading, motion, or other paper is not signed, it will be stricken unless signed promptly after this omission is called to the attention of the pleader. Sanctions, including attorneys' fees, are mandatory for documents violating Rule 11 and may be imposed by the court sua sponte.[35]

§ 7.6 Denials

Although a general denial is sufficient to controvert any of the averments in the complaint, it is subject to Rule 11's certification requirements.[36] Therefore, in most cases specific denials of matters in contention should be used, since it is unlikely that every averment, including jurisdiction, will be subject to a denial.[37] The amount of detail given in an answer often depends on counsel's overall strategy concerning the case. As a general rule, most answers supply minimal information except as to affirmative defenses.

Qualified denials which admit part of an allegation are frequently used in drafting. However, counsel should avoid denials containing negative pregnants in which only a minor part of an allegation is denied, thereby implicitly admitting the remainder.[38] For example, denying that all of the identified transactions occurred may be read to admit that some did occur. Although alleging insufficient knowledge to admit or deny an averment is not prohibited, such allegations may run afoul of Rule 11 if the information is available. Denials based on information and belief are common in business litigation when hearsay

---

[31] *Id.; see* Frederic P. Wiedersum Assocs. v. National Homes Constr. Corp., 540 F.2d 62, 65 (2d Cir. 1976); 3 Moore's Federal Practice ¶ 15.08[7].

[32] *See* White v. Arco/Polymers, Inc., 720 F.2d 1391, 1396 (5th Cir. 1983); Genusa v. City of Peoria, 619 F.2d 1203, 1208 (7th Cir. 1980).

[33] Fed. R. Civ. P. 11; *see, e.g.*, Fed. R. Civ. P. 23.1 (requiring verification of derivative actions by shareholders).

[34] Fed. R. Civ. P. 11.

[35] See **ch. 28**.

[36] Mann v. Smith, 796 F.2d 79, 86 (5th Cir. 1986).

[37] *See* 2A Moore's Federal Practice ¶ 8.23.

[38] *See id.* ¶ 8.24.

is the main source used by the person signing the complaint. In rare instances, an answer may invoke the party's Fifth Amendment right against self incrimination.[39]

All allegations of the complaint which are not denied, except for the amount of damages, are considered admitted.[40] On the other hand, a plaintiff is not required to deny an affirmative defense unless ordered by the court.[41] However, an answer or Rule 12 motion must be filed to preserve defenses to a counter-claim, cross-claim, or third party claim.[42]

§ 7.7 Affirmative Defenses

A general denial does not raise matters constituting an avoidance or affirmative defenses which must be specifically pleaded under Rule 8(c).[43] Defenses which must be pleaded include accord and satisfaction, arbitration and award, assumption of risk, contributory negligence, discharge in bankruptcy, duress, estoppel, failure of consideration, fraud, illegality, injury by fellow servant, laches, license, payment, release, res judicata, statute of frauds, statute of limitations, and waiver. A party who challenges the capacity of any party also must do so by specific negative averment which includes supporting particulars within the pleader's knowledge.[44] Determining whether a contention is an affirmative defense in a diversity action is a matter of state law, but the Federal Rules specify the manner and time in which such defenses are raised.[45]

Failure to plead affirmative defenses usually results in their waiver[46] unless leave to amend has been granted,[47] or the issue is raised when the opponent has sufficient time and is not prejudiced in its ability to respond,[48] or the defense is tried by consent under Rule 15(b). For example, a statutory limitation on damages awarded against health care providers was not applied when that defense was not raised until several months after entry of judgment.[49] However,

---

[39] See § **18.19**.

[40] Fed. R. Civ. P. 8(d); *see* 2A Moore's Federal Practice ¶ 8.29.

[41] Fed. R. Civ. P. 7(a), 8(d); 2A Moore's Federal Practice ¶ 8.29.

[42] *Id.*

[43] Trinity Carton Co. v. Falstaff Brewing Corp., 767 F.2d 184, 193–94 (5th Cir. 1985), *cert. denied,* ____ U.S. ____, 106 S. Ct. 1202 (1986); Jackson v. Seaboard Coastline R.R., 678 F.2d 992, 1010–11 (11th Cir. 1982).

[44] Fed. R. Civ. P. 9(a); Ralston Oil & Gas Co. v. Gensco, Inc., 706 F.2d 685, 692 (5th Cir. 1983).

[45] Troxler v. Owens-Illinois, Inc., 717 F.2d 530, 532 (11th Cir. 1983).

[46] Davis v. Bryan, 810 F.2d 42, 44–45 (2d Cir. 1987); Marine Overseas Servs. v. Crossocean Shipping, 791 F.2d 1227, 1233 (5th Cir. 1986).

[47] Trinity Carton Co. v. Falstaff Brewing Corp., 767 F.2d 184, 194 (5th Cir. 1985), *cert. denied,* ____ U.S. ____, 106 S. Ct. 1202 (1986); *see generally* 2A Moore's Federal Practice § 8.27[3].

[48] Lucas v. United States, 807 F.2d 414, 417–18 (5th Cir. 1986); see § **16.4**.

[49] *See* Ingraham v. United States, 808 F.2d 1075, 1078–79 (5th Cir. 1987).

a defendant can resort to a timely Rule 12 or summary judgment motion in lieu of filing any answer, thereby not waiving its right to raise any applicable affirmative defense.

Courts differ over whether res judicata can be raised sua sponte by the judge in the interest of judicial economy.[50] Even those courts which permit an untimely res judicata defense usually limit the circumstances in which a waiver will be averted.[51] Similarly, courts split as to whether a defendant can move for summary judgment on the basis of an affirmative defense omitted from the answer.[52]

§ 7.8 Statute of Limitations Problems

The requirements of state law are extremely important in diversity cases, since the federal court applies the state's statute of limitations[53] and follows state substantive law concerning when the action commences.[54] Thus, when the act of service is an integral part of the state statue of limitations, a federal court requires service before the statute is tolled. In other words, Rule 3's provision that the filing of an action commences the suit is ineffective in diversity cases when the state provides that the summons must be served within the statutory period.[55] As a result, counsel cannot rely on Rule 3 in diversity cases without reviewing the state commencement statute to determine if it requires service in addition to filing.

Another issue is whether an action which has been dismissed for jurisdictional reasons tolls the statute of limitations when a new action based on the same incident is untimely filed in state court. In diversity cases, this issue may be resolved by determining whether the state has a savings provision which mitigates the usual rule that the new action is untimely.[56] However, such savings statutes are usually interpreted strictly and may be unavailing in a given action.[57] The circuits vary as to whether the statute of limitations can be tolled when the

---

[50] *Compare* Savings & Profit Sharing Fund of Sears Employees v. Gago, 717 F.2d 1038, 1039 n.3 (7th Cir. 1983) *and* Hifai v. Shell Oil Co., 704 F.2d 1425, 1428 (9th Cir. 1983) (waived if not raised) *with* Nagle v. Lee, 807 F.2d 435, 438–39 (5th Cir. 1987) *and* Lesher v. Lavrich, 784 F.2d 193, 195 (6th Cir. 1986) (defense can be raised sua sponte or untimely).

[51] *See* Carbonell v. Los Angeles Dep't of Health & Human Resources, 772 F.2d 185, 189 (5th Cir. 1985).

[52] 2A Moore's Federal Practice ¶ 8.28.

[53] Guaranty Trust Co. v. York, 326 U.S. 99, 110–12 (1945); see §§ **2.23, 5.4**.

[54] Walker v. Armco Steel Corp., 446 U.S. 740, 748–53 (1980).

[55] See § **5.4**.

[56] *See, e.g.,* Carter v. Washington Metropolitan Area Transit Auth., 764 F.2d 854, 855–57 (D.C. Cir. 1985).

[57] *See id.;* Cross v. General Motors Corp., 778 F.2d 468, 470 (8th Cir. 1985), *cert. denied,* ____ U.S. ____, 106 S. Ct. 2893 (1986).

action is dismissed in state court because of the exclusive jurisdiction of federal court.[58]

§ 7.9 Counterclaims

A plaintiff must always consider the availability of counterclaims when bringing suit. Permissive counterclaims must meet federal jurisdictional requirements,[59] except for setoffs.[60] Compulsory counterclaims are within the court's ancillary jurisdiction.[61] The existence of federal counterclaims alleging violations of RICO, federal antitrust acts, or federal securities acts may in given cases make a state court a more desirable forum. Counterclaims can also exceed the amount sought in the original pleading or request a different type of remedy, such as an injunction,[62] except that counterclaims against the United States are limited by law.[63] A counterclaim can assert a defense arising out of the transaction even if the party is barred from obtaining affirmative relief by the statute of limitations.[64]

§ 7.10 Distinguishing Compulsory from Permissive Counterclaims

Counterclaims are either compulsory or permissive. It is important to distinguish them because of differences in jurisdictional requirements as well as whether the counterclaim is barred if not brought in the original action.

Compulsory counterclaims are claims brought against the opposing party which arise out of the transaction or occurrence that is the subject matter of the opposing party's claim; they do not require the presence of third parties over whom the court cannot acquire jurisdiction.[65] *Permissive counterclaims* are claims against an opposing party which do not arise out of the transaction or occurrence being litigated.[66] Counterclaims maturing or acquired after pleading

---

[58] *See* Bailey v. Carnival Cruise Lines, Inc., 774 F.2d 1577, 1579–81 (11th Cir. 1985) (discussing cases).

[59] McCaffrey v. Rex Motor Transp., Inc., 672 F.2d 246, 248 (1st Cir. 1982); Federman v. Empire Fire & Marine Ins. Co., 597 F.2d 798, 812 (2d Cir. 1979); *see generally* 3 Moore's Federal Practice ¶ 13.19.

[60] 3 Moore's Federal Practice ¶ 13.19[1].

[61] Baker v. Gold Seal Liquors, Inc., 417 U.S. 467, 469 n.1 (1974); Nationwide Mut. Fire Ins. v. T & D Cottage Auto Parts & Serv., Inc., 705 F.2d 685, 687 (3d Cir. 1983); see § **2.26**.

[62] Fed. R. Civ. P. 13(c).

[63] Fed. R. Civ. P. 13(d); *see generally* 3 Moore's Federal Practice ¶ 13.26.

[64] 3 Moore's Federal Practice ¶ 13.11; *see* Stone v. White, 301 U.S. 532, 538 (1937).

[65] Fed. R. Civ. P. 13(a).

[66] Fed. R. Civ. P. 13(b).

may, with the permission of the court, be asserted by supplemental pleading[67] and are not considered compulsory, even if they arise out of the same transaction.[68]

The court has discretion to permit a party to amend its pleadings to add a counterclaim if it has failed to file one through oversight, inadvertence, excusable neglect, or when justice requires.[69] However, if a considerable amount of time passes before the counterclaim is raised in an amended complaint or pretrial memorandum, a denial to permit the counterclaim is not considered an abuse of discretion.[70]

Compulsory counterclaims must be pleaded, or they are barred.[71] The only exceptions are if (1) at the time the action was commenced, the claim was the subject of another pending action or (2) the opposing party brought suit upon its claim by attachment or other process which did not result in personal jurisdiction concerning the claim and no counterclaim is asserted.[72] A counterclaim is also not required in response to a Rule 12 motion, because such a motion is not a pleading as defined in Rule 7.[73] Any counterclaim should be specifically identified, since a reply is mandatory only if it is so denominated.[74]

If a party institutes a second action based on a compulsory counterclaim in a pending action, courts can transfer, stay, or consolidate the actions.[75] The court's dismissal of an action because it should have been stated as a compulsory counterclaim in earlier litigation is reviewed de novo, since it is a matter of law, not discretion.[76] In determining whether a counterclaim is compulsory, several circuits use the logical relationship test to determine if the same operative facts serve as the basis of both claims or if the aggregate core of facts upon which the claim rests activates additional legal rights.[77] Other circuits require greater identity of fact and law.[78]

---

[67] Fed. R. Civ. P. 13(e).

[68] Young v. City of New Orleans, 751 F.2d 794, 801 (5th Cir. 1985); *see* 6 Federal Practice and Procedure § 1411, at 55.

[69] Fed. R. Civ. P. 13(f).

[70] *See* FDIC v. Staudinger, 797 F.2d 908, 911 (10th Cir. 1986); Imperial Enters., Inc. v. Fireman's Fund Ins. Co., 535 F.2d 287, 293 (5th Cir. 1976).

[71] Baker v. Gold Seal Liquors, Inc., 417 U.S. 467, 469 (1974).

[72] Fed. R. Civ. P. 13(a).

[73] United States v. Snider, 779 F.2d 1151, 1157 (6th Cir. 1985).

[74] Fed. R. Civ. P. 7(a).

[75] *See generally,* 3 Moore's Federal Practice ¶ 13.14[2]; 6 Federal Practice and Procedure § 1418.

[76] Republic Health Corp. v. Lifemark Hosps. of Fla., Inc., 755 F.2d 1453, 1454 (11th Cir. 1985); Xerox Corp. v. SCM Corp., 576 F.2d 1057, 1058 n.1 (3d Cir. 1978).

[77] Republic Health Corp. v. Lifemark Hosps. of Fla., Inc., 755 F.2d 1453, 1455 (11th Cir. 1985) (quoting Plant v. Blazer Financial Servs., Inc., 598 F.2d 1357, 1361 (5th Cir. 1979)); United States v. Aquavella, 615 F.2d 12, 22 (2d Cir. 1979); *see* Moore v. New York Cotton Exch., 270 U.S. 593, 610 (1926) (interpreting former Equity Rule 30).

[78] *See generally* 6 Federal Practice and Procedure § 1410, at 42.

§ 7.11 Cross-Claims

Cross-claims differ from counterclaims in that they are claims by one party against a co-party rather than against an opposing party. Cross-claims do not need any independent jurisdictional basis, since they are considered ancillary to the original claim.[79] Cross-claims may be brought concerning the transaction or occurrence that is the subject matter of the original action or a counterclaim or relating to any property that is the subject matter of the original action or a counterclaim or relating to any property that is the subject matter of the original action.[80] Usually, a cross-claim asserts that the co-party is liable for all or part of the original claim; it may resemble an indemnity action. Judgment on a counterclaim or cross-claim may be rendered even if the claims of the opposing party have been dismissed.[81]

§ 7.12 Service of Counterclaims and Cross-Claims

Service of counterclaims and cross-claims follows Rule 5 procedure, and personal service is not required if the party served has appeared in the action.[82] Persons other than those originally sued may be joined as parties to a counterclaim or cross-claim in accordance with Rules 19 and 20.[83] However, Rule 13(h) does not permit an additional party to be joined if the claim is directed solely against the new party and asserts no rights against an original party.[84]

§ 7.13 Third Party Practice

A defendant may become a third party plaintiff against any person not a party to the action who is or may be liable to it for all or part of the plaintiff's claim.[85] This procedure is referred to as *impleader* and eliminates the need for the defendant to bring a separate action against a third individual who may be secondarily or derivatively liable to the defendant.[86] A third party complaint is not appropriate for a related claim, since the claim must be derivatively based on the original plaintiff's claims.[87] However, a third party complaint can be used to

---

[79] McDonald v. Oliver, 642 F.2d 169, 172 (5th Cir. 1981); 3 Moore's Federal Practice ¶ 13.36.

[80] Fed. R. Civ. P. 13(g).

[81] Fed. R. Civ. P. 13(i).

[82] 3 Moore's Federal Procedure ¶ 13.10.

[83] Fed. R. Civ. P. 13(h).

[84] 3 Moore's Federal Practice ¶ 13.39.

[85] Fed. R. Civ. P. 13(a).

[86] *See generally* 6 Federal Practice and Procedure § 1442, at 202–03.

[87] United States v. One 1977 Mercedes Benz, 708 F.2d 444, 452 (9th Cir. 1983), *cert. denied.*, 464 U.S. 1071 (1984); *see generally* 6 Federal Practice and Procedure § 1446.

assert affirmative claims of damages in excess of the original prayer and may raise claims having a different legal nature than the original claim, as long as they arise out of the same operative facts.[88]

Third party claims can be based upon indemnity, subrogation, breach of warranty, contribution between joint tortfeasors, and, in some cases, liability of an insurer.[89] Sometimes a defendant may wish to implead an existing party to the action. Although Rule 14 applies only to nonparties, courts will either sever the claim so that impleader and consolidation reunite the action or permit the claim directly by liberally construing Rule 14.[90]

The court's decision as to whether to implead a third party defendant is reviewed for abuse of discretion.[91] Denial of an application for impleader has been upheld when it would disadvantage the existing action.[92] Any party can move to strike the third party claim or for its severance or separate trial, and the court has power to strike an unmeritorious third party complaint, whether or not it was brought by right.[93] The court can also enter partial judgment, which prohibits nonsettling defendants from bringing third party claims against settling defendants.[94]

Third party complaints do not require separate jurisdictional allegations, and most courts consider such claims to fall within their ancillary jurisdiction.[95] Jurisdiction problems do exist when a third party is impleaded as liable to the plaintiff rather than the defendant and no diversity is present between the plaintiff and the third party.[96] Similarly, the Supreme Court has held that a plaintiff cannot amend the complaint to add a claim against a third party defendant without an independent basis of jurisdiction.[97] Courts differ as to whether jurisdictional requirements must be met for claims of third party defendants against the plaintiff.[98]

§ 7.14 Third Party Procedure

Third party procedure merely identifies how such claims are made and does not create any substantive right to indemnity or contribution when it would not

---

[88] 3 Moore's Federal Practice ¶ 14.07[1], [2].

[89] *See generally id.* ¶¶ 14.10–14.12.

[90] *Id.* § 14.14.

[91] Kenneth Leventhal & Co. v. Joyner Wholesale Co., 736 F.2d 29, 31 (2d Cir. 1984); *see generally* 6 Federal Practice and Procedure § 1443.

[92] Southwest Administrators, Inc. v. Rozay's Transfer, 791 F.2d 769, 777 (9th Cir. 1986).

[93] 6 Federal Practice and Procedure § 1460.

[94] McDonald v. Union Carbide Corp., 734 F.2d 182, 184 (5th Cir. 1984).

[95] 3 Moore's Federal Practice ¶ 14.26.

[96] *Id.*

[97] Owen Equip. & Erection Co. v. Kroger, 437 U.S. 365, 377 (1978).

[98] *See generally* 3 Moore's Federal Practice ¶ 14.27[2].

otherwise exist.[99] A third party complaint should be served no later than 10 days after service of the pleader's original answer. Otherwise, leave must be obtained on motion, and all parties to the action must be notified.[100] Local rules should be consulted, since they may prohibit bringing complaints after a fixed period of time, such as six months, without a showing of special circumstances.[101] Service is dictated by Rule 4 rather than Rule 5.

The third party defendant follows Rule 12 timing for its response.[102] Compulsory counterclaims or cross-claims and defenses must be raised against third party plaintiffs as well as any defenses the third party plaintiff has to the plaintiff's claim.[103] In addition, the third party defendant may assert permissive counterclaims, as well as any claim against the plaintiff arising out of the plaintiff's claim against the third party plaintiff.[104] However, the third party defendant cannot assert a setoff against the plaintiff unless the plaintiff asserts a claim against it.[105] A plaintiff may also bring a third party claim relating to a counterclaim asserted against it.[106] The statute of limtations does not bar the joinder of a third party defendant for contribution or indemnity.[107]

§ 7.15 Jury Demands

State practitioners often fall victim to Rule 38(b)'s requirement that a party must serve its demand for a jury trial not later than 10 days after the service of the last pleading directed to the jury issue. Since some state court systems offer much greater flexibility as to when the jury can first be requested, counsel who are not familiar with the federal rules often discover that they have inadvertently waived their clients' right to a trial by jury. Rule 39(b) gives the court discretion to order a trial by jury upon motion of a party, despite the lack of a timely demand. However, many federal judges are well known for denying Rule 39 motions based solely on the ground of untimeliness.[108] Moreover, counsel cannot revive a jury request by amending the complaint if this right has been previously waived,[109] even when the amendment follows a dismissal.[110] The only exception

---

99 *Id.* ¶ 14.03.

100 Fed. R. Civ. P. 14(a).

101 *See, e.g.*, S.D.N.Y. Local R. 3(k).

102 Fed. R. Civ. P. 14(a).

103 *Id.*

104 *Id.*

105 3 Moore's Federal Practice ¶ 13.06.

106 Fed. R. Civ. P. 14(b).

107 See 3 Moore's Federal Practice ¶ 14.09.

108 *See* 9 Federal Practice and Procedure § 2334, at 115–16.

109 Fredieu v. Rowan Co., 738 F.2d 651, 653 (5th Cir. 1984); Bell v. Cameron Meadows Land Co., 669 F.2d 1278, 1285 (9th Cir. 1982); Walton v. Eaton Corp., 563 F.2d 66, 71 (3d Cir. 1977) (en banc); 5 Moore's Federal Practice ¶ 38.39[2], at 38-353 (2d ed. 1985).

110 Cardio-Medical Assocs. v. Crozer-Chester Medical Center, 721 F.2d 68, 76 (3d Cir. 1983).

to this general rule is when the amended pleading raises new issues not asserted in the original pleading.[111] Therefore, counsel must be sure to make a timely demand for a jury to avoid a bench trial.

On the other hand, a jury trial should not be blindly demanded without analyzing whether it is really desired, because the demand cannot be withdrawn without the consent of all of the parties.[112] In other words, a party can rely on its opponent's jury demand to preserve its own right to a jury trial.[113] Even if one party has withdrawn the demand without apparent objection, when the remaining party immediately demands a jury, it has been permitted.[114]

§ 7.16 Procedural Requirements

Merely checking the jury demand box on the civil cover sheet and timely serving it on the opposing party is considered insufficient by many courts to meet the requirements of Rule 38(b).[115] It is plain that such a procedure is not the preferred method of compliance and is fraught with danger for the party relying on it.[116] In other words, if the party receiving such a cover sheet does not serve a jury demand on the assumption that opposing counsel's demand is valid, some courts will consider any later demand as untimely.

Local rules should be consulted in determining the exact form of the jury request. However local rules which add requirements not found in Rule 38 are not valid.[117] For instance, if a timely request is made, the fact that the demand is not repeated in the jury caption is not grounds for denying a jury trial.[118]

The preferred practice is to write the demand on the first page of the pleading.[119] However, the demand is valid even if made on the last page of the pleading.[120] A defendant should be careful when the request is attached to a counterclaim, since the plaintiff may argue that the defendant has waived a jury

---

[111] *See* 5 Moore's Federal Practice ¶ 38.39[2], at 38-354.

[112] Fed. R. Civ. P. 38(d).

[113] Gargiulo v. Delsole, 769 F.2d 77, 79 (2d Cir. 1985); 5 Moore's Federal Practice ¶ 38.43.

[114] *See* Nimrod Marketing (Overseas) v. Texas Energy Inv. Corp., 769 F.2d 1076, 1079 (5th Cir. 1985), *cert. denied,* _____ U.S. _____, 106 S. Ct. 1266 (1986).

[115] Wall v. National R.R. Passenger Corp., 718 F.2d 906, 909 (9th Cir. 1983); Cochran v. Birkel, 651 F.2d 1219, 1221 n.4 (6th Cir. 1981), *cert. denied,* 454 U.S. 1152 (1982); Omawale v. WBZ, 610 F.2d 20 ,22 (1st Cir. 1979); *see also* Pinemont Bank v. Belk, 722 F.2d 232, 235 (5th Cir. 1984); *see generally* Annotation, *Sufficiency of Demand for Jury Trial under Rule 38(b) of Federal Rules of Civil Procedure,* 73 A.L.R. Fed. 698 (1985).

[116] Pinemont Bank v. Belk, 722 F.2d 232, 235 (5th Cir. 1984)

[117] *See* Pradier v. Elespuru, 641 F.2d 808, 811 (9th Cir. 1981).

[118] *Id.*

[119] Gargiulo v. Delsole, 769 F.2d 77, 78 (2d Cir. 1985); 5 Moore's Federal Practice ¶ 38.40, at 38-362 (2d ed. 1985).

[120] Gargiulo v. Delsole, 769 F.2d 77, 78 (2d Cir. 1985).

on any separate issues set out in the complaint.[121] To avoid such a possibility, the demand should specifically request trial by jury of all issues in the pleadings.[122]

§ 7.17 Untimely Jury Requests

Courts vary as to the standard applicable to the court's exercise of discretion to grant an untimely jury request. For example, several circuits require a motion for jury trial to be granted in the absence of strong and compelling reasons to the contrary.[123] Factors considered in such an analysis include:

1. Whether the case involves issues which are best tried to a jury
2. Whether granting the motion would disrupt the court's schedule or that of the adverse party
3. The degree of prejudice to the adverse party
4. The length of the delay before requesting a jury trial, and
5. The reason for the movant's tardiness in requesting a jury trial.[124]

Inadvertence or neglect are considered insufficient excuses to obtain relief from waiver in many courts.[125] Even in those circuits which consider oversight an excuse, it is not an abuse of discretion to deny a Rule 39(b) motion based on mere inadvertence.[126]

Unlike the traditional test of waiver of a constitutional right which requires an intentional relinquishment or abandonment of a known right, Rule 38(d) is based on the premise that a jury trial is waived unless a timely demand is filed.[127] There is some dispute whether the same waiver standard applies to pro se litigants.[128]

---

[121] *See, e.g.*, Phillips v. Kaplus, 764 F.2d 807, 811 (11th Cir. 1985), *cert. denied*, _____ U.S. _____, 106 S. Ct. 802 (1986).

[122] *See generally* 5 Moore's Federal Practice ¶ 38.39[2].

[123] Parrott v. Wilson, 707 F.2d 1262, 1267 (11th Cir.), *cert. denied*, 464 U.S. 936 (1983); Pinemont Bank v. Belk, 722 F.2d 232, 236 (5th Cir. 1984).

[124] Parrot v. Wilson, 707 F.2d 1262, 1267 (11th Cir.), *cert. denied*, 464 U.S. 936 (1983).

[125] *See e.g.*, Blau v. Del Monte Corp., 748 F.2d 1348, 1357 (9th Cir. 1984); Littlefield v. Fort Dodge Messenger, 614 F.2d 581, 585 (8th Cir. 1980); Noonan v. Cunard S.S. Co., 375 F.2d 69, 70 (2d Cir. 1967).

[126] Misco, Inc. v. United States Steel Corp., 784 F.2d 198, 205 (6th Cir. 1986); Bellmore v. Mobil Oil Corp., 783 F.2d 300, 307 (2d Cir. 1986); Fredieu v. Rowan Cos., 738 F.2d 651, 654 (5th Cir. 1984); Parrott v. Wilson, 707 F.2d 1262, 1267 (11th Cir.), *cert. denied*, 464 U.S. 936 (1983).

[127] Washington v. New York City Bd. of Estimate, 709 F.2d 792, 797 (2d Cir.), *cert. denied*, 464 U.S. 1013 (1983).

[128] *Compare id.* at 797–98 (waiver) *with* Lewis v. Thigpen, 767 F.2d 252, 258–59 & n.10 (5th Cir. 1985) (no waiver when claim of ignorance of procedures is credible).

§ 7.18 Waiver of Timely Jury Requests

If a jury trial is timely demanded, Rule 39(a)(1) requires that the parties or their attorneys of record file a written stipulation with the court or orally stipulate in open court on the record if they consent to a bench trial. In the absence of a stipulation, waiver of a jury trial is not lightly inferred, because the right to a jury trial is fundamental.[129] Plaintiffs are not required to walk out of the courtroom rather than proceed with a nonjury trial in order to preserve their objection to the judge's finding of waiver.[130] However, the circuits are split as to whether the right to a jury trial can be waived by the conduct of the parties.[131] Therefore, mere acquiescence to a bench trial effects a waiver in some courts.[132]

§ 7.19 Pleadings Checklist

Requirement of Particularity

1. Does Rule 9(b) apply?
2. Does circuit require some degree of specificity?

Requirement of Specificity

1. Is standing to sue an issue?
2. Does litigation involve alleged violation of civil rights?
3. Is a RICO claim included?
4. Is a conspiracy alleged?
5. Is fraud alleged?
6. Are special damages requested?

Form and Substance of Allegations

1. Has jurisdictional basis been alleged?

---

[129] Garguilo v. Delsole, 769 F.2d 77, 79 (2d Cir. 1985).

[130] *Id.*

[131] United States v. 1966 Beechcraft Aircraft Model King Air, 777 F.2d 947, 951 (4th Cir. 1985); *see generally* 9 Federal Practice and Procedure § 2321.

[132] United States v. 1966 Beechcraft Aircraft Model King Air, 777 F.2d 947, 951 (4th Cir. 1985); Southland Reship Inc. v. Flegel, 534 F.2d 639, 645 (5th Cir. 1976); *but see* Palmer v. United States, 652 F.2d 893, 896 (9th Cir. 1981); DeGioia v. United States Lines Co., 304 F.2d 421, 424 n.1 (2d Cir. 1962).

2. In diversity action does complaint show:
   a. The citizenship of individuals?
   b. The place of incorporation and principal place of business for all corporations?
   c. Absence of Does, or demonstrate that Does are sham?
   d. The jurisdictional amount of damages (exceeds $10,000)?
3. Is fraudulent concealment or other factual matter averred to survive statute of limitations attack on pleadings?
4. Are separate counts stated for different transactions or legal theories?
5. Are sources of statements adopted by reference attached or disclosed?
6. Is verification required?
   a. Is suit a shareholder's derivative action?

Denials

1. Is a general denial appropriate?
   a. Are all the allegations controverted?
2. Should a specific denial be used:
   a. As to part of the allegation?
   b. As to an entire allegation?
3. Should the fifth amendment be pleaded?
4. Is answer filed within 20 days (Rule 12 timing)?

Affirmative Defenses

1. Have any of the following affirmative defenses been stated which must appear in answer?

   Accord and satisfaction
   Arbitration and award
   Assumption of risk
   Contributory negligence
   Discharge in bankruptcy
   Duress
   Estoppel
   Failure of consideration
   Fraud
   Illegality
   Injury by fellow servant
   Laches
   License
   Payment
   Release
   Res judicata
   Statute of frauds
   Statute of limitations
   Waiver
2. Has capacity been specifically challenged?
3. Are any of the above defenses subject to a Rule 12 challenge (see **ch. 14**)?

Other Pleadings

1. Is a counterclaim appropriate against an opposing party?
   a. Is counterclaim compulsory (arising out of same transaction or occurrence as claim)?
   b. Is counterclaim permissive (other transactions)?
2. Is cross-claim appropriate against co-party?
   a. Does claim relate to subject matter of action or counterclaim?
3. Is a third party claim appropriate against one who is not a party?
   a. Is a third party liable for all or part of the plaintiff's claim?
   b. Has complaint been filed within 10 days after answer was served?
   c. If complaint is untimely, has leave of court been granted?
4. Is supplemental pleading appropriate for later claim?
5. Is an amended pleading necessary (see **ch. 8**)?

Jury Demand

1. Has a jury been demanded:
   a. In a pleading?
   b. No later than 10 days after service of the last pleading directed to the jury issue?
2. If jury request is timely, has Rule 39(b) motion been made?
   a. Is there a reason for waiver beyond mere ignorance of rule?

Rule 11

1. After reasonable inquiry, can the attorney certify that the pleadings are well grounded in law and fact and not brought for an improper purpose?

CHAPTER 8

AMENDMENTS

§ 8.1 Amendments

The Federal Rules permit liberal use of amendments in order to facilitate the determination of claims on the merits and to prevent litigation from becoming a technical exercise in the fine points of pleading.[1] Pleadings are construed to do substantial justice,[2] and mere technical defects do not provide a basis for dismissal.[3] Rule 15(a) provides that a party may amend its pleading once as a

[1] Jones v. Louisiana, 764 F.2d 1183, 1185 (5th Cir. 1985).

[2] Fed. R. Cir. P. 8(f).

[3] Jones v. Louisiana, 764 F.2d 1183, 1185 (5th Cir. 1985).

matter of course at any time before a responsive pleading is served, or within 20 days after the service of a pleading not requiring a response. Otherwise, a party may amend its pleading only by leave of court or by written consent of the adverse party. The rule specifically requires that leave shall be freely granted when justice so requires.

§ 8.2 Denying Amendments

Most litigation concerning Rule 15(a) revolves around the extent of the court's discretion to deny amendments. The leading case in this area is *Foman v. Davis.*[4] *Foman* requires that leave to amend be freely granted, unless there has been undue delay, bad faith, or dilatory motive on the part of the movant, repeated failure to cure deficiencies by amendments previously allowed, or undue prejudice to the opposing party, or if the amendment is futile.[5] As a result of the *Foman* standard, courts have granted amendments liberally,[6] in effect placing the burden of showing why the amendment should not be granted on the nonmovant.[7] At least one circuit even considers the prejudice to the movant as well as the prejudice to the opponent if the motion is denied.[8]

Administrative pleadings are also easily amended.[9] Similarly, leave to amend in bankruptcy cases is freely granted when the purpose is to cure a defect in the claim, describe the claim with greater particularity, or plead a new theory of recovery on the facts already set forth.[10] The discretion whether to grant leave to file a supplemental pleading has been considered comparable to that exercised for leave to amend.[11]

---

[4] 371 U.S. 178 (1962).

[5] *Id.* at 182.

[6] *See generally* 3 J. Moore *et al.*, Moore's Federal Practice ¶ 15.08[2] (2d ed. 1985) [hereinafter Moore's Federal Practice]; 6 C. Wright & A. Miller, Federal Practice and Procedure § 1473 (1971) [hereinafter Federal Practice and Procedure].

[7] *See* Senza-Gel Corp v. Seiffhart, 803 F.2d 661, 666 (Fed. Cir. 1986) (patent appeal interpreting 9th Cir. procedural law).

[8] Stevens v. Gay, 792 F.2d 1000, 1003 (11th Cir. 1986).

[9] Yaffe Iron & Metal Co. v. United States Envt'l Protection Agency, 774 F.2d 1008, 1012 (10th Cir. 1985); Mineral Indus. & Heavy Constr. Group v. OSHRC, 639 F.2d 1289, 1292 (5th Cir. 1981).

[10] LeaseAmerica Corp. v. Eckel, 710 F.2d 1470, 1473 (10th Cir. 1983); *In re* Commonwealth Corp., 617 F.2d 415, 420 (5th Cir. 1980).

[11] Lewis v. Knutson, 699 F.2d 230, 239 (5th Cir. 1983); *see* Otis Clapp & Son, Inc. v. Filmore Vitamin Co., 754 F.2d 738, 743 (9th Cir. 1985); *see generally* 6 Federal Practice & Procedure § 1504.

§ 8.3 Delay

Mere delay does not support a denial of an amendment if no prejudice exists.[12] However, delay is a relevant factor in assessing prejudice,[13] and undue delay can be a basis for denial.[14] The delay must be in the actual proceeding, not in bringing the suit.[15] Some courts appear to view long time delays as imputing prejudice.[16] In other words, at some point, the delay becomes undue, placing an unwarranted burden on the court, or becomes prejudicial, placing an unfair burden on the opposing party.[17] Several circuits place the burden of showing a valid reason for the neglect and delay upon the movant if considerable time has elapsed between the filing of the complaint and the motion to amend.[18] Therefore, unjustifiable delay can go beyond excusable neglect even in the absence of bad faith.[19] Indeed, delay itself can be considered evidence of bad faith.[20] At a minimum, no party should wait to file an amendment for a significant amount of time after the court has actually warned it that a motion to amend is required.[21]

The closer to trial, the more likely it is that a denial to amend will be upheld on appeal.[22] Similarly, an amendment often is denied if it would result in reopening

---

[12] Moore v. City of Paducah, 790 F.2d 557, 559–62 (6th Cir. 1986); Howze v. Jones & Laughlin Steel Corp., 750 F.2d 1208, 1212 (3d Cir. 1984); United States v. Webb. 665 F.2d 977, 980 (9th Cir. 1981); Buder v. Merrill, Lynch, Pierce, Fenner & Smith, 644 F.2d 690, 694 (8th Cir. 1981); *see generally* 3 Moore's Federal Practice ¶ 15.08[4].

[13] *See, e.g.,* Loehr v. Ventura County Community College Dist., 743 F.2d 1310, 1320 (9th Cir. 1984).

[14] Isaac v. Harvard Univ., 769 F.2d 817, 829 (1st Cir. 1985).

[15] Boileau v. Bethlehem Steel Corp., 730 F.2d 929, 939 (3d Cir.), *cert. denied,* 469 U.S. 871 (1984).

[16] *See, e.g.,* Serrano Medina v. United States, 709 F.2d 104, 106 (1st Cir. 1983) (delay of more than 2 years); Evans v. Syracuse City School Dist., 704 F.2d 44, 47 (2d Cir. 1983) (delay of two years and nine months); Daly v. Sprague, 675 F.2d 716, 723 (5th Cir. 1982) (16-month delay), *cert. denied,* 460 U.S. 1047 (1983).

[17] Adams v. Gould, Inc., 739 F.2d 858, 868 (3d Cir. 1984), *cert. denied,* 469 U.S. 1122 (1985).

[18] Stephanischen v. Merchants Despatch Transp. Corp., 722 F.2d 922, 933 (1st Cir. 1983); Best Canvas Prods. & Supplies, Inc. v. Ploof Truck Lines, Inc., 713 F.2d 618, 623 (11th Cir. 1983); Freeman v. Continental Gin Co., 381 F.2d 459, 469 (5th Cir. 1967).

[19] Daves v. Payless Cashways, Inc., 661 F.2d 1022 (5th Cir. 1981) (19-month delay).

[20] Adams v. Gould Inc., 739 F.2d 858, 868 (3d Cir. 1984), *cert. denied,* 469 U.S. 1122 (1985); 6 Federal Practice and Procedure § 1488.

[21] *See* Ellis v. United States Postal Serv., 784 F.2d 835, 838 (7th Cir. 1986); Best Canvas Prods. & Supplies, Inc. v. Ploof Truck Lines, Inc., 713 F.2d 618, 623 (11th Cir. 1983).

[22] *See, e.g.,* Colmenares Vivas v. Sun Alliance Ins. Co., 807 F.2d 1102, 1108 (1st Cir. 1986) (six days before trial); Brackin Tie, Lumber & Chip Co. v. McLarty Farms, Inc., 704 F.2d 585, 586–7 (11th Cir. 1983) (three days before trial); Daves v. Payless Cashways, Inc., 661 F.2d 1022,

discovery after it has essentially been completed[23] or if it is submitted after a summary judgment motion has been filed[24] or granted.[25] The nonmovant's own delay in responding to discovery can be considered in weighing prejudice,[26] but a late motion for summary judgment or dismissal does not in itself justify an excessive delay in moving to amend.[27] Even if the movant alleges that no further discovery is necessary, courts can consider whether the amendment would affect trial strategy and tactics.[28] If the amendment is viewed as a means to force a favorable settlement by abusive use of the discovery process[29] or as a means to circumvent the district court's denial of a jury trial,[30] a denial is proper. However, in the absence of diversity, a plaintiff has been permitted to elect to proceed in admiralty, in effect withdrawing its right to a jury trial under a Jones Act claim, even though that amendment defeated the defendant's ability to obtain a jury trial.[31]

Some courts require that an amendment be tendered no later than the time of pretrial in the absence of any compelling reason for the delay.[32] Other courts allow amendments made as late as the day of trial if there is no prejudice to the opposing party.[33] Since practice is not entirely consistent, counsel should always move to amend as soon as the information supporting the amendment becomes known.

1024 (5th Cir. 1981) (eve of trial); *cf* United States v. City of Twin Falls, 806 F.2d 862, 874–76 (9th Cir. 1986) (during trial).

[23] Dart Indus., Inc. v. Plunkett Co. of Okla., 704 F.2d 496, 500 (10th Cir. 1983).

[24] *See, e.g.,* Matsumoto v. Republic Ins. Co., 792 F.2d 869, 872 (9th Cir. 1986); Local 472 of Plumbing & Pipefitting Indus. v. Georgia Power Co., 684 F.2d 721, 724 (11th Cir. 1982).

[25] *See, e.g.,* Williamsburg Wax Museum v. Historic Figures, Inc., 810 F.2d 243, 247 (D.C. Cir. 1987); Nguyen v. United States, 792 F.2d 1500, 1503 (9th Cir. 1986); Union Planters National Leasing, Inc. v. Woods, 687 F.2d 117, 121 (5th Cir. 1982); *see generally* 10 Federal Practice and Procedure § 2712 (2d ed. 1983).

[26] *See* Washington v. New York City Bd. of Estimate, 709 F.2d 792, 796 (2d Cir. 1983), *cert. denied,* 464 U.S. 1013 (1984).

[27] Andrews v. Bechtel Power Corp., 780 F.2d 124, 139 (1st Cir. 1985), *cert. denied,* ____ U.S. ____, 106 S. Ct. 2896 (1986).

[28] Tiernan v. Blyth, Eastman, Dillon & Co., 719 F.2d 1, 4 (1st Cir. 1983).

[29] Barrows v. Forest Laboratories, Inc., 742 F.2d 54, 58 (2d Cir. 1984).

[30] Earlie v. Jacobs, 745 F.2d 342, 345 (5th Cir. 1984).

[31] Rachal v. Ingram Corp., 795 F.2d 1210, 1215–17 (5th Cir. 1986).

[32] Nevels v. Ford Motor Co., 439 F.2d 251, 257 (5th Cir. 1971), *quoted with approval in* Evans v. Syracuse City School Dist., 704 F.2d 44, 47 (2d Cir. 1983). *But see* Guthrie v. J.C. Penney Co., 803 F.2d 202, 210 (5th Cir. 1986) (affirming amendment which added statute of limitations defense 11 days before trial).

[33] *See* Sweetheart Plastics, Inc. v. Detroit Forming, Inc., 743 F.2d 1039, 1044 (4th Cir. 1984).

§ 8.4 Amendments to Defeat Jurisdiction

Courts usually deny amendments which defeat diversity jurisdiction, unless the party being added is indispensable.[34] This usually occurs when the case has been removed and the plaintiff attempts to add a nondiverse party. The court often evaluates the plaintiff's motive in determining whether to permit such an amendment.[35]

§ 8.5 Successive or Futile Amendments

Leave to amend is given freely but not indefinitely.[36] There does not appear to be any particular number beyond which no further amendment is allowed, but appellate courts have affirmed denials when the complaint has previously been amended two[37] or three times.[38]

If the complaint as amended would be subject to dismissal, no abuse of discretion occurs if the proposed amendment is denied.[39] Therefore, an amendment will be denied if it attempts to state a claim which is insufficient as a matter of law.[40] However, if no other ground is presented to support denial of an amendment and the amendment states a claim, it must be granted.[41] In other words, if the district court is incorrect that the amendment does not state a claim, its denial of an amendment will be reversed.[42]

---

[34] *See, e.g.,* Faser v. Sears, Roebuck & Co., 674 F.2d 856, 859 (11th Cir. 1982); *see generally* 1A Moore's Federal Practice ¶ 0.161[1.-3]; see also § **9.3**.

[35] *See* Desert Empire Bank v. Insurance Co. of N. Am., 623 F.2d 1371, 1376 (9th Cir. 1980) (permitting amendment).

[36] DeBry v. Transamerica Corp., 601 F.2d 480, 492 (10th Cir. 1979).

[37] Hayduk v. Lanna, 775 F.2d 441, 445 (1st Cir. 1985), *cert. denied,* ____ U.S. ____, 106 S. Ct. 1790 (1986).

[38] A.E. v. Mitchell, 724 F.2d 864, 868 (10th Cir. 1983); Armstrong v. McAlpin, 699 F.2d 79, 94 (2d Cir. 1983); Gordon v. Terry, 684 F.2d 736, 739 (11th Cir. 1982), *cert. denied,* 459 U.S. 1203 (1983).

[39] Halliburton & Assocs. v. Henderson, Few & Co., 774 F.2d 441, 444 (11th Cir. 1985); Glick v. Koenig, 766 F.2d 265, 268 (7th Cir. 1985); Addington v. Farmer's Elevator Mut. Ins. Co., 650 F.2d 663, 667 (5th Cir.), *cert. denied,* 454 U.S. 1098 (1981); *see generally* 6 Federal Practice and Procedure § 1487.

[40] *See, e.g.,* Sooner Prods. Co. v. McBride, 708 F.2d 510, 512 (10th Cir. 1983); *see generally* 6 Federal Practice and Procedure § 1487.

[41] *See* Keniston v. Roberts, 717 F.2d 1295, 1302 (9th Cir. 1983).

[42] Jamieson v. Shaw, 772 F.2d 1205, 1209 (5th Cir. 1985); *see* Moffatt Enters., Inc. v. Borden Inc., 807 F.2d 1169, 1177 (3d Cir. 1986) (reversed denial of amendment which was based on erroneous grant of summary judgment).

§ 8.6 Amendments by Defendants

Although amendment of pleadings is usually requested by the plaintiff, a defendant may wish to amend to assert an affirmative defense or a counterclaim which has not been previously pleaded.[43] In fact, if an affirmative defense is not raised in the pleadings, unless it is tried with the implied consent of the parties, an amendment is the only way to preserve the defense.[44] In assessing whether to allow an affirmative defense, some courts balance the length of the delay against the resulting prejudice, requiring less prejudice as the period of unexplained delay lengthens.[45] Although affirming a late amendment, the Sixth Circuit upheld an award of litigation costs to the plaintiff, since a timely assertion of the defense would have resulted in an early termination of the case.[46]

§ 8.7 Procedural Requirements

No particular procedure is set out in Rule 15 for requesting leave to amend, and various methods have been recognized as sufficient.[47] For example, the Ninth Circuit construed a request in a brief opposing a motion to dismiss as sufficient to entitle the plaintiff to amend as of right when no responsive pleading had been filed.[48] Similarly, the Fifth Circuit interpreted the plaintiff's revised theory in its memorandum in opposition to summary judgment as a motion to amend the pleadings.[49] However, other courts are quite formal and require a motion which is made in writing and sets forth with particularity the reasons for the amendment.[50]

Several circuits require the proposed amendment to be submitted to the trial court.[51] Even if not required, this is the better practice in order to ensure that the

---

[43] *See, e.g.*, Tokio Marine & Fire Ins. Co. v. Employers Ins. of Wausau, 786 F.2d 101, 103 (2d Cir. 1986).

[44] Depositors Trust Co. v. Slobusky, 692 F.2d 205, 208 (1st Cir. 1982).

[45] *See* Evans v. Syracuse City School Dist., 704 F.2d 44, 47 (2d Cir. 1983).

[46] Adkins v. International Union of Elec., Radio & Mach. Workers, 769 F.2d 330, 334 (6th Cir. 1985).

[47] Tefft v. Seward, 689 F.2d 637, 639 (6th Cir. 1982); *see generally* 6 Federal Practice and Procedure § 1485.

[48] Nolen v. Fitzharris, 450 F.2d 958, 958–59 (9th Cir. 1971).

[49] Sherman v. Hallbauer, 455 F.2d 1236, 1242 (5th Cir. 1972).

[50] *See* Wolgin v. Simon, 722 F.2d 389, 394–95 (8th Cir. 1983) (refusing to construe request in opposition to motion to dismiss as a motion for leave to amend).

[51] *See id.* at 395; Otto v. Variable Annuity Life Ins. Co., 808 F.2d 512, 524–25 (7th Cir. 1986); *see generally* 6 Federal Practice and Procedure § 1485.

court has all the relevant information before it when exercising its discretion.[52] At a minimum, the theories underlying the amendment should be spelled out so the appellate court can determine whether the amendment would correct the deficiencies in the complaint,[53] although amendments adding closely related claims and parties may speak for themselves.[54] Some circuits are more lenient regarding amendments by pro se plaintiffs, even remanding for amendments to add or change parties absent such a request.[55]

The trial court must also justify its denial of the proposed amendment.[56] As a result, some circuits require the district judge to give a statement of reasons for the denial, unless the reasons are apparent or the amendment would be futile.[57] Counsel should request such a statement, even if it is not required.

§ 8.8 Amendments as of Right

Rule 15(a) provides that a party may amend its pleading once as a matter of course at any time before a responsive pleading is served or if a responsive pleading is not permitted within 20 days after service. It is well established that neither a motion to dismiss nor a motion for summary judgment is a responsive pleading within the meaning of Rule 15.[58] Therefore, an amendment as of right can be made after such a motion is filed.[59] However, courts differ as to whether the ability to amend as of right survives the granting of either of these motions.[60]

---

[52] Twohy v. First Nat'l Bank of Chicago, 758 F.2d 1185, 1197 (7th Cir. 1985); 3 Moore's Federal Practice § 15.12.

[53] *See, e.g.*, Zaidi v. Ehrlich, 732 F.2d 1218, 1220 (5th Cir. 1984); Triplett v. LeFlore County, 712 F.2d 444, 446–47 (10th Cir. 1983).

[54] *See* Halliburton & Assocs. v. Henderson, Few & Co., 774 F.2d 441, 444 (11th Cir. 1985).

[55] *See, e.g.*, Wilborn v. Escalderon, 789 F.2d 1328, 1332 (9th Cir. 1986); Berndt v. Tennessee, 796 F.2d 879, 882 (6th Cir. 1986); Wilger v. Department of Pensions & Sec., 593 F.2d 12, 13 (5th Cir. 1979).

[56] Foman v. Davis, 371 U.S. 178, 182 (1962).

[57] *See, e.g.*, Cornwall v. United States Constr. Mfg., Inc., 800 F.2d 250, 253 (Fed. Cir. 1986) (interpreting 11th Circuit law); Loehr v. Ventura County Community College Dist., 743 F.2d 1310, 1319 (9th Cir. 1984).

[58] Zaidi v. Ehrlich, 732 F.2d 1218, 1220 (5th Cir. 1984); Labatt v. Twomey, 513 F.2d 641, 651 (7th Cir. 1975); 6 Federal Practice and Procedure § 1483.

[59] Zaidi v. Ehrlich, 732 F.2d 1218, 1220 (5th Cir. 1984); Le Grand v. Evan, 702 F.2d 415, 417 (2d Cir. 1983).

[60] *Compare* Jafree v. Barber, 689 F.2d. 640, 642 n.2 (7th Cir. 1982) (right survives dismissal) *with* Czeremcha v. International Ass'n of Mach. & Aerospace Workers, 724 F.2d 1552, 1556 (11th Cir. 1984), Elfenbein v. Gulf & W. Indus., Inc., 590 F.2d 445, 448 n.2 (2d Cir. 1978) *and* United

Some courts distinguish dismissal of the complaint and dismissal of the action.[61] In other words, some circuits consider that, after judgement has been entered, there is nothing left to amend. In these circuits, a motion requesting that the judgment be set aside or vacated pursuant to Rules 59(e) or 60(b) is a prerequisite for an amendment,[62] although, if granted, a motion for leave to amend is liberally construed.[63] If leave to amend is sought after dismissal, the district court need not allow an amendment that does not cure the defects that led to dismissal.[64]

Counsel should never request leave to amend when an amendment as of right is proper. Although most courts analyze such requests as if the request were made as of right,[65] a few older cases view the request as waiving the right to amend as a matter of course.[66] Courts usually grant leave to amend following dismissal of a complaint for failure to state a claim when there is any likelihood of correcting the defect.[67] Similarly, pro se plaintiffs usually are given an opportunity to amend before their complaints are dismissed for failure to state a cause of action.[68] Several circuits do not affirm Rule 12(b)(6) dismissals unless it is clear that the complaints could not be saved by any amendment.[69] In the absence of a declared or apparent reason, an outright refusal to grant leave to amend is an abuse of discretion.[70]

Steelworkers v. American Int'l Alum. Corp., 334 F.2d 147, 150 n.4 (5th Cir. 1964) (right dissolves after dismissal); *see generally* 3 Moore's Federal Practice ¶ 15.07[2].

[61] *See, e.g.,* Car Carriers, Inc. v. Ford Motor Co., 745 F.2d 1101, 1111 (7th Cir. 1984), *cert. denied,* 470 U.S. 1054 (1985) (permitting an amendment as of right if only the complaint is dismissed, but not if the action is dismissed).

[62] *See, e.g.,* Johnson v. Levy Org. Dev. Co., 789 F.2d 601, 611 (7th Cir. 1986); Cooper v. Shumway, 780 F.2d 27, 29 (10th Cir. 1985); *see generally* 6 Federal Practice and Procedure § 1489.

[63] *See* Czeremcha v. International Ass'n of Mach. & Aerospace Workers, 724 F.2d 1552, 1556 (11th Cir. 1984); *see also* Triplett v. LeFlore County, 712 F.2d 444, 446 (10th Cir. 1983).

[64] Czeremcha v. International Ass'n of Mach. & Aerospace Workers, 724 F.2d 1552, 1556 (11th Cir. 1984); Textor v. Board of Regents of N. Ill. Univ., 711 F.2d 1387, 1391 (7th Cir. 1983).

[65] *See, e.g.,* Wright v. Newsome, 795 F.2d 964, 967 (11th Cir. 1986).

[66] *Compare* Zaidi v. Ehrlich, 732 F.2d 1218, 1220 (5th Cir. 1984) *and* Washington v. New York City Bd. of Estimate, 709 F.2d 792, 795–96 (2d Cir.), *cert. denied,* 464 U.S. 1013 (1983) *with* Vars v. International Bhd. of Boilermakers, 204 F.Supp. 245, 246 (D. Conn. 1962).

[67] *See* Hall v. City of Santa Barbara, 797 F.2d 1493, 1496 (9th Cir. 1986); Triplett v. LeFlore County, 712 F.2d 444, 446 (10th Cir. 1983); Thomas v. Farmville Mfg. Co., 705 F.2d 1307, 1307–08 (11th Cir. 1983); *see generally* 3 Moore's Federal Practice ¶ 15.10.

[68] *See generally* 5 Federal Practice and Procedure § 1202.

[69] Kelson v. City of Springfield, 767 F.2d 651, 656 (9th Cir. 1985); *see* O'Quinn v. Manuel, 773 F.2d 605, 610 (5th Cir. 1985) (remanding when dismissal was from first complaint).

[70] Foman v. Davis, 371 U.S. 178, 182 (1962); Thomas v. Farmville Mfg. Co., 705 F.2d 1307, 1307–08 (11th Cir. 1983).

§ 8.9 Reviewing Dismissals

The district court's ruling concerning a motion to amend a complaint is reviewed for abuse of discretion.[71] As a practical matter, if the trial court allows the amendment, it is unlikely that this decision will be reversed on appeal.[72] On the other hand, *Foman*[73] restricts the scope of the district court's discretion to deny the amendment.

The appealability of a dismissal of the complaint is a matter of disagreement among the circuits. The Second Circuit holds that the dismissal of a complaint, unless leave to amend is explicitly granted, constitutes a final appealable order.[74] Other circuits distinguish between a dismissal of the complaint and a dismissal of the action. Dismissal of the complaint is not final unless the trial court makes clear that the action cannot be saved by amendment.[75] An intermediary approach giving the plaintiff the choice of pursuing a permissive right to amend the complaint or treating the order as final is followed by several other circuits.[76] The denial of leave to amend is normally a nonappealable interlocutory order[77] which is only reviewable on appeal from a final order or judgment.[78]

When the action is dismissed, the plaintiff can either appeal or move for relief under Rules 59(e) or 60(b) on the basis of a proposed amendment.[79] Rule 59 provides for motions to alter or amend the judgment, and Rule 60 outlines grounds on which a party can move for relief from a final judgment. Several circuits review the Rule 59(e) motion as if judgment had not been entered and the court were ruling solely on Rule 15 factors which encourage liberal use of

---

[71] Zenith Radio Corp. v. Hazeltine Research, Inc., 401 U.S. 321, 330 (1971); Daly v. Sprague, 675 F.2d 716, 723 (5th Cir. 1982), *cert. denied,* 460 U.S. 1047 (1983).

[72] *See, e.g.,* Smith v. Town of Clarkton, 682 F.2d 1055, 1059 (4th Cir. 1982) (affirmed when amendment was allowed five weeks before trial).

[73] Foman v. Davis, 371 U.S. 178 (1962). See § **8.2**.

[74] Elfenbein v. Gulf & W. Ind., Inc., 590 F.2d 445, 448 (2d Cir. 1978).

[75] Dist. Council 47, American Fed'n of State, County & Municipal Employees v. Bradley, 795 F.2d 310, 316 (3d Cir. 1986); Azar v. Conley, 480 F.2d 220, 222–23 (6th Cir. 1973); Ruby v. Secretary of United States Navy, 365 F.2d 385, 387 (9th Cir. 1966).

[76] Czeremcha v. International Ass'n of Mach. & Aerospace Workers, 724 F.2d 1552, 1556 (11th Cir. 1984); United States v. Mayton, 335 F.2d 153, 158 n.12 (5th Cir. 1964).

[77] Czeremcha v. International Ass'n of Mach. & Aerospace Workers, 724 F.2d 1552, 1556 (11th Cir. 1984); Wells v. South Main Bank, 532 F.2d 1005, 1006 (5th Cir. 1976).

[78] Czeremcha v. International Ass'n of Mach. & Aerospace Workers, 724 F.2d 1552, 1556 (11th Cir. 1984).

[79] Car Carriers, Inc. v. Ford Motor Co., 745 F.2d 1101, 1111 (7th Cir. 1984), *cert. denied,* 470 U.S. 1054 (1985); Czeremcha v. International Ass'n of Mach. & Aerospace Workers, 724 F.2d 1552, 1556 (11th Cir. 1984); 3 Moore's Federal Practice ¶¶ 15.07[2], 15.10; 6 Federal Practice and Procedure § 1489.

amendments.[80] Other circuits interpret Rule 15 more restrictively in post-judgment situations and consider delay in presenting amendments as a valid reason to deny them.[81] If the only proffered reasons for not raising affirmative defenses until after the verdict is that counsel did not expect to lose, it is not abuse of discretion to deny the amendment.[82]

§ 8.10 Rule 11 Sanctions

Rule 11 sanctions apply to amendments as well as to other types of pleadings and motions. Therefore, counsel must be careful that the amendment has a basis in law and that the allegations have some factual basis to avoid assessment of monetary awards against counsel, even in the absence of any bad faith.[83] Similarly, even if leave to amend is granted, the court can assess the additional costs of litigating the new issues against the party asserting them.[84]

§ 8.11 Relation Back

Rule 15(c) sets out the criteria for determining when an amendment relates back to the date of the original pleading. Relation back is critical if the statute of limitations has run before the amendment is filed, because it is the only way to add a new party[85] or a new claim against a named party. The rule was enacted to avoid the harsh consequences that can result from a rigid application of the statute of limitations.[86] However, the Supreme Court has strictly construed this doctrine insofar as notice must be provided within the statutory limitations period.[87]

---

[80] Adams v. Gould Inc., 739 F.2d 858, 864 (3d Cir. 1984), *cert. denied,* 469 U.S. 1122 (1985); Dussouy v. Gulf Coast Inv. Corp., 660 F.2d 594, 597–98 (5th Cir. 1981).

[81] *See* Twohy v. First Nat'l Bank of Chicago, 758 F.2d 1185, 1196 (7th Cir. 1985); Ondis v. Barrows, 538 F.2d 904, 909 (1st Cir. 1976); Jackson v. American Bar Ass'n, 538 F.2d 829, 833 (9th Cir. 1976).

[82] Trinity Carton Co. v. Falstaff Brewing Corp., 767 F.2d 184, 194 (5th Cir. 1985), *cert. denied,* ____ U.S. ____, 106 S. Ct. 1202 (1986).

[83] Rodgers v. Lincoln Towing Serv., Inc., 771 F.2d 194, 204–06 (7th Cir. 1985); see **ch. 28.**

[84] Adkins v. International Union of Elec., Radio & Mach. Workers, 769 F.2d 330, 334 (6th Cir. 1985).

[85] Korn v. Royal Caribbean Cruise Line, Inc., 724 F.2d 1397, 1399 (9th Cir. 1984).

[86] Employees Sav. Plan of Mobil Oil Corp. v. Vickery, 99 F.R.D. 138, 142 (S.D.N.Y 1983); *see generally* 6 Federal Practice and Procedure §§ 1496, 1497.

[87] Schiavone v. Fortune, ____ U.S. ____, 106 S. Ct. 2379, 2384–85 (1986).

§ 8.12 Rule 15(c) Criteria

Relation back applies both to new claims and to new parties. In order for the doctrine to apply, the following four factors must be satisfied:

1. The basic claim or defense must arise out of the conduct, transaction, or occurrence set forth or attempted to be set forth in the original pleading
2. The party to be brought in must have received such notice of the action that it will not be prejudiced in maintaining its defense on the merits
3. That party must or should have known that, but for a mistake concerning identity, the action would have been brought against it
4. The second and third requirements must have been fulfilled within the prescribed limitations period.[88]

Resolution of these issues involves inherently factual determinations, and a complete factual record is required.[89] The appellate court reviews relation back questions by an abuse of discretion standard.[90] Therefore, these issues usually are won or lost before the trial judge.

Courts usually construe liberally whether the claim arose out of the same conduct, transaction, or occurrence, especially when the amendment does not add a new cause of action but merely makes defective allegations more definite.[91] Thus, a claim seeking recovery for shipments made before those identified in the original complaint was permitted on the theory that the original complaint put the defendant on notice of all unpaid shipping services.[92] On the other hand, an amendment alleging a coverup did not relate back to the original negligence claim.[93] Unfair surprise and prejudice are significant factors in determining whether a new claim will relate back.[94]

---

[88] *Id.; see* Fed. R. Civ. P. 15(c).

[89] Serrano v. Torres, 764 F.2d 47, 49 (1st Cir. 1985); Johnson v. Bechtel Assocs. Prof. Corp., 717 F.2d 574, 585 (D.C. Cir. 1983), *cert. denied,* 464 U.S. 1070 (1984); Ringrose v. Engelberg Huller Co., 692 F.2d 403, 405 (6th Cir. 1982).

[90] Korn v. Royal Caribbean Cruise Line, Inc., 724 F.2d 1397, 1399 (9th Cir. 1984).

[91] Siegel v. Converters Transp., Inc., 714 F.2d 213, 216 (2d Cir. 1983).

[92] *Id.*

[93] Fuller v. Marx, 724 F.2d 717, 720 (8th Cir. 1984).

[94] *See Id.;* Clipper Express v. Rocky Mountain Motor Tariff Bureau, Inc., 690 F.2d 1240, 1259 n.29 (9th Cir. 1982), *cert. denied,* 459 U.S. 1227 (1983); Rosenberg v. Martin, 478 F.2d 520, 526 (2d Cir.), *cert. denied,* 414 U.S. 872 (1973).

§ 8.13 Notice

Courts vary on how strictly they require compliance with the notice provisions of Rule 15(c).[95] Some courts have permitted an identity of interest exception to Rule 15 to substitute a party who has not received notice for one who has, when the two are united in interest.[96] Other circuits allow relation back to correct misnomers only if the provisions of Rule 15 are met.[97] The misnomer concept has been held inapplicable to substitute the United States as a defendant for one of its governmental agencies.[98] Misspellings generally may be corrected without strict adherence to Rule 15.[99]

Notice during the limitations period usually is the stumbling block to adding new parties.[100] The Supreme Court has refused to engraft an extension of the limitations period for the service of a timely filed complaint.[101] Therefore, for relation back to be permitted, notice during the limitations period is required, even if the action is commenced by filing.[102] Notice of the incident giving rise to the action is insufficient.[103] Thus, counsel must be careful to serve the defendant within the statutory period if any question exists that the party is not correctly named.

Notice to the defendant does not have to be formal.[104] Knowledge can be imputed to a new defendant through its attorney who also represented the party originally sued.[105] It can also be imputed by notifying the new defendant's agent for claims that a suit has been filed.[106] The fact that the proposed defendant submitted an affidavit in the original action also evidenced notice.[107]

The requirement that the party added must be chargeable with knowledge that, but for a mistake, the action would have been brought against it can also be demonstrated in a variety of ways, including whether the proposed defendant is a

---

[95] *See, e.g., Note, The Relation Back of Claims Against Third-Party Defendants,* 7 Cardoza L. Rev. 281 (1985) (discussing New York and federal law).

[96] *See* Schiavone v. Fortune, ____ U.S. ____, 106 S. Ct. 2379, 2384 (1986); 3 Moore's Federal Practice ¶ 15.15[4.-1].

[97] *See, e.g.,* Watson v. Unipress, Inc., 733 F.2d 1386, 1390 (10th Cir. 1984).

[98] Hughes v. United States, 701 F.2d 56, 58 (7th Cir. 1982) (Federal Tort Claims Action).

[99] Ingram v. Kumar, 585 F.2d 566, 570 (2d Cir. 1978), *cert. denied,* 440 U.S. 940 (1979).

[100] *See, e.g.,* Hughes v. United States, 701 F.2d 56, 58 (7th Cir. 1982).

[101] Schiavone v. Fortune, ____ U.S. ____, 106 S. Ct. 2379, 2385 (1986).

[102] *Id.*

[103] Korn v. Royal Caribbean Cruise Line, Inc., 724 F.2d 1397, 1400 (9th Cir. 1984).

[104] *Id.* at 1399.

[105] Kirk v. Cronvich, 629 F.2d 404, 408 (5th Cir. 1980).

[106] Korn v. Royal Caribbean Cruise Line, Inc., 724 F.2d 1397, 1401 (9th Cir. 1984).

[107] Eakins v. Reed, 710 F.2d 184, 188 (4th Cir. 1983).

successor in interest to the named defendant[108] or has refused to respond to discovery which would have revealed the mistake.[109] However, when a plaintiff failed to amend its complaint after being notified of the mistake, an unnamed party was entitled to conclude that it was not named because of strategic reasons rather than mistake, thereby precluding relation back of a later amendment.[110]

§ 8.14 Notice to the United States

Notice to the United States of any or its agencies or officers is satisfied by the delivery or mailing of process to the United States Attorney, his designee, or the Attorney General of the United States, or to an agency or officer who would have been a proper defendant if named.[111] If the government does not receive notice of the proceedings until after the statute of limitations has expired, no amendment adding the United States as a defendant is allowed.[112] However, when the United States was not originally named as a party, service on the United States Attorney during the statutory period was sufficient to permit relation back of the amendment naming the United States as a defendant.[113] Some courts will not impute knowledge of the suit by a government agency to the United States Attorney.[114]

The most liberal case permitting addition of the United States as a defendant occurred in the context of a pro se prisoner's action. A federal tort claims action was submitted to the clerk, who mistakenly returned it to the defendant without filing it, with instructions to submit it on forms dealing with civil rights actions which required the Attorney General to be named as defendant. When the defendant later tried to add the United States, he was beyond the statutory limitations period. The Fourth Circuit refused to be bound by strict Rule 15(c) analysis, since the mistake was clearly the result of the clerk's office and no prejudice to the United States had been suggested.[115] However, counsel should anticipate that the notice requirement will be strictly construed when the United States is the defendant.

---

[108] 6 Federal Practice and Procedure § 1499.

[109] *See* Photolab Corp. v. Simplex Specialty Co., 806 F.2d 807, 811 (8th Cir. 1986).

[110] Kilkenny v. Arco Marine Inc., 800 F.2d 853, 857 (9th Cir. 1986).

[111] Fed. R. Civ. P. 15(c).

[112] Weisgal v. Smith, 774 F.2d 1277, 1279 (4th Cir. 1985); Hughes v. United States, 701 F.2d 56, 58–59 (7th Cir. 1982); Carr v. Veterans Admin., 522 F.2d 1355, 1358 (5th Cir. 1975).

[113] Edwards v. United States, 755 F.2d 1155, 1157 (5th Cir. 1985).

[114] *See* Williams v. United States, 711 F.2d 893, 898 (9th Cir. 1983).

[115] Owens-El v. United States Attorney Gen., 759 F.2d 349, 350 (4th Cir. 1985).

§ 8.15 Amendments Changing Plaintiffs

Although Rule 15 specifically refers to amendments concerning defendants, it also applies to amendments changing plaintiffs.[116] A few circuits severely limit joinder by requiring that a defendant must have had fair notice of the existence of the new party and its claim.[117] In these circuits, it does not matter that no showing of specific prejudice exists.[118] In general, notice from a previous complaint is seldom adequate when substituting plaintiffs, unless the change merely brings in the real party in interest or accomplishes some similar technical result.[119] However, some courts allow amendments changing plaintiffs to relate back if the relief sought in the amended complaint is identical to that demanded originally, despite the lack of notice.[120] Other courts permit such amendments as long as no actual prejudice results to the defendant.[121] Courts often focus on whether the new and old plaintiffs have an identity of interest.[122] If the wrong party brought the action because of its own inexcusable neglect, some courts will not allow substitution.[123]

§ 8.16 Does and Relation Back

More than 30 states allow plaintiffs to use some form of Doe pleading.[124] Many such provisions are more liberal than Rule 15(c) in permitting defendants to be added after the applicable statute of limitations has run.[125] A plaintiff who resides in a jurisdiction allowing Doe pleading must carefully consider potential statute of limitations problems when deciding in which forum to litigate. If the matter is heard in state court, the plaintiff can name several Does in the

---

[116] Raynor Bros. v. American Cyanamid Co., 695 F.2d 382, 384 (9th Cir. 1982); Leachman v. Beech Aircraft Corp., 694 F.2d 1301, 1308 (D.C. Cir. 1982); *see* 3 Moore's Federal Practice ¶ 15.15[4.-2].

[117] Leachman v. Beech Aircraft Corp., 694 F.2d 1301, 1308 (D.C. Cir. 1982); Williams v. United States, 405 F.2d 234, 238 (5th Cir. 1968).

[118] Leachman v. Beech Aircraft Corp., 694 F.2d 1301, 1309 (D.C. Cir. 1982).

[119] Besig v. Dolphin Boating & Swimming Club, 683 F.2d 1271, 1278 (9th Cir. 1982).

[120] *E.g., id.*

[121] *See, e.g.,* Wadsworth v. United States Postal Serv., 511 F.2d 64, 67 (7th Cir. 1975); *see generally* 6 Federal Practice and Procedure § 1501.

[122] Raynor Bros. v. American Cyanamid Co., 695 F.2d 382, 384 (9th Cir. 1982); Staren v. American Nat'l Bank & Trust Co., 529 F.2d 1257, 1263 (7th Cir. 1976); *see generally* 3 Moore's Federal Practice ¶ 15.15[4.-1]; 6 Federal Practice and Procedure § 1501 & n.33.

[123] Leachman v. Beech Aircraft Corp., 694 F.2d 1301, 1310 n.7 (D.C. Cir. 1982).

[124] *See* extensive list in Comment, *Doe Defendants and Other State Relation Back Doctrines in Federal Diversity Cases,* 35 Stanford L. Rev. 297, 300 n.14 (1983).

[125] *E.g.,* Cal. Civ. Proc. Code § 474 (West 1979); N.Y. Civ. Prac. L. & R. 1024 (McKinney 1976).

complaint and not worry about any statute of limitations bar when later substituting their true identities. In contrast, Doe pleading is frowned upon in federal court, because it typically destroys complete diversity.[126] No federal statute or rule specifically countenances the naming of fictitious parties in a lawsuit.[127] Some district courts will not even accept a complaint which names Doe defendants.

If a plaintiff chooses federal court and later wishes to add a new defendant, the applicability of the state Doe practice and relation back procedure can become an issue. This problem can also arise when a federal action which has pendent state claims naming Does is removed by the defendant from state court.[128] Courts have split on whether the state law of Federal Rule 15 should be applied,[129] depending upon whether the state law is considered procedural[130] or substantive.[131] If the state statute is not substantive, Rule 15(c) applies. Only if the state statute is not substantive does it override Rule 15's requirements. It has been argued that Doe practice and state relation back principles are always substantive because they effectively extend the state's statute of limitations,[132] but this is clearly not a universally held position.[133] However, the Ninth Circuit, which faces numerous relation back issues caused by California's liberal Doe practice, has held that California law rather than Rule 15(c) applies to relation back claims, since California has effectively extended its statute of limitations three years past the commencement of the action as to defendants named as Does.[134] On the other hand, this holding appears to be limited to actions in which strict compliance with Doe procedure is followed, which requires the Doe to appear in the federal complaint and be dismissed in favor of the newly identified defen-

---

[126] *See generally* Comment, *Doe Defendants and Other State Relation Back Doctrines in Federal Diversity Cases,* 35 Stanford L. Rev. 297, 304–06 (1983); §§ **2.18, 3.11.**

[127] Watson v. Unipress, Inc., 733 F.2d 1386, 1388 (10th Cir. 1984).

[128] 28 U.S.C. 1441(c) (1982); *see, e.g.,* Anderson v. Allstate Ins. Co., 630 F.2d 677, 679–80 (9th Cir. 1980).

[129] *See* Comment, *Doe Defendants and Other State Relation Back Doctrines in Federal Diversity Cases,* 35 Stanford L. Rev. 297, 307–08 (1983); *see also* Vickers, *Procedural Defenses Available to the New Party-Defendant: The Necessity of Obtaining Leave to Amend and Relation Back,* 17 Akron L. Rev. 1 (1983) (analyzing Ohio and Federal Rules).

[130] *E.g.,* Royal Indem. Co. v. Petrozzino, 598 F.2d 816, 820 (3d Cir. 1979).

[131] *E.g.,* Marshall v. Mulrenin, 508 F.2d 39, 44 (1st Cir. 1974).

[132] Comment, *Doe Defendants and Other State Relation Back Doctrines in Federal Diversity Cases,* 35 Stanford L. Rev. 297, 314–18 (1983).

[133] *See* Johansen v. E.I. Du Pont de Nemours & Co., 810 F.2d 1377, 1380 (5th Cir. 1987) (federal rather than Texas relation back rule applies); Talbert v. Kelly, 799 F.2d 62, 66 n.1 (3d Cir. 1986) (New Jersey's John Doe practice does not extend statute of limitations in diversity cases); see also extensive discussion in Ringrose v. Engelberg Huller Co., Inc., 692 F.2d 403, 406–12 (6th Cir. 1982) (Jones, J., concurring).

[134] Lindley v. General Elec. Co., 780 F.2d 797, 800 (9th Cir.), *cert. denied,* _____ U.S. _____, 106 S. Ct. 2926 (1986).

dant. However, Does would be present in diversity cases only if not dismissed due to oversight or in those few actions in which removal is not based on diversity.[135] If the amendment in issue preceded removal, state law has been used to determine that it is time-barred.[136] Counsel should be aware that even if state law is applied, this does not ensure that the amendment will relate back, since Doe statutes protect the plaintiff only when adding newly discovered defendants, not when adding individuals whose names and connection with the incident were previously known.[137]

§ 8.17 Supplemental Pleadings

Relation back issues can also arise in the context of a supplemental pleading which adds transactions, occurrences, or events which have happened since the original pleading. Usually statute of limitations questions are unlikely in this context, since the events occurred after the commencement of suit. If a statute of limitations problem is raised, as long as the original pleading gave notice that the alleged wrongful conduct was of a continuing nature, the supplemental pleading will relate back to the original complaint.[138]

§ 8.18 Amendment Checklist

Procedural Considerations

1. Can the amendment be served as a matter of course?
- **a.** Is it the first amendment served before receipt of a responsive pleading?
- **b.** Is amendment made within 20 days of serving a pleading which does not require a response?

2. Has leave of court been sought to serve any other amendment?
- **a.** How has request been made?
  - **(1)** Motion is preferred method.
- **b.** Does amendment accompany motion?

---

[135] *See* CTS Printex, Inc. v. American Motorists Ins. Co., 639 F. Supp. 1272, 1275–78 (N.D. Cal. 1986); **ch. 3**.

[136] Anderson v. Allstate Ins. Co., 630 F.2d 677, 682 (9th Cir. 1980); Witherow v. Firestone Tire & Rubber Co., 530 F.2d 160, 168–69 (3d Cir. 1976).

[137] *See, e.g.*, Anderson v. Allstate Ins. Co., 630 F.2d 677, 682 (9th Cir. 1980).

[138] William Inglis & Sons Baking Co. v. ITT Continental Baking Co., 668 F.2d 1014, 1053–54 (9th Cir. 1981), *cert. denied*, 459 U.S. 825 (1982); *see* 6 Federal Practice and Procedure § 1508.

Criteria for Amendments

1. Leave to serve amendment will be freely granted, unless:

- **a.** There has been undue delay in seeking the amendment.
  - **(1)** What is the length of time before the amendment was sought?
  - **(2)** How close is the case to trial?
  - **(3)** What is the current stage of discovery?
  - **(4)** Has any dispositive motion been filed or granted?
- **b.** The amendment has been brought in bad faith.
- **c.** There is dilatory motive for bringing the amendment.
- **d.** There have been repeated failures to cure deficiencies in the pleading.
- **e.** The amendment is futile
- **f.** The other side will be prejudiced if the amendment is granted.

Relation Back of Amendment to the Original Pleading

1. Does amendment arise out of same conduct, transaction or occurrence as the pleading?

2. Has opponent received notice of the action so it will not be prejudiced?

3. Should opponent know that, but for mistake, action would have been brought against it?

4. Did notice required by 2 and 3 fall within the statute of limitations period?

- **a.** Was the notice actual or constructive?
- **b.** Was there an identity of interest between the new and existing party?
- **c.** Was there notice of the complaint, not only of the underlying incident?

5. What is the effect of Doe pleading?

- **a.** Check whether Rule 15 or state law concerning relation back applies.

CHAPTER 9

PARTY PRACTICE

§ 9.1 Party Issues Generally

Various rules control the addition, deletion, or substitution of parties. Questions of capacity, joinder, indispensable parties, intervention, interpleader, and substitution each raise separate considerations. Courts usually view party problems pragmatically, as exemplified by Rule 21, which permits parties to be dropped or added at any stage on terms that are just and prevents misjoinder from being a ground for dismissal. Another theme which runs through party litigation is ensuring that relief has been timely requested.

§ 9.2 Capacity of Parties and Real Party in Interest

Rule 17 governs the general requirements concerning parties. Although an action must be prosecuted in the name of the real party in interest, it will not be dismissed on that ground until a reasonable time after objection has passed without ratification, joinder, or substitution by the real party in interest.[1] The commencement of the original action is the relevant date for statute of limitation purposes.[2] Executors, administrators, guardians, bailees, trustees of an express trust, parties with whom or in whose name a third party beneficiary contract has been made, or parties authorized by statute can sue in their own names.[3] This has generated controversy concerning the ability of a party to create diversity jurisdiction when it would not otherwise be available.[4] However, waiting to assert a real party in interest defense until trial may backfire, because the court has discretion under Rule 21 to add a party at any stage of the proceedings.[5]

Rule 17(b) provides that the capacity of an individual to sue or be sued, other than one acting in a representative capacity, is determined by domicile; corporate capacity is determined by the law under which the corporation was organized.[6] In most other cases, capacity is determined by the law of the state in which the district court sits. One exception is that a partnership or other unincorporated association may sue or be sued in its common name to enforce a substantive right existing under the Constitution or laws of the United States even if this is not permitted by state law. Second, the capacity of a receiver appointed by a court of the United States is governed by statute.[7] Rule 17(c) permits infants or incompetent persons to sue through a representative or guardian ad litem.

§ 9.3 Compulsory Joinder

Joinder of parties, like joinder of claims, is either compulsory or permissive. Rule 19 concerns compulsory joinder of persons who are needed for just adjudication.[8] It contains a two-step analysis:

---

[1] Fed. R. Civ. P. 17(a).

[2] *Id.*

[3] *Id.*

[4] *See, e.g.*, Note, *Civil Procedure—The Appointment of an Administrator for a Decedent's Estate to Create Diversity of Citizenship—Krier-Hawthorne v. Beam,* 21 Wake Forest L. Rev. 489 (1986); *see generally* 3A J. Moore *et al.*, Moore's Federal Practice ¶ 17.04 (2d ed. 1986) [hereinafter Moore's Federal Practice]; § **2.17**.

[5] *See, e.g.*, Thor Power Tool Co. v. Weintraub, 791 F.2d 579, 582–83 (7th Cir. 1986).

[6] Fed. R. Civ. P. 17(b).

[7] *Id.*; 28 U.S.C. §§ 754, 959(a) (1982).

[8] *See generally,* Freer, *Rethinking Compulsory Joinder: A Proposal to Restructure Federal Rule 19,* 60 N.Y.U. L. Rev. 1061 (1985).

1. To determine under Rule 19(a) if a person should be joined and
2. If so, how to proceed pursuant to Rule 19(b) if joinder is not feasible.[9]

As a result, Rule 19(b) does not apply until Rule 19(a) has been considered.[10] Rule 19(a) requires joinder if, in the absence of that person, complete relief cannot be granted to the existing parties or if the disposition of the action without joinder practically impairs the absent individual's ability to protect her interest in the action or leaves any party subject to multiple or inconsistent obligations. These factors must be reviewed in light of pragmatic concerns, primarily the effect of nonjoinder on the parties and litigation.[11] A necessary party who refuses to join as a plaintiff may be made a defendant under the involuntary plaintiff doctrine.[12]

If a person cannot be made a party, usually due to lack of personal or subject matter jurisdiction or statute of limitations problems, Rule 19(b) requires the court to determine in equity and good conscience whether to dismiss the case or proceed to judgment. The factors which the court considers include the extent of prejudice, means of lessening prejudice, adequacy of any judgment rendered, and the plaintiff's remedy if the action is dismissed.[13]

A corporation is an indispensable party in a derivative action brought by one of its shareholders.[14] Similarly, a parent or subsidiary corporation may be an indispensable party if liability is dependent on the acts of the absent corporation.[15] In contract rescission actions, numerous cases require all parties to the contract and others having a substantial interest in it to be joined.[16] If an indispensable party is not amenable to service in the district where the litigation is pending, the court has discretion to transfer the case to a district where process is available.[17]

---

[9] *See generally* 3A Moore's Federal Practice ¶ 19.07-1[0].

[10] Aguilar v. Los Angeles County, 751 F.2d 1089, 1092 (9th Cir.), *cert. denied,* 471 U.S. 1125 (1985).

[11] Kelly v. Commercial Union Ins. Co., 709 F.2d 973, 978 (5th Cir. 1983); CTI-Container Leasing Corp. v. Uiterwyk Corp., 685 F.2d 1284, 1290 (11th Cir. 1982), *cert. denied,* 459 U.S. 1173 (1983).

[12] *See generally* 3A Moore's Federal Practice ¶ 19.06.

[13] *See generally* Provident Tradesmens Bank & Trust Co. v. Patterson, 390 U.S. 102, 109–11, 118–19 (1968).

[14] Liddy v. Urbanek, 707 F.2d 1222, 1224 (11th Cir. 1983); *see* Ross v. Bernhard, 396 U.S. 531, 538 (1970).

[15] *See* H.D. Corp. of Puerto Rico v. Ford Motor Co., 791 F.2d 987, 993 (1st Cir. 1986); Freeman v. Northwest Acceptance Corp., 754 F.2d 553, 559 (5th Cir. 1985); Envirotech Corp. v. Bethlehem Steel Corp., 729 F.2d 70, 75–77 (2d Cir. 1984).

[16] Naartex Consulting Corp. v. Watt, 722 F.2d 779, 788 (D.C. Cir. 1983), *cert. denied,* 467 U.S. 1210 (1984) (extensive citations).

[17] 28 U.S.C. §§ 1631 (1982); *see* Sierra Club v. Leathers, 754 F.2d 952, 955 (11th Cir. 1985).

§ 9.4 —Procedural Requirements

Joinder is determined by federal law in diversity[18] as well as federal actions. Technically, other than in class actions, counsel is required to state in the complaint the names of any known necessary parties who are not joined and the reasons for their absence.[19] The defendant should raise the absence of an indispensable party in a Rule 12(b)(7) motion,[20] but failure to do so does not waive the defense.[21] Since a nondiverse indispensable party defeats jurisdiction, a plaintiff may hold back from joining an indispensable party and raise that defect for the first time on appeal to avoid the effect of an adverse judgment.[22] Rule 11 sanctions should be sought in such cases.[23]

Decisions applying Rule 19(b) criteria are reviewed under an abuse of discretion standard.[24] Counsel should request findings on the individual factors weighed, because an appellate court may remand for such a statement if the basis for the district court's decision is unclear.[25]

§ 9.5 Permissive Joinder

Rule 20 authorizes permissive joinder of plaintiffs who assert any right to relief jointly, severally, or in the alternative arising out of the same transaction, occurrence, or series of transactions or occurrences when any question of law or fact common to all these persons will arise in the action. This same test is used for joinder of claims asserted against defendants. A plaintiff or defendant need not be interested in obtaining or defending against all the relief demanded, and the court can order separate trials when appropriate.[26]

---

[18] Provident Tradesmens Bank & Trust Co. v. Patterson, 390 U.S. 102, 125 n.22 (1968); Tick v. Cohen, 787 F.2d 1490, 1493 (11th Cir. 1986).

[19] Fed. R. Civ. P.19(c), (d).

[20] See § **14.53**.

[21] *See* Fed. R. Civ. P. 12(h)(2); Provident Tradesmens Bank & Trust Co. v. Patterson, 390 U.S. 102, 109 (1968); Pickle v. International Oilfield Divers, Inc., 791 F.2d 1237, 1242 (5th Cir. 1986), *cert. denied,* _____ U.S. _____, 107 S. Ct. 939 (1987).

[22] *See* County Sanitation Dist. No. 2 v. Inland Container Corp., 803 F.2d 1074, 1079–80 (9th Cir. 1986) (Noonan, J., dissenting).

[23] See **ch. 28**.

[24] Cloverleaf Standardbred Owners Ass'n, Inc. v. National Bank, 699 F.2d 1274, 1276 (D.C. Cir. 1983); Walsh v. Centeio, 692 F.2d 1239, 1241–43 (9th Cir. 1982).

[25] *See, e.g.*, Bakia v. County of Los Angeles, 687 F.2d 299, 302 (9th Cir. 1982); *cf.* Steel Valley Auth. v. Union Switch & Signal Div., 809 F.2d 1006, 1010 (3d Cir. 1987) (when district court did not make explicit Rule 19 determination, appellate court engaged in independent analysis of indispensability).

[26] Fed. R. Civ. P. 20(a), (b).

Misjoinder of parties is not ground for dismissal of an action, and the court may add or drop parties sua sponte or on motion, on terms that are just.[27] Such dismissals are not construed as dismissals for failure to state a claim,[28] because Rule 21 focuses on parties, not claims.[29] When counsel adds a party, statute of limitations problems may bar the new claim unless the amendment relates back to the original commencement of the action.[30]

§ 9.6 Interpleader

Interpleader permits a plaintiff to join individuals asserting mutually exclusive claims, which may expose it to double or multiple claims.[31] To justify interpleader, the stakeholder must have a real and reasonable fear of double liability or vexatious, conflicting claims.[32] Rule 22 permits interpleader regardless of whether the claims or titles on which the claims depend do not have a common origin or are not identical but are adverse to and independent of one another, or whether the plaintiff alleges that it is not liable in whole or in part to any or all of the claimants. In the usual interpleader action, the plaintiff holds money or property which belongs to another, and a dispute exists concerning the rightful owner.[33] In many cases, the stakeholder is an insurance company or surety on a bond. Defendants can obtain interpleader by way of cross-claim or counterclaim.[34]

Because Rule 22 interpleader is not an independent source of jurisdiction, in diversity cases complete diversity is required.[35] On the other hand, statutory interpleader, which is governed by 28 U.S.C. § 1335, provides an alternative remedy which requires only minimal rather than complete diversity and a disputed amount of $500.[36] Interpleader jurisdiction is determined at the time the suit is filed and subsequent events do not divest the court of jurisdiction.[37]

---

[27] Fed. R. Civ. P. 21.

[28] See §§ **14.41–14.52**.

[29] *See* Lampliter Dinner Theater, Inc. v. Liberty Mut. Ins. Co., 792 F.2d 1036, 1045 n.10 (11th Cir. 1986).

[30] See § **8.11**.

[31] Fed. R. Civ. P. 22; 28 U.S.C. § 1335 (1982).

[32] Indianapolis Colts v. Mayor of Baltimore, 741 F.2d 954, 957 (7th Cir. 1984), *cert. denied,* 470 U.S. 1052 (1985); Fonseca v. Regan, 734 F.2d 944, 950 (2d Cir.), *cert. denied,* 469 U.S. 882 (1984); Dunbar v. United States, 502 F.2d 506, 510–11 (5th Cir. 1974).

[33] *See generally* 3A Moore's Federal Practice ¶ 22.02[1].

[34] Fed. R. Civ. P. 22(1).

[35] *See generally* 3A Moore's Federal Practice ¶ 22.04[2.-1].

[36] See § **2.13**.

[37] Walker v. Pritzker, 705 F.2d 942, 944 (7th Cir. 1983).

Service is made pursuant to Rule 4.[38] Unlike Rule 22, which follows general venue rules, venue in statutory interpleader is proper in any district in which one or more claimants reside.[39] In a given case, interpleader may be initiated as a counterclaim.

The party seeking interpleader initiates the process by moving to deposit the disputed fund with the court and be discharged from litigation.[40] After the stakeholder is discharged or determined to be an interested party, the dispute focuses on the merits of the individual claims. In appropriate cases, an injunction can be granted to prevent further litigation against a dismissed stakeholder. For example, when a claimant sued an insured party, the insurance company filed a federal interpleader action and deposited the limits of its coverage with the court. A default judgment which was obtained in a state suit by the claimant against the insurance company based solely on the policy was held to be subject to the interpleader action and properly stayed by the federal court.[41]

A judgment is final in an interpleader action when the court determines the claimants are entitled to the money and the amount due each claimant.[42] Review of the propriety of a court's ruling concerning interpleader is de novo when the issue is solely legal.[43]

§ 9.7 Intervention

Rule 24 provides for intervention of right and permissive intervention. Courts frequently focus on questions relating to the scope and nature of intervention in cases involving the approval of consent decrees or stipulations in employment discrimination suits.[44] Intervention may also be used in class actions, but it is even applicable to such mundane matters as a lawyer's intervention in a former client's personal injury action in order to protect the attorney's rights under a contingent fee contract.[45]

Intervention of right occurs when

1. A statute of the United States confers an unconstitutional right to intervene or

---

[38] 3A Moore's Federal Practice ¶ 22.04[2.-2].

[39] 28 U.S.C. § 1397 (1982).

[40] 3A Moore's Federal Practice ¶ 22.02[1].

[41] Illinois Employers Ins. v. Mihalcik, 801 F.2d 949, 951 (7th Cir. 1986).

[42] *In re* Sinking of M/V Ukola, 806 F.2d 1, 3 (1st Cir. 1986).

[43] Indianapolis Colts v. Mayor of Baltimore, 741 F.2d 954, 956 (7th Cir. 1984), *cert. denied,* 470 U.S. 1052 (1985).

[44] Kirkland v. New York State Dep't of Correctional Servs., 711 F.2d 1117, 1125 (2d Cir. 1983), *cert. denied,* 465 U.S. 1005 (1984).

[45] *See* Keith v. St. George Packing Co., 806 F.2d 525, 526 (5th Cir. 1986).

2. **(a)** When the applicant has an interest in the subject matter of the litigation
   (b) The interest will be impaired by disposition of the action without the applicant's involvement, and
   (c) The applicant's interest is not represented adequately by one of the existing parties to the action.[46]

The interest requirement is usually interpreted as requiring a direct and substantial interest.[47] Inadequacy can be shown if the representative has an adverse interest to the applicant, has failed to represent the applicant's interest, or has engaged in collusion with an opposing party.[48] The extent of showing as to inadequacy has generated controversy when the government is the representative.[49] Generally, counsel should request permissive intervention as an alternative to intervention of right whenever the basis for intervention is unclear.

Permissive intervention is authorized when a statute confers a conditional right to intervene or when an applicant's claim or defense and the main action have a question of law or fact in common. Permissive intervenors must have independent jurisdictional grounds to become a party to the action.[50] However, Rule 24(b) permits governmental officers or agencies to intervene concerning statutes, orders, or regulations administered by them, although limited intervention does not preclude the government from fulfilling its statutory duty to pursue a separate enforcement action.[51] Since permissive intervention is a discretionary ruling, in which the court considers whether the intervention will unduly delay

---

[46] Fed. R. Civ. P. 24(a)(2); Keith v. Daley, 764 F.2d 1265, 1268 (7th Cir.), *cert. denied,* ___ U.S. ___, 106 S. Ct. 383 (1985); Smith v. Pangilinan, 651 F.2d 1320, 1323–24 (9th Cir. 1981); *see* Restor-A-Dent Dental Labs., Inc. v. Certified Alloy Prods., Inc., 725 F.2d 871, 874 (2d Cir. 1984).

[47] Restor-A-Dent Dental Labs., Inc. v. Certified Alloy Prods., Inc., 725 F.2d 871, 874 (2d Cir. 1984); *see generally* Meridian Homes Corp. v. Nicholas W. Prassas & Co., 683 F.2d 201, 203–05 (7th Cir. 1982); 3B Moore's Federal Practice ¶ 24.07[2].

[48] Sanguine, Ltd. v. United States Dep't of Interior, 736 F.2d 1416, 1419 (10th Cir. 1984); *see generally* 7C C. Wright, A. Miller, *et al.,* Federal Practice and Procedure § 1909 (2d ed. 1986) [hereinafter Federal Practice and Procedure].

[49] *Compare* United States v. Stringfellow, 783 F.2d 821, 827 (9th Cir. 1986) (minimal showing), *vacated on other grounds,* ___ U.S. ___, 107 S. Ct. 1177 (1987) *with* United States v. Hooker Chem. & Plastics Corp., 749 F.2d 968, 987 (2d Cir. 1984) (strong showing); *see generally* Fox, *Hooker Chemicals: Closing the Courthouse Door to Intervenors,* 61 Chi.-Kent L. Rev. 93 (1985); *cf.* Pub. L. No. 99-499, 100 Stat. 1613 (1986) (Superfund Amendments and Authorization Act of 1986 permits affected groups to intervene as of right in hazardous waste litigation).

[50] Harris v. Amoco Prod. Co., 768 F.2d 669, 675 (5th Cir. 1985), *cert. denied,* ___ U.S. ___, 106 S. Ct. 1186 (1986); *see generally* 7C Federal Practice and Procedure § 1917; see § **2.26**.

[51] *See* Secretary of Labor v. Fitzsimmons, 805 F.2d 682, 694–96 (7th Cir. 1986) (reviewing caselaw).

or prejudice the adjudication of the rights of the original parties,[52] the district court's decision. can be overturned only for abuse of discretion.[53] The Fifth Circuit has noted that it has never reversed a denial of permissive intervention and that such decisions are extremely rare.[54]

§ 9.8 —Timeliness and Risks of Intervention

Rule 24 requires that all motions for intervention must be timely,[55] and untimeliness is frequently raised as a bar to intervention. A denial for untimeliness is a discretionary ruling, regardless of whether permissive intervention or intervention of right is being claimed.[56] Timeliness is determined by the totality of circumstances,[57] but factors considered include

1. The length of time the intervenor knew or should have known of its interest in the case
2. The prejudice to the original parties cause by the delay
3. The resulting prejudice to the intervenor if the motion is denied, and
4. Any unusual circumstances.[58]

Motions to intervene at the appellate level usually are considered untimely unless sought in an exceptional case for imperative reasons.[59]

Intervention carries the risks that the intervenor will be treated as a party for all purposes and that claims concerning the adverse party can be completely litigated.[60] In other words, the price of intervention is the possibility that a

---

[52] Fed. R. Civ. P. 24(b); *see generally* 3B Moore's Federal Practice ¶ 24.10[4].

[53] United States v. American Cyanamid Co., 719 F.2d 558, 563 (2d Cir. 1983), *cert. denied,* 465 U.S. 1101 (1984).

[54] Kneeland v. National Collegiate Athletic Ass'n, 806 F.2d 1285, 1289–90 (5th Cir. 1987).

[55] *See generally* 3B Moore's Federal Practice ¶ 24.13 (2d ed. 1985).

[56] United States v. Jefferson County, 720 F.2d 1511, 1516 (11th Cir. 1983); *see* United Airlines, Inc. v. McDonald, 432 U.S. 385, 387 (1977); NAACP v. New York, 413 U.S. 345, 365–66 (1973); United States v. $129,374 in U.S. Currency, 769 F.2d 583, 585 (9th Cir. 1985), *cert. denied,* ____ U.S. ____, 106 S. Ct. 863 (1986); Holland v. Sterling Enters., Inc., 777 F.2d 1288, 1293 (7th Cir. 1985); *see generally* 3B Moore's Federal Practice ¶ 24.13; 7C Federal Practice and Procedure § 1916.

[57] NAACP v. New York, 413 U.S. 345, 365–66 (1973).

[58] United States v. Jefferson County, 720 F.2d 1511, 1516 (11th Cir. 1983); United States v. Kemper Money Market Fund, Inc., 704 F.2d 389, 391 (7th Cir. 1983); Stallworth v. Monsanto Co., 558 F.2d 257, 264–66 (5th Cir. 1977).

[59] Amalgamated Transit Union Int'l v. Donovan, 771 F.2d 1551, 1552–53 (D.C. Cir. 1985), *cert. denied,* ____ U.S. ____, 106 S. Ct. 1262 (1986).

[60] District of Columbia v. Merit Sys. Protection Bd., 762 F.2d 129, 132 (D.C. Cir. 1985); 3B Moore's Federal Practice ¶ 24.16[6] (2d ed. 1985).

plaintiff will be able to obtain relief against an intervenor defendant even if the original defendant is eliminated from the lawsuit.[61] However, the extent to which an intervenor can broaden the scope of litigation by asserting additional claims is unclear, particularly when the original plaintiffs drop out, leaving only an intervenor plaintiff.[62]

§ 9.9 —Procedural Requirements

Rule 24(c) requires a person desiring to intervene to serve a motion upon the parties as provided in Rule 5. The grounds for the motion must be stated, and the motion is accompanied by a pleading setting forth the claim or defense for which intervention is sought. Most courts disregard nonprejudicial technical defects,[63] but a few require strict adherence to the rule.[64] A memorandum without any supporting claim, cross-claim, or counterclaim has been rejected as support for intervention.[65] In evaluating the motion to intervene, nonconclusory allegations of the motion and pleading are accepted as true.[66]

Sometimes a court will permit a nonparty to participate informally in the proceedings. If counsel wishes to preserve the option of appealing from the judgment, it is safer to intervene formally.[67] An order granting intervention cannot be appealed until the termination of the action.[68] The denial of a Rule 24(a) motion requesting intervention of right is a final appealable order;[69] a denial of permissive intervention is not appealable unless there is an abuse of discretion.[70] However, the Supreme Court has refused to permit an immediate appeal of the denial of intervention of right coupled with a grant of permissive

---

[61] District of Columbia v. Merit Sys. Protection Bd., 762 F.2d 129, 132 (D.C. Cir. 1985).

[62] *See* Harris v. Amoco Prod. Co., 768 F.2d 669, 675–76 (5th Cir. 1985), *cert. denied*, ____ U.S. ____, 106 S. Ct. 1186 (1986).

[63] Piambino v. Bailey, 757 F.2d 1112, 1121 (11th Cir. 1985), *cert. denied*, ____ U.S. ____, 106 S. Ct. 2889 (1986).

[64] *See, e.g.*, Abramson v. Pennwood Inv. Corp., 392 F.2d 759, 761–62 (2d Cir. 1968).

[65] Shevlin v. Schewe, 809 F.2d 447, 449–50 (7th Cir. 1987).

[66] Lake Inv. Dev. Group v. Egidi Dev. Group, Inc., 715 F.2d 1256, 1258 (7th Cir. 1983); United States v. AT&T, 642 F.2d 1285, 1291 (D.C. Cir. 1980).

[67] *See, e.g.*, Hispanic Society v. New York City Police Dep't, 806 F.2d 1147, 1152–54 (2d Cir. 1986) (no formal motion to intervene); United States v. LTV Corp., 746 F.2d 51, 53–55 (D.C. Cir. 1984) (declined to intervene).

[68] 3B Moore's Federal Practice ¶ 24.15.

[69] Brotherhood of R.R. Trainmen v. Baltimore & O. R.R., 331 U.S. 519, 524 (1947); Sellers v. United States, 709 F.2d 1469, 1471 (11th Cir. 1983).

[70] Brotherhood of R.R. Trainmen v. Baltimore & O. R.R., 331 U.S. 519, 524–25 (1947); Woolen v. Surtran Taxicabs, Inc., 684 F.2d 324, 330–32 (5th Cir. 1982); *see* 3B Moore's Federal Practice ¶ 24.15.

intervention subject to conditions.[71] The denial of intervention as of right is a legal issue reviewed de novo, except as to the discretionary issue of timeliness.[72]

§ 9.10 Substitution of Parties

Rule 25 provides for substitution of parties in the event of death or incompetency. The rule is procedural and does not affect whether the action substantively survives the event.[73] The timing of the substitution is fairly flexible; it is not tied to the date of death but to the date when the death or incompetency is suggested upon the record by service of a statement concerning its factual basis. The substitution must be made within 90 days of the filing of the statement, although the court has discretion within that period to grant an extension.[74] It is safer to substitute the proper party or representative in a timely manner, because the court has discretion to deny the motion.

In case of transfer of interest, substitution is not required unless the court upon motion directs a substitution or joinder of the new party.[75] A public officer is automatically substituted for a predecessor who was sued in an official capacity.[76] While Rule 25 does not specifically mention corporate dissolutions, they appear to be considered as a transfer of interest under Rule 25(c) rather than as the death of a party.[77]

§ 9.11 Party Checklist

Substitution

1. Is joinder or substitution of a real party in interest required pursuant to Rule 17(a)?

a. Reasonable time for correction is allowed after objection.

---

[71] Stringfellow v. Concerned Neighbors in Action, _____ U.S. _____, 107 S. Ct. 1177 (1987).

[72] United States v. $129,374 in U.S. Currency, 769 F.2d 583, 585 (9th Cir. 1985), *cert. denied,* _____ U.S. _____, 106 S. Ct. 863 (1986); *see* United States v. City of Philadelphia, 798 F.2d 81, 90 (3d Cir. 1986).

[73] *See generally* 3B Moore's Federal Practice ¶ 25.04[1].

[74] Fed. R. Civ. P. 6(e).

[75] Fed. R. Civ. P. 25(c).

[76] Fed. R. Civ. P. 25(d).

[77] *See generally* 3B Moore's Federal Practice ¶ 25.10.

2. Is substitution required due to death or incompetency of a party pursuant to Rule 25?
   a. Substitution is required within 90 days of service of a statement suggesting the fact of the death or incompetency.

Necessary and Indispensable Parties

1. Is every necessary or indispensable party joined?
2. Is a nonjoined party considered necessary?
   a. Can complete relief not be granted in the person's absence?
   b. Does failure to join the person impair that individual's ability to protect his or her interest?
   c. Does failure to join the person subject that individual to multiple or inconsistent obligations?
3. Is a necessary party considered indispensable?
   a. Should the action be dismissed if the necessary party cannot be joined?
      (1) What is the extent of prejudice to absent person?
      (2) Do any means exist to lessen prejudice?
      (3) What is the adequacy of any judgment rendered in the person's absence?
      (4) What is the plaintiff's remedy if the action is dismissed?
4. Defense should be raised by Rule 12(b)(7) motion (see § **14.53**).
   a. No timing restriction on raising defense.

Interpleader

1. Is interpleader appropriate?
   a. Is money held which is subject to multiple claims?
2. Should interpleader be sought under Rule 22?
   a. Does federal jurisdiction exist?
3. Is statutory interpleader appropriate under 28 U.S.C. § 1335?
   a. Does party filing action hold $500 or more?
   b. Does minimum diversity exist between adverse claimants (i.e., are at least two diverse)?
4. Has a motion been made to deposit the disputed fund?
5. Have the parties been served pursuant to Rule 4? (see **ch. 5**)

Intervention

1. Is intervention of right appropriate?
   a. Is intervention provided by statute?
   b. Does applicant have an interest in litigation:
      (1) Which will be impaired and
      (2) Is inadequately represented by present parties?
2. Is permissive intervention appropriate?
   a. Is a conditional right to intervene provided by statute?
   b. Is a governmental officer or agency intervening concerning rules being challenged?
   c. Does the applicant's claim or defense have a common question of law or fact with main action?
   d. Does an independent jurisdictional basis exist?
3. Is the motion to intervene timely?
4. Is interlocutory review likely to be granted?
   a. Is appeal taken from denial of intervention of right?
   b. Is mandamus likely to be granted for denial of permissive intervention or qualified grant of intervention?

CHAPTER 10

CLASS ACTIONS

§ 10.1 Overview

Class action litigation generates fierce battles which utilize every procedural weapon available in the Federal Rules. Entire volumes have been written concerning class actions,[1] and the few pages in this text can barely raise the

[1] *See generally* H. Newberg, 1–5 Newberg on Class Actions (2d ed. 1985) [hereinafter Newberg on Class Actions]; *see also* 3B J. Moore *et al.,* Moore's Federal Practice ch. 23 (2d ed. 1987) [hereinafter Moore's Federal Practice]; 7A & 7B C. Wright, A. Miller *et al.,* Federal Practice and Procedure (2d ed. 1986) [hereinafter Federal Practice and Procedure]; Solovy, *et al., Class Action Controversies,* in 1 Current Problems in Federal Civil Practice 1986 (PLI Handbook No. 318).

panoply of issues, let alone analyze them. Like antitrust and securities law, class action practice has spawned its own specialized bar due to the complexities and overwhelming nature of such litigation.

As a general rule, it is foolhardy for anyone other than an experienced class action practitioner to file a Rule 23 action. However, counsel may become involved in a class action in a variety of ways. For example, if an individual suit is later enjoined by or (some might say) preempted by a class action, a decision must be made to become part of the class, intervene, or, if the option is available, opt out of the class. Counsel who represent defendants targeted in a class action because their conduct affected numerous individuals must determine whether to oppose class certification and whether it is necessary to associate a firm specializing in class action practice. Counsel may also be approached by class members who object to a proposed class action settlement. This chapter is aimed at familiarizing counsel with class actions issues so they can determine if they have the time and resources to undertake the prosecution or defense of such actions.

§ 10.2 Current Sentiment Concerning Class Actions

Class actions have been alternatively lauded and vilified.[2] Their purpose is to avoid duplication and inconsistent judgments, as well as to redress small injuries affecting a large group which otherwise would be uneconomical to litigate. However, they have the potential to be strike suits promoted by attorneys who are more interested in their own fees than in the outcome for the class members.[3]

It sometimes appears that no one likes class actions in federal court except for named class action plaintiffs and their lawyers. Although judges have varying views concerning class actions, the major judicial concern is the amount of resources which must be committed by the court to such litigation. Class actions are not even uniformly loved by other plaintiffs' lawyers because attorneys who have significant individual cases may find themselves squeezed out of any role in strategy or discovery of the case by the judge or the plaintiffs' steering committee which metes out work. The question of attorneys' fees aside, in a given case, this may disadvantage an individual litigant who is ready to go to trial much earlier than the class action can be heard. Therefore, not all plaintiffs or plaintiff's lawyers embrace class actions, because they believe they could do better by litigating alone.[4]

---

[2] *See, e.g.*, Miller, *Of Frankenstein Monsters and Shining Knights: Myth, Realty, and the "Class Action Problem,"* 92 Harv. L. Rev. 664 (1979); *see also* Banoff & Duvall, *The Class Action As A Mechanism For Enforcing The Federal Securities Laws: An Empirical Study of The Burdens Imposed,* 31 Wayne L. Rev. 1 (1984).

[3] *See* Piambino v. Bailey, 757 F.2d 1112, 1143 (11th Cir. 1985), *cert. denied,* ____ U.S. ____, 106 S. Ct. 2889 (1986).

[4] *See, e.g.*, Trangsrud, *Joinder Alternatives in Mass Tort Litigation,* 70 Cornell L. Rev. 779, 816–24 (1985).

Defendants do not like class actions because they can be enormously expensive, both in lawyers' fees and potential recovery. Defense counsel usually view class certification as the primary battlefield, since it is rare for class actions actually to reach trial. Defendants often have a strong incentive to settle cheaply with the named representatives before certification. Generally, defense strategy is to attempt to dispose of the class action aspect of the case in order to return to fighting individual claims. However, if the collateral estoppel effect of even a single judgment against a defendant will control in similar litigation, a defendant may prefer to fight in one forum than in many. This is particularly true when punitive damages are alleged. In fact, both Johns-Manville and A.H. Robins Company filed for bankruptcy when they were unable to consolidate litigation against them into mandatory class actions. Courts are currently split as to whether to permit class claims in bankruptcy.[5]

Therefore, the class action lawyer must be willing to meet the disapprobation of the bar and bench in the quest for class action status. Rather than being defensive, most class action specialists are confident that such litigation is the only way to reimburse minor claims and the fairest way to provide for all litigants, given limited resources of a defendant,[6] despite the possibility that some plaintiffs may receive less than they would if their cases were tried separately.

§ 10.3 Ethical Concerns

Class actions raise a host of ethical issues, including counsel's personal interest in the litigation, conflicts due to prior representation, sources of funding of the class action and repayment, solicitation of the named representative, and attorneys' fees in class settlement.[7] An attorney is prohibited not only from representing a class but also from serving as a class representative when a conflict exists due to prior employment.[8] Both plaintiffs' and defendants' lead

---

[5] *See In re* GAC Corp., 681 F.2d 1295, 1298–99 (11th Cir. 1982) (discussing cases); *see generally* Note, *Class Actions in Bankruptcy,* 64 Tex. L. Rev. 791 (1985); Note, *Strategic Bankruptcies: Class Actions, Classification & the Dalkon Shield Cases,* 7 Cardozo L. Rev. 817 (1986).

[6] *See, e.g., Wright & Colussi, The Successful Use of the Class Action Device in the Management of the Skywalk Tort Litigation,* 52 U.M.K.C. L. Rev. 141 (1984).

[7] *See generally* 3 Newberg on Class Actions ch. 15; Dam, *Class Actions: Efficiency, Compensation, Deterrence and Conflict of Interest,* 4 J. Legal Stud. 47 (1975); Garth, *Conflict and Dissent in Class Actions: A Suggested Perspective,* 77 Nw. U. L. Rev. 492 (1982); Rhode, *Class Conflicts in Class Actions,* 34 Stan. L. Rev. 1183 (1982); Underwood, *Legal Ethics and Class Actions: Problems, Tactics and Judicial Responses,* 71 Ky. L.J. 787 (1982); Note, *Abuse in Plaintiff Class Action Settlements: The Need for a Guardian During Pretrial Settlement Negotiations,* 84 Mich. L. Rev. 308 (1985); Note, *Conflicts of Interest in Class Action Representation Vis-A-Vis Class Representative and Class Counsel,* 33 Wayne L. Rev. 141 (1986).

[8] Doe v. A Corp., 709 F.2d 1043, 1047 (5th Cir. 1983).

counsel can be removed for ethical violations,[9] and fines or disallowance of attorneys' fees have been ordered in appropriate cases.[10] Attempts to disqualify counsel or deny certification based on counsel's financing of class expenses have met with mixed responses.[11] Counsel has always been permitted to pay expenses for indigent clients; however, the same is not true for other clients. The A.B.A. Model Rules of Professional Conduct now generally permit counsel to advance fees, with repayment contingent on the outcome of litigation,[12] but many states have not yet adopted these rules.

§ 10.4 General Limitations on Federal Class Actions

The Supreme Court has limited the availability of class actions in federal court. Consumer litigation, which has probably generated most of the good press received by class action litigation, is usually unavailable in federal court in diversity cases, since each class member must satisfy the $10,000 jurisdictional amount as to its claim.[13] Similarly, in federal actions based on the Truth in Lending Act[14] or the Magnuson-Moss Act,[15] the cost of notice may be prohibitive.[16] In Title VII cases, the Supreme Court has rejected the across-the-board rule, which permitted any victim of racial discrimination to maintain an attack on all practices allegedly fostering racial discrimination without inquiring whether Rule 23(a) prerequisites had been met.[17] In addition, the Court has approved a class action settlement which included a complete waiver of statutory fees,[18] even though this practice arguably decreases the willingness of lawyers to accept civil rights cases.

---

[9] *See* Kleiner v. First Nat'l Bank of Atlanta, 751 F.2d 1193, 1210 (11th Cir. 1985) (defense counsel); Piambino v. Bailey, 757 F.2d 1112, 1146 (11th Cir. 1985), *cert. denied,* ____ U.S. ____, 106 S. Ct. 2889 (1986) (plaintiff's counsel).

[10] See § **10.14**.

[11] *See generally* 1 Newberg on Class Actions § 3.37; Underwood, *Legal Ethics and Class Actions: Problems, Tactics and Judicial Responses,* 71 Ky. L.J. 787 (1982); Comment, *Class Certification: Relevance of Plaintiff's Finances and Fee Arrangements with Counsel,* 40 Pitt. L. Rev. 70 (1978).

[12] Model Rules of Professional Conduct Rule 1.8(e)(1) (1983).

[13] Zahn v. International Paper Co., 414 U.S. 291, 301 (1973).

[14] 15 U.S.C. § 1601 *et. seq.* (1982); *see generally* 3 Newberg on Class Actions §§ 21.01–21.27.

[15] 15 U.S.C. § 2301 *et seq.* (1982); *see generally* 3 Newberg on Class Actions § 21.29.

[16] *See, e.g.,* Walsh v. Ford Motor Co., 807 F.2d 1000, 1003 (D.C. Cir. 1986) (several million absentee class members).

[17] General Tel. Co. v. Falcon, 457 U.S. 147, 160 (1982); *see* Rossini v. Ogilvy & Mather, Inc., 798 F.2d 590, 597–98 (2d Cir. 1986) (discussing how *Falcon* has been interpreted by the circuits); *see also* Note, *Certifying Classes and Subclasses in Title VII Suits,* 99 Harv. L. Rev. 619 (1986).

[18] Evans v. Jeff D., ____ U.S. ____, 106 S. Ct. 1531, 1538 (1986).

§ 10.5 Preliminary Considerations Concerning Class Actions

Diversity in class actions is established if the named plaintiffs have different citizenship than the defendants.[19] Therefore, a nondiverse named plaintiff will be replaced by an appropriate class member having diversity. Intervention of right by a nondiverse plaintiff will not destroy diversity.[20] Standing[21] and mootness[22] questions may also arise in class actions. In addition, class actions which order or have the practical effect of enjoining litigation in state courts also raise problems of application of the Anti-Injunction Act.[23]

Other preliminary matters which arise in determining both the desirability and the feasibility of bringing a multistate class action include personal jurisdiction and choice of law questions. In *Phillips Petroleum Co. v. Shutts,*[24] the Supreme Court permitted a nationwide class despite the inclusion of individual plaintiffs who lacked minimum contacts with the forum but prohibited the forum from applying its own law to such class members. This decision has left many unanswered questions such as its application to mandatory classes in which an individual is not permitted to opt out,[25] an issue which can be critical if certification is sought for a mandatory class in a mass torts action when punitive damages are alleged. In general, attempts to certify mass torts actions have not fared well in federal court.[26]

Usually the statute of limitations is not a problem in class actions. The Supreme Court has held that the filing of a class action tolls the statute of limitations for individual complaints.[27] Once class certification is denied, class members may file their own suits or intervene as plaintiffs in the pending

---

[19] Synder v. Harris, 394 U.S. 332, 340 (1969); Supreme Tribe of Ben-Hur v. Cauble, 255 U.S. 356, 366 (1921).

[20] *See* 7A Federal Practice and Procedure § 1756; § **2.26**.

[21] *See generally* 1 Newberg on Class Actions §§ 2.05–2.10; 7A Federal Practice and Procedure § 1785.1.

[22] *See* United States Parole Comm'n v. Geraghty, 445 U.S. 388, 396 (1980); Davis v. Ball Memorial Hosp. Ass'n, Inc., 753 F.2d 1410, 1416–17 (7th Cir. 1985); *see generally* 1 Newberg on Class Actions §§ 2.12–2.33.

[23] 28 U.S.C. § 2283 (1982); *see, e.g., In re* School Asbestos Litig., 789 F.2d 996, 1002 (3d Cir.), *cert. denied,* ___ U.S. ___, 107 S. Ct. 318 (1986); *In re* Federal Skywalk Cases, 680 F.2d 1175, 1180–83 (8th Cir.), *cert. denied,* 459 U.S. 988 (1982); *cf. In re* Baldwin-United Corp., 770 F.2d 328, 335 (2d Cir. 1985).

[24] 472 U.S. 797 (1985).

[25] *See generally* Miller & Crump, *Jurisdiction and Choice of Law in Multistate Class Actions After Phillips Petroleum Co. v. Shutts,* 96 Yale L.J. 1 (1986).

[26] *See, e.g., In re* Northern Dist. of Cal. "Dalkon Shield" IUD Prods. Liability Litig., 693 F.2d 847 (9th Cir. 1982), *cert. denied,* 459 U.S. 1171 (1983); *In re* Federal Skywalk Cases, 680 F.2d 1175 (8th Cir.), *cert. denied,* 459 U.S. 988 (1982); *see generally,* Note, *Class Certification in Mass Accident Cases Under Rule 23(b)(1),* 96 Harv. L. Rev. 1143 (1983).

[27] American Pipe & Constr. Co. v. Utah, 414 U.S. 538, 552–53 (1974).

action.[28] However, tolling questions are not always obvious, because the Supreme Court has rejected a uniform federal rule when state law supplies the statute of limitations.[29] Similarly, the general rule is that a class action judgment binds class members who have been adequately represented, but claims not litigated as part of the class decision are not precluded.[30]

§ 10.6 Prerequisites

Rule 23 lists four prerequisites to bringing a class action:

1. The class is so numerous that joinder of all members is impracticable[31]
2. There are questions of law or fact common to the class[32]
3. The claims or defenses of the representative parties are typical of the class,[33] and
4. The representative parties will fairly and adequately protect the interests of the class.[34]

These requirements are known as *numerosity, commonality, typicality,* and *adequacy of representation*. Each criterion must be satisfied in order to maintain an action pursuant to Rule 23(b), although typicality is often merged with commonality[35] and adequacy of representation.[36]

Courts vary as to how many individuals must be affected to satisfy numerosity, but it is unlikely that fewer than 20 will be considered numerous, and even fewer than 100 can evoke mixed responses.[37] The class representative must be a

---

[28] Crown, Cork & Seal Co. v. Parker, 462 U.S. 345, 354 (1983).

[29] Chardon v. Soto, 462 U.S. 650, 662 (1983).

[30] *See* Cooper v. Federal Reserve Bank, 467 U.S. 867, 880 (1984); *see generally* 3 Newberg on Class Actions §§ 16.20–16.25.

[31] *See generally* 1 Newberg on Class Actions §§ 3.03–3.09; 3B Moore's Federal Practice ¶ 23.05; 7A Federal Practice and Procedure § 1762.

[32] *See generally* 1 Newberg on Class Actions §§ 3.10–3.12; 3B Moore's Federal Practice ¶ 23.06; 7A Federal Practice and Procedure § 1763.

[33] *See generally* 1 Newberg on Class Actions §§ 3.13–3.20; 3B Moore's Federal Practice ¶ 23.06-2; 7A Federal Practice and Procedure § 1764.

[34] *See generally* 1 Newberg on Class Actions §§ 3.21–3.28; 3B Moore's Federal Practice ¶ 23.07; 7A Federal Practice and Procedure §§ 1765–1770.

[35] General Tel. Co. v. Falcon, 457 U.S. 147, 157 & n.13 (1982); 1 Newberg on Class Actions § 3.13.

[36] Appleyard v. Wallace, 754 F.2d 955, 958 (11th Cir. 1985); *see* 1 Newberg on Class Actions § 3.22 (2d ed. 1985); 3B Moore's Federal Practice ¶ 23.06-2; *cf.* De La Fuente v. Stokely-Van Camp, Inc., 713 F.2d 225, 232 (7th Cir. 1983).

[37] *See* 3B Moore's Federal Practice ¶ 23.05[1]; *see also* 1 Newberg on Class Actions § 3.05.

class member in order to satisfy standing and adequacy of representation.[38] However, in a given case, a new class representative can be designated[39] or permitted to intervene, even after an appellate court has vacated class findings due to inadequate representation.[40]

Adequacy is determined by reference to both the class representative and the class counsel.[41] Therefore, lack of experience or competence of the attorney for the proposed class are factors to be considered.[42] A dismissal for inadequacy has been affirmed when a representative failed to make a timely motion for class status.[43] Refusal to answer proper discovery questions is also ground for concluding that a representative is inadequate.[44] Conflict of interest between class members can result in inadequate representation.[45] Significant disagreement within the class has been reason to deny certification for lack of typicality and adequacy of representation when a realistic possibility of antagonism exists, even in the absence of hard evidence on the issue.[46] Similarly, the antagonism of counsel for different subclasses was considered relevant in decertifying a subclass.[47] Proof of financial resources has not been required in the absence of any reason to believe that there are inadequate resources to litigate,[48] but some courts do consider the financial ability of the plaintiff as relevant.[49]

§ 10.7 Rule 23(b)(1) Actions

A Rule 23(b)(1) class exists if the prosecution of separate actions by or against individual members of the class would create a risk of inconsistent or varying

---

38 1 Newberg on Class Actions § 3.19; 3B Moore's Federal Practice ¶ 23.04[2]; 7A Federal Practice and Procedure § 1761.

39 *See* Satterwhite v. City of Greenville, 634 F.2d 231 (5th Cir. 1981) (en banc), *vacated on other grounds,* 445 U.S. 940 (1980).

40 Goodman v. Lukens Steel Co., 777 F.2d 113, 124 (3d Cir. 1985), *cert. granted,* _____ U.S. _____, 107 S. Ct. 568 (1986).

41 3B Moore's Federal Practice ¶ 23.07[1].

42 *See, e.g.,* McGowan v. Faulkner Concrete Pipe Co., 659 F.2d 554, 559 (5th Cir. 1981).

43 *See* East Tex. Motor Freight Sys., Inc. v. Rodriguez, 431 U.S. 395, 404 (1977); *see generally* 1 Newberg on Class Actions § 3.43.

44 Kline v. Wolf, 702 F.2d 400, 403 (2d Cir. 1983).

45 *See* Sosna v. Iowa, 419 U.S. 393, 403 (1975); Secretary of Labor v. Fitzsimmons, 805 F.2d 682, 697–99 (7th Cir. 1986); Note, *Conflicts in Class Actions and Protection of Absentee Class Members,* 91 Yale L.J. 590 (1980).

46 Horton v. Goose Creek Indep. School Dist., 677 F.2d 471, 489 (5th Cir. 1982), *cert. denied,* 463 U.S. 1207 (1983) (discussing cases); *cf.* Hansberry v. Lee, 311 U.S. 32, 44–45 (1940) (class members can't be bound by judgment when disagreement indicated inadequate representation).

47 Hervey v. City of Little Rock, 787 F.2d 1223, 1227 (8th Cir. 1986).

48 *See, e.g.,* Horton v. Goose Creek Indep. School Dist., 677 F.2d 471, 489 n. 46 (5th Cir. 1982), *cert. denied,* 463 U.S. 1207 (1983).

49 *See* McGowan v. Faulkner Concrete Pipe Co., 659 F.2d 554, 558–59 (5th Cir. 1981) (important, but not determinative); *see generally* 1 Newberg on Class Actions § 3.37.

adjudications as to individual class members which would establish incompatible standards of conduct for the party opposing the class, or individual adjudications which would in effect be dispositive of the interests of nonparties or substantially impair or impede their ability to protect their interests.[50]

Rule 23(b)(1) has been compared to the determination of indispensable parties under Rule 19.[51] Several circuits view a request for money damages as not normally imposing a danger of incompatible standards of conduct.[52] Rule 23(b)(1) actions have been certified when a limited fund exists which must satisfy all plaintiffs' judgments.[53] In mass tort cases, the *limited fund theory* has been propounded with varying success, on the rationale that punitive or compensatory damages would result in exhaustion of the defendant's resources in the first cases.[54] Even if this theory is found to support certification, the record and factual findings must be adequate or the certification will be reversed.[55]

§ 10.8 Rule 23(b)(2) Actions

Actions pursuant to Rule 23(b)(2) are appropriate when the class seeks injunctive or declaratory relief with respect to the class as a whole because the defendant has acted or refused to act on grounds generally applicable to the class.[56] Since the injuries suffered are group as opposed to individual injuries,[57] Rule 23(b)(2) classes, by their very nature, are considered homogeneous, without any conflicting interests between the class members.[58] Title VII and other civil rights actions requesting injunctive relief are prime candidates for

---

[50] *See generally* Newberg on Class Actions §§ 4.03–4.10; 3B Moore's Federal Practice ¶ 23.35; 7A Federal Practice and Procedure §§ 1772–1774.

[51] 7A Federal Practice and Procedure § 1772.

[52] *See* Zimmerman v. Bell, 800 F.2d 386, 389 (4th Cir. 1986); Green v. Occidental Petroleum Corp., 541 F.2d 1335, 1340 n.10 (9th Cir. 1976).

[53] *See* 7A Federal Practice and Procedure § 1774.

[54] *Compare In re* Northern Dist. of Cal. "Dalkon Shield" IUD Prods. Liability Litig., 693 F.2d 847, 851–52 (9th Cir. 1982), *cert. denied,* 459 U.S. 1171 (1983) *with* Jenkins v. Raymark Indus., Inc., 782 F.2d 468, 473–75 (5th Cir. 1986); *In re* "Agent Orange" Prod. Liability Litig., 100 F.R.D. 718, 720 (E.D.N.Y. 1983), *mandamus denied,* 725 F.2d 858 (2d Cir.), *cert. denied,* 465 U.S. 1067 (1984); *see generally* Note, *Class Certification in Mass Accident Cases Under Rule 23(b)(1),* 96 Harv. L. Rev. 1143 (1983); *see also* 3 Newberg on Class Actions ch. 17 for detailed class action procedures in mass torts cases.

[55] *See In re* School Asbestos Litig., 789 F.2d 996, 1005 (3d Cir.), *cert. denied,* ____ U.S. ____, 107 S. Ct. 318 (1986).

[56] *See generally* 1 Newberg on Class Actions §§ 4.11–4.19; 3B Moore's Federal Practice ¶ 23.40; 7A Federal Practice and Procedure §§ 1775–1776.

[57] *See* Comment, *Notice in Rule 23(b)(2) Class Actions for Monetary Relief: Johnson v. General Motors Corp.,* 128 U. Pa. L. Rev. 1236, 1252–53 (1980).

[58] Wetzel v. Liberty Mut. Ins. Co., 508 F.2d 239, 256 (3d Cir.), *cert. denied,* 421 U.S. 1011 (1975).

Rule 23(b)(2) certification.[59] Most class actions involve plaintiff classes; defendants have had mixed results in attempting certification under Rule 23(b)(2) in litigation seeking declaratory or injunctive relief.[60]

Members of a Rule 23(b)(2) class are not ordinarily entitled to individual notice,[61] and courts split concerning whether an individual can opt out of a Rule 23(b)(2) class.[62] This problem usually occurs in hybrid actions which seek both individual monetary relief and a classwide injunction. However, even in circuits which do not provide an absolute right to opt out, the judge has discretion to permit that procedure.[63] Such opt-outs may not be permitted at certification but only at the monetary relief stage of the suit.[64]

§ 10.9 Rule 23(b)(3) Actions

Rule 23(b)(3) is the most frequently employed type of class action, because it can encompass any action in which common questions of law or fact predominate. A Rule 23(b)(3) action requires

1. Common questions of law or fact
2. Class questions which predominate over individual questions, and
3. Superiority of the class action to other available methods for the fair and efficient adjudication of the controversy.[65]

Rule 23(b)(3) sets forth the following criteria for determining whether the action should be certified:

1. The interests of the members of the class in individually controlling the prosecution or defense of separate actions

---

[59] *See* 7A Federal Practice and Procedure § 1776.

[60] *See, e.g.*, Thompson v. Board of Educ., 709 F.2d 1200, 1203–04 (6th Cir. 1983); *see generally,* 7A Federal Practice and Procedure § 1775; Comment, *Certification of Defendant Classes Under Rule 23(b)(2),* 84 Colum L. Rev. 1371 (1984); Comment, *Defendant Class Actions and Federal Civil Rights Litigation,* 33 UCLA L. Rev. 283 (1985).

[61] Holmes v. Continental Can Co., 706 F.2d 1144, 1156 (11th Cir. 1983); 1 Newberg on Class Actions § 4.20; 3B Moore's Federal Practice ¶ 23.40[4].

[62] Holmes v. Continental Can Co., 706 F.2d 1144 (11th Cir. 1983) (discussing cases).

[63] *Id.*; Penson v. Terminal Transport Co., 634 F.2d 989, 995 (5th Cir. 1981).

[64] *See* Cox v. American Cast Iron Pipe Co., 784 F.2d 1546, 1554 (11th Cir.), *cert. denied,* ____ U.S. ____, 107 S. Ct. 274 (1986).

[65] *See generally* 1 Newberg on Class Actions §§ 4.23–4.32; 3B Moore's Federal Practice ¶ 23.45; 7A Federal Practice and Procedure §§ 1777.

2. The extent and nature of any relevant litigation already commenced by or against class members
3. The desirability or undesirability of litigating the claims in the particular forum, and
4. The difficulties involved in managing the class.

Defendant class actions can be certified under Rule 23(b)(3) but are rare.[66]

Manageability becomes a particular problem in Rule 23(b)(3) class actions if thousands of individual damage trials must be held.[67] Courts are flexible in assuring manageability. For example, the use of a classwide injury and damages trial by a jury which was bifurcated from individual damage proceedings held before a magistrate has been permitted.[68] Alternatives to class actions considered when assessing superiority include test case litigation, joinder, consolidation, and intervention.[69] The availability of counterclaims against individual class members has generated substantial controversy, and to the extent permitted raises questions of manageability.[70]

§ 10.10 Procedures for Class Certification and Management

Most federal judges hearing a class action refer to at least some of the class action procedures outlined in Part III of the second edition of the Manual for Complex Litigation to ensure that the action does not proceed as a headless horseman. The complaint must demonstrate that each of the elements necessary to maintain the class exists,[71] although Rule 15 amendments may be used to correct defective allegations.[72] Local rules should also be consulted for specific class action pleading and practice requirements. Certification must be sought as soon as practicable, and some district courts have adopted time limits within which a certification motion must be filed.[73] On the other had, Rule 23 sets no deadline by which the court must act.[74] The court has a great deal of discretion to make

---

[66] *See generally* 1 Newberg on Class Actions §§ 4.48–4.61.

[67] Abrams v. Interco Inc., 719 F.2d 23, 31 (2d Cir. 1983).

[68] *See* Greenhaw v. Lubbock County Beverage Ass'n, 721 F.2d 1019, 1025 (5th Cir. 1983), *overruled an other grounds by* International Woodworkers v. Champion Int'l Corp., 790 F.2d 1174, 1181 n.8 (5th Cir.), *aff'd sub nom.* Crawford Fitting Co. v. J.T. Gibbons, _____ U.S. _____, 107 S. Ct. 2494, 55 U.S.L.W. 4820 (June 15, 1987).

[69] *See generally* 1 Newberg on Class Actions § 4.27.

[70] *See generally id.* § 4.34.

[71] *See generally id.* §§ 6.18–6.24.

[72] 3B Moore's Federal Practice ¶ 23.02-2.

[73] *See, e.g.*, McCarthy v. Kleindienst, 741 F.2d 1406, 1411–12 (D.C. Cir. 1984) (discussing 90-day rule); *see generally* 2 Newberg on Class Actions §§ 7.13–7.15.

[74] Montelongo v. Meese, 803 F.2d 1341, 1351 (5th Cir. 1986).

whatever orders it deems appropriate.[75] However, any restriction on communications by counsel with unnamed class members is quite limited and must be based on a clear record and specific findings reflecting a weighing of the need for the limitation against the potential interference with the parties' rights.[76]

It is unusual for certification to be ordered on the pleadings,[77] and a hearing is required whenever serious questions are raised concerning the propriety of a class action.[78] However, failure to hold a hearing may be waived as an issue if a hearing is never requested, or the failure may be treated as harmless error.[79] At the hearing, the plaintiff has the burden to demonstrate the appropriateness of class certification without reference to the merits of the underlying case.[80] It is rarely appropriate for a court to delay the certification decision until after a trial on the merits,[81] but Rule 12 and 56 motions can be heard before certification. Certification may be sought with respect to particular issues or may include subclasses which are treated as classes.[82]

Certification rulings are reviewed for abuse of discretion.[83] The court also has discretion to decertify a class.[84] However, it need not decertify when it later appears that the named plaintiffs were not class members or when subsequent events at trial undermine the named plaintiffs' individual claims, as long as the initial certification was proper.[85] Although Rule 23(e) provides that notice of a proposed dismissal must be provided to class members, some circuits dismiss for lack of prosecution without notice.[86]

---

[75] *See* Fed. R. Civ. P. 23(d); *see generally* 3B Moore's Federal Practice ¶ 23.70; 7B Federal Practice and Procedure §§ 1791–1796.

[76] Gulf Oil Co. v. Bernard, 452 U.S. 89, 90 (1981); *see* Domingo v. New England Fish Co., 727 F.2d 1429, 1438–41 (9th Cir. 1984), *modified on other grounds,* 742 F.2d 520 (9th Cir. 1984).

[77] *See, e.g.,* Stewart v. Winter, 669 F.2d 328, 332 (5th Cir. 1982).

[78] *See, e.g.,* Bradford v. Sears, Roebuck & Co., 673 F.2d 792 (5th Cir. 1982).

[79] *See* Merrill v. SMU, 806 F.2d 600, 609 (5th Cir. 1986).

[80] Eisen v. Carlisle & Jacquelin, 417 U.S. 156, 177 (1974); 3B Moore's Federal Practice ¶ 23.02-2.

[81] Paxton v. Union Nat'l Bank, 688 F.2d 552, 558 (8th Cir. 1982), *cert. denied,* 460 U.S. 1083 (1983); *see* Eisen v. Carlisle & Jacquelin, 417 U.S. 156, 177–78 (1974); Note, *Reopening the Debate: Postjudgment Certification in Rule 23(b)(3) Class Actions,* 66 Cornell L. Rev. 1218 (1981).

[82] Fed. R. Civ. P. 23(c)(4); *see generally* 7B Federal Practice and Procedure § 1790.

[83] Secretary of Labor v. Fitzsimmons, 805 F.2d 682, 697 (7th Cir. 1986); Watson v. Fort Worth Bank & Trust, 798 F.2d 791, 795 (5th Cir. 1986); Abrams v. Interco Inc., 719 F.2d 23, 27–28 (2d Cir. 1983).

[84] General Tel. Co. v. Falcon, 457 U.S. 147, 160 (1982).

[85] East Tex. Motor Freight Sys., Inc. v. Rodriguez, 431 U.S. 395, 406 n.12 (1977); Franks v. Bowman Transp. Co., 424 U.S. 747, 752–57 (1976).

[86] *See, e.g.,* Jones v. Caddo Parrish School Bd., 704 F.2d 206, 214–15 (5th Cir. 1983) (without prejudice).

When class actions overlap with litigation pending in other districts, they are prime candidates for multidistrict coordination under 28 U.S.C. § 1407[87] or change of venue under 28 U.S.C. § 1404(a).[88] In some cases, it may be appropriate to enjoin other actions in state or federal court.[89]

§ 10.11 Discovery in Class Actions

Discovery in connection with class certification motions is discretionary,[90] but in most cases, it is proper and even necessary in order to determine whether the prerequisites of Rule 23 are satisfied.[91] Counsel should anticipate that such discovery will not be unlimited and that discovery on the merits may be stayed while the certification question is pending.[92] Discovery from the named representatives is particularly important in assessing typicality and adequacy of class representation.[93] Such discovery focuses on the uniqueness of the representative and any potential conflicts which exist between that individual and other class members.

The propriety of discovery from unnamed class members has generated debate, because if such members are treated as parties, the requirement of answering lengthy interrogatories may be used to force members to opt out or suffer dismissal. On the other hand, the only way to determine the true commonality of the class in some actions is through such discovery. Most courts require some showing of need before party discovery of unnamed class members is permitted.[94] There is disagreement whether dismissal of unnamed class members is appropriate as a discovery sanction.[95]

---

[87] *See generally* 2 Newberg on Class Actions §§ 9.13–9.18; see § **6.11**.

[88] *See* 2 Newberg on Class Actions §§ 9.19–9.20; see § **6.7**.

[89] *See* 2 Newberg on Class Actions §§ 9.25–9.26; see § **10.5**.

[90] Stewart v. Winter, 669 F.2d 328, 331 (5th Cir. 1982); Kamm v. California City Dev. Co., 509 F.2d 205, 209 (9th Cir. 1975).

[91] Stewart v. Winter, 669 F.2d 328, 331 (5th Cir. 1982); Sirota v. Solitron Devices, Inc., 673 F.2d 566, 571–72 (2d Cir.), *cert. denied,* 459 U.S. 838 (1982).

[92] *See, e.g.,* Stewart v. Winter, 669 F.2d 328, 331 (5th Cir. 1982) (proper to deny sweeping request re merits).

[93] *See generally* 2 Newberg on Class Actions § 7.08.

[94] *See* Dellums v. Powell, 566 F.2d 231, 236 (D.C. Cir. 1977); Brennan v. Midwestern United Life Ins. Co., 450 F.2d 999, 1005 (7th Cir. 1971), *cert. denied,* 405 U.S. 921 (1972); *see generally* 3 Newberg on Class Actions § 16.03.

[95] *Compare* Brennan v. Midwestern United Life Ins. Co., 450 F.2d 999, 1005 (7th Cir. 1971), *cert. denied,* 405 U.S. 921 (1972) (affirming dismissal) *with* Cox v. American Cast Iron Pipe Co., 784 F.2d 1546, 1556–57 (11th Cir.), *cert. denied,* ____ U.S. ____, 107 S. Ct. 274 (1986) (rejecting *Brennan*).

§ 10.12 Notice in Rule 23(b)(3) Actions

Rule 23(c)(2) requires notice to be given in Rule 23(b)(3) actions that (1) the court will exclude the absent class member from the class if he so requests by a specified date; (2) if the absentee fails to make a request to opt out, that individual will be included in the judgment; and (3) if the absentee does not request exclusion, he may enter an appearance through counsel.[96] It is well settled that a Rule 23(b)(3) action requires notice in the form best suited to reaching the class members, and its cost must ordinarily be borne by the plaintiff, even if that notice has the practical result of not being affordable.[97] Therefore, notice must be mailed individually to all Rule 23(b)(3) class members whose names and addresses may be ascertained through reasonable means.[98] Individual mailing to a last known address, with or without supplemental newspaper publication, is appropriate.[99] However, notice to a street name addresses with a request that it be forwarded to the beneficial holder of securities, but without an offer to defray expenses, has been disapproved.[100] Some flexibility exists in requiring the defendant to assist in class notifications in exceptional circumstances when such notice is less difficult or expensive.[101]

Notice usually is not distributed until after class certification, unless the court is proceeding under Rule 23(d)(2), which permits discretionary notice whenever appropriate.[102] The court can design the notice; however, the plaintiff usually prepares the draft for the court's approval, at which time the defendant has an opportunity to object or suggest changes. The notice must be neutral and must fairly apprise the prospective members of the proposed settlement and options that are open in connection with the proceedings, but often it is quite general.[103] Notice on court stationary or signed by a judicial officer is considered improper in some circuits.[104] The issue of simultaneous notification of class members concerning the class determination and a proposed settlement has generated debate because of the potential for collusion or improper pressure, but generally

---

[96] *See generally* 2 Newberg on Class Actions ch. 8; 3B Moore's Federal Practice ¶ 23.55; 7B Federal Practice and Procedure §§ 1786–1788.

[97] Eisen v. Carlisle & Jacquelin, 417 U.S. 156, 176 (1974).

[98] *Id.* at 173.

[99] *See* Weinberger v. Kendrick, 698 F.2d 61, 71 (2d Cir. 1982), *cert. denied,* 464 U.S. 818 (1983).

[100] *In re* Franklin Nat'l Bank Secs. Litig., 574 F.2d 662, 669–70, *modified on other grounds,* 599 F.2d 1109 (2d Cir. 1978).

[101] *See* Oppenheimer Fund, Inc. v. Sanders, 437 U.S. 340, 356–59 (1978); Malchman v. Davis, 706 F.2d 426, 435 (2d Cir. 1983).

[102] *See generally* 2 Newberg on Class Actions § 8.15.

[103] Weinberger v. Kendrick, 698 F.2d 61, 70 (2d Cir. 1982), *cert. denied,* 464 U.S. 818 (1983); *see, e.g.,* Manual For Complex Litigation § 41.41 (2d ed. 1985) [hereinafter Manual for Complex Litigation] (Sample Notice Form); 2 Newberg on Class Actions App. 8-1 (Illustrative Rule 23(c)(2) Notice).

[104] *See, e.g.,* Woods v. New York Life Ins. Co., 686 F.2d 578, 581 (7th Cir. 1982).

no per se prohibition exists against this practice.[105] Usually a proof of claim form is not included with the notice of certification but is required once liability and class damages have been ascertained.[106]

§ 10.13 Class Action Settlements

A variety of issues must be considered by counsel in negotiating class action settlements, ranging from ethical and practical questions concerning precertification settlements to defending the settlement from a vocal minority which dissents from its terms.[107] One of the most controversial issues in class action litigation is whether temporary settlement classes should be recognized in a precertification settlement.[108] This practice is viewed cautiously but currently is not banned.[109] Rule 23(e) requires approval of the court for any compromise, even if the action has not yet been certified.[110] The Manual For Complex Litigation, second edition, proposes a two-step process for review of class settlements in which a preliminary evaluation of fairness is made, informally or through briefs and a hearing, followed by a formal fairness hearing if the settlement appears appropriate.[111]

The basic considerations whether any settlement is fair, reasonable and adequate require (1) a comparison of the terms of the compromise with the likely rewards of litigation,[112] and (2) a determination of whether arm's length negotiations were held by experienced plaintiff's counsel who engaged in any necessary discovery.[113] The Second Circuit has set forth various factors which are relevant in determining fairness of a settlement, including:

1. The complexity, expenses and likely duration of the litigation
2. The reaction of the class to the settlement
3. The stage of the proceedings and the amount of discovery completed
4. The risks of establishing liability

---

[105] *See* Weinberger v. Kendrick, 698 F.2d 61, 72 (2d Cir. 1982), *cert. denied,* 464 U.S. 818 (1983); *In re* Beef Indus. Antitrust Litig., 607 F.2d 167, 173–78 (5th Cir. 1979), *cert. denied,* 452 U.S. 905 (1981); Marshall v. Holiday Magic, Inc., 550 F.2d 1173, 1176 (9th Cir. 1977).

[106] *See* 7A Federal Practice and Procedure § 1787.

[107] *See generally* 2 Newberg on Class Actions ch. 11.

[108] *In re* Beef Indus. Antitrust Litig., 607 F.2d 167 (5th Cir. 1979), *cert. denied,* 452 U.S. 905 (1981); *see* Manual For Complex Litigation § 30.45.

[109] *See* Manual for Complex Litigation § 30.45.

[110] Sosna v. Iowa, 419 U.S. 393, 399 n.8 (1975).

[111] Manual for Complex Litigation § 30.44.

[112] Protective Comm. for Indep. Stockholders of TMT Trailer Ferry, Inc. v. Anderson, 390 U.S. 414, 424–25 (1968).

[113] Weinberger v. Kendrick, 698 F.2d 61, 73 (2d Cir. 1982), *cert. denied,* 464 U.S. 818 (1983).

5. The risks of establishing damages
6. The risks of maintaining the class action through the trial
7. The ability of the defendants to withstand a greater judgment
8. The range of reasonableness of the settlement fund in light of the best possible recovery, and
9. The range of reasonableness of the settlement fund to a possible recovery in light of all the attendant risks of litigation.[114]

Other circuits have similar formulations.[115] Because these are factual determinations for the judge, the disposition of a proposed class action settlement is accorded considerable deference.[116] Therefore, it is not necessarily an abuse of discretion for the judge to accept a settlement over the objections of the named representatives[117] or a substantial minority of known class members.[118] However, the judge must explore the relevant factors and hold a hearing if any doubts exist rather than relying completely on a magistrate's report.[119] The judge also cannot implement a forced settlement over the objections of the plaintiffs.[120]

When preferential treatment of the named plaintiffs is provided in the settlement, a substantial burden falls upon the proponents of the settlement to demonstrate its fairness.[121] Other suspicious factors include a high number of objectors, filing a proposed decree early in the case or before significant discovery, or an allegation that the attorneys have sacrificed their clients' interests to assure themselves of receiving sizable attorneys' fees.[122]

An opt-out feature is rarely provided in a class action settlement, and it is not required because the notice of certification and fairness hearing answer any due process concerns.[123] Rule 23(e) provides for notice concerning any proposed

---

[114] City of Detroit v. Grinnell Corp., 495 F.2d 448, 465 (2d Cir. 1974).

[115] *See, e.g.,* Bennett v. Behring Corp., 737 F.2d 982, 986 (11th Cir. 1984); *In re* Flight Transp. Corp. Secs. Litig., 730 F.2d 1128, 1135 (8th Cir. 1984); Gautreaux v. Pierce, 690 F.2d 616, 631 (7th Cir. 1982); Officers for Justice v. Civil Serv. Comm'n, 688 F.2d 615, 625 (9th Cir. 1982), *cert. denied,* 459 U.S. 1217 (1983); Parker v. Anderson, 667 F.2d 1204, 1209 (5th Cir.), *cert. denied,* 459 U.S. 828 (1982); *see also* Manual for Complex Litigation § 30.41.

[116] Malchman v. Davis, 706 F.2d 426, 434 (2d Cir. 1983); Officers for Justice v. Civil Serv. Comm'n, 688 F.2d 615, 626 (9th Cir. 1982), *cert. denied,* 459 U.S. 1217 (1983).

[117] Clark Equip. Co. v. International Union, Allied Indus. Workers, 803 F.2d 878, 880 (6th Cir. 1986).

[118] *See, e.g.,* Salinas v. Roadway Express, Inc., 802 F.2d 787, 790 (5th Cir. 1986) (34% filed objections).

[119] Malchman v. Davis, 706 F.2d 426, 434 (2d Cir. 1983).

[120] Kline v. Wolf, 702 F.2d 400, 404–05 (2d Cir. 1983).

[121] Holmes v. Continental Can Co., 706 F.2d 1144, 1147 (11th Cir. 1983).

[122] EEOC v. Hiram Walker & Sons, Inc., 768 F.2d 884, 890–91 (7th Cir. 1985), *cert. denied,* ____ U.S. ____, 106 S. Ct. 3293 (1986).

[123] Officers for Justice v. Civil Serv. Comm'n, 688 F.2d 615, 634–35 (9th Cir. 1982), *cert. denied,* 459 U.S. 1217 (1983).

dismissal or compromise, but the type of notice is discretionary.[124] Notice by publication, posting, and selected individual delivery in lieu of individual notice have all been approved.[125] The court even has discretion not to give notice.[126] Although dissenters can obtain private counsel, the court has no authority to appoint counsel at the opposing party's expense prior to any determination of liability.[127]

§ 10.14 Attorneys' Fees

Attorneys' fees are a sore point in class action litigation. A few circuits have prohibited the simultaneous negotiation of settlement and fees and recommend that any discussion of fees wait until after settlement of the merits.[128] Other circuits are cautious about approving such fees.[129] The Supreme Court recently permitted a settlement in which simultaneous negotiations in a civil rights action resulted in a waiver of attorneys' fees and expenses in exchange for a favorable compromise on the merits.[130] Therefore, in actions in which fees are authorized by statute, it is likely to become commonplace for defendants to request fee waivers as part of any settlements unless prohibited by court practice or local ethical rulings. Questions have also been raised about the practice of agreeing not to oppose a reasonable amount of attorneys' fees up to a specified sum, often called *clear sailing clauses*. Mere silence as to fees in a settlement agreement has not been construed as a waiver if fees are permitted by statute.[131]

Attorneys' fees for successful class litigation are available under a common fund theory or if authorized by statute.[132] At least 131 attorneys' fees shifting statutes currently exist.[133] The amount of attorneys' fees awarded in successful class litigation differs greatly, and each circuit has its own formula for

---

[124] *See generally* 2 Newberg on Class Actions § 8.18.

[125] *See, e.g.*, Handschu v. Special Servs. Div., 787 F.2d 828, 833 (2d Cir. 1986); Walsh v. Great Atl. & Pac. Tea Co., 726 F.2d 956, 963 (3d Cir. 1983); Franks v. Kroger Co., 649 F.2d 1216, 1222–23 (6th Cir. 1981).

[126] 2 Newberg on Class Actions § 8.18.

[127] *See* Walsh v. Great Atl. & Pac. Tea Co., 726 F.2d 956, 964 (3d Cir. 1983); Mandujano v. Basic Vegetable Prods., Inc., 541 F.2d 832, 835 n.6 (9th Cir. 1976).

[128] Prandini v. National Tea Co., 557 F.2d 1015, 1021 (3d Cir. 1977); Mendoza v. United States, 623 F.2d 1338, 1353 (9th Cir. 1980), *cert. denied,* 450 U.S. 912 (1981); *see generally* 3 Newberg on Class Actions § 15.31.

[129] Malchman v. Davis, 761 F.2d 893, 904–05 (2d Cir. 1985), *cert. denied,* ___ U.S. ___, 106 S. Ct. 1798 (1986).

[130] Evans v. Jeff D., ___ U.S. ___, 106 S. Ct. 1531, 1538 (1986).

[131] 3 Newberg on Class Actions § 15.35.

[132] *See generally id.* §§ 14.01–14.03.

[133] *See* 9 Att'y Fee Awards Rep. 2-3 (1986); Coulter v. Tennessee, 805 F.2d 146, 152–55 app. A (6th Cir. 1986).

determining such fees.[134] Most circuits have adopted some variation of the *lodestar rule,* which requires the hours spent to be calculated as the start of any fee application, multiplied by a reasonable billing rate, with a multiplier concerning contingency and quality.[135] However, the efficacy of the lodestar rule is currently being questioned because of its potential for encouraging excessive billing and discouraging early settlements.[136] Regardless of the method used to calculate the award, the necessity of keeping thorough, contemporaneous records cannot be overstated, because their absence may result in significant reduction of claimed fees and expenses. Indeed, the Sixth Circuit reversed an award of attorneys' fees when the district court did not determine the reasonableness of the fees but granted the requested amount based solely on a procedural default for failure to file a timely opposition imposed by a local rule.[137]

Ethical violations by class counsel can be considered when apportioning attorneys' fees. Attorneys' fees following the ethical breach have been disallowed,[138] and in some cases, forfeiture of all pay has been required.[139] Similarly, attorneys' fees and expenses were ordered to be repaid when they resulted from a collusive settlement, and the lead counsel was removed pursuant to the court's supervisory powers.[140]

§ 10.15 Dismissals

Rule 23(e) provides that the court must approve the voluntary dismissal of a class action. Because this provision apparently applies regardless of whether the class has been certified,[141] a plaintiff who wishes to settle its own claim may find that it cannot unburden itself of the obligation to pursue the class action without

---

[134] *See generally* 3B Moore's Federal Practice ¶ 23.91; 7B Federal Practice and Procedure § 1803.

[135] *See* Evans v. Jeff D., ____ U.S. ____, 106 S. Ct. 1531, 1542 (1986); Lindy Bros. Builders, Inc. v. American Radiator & Standard Sanitary Corp., 487 F.2d 161, 166–69 (3d Cir. 1973); *see also* Manual for Complex Litigation § 24.12; *see generally* A. Miller, Attorneys' Fees in Class Actions (1980).

[136] *See generally* Coffee, *Understanding the Plaintiff's Attorney: The Implications of Economic Theory for Private Enforcement of Law Through Class and Derivative Actions,* 86 Colum L. Rev. 669, & 675 n.17 (1986).

[137] Jordan v. Mark IV Hair Styles, Inc., 806 F.2d 695, 696–98 (6th Cir. 1986).

[138] *In re* Eastern Sugar Antitrust Litig., 697 F.2d 524, 533 (3d Cir. 1982); *In re* Chicago & W. Towns Ry., 230 F.2d 364, 369 (7th Cir.), *cert. denied,* 351 U.S. 943 (1956).

[139] *In re* New York, New Haven & Hartford R.R., 567 F.2d 166, 176 (2d Cir.), *cert. denied,* 434 U.S. 833 (1977).

[140] Piambino v. Bailey, 757 F.2d 1112, 1146 (11th Cir. 1985), *cert. denied,* ____ U.S. ____, 106 S. Ct. 2889 (1986).

[141] Glidden v. Chromalloy Am. Corp., 808 F.2d 621, 625–27 (7th Cir. 1986); *see generally* 2 Newberg on Class Actions § 11.63.

giving notice to the class.[142] Therefore, using a class action simply to obtain a higher settlement can be risky. Courts do have the discretion to approve dismissals before certification without notice.[143]

§ 10.16 Intervention

Intervention can be sought in a class action subject to Rule 24.[144] Although intervention has the benefit of obtaining direct representation for an unnamed class member, it also may expose such a member to payment of costs for unsuccessful litigation and to discovery as a party.[145] Merely entering an appearance of counsel may not have this result, but it probably will not provide the unnamed class member with standing to appeal.[146]

Individual class members are entitled to intervene of right when their interests are not adequately represented;[147] otherwise, permissive intervention must be sought.[148] Intervention must be timely and must follow Rule 24(c) procedures.[149] Delays of four and six years before moving to intervene in a class action have been found untimely.[150] Intervention has even been denied partially because of a lengthy failure of the applicants to serve a copy of their motion upon the parties to the action.[151]

Intervention generally is permitted after the class certification has been denied or judgment entered so that the denial can be appealed.[152] However, if parties excluded from the class definition do not timely intervene to challenge their exclusion, they will lack standing to raise this issue on appeal.[153] Intervention after entry of a settlement decree has been permitted,[154] although several circuits have considered intervention after entry of a consent decree to be extraordinary.[155] For example, if intervention is not sought until well after it is

---

[142] 2 Newberg on Class Actions § 11.69.

[143] *Id.* § 11.70; Glidden v. Chromalloy Am. Corp., 808 F.2d 621, 627–28 (7th Cir. 1986).

[144] *See generally* 3 Newberg on Class Actions §§ 16.06–16.12; 3B Moore's Federal Practice ¶ 23.90; 7B Federal Practice and Procedure § 1779; §§ **9.6–9.9**.

[145] *See* 3 Newberg on Class Actions § 16.13, at 310.

[146] *See In re* Fine Paper Antitrust Litig., 695 F.2d 494, 499 (3d Cir. 1982) (eliminated class members must intervene to appeal); *see* § **9.9**.

[147] Kleiner v. First Nat'l Bank of Atlanta, 751 F.2d 1193, 1202 (11th Cir. 1985).

[148] See § **9.7**.

[149] See § **9.8**.

[150] Lelsz v. Kavanagh, 710 F.2d 1040, 1047–48 (5th Cir. 1983).

[151] McCarthy v. Kleindienst, 741 F.2d 1406, 1416 (D.C. Cir. 1984).

[152] 3 Newberg on Class Actions § 16.11.

[153] *See In re* Fine Paper Antitrust Litig., 695 F.2d 494, 499 (3d Cir. 1982).

[154] United Airlines, Inc. v. McDonald, 432 U.S. 385, 394 (1977).

[155] *See, e.g.*, Jones v. Caddo Parish School Bd., 704 F.2d 206, 221 (5th Cir. 1983); Alaniz v. Tillie Lewis Foods, 572 F.2d 657, 659 (9th Cir.), *cert. denied*, 439 U.S. 837 (1978).

obvious that the intervenors are not class members, a denial is appropriate.[156] A few circuits have suggested that, when inadequacy of class representation requires class findings to be vacated, intervention by a qualified representative should be sought so that the findings may be reinstated.[157]

§ 10.17 Review of Decisions Concerning Class Action Issues

Class issues rarely can be reviewed prior to final judgment.[158] The collateral order doctrine is not usually applicable to class issues.[159] In addition, the Supreme Court has held that a denial of class certification cannot be appealed as collateral orders prior to final judgment.[160] Such appeals have been denied even when sought under the guise of a Rule 54(b) judgment,[161] although certification of a denial by the district judge is still available when appropriate under 28 U.S.C. § 1292(b).[162] Similarly, certification from the court's order raises all questions of law necessary to the proper disposition of the appeal.[163]

Appellate courts have also denied review of an order deferring certification.[164] However, the Seventh Circuit has held that Rule 23(e) prevents a summary judgment from being final when the district judge has deferred certification.[165]

Questions concerning reviewability of issues arising in class actions have met with varying success when they are part of an order concerning injunctive

---

[156] *In re* Fine Paper Antitrust Litig., 695 F.2d 494, 501 (3d Cir. 1982).

[157] Goodman v. Lukens Steel Co., 777 F.2d 113, 124 (3d Cir. 1985), *cert. granted,* ——— U.S. ———, 107 S. Ct. 568 (1986); Hill v. Western Elec. Co., 672 F.2d 381, 387 (4th Cir.), *cert. denied,* 459 U.S. 981 (1982); *see* Note, *Reinstating Vacated Findings in Employment Discrimination Class Actions: Reconciling General Telephone Co. v. Falcon with Hill v. Western Electric Co.,* 1983 Duke L.J. 821.

[158] *See generally* 2 Newberg on Class Actions §§ 7.38–7.46; 3B Moore's Federal Practice ¶ 23.97; 7B Federal Practice and Procedure §§ 1802–1803.

[159] *Compare* Oppenheimer Fund, Inc. v. Sanders, 437 U.S. 340, 356 (1978); Eisen v. Carlisle & Jacquelin, 417 U.S. 156, 169–72 (1974); *In re* Victor Technologies Secs. Litig., 792 F.2d 862, 864 (9th Cir. 1986) (permitting appeal) *with* Coopers & Lybrand v. Livesay, 437 U.S. 463, 477 (1978); Rodriguez v. Banco Central, 790 F.2d 172, 176–80 (1st Cir. 1986) *and* Lusardi v. Xerox Corp., 747 F.2d 174, 176–78 (3d Cir. 1984) (denying appeal).

[160] Coopers & Lybrand v. Livesay, 437 U.S. 463, 477 (1978).

[161] Minority Police Officers Ass'n v. City of South Bend, 721 F.2d 197, 201 (11th Cir. 1983).

[162] Deposit Guaranty Nat'l Bank v. Roper, 445 U.S. 326, 336 (1980).

[163] Walsh v. Ford Motor Co., 807 F.2d 1000, 1002 n.2 (D.C. Cir. 1986); *In re* Flight Transp. Corp. Secs. Litig., 730 F.2d 1128, 1133 n.6 (8th Cir. 1984).

[164] Rodriguez v. Banco Central, 790 F.2d 172, 177–80 (1st Cir. 1986).

[165] Glidden v Chromalloy Am. Corp. 808 F.2d 621, 628 (7th Cir. 1986).

relief.[166] Because intervention is distinct from class issues, a denial of intervention as of right in a class action is appealable.[167]

§ 10.18 Derivative Actions by Shareholders

The requirements for derivative actions by shareholders are provided in Rule 23.1.[168] In diversity actions, the characterization of the litigation as derivative or direct is a question of state law, but Rule 23.1 governs procedural requirements once the claim is considered derivative.[169]

Derivative actions are brought by one or more shareholders to enforce a right of a corporation or unincorporated association when that organization fails to enforce a right which it may properly assert.[170] The corporation is an indispensable party in a derivative action brought by its shareholders[171] and will be realigned according to its real interest for purposes of diversity.[172]

Rule 23.1 requires the complaint to allege (1) that the plaintiff was a shareholder or member at the time of the transaction in question or later received the requisite interest by operation of law and (2) that the action is not a collusive one to confer federal jurisdiction. The plaintiff must also allege with particularity the efforts, if any, made to obtain the desired action from the appropriate corporate authorities or shareholders and the reasons for any failure to obtain the action or for not making the effort. Verification is necessary even if the basis of the complaint is reliance on advice from one's attorney.[173] The district court may impose state requirements for posting of security in diversity cases, which has the effect of discouraging actions by small shareholders.[174] Derivative suits are difficult to win, because the corporation's refusal to comply with the plaintiff's request based on its honest business judgment provides a formidable defense.[175]

---

[166] *See* Gardner v. Westinghouse Broadcasting Co., 437 U.S. 478, 482; Shanks v. City of Dallas, 752 F.2d 1092, 1095–96 (5th Cir. 1985); Kershner v. Mazurkiewicz, 670 F.2d 440, 446–49 (3d Cir. 1982) (discussing cases).

[167] Woolen v. Surtran Taxicabs, Inc., 684 F.2d 324, 330–31 (5th Cir. 1982).

[168] *See generally* 4 Newberg on Class Actions §§ 22.81–22.96; 3B Moore's Federal Practice ch. 23.1; 7C Federal Practice and Procedure §§ 1821–1841.

[169] Sax v. World Wide Press, Inc., 809 F.2d 610, 613 (9th Cir. 1987).

[170] Fed. R. Civ. P. 23.1; Daily Income Fund, Inc. v. Fox, 464 U.S. 523, 533–34 (1984).

[171] Ross v. Bernhard, 396 U.S. 531, 538 (1970).

[172] Smith v. Sperling, 354 U.S. 91, 97–98 (1957); Liddy v. Urbanek, 707 F.2d 1222, 1224–25 (11th Cir. 1983); *see* 3B Moore's Federal Practice ¶ 23.1.21[1]; 7C Federal Practice and Procedure § 1822.

[173] Surowitz v. Hilton Hotels Corp., 383 U.S. 363, 371–72 (1966); *see* 7C Federal Practice and Procedure § 1827.

[174] *See generally* 3B Moore's Federal Practice ¶ 23.1.15[3]; 7C Federal Practice and Procedure § 1835.

[175] *See* Maher v. Zapata Corp., 714 F.2d 436, 456 (5th Cir. 1983); *see generally* 7C Federal Practice and Procedure § 1831.

A derivative action cannot be maintained if the plaintiff does not fairly and adequately represent the interest of the shareholders or members similarly situated in enforcing the right in question.[176] Fair representation requires an experienced plaintiff's attorney and a plaintiff who does not have interests antagonistic to the class.[177] Antagonism involves a variety of factors, including economic conflict between representative and class, the remedy sought by the plaintiff, indications that the named plaintiff is not the driving force behind the litigation, the plaintiff's unfamiliarity with the litigation, other litigation pending between the plaintiff and defendants, the relative magnitude of the plaintiff's personal interests compared with her interest in the derivative action, the plaintiff's vindictiveness toward the defendants, and the degree of support the plaintiff received from the shareholders represented.[178]

Any dismissal or compromise of a derivative action must be approved by the court, with notice given in the manner the court directs.[179] Settlement may range from payment of cash to selection of new management,[180] and the absence of monetary consideration does not by itself render a settlement unfair.[181] Attorneys' fees and costs have been awarded to successful litigants in derivative actions.[182]

§ 10.19 Class Actions Relating to Unincorporated Associations

Rule 23.2 provides that an action brought by or against the members of an unincorporated association as a class may be maintained only if the representative parties fairly and adequately protect the interests of the association and its members. Any dismissal or compromise must be approved by the court pursuant to Rule 23(e).[183] Class action treatment is beneficial in litigation involving an unincorporated association because of advantageous rules concerning diversity, personal jurisdiction, service of process, and venue.[184]

---

[176] Fed. R. Civ. P. 23.1; *see generally* 4 Newberg on Class Actions § 22.87; 7C Federal Practice and Procedure § 1833.

[177] Vanderbilt v. Geo-Energy Ltd., 725 F.2d 204, 207 (3d Cir. 1983).

[178] *Id.*

[179] Fed. R. Civ. P. 23.1; Maher v. Zapata Corp., 714 F.2d 436, 450 (5th Cir. 1983); Papilsky v. Berndt, 466 F.2d 251, 258 (2d Cir.), *cert. denied,* 409 U.S. 1077 (1972); 4 Newberg on Class Actions § 22.96; 3B Moore's Federal Practice ¶ 23.1.24; 7C Federal Practice and Procedure § 1839.

[180] *See* 4 Newberg on Class Actions § 22.95.

[181] *See* Maher v. Zapata Corp., 714 F.2d 436, 466–67 (5th Cir. 1983).

[182] *See generally* 3B Moore's Federal Practice ¶ 23.1.25; 7C Federal Practice and Procedure § 1841.

[183] See **§ 10.13**.

[184] 7C Federal Practice and Procedure § 18.61.

CHAPTER 11

PROVISIONAL RELIEF

§ 11.1 Overview of Injunctive Relief

Often in litigation, immediate judicial action is necessary to prevent a successful verdict from being a meaningless gesture. Almost any type of action not wholly compensable by money damages is a possibility for injunctive relief,[1] but the prime candidates are patent and trademark infringement actions, civil rights litigation,[2] and takeover litigation.[3] Counsel must be careful to follow federal procedures for obtaining and employing injunctive relief. Rule 65 controls in diversity as well as federal cases, except when an act of Congress states otherwise.[4]

---

[1] Sampson v. Murray, 415 U.S. 61, 90 (1974); Cunningham v. Adams, 808 F.2d 815, 821 (11th Cir. 1987).

[2] *See generally* O. Fiss, The Civil Rights Injunction (1978).

[3] *See* Nussbaum, *Preliminary Injunctions in the Federal Courts: General Standards and their Recent Application in Corporate Takeover Battles,* 1 Current Problems In Federal Civil Practice 1986 at 699–766 (PLI Handbook No. 318).

[4] *See* Fed. R. Civ. P. 65(e) exempting 28 U.S.C. §§ 2361 and 2284 from Rule 65 procedures.

§ 11.2 Temporary Restraining Orders

The temporary restraining order (TRO) is designed to keep the status quo until the court can determine the merits of the underlying dispute.[5] It is not unusual that the first indication of a lawsuit will be a call from opposing counsel giving notice of a hearing to obtain a TRO or the service of a complaint with the TRO.

Rule 65(b) provides that a TRO may be granted without written or oral notice to the adverse party or his attorney only if (1) it clearly appears from specific facts shown by affidavit or verified complaint that immediate and irreparable injury, loss, or damage will result to the applicant before the opposition can be heard, and (2) the applicant's attorney certifies in writing the efforts, if any, which have been made to give notice and why notice should not be required. Local court rules have virtually eliminated the complete absence of notice because they require 4- to 24-hours' notice in the absence of exceptional circumstances. However, if the client is not currently represented by counsel or has inadequate procedures for immediately reaching counsel, such notice may be unavailing. Other reasons for ex parte TRO hearings are that the identity of the adverse party is unknown, the known party cannot be located in time for a hearing, or in rare circumstances, notice would frustrate the purpose of the action.[6]

Rule 65(b) requires that if a TRO is granted without notice, it must define the injury and state why the injury is irreparable and why the TRO is granted without notice. TROs expire at the time set by the court but cannot exceed ten days. For good cause shown within the period, the TRO can be extended for another ten days, unless the party against whom the order is directed consents to a longer extension. If the TRO is granted without notice, the motion for a preliminary injunction is set for the earliest possible hearing and takes precedence over other matters. The adverse party may also move on two days' notice, or less if prescribed by the court, for a modification or dissolution of the TRO.

§ 11.3 Preliminary Injunctions

A preliminary injunction cannot be granted without notice.[7] Rule 65(a)(2) provides that the court may order the trial on the merits advanced and consolidated with the hearing on the preliminary injunction. Even if consolidation is not ordered, any evidence presented at the hearing which would be admissible at

---

[5] *See* Granny Goose Foods, Inc. v. Brotherhood of Teamsters & Auto Truck Drivers, 415 U.S. 423, 438–39 (1974).

[6] American Can Co. v. Mansukhani, 742 F.2d 314, 322–23 (7th Cir. 1984); *see In re* Vuitton et Fils S.A., 606 F.2d 1, 5 (2d Cir. 1979).

[7] Fed. R. Civ. P. 65(a)(1).

trial need not be repeated at a bench trial.[8] Notice of consolidation must be sufficient to give the parties adequate opportunity to present their cases.[9] The notice must also be clear and unambiguous so that the parties have an opportunity to object or suggest special procedures.[10] If appropriate notice is given, a court's order of consolidation will not be overturned absent a showing of substantial prejudice in the sense that a party was not allowed to present material evidence.[11] If notice is not given of the consolidation and counsel declines an opportunity for a rehearing, this defect is waived on appeal.[12] However, any consolidation must follow the rules of procedure and cannot incorporate a summary jury trial as used in alternative dispute resolution.[13]

§ 11.4 Criteria for Granting an Injunction

Since injunctive relief is considered an extraordinary remedy, counsel cannot assume it will be granted merely because the equities appear to favor his position. Each circuit has its own exact formulation of what criteria support preliminary injunctive relief.[14] However, all circuits include the likelihood of success on the merits and a showing of irreparable injury which cannot be remedied with money damages.[15] An evaluation of public interest factors[16] and balancing of the hardships to the parties[17] are considered to some degree in most

---

[8] Fed. R. Civ. P. 65(a)(2).

[9] University of Tex. v. Camenisch, 451 U.S. 390, 395 (1981); Abraham Zion Corp. v. Lebow, 761 F.2d 93, 101 (2d Cir. 1985); 7, pt.2 J. Moore, *et al.*, Moore's Federal Practice ¶ 65.04[4] (2d ed. 1986) [hereinafter Moore's Federal Practice].

[10] University of Tex. v. Camenisch, 451 U.S. 390, 395 (1981).

[11] Abraham Zion Corp. v. Lebow, 761 F.2d 93, 101 (2d Cir. 1985); Eli Lilly & Co. v. Generix Drug Sales, Inc., 460 F.2d 1096, 1106–07 (5th Cir. 1972); *see* Paris v. United States Dep't of Housing & Urban Dev., 713 F.2d 1341, 1346 (7th Cir. 1983); *cf.* Berry v. Bean, 796 F.2d 713, 719 (4th Cir. 1986) (further evidence would be a useless gesture).

[12] Channel Home Centers v. Grossman, 795 F.2d 291, 298 (3d Cir. 1986).

[13] Proimos v. Fair Automotive Repair, Inc., 808 F.2d 1273, 1277 (7th Cir. 1987); see § **16.3**.

[14] *See* Brosnahan, Lazarus & Reilly, *Obtaining A Preliminary Injunction and Temporary Restraining Order in the Ninth Circuit,* 1 Current Problems in Federal Civil Practice 1986, at 767–88 (PLI Handbook No. 318); Wolf, *Preliminary Injunctions: The Varying Standards,* 7 W. New Eng. L. Rev. 173 (1984) (discussing case law in each circuit).

[15] *See* Brown v. Chote, 411 U.S. 452, 456 (1973).

[16] *See* Sampson v. Murray, 415 U.S. 61, 83–84 (1974); Mississippi Power & Light v. United Gas Pipe Line, 760 F.2d 618, 625–26 (5th Cir. 1985); *cf.* Amoco Production Co. v. Village of Gambell, ____ U.S. ____, 107 S. Ct. 1396, 1404–05 (1987) (although public interest should be considered, irreparable damage cannot be presumed by agency failure to comply with law).

[17] *See, e.g.*, National Wildlife Fed'n v. Coston, 773 F.2d 1513, 1517 (9th Cir. 1985); Zardui-Quintana v. Richard, 768 F.2d 1213, 1216 (11th Cir. 1985); LeBeau v. Spirito, 703 F.2d 639, 642

circuits. A few circuits employ alternative tests, giving the applicant a chance to qualify under either formulation.[18] The Seventh Circuit has even stated the standard for relief as a mathematical formula,[19] although this rendition did not change the circuit's traditional approach to granting preliminary injunctive relief.[20] In some circuits, irreparable injury is determined before any of the other factors, since its absence defeats injunctive relief.[21] Due to the importance of demonstrating irreparable harm, counsel must be prepared to show why money damages are not adequate for the alleged injury.[22]

The courts consider the same criteria for both prohibitory and mandatory preliminary injunctions but are more cautious in granting mandatory injunctions.[23] If modification is sought, the defendant bears the burden of proof[24] to demonstrate that changed circumstances make the continuation of any injunction inequitable,[25] but courts apply a more lenient standard of changed circumstances in modifying preliminary injunctions than in granting final injunctive relief.[26]

§ 11.5 Procedural Requirements and Enforcement

Although an evidentiary hearing may be necessary if the affidavits are disputed,[27] it is proper to grant preliminary injunctive relief on the affidavits

(1st Cir. 1983); Wesley-Jessen Div. v. Bausch & Lomb Inc., 698 F.2d 862, 864 (7th Cir. 1983); United States v. Price, 688 F.2d 204, 211 (3d Cir. 1982); Dataphase Sys., Inc. v. C L Sys., Inc., 640 F.2d 109, 113 (8th Cir. 1981) (en banc); Canal Auth. v. Callaway, 489 F.2d 567, 572 (5th Cir. 1974).

[18] *See, e.g.*, Loveridge v. Pendelton Woolen Mills, Inc., 788 F.2d 914, 916 (2d Cir. 1986); *see also* First Brands Corp. v. Fred Meyer, Inc., 809 F.2d 1378, 1381 (9th Cir. 1987) (validity of Ninth Circuit's alternative formulation may be questionable in light of Amoco Production Co. v. Village of Gambell, ____ U.S. ____, 107 S. Ct. 1396 (1987)).

[19] American Hosp. Supply Corp. v. Hospital Prods. Ltd., 780 F.2d 589, 593 (7th Cir. 1986), *questioned in* Brunswick Corp. v. Jones, 784 F.2d 271, 274 n.1 (7th Cir. 1986) *and* Lawson Prods., Inc. v. Avnet, Inc., 782 F.2d 1429, 1433–37 (7th Cir. 1986).

[20] Schultz v. Frisby, 807 F.2d 1339, 1343 (7th Cir. 1986).

[21] *See, e.g.*, Arthur Guinness & Sons, PLC v. Sterling Publishing Co., 732 F.2d 1095, 1099 (2d Cir. 1984).

[22] *See, e.g.*, ECRI, v. McGraw-Hill, Inc., 809 F.2d 223, 226 (3d Cir. 1987).

[23] *See* 7, pt.2 Moore's Federal Practice ¶ 65.04[1].

[24] Stewart v. General Motors Corp., 756 F.2d 1285, 1291 (7th Cir. 1985); International Bhd. of Teamsters v. Western Pa. Motor Carriers Ass'n, 660 F.2d 76, 85 (3d Cir. 1981).

[25] Winterland Concessions Co. v. Trela, 735 F.2d 257, 260 (7th Cir. 1984); Merrell-National Laboratories, Inc. v. Zenith Laboratories, Inc., 579 F.2d 786, 791 (3d Cir. 1978); *see* United States v. United Shoe Mach. Corp., 391 U.S. 244, 248 (1968).

[26] Movie Sys., Inc. v. Mad Minneapolis Audio Distrib., 717 F.2d 427, 430 (8th Cir. 1983); *see generally* 7, pt.2 Moore's Federal Practice ¶ 65.07.

[27] D.E.C. v. Emulex Corp., 805 F.2d 380, 382–83 & n.5 (Fed. Cir. 1986); *see* 7, pt.2 Moore's Federal Practice ¶ 65.04[3].

alone,[28] and most TROs and preliminary injunctions are granted without live testimony. Some local rules require counsel to have witnesses present, but the court usually does not request that they be called. It is preferable to draft affidavits upon personal knowledge, containing matters that are admissible in evidence; however, courts appear to accept affidavits that would not be sufficient in a summary judgment context.[29]

Every order granting an injunction or TRO must (1) set forth the reasons for its issuance, (2) provide specific terms, and (3) describe in reasonable detail, not by reference to other documents, the act or acts sought to be restrained.[30] The judge is required to issue findings of fact and conclusions of law concerning the granting or denial of interlocutory injunctions.[31] A complete departure from the basic procedural requirements may result in the injunctions being vacated.[32]

Rule 65(d) limits the enforceability of the injunction or TRO to parties to the action, their officers, agents, servants, employees, and attorneys, and to those persons in active concert or participation with them who receive actual notice of the order.[33] Violation of an injunctive order is usually treated as a contempt of court.[34]

§ 11.6 Security

No TRO or injunction issues without security,[35] unless the applicant is the United States or one of its officers or agencies.[36] The bond is intended to cover any costs or damages of a party wrongfully enjoined or restrained. Local rules often provide for nominal sums, which can be increased if the judge so provides. If counsel believes the injunction is improper and will cause substantial injury, the amount of the expected loss should be documented to the extent possible, because the court-ordered bond will be the only available remedy unless the suit

---

[28] *See, e.g.*, SEC v. Frank, 388 F.2d 486, 490–91 (2d Cir. 1968); 7, pt.2 Moore's Federal Practice ¶ 65.04[3].

[29] *See* Asseo v. Pan American Grain Co., 805 F.2d 23, 26 (1st Cir. 1986); 7, pt.2 Moore's Federal Practice ¶ 65.04[3].

[30] Fed. R. Civ. P. 65(d).

[31] Fed. R. Civ. P. 52(a).

[32] *See* D.E.C. v. Emulex Corp., 805 F.2d 380, 383 (Fed. Cir. 1986); *cf.* Thomas v. Brock, 810 F.2d 448, 450 (4th Cir. 1987) (striking paragraph referring to 22-page findings of fact and conclusions of law).

[33] *See, e.g.*, Zenith Radio Corp. v. Hazeltine Research, Inc., 395 U.S. 100, 112 (1969); Waffenschmidt v. MacKay, 763 F.2d 711, 727 (5th Cir. 1985), *cert. denied*, ____ U.S. ____, 106 S. Ct. 794 (1986); Annot., 61 A.L.R. Fed. 482 (1983).

[34] *See generally* 7, pt.2 Moore's Federal Practice ¶ 65.02[3]; **ch. 31**.

[35] *See generally* Note, *Recovery for Wrongful Interlocutory Injunctions Under Rule 65(c)*, 99 Harv. L. Rev. 828 (1986).

[36] Fed. R. Civ. P. 65(c).

is prosecuted maliciously and without probable cause.[37] Counsel should contact a surety before the hearing, because it is useless to have relief granted if the mechanisms for its enforcement are not immediately available.

§ 11.7 Reviewing Injunctive Orders

28 U.S.C. § 1292(a)(1) specifically provides for appeal of interlocutory orders granting, continuing, modifying, refusing, or dissolving injunctions or refusing to dissolve or modify injunctions. Because most other interlocutory orders cannot be appealed, litigants often attempt to portray them as orders affecting injunctive relief so that they can obtain immediate appellate review. Such efforts have met with varying success.[38] Even the Supreme Court has indicated that the order must have a serious, perhaps irreparable consequence and must be effectually challenged only by an immediate appeal to fall within § 1292(a)(1).[39] The Court has also held that refusal to grant a TRO is not appealable.[40] However, appeals of TROs have been granted when their denial effectively decided the merits of the case.[41] If an appeal is sought, it may be necessary to obtain a stay pending appeal from the district judge or, if denied below, from the appellate court.[42] If a request for an expedited appeal is desired,[43] counsel should consult the local appellate rules for the correct procedures.

The standard of review depends on the function of the court, with factual decisions being reviewed as clearly erroneous[44] and questions of law reviewed de novo.[45] Since the decision to grant a preliminary injunction is discretionary, the

---

[37] *See* 7, pt.2 Moore's Federal Practice ¶ 65.10[1]; Note, *Recovery for Wrongful Interlocutory Injunctions Under Rule 65(c),* 99 Harv. L. Rev. 828 (1986).

[38] *See, e.g.*, Carson v. American Brands, Inc., 450 U.S. 79, 84 (1981); I.A.M. Nat'l Pension Fund v. Cooper Indus., Inc., 789 F.2d 21, 23–25 (D.C. Cir. 1986), *cert. denied,* ___ U.S. ___, 107 S. Ct. 473 (1986); Samayoa v. Chicago Bd. of Educ., 783 F.2d 102, 103–04 (7th Cir. 1986); Cable Holdings of Battlefield, Inc. v. Cooke, 764 F.2d 1466, 1471 (11th Cir. 1985); Sentry Life Ins. Co. v. Borad, 759 F.2d 695, 697–98 (9th Cir. 1985); Lucas v. Bolivar County, 756 F.2d 1230, 1235 (5th Cir. 1985).

[39] Stringfellow v. Concerned Neighbors in Action, ___ U.S. ___, 107 S. Ct. 1177, 1184 (1987); Carson v. American Brands, Inc., 450 U.S. 79, 84 (1981).

[40] Office of Personnel Mgmt. v. American Fed'n of Gov't Employees, ___ U.S. ___, 105 S. Ct. 3467, 3470 (1985); *cf.* General Motors Corp. v. Gibson Chem. & Oil Corp., 786 F.2d 105, 108 (2d Cir. 1986) (grant of TRO not appealable).

[41] *See* Graham v. Teledyne-Continental Motors, Inc., 805 F.2d 1386, 1388 (9th Cir. 1986).

[42] *See* Fed. R. Civ. P. 62(c); Fed. R. App. P. 8; Lopez v. Heckler, 713 F.2d 1432, 1435 (9th Cir. 1983); Ruiz v. Estelle, 666 F.2d 854, 856–57 (5th Cir. 1982).

[43] *See* Fed. R. App. P. 2.

[44] *See* Anderson v. City of Bessemer City, 470 U.S. 564, 573–76 (1985).

[45] *See, e.g.*, Stormy Clime, Ltd. v. Progroup, Inc., 809 F.2d 971, 974 (2d Cir. 1987); Plains Cotton Co-op. v. Goodpasture Computer Serv., 807 F.2d 1256, 1259 (5th Cir. 1987); United States v. McConney, 728 F.2d 1195, 1203 (9th Cir.) (en banc), *cert. denied,* 469 U.S. 824 (1984).

general review is for abuse of discretion.[46] TROs are also reviewed on an abuse discretion standard.[47] The Second Circuit has permitted de novo review when there has been no evidentiary hearing and the decision below was based entirely upon legal arguments and papers submitted to the court,[48] but this approach has not been adopted by other circuits.[49]

Abuse of discretion can be found if the judge (1) applies incorrect substantive law or preliminary injunction standards, (2) makes clearly erroneous findings of fact, or (3) applies the preliminary injunction standard in a manner that results in abuse of discretion.[50] The issuance of an injunction which directly conflicted with an injunction issued by another federal court has been considered an abuse of discretion.[51]

§ 11.8 Seizure of Property

Rule 64 governs the seizure of persons or property during an action for the purpose of ultimately securing satisfaction of any judgment rendered. All remedies permitted by the law of the state in which the district court is held are available after commencement of the action, except in those rare instances when a United States statute is applicable. The scope and procedures of provisional remedies vary significantly among the states; the rule neither creates nor authorizes provisional remedies but simply permits their use in accordance with state law.[52] Remedies available pursuant to Rule 64 include arrest, attachment, garnishment, replevin, sequestration, and other corresponding or equivalent remedies, however designated and regardless of whether state procedure requires the remedy to be obtained by an independent action.[53] In removed cases, valid attachments or sequestrations stand after removal,[54] although the removed action is then subject to the provisions of the federal rules.[55]

---

[46] *See, e.g.*, Doran v. Salem Inn, Inc., 422 U.S. 922, 931–32 (1975); Oakland Tribune, Inc. v. Chronicle Publishing Co., 762 F.2d 1374, 1376 (9th Cir. 1985).

[47] American Can Co. v. Mansukhani, 742 F.2d 314, 321 (7th Cir. 1984); Majd-Pour v. Georgiana Community Hosp., 724 F.2d 901, 902 (11th Cir. 1984).

[48] Norlin Corp. v. Rooney, Pace Inc., 744 F.2d 255, 260–61 (2d Cir. 1984).

[49] *See* Lawson Prod., Inc. v. Avnet, Inc., 782 F.2d 1429, 1439 (7th Cir. 1986).

[50] Zepeda v. United States I.N.S., 753 F.2d 719, 724 (9th Cir. 1983); *see* American Can Co. v. Mansukhani, 742 F.2d 314, 326 (7th Cir. 1984); Coca-Cola Co. v. Tropicana Prods., Inc., 690 F.2d 312, 315–16 (2d Cir. 1982); United States v. Price, 688 F.2d 204, 211 (3d Cir. 1982); *see also* Anderson v. City of Bessemer City, 470 U.S. 564, 576 (1985).

[51] Feller v. Brock, 802 F.2d 722, 730–31 (4th Cir. 1986).

[52] 7 Moore's Federal Practice ¶ 64.04[3].

[53] Fed. R. Civ. P. 64.

[54] 28 U.S.C. § 1450 (1982); 7 Moore's Federal Practice ¶ 64.06[1].

[55] Fed. R. Civ. P. 64, 81(c).

Process for the seizure is issued by the district court and served pursuant to Rule 4(f) for parties within the territorial limits of the state in which the district court sits or Rule 4(e) for a party not found within the state. Quasi in rem jurisdiction over the property seized supports a valid judgment against it but does not by itself support an in personam judgment against the party.[56]

Most orders granting or denying provisional remedies cannot be appealed before the conclusion of the action.[57] However, the vacating of a provisional remedy on motion of a defendant has been treated as appealable under the collateral order doctrine.[58]

§ 11.9 Receivers

Rule 66 governs the appointment of equity receivers and eliminates the plaintiff's ability to voluntarily dismiss an action without court order if a receiver has been appointed. The rule does not apply to bankruptcy cases.[59] Receivers are appointed to take custody and control of property, to preserve it during litigation concerning its disposal.[60] Receivers may be requested by stockholders, mortgagees or lienholders, or creditors as well as by the government to administer an insolvent national bank.[61]

An application to appoint a receiver commences the process and, if filed at the initiation of the action, should be accompanied by a verified complaint.[62] Generally, the procedures followed are similar to those applied in obtaining injunctions, although they require less formality. A receiver is appointed only if some necessity compels this procedure, such as a debtor's inability to meet its expenses or likely dissipation of corporate assets.[63] Several statutes contain restrictions on who can be appointed as receivers.[64] Receivers are subject to state law concerning the management of property.[65]

Appeals from interlocutory orders appointing receivers, refusing to wind up receiverships or to take steps to accomplish the purposes of the receivership are specifically authorized by 28 U.S.C. § 1292(a)(2). Other orders concerning

---

[56] 7 Moore's Federal Practice ¶ 64.09[3], [4]; see § **4.9**.

[57] *See, e.g.*, Perpetual Am. Bank v. Terrestrial Sys., Inc., 811 F.2d 504, 505–06 (9th Cir. 1987); 7 Moore's Federal Practice ¶ 64.10.

[58] *Id.; see* Swift & Co. Packers v. Compania Colombiana Del Caribe, 339 U.S. 684, 688–89 (1950); Britton v. Howard Sav. Bank, 727 F.2d 315, 320–22 (3d Cir. 1984); Brastex Corp. v. Allen Int'l Inc., 702 F.2d 326, 329 (2d Cir. 1983).

[59] 7, pt.2 Moore's Federal Practice ¶ 66.02.

[60] *Id.* ¶ 66.03.

[61] *See generally id.* ¶ 66.09[1].

[62] *See generally id.* ¶ 66.04[1].

[63] *Id.* ¶ 66.05[1].

[64] *See* 28 U.S.C. §§ 458, 957, 958 (1982 & Supp. III 1985).

[65] 28 U.S.C. § 959(b) (1982).

receivers are usually not appealable until the termination of the action.[66] Decisions concerning the supervision of an equitable receivership are reviewed for abuse of discretion.[67] Reversals are rare due to the district court's broad discretion, which even permits it to avoid formalities by using summary proceedings.[68]

§ 11.10 Securities and Deposits

Rule 65.1 provides that when security is given in the form of a bond, stipulation, or other undertaking given by a surety, the surety submits itself to the jurisdiction of the court. The clerk is the agent for the surety for service of process of any papers concerning liability on the undertaking. Such liability may be enforced on motion without the necessity for an independent action.[69] Sureties are common in pretrial practice to guarantee security for TROs, injunctions, attachments and derivative actions.

Rule 67 permits a party to deposit with the court all or part of a sum of money or item capable of delivery which is the subject of an action. Notice of the deposit must be given to every other party, and the court must approve the deposit. Usually, this procedure is used in connection with interpleader in which the party depositing the contested sum has no stake in the ultimate outcome between contesting litigants;[70] however, Rule 67 also encompasses cases in which the party claims all or part of the disputed sum. Money deposited under the rule must be placed in interest-bearing accounts or invested in interest-bearing instruments approved by the court.

§ 11.11 Provisional Relief Checklist

Temporary Restraining Orders (TROs)

1. Is immediate court action required to retain the status quo?
2. Will obtaining a TRO enhance counsel's ability to litigate the preliminary injunction?
3. Is the complaint verified or accompanied by affidavit?

---

[66] 7, pt.2 Moore's Federal Practice ¶ 66.04[3].

[67] SEC v. Hardy, 803 F.2d 1034, 1037 (9th Cir. 1986); SEC v. Safety Finance Serv., Inc., 674 F.2d 368, 372–73 (5th Cir. 1982).

[68] SEC v. Hardy, 803 F.2d 1034, 1040 (9th Cir. 1986).

[69] Fed. R. Civ. P. 65.1.

[70] See § **9.6**.

4. Has security been obtained?
5. Has opposing party been notified?
   a. If notice has not been given, will irreparable injury, loss or damage occur before the opposition can be heard?
   b. Has the attorney certified what efforts have been made regarding notice or why no notice should be required?
   c. Do local rules require a specific amount of notice?
   d. If the TRO was granted without notice, does it state the nature of the injury, why it is irreparable, and why it was granted without notice?
6. Does the TRO contain:
   a. The reasons for its issuance?
   b. Reasonable detail concerning the acts restrained?
7. Should an extension be sought to increase the 10-day limit of the TRO another 10 days?
   a. Will the opponent consent to a longer extension?
8. Should modification or dissolution of the TRO be requested?
   a. Has two days' notice been given?

Preliminary Injunctions

1. Has notice been given?
2. Is consolidation of the injunction hearing with the merits appropriate?
3. Do the criteria for granting a preliminary injunction exist?
   a. Is there a likelihood of success on the merits?
   b. Is there irreparable injury beyond money damages?
   c. What, if any, public interest factors exist?
   d. What is the balancing of hardship to the parties?
4. Has the appropriate proof been obtained?
   a. Have affidavits been signed?
   b. Are witnesses required or permitted at the hearing?
5. Does the injunction order contain:
   a. The reasons for its issuance.
   b. Reasonable detail concerning the acts restrained.
6. Has security been obtained?
7. Is an interlocutory appeal necessary?

Seizure of Property

1. Have state procedures been followed?

Equity Receivers

1. Is appointment of an equity receiver desirable to preserve assets during litigation concerning their disposal?

Sureties

1. Is a surety required for such purposes as obtaining a TRO or preliminary injunction or for instituting a derivative action?
2. Is a motion to enforce a surety obligation appropriate?
3. Has the court clerk been served as the surety's agent for service of process?

CHAPTER 12

DEFAULTS AND VOLUNTARY DISMISSALS

§ 12.1 Overview of Defaults

If counsel does not submit a timely answer or Rule 12 motion or otherwise fails to defend the action, a default can be entered under Rule 55. Unless a party is already in default when counsel agrees to undertake its representation, a default is usually easily avoided by calling opposing counsel for an extension to answer or obtaining additional time from the court. Technical defaults are not favored, and if the defendant has responded to any preliminary motion or merely missed a filing deadline, a denial of a default is proper.[1] Failure to order a default was not an abuse of discretion when the plaintiff did not request it until trial, even though the individual defendant had not responded for two years.[2] However, courts have upheld defaults when pleadings were not filed after extensions had been granted.[3] A default is not proper if no personal jurisdiction exists over the

[1] Educational Servs. v. Maryland State Bd. for Higher Educ., 710 F.2d 170, 176–77 (4th Cir. 1983); Meehan v. Snow, 652 F.2d 274, 277 (2d Cir. 1981); *see* Passarella v. Hilton Int'l Co., 810 F.2d 674, 675 (7th Cir. 1987) (trial on merits favored over default).

[2] *See* Swink v. City of Pagedale, 810 F.2d 791, 792 (8th Cir. 1987).

[3] *See, e.g.*, Chrysler Credit Corp. v. Macino, 710 F.2d 363, 365 (7th Cir. 1983).

defendant.[4] Defaults against military personnel are limited by the Soldiers' and Sailors' Civil Relief Act.[5]

Although most defaults concern failures to respond initially to a complaint, Rule 55 is sometimes cited when a Rule 37 discovery failure has resulted in a default.[6] Rule 55(e) prohibits default judgments against the United States, unless the claimant establishes a claim or right to relief by evidence satisfactory to the court. A split exists as to whether such defaults can be entered for procedural violations other than total failure to respond.[7]

§ 12.2 Default Hearings

Rule 55(b)(2) provides for a hearing if necessary, including a trial by jury. It is rare that a jury on damages is required by statute.[8] A hearing as to damages is usually considered necessary unless the amount claimed is a liquidated sum or can be mathematically calculated.[9] A party who has appeared in the action is entitled to three days' notice of the hearing.[10] For purposes of this rule, appearance is interpreted broadly and includes a defaulting party who has indicated to the moving party a clear purpose to defend the suit.[11] At the hearing, all factual allegations of the complaint except those relating to damages are accepted as true,[12] although the court has discretion to require proof of necessary facts and can determine that a valid cause of action has not been stated.[13]

---

[4] Broadcast Music, Inc. v. M.T.S. Enters., 811 F.2d 278, 281 (5th Cir. 1987); 10 C. Wright, A. Miller, *et al.*, Federal Practice and Procedure § 2695 (2d ed. 1983) [hereinafter Federal Practice and Procedure].

[5] 50 U.S.C. App. § 501 *et seq.* (1982); 6 J. Moore *et al.*, Moore's Federal Practice ¶ 55.13 (2d ed. 1986) [hereinafter Moore's Federal Practice].

[6] *See, e.g.*, Brock v. Unique Racquetball & Health Clubs, Inc., 786 F.2d 61, 64 (2d Cir. 1986); **§ 29.10**.

[7] *Compare* Marziliano v. Heckler, 728 F.2d 151, 157 (2d Cir. 1984) (permitting procedural default) *with* Campbell v. Eastland, 307 F.2d 478, 490–91 (5th Cir. 1962), *cert. denied,* 371 U.S. 955 (1963) *and* Giampaoli v. Califano, 628 F.2d 1190, 1193 (9th Cir. 1980) (prohibiting procedural default); *see* 10 Federal Practice and Procedure § 2072, at 548 (better rule to prohibit procedural defaults).

[8] *See* 6 Moore's Federal Practice ¶ 55.07.

[9] Hunt v. Inter-Globe Energy, Inc., 770 F.2d 145, 148 (10th Cir. 1985).

[10] Fed. R. Civ. P. 55(b)(2).

[11] Muniz v. Vidal, 739 F.2d 699, 700 (1st Cir. 1984); H. F. Livermore Corp. v. Aktiengesellschaft Gebruder Loepfe, 432 F.2d 689, 691 (D.C. Cir. 1970); 10 Federal Practice and Procedure § 2686.

[12] Au Bon Pain Corp. v. Artect Inc., 653 F.2d 61, 65 (2d Cir. 1981); 10 Federal Practice and Procedure § 2688.

[13] Au Bon Pain Corp. v. Artect Inc., 653 F.2d 61, 65 (2d Cir. 1981).

§ 12.3 Vacating Defaults

To vacate a default, counsel must bring a motion pursuant to Rule 55(c) before judgment is entered or a Rule 60(b) motion after final judgment. The standards for both motions are usually treated interchangeably and require a showing of good cause or excusable neglect. Specifically, the defaulting party must demonstrate a lack of willfulness, absence of prejudice to its adversary, and the existence of a meritorious defense.[14] The affidavits supporting the motion must allege underlying facts; sworn conclusory statements have been considered insufficient to reopen a default.[15] There is disagreement concerning which party bears the burden of proof to establish whether or not the district court had personal jurisdiction when it entered judgment.[16]

Counsel must make an affirmative showing of a defense that is likely to be successful and cannot rely on a general denial of the plaintiff's claim.[17] The mere fact that a significant amount of money is awarded by virtue of the default is a factor to be considered, but it does not always ensure that a default will be vacated in the absence of a good excuse.[18] Good cause also will not be found if the decision to allow the entry of the default is considered a tactical matter.[19] However, willfulness may be found lacking if the plaintiffs did not inquire, by mail or otherwise, about the defendant's intention before proceeding ex parte with the default.[20]

The denial of a motion to reopen is reviewed for abuse of discretion[21] and does not raise the merits of the underlying judgment, but only the validity of the denial.[22] In other words, an error which would result in reversal of the default on appeal may not constitute abuse of discretion which requires the default to be set

---

[14] *See* United States v. $55,518.05 in U.S. Currency, 728 F.2d 192, 195 (3d Cir. 1984); Chrysler Credit Corp. v. Macino, 710 F.2d 363, 367 (7th Cir. 1983); United Coin Meter Co. v. Seaboard Coastline R.R., 705 F.2d 839, 845 (6th Cir. 1983); *see also* Davis v. Musler, 713 F.2d 907, 915 (2d Cir. 1983); *see generally* 10 Federal Practice and Procedure § 2692; Project, *Relief from Default Judgments under Rule 60(b) — A Study of Federal Case Law,* 49 Fordham L. Rev. 956 (1981).

[15] Sony Corp. v. Elm State Elecs., Inc., 800 F.2d 317, 320–21 (2d Cir. 1986); United States v. $55,518.05 in U.S. Currency, 728 F.2d 192, 196–97 (3d Cir. 1984).

[16] *See* Bally Export Corp. v. Balicar, Ltd., 804 F.2d 398, 401 (7th Cir. 1986).

[17] Solaroll Shade & Shutter Corp. v. Bio-Energy Sys., Inc., 803 F.2d 1130, 1133 (11th Cir. 1986); United States v. One 1978 Piper Navajo PA-31 Aircraft, 748 F.2d 316, 319 (5th Cir. 1984).

[18] *See* C.K.S. Eng'rs, Inc. v. White Mountain Gypsum Co., 726 F.2d 1202, 1208 (7th Cir. 1984) ($600,000 default upheld).

[19] *See* Wells v. Rockefeller, 728 F.2d 209, 214 (3d Cir. 1984), *cert. denied,* 471 U.S. 1107 (1985).

[20] *See* Bieganek v. Taylor, 801 F.2d 879, 882 (7th Cir. 1986).

[21] *See* Chrysler Credit Corp. v. Macino, 710 F.2d 363, 367 (7th Cir. 1983); Traguth v. Zuck, 710 F.2d 90, 94 (2d Cir. 1983).

[22] Williams v. New Orleans Pub. Serv., Inc., 728 F.2d 730, 733–34 (5th Cir. 1984); Davis v. Musler, 713 F.2d 907, 912 (2d Cir. 1983).

aside.[23] Therefore, when counsel has notice of the default, a direct appeal should also be filed. Such an appeal must be timely, because a Rule 60(b) motion does not toll the 30-day time limit for taking an appeal from the underlying judgment.[24] A few courts are more liberal in reviewing Rule 55(c) motions than Rule 60(b) motions on the theory that Rule 60 is an exceptional remedy,[25] but most consider that an abuse of discretion under Rule 60(b) need not be glaring to justify reversal of a district court order denying a motion to vacate a default judgment.[26]

§ 12.4 Voluntary Dismissals

Rule 41(a) delineates two categories of voluntary dismissal, (1) by plaintiff or by stipulation and (2) by court order. Probably the most common use of voluntary dismissals in federal and state court is in conjunction with settlements, when the parties file a stipulation listing the agreed upon terms and dismissing the action with prejudice. Dismissal by notice occurs when the plaintiff unilaterally dismisses its case, usually without prejudice. The most frequently litigated areas concerning such dismissals are (1) whether the court is required to approve the dismissal, (2) whether the court should grant or deny the dismissal, (3) what conditions should be imposed upon the dismissal, and (4) whether the dismissal should be with or without prejudice.

A plaintiff may choose to dismiss for a variety of reasons including a desire to add nondiverse parties to the action or join in ongoing litigation in state court, a failure of anticipated proof, or simply as a means of returning a removed action to state court, where any refiled complaint will be drafted so as to defeat any further removal. No action should be voluntarily dismissed without considering the statute of limitations; any future complaint will have to be timely filed, because the dismissed action is treated as if it never existed,[27] unless a state tolling statute provides otherwise.[28]

Although Rule 41(a) applies to dismissal of the action, not dismissal of claims or parties, courts usually interpret incorrectly designated dismissals as Rule 15

---

[23] *See, e.g.*, Williams v. New Orleans Pub. Serv., Inc., 728 F.2d 730, 736 (5th Cir. 1984).

[24] Browder v. Director, Ill. Dep't of Corrections, 434 U.S. 257, 263 n.7 (1978); Inryco, Inc. v. Metropolitan Eng'g Co., 708 F.2d 1225, 1232 (7th Cir.), *cert. denied*, 464 U.S. 937 (1983).

[25] *See* C.K.S. Eng'rs, Inc. v. White Mountain Gypsum Co., 726 F.2d 1202, 1205–06 (7th Cir. 1984).

[26] Davis v. Musler, 713 F.2d 907, 913 (2d Cir. 1983); Keegel v. Key West & Caribbean Trading Co., 627 F.2d 372, 374 (D.C. Cir. 1980); *see* Williams v. New Orleans Pub. Serv., Inc., 728 F.2d 730, 734 (5th Cir. 1984) (slight abuse justifies reversal of default); United States v. $55,518.05 in U.S. Currency, 728 F.2d 192, 194–95 (3d Cir. 1984) (doubtful cases resolved in favor of vacating default).

[27] Ford v. Sharp, 758 F.2d 1018, 1023–24 (5th Cir. 1985).

[28] *See* 5 Moore's Federal Practice ¶ 41.05[2].

amendments,[29] Rule 21 misjoinder motions,[30] or motions pursuant to the court's inherent powers.[31] Rule 41(c) provides that counterclaims, cross-claims, and third party claims are also subject to voluntary dismissal.

§ 12.5 Dismissal as of Right

Although state practice varies regarding the amount of time, the plaintiff retains an absolute right to dismiss its action in federal court; even diversity actions fall within the ambit of Rule 41(a)(1).[32] Rule 41(a)(1) limits noticed dismissals to the time before service by the adverse party of an answer or motion for summary judgment, or to any time by stipulation. Counterclaims, cross-claims, and third party complaints can be dismissed before a responsive pleading is served, or if none is required, before the introduction of evidence at the trial or hearing.[33] This permits a plaintiff who has included a counterclaim in its response to wait until before trial to enter a voluntarily dismissal by notice.[34] Rule 41(a) does not apply to class actions or cases in which receivers have been appointed or if it conflicts with a federal statute.[35]

The plaintiff terminates the actions by filing a notice of dismissal or stipulation without the need for any further court order.[36] In other words, a court cannot refuse to allow the dismissal to be filed.[37] Oral stipulations have been enforced in limited circumstances, but they can be risky.[38] The rule states that voluntary dismissals are without prejudice unless otherwise stated in the notice of appeal or stipulation. However, Rule 41(a)(1) sets forth a *two-dismissal rule* which deems a dismissal to be with prejudice if the plaintiff has previously dismissed the complaint in any state or federal court. Court-ordered or stipulated dismissals do not activate the two-dismissal rule, but there is some question whether such a dismissal triggers the rule when a later noticed dismissal is entered.[39]

---

[29] *See id.* ¶ 41.06-1; **ch. 8**.

[30] *See* 5 Moore's Federal Practice ¶ 41.05[2]; **ch. 9**.

[31] 9 Federal Practice and Procedure § 2362 (1971).

[32] *See* 5 Moore's Federal Practice ¶ 41.01-1.

[33] Fed. R. Civ. P. 41(c).

[34] 5 Moore's Federal Practice ¶ 41.15.

[35] *See generally id.* at ¶ 41.03; 9 Federal Practice and Procedure § 2363 (1971).

[36] Scam Instrument Corp. v. C.D.C., 458 F.2d 885, 888 (7th Cir. 1972);5 Moore's Federal Practice ¶ 41.02[2]; 9 Federal Practice and Procedure § 2363 (1971).

[37] *See* Foss v. Federal Intermediate Credit Bank, 808 F.2d 657, 659–60 (8th Cir. 1986).

[38] *See* Ocean Drilling & Exploration Co. v. Mont Boat Rental Servs., Inc., 799 F.2d 213, 218 (5th Cir. 1986).

[39] *See* 5 Moore's Federal Practice ¶ 41.04; 9 Federal Practice and Procedure §§ 2363, 2367 (1971).

Rule 41(a)(1) provides that summary judgment as well as an answer cuts off the plaintiff's right to a voluntary dismissal. There has been some question whether a Rule 12(b)(6) motion should also be considered as limiting the plaintiff's right to dismiss, even when it has not been converted to a summary judgment motion.[40] Rarely is any other type of motion viewed as limiting the plaintiff's ability to dismiss.[41]

The court cannot impose conditions on a dismissal which is taken as of right.[42] However, Rule 41(d) provides that, if a plaintiff who has dismissed an action in any court refiles it, the court may order it to pay the costs of the action previously dismissed and stay the proceedings of the new action until it has complied with the order.[43]

§ 12.6 Court-Ordered Dismissals

If the plaintiff cannot voluntarily dismiss as of right, it must move for dismissal. Rule 41(a)(2) gives the court discretion to deny or condition the dismissal in whatever manner it deems proper. Counsel can assume that costs and, often, attorneys' fees will be assessed against the plaintiff as a condition of granting the dismissal or permitting later refiling of the action.[44] In fact, a refusal to award such costs may be considered an abuse of discretion.[45] The only costs which typically are not awarded relate to items which can be used in later litigation.[46] However, the court may still determine that payment of expenses does not eliminate the prejudice to the defendant in a given case and may either impose other conditions or refuse to grant the dismissal.

Reasons for denying the motion vary. Often involved are cases in which the dismissal is sought during or on the eve of trial or after extended discovery resulting in the filing or granting of a summary judgment motion. Even the denial of a proposed dismissal with prejudice may not be considered an abuse of discretion in a multiparty action.[47] On the other hand, prejudice to an opposing party will not be found merely because the plaintiff gains some strategic advantage from the dismissal.[48] Similarly, prejudice is something other than the

---

[40] *See* 5 Moore's Federal Practice ¶ 41.02[3].

[41] *See id.;* 9 Federal Practice and Procedure § 2363 (1971).

[42] *See generally* 5 Moore's Federal Practice ¶ 41.02[4].

[43] *Id.* ¶ 41.16.

[44] *See* 5 Moore's Federal Practice ¶ 41.06; 9 Federal Practice and Procedure § 2366 (1971).

[45] *See* Kern v. TXO Prod. Corp., 738 F.2d 968, 972 (8th Cir. 1984).

[46] *See, e.g.*, United States v. Outboard Marine Corp., 789 F.2d 497, 506–07 (7th Cir.), *cert. denied,* ____ U.S. ____, 107 S. Ct. 457 (1986).

[47] *See* 5 Moore's Federal Practice ¶ 41.05[2].

[48] *See id.* ¶ 41.05[1]; 9 Federal Practice and Procedure § 2364 (1971).

necessity that the defendant may face the prospect of a second lawsuit, because requiring payment of costs and expenses eliminates that harm.[49]

Rule 41(a)(2) provides that court-ordered dismissals are without prejudice unless otherwise specified. Counsel must be careful not to agree to the dismissal of some claims with prejudice if it would bar the litigation of other claims on res judicata principles, unless the record is clear that the parties have agreed that the plaintiff may split its claims.[50] A court cannot dismiss with prejudice when the plaintiff has requested a dismissal without prejudice unless it gives the plaintiff notice and an opportunity to proceed with the litigation.[51] The plaintiff also has the option of refusing a voluntary dismissal if the conditions imposed are too onerous.[52]

Rule 41(a)(2) also requires that, if the defendant has pleaded any counterclaim prior to the dismissal motion, the action will not be dismissed over the defendant's objection unless the court can retain jurisdiction over the counterclaim. This provision is limited to the rare cases in which a permissive counterclaim, such as a setoff, has no independent jurisdictional basis.[53]

§ 12.7 Appeals from Voluntary Dismissals

The plaintiff usually cannot appeal from a voluntary dismissal, because such a dismissal is not an involuntary adverse judgment.[54] Therefore, a voluntary dismissal taken as of right can be reviewed only to challenge the validity of the stipulation or the opposing party's failure to comply with its provisions.[55] If the dismissal has been entered, a party who wishes to challenge it can bring either a Rule 59(e) or a Rule 60(b) motion to reopen the judgment and then appeal from any denial.[56] A defendant can appeal from a dismissal to which it has objected. The refusal of the court to grant a dismissal under Rule 41(a)(2) can be challenged only at the conclusion of the action.[57]

---

[49] Conafay v. Wyeth Laboratories, 793 F.2d 350, 353 (D.C. Cir. 1986); Kern v. TXO Prod. Corp., 738 F.2d 968, 971 (8th Cir. 1984).

[50] *See* Calderon Rosado v. G.E. Circuit Breakers, Inc., 805 F.2d 1085, 1086–87 (1st Cir. 1986).

[51] Andes v. Versant Corp., 788 F.2d 1033, 1037 (4th Cir. 1986).

[52] Lau v. Glendora Unified School Dist., 792 F.2d 929, 930 (9th Cir. 1986); GAF Corp. v. Transamerica Ins. Co., 665 F.2d 364, 367–68 (D.C. Cir. 1981); 9 Federal Practice and Procedure § 2366 (1971).

[53] *See* 5 Moore's Federal Practice ¶ 41.09; 9 Federal Practice and Procedure § 2365 (1971).

[54] Wickland Oil Terminals v. Asarco, Inc., 792 F.2d 887, 893 (9th Cir. 1986); *see* Studstill v. Borg Warner Leasing, 806 F.2d 1005, 1008 (11th Cir. 1986).

[55] *See generally* 5 Moore's Federal Practice ¶ 41.02[6].

[56] *Id.*

[57] *See id.* ¶ 41.05[3]; 9 Federal Practice and Procedure § 2376 (1971).

It is very risky to refuse to proceed with the action, thereby suffering a Rule 41(b) dismissal for failure to prosecute in order to challenge the denial of a Rule 41(a)(2) dismissal.[58] Similarly, although a plaintiff may be able to obtain review of onerous conditions by refusing to comply thereby enabling the court to dismiss with rather than without prejudice,[59] this method of appeal is perilous because the court's ruling concerning a discretionary dismissal will be reversed only for abuse of discretion.[60] When the conditional dismissal is without prejudice, courts vary as to its appealability.[61]

Reversals of dismissals without prejudice are rare, because the district court abuses its discretion only when the defendant will suffer plain legal prejudice as a result of the dismissal.[62] Factors considered in this determination include the defendant's effort and expense in preparing for trial, excessive delay and lack of diligence by the plaintiff in prosecuting the action, insufficient explanation for the need to take a dismissal, and the presence of a summary judgment motion.[63] In contrast, the court's refusal to grant a voluntary dismissal may be an abuse of discretion in the absence of any stated reason of the district court for the denial.[64]

§ 12.8 Default and Voluntary Dismissal Checklist

Defaults
Default Criteria

1. Is the default appropriate?
   a. Have 20 days passed without an answer?
   b. Is the default being imposed as a court ordered sanction?
2. Is the default merely a technical failure which is likely to be vacated?

---

[58] Kern Oil & Refining Co. v. Tenneco Oil Co., 792 F.2d 1380, 1389 (9th Cir. 1986).

[59] *See* Lau v. Glendora Unified School Dist., 792 F.2d 929, 930 n.2 (9th Cir. 1986).

[60] United States v. Outboard Marine Corp., 789 F.2d 497, 502 (7th Cir.), *cert. denied,* _____ U.S. _____, 107 S. Ct. 457 (1986). 5 Moore's Federal Practice ¶ 41.05[1]; 9 Federal Practice and Procedure § 2364 (1971).

[61] Unioil, Inc. v. E.F. Hutton & Co., 809 F.2d 548, 555–56 (9th Cir. 1986) (permitting appeal after surveying case law); *see In re* Union Carbide Corp. Gas Plant Disaster, 809 F.2d 195, 203 (2d Cir. 1987); Fassett v. Delta Kappa Epsilon, 807 F.2d 1150, 1155 (3d Cir. 1986) (permitting appeal); *see generally* 5 Moore's Federal Practice ¶ 41.05[3].

[62] United States v. Outboard Marine Corp., 789 F.2d 497, 503 (7th Cir.), *cert. denied,* _____ U.S. _____, 107 S. Ct. 457 (1986).

[63] *Id.*

[64] Conafay v. Wyeth Laboratories, 793 F.2d 350, 352–54 (D.C. Cir. 1986).

3. Have the appropriate procedures been followed concerning any defendant who is in the military?

Default Hearing

1. Has three days' notice been given to the defendant who has appeared or signified an intention to appear?
2. Is a jury required by statute?
3. Has a hearing been set for damages other than liquidated sums or those which can be calculated mathematically?
4. Has the plaintiff proven the extent of damages?
5. If the defaulting defendant is the United States, has the plaintiff proven liability and damages?

Vacating Default

1. Has a Rule 55(c) motion been made before judgment?
2. Has a Rule 60(b) motion been made after judgment?
3. What good cause or excusable neglect can be shown for the default?
   a. Is there lack of willfulness by the defendant?
   b. Is there an absence of prejudice to the opponent if the default is vacated?
   c. Does a meritorious defense exist to the action?
4. **Warning**: The defendant must timely appeal from the underlying judgment as well as from the denial to vacate the default since the latter appeal does not raise the validity of original judgment.

Voluntary Dismissals

Dismissals of Right

1. Is the dismissal of the complaint entered before service of the defendant's answer or summary judgment motion?
2. Is the dismissal entered by stipulation if taken at another time?
3. Is the dismissal of the counterclaim, cross claim or third party complaint entered before a responsive pleading is made, or if none is required, before evidence is adduced at trial?
4. Has the notice of dismissal or stipulation been filed?
5. Is the dismissal without prejudice?
   a. Does the dismissal state otherwise?

b. Is the dismissal subject to "two dismissal rule," which provides that the dismissal is with prejudice if a previous voluntary dismissal has been entered in state or federal court?

Court-Ordered Dismissals

1. What conditions are likely to be ordered?

  a. What are the costs and attorneys' fees incurred by the opponent?

  b. Will the court refuse to dismiss without prejudice?

    1. Unless otherwise stated, any dismissal is without prejudice.

2. Has the plaintiff been given an opportunity to oppose any onerous condition?

3. Is the court likely to deny the request for dismissal?

  a. What is the prejudice to the opponent if the case is dismissed?

  b. How close is the dismissal to trial?

Reviewing Dismissals

1. **Warning**: A plaintiff generally cannot appeal from a voluntary dismissal.

  a. Move to vacate judgment and appeal from any denial.

  b. While possible, it is dangerous to refuse to comply with court ordered conditions to obtain an involuntary dismissal from which an appeal can be taken.

PART III

WINNING THE CASE THROUGH EFFECTIVE MOTIONS AND PRETRIAL PRACTICE

CHAPTER 13

EFFECTIVE MOTION PRACTICE

§ 13.1 Introduction

Because most civil actions in federal as well as state courts are disposed of by the court or settled by the parties before trial, pretrial practice has become the main arena in which litigators battle for advantage, with motions as their weapons of choice. Motions come in infinite variety, each having its own procedures and consequences. Undoubtedly, most subjects discussed in this book have been the subject of pretrial motions, because Rule 7(b)(1) requires that any application to the court for an order must be made by motion. Motions can terminate an action on jurisdictional or forum non conveniens grounds or for improper venue, failure to state a claim, discovery abuse, failure to prosecute, or failure to obey court orders. They can be used to transfer the action to a district court in another state, determine whether an amendment relates back to the filing of the original complaint, resolve discovery disputes, educate the judge, or simply delay the proceedings.

The importance of federal motion practice cannot be overstated, because even motions which are not dispositive may have lasting ramifications affecting any later trial or settlement. Indeed, the very existence of a pending motion may result in settlement. However, motions should not be employed lightly, because their improper use may result in an award of expenses and attorneys' fees to the opposing party.[1] Moreover, losing a motion may be worse than never having brought it in the first place. Not only is the issue resolved against the party, but opposing counsel has been forced to spend time and money necessary to analyze the case in order to defeat the motion. Therefore, unsuccessful motions may make the case more difficult to settle. Similarly, the motion may have revealed counsel's litigation strategy, negating any element of surprise if the case is eventually tried.

Strategic concerns regarding individual motions are included in this book in the discussion of each subject to which they relate. However, counsel should avoid thinking of motions in a piecemeal fashion, because they can be used effectively to structure the entire case.[2] For example, merely reacting to a Rule 12 deadline ignores the possibility of alternative transfer or forum non conveniens motions. Not realizing that opposing counsel must serve a complaint within 120 days may result in waiver of a service issue which could have completely terminated the litigation if the statute of limitation bars refiling of the complaint. Deciding shortly before trial to bring a summary judgment motion denies counsel the ability to focus discovery requests on material needed to support the motion. If the case is to be tried rather than settled, defense counsel should not overlook a motion requesting that liability be bifurcated from damages,[3] because this traditionally produces lower awards. If not provided for in the final pretrial statement, counsel should determine the appropriateness of requesting in limine evidentiary rulings prior to trial.

The best way to implement a cohesive pretrial plan is to decide at the inception of litigation which motions are pertinent and what discovery or other legal or factual support is necessary in order ultimately to win them. This game plan[4] should be updated whenever events suggest additional relevant motions. **Section 13.9** lists some of the most frequently used motions as a guideline for analyzing an individual case. Obviously, some cases will generate more motions than others, and torturing facts to make them fit a particular motion is undoubtedly a sign that the motion is inappropriate and may result in the imposition of Rule 11 sanctions.[5] On the other hand, simply ignoring a motion out of ignorance or inability to recognize how it might benefit the overall litigation posture of the case is a disservice to the client.

---

[1] *E.g.*, Fed. R. Civ. P. 11, 37(a)(4).

[2] *See, e.g.*, Faruki, *The Practical Use of Motions to Structure a Complex Civil Case,* 41 Ohio St. L.J. 107 (1980); McElroy, *Federal Pre-Trial Procedure in an Antitrust Suit,* 31 Sw. L.J. 649 (1977).

[3] Fed. R. Civ. P. 42(b); § 16.3.

[4] See also § **17.2** regarding a discovery plan.

[5] See **ch. 28**.

§ 13.2 Procedural Requirements

Rules 5, 6, and 7 apply generally to motion practice. Rule 7(b)(1) requires a motion not made during a hearing or trial to be in writing and to state with particularity its grounds and the relief or order sought. A motion may be combined with a written notice which sets forth the hearing date. Rule 5(a) provides that every motion which is not heard ex parte must be served upon each party who is not in default for failure to appear. Noticed motions must be filed with the court shortly after service; local rules usually require that an affidavit of service also be filed. Motions generally are filed with the district court, but judges may permit papers to be filed with them.[6]

Local rules must always be consulted in motion practice, because their violation can result in the automatic denial or granting of the motion. Not filing a memorandum of law in support of a motion is sufficient ground for denying a motion in many districts. Similarly, failure to file an opposition to a motion can result in the motion's being granted. Having motion papers returned for violation of local court rules is costly, and even if the refiled motion is timely, it probably will be heard at a later date which may not be tactically as advantageous.

Many judges also have their own rules, which are separately available or included as part of the pretrial scheduling order. Furthermore, counsel can assume that most judges are not willing to waive provisions of the local rules. In some districts, improperly formatted motions never even get beyond the clerk's office, which bounces back papers along with a standardized form indicating the reasons why the motion is being returned. The reasons can be as arcane as not having a table of contents, not numbering exhibits to show their number above or below the page number, or not typing the name of the document on every page. After reading the local rules, if counsel is still unsure of the proper format, either call the clerk's office, go there and look at some filed motions or ask colleagues who have practiced in the local federal court to send a copy of documents they have filed. Bender's *Federal Practice Forms* is a multivolume work which can be consulted for general formatting of any pleading or motion. It is also useful to collect precedent files containing federal court pleadings, motions, and discovery.

§ 13.3 Service

If a party is represented by counsel, its attorney must be served unless the court orders service upon the party.[7] Rule 5(b) permits service by delivery or mail.

---

[6] Fed. R. Civ. P. 6(e).

[7] Fed. R. Civ. P. 5(b).

Service by delivery is effectuated by giving a copy of the motion to the attorney or party or leaving it at the individual's office with a clerk or another person in charge or, if there is no one in charge, leaving it in a conspicuous place. If the individual to be served has no office or if the office is closed, the motion may be left at the person's dwelling with some person of suitable age and discretion residing there. Service by mail is complete upon mailing.[8] Rule 6(e) requires that when a paper is served by mail, three days must be added to any prescribed period for response.

§ 13.4 Timing and Notice

The timing of Rule 12 motions and the notice provision of Rule 56 motions are dictated by the federal rules;[9] the timing and notice of most other motions is governed solely by local rules or tactical concerns. It is essential that counsel read the local rules related to motion practice shortly after commencing the action to ensure that any proffered motion is timely and in accord with whatever requirements the rules mandate. Learning that motions related to discovery must be filed within 30 days of the event triggering them or 10 days after the discovery cutoff is futile if that date has already passed. Similarly, many judges require summary judgment motions to be brought as long as 45 days before trial.

Written motions which are not heard ex parte must be served not later than five days before the time specified for the hearing, unless a different time is fixed by rule or court order.[10] Affidavits are served with the motion they support, and opposing affidavits may be served no later than one day before the hearing, unless otherwise permitted.[11] The federal rules specifically provide 10 days' notice of summary judgment motions.[12] However, many courts require 15 to 21 days' notice for all motions in order to guarantee that they are adequately briefed. Rule 6(a) has been modified to exclude weekends and legal holidays from computation when the period prescribed by the rules is less than 11 days. Such notice provisions help to discourage the overused ploy of personally serving papers on a Friday afternoon in the hope that they will not be noticed until Monday or will ruin opposing counsel's weekend. Local rules may also require that an opposition or reply be filed within a given time.

The court has discretion to enlarge most timing and notice requirements in the federal or local rules. However, the timing of Rules 59(e) and 60(b) concerning reopening judgments and 74(a) regarding appeals from the rulings of magistrates cannot be lengthened. Rule 6(b)(1) permits applications to extend time to be

---

[8] *Id.*

[9] See §§ **14.3, 15.3**.

[10] Fed. R. Civ. P. 6(d).

[11] *Id.*

[12] Fed. R. Civ. P. 56(c).

made with or without motion or notice if the request occurs during the prescribed period. Otherwise, Rule 6(b)(2) requires a motion establishing that the failure to act before the expiration of the specified time was a result of excusable neglect.

Counsel should also determine if an oral hearing is generally set or must be specifically requested. Oral argument should never be waived unless the judge is completely hostile to setting a hearing. In courts permitting oral hearings, counsel must determine the earliest appropriate date when the motion can be heard, which must be included in the notice of motion. In a given case, it may also be desirable to clear the date with opposing counsel. Some courts hear motions on any day; other judges assign a specific day each week to hear motions. This may result in the judge's having a full calendar and limiting the amount of time for argument as well as preventing counsel from offering testimony in support of the motion. If a live hearing is desired, it should always be specifically requested.

§ 13.5 Citing Appropriate Law

Practitioners in diversity cases who are unfamiliar with federal practice often cite state cases in their motions. Although state law is determinative on substantive matters, procedural matters are governed by the federal rules, and, therefore, federal cases should be cited, even if the state law is identical. Any federal case law interpreting a state statute should be cited in preference to state cases. For example, in California, the state long-arm statute[13] permits jurisdiction to the extent allowed by the United States Constitution. As a result, the Ninth Circuit has evolved its own method of analyzing due process issues, which it applies to California cases.[14] Arguing California law in a Rule 12(b)(2) motion is not helpful, because federal court can interpret due process without any reference to state law. In such a situation, counsel should cite federal cases exclusively, unless a state case exists with substantially similar facts.

If the motion involves interpretation of state law, decisions of the state supreme court and state appellate courts should be cited. However, there may be issues which are unresolved in state court but which have been interpreted in a particular way by federal case law. If so, the federal position is determinative. However, counsel may be able to argue that later state decisions indicate that the state supreme court would not agree with the federal interpretation of its substantive law.

When choosing which cases to cite, the order of preference is usually as follows: United States Supreme Court, the circuit in which the litigation is proceeding, other circuits, district courts in the relevant circuit, and other

---

[13] Cal. Code Civ. P. § 410.10 (West 1973).

[14] See § **4.11**.

district courts. The Eleventh Circuit adopted as binding all precedent of the former Fifth Circuit handed down prior to October 1, 1981.[15] District court citations are most valuable when authored by the judge deciding the motion or another judge in the district in which the case is pending. However, Federal Supplement and Federal Rules Decisions citations from far-flung districts often are the only support for discovery motions. This results from counsel's inability to obtain an interlocutory appeal of most discovery orders. Therefore, many pretrial issues are never decided by circuit courts because the case settles or the issue is not important enough to be briefed on appeal.

§ 13.6 Researching Federal Law

The first step in researching a motion or opposition is to read the particular statute or rule which authorizes the motion in order to determine any stated criteria for deciding the motion and the type of evidentiary showing required. Researching federal and state law has been vastly simplified by access to computerized sources. However, even computerized research can be more efficient if counsel has some background concerning the disputed issue, as anyone is well aware whose search has dumped out hundreds of cases, no cases, or one case having nothing to do with the problem. This book is intended to assist in the initial research process by identifying citations to case law in several of the larger circuits as well as by providing specific references to *Moore's Federal Practice* and Wright and Miller's *Federal Practice and Procedure.* Both of these multivolume treatises have extensive references to case law in every circuit and should be the starting point of in-depth research. A multivolume set entitled *Federal Litigation Guide,* which focuses on strategic concerns, is also available. Weinstein's *Evidence* is another multivolume treatise which should be consulted regarding evidentiary matters such as privilege. On occasion, an annotation in *American Law Reports Federal* will be directly on point. *Federal Practice Digests* (3d edition) lists cases under West's headnoting system. *Federal Rules Digest* (3d edition) summarizes cases by reference to the appropriate federal rule. The *United States Code Annotated* contains annotations on the federal rules as well as substantive law. Law review articles can also be helpful when the state of the law is unresolved, and they suggest sound arguments which may support counsel's position.

Once relevant cases have been identified, they must be read, regardless of the high esteem in which counsel holds the author who originally cited them. The case may stand for the proposition for which it is cited and still be unhelpful because of its factual context or holding. The next step is to Shepardize cases manually or by computer, not only to check that they are still valid law but also to identify other cases which may be even more significant.

---

[15] Bonner v. City of Prichard, 661 F.2d 1206, 1209 (11th Cir. 1981).

Practitioners who anticipate appearing regularly in federal court should consider attending a federal practice institute. For example, the California Continuing Education of the Bar (C.E.B.) sponsors such an event yearly at which practitioners not only hear panel discussions but also receive program materials of several hundred pages which cover general practice issues as well as circuit precedent. Practicing Law Institute also sponsors civil litigation practice seminars and publishes extended pamphlets containing articles on the topics presented.

Lawyers practicing regularly in federal court often subscribe to the *Federal Litigator,* which digests recent cases as well as presenting articles of interest to practitioners. *Federal Civil Procedure Abstracts* digests law review articles on civil procedure and evidentiary matters. The *Federal Practice Advisory* also highlights developments in federal practice. Some state-oriented publications, such as the California C.E.B. *Civil Litigation Reporter,* report federal cases in the local circuit as well as state cases. On occasion, such publications as *The Practical Lawyer, Trial,* and *Litigation* have articles focusing on pretrial problems. Specialized reporters also exist in a variety of substantive areas and in such fields as class action litigation.

§ 13.7 Writing Memorandum of Points and Authorities

Poorly written memoranda can result in losing a motion which could have been won. Since judges have only a limited time to spend on motion practice, counsel's memorandum supporting or opposing a motion must focus the issues raised, discuss them succinctly, and weave in appropriate references to authorities which are factually and legally on point. Verbose, poorly organized, or confusing memoranda are as ineffective as those which have numerous headings followed by a case quotation and a string citation. Putting together a memorandum requires counsel to determine which issues are really important and which cases are most persuasive as well as to write a well crafted argument. The goal is to persuade the judge without exaggerating the facts or law, because overstatement is easy for opposing counsel to target and use to damage the memorandum's credibility. In constructing the motion, a strong factual opening statement should be followed by counsel's strongest or most interesting argument. However, care must be taken that the rest of the memo does not fall flat. If affidavits are required or helpful to focus the issues, they should be submitted with the motion. Supporting exhibits should also be selected carefully and should be short enough so that the judge might actually read them.

There are many sources for ideas about how to structure arguments and write clearly, including references recommended in appellate cases by judges who are tired of reading poorly framed briefs.[16] Although some focus on appellate

[16] *See, e.g.,* Zaidi v. Ehrlich, 732 F.2d 1218, 1220 (5th Cir. 1984).

writing or are written primarily for law students, they offer suggestions which also apply to federal motion practice. The following books are devoted to writing:

N. Brand & J. White, *Legal Writing, The Strategy of Persuasion* (1976)

J. Dernbach & R. Singleton, *A Practical Guide to Legal Writing & Legal Method* (1981)

R. Flesch, *How to Write Plain English* (1979)

M. Fontham, *Written and Oral Advocacy* (1985)

M. Moskovitz, *Winning an Appeal* (1983)

M. Pittoni, *Brief Writing and Argumentation* (3d ed. 1967)

W. Strunk & E.B. White, *The Elements of Style* (3d ed. 1979)

R. Wydick, *Plain English for Lawyers* (2d ed. 1985)

Other references include:

R. Haydock, D. Herr, & J. Stempel, *Fundamentals of Pretrial Litigation* chs. 10 and 13 (1985)

Gibson, *Effective Legal Writing and Speaking,* 36 Bus Law. 1 (Nov. 1980)

Gobold, *Twenty Pages and Twenty Minutes—Effective Advocacy,* 30 S.W.L.J. 801 (1976)

Katz and Felshman, *Lawyers' Language—Some Suggestions for Incorporating Techniques of Advocacy Into the Appellate Brief,* 9 L. Contemp. L. 127 (1983)

Kolin and Marquardt, *Research on Legal Writing: A Bibliography,* 78 Law Library J. 493 (1986)

Tate, *Federal Appellate Advocacy in the 1980s,* 5 Am. J. Trial Advocacy 63 (1981).

Local rules should always be consulted for stylistic quirks or preferred citation format. Otherwise, *A Uniform System of Citation* (14th ed. 1986) should be used for citation form.

§ 13.8 Ethical Considerations

Motions are often used to gain strategic advantage as well as to determine issues in the case. Rule 11[17] now requires counsel to certify that all motions and other

---

[17] See **ch. 28**.

papers are well grounded in fact, warranted by existing law or a good faith argument for the extension, modification, or reversal of existing law, and not interposed for any improper purpose such as to harass or to cause unnecessary delay or needless increase in the cost of litigation. Violations of this certification result in sanctions, which consist mainly of reimbursing the opposing party's attorneys' fees. Therefore, bringing or opposing a motion should be viewed not only as a tactical decision but also as a question of counsel's responsibility under Rule 11 and the appropriate ethical codes. Foe example, failure to cite controlling authority which contradicts the cases or theory which counsel relies upon may be viewed as both a Rule 11 and an ethical violation, [18] as is bringing a motion for improper purposes.[19]

In general, Rule 11 is being used to curtail "sharp practices" by providing an enforcement mechanism for both unethical and objectively unreasonable conduct by counsel. Although Rule 11 does not cover every ethical violation, it provides an objective standard which judges can apply instead of relying on infrequently used bar disciplinary actions. It is no longer uncommon for district and appellate court judges to admonish counsel for violation of their Rule 11 obligations even when other penalties are not imposed. As a practical matter, the possibility of being rebuked in such a manner is rapidly becoming an effective means of promoting a higher standard of ethics in federal motion practice as well as discouraging bogus motions and oppositions.

§ 13.9 List of Frequently Used Federal Motions

Determining which motion to bring depends on several factors including:

1. Knowledge of the existence of the motion
2. Knowledge of any timing or other requirements
3. An understanding of the relationship between the chosen motion and other motions which can be brought concurrently or sequentially, and
4. An evaluation of the relative benefits of winning the motion versus the economic and strategic costs of losing it.

When structuring the case by use of appropriate motions, counsel should consider the availability of the following regularly used federal motions, which are cross-referenced to the sections in which they are discussed in greater detail.

---

[18] Model Rules of Professional Conduct Rule 3.3(a)(3) (1983); Model Code of Professional Responsibility, DR 7-106(B)(1) (1980).

[19] *See* Model Code of Professional Responsibility DR 7-102(A)(1), (2) (1980); *cf.* Model Rules of Professional Conduct Rule 3.4(d) (1983) (prohibiting making frivolous discovery request or opposition).

Motions Challenging The Existence or Exercise of Subject Matter Jurisdiction

1. Rule 12(b)(1) dismissal motion (can be brought with Rule 12 motions, but never waived; untimely motions brought pursuant to 12(h)(3)) (see **ch. 2** and §§ **14.8–14.16**)
2. Motion challenging standing (see § **2.3**)
3. Motion to abstain from exercising jurisdiction (should be brought early, but no time restriction) (see § **2.6**)
4. Motion to stay pending litigation (should be brought early, but no time restriction) (see § **2.6**)
5. Motion to remand removed case (subject to waiver if defect is technical rather than going to absence of subject matter) (see § **3.16**)
6. Motion to dismiss ancillary or pendent claims (see §§ **2.25–2.30**)

Challenging Personal Jurisdiction

1. Rule 12(b)(2) motion (Rule 12 timing, subject to waiver) (see **ch. 4** and §§ **14.17–14.31**)
2. 28 U.S.C. § 1631 motion to transfer without jurisdiction (often brought in response to 12(b)(2) motion, no timing restriction) (see §§ **6.9** and **14.30**)

Challenging Improper or Inconvenient Venue

1. Rule 12(b)(3) dismissal motion (Rule 12 timing, subject to waiver) (see §§ **14.31–14.37**)
2. 28 U.S.C. § 1406(a) dismissal or transfer motion for improper venue (Rule 12 timing, subject to waiver) (see § **6.9**)
3. 28 U.S.C. § 1404(a) motion to transfer for convenience of witnesses (often brought alternatively to Rule 12(b)(2) or (3) motion, no timing restriction) (see §§ **6.7 and 6.8**)
4. Forum Non Conveniens dismissal motion (should be brought early, often brought alternatively to Rule 12(b)(2) motion, but has no timing restriction) (see §§ **6.15–6.21**)

Challenging Service of Complaint

1. Rule 12(b)(4) dismissal for insufficiency of process, (motion is rarely applicable; Rule 12 timing, subject to waiver) (see **ch. 5** and § **14.38**)

2. Rule 12(b)(5) dismissal for insufficiency of service of process (Rule 12 timing, subject to waiver) (see **ch. 5** and §§ **14.38–14.40**)
3. Rule 4(j) motion to dismiss for failure to serve within 120 days (no timing restriction, but subject to waiver) (see §§ **5.11–5.12**)

Challenging the Claim

1. Rule 12(b)(6) dismissal for failure to state a claim, (Rule 12 timing, but no waiver - late motion may be treated as 12(c) motion; 12(b)(6) motion can be brought alternatively as summary judgment motion) (see §§ **14.41–14.52**)
2. Rule 9 dismissal for failure to plead with particularity (often brought as a Rule 12(b)(6) motion) (see §§ **7.3** and **14.41–14.52**)
3. Rule 12(c) motion for judgment on the pleadings (only timing restriction is that it cannot delay trial; may be treated as summary judgment motion) (see §§ **14.54** and **14.55**)
4. Rule 56 motion for summary judgment (10-days' notice) (see **ch. 15**)

Discovery Motions

1. Rule 26(b)(4) motion for deposition of expert (see **ch. 20**)
2. Rule 26(c) motion for protective order (see **ch. 19**)
3. Rule 26(f) motion for discovery conference (see § **19.1**)
4. Rule 28 motion for commission or letter rogatory regarding international discovery (see § **22.3**)
5. Rule 34 motion to preserve documents (see § **25.8**)
6. Rule 35(a) motion for mental or physical examination (see § **25.11**)
7. Rule 36 motion to confirm or withdraw admission (see §§ **26.6** and **26.7**)
8. Rule 37 motion to compel discovery (see **ch. 29**)
9. Rule 45 motion to quash subpoena (see **ch. 21**)

Discovery and Pretrial Sanctions Motions

1. Attorneys' fees: Rules 11, 16(f), and 37, 28 U.S.C. § 1927, inherent powers, local rules (see **chs. 27–31**)
2. Dismissals and defaults: Rules 16(f), 37, and 41(b), inherent powers, local rules (see **chs. 27–31**)
3. Other sanctions: Rules 16(f), 37, and 41(b), inherent powers, local rules, criminal contempt, civil contempt, fines (see **chs. 27–31**)

Other Motions

1. Rule 6(b) motion to enlarge timing (see passim)
2. Rule 12(b)(7) motion to dismiss for failure to join indispensable party (Rule 12 timing, but not subject to waiver) (see §§ **9.3** and **14.53**)
3. Rule 12(e) motion for more definite statement (Rule 12 timing, subject to waiver; disfavored motion) (see § **14.58**)
4. Rule 12(f) motion to strike (20 days after pleading served requiring response; disfavored motion) (see §§ **14.59** and **14.60**)
5. Rule 13 motions to add or dismiss counterclaim or cross-claim (see §§ **7.9–7.12**)
6. Rule 14 motions to add or dismiss third party complaint (see §§ **7.13** and **7.14**)
7. Rule 15(a) motion to amend pleadings (see **ch. 8**)
8. Rule 21 motions to add or drop parties (see **ch. 9**)
9. Rules 22 & 67 motions concerning interpleader (see § **9.6**)
10. Rule 23 class action motions (see **ch. 10**):
    - **a.** Certification (must be brought as practicable)
    - **b.** Motion challenging settlement, and
    - **c.** Motion for attorney's fees
11. Rule 23.1 motions challenging derivative shareholders' action (see § **10.18**)
12. Rule 24 motions requesting or challenging intervention (see §§ **9.7–9.9**)
13. Rule 25 motion to substitute parties (see § **9.10**)
14. Rule 39(b) motion to request a jury trial which has been previously waived (see §§ **3.22** and **7.17**)
15. Rule 41(a) motion to voluntarily dismiss (see § **12.6**)
16. Rule 42 motion to bifurcate or consolidate (see § **16.3**)
17. Rule 53 motion to refer matter to master (see §§ **16.15** and **16.16**)
18. Rule 55 motion for default or to reopen default (see § **12.3**)
19. Rule 59(e) motion to alter or amend judgment (see § **12.3** and passim)
20. Rule 60(b) motion for relief from judgment (see § **12.3** and passim)
21. Rule 64 motions challenging provisional remedies (see § **11.8**)
22. Rule 65 motion for TRO or injunction (see **ch. 11**)
23. Rule 65.1 motion to proceed against sureties (see § **11.10**)
24. Rule 66 motion to appoint receiver (see § **11.9**)
25. Rule 72 motion to refer matter to magistrate (see §§ **16.10–16.14**)

26. Pretrial in limine evidentiary motions (see § **16.3**)
27. Motion enforcing settlement (see § **16.7**)
28. Motion disqualifying judge (see § **16.8**)
29. Motion disqualifying opposing counsel (see § **16.9**)
30. Motion enforcing or staying arbitration (see § **1.12**)

CHAPTER 14

RULE 12 MOTIONS

PRELIMINARY MATTERS

§ 14.1 Factors To Be Considered by Moving Party

Rule 12 is a powerful weapon which enables the defendant to control the litigation from its onset by bringing any of ten motions, nine of which delay the timing for answering the complaint. Not only can these motions set the tone of the litigation by clarifying the plaintiff's theory of the case, delaying discovery on the merits, or transferring the case to a more favorable forum but, in addition, several of the motions can result in a speedy judgment or a dismissal which absolutely or effectively terminates litigation. Referring to Rule 12 practice may be misleading since each of the motions has its own evidentiary and substantive requirements and results in a different type of order.

Since some of the Rule 12 motions are considered to be merely dilatory, rather than affecting the ultimate disposition of the case, courts are usually not favorably disposed to these motions. Even those Rule 12 motions which result in termination are considered by some to be based on technicalities rather than the merits of the action. Conversely, Rule 12 motions which affect the merits through conversion to summary judgment are difficult to win because they shortcut the plaintiff's ability to obtain discovery and a jury trial. Moreover, notice pleading and the liberal amendment policy embodied in the federal rules fosters the policy of not rejecting pleadings for failure to state a claim "by sweeping aside the hypertechnical pleading rules that once defeated many an unwary but meritorious claimant . . . ."[1] Thus, in order to obtain favorable Rule 12 ruling, counsel must satisfy exacting requirements.

Since all but three of the Rule 12 motions must be brought early in the action, counsel must not only be aware of the rule as an alternative to pleading but also must seriously consider at the commencement of litigation whether any Rule 12 defenses which are subject to waiver are applicable. In essence, Rule 12 should be viewed as a framework for analyzing the complaint. Although the rule is designed to shake out cases which do not belong in federal court on procedural and substantive grounds, it also ensures that a defendant cannot bring a series of motions merely to delay the proceedings. However, meeting the early deadline can be both time-consuming and costly at a point in time when counsel knows very little about the action.

Although Rule 12 motions should not be brought routinely, they also should not be overlooked, or at a later point in the litigation counsel may discover that the best defense to the action has already been lost. Assuming that the motion is unlikely to be granted before discovery begs the question, because a few of the Rule 12 motions look solely to the pleadings, and other Rule 12 motions can be filed with a request for the discovery necessary to support them. In addition, since motions challenging personal jurisdiction and venue usually focus on the defendant rather than the plaintiff, discovery is not necessary to document such allegations.

An important benefit of bringing a Rule 12 motion is the possibility of limiting discovery on the merits of the action until after the resolution of the motion. Courts will generally grant a stay of discovery if the motion is potentially dispositive of the action, for example, a challenge to the court's personal or subject matter jurisdiction or the existence of a claim for which relief can be granted. Therefore, the Rule 12 motion enables counsel not only to avoid answering the complaint, but also to avoid costly and possibly embarrassing discovery. Obviously, if the motion is successful, it is a relatively inexpensive and immediate victory. However, even if the motion is denied, additional time has been gained in which to determine strategy.

The only defenses which cannot be waived if brought sequentially are lack of subject matter jurisdiction, failure to state a claim for which relief can be granted, and failure to join an indispensable party. Of course, these motions can be brought together with the Rule 12 motions, which is desirable if they can be quickly researched, because they can terminate the litigation. In particular, the Rule 12(b)(6) motion for failure to state a claim should be timely brought. No discovery is required, because the motion is based strictly on the pleadings. If no

[1] Auster Oil & Gas, Inc. v. Stream, 764 F.2d 381, 386 (5th Cir. 1985).

other Rule 12 motion is applicable, the defendant must answer the complaint unless the 12(b)(6) motion is timely brought. Moreover, counsel may decide that the motion has a better chance of succeeding before an answer is filed or discovery begins on the merits of the action, because the plaintiff may obtain information which enables it to add new causes of action. At a minimum, if early settlement is desirable, the defendant may not wish to reveal any factual matter necessary to the answer before the motion is decided.

As with all motions, counsel must decide if a valid factual basis exists for bringing the motion or suffer the possible penalties of sanctions being levied under Rule 11.[2] Similarly, the cost effectiveness of the motion must be considered. Will it really terminate the litigation or encourage early settlement or will it result only in delay and substantial bills to the client? Needless to say, if the motion has merit, strategic reasons may favor bringing it, even though the chance of ultimate success is not overwhelming. However, in such cases, counsel should remember that some federal judges are not favorably inclined toward motions which are aimed primarily at educating them. Since all aspects of the case are controlled by one judge, a dilatory motion may result in the court's being unfavorably impressed with counsel and more likely to deny favorable discretionary rulings or, worse, more willing to sanction counsel if requested. Thus, if a Rule 12(b)(6) motion challenges a point which can be easily corrected, it is better practice to call opposing counsel and stipulate to an amendment. On the other hand, if the complaint is hopelessly drafted, even though it can be salvaged, a motion will bring the opposing counsel's sloppiness to the attention of the court. Indeed, if the amended complaint is equally poorly drawn, a second motion may be in order. After several unsuccessful attempts to amend, a court can fairly assume that the complaint cannot be amended to state a claim.[3] Dismissal of a complaint, even if without prejudice, is a potent remedy, because it often pushes the plaintiff beyond the applicable statute of limitations period. Of course, in moving to dismiss, the possibility of appeal must always be considered, because disposition on the merits is preferred over technical dismissals. Thus, counsel should also evaluate whether the decision will stand on appeal. However, a successful result in the trial court may, as a practical matter, end the case or encourage settlement on terms extremely favorable for the defendant.

§ 14.2 Factors To Be Considered by Defending Party

If counsel has been served with a Rule 12 motion, the first step is to determine its exact nature. If it is to strike unnecessary language in the complaint or for a more

---

[2] *See, e.g.*, Lucha, Inc. v. Goeglein, 575 F. Supp. 785, 788 E.D. Mo. 1983) (sanctions imposed for baseless motion to dismiss); see **ch. 28**.

[3] See **ch. 8**.

definite statement, the outcome of the motion may not be significant. Similarly, if a defect in service is being claimed, it may be feasible to serve the defendant again without running afoul of statute of limitations problems. On the other hand, if the result of the motion will be a dismissal which effectively terminates the litigation, counsel's response must be effective and raise all appropriate objections in order to ensure that the case will not be prematurely aborted. Second, counsel should determine whether the motion has been timely brought, because all but three of the Rule 12 motions are waived if not brought within the appropriate period. Third, a continuance of the hearing and time to respond should be sought if the motion is one which can be defeated only after discovery. Alternatively, if counsel believes the motion is likely to be denied, but additional discovery is necessary to ensure that result, consider indicating the exact nature of any additional discovery in the opposition. For example, in a response to a motion challenging personal jurisdiction over the defendant, the plaintiff can include a request for discovery concerning the defendant's contacts with the forum in the event that the court is inclined to grant the motion.

In responding to any Rule 12 motion, counsel must decide what information the court is entitled to review in reaching its decision. Care must be taken to view each Rule 12 motion separately, because the motions have entirely different standards of proof and evidentiary requirements. For example it could be a costly mistake to submit affidavits in response to a Rule 12(b)(6) or 12(c) motion, because they can be considered only if the court converts the motion into one for summary judgment. Thus, by such a response, counsel has in essence requested a resolution on the merits rather than on the pleadings. On the other hand, the plaintiff must respond to affidavits submitted with a 12(b)(2) motion challenging personal jurisdiction in order to withstand the motion.

Counsel should also consult the local court rules to determine whether a written opposition must be served, because failure to respond may waive counsel's right to object to the requested relief. There is disagreement as to whether a dismissal or entry of an adverse summary judgment is proper on the technical grounds that a response was not filed.[4] If the court relies on such a rule, it can dismiss only the claims to which the motion is addressed, not the entire action.[5] However, it is much safer to determine the rules in advance than to be forced to argue their inapplicability or inequitable outcome after failing to comply with them.

If a frivolous Rule 12 motion is brought, counsel can consider requesting sanctions under Rule 11.[6] Rule 11 is applicable even if the motion is not

---

[4] *Compare* Jacobsen v. Fuller, 790 F.2d 1362, 1364 (9th Cir. 1986) *and* Tarpley v. Green, 684 F.2d 1, 6, 7 (D.C. Cir. 1982) (affirming terminations) *with* Dixie Stevedores, Inc. v. Marinic Maritime, Ltd., 778 F.2d 670, 672–73 (11th Cir. 1985); John v. Louisiana, 757 F.2d 698, 707–09 (5th Cir. 1985); *and* Maggette v. Dalsheim, 709 F.2d 800, 802 (2d Cir. 1983) (reversing terminations); *see also* Greene v. Union Mut. Life Ins. Co. of Am., 764 F.2d 19, 22–23 (1st Cir. 1985) (remanding dismissed action for Rule 60(b) consideration).

[5] Greene v. Union Mut. Life Ins. Co. of Am., 764 F.2d 19, 22 (1st Cir. 1985).

[6] *See, e.g.*, Lucha, Inc. v. Goeglein, 575 F. Supp. 785, 788 (E.D. Mo. 1983).

frivolous but is brought only for delay or to unnecessarily increase the cost of litigation.[7] However, since Rule 11 deters a wealthy defendant from drowning its opponent in a sea of paper motions, plaintiffs must treat all Rule 12 motions seriously because a defendant has decided to move despite the risk of sanctions.

§ 14.3 Timing

Rule 12(a) provides that a defendant must serve its answer within 20 days after the service of the summons and complaint, unless service is made under Rule 4(e) and prescribes a different time. A party served with a cross-claim has 20 days to answer after service, and a reply to a counterclaim in the answer is due within 20 days after service of the answer or court order directing the answer unless the order otherwise directs. The United States has 60 days rather than 20 days for its answer to a complaint, cross-claim or reply to a counterclaim. These times can be modified only by the court; thus, approval of any stipulation extending time is required. If an extension has been allowed for filing a responsive pleading, it applies to the motion as well,[8] but to be safe, any stipulation or order should be drafted explicitly to include time to answer or otherwise respond.

Service of a Rule 12 motion alters the time to answer. Unless a different time is fixed by the court, a responsive pleading is not required until 10 days after the court notifies the party that the motion is denied or postponed until trial. Although nothing in the rule prohibits the filing of a motion to dismiss with an answer,[9] usually there is no advantage to filing an answer until the motion is denied. If the court grants a motion for a more definite statement, the responsive pleading must be served within 10 days after the service of the more definite statement. No provision for extension is provided concerning the grant of a motion to strike. This omission has been viewed as unintended and has not resulted in any technical defaults.[10] Since a party's time to respond is not extended by the fact that a codefendant has moved to dismiss, a default can be granted against the nonresponding coparty.[11] Although the rule is silent as to whether counsel must answer causes of actions not encompassed in its Rule 12 motion, in practice, defaults are not granted in such cases.

If the plaintiff amends the complaint, the defendant can replead but is required to answer only new material in the complaint. Similarly, the amended complaint does not revive the defendant's right to bring Rule 12 motions on grounds already

---

[7] See **ch. 28**.

[8] Bechtel v. Liberty Nat'l Bank, 534 F.2d 1335, 1341 (9th Cir. 1976).

[9] Beary v. West Pub. Co., 763 F.2d 66, 68 (2d Cir.), *cert. denied,* _____ U.S. _____, 106 S. Ct. 232 (1985).

[10] *See* 5 C. Wright, A. Miller, *et al.,* Federal Practice and Procedure § 1346, at 532 (1969) [hereinafter Federal Practice and Procedure].

[11] *See id.* § 1346, at 167 (Supp. 1985).

waived. Of course, additional Rule 12 motions can be directed at new matters in the complaint.[12] Motions pending before the complaint is amended should be reasserted or the court notified of counsel's intention to direct them to the amended pleadings.

§ 14.4 Procedure

Rule 12(b) requires that every defense be asserted in the responsive pleading except for those brought by Rule 12(b)(1)-(7). Thus, even those defenses which are permitted by Rule 12(b)(1)-(7) can be raised in the answer, although this procedure is usually not followed in favor of bringing an immediate motion.

Often the party needs discovery in order to support the motion. If so, the discovery should be requested before or at the same time as the motion. An extension to respond to the complaint or supplement the motion should also be requested while discovery concerning the motion is outstanding. Similarly, the plaintiff should request additional time to respond to the motion as well as a postponement of the hearing if other discovery is necessary. In order to preserve the discovery issue for appeal, the reason for such requests should be spelled out in the motion and accompanied by the specific discovery requests. The defendant should consider moving to limit outstanding discovery to the matters encompassed in the motion. Often the court is amenable to such limitations if successful resolution of the motion will result in the termination of litigation in federal court.[13]

Since the defendant has only 10 days to serve its answer after denial of the motion, counsel should consider immediately requesting additional time if the ruling is made orally, because the court must approve any stipulation to extend time under Rule 12(a). Any written stipulation entered before the defendant has answered or brought a Rule 12 motion should refer to additional time to respond rather than to answer, to avoid claims that the time was granted solely for the defendant to answer the complaint or that the defendant waived any jurisdictional defense in agreeing to the stipulation.[14] Conversely, the plaintiff must ensure that the stipulation does not inadvertently permit an extension of any statute of limitations which applies to potential counterclaims available to the defendant.[15]

---

[12] *Id.* § 1347.

[13] See **ch. 19**.

[14] *See, e.g.*, Browne, *The Leave to Plead as a Waiver of the Jurisdictional Defenses*, 32 Clev. St. L. Rev. 431 (1983–84) (analysis of Ohio Rules, which are patterned after Federal Rules).

[15] *See* Sea-Land Serv., Inc. v. R.V. D'Alfonso Co., 727 F.2d 1, 2–3 (1st Cir. 1984) (stipulation allowing additional time to answer extended statute of limitations for defendant's counterclaim).

§ 14.5 Preliminary Hearings

Rule 12(d) authorizes that defenses enumerated in Rule 12(b)(1)-(7) and 12(c) shall be heard and determined before trial on application of any party, unless the court orders the hearing deferred until the trial. It does not matter whether the defenses are raised by pleading or motion for purposes of these sections. Usually, the only motions deferred are those which intertwine with the merits of the action.[16] Affirmative defenses not within Rule 12(b)(1)–(7) are technically not within this provision, but courts have the power to consider pretrial motions pursuant to their inherent powers.

§ 14.6 Sua Sponte Dismissals

The court on its own initiative can note the inadequacy of a complaint under Rule 12(b) and dismiss it for failure to state a claim,[17] failure to join an indispensable party,[18] or for lack of subject matter jurisdiction. A subject matter dismissal in an in forma pauperis action can even be granted before issuance of a summons or other procedural requirements.[19]

The procedural requirements vary concerning sua sponte dismissals for failure to state a claim. Several circuits require service of the complaint and notice to all parties of any proposed dismissal with prejudice, as well as an opportunity to respond.[20] If the dismissal is without prejudice, at least one circuit requires only that the court allow some opportunity for the plaintiff to amend the complaint or respond to the proposed dismissal.[21] Other circuits require issuance and service of process, as well as notification to the plaintiff to permit written argument or amendment.[22] If the court sua sponte dismisses the complaint after service, several circuits do not require a hearing as long as

---

[16] *See* 2A J. Moore *et al.*, Moore's Federal Practice ¶ 12.16 (2d ed. 1986) [hereinafter Moore's Federal Practice].

[17] See extensive citations in Shawnee Int'l, N.V. v. Hondo Drilling Co., 742 F.2d 234, 236 (5th Cir. 1984); *see also* Martin-Trigona v. Stewart, 691 F.2d 856, 858 (8th Cir. 1982).

[18] Provident Tradesmens Bank & Trust Co. v. Patterson, 390 U.S. 102, 110 (1968).

[19] Franklin v. Oregon State Welfare Div., 662 F.2d 1337, 1342 (9th Cir. 1981).

[20] *E.g.*, Franklin v. Murphy, 745 F.2d 1221, 1226 (9th Cir. 1984); Salibra v. Supreme Court of Ohio, 730 F.2d 1059, 1062 (6th Cir.), *cert. denied*, 469 U.S. 917 (1984); *see also* Square D. Co. v. Niagara Frontier Tariff Bureau, Inc., 760 F.2d 1347, 1365 (2d Cir. 1985), *aff'd on other grounds*, ___ U.S. ___, 106 S. Ct. 1922 (1986); Literature, Inc. v. Quinn, 482 F.2d 372, 374 (1st Cir. 1973).

[21] Morrison v. Tomano, 755 F.2d 515, 517 (6th Cir. 1985).

[22] Franklin v. Oregon State Welfare Div., 662 F.2d 1337, 1341 (9th Cir. 1981); *cf.* Nichols v. Schubert, 499 F.2d 946, 947 (7th Cir. 1974) (service required).

sufficient basis for the court's action appears from the pleadings.[23] Similarly, a court can dismiss an action sua sponte under Rule 12(c) when the parties have had an opportunity to be heard on the legal issues in the case.[24]

§ 14.7 Pro Se In Forma Pauperis Dismissals

One context in which the court's sua sponte power to dismiss a case is frequently litigated is when the judge dismisses a pro se action as frivolous or malicious under 28 U.S.C. § 1915. This section embodies a delicate balance between the free access to the courts granted to indigent litigants and the need to curb abuses necessarily associated with in forma pauperis litigation.[25] Most circuits have accorded trial courts broad discretion to dismiss complaints as frivolous,[26] although arbitrary rulings are reversed.[27] Whether the dismissal is with prejudice is unclear, but such dismissals appear to be reserved for cases in which bad faith, litigiousness, or manipulative tactics exist.[28] The court can also restrict access to the courts for frequent filings of frivolous, repetitious lawsuits,[29] and can assign Rule 11 sanctions to pro se litigants.[30]

Pro se complaints, however inartfully pleaded, are held to less stringent standards than formal pleadings drafted by lawyers.[31] The allegations in pro se complaints are taken as true and construed in favor of the plaintiff for this determination.[32] Although the court has the power to appoint counsel for indigent civil litigant cases,[33] this is rarely done, and some circuits view § 1915(d) as not authorizing appointment without compensation.[34]

---

[23] *See* Leonhard v. United States, 633 F.2d 599, 609 n.11 (2d Cir. 1980), *cert. denied,* 451 U.S. 908 (1981); Bryson v. Brand Insulations, Inc., 621 F.2d 556, 559 (3d Cir. 1980); Tamari v. Bache & Co., (Lebanon) S.A.L., 565 F.2d 1194, 1198 (7th Cir. 1977), *cert. denied,* 435 U.S. 905 (1978).

[24] Flora v. Home Fed. Sav. & Loan Ass'n, 685 F.2d 209, 211 (7th Cir. 1982).

[25] Jones v. Morris, 777 F.2d 1277, 1279 (7th Cir. 1985); Phillips v. Mashburn, 746 F.2d 782, 784 (11th Cir. 1984).

[26] Malone v. Colyer, 710 F.2d 258, 260 (6th Cir. 1983); *see* Green v. McKaskle, 788 F.2d 1116, 1119 (5th Cir. 1986); Anderson v. Coughlin, 700 F.2d 37, 42 (2d Cir. 1983).

[27] Malone v. Colyer, 710 F.2d 258, 260 (6th Cir. 1983).

[28] *See* Lay v. Justices—Middle Dist. Court, 811 F.2d 285, 286 (5th Cir. 1987); Camp v. Oliver, 798 F.2d 434, 437–38 (11th Cir. 1986); Harris v. Cuyler, 664 F.2d 388, 390–91 (3d Cir. 1981).

[29] *See* Procup v. Strickland, 792 F.2d 1069, 1072–74 (11th Cir. 1986); Urban v. United Nations, 768 F.2d 1497, 1499–1500 (D.C. Cir. 1985).

[30] Cotner v. Hopkins, 795 F.2d 900, 902 (10th Cir. 1986).

[31] Hughes v. Rowe, 499 U.S. 5, 9 (1980) (per curiam) (quoting Haines v. Kerner, 404 U.S. 519, 520 (1972)); see **ch. 7**.

[32] Westlake v. Lucas, 537 F.2d 857, 858 (6th Cir. 1976).

[33] *See* Hodge v. Police Officers, 802 F.2d 58, 60–62 (2d Cir. 1986); Cookish v. Cunningham, 787 F.2d 1, 2 (1st Cir. 1986) (extensive citations); *see also* Jackson v. Dallas Police Dep't, 811 F.2d 260, 262 (5th Cir. 1986) (appointment of counsel in exceptional cases).

[34] *See* United States v. 30.64 Acres of Land, 795 F.2d 796, 798–802 (9th Cir. 1986).

The standard for determining frivolousness varies among the circuits. Several circuits use the 12(b)(6) standard of allowing a dismissal only if it appears beyond doubt that the plaintiff can prove no set of facts in support of the claim.[35] A few circuits determine whether the action has arguable substance in law and fact.[36] Still others consider whether a plaintiff can make a rational argument on the law and facts in support of the claim.[37] The Fifth Circuit has articulated three different standards for dismissal: (1) the 12(b)(6) standard; (2) whether the plaintiff's realistic chances of ultimate success are slight; and (3) whether the complaint has no arguable merit in law or fact.[38] Although those circuits which define frivolousness differently from the 12(b)(6) standard appear to permit dismissals of complaints which state a claim,[39] most cases cited for this proposition can be fitted into traditional 12(b)(6) procedure. For example, a complaint can be dismissed under 12(b)(6) if it merely recites bare legal conclusions without supporting facts or if the allegations are contradicted by facts which are judicially noticed.[40] Similarly, dismissal is proper when the defense is complete and obvious from the face of the pleadings or the court's own records.[41] On the other hand, the Fifth Circuit has emphasized that § 1915(d) determinations should not be confused with determinations made under the federal rules[42] and has even adopted procedures to determine the merit of the complaint, including a preservice questionnaire sent to prisoners and, when appropriate, an evidentiary hearing held before a magistrate.[43] If a hearing is held, the only credibility determination which is permitted concerns the inherent plausibility of the allegations based on objective factors, not the demeanor of witnesses or the witness's prior criminal record.[44] Therefore, if the parties differ as to their version of the facts, that conflict is to be determined by the ultimate trier of fact, unless the allegations are almost impossible to prove or conflict with judicially noticed facts.[45]

---

[35] *See* Massop v. Coughlin, 770 F.2d 299, 301 (2d Cir. 1985); Phillips v. Mashburn, 746 F.2d 782, 784 (11th Cir. 1984); Horsey v. Asher, 741 F.2d 209, 211 (8th Cir. 1984); Malone v. Culyer, 710 F.2d 258, 260 (6th Cir. 1983).

[36] Brandon v. D.C. Bd. of Parole, 734 F.2d 56, 59 (D.C. Cir. 1984), *cert. denied,* 469 U.S. 1127 (1985); Franklin v. Murphy, 745 F.2d 1221, 1227 (9th Cir. 1984); Boyce v. Alizaduh, 595 F.2d 948, 952 (4th Cir. 1979).

[37] Jones v. Morris, 777 F.2d 1277, 1278–79 (7th Cir. 1985); Wiggins v. New Mexico State Supreme Court Clerk, 664 F.2d 812, 815 (10th Cir. 1981), *cert. denied,* 459 U.S. 840 (1982).

[38] Green v. McKaskle, 788 F.2d 1116, 1120 (5th Cir. 1986).

[39] Franklin v. Murphy, 745 F.2d 1221, 1228 (9th Cir. 1984).

[40] *See, e.g.,* Taylor v. Gibson, 529 F.2d 709, 717 (5th Cir. 1976).

[41] Franklin v. Murphy, 745 F.2d 1221, 1228 (9th Cir. 1984); *see* 2A Moore's Federal Practice ¶ 2.07[2.-5].

[42] Green v. McKaskle, 788 F.2d 1116, 1120 (5th Cir. 1986).

[43] Cay v. Estelle, 789 F.2d 318, 323 (5th Cir. 1986).

[44] *Id.* at 326–27.

[45] *Id.* at 327.

If the court finds the complaint is frivolous, most circuits permit dismissal of the action prior to service of process.[46] Complaints can be dismissed under § 1915 prior to service even in circuits requiring service for complaints other than those filed in forma pauperis.[47] However, the court usually requires service of process and the defendant's answer before making such a decision.[48] Several circuits strongly disfavor sua sponte dismissals of pro se prisoner petitions before service and filing of a response.[49] Similarly, lack of personal jurisdiction and venue have been considered insufficient reason to refuse in forma pauperis status, since they are waivable defenses.[50] A number of circuits request the district court to prepare a statement of reasons for dismissal unless the basis is evident on the face of the complaint.[51]

SUBJECT MATTER JURISDICTION

§ 14.8 Motions Challenging Subject Matter Jurisdiction

A motion to dismiss for lack of subject matter jurisdiction can either attack the allegations of the complaint or be a "speaking motion" attacking the existence of jurisdiction in fact.[52] Depending upon the nature of the jurisdictional attack, the district court has the power to dismiss for lack of subject matter jurisdiction on the basis of the complaint alone; the complaint supplemented by undisputed facts evidenced in the record; or the complaint supplemented by undisputed facts plus the court's resolution of disputed facts.[53] If the jurisdictional challenge does not implicate the merits of the action, jurisdiction must be established both facially

---

[46] Harris v. Johnson, 784 F.2d 222, 223–34 (6th Cir. 1986); McCone v. Holiday Inn Convention Center, 797 F.2d 853, 854 (10th Cir. 1986); Phillips v. Mashburn, 746 F.2d 782, 784 (11th Cir. 1984); Franklin v. Murphy, 745 F.2d 1221, 1226 (9th Cir. 1984); LeGrand v. Evan, 702 F.2d 415, 417 (2d Cir. 1983); Martin-Trigona v. Stewart, 691 F.2d 856, 857 (8th Cir. 1982) (per curiam); Hogan v. Midland County Comm'rs Court, 680 F.2d 1101, 1102 (5th Cir. 1982).

[47] Spruytte v. Walters, 753 F.2d 498, 500 (6th Cir. 1985), *cert. denied,* ____ U.S. ____, 106 S. Ct. 788 (1986).

[48] Phillips v. Mashburn, 746 F.2d 782, 784 (11th Cir. 1984); Anderson v. Coughlin, 700 F.2d 37, 41 (2d Cir. 1983).

[49] Munz v. Parr, 758 F.2d 1254, 1258 (8th Cir. 1985); Salibra v. Supreme Court of Ohio, 730 F.2d 1059, 1062 (6th Cir.), *cert. denied,* 469 U.S. 917 (1984); Bayron v. Trudeau, 702 F.2d 43, 45 (2d Cir. 1983).

[50] *See* Anger v. Revco Drug Co., 791 F.2d 956, 957 (D.C. Cir. 1986) (personal jurisdiction); Sinwell v. Shapp, 536 F.2d 15, 19 (3d Cir. 1976) (venue).

[51] *E.g.,* Cay v. Estelle, 789 F.2d 318, 327 (5th Cir. 1986); Levoy v. Mills, 788 F.2d 1437, 1439 (10th Cir. 1986); Jones v. Morris, 777 F.2d 1277, 1281 (7th Cir. 1985); Sills v. Bureau of Prisons, 761 F.2d 792, 796 (D.C. Cir. 1985).

[52] Land v. Dollar, 330 U.S. 731, 735 n.4 (1947).

[53] Lewis v. Knutson, 699 F.2d 230, 237 (5th Cir. 1983).

and factually before the district court can address the merits.[54] No right to a jury trial exists on purely jurisdictional matters.[55]

Since federal court has limited jurisdiction, it is presumed that no subject matter jurisdiction exists until the party invoking it establishes otherwise.[56] In fact, a federal court has the power and obligation to inquire into jurisdiction whenever it appears to be lacking.[57] Thus, even if counsel does not file a timely Rule 12(b)(1) motion, the lack of subject matter jurisdiction can be raised by a party or sua sponte by the court at any time in the proceedings.[58] If the motion is untimely under Rule 12, it will be considered as a suggestion that the court lacks jurisdiction pursuant to Rule 12(h)(3). A successful Rule 12(b)(1) motion will terminate an action in federal court action without any consideration of its merits. Although the action can be refiled in an appropriate state forum, often the statute of limitations or logistical problems result in the dismissal's effectively ending the litigation.

§ 14.9 Facial Attacks

A facial attack on jurisdiction challenges whether the plaintiff has stated facts upon which subject matter jurisdiction can be based. For purposes of this motion, all facts alleged in the complaint are assumed to be true,[59] and the allegations of the complaint are construed favorably to the pleader.[60] For example, jurisdiction was found to exist in an F.I.C.A. wrongful death action which alleged intentional acts rather than negligent conduct within the scope of employment.[61] The appellate court reviews facial determinations of subject matter jurisdiction de novo.[62]

In effect, the plaintiff confronting a facial jurisdictional attack is afforded the same procedural protections as if the motions were given Rule 12(b)(6)

---

[54] Gross v. Hougland, 712 F.2d 1034, 1036 (6th Cir. 1983), *cert. denied,* 465 U.S. 1025 (1984); Lewis v. Knutson, 699 F.2d 230, 237 (5th Cir. 1983).

[55] Williamson v. Tucker, 645 F.2d 404, 413 (5th Cir.), *cert. denied,* 454 U.S. 897 (1981); *see generally* 1 Moore's Federal Practice ¶ 0.92[4].

[56] Fitzgerald v. Seaboard Sys. R.R., 760 F.2d 1249, 1251 (11th Cir. 1985); Basso v. Utah Power & Light Co., 495 F.2d 906, 909 (10th Cir. 1974).

[57] Philbrook v. Glodgett, 421 U.S. 707, 721 (1975).

[58] Fed. R. Civ. P. 12(h)(3); *see, e.g.,* Freeman v. Northwest Acceptance Corp., 754 F.2d 553, 555 (5th Cir. 1985).

[59] Adams v. Bain, 697 F.2d 1213, 1219 (4th Cir. 1982); Chatham Condo. Ass'ns v. Century Village, Inc., 597 F.2d 1002, 1012 (5th Cir. 1979).

[60] Scheuer v. Rhodes, 416 U.S. 232, 236 (1974).

[61] *See, e.g.,* Hoston v. Silbert, 681 F.2d 876, 878 (D.C. Cir. 1982) (per curiam).

[62] Medical Fund-Philadelphia Geriatric Center v. Heckler, 804 F.2d 33, 36 (3d Cir. 1986); City of Las Vegas v. Clark County, 755 F.2d 697, 701 (9th Cir. 1985).

consideration.[63] However, it is improper to convert a Rule 12(b)(1) motion into one for summary judgment when subject matter is lacking, since the lack of subject matter is a defense not going to the merits of the claim.[64] Thus, a lack of diversity is not a ground for summary judgment[65] but for dismissal under Rule 12(b)(1), which permits the claim to be refiled in any court having subject matter jurisdiction.[66]

§ 14.10 Amendments

Although the factual allegations supporting diversity jurisdiction are quite simple, failure to properly plead diversity is a common problem in federal court. The party asserting jurisdiction bears the burden of pleading the grounds upon which the court's jurisdiction depends.[67] An allegation that the parties are residents of particular states does not satisfy the requirement for diversity, because domicile must be asserted.[68] Moreover, allegations regarding the citizenship of a corporation must set out the principal place of business as well as the state of incorporation.[69]

The liberal amendment policy of Rule 15 ensures that a poorly drafted complaint will not be dismissed if it can be amended easily to solve the jurisdiction problem.[70] Therefore, if residency rather than citizenship is alleged, the complaint will be dismissed only if an amendment cannot establish complete diversity. Similarly, a plaintiff whose damages exceeded the jurisdictional limits of the Tucker Act was given the opportunity to waive any claims in excess of $10,000 before the district court transferred the case to the Court of Claims.[71] Defective allegations can be amended in the appellate court as well as in the district court.[72] However, appellate courts usually remand on this issue rather

---

[63] Adams v. Bain, 697 F.2d 1213, 1219 (4th Cir. 1982).

[64] Capitol Indus.-EMI, Inc. v. Bennett, 681 F.2d 1107, 1118 (9th Cir.), *cert. denied,* 459 U.S. 1087 (1982).

[65] Prakash v. American Univ., 727 F.2d 1174, 1181 (D.C. Cir. 1984).

[66] *See* Spiegel v. Continental Ill. Nat'l Bank, 790 F.2d 638, 645 (7th Cir.), *cert. denied,* ___ U.S. ___, 107 S. Ct. 579 (1986).

[67] Fed. R. Civ. P. 8(a)(1); McNutt v. General Motors Acceptance Corp., 298 U.S. 178, 189 (1936); Lew v. Moss, 797 F.2d 747, 751 (9th Cir. 1986); Nadler v. American Motors Sales Corp., 764 F.2d 409, 412 (5th Cir. 1985); *see generally* 13B Federal Practice and Procedure § 3611 (2d ed. 1984).

[68] 28 U.S.C. § 1332 (1982); Nadler v. American Motors Sales Corp., 764 F.2d 409, 412 (5th Cir. 1985).

[69] 28 U.S.C. § 1332(c) (1982); Nadler v. American Motors Sales Corp., 764 F.2d 409, 412 (5th Cir. 1985); *see* District of Columbia v. Transamerica Ins. Co., 797 F.2d 1041, 1044 (D.C. Cir. 1986); 2A Moore's Federal Practice ¶ 8.10.

[70] *See generally* 5 Federal Practice and Procedure § 1350.

[71] Goble v. Marsh, 684 F.2d 12, 17 (D.C. Cir. 1982).

[72] 28 U.S.C. § 1653 (1982); *see* Nadler v. American Motors Sales Corp., 764 F.2d 409, 413 (5th Cir. 1985).

than take evidence[73] and have the power to dismiss the complaint.[74] If the amended allegations are not contested, jurisdiction is deemed proper, despite the plaintiff's usual burden of alleging and proving jurisdiction.[75]

If no amendment is made which can withstand a subject matter jurisdictional attack, arguing additional bases for jurisdiction will not be permitted on appeal.[76] For example, a diversity allegation could be corrected on appeal, but the addition of a federal claim to support jurisdiction in the absence of diversity would not be allowed. Amendments also cannot be used to create jurisdiction retroactively when it did not exist previously.[77] The jurisdictional allegations in pro se complaints are held to less stringent standards than pleadings drafted by counsel.[78]

§ 14.11 Challenges to the Jurisdictional Allegations

As with facial attacks, the party asserting jurisdiction has the burden of proving that it exists.[79] Similarly, when a subject matter challenge is interposed on an application for a preliminary injunction, the plaintiff must adequately establish that there is a reasonable probability of ultimate success upon the question of jurisdiction when the action is tried on the merits.[80]

However, there are critical procedural differences between motions which attack the sufficiency of the jurisdictional allegations and those which challenge the truth of the jurisdictional allegations. For example, no presumptive truthfulness attaches to a plaintiff's allegations which are factually challenged.[81] Thus, if the defendant contests the plaintiff's jurisdictional allegations under oath, the plaintiff must respond to the defendant's factual assertions by affidavits or other sworn proofs.[82] If materials outside the pleadings are considered, at least one circuit requires the court to inform the parties and set a schedule if the parties

---

[73] Illinois Cent. Gulf R.R. v. Pargas, Inc., 706 F.2d 633, 638 (5th Cir. 1983).

[74] *See* Jason's Foods Inc. v. Peter Eckrich & Sons, Inc., 768 F.2d 189, 190–91 (7th Cir. 1985).

[75] District of Columbia v. Transamerica Ins. Co., 797 F.2d 1041, 1044 (D.C. Cir. 1986); *see* 13B Federal Practice and Procedure § 3611 (2d ed. 1984); 3 Moore's Federal Practice ¶ 15.09.

[76] *See, e.g.*, Kearson v. Southern Bell Tel. & Tel. Co., 763 F.2d 405, 407 (11th Cir. 1985), *cert. denied*, ___ U.S. ___, 106 S. Ct. 817 (1986).

[77] Aetna Casualty & Sur. Co. v. Hillman, 796 F.2d 770, 775 (5th Cir. 1986); Field v. Volkswagenwerk AG, 626 F.2d 293, 306 (3d Cir. 1980).

[78] Mann v. City of Tucson, Dep't of Police, 782 F.2d 790, 794 (9th Cir. 1986); *see* Haines v. Kerner, 404 U.S. 519, 520 (1972) (per curiam).

[79] Thornhill Pub. Co. v. G.T.&E. Corp., 594 F.2d 730, 733 (9th Cir. 1979); Mortensen v. First Fed. Sav. & Loan Ass'n, 549 F.2d 884, 891 (3d Cir. 1977).

[80] Majd-Pour v. Georgiana Community Hosp., Inc., 724 F.2d 901, 902 (11th Cir. 1984); Industrial Elec. Corp. v. Cline, 330 F.2d 480, 482 (3d Cir. 1964).

[81] Mortensen v. First Fed. Sav. & Loan Ass'n, 549 F.2d 884, 891 (3d Cir. 1977).

[82] Seglin v. Esau, 769 F.2d 1274, 1277 n.1 (7th Cir. 1985); International Ass'n of Machinists v. Northwest Airlines, Inc., 673 F.2d 700, 711–12 (3d Cir. 1982).

wish to submit additional affidavits and documents.[83] Although the standard for admitting such evidence is rarely discussed, the Second Circuit has required that evidence submitted outside the pleadings be competent and admissible under the same standards as summary judgment materials.[84]

When the content of a jurisdictional allegation is at issue, the trial court can go beyond the complaint and can also hold an evidentiary hearing before trial.[85] Such hearings are held in order to assess credibility of the witnesses when the facts are disputed.[86] Counsel should ask for a hearing if the court does not schedule one in order to avoid the possibility of waiver. For example, it was not considered error to hold no hearing when the evidentiary submissions of the parties were not limited and the plaintiff had not requested one.[87]

Evidence, including affidavits, depositions, and live testimony, can be received at the hearing without converting the proceeding to a summary judgment.[88] The court can weigh the evidence to resolve factual issues necessary to determine its jurisdiction, and its findings must be accepted on appeal unless they are clearly erroneous.[89] Although Rule 42(a) provides that findings of fact are unnecessary under Rule 12, counsel should request findings of fact and law whenever the court's decision is based on a complex record to avoid appellate review being hindered by an unclear record.[90]

§ 14.12 Jurisdictional Challenges Which Implicate the Merits

Jurisdictional dismissals of cases in which jurisdiction is dependent upon an element of the claim were restricted by the Supreme Court in *Bell v. Hood*[91] to

---

[83] Gordon v. National Youth Work Alliance, 675 F.2d 356, 361 (D.C. Cir. 1982); *see* Rogers v. Stratton Indus., Inc., 798 F.2d 913, 918 (6th Cir. 1986) (manner of considering outside material must be fair).

[84] Kamen v. AT&T Co., 791 F.2d 1006, 1011 (2d Cir. 1986).

[85] Augustine v. United States, 704 F.2d 1074, 1077 (9th Cir. 1983); Williamson v. Tucker, 645 F.2d 404, 413 (5th Cir.), *cert. denied,* 454 U.S. 897 (1981); *see* 5 Federal Practice and Procedure § 1350.

[86] *E.g.*, Prakash v. American Univ., 727 F.2d 1174, 1180 (D.C. Cir. 1984); Williamson v. Tucker, 645 F.2d 404, 414 (5th Cir.), *cert. denied,* 454 U.S. 897 (1981).

[87] O'Toole v. Arlington Trust Co., 681 F.2d 94, 98 (1st Cir. 1982).

[88] Adams v. Bain, 697 F.2d 1213, 1219 (4th Cir. 1982); *see also* Mortensen v. First Fed. Sav. & Loan Ass'n, 549 F.2d 884, 891 (3d Cir. 1977).

[89] Blakemore v. Missouri Pac. R.R., 789 F.2d 616, 618 (8th Cir. 1986); Williamson v. Tucker, 645 F.2d 404, 413 (5th Cir.), *cert. denied,* 454 U.S. 897 (1981); Krasnov v. Dinan, 465 F.2d 1298, 1302–03 (3d Cir. 1972); *see* Lew v. Moss, 797 F.2d 747, 750 (9th Cir. 1986); *cf.* Anderson v. City of Bessemer City, 470 U.S. 564, 573 (1985) (Rule 52(a) findings).

[90] *See* Societe de Conditionnement en Aluminum v. Hunter Eng'g, 655 F.2d 938, 942 (9th Cir. 1981); Williamson v. Tucker, 645 F.2d 404, 410–11 (5th Cir.), *cert. denied,* 454 U.S. 897 (1981).

[91] 327 U.S. 678 (1946).

actions in which the "alleged claim under the Constitution or federal statutes clearly appears to be immaterial and made solely for the purpose of obtaining jurisdiction or where such a claim is wholly unsubstantial and frivolous."[92] A claim is insubstantial if previous decisions foreclose the subject and leave no room for any inferences supporting jurisdiction.[93] If there is any plausible foundation for the claim, jurisdiction exists.[94] The rationale enunciated in *Bell* for federal question jurisdiction has been extended to admiralty cases.[95]

Subject matter jurisdiction in cases implicating the merits does not depend on the plaintiffs' ability to prove the elements of their cause of action. They must merely demonstrate that the matter in controversy arose under the Constitution or laws of the United States.[96] Whether the complaint states a cause of action on which relief can be granted is a question of law which must be decided after, not before, the court has assumed jurisdiction, because a dismissal on that basis would be on the merits and not for want of jurisdiction.[97] Thus, jurisdiction is not defeated by the possibility that the plaintiff might fail to state a cause of action on which it can recover.[98] In other words, the jurisdictional issue is not whether a plaintiff will ultimately prevail, but whether the claimant is entitled to offer evidence to support the claims even if recovery appears very remote.[99] Indeed, the Ninth Circuit has flatly stated that jurisdictional dismissals in cases premised on federal question jurisdiction are exceptional and are not granted merely because the plaintiff does not have a cause of action.[100]

§ 14.13 Intertwining of Jurisdiction with the Merits

The court's determination of genuinely disputed jurisdictional facts is considered inappropriate when "the jurisdictional issue and substantive issues are so intertwined that the question of jurisdiction is dependent on the resolution of factual issues going to the merits."[101] Whether this intermesh exists is determined by a case-by-case analysis.[102] Intertwining usually occurs when a statute

---

[92] *Id.* at 682.

[93] Hagans v. Lavine, 415 U.S. 528, 538 (1973); *see* Duke Power Co. v. Carolina Envtl. Study Group, Inc., 438 U.S. 59, 70–71 (1978).

[94] New Orleans Pub. Serv. v. City of New Orleans, 782 F.2d 1236, 1241 (5th Cir.) *vacated in part on other grounds,* 798 F.2d 858 (5th Cir. 1986); 13 Federal Practice and Procedure § 3564 (2d ed. 1984).

[95] Marine Coatings of Ala., Inc. v. United States, 792 F.2d 1565, 1567 (11th Cir. 1986).

[96] Ortiz de Arroyo v. Barcelo, 765 F.2d 275, 279 (1st Cir. 1985).

[97] Bell v. Hood, 327 U.S. 678, 682 (1946).

[98] *Id., quoted in* Hagans v. Lavine, 415 U.S. 528, at 542 (1973).

[99] Scheuer v. Rhodes, 416 U.S. 232, 236 (1973).

[100] Sun Valley Gasoline, Inc. v. Ernst Enters., Inc., 711 F.2d 138, 140 (9th Cir. 1983).

[101] Augustine v. United States, 704 F.2d 1074, 1077 (9th Cir. 1983).

[102] Timberlane Lumber Co. v. Bank of Am., 749 F.2d 1378, 1382 (9th Cir. 1984), *cert. denied,* _____ U.S. _____, 105 S. Ct. 3514 (1985).

provides the basis for both the subject matter jurisdiction and the plaintiff's substantive claim.[103]

If intertwining occurs, jurisdictional findings are deferred to a plenary trial in which the entire record is examined.[104] Thus, the jurisdictional inquiry is limited to facial scrutiny, and the factual scrutiny is reserved for the merits of the case.[105] The Ninth Circuit has even held that summary judgment standards should be employed in ruling on a jurisdictional motion involving factual issues which go to the merits. In other words, the moving party should prevail only if the material jurisdictional facts are not in dispute and the movant is entitled to prevail as a matter of law.[106] Moreover, if the question of jurisdiction is dependent on a decision of the merits, some authority exists supporting a party's right to have the jurisdictional issue submitted to the jury rather than to have the court resolve those factual issues.[107] Of course, in appropriate cases, the court can either dismiss such an action if it fails to state a claim or grant summary judgment to the opposing party.

§ 14.14 Comparing Rule 12(b)(1) with Rule 12(b)(6) Dismissals

When the jurisdictional issue and the merits overlap, it is often confusing to identify whether a dismissal is based on Rule 12(b)(1) or is actually a determination that the plaintiff has failed to state a claim.[108] The court does have jurisdiction to proceed to a decision on the merits of the case if the attack on jurisdiction requires the court to consider the merits.[109] If the case survives the facial jurisdictional attack, then a Rule 12(b)(6) motion can be entertained.[110]

---

[103] Clark v. Tarrant County, Tex., 798 F.2d 736, 742 (5th Cir. 1986); Sun Valley Gasoline, Inc. v. Ernst Enters., Inc., 711 F.2d 138, 139 (9th Cir. 1983).

[104] International Ass'n of Machinists v. Northwest Airlines, Inc., 673 F.2d 700, 711–12 (3d Cir. 1982); *see* Augustine v. United States, 704 F.2d 1074, 1077 (9th Cir. 1983).

[105] Lewis v. Knutson, 699 F.2d 230, 237 (5th Cir. 1983); Adams v. Bain, 697 F.2d 1213, 1219 (4th Cir. 1982); Eaton v. Dorchester Dev., Inc., 692 F.2d 727, 733 (11th Cir. 1982); Chatham Condo. Ass'ns v. Century Village, Inc., 597 F.2d 1002, 1011 (5th Cir. 1979); *see* Bell v. Hood, 327 U.S. 678, 682 (1945); *See generally* 2A Moore's Federal Practice ¶ 12.16.

[106] Augustine v. United States, 704 F.2d 1074, 1079 (9th Cir. 1983).

[107] Thornhill Pub. Co. v. G.T.&E. Corp., 594 F.2d 730, 735 (9th Cir. 1979). *See generally* 5 Moore's Federal Practice ¶ 38.36; Note, *The Right to a Jury Trial for Jurisdictional Issues,* 6 Cardoza L. Rev. 149 (1984). *But see* Menchaca v. Chrysler Credit Corp., 613 F.2d 507, 511–13 (5th Cir. 1980).

[108] *See, e.g.,* Carter v. Norfolk Community Hosp. Ass'n, 761 F.2d 970, 974 (4th Cir. 1985); AVC Nederland B.V. v. Atrium Inv. Partnership, 740 F.2d 148, 52–53 (2d Cir. 1984); *cf.* Rollins Envtl. Servs., Inc. v. Parish of St. James, 775 F.2d 627, 632 (5th Cir. 1985) (subject matter dismissal treated by appellate court as failure to state claim).

[109] Land v. Dollar, 330 U.S. 731, 739 (1947); Thornhill Pub. Co. v. G.T.&E. Corp. 594 F.2d 730, 734 (9th Cir. 1979).

[110] Lewis v. Knutson, 699 F.2d 230, 237 (5th Cir. 1983).

As long as the jurisdictional claim is not so patently frivolous that it does not involve a federal controversy, any dismissal will be based on Rule 12(b)(6) rather than 12(b)(1), and counsel should draft the order accordingly.[111] If discovery materials are relied upon in such a determination, the motion must be converted to one for summary judgment,[112] with the requisite notice requirements.[113] On the other hand, if the dismissal can be based on lack of subject matter jurisdiction as well as on failure to state a claim, the court will dismiss only on the jurisdictional ground, because in essence this is a dismissal without prejudice.[114]

§ 14.15 Differences between Rule 12(b)(1) and 12(b)(6) Resolutions

If the motion can be resolved either by Rule 12(b)(1) or 12(b)(6), counsel should bring it alternatively.[115] However, it must be remembered that the two motions are quite distinctive. In practice, treating indirect attacks on the merits as 12(b)(6) motions rather than 12(b)(1) motions provides more protection to the plaintiff.[116] In Rule 12(b)(1) motions, the burden is on the party seeking to invoke the jurisdiction of the court, while in Rule 12(b)(6) motions the burden is on the defendant to show beyond doubt that no claim exists.[117] If a 12(b)(6) motion is converted to a summary judgment motion, the court must deny the motion if a genuine issue of material fact exists, while it can resolve factual disputes in a 12(b)(1) motion.[118] On the other hand, a subject matter dismissal affects only the right to be heard in federal court, but a dismissal for failure to state a claim precludes refiling of the same action in any forum.[119] Thus, a dismissal for lack of subject matter jurisdiction is not a disposition on the merits and therefore not res judicata when the plaintiff refiles the action in an

---

[111] *See* Chiplin Enters., Inc. v. City of Lebanon, 712 F.2d 1524, 1528–29 (1st Cir. 1983); Eaton v. Dorchester Dev., Inc., 692 F.2d 727, 733 (11th Cir. 1982).

[112] *See* JM Mechanical Corp. v. United States, 716 F.2d 190, 197 (3d Cir. 1983); Murphy v. Inexco Oil Co., 611 F.2d 570, 573 (5th Cir. 1980).

[113] Marine Coatings of Ala., Inc. v. United States, 792 F.2d 1565, 1567–68 (11th Cir. 1986).

[114] Voisin's Oyster House, Inc. v. Guidry, 799 F.2d 183, 188 (5th Cir. 1986); Boda v. United States, 698 F.2d 1174, 1177, n.4 (11th Cir. 1983); *See* 5 Federal Practice and Procedure § 1350.

[115] *Cf.* Malak v. Associated Physicians, Inc., 784 F.2d 277, 279 (7th Cir. 1986) (when federal claim not substantial, 12(b)(1) motion should be treated as 12(b)(6) motion).

[116] *Id.* at 280.

[117] *Compare* McNutt v. General Motors Acceptance Corp., 298 U.S. 178, 182–83 (1936) *with* Conley v. Gibson, 355 U.S. 41, 45–46 (1957).

[118] Rogers v. Stratton Indus., Inc., 798 F.2d 913, 915 (6th Cir. 1986).

[119] Daigle v. Opelousas Health Care, Inc., 774 F.2d 1344, 1348 (5th Cir. 1985); 2A Moore's Federal Practice ¶ 12.07[2.1].

appropriate forum.[120] Similarly, a dismissal based on lack of standing is considered quasijurisdictional and therefore not a bar to asserting another theory of relief based upon the same operative facts.[121]

However, even if the subject matter dismissal is without prejudice because not on the merits, it may result in the suit's being untimely filed in the proper jurisdiction. Such consequences do not turn the decision into one on the merits or supply grounds for finding an abuse of discretion if the trial court denies the plaintiff's Rule 60(b) motion to set aside the dismissal.[122] The possibility that the statute of limitations would prevent the commencement of a new action in state court cannot confer jurisdiction on federal court in the absence of a showing of diversity.[123]

When in doubt about the basis of the dismissal, clarification should be requested to identify the dismissal as falling within Rule 12(b)(1) or 12(b)(6). For example, a statute of limitations defense is usually raised under Rule 12(b)(6),[124] but statutes of limitations can be jurisdictional in many suits against the federal government[125] and therefore would be raised by 12(b)(1) motion. Some circuits consider a challenge based on a forum selection clause as within Rule 12(b)(6) rather than 12(b)(1) or 12(b)(3), viewing the clause as a stipulation requesting that the court decline to exercise its jurisdiction.[126]

§ 14.16 Discovery of Jurisdictional Facts

Federal courts clearly have the power to order discovery on jurisdictional issues.[127] Since the pleadings may not reveal whether the court has jurisdiction, if discovery is necessary, it should be timely requested.[128] Some courts view jurisdictional discovery as a form of qualified right rather than completely

---

[120] Indium Corp. of Am. v. Semi-Alloys, Inc., 781 F.2d 879, 883 (Fed. Cir. 1985), *cert. denied,* ____ U.S. ____, 107 S. Ct. 84 (1986); Daigle v. Opelousas Health Care, Inc., 774 F.2d 1344, 1348 (5th Cir. 1985); Prakash v. American Univ., 727 F.2d 1174, 1182 (D.C. Cir. 1984).

[121] McCarney v. Ford Motor Co., 657 F.2d 230, 234 (8th Cir. 1981).

[122] Verret v. Elliot Equip. Corp., 734 F.2d 235, 238 (5th Cir. 1984).

[123] Gilbert v. David, 235 U.S. 561, 568 (1915); Freeman v. Northwest Acceptance Corp., 754 F.2d 553, 560 (5th Cir. 1985).

[124] Gordon v. National Youth Work Alliance, 675 F.2d 356, 360 (D.C. Cir. 1982).

[125] Crawford v. United States, 796 F.2d 924, 927 (7th Cir. 1986).

[126] *See, e.g.,* LFC Lessors, Inc. v. Pacific Sewer Maintenance Corp., 739 F.2d 4, 7 (1st Cir. 1984).

[127] *See* Oppenheimer Fund, Inc. v. Sanders, 437 U.S. 340, 351 n.13 (1978).

[128] *See* Eaton v. Dorchester Dev., Inc., 692 F.2d 727, 729 (11th Cir. 1982); *see generally* 8 Federal Practice and Procedure § 2009.

discretionary.[129] Dismissals prior to discovery are granted sparingly,[130] and dismissals without permitting reasonable discovery have been reversed as an abuse of discretion.[131] On the other hand, a dismissal was upheld when adequate time was given to complete discovery and the jurisdictional facts were fully developed and placed before the court during an adversary hearing.[132]

Counsel must be careful that the pleadings allege sufficient facts regarding jurisdiction, or the court may deny discovery on the theory that plaintiff has not met its initial burden.[133] In addition, the party asserting jurisdiction cannot rest on the pleadings when jurisdictional facts are challenged but must discover facts supporting its claim. The party opposing jurisdiction is equally free to use discovery in its attempt to dismiss the action.

PERSONAL JURISDICTION

§ 14.17 Challenging Personal Jurisdiction

A defendant can challenge personal jurisdiction by bringing a motion to dismiss under Rule 12. This replaces the motion to quash as the proper means of challenging personal jurisdiction in federal court. In other words, limited or special appearances required in many states to avoid waiving a defense based on lack of personal jurisdiction do not exist in federal court. Therefore, a party can appear and challenge personal jurisdiction as well as raising other defenses, as long as proper Rule 12 procedure is followed. While incorrect nomenclature is not fatal to a motion if it meets the other requirements of Rule 12, sloppy practice identifies the practitioner as someone unfamiliar with the federal rules and therefore a target for procedural motions. Moreover, many federal judges will not hesitate to impose sanctions when counsel ignores the federal or local rules.

---

[129] *See* Eaton v. Dorchester Dev., Inc., 692 F.2d 727, 729–30 (11th Cir. 1982); Kamen v. AT&T Co., 791 F.2d 1006, 1011 (2d Cir. 1986) (discovery permitted when facts are peculiarly within knowledge of opposing party); *see generally* Note, *The Use of Discovery to Obtain Jurisdictional Facts,* 59 Va. L. Rev. 533, 546–47 (1973).

[130] Chatham Condo. Ass'ns v. Century Village, Inc., 597 F.2d 1002, 1012 (5th Cir. 1979); *see* Hospital Bldg. Co. v. Trustees of Rex Hosp., 425 U.S. 738, 746–47 (1976).

[131] *See, e.g.,* Majd-Pour v. Georgiana Community Hosp., Inc., 724 F.2d 901, 903 (11th Cir. 1984).

[132] Chatham Condo. Ass'ns v. Century Village, Inc., 597 F.2d 1002, 1012 (5th Cir. 1979) (antitrust action).

[133] *E.g.,* United Presbyterian Church in the U.S.A. v. Reagan, 738 F.2d 1375, 1382–83 (D.C. Cir. 1984); *cf.* Naartex Consulting Corp. v. Watt, 722 F.2d 779, 788 (D.C. Cir. 1983), *cert. denied,* 467 U.S. 1210 (1984) (denied additional discovery when no allegations of specific facts regarding personal jurisdiction).

§ 14.18 Requirements of Rule 12(b)(2) Motions

The court has quite a bit of procedural leeway in determining the motion. It may receive affidavits, grant discovery, or conduct a preliminary hearing on the merits.[134] Besides affidavits, interrogatories, depositions, oral testimony, or any recognized discovery method can be used to resolve the issue of personal jurisdiction.[135]

§ 14.19 Burden of Proof

The plaintiff bears the burden of establishing that the court has personal jurisdiction over the defendant.[136] This burden cannot be shifted to the party challenging jurisdiction,[137] although some question has been raised whether the discussion of reasonableness in *Burger King Corp. v. Rudzewicz*[138] shifts the burden to the defendant to show unreasonableness once minimum contacts are found to exist.[139] If the plaintiff relies upon a contract to establish minimum contacts of the defendant with the forum, it has the burden of producing a copy of the entire contract, or at the least proffering an explanation for its absence.[140]

For a plaintiff to prevail on summary judgment when the defendant contests personal jurisdiction, its burden is to show that there is no genuine issue as to any material fact on the jurisdictional question.[141] However, a motion to dismiss pursuant to Rule 12(b)(2) is a more appropriate procedural vehicle than a motion for summary judgment.[142] Unlike summary judgment, which is res judicata as to

---

[134] Visual Sciences, Inc. v. Integrated Communications, Inc., 660 F.2d 56, 58 (2d Cir. 1981); Welsh v. Gibbs, 631 F.2d 436, 438–39 (6th Cir. 1980), *cert. denied,* 450 U.S. 981 (1981); Data Disc, Inc. v. Systems Technology Assocs., Inc., 557 F.2d 1280, 1285 (9th Cir. 1977); 4 Moore's Federal Practice ¶ 26.56[6].

[135] Thompson v. Chrysler Motors Corp., 755 F.2d 1162, 1165 (5th Cir. 1985).

[136] Reuber v. United States, 787 F.2d 599, 599 (D.C. Cir. 1986); Hoffritz for Cutlery, Inc. v. Amajac, Ltd., 763 F.2d 55, 57 (2d Cir. 1985); Thompson v. Chrysler Motors Corp., 755 F.2d 1162, 1165 (5th Cir. 1985); Behagen v. Amateur Basketball Ass'n of U.S.A., 744 F.2d 731, 733 (10th Cir. 1984), *cert. denied,* 471 U.S. 1010 (1985); *see* McNutt v. General Motors Acceptance Corp., 298 U.S. 178, 189 (1936); 2A Moore's Federal Practice ¶ 12.07[2.–2], at 12–55.

[137] Institutional Food Marketing Assocs. v. Golden State Strawberries, Inc., 747 F.2d 448, 452 (8th Cir. 1984).

[138] 471 U.S. 462 (1985).

[139] *See id.* at 476–78; Knudsen, *Keeton, Calder, Helicopteros and Burger King—International Shoe's Most Recent Progeny,* 39 U. Miami L. Rev. 809, 839–40 (1985); *compare* Asahi Metal Indus. Co. v. Superior Ct., ____ U.S. ____, 107 S. Ct. 1026 (1987) (finding unreasonableness without discussing burden of proof).

[140] Time Share Vacation Club v. Atlantic Resorts, Ltd., 735 F.2d 61, 65 (3d Cir. 1984).

[141] Beacon Enters., Inc. v. Menzies, 715 F.2d 757, 763 (2d Cir. 1983).

[142] *Id.* at 762 n.5; *see* 10 Federal Practice and Procedure § 2713.

the merits of the action, a dismissal based on lack of personal jurisdiction is only res judicata as to the jurisdictional question.[143] Thus, if the state court determines it has no personal jurisdiction over the defendant, the doctrine of res judicata bars further litigation of the matter in any federal district court sitting in the state.[144] On the other hand, a federal court which decides it has no jurisdiction over the defendant is incorrect if it dismisses the complaint with prejudice, since the case can be brought in any forum where personal jurisdiction does exist.[145]

§ 14.20 Prima Facie Showing

When the court decides the issue of personal jurisdiction without an evidentiary hearing, the plaintiff need show only a prima facie case.[146] The uncontradicted allegations of the complaint must be taken as true, and any conflicts in the facts must be resolved in favor of the plaintiff for purposes of determining whether a prima facie case has been established.[147] Facts alleged in the complaint which are controverted by an affidavit are not taken as true.[148] If the plaintiff fails to answer the defendant's affidavits, resting only on conclusory allegations in the complaint, it has failed to carry the burden of showing that personal jurisdiction exists.[149] When the parties present conflicting affidavits, all factual disputes are resolved in the plaintiff's favor, and the plaintiff's prima facie showing is sufficient notwithstanding the contrary presentation by the moving party.[150]

---

[143] *See* Underwriters Nat'l Assurance Inc. v. North Carolina Life & Accident & Health Ins. Guaranty Ass'n, 455 U.S. 691, 706, 713–14 (1982); Rubaii v. Lakewood Pipe of Tex., Inc., 695 F.2d 541, 543 (11th Cir. 1983).

[144] Rubaii v. Lakewood Pipe of Tex., Inc., 695 F.2d 541, 543 (11th Cir. 1983).

[145] *See* Grigsby v. CMI Corp., 765 F.2d 1369, 1372 n.5 (9th Cir. 1985).

[146] Hoffritz for Cutlery, Inc. v. Amajac, Ltd., 763 F.2d 55, 57 (2d Cir. 1985); Nelson by Carson v. Park Indus., Inc., 717 F.2d 1120, 1123 (7th Cir. 1983), *cert. denied,* 465 U.S. 1024 (1984); Data Disc, Inc. v. Systems Technology Assocs., Inc., 557 F.2d 1280, 1285 & n.2 (9th Cir. 1977); 2A Moore's Federal Practice ¶ 12.07[2.–2].

[147] Marine Midland Bank, N.A. v. Miller, 664 F.2d 899, 903 (2d Cir. 1981); Data Disc, Inc. v. Systems Technology Assocs., Inc., 557 F.2d 1280, 1285 (9th Cir. 1977).

[148] Hoffritz for Cutlery, Inc. v. Amajac, Ltd., 763 F.2d 55, 57 (2d Cir. 1985); Wolf v. Richmond County Hosp. Auth., 745 F.2d 904, 908 (4th Cir. 1984), *cert. denied,* ____ U.S. ____, 106 S. Ct. 83 (1985); Black v. Acme Markets, Inc., 564 F.2d 681, 683 n.3 (5th Cir. 1977).

[149] Geist v. Martin, 675 F.2d 859, 862 (7th Cir. 1982); *see* Stranahan Gear Co. v. NL Indus., Inc., 800 F.2d 53, 58 (3d Cir. 1986); Weller v. Cromwell Oil Co., 504 F.2d 927, 929–30 (6th Cir. 1974).

[150] Behagen v. Amateur Basketball Ass'n of U.S.A., 744 F.2d 731, 733 (10th Cir. 1984), *cert. denied,* 471 U.S. 1010 (1985); Brown v. Flowers Indus., Inc., 688 F.2d 328, 332 (5th Cir. 1982), *cert. denied,* 460 U.S. 1023 (1983); Marine Midland Bank, N.A. v. Miller, 664 F.2d 899, 904 (2d Cir. 1981), Neiman v. Rudolf Wolff & Co., 619 F.2d 1189, 1190 (7th Cir.), *cert. denied,* 449 U.S. 920 (1980); Data Disc, Inc. v. Systems Technology Assocs., Inc., 557 F.2d 1280, 1285 (9th Cir. 1977).

However, the plaintiff must respond with actual proofs, not mere allegations. Thus, conclusory affidavits which parrot and restate allegations in the complaint without identifying particular defendants and without factual content do not sustain the plaintiff's burden.[151] If an affidavit has been filed by a party but never received by the opponent, any order concerning jurisdiction is inappropriate until the party can respond to the factual allegations.[152] The filing of affidavits does not convert the motion into one for summary judgment, because outside materials can be considered for purposes of resolving jurisdictional disputes.[153] Even if the plaintiff survives a Rule 12(b)(2) motion through its prima facie showing, jurisdiction must be established at trial by a preponderance of the evidence.[154]

§ 14.21 Evidentiary Hearings

If the plaintiff makes a prima facie case that personal jurisdiction exists, the only way the court can grant the motion to dismiss before trial is to hold a full evidentiary hearing on the issue, at which the plaintiff must establish jurisdictional facts by a preponderance of the evidence.[155] This hearing occurs after the appropriate discovery has taken place.[156] Similarly, if personal jurisdiction is challenged on a motion for preliminary injunction, a prima facie case does not suffice, because the court must have in personam jurisdiction before it can validly enter an interlocutory injunction against a defendant[157] and lacks power to grant an interlocutory or final injunction against a party over whom it has not acquired valid jurisdiction.[158] Thus, in such cases, a full hearing may be required to determine whether the plaintiff has a reasonable probability of ultimate success on the question of jurisdiction.[159]

---

[151] Time Share Vacation Club v. Atlantic Resorts, Ltd., 735 F.2d 61, 66–67 & n.9 (3d Cir. 1984); *cf.* Butcher's Union Local No. 498 v. SDC Inv., Inc., 788 F.2d 535, 540 (9th Cir. 1986) (neither original nor amended complaint's nonspecific language satisfied burden of showing minimum contacts regarding RICO claim).

[152] *See* Naulty v. Fuinch, 686 F.2d 190, 191 (3d Cir. 1982).

[153] Attwell v. LaSalle Nat'l Bank, 607 F.2d 1157, 1161 (5th Cir. 1979).

[154] Travelers Indem. Co. v. Calvert Fire Ins. Co., 798 F.2d 826, 831 (5th Cir. 1986); Marine Midland Bank, N.A. v. Miller, 664 F.2d 899, 904 (2d Cir. 1981); Data Disc, Inc. v. Systems Technology Assocs., Inc., 557 F.2d 1280, 1285 n.2 (9th Cir. 1977).

[155] *See* Handley v. Indiana & Mich. Elec. Co., 732 F.2d 1265, 1270 (6th Cir. 1984); Marine Midland Bank, N.A. v. Miller, 664 F.2d 899, 904 (2d Cir. 1981); Data Disc, Inc. v. Systems Technology Assocs., Inc., 557 F.2d 1280, 1285 (9th Cir. 1977); 2A Moore's Federal Practice ¶ 12.07[2.–2].

[156] Volkswagenwerk Aktiengesellschaft v. Beech Aircraft Corp., 751 F.2d 117, 120 (2d Cir. 1984).

[157] Visual Sciences, Inc. v. Integrated Communications, Inc., 660 F.2d 56, 59 (2d Cir. 1981); see **ch. 11**.

[158] Enterprise Int'l v. Corporacion Estatal Petrolere, 762 F.2d 464, 470 (5th Cir. 1985).

[159] *Id.* at 471; Visual Sciences, Inc. v. Integrated Communications, Inc., 660 F.2d 56, 59 (2d Cir. 1981).

§ 14.22 Intertwining of Personal Jurisdiction and the Merits

Only if the jurisdictional issue is closely intertwined with the merits of the case must a decision on personal jurisdiction be postponed until trial.[160] If at trial the defendant challenges the jurisdictional facts, the plaintiff must then prove jurisdiction by a preponderance of the evidence.[161]

§ 14.23 Discovery Concerning Personal Jurisdiction

If the plaintiff's claim is not clearly frivolous, the district court must ordinarily allow discovery on jurisdiction in order to aid the plaintiff in discharging its burden.[162] Jurisdictional discovery is considered within the trial court's discretion and will not be disturbed unless a clear abuse is shown.[163] No discovery is required if the record establishes that the defendant did not commit an act covered by the long-arm statute[164] or that no dispute exists about the relevant facts.[165] Similarly, if the contacts to be discovered are not relevant to the assertion of specific jurisdiction at issue, the request need not be granted.[166] The court is not required to defer ruling on a jurisdictional question until all discovery is completed, as long as an opportunity for discovery has been provided.[167] Therefore, if counsel does not move to compel further discovery responses with reasonable dispatch, the district court can refuse to stay its jurisdictional ruling.[168]

Requests for discovery should be specific, as a denial can be upheld on appeal if the court views counsels' statements that they "believe" discovery will establish contacts as speculative.[169] Counsel should consider limiting discovery requests to the jurisdictional matter, because a Rule 26(c) protective order is appropriate to prevent far-ranging general discovery, and a limited request normally is granted.[170] Conversely, the party challenging personal jurisdiction

---

[160] Wolf v. Richmond County Hosp. Auth., 745 F.2d 904, 908 (4th Cir. 1984), *cert. denied,* ____ U.S. ____, 106 S. Ct. 83 (1985); *see* 2A Moore's Federal Practice ¶ 12.16.

[161] Visual Sciences, Inc. v. Integrated Communications, Inc., 660 F.2d 56, 58 (2d Cir. 1981).

[162] Nehemiah v. Athletics Congress of U.S.A., 765 F.2d 42, 48 (3d Cir. 1985); *see* Insurance Corp. of Ireland, Ltd. v. Compagnie Des Bauxites De Guinee, 456 U.S. 694, 707–09 (1982).

[163] Patterson v. Dietze, Inc., 764 F.2d 1145, 1148 (5th Cir. 1985).

[164] Wyatt v. Kaplan, 712 F.2d 1002, 1003 (5th Cir. 1983).

[165] Patterson v. Dietze, Inc., 764 F.2d 1145, 1147–48 (5th Cir. 1985).

[166] *Id.* at 1148.

[167] *Id.* at 1147 n.4.

[168] Reuber v. United States, 787 F.2d 599, 600–01 (D.C. Cir. 1986).

[169] *See* Butcher's Union Local No. 498 v. SDC Inv., Inc., 788 F.2d 535, 540 (9th Cir. 1986).

[170] *See* Wyatt v. Kaplan, 686 F.2d 276, 283 n.14 (5th Cir. 1982); **ch. 19**.

should move for a protective order if discovery beyond the jurisdictional issue is sought, because such discovery will be unnecessary if the case is dismissed.

§ 14.24 Sequence of Personal Jurisdiction Motions

The question of personal jurisdiction, which goes to the court's power to exercise control over the parties, typically is decided in advance of venue, which is primarily a matter of choosing a convenient forum.[171] However, when there is justification for doing so, a court may reverse the normal order.[172] For example, forum non conveniens dismissals have been upheld despite the district court's decision deferring the personal jurisdiction challenge until after the resolution of the forum non conveniens motion.[173] On the other hand, subject matter jurisdiction is usually decided prior to resolving personal jurisdiction questions.[174]

§ 14.25 Sanctions Concerning Personal Jurisdiction Issues

One question which sometimes arises is whether a court can impose sanctions on a defendant who violates a court order concerning discovery. The Supreme Court in *Insurance Corp. of Ireland v. Compagnie Des Bauxites De Guinee*[175] noted that, by submitting to the jurisdiction of the court for the limited purpose of challenging jurisdiction, the defendant agrees to abide by the court's determination concerning jurisdiction and can be sanctioned under Rule 37 for violation of any order relevant to that issue.[176] Therefore, a defendant may be estopped from raising the defense of personal jurisdiction as a discovery sanction, and such jurisdiction can be presumed.[177] However, since the presumption of personal jurisdiction in *Insurance Corp. of Ireland* was approved in part because the claim was not frivolous,[178] it may still be an open issue whether such sanctions are justified when personal jurisdiction is more questionable. If personal jurisdiction is presumed as a sanction, that order is reversed only if the district court has abused its discretion.[179]

A district court may dismiss a complaint because the plaintiff failed to file an opposition to the Rule 12(b)(2) motion in violation of the court's order or a local

---

[171] Leroy v. Great W. United Corp., 443 U.S. 173, 180 (1978).

[172] *Id.*

[173] *See* Kryvicky v. Scandinavian Airlines Sys., 807 F.2d 514, 516–17 (6th Cir. 1986).

[174] Allen v. Ferguson, 791 F.2d 611, 615–16 (7th Cir. 1986).

[175] 456 U.S. 694 (1982).

[176] *Id.* at 706–09.

[177] *Id.* at 704–05.

[178] *Id.* at 708.

[179] *Id.* at 707.

rule. Sanctions for violations of such court orders are also reviewed for abuse of discretion.[180] However, there is some dispute whether a local rule which is more restrictive that the appropriate federal rule can form the sole basis for dismissal.[181] If the dismissal for failure to follow the rule or order is improper, the appellate court can proceed to determine the personal jurisdiction issue if an appropriate record was made below.[182]

§ 14.26 Waiving Personal Jurisdiction as a Defense

The defense of personal jurisdiction can be waived in a variety of ways other than as a discovery sanction, including failing to bring a timely Rule 12(b)(2) motion, specifically agreeing in a contract to jurisdiction, implicitly agreeing to jurisdiction in an arbitration clause, and stipulating to jurisdiction.[183] The defense can also be waived by submission of the action to the factfinder[184] or by failing to raise the issue in a pretrial statement.[185] The most common form of waiver is failure to assert the defense in a timely manner in the district court. This failure is considered to confer jurisdiction by consent.[186] Merely objecting to service of process or venue does not preserve the issue of personal jurisdiction.[187]

Since there are no special appearances in federal court, a defendant does not waive an attack on personal jurisdiction by appearing, as long as it contests the court's personal jurisdiction in a timely manner.[188] Obtaining extensions of time or engaging in discovery before answering does not waive the defense.[189] On the other hand, when a defendant attended numerous depositions and waited several years before filing his motion, even though he had not filed any responsive

---

[180] *See, e.g.*, Mangual v. General Battery Corp., 710 F.2d 15, 18 (1st Cir. 1983).

[181] *Cf.* Dixie Stevedores, Inc. v. Marinic Maritime, Ltd., 778 F.2d 670, 672–73 (11th Cir. 1985); John v. Louisiana, 757 F.2d 698, 707–09 (5th Cir. 1985) (summary judgment inappropriate for mere violation of local rule).

[182] *See* Mangual v. General Battery Corp., 710 F.2d 15, 18 (1st Cir. 1983).

[183] Insurance Corp. of Ireland, Ltd. v. Compagnie Des Bauxites De Guinee, 456 U.S. 694, 704–05 (1982).

[184] Shawmut Boston Int'l Banking Corp. v. Duque-Pena, 767 F.2d 1504, 1506–07 (11th Cir. 1985).

[185] *See* Trans-Asiatic Oil Ltd. S.A. v. Apex Oil Co., 804 F.2d 773, 778–79 (1st Cir. 1986).

[186] Harris Corp. v. National Iranian Radio & Television, 691 F.2d 1344, 1353 n.18 (11th Cir. 1982).

[187] Chilicky v. Schweiker, 796 F.2d 1131, 1136 (9th Cir. 1986) (process); Harris Corp. v. National Iranian Radio & Television, 691 F.2d 1344, 1353 (11th Cir. 1982) (process); Myers v. American Dental Ass'n, 695 F.2d 716, 720 (3d Cir. 1982), *cert. denied,* 462 U.S. 1106 (1983) (venue); *see generally* 2A Moore's Federal Practice ¶ 12.23.

[188] Marcial Ucin, S.A. v. SS Galicia, 723 F.2d 994, 997 (1st Cir. 1983); *see generally* 2A Moore's Federal Practice ¶ 12.12. *But see* Benny v. Pipes, 799 F.2d 489, 492 (9th Cir. 1986) (general appearance waives personal jurisdiction).

[189] Benny v. Pipes, 799 F.2d 489, 492–93 (9th Cir. 1986); 2A Moore's Federal Practice ¶ 12.12.

pleading prior to that time, his conduct was sufficiently dilatory to constitute a waiver of the defense.[190]

A party's removal of an action to federal court does not act as a waiver of its defense of lack of personal jurisdiction, because pursuit of inconsistent defenses prior to trial is clearly permissible.[191] However, actions taken in state court prior to removal can waive the defense.[192] Similarly, if after removing the case the party answers without asserting any deficiency in personal jurisdiction and participates in the case before filing its motion, it waives any challenge to personal jurisdiction.[193] Waiver has also been found when a defendant participated in a preliminary injunction hearing[194] and when the defendant requested transfer to the district it later claimed lacked jurisdiction.[195] Inaction by the defendants has not yet been equated with participation, even when the plaintiffs argued that the defendants took no action because they hoped for a favorable decision in a related case.[196] It is unclear whether a party can waive a waiver of the defense of personal jurisdiction.[197]

§ 14.27 Effect of Counterclaims on Waiver

One waiver issue which has arisen with some frequency is whether the defendant waives the right to challenge personal jurisdiction by pleading a counterclaim. Although courts generally agree that filing a compulsory counterclaim does not waive the defense,[198] pleading a permissive counterclaim can constitute a waiver in certain circumstances. Usually, if the motion is brought prior to filing the counterclaim, no waiver is found.[199] Similarly, the circuits now appear to agree that both a counterclaim and an answer which sets up a jurisdictional defense may be filed concurrently without waiving the defense.[200] However,

---

[190] *Id.; see* Broadcast Music, Inc. v. M.T.S. Enters., Inc., 811 F.2d 278, 281 (5th Cir. 1987) (actions of counsel constituted appearance).

[191] Holzsager v. Valley Hosp., 646 F.2d 792, 796 (2d Cir. 1981).

[192] Fields v. Sedgwick Associated Risks, Ltd., 796 F.2d 299, 300–01 (9th Cir. 1986) (finding no waiver when motion in state court was deemed a limited appearance).

[193] Golden v. Cox Furniture Mfg. Co., 683 F.2d 115, 119 (5th Cir. 1982).

[194] Wyrough & Loser, Inc. v. Pelmor Laboratories, Inc., 376 F.2d 543, 547 (3d Cir. 1967).

[195] Liaw Su Teng v. Skaarup Shipping Corp., 743 F.2d 1140, 1149 (5th Cir. 1984).

[196] *In re* Arthur Treacher's Franchisee Litig., 92 F.R.D. 398, 414 (E.D. Pa. 1981).

[197] *See* Giotis v. Apollo of the Ozarks, Inc., 800 F.2d 660, 663–64 (7th Cir. 1986) (analyzing but not resolving issue).

[198] Gates Learjet Corp. v. Jensen, 743 F.2d 1325, 1330 n.1 (9th Cir. 1984), *cert. denied,* 471 U.S. 1066 (1985); Hasse v. American Photograph Corp., 299 F.2d 666, 668–69 (10th Cir. 1962).

[199] Gates Learjet Corp. v. Jensen, 743 F.2d 1325, 1330 n.1 (9th Cir. 1984), *cert. denied,* 471 U.S. 1066 (1985); Neifeld v. Steinberg, 438 F.2d 423, 428 n.10 (3d Cir. 1971).

[200] *See* Chase v. Pan-Pacific Broadcasting, Inc., 750 F.2d 131, 132 (D.C. Cir. 1984); Gates Learjet Corp. v. Jensen, 743 F.2d 1325, 1330 n.1 (9th Cir. 1984), *cert. denied,* 471 U.S. 1066 (1985); *In re* Arthur Treacher's Franchisee Litig. 92 F.R.D. 398, 413 (E.D. Pa. 1981).

courts currently disagree whether the assertion of a permissive counterclaim constitutes a waiver of personal jurisdiction when the motion is brought after the filing of the counterclaim.[201] One factor considered as negating waiver is the defendant's valid withdrawal of the counterclaim without leave of court.[202] Another factor is the nature of the counterclaim.[203]

§ 14.28 Collateral Attacks on Judgments Entered without Personal Jurisdiction

A judgment entered by the court without personal jurisdiction over the parties is void[204] and has no res judicata effect.[205] Thus, a party can fail to appear, and any default entered will be set aside in the absence of personal jurisdiction.[206] If such a default judgment is attacked when the plaintiff attempts to enforce it in federal court, the proper way to raise the issue is to answer the complaint and raise lack of personal jurisdiction as an affirmative defense.[207] A Rule 12(b)(2) motion is not appropriate as long as there is personal jurisdiction in the court in which the judgment is being enforced. Similarly, a Rule 12(b)(6) motion in such circumstances is correct only if the defense is obvious on the face of the complaint.

However, counsel must distinguish failing to appear from appearing in the court which rendered judgment and failing to raise the personal jurisdiction defense. If the defense is waived, it cannot be raised collaterally in the court enforcing the judgment.[208]

§ 14.29 Review of Personal Jurisdiction Issues

A district court's determination that personal jurisdiction can be properly exercised is a question of law which is reviewed de novo when the underlying facts are undisputed.[209] When the district court has decided the issue without an

---

[201] *Compare* North Branch Prods., Inc. v. Fisher, 284 F.2d 611, 615 (D.C. Cir. 1960) (waiver), *with* Gates Learjet Corp. v. Jensen, 743 F.2d 1325, 1330 n.1 (9th Cir. 1984), *cert. denied,* 471 U.S. 1066 (1985) (no waiver); *see* Bayou Steel Corp. v. M/V Amstelvoorn, 809 F.2d 1147, 1149 (5th Cir. 1987) (counterclaim, cross-claim, or third party action does not waive objection).

[202] Neifeld v. Steinberg, 438 F.2d 423, 427 (3d Cir. 1971).

[203] Cargill, Inc. v. Sabine Trading & Shipping Co., 756 F.2d 224, 226–30 (2d Cir. 1985) (counterclaim arising out of an allegedly improper attachment of the defendant's property did not subject him to full in personam jurisdiction).

[204] Pacific Atl. Trading Co. v. M/V Main Express, 758 F.2d 1325, 1331 (9th Cir. 1985).

[205] Americana Fabrics, Inc. v. L & L Textiles, Inc., 754 F.2d 1524, 1531 (9th Cir. 1985).

[206] *Id.*

[207] Hudson Drydocks Inc. v. Wyatt Yachts Inc., 760 F.2d 1144, 1146 n.3 (11th Cir. 1985).

[208] Americana Fabrics, Inc. v. L & L Textiles, Inc., 754 F.2d 1524, 1531 (9th Cir. 1985).

[209] Pacific Atl. Trading Co. v. M/V Main Express, 758 F.2d 1325, 1326 (9th Cir. 1985); *see* Cutco Indus., Inc. v. Naughton, 806 F.2d 361, 365 (2d Cir. 1986).

evidentiary hearing, the appellate court can review the affidavits and discovery material submitted to determine independently if a prima facie showing of jurisdictional facts was established.[210]

Findings of fact made pursuant to a hearing are reviewed under the clearly erroneous standard.[211] An appeal can be taken immediately if the finding of lack of jurisdiction results in a dismissal of the action. If it results only in dismissal of one party to existing litigation, an appeal is proper only if a Rule 54(b) order certifying the judgment is entered. When the court holds that personal jurisdiction is present, the issue usually cannot be appealed until the end of the litigation. Earlier review is possible only in the unusual cases when an interlocutory appeal is certified due to the centrality of the personal jurisdiction issue to the action[212] or a writ of mandamus is deemed appropriate.

§ 14.30 Alternatives to a Personal Jurisdiction Dismissal

Because dismissal is considered a drastic remedy, courts often peruse the complaint carefully to see if any alternative exists. For example, when discovery materials suggested that personal jurisdiction would be proper if the plaintiffs added a strict liability claim, the court vacated the judgment to allow the complaint to be amended.[213]

In general, it is quite difficult to obtain an outright dismissal due to the absence of personal jurisdiction, as long as jurisdiction is proper in some location in the United States. Several statutes can be used as support for a transfer rather than a dismissal. 28 U.S.C. § 1631 provides that a transfer for lack of jurisdiction is appropriate if the court finds it to be in the interest of justice, and such transfers do not affect the original filing date of the complaint. The court can refuse to dismiss on grounds of lack of personal jurisdiction, because the defendant could have sought a transfer under 28 U.S.C. § 1404(a) for change of venue rather than seeking an outright dismissal.[214] Such transfers are appropriate even if personal jurisdiction is lacking in the jurisdiction where the case was originally brought.[215] Therefore, if a plaintiff brings an action in a federal court

---

[210] Jenkins v. Whittaker Corp., 785 F.2d 720, 723 (9th Cir.), *cert. denied,* ___ U.S. ___, 107 S. Ct. 324 (1986).

[211] *Id.*

[212] *See* 28 U.S.C. § 1292(b)(1982); *e.g.*, Growden v. Ed Bowlin & Assocs., Inc., 733 F.2d 1149, 1150 (5th Cir. 1984); Army Times Pub. Co. v. Watts, 730 F.2d 1398, 1399 (11th Cir. 1984).

[213] Thompson v. Chrysler Motors Corp., 755 F.2d 1162, 1173 (5th Cir. 1985).

[214] *See, e.g.*, Handley v. Indiana & Mich. Elec. Co., 732 F.2d 1265, 1272 (6th Cir. 1984).

[215] *See, e.g.*, Cote v. Wadel, 796 F.2d 981, 984–85 (7th Cir. 1986); Dollar Sav. Bank v. First Sec. Bank of Utah, 746 F.2d 208, 214 (3d Cir. 1984); *see* 15 Federal Practice and Procedure § 3827, at 264–66 (2d ed. 1986).

lacking personal jurisdiction and it is transferred under § 1404(a) to a court having jurisdiction and venue, a valid dismissal with prejudice can be entered if the plaintiff refuses to appear in the transferee forum.[216] The court also has the power to transfer the action under 28 U.S.C. § 1406(a), which governs improper venue, to a district where personal jurisdiction may be obtained.[217] Often courts do not distinguish under which statute the transfer is being granted, and all transfers based on lack of personal jurisdiction are subject to the requirement that the choice of law of the transferee jurisdiction applies.[218]

A transfer should always be requested by the plaintiff, if the statute of limitations will prevent the suit from being brought in the appropriate forum after dismissal. Although some states have statutes which extend the limitation period for cases dismissed for lack of jurisdiction,[219] their availability is hardly to be relied upon. However, even relying on transfer statutes can be risky, because a denial of a transfer motion is decided on an abuse of discretion standard.[220] Therefore, a district court's decision to dismiss rather than transfer after the expiration of the statute of limitations has been upheld on appeal.[221]

If a substantial probability exists that the case will be dismissed from federal court, the plaintiff should also consider bringing a protective suit in an alternative state court where jurisdiction is proper, if service can be delayed until after the personal jurisdiction issue is decided. The state case should be filed before the statute has run to avoid the dilemma of discovering that neither the state nor the federal action falls within any state tolling provision.[222] Similarly, a plaintiff can also file in two different federal districts when personal jurisdiction is questionable in the desired forum. However, in such circumstances, a court may refuse to follow the rule giving priority to the first court in which jurisdiction attaches,[223] thus denying whatever choice of law advantage the plaintiff hoped to gain by filing in the original jurisdiction.

---

[216] *See* Morris by Rector v. Peterson, 759 F.2d 809, 812 (10th Cir. 1985).

[217] Goldlawr, Inc. v. Heiman, 369 U.S. 463, 467 (1962).

[218] 15 Federal Practice and Procedure § 3827 (2d ed. 1986).

[219] *E.g.*, Ill. Rev. Stat. ch. 110, ¶ 213–217 (1983) applied to action involving forum selection clause in Andrews v. Heinold Commodities, Inc., 771 F.2d 184, 187–88 (7th Cir. 1985).

[220] Cote v. Wadel, 796 F.2d 981, 985 (7th Cir. 1986); *see* Piper Aircraft Co. v. Reyno, 454 U.S. 235, 237 (1981).

[221] *E.g.*, Cote v. Wadel, 796 F.2d 981, 985 (7th Cir. 1986).

[222] *See, e.g.*, Cook v. G.D. Searle & Co., 759 F.2d 800, 805 (10th Cir. 1985) (action filed during pendency of original case found untimely after original case dismissed, because state savings statute applied only to cases brought after dismissal and not during pendency of original action).

[223] *See* Orthmann v. Apple River Campground, 765 F.2d 119, 120–21 (8th Cir. 1985) (dismissed appeal challenging lack of personal jurisdiction to allow action to continue in another district where personal jurisdiction clearly existed).

VENUE

§ 14.31 Comparing Venue and Personal Jurisdiction Motions

The underlying reasons for bringing improper venue motions are either the defendant's desire to change the location of the litigation for choice of law or convenience reasons or to bar any refiled action on statute of limitations grounds. Usually an attack on venue is part of a more inclusive motion to dismiss based on lack of personal jurisdiction. When counsel contemplates raising one of these issues, it is wise also to consider the other, because questions of venue are often intertwined with those of personal jurisdiction. However, merely raising an objection to venue does not raise the defense of lack of personal jurisdiction, even when those issues are related,[224] because there is a fundamental distinction between jurisdiction and venue.[225] Lack of subject matter jurisdiction or personal jurisdiction goes to the court's power to consider the suit on the merits, while venue merely concerns the place where the suit should be heard for the convenience of the litigants.[226] Thus, venue is not a jurisdictional prerequisite, and its presence or absence does not affect a court's authority to adjudicate.[227]

§ 14.32 Burden of Demonstrating Proper Venue

Confusion between venue and jurisdiction has resulted in a disagreement among the circuits as to which party has the burden in a motion to dismiss for improper venue. Most courts hold that the plaintiff has the burden to establish proper venue in response to a Rule 12(b) motion.[228] However, a few courts require the movant to shoulder the burden of proving that venue is improper.[229] Unlike jurisdiction, venue is not required to be alleged in the complaint.[230] Evidence outside the pleadings can be considered in a Rule 12(b)(3) motion.[231]

---

[224] Myers v. American Dental Ass'n, 695 F.2d 716, 720 (3d Cir. 1982), *cert. denied,* 462 U.S. 1106 (1983).

[225] See § **6.1**.

[226] *See* Leroy v. Great W. United Corp., 443 U.S. 173, 180 (1978); Panhandle E. Pipe Line Co. v. Federal Power Comm'n, 324 U.S. 635, 638–39 (1945); Neirbo Co. v. Bethlehem Shipbuilding Corp., 308 U.S. 165, 167–68 (1939).

[227] Harris Corp. v. National Iranian Radio & Television, 691 F.2d 1344, 1349 (5th Cir. 1982); *see* Neirbo Co. v. Bethlehem Shipbuilding Corp., 308 U.S. 165, 167–68 (1939).

[228] *See generally* 15 Federal Practice and Procedure § 3826, at 259 (2d ed. 1986).

[229] *E.g.*, Myers v. American Dental Ass'n, 695 F.2d 716, 724 (3d Cir. 1982), *cert. denied,* 462 U.S. 1106 (1983); *see generally* 1 Moore's Federal Practice ¶ 0.140[1.–4], at 1319–20.

[230] 15 Federal Practice and Procedure § 3826 (2d ed. 1986).

[231] *See generally* 2A Moore's Federal Practice ¶ 12.09[3].

§ 14.33 Plaintiffs' Alternatives When Responding to Rule 12(b)(3) Motions

Courts rarely grant outright dismissals for improper venue, since the action can be transferred to a court where jurisdiction is proper under 28 U.S.C. § 1406(a) or, alternatively, transferred for the convenience of parties and witnesses under 28 U.S.C. § 1404(a).[232] The Supreme Court has recognized that these statutes were broadly designed to allow transfer instead of dismissal.[233] Therefore, a plaintiff responding to a Rule 12(b)(3) motion should also consider requesting a transfer in the interest of justice under 28 U.S.C. § 1406(a) as an alternative to the judge's dismissing the action. In general, plaintiffs facing a Rule 12(b)(3) motion when the underlying action is still timely have several alternatives:

1. Voluntarily dismiss the action in the improper forum and refile in a proper forum
2. Fight the motion and appeal from a dismissal, thereby risking that the statute of limitations will run in the interim if the dismissal is affirmed
3. Fight the motion and refile after a dismissal, or
4. Fight the motion, alternatively requesting a § 1406(a) transfer in lieu of dismissal, and either refile or appeal if the action is dismissed.

If the action would be barred if refiled, it is imperative to request a transfer under § 1406(a) in lieu of dismissal, because the transfer preserves the original filing date.

§ 14.34 Defendants' Alternatives to Rule 12(b)(3) Motions

Defendants should consider bringing their Rule 12(b)(3) motions together with a motion to transfer for the convenience of parties and witnesses. Improper venue can also be raised in a defendant's answer, but there is usually no strategic reason to do so. Although a § 1404(a) motion is not waived by bringing it after the Rule 12 motion,[234] it may appear to be a strategic afterthought, and the court will probably be more receptive if these motions are brought at the same time. However, since a § 1404(a) transfer does not change the choice of law, if that is the defendant's actual goal, it may be better to hold the § 1404(a) motion in abeyance so that the judge does not have an easy way out of deciding the improper venue issue. Defendants should not suggest a § 1406(a) transfer

---

[232] See §§ **6.6–6.9**.

[233] Van Dusen v. Barrack, 376 U.S. 612, 634 (1964).

[234] 1 Moore's Federal Practice ¶ 0.145[4–3]; 15 Federal Practice and Procedure § 3844.

motion, because some courts will dismiss when the plaintiff's venue choice is unreasonable. Even if the plaintiff requests a § 1406(a) transfer, the court can still order a dismissal if it finds that it is not in the interest of justice to transfer the case.[235] If a court dismisses rather than transfers an action, that decision is reviewed on an abuse of discretion standard.[236]

§ 14.35 Sequence of Venue Motions

The question of personal jurisdiction, which goes to the court's power to exercise control over the parties, typically is decided in advance of venue, which is primarily a matter of choosing a convenient forum.[237] However, when there is justification for doing so, a court can reverse the normal order.[238] Thus, if venue is critical, counsel should request that it be considered first.

§ 14.36 Waiving the Defense of Improper Venue

Generally, venue provisions protect the defendant against the risk that a plaintiff will select an unfair or inconvenient place of trial.[239] Therefore, venue is considered a personal privilege which is waived if not raised in a timely manner in the district court.[240] In addition, this defense can be waived expressly by contract or by conduct amounting to waiver as a matter of law.[241] Conversely, a plaintiff who brings a suit in an improper district relinquishes the right to object to venue.[242] If the defendant has not filed a responsive pleading, there is a split as to whether a judge can sua sponte raise the issue of defective venue.[243] Even courts permitting the judge to raise the issue require the defendant to be notified

---

[235] *See* Noxell Corp. v. Firehouse No. 1 Bar-B-Que Rest., 760 F.2d 312, 317 (D.C. Cir. 1985); Dubin v. United States, 380 F.2d 813, 816 n.5 (5th Cir. 1967).

[236] Costlow v. Weeks, 790 F.2d 1486, 1488 (9th Cir. 1986).

[237] Leroy v. Great W. United Corp., 443 U.S. 173, 180 (1978).

[238] *Id.*

[239] Leroy v. Great W. United Corp., 443 U.S. 173, 184 (1978).

[240] Harris Corp. v. National Iranian Radio & Television, 691 F.2d 1344, 1349 (5th Cir. 1982); *see* Leroy v. Great W. United Corp., 443 U.S. 173, 180 (1979); *see generally* 15 Federal Practice and Procedure § 3829.

[241] Manley v. Engram, 755 F.2d 1463, 1468 (11th Cir. 1985); *see* Neirbo Co. v. Bethlehem Shipbuilding Corp., 308 U.S. 165, 168 (1939); 15 Federal Practice and Procedure § 3803.1 (2d ed. 1986).

[242] Olberding v. Illinois Cent. Ry., 346 U.S. 338, 340 (1953).

[243] *Compare* Costlow v. Weeks, 790 F.2d 1486, 1488 (9th Cir. 1986) (affirming sua sponte dismissal) *with* Sinwell v. Shapp, 536 F.2d 15, 19 (3d Cir. 1976) (sua sponte dismissal inappropriate).

so it can decide whether to waive the issue.[244] However, the district court cannot raise the venue issue once it has been waived.[245]

Once venue is waived by the parties, any defect is cured, and a transfer under § 28 U.S.C. 1406(a) to a court having proper venue is no longer available.[246] However, transfer by a plaintiff has been permitted when the reason for the defect was the defendant's failure to disclose his true permanent residence despite diligent attempts of the plaintiff to ascertain the proper venue.[247] The only limitation on a defendant's waiving venue defects is that it cannot agree to a § 1404(a) transfer to a district in which venue is improper.[248]

§ 14.37 Reviewing Venue Decisions

Venue decisions are interlocutory orders and therefore cannot generally be reviewed until the end of an action. A denial of dismissal for improper venue rarely is reviewed pursuant to a writ of mandate.[249]

PROCESS AND SERVICE OF PROCESS

§ 14.38 Rule 12(b)(4) and 12(b)(5) Motions

Motions to dismiss for insufficient process or service of process are often brought together with motions challenging personal jurisdiction, because "it is axiomatic that in order for there to be in personam jurisdiction there must be valid service of process."[250] In other words, service of process is the physical means by which jurisdiction is asserted.[251] Most motions challenging process are brought under Rule 12(b)(5), which attacks the mode of delivery or the absence of service.[252] Rule 12(b)(4) motions are fairly rare, because they

---

[244] Costlow v. Weeks, 790 F.2d 1486, 1488 (9th Cir. 1986).

[245] *Id.*; Concession Consultants, Inc. v. Mirisch, 355 F.2d 369, 371 (2d Cir. 1966).

[246] Manley v. Engram, 755 F.2d 1463, 1468 (11th Cir. 1985).

[247] *Id.* at 1471.

[248] Hoffman v. Blaski, 363 U.S. 335, 342–44 (1960).

[249] 28 U.S.C. § 1651(a) (1982); *see, e.g., In re* Cordis Corp., 769 F.2d 733, 736–37 (Fed. Cir. 1985) (patent action).

[250] Attwell v. LaSalle Nat'l Bank, 607 F.2d 1157, 1159 (5th Cir. 1979); *see* Mullane v. Central Hanover Bank & Trust Co., 339 U.S. 306, 312–15 (1950).

[251] Terry v. Raymond Int'l, Inc., 658 F.2d 398, 401 (5th Cir. 1981), *cert. denied,* 456 U.S. 928 (1982).

[252] 5 Federal Practice and Procedure § 1353.

concern only the propriety of the form of the process.[253] Counsel should not confuse motions challenging process with motions challenging personal jurisdiction, because a Rule 12(b)(5) motion is generally not considered as raising the defense of lack of personal jurisdiction.[254]

§ 14.39 Challenging Process

Once the validity of service is contested by a Rule 12 motion, the party who has effected service has the burden to demonstrate its validity.[255] The process server's return provides a prima facie case that service was made as stated but can be controverted by affidavit.[256] Counter affidavits and discovery material can also be used to support or attack the motion.[257]

Although the motion challenging process must be made prior to a responsive pleading,[258] there is authority that a judge can dismiss sua sponte for service defects.[259] Dismissal is not considered appropriate when a reasonable prospect exists that service can be obtained.[260] It is doubtful that a judge can initiate a dismissal if the defendant has actually answered or otherwise participated in the proceedings, because the defense of ineffective process can be waived.[261] Waiver can also occur due to preanswer motions, and it is wise, when requesting additional time to reply to the complaint, to include language indicating that no affirmative defenses are waived to ensure that they are not treated as general appearances.[262] Because Rule 4 is usually liberally construed, as long as a party receives sufficient notice of the complaint,[263] generally technical defects in

---

[253] *Id.*

[254] *See, e.g.*, Chilicky v. Schweiker, 769 F.2d 1131, 1136 (9th Cir. 1986); Harris Corp. v. National Iranian Radio & Television, 691 F.2d 1344, 1353 (11th Cir. 1982).

[255] Saez Rivera v. Nissan Mfg. Co., 788 F.2d 819, 821 n.2 (1st Cir. 1986); Norlock v. City of Garland, 768 F.2d 654, 656 (5th Cir. 1985); 5 Federal Practice and Procedure § 1353, at 582.

[256] 5 Federal Practice and Procedure § 1353; *see* Mechanical Appliance Co. v. Castleman, 215 U.S. 437, 445 (1910).

[257] *Id.*

[258] Fed. R. Civ. P. 12(a).

[259] Redding v. Essex Crane Rental Corp. of Ala., 752 F.2d 1077, 1078 (5th Cir. 1985); Novak v. World Bank, 703 F.2d 1305, 1310 (D.C. Cir. 1983).

[260] Montalbano v. Easco Hand Tools, Inc., 766 F.2d 737, 740 (2d Cir. 1985); Novak v. World Bank, 703 F.2d 1305, 1310 (D.C. Cir. 1983).

[261] Fed. R. Civ. P. 12(h)(1); *see* Photolab Corp. v. Simplex Specialty Co., 806 F.2d 807, 810–11 (8th Cir. 1986) (waiver of improper service under Hague Convention).

[262] *See* Benny v. Pipes, 799 F.2d 489, 493 (9th Cir. 1986) (no waiver but close question when three motions to extend time to answer had been filed).

[263] United Food & Commercial Workers Union v. Alpha Beta Co., 736 F.2d 1371, 1382 (9th Cir. 1984); FTC v. Compagnie de Saint-Gobain-Pont-A-Mousson, 636 F.2d 1300, 1312 (D.C. Cir. 1980); *see generally* 4 Federal Practice and Procedure § 1083.

summons concerning time to answer are deemed cured by the defendant's response to the complaint.[264]

When the service is improper, the court must decide whether it should be cured by issuing a new summons.[265] Rule 4(h) gives the court discretion to permit amendment of service, unless it would materially prejudice the other party. This section has been used to cure defects existing at the time of removal.[266] Rule 4(j) now requires dismissal if service is not made within 120 days after filing, unless there is good cause for the delay, and is rapidly becoming the most litigated process motion.[267] In general, counsel must assume that dismissals based on the service of insufficient process will usually be affirmed.[268]

The case law is clear that a dismissal for improper service is without prejudice to refiling the case,[269] although it precludes relitigating matters concerning service actually decided in the first litigation.[270] Therefore, dismissals are usually sought only when they result in time barring of the case.

§ 14.40 Defendant's Alternatives When Faced with Faulty Service

A defendant who has been improperly served must decide whether to default or to respond with a Rule 12 motion. The safer procedure is to respond with a motion because a court can refuse to set aside a default if it believes service was proper.[271] On the other hand, if service is void a defendant need not answer since the court is without jurisdiction, and any default will be set aside.[272]

---

[264] United Food & Commercial Workers Union v. Alpha Beta Co., 736 F.2d 1371, 1382 (9th Cir. 1984); FTC v. Compagnie de Saint-Gobain-Pont-A-Mousson, 636 F.2d 1300, 1312 (D.C. Cir. 1980); *see generally* 2 Moore's Federal Practice ¶ 4.02[3]; 4 Federal Practice and Procedure § 1088.

[265] Fluor Eng'rs & Constructors, Inc v. South Pac. Transp. Co., 753 F.2d 444, 449 (5th Cir. 1985); Vorhees v. Fischer & Krecke, 687 F.2d 574, 576 (4th Cir. 1983); Alexander v. Unification Church, 634 F.2d 673, 675 (2d Cir. 1980).

[266] *See* Micromedia v. Automated Broadcast Controls, 799 F.2d 230, 233 (5th Cir. 1986).

[267] See§§ **5.11–5.12**.

[268] *See, e.g., In re* Agent Orange Prod. Liability Litig., 787 F.2d 822, 824 (2d Cir. 1986); Norlock v. City of Garland, 768 F.2d 654, 657 (5th Cir. 1985).

[269] Saez Rivera v. Nissan Mfg. Co., 788 F.2d 819, 821 (1st Cir. 1986).

[270] *Id.* 2A Moore's Federal Practice ¶ 12.14, at 12–100.

[271] *See, e.g.,* Benny v. Pipes, 799 F.2d 489, 493 (9th Cir. 1986); FDIC v. Schaffer, 731 F.2d 1134, 1135 (4th Cir. 1984).

[272] Armco, Inc. v. Penrod-Stauffer Bldg. Sys., Inc., 733 F.2d 1087, 1089 (4th Cir. 1984).

FAILURE TO STATE A CLAIM

§ 14.41 Rule 12(b)(6) Overview

Rule 12(b)(6) provides that a party may move to dismiss on the grounds that the complaint fails to state a claim. Many courts view the motion with disfavor,[273] and such dismissals have been called a "precarious disposition with a high mortality rate."[274] The difficulty of obtaining a Rule 12(b)(6) dismissal arises from the interplay of several factors, including the strict requirements applicable to such motions, the policies underlying notice pleading, and the liberal standard for granting amendments.[275] As a practical matter, such dismissals are granted only in cases in which a plaintiff's allegations show on the face of the complaint that there is some insuperable bar to relief, or that the plaintiff's theory of recovery is premised on a legal doctrine which is incorrect as a matter of law.[276] On the other hand, the defendant should not assume that a Rule 12(b)(6) motion is always a waste of time and money, because it provides an immediate opportunity for a defendant to control, delay, or terminate the litigation, as well as to educate the judge on complex issues of law. Because the motion need not be granted or denied in toto but can be granted as to only part of a complaint, it can benefit the defendant even if it does not terminate the action.[277]

§ 14.42 The 12(b)(6) Standard

The threshold of sufficiency that a complaint must meet to survive a motion to dismiss for failure to state a claim is exceedingly low.[278] A Rule 12(b)(6) dismissal is not granted "unless it appears beyond doubt that the plaintiff can prove no set of facts in support of his claim which would entitle him to relief."[279] In other words, the court must find beyond doubt that there is no set of facts favorable to the plaintiff and suggested by the complaint upon which any form of

---

[273] *E.g.,* Doe v. United States Dep't of Justice, 753 F.2d 1092, 1102 (D.C. Cir. 1985); Kaiser Aluminum & Chem. Sales, Inc. v. Avondale Shipyards, Inc., 677 F.2d 1045, 1050 (5th Cir. 1982), *cert. denied,* 459 U.S. 1105 (1983).

[274] Kaiser Aluminum & Chem. Sales, Inc. v. Avondale Shipyards, Inc., 677 F.2d 1045, 1050 (5th Cir. 1982), *cert. denied,* 459 U.S. 1105 (1983) (quoting Barber v. Motor Vessel "Blue Cat," 372 F.2d 626, 627 (5th Cir. 1967)).

[275] See §§ **7.2, 8.8** and **8.9**.

[276] *E.g.,* Clark v. Amoco Prod. Co., 794 F.2d 967, 970 (5th Cir. 1986); Garrison v. Heublein, Inc., 673 F.2d 189, 190 (7th Cir. 1982).

[277] *See, e.g.,* Decker v. Massey-Ferguson, Ltd., 681 F.2d 111, 115 (2d Cir. 1982); Fielding v. Brebbia, 399 F.2d 1003, 1006 (D.C. Cir. 1968).

[278] Quality Foods v. Latin Am. Agribusiness Dev. Corp., 711 F.2d 989, 995 (11th Cir. 1983).

[279] Conley v. Gibson, 355 U.S. 41, 45–46 (1957).

relief can be granted.[280] This standard applies to every type of claim,[281] including diversity cases, since federal rather than state law requirements for a Rule 12(b)(6) dismissal apply.[282] Although a court may hesitate to dismiss an antitrust action which requires nothing more than notice pleading,[283] a motion to dismiss is granted if no reasonable prospect exists that the plaintiff can make out a cause of action from the events related in the complaint.[284]

In evaluating the complaint, only its legal sufficiency is considered, not the weight of the evidence which might be offered in support thereof.[285] The complaint cannot be dismissed merely because the court doubts that a plaintiff will be able to prove all of the necessary factual allegations[286] or because the possibility of recovery is remote.[287]

The complaint is liberally construed, with all factual allegations deemed to be true.[288] The allegations in the complaint, together with their reasonable inferences, are viewed in the light most favorable to the plaintiff in determining whether any reasonable reading of the pleadings states a claim.[289] Any doubts are resolved in favor of the pleader.[290] On the other hand, conclusionary allegations in the complaint are not required to be accepted as true,[291] and the court must not assume plaintiffs can prove facts not alleged or that defendants have violated the law in ways not pleaded.[292] Legal conclusions are also not accepted as true.[293] Pro se complaints are read liberally;[294] however, as the Fourth Circuit has noted, district court judges are not mind readers.[295]

---

[280] Cowin v. Bresler, 741 F.2d 410, 413–14 & n.3 (D.C. Cir. 1984).

[281] McLain v. Real Estate Bd. of New Orleans, Inc., 444 U.S. 232, 246 (1980) (Sherman Act case).

[282] Church of Scientology of Cal. v. Flynn, 744 F.2d 694, 696 n.2 (9th Cir. 1984); *see* 5 Federal Practice and Procedure § 1357 (Supp. 1985).

[283] Quality Foods v. Latin Am. Agribusiness Dev. Corp., 711 F.2d 989, 995 (11th Cir. 1983).

[284] McLain v. Real Estate Bd. of New Orleans, Inc., 444 U.S. 232, 246 (1980); Brillhart v. Mutual Med. Ins., Inc., 768 F.2d 196, 198 (7th Cir. 1985).

[285] Geisler v. Petrocelli, 616 F.2d 636, 639 (2d Cir. 1980).

[286] Bennett v. Berg, 685 F.2d 1053, 1058 (8th Cir. 1982), *cert. denied,* 464 U.S. 1008 (1983).

[287] Scheuer v. Rhodes, 416 U.S. 232, 236 (1974).

[288] Miree v. DeKalb County, 433 U.S. 25, 27 n.2 (1977).

[289] Estate of Bailey by Oare v. County of York, 768 F.2d 503, 506 (3d Cir. 1985).

[290] *See* Hospital Bldg. Co. v. Trustees of Rex Hosp., 425 U.S. 738, 740 (1976).

[291] Seglin v. Esau, 769 F.2d 1274, 1283 (7th Cir. 1985); Cowin v. Bresler, 741 F.2d 410, 413–14 & n.3 (D.C. Cir. 1984); Kaiser Aluminum & Chem. Sales, Inc. v. Avondale Shipyards, Inc., 677 F.2d 1045, 1050 (5th Cir. 1982); *cert. denied,* 459 U.S. 1105 (1983).

[292] Associated Gen. Contractors of Cal., Inc. v. California State Council of Carpenters, 459 U.S. 519, 526 (1983).

[293] Prudential Ins. Co. of Am. v. Sipula, 776 F.2d 157, 159 (7th Cir. 1985); Solis-Ramirez v. United States Dep't of Justice, 758 F.2d 1426, 1429 (11th Cir. 1985); Associated Builders, Inc. v. Alabama Power Co., 505 F.2d 97, 99 (5th Cir. 1974).

[294] Haines v. Kerner, 404 U.S. 519, 520–21 (1972) (per curiam).

[295] Beaudett v. City of Hampton, 775 F.2d 1274, 1278 (4th Cir. 1985), *cert. denied,* _____ U.S. _____, 106 S. Ct. 1475 (1986).

§ 14.43 Effect of Notice Pleading on Rule 12(b)(6) Motions

Notice pleading is a barrier to Rule 12(b)(6) dismissals.[296] Rule 8(a)(2) requires only a short and plain statement of the claim showing that the pleader is entitled to relief, unless particularity in pleading is mandated by Rule 9. In addition, Rule 8(f) mandates that pleadings should be construed to do substantial justice. Therefore, the complaint need only give the defendant fair notice of what the plaintiff's claim is and the grounds upon which it rests.[297] The "Federal Rules reject the approach that pleading is a game of skill in which one misstep by counsel may be decisive to the outcome and accept the principle that the purpose of pleading is to facilitate a proper decision on the merits."[298] This philosophy assumes that the discovery process bears the burden of filling in the details.[299] Even pleadings based on "information and belief" have withstood a 12(b)(6) motion when the information pleaded was not peculiarly within the knowledge of the party.[300]

All complaints not subject to Rule 9 specificity need show only a prima facie case which is pleaded with enough data to identify each element of the alleged violation.[301] Mere vagueness or lack of detail is not sufficient to permit dismissal of a complaint,[302] although the failure to intimate any facts underlying the claims justifies dismissal.[303] Similarly, conclusory allegations without any facts are considered to be legal conclusions which can be disregarded.[304] In a conspiracy case, it is not enough to simply aver that a conspiracy existed; the defendant must be informed of the nature of the conspiracy which is alleged.[305]

Because a complaint is read liberally, a party need not plead specific legal theories, as long as the defendant receives notice as to what is in issue.[306] In other words, if the facts support some other theory than that pleaded, the

---

[296] See § **7.2**.

[297] Conley v. Gibson, 355 U.S. 41, 47 (1957).

[298] *Id.*

[299] *See, e.g.*, Morrison v. City of Baton Rouge, 761 F.2d 242, 244 (5th Cir. 1985).

[300] *See* Perington Wholesale, Inc. v. Burger King Corp., 631 F.2d 1369, 1372 (10th Cir. 1979).

[301] Quality Foods v. Latin Am. Agribusiness Dev. Corp., 711 F.2d 989, 995 (11th Cir. 1983); 5 Federal Practice and Procedure § 1228, at 170.

[302] Strauss v. City of Chicago, 760 F.2d 765, 767 (7th Cir. 1985); *see generally* 2A Moore's Federal Practice ¶ 12.08, at 2274, 2285.

[303] Strauss v. City of Chicago, 760 F.2d 765, 767 (7th Cir. 1985); *see* Lombard's Inc. v. Prince Mfg., Inc., 753 F.2d 974, 975 (11th Cir. 1985), *cert. denied,* ___ U.S. ___, 106 S. Ct. 851 (1986).

[304] Strauss v. City of Chicago, 760 F.2d 765, 767–68 (7th Cir. 1985) (1983 action); Quality Foods v. Latin Am. Agribusiness Dev. Corp., 711 F.2d 989, 995 (11th Cir. 1983) (antitrust action); *see generally* 5 Federal Practice and Procedure § 1228.

[305] Fullman v. Graddick, 739 F.2d 553, 557 (11th Cir. 1984); *see* Ostrer v. Aronwald, 567 F.2d 551, 553 (2d Cir. 1977); *see generally* 2A Moore's Federal Practice ¶ 8.17[5] (2d ed. 1986).

[306] American Timber & Trading Co. v. First Nat'l Bank of Or., 690 F.2d 781, 786 (9th Cir. 1982).

complaint will not be dismissed.[307] Similarly, pleading facts not necessary to state a claim is not ground for dismissal if facts supporting a valid legal theory are alleged as well as those alleging an invalid theory.[308] Some courts view it as their duty to determine whether the facts set forth justify taking jurisdiction on grounds other than those pleaded artistically.[309] However, it is better to draft the complaint carefully to state each element of the action than to rely on the generosity of the judge who interprets it.

§ 14.44 Requirements of Particularity

Courts are more likely to grant a Rule 12(b)(6) motion when the complaint is subject to Rule 9, which requires certain matters, such as capacity, fraud or mistake, denials of conditions precedent, and special damages, to be pleaded with particularity.[310] For example, if any facts demonstrating scienter cannot be alleged in a securities fraud case, the complaint can be properly dismissed with prejudice.[311] Every circuit has articulated a requirement of particularity of pleading regarding civil rights complaints.[312] Thus, in a civil rights action brought under 42 U.S.C. § 1983, merely alleging that the defendants have violated the plaintiffs' rights without any facts supporting the allegation falls short of the minimum standards upon which a claim of denial of constitutional rights must rest.[313] Similarly, if judicial immunity or prosecutorial immunity is involved, the plaintiff must allege with particularity the facts supporting the contention that a plea of immunity cannot be sustained.[314] When pleading special damages, actual pecuniary loss, rather than an unsubstantiated dollar amount, must be pleaded.[315] However, a complaint will not be dismissed merely because the requested damages are higher than the plaintiff can recover.[316]

---

[307] Electrical Constr. & Maint. Co. v. Maeda Pac. Corp., 764 F.2d 619, 623 (9th Cir. 1985); *see generally* 5 Federal Practice and Procedure § 1357, at 601–03.

[308] Athens Newspapers, Inc. v. Jefferson Standard Life Ins. Co., 729 F.2d 1412, 1417 (11th Cir. 1984).

[309] Yoder v. Orthomolecular Nutrition Inst., Inc., 751 F.2d 555, 558 (2d Cir. 1985).

[310] See § **7.3**.

[311] SEC v. Seaboard Corp., 677 F.2d 1315, 1316 (9th Cir. 1982); *see* Zerman v. Ball, 735 F.2d 15, 22 (2d Cir. 1984).

[312] Morrison v. City of Baton Rouge, 761 F.2d 242, 244 (5th Cir. 1985) (quoting Hobson v. Wilson, 737 F.2d 1, 30 (D.C. Cir. 1984), *cert. denied,* 470 U.S. 1084 (1985)); *see generally* 2A Moore's Federal Practice ¶ 8.17 [4]; Wingate, *A Special Pleading Rule for Civil Rights Complaints: A Step Forward or a Step Back?,* 49 Mo. L. Rev. 677 (1984).

[313] Kaylor v. Fields, 661 F.2d 1177, 1183 (8th Cir. 1981); *see* Fullman v. Graddick, 739 F.2d 553, 556–57 (11th Cir. 1984).

[314] Smith v. Nixon, 807 F.2d 197, 200 (D.C. Cir. 1986); Morrison v. City of Baton Rouge, 761 F.2d 242, 244–45 (5th Cir. 1985).

[315] Action Repair, Inc. v. A.B.C. Inc., 776 F.2d 143, 149–50 (7th Cir. 1985).

[316] Fort Howard Paper Co. v. William D. Witter, Inc., 787 F.2d 784, 794 (2d Cir. 1986).

Even if Rule 9 specificity is required, the facts themselves need not be spelled out with exactitude, nor must recovery appear imminent to survive the motion.[317] However, the claim must set forth more than conclusory allegations or subjective characterizations.[318] In other words, minimal facts as to who did what to whom are required.[319]

§ 14.45 Discovery

Although it is generally true that what may amount to summary judgment should not be granted until after discovery,[320] if discovery would be fruitless to cure the defect in stating a claim, it is properly denied.[321] Discovery is not usually considered necessary when the allegations in the complaint are disposed of on legal grounds.[322] Therefore, if the plaintiff cannot set forth facts that could possibly warrant relief, dismissal in the absence of discovery is proper.[323] Discovery has been denied when the dismissal was based on the lack of specificity of the allegations as to when and where the acts took place and what acts were committed, though such dismissals are usually granted without prejudice to refiling an amended complaint.[324] As one court aptly noted, discovery "is not a device to enable a plaintiff to make a case when his complaint has failed to state a claim."[325] If a motion to dismiss is pending, the defendant should consider requesting a protective order suspending discovery until the disposition of the motion. The imposition of discovery limitations is reviewed on an abuse of discretion standard.[326] Counsel should be aware that if a complaint barely survives a motion to dismiss and the court suspects that the allegations are a ploy to obtain discovery unrelated to the action, it can assume a managerial role concerning discovery and call for an early summary judgment motion.[327]

---

[317] *See* United States v. Employing Plasterers Ass'n of Chicago, 347 U.S. 186, 188–89 (1954); Quality Foods v. Latin Am. Agribusiness Dev. Corp., 711 F.2d 989, 995 (11th Cir. 1983).

[318] Serrano v. Torres, 764 F.2d 47, 48–49 (1st Cir. 1985).

[319] *Id.*

[320] *See* 6 Moore's Federal Practice ¶ 56.24.

[321] SEC v. Seaboard Corp., 677 F.2d 1315, 1317 (9th Cir. 1982).

[322] Kaylor v. Fields, 661 F.2d 1177, 1184 (8th Cir. 1981).

[323] Wade v. Johnson Controls, Inc., 693 F.2d 19, 20 (2d Cir. 1982).

[324] Kaylor v. Fields, 661 F.2d 1177, 1184 (8th Cir. 1981).

[325] *Id.*

[326] Lombard's Inc. v. Prince Mfg., Inc., 753 F.2d 974, 976 (11th Cir. 1985), *cert. denied,* ____ U.S. ____, 106 S. Ct. 851 (1986); Florsheim Shoe Co. v. United States, 744 F.2d 787, 797 (Fed. Cir. 1984); *see* Wood v. McEwen, 644 F.2d 797, 801–02 (9th Cir. 1981), *cert. denied,* 455 U.S. 942 (1982).

[327] Quality Foods v. Latin Am. Agribusiness Dev. Corp., 711 F.2d 989, 999 (11th Cir. 1983).

§ 14.46 Timing

Rule 12(b)(6) motions are made before pleading.[328] However, the defense of a failure to state a claim is not waived even if the motion is brought later, regardless of whether the defense was raised in the answer. This has led to some inconsistency in treatment of late 12(b)(6) motions. Some courts indicate that a later motion can be treated as one for judgment on the pleadings, because this harmonizes with the provision of Rule 12(h)(2) which permits a Rule 12(c) motion to raise the defense of failure to state a claim.[329] A few older cases have accepted late 12(b) motions, holding that the timing provision of Rule 12(b) is not mandatory as to such motions.[330] The court has the power to hear such a motion, no matter what it is called,[331] and the defendant can even wait until trial before raising the objection.[332] A Rule 12(b)(6) motion does not act as a responsive pleading which cuts off the plaintiff's right to voluntarily amend its complaint.[333]

§ 14.47 Consideration of Outside Materials

Unless the court converts the Rule 12(b)(6) motion into a summary judgment motion,[334] it must exclude any facts presented in the parties' briefs and exhibits or through discovery material,[335] because material outside the pleadings cannot be considered under Rule 12(b)(6). Therefore, when attempting to incorporate allegations from other documents into the pleadings in order to withstand a dismissal, counsel must be careful to clarify which statements are incorporated. Merely referring to a lengthy document is not sufficient,[336] and exhibits incorporated into a pleading must be attached.[337] Documents which are attached

---

[328] See § **14.3**.

[329] Maggette v. Dalsheim, 709 F.2d 800, 801 (2d Cir. 1983); Aldabe v. Aldabe, 616 F.2d 1089, 1093 (9th Cir. 1980); see § **14.54**.

[330] *E.g.*, Majerus v. Walk, 275 F. Supp. 952, 954–55 (D. Minn. 1967) (12(b)(2) motion).

[331] *But see* Orange Theatre Corp. v. Rayherstz Amusement Corp., 139 F.2d 871, 874 (3d Cir.), *cert. denied,* 322 U.S. 740 (1944).

[332] Fed. R. Civ. P. 12(h)(2).

[333] McCrary v. Poythress, 638 F.2d 1308, 1314 (5th Cir.), *cert. denied,* 454 U.S. 865 (1981).

[334] See § **15.25**.

[335] Powe v. City of Chicago, 664 F.2d 639, 642 (7th Cir. 1981).

[336] Shelter Mut. Ins. Co. v. Public Water Supply Dist. No. 7, 747 F.2d 1195, 1198 (8th Cir. 1984); Levitch v. C.B.S., Inc., 94 F.R.D. 292, 294 (S.D.N.Y. 1982), *aff'd,* 697 F.2d 495 (2d Cir. 1983).

[337] Fed. R. Civ. P. 10(c); Goldman v. Belden, 754 F.2d 1059, 1066 (2d Cir. 1985); Shelter Mut. Ins. Co. v. Public Water Supply Dist. No. 7, 747 F.2d 1195, 1198 (8th Cir. 1984).

to the complaint can be considered in the 12(b)(6) setting.[338] A court can also take judicial notice of facts outside the pleadings.[339]

Conversion to summary judgment is authorized by Rule 12(b)(6), but the procedural requirements of Rule 56, including notice, must be met.[340] If the judge does not comply with the requirements of Rule 56 and does not refer to or rely on matters outside the pleadings, any dismissal will be reviewed under Rule 12, even if the district court referred to the disposition as a summary judgment.[341] If a district court considers matters extraneous to the pleadings while treating the motion as one to dismiss, it commits reversible error.[342] However, on appeal, such dispositions can be salvaged if they meet all of the procedural and substantive requirements of summary judgment orders[343] or if the appellate court is requested to ignore the extraneous material and uphold the 12(b)(6) dismissal without reference to matters outside the complaint.[344] The most common way in which practitioners inadvertently convert a Rule 12(b)(6) motion into a summary judgment motion is by including affidavits with the motion or opposition. This can result in conversion by the judge to a motion for summary judgment, and the appellate court may consider any irregularity concerning the notice as harmless error.[345]

§ 14.48 Affirmative Defenses

Generally, the existence of an affirmative defense will not support a motion to dismiss. Nevertheless, a complaint can be dismissed under Rule 12(b)(6) when its own allegations indicate the existence of an affirmative defense on the face of the complaint.[346] Thus, a statute of limitations defense can be raised on a motion

---

[338] Solis-Ramirez v. United States Dep't of Justice, 758 F.2d 1426, 1430 (11th Cir. 1985); Beneficial Life Ins. Co. v. Knobelauch, 653 F.2d 393, 395 (9th Cir. 1981); 2A Moore's Federal Practice ¶ 12.07[2.–5], at 12–69.

[339] Mack v. South Bay Beer Distribs., Inc., 798 F.2d 1279, 1282 (9th Cir. 1986); 5 Federal Practice and Procedure § 1363, at 659–60.

[340] See § **15.25**.

[341] *See* Childers v. Independent School Dist. No. 1, 676 F.2d 1338, 1340 (10th Cir. 1982); § **15.28**.

[342] Carter v. Stanton, 405 U.S. 669, 671 (1972); Bonilla v. Oakland Scavenger Co., 697 F.2d 1297, 1301 (9th Cir. 1982), *cert. denied,* 467 U.S. 1251 (1984).

[343] Jackson v. Procunier, 789 F.2d 307, 310 (5th Cir. 1986); Ryder Energy Distrib. Corp. v. Merrill Lynch Commodities, Inc., 748 F.2d 774, 779 (2d Cir. 1984); Estate of Smith v. Tarrant County Hosp. Dist., 691 F.2d 207, 208 (5th Cir. 1982).

[344] Ryder Energy Distrib. Corp. v. Merrill Lynch Commodities, Inc., 748 F.2d 774, 779 (2d Cir. 1984); Chicago-Midwest Meat Ass'n v. City of Evanston, 589 F.2d 278, 282 (7th Cir. 1978), *cert. denied,* 442 U.S. 946 (1979).

[345] *See, e.g.,* Nichols v. United States, 796 F.2d 361, 364 (10th Cir. 1986); § **15.25**.

[346] Quiller v. Barclays American/Credit, Inc., 727 F.2d 1067, 1069 (11th Cir. 1984), *cert. denied,* ____ U.S. ____, 106 S. Ct. 1992 (1986).

to dismiss under Rule 12(b)(6) when the complaint shows on its face that the limitations period has run,[347] unless fraudulent concealment is adequately pleaded[348] or state law permits late filing.[349] In contrast, a statute of limitations defense must be raised by summary judgment motion when the alleged failure to comply does not appear on the face of the complaint.[350]

Res judicata is not a defense under Rule 12(b) but is an affirmative defense which should be raised under Rule 8(c).[351] However, several courts have allowed a party to raise a res judicata defense by motion rather than by answer when the existence of the defense can be judged by the face of the complaint.[352] Care should be taken to identify the defense specifically in the motion, or it is waived. For example, a motion alleging a failure to exhaust state administrative remedies was not sufficient to raise res judicata as an affirmative defense.[353] Other affirmative defenses which have been raised by motion to dismiss include assumption of risk, contributory negligence, estoppel, immunity, privilege, and the statute of frauds.[354] A Rule 23 motion claiming failure to state a class action is not considered a motion for failure to state a claim.[355]

§ 14.49 Effect of Rule 12 Dismissals

A Rule 12(b)(6) dismissal is with prejudice, unless the order specifically states otherwise.[356] Therefore, counsel must request that the dismissal be without prejudice if leave to amend the complaint is desired.[357] If the original statute of limitations has run, the plaintiff should request that any dismissal be conditioned on a failure to amend to correct the deficiency in the complaint,[358] since the original complaint is treated as if it never existed.[359] If it appears clear that the

---

[347] Duncan v. Leeds, 742 F.2d 989, 991 (6th Cir. 1984); Avco Corp. v. Precision Air Parts, Inc., 676 F.2d 494, 495 (11th Cir.), *cert. denied,* 459 U.S. 1037 (1982).

[348] Duncan v. Leeds, 742 F.2d 989, 992 (6th Cir. 1984).

[349] *See* Yarber v. Allstate Ins. Co., 674 F.2d 232, 233 (4th Cir. 1982) (limitations period extended after voluntary nonsuit).

[350] Avco Corp. v. Precision Air Parts, Inc., 676 F.2d 494, 495 (11th Cir.), *cert. denied,* 459 U.S. 1037 (1982).

[351] Concordia v. Bendekovic, 693 F.2d 1073, 1075 (11th Cir. 1982); see **§ 7.7**.

[352] *Id.;* Guam Inv. Co. v. Central Bldg., Inc., 288 F.2d 19, 24 (9th Cir. 1961).

[353] Nevels v. Hanlon, 656 F.2d 372, 376 (8th Cir. 1981).

[354] *See generally* 5 Federal Practice and Procedure § 1357.

[355] Miller v. Mackey Int'l, Inc., 452 F.2d 424, 427–28 (5th Cir. 1971).

[356] Carter v. Norfolk Community Hosp. Ass'n, 761 F.2d 970, 974 (4th Cir. 1985).

[357] *See* Shelter Mut. Ins. Co. v. Public Water Supply Dist. No. 7, 747 F.2d 1195, 1198 (8th Cir. 1984); **ch. 8**.

[358] *See, e.g.,* Doe v. United States Dep't of Justice, 753 F.2d 1092, 1104 (D.C. Cir. 1985); *see generally* 2A Moore's Federal Practice ¶ 12.08.

[359] Cardio-Medical Assocs. v. Crozer-Chester Medical Center, 721 F.2d 68, 77 (3d Cir. 1983).

complaint cannot be successfully amended, the court will not abuse its discretion by dismissing the complaint with prejudice.[360] Similarly, if the plaintiff has already amended the complaint, the court is not required to permit numerous attempts to plead a sufficient cause of action.[361] Although it has been suggested that one amendment should be allowed regardless of how unpromising the complaint looks,[362] a dismissal was affirmed when the plaintiff failed to amend the complaint after being warned by the trial judge that an amendment was necessary.[363] Rule 15 requires a finding that any amendment not as of right be in the interest of justice. As a result, a denial of an amendment is reviewed on an abuse of discretion standard.[364]

Although Rule 12(b)(6) is technically not res judicata because it does not reach the merits of the action, it does bar the party from bringing an amended complaint which is substantially the same as the original.[365] In other words, it is an adjudication on the merits insofar as bringing the identical claim is concerned.[366] If the motion is treated as one of the underlying merits of the action, the court must give notice that it is being converted into a summary judgment motion.[367]

§ 14.50 Local Rules

Local rules must be carefully considered in Rule 12(b)(6) practice. For example, in some courts, if a motion is not briefed, it is deemed withdrawn.[368] Similarly, if no opposition is filed, local rules may provide that the motion is considered to be unopposed.[369] If so, it is discretionary with the court as to whether to waive such

---

[360] Foman v. Davis, 371 U.S. 178, 182 (1962).

[361] Decker v. Massey-Ferguson, Ltd., 681 F.2d 111, 115 (2d Cir. 1982); see § **8.5**.

[362] 5 Federal Practice and Procedure § 1357, at 614; *see* Schreiber Distrib. v. Serv-Well Furniture Co., 806 F.2d 1393, 1401 (9th Cir. 1986) (leave to amend should be granted unless pleading could not possibly cure the deficiency).

[363] Friedlander v. Nims, 775 F.2d 810, 813 (11th Cir. 1985).

[364] Auster Oil & Gas, Inc. v. Stream, 764 F.2d 381, 386 (5th Cir. 1985); *see* Foman v. Davis, 371 U.S. 178, 182 (1962).

[365] Johnsrud v. Carter, 620 F.2d 29, 32–33 (3d Cir. 1980); *see generally* 5 Federal Practice and Procedure § 1357, at 614–15.

[366] *See* Montana v. United States, 440 U.S. 147, 153 (1979); Cannon v. Loyola Univ. of Chicago, 784 F.2d 777, 780 (7th Cir. 1986), *cert. denied,* ___ U.S. ___, 107 S. Ct. 880 (1987); Cook v. Peter Kiewit Sons Co., 775 F.2d 1030, 1035 (9th Cir. 1985), *cert. denied,* ___ U.S. ___, 106 S. Ct. 2919 (1986).

[367] See § **15.25**.

[368] *See, e.g.,* Henz v. Superior Trucking Co., 96 F.R.D. 219, 220 (M.D. Pa. 1982) (M.D. Pa. Rule 401.5).

[369] *E.g.,* Greene v. Union Mut. Life Ins. Co of Am., 764 F.2d 19, 21 (1st Cir. 1985).

provisions.[370] In jurisdictions not automatically granting hearings for 12(b)(6) motions, the party must request an oral hearing to avoid waiving it.[371]

The major problem arising from the application of local rules is whether a plaintiff who fails to submit any response to a dismissal motion can be dismissed for its default.[372] The Second Circuit has held that, if the pleadings will withstand the motion, failure to respond is not cause for dismissal,[373] and the D.C. Circuit has considered such a dismissal an abuse of discretion in the absence of bad faith or callous disregard.[374] Some circuits require pro se defendants to be notified of the consequences of failing to respond.[375] However, it cannot be assumed that all circuits are as forgiving.[376]

§ 14.51 Appellate Review

A dismissal under Rule 12(b)(6) is freely reviewable as a question of law.[377] Findings of fact and conclusions of law are not required under Rule 12. However, counsel should consider requesting them if they are essential for appeal. Indeed, some local court rules require findings of fact, and appellate courts have strongly encouraged district courts to create such a record in complex cases.[378]

§ 14.52 Sanctions for Improper Rule 12(b)(6) Motions or Responses

In deciding whether to bring a motion to dismiss or to oppose it, counsel must keep in mind the provisions of Rule 11 which require certification that the motion is not brought for any improper purposes. In addition, if the court finds that the motion or response is frivolous, attorneys' fees will be awarded.[379] Bad

---

[370] *See, e.g.*, Bangert v. Harris, 553 F. Supp. 235, 237 (M.D. Pa. 1982).

[371] Biesenbach v. Guenther, 588 F.2d 400, 402 (3d Cir. 1978).

[372] *See, e.g.*, S.D.N.Y. Civ. R. 3(b).

[373] Maggette v. Dalsheim, 709 F.2d 800, 802 (2d Cir. 1983).

[374] Robbins v. Reagan, 780 F.2d 37, 52 (D.C. Cir. 1985) (upholding the dismissal on different grounds). *But see* Tarpley v. Green, 684 F.2d 1, 6–7 & n.15 (D.C. Cir. 1982) (summary judgment granted for violation of local rule).

[375] Maggette v. Dalsheim, 709 F.2d 800, 802 (2d Cir. 1983).

[376] *See, e.g.*, Jacobsen v. Filler, 790 F.2d 1362, 1364 (9th Cir. 1986); Greene v. Union Mut. Life Ins. Co. of Am., 764 F.2d 19, 21 (1st Cir. 1985).

[377] Morgan v. City of Rawlins, 792 F.2d 975, 978 (10th Cir. 1986); Church of Scientology of Cal. v. Flynn, 744 F.2d 694, 695 (9th Cir. 1984).

[378] *See, e.g.*, Martin v. Mogan Drive Away, Inc., 665 F.2d 598, 607 (5th Cir.), *cert. denied,* 458 U.S. 1122 (1982).

[379] *See, e.g.*, Huettig & Schromm, Inc. v. Landscape Contractors Council of N. Cal., 790 F.2d 1421, 1427 (9th Cir. 1986) (experienced labor lawyers knew pleadings did not state valid

faith is not required for a Rule 11 sanction, and counsel as well as the client can be ordered to pay.

INDISPENSABLE PARTIES

§ 14.53 Rule 12(b)(7) Motions

Rule 12(b)(7) motions permit defendants to move for a dismissal based on the absence of a party considered indispensable under Rule 19.[380] Courts generally permit speaking motions under Rule 12(b)(7),[381] and to the extent that such a motion is transformed into a motion to dismiss for failure to state a claim, it may be converted into a motion for summary judgment when matters outside the pleadings are presented.[382] Although a 12(b)(7) motion should be timely made, because it can result in the action's being terminated, the absence of an indispensable party cannot be waived.[383]

Decisions applying Rule 19(b) criteria are reviewed under an abuse of discretion standard.[384] Findings should be requested as to the individual factors weighed, and an appellate court may remand for such a statement if the basis for the district court's decision is unclear.[385] A dismissal for failure to join a party under Rule 19 does not operate as an adjudication upon the merits.[386] If an indispensable party is not amenable to service in the district where the litigation is pending, one alternative to dismissal is to transfer the case to a district where process is available.[387] However, a more common difficulty is that the joinder of the required party destroys diversity jurisdiction.

---

claim); Cannon v. Loyola Univ. of Chicago, 784 F.2d 777, 782 (7th Cir. 1986) (claim barred by res judicata), *cert. denied,* ____ U.S. ____ 107 S. Ct. 880 (1987); see **ch. 28**.

[380] *See generally* Freer, *Rethinking Compulsory Joinder: A Proposal to Restructure Federal Rule 19,* 60 N.Y.U. L. Rev. 1061 (1985); § **9.3**.

[381] *See* 5 Federal Practice and Procedure §§ 1364, 1366; 2A Moore's Federal Practice ¶ 12.09[3].

[382] Japan Petroleum Co. (Nigeria) v. Ashland Oil, Inc., 456 F. Supp. 831, 837 (D. Del. 1978).

[383] *See* Fed. R. Civ. P. 12(h)(2); Provident Tradesmens Bank & Trust Co. v. Patterson, 390 U.S. 102, 109 (1968); Pickle v. Int'l Oilfield Divers, Inc., 791 F.2d 1237, 1241 (5th Cir. 1986), *cert. denied,* ____ U.S. ____, 107 S. Ct. 939 (1987).

[384] Cloverleaf Standardbred Owners Ass'n v. National Bank, 699 F.2d 1274, 1276 (D.C. Cir. 1983); Walsh v. Centeio, 692 F.2d 1239, 1241–43 (9th Cir. 1982).

[385] *See, e.g.,* Bakia v. County of Los Angeles, 687 F.2d 299, 302 (9th Cir. 1982).

[386] Cloverleaf Standardbred Owners Ass'n v. National Bank, 699 F.2d 1274 (D.C. Cir. 1983).

[387] *See* Sierra Club v. Leathers, 754 F.2d 952, 954–55 (11th Cir. 1985); see §§ **6.6–6.9**.

JUDGMENT ON THE PLEADINGS

§ 14.54 Rule 12(c) Motions

Rule 12(c) provides that any party may move for judgment on the pleadings. The movant must clearly establish that no material factual issue remains and that it is entitled to judgment as a matter of law.[388] Rule 12(c) motions are fairly rare, because they largely duplicate Rule 12(b)(6) and summary judgment motions. Indeed, most 12(c) motions occur when the party has not moved under Rule 12(b)(6) in a timely fashion, and the motion is considered proper under Rule 12(c).[389] Unlike most Rule 12(b) motions which are brought in lieu of answering the complaint, Rule 12(c) motions cannot be brought until the pleadings are closed, and the only timing requirement is that the motion does not delay the trial.

§ 14.55 Rule 12(c) Procedural Requirements

For purposes of this motion, all well pleaded material allegations of the opponent's motion are taken as true.[390] The movant cannot have judgment granted against it merely by bringing the motion, although both parties may stipulate that the facts are true and simultaneously move for a judgment on the pleadings.[391] The only matters which can be considered outside the pleadings are facts which can be judicially noticed by the court. However, similar to Rule 12(b)(6) motions, Rule 12(c) motions can be converted to a motion for summary judgment if the court has given notice that the motion will be so treated.[392] Thus, counsel must be careful about submitting affidavits to the court if summary judgment treatment is not desired.[393] If the motion is converted, Rule 56 procedures must be followed.[394] The standard of review for Rule 12(c) motions is identical to that for Rule 12(b)(6) motions.[395]

---

388 Flora v. Home Fed. Sav. & Loan Ass'n, 685 F.2d 209, 211 (7th Cir. 1982).

389 *See* Maggette v. Dalsheim, 709 F.2d 800, 801 (2d Cir. 1983); Aldabe v. Aldabe, 616 F.2d 1089, 1093 (9th Cir. 1980); *see also* Wagner v. Higgens, 754 F.2d 186, 188 (6th Cir. 1985).

390 Beal v. Missouri Pac. R.R., 312 U.S. 45, 51 (1941); Republic Steel Corp. v. Pennsylvania Eng'g Corp., 785 F.2d 174, 177 n.2 (7th Cir. 1986).

391 *See* 5 Federal Practice and Procedure § 1370, at 704.

392 Fed. R. Civ. P. 12(c); Maggette v. Dalsheim, 709 F.2d 801, 802 (2d Cir. 1983).

393 *See, e.g.*, Republic Steel Corp. v. Pennsylvania Eng'g Corp., 785 F.2d 174, 178 (7th Cir. 1986).

394 Falls Riverway Realty Inc. v. City of Niagara Falls, 754 F.2d 49, 53–54 (2d Cir. 1985).

395 Ryder Energy Distrib. Corp. v. Merrill Lynch Commodities, Inc., 748 F.2d 774, 778 n.3 (2d Cir. 1984); *see also* Republic Steel Corp. v. Pennsylvania Eng'g Corp., 785 F.2d 174, 177 n.2 (7th Cir. 1986).

As with other motions, counsel must be careful to comply with local rules to avoid a dismissal or default for failure to respond to the motion,[396] although some circuits do not permit the suit to be terminated when the pleadings alone withstand the motion.[397] Pro se parties may also be entitled to notice of the consequences of failing to respond in some circuits.[398]

MORE DEFINITE STATEMENTS

§ 14.56 More Definite Statements

Rule 12(e) authorizes a party to move for a more definite statement if the pleading to which it must respond is so vague or ambiguous that it cannot reasonably frame the responsive pleading. Most courts view this motion with disfavor, due to the liberal notice pleading permitted by the rules, and the fact that discovery enables the party to learn the specifics of the complaint. As a strategic matter, the motion does little other than to delay the time to answer and should only be brought when the complaint is unintelligible and opposing counsel refuses to amend.

§ 14.57 Factors Considered in Granting the Rule 12(e) Motion

More definite statements have been required when the complaint is extremely general as to standing[399] or facts which must be pleaded with particularity under Rule 9(b), such as fraud or special damages.[400] Courts disagree whether a Rule 12(e) motion is appropriate to require the date of a claim to be specified for purposes of a statute of limitations defense.[401]

The judge can require an amendment to the complaint in lieu of granting the motion or order the requisite information to be supplied by affidavits.[402] Sometimes, courts grant a motion for more definite statement instead of

---

[396] *See, e.g.*, S.D.N.Y. Civ. R. 3(b).

[397] Maggette v. Dalsheim, 709 F.2d 800, 802 (2d Cir. 1983).

[398] *Id.; cf.* Lewis v. Faulkner, 689 F.2d 100, 102 (7th Cir. 1982); Davis v. Zahradnick, 600 F.2d 458, 460 (4th Cir. 1979) (per curiam); Hudson v. Hardy, 412 F.2d 1091, 1094 (D.C. Cir. 1968) (per curiam) (notice for summary judgment motions).

[399] *See* Havens Realty Corp. v. Coleman, 455 U.S. 363, 377–78 (1982).

[400] *See* 5 Federal Practice and Procedure § 1376.

[401] *Id.*

[402] *See, e.g.*, Warth v. Seldin, 422 U.S. 490, 501–02 (1975) (standing).

dismissing a complaint,[403] in essence converting a Rule 12(b)(6) motion into a request for a more definite statement because the complaint is poorly drafted.[404] Because bills of particulars, which became part of the pleadings they clarified, no longer exist in federal practice, courts automatically convert such requests into motions for more definite statements.[405]

§ 14.58 Rule 12(e) Procedures

In order to obtain a more definite statement, the movant must indicate the defects in the pleading and the details desired. Because the burden is on the movant, the motion will be denied if outside information is available which enables that party to frame a responsive pleading.[406] Affidavits are usually not required in support of the motion.[407]

Rule 12(e) provides that any statement ordered must be obeyed within 10 days after notice or within the time fixed by such order as the court deems just. Therefore, counsel should request that the court order provide for dismissal if the statement is not timely. This avoids having to move for sanctions. However, the violation of the court order must be willful for dismissal to be appropriate.[408]

MOTIONS TO STRIKE

§ 14.59 Motions to Strike

Rule 12(f) authorizes the court to strike any insufficient defense or any redundant, immaterial, impertinent, or scandalous matter. The motion must be made before responding to the pleading or within 20 days after service of the pleading if no response is permitted. The rule also provides that the court may strike the matter on its own initiative at any time. No hearing need be granted if the matter is not complicated.[409] Motions to strike a defense are generally disfavored and usually have no strategic value, unless counsel is attempting to restrict the ability of the press to quote from scandalous pleadings.

---

403 *See* Quality Foods v. Latin Am. Agribusiness Dev. Corp., 711 F.2d 989, 998 (11th Cir. 1983).

404 5 Federal Practice and Procedure § 1376, at 734 (1969).

405 *Id.* at § 1378; *see generally,* 2A J. Moore & J. Lucas, Moore's Federal Practice ¶ 12.17.

406 5 Federal Practice and Procedure § 1378, at 770.

407 *Id.*

408 See **ch. 30**.

409 United States v. 416.81 Acres of Land, 514 F.2d 627, 631 (7th Cir. 1975).

§ 14.60 Factors in Obtaining Rule 12(f) Orders

Rule 12(f) motions are proper when a defense is insufficient as a matter of law,[410] such as when the statute of limitations is pleaded in a way which reveals its inapplicability to the given case.[411] A motion to strike has also been used to strike the prayer of damages when it was beyond the amount authorized by law[412] and to challenge an improper request for punitive damages or attorneys' fees.[413] However, some courts frown upon using a motion to strike to challenge prayers for attorneys' fees or punitive damages when they are clearly impermissible and consider a motion for failure to state a claim the appropriate procedure.[414] Such courts may simply deny the 12(f) motion as being inapplicable[415] rather than automatically converting it to a Rule 12(b)(6) motion. Therefore, it may be safer to alternatively caption such a motion.

Often a court will not grant a valid motion to strike on the ground that no prejudice exists to the movant if the motion is denied.[416] However, many courts have stricken unnecessary evidentiary detail from pleading and such decisions are not reversed unless found to be an abuse of discretion.[417]

The motion to strike is limited to pleadings. Thus, it is error to strike a motion under this rule.[418] If factual questions going to the merits of the action need resolution, the motion to strike is also inappropriate, and partial summary judgment should be requested. However, this procedure may not be worth the effort.[419]

If the grant of the motion does not result in a final order, no appeal will be allowed until the case is ultimately terminated. Similarly, the denial of such a motion is never final.[420]

---

[410] Kaiser Aluminum & Chem. Sales, Inc. v. Avondale Shipyards, Inc., 677 F.2d 1045, 1057 (5th Cir. 1982), *cert. denied,* 459 U.S. 1105 (1983); Lundsford v. United States, 570 F.2d 221, 228 (8th Cir. 1977).

[411] *See* Kaiser Aluminum & Chem. Sales, Inc. v. Avondale Shipyards, Inc., 677 F.2d 1045, 1057 (5th Cir. 1982), *cert. denied,* 459 U.S. 1105 (1983); Brohan *ex rel.* Brohan v. Volkswagen Mfg. Corp., 97 F.R.D. 46, 50 (E.D.N.Y. 1983).

[412] See Tapley v. Lockwood Green Eng'rs, Inc., 502 F.2d 559, 560 (8th Cir. 1974).

[413] *See* 2A Moore's Federal Practice ¶ 12.21[1].

[414] *See, e.g.,* Professional Asset Mgmt., Inc. v. Penn Square Bank, 566 F. Supp. 134, 136 (W.D. Okla. 1983); Pierson v. Dean, Witter, Reynolds, Inc., 551 F. Supp. 497, 504 (C.D. Ill. 1982).

[415] *See, e.g.,* Massachusetts v. Russell Stover Candies, 541 F. Supp. 143, 145 (D. Mass. 1982).

[416] *See* 5 Federal Practice and Procedure §§ 1381, 1382.

[417] *In re* Beef Indus. Antitrust Litig., 600 F.2d 1148, 1169 (5th Cir. 1979).

[418] Sidney-Vinstein v. A.H. Robins Co., 697 F.2d 880, 886 (9th Cir. 1983).

[419] *See* 5 Federal Practice and Procedure § 1381, at 804; § **15.26**.

[420] *See generally* 5 Federal Practice and Procedure § 1381, at 805.

CONSOLIDATION AND WAIVER OF DEFENSES

§ 14.61 Waiver of Rule 12 Motions

Rule 12(g) and (h) set out the requirements of consolidation and waiver of defenses. The defenses of lack of personal jurisdiction, improper venue, and insufficiency of process or service of process are waived if not made by a Rule 12 motion or included in a responsive pleading or an amendment made as a matter of course under Rule 15(a).[421] In addition, parties are barred from raising any of those defenses, as well as from bringing motions to strike or for more definite statements if they were omitted from the Rule 12 motion. The defenses of failure to state a claim, failure to join an indispensable party under Rule 19, and lack of subject matter jurisdiction are not affected by the Rule 12 timing. Although a party does not waive its right to move to dismiss if it files its Rule 12 motion along with an answer, usually there is no advantage to filing the answer until the motion is denied.

These provisions effectively prevent a party from bringing sequential motions under Rule 12(b)(2)–(5), 12(e), and 12(f). In contrast, the defendant may raise personal jurisdiction, venue, and process issues before bringing a motion for failure to state a claim, failure to join an indispensable party, or lack of subject matter jurisdiction, because the latter three defenses are never waived. Indeed, such defenses may even be raised sua sponte by the court[422] or for the first time on appeal.[423] For example, if an indispensable party is not diverse, the lack of subject matter jurisdiction can be raised at any time.[424]

§ 14.62 Untimely Responses

The application of waiver to a party who has not filed any response within 20 days is not totally settled. Usually a party in default is considered to have waived Rule 12 defenses.[425] Therefore, some courts view any response filed beyond 20 days as untimely under Rule 12 even if it is the party's initial response.[426] Other

---

[421] Beary v. West Pub. Co., 763 F.2d 66, 68 (2d Cir.), *cert. denied,* ____ U.S. ____, 106 S. Ct. 232 (1985).

[422] Rauch v. Day & Night Mfg. Corp., 576 F.2d 697, 699–700 (6th Cir. 1978).

[423] *See, e.g.,* Freeman v. Northwest Acceptance Corp., 754 F.2d 553, 559 (5th Cir. 1985).

[424] *Id.* at 560.

[425] *See generally* 5 Federal Practice and Procedure § 1391, at 856.

[426] Farmers Elevator Mut. Ins. Co. v. Carl J. Austad & Sons, Inc., 343 F.2d 7, 12 (8th Cir. 1965); 5 Federal Practice and Procedure § 1391, at 856.

courts permit the assertion of a Rule 12 defense when the plaintiff's first response raises the issue, even if the motion is filed after the time permitted under Rule 12(a), on the theory that the timing requirements affect the filing of pleadings, not the issue of waiver.[427] The failure of a defendant to assert the defense of lack of personal jurisdiction is not considered a waiver at any time before its voluntary appearance, nor does the 20-day period prescribed by Rule 12 commence to run prior to an appearance.[428] A few circuits even grant the district court judge discretion to allow the defendant to amend its original motion to dismiss before the hearing or responsive pleading is filed in order to include additional Rule 12 defenses.[429]

Defenses subject to waiver cannot be raised for the first time on appeal, because they must be presented to the district court.[430] Moreover, the court can reject any Rule 12 defense which has been waived even if opposing counsel does not object to its untimely injection into the action.[431] Although the court has the power to enforce a waiver sua sponte, it cannot sua sponte raise a Rule 12 defense which has been waived by the defendant.[432] Therefore care must be taken to raise all waivable Rule 12 defenses at the appropriate time, or they will be lost. Similarly, each of the defenses raised should be fully briefed, both in the district court and on appeal, because omitted or briefly mentioned issues may be considered as waived.[433]

§ 14.63 Comparing Rule 12 Defenses with Affirmative Defenses

Rule 12 waivers should not be confused with waivers of affirmative defenses.[434] A defendant can raise an affirmative defense, such as statute of limitations, on

---

[427] Bechtel v. Liberty Nat'l Bank, 534 F.2d 1335, 1341 (9th Cir. 1976); Foss v. Klapka, 95 F.R.D. 521, 522–23 (E.D. Pa. 1982); 5 Federal Practice and Procedure § 1391, at 856.

[428] Orange Theatre Corp. v. Rayherstz Amusement Corp., 139 F.2d 871, 873 (3d Cir.), *cert. denied,* 322 U.S. 740 (1944).

[429] Bechtel v. Liberty Nat'l Bank, 534 F.2d 1335, 1341 (9th Cir. 1976); MacNeil v. Whittemore, 254 F.2d 820, 821 (2d Cir. 1958).

[430] *E.g.,* Harris Corp. v. National Iranian Radio & Television, 691 F.2d 1344, 1353 (11th Cir. 1982).

[431] Myers v. American Dental Ass'n, 695 F.2d 716, 720–21 (3d Cir. 1982), *cert. denied,* 462 U.S. 1106 (1983) (personal jurisdiction); Lockett v. General Fin. Loan Co., 623 F.2d 1128, 1132 n.5 (5th Cir. 1980) (personal jurisdiction and service of process); Pila v. G.R. Leasing & Rental Corp., 551 F.2d 941, 943 (1st Cir. 1977) (service of process).

[432] Rauch v. Day & Night Mfg. Corp., 576 F.2d 697, 698 (6th Cir. 1978).

[433] *See* Adden v. Middlebrooks, 688 F.2d 1147, 1157 (5th Cir. 1982); Shuford v. Anderson, 352 F.2d 755, 765 (10th Cir. 1965), *cert. denied,* 383 U.S. 935 (1966).

[434] See § **7.7**.

appeal if its Rule 12 motion results in a dismissal, as long as no answer was filed in the district court. In other words, a party does not fall within Rule 8(c)'s requirement that affirmative defenses must be raised unless a responsive pleading is filed. Moreover, there is no requirement under Rule 12 to affirmatively raise the statute of limitations defense by motion.[435] Although affirmative defenses should also be timely pleaded in order to avoid waiver, if a party introduces evidence at trial in support of the waived defense without objection by opposing counsel, the defense is considered as tried with the implied consent of the parties.[436]

§ 14.64 Subsequently Acquired Defenses and Amendments

Only defenses which are available when the Rule 12 motion is brought are subject to waiver. If some factual issue becomes known after the motion is no longer timely, it can still be raised.[437] Similarly, if a legal issue becomes available at a later time, it is not waived.[438] Since the rule mentions only amendments as a matter of course, amendments by leave of the court do not revive a waived defense.[439] For example, if the plaintiff amends the complaint, the defendant cannot assert a personal jurisdiction defense which was not timely filed in response to the original complaint.[440]

§ 14.65 Waiver of Sovereign Immunity

Unlike other subject matter defenses which cannot be waived, the statute governing sovereign immunity of a foreign state provides for waiver which can

---

[435] Serrano v. Torres, 764 F.2d 47, 49 (1st Cir. 1985).

[436] Okeson v. Tolley School Dist. No. 25, 760 F.2d 864, 867, *rev'd on other grounds,* 766 F.2d 378 (8th Cir. 1985); Jones v. Miles, 656 F.2d 103, 107 n.7 (5th Cir. 1981); *see* Giotis v. Apollo of the Ozarks, Inc., 800 F.2d 660, 663–64 (7th Cir. 1986) (distinguishing affirmative defenses from Rule 12 defenses); § **16.4**.

[437] *See, e.g.,* Glater v. Eli Lilly & Co., 712 F.2d 735, 738 (1st Cir. 1983); *see* 5 Federal Practice and Procedure § 1391, at 853–54.

[438] Holzsager v. Valley Hosp., 646 F.2d 792, 796 (2d Cir. 1981).

[439] Glater v. Eli Lilly & Co., 712 F.2d 735, 738 (1st Cir. 1983); Konisberg v. Shute, 435 F.2d 551, 552 (3d Cir. 1970) (per curiam); *see generally* 5 Federal Practice and Procedure § 1391, at 855.

[440] Rowley v. McMillan, 502 F.2d 1326, 1332 (4th Cir. 1974); Brohan *ex rel.* Brohan v. Volkswagen Mfg. Corp., 97 F.R.D. 46, 48 (E.D.N.Y. 1983).

be either explicit or implied.[441] The legislative history indicates that an implicit waiver occurs when a responsive pleading is filed without raising the defense.[442] Thus, no automatic waiver occurs when motions were brought but no pleading filed.[443] Of course, the character of the sovereign's participation in the litigation can constitute a waiver, and the court can require the assertion or abandonment of the defense prior to submission of an answer.[444]

§ 14.66 Nonspecified Defenses

Defenses not specifically enumerated in Rule 12 have not been eliminated and should be raised in the answer or brought by motions such as to stay an action due to the pendency of other suits or to obtain security for costs.[445] Similarly, motions to change venue under 28 U.S.C. § 1404(a) or to dismiss under the doctrine of forum non conveniens are not waived if brought outside the Rule 12 framework,[446] although they can also be joined with any Rule 12 defenses.

DISMISSALS

§ 14.67 Appeals from Dismissals

Counsel facing a dismissal should always inquire if it is a final ruling or whether the complaint can be saved by an amendment. An order dismissing a complaint but not the underlying action is ordinarily not considered a final order and is, therefore, not appealable under 28 U.S.C. § 1291.[447] However, in some circuits, if the plaintiff intends to stand on the allegations of the complaint, the dismissal is treated as final.[448] On the other hand, even if the judge fails to dismiss the

---

[441] 28 U.S.C. §§ 1330, 1605(a)(1) (1982); *see* Verlinden B.V. v. Central Bank of Nigeria, 461 U.S. 480, 485 n.5 (1983); Canadian Overseas v. Compania de Acero, 727 F.2d 274, 277 (2d Cir. 1984); *see generally Special Issue: The Foreign Sovereign Immunities Act Ten Years Later,* 19 Vand. J. Transnat'l L. 1–179 (1986).

[442] H.R. Rep. No. 1487, 94th Cong., 2d Sess., *reprinted in* 1976 U.S. Code Cong. & Admin. News 6604, 6617.

[443] Canadian Overseas v. Compania de Acero, 727 F.2d 274, 278 (2d Cir. 1984).

[444] *Id.*

[445] *See* 2A Moore's Federal Practice ¶ 12.07[4].

[446] Leif Hoegh & Co. v. Alpha Motor Ways, Inc., 534 F. Supp. 624, 626 (S.D.N.Y. 1982) (venue); Snam Progetti S.P.A. v. Lauro Lines, 387 F. Supp. 322, 323 (S.D.N.Y. 1974) (forum non conveniens); see §§ **6.7, 6.15**.

[447] *See, e.g.,* California v. Harvier, 700 F.2d 1217, 1218 (9th Cir.), *cert. denied,* 464 U.S. 820 (1983).

[448] *See* Bradshaw v. G.M. Corp., 805 F.2d 110, 112 n.1 (3d Cir. 1986).

action, the order will be final if the complaint is dismissed without leave to amend.[449] If an action is dismissed as to all of the defendants who have been served and only unserved defendants remain, the order is considered final for the purpose of perfecting an appeal, because there is no reason to assume that there will be further adjudication.[450] A dismissal order which actually only stays the proceedings is generally not appealable.[451]

§ 14.68 Review of Nonfinal Orders

If the Rule 12 order is not final, litigants rarely will be able to obtain interlocutory review, although the following procedures may be available in a given action. First, in the case of multiple claims or parties, a partial dismissal can be entered as a final judgment if the judge certifies pursuant to Rule 54(b) that there is no reason to delay entry of judgment.[452] Even if a Rule 54(b) certification is not issued, an interlocutory appeal will be heard if the judgment becomes final prior to disposition of the appeal.[453] Second, the judge can certify the decision under 28 U.S.C. § 1292(b) if it affects a controlling question of law when there is substantial ground for difference of opinion. However, although the district court judge certifies the appeal, an appellate court may still dismiss it as improvidently granted. For example, a denial of a dismissal for want of subject matter jurisdiction was remanded because of the multitude of factual possibilities which generated a kaleidoscope of hypothetical legal issues.[454]

The ruling may also fall within the collateral order doctrine pursuant to *Cohen v. Beneficial Industrial Loan Corp.*[455] and its progeny. The *Cohen* standard permits review if the order (1) conclusively determines the controversy, (2) resolves an important issue completely separate from the merits, and (3) is effectively unreviewable on appeal from a final judgment.[456] Usually the issue in

---

[449] Whittington v. Whittington, 733 F.2d 620, 621 (9th Cir. 1984).

[450] Patchick v. Kensington Pub. Corp., 743 F.2d 675, 677 (9th Cir. 1984); *see* Leonhard v. United States, 633 F.2d 599, 608 (2d Cir. 1980), *cert. denied,* 451 U.S. 908 (1981) (final for Rule 54(b) purposes).

[451] *See* Intermedics Infusaid, Inc. v. Regents of Univ. of Minn., 804 F.2d 129, 134 (Fed. Cir. 1986); Microsoftware Computer Sys., Inc. v. Ontel Corp., 686 F.2d 531, 534 (7th Cir. 1982).

[452] *See* Thompson v. Betts, 754 F.2d 1243, 1245–46 (5th Cir. 1985) and cases cited therein.

[453] *See* Sandidge v. Salem Offshore Drilling Co., 764 F.2d 252, 255 (5th Cir. 1985); Gillis v. United States Dep't of Health & Human Serv., 759 F.2d 565, 569 (6th Cir. 1985) and cases cited therein.

[454] International Soc'y for Krishna Consciousness, Inc. v. Air Canada, 727 F.2d 253, 256 (2d Cir. 1984).

[455] 337 U.S. 541 (1949).

[456] *Id.* at 546–47; *see* Mitchell v. Forsyth, _____ U.S. _____, 105 S. Ct. 2806, 2815 (1985).

dispute must involve an unsettled area of law,[457] and some circuits absolutely require this element.[458] These criteria are often referred to as *separability, finality, urgency,* and *importance.*[459]

Finally, a litigant can resort to mandamus.[460] However, because mandamus applies only in extraordinary situations, such as when the court has exceeded its jurisdiction or refused to act when it has a duty to do so,[461] a mere abuse of discretion is not sufficient to obtain review.[462]

§ 14.69 Reviewing Denials of Dismissals

As a general rule, denials of motions to dismiss are not appealable, even when the motion is based on jurisdictional grounds.[463] Attempts to have a denial of a Rule 12(b)(6) motion reviewed under the collateral order doctrine generally meet with failure, because the issues raised are not usually separate from the merits of the defense and would be effectively reviewable on appeal.[464] One type of issue which appellate courts will review is the denial of a motion to dismiss based on a ruling that the defendant is not entitled to absolute immunity[465] or qualified immunity to the extent that it turns on an issue of law.[466] On the other hand, in the absence of a Rule 54(b) certification, a dismissal based on granting the immunity defense is not reviewable until the disposition of the entire action.[467] Some authority also exists for permitting review of an otherwise unreviewable denial if it is part of an order granting or denying preliminary injunctive relief.[468] In addition, certification of the order may be appropriate under 28 U.S.C. § 1292(b), although the appellate court can still refuse the appeal.[469]

---

457 *See, e.g.,* Nixon v. Fitzgerald, 457 U.S. 731, 742 (1982); Cohen v. Beneficial Indus. Loan Corp., 337 U.S. 541, 547 (1949).

458 *See In re* Contintental Inv. Corp., 637 F.2d 1, 4 (1st Cir. 1980).

459 *See id.*

460 28 U.S.C. § 1651(a) (1982).

461 Allied Chem. Corp. v. Daiflon, Inc., 449 U.S. 33, 34–35 (1980) (per curiam).

462 *Id.* at 36; Will v. Calvert Fire Ins. Co., 437 U.S. 655, 665–66 (1978).

463 Catlin v. United States, 324 U.S. 229, 236 (1945); Texaco, Inc. v. Cottage Hill Operating Co., 709 F.2d 452, 453 (7th Cir. 1983).

464 *E.g.,* Spiess v. C. Itoh & Co., 725 F.2d 970, 974–75 (5th Cir.), *cert. denied,* 469 U.S. 812 (1984).

465 *E.g.,* McDonald v. Smith, 472 U.S. 479, 482 n.3 (1985); Nixon v. Fitzgerald, 457 U.S. 731, 742–43 (1982).

466 Mitchell v. Forsyth, ____ U.S. ____, 105 S. Ct. 2806, 2817 (1985).

467 Thompson v. Betts, 754 F.2d 1243, 1245 (5th Cir. 1985).

468 Noxell Corp. v. Firehouse No. 1 Bar-B-Que Restaurant, 760 F.2d 312, 315 (D.C. Cir. 1985) (personal jurisdiction and improper venue reviewable); Helzberg's Diamond Shops v. Valley West Des Moines Shopping Center, Inc., 564 F.2d 816, 818 (8th Cir. 1977).

469 *See* Isra Fruit Ltd v. Agrexco Agr. Export Co., 804 F.2d 24, 25–26 (2d Cir. 1986).

§ 14.70 Reopening Dismissals

If the action has been dismissed for some technical violation, such as failing to respond within the given time allowed by local rules, the plaintiff should move under Rule 60(b) for relief from judgment on the ground of excusable neglect. If this is denied, the appeal of the denial is determined on an abuse of discretion standard.[470] An appeal should also be taken from the dismissal, because this is the only way to challenge from the underlying order.[471] Such an appeal must be timely, because the Rule 60(b) motion does not extend the time to appeal.[472] Counsel cannot assume that even technical failures will be excused, and such dismissals have been affirmed, because a district court is entitled to insist upon compliance with its local rules.[473] If only a portion of the complaint is dismissed, the reconsideration does not fall within Rule 60 but is based on the court's inherent power to afford relief. Thus, excusable neglect need not be shown, and relief will be granted as justice requires, which is considered a more flexible standard.[474]

§ 14.71 Untimely Amendments

If a Rule 12(b)(6) motion has been granted with prejudice, the plaintiff has several options concerning the proffer of an untimely amendment, including filing a Rule 59(e) motion to alter or amend the judgment or moving to reopen under Rule 60(b)(1) alleging that the judgment was entered through mistake or inadvertence of the trial court.[475] Usually, at least one amendment will be granted, unless it is futile.[476] If a timely motion to amend the judgment is filed, counsel should proffer the amended complaint with the motion or, at a minimum, indicate the exact nature of the amendment. If not, the denial of an amendment may be upheld on appeal.[477] If the plaintiff elects to stand on the complaint and appeal rather than attempting to amend in the district court, arguing on appeal that an amendment should have been granted will be unavailing.[478]

---

[470] Browder v. Director, Ill. Dep't of Corrections, 434 U.S. 257, 263 n.7 (1978).

[471] *Id.*

[472] *Id.;* Huff v. International Longshoremen's Ass'n, 799 F.2d 1087, 1089–91 (5th Cir. 1986).

[473] *E.g.*, Corey v. Mast Road Grain & Bldg. Materials Co., 738 F.2d 11, 12 (1st Cir. 1984).

[474] Greene v. Union Mut. Ins. Co. of Am., 764 F.2d 19, 22–23 (1st Cir. 1985).

[475] *See* Strauss v. City of Chicago, 760 F.2d 765, 770 (7th Cir. 1985); McCrary v. Poythress, 638 F.2d 1308, 1314–15 (5th Cir.), *cert. denied,* 454 U.S. 865 (1981); *see generally* 3 Moore's Federal Practice ¶ 15.07[2], at 15–51.

[476] Foman v. Davis, 371 U.S. 178, 182 (1962); see **ch. 8**.

[477] *See* Twohy v. First Nat'l Bank of Chicago, 758 F.2d 1185, 1196–97 (7th Cir. 1985).

[478] *See, e.g.*, Strauss v. City of Chicago, 760 F.2d 765, 767 (7th Cir. 1985); Biesenbach v. Guenther, 588 F.2d 400, 403 (3d Cir. 1978).

CHECKLIST

§ 14.72 Rule 12 Checklist

12(b) Procedure and Timing

1. Has the motion been filed by the defendant within 20 days after service, or within 60 days if the defendant is the United States?
2. Has the appropriate notice of motion been given, which requires at least 10 days if the motion is alternatively captioned as one for summary judgment?
3. Has any stipulation extending time been drafted to specify that additional time is to "answer or otherwise respond"?
4. Has any extension to respond been approved by the court?
5. Has the answer been served within 10 days after notice of the denial of any 12(b) motion?
6. Is there any strategic benefit in raising the Rule 12(b) defense in the answer rather than by motion?
7. Is the defense subject to waiver if untimely (i.e., all Rule 12 defenses except
    - **a.** Subject matter jurisdiction
    - **b.** Failure to state a claim; and
    - **c.** Absence of an indispensable party)?
8. Is it necessary to request a hearing?
9. **Warning:** Check local court rules regarding any requirements concerning memoranda and oppositions to avoid the motion being denied or granted on technical grounds.

12(b)(1) Subject Matter Dismissals (see ch. 2)

1. Has the party asserting jurisdiction met the burden of showing its existence?
2. Does the motion raise a facial attack on the existence of jurisdiction (i.e., no evidence is permitted, facts in complaint are presumed true)?
3. Does the motion attack plaintiff's jurisdictional allegations?
    - **a.** Have controverting affidavits and evidence been submitted with the motion or response?
    - **b.** Is discovery of jurisdictional facts necessary?

4. Is jurisdiction intertwined with the merits of the action?
   a. Court must assume jurisdiction unless the claims are insubstantial and frivolous.
   b. Is dismissal entered pursuant to Rule 12(b)(6) or 12(b)(1)?
      (1) Obtain clarification if necessary.
5. If the dismissal was obtained on jurisdictional grounds, the action can be refiled in any appropriate forum.
   a. Does the refiled complaint face statute of limitations problems?
      (1) Is there a tolling statute?
6. If the motion is untimely under Rule 12, has it been designated as a Rule 12(h)(3) suggestion that jurisdiction is lacking?
7. Should the defendant seek a protective order barring discovery on the merits of the action during the pendency of the motion?
8. **Warning:** Since a subject matter attack can be raised by the defendant or the court at any time, the plaintiff who affirmatively seeks a federal forum must be certain that jurisdiction exists in order to avoid any statute of limitations problems.

12(b)(2) Personal Jurisdiction Dismissals (see ch. 4)

1. Has counsel used the proper motion to challenge personal jurisdiction?
   a. Papers should be entitled as 12(b)(2) motion, not as motion to quash personal justification.
   b. There are no special appearances in federal court.
2. Has the plaintiff met burden of showing that personal jurisdiction exists over the defendant?
3. Is discovery necessary concerning the jurisdictional facts?
4. Have affidavits and evidence been submitted with the motion or response?
5. Has the defendant waived its Rule 12(b)(2) objection?
   a. Has the defendant's conduct been inconsistent with its assertion of the defense?
   b. Was the defendant's Rule 12 motion untimely?
   c. Does the contract at issue provide for the assertion of jurisdiction in the forum?
   d. What is the effect of the defendant's assertion of a permissive counterclaim?
   e. Can personal jurisdiction be presumed as a Rule 37 sanction?

6. Should a hearing be requested?
   a. If no evidentiary hearing is held, the plaintiff need only show a prima facie case before trial, but personal jurisdiction must be proved by a preponderance standard at trial.
7. Alternative Motions
   a. Motion to transfer under 28 U.S.C. § 1631 (see § **6.9**)
   b. Motion to transfer under 28 U.S.C. § 1404(a) (see §§ **6.7–6.8**)
   c. Motion to transfer under 28 U.S.C. § 1406(a) (see § **6.9**)
   d. Forum non conveniens motion if the action concerns any foreign parties or claims (see §§ **6.15–6.17**)
8. **Warning:** Permitting a default to be taken and raising a collateral attack on the judgment for lack of personal jurisdiction is risky.

12(b)(3) Venue Dismissals (see §§ 6.1–6.6)

1. Is the motion worth bringing?
   a. Do choice of law considerations mandate bringing the motion?
   b. Will the complaint be untimely if refiled?
2. Have affidavits and evidence been submitted with the motion or response?
3. What is the best alternative for the plaintiff in responding to the motion?
   a. Should the complaint be voluntarily dismissed and refiled?
   b. Should the plaintiff fight the motion and appeal from any dismissal?
   c. Should the plaintiff fight the motion and refile the complaint?
   d. Should the plaintiff request a 1404(a) or 1406(a) transfer?
4. Has the defendant waived the defense?

12(b)(4) and (5) Process Dismissals (see ch. 5)

1. Is the motion worth bringing in connection with 12(b)(2) attack?
2. Would the dismissal result in the complaint being untimely when it is refiled?
3. Generally Rule 12(b)(4) motions are rarely appropriate; most motions challenging process are Rule 12(b)(5) motions.
4. Have affidavits and evidence been submitted with the motion or response?
   a. What proof is necessary to controvert the process server's return?
5. Alternative motion
   a. Rule 4(j) dismissal for failing to serve within 120 days (see § **5.12**)

6. **Warning:** Permitting a default to be taken and raising a collateral attack on the judgment for improper service is risky.

12(b)(6) Dismissals for Failure to State a Claim

1. Is the attack aimed solely at the pleadings?
   a. Only exhibits attached to complaint can be considered.
   b. The pleadings can be contradicted only by judicially noticed facts.
   c. No affidavits can be considered.
   d. No discovery is necessary.
   e. Well-pleaded facts are assumed to be true.
   f. Doubts are resolved in the pleader's favor.
2. Has the standard for granting a Rule 12(b)(6) motion been met?
   a. Is it beyond doubt that no set of facts supports the claim?
   b. Do the facts support any legal theory, even if not raised by the pleadings?
   c. Is Rule 9 specificity required?
3. Is the court likely to require a Rule 12(e) more definite statement as an alternative to dismissal?
4. Is the court likely to grant an amendment which will correct any deficiency in the complaint?
   a. The plaintiff must request an amendment if it faces statute of limitations problems concerning any refiled complaint.
5. If the Rule 12(b)(6) motion is untimely, has it alternatively been titled as a Rule 12(c) motion?
6. Has conversion to summary judgment been sought (see § **15.25**).
   a. Has 10-days actual or constructive notice been given to the opponent?
   b. Is discovery necessary to respond to the converted motion?
      (1) Is a Rule 56(f) affidavit for a continuance to obtain discovery necessary?
7. Dismissal precludes the plaintiff from bringing the same action in any forum.
8. **Warning:** Submission of affidavits by any party may lead to consideration of the motion as one for summary judgment.

12(b)(7) Motion to Dismiss for Absence of an Indispensable Party (see § 9.3)

1. Is the absent party necessary?

2. If joinder is not feasible, should the court dismiss or proceed to judgment?
3. Have affidavits and evidence been submitted with the motion or response?
4. There is no waiver if an untimely motion is brought.
5. **Warning:** The plaintiff must be certain that indispensable parties are joined since their absence can be raised at any time.

12(c) Motion for Judgment on the Pleadings

1. Has the motion been submitted after the pleadings are closed?
   - **a.** Will the motion delay the trial?
2. Is the attack aimed solely at the pleadings?
   - **a.** No discovery materials can be considered.
   - **b.** No outside evidence, except exhibits attached to complaint, can be considered.
   - **c.** The pleadings can be contradicted only by judicial notice.
   - **d.** Well-pleaded facts are assumed true.
3. Has conversion to summary judgment been sought (see § **15.25**)?
   - **a.** Has 10-days actual or constructive notice been given to the opponent?
   - **b.** Is discovery necessary to respond to the converted motion?
     - **(1)** Is a Rule 56(f) affidavit for a continuance to obtain discovery necessary?
4. **Warning:** Submission of affidavits by any party may lead to consideration of the motion as one for summary judgment.

12(e) Motion for More Definite Statement

1. Since the motion is disfavored, are there particular facts which make it likely to be granted?
2. Has the motion been submitted before the response is due?
3. Are the pleadings so vague and ambiguous that a response cannot be drafted?
4. Does the motion point out the defects in the complaint?
5. Does the motion point out what details are desired?
6. Has the statement been served within 10 days after the opponent has been notified that it is required?

7. Has a conditional sanction been requested if the statement is not timely served?

12(f) Motion to Strike

1. Since the motion is disfavored, are there particular facts which make it likely to be granted?
2. Has the motion been served before the response is due?
3. Has the motion been served within 20 days of receiving the pleading if no response is due?
4. Has the court ordered the material to be struck sua sponte?
5. Does the motion challenge an insufficient defense?
6. Does the motion challenge any redundant, immaterial, impertinent, or scandalous matter?
7. If the motion requests that attorneys' fees be stricken is it alternatively entitled as a Rule 12(b)(6) motion?

Reopening Dismissals (see §§ 8.9, 12.3, and 14.70)

1. Has reconsideration been requested before the dismissal is entered?
2. Has a Rule 60(b) motion been filed after the dismissal is entered?
   - **a.** Does mistake, inadvertence, surprise or excusable neglect exist?
   - **b.** Is there any other reason justifying relief from the judgment?
   - **c.** Will the opposing party be prejudiced if the judgment is reopened?
   - **d.** Is the claim meritorious?
3. **Warning:** The underlying dismissal must be timely appealed, since the Rule 60(b) motion does not raise the validity of the original judgment.

Reviewing Dismissal Rulings

1. Has an appeal been filed if the dismissal terminates the action?
2. Has a Rule 54(b) certificate been entered to permit appeal of a partial dismissal?
3. Is the denial of a dismissal likely to be reviewed as:
   - **a.** A writ of mandamus?
   - **b.** A certification by the judge under 28 U.S.C. § 1292(b)?
   - **c.** A collateral order which is separate from the merits of the action and involves an important issue of law?

Rule 11

1. Does a Rule 11 basis in law or fact exist for the Rule 12 motion or opposition?
2. Is the motion or opposition brought for an improper purpose such as to harass or to cause unnecessary delay or needless increase in the cost of litigation?

CHAPTER 15

SUMMARY JUDGMENT

§ 15.1 Strategic Overview for Moving Party

Summary judgment is designed to meet two very different goals: (1) avoiding useless trials on meritless cases and (2) resolving cases in which the parties do not dispute the facts, but only their legal significance. Summary judgment promotes judicial economy by ensuring the speedy and expeditious disposition of such cases, thus, preventing vexation and delay. It enables the court to determine whether the curtain should rise and the trial proceed.[1] Summary judgment has been described as both "Damoclean and lethal. It can serve as a quick sword untangling the Gordian knot of litigation,"[2] because it denies the losing party an opportunity to have a jury and has res judicata effect in subsequent litigation.

In practice, summary judgment is a much misunderstood motion. Some attorneys routinely bring summary judgment motions and complain that they are rarely granted. Other attorneys refuse to bring summary judgment motions, assuming that they are never granted. Neither extreme is correct. Summary judgment is granted more often than many practitioners believe, but clearly it is not suitable in every case.[3] The reason for this is simple: because summary judgment is such a drastic remedy, the standard for granting the motion is very stringent and rigorously enforced. Thus, unless the movant can show both that no material issue of fact is in dispute and that it is entitled to summary judgment as a matter of law, summary judgment is not granted. Further, some circuits have demonstrated more antipathy to granting summary judgment than others,[4] although the Supreme Court has recently become quite hospitable to summary judgment, stating that it is "properly regarded not as a disfavored procedural shortcut, but rather as an integral part of the Federal Rules as a whole . . . ."[5]

---

[1] Patrick v. LeFevre, 745 F.2d 153, 158 (2d Cir. 1984).

[2] Nicholas Acoustics & Specialty Co. v. H & M Constr. Co., 695 F.2d 839, 844 (5th Cir. 1983).

[3] *Compare* Schwarzer, *Summary Judgment Under the Federal Rules: Defining Genuine Issues of Material Fact,* 99 F.R.D. 465, 467 n.9 (1984) (reported decisions give distorted view of reversal rate for summary judgment, because affirmed cases often result in nonpublished decisions) *with* Sonenshein, *State of Mind and Credibility in the Summary Judgment Context: A Better Approach,* 78 Nw. U.L. Rev. 774, 776 (1984) (summary judgment does not reduce court congestion) *and* McLauchlan, *An Empirical Study of the Federal Summary Judgment Rule,* 6 J. Legal Stud. 427, 458 (1977) (summary judgment does not dispose of a very large proportion of cases).

[4] *E.g., compare* Snell v. United States, 680 F.2d 545, 547 (8th Cir.), *cert. denied,* 459 U.S. 989 (1982) (this circuit has repeatedly emphasized the drastic nature of summary judgment) *with* Brachtl, *Has Summary Judgment Been Eliminated in the Second Circuit?,* 46 Brooklyn L. Rev. 565 (1980) (generally noting that earlier antipathy to summary judgment has dissipated in the Second Circuit); *see also* Irvin v. Griffin Corp., 808 F.2d 802, 807 (11th Cir. 1987) (refusing to reverse a denial of summary judgment, because the trial court has wide discretion not to grant summary judgment whenever it believes it would be just to proceed to trial).

[5] Celotex Corp. v. Catrett, _____ U.S. _____, 106 S. Ct. 2548, 2555 (1986); *see also Second Cir. Comm. on the Pretrial Phase of Civil Litigation, Final Report June 1986,* 2 Current Problems in Federal Civil Practice 1986, 637, 656–57 (PLI Handbook No. 319) (noting that reversals of summary judgment notions did differ significantly from reversal rates for civil cases generally in Second Circuit).

Therefore, when considering a summary judgment motion, counsel should realistically assess the cost effectiveness of bringing the motion. The following questions should be considered:

1. What is the likelihood of success?
2. Does this case neatly fit the summary judgment standard?
3. Is it desirable to educate the judge about complex issues as a way of ensuring more thoughtful trial rulings, even though the chances of actually winning at this stage are uncertain?
4. Will merely bringing a summary judgment motion move the opposing party to a more realistic settlement posture at an earlier time frame than would otherwise occur?
5. Will the motion telegraph the weaknesses in opposing counsel's case at a time when they can be corrected?
6. Will it reveal counsel's own strategy earlier than would otherwise occur?
7. Is an early motion desirable for smoking out the adverse party's legal and factual positions?
8. Will it be useful to pin down the testimony of witnesses?
9. Is the motion only being brought to demonstrate that counsel is actively pursuing the client's interests?[6]

Also consider the judge's attitude toward summary judgment:

1. Will the judge be annoyed if the motion is not a clear winner?
2. Will the motion be referred to a magistrate to recommend a ruling, thereby eliminating any educative effect?[7]
3. Will the judge defer ruling until shortly before trial, thereby encouraging settlement talks because no expense will be saved in trial preparation?

It may prove useful to read the judge's previously reported summary judgment opinions in deciding how best to proceed. Those decisions will be easily accessible through computerized research.

However, even assuming that the judge grants summary judgment, is it a judgment which will stand on appeal? If not, the summary judgment may prove exceedingly costly, not only due to additional expense, but also because of

---

[6] A survey of state court judges in Minnesota indicated that more than one-third of the responding judges believe that, at least half the time, attorneys bring summary judgment motions simply to show their clients they are doing something. Pielemeier, *Summary Judgment in Minnesota: A Search For Patterns,* 7 William Mitchell L. Rev. 147, 150 n.18 (1981).

[7] Under 28 U.S.C. § 636(b)(1)(B) (1982), a judge may refer a motion for summary judgment to a magistrate to conduct hearings and submit proposed findings of fact and recommendations for disposition of the motion. The court may accept, reject, or modify the recommendation and must make a de novo determination of any recommendation as to which objections are made. See §§ **16.11–16.12**.

inevitable delay and the difficulty of trying the case when witnesses have scattered or totally forgotten the facts.[8] The type of case being litigated must be factored into this assessment. Summary judgment is rarely appropriate when issues such as intent or reasonableness of conduct are critical, because such factual questions are often disputed and can rarely be decided as a matter of law. On the other hand, cases which rely mainly on documents or in which the parties agree on the facts are good candidates for summary judgment. In fact, in many cases, the only dispute concerns legal, not factual, contentions.

Even if summary judgment is not feasible, consider whether partial summary judgment would be beneficial. Issues which are adjudicated before trial can shape and considerably simplify trial presentation. However, the absence of such issues may interfere with the coherent or dramatic presentation of the case. For example, lower damages may be awarded to a plaintiff who does not offer evidence on liability. Indeed, the jurors may resent the party who appears to be preventing them from learning all of the facts.

An early assessment of the desirability of bringing a summary judgment motion is not an academic question. Preparing a summary judgment motion is both expensive and time consuming. Not only must the law be fully researched, but in essence counsel must prepare for trial by organizing the facts, sifting through discovery materials, obtaining affidavits, and, in some districts, drafting statements of undisputed facts, conclusions of law, and proposed judgments. A client may want to forgo bringing a valid summary judgment motion or limit expenditures for the motion solely because of cost factors. However, an inexpensive, sloppily drafted summary judgment motion is probably doomed to failure, because the movant has the difficult burden of establishing that no genuine issue of material fact exists. When summary judgment is truly appropriate, the client should be reminded that trying the case will be even more expensive. In practice, the additional cost of drafting a summary judgment motion may be minimal in courts where counsel must draft elaborate pretrial statements of fact and law.

The decision to bring a summary judgment motion should also be made early in the case in order to maximize the value of discovery. The possibility of winning a summary judgment motion can be greatly enhanced by the effective use of depositions, interrogatories, and requests for admissions. Local court rules and court-ordered cutoff dates for motions may affect the timing, because summary judgment motions must be brought at least 45 days before trial in some districts.[9]

Counsel should also note that, although summary judgment has often been considered a prime weapon in the arsenal of the paper war, it can no longer be so

---

[8] *See, e.g.*, Stamper, *Rule 56: Using Summary Judgment Motions*, 7 Litigation 36, 38 (Spring 1981).

[9] *See, e.g.*, Kennedy v. City of Cleveland, 797 F.2d 297, 301 (6th Cir. 1986) (approving cutoff dates for discovery and summary judgment motions); Eagle v. AT&T Co., 769 F.2d 541, 548 (9th Cir. 1985) (pretrial conference order's cutoff precluded new theory raised in summary judgment motion), *cert. denied*, ___ U.S. ___, 106 S. Ct. 1465 (1986); N.D. Tex. R. 5.2(a) (motion must be filed 45 days before trial).

regarded. Rule 11 now mandates that an attorney must certify that the motion is not brought for improper purposes such as harassment or delay or to needlessly increase the cost of litigation, and violation of this requirement can result in sanctions.[10] Therefore, care must be taken that the purpose for the motion, whether it be to educate the judge, discover the opponent's case, or retard the progress of a suit, is not considered improper.[11] In other words, there should be more than a faint hope for a quick victory. Thus, filing a summary judgment motion entails varying risks, but the reward of winning the motion is the immediate termination of the action.

§ 15.2 Strategic Overview for Defending Party

The party defending against a summary judgment motion has entirely different strategic concerns. The defense need only raise a genuine issue of material fact to defeat summary judgment. Thus, obfuscation has often been the easiest strategy, because judges do not grant summary judgment unless they are clearly convinced that no genuine issue of fact exists. Such tactics must be viewed skeptically, because judges are rightly hostile to these ploys. In extreme cases, counsel may be sanctioned if a supporting affidavit is interposed in bad faith.[12] Judges are not hesitant to rely on Rule 11 to impose sanctions for any response which is submitted for an improper purpose. If a valid defense to summary judgment exists, it should be clearly identified. At a minimum, sloppy lawyering may result in unfavorable rulings on discretionary evidentiary issues at trial if the judge is disenchanted with counsel's overall performance.

Defeating summary judgment is fairly easy in most cases, but care should be taken in preparing a response, because poorly drafted affidavits will return to haunt witnesses during cross-examination at trial. Moreover, when opposing a summary judgment motion, never merely answer the movant's contentions. Instead, analyze the case to determine the disputed factual and legal issues, regardless of whether they have been mentioned in the moving papers. Although a single material factual issue will defeat the motion, if any possibility exists that motion will be granted, all factual and legal grounds for opposing summary judgment must be argued to the district judge in order to avoid waiver on appeal.

Preparing summary judgment motions or oppositions may appear onerous, but there are always some benefits. If the motion is successful, trial is avoided; if the motion is denied, the case is more fully prepared for trial or realistic settlement discussions.

---

[10] Fed. R. Civ. P. 11; *see, e.g.*, Mossman v. Roadway Express, Inc., 789 F.2d 804, 806 (9th Cir. 1986) (Rule 11 appropriate for unsupported Rule 56 motion, but attorneys fees should be limited because of provoking behavior of plaintiff's counsel); Frazier v. Cast, 771 F.2d 259, 265 (7th Cir. 1985) (argument without factual foundation); see **ch. 28**.

[11] *See* Professional Mgrs. v. Fawer, Brian, Hardy & Zatzkis, 799 F.2d 218, 221–22 (5th Cir. 1986).

[12] Fed. R. Civ. P. 56(g).

§ 15.3 Notice Requirements

A summary judgment motion can be brought by a defending party at any time;[13] a claimant must wait 20 days after commencement of the suit or after service of an adverse summary judgment motion.[14] Thus, a defendant has a timing advantage which may result in consideration of summary judgment before the complaint is answered or discovery has begun in those cases in which a Rule 12 motion is tendered which is alternatively captioned as a Rule 56 motion. Under Rule 12(a), timely submission of the motion extends the time to answer. It is not uncommon for the complaint to remain unanswered until the resolution of the motion. If so, an affirmative defense may be raised by a summary judgment motion prior to the filing of an answer, although the defense is not suggested by the complaint.[15] Of course, if an affirmative defense is not timely raised by way of the pleadings or a Rule 12 motion, it is waived and cannot be asserted in the summary judgment motion without obtaining permission from the court.[16] As a practical matter, only in rare cases will the motion be granted before any discovery takes place[17] or, in a class action, before a class is certified.[18]

A claimant has one potential timing advantage—a summary judgment motion can technically be served at the same time as the complaint, because the 20-day waiting period runs from the filing of the complaint, not its service. Although a court will no doubt grant an extension to answer the motion or defer its consideration until well after the complaint is answered, this shock tactic may, in an appropriate case, accelerate an anticipated settlement.

Rule 56 requires a written motion[19] which must be served at least 10 days before the hearing.[20] Any affidavits used to support the summary judgment must be served with the motion.[21] In those circuits not requiring oral hearings, 10 days must elapse before judgment is entered, and, in a few circuits, notice must

---

[13] Fed. R. Civ. P. 56(b).

[14] Fed. R. Civ. P. 56(a).

[15] *E.g.*, Jordan v. Kelly, 728 F.2d 1, 3–4 (1st Cir. 1984); 10A C. Wright, A. Miller, *et al.*, Federal Practice and Procedure § 2734, at 426 (2d ed. 1983) [hereinafter Federal Practice and Procedure].

[16] Baker v. Chicago Fire & Burglary Detection, Inc., 489 F.2d 953, 955 (7th Cir. 1973); see **§ 7.7**.

[17] See §§ **15.22–15.24**.

[18] *See, e.g.*, Wright v. Schock, 742 F.2d 541, 543 (9th Cir. 1984) (extensive citations); **see § 10.11**.

[19] Cool Fuel, Inc. v. Connett, 685 F.2d 309, 311 (9th Cir. 1982); Hanson v. Polk County Land, Inc., 608 F.2d 129, 131 (5th Cir. 1979).

[20] For procedural requirements, *see generally* 6 J. Moore *et al.*, Moore's Federal Practice ¶ 56.14 (2d ed. 1986) [hereinafter Moore's Federal Practice]; 10A Federal Practice and Procedure § 2719.

[21] Fed. R. Civ. P. 6(d); CIA Petrolera Caribe, Inc. v. Arco Caribbean, Inc., 754 F.2d 404, 409 (1st Cir. 1985).

be given that the motion and all materials supporting or opposing it will be taken under advisement as of a certain day.[22] Local rules may provide for as much as 28 days' notice.[23] Similarly, while Rule 56 provides that the adverse party may serve opposing affidavits prior to the day of hearing, local court rules vary as to when oppositions are due.[24] Reply briefs may also be specifically provided for in such rules.[25] In some districts a continuance of the hearing automatically extends the time for filing opposing papers and reply briefs.[26] Parties can also stipulate to later filings. However, counsel should always consult the local rules, because stipulations are only effective in many districts when approved by the judge.

In complicated cases, counsel should consider requesting that an expanded briefing schedule for the motion be included in the scheduling or pretrial orders mandated by Rule 16.[27] Lengthy briefing schedules are common in complex litigation.[28] Failure to submit materials within the designated period can result in the judge's refusing to consider the untimely filings or giving additional time to the opposing counsel to respond.[29] Any extension must be sought prior to the motion's return date.[30] Counsel can argue that its inaction resulted from excusable neglect,[31] but the court's refusal to consider the untimely materials is unlikely to be considered an abuse of discretion even if it results in a grant of summary judgment.[32]

Courts have consistently held that a trial judge who does not comply with the advance notice and response provisions of Rule 56(c) has no power to enter

---

[22] *Compare* Grigoleit Co. v. United Rubber, Local No. 270, 769 F.2d 434, 437 (7th Cir. 1985) *and* Cowgill v. Raymark Indus., Inc., 780 F.2d 324, 329 (3d Cir. 1985) *and* Daniels v. Morris, 746 F.2d 271, 275 (5th Cir. 1984) (10 days must elapse) *with* Milburn v. United States, 734 F.2d 762, 765 (11th Cir. 1984) (explicit notice).

[23] *E.g.*, N.D. Cal. R. 220.2 (28 days for all motions); N.D. Tex. R. 5.1(e)(20 days).

[24] *E.g.*, S.D. & E.D.N.Y. Rule 3(c)(2) (three days before return date); C.D. Cal. R. 7.6 (seven days after service of motion).

[25] *E.g.*, C.D. Cal. R. 7.7 (four days after service of opposition).

[26] *E.g.*, C.D. Cal. R. 7.8.

[27] *See, e.g.*, Miller v. Solem, 728 F.2d 1020, 1023 (8th Cir.), *cert. denied,* 469 U.S. 841 (1984) (order granted 33 days for opposition, which was extended another six weeks, and 18 days for reply); Indiana Port Comm'n v. Bethlehem Steel Corp., 702 F.2d 107, 111 (7th Cir. 1983) (when the court allowed 33 days in the pretrial order for a response, the timing could not be shortened without notice); see §§ **16.2–16.4**.

[28] *See, e.g.*, Zenith Radio Corp. v. Matsushita Elec. Indus. Co., 478 F. Supp. 889, 952 (E.D. Pa. 1979) (Pretrial Order No. 154 setting forth briefing scheduling).

[29] *See* Pfeil v. Rogers, 757 F.2d 850, 858 (7th Cir. 1985), *cert. denied,* ____ U.S. ____, 106 S. Ct. 1513 (1986); CIA Petrolera Caribe, Inc. v. Arco Caribbean, Inc., 754 F.2d 404, 409 (1st Cir. 1985).

[30] Davidson v. Keenan, 740 F.2d 129, 131–32 (2d Cir. 1984).

[31] Fed. R. Civ. P. 6(b)(2); *see* Hooks v. Hooks, 771 F.2d 935, 946 (6th Cir. 1985).

[32] *See* Davidson v. Keenan, 740 F.2d 129, 131–32 (2d Cir. 1984).

summary judgment.[33] Although harmless error[34] and waiver doctrines[35] may apply to notice problems, some circuits limit such exceptions to extraordinary cases.[36] In pro se cases when the plaintiff is a prisoner, several circuits require that the plaintiff must be explicitly notified by the court or opposing counsel not only that the motion is being filed, but also that any factual assertion in the movant's affidavits will be accepted by the district judge as being true unless the plaintiff submits his own affidavits or other documentary evidence contradicting the assertion.[37]

§ 15.4 Granting Summary Judgment to the Opposing Party

Despite the requirements for notice, if one party moves for summary judgment and, at the hearing, it appears that there is no genuine dispute respecting a material fact essential to the proof of the movant's case and that the case cannot be proved if a trial should be held, the court may sua sponte grant summary judgment to the nonmoving party.[38] Thus, technically no cross-motion for summary judgment is necessary. This explains why some courts appear to allow oral notice of a motion at the hearing. However, it is always better practice to submit a cross-motion in which counsel's theory of the case is thoroughly explored, because courts are rightly hesitant to grant summary judgment to the nonmovant without ensuring adequate opportunity for the opponent to be

---

[33] Indiana Port Comm'n v. Bethlehem Steel Corp., 702 F.2d 107, 111 (7th Cir. 1983); *see* Anthuis v. Colt Indus. Operating Corp., 789 F.2d 207, 211–12 (3d Cir. 1986); Finn v. Gunter, 722 F.2d 711, 713 (11th Cir. 1984); Winbourne v. Eastern Airlines, Inc., 632 F.2d 219, 223 (2d Cir. 1980). *But see* Portsmouth Square, Inc. v. Shareholders Protective Comm., 770 F.2d 866, 869 (9th Cir. 1985).

[34] Western Fire Ins. Co. v. Copeland, 786 F.2d 649, 653 (5th Cir. 1986); Hoopes v. Equifax, Inc., 611 F.2d 134, 136 (6th Cir. 1979); Ikerd v. Lapworth, 435 F.2d 197, 203 (7th Cir. 1970).

[35] Trustees of Sabine Area Carpenters' Health & Welfare Fund v. Don Lightfoot Home Builder, Inc., 704 F.2d 822, 828 (5th Cir. 1983); Spence v. Latting, 512 F.2d 93, 97 (10th Cir. 1975), *cert. denied,* 423 U.S. 896 (1976).

[36] *E.g.*, Gutwein v. Roche Laboratories, 739 F.2d 93, 95 (2d Cir. 1984); *see* Marshall v. City of Cape Coral, 797 F.2d 1555, 1562–63 (11th Cir. 1986).

[37] Lewis v. Faulkner, 689 F.2d 100, 102 (7th Cir. 1982); *see also* Moore v. Florida, 703 F.2d 516, 519–21 (11th Cir. 1983); Davis v. Zahradnick, 600 F.2d 458, 460 (4th Cir. 1979); Hudson v. Hardy, 412 F.2d 1091, 1094 (D.C. Cir. 1968). *But see* Jacobsen v. Filler, 790 F.2d 1362, 1364–67 (9th Cir. 1986) (does not apply to nonprisoner pro se litigants).

[38] *E.g.*, Pueblo of Santa Ana v. Mountain States Tel. & Tel. Co., 734 F.2d 1402, 1408 (10th Cir. 1984), *rev'd on other grounds,* ______ U.S. ______, 105 S. Ct. 2587 (1985); Project Release v. Prevost, 722 F.2d 960, 969 (2d Cir. 1983); Cool Fuel, Inc. v. Connett, 685 F.2d 309, 311 (9th Cir. 1982); *see generally* 6 Moore's Federal Practice ¶ 56.12 (2d ed. 1986); 10A Federal Practice and Procedure § 2720.

heard.[39] Courts usually allow the original movant additional time to supplement the record before granting judgment to the nonmovant.[40]

§ 15.5 Sua Sponte Summary Judgment

There is authority permitting courts to enter judgment sua sponte even though no party has requested summary judgment.[41] This practice is appropriate as long as the losing party is given notice and opportunity to respond.[42] Such sua sponte action is usually taken when a Rule 12 motion or a partial summary judgment motion is pending.[43] Counsel should be aware that some judges are not hesitant to utilize Rule 16 as an alternative method for granting summary judgment. For example, the Eleventh Circuit gratuitously suggested that the district court possesses power under Rule 16 to summarily decide a case without trial if no issue of material fact exists.[44] Other courts have indicated that the trial judge has power to compel the parties to agree to all facts without dispute.[45] The Ninth Circuit has even permitted the sua sponte granting of summary judgment when no triable issue exists at the end of the pretrial conference.[46] Thus, consistent with Rule 56(c), a judge may give notice that the final pretrial statement will be given preclusive effect and may review the evidence so presented in a manner closely analogous to a directed verdict.[47] However, the judge cannot force the parties to submit their evidence to determine if a directed verdict is appropriate

---

[39] *See generally* 6 Moore's Federal Practice ¶ 56.12; 10A Federal Practice and Procedure § 2720.

[40] *E.g.*, King v. Wells, 94 F.R.D. 675, 687 (E.D. Mich. 1982).

[41] Celotex Corp. v. Catrett, _____ U.S. _____, 106 S. Ct. 2548, 2554 (1986); Portsmouth Square, Inc. v. Shareholders Protective Comm., 770 F.2d 866, 869 (9th Cir. 1985); Yashon v. Gregory, 737 F.2d 547, 552 (6th Cir. 1984); *But see* Clark v. Tarrant County, Tex., 798 F.2d 736, 741 (5th Cir. 1986) (summary judgment cannot be granted to a party who has not requested it).

[42] Celotex Corp. v. Catrett, _____ U.S. _____, 106 S. Ct. 2548, 2554 (1986); 6 Moore's Federal Practice ¶ 56.12, at 56-338 to 56-339; 10A Federal Practice and Procedure § 2720, at 27–29; *see also* Stewart v. Credit Bureau, Inc., 734 F.2d 47, 53 (D.C. Cir. 1984) (reversing summary judgment granted on issue different from that raised by the movant).

[43] *See, e.g.*, Malak v. Associated Physicians, Inc., 784 F.2d 277, 279 (7th Cir. 1986) (codefendants motion); Williams v. City of St. Louis, 783 F.2d 114, 116 (8th Cir. 1986); Flores v. Heckler, 755 F.2d 401, 403 (5th Cir. 1985) (harmless error).

[44] Diaz v. Schwerman Trucking Co., 709 F.2d 1371, 1375 n.6 (11th Cir. 1983); see § **16.3**.

[45] Holcolm v. Aetna Life Ins. Co., 255 F.2d 577, 580–81 (10th Cir.), *cert. denied,* 358 U.S. 879 (1958); *See* 6 Federal Practice and Procedure §§ 1525, 1527.

[46] Portsmouth Square, Inc. v. Shareholders Protective Comm., 770 F.2d 866, 869–70 (9th Cir. 1985).

[47] *In re* Japanese Elec. Prods., 723 F.2d 238, 258 (3d Cir. 1983), *rev'd on other grounds sub nom.* Matsushita Elec. Indus. Co. v. Zenith Radio, _____ U.S. _____, 106 S. Ct. 1348 (1986); 2 P. Areeda & D. Turner, Antitrust Law ¶ 316, at 61 (1978).

when summary judgment is not proper[48] or to support a summary judgment by reference to a procedurally defective pretrial order.[49] If no notice is given, an in limine motion cannot be treated as a summary judgment motion.[50] Counsel can anticipate that judges who view themselves as case managers will invite summary judgment motions whenever they deem them to be appropriate.

§ 15.6 Summary Judgment Standard

The standard for granting summary judgment is clearly stated in Rule 56(c), which requires that "there is no genuine issue as to any material fact and that the moving party is entitled to a judgment as a matter of law." This standard applies in diversity cases as well as in federal actions.[51] Thus, never bring a summary judgment motion, without asking (1) whether there is any genuine factual issue, and (2) whether that issue affects a material fact. Genuine issues are often referred to as those sustained by substantial or significantly probative evidence, in contrast to issues raised by slight or merely colorable evidence, a scintilla, or unadorned speculation.[52] Therefore, the mere possibility that a factual dispute may exist is not sufficient to defeat summary judgment.[53] Material facts are those which necessarily affect the outcome of the case.[54] A material issue of genuine fact would exist if the facts proved would constitute a legal claim or defense.[55] Unfortunately, "the law provides no magical talisman or compass that will serve as an unerring guide to determine when a material issue of fact is presented."[56] When the movant has the burden on an issue at trial, the showing

---

[48] Williams v. Georgia Dep't of Human Resources, 789 F.2d 881, 882–83 (11th Cir. 1986).

[49] Miera v. First See, Bank of Utah, N.A., 776 F.2d 902, 906 (10th Cir. 1985).

[50] Brobst v. Columbus Servs. Int'l, 761 F.2d 148, 154 (3d Cir. 1985).

[51] Reinke v. O'Connor, 790 F.2d 850, 851 (11th Cir. 1986); Reid v. Sears Roebuck & Co., 790 F.2d 453, 459 (6th Cir. 1986); Bank of Cal. v. Opie, 663 F.2d 977, 979 (9th Cir. 1981); 10 Federal Practice and Procedure § 2712, at 591.

[52] *See* Anderson v. Liberty Lobby, Inc., ____ U.S. ____, 106 S. Ct. 2505, 2510–12 (1986); Professional Mgrs. v. Fawer, Brian, Hardy & Zatzkis, 799 F.2d 218, 222 (5th Cir. 1986); Ground Saucer Watch, Inc. v. CIA, 692 F.2d 770, 772 (D.C. Cir. 1981); Union Planters Nat'l Leasing, Inc. v. Woods, 687 F.2d 117, 119 (5th Cir. 1982); Fireman's Ins. Co. v. DuFresne, 676 F.2d 965, 969 (3d Cir. 1982); British Airways Bd. v. Boeing Co., 585 F.2d 946, 952 (9th Cir. 1978), *cert. denied,* 440 U.S. 981 (1979).

[53] Anderson v. Liberty Lobby, Inc., ____ U.S. ____, 106 S. Ct. 2505, 2510–12 (1986); Linhart v. Glatfelter, 771 F.2d 1004, 1008 (7th Cir. 1985); United States v. One Tintoretto Painting, 691 F.2d 603, 606 (2d Cir. 1982).

[54] Anderson v. Liberty Lobby, Inc., ____ U.S. ____, 106 S. Ct. 2505, 2510 (1986); St. Amant v. Benoit, 806 F.2d 1294, 1297 (5th Cir. 1987); Wainwright Bank & Trust Co. v. Railroadmens Fed. Sav. & Loan Ass'n, 806 F.2d 146, 149 (7th Cir. 1986).

[55] *E.g.,* First Nat'l Bank Co. v. Ins. Co. of N. Am., 606 F.2d 760, 766 (7th Cir. 1979).

[56] American Mfrs. Mut. Ins. Co. v. American Broadcasting-Paramount Theatres, Inc., 388 F.2d 272, 279 (2d Cir. 1967).

must be sufficient for the court to hold that no reasonable trier of fact could find other than for that party.[57] When the moving party does not have the burden at trial, the Supreme Court has stated that, if the record taken as a whole could not lead a reasonable trier of fact to find for the nonmoving party, no genuine issue of material fact exists.[58] The judge must also consider the substantive evidentiary standard of proof when ruling on a summary judgment motion.[59] Thus, if a civil case is to be determined by a clear and convincing standard, the trial judge must determine if a "fair minded jury" could return a verdict for the plaintiff based on the convincing clarity of the evidence.[60]

In determining summary judgment, the court views the evidence in the light most favorable to the opposing party.[61] Similarly, the court must give the opposing party the benefit of all factual inferences or ambiguities drawn from the evidence.[62] If differing inferences can be drawn from the undisputed evidence, summary judgment is inappropriate.[63] Thus, if conduct may be interpreted in two ways, one supporting the motion and the other controverting the motion, summary judgment must be denied.[64] For example, in a libel case, although no dispute may exist concerning the written article, if the words are capable of more than one meaning, only one of which is defamatory, summary judgment cannot be granted.[65] However, only reasonable inferences can defeat summary judgment.[66]

---

[57] Calderone v. United States, 799 F.2d 254, 259 (6th Cir. 1986) (quoting Judge Schwarzer's thoughtful article, *Summary Judgment Under the Federal Rules: Defining Genuine Issues of Material Fact,* 99 F.R.D. 465 (1984)).

[58] Anderson v. Liberty Lobby, Inc., ____ U.S. ____, 106 S. Ct. 2505, 2510–11 (1986); Matsushita Elec. Indus. Co. v. Zenith Radio, ____ U.S. ____, 106 S. Ct. 1348, 1356 (1986).

[59] Anderson v. Liberty Lobby, Inc., ____ U.S. ____, 106 S. Ct. 2505, 2512–13 (1986).

[60] *Id.*

[61] Adickes v. S.H. Kress & Co., 398 U.S. 144, 157 (1970); United States v. Diebold, Inc., 369 U.S. 654, 655 (1962) (per curiam).

[62] Adickes v. S.H. Kress & Co., 398 U.S. 144, 158–59 (1970); United States v. One Tintoretto Painting, 691 F.2d 603, 606 (2d Cir. 1982).

[63] Barnes v. Arden Mayfair, Inc., 759 F.2d 676, 681 (9th Cir. 1985); Daly v. Sprague, 675 F.2d 716, 725 (5th Cir. 1982), *cert. denied,* 460 U.S. 1047 (1983).

[64] Avery v. County of Burke, 660 F.2d 111, 115–16 (4th Cir. 1981); *see* TSC Indus., Inc. v. Northway, Inc., 426 U.S. 438, 450 (1976); Greenberg v. F.D.A., 803 F.2d 1213, 1216 (D.C. Cir. 1986).

[65] Hallmark Builders, Inc. v. Gaylord Broadcasting Co., 733 F.2d 1461, 1463 (11th Cir. 1984); Fitzgerald v. Penthouse Int'l, Ltd., 639 F.2d 1076, 1079 (4th Cir. 1981), *cert. denied,* 460 U.S. 1024 (1983).

[66] Richoux v. Armstrong Cork Corp., 777 F.2d 296, 297–98 (5th Cir. 1985); Barnes v. Arden Mayfair, Inc., 759 F.2d 676, 680–81 (9th Cir. 1985); Thrasher v. State Farm Fire & Casualty Co., 734 F.2d 637, 639 (11th Cir. 1984); *see* Matsushita Elec. Indus. Co. v. Zenith Radio, ____ U.S. ____, 106 S. Ct. 1348, 1357 (1986).

§ 15.7 Burden of Proof

The movant's burden of proof to show that no genuine issue of material fact exists has been clarified in connection with issues on which the nonmoving party has the ultimate burden of persuasion at trial. In *Celotex v. Catrett,*[67] the Supreme Court ruled that summary judgment can be granted against a party who has been afforded discovery but fails to make a showing sufficient to establish the existence of an essential element on which it bears the burden of proof at trial.[68] In such cases, there is no requirement that the moving party support its motion with affidavits or other similar materials negating the opponent's claim. Instead, summary judgment is properly based upon discovery materials showing an absence of evidence to support the nonmoving party's case.[69] The court can also grant summary judgment based solely on the materials submitted by the opponent of the motion.[70] Similarly, evidence from any source will defeat a summary judgment motion if it creates a genuine issue of material fact, regardless of how many affidavits are filed by the movant.

Since summary judgment is a drastic remedy, any doubts concerning the existence of genuine issues of material fact are resolved against the moving party.[71] Courts which have viewed summary judgment as a "disfavored" motion often state that it should be granted only when the movant establishes a clear, uncontestable right to judgment.[72] However, such attitudes may soften with the Supreme Court's recent reminder that Rule 56 must be construed with due regard not only for the rights of those asserting adequate claims and defenses to have a jury trial, but also for the rights of those opposing such claims and defenses to demonstrate their lack of factual basis.[73]

§ 15.8 Statement of Uncontroverted Facts

In order to help the court determine if summary judgment is appropriate, many districts now require that the movant file a separate document which contains a concise statement of uncontroverted facts as to which the party contends there is

---

[67] ____ U.S. ____, 106 S. Ct. 2548 (1986); *cf.* Thornbrough v. Columbus & Greenville R. Co., 760 F.2d 633, 641 n.9 (5th Cir. 1986) (discussing relationship of prima facie case and summary judgment in employment discrimination case).

[68] Celotex Corp. v. Catrett, ____ U.S. ____, 106 S. Ct. 2548, 2552–53 (1986).

[69] *Id.; see also* Murray v. Xerox Corp., 811 F.2d 118, 122 (2d Cir. 1987) (judgment mandated when plaintiff failed to offer evidence of fraudulent intent).

[70] *In re* Japanese Elec. Prods., 723 F.2d 238, 258 (3d Cir. 1983), *rev'd on other grounds sub nom.* Matsushita Elec. Indus. Co. v. Zenith Radio, ____ U.S. ____, 106 S. Ct. 1348 (1986).

[71] Continental Ins. Co. v. Bodie, 682 F.2d 436, 438 (3d Cir. 1982).

[72] Tele-Radio Sys. Ltd. v. De Forest Elecs., Inc., 92 F.R.D. 371, 373 (D.N.J. 1981); *see* Ledwith v. Douglas, 568 F.2d 117, 119 (8th Cir. 1978).

[73] Celotex Corp. v. Catrett, ____ U.S. ____, 106 S. Ct. 2548, 2555 (1986).

no genuine issue.[74] The major difficulty with drafting such statements is that counsel must include every fact necessary to sustain the judgment. Merely stating ultimate factual conclusions is not considered sufficient by many judges. Therefore, most statements resemble the detailed findings of fact filed by judges pursuant to Rule 52 in nonjury actions. If the pretrial statement is due before the summary judgment motion, it should be written to simplify drafting the Rule 56 required factual statement. It is often useful to indicate the source of the nondisputed fact even if not required by local rules. In this way, the court is provided with an easy-to-consult reference work which favors counsel's position. For example, in a wrongful discharge or Title VII case, when the plaintiff alleges that he was discharged for discriminatory reasons, one undisputed fact and its source might be stated as follows:

Undisputed Fact	Source
J. Jones (Plaintiff) was often absent from work	Jones's deposition p. 227, lines 4–22; Affidavit of Jones's supervisor, T. Smith

It is essential that counsel consult the local court rules before filing the motion, because the court can deny summary judgment solely on the ground that a party failed to file a statement of undisputed facts or that its statement was wholly insufficient.[75] Similarly, some districts also require the movant to submit undisputed conclusions of law and a proposed judgment in addition to the points and authorities supporting the motion. Such requirements increase the difficulty of drafting the motion, but they are important to avoid a technical denial and also because judges granting summary judgment often adopt or modify portions of these documents as their findings of fact and conclusions of law. Thus, counsel may be creating the appellate record. While appellate courts indicate that the judge's findings are desirable, their presence does not change the standard of review which requires the appellate court to determine for itself whether an issue of material fact exists.[76]

The statement of undisputed facts and law should be written cogently, concisely, and as favorably to counsel's position as is realistically supportable. Overstatement is an easy target for opposing counsel, and the judge will question the entire motion if it appears that the movant is distorting the facts. Moreover, even if judgment is granted, an appellate court may focus on a particular misrepresentation as ground for reversal. Similarly, the legal memorandum supporting the motion should be organized to highlight the facts without misrepresenting them. A factual statement should precede the legal argument and is often the most important part of the points and authorities. The critical facts should be woven into a graphic picture supporting counsel's theory of the

[74] *E.g.*, C.D. Cal. R. 7.14.1; S.D. & E.D.N.Y. R. 3(g); D.C. R. 1–9(i).

[75] *See, e.g.*, D.C. R. 1–9(i); C.D. Cal. R. 7.9; S.D. & E.D.N.Y. R. 3(g).

[76] Shook v. United States, 713 F.2d 662, 665 (11th Cir. 1983); see § **15.28**.

case. Furthermore, the statement should enable the judge to ignore any red herrings which opposing counsel attempts to raise. The introduction should be long enough to include all the key facts but not so long that it is merely a rambling chronology rather than a well crafted piece of advocacy. The factual statement should be followed by the strongest legal argument. In other words, summary judgment is not a motion which is won by overwhelming the judge with unrelated legal theories which cumulatively favor counsel's position. The motion is usually won or lost by the judge's reaction to the facts in the context of counsel's first legal argument.

§ 15.9 Defeating a Summary Judgment Motion

Rule 56(e) provides that the party opposing summary judgment may not rest on mere allegations or denials in its pleadings but must respond with affidavits or other evidentiary material which set forth "specific facts" showing the existence of a genuine issue for trial.[77] Thus, the court clearly has the power to pierce the pleadings in assessing whether a factual dispute exists. Some practitioners and judges mistakenly believe that when no opposing affidavit is filed, summary judgment is automatically required.[78] Conversely, other courts do not grant summary judgment without reviewing the pleadings or legal memoranda for factual issues when the nonmovant files no evidence controverting the factual assertions of the movant.[79] This confusion arises because parties can rest on their pleadings as long as the "movant's papers are insufficient on their face or themselves demonstrate the existence of a material issue of fact."[80] In other words, the adverse party need not submit any evidentiary material until the movant meets its initial burden of showing that no genuine issue of fact exists.[81] Thus, the evidentiary materials submitted by the movant may require denial of the motion even though nothing was submitted by the opposing party.[82]

The leading case on this point is *Adickes v. S.H. Kress & Co.*,[83] in which the Supreme Court reversed the grant of summary judgment on a conspiracy

---

[77] *See, e.g.*, Tarpley v. Greene, 684 F.2d 1, 6–7 (D.C. Cir. 1982); Security Nat'l Bank v. Belleville Livestock Comm'n Co., 619 F.2d 840, 846–47 (10th Cir. 1980).

[78] *See, e.g.*, Yorger v. Pittsburgh Corning Corp., 733 F.2d 1215, 1221–22 (7th Cir. 1984) (court could not accept as an absolute requirement that a party opposing a motion for summary judgment must file an affidavit in order to preserve issues adequately mentioned in the response and elsewhere); Thornton v. Evans, 692 F.2d 1064, 1074 (7th Cir. 1982) (district court granted judgment because plaintiff rested on his pleadings; appellate court reversed, because summary judgment was not appropriate).

[79] *See, e.g.*, Thompson v. Johns-Manville Sales Corp., 714 F.2d 581, 582 (5th Cir. 1983), *cert. denied*, 465 U.S. 1102 (1984).

[80] Hamilton v. Keystone Tankship Corp., 539 F.2d 684, 686 (9th Cir. 1976) (per curiam).

[81] Adickes v. S.H. Kress & Co., 398 U.S. 144, 159–161 (1970); Egger v. Phillips, 710 F.2d 292, 296 (7th Cir.), *cert. denied*, 464 U.S. 918 (1983).

[82] *E.g.*, Thornton v. Evans, 692 F.2d 1064, 1074–75 (7th Cir. 1982).

[83] 398 U.S. 144 (1970).

allegation despite the fact that the adverse party submitted no affidavit on this issue. Summary judgment was inappropriate because the movant did not defeat every theory of conspiracy in its own affidavits. The validity of the conspiracy allegation depended upon whether a policeman was in the store at the time Adickes was denied food service by a Kress employee. Kress argued that Adickes had to submit proof that a policeman was present, which she had not done. However, Kress's affidavits failed to foreclose the possibility that a policeman was present in the store. In other words, when the moving party did not prove the absence of an issue raised by the pleadings, no opposing evidential material was necessary.[84] Although recent Supreme Court rulings have not overruled *Adickes,* they should be read as limiting its usefulness in those cases in which the nonmovant has the burden of proof at trial.[85]

Of course, the nonmoving party can usually easily avoid this problem by submitting evidence controverting the movant's factual offering rather than merely resting on its pleadings. As the court in *Adickes* pointed out, "[e]ven though not essential here to defeat respondent's motion, the submission of such an affidavit would have been the preferable course for petitioner's counsel to have followed."[86] Therefore, it is always prudent to respond to a summary judgment motion, even if counsel believes the movant failed to sustain its initial burden.[87]

§ 15.10 Proving Disputed Facts

If the movant meets its initial burden, the opposing party must respond with evidentiary proof[88] and do more than simply show that there is some "metaphysical doubt" as to the material facts.[89] The opponent cannot simply rely on conclusory statements, bare assertions, or references to phantom documents or merely dismiss the moving affidavit as incredible.[90] Moreover, opposing counsel cannot manufacture issues by protesting in legal memoranda, statement of

---

[84] McWhirter Distrib. Co. v. Texaco, Inc., 668 F.2d 511, 519 (Temp. Emer. Ct. App. 1981).

[85] *See* Celotex Corp. v. Catrett, ____ U.S. ____, 106 S. Ct. 2548, 2554 (1986); *see also* Anderson v. Liberty Lobby, Inc., ____ U.S. ____, 106 S. Ct. 2505, 2509 (1986); Boies, *Summary Judgment,* 1 Current Problems in Federal Civil Practice 1986, at 111 (PLI Handbook No. 318); Vanyo & Scott, *The Benefit of the Burden: The Supreme Court's Recent Clarification of the Standards Governing Summary Judgment,* 1 Current Problems in Civil Practice 1986, at 173 (PLI Handbook No. 318).

[86] Adickes v. S.H. Kress & Co., 398 U.S. 144, 160-1 (1970).

[87] Egger v. Phillips, 710 F.2d 292, 296 (7th Cir.), *cert. denied,* 464 U.S. 918 (1983); *see* 6, pt. 2 J. Moore & J. Wicker, Moore's Federal Practice ¶ 56.22[2], at 56-1341 to 44 (2d ed. 1985).

[88] Adickes v. S.H. Kress & Co., 398 U.S. 144, 160 (1970).

[89] Matsushita Elec. Indus. Co. v. Zenith Radio, ____ U.S. ____, 106 S. Ct. 1348, 1356 (1986).

[90] Connick v. T.I.A.A., 784 F.2d 1018, 1020 (9th Cir. 1986), *cert. denied,* ____ U.S. ____, 107 S. Ct. 74 (1986); Howard v. City of Greenwood, 783 F.2d 1311, 1315 (5th Cir. 1986); Wyler v. United States, 725 F.2d 156, 160 (2d Cir. 1983); Fireman's Ins. Co. v. DuFresne, 676 F.2d 965, 969 (3d Cir. 1982).

contested facts, or at oral argument that facts are in dispute.[91] For example, in the *Adickes* case, if Kress had submitted affidavits from the police denying their presence in the store, the plaintiff would have had to submit either an affidavit of someone who saw the policeman in the store or an affidavit pursuant to Rule 56(f) explaining why she could not submit evidence establishing the policeman's presence.[92]

When expert testimony is necessary to prevail at trial, if an expert affidavit is submitted by the movant, the opposing party must also submit an expert affidavit in order to create a material factual issue.[93] Courts vary as to the amount of specificity which must be shown concerning both an expert's opinion and the factual basis underlying it.[94] The Supreme Court recently added to the confusion when it affirmed a grant of summary judgment by disregarding an expert's affidavit which it described as having little probative value.[95] It is always safer to state the basis for the expert's conclusion than gamble that the court will request supplementation instead of dismissing the affidavit as conclusory.[96] The expert's opinion must be based on information which is reasonably relied upon by experts in the particular field,[97] and the affiant's competence as an expert must be established.[98] Similarly, even if the plaintiff's affidavit is considered on the issue of causation of an injury, it must set forth specific facts and demonstrate the percipient witness's competency to testify about the accident.[99]

Rather than merely controverting the movant's facts, the opponent's affidavit should also include any additional disputed issues of fact or law; failure to do so will act as a waiver if the summary judgment is granted. If summary judgment is denied, the facts may be developed at trial without regard to the statement of genuine issues.

---

[91] Helmich v. Kennedy, 796 F.2d 1441, 1443 (11th Cir. 1986); Bryson v. Royal Business Group, 763 F.2d 491, 494 (1st Cir. 1985); Zanghi v. Incorporated Village of Old Brookville, 752 F.2d 42, 47 (2d Cir. 1985); VARIG Airlines v. Walter Kidde & Co., Inc., 690 F.2d 1235, 1238 (9th Cir. 1982); Frito-Lay of Puerto Rico, Inc. v. Canas, 92 F.R.D. 384, 391 (D.P.R. 1981).

[92] Adickes v. S.H. Kress & Co., 398 U.S. 144, 160 (1970).

[93] *See, e.g.*, Sitts v. United States, 811 F.2d 736, 740–42 (2d Cir. 1987); Gans v. Mundy, 762 F.2d 338, 343 (3d Cir.), *cert. denied*, ____ U.S. ____, 106 S. Ct. 537 (1985); Bowers v. DeVito, 686 F.2d 616, 617 (7th Cir. 1982); Jones v. Wike, 654 F.2d 1129, 1130 (5th Cir. 1981).

[94] *See* Fed. R. Evid. 703; *compare* Bulthuis v. Rexall Corp., 789 F.2d 1315, 1318 (9th Cir. 1986) (when basis for conclusion is stated, court can require factual reasoning disclosed) *with* Reinke v. O'Connor, 790 F.2d 850, 850–52 (11th Cir. 1986) (affidavit stating doctor was not guilty of malpractice insufficient to trigger duty to respond).

[95] Matsushita Elec. Indus. Co. v. Zenith Radio, ____ U.S. ____, 106 S. Ct. 1348, 1360 n.19 (1986); *see* Akerman v. Oryx Communications, Inc., 810 F.2d 336, 343 (2d Cir. 1987) (unreliable and inconsistent statistical studies disregarded).

[96] *See, e.g.*, Coats & Clark, Inc. v. Gay, 755 F.2d 1506 (11th Cir.), *cert. denied*, ____ U.S. ____, 106 S. Ct. 231 (1985) (speculative affidavit of expert disregarded in granting summary judgment).

[97] Fed. R. Evid. 703; *see, e.g.*, Bulthuis v. Rexall Corp., 789 F.2d 1315, 1318 (9th Cir. 1986).

[98] American Key Corp. v. Cole Nat'l Corp., 762 F.2d 1569, 1580 (11th Cir. 1985).

[99] Bushman v. Halm, 798 F.2d 651, 660 (3d Cir. 1986).

Affidavits must be carefully drafted to pinpoint factual disputes. For example, in an age discrimination case, a plaintiff who was untimely in filing his complaint with the EEOC attempted to create a factual issue by showing that his employer failed to post notice of his right to sue in a conspicuous place as required. The plaintiff's affidavit indicated that he never saw the notice. Summary judgment was granted and upheld on appeal, because this assertion was not the equivalent of stating that the notice was not conspicuously posted.[100]

§ 15.11 Court's Role in Determining Issues of Fact

Courts differ as to the duty of the trial judge to search through discovery materials on file to determine if an issue of fact exists when the nonmovant fails to submit any response or files an inadequate opposition and summary judgment is otherwise appropriate.[101] For example, it appears that at least one circuit requires the trial judge to examine all materials on file, even if the nonmovant failed to respond to the motion.[102] Other circuits consider such a review discretionary.[103] Similarly, appellate courts have varying reactions to cases in which the parties submit vague papers inadequately identifying the issues or rely on voluminous depositions without clarifying affidavits.[104] One judge criticized the anomalous result of reversing a summary judgment when the voluminous record raised factual ambiguities, because "largely as a consequence of less than adequate lawyering, a result has been achieved that might not otherwise have been obtained."[105] Clearly, no counsel wishes to be so identified by the court. Moreover, parties opposing summary judgment cannot always rely on the appellate court to bail them out. For example, at least one court has stated that "[r]eversal should not occur because of confusion in the record;"[106] another has

---

[100] Posey v. Skyline Corp., 702 F.2d 102, 106 (7th Cir.), *cert. denied,* 464 U.S. 960 (1983); *cf.* Hansen v. Prentice-Hall Inc., 788 F.2d 892, 893–94 (2d Cir.), *cert. denied,* ____ U.S. ____, 107 S. Ct. 178 (1986) (statement that affiant believed he provided notice not sufficient to allege notice).

[101] *See generally* Note, *Court Examination of the Discovery File on a Motion for Summary Judgment,* 79 Mich. L. Rev. 321 (1980); *see also* Fullman v. Graddick, 739 F.2d 553, 557 (11th Cir. 1984).

[102] Smith v. Hudson, 600 F.2d 60, 65 (6th Cir.), *cert. dismissed,* 444 U.S. 986 (1979); *see also* Yorger v. Pittsburgh Corning Corp., 733 F.2d 1215, 1221 n.5 (7th Cir. 1984) (voluminous deposition considered to supplement inadequate response).

[103] *See, e.g.,* Kaszuk v. Bakery & Confectionery Union, 791 F.2d 548, 558 (7th Cir. 1986) (no obligation to comb the record for evidence contradicting the movant's affidavit); Downes v. Beach, 587 F.2d 469, 472 (10th Cir. 1978).

[104] *See, e.g.,* John v. Louisiana, 757 F.2d 698, 711–12 (5th Cir. 1985).

[105] Peterson v. Lehigh Valley Dist. Council, 676 F.2d 81, 91 (3d Cir. 1982) (Garth, J., concurring in part).

[106] VARIG Airlines v. Walter Kidde & Co., Inc., 690 F.2d 1235, 1238 (9th Cir. 1982).

noted that a party may not prevail in opposition to a motion for summary judgment by simply overwhelming the district court with a miscellany of unorganized documentation.[107] To avoid summary judgment, a party "must do more than whet the curiosity of the court; he must support vague accusation and surmise with concrete particulars."[108] Courts have even stated that the party opposing summary judgment must fully disclose evidence that it will rely on at trial to establish a genuine issue of material fact.[109]

§ 15.12 Statement of Genuine Issues

Due to the perceived inadequate factual record presented by many lawyers in response to summary judgment motions, courts have begun to require that the nonmovant cite specific page references to the documentary evidence and deposition testimony supporting its contentions. For example, the First Circuit chastised plaintiff's counsel for filing barely adequate summary judgment papers in the district court and then drafting a lengthy factually detailed brief on appeal.[110] The movant argued that the plaintiff's failure to cite specific evidence freed the judge from any obligation to search the record. Although the First Circuit found this principle appealing and noted that it was irresponsible of counsel to neglect to file affidavits or citation to a sizable or complex record pointing out the factual disputes, it held that Rule 56(c) did not limit the court's examination to issues raised in affidavits or to the record pinpointed in the parties' memoranda. Thus, if a deposition is merely filed as opposed to being singled out by counsel, it must still be reviewed.[111]

However, the First Circuit proposed several alternatives to prevent trial judges from being unfairly sandbagged. First, it noted the Fifth Circuit's suggestion that, in fairly large or complicated cases, the trial court cannot read the entire record because "[j]udges are not ferrets!"[112] Second, it recommended that a district court handle a sprawling record by ordering the movant to provide a list of undisputed facts, supported by appropriate record citations, and the opposing party to provide a counter list of genuine material factual issues also supported

---

[107] Zoslaw v. MCA Distrib. Corp., 693 F.2d 870, 883 (9th Cir. 1982), *cert. denied,* 460 U.S. 1085 (1983).

[108] Applegate v. Top Assocs., Inc., 425 F.2d 92, 96 (2d Cir. 1970).

[109] City of Warrensburg v. RCA Corp., 550 F. Supp. 1364, 1370 (W.D. Mo. 1982) (citing extensively to Moore's Federal Practice).

[110] Stephanischen v. Merchants Despatch Transp. Corp., 722 F.2d 922–27 (1st Cir. 1983).

[111] *Id.* at 930; *see also* Higgenbotham v. Ochsner Found. Hosp., 607 F.2d 653, 656–57 (5th Cir. 1979).

[112] Nicholas Acoustics & Specialty Co. v. H & M Constr. Co., 695 F.2d 839, 846–47 (5th Cir. 1983).

by citation to the record. Once so warned, a party's failure to comply would, when appropriate, be a ground for judgment against that party.[113] Furthermore, the First Circuit recommended that district judges in Massachusetts might consider local rules similar to Rule 3(g), enacted by the Southern District of New York, which requires such statements and provides that "[a]ll material facts set forth in the statement required to be served by the moving party will be deemed to be admitted unless controverted by the statement required to be served by the opposing party."

Many districts currently have enacted rules which provide for such waivers, and it is likely that this trend will continue in order to "clear away the fog that so often hangs over the early stages of litigation."[114] Such rules limit or completely eliminate the judge's responsibility to sift through routine discovery. However, a split appears to be developing as to whether the violation of a local rule can be the sole reason authorizing summary judgment.[115] Similarly, courts appear hesitant to find that a filed statement is so inadequate under the local rules as to permit summary judgment.[116] Of course, in many districts, routine discovery is filed only if ordered by the court so that the court would not have any discovery material before it to review unless specifically submitted by the parties.

In general, counsel should assume that rambling assertions in briefs citing generally to voluminous depositions or documents no longer suffice to defeat summary judgment motions. When drafting statements of disputed facts, counsel should focus on ultimate factual disputes rather than laying out the entire case to be proved at trial. Unlike the movant, counsel's task is solely to raise factual issues, not to prove the case as a matter of law. However, it usually is necessary to indicate supporting factual data. For example, in the statement of undisputed facts in the wrongful discharge case mentioned in § **15.8**, the ultimate factual dispute is whether the plaintiff was fired for discriminatory reasons. Merely stating this conclusion is not sufficient to create a factual issue, unless the evidentiary facts or inferences support the assertion. Thus, one way to controvert the defendant's position that plaintiff was fired for his continued absence might be as follows:

---

[113] Stephanischen v. Merchants Despatch Transp. Corp., 722 F.2d 922, 931 (1st Cir. 1983); *see* NRM Corp. v. Hercules Inc., 758 F.2d 676, 680 (D.C. Cir. 1985) (failure to allege factual dispute statement to genuine issues precluded review).

[114] SEC v. Research Automation Corp., 585 F.2d 31, 34 n.6 (2d Cir. 1978). At least 30 district courts currently have such rules, which are listed in Note, *Court Examination of the Discovery File on a Motion for Summary Judgment,* 79 Mich. L. Rev. 321, 325 n.19 (1980).

[115] *Compare* Dixie Stevedores, Inc. v. Marinic Maritime, Ltd., 778 F.2d 670, 672–73 (11th Cir. 1985); John v. Louisiana, 757 F.2d 698, 707–09 (5th Cir. 1985) (violation of local rules does not support summary judgment when record does not support it) *with* Jacobsen v. Filler, 790 F.2d 1362, 1364 (9th Cir. 1986) *and* Tarpley v. Green, 684 F.2d 1, 6–7 (D.C. Cir. 1982) (local rule violation can result in partial or total summary judgment against the nonmovant).

[116] *See* Greenberg v. F.D.A., 803 F.2d 1213, 1219 (D.C. Cir. 1986).

Disputed Fact	Source
When he was fired, Jones was one of three minority employees out of a total work force of 257.	Answer to Request for Admission No. 12
Tim Smith, a nonminority employee with the same seniority as Jones, was absent more often than Jones but was given a warning rather than being fired.	Smith's deposition, p. 10, lines 1–20; p. 12, lines 5–30; Answer to Interrogatory No. 17

In other words, a reasonable inference from these facts would be that Jones was treated differently from Smith due to his minority status. In order to combat this issue, the movant would have to show facts which would indicate as a matter of law that the reason for the difference in treatment was not based on Jones's minority status.

While statements of controverted facts and law are often viewed as busy work by attorneys, they serve two valuable functions: (1) they ensure that rulings on summary judgment motions adequately reflect the state of the record, and (2) even if summary judgment is denied, they force refinement of the issues for trial.

§ 15.13 Cross Motions for Summary Judgment

While most litigators consider summary judgment a defendant's tool, cross motions for summary judgment can be brought. The fact that both sides move for summary judgment does not change the normal standard for judging such motions. The court must consider each motion separately to determine whether any genuine issue of material fact exists, because neither side concedes the truthfulness of its adversary's evidence other than for the purpose of its own motion.[117] This is appropriate, because one side may be requesting summary judgment on an affirmative defense and the other on the merits of the underlying action. Thus, a party who has brought a summary judgment motion may still assert that issues of fact exist which prevent summary judgment from being granted against it.[118] The court is not required to grant summary judgment to either of the parties and may deny both motions.[119] However, if both parties are proceeding on the same legal theory and rely on the same material facts, this clearly signals that the case is ripe for summary judgment.[120]

[117] Chambers v. McLean Trucking Co., 550 F. Supp. 1335, 1338 (M.D.N.C. 1981); *see generally* 10A Federal Practice and Procedure § 2720; 6 Moore's Federal Practice ¶ 56.13.

[118] Hotel Del Coronado Corp. v. Foodservice Equip., 783 F.2d 1323, 1325 n.1 (9th Cir. 1986); Schwabenbauer v. Board of Educ., 667 F.2d 305, 313 (2d Cir. 1981); Vetter v. Frosch, 599 F.2d 630, 632 (5th Cir. 1979).

[119] *E.g.*, Shook v. United States, 713 F.2d 662, 665 (11th Cir. 1983); Schwabenbauer v. Board of Educ., 667 F.2d 305, 313 (2d Cir. 1981).

[120] Shook v. United States, 713 F.2d 662, 665 (11th Cir. 1983); *see* Bencivenga v. Western Pa. Teamsters, 763 F.2d 574, 576 (3d Cir. 1985).

In nonjury cases, if both parties move for summary judgment and the court finds that factual issues exist which have been fully developed at the hearing, counsel runs the risk of having the court decide the factual issues on the record. In effect, the court treats the case as if it has been tried on a stipulated record.[121] However, this risk exists even if only one party moves for summary judgment in a nonjury action.[122] Since such cases are actually tried rather than being resolved by summary judgment, the factual findings of the court will be overturned only if they are clearly erroneous.[123] If a judicial determination on the record is desired, it is better to indicate that the judge can decide any disputed facts, because the appellate court may otherwise remand if summary judgment is clearly not proper.[124]

§ 15.14 Credibility

In determining whether to grant summary judgment, the court can decide only whether a factual issue exists; it cannot resolve any factual disputes which do exist.[125] Stated another way, the key is issue finding, not issue resolution.[126] Therefore, the judge cannot determine credibility or weigh conflicting affidavits.[127] Holding an evidentiary hearing rarely is proper, because the judge cannot determine credibility.[128] Nor can the judge disbelieve good faith statements of experts contained in depositions or affidavits.[129] Rule 56 simply does not permit trial by affidavit.[130] Whenever credibility is critical, courts find that

---

[121] Lac Courte Oreilles Band v. Voigt, 700 F.2d 341, 349 (7th Cir.), *cert. denied,* 464 U.S. 805 (1983); Vetter v. Frosch, 599 F.2d 630, 632 (5th Cir. 1979); Starsky v. Williams, 512 F.2d 109, 113 (9th Cir. 1975).

[122] *See* United States v. U.S. Gypsum Co., 340 U.S. 76, 87–88 (1950).

[123] Lac Courte Oreilles Band v. Voigt, 700 F.2d 341, 349 (7th Cir.), *cert. denied,* 464 U.S. 805 (1983); 10A Federal Practice and Procedure § 2720.

[124] Boston Five Cents Sav. Bank v. Department of Housing & Urban Dev., 768 F.2d 5, 12 (1st Cir. 1985); see extensive discussion in John v. Louisiana, 757 F.2d 698, 703–06 (5th Cir. 1985).

[125] Anderson v. Liberty Lobby, Inc., ____ U.S. ____, 106 S. Ct. 2505, 2511 (1986); Lemelson v. TRW, 760 F.2d 1254, 1260–61 (Fed. Cir. 1985); *see generally* 6 pt 2 Moore's Federal Practice ¶¶ 56.15[4], 56.17; 10A Federal Practice and Procedure §§ 2726, 2729–33.

[126] United States v. One Tintoretto Painting, 691 F.2d 603, 606 (2d Cir. 1982).

[127] Warrior Tombigbee Transp. Co. v. M/V Nan Fung, 695 F.2d 1294, 1299 (11th Cir. 1983); *In re* Atlas Concrete Pipe, Inc., 668 F.2d 905, 909 (6th Cir. 1982).

[128] See extensive discussion concerning availability of Fed. R. Civ. P. 43(e) hearing in Stewart v. RCA Corp., 790 F.2d 624, 628–29 (7th Cir. 1986); *see also* Smith v. City of Pittsburgh, 764 F.2d 188, 192 (3d Cir.), *cert. denied,* ____ U.S. ____, 106 S. Ct. 349 (1985) (no evidentiary hearing allowed).

[129] Federal Labs., Inc. v. Barringer Research, Ltd., 696 F.2d 271, 274 (3d Cir. 1982). *But see* Matsushita Elec. Indus. Co. v. Zenith Radio, ____ U.S. ____, 106 S. Ct. 1348, 1360 n.19 (1986) (antitrust action).

[130] Anderson v. Liberty Lobby, Inc., ____ U.S. ____, 106 S. Ct. 2505, 2513 (1986); Poller v. CBS, Inc., 368 U.S. 464, 473 (1962).

summary judgment is particularly inappropriate.[131] Therefore, it is quite difficult to obtain summary judgment when intent, reasonableness, motive, or any subjective feelings are in issue.[132] Thus, courts are often hesitant to grant summary judgment in cases involving securities fraud,[133] antitrust,[134] negligence,[135] and Title VII actions.[136]

However, summary judgment should be considered in antitrust cases, even when conspiracies are alleged, due to the recent change in Supreme Court case law. Previously, *Poller v. Columbia Broadcasting System, Inc.*[137] was repeatedly quoted by plaintiffs to defeat summary judgment in antitrust cases. *Poller* stated that "summary procedures should be used sparingly in complex antitrust litigation where motive and intent play leading roles, the proof is largely in the hands of the alleged conspirators, and hostile witnesses thicken the plot."[138] Although the Supreme Court subsequently upheld summary judgment in *First National Bank v. Cities Services Co.*, an antitrust conspiracy case, by citing an "absence of any significant probative evidence tending to support the complaint,"[139] summary judgment was still considered a rarity in antitrust

---

[131] *Id.*; Sartor v. Arkansas Natural Gas Corp., 321 U.S. 620, 627–28 (1944); *see generally* Sonenshein, *State of Mind and Credibility in the Summary Judgment Context: A Better Approach,* 78 Nw. U.L. Rev. 774 (1983). *But see* Pelphrey v. United States, 674 F.2d 243, 247–48 (4th Cir. 1982) (rejecting position that uncontradicted affidavit of interested witness cannot support summary judgment).

[132] Patrick v. LeFevre, 745 F.2d 153, 159 (2d Cir. 1984) (inappropriate when state of mind, motive, sincerity, or conscience are squarely implicated); McGee v. Hester, 724 F.2d 89, 91 (8th Cir. 1983) (notoriously inappropriate when intent, good faith, and other subjective feelings play dominant roles); Gracyalny v. Westinghouse Elec. Corp., 723 F.2d 1311, 1316 (7th Cir. 1983) (reasonableness, foreseeability, and proximate causation lend themselves to jury determination); Northrop Corp. v. McDonnell Douglas Corp., 705 F.2d 1030, 1050 (9th Cir.), *cert. denied,* 464 U.S. 849 (1983) (disfavored when motive in issue); National Union Fire Ins. Co. v. Argonaut Ins. Co., 701 F.2d 95, 97 (9th Cir. 1983) (any ambiguity in contract raises question of intent); Thornton v. Evans, 692 F.2d 1064, 1075 (7th Cir. 1982) (hesitant to grant summary judgment on subjective matters such as knowledge).

[133] Wechsler v. Steinberg, 733 F.2d 1054, 1058–59 (2d Cir. 1984) (scienter usually inappropriate for disposition on summary judgment); Gieringer v. Silverman, 731 F.2d 1272, 1277 (7th Cir. 1984) (restricted availability of summary judgment in securities cases because motive and intent usually involved).

[134] Poller v. Columbia Broadcasting System, Inc., 368 U.S. 464, 473 (1962); *see generally* Note, *Conscious Parallelism: The Business Judgment Defense in a Summary Judgment Context,* 35 Hastings L.J. 115 (1983); Rogers, *Summary Judgment in Antitrust Conspiracy Litigation,* 10 Loy. U. Chi. L.J. 667 (1979).

[135] Ashby v. Hustler Magazine, Inc., 802 F.2d 856, 858 (6th Cir. 1986); Gracyalny v. Westinghouse Elec. Corp., 723 F.2d 1311, 1315 (7th Cir. 1983); Cook v. Banker Equip. Eng'g Co., 582 F.2d 862, 865 (4th Cir. 1978).

[136] Trevino v. Celanese Corp., 701 F.2d 397, 407 (5th Cir. 1983) (ordinarily summary disposition of Title VII cases is not favored); McKenzie v. Sawyer, 684 F.2d 62, 67 (D.C. Cir. 1982) (factual disputes involved in most Title VII cases preclude summary judgment).

[137] 368 U.S. 464 (1962).

[138] *Id.* at 473.

[139] 391 U.S. 253, 290 (1968).

litigation. However, the latest Supreme Court pronouncement has come full circle and appears to make summary judgment easier to obtain in antitrust actions than in other cases. In *Matsushita Electric Industries Co. v. Zenith Radio,*[140] the Court indicated that the trial judge should decide competing inferences from ambiguous evidence in antitrust cases. Appellate courts are grappling with the extent that this task involves resolving facts.[141] Moreover, if the factual context renders its case implausible, an antitrust plaintiff must come forward with more persuasive evidence to support its claim than would otherwise be necessary.[142] Such language will no doubt result in more summary judgment motions being carefully considered in antitrust cases.

Similarly, in other types of cases in which credibility is often critical, summary judgment may be applicable in a specific factual context.[143] The Supreme Court has noted that summary judgment is available even in libel cases in which state of mind is in issue as long as the plaintiff offers no concrete, affirmative evidence which would support a jury verdict.[144] Likewise, even in a case alleging discrimination, summary judgment will be affirmed when the plaintiff's case is wholly empty[145] or relies only on the attenuated possibility that a jury would infer a discriminatory motive.[146] If the opposing party's only possibility of raising a factual dispute rests on impeachment, "neither a desire to cross-examine an affiant nor an unspecified hope of undermining his or her credibility suffices to avert summary judgment."[147] However, if reasonable

---

[140] Matsushita Elec. Indus. Co. v. Zenith Radio, ____ U.S. ____, 106 S. Ct. 1348, 1357–62 (1986).

[141] T.W. Elec. Serv. Inc. v. Pacific Elec. Contractors Ass'n, 809 F.2d 626, 631 & n.3 (9th Cir. 1987).

[142] Matsushita Elec. Indus. Co. v. Zenith Radio, ____ U.S. ____, 106 S. Ct. 1348, 1356 (1986); *see, e.g.,* Richards v. Neilsen Freight Lines, 810 F.2d 898, 902 (9th Cir. 1987); *cf.* Akerman v. Oryx Communications, Inc., 810 F.2d 336, 343 (2d Cir. 1987) (summary judgment affirmed re Securities Act violation based on internally inconsistent study).

[143] *E.g.,* SRI Int'l v. Matsushita Elec. Corp. of Am., 775 F.2d 1107, 1116 (Fed. Cir. 1985) (summary judgment in patent case); LeFevre v. Spacecom, 771 F.2d 421, 424 (10th Cir. 1985) (summary judgment appropriate when sheer speculation as to motive); Prinzi v. Keydrel Co., 738 F.2d 707, 708–09 (5th Cir. 1984) (summary judgment affirmed in Jones Act case); Adams v. Union Carbide Corp., *cert. denied,* 737 F.2d 1453, 1458 (6th Cir.), 469 U.S. 1062 (1984) (summary judgment in negligence action affirmed); Nelson v. International Paint Co., 734 F.2d 1084, 1092 (5th Cir. 1984) (question of whether subsidiary is alter ego of its parent may be decided by summary judgment when there is lack of sufficient evidence to place alter ego in dispute); Vaughn v. Teledyne, Inc., 628 F.2d 1214, 1220 (9th Cir. 1980) (reasonable inferences defeated claim of scienter).

[144] Anderson v. Liberty Lobby, Inc., ____ U.S. ____, 106 S. Ct. 2505, 2514 (1986).

[145] Huhn v. Koehring Co., 718 F.2d 239, 245 (7th Cir. 1983); *see* Slaughter v. Allstate Ins. Co., 803 F.2d 857, 861 (5th Cir. 1986).

[146] Ross v. Communications Satellite Corp., 759 F.2d 355, 365 (4th Cir. 1985); Parker v. FNMA, 741 F.2d 975, 980 (7th Cir. 1984); Pace v. Southern Ry. Sys., 701 F.2d 1383, 1391 (11th Cir.), *cert. denied,* 464 U.S. 1018 (1983).

[147] National Union Fire Ins. Co. v. Argonaut Ins. Co., 701 F.2d 95, 97 (9th Cir. 1983); *see also* Haase v. Webster, 807 F.2d 208, 212 (D.C. Cir. 1986); Boruski v. United States, 803 F.2d 1421,

inferences can be drawn from the movant's own affidavits which support the nonmovant's position on credibility, summary judgment will be denied. Therefore, although the possibility of obtaining summary judgment in such cases should not be discounted, careful analysis of the opponent's proof is necessary to determine whether or not a motion will be successful.

§ 15.15 Proof

Technically, a summary judgment motion may be filed without any supporting affidavits.[148] The judge is specifically authorized to consider the pleadings, depositions, and answers to interrogatories and admissions on file together with affidavits, if any, in determining whether judgment is appropriate.[149] Summary judgment is even proper in the absence of any evidence submitted by the moving party, if the nonmovant who has the ultimate burden at trial cannot produce evidence of an essential element.[150] However, it is usually extremely difficult to establish the absence of a genuine issue of material fact without some evidentiary support, whether by means of affidavit or discovery materials, unless the parties stipulate to the factual record or the nonmovant stipulates that no facts are in dispute. Moreover, affidavits should be submitted in addition to discovery materials, because they focus on the material factual questions which can otherwise be established only by extensive deposition excerpts.

§ 15.16 Preparing Affidavits and Declarations

Although Rule 56 refers only to affidavits, declarations under penalty of perjury are permitted.[151] The subscription suggested by 28 U.S.C. § 1746 for an unsworn declaration executed in the United States is as follows:

I declare (or certify, verify, or state) under penalty of perjury that the foregoing is true and correct. Executed on (date).

(Signature)

1428 (7th Cir. 1986); Pelphrey v. United States, 674 F.2d 243, 247–48 (4th Cir. 1982); Soar v. National Football League Player's Ass'n, 550 F.2d 1287, 1289 n.4 (1st Cir. 1977).

[148] Fed. R. Civ. P. 56(a) (b); Celotex Corp. v. Catrett, ____ U.S. ____, 106 S. Ct. 2548, 2553 (1986).

[149] Fed. R. Civ. P. 56(c); Celotex Corp. v. Catrett, ____ U.S. ____, 106 S. Ct. 2548, 2553–54 (1986); Adickes v. S.H. Kress & Co., 398 U.S. 144, 159–60 (1970).

[150] Celotex Corp. v. Catrett, ____ U.S. ____, 106 S. Ct. 2548, 2552–53 (1986); Fontonot v. Upjohn Co., 780 F.2d 1190, 1194–98 (5th Cir. 1986); American Nurses' Ass'n v. Illinois, 783 F.2d 716, 729 (7th Cir. 1986).

[151] 28 U.S.C. § 1746 (1982); *cf.* Steinle v. Warren, 765 F.2d 95, 100 (7th Cir. 1985) (affidavit in proper form ignored).

A verified pleading or exhibit may be considered as an affidavit for purposes of opposing a summary judgment motion.[152]

In drafting affidavits, counsel should be aware that conclusive assertions of ultimate facts or legal opinions are given little weight in determining whether a genuine issue of fact exists.[153] Because affidavits must be based on personal knowledge, prefatory statements such as "I am informed" or "on information and belief" are not sufficient.[154] Therefore, the following type of language should be included in either the first or last paragraph of the affidavit:

If called as a witness, I could competently testify to the following (foregoing) facts from my own personal knowledge.

As a practical matter, the requirement of personal knowledge virtually eliminates affidavits by attorneys, because an affidavit cannot be submitted in support of a summary judgment motion unless the attorney knows the facts underlying the dispute,[155] which is unlikely in view of conflict of interest requirements. However, an in-house attorney's affidavit may be appropriate to authenticate documents or establish their foundation as business records if counsel has personal knowledge of the company's recordkeeping procedures.[156] Counsel should also be aware of an easily overlooked provision of Rule 56(e) which requires that sworn or certified copies of documents referred to in affidavits be attached thereto.[157]

---

[152] Hooks v. Hooks, 771 F.2d 935, 946 (6th Cir. 1985); Lew v. Kona Hosp., 754 F.2d 1420 (9th Cir. 1985) (verified complaint); Spear v. Dayton's, 733 F.2d 554, 555 (8th Cir. 1984) (verified exhibit attached to complaint); Enquip, Inc. v. Smith-McDonald Corp., 655 F.2d 115, 119 (7th Cir. 1981) (verified answer).

[153] *E.g.*, Pfeil v. Rogers, 757 F.2d 850, 862 (7th Cir. 1985), *cert. denied*, ____ U.S. ____, 106 S. Ct. 1513 (1986); Maldonado v. Ramirez, 757 F.2d 48, 50–51 (3d Cir. 1985); Yorger v. Pittsburgh Corning Corp., 733 F.2d 1215, 1222 (7th Cir. 1984); Miller v. Solem, 728 F.2d 1020, 1024 (8th Cir.), *cert. denied*, 469 U.S. 841 (1984); Cheesebrough-Pond's Inc. v. Faberge, Inc., 666 F.2d 393, 397–98 (9th Cir.), *cert. denied*, 459 U.S. 967 (1982); 10A Federal Practice and Procedure § 2727, at 157–59.

[154] Automatic Radio Mfg. v. Hazeltine, 339 U.S. 827, 831 (1950); Camfield Tires, Inc. v. Michelin Tire Corp., 719 F.2d 1361, 1367 (8th Cir. 1983); Londrigan v. F.B.I., 670 F.2d 1164, 1174–75 (D.C. Cir. 1981); 6 pt 2 Moore's Federal Practice ¶ 56.22[1].

[155] *E.g.*, Beyah v. Coughlin, 789 F.2d 986, 989 (2d Cir. 1986); Equia v. Tompkins, 756 F.2d 1130, 1136 (5th Cir. 1985); *see generally* Garvey, *The Attorney's Affidavit in Litigation Proceedings*, 31 Stanford L. Rev. 191 (1979).

[156] Pacific Serv. Stations Co. v. Mobil Oil Corp., 689 F.2d 1055, 1061 (Temp. Emer. Ct. App. 1982); *cf.* Sitts v. United States, 811 F.2d 736, 742 (2d Cir. 1987) (attorney affidavit when motion premised on procedural fact within personal knowledge of attorney).

[157] *See* United States v. Stribling Flying Serv., 734 F.2d 221, 224 (5th Cir. 1984) (refused to reverse summary judgment when document supporting affidavit was inadvertently not attached because it was included in pleadings).

§ 15.17 Other Supporting Evidence

Although Rule 56(c) refers only to depositions, answers to interrogatories, admissions, and affidavits, any material which is admissible at trial can support a summary judgment motion.[158] Apparently the Supreme Court has sanctioned the use of inadmissible evidence by the nonmovant to defeat summary judgment, but materials submitted by the movant are still likely to be required in admissible form.[159] The most frequently applicable objection to the content of affidavits or discovery materials is hearsay, which is inadmissible to support the motion unless it falls within some exception under the Federal Rules of Evidence.[160] Of course, failure to make an objection waives the party's right to contest the evidence both before the trial court and on appeal.[161] If an affidavit or other supporting material is defective or submitted untimely, opposing counsel should move to strike the inadmissible portion, or if appropriate, the entire affidavit.[162]

§ 15.18 Depositions

In addition to affidavits, depositions are frequently submitted in support of the parties' summary judgment positions. Most courts consider depositions more reliable than affidavits. Thus, ambiguities in an affidavit will not defeat summary judgment if they can be resolved by deposition testimony.[163] Deposition excerpts are admissible even if taken before joinder of the nonmovant and therefore not subjected to cross-examination, because the testimony is sworn

---

[158] Victoria L. by Carol A. v. District School Bd., 741 F.2d 369, 373 (11th Cir. 1984); *see generally* 10A Federal Practice and Procedure § 2721; 6 Moore's Federal Practice ¶ 56.11.

[159] *Compare* Celotex Corp. v. Catrett, ____ U.S. ____, 106 S. Ct. 2548, 2553–54 (1986); Bushman v. Halm, 798 F.2d 651, 654–55 & n.5 (3d Cir. 1986) (inadmissible evidence for rebuttal); *with* Martz v. Union Labor Life Ins. Co., 757 F.2d 135, 138 (7th Cir. 1985); Union Planters Nat'l Leasing v. Woods, 687 F.2d 117, 119 (5th Cir. 1982); Applegate v. Top Assocs., Inc., 425 F.2d 92, 97 (2d Cir. 1970) (admissible evidence necessary to support summary judgment).

[160] *See, e.g.*, Adickes v. S.H. Kress & Co., 398 U.S. 144, 159 n.19 (1970); Pink Supply Corp. v. Hiebert, Inc., 788 F.2d 1313, 1319 (8th Cir. 1986); Finn v. Consol Rail Corp., 782 F.2d 13, 16–17 (1st Cir. 1986); Burlington Coat Factory Warehouse v. Esprit de Corps., 769 F.2d 919, 924 (2d Cir. 1985); Pfeil v. Rogers, 757 F.2d 850, 860, 863 (7th Cir. 1985), *cert. denied,* ____ U.S. ____, 106 S. Ct. 1513 (1986); Southmark Properties v. Charles House Corp., 742 F.2d 862, 875 (5th Cir. 1984); Blair Foods, Inc. v. Ranchers Cotton Oil, 610 F.2d 665, 667 (9th Cir. 1980).

[161] McCloud River R.R. v. Sabine River Forest Prods., Inc., 735 F.2d 879, 882 (5th Cir. 1984).

[162] United States v. Hodges X-Ray, Inc., 759 F.2d 557, 561 (6th Cir. 1985); Buchanan v. Stanships Inc., 744 F.2d 1070, 1076 n.6 (5th Cir. 1984); Fitzgerald v. Penthouse Int'l Ltd., 639 F.2d 1076, 1078 n.3 (4th Cir. 1981), *cert. denied,* 460 U.S. 1024 (1983).

[163] Shearer v. Homestake Mining Co., 557 F. Supp. 549, 558 n.5 (D.S.D. 1983), *aff'd,* 727 F.2d 707 (8th Cir. 1984); 10A Federal Practice and Procedure § 2722.

and serves as the equivalent of an affidavit.[164] On occasion, the nonmovant's affidavit attempts to contradict deposition testimony in order to create a factual issue. Courts vary as to whether to admit such affidavits, because they automatically defeat summary judgment.[165] The policy rationale for excluding such affidavits is that, if testimony under oath can be abandoned by filing an affidavit, no case would be appropriate for summary judgment. Those courts which do not have a per se rule excluding such affidavits look to the following factors in determining their admissibility: when the affidavit is filed, whether the deposition was signed, the nature and extent of the conflict between the affidavit and deposition, and the reason advanced as justifying the difference in content.[166] If the affiant was confused at the deposition and explains that aspect of the testimony or if the affiant lacked access to material facts which were later discovered, the affidavit is not considered a sham.[167] A contradictory affidavit of a disinterested witness is also less likely to be considered a sham.[168] If an affidavit is submitted in bad faith, sanctions can be imposed under Rule 56(g), which authorizes not only the imposition of attorney's fees, but also a finding that the offending party or attorney is guilty of contempt. Rule 11 sanctions may also be invoked for sham affidavits.

§ 15.19 Interrogatories and Admissions

Although interrogatory answers can be considered by the judge in rendering summary judgment, requests for admission are usually much more useful. Indeed, the requests should be drafted with summary judgment in mind, because such admissions are conclusive and therefore cannot be contradicted.[169] In fact, if an opponent fails to answer, object, or otherwise respond to requests for

---

[164] Hoover v. Switlik Parachute Co., 663 F.2d 964, 967 (9th Cir. 1981).

[165] *Compare* Kennett-Murray Corp. v. Bone, 622 F.2d 887, 893–94 (5th Cir. 1980) (genuine issue can be raised by contradictory affidavit when inconsistency explanatory of confused record and not inherently inconsistent) *and* Dudo v. Schaffer, 91 F.R.D. 128, 132–33 (E.D. Pa. 1981) (considering later affidavit is discretionary) *and* 6 pt 2 Moore's Federal Practice ¶ 56.22[1], at 56-1325 to 56-1326 (court must consider later affidavit) *with* Franks v. Nimmo, 796 F.2d 1230, 1237 (10th Cir. 1986) *and* Reid v. Sears, Roebuck & Co., 790 F.2d 453, 460 (6th Cir. 1986) *and* Babrocky v. Jewell Food Co., 773 F.2d 857, 861 (7th Cir. 1985) *and* Foster v. Arcata Assocs., Inc., 772 F.2d 1453, 1462 (9th Cir. 1985), *cert. denied,* ____ U.S. ____, 106 S. Ct. 1267 (1986) *and* Barwick v. Celotex Corp., 736 F.2d 946, 960 (4th Cir. 1984) *and* Van T. Jinkins & Assoc. v. U.S. Indus., 736 F.2d 656, 657–58 (11th Cir. 1984) *and* Camfield Tires, Inc. v. Michelin Tire Corp., 719 F.2d 1361, 1364–66 (8th Cir. 1983); Radobenko v. Automated Equip. Corp., 520 F.2d 540, 544 (9th Cir. 1975); *and* Perma Research & Dev. Co. v. Singer Co., 410 F.2d 572, 578 (2d Cir. 1969) (all ignoring sham contradictory affidavits).

[166] Dudo v. Schaffer, 91 F.R.D. 128, 132–33 (E.D. Pa. 1981).

[167] Miller v. A.H. Robbins Co., 766 F.2d 1102, 1104 (7th Cir. 1985).

[168] *See* Lane v. Celotex Corp., 782 F.2d 1526, 1530 (11th Cir. 1986).

[169] Fed. R. Civ. P. 36(b); see **ch. 26**.

admission, the facts are admitted for purposes of the litigation, unless the court, in its discretion, permits the admissions to be withdrawn.[170] Thus, judicious use of Rule 36 when confronted with a sloppy opponent or one who has not carefully studied the case may result in summary judgment being granted. Pretrial statements can also be used to focus issues for summary judgment and to create a record of undisputed facts.[171] Indeed, if an issue is not raised in the Rule 16 pretrial order, it cannot be raised in a summary judgment motion.[172] Counsel should also consider the applicability of judicial notice in a summary judgment context.

§ 15.20 Documents

Documents also provide support for summary judgment papers.[173] Counsel must not only authenticate the documents submitted, but also must establish that the contents of the documents are used for nonhearsay purposes or meet hearsay exceptions.[174] Some courts consider a document authenticated merely if it was produced from the opposing party's files.[175] However, other courts may require a more detailed showing.[176] Similarly, documents produced from the party's own files must also be authenticated.[177] Authentication is often obtained through requests for admissions or in pretrial orders.

Potential hearsay problems must also be resolved before a document is considered. For example, when relying on business records, a foundation for

---

[170] Fed. R. Civ. P. 36(a), (b); *see, e.g.*, Donovan v. Carls Drug Co., 703 F.2d 650, 651–52 (2d Cir. 1983); Luick v. Graybar Elec. Co., 473 F.2d 1360, 1361 (8th Cir. 1973); Milene Music Inc. v. Gotauco, 551 F. Supp. 1288, 1292 (D.R.I. 1982).

[171] *E.g., In re* Japanese Elec. Prods., 723 F.2d 238, 257–59 (3d Cir. 1983), *rev'd on other grounds sub nom.* Matsushita Elec. Indus. Co. v. Zenith Radio, ____ U.S. ____, 106 S. Ct. 1348 (1986). *See* Fed. R. Civ. P. 16(c) and (e); see **ch. 16**.

[172] Southern Cal. Retail Clerk's Union v. Bjorklund, 728 F.2d 1262, 1264 (9th Cir. 1984); see **§ 16.4**.

[173] Davis v. CIA, 711 F.2d 858, 860–61 (8th Cir. 1983), *cert. denied,* 465 U.S. 1035 (1984) (letter contradicting claims in affidavit created factual issue); Western Transp. Co. v. Wilson & Co., 682 F.2d 1227, 1232 (7th Cir. 1982) (invoices attached to conclusory affidavit raised factual issue); Enquip, Inc. v. Smith-McDonald Corp., 655 F.2d 115, 119 (7th Cir. 1981) (documents sufficient to alert court of disputed fact).

[174] Zoslaw v. MCA Distrib. Corp., 693 F.2d 870, 883 (9th Cir. 1982), *cert. denied,* 460 U.S. 1085 (1983) (documents must be authenticated to defeat summary judgment motion); *see, e.g.*, Doe v. N.Y.U., 666 F.2d 761, 779 (2d Cir. 1981) (records and reports submitted without verification probably would be admissible at trial as business records if authenticated).

[175] *See* Anderson v. Cramlet, 789 F.2d 840, 845 (10th Cir. 1986).

[176] *See In re* Japanese Elec. Prods., 723 F.2d 238, 284–86 (3d Cir. 1983), *rev'd on other grounds sub nom.* Matsushita Elec. Indus. Co. v. Zenith Radio, ____ U.S. ____, 106 S. Ct. 1348 (1986).

[177] *See* Flaherty v. Coughlin, 713 F.2d 10, 14 (2d Cir. 1983) (because verification can easily be supplied, there is little reason not to require it as a prerequisite to granting summary judgment).

such documents pursuant to Rule 803(6) of the Federal Rules of Evidence must be provided.[178] Usually an affidavit, deposition testimony, admissions, or a pretrial order suffices to establish the business record's admissibility. In documentary cases, it is common to have a custodian of records depositions to ensure admissibility. If counsel is relying on the co-conspirators exception, preliminary requirements concerning the establishment of the conspiracy apply in civil as well as criminal cases.[179] Privileged documents cannot be relied upon by the court in determining summary judgment unless the opposing party is given an edited, sanitized, or summarized version of the materials.[180] Although some courts liberally construe the nonmovant's supporting evidence, all counsel should be aware of evidentiary requirements when submitting materials rather than relying on the court to excuse oversights.[181]

§ 15.21 Factual Appendix

The proof submitted by the parties is critical in determining whether summary judgment is appropriate. Therefore, it is not uncommon for the factual appendix to a summary judgment motion to be voluminous. However, submitting boxes of unfocused materials to the judge in support of the motion is unlikely to result in summary judgment's being granted. Such submissions sometimes ensure that the motion will be denied merely because the judge will not wade through the materials. Make sure to quote or cite the essential language in the statement of the facts, even if this necessitates extensive deposition excerpts. As previously mentioned, a well-written factual statement supported by detailed citations to the factual appendix is probably the most important part of any summary judgment motion, because it sets the tone of the entire motion and develops the themes which are essential to the arguments. Moreover, the relevant facts should also be cited at the appropriate places in counsel's legal argument. Remember, the judge is not interested in abstract legal concepts, but in specific reasons why

---

[178] *See* FDIC v. Roldan Fonseca, 795 F.2d 1103, 1110 (1st Cir. 1986) (rejecting photocopies of business records when no foundation established); see § **21.7**.

[179] World of Sleep, Inc. v. La-Z-Boy Chair Co., 756 F.2d 1467, 1474 (10th Cir.), *cert. denied,* ——— U.S. ———, 106 S. Ct. 77 (1985); Filco v. Amana Refrigeration, Inc., 709 F.2d 1257, 1267 (9th Cir.), *cert. dismissed,* 464 U.S. 956 (1983) (requiring independent evidence of the conspiracy to be shown). *Compare* Bourjaily v. United States, ——— U.S. ———, 107 S. Ct. 2775, 2780 (1987) (a criminal case which held that the coconspirator's statement can be considered in determining the primary fact of whether the conspiracy existed).

[180] Association for Reduction of Violence v. Hall, 734 F.2d 63, 67–68 (1st Cir. 1984).

[181] *Compare* Enquip Inc. v. Smith-McDonald Corp., 655 F.2d 115, 118 (7th Cir. 1981) (liberally construe nonmovant's defense in form and substance) *with* Macklin v. Butler, 553 F.2d 525, 528 n.1 (7th Cir. 1977) (exhibit submitted by movant which did not meet Rule 56(e) standard could not be relied upon by court); *and* United States v. Glass Nursing & Convalescent Homes, Inc., 550 F. Supp. 1149, 1154 (S.D. Ohio 1982) (nonmoving party cannot avoid summary judgment by tardy unsolicited submission of unsworn documents).

summary judgment should be granted or denied in this case. The court may ignore counsel's characterization of the law, but if it has any doubt about counsel's factual contentions, summary judgment will be denied. Similarly, filing every deposition taken will not necessarily defeat a summary judgment motion but will definitely annoy the judge. It is less costly to prepare a well documented defense than to pursue an appeal.

§ 15.22 Continuances to Obtain Affidavits or Discovery

Rule 56(f) provides that, when a party opposing the motion submits an affidavit specifying the reasons why evidence supporting its position is unavailable, the court may refuse to enter judgment, order a continuance for counsel to obtain affidavits or discovery, or make such other order as is just. The most common use of such affidavits is to obtain discovery, but Rule 56(f) may also justify consideration of tardy affidavits.[182] Due to the importance of the factual record, discovery is usually completed before a summary judgment motion is appropriate. However, when faced with an early summary judgment motion, a Rule 56(f) affidavit is required to demonstrate why additional discovery is necessary. Where there has been almost no discovery, even if summary judgment can be granted, most courts consider it the better course to deny the motion without prejudice to its renewal after discovery.[183] Similarly, some courts believe discovery should be granted as a matter of course when the facts are in the possession of the moving party.[184] Therefore, merely because summary judgment has been previously denied, this is not the law of the case, because the court is free to reconsider a renewed motion based upon substantial discovery of facts not before the court at the time of the original motion.[185] Thus, when summary judgment is premature, it is not necessarily foreclosed, because the movant may be able to establish its right to summary judgment on a more developed record.

§ 15.23 Rule 56(f) Affidavits

When requesting additional discovery under Rule 56(f), parties must in good faith demonstrate why they cannot respond to a summary judgment motion and how postponement of a ruling will enable them to establish a genuine issue of

---

[182] Buchanan v. Stanships, Inc., 744 F.2d 1070, 1074 (5th Cir. 1984).

[183] Martin Ice Cream Co. v. Chipwich, Inc., 554 F. Supp. 933, 936 (S.D.N.Y. 1983); 10A Federal Practice and Procedure § 2728, at 192.

[184] Sames v. Gable, 732 F.2d 49, 51 (3d Cir. 1984); *see also* Flaherty v. Coughlin, 713 F.2d 10, 13 (2d Cir. 1983) (caution in granting summary judgment when relevant discovery denied).

[185] Shearer v. Homestake Mining Co., 727 F.2d 707, 709 (8th Cir. 1984); Zell v. InterCapital Income Secs., Inc., 675 F.2d 1041, 1049 (9th Cir. 1982); Middle Atl. Utils. Co. v. S.M.W. Dev. Corp., 392 F.2d 380, 384 (2d Cir. 1968).

fact. In other words, specific facts must be set forth in the opponent's Rule 56(f) affidavit.[186] Counsel cannot simply rely on vague assertions that discovery will provide the necessary factual issues[187] or complain about insufficient time or resources to complete discovery.[188] Even stating that the facts are peculiarly within the knowledge of the opposing party is not sufficient if no information is suggested which establishes that allegation and it appears unlikely in the context of the case.[189] In general, a Rule 56(f) affidavit must demonstrate how additional time will enable the party to rebut the movant's allegations of no genuine issue of fact.[190] If the results of a continuance would be speculative, it is properly denied.[191] As the Third Circuit once observed:

> [T]o take advantage of this provision he must state by affidavit the reasons for his inability to do so and these reasons must be genuine and convincing to the court rather than merely colorable. It is not enough to rest upon the uncertainty which broods over all human affairs or to pose philosophic doubts regarding the conclusiveness of evidentiary facts. In the world of speculation such doubts have an honored place, but in the daily affairs of mankind and the intensely practical business of litigation they are put aside as conjectural.[192]

§ 15.24 Denying Discovery Requests

A party does not have an unlimited right to discovery prior to a hearing on the motion for summary judgment,[193] and a denial of discovery will be reversed only for an abuse of discretion.[194] There are few guidelines governing the exercise of

---

[186] Glen Eden Hosp. v. Blue Cross & Blue Shield, 740 F.2d 423, 427–30 (6th Cir. 1984); Korf v. Ball State Univ., 726 F.2d 1222, 1230 (7th Cir. 1984); Willmar Poultry Co. v. Morton-Norwich Prods., Inc., 520 F.2d 289, 297 (8th Cir. 1975), *cert. denied,* 424 U.S. 915 (1976); 10A Federal Practice and Procedure § 2740.

[187] Bettin v. Nelson, 744 F.2d 53, 58 (8th Cir. 1984); Wallace v. Brownell Pontiac-GMC Co., 703 F.2d 525, 527 (11th Cir. 1983); S.E.C. v. Spence & Green Chem. Co., 612 F.2d 896, 901 (5th Cir. 1980), *cert. denied,* 449 U.S. 1082 (1981).

[188] Fontenot v. Upjohn Co., 780 F.2d 1190, 1194 (5th Cir. 1986).

[189] *Id.*

[190] Hall v. Hawaii, 791 F.2d 759, 761 (9th Cir. 1986); Pasternak v. Lear Petroleum Exploration, Inc., 790 F.2d 828, 833 (10th Cir. 1986).

[191] Visa Int'l Serv. Ass'n v. Bancard Holders, 784 F.2d 1472, 1475 (9th Cir. 1986); Contemporary Mission, Inc. v. United States Postal Serv., 648 F.2d 97, 107 (2d Cir. 1981).

[192] Robin Constr. Co. v. United States, 345 F.2d 610, 614 (3d Cir. 1965).

[193] Amey, Inc. v. Gulf Abstract & Title, Inc., 758 F.2d 1486, 1506 (11th Cir. 1985), *cert. denied,* ―― U.S. ――, 106 S. Ct. 1513 (1986).

[194] Hotel & Restaurant Employees Union, Local 25 v. Attorney Gen., 804 F.2d 1256, 1269 (D.C. Cir. 1986); *In re* Bishop, Baldwin, Rewald, Dillingham & Wong, Inc., 779 F.2d 471, 475, 476 (9th Cir. 1985); Paul Kadair, Inc. v. Sony Corp. of Am., 694 F.2d 1017, 1029 (5th Cir. 1983).

the judge's discretion in deciding a Rule 56(f) request for further discovery, because the ruling is necessarily factually oriented.[195] Abuse of discretion in refusing to grant discovery has been found when access to the discovery is crucial[196] or when the case is complicated and the party opposing summary judgment does not have ready access to the information sought.[197] If important policy issues are raised by the complaint, the court will also allow discovery.[198]

Requesting discovery on immaterial issues does not satisfy the burden of indicating specific facts showing a genuine issue for trial.[199] For example, the court may properly stay discovery of the merits of the case, pending decision on questions of governmental immunity.[200] Similarly, when a strong statute of limitations or other affirmative defense exists, an early summary judgment motion should be considered. Since the determinative issue is quite narrow, counsel can request that discovery be curtailed on the rest of the action pending the outcome of the motion. In this way, extremely expensive discovery may be entirely avoided if the motion is granted. In fact, it has been suggested the court should consider the economic dimensions of the case every time a Rule 56(f) request is brought.[201]

When the facts necessary to defeat summary judgment are in the hands of the nonmovant, discovery is also considered to be irrelevant.[202] It is also unnecessary to grant discovery when the record indicates discovery would have been useless.[203] This is true even though general pretrial discovery has been curtailed.[204] Of course, even if voluminous documents have been produced, the particular facts may support additional discovery.[205] However, in national security cases, courts are more likely to refuse discovery on the theory that some sacrifice to the ideals of the full adversary system is inevitable.[206]

---

[195] Paul Kadair, Inc. v. Sony Corp. of Am., 694 F.2d 1017, 1029 (5th Cir. 1983).

[196] *See, e.g.*, Villante v. Department of Corrections, 786 F.2d 516, 523 (2d Cir. 1986); Zell v. InterCapital Income Secs., Inc., 675 F.2d 1041, 1049 (9th Cir. 1982); Parrish v. Board of Comm'rs, 533 F.2d 942, 948 (5th Cir. 1973).

[197] *See, e.g.*, Gary Plastic Packaging v. Merrill Lynch, Pierce, Fenner & Smith, Inc., 756 F.2d 230, 236–37 (2d Cir. 1985); Diaz v. A.T.&T., 752 F.2d 1356, 1362–64 (9th Cir. 1985); Littlejohn v. Shell Oil Co., 483 F.2d 1140, 1145–46 (5th Cir.) (en banc), *cert. denied,* 414 U.S. 1116 (1973).

[198] Pennsylvania v. General Pub. Utils. Corp., 710 F.2d 117, 121 (3d Cir. 1983) (Three Mile Island litigation concerning accident at nuclear facility).

[199] *E.g.*, Powers v. McGuigan, 769 F.2d 72, 76 (2d Cir. 1985).

[200] Chagnon v. Bell, 642, F.2d 1248, 1266 (D.C. Cir. 1980), *cert. denied,* 643 U.S. 911 (1981).

[201] Schwarzer, *Summary Judgment Under the Federal Rules: Defining Genuine Issues of Material Fact,* 99 F.R.D. 465, 483 (1984).

[202] Gieringer v. Silverman, 731 F.2d 1272, 1278 (7th Cir. 1984) (when the state of mind of the nonmovant was key to determining the statute of limitations questions, discovery was unnecessary).

[203] Wallace v. Brownell Pontiac-GMC Co., 703 F.2d 525, 528 (11th Cir. 1983).

[204] First Nat'l Bank v. Cities Serv. Co., 391 U.S. 253, 290–94 (1968).

[205] Schering Corp. v. Home Ins. Co., 712 F.2d 4, 10 (2d Cir. 1983) (stay of discovery after 74,000 pages of documents produced improper).

[206] Military Audit Project v. Casey, 656 F.2d 724, 751 (D.C. Cir. 1981).

Summary judgment will not usually be granted while discovery requests remain unanswered.[207] However, the outstanding requests must clearly be shown to be relevant to establishing a genuine factual issue. If they are vague or relate to peripheral issues, the Rule 56(f) request is properly denied.[208] The court can also deny the specific discovery request and substitute another procedure, such as allowing interrogatories instead of a deposition. However, if the resulting interrogatory answers are not sufficient and clearly demonstrate the need for a deposition, the originally requested discovery must be granted.[209]

When the party opposing summary judgment has obtained the requested discovery and has not asked for other discovery, it cannot argue that additional discovery is necessary to develop its claims.[210] Similarly, courts have refused to grant Rule 56(f) discovery on the ground that the party was dilatory in requesting discovery or failed to comply with the court's orders or when discovery was a "fishing expedition."[211] The following factors have been considered in determining whether Rule 56(f) discovery should be granted:

1. The length of the pendency of the case prior to the Rule 56(f) request
2. Whether and when the plaintiff could have anticipated its need for the requested discovery
3. The previous efforts, if any, made by the plaintiff to obtain the needed information, through formal discovery or otherwise
4. The degree and nature of discovery already undertaken
5. Any limitations placed upon discovery previously by the trial court
6. Any prior solicitation of or provisions for discovery by the trial court
7. Any warning the plaintiff might have had that, absent a speedier request, discovery might be denied and his claim might be dismissed, and
8. Whether the requested information was inaccessible to the plaintiff, for example, within the defendant's exclusive control, or whether alternative accessible sources existed but were forgone.[212]

---

[207] Cowan v. J.C. Penney Co., 790 F.2d 1529, 1532 (11th Cir. 1986); Sames v. Gable, 732 F.2d 49, 51 (3d Cir. 1984).

[208] City of Springfield v. Washington Pub. Power Supply Sys., 752 F.2d 1423, 1427 (9th Cir. 1985), *cert. denied,* ____ U.S. ____, 106 S. Ct. 792 (1986); Mid-South Grizzlies v. National Football League, 720 F.2d 772, 781 (3d Cir. 1983), *cert. denied,* 467 U.S. 1215 (1984); Paul Kadair, Inc. v. Sony Corp. of Am., 694 F.2d 1017, 1032 (5th Cir. 1983).

[209] Londrigan v. F.B.I., 670 F.2d 1164, 1175 (D.C. Cir. 1981).

[210] Moss v. Morgan Stanley Inc., 553 F. Supp. 1347, 1364 (S.D.N.Y. 1983), *aff'd,* 719 F.2d 5 (2d Cir. 1983), *cert. denied,* 465 U.S.1025 (1984).

[211] Paul Kadair, Inc. v. Sony Corp. of Am., 694 F.2d 1017, 1023–24 (5th Cir. 1983); *see, e.g.,* Pfeil v. Rogers, 757 F.2d 850, 857 (7th Cir. 1985), *cert. denied,* ____ U.S. ____, 106 S. Ct. 1513 (1986); Landmark Dev. Corp. v. Chambers Corp., 752 F.2d 369, 372–73 (9th Cir. 1985); Zerilli v. Smith, 656 F.2d 705, 716 (D.C. Cir. 1981); *see generally* 10A Federal Practice and Procedure § 2740, at 535; 6, pt 2 Moore's Federal Practice ¶ 56.24, at 1439.

[212] Paul Kadair, Inc. v. Sony Corp. of Am., 694 F.2d 1017, 1031 (5th Cir. 1983).

Often the improper granting of summary judgment arises from the nonmovant's failure to request a continuance or to file a Rule 56(f) affidavit specifying how the outstanding discovery requests will create a genuine issue of fact. Usually the only reason for such failures is that "I didn't think the judge would grant the motion."[213] Needless to say, the court will not be sympathetic to that response. In fact, most circuits require that a Rule 56(f) affidavit be filed in order to preserve the issue that summary judgment should have been delayed pending further discovery.[214] At a minimum, the party opposing summary judgment may be required to bear the costs on appeal when its inaction to request a continuance caused the appeal, and summary judgment can be considered appropriate if its procedural failings were "sufficiently egregious."[215] Further, merely moving for an extension of a discovery deadline is not the equivalent of a Rule 56(f) motion.[216] Oppositions to summary judgment motions, untimely affidavits, and motions to strike the movant's affidavit or to compel discovery have all been held insufficient under Rule 56(f).[217] It is also questionable whether a motion to defer consideration of summary judgment until after completion of discovery complies with Rule 56(f).[218] Finally, counsel should be aware that the mere filing of a Rule 56(f) affidavit does not automatically stay the summary judgment procedures.[219]

In order to maximize the possibility of obtaining a continuance, the actual discovery requests which are necessary to defeat summary judgment should be filed concurrently with the Rule 56(f) affidavit, and their relevance to the controverted issues should be explained. In this way, the judge can easily analyze the relevance of the submitted requests and may be more hesitant to deny the discovery than if faced with the affidavit alone. Likewise, the party opposing

---

[213] Tri-Hawaii, Inc. v. First Commerce Fin. Corp., 627 F.2d 991, 994 n.1 (9th Cir. 1980) (response to counsel at oral argument on appeal to query as to why no factual response or affidavit was filed).

[214] Burlington Coat Factory Warehouse v. Esprit de Corps, 769 F.2d 919, 926 (2d Cir. 1985); Mid-South Grizzlies v. National Football League, 720 F.2d 772, 780 (3d Cir. 1983), *cert. denied,* 467 U.S. 1215 (1984); Cassidy, Inc. v. Hantz, 717 F.2d 1233, 1235 (8th Cir. 1983); Zerilli v. Smith, 656 F.2d 705, 716 (D.C. Cir. 1981); Gray v. Udevitz, 656 F.2d 588, 592 (10th Cir. 1981); Tri-Hawaii, Inc. v. First Commerce Fin. Corp., 627 F.2d 991, 994 (9th Cir. 1980); Over the Road Drivers v. Transport Ins. Co., 637 F.2d 816, 821 (1st Cir. 1980). *But see* Hotel & Restaurant Employees Union, Local 25 v. Attorney Gen., 804 F.2d 1256, 1269 (D.C. Cir. 1986); Littlejohn v. Shell Oil Co., 483 F.2d 1140, 1146 (5th Cir.) (en banc), *cert. denied,* 414 U.S. 1116 (1973).

[215] Sames v. Gable, 732 F.2d 49, 52 n.3 (3d Cir. 1984).

[216] Anchor Motor Freight v. International Bhd. of Teamsters, 700 F.2d 1067, 1071 (6th Cir.), *cert. denied,* 464 U.S. 819 (1983).

[217] *See* Pasternak v. Lear Petroleum Exploration, Inc., 790 F.2d 828, 833 (10th Cir. 1986); Herbert v. Wicklund, 744 F.2d 218, 221–22 (1st Cir. 1984); Wallace v. Brownell Pontiac-GMC Co., 703 F.2d 525, 527 (11th Cir. 1983). *But see* Cowan v. J.C. Penney Co., 790 F.2d 1529, 1532 (11th Cir. 1986) (failure to file Rule 56(f) motion not controlling when court aware discovery was outstanding).

[218] Claus v. Gyorkey, 674 F.2d 427, 435 (5th Cir. 1982).

[219] Gieringer v. Silverman, 731 F.2d 1272, 1280 (7th Cir. 1984).

discovery should detail any substantive objections it has to the requests and indicate why they are irrelevant to the issues in question. For example, in an antitrust action in which summary judgment was granted by the trial court because of the absence of competition between the parties in any relevant market, the appellate court used the following format to analyze the relevance of the requested discovery:[220]

Request	Appellee's (Summary Judgment Movant's) Objection	Relevance to Competition Issue
#2–4, 6 All documents relating to formal meetings at which applicant's application was discussed	Beyond scope of issue	Irrelevant to competition issue—only relevant to objective standard issue

Thus, the Rule 56(f) response should effectively focus the court on the factual issues which are necessary to deciding the motion.

§ 15.25 Converting Motions to Dismiss into Summary Judgment Motions

Motions to dismiss brought under Rule 12(b)(6) for failure to state a claim and Rule 12(c) motions for judgment on the pleadings must be treated as summary judgment motions by the court, if matters outside the pleading are considered.[221] The possibility of conversion usually arises when one or more parties submit affidavits or other evidence in support of their positions concerning dismissal, although on occasion the judge will sua sponte consider filed discovery materials or evidence presented in previous motions when determining whether to dismiss the action. Since no outside materials can be considered in ruling on a Rule 12(b)(6) or 12(c) motion, the judge has two choices: (1) ignore the submitted materials and decide the Rule 12 motion or (2) consider them and convert the motion into one for summary judgment.[222] Practitioners sometimes assume that by unilaterally submitting outside material, the motion automatically becomes one for summary judgment. In fact, Rules 12(b)(6) and 12(c) both require this result only if matters outside the pleadings are presented

[220] *See* Mid-South Grizzlies v. National Football League, 720 F.2d 772, 780 n.5 (3d Cir. 1983), *cert. denied,* 467 U.S. 1215 (1984), which analyzed the relevance of the outstanding discovery requests using this format.

[221] Fed. R. Civ. P. 12(b)(6), 12(c); Carter v. Stanton, 405 U.S. 669, 671 (1972) (per curiam); *see* Goldman v. Belden, 754 F.2d 1059, 1066 (2d Cir. 1985) (once converted, judge must consider all evidence properly submitted).

[222] *See, e.g.,* Ware v. Associated Milk Producers, Inc., 614 F.2d 413, 414–15 (5th Cir. 1980).

to and not excluded by the court. Thus, the judge, not the parties, determines whether to convert the Rule 12 into a Rule 56 motion. If the judge refuses to consider outside materials and denies the motion to dismiss, a summary judgment motion following Rule 56 procedure can still be brought.

The most difficult problem facing the parties when the judge converts a Rule 12 motion into a Rule 56 motion is notice. Granting a motion to dismiss may not actually terminate litigation if the party can amend the complaint to state a viable cause of action. However, summary judgment deals a mortal blow to the action and, therefore, courts are particularly cautious to ensure the nonmovant every opportunity to marshal its proof in order to combat the motion.[223] Therefore, notice is critical to prevent the opposing party from first learning that the motion was considered as one for summary judgment when judgment is granted. As the Fifth Circuit once commented: "[t]he notice requirement of Rule 12 guarantees that the automatic change of a motion to dismiss into a motion for summary judgment will not be accomplished by an unforeseeable thrust with no chance to parry. Notice is ascendant and primary in the Federal Rules."[224] A movant's submission of evidence or even the court's statement that it has considered the record is not enough to supply the necessary notice. Many circuits require strict compliance with the 10-day notice provision of Rule 56 whenever a motion to dismiss is treated as a summary judgment motion,[225] although others have adopted a harmless error or waiver approach to notice problems which applies when no prejudice from the violation is apparent.[226]

The type of notice required is not entirely clear. Written notice is not necessary as long as the notice is explicit or the record adequately demonstrates that all counsel were aware that the motion would be treated as one for summary judgment.[227] However, when plaintiff is a prisoner acting pro se, written notice

---

[223] Georgia S. & Fl. Ry. v. Atlantic Coast Line R.R., 373 F.2d 493, 498 (5th Cir.), *cert. denied,* 389 U.S. 851 (1967); *cf.* Thoen v. United States, 765 F.2d 1110, 1113–15 (Fed. Cir. 1985) (notice of conversion required under Court of Claims Rules even without explicit provision).

[224] *Id.*

[225] *See, e.g.,* Selva & Sons, Inc. v. Nina Footwear, Inc., 705 F.2d 1316, 1322 (Fed. Cir. 1983); International Ass'n of Machinists v. United Technologies Corp., 704 F.2d 569, 572 (11th Cir. 1983); Winfrey v. Brewer, 570 F.2d 761, 764 (8th Cir. 1978); Davis v. Howard, 561 F.2d 565, 571 (5th Cir. 1977). The Second Circuit has indicated a preference for the strict rule but has never expressly rejected the harmless error approach. *In re* Bristol Indus. Corp., 690 F.2d 26, 29 (2d Cir. 1982). *See generally* 6 Moore's Federal Practice ¶ 56.14[1] (better practice to notify).

[226] *See, e.g.,* Moody v. Town of Weymouth, 805 F.2d 30, 31 (1st Cir. 1986); Denis v. Liberty Mut. Ins. Co., 791 F.2d 846, 850 (11th Cir. 1986); Kaestel v. Lockhart, 746 F.2d 1323, 1324 (8th Cir. 1984); Prospero Assoc. v. Burroughs Corp., 714 F.2d 1022, 1024–25 (10th Cir. 1983); Milwaukee Typographical Union No. 23 v. Newspaper, Inc., 639 F.2d 386, 391 (7th Cir.), *cert. denied,* 454 U.S. 838 (1981).

[227] *E.g.,* Gay v. Wall, 761 F.2d 175, 177 (4th Cir. 1985); Beacon Enters., Inc. v. Menzies, 715 F.2d 757, 767 (2d Cir. 1983); Prospero Assoc. v. Burroughs Corp., 714 F.2d 1022, 1024–25 (10th Cir. 1983); Davis v. Howard, 561 F.2d 565, 571 (5th Cir. 1977).

of the consequences of failing to respond with affidavits to an alternatively styled motion is usually required.[228] In other cases, the appellate court assesses the comments of the trial judge and the actions of the parties to determine whether the opponent knew the judge was converting the motion to dismiss into a summary judgment motion.[229] Thus, if the party against whom summary judgment is granted has itself submitted matters outside the pleadings, it is difficult to argue that it had no knowledge that the Rule 12(b)(6) motion would be considered as a summary judgment motion.[230] However, even in such circumstances, summary judgment has been reversed when the trial court gave no notice of when it would take the motion under advisement, gave no statement of reasons for its action, and labeled its ruling a dismissal, despite the fact that its order stated that the record had been considered.[231]

The safest way to have the court consider the motion to dismiss as a summary judgment is to entitle the motion alternatively as one for summary judgment in order to put opposing counsel on notice. Conversely, if affidavits are submitted by a Rule 12 movant, opposing counsel should move to strike the materials submitted outside the pleadings. In this way, the court will be aware that, if it considers the outside materials, it must give notice and a reasonable opportunity to respond. However, if the court grants summary judgment without formally denying the motion to strike or giving notice, and counsel does not controvert the accuracy of the opposing affidavits on appeal, the appellate court may find the absence of formal notice to be harmless error.[232] Simply stating in the opposition that the response is limited to the dismissal issue is a risky tactic when the motion is alternatively labeled as one for summary judgment. If the judge considers the opposing party's evidentiary materials at the hearing, counsel should request an opportunity to submit any additional materials considered necessary for a fair determination of the issue, as well as to submit any appropriate Rule 56(f) affidavit to obtain discovery.[233] If judgment is granted despite these precautions, reargument or reconsideration should be requested under Rule 59(e). A motion may also be appropriate under Rule 60(b), which requests relief from judgment on the basis of the previously excluded factual materials which counsel should submit concurrently with the Rule 59(e)

---

[228] Lewis v. Faulkner, 689 F.2d 100, 102 (7th Cir. 1982); *see also* Moore v. Florida, 703 F.2d 516, 519–21 (11th Cir. 1983); Davis v. Zahradnick, 600 F.2d 458, 460 (4th Cir. 1979); Hudson v. Hardy, 412 F.2d 1091, 1094 (D.C. Cir. 1968). *But see* Jacobsen v. Filler, 790 F.2d 1362, 1364–67 (9th Cir. 1986) (does not apply to non-prisoner pro se litigants).

[229] *E.g.*, Dayco Corp. v. Goodyear Tire & Rubber Co., 523 F.2d 389, 393 (6th Cir. 1975).

[230] *Id.* at 392–93; *see* Nichols v. United States, 796 F.2d 361, 364 (10th Cir. 1986); Villante v. Department of Corrections, 786 F.2d 516, 521 (2d Cir. 1986); Grove v. Mead School Dist. No. 354, 753 F.2d 1528, 1533 (9th Cir.), *cert. denied*, ___ U.S. ___, 106 S. Ct. 85 (1985); Property Mgmt. & Invs., Inc. v. Lewis, 752 F.2d 599, 604 (11th Cir. 1985).

[231] Milburn v. United States, 734 F.2d 762, 766 (11th Cir. 1984).

[232] Moody v. Town of Weymouth, 805 F.2d 30, 31 (1st Cir. 1986).

[233] *See* Gay v. Wall, 761 F.2d 175, 177 (4th Cir. 1985).

motion.[234] If counsel pursues none of these options, the claim of lack of notice may fall upon deaf appellate ears.[235]

§ 15.26 Partial Summary Judgment

Rule 56(d) provides that if judgment is not rendered upon the whole case or for all the relief asked, the judge has the power to determine material facts which are without substantial controversy. This procedure is generally known as partial summary judgment, even though no judgment is actually entered, because the surviving causes of action must be tried as to the remaining parties. Since the procedural requirements and standards for granting partial summary judgment are exactly the same as for summary judgment,[236] it is always advisable to determine whether adjudication of facts without substantial controversy will provide any advantage in trying the action. The benefit of such a ruling is that it can narrow the case to focus on the disputed issues without the necessity of introducing extraneous information which may be confusing or even prejudicial. If filed early in the litigation, it may eliminate the necessity of any discovery regarding such issues, or a favorable resolution on a particular issue may encourage a reasonable settlement. Of course, stipulations, requests for admissions, or Rule 16 pretrial orders may accomplish the same result more economically, since drafting partial summary judgment papers is as costly and time consuming as requesting summary judgment and as difficult to obtain. Further, if partial summary judgment is granted, it provides a built-in issue for appeal. Therefore, the most practical use of partial summary judgment is as an alternative request to summary judgment. Counsel should note that, under Rule 56(d), the judge is technically authorized to ascertain material facts without substantial controversy whenever the requested judgment is not granted. However, judges are loath to exercise this power without a prior request. Another situation in which partial summary judgment may be beneficial is in complex litigation when the parties will not agree to anything, rendering the normal means of cooperation ineffective. Finally, Rule 56(c) also provides for a interlocutory judgment on the issue of liability when a genuine issue as to the amount of damages exists.

Although partial summary judgment is the law of the case, a trial court is not inexorably bound by it.[237] Thus, the fact that partial summary judgment has been granted to a codefendant does not stop the remaining defendant from alleging the negligence of the dismissed party.[238] The order granting partial

---

[234] *See* Backlund v. Barnhart, 778 F.2d 1386, 1388 (9th Cir. 1985).

[235] Townsend v. Columbia Operations, 667 F.2d 844, 849–50 (9th Cir. 1982).

[236] *See* Finn v. Gunter, 722 F.2d 711, 712–13 (11th Cir. 1984).

[237] Golman v. Tesoro Drilling Corp., 700 F.2d 249, 253 (5th Cir. 1983).

[238] *Id.*

summary judgment is interlocutory and thus is considered to have no res judicata or collateral estoppel effect.[239]

Partial summary judgment should be distinguished from summary judgment on all or any part of the claim which is authorized by Rule 56(a) and (b). A common situation in which such a judgment should be requested is in a multiple party action when it results in a claimant's obtaining full relief against one but not all of the defendants or in a defendant being dismissed from the action. Similarly, if several claims are pending against a single defendant, summary judgment can be requested on one claim, although it does not terminate the entire action. The main reason why counsel must differentiate summary judgment rulings is to determine whether the order can or must be appealed immediately to preserve the issue so adjudicated.[240]

§ 15.27 Hearings

Rule 56 is silent as to any requirement for an oral hearing concerning summary judgment motions, although it refers to the motion's being served 10 days before the hearing. Rule 78 allows the court to determine motions without oral hearings, and Rule 83 states that courts may regulate their practice in any manner not inconsistent with the federal rules. As a result of these varied provisions, most circuits hold that oral argument is not required, reasoning that a hearing need not necessarily be oral.[241] In other words, consideration of the motion along with the response and supporting documents is deemed an adequate substitute for the Rule 56 hearing.[242] Most courts hold that there is no requirement that a court notify the party 10 days before deciding the motion as long as more than 10 days have elapsed since the motion was filed.[243] In general, a party desiring an oral hearing must file a request, and the decision to grant it is discretionary.[244] The request can be made in the summary judgment motion or in

---

[239] *Id.*; United States v. Horton, 622 F.2d 144, 148 (5th Cir. 1980). *But see In re* Falstaff Brewing Corp. Antitrust Litig., 441 F. Supp. 62, 66 (E.D. Mo. 1977) (partial summary judgment acts as estoppel in the pending action).

[240] See § **15.29**.

[241] Grigoleit Co. v. United Rubber, Local No. 270, 769 F.2d 434, 437 (7th Cir. 1985); CIA Petrolera Caribe, Inc. v. Arco Caribbean, Inc., 754 F.2d 404, 411 (1985) (extensive citations); Hamman v. Southwestern Gas Pipeline, Inc., 721 F.2d 140, 142 (5th Cir. 1983); Moore v. Florida, 703 F.2d 516, 519 (11th Cir. 1983); Spark v. Catholic Univ., 510 F.2d 1277, 1280 (D.C. Cir. 1975); Parish v. Howard, 459 F.2d 616, 620 (8th Cir. 1972).

[242] Milburn v. United States, 734 F.2d 762, 766 (11th Cir. 1984).

[243] Grigoleit Co. v. United Rubber, Local No. 270, 769 F.2d 434, 437 (7th Cir. 1985); *see* Cowgill v. Raymark Indus., Inc., 780 F.2d 324, 329 (3d Cir. 1985); Daniels v. Morris, 746 F.2d 271, 275 (5th Cir. 1984); *cf.* Donaldson v. Clark, 786 F.2d 1570, 1575 (11th Cir. 1986) (seven days for submissions not notice enough).

[244] *See* Bratt v. I.B.M., 785 F.2d 352, 363 (1st Cir. 1986); Shearer v. Homestake Mining Co., 727 F.2d 707, 709 (8th Cir. 1984).

a separate motion in limine. Only the Ninth Circuit has held that district court may not by rule or otherwise preclude a party from requesting oral argument nor deny such a request when made by a party opposing the motion unless summary judgment is denied. However, even the Ninth Circuit recognizes that a failure to request a hearing may result in a waiver.[245]

Local court rules concerning Rule 56 hearings also vary. Some require a request to ensure that an oral argument is granted.[246] Others specifically state that the court may determine the motion without oral hearing,[247] while still others require a hearing unless waived by all parties.[248] Therefore, local practice must be consulted whenever counsel wishes to argue the motion. Most circuits encourage oral hearings in all but the most simple cases.[249] Indeed, argument is particularly suited to summary judgment motions, because the judge's factual questions can be addressed, and, if necessary, a party can request that it be allowed to submit supplemental materials to prove or disprove the existence of a genuine issue of fact. If a hearing is permitted, consider submitting on the papers and supporting factual material only if the trial judge is particularly hostile to oral argument.

§ 15.28 Review of Summary Judgment Rulings

The judgment entered by a grant of summary judgment is immediately appealable if it terminates the entire action. The order granting summary judgment is also appealable if it has the practical effect of terminating the action,[250] even if a ministerial act is required to implement it.[251] The appellate court must conduct a de novo review of the facts supporting summary judgment, applying the same legal standards which control the district court's ruling.[252] Thus, the respondent has the burden of showing the absence of a genuine issue of fact, and for these

---

[245] Fernhoff v. Tahoe Regional Planning Agency, 803 F.2d 979, 983 (9th Cir. 1986) (waiver); Dredge Corp. v. Penny, 338 F.2d 456, 461–62 (9th Cir. 1964) (rule cannot preclude oral argument).

[246] *E.g.*, McMillan v. City of Rockmart, 653 F.2d 907, 911 (5th Cir. 1981) (hearing was not required under N.D. Ga. Rule 91.3 when not requested); *see also* D. Mass. R. 12(c)(1).

[247] *E.g.*, S.D. & E.D.N.Y. R. 3(i).

[248] *E.g.*, Nev. R. 16(g).

[249] Parish v. Howard, 459 F.2d 616, 620 (8th Cir. 1972); *see also* Season-All Indus., Inc. v. Turkiye Sise Ve Cam Fabrikalari, A.S., 425 F.2d 34, 39–40 (3d Cir. 1970).

[250] Ardoin v. J. Ray McDermott & Co., 641 F.2d 277, 278 (5th Cir. 1981); *see* Gillespie v. United States Steel, 379 U.S. 148 (1964); Baltimore Orioles v. Major League Baseball Players, 805 F.2d 663, 666–67 (7th Cir. 1986); *see generally* 10 Federal Practice and Procedure § 2715.

[251] United States v. Brook Contracting Corp., 759 F.2d 320, 323 (3d Cir. 1985); Parks v. Pavkovic, 753 F.2d 1397, 1401 (7th Cir.), *cert. denied,* ___ U.S. ___, 106 S. Ct. 246 (1985).

[252] Thrasher v. State Farm Fire & Casualty Co., 734 F.2d 637, 638 (11th Cir. 1984); Roberts v. Elaine Powers Figure Salons, Inc., 708 F.2d 1476, 1478 (9th Cir. 1983); Daly v. Sprague, 675 F.2d 716, 724 n.10 (5th Cir. 1982), *cert. denied,* 460 U.S. 1047 (1983).

purposes, the evidence is viewed in the light most favorable to the party opposing the motion.[253] However, if evidence was excluded which the opponent claims would have defeated summary judgment, the standard governing the review depends upon the nature of the particular evidentiary ruling. In other words, when the ruling is factual, the clearly erroneous standard applies; when the ruling is discretionary, the abuse of discretion standard applies; and when there is a legally set standard, the appellate court will undertake a plenary review of the ruling.[254] Since judges are not required to make findings of fact when granting summary judgment motions,[255] any submitted findings of fact and conclusions of law, while extremely helpful, are entitled to no deference on appeal.[256] However, a case may be remanded if the reasons underlying the decision are opaque.[257] If the trial court converted a Rule 12 motion to one for summary judgment, any appellate review will be based on the standard for summary judgment, even if Rule 12 was cited when the complaint was dismissed.[258] Conversely, if a summary judgment was granted which was really a Rule 12 dismissal, it will be reviewed as a dismissal.[259]

A denial of a summary judgment is not appealable because it is not a final decision as required by 28 U.S.C. § 1291; the judge merely preserves the status quo by denying the motion. Such interlocutory appeals are prohibited in order to prevent piecemeal litigation and eliminate delays.[260] The only interlocutory orders which are appealable are those authorized by statute. Thus, the grant or denial of an injunction by summary judgment will be appealable because it falls within 28 U.S.C. § 1292(a)(1). But when summary judgment is denied on a request for injunctive relief, that order is not appealable.[261] However, when the denial of summary judgment or grant of partial summary judgment effectively

---

253 Adickes v. S.H. Kress & Co., 398 U.S. 144, 157 (1970).

254 *In re* Japanese Elecs. Prods., 723 F.2d 238, 257 (3d Cir. 1983), *rev'd on other grounds sub nom.* Matsushita Elec. Indus. Co. v. Zenith Radio, ____ U.S. ____, 106 S. Ct. 1348 (1986).

255 Fed. R. Civ. P. 52(a); Anderson v. Liberty Lobby, Inc., ____ U.S. ____, 106 S. Ct. 2505 (1986).

256 SEC v. Seaboard Corp., 677 F.2d 1315 (9th Cir. 1982).

257 *E.g.*, Carter v. Stanton, 405 U.S. 669, 671 (1972); see discussion in Clay v. Equifax, Inc., 762 F.2d 952, 956–58 (11th Cir. 1985); *see also* Anthuis v. Colt Indus. Operating Corp., 789 F.2d 207, 213–14 (3d Cir. 1986) (requesting statement of reasons if trial court granted summary judgment in complex cases).

258 Romero v. International Terminal Operating Co., 358 U.S. 354, 357 n.4 (1959); McKinney v. Dole, 765 F.2d 1129, 1134 (D.C. Cir. 1985); Grand Union Co. v. Cord Meyer Dev. Corp., 735 F.2d 714, 716–17 (2d Cir. 1984).

259 Rutherford v. United States, 702 F.2d 580, 581 n.1 (5th Cir. 1983); *see* Baptiste v. Sennet & Krumholz, 788 F.2d 910, 911 (2d Cir. 1986) (when no notice to convert motion to summary judgment, affidavits would be disregarded and motion tested by 12(b)(6) standard).

260 *See, e.g.*, Firestone Tire & Rubber Co. v. Risjord, 449 U.S. 368, 373–74 (1981); *In re* Smith, 735 F.2d 459, 461 (11th Cir. 1984); *In re* Corrugated Container Antitrust Litig., 694 F.2d 1041, 1043 (5th Cir. 1983); *see generally* 10 Federal Practice and Procedure § 2715; 6, pt 2 Moore's Federal Practice ¶ 56.20[2].

261 Switzerland Cheese Ass'n v. E. Horne's Market, Inc., 385 U.S. 23, 25 (1966).

decides whether an injunction will issue, it is appealable under 28 U.S.C. § 1292(a)(1), if the order has serious consequences and can be effectively challenged only by immediate appeal.[262]

On occasion, the denial of summary judgment will conclusively determine an important question which is completely separate from the merits of the action and which is effectively unreviewable on appeal from the final judgment. In such cases, the order is immediately appealable under the collateral order doctrine of *Cohen v. Beneficial Industrial Loan Corp.*[263] Issues which have been held appealable include absolute immunity[264] and qualified immunity to the extent that it turns on an issue of law.[265] Interlocutory appeal is also authorized by 28 U.S.C. § 1292(b). However, such appeals require the judge to certify both that the order involves a controlling question of law as to which there is substantial ground for differences of opinion and that an immediate appeal will materially advance the ultimate termination of the litigation. In other words, the judge, not the party, determines that the order is immediately appealable. A party can also attempt to have a summary judgment ruling reviewed by way of a writ of mandamus under the All Writs Statute.[266] However, such writs are rarely granted, even when the court's ruling is incorrect.[267]

The party against whom summary judgment has been granted should request reconsideration of the motion from the district court before entry of judgment, although this does not ensure that the district court will reopen the case if an appropriate excuse for any belated submission is not offered.[268] Merely repeating already rejected arguments to the court will not result in the summary judgment's being denied.[269] However, the losing party must present any new factual or legal issue to the district court in order to preserve them for appeal,[270] and no supporting evidence can be presented to the appellate court unless

---

[262] *See* Carson v. American Brands, Inc., 450 U.S. 79, 84–85 (1981); Brown v. Kerr-McGee Chem. Corp., 767 F.2d 1234, 1239 (7th Cir. 1985), *cert. denied,* ____ U.S. ____, 106 S. Ct. 882 (1986); Presinzano v. Hoffman-LaRoche, Inc., 726 F.2d 105, 109 (3d Cir. 1984); Weiss v. Duberstein, 445 F.2d 1297, 1299 (2d Cir. 1971).

[263] 337 U.S. 541, 546–47 (1949); *see* Richardson-Merrell Inc. v. Koller, ____ U.S. ____, 105 S. Ct. 2757, 2761 (1985).

[264] Nixon v. Fitzgerald, 457 U.S. 731, 742 (1982).

[265] Mitchell v. Forsyth, ____ U.S. ____, 105 S. Ct. 2806, 2817 (1985); *cf.* Group Health Inc. v. Blue Cross Ass'n, 793 F.2d 491, 497 (2d Cir. 1986) (refusing review when immunity issues intertwined with merits). *But see* Chicago & N. W. Transp. Co. v. Ulery, 787 F.2d 1239, 1240–41 (8th Cir. 1986) (not immediately reviewable when immunity concerned private party rather than public official).

[266] 28 U.S.C. § 1651 (1982).

[267] *In re* Puerto Rico Elec. Power Auth., 687 F.2d 501, 504 (1st Cir. 1982).

[268] Refrigeration Sales Co. v. Mitchell-Jackson, Inc., 770 F.2d 98, 100 (7th Cir. 1985).

[269] *See, e.g.,* Frito-Lay of Puerto Rico v. Canas, 92 F.R.D. 384, 390 (D.P.R. 1981).

[270] Singleton v. Wulff, 428 U.S. 106, 120 (1976); Yorger v. Pittsburgh Corning Corp., 733 F.2d 1215, 1220–21 (7th Cir. 1984); Hargrave v. Fibreboard Corp., 710 F.2d 1154, 1164 (5th Cir. 1983). *But see* 6, pt 2 Moore's Federal Practice ¶ 56.27[1], at 56-1557.

submitted below.[271] On the other hand, the court of appeals can uphold a grant of summary judgment on different legal grounds than those relied upon by the district court, because it can affirm a case on any grounds supported in the record.[272]

Sometimes, a party asks the court to alter, amend, or vacate judgment pursuant to Rule 59(e) when, in effect, it is requesting a reversal of summary judgment. This is not a proper use of such motions. As one court noted, "[s]ince the plaintiff has brought up nothing new—except his displeasure—this Court has no proper basis upon which to alter or amend the order previously entered. The judgment may indeed be based upon an erroneous view of the law, but if so, the proper recourse is appeal—not reargument."[273] Moreover, the court's denial of a motion to alter or amend judgment is reviewed only for abuse of discretion.[274] Similarly, if a motion for reconsideration is brought under Rule 60(b), the moving party must fit within the exceptions provided by the rule,[275] and the court's denial of the motion will be overturned only for an abuse of discretion.[276]

§ 15.29 Rule 54(b) Orders

Another issue which often arises is the timing of an appeal from a partial summary judgment order. Such an appeal is premature even if a claim is determined against a party, unless the judge certifies the case under Rule 54(b), which provides that when more than one claim is presented or when multiple parties are involved, "the court may direct the entry of a final judgment as to one or more but fewer than all the claims or parties only upon an express determination that there is no just reason for delay and upon an express direction for entry of judgment." In other words, the partial summary judgment must be final under 28 U.S.C. § 1291. If not, it still remains an interlocutory decree which cannot be appealed even if the judge mistakenly enters a Rule 54(b) certification.[277]

---

[271] Drexel v. Union Prescription Centers, Inc., 582 F.2d 781, 784 n.4 (3d Cir. 1978).

[272] Helvering v. Gowran, 302 U.S. 238, 245–46 (1937); Sally Beauty Co. v. Nexxus Prods. Co., 801 F.2d 1001, 1005 (7th Cir. 1986); Alcaraz v. Block, 746 F.2d 593, 602 (9th Cir. 1984); *see generally* 10 Federal Practice and Procedure § 2716, at 658; 6, pt 2 Moore's Federal Practice ¶ 56.27(1), at 56-1561.

[273] Durkin v. Taylor, 444 F. Supp. 879, 889 (E.D. Va. 1977); *see* Backlund v. Barnhart, 778 F.2d 1386, 1388 (9th Cir. 1985); *cf.* American Home Assurance v. Glenn Estess & Assoc., 763 F.2d 1237, 1238–39 (11th Cir. 1985) (affirming denial of Rule 59(e) motion which raised new summary judgment issue).

[274] Batterton v. Texas Gen. Land Office, 783 F.2d 1220, 1225 (5th Cir.), *cert. denied,* ____ U.S. ____, 107 S. Ct. 316 (1986).

[275] Backlund v. Barnhart, 778 F.2d 1386, 1388 (9th Cir. 1985).

[276] Hibernia Nat'l Bank v. Administracion Central Sociedad Anonima, 776 F.2d 1277, 1281 (5th Cir. 1985).

[277] Curtis-Wright Corp. v. General Elec. Co., 446 U.S. 1, 7 (1980); *see* Hayden v. McDonald, 719 F.2d 266, 269–70 (8th Cir. 1983); Behring Int'l, Inc. v. Imperial Iranian Air Force, 712 F.2d 45,

Conversely, if the judge does not certify the partial summary judgment, it also cannot be appealed until the case is finally decided. Most circuits are hostile to routinely filed Rule 54(b) orders[278] and require a reasoned explanation for the certification to be effective.[279]

Some commentators suggest that a "partial summary adjudication" under Rule 56(d) should not be labeled as a judgment in order to avoid confusion with final appealable judgments entered under Rule 54(b).[280] In other words, when multiple parties are litigants or multiple claims are pending, if summary judgment does not terminate the entire action, the order can still be immediately appealed under Rule 54(b) if it results in adjudicating the entire claim of one party or one claim as to all parties. However, any partial adjudication not meeting the above criteria remains interlocutory. If a Rule 54(b) order is not entered, the only possibility for review prior to the action is by way of a writ or interlocutory appeal under 28 U.S.C. § 1292(b). Since the judge must certify interlocutory appeals, they occur rarely, and then mainly in multiparty cases involving complex litigation or novel legal theories. Counsel should be careful in ascertaining whether the appeal is certified under Rule 54(b) or is an interlocutory appeal, since these are often confused by both the bench and the bar.[281]

In general, counsel should be aware that the timing of an appeal is critical. An appeal which is premature will be dismissed by the appellate court,[282] but waiting to appeal until the entire case is resolved may result in an appeal's being dismissed as untimely, if the earlier ruling is considered a final order.[283] Therefore, care must be taken to determine the exact nature of every summary judgment ruling.

---

47 (3d Cir. 1983); Rudd Constr. Equip. Co. v. Home Ins. Co., 711 F.2d 54, 56 (6th Cir. 1983); Wheeler Mach. Co. v. Mountain States Mineral Enters., Inc., 696 F.2d 787, 789 (10th Cir. 1983).

[278] *E.g.*, United States Gen., Inc. v. Albert, 792 F.2d 678, 680–83 (7th Cir. 1986); Frank Briscoe Co. v. Morrison-Knudsen Co., 776 F.2d 1414, 1416 (9th Cir. 1985); Aaro Inc. v. Daewoo Int'l Corp., 755 F.2d 1398, 1400 (11th Cir. 1985); Veach v. Vinyl Improvement Prods. Co., 700 F.2d 1390 (Fed. Cir. 1983); *see* 10 Federal Practice and Procedure § 2715.

[279] *See* Ansam Assoc., Inc. v. Cola Petroleum Ltd., 760 F.2d 442, 445 (2d Cir. 1985); Pahlavi v. Palandjian, 744 F.2d 902, 905 n.6 (1st Cir. 1984) (extensive citations to other circuits).

[280] 10A Federal Practice and Procedure § 2737, at 464–5 (2d ed. 1983).

[281] *E.g.*, DeMelo v. Woolsey Marine Ind., 677 F.2d 1030, 1032–4 (4th Cir. 1982); Ford Motor Credit Co. v. S.E. Barnhart & Sons, Inc., 664 F.2d 377, 379–380 (3d Cir. 1981); Local P-171 v. Thompson Farms Co., 642 F.2d 1065, 1068 (7th Cir. 1981).

[282] Griggs v. Provident Consumer Discount Co., 459 U.S. 56, 61 (1982) (premature notice self-destructs); *cf.* Curtiss-Wright v. General Elec., 446 U.S. 1, 10 (1980) (appellate court should scrutinize order to prevent piecemeal appeal); Jack Walters & Sons Corp. v. Morton Bldg., Inc., 737 F.2d 698, 701 (7th Cir.), *cert. denied,* 469 U.S. 1018 (1984) (trial judges do not have carte blanche to certify partial dispositions under Rule 54(b).

[283] 10 C. Wright, A. Miller & M. Kane, Federal Practice & Procedure § 2715, at 642 (2d ed. 1983); *see* Marane Inc. v. McDonald's Corp., 755 F.2d 106, 110–112 (7th Cir. 1985) and Peake v. First Nat. Bank and Trust Co., 717 F.2d 1016, 1019–20 (6th Cir. 1983) (confusion between Rule 59(e) and Rule 60(b) motion resulted in dismissal of summary judgment appeal).

§ 15.30 Consequences of Summary Judgment Motions and Orders

The relationship between summary judgment and other procedures should always be considered in deciding whether to bring the motion. For example, a plaintiff's right voluntarily to dismiss an action without prejudice under Rule 41(a) is terminated by the defendant's answering the complaint or filing a summary judgment motion. Therefore, the plaintiff must obtain a court order to dismiss the action without prejudice after the motion has been filed, even if the defendant has not answered. Thus, by filing a summary judgment motion, the defendant can prohibit the plaintiff from forum shopping, because the plaintiff's option to refile the action in state court before the motion is decided has been foreclosed. Usually this situation arises when a Rule 12 motion has been timely submitted and is alternatively entitled a summary judgment motion.

The denial of a motion to dismiss does not preclude the district court from later granting summary judgment.[284] Similarly, a denial by one judge of a summary judgment motion does not prevent a different judge or magistrate from granting the motion.[285] Bringing an unsuccessful summary judgment motion also has no adverse effect on the right to move for a directed verdict at trial. Although both motions are intended to save the time, money, and effort of a needless trial when there is no genuine issue of material fact,[286] a denial of summary judgment does not foreclose the granting of a directed verdict, even if the evidence presented is virtually identical.[287] The denial of summary judgment merely affirms that a factual issue exists and is not a determination on the merits.[288] In fact, judges occasionally lament that the party opposing the summary judgment motion will undoubtedly lose at trial if no additional evidence is presented.[289] However, many courts grant summary judgment whenever a directed verdict would be appropriate,[290] and the Supreme Court has

---

[284] Cameo Convalescent Center, Inc. v. Percy, 800 F.2d 108, 110 (7th Cir. 1986).

[285] Shouse v. Ljunggren, 792 F.2d 902, 904 (9th Cir. 1986).

[286] Catts Co. v. Gulf Ins. Co., 723 F.2d 1494, 1502 (10th Cir. 1983); *see generally* Currie, *Thoughts on Directed Verdict and Summary Judgments,* 45 U. Chi. L. Rev. 72 (1977).

[287] *Id.;* Matthews v. Ashland Chem., Inc., 770 F.2d 1303, 1307 (5th Cir. 1985).

[288] See 10 Federal Practice and Procedure § 2712, at 587.

[289] *E.g.*, Backes v. Valspar Corp., 783 F.2d 77, 78–79 (7th Cir. 1986); Byrd v. Roadway Express, Inc., 687 F.2d 85, 87 (5th Cir. 1982); Doe v. N.Y.U., 666 F.2d 761, 779 (2d Cir. 1981).

[290] *E.g.*, Professional Mgrs. v. Fawer, Brian, Hardy & Zatzkis, 799 F.2d 218, 223 (5th Cir. 1986); Bushman v. Halm, 798 F.2d 651, 657 (3d Cir. 1986); Barwick v. Celotex Corp., 736 F.2d 946, 962–63 (4th Cir. 1984); National Indus., Inc. v. Republic Nat'l Life Ins. Co., 677 F.2d 1258, 1265 (9th Cir. 1982); Ambook Enters. v. Time, Inc., 612 F.2d 604, 611 (2d Cir. 1979), *cert. dismissed,* 448 U.S. 914 (1980); *see generally* Sonenshein, *State of Mind and Credibility in the Summary Judgment Context: A Better Approach,* 78 Nw. U.L. Rev. 774, 783–85 (1983) (arguing standard for deciding both motions should be the same).

recently adopted this view.[291] Counsel should also be aware that while summary judgment is governed by federal procedure, a few circuits apply state directed verdict procedures in diversity cases.[292]

When summary judgment is granted, the ruling has lasting consequences. In any future litigation, the judgment has both res judicata[293] and collateral estoppel[294] effects, because Rule 56 requires deciding the case on its merits.[295] Conversely, the party opposing summary judgment should recognize that because Rule 56 reaches the merits of an action, the court cannot grant a summary judgment motion if it determines that subject matter or personal jurisdiction is lacking.[296] In general, familiarity with summary judgment procedures will enhance counsel's ability to obtain judgment or defeat the motion.

§ 15.31 Summary Judgment Checklist

Procedural Requirements

1. Is the motion timely?
   - **a.** Has the claimant waited 20 days after commencement of the action?
   - **b.** Do local rules or the pretrial order provide a cutoff date for motions?

2. Has the appropriate notice of the motion been given?
   - **a.** Has 10-days notice been provided?
   - **b.** If the summary judgment motion has been converted from a Rule 12(b)(6) or 12(c) motion has 10-days actual or constructive notice been given?
   - **c.** Do local rules or the pretrial orders provide for longer notice requirements?

---

[291] Anderson v. Liberty Lobby, Inc., ____ U.S. ____, 106 S. Ct. 2505, 2511–12 (1986); *see* Matsushita Elec. Indus. Co. v. Zenith Radio, ____ U.S. ____, 106 S. Ct. 1348, 1356 (1986) (no genuine issue when record taken as a whole could not lead a rational trier of fact to find for the nonmoving party).

[292] Horton v. Miller Chem. Co., 776 F.2d 1351, 1355 (7th Cir. 1985), *cert. denied,* ____ U.S. ____, 106 S. Ct. 1641 (1986); Garrison v. Jervis B. Webb Co., 583 F.2d 258, 261 n.4 (6th Cir. 1978).

[293] Spiegel v. Continental Ill. Nat'l Bank, 790 F.2d 638, 645 (7th Cir.), *cert. denied,* ____ U.S. ____, 107 S. Ct. 579 (1986); Hubicki v. ACF Indus., Inc., 484 F.2d 519, 523 (3d Cir. 1973).

[294] Wilson v. Retail Credit Co., 474 F.2d 1260, 1261 (5th Cir. 1973).

[295] Finn v. Gunter, 722 F.2d 711, 713 (11th Cir. 1984).

[296] Capitol Indus.—EMI, Inc. v. Bennett, 681 F.2d 1107, 1118 (9th Cir.), *cert. denied,* 459 U.S. 1087 (1982) (subject matter jurisdiction); 10 Federal Practice and Procedure § 2713 at 608 (personal jurisdiction).

3. What, if any, materials are submitted with the written motion or opposition?
    a. Although affidavits are not required, they are desirable to focus the issues.
    b. Discovery materials, pleadings, or other evidentiary support are permitted.
        (1) Have documents been authenticated and business records foundation established?
        (2) Is a certified copy of any relevant deposition excerpt being submitted?
4. Have local rules been checked for specific requirements concerning the need for and timing of any:
    a. Supporting memorandum, opposition, or reply?
    b. Factual appendix?
    c. Statement of uncontroverted facts?
    d. Proposed findings of law and fact?
    e. Proposed order?
    f. Statement of genuine issues?
5. Has an oral hearing been requested, if not automatically provided?
6. **Warning:** Failure to follow local rules may result in the motion being granted or denied on technical grounds.

Summary Judgment Standard

1. Has the standard for granting summary judgment been met?
    a. Is there no genuine issue as to any material fact?
    b. Is the movant entitled to summary judgment as a matter of law?
    c. If the movant does not have the burden at trial, could the record not lead a reasonable trier of fact to find for the nonmoving party?
    d. Has the substantive burden of proof been considered (e.g., clear and convincing evidence of fraud or malice)?
2. If credibility is at issue, what facts make summary judgment appropriate?
3. Is summary judgment appropriate when the evidence is viewed in the light most favorable to the opposing party?
4. Is summary judgment appropriate when the opponent is given the benefit of inferences or ambiguities in the evidence?

Partial Summary Judgment

1. Are there any material facts which are without substantial controversy?

2. Is there any strategic reason to request a partial judgment which does not completely resolve any single claim or terminate a party?
   a. Can the issue be eliminated by the Rule 16 pretrial order? (see **ch. 16**)
   b. Can the issue be eliminated by Rule 36 admissions? (see **ch. 26**)

Discovery

1. Has discovery been substantially completed before submission of the motion?
2. Are there any outstanding discovery requests relevant to the motion?
3. Has a Rule 56(f) affidavit been filed?
   a. Is a continuance necessary for the nonmovant to obtain discovery or supporting affidavits?
   b. Can the Rule 56(f) affidavit make a good faith showing of how a postponement will result in that party's being able to demonstrate a genuine issue of material fact?
   c. Is the Rule 56(f) request likely to be denied because the proposed discovery is untimely or irrelevant to the summary judgment issue?
   d. Has any requested discovery been filed concurrently with the Rule 56(f) affidavit?

Reopening Judgment (see §§ 7.2, 8.8, 8.9, and 14.70)

1. Should a reconsideration be requested before the judgment is entered?
2. Should a Rule 60(b) motion be filed after the judgment is entered?
   a. Does mistake, inadvertence, surprise, or excusable neglect exist?
   b. Is there any other reason justifying relief from the judgment?
   c. Will the opposing party be prejudiced if the judgment is reopened?
   d. Is there a meritorious defense to the merits of the claim?
3. **Warning:** The underlying judgment must be timely appealed, because the Rule 60(b) motion does not raise its validity.
4. Is a Rule 59(e) motion to alter or amend the judgment appropriate?

Appellate Review

1. Has an appeal been filed if the judgment terminates the action?
2. Has a Rule 54(b) certificate been entered to permit appeal of a partial judgment which terminates a claim or party?
3. Is the denial of summary judgment likely to be reviewed as:
   a. A writ of mandamus?

b. A certification by the judge under 28 U.S.C. § 1292(b)?

c. A collateral order which is separate from the merits of the action and involves an important issue of law?

Rule 11

1. Does a Rule 11 basis in law or fact exist for the summary judgment motion or opposition?
2. Is the motion or opposition brought for an improper purpose such as to harass or to cause unnecessary delay or needless increase in the cost of litigation?

CHAPTER 16

OTHER PRETRIAL CONCERNS

§ 16.1 Rule 16 Overview

Pretrial practice pursuant to Rule 16 and the myriad of local district court rules are a source of frustration for many diversity practitioners who consider such requirements overly complex formalistic rituals designed to bedevil those not initiated in the fine points of federal practice. Although viewing Rule 16 as a field strewn with landmines waiting to explode at counsel's first misstep may be an exaggeration, it can be a costly mistake cavalierly to ignore even the pettiest of local rules. Complete demystification concerning pretrial procedures requires a thorough reading of local rules; each district follows its own procedures, and individual judges may opt for their own rules. However, the following discussion of what judges expect from Rule 16 practice and where lawyers go astray should hearten those who view Rule 16 as a test of their resolve to litigate in federal court.

Generally, practitioners will survive and even profit from pretrial practice rules if they view them as catering to the individual judge's concept of case management. Rule 16(a) provides for pretrial conferences for the following specific purposes:

1. Expediting the disposition of the action
2. Establishing early and continuing control so the case will not be protracted because of lack of management
3. Discouraging wasteful pretrial activities
4. Improving the quality of the trial through more thorough preparation, and
5. Facilitating settlement of the case.

This statement of objectives is meant to encourage judges to manage cases aggressively and legitimatize the goal of facilitating settlements. Therefore, regardless of one's position concerning the desirability of managerial judges,[1] it is clear that Rule 16 provides the framework within which a judge can expedite discovery, dispositions, and trials. As a practical matter, trial judges are aware of continuing record filings in federal court and receive their own statistical reports on a regular basis. In other words, they know the extent of their caseloads and the approximate number of cases which must be terminated in order to keep their calendars current. The apocryphal story of the district judge who was not given the nod to the circuit court because of his constantly backlogged calendar is an indication of the seriousness with which judges currently view their managerial responsibilities. In this context, local rules and status conferences are designed to ensure that cases do not get lost. Moreover, the rapid pace established by discovery and motion cutoffs as well as other pretrial procedural requirements help to separate quickly cases which will be tried from those which will be settled.

In general, the theme unifying federal pretrial practice is simply that all requirements, big and small, must be taken seriously. Unlike some state courts, where a missed appearance is barely noticed by the master calendar judge, failure to attend even a preliminary status conference before the federal judge assigned to the case can result in serious sanctions. Similarly, if the judge is serious about discovery or motions cutoffs, counsel must assume that any extensions will require documentation concerning counsel's diligence and, when relevant, details concerning the adversary's resistance. As one judge has noted, when a judge prepares a lengthy procedural order, he is generally fond of it.[2] Therefore, it should be read and followed exactly, even if some of the requirements may appear to have no significance other than to create work. For

[1] *See generally,* Elliott, *Managerial Judging and the Evolution of Procedure,* 53 U. Chi. L. Rev. 306 (1986); Reznik, *Failing Faith: Adjudicatory Procedure in Decline,* 53 Chi. L. Rev. 494 (1986); Reznik, *Managerial Judges,* 91 Harv. L. Rev. 374 (1982).

[2] Kozinski, *10 Principles for the New Federal Practice,* 31 Fed. Bar News & J. 16, 18 (Jan. 1984).

example, if the judge wants exhibits appended to the pretrial statement and marked in a particular way, counsel should not be surprised to face sanctions for failure to follow the stated format. More significantly, failure to identify required witnesses or exhibits can result in their exclusion from trial. Similarly, an issue which is omitted from the pretrial statement may be foreclosed from being raised in a summary judgment motion or at trial.

Although time consuming and expensive, federal pretrial procedures can also pose opportunities to enhance the trial posture or settlement value of the action. Indeed, a sloppy lawyer may find that settlement is the only option after the pretrial order is entered, because there is virtually no case left to try. Some lawyers believe that the mere presence of Rule 16 encourages settlement, because compliance requires counsel virtually to complete trial preparation. Certainly the cost of preparing the Rule 16 statement which is required in many districts is a consideration in determining when to settle and at what price.

§ 16.2 Scheduling and Planning

In all actions, other than those exempted by local rule, the judge or magistrate must hold a scheduling conference and enter a scheduling order. The conference can be by telephone, mail, or other suitable means, as well as in person. The resulting scheduling order must be entered within 120 days after filing of the complaint, and limits the time (1) to join other parties and amend the pleadings, (2) to file and hear motions, and (3) to complete discovery. It will also include (4) the date or dates for conferences before trial, a final pretrial conference, and trial, and (5) any other matters appropriate in the circumstances of the case.

The timing of the scheduling order presents several difficulties. First, it assumes prompt service of the complaint on the defendants. Since counsel usually has 120 days to serve a timely complaint,[3] the 120 days after filing may not afford much if any time to the defendant to be ready to prepare a useful scheduling order. Second, since the entry of the scheduling order falls upon the judge rather than counsel, it is not unheard of that either pro forma scheduling order or no scheduling order is timely entered. Often the order recites general cutoffs, such as the filing of all discovery motions 10 days after the discovery cutoff or of summary judgment motions no later than 45 days prior to trial. Requirements for designating exhibits and deposition testimony as well as trial briefs may also be included.

As with all Rule 16 requirements, counsel must consult the local rules to determine what if any scheduling responsibilities have been delegated to the parties. In some districts a conference between counsel to discuss scheduling issues is mandated, and counsel may even be required to prepare a report which is sent to the court for purposes of entering the scheduling order or holding a

---

[3] See § **5.11**.

status conference. The rules may even require early exchange of documents and a preliminary deposition schedule.

Since Rule 16(b) provides that the scheduling order can be modified upon a showing of good cause, many counsel do not take the order seriously. However, counsel cannot assume that, merely because both parties are willing to stipulate to extensions of cutoff dates, the court will agree. Since the pretrial order controls the subsequent course of the action unless modified,[4] late submission of a summary judgment motion was properly denied as untimely when no modification was sought.[5] Similarly, summary judgment has been granted when failure to timely designate witnesses as required in the pretrial order resulted in their preclusion.[6] Therefore, rather than randomly selecting cutoff dates, counsel should view the order as an incentive to start effective discovery and motion planning.[7] First, this notifies opposing counsel and the court that the case will be diligently pursued. Second, it ensures that the proper amount of time is allocated for discovery. Third, if the case appears to involve complicated issues or massive discovery, it puts the court on notice that the case may require special attention. Even if the action is relatively simple, a well thought out scheduling order gives counsel a good idea of how much time the case will ultimately consume.

§ 16.3 Subjects To Be Discussed at Pretrial Conferences

Rule 16(c) sets forth the following 11 topics to be discussed at pretrials:

1. The formulation and simplification of the issues, including the elimination of frivolous claims or defenses
2. The necessity or desirability of amendments to the pleadings
3. The possibility of obtaining admissions of fact and documents which will avoid unnecessary proof, stipulations regarding the authenticity of documents, and advance rulings from the court on the admissibility of evidence
4. The avoidance of unnecessary proof and cumulative evidence
5. The identification of witnesses and documents, the need and schedule for filing and exchanging pretrial briefs, and the date or dates for further conferences and for trial
6. The advisability of referring matters to a magistrate or master
7. The possibility of settlement or the use of extrajudicial procedures to resolve the dispute

---

[4] Fed. R. Civ. P. 16(e); United States v. First Nat'l Bank, 652 F.2d 882, 887 (9th Cir. 1981); Hodges v. United States, 597 F.2d 1014, 1017–18 (5th Cir. 1979).

[5] U.S. Dominator, Inc. v. Factory Ship Robert E. Resoff, 768 F.2d 1099, 1104 (9th Cir. 1985).

[6] Rabb v. Amatex Corp., 769 F.2d 996, 999–1000 (4th Cir. 1985).

[7] See §§ **13.1, 17.2**.

8. The form and substance of the pretrial order
9. The disposition of pending motions
10. The need for adopting special procedures for managing potentially difficult or protracted actions that may involve complex issues, multiple parties, difficult legal questions, or unusual proof problems, and
11. Such other matters as may aid in the disposition of the action.

In order to ensure that the conference is not an empty formality, Rule 16(c) also requires that one of the attorneys for each party present must have authority to enter into stipulations and to make admissions regarding all matters that the participants may reasonably anticipate being discussed. The listing of approved topics is designed to encourage early and vigorous case management by the judge. Obviously, a judge cannot be forced to discuss these issues, but more judges and magistrates are using Rule 16(c) to encourage dispositions as well as to streamline trial presentation. In essence, a judge can invite motions or require offers of proof which may form the basis of a summary judgment or other dispositive ruling.[8] In a given case, the judge may also refer to *The Manual for Complex Litigation Second* to implement pretrial procedures. At the other extreme, Rule 16 authorizes a judge to require a pro se litigant to submit his direct examination to the court and opposing counsel prior to trial.[9]

The mention of extrajudicial procedures to resolve the dispute can encompass the summary jury trial,[10] other methods of alternative dispute resolution,[11] or aggressive use of special masters.[12] Certainly, some judges are becoming more

---

[8] *See, e.g.,* Portsmouth Square, Inc. v. Shareholders Protective Comm., 770 F.2d 866, 869–70 (9th Cir. 1985) (affirming sua sponte summary judgment entered at final pretrial conference); see § **15.5**.

[9] Miller v. Los Angeles County Bd. of Educ., 799 F.2d 486, 487–88 (9th Cir. 1986).

[10] *See generally* Burnett, *An Advisory Summary "Trial" Procedure As a Useful Pretrial Method to Promote Settlement of Civil Cases,* 32 Fed. Bar. News & J. 290 (Sept. 1985); Lambros, *The Judge's Role in Fostering Voluntary Settlements,* 29 Villanova L. Rev. 1363 (1984); Lambros, *The Summary Jury Trial and Other Alternative Methods of Dispute Resolution,* 103 F.R.D. 461 (1984); Posner, *The Summary Jury Trial and Other Methods of Alternative Dispute Resolution: Some Cautionary Observations,* 53 U. Chi. L. Rev. 366 (1986).

[11] *See, e.g.,* Alschuler, *Mediation With a Mugger: The Shortage of Adjudicative Services and the Need for a Two-Tier Trial System in Civil Cases,* 99 Harv. L. Rev. 1808 (1986); Levin & Golash, *Alternative Dispute Resolution in Federal District Courts,* 37 U. Fla. L. Rev. 29 (1985); Lieberman & Henry, *Lessons from the Alternative Dispute Resolution Movement,* 53 U. Chi. L. Rev. 424 (1986); McMillan & Siegel, *Creating A Fast-Track Alternative Under the Federal Rules of Civil Procedure,* 60 Notre Dame L. Rev. 431 (1985); Peckham, *A Judicial Response to the Cost of Litigation (sic): Case Management, Two-Stage Discovery Planning and Alternative Dispute Resolution,* 37 Rutgers L. Rev. 253 (1985); *see also* 2 Current Problems in Federal Civil Practice 1986, PLI Handbook No. 319.

[12] *See, e.g.,* Brazil, *Special Masters in Complex Cases: Extending the Judiciary or Reshaping Adjudication,* 53 U. Chi. L. Rev. 394 (1986); McGovern, *Toward a Functional Approach for Managing Complex Litigation,* 53 U. Chi. L. Rev. 440 (1986); Schuck, *The Role of Judges in Settling Complex Cases: The Agent Orange Example,* 53 U. Chi. L. Rev. 337 (1986).

involved in settlement negotiations.[13] Indeed, a recent survey indicates that counsel want federal judges to be more actively involved,[14] although mandatory settlement conferences can raise their own issues of fairness and effectiveness.[15] A few local rules may even require mediation or arbitration for diversity cases or all litigation requesting damages below a given amount. One local rule which required a defendant who rejects a proposed mediation award to pay actual costs unless the verdict at trial is more than 10 percent below the evaluation has been upheld.[16]

Rather than letting the judge dominate the pretrial conference, counsel should use Rule 16 aggressively. For example, such discretionary issues as bifurcation[17] and consolidation[18] can be raised at a Rule 16 conference.[19] Indeed, consolidation has been described as part of a trial court's inherent managerial power.[20] Typically, this issue would be raised by a plaintiff because consolidation is considered to favor plaintiffs on liability issues.[21] A defendant should consider whether bifurcation is appropriate, because surveys indicate that personal injury defendants fare better at bifurcated trials.[22] Bifurcation is permissible in diversity cases even if state law prohibits a bifurcated trial.[23] As part of comprehensive Rule 16 strategy, all parties should consider the benefit of in limine rulings concerning evidentiary issues which will be significant at trial. Another advantage of effective Rule 16 practice is to provide a list of uncontested matters which do not have to be proved at trial.[24]

---

[13] *See, e.g.*, Galanter, *". . . A Settlement Judge, Not a Trial Judge:" Judicial Mediation in the United States,* 12 J.L. & Soc'y 1 (1985); Schiller & Wall, *Judicial Settlement Techniques,* 5 Am. J. Trial Advocacy 39 (1981); Schuck, *The Role of Judges in Settling Complex Cases: The Agent Orange Example,* 53 U. Chi. L. Rev. 337 (1986).

[14] Brazil, *What Lawyers Want From Judges in the Settlement Arena,* 106 F.R.D. 85 (1986).

[15] *See, e.g.*, Menkel-Meadow, *For and Against Settlement: Uses and Abuses of the Mandatory Settlement Conference,* 33 UCLA L. Rev. 485 (1985); Reznik, *Managerial Judges,* 96 Harv. L. Rev. 374, 432–35 (1982); Note, *Judicial Authority in the Settlement of Federal Civil Cases,* 42 Wash. & Lee L. Rev. 171 (1985).

[16] Rhea v. Massey-Ferguson, Inc., 767 F.2d 266, 268–69 (6th Cir. 1985).

[17] Fed. R. Civ. P. 42(b).

[18] Fed. R. Civ. P. 42(a).

[19] *See generally* J. Fischer, Federal Trial Procedure Handbook ch. 3 (1985).

[20] Hendrix v. Raybestos-Manhattan, Inc., 776 F.2d 1492, 1495 (11th Cir. 1985); *see* Landis v. North Am. Co., 299 U.S. 248, 254–55 (1936).

[21] *See* McGovern, *Toward a Functional Approach for Managing Complex Litigation,* 53 U. Chi. L. Rev. 440, 450–51 (1986).

[22] *See* Rosales v. Honda Motor Co., 726 F.2d 259, 261 (5th Cir. 1984) (citing 9 C. Wright & A. Miller, Federal Practice and Procedure § 2390 (1970) [hereinafter Federal Practice and Procedure]).

[23] Sellers v. Baisier, 792 F.2d 690, 694 (7th Cir. 1986); Rosales v. Honda Motor Co., 726 F.2d 259, 262 (5th Cir. 1984).

[24] Shell Oil Co. v. M/T Gilda, 790 F.2d 1209, 1215 (5th Cir. 1986); United States v. First Nat'l Bank, 652 F.2d 882, 886 (9th Cir. 1981).

The final pretrial conference is usually held within two weeks of trial. Rule 16(d) provides that it must be attended by at least one of the attorneys who will conduct the trial and by any unrepresented parties. The conference is designed to formulate the final plan for trial, including the method of facilitating the admission of evidence. Often foundational problems are resolved at the pretrial conference, vastly simplifying the introduction of exhibits and deposition testimony at trial.[25] If the court imposes any time limitations on trial testimony as a result of pretrial discussions, counsel must be careful to note any objections both then and at trial to preserve this issue for appeal.[26]

§ 16.4 Pretrial Orders

A pretrial order is supposed to be entered after every Rule 16 conference. As a practical matter, status conferences often do not result in formal orders, and a final pretrial order may not be entered if no agreement can be reached in defining the issues.[27] Rule 16 does not specify who drafts the order, and practice varies as to whether the judge, the plaintiff, or the parties jointly prepare the order. If one party prepares the order, an opportunity for objections will be offered. The early pretrial statements generally flesh out the timing of motions and discovery and set forth the requirements of the final pretrial order.[28]

The final pretrial order usually is a result of pretrial statements submitted by the parties, either individually or jointly, depending upon local rules. Some districts require great detail including statements of contested and uncontested facts and law, a witness list which describes the proposed testimony of recipient and expert witnesses, and an exhibit list. Such rules often provide that witnesses and exhibits not listed can be excluded at trial unless offered solely for rebuttal. Since the pretrial order controls the subsequent course of the action unless modified by a subsequent order, it is proper to exclude omitted witnesses, documents, or issues, even in the absence of a local rule to that effect. Although local rule requiring a detailed pretrial statement was invalidated as being contrary to the previous version of Rule 16,[29] the current positive attitude toward judicial management combined with the broad rewording of Rule 16 dooms most local rule challenges.

---

[25] *See* J. Fischer, Federal Trial Procedure Handbook ch. 4 (1985).

[26] *See* Johnson v. Ashby, 808 F.2d 676, 678–79 (8th Cir. 1987); *cf.* Flaminio v. Honda Motor Co., 733 F.2d 463, 473 (7th Cir. 1984) (disapproving rigid timekeeping limitation).

[27] MCI Communications v. AT&T Co., 708 F.2d 1081, 1170 (7th Cir.), *cert. denied,* 464 U.S. 891 (1983).

[28] *See, e.g.,* Hardy v. Johns-Manville Sales Corp., 681 F.2d 334, 349 (5th Cir. 1982) (asbestos cases); Zenith Radio Corp. v. Matsushita Elec. Indus. Co., 478 F. Supp. 889, 946–60 (E.D. Pa. 1979) (extensive pretrial scheduling order in complex litigation).

[29] McCargo v. Hedrick, 545 F.2d 393, 401 (4th Cir. 1976).

Omissions from the pretrial order can be critical at trial when counsel wishes to present the new evidence or theory. Courts agree that issues raised in the pretrial order supersede those presented in the original pleadings.[30] Therefore, the appropriateness of permitting a new theory to be argued at trial can depend on whether the pretrial order gives full and fair disclosure of the issue.[31] Although courts interpret pretrial memoranda broadly,[32] it is counsel's responsibility to specify clearly all contested issues. Rule 16(e) provides that the final pretrial order can be modified only to prevent manifest injustice, and this generally means that if a claim or issue is omitted from the order, it is waived.[33]

The reason for such strict adherence to the pretrial order is to avoid trial by ambush and encourage timely trial preparation. However, courts are not consistent in treating omitted evidence or issues. A few circuits view the manifest injustice standard strictly to uphold the denial of a later amendment even in the absence of prejudice or surprise, if the issue was known at the time of the pretrial.[34] Other circuits appear to give great deference to the trial judge's decision concerning admission of evidence not included in the pretrial order.[35] Several circuits permit amendment to the pretrial order at trial based on evaluation of the following criteria: (1) the prejudice or surprise in fact to the nonmoving party, (2) the ability of that party to cure the prejudice, (3) the extent to which the waiver of the rule would disrupt the orderly and efficient trial of the case, and (4) bad faith or willfulness on the part of the movant.[36] Thus, when an unlisted witness was newly discovered, it was an abuse of discretion to refuse to amend the pretrial order to permit his testimony.[37]

At the first indication that new evidence or a new theory will be posted, counsel should immediately object, and if the court appears willing to admit the disputed evidence a continuance or recess should be sought. An objection is particularly important, since its absence permits the court to consider the issue

---

[30] *See, e.g.,* United States v. Hougham, 364 U.S. 310, 315–16 (1960); Erff v. Markhon Indus., Inc., 781 F.2d 613, 617 (7th Cir. 1986); Howard v. Kerr Glass Mfg. Co., 699 F.2d 330, 333 (6th Cir. 1983).

[31] *See, e.g.,* Erff v. Markhon Indus., Inc., 781 F.2d 613, 616–18 (7th Cir. 1986); *see* Acorn v. City of Phoenix, 798 F.2d 1260, 1272 (9th Cir. 1986).

[32] *See* Scutieri v. Paige, 808 F.2d 785, 792–93 (11th Cir. 1987).

[33] Swift v. State Farm Mut. Auto. Ins. Co., 796 F.2d 120, 123 (5th Cir. 1986).

[34] Trinity Carton Co. v. Falstaff Brewing Corp., 767 F.2d 184, 192 n.13 (5th Cir. 1985), *cert. denied,* ____ U.S. ____, 106 S. Ct. 1202 (1986).

[35] *See, e.g.,* Woods v. Burlington N. R.R., 768 F.2d 1287, 1290 (11th Cir. 1985), *rev'd on other grounds,* ____ U.S. ____, ____ S. Ct. ____ (1987); Robert v. Conti Carriers & Terminals, Inc., 692 F.2d 22, 24 (5th Cir. 1982).

[36] Joy Mfg. Co. v. Sola Basic Indus., Inc., 697 F.2d 104, 109 (3d Cir. 1982); Smith v. Ford Motor Co., 626 F.2d 784, 797 (10th Cir. 1980), *cert. denied,* 450 U.S. 918 (1981); *see* Adalman v. Baker, Watts & Co., 807 F.2d 359, 369 (4th Cir. 1986); Hale v. Firestone Tire & Rubber Co., 756 F.2d 1322, 1335 (8th Cir. 1985); McFadden v. Sanchez, 710 F.2d 907, 911 (2d Cir.), *cert. denied,* 464 U.S. 961 (1983); §§ **20.15, 30.10**.

[37] Dabney v. Montgomery Ward & Co., 692 F.2d 49, 51–52 (8th Cir. 1982), *cert. denied,* 461 U.S. 957 (1983).

as tried by the implied consent of the parties.[38] In other words, a court does not abuse its discretion in allowing evidence on a new theory when the opposing party fails to object or to claim surprise when the evidence presented at trial plainly raises the new issue.[39]

§ 16.5 Rule 16(f) Sanctions

Rule 16(f) authorizes a judge to impose sanctions on a party who fails to obey a scheduling or pretrial order. This topic is discussed in connection with sanctions in § **30.10**. In general, Rule 16 sanctions are appropriate if no appearance is made on behalf of a party at a scheduling or pretrial conference, or if a party or party's attorney is substantially unprepared to participate in the conference, or if a party or party's attorney fails to participate in good faith. Rule 16(f) penalties can be assessed on the court's own initiative or upon motion. The judge can resort to most sanctions available under Rule 37, including terminating the case, precluding evidence or issues, and imposing other evidentiary consequences related to the noncompliance. In addition, the reasonable expenses incurred because of the noncompliance, including attorneys' fees, must be reimbursed to the opposing party, unless noncompliance was substantially justified or other circumstances make an award of expenses unjust. The Second Circuit has held that implied orders do not justify sanctions under Rule 16(f).[40] Rule 16(f) also does not support sanctions for failure to settle a case before rather than during trial.[41] In some circuits, pro se litigants must be explicitly told of any failings in their pretrial statements to justify exclusion of evidence at trial pursuant to Rule 16(f).[42] However, when a pro se plaintiff was warned that the action would be dismissed if the pretrial statement was not amended within 10 days, a Rule 16(f) dismissal was proper.[43]

§ 16.6 Settlement Considerations

Although a discussion of negotiating techniques is outside the scope of this chapter,[44] some general observations can be made. First, most cases settle.

---

[38] Fed. R. Civ. P. 15(b); *see* Mechmetals Corp. v. Telex Computer Prods., Inc., 709 F.2d 1287, 1294 (9th Cir. 1983); Carlyle v. United States, 674 F.2d 554, 556 (6th Cir. 1982).

[39] Emmons v. Southern Pac. Transp. Co., 701 F.2d 1112, 1118 (5th Cir. 1983); *see* Bradford Trust Co. v. Merrill Lynch, Pierce, Fenner & Smith, Inc., 805 F.2d 49, 52–54 (2d Cir. 1986).

[40] Salahuddin v. Harris, 782 F.2d 1127, 1133 (2d Cir. 1986).

[41] Kothe v. Smith, 771 F.2d 667, 669 (2d Cir. 1985).

[42] *See, e.g.*, Carter v. Hutto, 781 F.2d 1028, 1032–33 (4th Cir. 1986) (pro se litigant).

[43] Burgs v. Sissel, 745 F.2d 526, 528 (8th Cir. 1984).

[44] *See, e.g.*, R. Fisher & W. Ury, Getting to Yes (1981); R. Haydock, Negotiation Practice (1984); H. Raiffa, The Art and Science of Negotiation (1982); G. Williams, Legal Negotiation and

Second, effective settlement technique depends on a thorough knowledge of the strengths and weaknesses of the case and an understanding of what is important to the parties. Third, client control is undermined by early unrealistic estimates of what the case is worth. Fourth, the timing of settlement discussions can be key to their outcome. Fifth, alternative dispute resolution methods may be desirable to expedite settlement.[45] Sixth, final offers usually aren't. Seventh, settlement by individual parties in multiparty litigation should not be lightly entered.[46] Eighth, it is to counsel's advantage to make the judge or magistrate an ally in settlement discussions.

Rule 68 settlement offers should also be considered in formulating settlement strategy. Such offers limit the costs which a plaintiff can recover after rejection of the offer. The Rule 68 offer must state that judgment may be taken against the defending party on the terms specified in the offer, with costs then accrued. The defendant is required to make the offer more than 10 days before the trial begins and serve it upon the adverse party. If within 10 days after service, the adverse party serves written notice that the offer is accepted, this is filed with the court and judgment is entered. An unaccepted offer is deemed withdrawn, and evidence thereof is not admissible at trial. A subsequent offer is permitted. If the judgment finally obtained by the offeree is not more favorable than the offer, the offeree must pay the costs incurred after the making of the offer. A Rule 68 offer can also be made if liability has been determined, but the amount or extent remains to be determined. In such cases the offer must be served no less than 10 days prior to the commencement of hearings to determine the amount or extent of liability.

Currently Rule 68 is a significant factor only in litigation in which the statutory definition of costs includes attorneys' fees,[47] because a plaintiff would be denied attorneys' fees for any work undertaken after the rejection of the Rule 68 offer which is more favorable than the relief ultimately recovered.[48] In other words, when Rule 68 applies, it has been considered mandatory, leaving no room for discretion to award costs pursuant to Rule 54(d).[49] However, even those

---

Settlement (1983); Gifford, *A Context-Based Theory of Strategy Selection in Legal Negotiation,* 46 Ohio St. L.J. 41 (1985); Menkel-Meadow, *Legal Negotiation: A Study of Strategies in Search of a Theory,* 1983 A.B. Found. Res. J. 905; Menkel-Meadow, *Toward Another View of Legal Negotiation: The Structure of Problem Solving,* 31 UCLA L. Rev. 754 (1984); White, *Machiavelli and the Bar: Ethical Limitations on Lying in Negotiation,* 1980 A.B. Found. Res. J. 926.

[45] See § **16.3**.

[46] *See, e.g.,* Booth v. Mary Carter Paint Co., 202 So. 2d 8, 10–11 (Fla. 1967) and its progeny; *see also* Irvin v. Griffin Corp., 808 F.2d 802, 804–07 (11th Cir. 1987) (effect of release on other parties).

[47] Marek v. Chesny, ____ U.S. ____, 105 S. Ct. 3012, 3017 (1985) (civil rights statute); *see id.* at 3036–39 (Brennan, J., dissenting) for Appendix listing statutes awarding attorneys' fees.

[48] *See* Grosvenor v. Brienen, 801 F.2d 944, 946–48 (7th Cir. 1986) (only post-offer attorneys' fees, not pre-offer fees affected).

[49] *See, e.g.,* Johnston v. Penrod Drilling Co, 803 F.2d 867, 869–70 (5th Cir. 1986); Grosvenor v. Brienen, 801 F.2d 944, 945–46 (7th Cir. 1986); Liberty Mut. Ins. Co. v. EEOC 691 F.2d 438, 442 (9th Cir. 1982); *see also* Delta Air Lines, Inc. v. August, 450 U.S. 346, 351–56 (1981).

courts which view Rule 68 as requiring the plaintiff to reimburse the defendant's post-offer costs have not interpreted Rule 68 to mandate payment of the defendant's post-offer attorneys' fees.[50]

In most cases not involving attorneys' fees, Rule 68 is not a major factor in settlement negotiations, because the monetary penalty of paying costs is relatively minor. Rule 68's effect is also limited to relatively few cases, because it does not apply when the plaintiff loses at trial,[51] but only when it wins a verdict less than that offered. Furthermore, Rule 68 is inapplicable to any offer made by the plaintiff. In addition, because the offer must be written and served, a defendant cannot turn an oral settlement offer made at a Rule 16 conference into a binding Rule 68 offer.[52] Its application to cases of joint offer of judgment is complicated when one party settles or only one party is held liable at trial.[53]

There is usually no strategic disadvantage to a defendant to make a Rule 68 offer, although as mentioned, its importance is restricted to cases in which attorneys' fees are included as costs. Plaintiffs in such litigation, including civil rights actions, must seriously evaluate the offer and determine the likely outcome at trial.[54] When considering an offer, the plaintiff should also consult local rules, because a few go beyond Rule 68 to include attorneys' fees. Although the validity of such local rules may be questionable, to date they have not been challenged. Proposals have been offered to modify Rule 68 to make it applicable to more cases. Considerable debate has been generated concerning revision, but currently no agreement has been reached as to a fair and effective way to redefine Rule 68 offers.[55]

§ 16.7 Enforcement of Settlement Agreements

Courts have inherent powers to enforce settlement agreements,[56] either by requiring specific performance[57] or awarding damages.[58] However, judges do not have power to impose a settlement agreement when the parties have not

---

[50] *See* Crossman v. Marcoccio, 806 F.2d 329, 330–34 (1st Cir. 1986).

[51] Delta Air Lines, Inc. v. August, 450 U.S. 346, 351 (1981).

[52] Grosvenor v. Brienen, 801 F.2d 944, 948–49 (7th Cir. 1986).

[53] *See* Johnston v. Penrod Drilling Co., 803 F.2d 867, 869–71 (5th Cir. 1986).

[54] *See, e.g., Verdicts and Settlements,* published monthly.

[55] *See generally* Note, *Federal Rule of Civil Procedure 68: "Settling" The Difference In The Proposed Amendments To The Offer Of Settlement Rule,* 7 Cardozo L. Rev. 1141 (1986); Note, *Rule 68: An Offer You Can't Afford to Refuse,* 37 Rutgers L. Rev. 373 (1985).

[56] White Farm Equip. Co. v. Kupcho, 792 F.2d 526, 529 (5th Cir. 1986); *In re* Suchy, 786 F.2d 900, 902–03 (9th Cir. 1985).

[57] TNT Marketing, Inc. v. Agresti, 796 F.2d 276, 278 (9th Cir. 1986); Pennwalt Corp. v. Plough, Inc., 676 F.2d 77, 80 (3d Cir. 1982).

[58] TNT Marketing, Inc. v. Agresti, 796 F.2d 276, 278 (9th Cir. 1986); Village of Kaktovik v. Watt, 689 F.2d 222, 230 (D.C. Cir. 1982); Hobbs & Co. v. American Investors Mgmt., Inc., 576 F.2d 29, 33 & n.7 (3d Cir. 1978).

agreed.[59] In diversity cases, state law defines the attorney's authority to settle the action, while in federal actions, federal law applies.[60] Attorneys do not possess inherent authority to compromise a claim by virtue of their representation of the client alone.[61] In some situations, the attorney has apparent authority to settle claims because of the client's representations to the opposing party. A third party who reaches an agreement with the attorney having apparent authority is entitled to enforce it even if the attorney was acting contrary to the client's express instructions.[62] The client's remedy in this situation is a malpractice claim against its attorney.[63] Some circuits require a hearing on the disputed issues concerning the validity and scope of the agreement.[64]

§ 16.8 Disqualification of Judges

Unlike some state court systems which basically permit one free chance to disqualify a judge,[65] in the federal system recusal is an exceptional remedy.[66] It is difficult to reverse a judge's denial of a recusal motion, because this issue is reviewed for abuse of discretion.[67] Some circuits review recusal rulings by way of a writ of mandamus.[68]

Two statutes govern questions of recusal.[69] 28 U.S.C. § 144 provides that whenever a party files a timely affidavit and the judge has a personal bias or prejudice against the party or in favor of any adverse party, recusal is required. The attorney must submit a certificate of good faith when bringing a § 144 motion. Timeliness is judged by a standard of reasonableness in the circumstances, which includes such factors as filing of pretrial motions after learning of

---

[59] Ozyagcilar v. Davis, 701 F.2d 306, 308 (4th Cir. 1983); *see* United States v. Ward Baking Co., 376 U.S. 327, 333 (1964); Cheyenne River Sioux Tribe v. United States, 806 F.2d 1046, 1050–52 (Fed. Cir. 1986).

[60] Edwards v. Born, Inc., 792 F.2d 387, 389 (3d Cir. 1986); *see* Mid-South Towing Co. v. Har-Win, Inc., 733 F.2d 386, 389 (5th Cir. 1984) (applies federal law in maritime claim); Glazer v. J.C. Bradford & Co., 616 F.2d 167, 169 (5th Cir. 1980) (applies state law in diversity).

[61] Edwards v. Born, Inc., 792 F.2d 387, 390 (3d Cir. 1986); Luis C. Forteza e Hijos, Inc. v. Mills, 534 F.2d 415, 418 (1st Cir. 1976).

[62] Capital Dredge & Dock Corp. v. City of Detroit, 800 F.2d 525, 530 (6th Cir. 1986); Edwards v. Born, Inc., 792 F.2d 387, 390 (3d Cir. 1986); *see* Restatement (Second) of Agency § 27 (1958); Spiegel, *Lawyering and Client Decisionmaking: Informed Consent and the Legal Profession,* 128 U. Pa. L. Rev. 41 (1979).

[63] Capital Dredge & Dock Corp. v. City of Detroit, 800 F.2d 525, 530 (6th Cir. 1986).

[64] *See* Mid-South Towing Co. v. Har-Win, Inc., 733 F.2d 386, 390–91 (5th Cir. 1984); Autera v. Robinson, 419 F.2d 1197, 1200–03 (D.C. Cir. 1969).

[65] *See, e.g.,* Cal. Civ. Proc. Code § 170.6 (West 1982 & Supp. 1987).

[66] *See generally* J. Fischer, Federal Trial Procedure Handbook ch. 1 (1985).

[67] United States v. Probst, 792 F.2d 111, 113 (8th Cir. 1986); *In re* City of Houston, 745 F.2d 925, 927 (5th Cir. 1984).

[68] *See, e.g, In re* Placid Oil Co., 802 F.2d 783, 786 (5th Cir. 1986).

[69] 28 U.S.C. §§ 144 & 455 (1982).

the asserted bias.[70] 28 U.S.C. § 455 is more comprehensive and does not specifically mention any procedural requirements, although some courts consider timeliness.[71] Section 455 requires disqualification when a judge's or magistrate's impartiality might reasonably be questioned[72] or if the judge or magistrate has a personal bias or prejudice concerning a party or personal knowledge of disputed facts.[73] Pursuant to this section, even the appearance of partiality requires recusal.[74] However, disqualification has been denied when a party claimed that the judge's attempts to encourage a settlement by indicating an evaluation of the case gave rise to an appearance of bias.[75] Financial interest is also often cited as a reason for recusal under § 455, but courts are unwilling to require recusal in every case in which a judge owns stock of a company in the same industry as one of the parties.[76]

§ 16.9 Disqualification of Counsel

Modern law practice results in an infinite variety of ways in which counsel may have a conflict of interest.[77] Although every firm or practitioner should have a system in place to spot conflicts and, if feasible, to obtain permission from each of the involved parties, it is not uncommon for a potential conflict to escape notice until the litigation is underway. Moreover, some of the ethical rules governing conflicts are vague enough to leave room for varying interpretations about when disqualification is required. The disqualification issue also has strategic importance in that a decision to disqualify[78] or not disqualify[79] a lawyer is not subject to interlocutory appeal, virtually making the district court's ruling unreviewable for the lawyer who can no longer represent the client or the party alleging a conflict who loses and then settles the case. A writ of mandamus may

---

[70] *See, e.g.*, Franks v. Nimmo, 796 F.2d 1230, 1234 (10th Cir. 1986); Smith v. Danyo, 585 F.2d 83, 86 (3d Cir. 1978).

[71] *See* United States v. Hines, 696 F.2d 722, 729 (10th Cir. 1982); *In re* IBM Corp., 618 F.2d 923, 932–33 (2d Cir. 1980).

[72] 28 U.S.C. § 455(a) (1982).

[73] *Id.* § 455(b)(1).

[74] *See* Pepsico, Inc. v. McMillen, 764 F.2d 458, 460 (7th Cir. 1985); 28 U.S.C. § 455(a) (1982).

[75] *See* Franks v. Nimmo, 796 F.2d 1230, 1235 (10th Cir. 1986); Johnson v. Trueblood, 629 F.2d 287, 291 (3d Cir. 1980), *cert. denied*, 450 U.S. 999 (1981).

[76] *See In re* Placid Oil Co., 802 F.2d 783, 786 (5th Cir. 1986).

[77] *See generally* Note, *Attorney Disqualification For a Conflict of Interest in Federal Civil Litigation: A Confusing Body of Law in Need of Organization*, 30 Villanova L. Rev. 463 (1985); *Developments in the Law—Conflicts of Interest in the Legal Profession*, 94 Harv. L. Rev. 1244 (1981).

[78] Richardson-Merrell Inc. v. Koller, 472 U.S. 424, 430 (1985).

[79] Firestone Tire & Rubber Co. v. Risjord, 449 U.S. 368, 377 (1981).

still be sought,[80] but it is rarely granted.[81] Moreover, the district court's decision is reversed only for abuse of discretion.[82]

As a matter of professional responsibility, an attorney owes a duty to the client which includes an obligation not to divulge confidential communications from the client and not to accept representation of a person whose interests are opposed to those of the client.[83] Representation against an existing client is usually considered prima facie improper without the consent of all involved.[84]

The attorney's obligations do not necessarily end at the conclusion of the relationship, because representation of a former client may result in the attorney's potentially being in a position to use privileged information in a current matter.[85] The former client expressly or impliedly consents to the adverse representation.[86] Otherwise, the attorney will be disqualified if the former client shows that matters embraced within the pending litigation are substantially related to the previous representation.[87] An exception exists in class action litigation when an attorney for the class has been permitted to represent either the dissenters against a proposed settlement or the majority against the dissenting class members.[88] Similarly, when a member or associate of a law firm or government legal department changes jobs, and the firm or lawyer is retained by an adversary of a client of the former employer, disqualification can be avoided by showing that effective measures were taken to prevent confidences from being received by the lawyers handling the new matter.[89] However, the substantial relationship test applies when the law firm itself changes sides.[90] The rebuttability of the substantial relationship presumption is a matter of disagreement, although the

---

[80] *See* Richardson-Merrell Inc. v. Koller, 472 U.S. 424, 435 (1985); *In re* American Cable Publications, Inc., 768 F.2d 1194, 1195 (10th Cir. 1985).

[81] *See, e.g., In re* Ford Motor Co., 751 F.2d 274, 275 (8th Cir. 1984).

[82] Trust Corp. of Mont. v. Piper Aircraft Corp., 701 F.2d 85, 87 (9th Cir. 1983).

[83] *In re* "Agent Orange" Prod. Liability Litig., 800 F.2d 14, 17 (2d Cir. 1986); *see, e.g.,* Model Code of Professional Responsibility Canon 9, EC 4-1, 5-2; DR 5-105 (1980).

[84] *See* Cinema 5, Ltd. v. Cinerama, Inc., 528 F.2d 1384, 1387 (2d Cir. 1976).

[85] *In re* "Agent Orange" Prod. Liability Litig., 800 F.2d 14, 17 (2d Cir. 1986); *see also In re* Corn Derivatives Antitrust Litig., 748 F.2d 157, 161 (3d Cir. 1984), *cert. denied,* ___ U.S. ___, 105 S. Ct. 2702 (1985).

[86] Trust Corp. of Mont. v. Piper Aircraft Corp., 701 F.2d 85, 87 (9th Cir. 1983); *In re* Yarn Processing Patent Validity Litig., 530 F.2d 83, 89 (5th Cir. 1976).

[87] *See, e.g.,* Analytica, Inc. v. NPD Research, Inc., 708 F.2d 1263, 1266–67 (7th Cir. 1983); Trone v. Smith, 621 F.2d 994, 998 (9th Cir. 1980); Fund of Funds, Ltd. v. Arthur Andersen & Co., 567 F.2d 225, 235 (2d Cir. 1977); Richardson v. Hamilton Int'l Corp., 469 F.2d 1382, 1385 (3d Cir. 1972); Model Rules of Professional Conduct Rule 1.9 (1983).

[88] *See In re* "Agent Orange" Prod. Liability Litig., 800 F.2d 14, 19 (2d Cir. 1986).

[89] Analytica, Inc v. NPD Research, Inc., 708 F.2d 1263, 1267 (7th Cir. 1983); Armstrong v. McAlpin, 625 F.2d 433, 445 (2d Cir. 1980) (en banc), *vacated on other grounds,* 449 U.S. 1106 (1981); *see generally* Comment, *Disqualification of Counsel: Adverse Interest and Revolving Doors,* 81 Colum. L. Rev. 199 (1981); *see* Model Rules of Professional Conduct Rules 1.9, 1.10 (1983); Annot., 51 A.L.R. Fed. 678 (1981).

[90] Analytica, Inc. v. NPD Research, Inc., 708 F.2d 1263, 1267 (7th Cir. 1983).

majority of courts appear not to permit rebuttal.[91] In evaluating disqualification motions, some circuits look to whether the violation tends to taint the underlying trial.[92] Taint in this context need be only potential rather than actual.[93] Engaging in ex party contacts with an employee of the adversary who is engaged in litigation preparation has resulted in disqualification of the offending lawyer.[94]

Disqualification motions have also arisen when a lawyer is represented by partners in the same firm. As long as the lawyer being represented is a litigant, courts agree that this is proper.[95] In addition, if after undertaking representation of a client, the lawyer or another lawyer in the firm believes she may be called as a witness other than on behalf of the client, withdrawal is not required unless the testimony may be prejudicial to the client,[96] except in minor matters or when withdrawal would work a substantial hardship on the client.[97] An attorney's conflict of interest has also been considered a factor in assessing any sanctions against the party for an ensuing discovery or pretrial violation.[98] A law firm improperly resisting a disqualification motion can itself be sanctioned by being required to pay the fees and expenses of its adversary in obtaining the disqualification.[99]

§ 16.10 Federal Magistrates Practice

Magistrates are a well recognized feature of federal pretrial litigation,[100] and in many districts they are regarded as indispensable. However, their use varies significantly among district courts and among judges in any given district.

---

[91] *See generally* Note, *Attorney Disqualification For a Conflict of Interest in Federal Civil Litigation: A Confusing Body of Law in Need of Organization,* 30 Villanova L. Rev. 463, 480 & n.55 (1985).

[92] Board of Educ. v. Nyquist, 590 F.2d 1241, 1246 (2d Cir. 1979).

[93] *See, e.g., In re* Yarn Processing Patent Validity Litig., 530 F.2d 83, 89 (5th Cir. 1976).

[94] *See* American Protection Ins. Co. v. MGM Grand Hotel-Las Vegas, Inc., 765 F.2d 925, 926 (9th Cir. 1985) (dismissing review of disqualification on jurisdictional grounds); Note, *Discovery of the Nontestifying Expert Witness' Identity Under the Federal Rules of Civil Procedure: You Can't Tell the Players Without a Program,* 37 Hastings L.J. 201, 215–18 (1985).

[95] *See In re* American Cable Publications, Inc. 768 F.2d 1194, 1195 (10th Cir. 1985); Bottaro v. Hatton Assocs., 680 F.2d 895, 897–98 (2d Cir. 1982); Model Rules of Professional Conduct Rule 3.7(b) (1983).

[96] Model Code of Professional Responsibility DR 5-102(B) (1980); Model Rules of Professional Conduct Rule 3.7 (1983).

[97] *See* Model Code of Professional Responsibility Dr. 5-101(B) (1980).

[98] Gutting v. Falstaff Brewing Corp., 710 F.2d 1309, 1315 (8th Cir. 1983).

[99] *See* Analytica, Inc. v. NPD Research, Inc., 708 F.2d 1263, 1270 (7th Cir. 1983) (bad faith); *see also* Fed. Rule Civ. P. 11; **ch. 28**.

[100] *See generally* K. Sinclair, Practice Before Federal Magistrates (1987); 7, pt. 2 J. Moore *et al.,* Moore's Federal Practice ¶ 72.01–.05 (2d ed. 1986) [hereinafter Moore's Federal Practice]; 12 Federal Practice and Procedure §§ 3076.1–.9 (2d ed. Supp. 1986); Silberman, *Masters and Magistrates, Part II: The American Analogue,* 50 N.Y.U. L. Rev. 1297 (1975).

Standing orders exist in some districts to refer all pretrial discovery matters and nondispositive motions to magistrates. In other districts standing orders may be more narrowly focused on certain categories of cases such as habeas corpus or social security actions. In the absence of local rules, individual judges may have their own general standing orders or may choose to refer individual matters to a magistrate.

The extent to which references are requested by the parties or initiated by a judge regardless of the party's consent depends upon individual perceptions concerning the benefits of using magistrates. Magistrates have been used successfully in some districts to conduct pretrial conferences and to facilitate settlement negotiations.[101] Probably their most significant use occurs regarding discovery, since many judges do not want to become embroiled in the internecine warfare generated by discovery practice. Practitioners also may want someone other than the judge reviewing such issues, fearing that the judge may become partial to the adversary's attorneys or prejudge the facts as a result of information gleaned from discovery hearings. Moreover, in the discovery context, obtaining a speedy resolution can often be as important as the content of what is decided. In addition, there is little encouragement to appeal from a magistrate's discovery ruling, because with minor exception judges tend to uphold them, in part because they are usually affirmed unless clearly erroneous.[102]

There is less agreement on the value of the court referring dispositive motions to magistrates for a report and recommendation. First, as a practical matter, the losing party always appeals to the judge when the recommendation concerns a dispositive matter. Therefore, the reference invariably involves some duplication. Second, it is not clear that judges regularly adopt the magistrate's recommendations. Indeed, some practitioners view the magistrate's findings as offering no prediction regarding the judge's ruling. Since experiences with magistrates differ greatly, it is always helpful to learn something about the individual district court judge's track record on upholding the magistrate's decisions.

§ 16.11 Authority of Magistrates

Magistrates are full-time judicial appointees who by statute[103] and rule[104] have authority to decide any civil nondispositive motions and to hold hearings and submit findings of fact and recommendations concerning dispositive motions.

---

[101] *See generally* Burnett, *Practical, Innovative and Progressive Utilization of United States Magistrates to Improve the Administration of Justice in the United States District Courts*, 28 Howard L.J. 293 (1985).

[102] 28 U.S.C. § 636(b)(1)(A) (1982).

[103] 28 U.S.C. § 636 (1982 & Supp. III 1985).

[104] Fed. R. Civ. P. 72–76.

References for motions are valid regardless of the consent of the parties,[105] although in a given case, a party may request that a magistrate be appointed.

Dispositive motions include motions for injunctive relief, for judgment on the pleadings, for summary judgment, to dismiss or quash an indictment or information made by the defendant, to suppress evidence in a criminal case, to dismiss or to permit maintenance of a class action, to dismiss for failure to state a claim upon which relief can be granted, and to involuntarily dismiss an action. A motion for leave to amend has been treated as a nondispositive motion, even though its denial resulted in the claim being untimely.[106] However, the court can refer a nondispositive motion for report rather than for decision, if it considers the issue to be significant or sensitive.

§ 16.12 Objections to Magistrate's Rulings

Within 10 days of entry of order, a party may object to a magistrate's ruling on a nondispositive matter.[107] Because it is unclear whether additional time is permitted when the court has mailed its ruling, prompt service of objections is advised.[108] Parties are given 10 days after service of findings and recommendation concerning dispositive matters to serve and file written objections.[109] Moving for reconsideration before the magistrate may be risky, because there is no indication that this motion tolls the 10-day objection period. Courts do have the power to extend the 10-day objection period upon request,[110] but it is safer to request enlargement before rather than after the period has expired.

There is no required format for objections, but in the absence of a local rule on this issue, it has been suggested that they be delineated clearly as "Objections to Decision of U.S. Magistrate" and be accompanied by a memorandum noting the specific reason for each individual objection.[111] Similarly, no procedures are mentioned for responding to objections for nondispositive motions, although this is clearly permitted. Although Rule 72(b) specifically mentions responses to objections as to dispositive matters, no particular format is specified.

Nondispositive matters referred for decision are rarely overturned because reconsideration is granted only when the ruling is clearly erroneous or contrary to law.[112] Dispositive motions and nondispositive motions referred solely for

---

[105] *See, e.g.*, Orpiano v. Johnson, 687 F.2d 44, 46 (4th Cir. 1982).

[106] *See* U.S. Dominator, Inc. v. Factory Ship Robert E. Resoff, 768 F.2d 1099, 1102 n.1 (9th Cir. 1985).

[107] Fed. R. Civ. P. 72(a).

[108] *See* 7, pt. 2 Moore's Federal Practice ¶ 72.03[6.-4].

[109] 28 U.S.C., § 636(b)(1)(C) (1982); Fed. R. Civ. P. 72(b).

[110] Grandison v. Moore, 786 F.2d 146, 148 (3d Cir. 1986).

[111] 7, pt. 2 Moore's Federal Practice ¶ 72.03[6.-5].

[112] 28 U.S.C. § 636(b)(1)(A) (1982).

recommendation are reviewed de novo as to those portions of the report, findings, or recommendations to which objection has been made.[113] The judge may accept, reject, or modify, in whole or in part, the findings or recommendations of the magistrate as well as receive further evidence or recommit the matter to the magistrate with instructions.[114] De novo review in this context does not mandate a new hearing but only a review of the record. [115] However, it would rarely be appropriate for the court to disregard a magistrate's finding which involves the credibility of a witness.[116]

In the absence of objections, the court has the power to review any issue but is not required to do so.[117] Similarly, a complete review of the transcript of the hearing was not required when the general objection raised concerned the bias of the magistrate, not any specific portion of the report.[118] Indeed, the Supreme Court has upheld the right of courts of appeals to establish a rule that the failure to file timely objections to the magistrate's report waives the party's right to appeal the district court's judgment.[119] Rules adopted by at least six circuits provide waiver of both legal and factual issues,[120] although a few circuits restrict waiver to factual matters.[121] The only restriction on enforcing such rules is that they must give clear notice to the litigants and an opportunity to seek an extension of time for filing objections before a waiver can be found.[122] A few circuits require magistrates to advise litigants of the requirement that objections must be specific and filed within 10 days and that the failure to file objections waives the right to appeal.[123]

§ 16.13 References for Trial

Parties can also consent to a magistrate's conducting any or all proceedings in a jury or nonjury civil matter pursuant to 28 U.S.C. § 636(c)(1), a provision which

---

[113] *Id.* § 636(b)(1)(C).

[114] *Id.*

[115] United States v. Raddatz, 447 U.S. 667, 675 (1980).

[116] *Id.* at n.7 (1980); United States v. Marshall, 609 F.2d 152, 155 (5th Cir. 1980); Bennerson v. Joseph, 583 F.2d 633, 641 (3d Cir. 1978).

[117] Thomas v. Arn, ___ U.S. ___, 106 S. Ct. 466, 474 (1985); Delgado v. Bowen, 782 F.2d 79, 81–82 (7th Cir. 1986).

[118] Goney v. Clark, 749 F.2d 5, 6–7 (3d Cir. 1984).

[119] Thomas v. Arn, ___ U.S. ___, 106 S. Ct. 466, 475 (1985).

[120] *See* Video Views, Inc. v. Studio 21, Ltd., 797 F.2d 538, 539 (7th Cir. 1986) (listing circuits).

[121] Nash v. Black, 781 F.2d 665, 667 (8th Cir. 1986); Britt v. Simi Valley Unified School Dist., 708 F.2d 452, 454 (9th Cir. 1983); Nettles v. Wainwright, 677 F.2d 404, 410 (5th Cir. 1982) (en banc).

[122] Thomas v. Arn, ___ U.S. ___, 106 S. Ct. 466, 475 (1985); *see* Welch v. Heckler, 808 F.2d 264, 266 (3d Cir. 1986) (waiver inappropriate when magistrate's notice indicated exceptions were permissive rather than mandatory).

[123] *See, e.g.*, United States v. Valencia-Copete, 792 F.2d 4, 6 (1st Cir. 1986); Wright v. Collins, 766 F.2d 841, 845–47 (4th Cir. 1985); United States v. Walters, 638 F.2d 947, 950 (6th Cir. 1981).

has been held constitutional by each of the circuits in which this issue has been raised.[124] One advantage of such a reference is that, in many districts, it ensures an earlier trial date than would be possible before a judge. Another advantage perceived by some diversity practitioners is that some magistrates are considered to be less formal than federal court judges. Additionally, a magistrate may be as highly regarded by litigators as the assigned judge, especially in those districts where the selection process has resulted in the appointment of experienced lawyers with impeccable qualifications.

The consent to trial before a magistrate is usually worded so that it encompasses dispositive motions as well as the trial. The consent must be explicit.[125] Therefore, absence of consent by additional defendants named in an amended complaint resulted in depriving the magistrate of authority to grant a dismissal, even though the plaintiff rather than the defendant challenged the magistrate's jurisdiction.[126] Although it is good practice to have both parties execute a written consent form for trial references, its absence is not jurisdictional as long as the parties agree to having the magistrate preside at trial.[127] The Fifth Circuit now requires a magistrate to inquire whether each party has filed consent to the magistrate's presiding at the trial before commencing the trial.[128] Unlike nonconsensual references, which can be withdrawn by the judge upon pleasure, once a case has been referred with the consent of the parties, the reference can be withdrawn by the district court only for good cause shown on its own motion or, under extraordinary circumstances, shown by any party.[129] Factual findings by the magistrate for § 636(c) references will be upheld unless clearly erroneous.[130]

The court can make a nonconsensual reference for a nonjury trial by a showing that some exceptional condition requires it.[131] In addition, the judge may refer a Title VII action to a magistrate acting as a special master, without exceptional conditions or consent of the parties, if the case has not been set for trial within

---

[124] *See, e.g.*, K.M.C. Co. v. Irving Trust Co., 757 F.2d 752, 755 n.1 (6th Cir. 1985); Gairola v. Virginia Dep't of General Servs., 753 F.2d 1281, 1284–85 (4th Cir. 1985) (listing circuits); *see generally* Note, *Federal Magistrates and the Principles of Article III*, 97 Harv. L. Rev. 1947 (1984); Note, *United States Magistrates Hearing Civil Cases: The Constitutionality of Rendering Final Judgments After Northern Pipeline Construction Co. v. Marathon Pipe Line Co.*, 59 Notre Dame L. Rev. 897 (1984).

[125] Caprera v. Jacobs, 790 F.2d 442, 445 (5th Cir. 1986); Geaney v. Carlson, 776 F.2d 140, 142 (7th Cir. 1985); Alaniz v. California Processors, Inc., 690 F.2d 717, 720 (9th Cir. 1982).

[126] Caprera v. Jacobs, 790 F.2d 442, 445 (5th Cir. 1986).

[127] *See* Parks v. Collins, 736 F.2d 313, 314–15 (5th Cir. 1984).

[128] Archie v. Christian, 808 F.2d 1132, 1137 (5th Cir. 1987) (en banc).

[129] 28 U.S.C. § 636(c)(6) (1982); Fellman v. Fireman's Fund Ins. Co., 735 F.2d 55, 58 (2d Cir. 1984).

[130] Fed. R. Civ. P. 52(a); C.I.T. Corp. v. Duncan Grading & Constr., Inc., 739 F.2d 359, 360 (8th Cir. 1984).

[131] 28 U.S.C. § 636(b)(2) (1982); Fed. R. Civ. P. 53(b); Brown v. Wesley's Quaker Maid, Inc., 771 F.2d 952, 954 (6th Cir. 1985).

120 days after issue has been joined.[132] Nonconsensual references for trial are also governed by the clearly erroneous standard.[133]

§ 16.14 Power of Magistrate to Sanction Litigants for Abusive Conduct

Section 636(e) restricts the magistrate's power to hold litigants in contempt for abusive behavior, disobedience, or resistance to its orders or acts which would be contemptuous if committed before the court. Such matters must be certified to the court for action. When the court has referred all discovery matters to the magistrate, sanctions motions are considered within the reference, although the magistrate cannot terminate the case as a discovery sanction but can only make a recommendation on that issue.[134] If the reference is more limited, a motion for sanctions occurring before the magistrate must be filed with the district court judge, who can refer it to the magistrate as either a dispositive or nondispositive motion, depending upon the egregiousness of the misconduct.

§ 16.15 Special Masters

Unlike magistrates, special masters can be private individuals assigned to complex matters pursuant to Rule 53. The judge may prefer a master to a magistrate because use of a special master means there will be no interference with precious court time and that expenses will be borne by the responsible parties.[135] The parties may prefer the master if no magistrate is available to hear the matters in dispute and if the proposed master is a well respected expert in the field.[136] When the reference is not consensual, issues arise concerning the appropriateness of the reference, the allocation of costs, and the standard of review.

Masters are compensated by the parties in a manner provided by the court. As a practical matter, this limits references to cases in which one or more of the parties can afford the large fees generally associated with such references.[137] Moreover, when the costs are not split evenly, concerns are raised about financial pressure on masters to favor the party paying their bills. Because references can

---

[132] 42 U.S.C. § 2000e-5(f)(5) (1982).

[133] Brown v. Wesley's Quaker Maid, Inc., 771 F.2d 952, 954–56 (6th Cir. 1985).

[134] 7, pt. 2 Moore's Federal Practice ¶ 72.04[2.-4].

[135] *See* Sherman & Kinnard, *Federal Court Discovery in the 80's—Making the Rules Work,* 95 F.R.D. 245, 275 (1983).

[136] *See generally* Brazil, *Special Masters in the Pretrial Development of Big Cases: Potential and Problems,* 1982 A.B.F. Res. J. 289.

[137] *See, e.g.,* Louisiana v. Mississippi, 466 U.S. 921, 922–23 (1984) (Burger, J., dissenting in part from compensation granted Special Master appointed by U.S. Supreme Court).

be nonconsensual, a question of unfairness may also arise if the party paying the costs wins the ultimate action and cannot recover expenses from its impecunious adversary.

§ 16.16 Rule 53 References

Rule 53 states that a reference to a master is the "exception and not the rule." It limits references without consent to complicated issues in jury actions and exceptional conditions in nonjury actions. The Supreme Court has narrowly interpreted the authority to appoint masters in nonjury cases, rejecting congestion of the court's docket, complexity of the referenced case, and anticipated length of trial as exceptional circumstances.[138]

Although Rule 53 was originally designed for reference of trial matters, reference of discovery proceedings is becoming common.[139] A reference of all pretrial and discovery matters may even be justified in a given case.[140] However, it has been argued that the court's inherent powers rather than Rule 53 provide the only authority to appoint masters for pretrial discovery.[141] Similarly, the reference of a summmary judgment motion running to several thousand pages was not considered unusual and therefore was improper pursuant to Rule 53(b), although not reversal error.[142] If a party objects to a reference, that fact should immediately be brought to the court's attention to avoid any issue of waiver on appeal.[143]

The court can designate a magistrate to serve as a master without the consent of the parties as long as the designation falls with Rule 53 requirements.[144] It can also designate the magistrate to act as a master with the consent of the parties, regardless of whether the reference would otherwise be appropriate under Rule 53.[145] In such cases, the magistrate's decisions are reviewed under the clearly erroneous standard,[146] and no compensation is awarded. Before agreeing to a

---

[138] La Buy v. Howes Leather, 352 U.S. 249, 256, 259 (1957).

[139] *See, e.g., In re* "Agent Orange" Prod. Liability Litig., 94 F.R.D. 173, 173–76 (E.D.N.Y. 1982) (detailed reference including payment); *see also* Lord, *Discovery Abuse: Appointing Special Masters,* 9 Hamline L. Rev. 63 (1986).

[140] *See, e.g., In re* Armco, Inc., 770 F.2d 103, 105 (8th Cir. 1985).

[141] *See generally* Brazil, *Referring Discovery Tasks to Special Masters: Is Rule 53 a Source of Authority and Restrictions?* 1983 A.B.F. Res. J. 143.

[142] Jack Walters & Sons Corp. v. Morton Bldg., Inc., 737 F.2d 698, 712–13 (7th Cir.), *cert. denied,* 469 U.S. 1018 (1984).

[143] 5A Moore's Federal Practice ¶ 53.05[3].

[144] 28 U.S.C. § 636(b)(2) (1982).

[145] *Id.*

[146] *See, e.g.,* Archambault v. United Computing Sys., Inc., 786 F.2d 1507, 1511 (11th Cir. 1986); Brown v. Wesley's Quaker Maid, Inc., 771 F.2d 952, 954 (6th Cir. 1985); National R.R. Passenger Corp. v. Koch Indus., Inc., 701 F.2d 108, 110 (10th Cir. 1983).

consensual reference to a magistrate as a master, counsel should be aware that a consensual reference to a magistrate serving as a master changes the standard of review for dispositive motions from de novo to clearly erroneous.[147]

In nonjury matters, the parties have 10 days from service of the notice of filing of the master's report to serve written objections,[148] plus three days because the notice is mailed. This time can be lengthened or shortened.[149] As with a magistrate, if matters are referred for recommendation rather than ruling, the court is not bound by the clearly erroneous standard on review.[150]

---

[147] *See* 7, pt. 2 Moore's Federal Practice ¶ 72.05.

[148] Fed. R. Civ. P. 53(e)(2).

[149] 5A Moore's Federal Practice ¶ 53.11.

[150] *See id.* ¶ 52.12[2], [4].

PART IV

DISCOVERY

CHAPTER 17

FEDERAL DISCOVERY OVERVIEW

§ 17.1 The Discovery Framework

Discovery is so ingrained in American litigation practice that attorneys automatically assume they are entitled to discovery without questioning how or why this has come about and whether unfettered discovery is the most effective or efficient way of preparing a case. The optimistic goal of self-executing discovery under the federal rules was adopted to promote justice and fairness and to eliminate what has been described as the sporting theory of litigation. There are many positive values associated with discovery, including the following overlapping goals:

1. Ascertaining the truth and preventing perjury by ensuring that witnesses are examined while their memories are fresh and when they have been exposed to less coaching
2. Preserving the testimony of witnesses in the event of their unavailability at trial
3. Obtaining facts which would otherwise not be accessible to the party
4. Safeguarding against surprise at trial
5. Ensuring that the merits will be reached by affording mutuality of information
6. Detecting sham claims and defenses
7. Generally facilitating preparation and trial, including narrowing of issues, and
8. Educating the parties, thereby fostering settlements which enable overloaded civil court systems to remain viable.

Generally, discovery provides a means for counsel to determine the merits of the action, to evaluate the witnesses and evidence for settlement purposes, and to present a cohesive theory of the case at trial. Some tension is inevitable between the competing goals of self-executing discovery with a willing exchange of information and the adversary system which requires counsel to zealously represent their clients' interests and resolve all disputes in their favor. However, the current emphasis on curtailing discovery abuse by imposing sanctions on lawyers and clients[1] should not deter practitioners from engaging in necessary discovery.

Although informal discovery is always available to litigants, the discovery procedures authorized by the federal rules are usually preferable. First, if any dispute arises, a party can resort immediately to a motion to compel and request appropriate sanctions. Second, evidentiary considerations may dictate that the information must be produced in admissible form, which is best obtained by custodian of records depositions, to preserve testimony, or requests for admissions. Third, nonparties often refuse to cooperate without a subpoena. Counsel should not ignore informal discovery but rather should use it to pinpoint information which can be obtained formally. Public records and requests under the Freedom of Information Act[2] can also be invaluable sources of discovery. Local rules should always be consulted when establishing a discovery game

---

[1] See **ch. 27**.

[2] 5 U.S.C. § 552 (1982 and Supp. III 1985); see §§ **17.6–17.10**.

plan, because some districts have created a hybrid form of discovery in which parties can face sanctions for failure to exchange relevant documents early in the litigation.

Discovery devices include oral and written depositions, interrogatories, requests to produce documents or other tangible items, requests for mental and physical examinations, and requests for entry on land. Requests for admissions are also available, but are useful to narrow issues for trial only after the information has been discovered. The determination of what type of discovery to undertake and in what order must be made on a case-by-case basis. For example, it is important to obtain testimony before the witness can compare notes with other individuals, work out a detailed theory of the case, or lose track of the information, an immediate deposition is warranted. On the other hand, especially in business or products liability litigation having voluminous documents and dealing with matters which occurred several years earlier, document production is a necessary prelude to other forms of discovery. Indeed, if an early deposition is taken, counsel may be faced with a Rule 26(c) motion for a protective order when a second deposition is deemed necessary after the documents have been analyzed. However, in business cases, an early deposition to determine the corporate structure and sources of computerized recordkeeping in the company may be desirable to specifically categorize requests for documents with specificity or identify potential deponents. In addition, *The Manual for Complex Litigation, Second,* suggests that counsel should inquire into facts that will affect the use of computerized data at trial either as direct evidence or as information relied upon by experts.[3]

The timing and amount of interrogatories propounded will depend in part on whether local rules have restrictions on the number of interrogatories which can be asked without a showing of good cause and the attitude of the assigned judge or magistrate as to their usefulness. Interrogatories which request the identity and location of percipient witnesses and documents are best used early in the litigation. Contention interrogatories, if ever useful, are usually saved until discovery is well underway.

§ 17.2 The Discovery Plan

Counsel should create a discovery plan for every case. Rule 16(b) requires a scheduling order to be entered within 120 days after filing the complaint which includes deadlines for discovery and motions.[4] However, this general framework is not a substitute for a detailed agenda which considers the specific types of discovery which are best suited to the individual action and which dovetails with

---

[3] Manual for Complex Litigation, Second § 21.446 (1985).

[4] See § **16.2**.

counsel's plans concerning motion practice.[5] In some types of litigation, this task is aided by the existence of suggested discovery checklists.[6] As discovery proceeds, counsel should consider requesting a magistrate's or special master's supervision if the discovery requests are massive or the adversary appears to be engaging in discovery abuse. Similarly, a Rule 26(f) conference to formalize a discovery plan may be appropriate.[7]

Generally, informal discovery for the plaintiff should start well before the initiation of the law suit, or counsel may run afoul of Rule 11 sanctions for the institution of a baseless lawsuit.[8] Both plaintiffs and defendants must carefully analyze the legal framework of the case in order to make the most of discovery. Randomly requesting documents and asking deponents anything that may have some relevance to the action is not the best method to prepare the case. Only if the theories of liability and potential defenses are understood early will counsel be focused enough to ensure the most efficient and productive use of discovery.

All types of information which are considered relevant should be listed by counsel, including the likely sources of such information as tangible items and witnesses and the identity of appropriate categories of documents. It can be useful in deciding what is relevant to refer to jury instructions which outline the elements and defenses related to the cause of action. Counsel should then determine what informal investigation can be undertaken, including initial identification of experts and the possibility of obtaining photographic and demonstrative evidence. Information which can be obtained through interrogatories should also be identified. This task may be aided by looking at pattern interrogatories or at any form interrogatories approved for use in state court. Before any deposition, counsel must fully analyze all of the relevant documents concerning the deponent, to make sure that the factual questions to be asked cover every theory of liability or defense. Near the end of discovery, contention interrogatories can be employed in conjunction with requests for admissions.[9] At that point, requests for admissions should also be used to eliminate evidentiary objections to documents intended to be introduced at trial as well as to eliminate issues for trial and to establish a record which can be used in support of a summary judgment motion.

The methods of discovery can be used in any sequence, and the fact that a party is conducting discovery does not delay any other party's discovery.[10] As a

---

[5] See § **13.1**.

[6] *See, e.g.*, Bender's Forms of Discovery (multivolume); D. Danner, Pattern Discovery Series (multivolume); M. Dombroff, *Discovery* (1986); Deposition Strategy, Law and Forms (multivolume); Howie, *Developing the Plaintiff's Discovery Plan in Mid-Air Collision Litigation,* 47 J. Air Law & Com. 797 (1982); Lack, *Defendant's Discovery Plan in Mid-Air Crash Litigation,* 47 J. Air L. & Com. 769 (1982); Romano & Taggert, *Anatomy of a Recreational Tort Case,* 5 Am. J. Trial Advoc. 457 (1982).

[7] See § **19.1**.

[8] See **ch. 28**.

[9] See §§ **24.1, 26.1**.

[10] Fed. R. Civ. P. 26(d).

practical matter, the defendant has the first opportunity to take depositions, since the plaintiff must obtain leave of court to take a deposition prior to 30 days after service of the complaint.[11] In most litigation, the logistical and manpower problems associated with taking simultaneously multiple depositions dictate that no more than one or two depositions will be taken at the same time. Even when each side serves deposition notices and subpoenas without advance consultation, deposition schedules rarely proceed without mutual changes agreed upon by the parties. Simple courtesy requires that scheduling be discussed before rather than after the deposition notice is served, unless the deponent is likely to disappear before service or the relationship between the parties is barely civil.

Although any discovery plan will require modification and additional discovery will be generated by information learned through ongoing discovery, the existence of a plan is important to keep counsel focused on how the discovery interrelates with the legal theories to be presented in motions and at trial. Without any plan, discovery tends to expand to the available time of all counsel involved. Having an analytical framework also helps to distinguish leads which concern important issues from those which are merely interesting. Similarly, the plan can be used to identify which issues are worth fighting about if discovery disintegrates into a paper war.

§ 17.3 Rule 26 Overview

Although relevance has been broadly interpreted in discovery settings, counsel should be aware of its limits and the various objections which can restrict access to otherwise relevant materials. In general, judges and litigants no longer close their eyes to discovery abuse, and sanctions are being assessed for some discovery practices which were previously considered within the range of zealous advocacy.[12] The court's inherent powers, as well as Rules 11, 16, 26, 37, and 41, provide authority for imposing sanctions concerning various aspects of discovery practice. Costs, fines, and attorneys' fees are now routinely levied against practitioners as well as their clients for abusive discovery tactics.[13] Courts are also assessing sanctions which affect the merits of the case, including dismissals and defaults for culpable discovery conduct. Even if sanctions are not warranted, the trial court now has the explicit power to curtail discovery under Rule 26(b)(1) and to manage the litigation process under Rule 16. Moreover, Rule 26(g) requires counsel to certify to the reasonableness of discovery requests and responses and the absence of any improper motive concerning their use. Counsel must consider the general framework of Rule 26 in relation to the

---

[11] Fed. R. Civ. P. 30(a); see § **23.5**.

[12] *See, e.g.*, ReMine & Gilbert, *Discovery—Abuses, Sanctions and Ethical Concerns*, 23 Trial 53 (Jan. 1987).

[13] See **ch. 27**.

overall managerial approach currently taken by judges[14] whenever discovery tactics are being evaluated.

§ 17.4 Applicability of Rule 26

Rule 26 applies to all civil proceedings filed in federal court except those limited categories of cases listed in Rule 81. Discovery is not mandatory in administrative proceedings, because it is not currently required by the Administrative Procedures Act.[15] However, some circuits review denials of administrative discovery for prejudice.[16] If an agency has adopted rules which provide for discovery, it is bound by those provisions, and the rules must comport with due process.[17] The use of discovery devices is also limited in summons proceedings,[18] where it has been described as the exception rather than the rule.[19] For example, a taxpayer must make a preliminary and substantial demonstration of abuse before even limited discovery will be allowed in a summons enforcement proceeding.[20] Similarly, discovery typically is denied in E.E.O.C. and S.E.C. subpoena enforcement actions.[21] Discovery is available in cases brought under the Freedom of Information Act to challenge the adequacy of the administrative agency's document search.[22]

§ 17.5 Rule 26(b) Discovery Standard

Rule 26(b)(1) provides that a party may obtain discovery regarding any non-privileged matter which is relevant to the subject matter of the action. The

---

[14] *See generally* Resnik, *Managerial Judges,* 96 Harv. L. Rev. 374 (1982).

[15] 5 U.S.C. § 551 *et seq.* (1982 & Supp. III 1985); *see generally* K. Davis, *Administrative Law Treatise* (2d ed. 1978); *see* Beef Nebraska, Inc. v. United States, 807 F.2d 712, 718–19 (8th Cir. 1986) (surveying case law); Silverman v. Commodity Futures Trading Comm'n, 549 F.2d 28, 33 (7th Cir. 1977) (no constitutional right to discovery in administrative proceedings).

[16] *See, e.g.,* Sims v. National Transp. Safety Bd., 662 F.2d 668, 671 (10th Cir. 1981) and cases cited therein.

[17] P.G.&E. Co. v. F.E.R.C., 746 F.2d 1383, 1388 (9th Cir. 1983); *see generally* Benkin, *More Ado About Prehearing Discovery at F.E.R.C.,* 6 Energy L.J. 1 (1985).

[18] United States v. Will, 671 F.2d 963, 968 (6th Cir. 1982); *see* Donaldson v. United States, 400 U.S. 517, 528–29 (1971).

[19] United States v. Lask, 703 F.2d 293, 300 (8th Cir.), *cert. denied,* 464 U.S. 829 (1983) (quoted in United States v. Ernst & Whinney, 750 F.2d 516, 520 (6th Cir. 1984)); *accord* United States v. Church of Scientology of Cal., 520 F.2d 818, 824 (9th Cir. 1975).

[20] United States v. Will, 671 F.2d 963, 968 (6th Cir. 1982); United States v. Claes, 747 F.2d 491, 496 (8th Cir. 1984); *see* Moutevelis v. United States, 727 F.2d 313, 315 (3d Cir. 1984).

[21] *See* EEOC v. K-Mart Corp., 694 F.2d 1055, 1067 (6th Cir. 1982).

[22] *See, e.g.,* Weisberg v. United States Dep't of Justice, 627 F.2d 365, 371 (D.C. Cir. 1980); see **§ 17.8**.

information can relate to the claim or defense of the party seeking discovery or of any other party. Discovery is not objectionable because the information sought is inadmissible at trial, as long as it appears reasonably calculated to lead to the discovery of admissible evidence. As a result, relevance for purposes of discovery is much broader than for trial. In addition, discovery concerning information useful to impeach a witness is proper, although there is some debate about whether a defendant's surveillance films of the plaintiff should be routinely discoverable.[23] Discovery concerning jurisdictional facts is also permitted[24] but can be denied when the complaint alleges no specific facts supporting jurisdiction.[25]

Because the parties are given great latitude in obtaining information which is not admissible at trial, often practitioners act as if they are entitled to every document in their opponent's files. However, relevance does have some boundaries. For example, discovery as to a party's wealth is not relevant without a punitive damage claim or some reason why it is related to the issue in dispute. Discovery of computer tapes and programs is sometimes restricted by courts when alternate forms of data are available.[26] Discovery of unnamed class members is usually severely limited in class action litigation,[27] and discovery concerning the merits of a suit is generally not appropriate in considering whether it can be maintained as a class action.[28] Post-complaint discovery can be denied in the absence of a supplemental pleading, unless the litigation concerns a continuing violation.[29] Insurance agreements are specifically made discoverable under Rule 26(b)(2) to eliminate the dispute which existed concerning their relevance to the merits of an action apart from their value for settlement purposes. However, the rule provides that insurance applications are not discoverable unless relevant to the subject matter of the dispute. Even if discovery is

---

[23] *See generally* 8 C. Wright and A. Miller, Federal Practice and Procedure § 2015 (1970) [hereinafter Federal Practice and Procedure].

[24] Oppenheimer Fund Inc. v. Sanders, 437 U.S. 340, 351 n.13 (1978); 4A J. Moore *et al.*, Moore's Federal Practice ¶ 30.53[5] (2d ed. 1983) [hereinafter Moore's Federal Practice].

[25] *See* United Presbyterian Church in the U.S.A. v. Reagan, 738 F.2d 1375, 1382–83 (D.C. Cir. 1984) (standing); Naartex Consulting Corp. v. Watt, 722 F.2d 779, 788 (D.C. Cir. 1983), *cert. denied,* 467 U.S. 1210 (1984) (denied further discovery on personal jurisdiction).

[26] *See, e.g.,* Williams v. Owens-Illinois, Inc., 665 F.2d 918, 933 (9th Cir.), *cert. denied,* 459 U.S. 971 (1982). *See generally* Note, *The Discovery and Use of Computerized Information: An Examination of Current Approaches,* 13 Pepperdine L. Rev. 405, 407 (1986). *But see* Manual for Complex Litigation § 21:446 (2d ed. 1985) (computer requests should be treated consistently with other requests).

[27] *See, e.g.,* Cox v. American Cast Iron Pipe, Co., 784 F.2d 1546, 1556 (11th Cir.), *cert. denied,* ____ U.S. ____, 107 S. Ct. 274 (1986); see **§ 10.11**.

[28] Eisen v. Carlisle & Jacquelin, 417 U.S. 156, 177 (1974); *see* Eggleston v. Chicago Journeymen Plumbers' Local Union No. 130, 657 F.2d 890, 895 (7th Cir. 1981), *cert. denied,* 455 U.S. 1017 (1982).

[29] *See, e.g.,* Carlson Cos., Inc. v. Sperry & Hutchinson Co., 374 F. Supp. 1080, 1100–04 (D. Minn. 1974).

permitted on an issue, conditions can be imposed by the court's granting of a protective order.[30]

§ 17.6 Freedom of Information Act Discovery

The Freedom of Information Act[31] (F.O.I.A.) can provide valuable discovery if data which is potentially useful to litigants has been previously submitted to or obtained by a governmental agency. Federal agencies receive several hundred thousand requests each year and grant access to most of the designated items.[32] Although the Supreme Court has noted that F.O.I.A. was "not intended to function as a private discovery tool,"[33] litigants as well as the general public are entitled to F.O.I.A. information, and the recent tendency to control discovery may fuel more F.O.I.A. requests.[34] Moreover, counsel for organizations which may submit information subject to F.O.I.A. requirements must be alert to the potential discoverability of such records, to ensure that they are protected to the extent permissible under F.O.I.A. exemptions.

F.O.I.A. has many potential discovery purposes, which include:

1. Obtaining information for a potential suit against the government
2. Obtaining information about a potential governmental proceeding against the requester
3. Obtaining agency-generated records for use in private litigation
4. Obtaining privately submitted agency records for use in private litigation
5. Obtaining agency records unavailable in discovery because they are arguably privileged
6. Obtaining irrelevant records
7. Obtaining an additional search for relevant records, and
8. Obtaining relevant agency records that are not adequately discoverable because of external limitations on discovery.[35]

F.O.I.A. is clearly the most feasible way of obtaining discovery before federal litigation is initiated due to the restrictions involved in obtaining information

---

[30] See **ch. 19**.

[31] 5 U.S.C. § 552 (1982 & Supp. III 1985).

[32] *See* Susman, *Risky Business: Protecting Government Contract Information Under the Freedom of Information Act,* 33 Fed. Bar News & J. 67 (Feb. 1986).

[33] N.L.R.B. v. Robbins Tire & Rubber Co., 437 U.S. 214, 242 (1978).

[34] *See generally* Tomlinson, *Use of the Freedom of Information Act for Discovery Purposes,* 43 Md. L. Rev. 119 (1984).

[35] *Id.* at 153–91.

pursuant to Rule 27.[36] In addition, there is no obligation to notify opposing counsel of the F.O.I.A. request; no restriction is placed on the use of F.O.I.A. documents, and the agency must decide within 10 days whether it will comply with the request.[37] An agency will also provide certified copies of records which are specifically identified, although this process can be quite lengthy.

§ 17.7 Procedures for Obtaining F.O.I.A. Records

A letter request to the office possessing the documents is sufficient if it indicates the category of documents desired and a willingness to bear the fees for searching and copying the records. Agency procedures and fees are published in the *Code of Federal Regulations* and the *Federal Register.* Current search charges and photocopying costs vary depending on the agency. A check to cover the anticipated cost should be enclosed with the request. If the volume of available material is unknown, counsel can ask to be notified if the cost will exceed a particular dollar amount. If a nationwide request is desired, that should be specified, or requests should be filed with each regional office which has desired information. The agency must decide within 10 days of receiving the request whether or not it will produce the records,[38] unless unusual circumstances exist to justify a 10-day extension.[39] The applicant must be given immediate notice of the agency's decision and the reasons for any denial.[40] If a request is denied, an appeal must be decided within 20 days after it is filed,[41] except if unusual circumstances require a 10-day extension.[42]

§ 17.8 F.O.I.A. Litigation

Counsel must exhaust administrative remedies before initiating a suit in district court to challenge a denial.[43] If a plaintiff has exhausted its administrative remedies only with respect to some aspects of its request, it cannot obtain concurrent review regarding the other portions of its request.[44] However, a suit

---

[36] See § **17.13**.

[37] *See* Gay, *Litigator's Guide to Using Government Sources and Freedom of Information Act,* 15 Brief 52, 53, 55 (Fall, 1985); *see also* Tomlinson, *Use of the Freedom of Information Act for Discovery Purposes,* 43 Md. L. Rev. 119, 153–91 (1984).

[38] 5 U.S.C. § 552(a)(6)(A)(i) (1982).

[39] *Id.* § 552(a)(6)(B).

[40] *Id.* § 552(a)(6)(A)(i).

[41] *Id.* § 552(a)(6)(A)(ii).

[42] *Id.* § 552(a)(6)(B).

[43] Stebbins v. Nationwide Mut. Ins. Co., 757 F.2d 364, 366 (D.C. Cir. 1985).

[44] Dettman v. United States Dep't of Justice, 802 F.2d 1472, 1477 (D.C. Cir. 1986).

can be filed immediately if the agency fails to meet any of its required deadlines.[45] Most suits are filed in Washington, D.C., because the vast majority of records requested are located there. However, although the Tennessee Valley Authority is a wholly owned federal corporation which is subject to F.O.I.A., suit cannot be brought against it in Washington, D.C., without a showing of personal jurisdiction there.[46]

The court reviews the agency's decision on a de novo standard.[47] The agency must demonstrate exceptional circumstances to convince the court that additional time is necessary to respond to the request.[48] Similarly, it has the burden of justifying the withholding of documents and can be required to create a "Vaughn" index which provides a detailed itemization of the records and the reasons for withholding them.[49] The judge has discretion to conduct an in camera review of the documents withheld.[50] However, if a sufficiently detailed affidavit has been provided, an in camera inspection may be unnecessary.[51] Factors considered as supporting an in camera review include judicial economy, the conclusory nature of the agency affidavits, bad faith on the part of the agency, disputes concerning the contents of the documents, whether the agency requests the inspection, and the strong public interest in disclosure.[52] Discovery is usually somewhat limited in F.O.I.A. actions, but the government as well as private litigants can use discovery which is relevant to the subject matter of the pending action.[53]

Summary judgment for the government may be appropriate in an F.O.I.A. action based on affidavits which contain reasonably detailed information sufficient to place the documents within an exempted category and which are not challenged by contrary evidence in the record or evidence of agency bad faith.[54] Summary judgment cannot be granted if the government affidavit merely claims a blanket exemption for the records at issue based solely on the character of the files in which the records are obtained.[55] Attorneys' fees are available if the complainant has substantially prevailed in F.O.I.A. action.[56]

---

[45] 5 U.S.C. § 552(a)(6)(C) (1982).

[46] *See* Jones v. Nuclear Regulatory Comm'n, 654 F. Supp. 130, 132 (D.D.C. 1987).

[47] 5 U.S.C. § 552(a)(4)(B) (1982).

[48] *Id.* § 552(a)(6)(C).

[49] Vaughn v. Rosen, 484 F.2d 820, 827 (D.C. Cir. 1973), *cert. denied,* 415 U.S. 977 (1974); *see generally* Tomlinson, *Use of the Freedom of Information Act for Discovery Purposes,* 43 Md. L. Rev. 119, 130–33 (1984).

[50] N.L.R.B. v. Robbins Tire & Rubber Co., 437 U.S. 214, 224 (1978).

[51] Donovan v. F.B.I., 806 F.2d 55, 59 (2d Cir. 1986).

[52] *Id.* (citing Allen v. CIA, 636 F.2d 1287, 1298–99 (D.C. Cir. 1980), *overruled on other grounds sub. nom.* Founding Church of Scientology v. Smith, 721 F.2d 828 (D.C. Cir. 1983)).

[53] *See* Weisberg v. Webster, 749 F.2d 864, 868 (D.C. Cir. 1984).

[54] Meeropol v. Meese, 790 F.2d 942, 958 (D.C. Cir. 1986).

[55] Crooker v. Bureau of Alcohol, Tobacco & Firearms, 789 F.2d 64, 65 (D.C. Cir. 1986).

[56] 5 U.S.C. § 552(a)(4)(E) (1982).

§ 17.9 Records Exempted from F.O.I.A. Production

The Freedom of Information Act provides nine categories of information exempted from disclosure.[57] In a discovery context, the most relevant exemptions are found in 5 U.S.C. §§ 552(b)(4) and (5). Section (b)(4) protects "trade secrets and confidential commercial or financial information obtained from a person and is privileged or confidential." This section applies to information which is submitted to the governmental by a private individual or entity. Determining what information is confidential has been a problem,[58] but a court-ordered[59] or stipulated[60] protective order concerning the information at issue appears to bar disclosure. Section (b)(5) exempts interagency or intraagency memoranda or letters which would not available by law to a party in litigation with the agency other than another agency. Information created by the government which is subject to executive privilege, attorney-client privilege, and work product immunity is protected under this exemption.[61] Other privileges have also received protection under exemption (b)(5), including a privilege for confidential statements made to air crash safety investigators.[62] Communications containing purely factual material are not typically within the purview of Exemption 5.[63] Because records can be exempted under this category as long as they are not "routinely" available, it is possible that certain privileged materials which have been or can be disclosed on other than a routine basis still are shielded from F.O.I.A. discovery.[64] The interrelation between F.O.I.A. exemptions and other statutes restricting access to information is not always clear. For example, considerable disagreement exists as to whether 26 U.S.C. § 6103 of the Internal Revenue Code supersedes F.O.I.A.[65]

---

[57] 5 U.S.C. § 552(b)(1)–(9) (1982); *see generally* J. Franklin & R. Bouchard, Guidebook to the Freedom of Information and Privacy Acts ch. 1 (1986); J. O'Reilly, Federal Information Disclosure ch. 9 (1986); J. Underwood, A Guide to Federal Discovery Rules § 13.03 (2d ed. 1985).

[58] *See, e.g.*, Greenberg v. F.D.A., 803 F.2d 1213, 1217–18 (D.C. Cir. 1986) (reversing summary judgment which held customer list exempt).

[59] *See* G.T.E. Sylvania, Inc. v. Consumer's Union, Inc., 445 U.S. 375, 386 (1980).

[60] FDIC v. Ernst & Ernst, 677 F.2d 230, 232 (2d Cir. 1982).

[61] *See* F.T.C. v. Grolier, 462 U.S. 19, 26–27 (1983); Federal Open Market Comm. of the Fed. Reserve Sys. v. Merrill, 443 U.S. 340, 361–63 (1979).

[62] United States v. Weber Aircraft Corp., 465 U.S. 792, 801 (1984).

[63] Julian v. United States Dep't of Justice, 806 F.2d 1411, 1419 (9th Cir. 1986).

[64] Durns v. Bureau of Prisons, 804 F.2d 701, 704 (D.C. Cir. 1986); *see* United States v. Weber Aircraft Corp., 465 U.S. 792, 799 & 802 n. 20 (1984); F.T.C. v. Grolier, 462 U.S. 19, 28 (1983). *But see* Julian v. United States Dep't of Justice, 806 F.2d 1411, 1418–20 & n. 5 (9th Cir. 1986).

[65] *See* Church of Scientology v. I.R.S., 792 F.2d 146, 149–50 (D.C. Cir. 1986) and cases cited therein; *see also* Church of Scientology v. I.R.S., 792 F.2d 153, 156–63 (D.C. Cir. 1986) (en banc) (interpreting definition in I.R.S. Code), *cert. granted*, ____ U.S. ____, 107 S. Ct. 947 (1987).

§ 17.10 Protecting Business Records Submitted to Agencies

Businesses which supply information to agencies often are concerned about retaining its confidentiality, because the extent of protection afforded by the exemptions is not self-evident, and little uniformity exists in defining even such commonly used terms as trade secrets.[66] Business clients should be sensitized to F.O.I.A. requirements so that they do not thoughtlessly submit unnecessary documents to the government. Often counsel can obtain the agreement of the government to treat particular data confidentially prior to submitting the requested documents.[67] A few statutes also exempt certain submitted information from F.O.I.A. discovery.[68] Court-ordered discovery can also be conditioned on the agency's according any document revealed confidential treatment.[69] Some attorneys attempt to have agencies inspect business documents at the business's premises rather than take possession of the information to avoid later F.O.I.A. discovery, because an agency has no duty to release documents which are not in its control.[70]

Although legislation is eventually expected to standardize procedures, currently each agency has its own rules for reviewing documents and providing notice to those individuals and businesses whose information has been requested. If an agency decides to release such records, the submitter can obtain judicial review under the Administrative Procedure Act.[71] In other words, although a Rule 34 order is ordinarily interlocutory and nonappealable,[72] an order compelling F.O.I.A. discovery is appealable as long as administrative remedies have been exhausted.[73] However, the agency's finding will be

---

[66] *See, e.g.*, Public Citizen Health Research Group v. F.D.A., 704 F.2d 1280, 1288–89 (D.C. Cir. 1983) (rejected restatement definition of trade secret). *But see* Ruckelshaus v. Monsanto Co., 467 U.S. 986, 1001–04 (1984) (adopted restatement definition of trade secret for Federal Insecticide, Fungicide and Rodenticide Act); *see generally* Susman, *Risky Business: Protecting Government Contract Information Under the Freedom of Information Act,* 33 Fed. Bar News & J. 67 (Feb. 1986).

[67] *See, e.g.*, S.E.C. Rules, 17 C.F.R. § 200.83 (1986); *see generally* Pedowitz, *Obtaining the Right Protective Order in Litigation with Private Parties and the Government and Blocking Disclosure of Confidential Information Furnished to the Government,* 4th Annual Civil Litigation Practice 471 (1985).

[68] *See, e.g.*, 15 U.S.C. §§ 18a(h), 1314(g) (1982) (related to antitrust and premerger data); 18 U.S.C. § 1905 (1982) (criminal penalty for improper disclosure); Chrysler Corp. v. Brown, 441 U.S. 281, 318 (1979) (trade secrets and other enumerated types of confidential information).

[69] *See* Phillips Petroleum Co. v. Pickens, 105 F.R.D. 545, 552 (N.D. Tex. 1985).

[70] Kissenger v. Reporters Comm. for Freedom of the Press, 445 U.S. 136, 150 (1980); *see* Forsham v. Harris, 445 U.S. 169, 184–85 (1980); Mackenzie, *Who Wants to Know?* California Law. 39, 40 (April 1985).

[71] 5 U.S.C. § 702 (Supp. III 1985).

[72] *In re* Steele, 799 F.2d 461, 464 (9th Cir. 1986).

[73] *Id.;* Green v. Department of Commerce, 618 F.2d 836, 841 (D.C. Cir. 1980).

overturned only if it is arbitrary, capricious, an abuse of discretion, or otherwise not in accordance with law.[74]

§ 17.11 Obtaining Discovery Regarding Criminal Cases

Although criminal and civil discovery have entirely different rules, there are several occasions when a criminal action may be relevant to civil litigation.[75] First, it is not unusual for a party or deponent to take the Fifth Amendment in a civil action because of the possibility of criminal liability. Second, grand jury testimony in a related criminal action may be sought by a civil litigant. Third, a civil litigant may attempt to obtain information which is not available in the related criminal action pending against the party.

Discovery strategy in a civil suit must consider the likelihood of a criminal action against the party. The law does not require postponement of civil discovery until the fear of criminal prosecution is gone; any limitation on discovery is within the court's discretion.[76] Similarly, a court can enter a protective order concerning information obtained in civil discovery.[77]

The consequences of invoking the privilege against self-incrimination are most severe for the party with the burden of proof. The Fifth Amendment is discussed in §§ **18.19–18.21** and **31.4**.

§ 17.12 Obtaining Grand Jury Transcripts

The problem of a civil litigant obtaining transcripts of federal criminal grand jury proceedings is addressed by Rule 6(e)(3)(i) of the Federal Rules of Criminal Procedure. Rule 6(e)(3)(D) provides that disclosure may be made when directed by a court preliminarily to or in connection with a judicial proceeding. A petition for disclosure must be filed in the district where the grand jury convened. Unless the hearing is held ex parte, which may occur when the practitioner is the government, the petitioner must serve written notice upon the attorney for the government, the parties to the judicial proceeding, and such other persons as the court may direct, and the court must afford those persons a reasonable opportunity to appear and be heard. Rule 6(e)(3)(E) specifies that, if the judicial proceeding giving rise to the petition is in a federal district court in another district, the court must transfer the matter to that court unless it can reasonably

[74] 5 U.S.C. § 706 (1982); *see* AT&T Information-Sys., Inc. v. G.S.A., 801 F.2d 1233, 1236 (D.C. Cir. 1987) (affidavits supplementing administrative record barred from review).

[75] *See generally* Note, *Using Equitable Powers to Coordinate Parallel Civil and Criminal Actions*, 98 Harv. L. Rev. 1023 (1985).

[76] Mid-America's Process Serv. v. Ellison, 767 F.2d 684, 687 (10th Cir. 1985); *see* SEC v. Dresser Indus., Inc., 628 F.2d 1368, 1375–76 (D.C. Cir.) (en banc), *cert. denied,* 449 U.S. 993 (1980).

[77] See **ch. 19**.

obtain sufficient knowledge of the proceeding to determine whether disclosure is proper. The transferee court must afford a reasonable opportunity for the notified individuals to appear and be heard. If the motion is transferred, if feasible, the court possessing the transcripts must transmit them to the court hearing the motion with a written evaluation of the need for continued grand jury secrecy.

The court determines whether or not to release the information by a showing of particularized need.[78] To meet this standard, the material must be necessary to avoid a possible injustice, the need for disclosure must be greater than the need for continued secrecy, and the request must be structured to disclose only material so needed.[79] Government attorneys as well as private litigants are subject to Rule 6(e) and must obtain an order to use grand jury materials to litigate civil cases against targets of criminal investigations.[80] However, Rule 6(e) does not require a prosecutor who conducted the original grand jury investigation to obtain a court order before using the grand jury materials in a civil suit.[81] There is some question whether disclosure of documents submitted to a grand jury must also meet the particularized need test.[82] Even if the court decides to release the information, it has discretion to determine at what point in the litigation the transcripts should be disclosed.[83]

One often cited justification for release of transcripts is to refresh a witness's recollection. Another is that immunized grand jury testimony provides the only source of discovery because the deponent has invoked the Fifth Amendment privilege against self-incrimination. However, the evidentiary value of grand jury transcripts at trial is questionable if the witness is not a party and does not testify, although several circuits allow an adverse inference to be drawn if a party's former employees have asserted the privilege.[84]

Sometimes grand jury testimony forms the basis of a prosecutor's request for documents which are subject to the attorney-client privilege or work product immunity. When the summoned party moves to quash the subpoena on these grounds, the response is that they are subject to the crime fraud exception.[85] In

---

[78] United States v. Sells Eng'g, Inc., 463 U.S. 418, 443 (1983).

[79] Douglas Oil Co. v. Petrol Stops Nw., 441 U.S. 211, 222 (1979); *see* United States v. Sells Eng'g, Inc., 463 U.S. 418, 443 (1983); *In re* Grand Jury Proceedings, GJ-76-4 & GJ-75-3, 800 F.2d 1293, 1298–1303 (4th Cir. 1986).

[80] United States v. Sells Eng'g, Inc., 463 U.S. 418, 427 (1983).

[81] United States v. John Doe, Inc. I, ____ U.S. ____, 107 S. Ct. 1656, 1660, 1662 (1987).

[82] *Compare In re* Grand Jury Proceedings, Miller Brewing Co., 687 F.2d 1079, 1089–90 (7th Cir. 1982) (no showing required) *with In re* Sealed Case, 801 F.2d 1379, 1381 (D.C. Cir. 1986) (must show particularized need).

[83] Douglas Oil Co. v. Petrol Stops Nw., 441 U.S. 211, 223, 230 (1979).

[84] *See* RAD Servs., Inc. v. Aetna Casualty & Sur. Co., 808 F.2d 271, 274–76 (3d Cir. 1986); Brink's Inc. v. City of New York, 717 F.2d 700, 708–10 (2d Cir. 1983); *cf.* Rosebud Sioux Tribe v. A&P Steel, Inc., 733 F.2d 509, 520–23 (8th Cir.), *cert. denied,* 469 U.S. 1072 (1984); see **§ 18.19**.

[85] See **§ 18.12**.

order to support this exception, the prosecutor will submit the protected materials to the judge for purposes of an in camera review. This procedure has been upheld in a number of circuits against claims that it effectively eliminates the subpoenaed party's ability to combat the prosecutor's showing.[86] Moreover, a few circuits do not require the judge to consider evidence submitted by the subpoenaed party in determining whether the grand jury materials demonstrate the applicability of the crime fraud exception.[87]

A civil litigant can appeal from a Rule 6(e) order, because it is considered a final decision,[88] but a reversal is appropriate only if a clear abuse of discretion is shown.[89]

§ 17.13 Discovery Prior to Instituting Suit

Rule 27 provides for depositions to perpetuate testimony prior to any action's being filed. Both oral depositions and depositions upon written interrogatories are permitted, as well as orders of the character provided for by Rules 34 and 35.[90] A person contemplating litigation has no absolute entitlement to early prefiling discovery.[91] Rule 27 cannot be used merely for discovery purposes but is limited to cases in which the an action cannot be presently brought and the court is satisfied that the discovery may prevent a failure or delay of justice.[92] Therefore, Rule 27 cannot be used to ascertain whom to sue or what claims a party may have.[93] Even the fact that a witness is ill or will become unavailable is not sufficient unless it can be shown that an action cannot be presently be brought.[94] It is rare that a petitioner is able to meet this standard. Although a person facing criminal charges may attempt to obtain the advantages of civil discovery under this rule, the court has discretion to deny such requests.[95] The types of actions in which Rule 27 discovery is available are usually those in which a potential defendant believes that some event will impede the presentation of an effective defense at a later date and an action for declaratory relief is not practical. For example, when neighbors complained about the harmful effect on their cattle of flourides emitted by an aluminum reduction plant, a petitioner

---

86 *See In re* Antitrust Grand Jury, 805 F.2d 155, 161 (6th Cir. 1986) (surveying case law).

87 *See Id.* at 167–68.

88 *See* Douglas Oil Co. v. Petrol Stops Nw., 441 U.S. 211, 232–33 (1979) (Rehnquist, J. concurring); *In re* Corrugated Container Antitrust Litig., 687 F.2d 52, 54 (5th Cir. 1982); *see generally* 9 Moore's Federal Practice ¶ 110.13[11].

89 Douglas Oil Co. v. Petrol Stops Nw., 441 U.S. 211, 223 (1979).

90 Fed. R. Civ. P. 27(a)(3).

91 *In re* Eisenberg, 654 F.2d 1107, 1112–13 (5th Cir. 1981).

92 Fed. R. Civ. P. 27(a)(1), (3).

93 *See* 8 Federal Practice and Procedure § 2071.

94 *Id.* § 2072.

95 *In re* Eisenberg, 654 F.2d 1107, 1112–14 (5th Cir. 1981).

was permitted to take a deposition, inspect land, and examine animals before they were sold, although no litigation was pending.[96]

To obtain Rule 27 discovery, a verified petition must be filed in the district of the residence of any expected adverse party which shows: (1) the petitioner expects to be a party to an action cognizable in a federal court but is presently unable to bring it or cause it to be brought; (2) the subject matter of the expected action and the petitioner's interest therein; (3) the facts which petitioner desires to establish by the proposed testimony and the reasons for desiring to perpetuate it; (4) the names or a description of the persons who are expected to be adverse parties and their addresses so far as known; and (5) the names and addresses of the persons to be examined and the substance of the testimony expected to be elicited. The petition must request an order authorizing the deposition to be taken.

Notice must be served upon each person named in the petition as an adverse party at least 20 days before the date of the hearing. If notice pursuant to Rule 4(d) cannot be made using due diligence, the court may order service by publication or otherwise and appoint an attorney to represent each person named and cross-examine the deponent.

Rule 27 depositions are treated no differently from other depositions for evidentiary purposes.[97] A Rule 27 order is immediately appealable[98] and is reviewed on an abuse of discretion standard.[99]

§ 17.14 Supplementation of Discovery Responses

A party has no duty to supplement completed discovery responses with later information unless the previous responses fall within the narrow categories detailed in Rule 26(e).[100]

The rule applies to all types of responses, including deposition testimony, requests for production, and interrogatories, and is not dependent on simultaneous supplementation of previous discovery answers.[101] Responses are required to be made seasonably, and a court can exclude documents or witnesses revealed after discovery or just prior to trial, if the responding party had previous knowledge of their existence.[102]

---

[96] Martin v. Reynolds Metals Corp., 297 F.2d 49 (9th Cir. 1961), *cited in* 8 Federal Practice and Procedure § 2072.

[97] *See* Fed. R. Civ. P. 27(a)(4).

[98] 8 Federal Practice and Procedure § 2072.

[99] Shore v. Acands, Inc., 644 F.2d 386, 388 (5th Cir. 1981).

[100] *See generally* Slomanson, *Supplementation of Discovery Responses in Federal Civil Procedure,* 17 San Diego L. Rev. 233 (1980); 8 Federal Practice and Procedure § 2049.

[101] Scott & Fetzer Co. v. Dile, 643 F.2d 670, 674 (9th Cir. 1981).

[102] *See, e.g.*, Havenfield Corp. v. H. & R. Block, Inc., 509 F.2d 1263, 1272 (8th Cir.), *cert. denied,* 421 U.S. 999 (1975).

Rule 26(e)(1) requires supplementation of information concerning the identity and location of persons having knowledge of discoverable matters, and the identity of each expert witness to be called at trial as well as the subject matter and substance of the expert's testimony. However, if no interrogatory or deposition questions have been posed on these subjects, no duty exists to reveal the information,[103] unless otherwise required by the court, such as in a Rule 16 pretrial statement.

A party is also under a duty to amend a prior response if later information reveals that: (1) the response was incorrect when made, or (2) although correct when made, it is no longer true and the circumstances are such that a failure to amend the response is in substance a knowing concealment.[104] Determining whether an answer was incorrect when made is somewhat difficult, because the court must evaluate whether ambiguous, incomplete, or grossly negligent responses were incorrect.[105] Furthermore, even a broadly worded question may be too narrow to create a duty to supplement. For example, at her deposition, a plaintiff testified that no one employed by the defendant had said, intimated, indicated, acknowledged or otherwise asserted to her that she had been discriminated against because of her age, while at trial the plaintiff and another witness testified that an employee of the defendant had intimated such information to the witness. Since the plaintiff had not been asked and did not testify that no employee of the defendant had intimated such information to anyone else, the deposition testimony was not false and did not require amendment.[106] There is also an absence of agreement as to what constitutes knowing concealment and the appropriate sanction for such a breach of Rule 26(e),[107] although at least one circuit reversed a judgment based on later found documents which were not revealed until admitted at trial.[108]

The duty to supplement responses can also be imposed by the court or stipulated by the parties.[109] Otherwise, a party must make a new request for supplementation of prior responses to obtain such information,[110] unless the court has imposed a limitation on the number of interrogatories which effectively prevents such updating.

---

[103] Slomanson, *Supplementation of Discovery Responses in Federal Civil Procedure,* 17 San Diego L. Rev. 233, 256–57 (1980).

[104] Fed. R. Civ. P. 26(e)(2).

[105] *E.g.,* Dudley v. South Jersey Metal, Inc., 555 F.2d 96, 99 (3d Cir. 1977); *see* Slomanson, *Supplementation of Discovery Responses in Federal Civil Procedure,* 17 San Diego L. Rev. 233, 272 (1980).

[106] O'Donnell v. Georgia Osteopathic Hosp., Inc., 748 F.2d 1543, 1548–49 (11th Cir. 1984).

[107] Slomanson, *Supplementation of Discovery Responses in Federal Civil Procedure,* 17 San Diego L. Rev. 233, 273 & n.237 (1980).

[108] Rozier v. Ford Motor Co., 573 F.2d 1332, 1342 (5th Cir. 1978).

[109] Fed. R. Civ. P. 26(e)(3).

[110] *Id.*

§ 17.15 Enforcing Rule 26(e) Obligations

Although Rule 26(g) imposes sanctions for signing an improper discovery request, response or objection, no sanction is specified for a violation of Rule 26(e).[111] The court has inherent power to impose a sanction.[112] Some courts may be reluctant to rely on this source of authority,[113] but sanctions have been imposed for Rule 26(e) violations. Usually a Rule 26(e) violation is alleged at trial when unanticipated evidence is offered by the opposing party. On appeal, the court determines whether admitting or prohibiting such evidence was an abuse of discretion,[114] recognizing that the district court has broad discretion to decide whether or not to impose any sanctions.[115] Some courts require prejudicial surprise to justify a reversal, as when a completely new issue or unidentified witness is allowed at trial.[116] Usually, exclusion of evidence under 26(e) is upheld only if some evasion or concealment, intentional or not, exists on the part of the litigant offering the evidence.[117]

If the court refuses to exclude evidence presented in violation of Rule 26(e), counsel should request a recess or continuance, as well as a summary of the anticipated evidence and an immediate deposition of any newly presented witness. Appellate courts view the absence of such requests as a factor justifying the trial judge's discretion to allow the evidence.[118] Decisions whether to exclude expert testimony under 26(e) often overlap with the party's violation of the Rule 16 pretrial order which usually includes the identity of all experts testifying at trial and the substance of their testimony.[119]

In general, counsel cannot rely on any consistent application of Rule 26(e) supplementation requirements and should attempt to obtain this type of information through the final pretrial order.

---

[111] *See* 8 Federal Practice and Procedure § 2050.

[112] Labadie Coal Co. v. Black, 672 F.2d 92, 95 (D.C. Cir. 1982); Campbell Indus. v. M/V Gemini, 619 F.2d 24, 27 (9th Cir. 1980).

[113] *See* 8 Federal Practice & Procedure § 2050, at 325–26.

[114] *See, e.g.,* Moore v. Boating Indus. Ass'ns, 754 F.2d 698, 715 (7th Cir.), *vacated on other grounds,* ____ U.S. ____, 106 S. Ct. 218 (1985); Bunch v. United States, 680 F.2d 1271, 1280 (9th Cir. 1982) (gross abuse).

[115] Moore v. Boating Indus. Ass'ns, 754 F.2d 698, 715 (7th Cir.), *vacated on other grounds,* ____ U.S. ____, 106 S. Ct. 218 (1985); Labadie Coal Co. v. Black, 672 F.2d 92, 95 (D.C. Cir. 1982); 8 Federal Practice & Procedure § 2050, at 326–27.

[116] *See, e.g.,* K.M.C. Co. v. Irving Trust Co., 757 F.2d 752, 765 (6th Cir. 1985); O'Donnell v. Georgia Osteopathic Hosp., Inc., 748 F.2d 1543, 1549 (11th Cir. 1984); Halphen v. Johns-Manville Sales Corp, 737 F.2d 462, 467 (5th Cir. 1984).

[117] Johnson v. H.K. Webster, Inc., 775 F.2d 1, 8 (1st Cir. 1985).

[118] *See, e.g.,* Johnson v. H.K. Webster, Inc., 775 F.2d 1, 8–9 (1st Cir. 1985); K.M.C. Co. v. Irving Trust Co., 757 F.2d 752, 766 (6th Cir. 1985); Berroyer v. Hertz, 672 F.2d 334, 338–39 & n.6 (3d Cir. 1982).

[119] *See, e.g.,* Johnson v. H.K. Webster, Inc., 775 F.2d 1, 4, 7 n.7 (1st Cir. 1985); Meyers v. Pennypack Woods Home Ownership Ass'n, 559 F.2d 894, 904–05 (3d Cir. 1977); *see* §§ **16.5, 20.15, 30.10**.

§ 17.16 Court's Discretion in Discovery Practice

Discovery practice results in a multitude of orders permitting, denying, or granting partial discovery. The district court has broad discretion in all discovery matters.[120] It can set discovery timetables[121] or refuse to permit discovery after the cutoff date,[122] even if that results in the exclusion of testimony at trial.[123] The court can deny requests for additional discovery if counsel had an adequate opportunity to obtain discovery or did not pursue discovery in a diligent manner.[124] Therefore, counsel must be ready to explain why the given time was insufficient in order to obtain any additional period for discovery. Merely relying on opposing counsel's acquiescence to extending discovery is risky, because the judge can refuse such stipulations. Cutoffs do not affect the admissibility of evidence obtained outside the discovery process.[125]

§ 17.17 Reviewing Discovery Orders

Obtaining review of discovery orders is difficult, because they are reviewed on an abuse of discretion standard, and some circuits reverse such orders only upon a showing of clear[126] or gross abuse of discretion which results in fundamental unfairness in the trial of the case.[127] However, there are some limits to the court's discretion. For example, when a plaintiff was unable to secure counsel and the defendant did not oppose a discovery extension, restriction of discovery beyond that permitted by local rules was an abuse of discretion.[128]

The difficulty in obtaining a reversal of a discovery order is compounded by the fact that it is an interlocutory order and therefore is not generally reviewable

---

[120] *See, e.g.*, American Key Corp. v. Cole Nat'l Corp., 762 F.2d 1569, 1576 (11th Cir. 1985); Brown-Bey v. United States, 720 F.2d 467, 470–71 (7th Cir. 1983); Data Disc, Inc. v. Systems Technology Assocs., Inc., 557 F.2d 1280, 1285 n.1 (9th Cir. 1977).

[121] *See, e.g.*, Ellis v. Brotherhood of Ry. Clerks, 685 F.2d 1065, 1071 (9th Cir. 1982), *rev'd in part on other grounds*, 466 U.S. 435 (1984).

[122] *See, e.g.*, Kennedy v. City of Cleveland, 797 F.2d 297, 301 (6th Cir. 1986); Otero v. Buslee, 695 F.2d 1244, 1247–48 (10th Cir. 1982).

[123] *See, e.g.*, Wilfing v. G.M. Corp., 685 F.2d 1049, 1051 (8th Cir. 1982) (deposition notices quashed).

[124] *See, e.g.*, Naartex Consulting Corp. v. Watt, 722 F.2d 779, 788 & n.15 (D.C. Cir. 1983), *cert. denied*, 467 U.S. 1210 (1984).

[125] Whittaker Corp. v. Execuair Corp., 736 F.2d 1341, 1347 (9th Cir. 1984).

[126] *E.g.*, United Presbyterian Church in the U.S.A. v. Reagan, 738 F.2d 1375, 1382 (D.C. Cir. 1984); Ellis v. Brotherhood of Ry. Clerks, 685 F.2d 1065, 1071 (9th Cir. 1982), *rev'd in part on other grounds*, 466 U.S. 435 (1984).

[127] Prow v. Medtronic, Inc., 770 F.2d 117, 122 (8th Cir. 1985); *see also* Brown-Bey v. United States, 720 F.2d 467, 471 (7th Cir. 1983) (reversal only if limitation is improvident and prejudices substantial rights).

[128] Howze v. Jones & Laughlin Steel Corp., 750 F.2d 1208, 1213 (3d Cir. 1984).

until the end of the litigation.[129] The only orders permitting discovery considered final for purposes of appeal are those enforcing a summons.[130] On appeal, after trial, it is unlikely that the discovery order will be found to have affected the outcome of the case, unless the judge virtually prohibited discovery.[131] Immediate appellate review can be obtained through mandamus or a certified interlocutory appeal or if the decision is considered a collateral order, but the possibility of success via such routes is quite slim. The best chance of obtaining review exists when the issue is not only important to the case, but also raises a significant question of law. As a practical matter, if the decision is important, counsel should take an appeal which is alternatively labelled a petition for mandamus. Although this does not ensure review, at least the appellate court is given an opportunity to invoke its jurisdiction under either theory.

§ 17.18 —Mandamus

A writ of mandamus[132] is considered a drastic remedy which should be invoked only in extraordinary circumstances.[133] The writ is traditionally used to confine a court to the lawful exercise of its prescribed jurisdiction or to compel it to exercise authority when it has a duty to do so.[134] The party seeking mandamus must show both that there is no other adequate means of relief and that the right to the writ is clear and indisputable.[135] When mandamus is requested regarding a claim of privilege, some courts will allow review only if the disclosure of the information renders impossible any meaningful appellate review of the claim and involves questions of substantial importance to the administration of justice.[136] A mere error by the district court is not sufficient to obtain a writ of mandamus, although it may suffice to obtain reversal on direct appeal.[137]

---

[129] Alexander v. United States, 201 U.S. 117, 121–22 (1906); Cipollone v. Liggett Group, Inc., 785 F.2d 1108, 1116 (3d Cir. 1986); Union Carbide Corp. v. U.S. Cutting Serv., Inc., 782 F.2d 710, 712 (7th Cir. 1986); BarclaysAmerican Corp. v. Kane, 746 F.2d 653, 654–55 (10th Cir. 1984); *In re* Underwriters at Lloyd's, 666 F.2d 55, 57–58 (4th Cir. 1981); *see generally* 9 Moore's Federal Practice ¶ 110.13[2] (2d ed. 1985); 8 Federal Practice and Procedure § 2006, at 29.

[130] *E.g.*, Reisman v. Caplin, 375 U.S. 440, 449 (1964) (order enforcing IRS summons is final appealable order).

[131] *See, e.g.*, Panola Land Buyers Ass'n v. Shuman, 762 F.2d 1550, 1558–59 (11th Cir. 1985) (summary judgment reversed when discovery curtailed on relevant issues); Shaklee Corp. v. Gunnell, 748 F.2d 548, 550 (10th Cir. 1984) (judgment reversed when court denied discovery as irrelevant and then permitted evidence on issue at trial).

[132] All Writs Act, 28 U.S.C. § 1651(a) (1982).

[133] Allied Chem. Corp. v. Daiflon, Inc., 449 U.S. 33, 34 (1980) (per curiam); Kerr v. United States Dist. Court, 426 U.S. 394, 402 (1976).

[134] *Id.*; Will v. United States, 389 U.S. 90, 95 (1967).

[135] Allied Chem. Corp. v. Daiflon, Inc., 449 U.S. 33, 35 (1980) (per curiam).

[136] BarclaysAmerican Corp. v. Kane, 746 F.2d 653, 654–55 (10th Cir. 1984); Iowa Beef Processors, Inc. v. Bagley, 601 F.2d 949, 956 (8th Cir. 1979).

[137] Allied Chem. Corp. v. Daiflon, Inc., 449 U.S. 33, 35 (1980) (per curiam).

§ 17.19 —Interlocutory Appeals and Collateral Orders

Interlocutory appeals are permitted when the district court certifies that the order involves a controlling question of law as to which there is substantial ground for disagreement and that an immediate appeal may materially advance the ultimate termination of the litigation.[138] Discovery orders fail this test, because they are rarely considered pivotal to the outcome of the case.[139]

The collateral order doctrine enunciated in *Cohen v. Beneficial Industrial Loan Corp.*[140] permits appeal for the category of orders which (1) conclusively determines the disputed question, (2) resolves an important issue completely separate from the merits of the action, and (3) is effectively unreviewable on appeal from final judgment.[141] Some courts also require that the appeal present a serious and unsettled question,[142] and this may be subsumed within the second criterion. Since most discovery orders touch on the merits of the underlying action, they do not fit within the collateral order doctrine. On the other hand, discovery orders directed to nonparties are sometimes reviewed as collateral orders,[143] or if resulting in sanctions, they are simply considered final orders.[144] However, the circuits disagree as to whether an attorney can immediately appeal a discovery sanction order.[145] The collateral order exception has also been used to obtain review by a party contesting an order to quashing a subpoena against a nonparty which is issued in a different court from that hearing the underlying case under the collateral order exception.[146]

§ 17.20 —Appealable Orders

Some discovery orders can result in interlocutory review. For example, if a party disobeys the order and is punished for criminal contempt or by the entry of final judgment, an appeal can be taken from those orders.[147] If the one who files the

---

[138] 28 U.S.C. § 1292(b) (1982).

[139] Cipollone v. Liggett Group, Inc., 785 F.2d 1108, 1118 n.14 (3d Cir. 1986); 8 Federal Practice and Procedure § 2006, at 31.

[140] 337 U.S. 541 (1949).

[141] Coopers & Lybrand v. Livesay, 437 U.S. 463, 468 (1978); Cohen v. Beneficial Indus. Loan Corp., 337 U.S. 541, 546–47 (1949).

[142] *E.g.*, Chavez v. Singer, 698 F.2d 420, 421 (10th Cir. 1983), *interpreting* Nixon v. Fitzgerald, 457 U.S. 731, 743 (1982).

[143] *See, e.g.*, Westmoreland v. CBS Inc., 770 F.2d 1168, 1172 (D.C. Cir. 1985). *But see* Alexander v. United States, 201 U.S. 117, 121 (1906); Estate of Domingo v. Republic of Philippines, 808 F.2d 1349, 1350–52 (9th Cir. 1987); Demasi v. Weiss, 669 F.2d 114, 122 (3d Cir. 1982).

[144] *See In re* Licht & Semonoff, 796 F.2d 564, 568–69 (1st Cir. 1986) (surveying case law).

[145] *See Id.* at 569–73 (surveying case law).

[146] *See, e.g.*, Heat & Control, Inc. v. Hester Indus., Inc., 785 F.2d 1017, 1021 (Fed. Cir. 1986).

[147] United States v. Ryan, 402 U.S. 530, 532–33 (1971); Cobbledick v. United States, 309 U.S. 323, 328 (1940); Union Carbide Corp. v. U.S. Cutting Serv., Inc., 782 F.2d 710, 712 (7th Cir. 1986).

motion to prohibit the production of allegedly privileged documents or testimony is not the person to whom the order is directed, an immediate appeal is proper, even though the third party has not been held in contempt.[148] Some circuits assume that clients are entitled to appeal as soon as their attorneys are required to produce documents,[149] while others permit an appeal only when contempt is unlikely as a practical matter.[150] A few require that an attorney be held in contempt before considering an appeal proper.[151]

§ 17.21 Discovery Alternatives Checklist

Freedom of Information Act (see §§ 17.6–17.10)

1. Have records been submitted to a public agency by or concerning a party?
2. Has any public agency created its own records concerning any issue or litigant in the pending matter?
3. Has a stipulation been obtained by the party submitting documents to exempt its records from disclosure?
4. Has the F.O.I.A. request been accompanied by a check or instructions concerning the cost of copying?
5. Have the nature of the records requested and the locations to be searched been sufficiently described?
6. Are certified copies of appropriate records necessary for litigation?
7. Were administrative remedies exhausted after the F.O.I.A. request was denied and before initiating suit in district court?

Obtaining Grand Jury Materials (see § 17.12)

1. Is Fed. R. Crim. P. 6(e) applicable?

---

[148] Perlman v. United States, 247 U.S. 7, 13 (1918); Castle v. Sangamo Weston, Inc., 744 F.2d 1464, 1465–66 (11th Cir. 1984).

[149] *E.g.*, *In re* Klein, 776 F.2d 628, 630–32 (7th Cir. 1985); *In re* Grand Jury Subpoena Served Upon Doe, 759 F.2d 968, 971 n.1 (2d Cir. 1985), *cert. denied*, ____ U.S. ____, 106 S. Ct. 1515 (1986).

[150] *E.g.*, *In re* Sealed Case, 655 F.2d 1298, 1301–02 (D.C. Cir. 1981); *see generally* Comment, *The Perlman Exception: Limitations Required by the Final Decision Rule,* 49 U. Chi. L. Rev. 198 (1982).

[151] *E.g.*, *In re* Grand Jury Proceedings (Vargas), 723 F.2d 1461, 1465–66 (10th Cir. 1983), *cert. denied*, 469 U.S. 819 (1984). *Contra In re* Sealed Case, 737 F.2d 94, 98 (D.C. Cir. 1984); *In re* Grand Jury Subpoena Duces Tecum Dated September 15, 1983 (Marc Rich & Co.), 731 F.2d 1032, 1036 n.3 (2d Cir. 1984); United States v. Jones, 696 F.2d 1069, 1071 (4th Cir. 1982).

2. Has the requestor petitioned in the district where the grand jury convened?
3. Can particularized need for the transcript or documents be shown?
4. Will the grand jury materials be admissible evidence or only provide information leading to evidence?

Rule 27 Discovery Prior to Instituting Suit (see § 17.13)

1. Is the case unable to be presently brought?
2. Will discovery prevent a failure of justice?
3. Has a verified petition been filed where the potential adverse party resides?
4. Has the required 20 days' notice been given?

Discovery Outside the United States (see ch. 22)

1. Will the court require the Hague Convention to be followed?
   a. Is a Letter of Request appropriate?
   b. Should a commission be requested?
   c. Should a consular official be requested?
2. Will the federal rules govern foreign discovery?
   a. Has notice been given concerning party discovery?
   b. Should a commission or letters rogatory be requested for nonparty discovery?
3. Can discovery of American nationals be enforced pursuant to 28 U.S.C. § 1783?
   a. Are the testimony or documents of nonparty witnesses not otherwise obtainable?

Rule 45 Discovery of Nonparties (see ch. 21)

1. Has a subpoena duces tecum been issued to permit the nonparty to be deposed and produce documents?
2. Was the subpoena issued in the district where the deposition will be held?
3. Has notice of the deposition been given to all parties before requesting the subpoena?
   a. Has proof of service of the notice been given to the clerk to permit issuance of the subpoena?
4. Have one day's witness fees been tendered?

5. Has the nonparty opposed the subpoena?
    a. Has the nonparty failed to obey due to improper service?
        (1) **Warning:** This is a risky tactic.
    b. Has the nonparty filed a motion to quash?
    c. Has the nonparty filed a motion to modify or condition the subpoena on payment of costs?
    d. Has the nonparty moved for a protective order?
    e. Has the nonparty objected to the subpoena?
        (1) This is the best alternative for a nonparty who does not want to produce documents.
        (2) Production may be conditioned on payment of costs.
        (3) The examining party must move for an order to obtain the documents.
6. If the nonparty produces documents at a custodian of records deposition, have the appropriate questions been asked so that the documents will be admissible at trial?

Rule 26 Discovery of Experts (see ch. 20)

1. Will the expert testify at trial?
    a. Have interrogatories been submitted requesting the expert's identity, as well as the subject matter and substance of the trial testimony?
    b. Has a deposition been ordered or stipulated?
    c. How much discovery of the experts' documents is obtainable?
    d. What public sources of information exist concerning the expert's opinion?
        (1) Has the expert previously testified?
        (2) Has the expert previously written about the topic in issue?
    e. What is the reasonable fee for the deposition?
2. Was the expert hired for litigation, but not to testify at trial?
    a. Can the expert's identity be obtained:
        (1) By asking who assists in drafting answers to interrogatories?
        (2) Courts split as to whether exceptionable circumstances as opposed to relevance must be shown to obtain the expert's identity.
    b. Can exceptional circumstances be demonstrated to obtain the expert's opinion?
3. Was the expert informally consulted concerning the litigation?
    a. If so, no discovery can be obtained.

4. Was the expert's information not acquired for litigation?
   a. If so, the information is freely discoverable, the courts often restrict discovery of experts who are strangers to the litigation.

Depositions (see ch. 23)

1. Which of the following types of deposition is most appropriate?
   a. An oral deposition
   b. A telephone deposition
   c. A taped or videotaped deposition
   d. Written questions read at the deposition
   e. A deposition upon written questions
   f. A corporate deposition
2. Has reasonable notice of the deposition been given?
   a. Has the plaintiff waited 30 days after serving the complaint, unless the defense has initiated earlier discovery?
3. If the examining party failed to attend or serve the absent nonparty with a subpoena, has an award of expenses been requested by parties who attended the deposition?
4. Beware that refreshing witness with documents may result in their discovery. (see § **18.17**)
5. Has a protective order been sought to terminate or limit any deposition which is conducted in bad faith or which is unreasonably embarrassing or oppressing to the deponent?
6. Has timely objection been made concerning errors or irregularities in the deposition procedures?
7. Have the following objections been raised at the deposition:
   a. Improper form of the question or answer?
   b. Impropriety concerning the oath?
   c. Impropriety concerning the conduct of the parties?
   d. Errors which could be obviated or cured by prompt presentation, including competency of a witness or competency, relevancy or materiality of testimony?
8. Is an instruction not to answer appropriate?
   a. Does the question call for privileged information?
   b. Is an instruction permitted for lack of relevancy?

Interrogatories (see ch. 24)

1. Have the local rules been consulted to determine any restrictions on the number of interrogatories which can be requested without court approval?

2. Have appropriate instructions and definitions been drafted?
3. If the interrogatories are based on standard or boilerplate questions, have they been modified to fit the action?
4. Have the answers and/or objections been served within 30 days, except by the defendant who has 45 days to respond after being served with the complaint?
   a. Has any extension been approved by the court?
5. Have the answers been verified by the party?
6. Have any objections been signed by the attorney?
7. Has each interrogatory been specifically objected to or answered?
8. Is it appropriate to respond by offering to produce business records?

Production of Documents and Tangible Items and Entry on Land (see ch. 25)

1. Should any agreement or order be immediately obtained before any document request is served to suspend the opponent's routine destruction of business documents?
2. Have computer data as well as documents been requested?
3. Is testing or sampling of tangible things appropriate?
4. Should an entry on land be requested?
5. Does the request specify each item or category with reasonable particularity?
6. Does the request include instructions and definitions?
7. Has a written response been served within 30 days, except by the defendant who has 45 days to respond after being served with the complaint?
   a. Has any extension been approved by the court?
8. Have the documents been produced as kept in the ordinary course of business or by requested category?

Mental or Physical Examination (see ch. 25)

1. If the opposing party will not stipulate to the examination, can good cause be shown?
2. Is the person to be examined a party or a person in the custody or control of a party?
3. Is the mental or physical condition being examined in controversy?
4. Is a physician conducting the examination?
5. Does the order specify the time, place, manner, and scope of the examination, including any conditions and the identity of the examining physician?

6. Should the report of the examining physician be requested?
   a. A request entitles the examiner to like reports previously or thereafter made by the examined party concerning the condition.
   b. A request waives any privilege regarding the testimony of those who have examined or may examine the party concerning the condition.
7. If a requested physician's report is not produced, has a motion to exclude the expert at trial been filed?

Requests for Admissions (see ch. 26)

1. Is it likely that the opponent will not realize that not answering the requests results in their admission?
2. Does each RFA include only one fact?
3. If documents will be introduced at trial, do RFAs provide the quickest means of providing a proper foundation?
4. Has the response been served within 30 days, except by a defendant who has 45 days to respond after being served with the complaint?
5. Has a reasonable inquiry been made before failing to admit or deny an RFA based on lack of information?
6. Has the party who made an unintended admission moved to withdraw it?
   a. What is the prejudice to the opponent if the admission is withdrawn?
   b. Will the court require manifest injustice to be shown to withdraw the admission, or only good cause?
7. Has counsel moved to recover reasonable expenses of proof, including attorneys' fees, for any RFA which had to be proved at trial due to its denial by the opponent?
   a. Was the original denial substantially justified?
   b. Will other circumstances make an award of expenses unjust?
8. **Warning:** Failure to answer RFAs acts as binding admission.

Supplementation of Discovery Responses (see §§ 17.14–17.15)

1. Is supplementation required by stipulation, Rule 26(e), or court order?
2. Did the response concern the identity and location of persons having discoverable information?
3. Did the response concern the identity of an expert trial witness, or the subject matter or substance of the expert's testimony?
4. Was the response incorrect when made?

5. Is the response no longer true, and failure to update it would result in knowing concealment?

Rules 11 and 26(g) (see ch. 28)

1. After reasonable inquiry, can the attorney or unrepresented party certify that the discovery request, response, or objection:
   a. Was warranted by existing law?
   b. Was not interposed for any improper purpose?
   c. Was not unreasonably or unduly burdensome or expensive, given the nature of the case?
2. After reasonable inquiry, can the attorney or unrepresented party certify that the discovery motion or opposition:
   a. Was well grounded in fact?
   b. Was warranted by existing law?
   c. Was not interposed for any improper purpose?
3. **Warning:** Check local rules for other restrictions on discovery or additional discovery requirements.

Reviewing Discovery Orders (see §§ 17.17–17.20)

1. Has the ruling been disobeyed, resulting in a finding of criminal contempt?
2. Is mandamus likely to be granted?
   a. Is the right to the writ clear and indisputable?
   b. Is there no other adequate means of relief?
   c. Was the district court's ruling beyond its jurisdiction?
   d. Did the district court have a duty to provide the requested action?
3. Is the judge likely to certify the ruling pursuant to 28 U.S.C. § 1292(b)?
   a. Does the ruling involve a controlling question of law?
   b. Is there substantial ground for disagreement concerning the disputed issue?
   c. Will an immediate appeal materially advance the termination of the litigation?
4. Is the ruling a collateral order which can be directly appealed?
   a. Did the order conclusively determine the disputed question?
   b. Did the order resolve an important issue completely separate from the merits of the action?
   c. Is the order effectively unreviewable on appeal from final judgment?
   d. Does the disputed issue present a serious and unsettled question?

§ 17.22 Discovery Objections Checklist

General Objections to Discovery

1. Irrelevant to the subject matter of the action or not reasonably calculated to lead to the discovery of admissible evidence
2. Protected by privilege
3. Protected by work product immunity
4. Unreasonably cumulative or duplicative or obtainable from some other source that is more convenient, less burdensome, or less expensive
5. Party seeking discovery has had ample opportunity by discovery in the action to obtain the information sought
6. Discovery is unduly burdensome or expensive, taking into account the needs of the case, the amount in controversy, limitations on the parties' resources, and the importance of the issues at stake in the litigation
7. Question or request is overbroad, vague, or ambiguous

Invalid Objections to Discovery

1. Calls for hearsay
2. Inadmissible in evidence
3. Document has not been authenticated
4. Best evidence rule
5. Question calls for an opinion
6. Subject matter of admission presents a genuine issue for trial

Motions for Protective Orders

1. The person or party must show how good cause for protection from discovery which would cause annoyance, embarrassment, oppression, or undue burden or expense.
2. A protective order can designate that
   - **a.** Discovery not be had
   - **b.** Discovery be had only on specified terms and conditions, including a designation of the time or place
   - **c.** Discovery be had by a method other than requested
   - **d.** Certain matters not be inquired into, or the scope of discovery be limited
   - **e.** Discovery be conducted only in the presence of persons designated by the court
   - **f.** A deposition be opened only by the court after being sealed

g. A trade secret or other confidential research, development, or commercial information not be disclosed or be disclosed only in a designated way

h. Parties simultaneously file specified documents or information enclosed in sealed envelopes to be opened as directed by the court.

Objections Concerning Depositions

1. The amount of notice was unreasonable.
2. A party failed to subpoena the nonparty deponent.
3. The deposition officer is subject to disqualification.
4. The recorded, videotaped, or telephone deposition required an order or stipulation.
5. The examination was being conducted in bad faith or so as to unreasonably annoy, embarrass, or oppress the witness.
6. An objection exists concerning the competence of the deponent, or the competence, relevance, or materiality of testimony which, if made at the deposition, would obviate or remove that ground for objection at trial.
7. An error or irregularity occurred in the manner of taking the deposition, the form of questions or answers, the oath or affirmation, or the conduct of the parties.
8. An error of any kind occurred which might be obviated, removed, or cured if promptly presented.

Objections Concerning Interrogatory Practice

1. The interrogatories were not directed to a party.
2. Contention interrogatories should be delayed until the pretrial.
3. The Rule 33(c) option to produce business records applies.
4. **Warning:** Blanket objections to interrogatories do not preserve any objection to specific questions.

Objections Concerning Production of Documents and Tangible Items, and Entry on Land

1. The request is not directed to a party.
2. The item or category is not described with reasonable particularity.
3. The document does not exist.
4. The document is not in the possession, custody or control of the party.
5. The inspection would interrupt an ongoing business.
6. The testing would result in the destruction of the evidence.

7. **Warning:** Blanket objections to the request do not preserve any objection to specific categories of documents.

Objections Concerning Mental or Physical Examinations

1. The mental or physical condition is not in controversy.
2. The movant lacks good cause to obtain the examination.
3. The person to be examined is not a party or a person in the custody or under the legal control of a party.
4. The person performing the examination is not a physician.
5. The attorney of the examined party is not permitted at the examination.

Objections Concerning Requests for Admissions

1. After reasonable inquiry, the party lacks sufficient information or knowledge to admit or deny the request.

§ 17.23 Timing and Procedure Checklist for Objections

Objection	Timing	Procedure
Taking deposition	Before deposition	Protective order or motion to quash by nonparty
Deposition question	At deposition	Objection or instruction not to answer (privilege) (relevance in some circuits)
Interrogatory set	Within 30 days (by defendant within 45 days after being served with the complaint)	Protective order
Interrogatory	Within 30 days (by defendant within 45 days after being served with the complaint)	Written objection; written offer to produce business records
Document production	Within 30 days (by defendant within 45 days after being served with the complaint)	Written objections
Mental or physical examination	Opposition to motion for exam	Written opposition

Objection	Timing	Procedure
Request for admission	Within 30 days (by defendant within 45 days after being served with the complaint)	Written objection
Subpoena duces tecum	Within 10 days or before compliance is due, if that date is earlier	Objection, motion to quash, or protective order

CHAPTER 18

PREVENTING DISCOVERY BY INVOKING PRIVILEGE

§ 18.1 Privilege

The single greatest hindrance to discovery is privilege. Because parties are not entitled to privileged materials, no discovery sanction can result from exercising an appropriate privilege. This chapter summarizes some of the most common privileges invoked in civil litigation as interpreted in federal practice[1] and suggests how to ensure that protectable material falls within a privilege as well as how to avoid waiver problems.

Counsel in diversity matters must always remember that Federal Rule of Evidence 501 provides that privilege is determined in accordance with state law with respect to an element of a claim or defense as to which state law supplies the rule of decision. Therefore, state rather than federal privilege law usually governs in diversity, unless the state cause of action applies federal law. As a result, in most diversity cases, attorney-client privilege is ruled by state law, while work product immunity is based on federal procedure. Federal Rule of Evidence 501 provides that the law of privilege applicable in federal matters is governed by the principles of the common law as they may be interpreted by the courts of the United States in the light of reason and experience. This vague definition results in a case-by-case analysis to determine the scope of any alleged federal privilege. When state and federal claims are joined which have conflicting rules of privilege, usually the federal rule is applied.[2]

When litigating privilege issues, counsel should always determine whether it is necessary to submit the allegedly privileged materials to the judge for in camera inspection. To the extent that courts regard the existence of a privilege as a factual determination under Federal Rule of Evidence 104(a), such decisions are subject to review under the clearly erroneous standard.[3]

§ 18.2 Attorney-Client Privilege

Attorney-client privilege is probably the most common privilege which is invoked to block discovery. The standard common law definition of *attorney-client privilege* is as follows: "(1) Where legal advice of any kind is sought (2) from a professional legal adviser in his capacity as such, (3) the communications relating to that purpose, (4) made in confidence (5) by the client, (6) are at his instance permanently protected (7) from disclosure by himself or by the legal adviser, (8) except if the protection be waived."[4] Communications from attorney

---

[1] For extensive treatment of privilege, see generally 2 J. Weinstein & M. Berger, Weinstein's Evidence ¶¶ 501–513 (1986); *Developments in the Law, Privileged Communications*, 98 Harv. L. Rev. 1450–1666 (1985); see also M. Graham, Handbook of Federal Evidence (2d ed. 1986); M. Larkin, Federal Testimonial Privileges (1986); D. Louisell & C. Mueller, Federal Evidence (1979); P. Rothstein, Federal Rules of Evidence (2d ed. 1986); S. Saltzburg & K. Redden, Federal Rules of Evidence Manual (4th ed. 1986).

[2] Von Bulow by Auersperg v. Von Bulow, 811 F.2d 136, 141 (2d Cir. 1987); *see* Memorial Hosp. v. Shadur, 664 F.2d 1058, 1061 n.3 (7th Cir. 1981); Perrignon v. Bergen Brunswig Corp., 77 F.R.D. 455, 458–59 (N.D. Cal. 1978).

[3] *See, e.g.*, United States v. Wilson, 798 F.2d 509, 512 (1st Cir. 1986).

[4] 8 Wigmore, Evidence § 2292, at 554 (McNaughton rev. 1961); *see generally* 24 C. Wright & K. Graham, Federal Practice and Procedure § 5473 (1986) [hereinafter Federal Practice and Procedure].

to client are also shielded by the privilege if they rest on confidential information obtained from the client.[5] The privilege belongs to the client but must be asserted by the attorney when applicable. Because the privilege extends only to confidential legal communications, such items as the identity of a client,[6] attorneys' fees,[7] and authentication of a client's handwriting[8] are not considered confidential. Although some courts prevent disclosure of unprivileged information which would necessarily reveal confidential communications,[9] such protection is rarely applicable.[10]

The burden of demonstrating the applicability of the privilege rests upon the party who invokes it,[11] although the confidentiality of a communication between the client and the attorney usually is presumed.[12] The increasingly popular discovery vehicle of deposing opposing counsel has recently been limited by the Eighth Circuit, which permits such a deposition only if (1) no other means exist to obtain the information than to depose opposing council; (2) the information sought is relevant and nonprivileged; and (3) the information is crucial to the preparation of the case.[13]

A party must make a timely objection to discovery as being privileged. Because a blanket claim of privilege is unacceptable, each objection must be separately identified.[14] For example, in order to sustain the burden of establishing a claim of privilege in response to a Rule 34 document request, the party must state with respect to each item or category why the documents are privileged rather than rely on a general objection.[15] A privilege log should be kept concerning documents withheld from discovery which identifies background information, such as date, author, addresses, and general topic, but does

---

[5] United States v. (Under Seal), 748 F.2d 871, 874 & n.5 (4th Cir. 1984); *In re* Sealed Case, 737 F.2d 94, 99 (D.C. Cir. 1984); *see* Upjohn v. United States, 449 U.S. 383, 390 (1981); Sedco Int'l, S.A. v. Cory, 683 F.2d 1201, 1205 (8th Cir.), *cert. denied,* 459 U.S. 1017 (1982); United States v. Amerada Hess Corp., 619 F.2d 980, 985–86 (3d Cir. 1980); *In re* Fischel, 557 F.2d 209, 211 (9th Cir. 1977); Proposed Fed. R. Evid. Supreme Court Standard 503(b).

[6] *See, e.g., In re* Shargel, 742 F.2d 61, 62 (2d Cir. 1984).

[7] *See, e.g., In re* Two Grand Jury Subpoenae Duces Tecum Dated August 21, 1985, 793 F.2d 69, 71–72 (2d Cir. 1986); Liew v. Breen, 640 F.2d 1046, 1049 (9th Cir. 1981).

[8] *In re* Grand Jury Proceedings (85 Misc. 140), 791 F.2d 663, 665 (8th Cir. 1986).

[9] *See id.*; *In re* Shargel, 742 F.2d 61, 63 (2d Cir. 1984); *In re* Witnesses Before Special March 1980 Grand Jury, 729 F.2d 489, 495 (7th Cir. 1984); Baird v. Koerner, 279 F.2d 623, 627 (9th Cir. 1960); *see generally*, Developments in the Law, *Privileged Communications,* 98 Harv. L. Rev. 1450, 1514–24 (1985).

[10] *See, e.g., In re* Grand Jury Subpoenas, 803 F.2d 493, 497–98 (9th Cir. 1986).

[11] *See* Hodges, Grant & Kaufmann v. United States, 768 F.2d 719, 721 n.7 (5th Cir. 1985) and cases cited therein.

[12] *See generally* 2 J. Weinstein & M. Berger, Weinstein's Evidence ¶ 503(a)(4)[01] (1986).

[13] Shelton v. American Motors Corp., 805 F.2d 1323, 1327 (8th Cir. 1986).

[14] *See, e.g.,* United States v. Keplinger, 776 F.2d 678, 700 n.13 (7th Cir. 1985), *cert. denied,* _____ U.S. _____, 106 S. Ct. 2919 (1986).

[15] Peat, Marwick, Mitchell & Co. v. West, 748 F.2d 540, 541–42 (10th Cir. 1984), *cert. denied,* 469 U.S. 1199 (1985); *see* 8 Federal Practice and Procedure § 2213.

not reveal the substance of the privileged material. However, counsel must explain the basis of the alleged privilege in response to a motion to compel, because the mere existence of a privilege log may not be enough to satisfy the burden of showing the documents are privileged.[16]

Only the communication is privileged, not the facts which are disclosed in the communication.[17] Therefore, it is often possible to attain the same information by deposition of the party or corporate employee, unless that person invokes the Fifth Amendment privilege against self-incrimination.[18] Of course, such discovery is likely to be costly, especially if the deponents are scattered. In determining privilege issues the court may wish to inspect the documents in camera, because the questions of privilege and waiver are factual by nature. It may be wise to request that the district judge issue findings of fact in order to avoid a remand on these issues if the appellate court believes the record is inadequate.[19]

§ 18.3 Corporate Attorney-Client Privilege

The application of the attorney-client privilege to corporations raises a myriad of issues which arise frequently in civil litigation. It is too late to begin considering privilege issues when the adversary requests the allegedly protected materials. Counsel must be aware of the dimensions of the privilege from the inception of the attorney-client relationship in order to ensure that conversations and documents fall within the privilege and do not become subject to waiver.

§ 18.4 —Employees Whose Communications Are Protected

A common attorney-client issue which arises in civil litigation is determining who is the client in a corporate setting.[20] *Upjohn Co. v. United States*[21] is the leading case in this area. *Upjohn* rejected the control group test which limits attorney-client privilege to those persons in the corporation who are in a position to control or take a substantial part in a decision which the corporation may take as a result of the attorney's advice. While the Court refused to adopt any

---

[16] BarclaysAmerican Corp. v. Kane, 746 F.2d 653, 656 (10th Cir. 1984).

[17] Upjohn Co. v. United States, 449 U.S. 383, 395–96 (1981).

[18] See §§ **18.19–18.21**.

[19] *See, e.g.*, Hodges, Grant & Kaufmann v. United States, 768 F.2d 719, 720 (5th Cir. 1985) (case remanded for factual findings).

[20] *See generally* Cody, *The Attorney-Client Privilege and the Work Product Immunity Doctrine For The Corporate Client,* 15 Balt. L. Rev. 251 (1986).

[21] 449 U.S. 383 (1981).

particular test in its place, it has de facto adopted a modified subject matter test.[22] The privilege appears to apply if

1. The employee's communication was made for the purpose of securing legal advice
2. The employee made the communication at the direction of his corporate superior
3. The superior made the request so that the corporation could secure legal advice
4. The subject matter of the communication is within the scope of the employee's corporate duties, and
5. The communication was not disseminated beyond those persons who, because of the corporate structure, need to know its contents.[23]

At a minimum, any serious in-house legal investigation should start with a written request or notation. Counsel should recommend that written policies be adopted to ensure that the proper steps are taken to protect the corporate client's privileged information. Written communications between employees and counsel should be kept in the legal files, or if not practicable, in separate files clearly marked as privileged and not randomly accessible. Employees must be made aware of the confidential nature of the communications in order to ensure against waiver. The privilege appears to cover both corporate employees who serve as in-house counsel and outside counsel.[24] It also may cover former as well as current employees.[25] In a related matter, Rule 4.2 of the A.B.A. Model Rules of Professional Conduct has been interpreted to forbid counsel from having any ex parte contact with any managerial level employees of its corporate opponent due to the implications of the *Upjohn* test.[26] Thus, it is arguable that ex parte contact is prohibited as to any employee for whom the attorney-client privilege now applies.

---

[22] *See* Diversified Indus. Inc. v. Meredith, 572 F.2d 596, 602, 609 (8th Cir. 1977) (en banc); Harper & Row Publishers, Inc. v. Decker, 423 F.2d 487, 491–92 (7th Cir. 1970), *aff'd per curiam by equally divided court,* 400 U.S. 348 (1971).

[23] *See* Diversified Indus. Inc. v. Meredith, 572 F.2d 596, 609 (8th Cir. 1977) (en banc); *see generally* 2 J. Weinstein & M. Berger, Weinstein's Evidence ¶ 503(b)[04] (1986).

[24] Upjohn Co. v. United States, 449 U.S. 383, 394–95 (1981); *In re* Sealed Case, 737 F.2d 94, 99 (D.C. Cir. 1984).

[25] *In re* Coordinated Pretrial Proceedings in Petroleum Prod. Antitrust Litig., 658 F.2d 1355, 1361 n.7 (9th Cir. 1981), *cert. denied,* 455 U.S. 990 (1982); *see* Upjohn Co. v. United States, 449 U.S. 383, 394 n.3, 397 n.6 (1981) (not deciding issue).

[26] *Cf.* Massa v. Eaton Corp., 109 F.R.D. 312, 313–15 (W.D. Mich. S.D. 1985) (Michigan's DR 7–104(A)(1), based on Model Rules Professional Conduct Rule 4.2, prohibits such ex parte contact). *But see* Wright by Wright v. Group Health Hosp., 103 Wash. 2d 192, 691 P.2d 564, 566–70 (1984) (en banc) (improper for employer to advise employees not to speak with plaintiffs' attorneys; limiting DR 7–104(A) to employees with managing authority to bind corporation).

Since *Upjohn* was based solely on the Federal Rules of Evidence, the control group test is still applicable in a diversity case if the relevant state law applies that standard. This poses a quandary for practioners in such jurisdictions as Illinois, which has reaffirmed the control group test.[27] Obviously, affected practitioners should structure their communications with corporate clients to adhere to the more stringent state test rather than speculate whether any potential litigation will have federal as well as state claims.[28]

§ 18.5 —Representing Current and Former Employees

One issue which often arises during depositions is whether a present or former corporate employee is represented by counsel for the corporation. The attorney representing the corporation must be sensitive to any conflict of interest problem inherent in representing both the employee and the employer, especially when the individual is a former employee. If representation is undertaken individually as well as in a corporate capacity, the record must be clear in order to establish an attorney-client relationship.[29] Thus, a formal appearance should be stated on the record. If corporate counsel does not intend individually to represent the employee, this should also be made clear. Even if an employee is not represented individually, the attorney should instruct the deponent not to answer questions which are protected by the attorney-client privilege pursuant to *Upjohn*.[30]

§ 18.6 —Distinguishing Business from Legal Advice

Another issue which arises in corporate litigation is whether the communication is made in a legal or business capacity.[31] Corporate employees who have legal and business functions are particularly vulnerable to a claim that information is not privileged and must make a clear showing that the communication was given in a legal capacity.[32] In other words, it is crucial to identify the nature of the communication from the outset. The privilege is also not applicable between a pension plan trustee and an attorney who advises the trustee regarding the administration of the plan.[33]

---

[27] Consolidation Coal Co. v. Bucyrus-Erie Co., 89 Ill. 2d 103, 432 N.E.2d 250, 257 (1982).

[28] *See generally* Note, *The Attorney-Client Privilege in the Corporate Context: The Intersection of Federal and Illinois Law,* 1984 U. Ill. L. Rev. 175.

[29] *See, e.g.*, United States v. Keplinger, 776 F.2d 678, 700 & n.14 (7th Cir. 1985) (subjective belief of representation and references to "your attorney" not sufficient), *cert. denied,* ___ U.S. ___, 106 S. Ct. 2919 (1986).

[30] 449 U.S. 383 (1981).

[31] *See, e.g.*, *In re* Grand Jury Subpoena Duces Tecum Dated September 15, 1983, 731 F.2d 1032, 1037 (2d Cir. 1984); United States v. Jones, 696 F.2d 1069, 1072 (4th Cir. 1982).

[32] *In re* Sealed Case, 737 F.2d 94, 99 (D.C. Cir. 1984).

[33] United States v. Evans, 796 F.2d 264, 265–66 (9th Cir. 1986).

§ 18.7 —Maintaining Confidentiality

It is also sometimes difficult to determine whether a communication is confidential in a corporate setting, because documents often get distributed. Although there is no magic distribution number at which a document loses confidentiality, it is extremely difficult to argue that distribution to more than 10 employees is required.[34] In general, the less distribution, the more likely it is that a claim of confidentiality can be sustained. It is essential that only employees who are necessary to making the communication or executing the attorney's advice are given access to privileged information. Even if the documents are not generally distributed, their subsequent accessibility may be viewed as waiving the privilege. Although at least one court did not require separate locked files for privileged documents,[35] such documents should be marked confidential and separated from general project files when feasible.

§ 18.8 —Waiver

Counsel must be vigilant to ensure that privileged materials are not made discoverable due to waiver.[36] Voluntary disclosure by the client to a third party destroys the confidentiality of the communication and therefore waives the privilege. When the privileged information is waived, not only is the specific communication subject to disclosure, but often all other communications relating to the same subject matter become discoverable.[37] For a solvent corporation, the power to waive the privilege rests with the corporation's current management, while for a corporation in bankruptcy, the trustee has the power to waive the privilege with respect to prebankruptcy communications.[38] Because the directors or officers may have an individual attorney-client privilege apart from the corporate privilege, some disputes center on whether the individuals can prevent the disclosure of the corporation.[39] In addition, the applicability of attorney-client privilege in stockholder actions is in flux.[40]

---

[34] *See, e.g.*, James Julian, Inc. v. Raytheon Co., 93 F.R.D. 138, 141 (D. Del. 1982) and cases cited therein.

[35] *Id.* at 141–42.

[36] *See generally* Marcus, *The Perils of Privilege: Waiver and the Litigator,* 84 Mich. L. Rev. 1605 (1986).

[37] United States v. Jones, 696 F.2d 1069, 1072 (4th Cir. 1982); *In re* Sealed Case, 676 F.2d 793, 809 (D.C. Cir. 1982); *see* Weil v. Investment/Indicators, Research & Mgmt., Inc., 647 F.2d 18, 24–25 (9th Cir. 1981); *see generally* 8 J. Wigmore, Evidence § 2327 (McNaughton rev. 1961); 8 Federal Practice and Procedure § 2016.

[38] Commodity Futures Trading Comm'n v. Weintraub, 471 U.S. 343, 348, 358 (1985).

[39] *See, e.g., In re* Bevill, Bresler & Schulman Asset Mgmt. Corp., 805 F.2d 120, 124–25 (3d Cir. 1986).

[40] *Compare* Garner v. Wolfinbarger, 430 F.2d 1093, 1103–04 (5th Cir. 1970), *cert. denied,* 401 U.S. 974 (1971) *with In re* LTV Sec. Litig., 89 F.R.D. 595, 606–08 (N.D. Tex. 1981); *see*

Selective disclosure for tactical purposes waives the privilege.[41] The only third parties to whom the privilege applies are those who have a common legal interest with respect to the subject matter of the communication.[42] Conversely, there is no privilege between joint clients as to matters of common interest, because no secrecy exists between them at the time of the communication.[43] The joint defense doctrine does protect statements made to an attorney by a codefendant for a common purpose related to the defense of both from being revealed to the opposing party.[44] However, information discussed at meetings with attorneys and clients of codefendants cannot be assured to remain privileged, if the court finds that the interests of the parties were adverse[45] or there is no evidence that the parties agreed to pursue a joint defense strategy.[46] In a given case, it may be appropriate to sign a stipulation concerning cooperation between defendants or even to obtain a pretrial order mandating such cooperation on the condition that attorney-client privilege or work product is not waived.

Courts may consider the privilege waived by voluntary disclosures to outsiders, such as auditors or underwriters, which are made for business purposes.[47] There is some dispute as to whether information given to the S.E.C. as part of its Voluntary Disclosure Program or to other administrative agencies based on internal corporate investigations undertaken to comply with government regulations should retain its privileged status.[48] The D.C. Circuit held that any attorney-client privilege was waived regarding information which was revealed to the S.E.C. to facilitate processing a corporation's registration statement.[49] When possible, counsel should require that such documents be

---

generally Saltzburg, *Corporate Attorney-Client Privilege in Shareholder Litigation and Similar Cases: Garner Revisited,* 12 Hofstra L. Rev. 817 (1984).

[41] United States v. Jones, 696 F.2d 1069, 1072 (4th Cir. 1982); *In re* Sealed Case, 676 F.2d 793, 808–09 (D.C. Cir. 1982).

[42] Hodges, Grant & Kaufmann v. United States, 768 F.2d 719, 721 (5th Cir. 1985).

[43] Eureka Inv. Corp. v. Chicago Title Ins. Co., 743 F.2d 932, 937 (D.C. Cir. 1984); *see* 8 J. Wigmore, Evidence § 2312 (McNaughton rev. 1961).

[44] United States v. Keplinger, 776 F.2d 678, 701 (7th Cir. 1985), *cert. denied,* ____ U.S. ____, 106 S. Ct. 2919 (1986).

[45] *See* United States v. Lopez, 777 F.2d 543, 552–53 (10th Cir. 1985) and cases cited therein.

[46] *See In re* Bevill, Bresler & Schulman Asset Mgmt. Corp., 805 F.2d 120, 126 (3d Cir. 1986).

[47] *In re* John Doe Corp., 675 F.2d 482, 488–89 (2d Cir. 1982).

[48] *See* Crisman & Mathews, *Limited Waiver of Attorney-Client Privilege and Work-Product Doctrine in Internal Corporate Investigations: An Emerging Corporate "Self-Evaluative" Privilege,* 21 Am. Crim. L. Rev. 123 (1983); Note, *The Limited Waiver Rule: Creation of an SEC-Corporation Privilege,* 36 Stanford L. Rev. 789 (1984); Comment, *Stuffing the Rabbit Back into the Hat: Limited Waiver of the Attorney-Client Privilege in an Administrative Investigation,* 130 U. Pa. L. Rev. 1198 (1982); *see also* Diversified Indus., Inc. v. Meredith, 572 F.2d 596, 611 (8th Cir. 1977) (en banc); T.I.A.A. v. Shamrock Broadcasting Co., 521 F. Supp. 638, 642 (S.D.N.Y. 1981).

[49] Permian Corp. v. United States, 665 F.2d 1214, 1219 (D.C. Cir. 1981); *see In re* Subpoenas Duces Tecum, 738 F.2d 1367, 1369–70 (D.C. Cir. 1984).

subpoenaed by the agency and produced under a protective order, stipulation, or other express reservation about their privileged status.[50]

Implied waiver of attorney-client privilege is found when the client places the attorney-client relationship directly at issue or when a client asserts reliance on an attorney's advice as an element of a claim or defense.[51] However, such waivers are usually limited to the relevant communications, and some courts require a showing that the material is vital to the claim or defense.[52]

§ 18.9 —Inadvertent Disclosure

In some cases counsel may be faced with a waiver argument concerning the inadvertent disclosure of privileged documents. Courts vary as to whether production of a privileged document automatically waives the attorney-client privilege.[53] Some courts look to the nature of the precautions taken to maintain confidentiality, while others consider the voluntariness of the disclosure rather than whether it was intentional.[54] The difference in approaches has been referred to as conduct analysis versus strict responsibility.[55]

Regardless of which standard the court applies, counsel must take precautions to screen all documents for privileged material, identify privileged documents, and remove them from documents being produced. A privilege log should be kept to identify documents considered protected from discovery. Counsel must protest the use of the inadvertently disclosed document in a timely fashion after learning about its production. Return of the document or the existing of the privileged portion of a partially privileged document should be requested. If necessary, counsel should move for a protective order. A deponent who is asked

---

[50] *See* T.I.A.A. v. Shamrock Broadcasting Co., 521 F. Supp. 638, 646 (S.D.N.Y. 1981).

[51] *See* GAB Business Servs., Inc. v. Syndicate 627, 809 F.2d 755, 762 (11th Cir. 1987); Sedco Int'l, S.A. v. Cory, 683 F.2d 1201, 1206 (8th Cir.), *cert. denied,* 459 U.S. 1017 (1982); *see* 8 J. Wigmore, Evidence § 2388, at 855 (McNaughton rev. 1961); Davidson & Voth, *Waiver of the Attorney-Client Privilege,* 64 Or. L. Rev. 637, 646–50 (1986); Thornburg, *Attorney-Client Privilege: Issue-Related Waivers,* 50 J. Air L. & Commerce 1039 (1985).

[52] *See* Zenith Radio Corp. v. United States, 764 F.2d 1577, 1579–80 (Fed. Cir. 1985).

[53] *See generally* Davidson & Voth, *Waiver of the Attorney-Client Privilege,* 64 Or. L. Rev. 637, 640–46 (1986); Grippando, *Attorney-Client Privilege: Implied Waiver Through Inadvertent Disclosure of Documents,* 39 U. Miami L. Rev. 511 (1985); Note, *Attorney-Client Privilege: The Necessity of Intent to Waive the Privilege in Inadvertent Disclosure Cases,* 18 Pac. L.J. 59 (1986); Note, *Inadvertent Disclosure of Documents Subject to the Attorney-Client Privilege,* 82 Mich. L. Rev. 598 (1983).

[54] *Compare* Transamerica Computer Co. v. I.B.M. Corp., 573 F.2d 646, 651 (9th Cir. 1978) (voluntary disclosure test) *with In re* Horowitz, 482 F.2d 72, 81–82 (2d Cir.), *cert. denied,* 414 U.S. 867 (1973) (emphasizing failure to take precautions).

[55] Grippando, *Attorney-Client Privilege: Implied Waiver Through Inadvertent Disclosure of Documents,* 39 U. Miami L. Rev. 511, 512 (1985).

questions about such a document should be instructed not to answer concerning privileged information.

Although most such disclosures occur when there is voluminous document production, inadvertent disclosures can occur when relatively small quantities of documents are not screened by trained professionals who are sensitive to privilege issues. Because the knowledge of the contents of such documents can never be suppressed, even if the court later rules that the documents cannot themselves be used, counsel must always be alert for misplaced privileged material appearing in even the most routine files.

§ 18.10 —Preexisting Documents

Preexisting documents which are given to the attorney are not protected by the privilege, unless the documents themselves are privileged from production.[56] However, the communication involved when the client gives the attorney the documents is protected. Documents which by their vary nature contemplate disclosure to third parties are not considered privileged because they are not considered confidential.[57] Thus, communications concerning information to be placed in a prospectus or income tax return have been held unprivileged.[58] Similarly, information supplied to a law firm to meet continuing I.R.S. requests for information are not privileged.[59] On the other hand, merely employing an attorney to research the possibility of filing public papers or seeking a tax ruling does not destroy the privilege if no further action is taken.[60] There is no separate federal accountant-client privilege[61] or work product immunity for tax information.[62]

§ 18.11 Experts and Attorney-Client Privilege

The only time an expert's work is covered by attorney-client privilege is when the expert's analysis is required by the attorney to understand the client's

[56] Fisher v. United States, 425 U.S. 391, 403–05 (1976); *In re* Grand Jury Proceedings, 632 F.2d 1033, 1042 (3d Cir. 1980).

[57] *E.g.*, United States v. Aronson, 781 F.2d 1580, 1581 (11th Cir. 1986).

[58] *In re* Grand Jury Proceedings, 727 F.2d 1352, 1358 (4th Cir. 1984) (prospectus not actually issued); United States v. Lawless, 709 F.2d 485, 488 (7th Cir. 1983) (information transmitted to attorney for tax return). *But see In re* Grand Jury Subpoena Duces Tecum Dated September 15, 1983, 731 F.2d 1032, 1037 (2d Cir. 1984) (possibility that information may ultimately be published does not vitiate privilege.).

[59] United States v. Windfelder, 790 F.2d 576, 580 (7th Cir. 1986).

[60] United States v. (Under Seal), 748 F.2d 871, 875–76 (4th Cir. 1984).

[61] Couch v. United States, 409 U.S. 322, 335 (1973).

[62] United States v. Arthur Young & Co., 465 U.S. 805, 817 (1984).

confidential communication.[63] Therefore, a psychiatrist who is hired by the lawyer to determine whether the client has a claim for emotional distress is covered by the attorney-client privilege. This is important, because any psychotherapist-patient privilege which may exist in a diversity action is usually waived by bringing a claim for emotional distress. Thus, if counsel decides not to call the doctor, such information is not discoverable, even if the other party can make a showing of exceptional circumstances which would otherwise result in the disclosure of an expert's opinion under Rule 26(b)(4). If the doctor is called as a witness, such opinions become discoverable, but anything said to the attorney concerning the existence of the claim is still privileged.

It is rare that an expert's opinion is covered by attorney-client privilege, because most experts do not interpret confidential communications of clients. An expert who analyzes a physical item such as a wheel in a products liability action or the client's preexisting business records in business litigation is protected from discovery solely by Rule 26(b)(4).[64]

§ 18.12 Crime-Fraud Exception to Attorney-Client Privilege

If a client's communication to counsel furthers an ongoing crime or fraud, it is not protected by the attorney-client privilege.[65] Such communications are excluded from the scope of privilege even if the attorney is unaware that the advice is sought in furtherance of the improper purpose.[66] To make a prima facie showing that the exception applies, there must be a violation shown which is sufficiently serious to defeat the privilege, and the court must find some valid relationship between the privileged material and the prima facie violation.[67] The Second Circuit requires a showing of probable cause to believe that a crime or fraud was committed and the communications were in furtherance thereof but considers that there is little practical difference between the two tests.[68] The burden is satisfied if evidence is offered that if believed by the trier of fact would

---

[63] 2 J. Weinstein & M. Berger, Weinstein's Evidence ¶ 503(a)(3)[01] (1986).

[64] See **ch. 20**.

[65] *See, e.g.*, Clark v. United States, 289 U. S. 1, 15 (1933); Craig v. A.H. Robins Co., 790 F.2d 1, 4 (1st Cir. 1986); *In re* Sealed Case, 754 F.2d 395, 399 (D.C. Cir. 1985); *In re* Grand Jury Subpoena Duces Tecum Dated September 15, 1983, 731 F.2d 1032, 1038 (2d Cir. 1984); *see generally* Fried, *Too High a Price for Truth; The Exception to the Attorney-Client Privilege for Contemplated Crimes and Frauds,* 64 N.C.L. Rev. 443 (1986); *Developments in the Law, Privileged Communications,* 98 Harv. L. Rev. 1450, 1509–14 (1985).

[66] *In re* Grand Jury Subpoena Duces Tecum Dated September 15, 1983, 731 F.2d 1032, 1038 (2d Cir. 1984); United States v. Hodge & Zweig, 548 F.2d 1347, 1354 (9th Cir. 1977).

[67] *In re* Sealed Case, 754 F.2d 395, 399 (D.C. Cir. 1985); *In re* Grand Jury Proceedings, 689 F.2d 1351, 1352 (11th Cir. 1982).

[68] *In re* Grand Jury Subpoena Duces Tecum Dated September 15, 1983, 731 F.2d 1032, 1039 (2d Cir. 1984).

establish the elements of an ongoing or imminent crime or fraud.[69] The burden has also been described as requiring more than a strong suspicion that a crime was committed but not as strong a showing as needed to effect an arrest or secure an indictment.[70] The crime-fraud exception is not applicable merely upon a showing that the client communicated with counsel while the client was engaged in criminal activity.[71]

In diversity cases, the existence of the crime fraud exception is determined by state law, but determining whether a prima facie showing of fraud has been made may be a question of federal law.[72] Procedures for in camara review of the disputed documents or evidence demonstrating a waiver are required in most circuits[73] and should always be requested when the privilege issue cannot be determined without the judge's reviewing the document in question. The trial court's ruling concerning the crime-fraud exception is reviewed on an abuse of discretion standard.[74]

§ 18.13 Work Product Immunity

Attorney-client privilege exists to protect the relationship between the client and counsel; work product is an immunity which protects the attorney from having the fruits of his labor appropriated by opposing counsel. Work product immunity promotes the adversary system by safeguarding the attorney's trial preparation.[75] It recognizes that, if such materials were discoverable on demand, much of what is now put down in writing would remain unwritten and that inefficiency, unfairness, and sharp practices would inevitably develop.[76] The work product doctrine originated in *Hickman v. Taylor,*[77] which has been substantially codified in Rule 26(b)(3), to protect trial preparation materials. The doctrine has been applied to administrative proceedings under the Administrative Procedures

---

[69] *In re* Sealed Case, 754 F.2d 395, 399 (D.C. Cir. 1985).

[70] *In re* Antitrust Grand Jury, 805 F.2d 155, 165 (6th Cir. 1986).

[71] *In re* Grand Jury Subpoenas Duces Tecum, 798 F.2d 32, 34 (2d Cir. 1986).

[72] Pritchard-Keang Nam Corp. v. Jaworski, 751 F.2d 277, 281 n.4 (8th Cir. 1984), *cert. dismissed,* _____ U.S. _____, 105 S. Ct. 3491 (1985); *cf.* Glovatorium, Inc. v. NCR Corp., 684 F.2d 658, 660 (9th Cir. 1982) (applying this standard in action alleging fraud).

[73] *See, e.g., In re* John Doe Corp., 675 F.2d 482, 489–91 (2d Cir. 1982); *see also In re* Antitrust Grand Jury, 805 F.2d 155, 168 (6th Cir. 1986) (surveying case law).

[74] *In re* Sealed Case, 754 F.2d 395, 400 (D.C. Cir. 1985); *In re* Berkley & Co., 629 F.2d 548, 553 (8th Cir. 1980). *But see* United States v. Zolin, 908 F.2d 1411, 1417–19 (9th Cir. 1987) (de novo review if mixed question of law and fact; also requiring independent evidence of crime or fraud other than privileged communication).

[75] *See generally* 8 Federal Practice and Procedure § 2024.

[76] Hickman v. Taylor, 329 U.S. 495, 511 (1947).

[77] 329 U.S. 495 (1947).

Act, although it is apparently not mandated in that setting.[78] Similarly, work product immunity exists in litigation under the Freedom of Information Act.[79] Work product immunity does not terminate at the end of the litigation, regardless of whether other related litigation is pending or contemplated.[80]

Work product immunity protects documents and tangible items which are prepared in anticipation of litigaion. Rule 26(b)(3) provides that such materials are obtainable only upon a showing that (1) the party has substantial need of the materials to prepare the case and (2) the party is unable without undue hardship to obtain the substantial equivalent of the materials by other means. Materials prepared in anticipation of litigation or for trial are protected whether created by or for the party or the party's representative, including an attorney, consultant, surety, indemnitor, insurer, or agent.[81]

The rule provides additional protection for opinion work product.[82] Even if the required showing has been made, the court "shall protect against disclosure of the mental impressions, conclusions, opinions, or legal theories of an attorney or other representative of a party concerning the litigation."[83] Although this language appears to be mandatory as to the attorney's mental processes, the Supreme Court in *Upjohn*[84] was unwilling to decide whether such material is always protected by the work product rule. *Upjohn* did note that, at a minimum, a stronger showing of necessity and unavailability must be made to disclose opinion work product than ordinary work product.[85]

Opinion work product includes notes evaluating a witness's testimony as well as legal analysis. It protects counsel's selective process of compiling documents from among voluminous files in preparation of litigation, including the mere acknowledgment of the existence of those documents.[86] It has even protected discussions that an attorney has with a nonparty deponent concerning the case,[87] although such conversations can be risky unless the deponent is a known ally. Computerized litigation support systems which index documents by subject

---

[78] *See* Sprague v. Director, Office of Workers' Comp. Programs, 688 F.2d 862, 869 n.16 (1st Cir. 1982).

[79] 5 U.S.C. § 552(b)(5) (1982); F.T.C. v. Grolier, Inc., 462 U.S. 19, 26–27 (1983).

[80] F.T.C. v. Grolier, Inc., 462 U.S. 19, 25–26 (1983).

[81] Fed. R. Civ. P. 26(b)(3).

[82] *See generally* Wolfson, *Opinion Work Product—Solving the Dilemma of Compelled Disclosure,* 64 Neb. L. Rev. 248 (1985); Note, *Protection of Opinion Work Product Under the Federal Rules of Civil Procedure,* 64 Va. L. Rev. 333 (1978); Special Project, *The Work Product Doctrine,* 68 Cornell L. Rev. 760 (1983).

[83] Fed. R. Civ. P. 26(b)(3).

[84] 449 U.S. 383 (1981).

[85] *Id.* at 401–02.

[86] Shelton v. American Motors Corp., 805 F.2d 1323, 1326 (8th Cir. 1986); *see* Sporck v. Peil, 759 F. 2d 312, 315 (3d Cir.), *cert. denied,* ____ U.S. ____, 106 S. Ct. 232 (1985).

[87] Ford v. Philips Elecs. Instruments Co., 82 F.R.D. 359, 360–61 (E.D. Pa. 1979); *see also Special Project, The Work Product Doctrine,* 68 Cornell L. Rev. 760, 817–29 (1983).

matter or contain summaries also have been considered opinion work product.[88] It is arguable that the very identity of documents in the database is work product, when not all documents are included. However, unprivileged documents placed in the system are freely discoverable upon a relevant document request.

§ 18.14 —Obtaining Work Product

The burden of establishing that a document is work product is on the party who asserts the claim, but the burden of showing that work product should be disclosed is on the party seeking its production.[89] Because work product must be created in anticipation of litigation, routine business investigations are not protected. This poses a problem to insurers who routinely investigate claims which may result in litigation. Usually such work product claims are treated on a case-by-case basis.[90]

As a general rule, discovery of work product is denied if a party can obtain the information by deposition.[91] Therefore, counsel must request the names of witnesses who have been interviewed and follow the normal discovery procedures before work product will be released.[92] Although undue hardship may be demonstrated if the witness cannot recall the events in question or is unavailable, a particularized showing must be made that no other individuals possess the needed information.[93] Excessive expense required to obtain the information contained in the work product because witnesses are located abroad may be considered as a factor in the undue hardship analysis, although the cost of a few depositions does not justify revealing the protected information.[94]

---

[88] *See generally* Poirier, Robb & Mosher, *Computer-Based Litigation Support Systems: The Discoverability Issue,* 54 UMKC L. Rev. 440 (1986); Sherman & Kinnard, *The Development, Discovery, and Use of Computer Support Systems in Achieving Efficiency in Litigation,* 79 Colum. L. Rev. 267, 268–69 (1979); Note, *Computer Discovery in Federal Litigation: Playing by the Rules,* 69 Georgetown L. J. 1465 (1981); Comment, *The Discovery and Use of Computerized Information: An Examination of Current Approaches,* 13 Pepperdine L.J. 405, 408–10 (1986).

[89] Hodges, Grant & Kaufmann v. United States, 768 F.2d 719, 721 (5th Cir. 1985).

[90] *See generally* Note, *Work Product Discovery in Insurance Litigation,* 18 Ind. L. Rev. 547 (1985).

[91] *In re* International Sys. & Controls Corp. Secs. Litig., 693 F.2d 1235, 1240 (5th Cir. 1982); 8 Federal Practice and Procedure § 2025 n.72.

[92] Castle v. Sangamo Weston, Inc., 744 F.2d 1464, 1467 (11th Cir. 1984).

[93] *In re* International Sys. & Controls Corp. Secs. Litig., 693 F.2d 1235, 1240–41 (5th Cir. 1982); *see* Xerox Corp. v. I.B.M. Corp., 79 F.R.D. 7, 9 (S.D.N.Y. 1977).

[94] *In re* International Sys. & Controls Corp. Secs. Litig., 693 F.2d 1235, 1241 (5th Cir. 1982) (original investigation at issue cost $1.5 million); *see* Castle v. Sangamo Weston, Inc., 744 F.2d 1464, 1467 (11th Cir. 1984).

§ 18.15 —Distinguishing Attorney-Client Privilege from Work Product

The attorney-client privilege should not be confused with work product immunity, because different rules apply to each concept. Attorney-client privilege covers the client's confidential communications, and the client is the holder of that privilege. Work product is the lawyer's immunity, which covers legal analysis as well as work which is created by others to aid the lawyer in the litigation. The client and the attorney are joint holders of the work product protection.[95] Although the attorney-client privilege is waived by disclosure to third parties, work product may be shown to friendly third parties without waiver, unless such disclosure is likely to make the materials available to the adverse party.[96] Therefore, counsel engaged in a joint trial or who have comon interests can share work product without waiving its protection.[97] However, some circuits hold that work product can be lost by limited disclosure to governmental agencies without any promise of confidentiality.[98]

§ 18.16 —Witness Statements

Witness statements are protected by work product immunity rather than by attorney-client privilege, unless the person giving the statement is the client or an employee who falls within the *Upjohn* standard. Rule 26(b)(3) defines witness statements as (1) a written statement signed, adopted, or approved by the person making it, or (2) a stenographic, mechanical, electrical, or other recording or transcription thereof which is a substantially verbatim recital of an oral statement by the person making it and contemporaneously recorded, and provides that such statements may be obtained by a party without any required showing. Similarly, a nonparty may request such a statement without any showing of need. If the request is refused, the person may move for a court order. Expenses are awarded in relation to the motion unless the court finds that opposition was substantially justified or that an award of expenses in unjust.[99] Counsel can request in an appropriate case that a deposition be taken before the statement is

---

[95] *In re* Doe, 662 F.2d 1073, 1079 (4th Cir. 1981), *cert. denied,* 455 U.S. 1000 (1982); *In re* Special September 1978 Grand Jury, 640 F.2d 49, 63 (7th Cir. 1980).

[96] United States v. AT&T, 642 F.2d 1285, 1299 (D.C. Cir. 1980); *see generally* 8.J. Wigmore, Evidence §§ 2327–28 (McNaughton rev. 1961).

[97] *See, e.g.*, Castle v. Sangamo Weston, Inc., 744 F.2d 1464, 1467 (11th Cir. 1984).

[98] *See, e.g., In re* Subpoenas Duces Tecum, 738 F.2d 1367, 1371–75 (D.C. Cir. 1984).

[99] Fed. R. Civ. P. 23(b)(3).

produced.[100] However, the court has no discretion to deny the request completely, although a denial may be harmless error if no prejudice is demonstrated.[101]

§ 18.17 —Refreshing Recollection with Protected Materials

It is often necessary or desirable to show protected documents to experts or other witnesses to refresh their recollection prior to testifying. Two common situations are (1) showing an expert protected information, such as legal analysis and (2) putting together preexisting documents for the witness to review. Although preexisting documents are not protected, the fact that the attorney has selected and ordered those documents, often culling them from a much larger universe, reflects counsel's mental impressions and legal opinions as to how the evidence in the documents relates to the issues involved in the litigation.[102]

Merely showing witness work product does not appear to waive the protection.[103] However, Rule 612 of the Federal Rules of Evidence provides that if a witness refreshes her memory before testifying, the court has discretion to require that the documents be produced if it determines that this is necessary in the interests of justice. Rule 612 does not specifically exempt privileged or otherwise protected documents from production if they have refreshed a witness's recollection. Therefore, some controversy exists concerning whether such documents should be subject to discovery.[104]

Waiver by refreshing recollection poses difficulties for counsel attempting to prepare a client for deposition. At deposition, one of the preliminary questions asked of every deponent is what documents were reviewed for purposes of testifying. If it is likely that showing documents to the deponent will result in their disclosure, counsel may forego sifting the documents or may not show the

---

[100] Miles v. M/V Mississippi Queen, 753 F.2d 1349, 1351 & n.3 (5th Cir. 1985); 4 J. Moore *et al.*, Moore's Federal Practice ¶ 26.65, at 26–397 (2d ed. 1984).

[101] Miles v. M/V Mississippi Queen, 753 F.2d 1349, 1352–53 (5th Cir. 1985).

[102] Sporck v. Peil, 759 F.2d 312, 315 (3d Cir.), *cert. denied,* ____ U.S. ____, 106 S. Ct. 232 (1985); James Julian, Inc. v. Raytheon Co., 93 F.R.D. 138, 144 (D. Del. 1982); Berkey Photo, Inc. v. Eastman Kodak Co., 74 F.R.D. 613, 616 (S.D.N.Y. 1977).

[103] Bogosian v. Gulf Oil Corp., 738 F.2d 587, 594 (3d Cir. 1984); United States v. AT&T, 642 F.2d 1285, 1299 (D.C. Cir. 1980); 3 J. Weinstein & M. Berger, Weinstein's Evidence ¶ 612[04] (1986).

[104] *See, e.g.,* 3 J. Weinstein & M. Berger, Weinstein's Evidence ¶ 612.[04] (1986); Davidson & Voth, *Waiver of the Attorney-Client Privilege,* 64 Or. L. Rev. 637, 657–66 (1986); Note, *Discovery of Attorney Work Product Reviewed by an Expert Witness,* 85 Colum. L. Rev. 812 (1985); Note, *Discovery Under the Federal Rules of Civil Procedure of Attorney Opinion Work Product Provided to an Expert Witness,* 53 Fordham L. Rev. 1159 (1985).

documents to the client, resulting in a less well-prepared deponent.[105] The Third Circuit has attempted to reconcile Rule 612 and Federal Rule of Evidence 26(b)(3) by limiting identification of documents chosen by counsel to those which result from opposing counsel's own selection of relevant questioning and the witness's subsequent admission that her answers were informed by documents reviewed.[106] In other words, counsel must identify the document to the deponent, rather than randomly fishing for documents which have been reviewed. As a prerequisite to revealing such work product, counsel must establish that the witness relied on the documents in testifying or that the documents influenced her testimony.[107] Similarly, the Third Circuit has protected materials prepared by attorneys which contained their legal theories and which were then used to help formulate an expert's opinions.[108] However, other courts have held that the use of privileged documents to refresh a witness's recollection waives the privilege on the theory that the cross-examiner is placed at an unfair disadvantage if the documents are not revealed.[109]

Unless this dispute has been resolved in the circuit where litigation is pending, the safest course is to sift through the documents in order to focus the issues but discuss their content generally with the party, rather than showing the witness any particular document. Of course, in some cases, proper preparation may require taking the risk of disclosure. Deponents should also be informed that any documents which are reviewed on their own will also be subject to disclosure at the discretion of the court if the documents actually refresh recollection.

§ 18.18 —Crime-Fraud Exception to Work Product

Work product can also be lost by application of the crime-fraud exception.[110] Some circuits even hold that the crime-fraud exception applies to opinion work product.[111] Other circuits protect the attorney's opinion work product from

---

[105] *See* Sporck v. Peil, 759 F.2d 312, 317 (3d Cir.), *cert. denied,* _____ U.S. _____, 106 S. Ct. 232 (1985).

[106] *Id.* at 318.

[107] *Id.*

[108] Bogosian v. Gulf Oil Corp., 738 F.2d 587, 595 (3d Cir. 1984).

[109] *See, e.g., In re* Comair Air Disaster Litig., 100 F.R.D. 350, 353 (E.D. Ky. 1983); James Julian, Inc. v. Raytheon Co., 93 F.R.D. 138, 145–46 (D. Del. 1982); Wheeling-Pittsburgh Steel Corp. v. Underwriters Laboratories, Inc., 81 F.R.D. 8, 10 (N.D. Ill. 1978); *see also* Berkey Photo, Inc. v. Eastman Kodak Co., 74 F.R.D. 613, 616 (S.D.N.Y. 1977) (prospective cases only).

[110] Craig v. A. H. Robins Co., 790 F.2d 1, 4 (1st Cir. 1986); *In re* International Sys. & Control Corp. Secs. Litig., 693 F.2d 1235, 1242 (5th Cir. 1982); *In re* John Doe Corp., 675 F.2d 482, 492 (2d Cir. 1982).

[111] *In re* Doe, 662 F.2d 1073, 1079 (4th Cir. 1981), *cert. denied,* 455 U.S. 1000 (1982); *In re* Sealed Case, 676 F.2d 793, 811 (D.C. Cir. 1982).

disclosure when the attorney is innocent of the client's fraud.[112] Similarly, work product can be vitiated by unethical conduct on the part of the attorney.[113] For example, when an attorney clandestinely recorded his conversations with witnesses without their consent, the immunity was deemed waived.[114] Indeed, this practice may be illegal in some states.[115] On the other hand, a witness has been permitted to be refreshed with an unethically obtained taped witness statement.[116] Of course, such conduct can result in counsel's being referred for disciplinary action.

§ 18.19 Fifth Amendment Considerations

The Fifth Amendment applies in civil cases whenever the answer might tend to subject the witness to criminal responsibility.[117] Securities fraud and antitrust actions are likely cases in which the privilege may be invoked, but it can also be claimed in any civil action in which liability is premised upon an act which constitutes an element of a crime or when questions to a witness would reveal evidence of a crime.[118] Because the privilege applies to pleadings and discovery as well as to trial,[119] counsel must be alert to any potential Fifth Amendment problems from the outset of litigation.

The privilege can be validly asserted whenever the witness has reasonable cause to fear danger from a direct answer.[120] The court will not speculate whether the witness will in fact be prosecuted[121] and has broad discretion in determining the merits of the claimed privilege.[122] It is still an open question

---

[112] *In re* Antitrust Grand Jury, 805 F.2d 155, 163–64 (6th Cir. 1986); *In re* Special September 1978 Grand Jury, 640 F.2d 49, 63 (7th Cir. 1980).

[113] *See* Moody v. I.R.S., 654 F.2d 795, 800 (D.C. Cir. 1981).

[114] Parrott v. Wilson, 707 F.2d 1262, 1270–72 (11th Cir.), *cert. denied,* 464 U.S. 936 (1983).

[115] *See, e.g.,* Cal. Penal Code § 632 (West. Supp. 1987), which applies to recording confidential communications without the consent of all parties.

[116] 20th Century Wear, Inc. v. Sanmark-Stardust Inc., 747 F.2d 81, 93 n.17 (2d Cir. 1984), *cert. denied,* 470 U.S. 1052 (1985).

[117] McCarthy v. Arndstein, 266 U.S. 34, 40 (1924).

[118] *See generally* Daskel, *Assertion of the Constitutional Privilege Against Self-Incrimination in Federal Civil Litigation: Rights and Remedies,* 64 Marq. L. Rev. 243 (1980); Heidt, *The Conjurer's Circle—The Fifth Amendment Privilege in Civil Cases,* 91 Yale L.J. 1062 (1982).

[119] *See, e.g.,* United States v. Kordel, 397 U.S. 1, 7 (1970) (interrogatory answers); National Acceptance Co. of Am. v. Bathalter, 705 F.2d 924, 927 (7th Cir. 1983) (pleadings).

[120] Hoffman v. United States, 341 U.S. 479, 486 (1951); *see* Kastigar v. United States, 406 U.S. 441, 444–45 (1972).

[121] United States v. Jones, 703 F.2d 473, 478 (10th Cir. 1983) and cases cited therein.

[122] United States v. Whittington, 786 F.2d 644, 646 (5th Cir. 1986).

whether the Fifth Amendment can be invoked to protect a witness from prosecution in a foreign country.[123] The threshold question regarding potential prosecution is whether the danger is real, rather than remote.[124] The answers alone need not support a conviction as long as they would furnish a link in the chain of evidence needed to prosecute the witness for a crime.[125] Blanket assertions of Fifth Amendment privilege are not appropriate unless the danger of self-incrimination is readily apparent, because the burden of proving that the danger exists lies on the claimant.[126]

A defendant's invocation of the privilege in response to allegations in the plaintiff's complaint is not deemed an admission of those allegations which entitles the plaintiff to judgment.[127] Similarly, most federal courts do not automatically dismiss a plaintiff's action for taking the Fifth Amendment in answer to discovery but do balance the interests of the parties.[128] A plaintiff or defendant often requests a stay of discovery as to the privileged information until any criminal proceedings are concluded.[129] Such decisions are within the trial court's discretion, because the law does not require postponement of civil discovery until fear of criminal prosecution is gone. Although the court can fashion a protective order concerning the privileged information, a party may not believe that this remedy effectively shields the information which is disclosed.[130] Parties invoking the privilege cannot use the Fifth Amendment to meet their burden of proof in civil proceedings.[131] However, in a taxpayer's refund action, the government was not permitted to obtain a dismissal based on the plaintiff's invocation of privilege when called as a hostile government

---

[123] *See* United States v. (Under Seal), 794 F.2d 920, 923–28 (4th Cir.), *stay of contempt granted sub nom.* Araneta v. United States, ______ U.S. ______, 107 S. Ct. 1, 2 (Burger, J.), *cert. denied,* ______ U.S. ______, 107 S. Ct. 331 (1986); *see also* Zicarelli v. New Jersey State Comm'n of Investigation, 406 U.S. 472, 478–81 (1972); *In re* Gilboe, 699 F.2d 71, 74 & n.2 (2d Cir. 1983).

[124] Zicarelli v. New Jersey State Comm'n of Investigation, 406 U.S. 472, 478–80 (1972); Mason v. United States, 244 U.S. 362, 365–67 (1917); *see* United States v. Joudis, 800 F.2d 159, 162 (7th Cir. 1986); *In re* Grand Jury Subpoena of Flanagan, 691 F.2d 116, 121 (2d Cir. 1982) (listing factors to be evaluated).

[125] Hoffman v. United States, 341 U.S. 479, 486 (1951).

[126] Steinbrecher v. Commissioner, 712 F.2d 195, 198 (5th Cir. 1983).

[127] National Acceptance Co. of Am. v. Bathalter, 705 F.2d 924, 932 (7th Cir. 1983); *see* Rogers v. Webster, 776 F.2d 607, 611 (6th Cir. 1985).

[128] *See, e.g.,* Black Panther Party v. Smith, 661 F.2d 1243, 1271–74 (D.C. Cir. 1981), *vacated as moot sub nom.* Moore v. Black Panther Party, 458 U.S. 1118 (1982); Wehling v. C.B.S., 608 F.2d 1084, 1088 (5th Cir. 1979); Campbell v. Gerrans, 592 F.2d 1054, 1058 (9th Cir. 1979) (applying balancing test); *see* Comment, *Plaintiff as Deponent: Invoking the Fifth Amendment,* 48 U. Chi. L. Rev. 158 (1981).

[129] See § **17.11**.

[130] *See, e.g.,* Mid-America's Process Serv. v. Ellison, 767 F.2d 684, 685–87 (10th Cir. 1985).

[131] *See* United States v. Rylander, 460 U.S. 752, 758 (1983); Hiley v. United States, 807 F.2d 623, 628 (7th Cir. 1986); Steinbrecher v. C.I.R., 712 F.2d 195, 198 (5th Cir. 1983).

witness.[132] If a party frustrates discovery by invoking the privilege and then elects to waive the privilege at trial to testify, opposing counsel should request that the court exclude the testimony. Even if the court denies the motion, it is likely to grant a request for a continuance to depose the witness.

The Fifth Amendment can be asserted in a variety of pretrial settings. For example, a party can refuse to answer interrogatories or requests for admissions based on the Fifth Amendment, or a corporate party's employees may refuse to provide the requested information on the basis of privilege.[133] Often a deponent will invoke the privilege. The Supreme Court has held that a civil deponent who has previously given immunized grand jury testimony can assert the Fifth Amendment in deposition when asked to confirm the previous testimony, as long as the deposition testimony is not also immunized.[134] As a practical matter, this can frustrate parties who wish to rely on the deponent's testimony but who are prohibited by evidentiary rules from introducing the previously immunized testimony at trial or in support of a summary judgment motion.[135] Similarly, documents of one party which are unauthenticated because the deponent invoked the privilege cannot be used at trial against another party without other evidence of authenticity.[136]

At best, parties who have been denied discovery on the basis of privilege can rely on the inference that the testimony subject to the privilege would be adverse to the witness, because the Fifth Amendment does not prohibit such inferences in civil actions.[137] Therefore, adverse inferences have been permitted when present and former employees took the Fifth Amendment.[138] However, a party cannot use the claim of privilege as a substitute for that individual's own relevant evidence.[139] A judge can exclude evidence that the privilege has been invoked on

---

[132] *See* Hiley v. United States, 807 F.2d 623, 628–29 (7th Cir. 1986).

[133] *See* Cooper, *Fifth Amendment Rights in Private Treble Damage Litigation,* 48 Antitrust L.J. 1381, 1392–95 (1979).

[134] Pillsbury Co. v. Conboy, 459 U.S. 248, 256–57 (1983).

[135] *See, e.g.,* Pillsbury Co. v. Conboy, 459 U.S. 248, 259 n.17 (1983) (citing Fed. R. Evid. 804(b)(1)); *In re* Corrugated Container Antitrust Litig., 756 F.2d 411, 414–16 (5th Cir. 1985) (immunized interview notes not permitted substantively or for impeachment of witness at trial).

[136] *See* Mayer v. Angelica, 790 F.2d 1315, 1340 (7th Cir. 1986).

[137] Baxter v. Palmigiano, 425 U.S. 308, 318 (1976); Pagel, Inc. v. SEC, 803 F.2d 942, 946–47 (8th Cir. 1986).

[138] RAD Servs., Inc. v. Aetna Casualty & Sur. Co., 808 F.2d 271, 275–77 (3d Cir. 1986); Rosebud Sioux Tribe v. A&P Steel, Inc., 733 F.2d 509, 520–21 (8th Cir.), *cert. denied,* 469 U.S. 1072 (1984); Brink's Inc. v. City of New York, 717 F.2d 700, 707–10 (2d Cir. 1983); *see* Heidt, *The Conjurer's Circle: The Fifth Amendment Privilege in Civil Cases,* 91 Yale L.J. 1062, 1119–22 (1982).

[139] United States v. Rylander, 460 U.S. 752, 761 (1983); *In re* Bevill, Bresler & Schulman Asset Mgmt. Corp., 805 F.2d 120, 126 (3d Cir. 1986).

the grounds of undue prejudice.[140] As a practical matter, the party who must rely on an adverse inference to meet its burden of proof on an issue may lose even if the factfinder is informed about the consequences of asserting the privilege.[141]

§ 18.20 —Obtaining Incriminating Documents

Ordinarily, the self-incrimination privilege does not protect business records.[142] Because preparation of business records is voluntary, no compulsion is present that would accord a Fifth Amendment privilege to their contents.[143] Therefore, taxpayers can be compelled by subpoena to produce their accountant's workpapers or the taxpayer's records in the accountant's possession.[144] Similarly, tape recordings concerning sales taxes have been found unprivileged.[145] Courts vary as to whether incriminating personal records are protected.[146]

Documents required to be kept by law are also unprivileged.[147] This category encompasses records that the government requires pursuant to its regulatory function which contain information that the regulated party would ordinarily keep and which have assumed public aspects.

---

[140] *See, e.g.*, Farace v. Independent Fire Ins. Co., 699 F.2d 204, 211 (5th Cir. 1983).

[141] *See, e.g.*, United States v. Huckaby, 776 F.2d 564, 568–70 (5th Cir.), *cert. denied*, ____ U.S. ____, 106 S. Ct. 1468 (1986) (judge in IRS subpoena enforcement action); *In re* Corrugated Container Antitrust Litig., 756 F.2d 411, 415–16 (5th Cir. 1985) (jury).

[142] United States v. Doe, 465 U.S. 605, 610 (1984); Fisher v. United States, 425 U.S. 391, 401 (1976); *see* United States v. Black, 767 F.2d 1334, 1340 (9th Cir.), *cert. denied*, ____ U.S. ____, 106 S. Ct. 574 (1985); *see generally* Alioto, *Documents and the Privilege Against Self-Incrimination*, 48 U. Pitt. L. Rev. 27 (1986); Note, *Abolition of Fifth Amendment Protection for the Content of Preexisting Documents: United States v. Doe*, 38 Sw. L.J. 1023 (1984).

[143] United States v. Doe, 465 U.S. 605, 610 (1984).

[144] Fisher v. United States, 425 U.S. 391, 409–10 (1976) (accountant's papers); United States v. Doe, 465 U.S. 605, 610–12 (1984) (own tax records).

[145] *In re* Proceedings Before the Aug. 6, 1984 Grand Jury, 767 F.2d 39, 41 (2d Cir. 1985).

[146] *Compare* United States v. (Under Seal), 745 F.2d 834, 839–40 (4th Cir. 1984), *vacated as moot*, 471 U.S. 1001 (1985); *and* United States v. Davis, 636 F.2d 1028, 1043 (5th Cir.), *cert. denied*, 454 U.S. 862 (1981) (recognizing privilege) *with In re* Grand Jury Proceedings, 626 F.2d 1051, 1054 (1st Cir. 1980) (no protection for personal business records); *see also* Cramer, *Back For the Brink: Boyd's Private Papers Protection and the Sole Proprietor's Business Records*, 21 Am. Bus. L.J. 367 (1984); Note, *On Claiming the Fifth Amendment For Mixed Purpose Documents: The Problem of Categorizing Documents as Personal or Corporate In a Business Setting*, 17 U.S.F. L. Rev. 333 (1983).

[147] *See* Grosso v. United States, 390 U.S. 62, 67–68 (1968); Shapiro v. United States, 335 U.S. 1, 32–33 (1948); *see generally* Saltzburg, *The Required Records Doctrine: Its Lessons for the Privilege Against Self-Incrimination*, 53 U. Chi. L. Rev. 6 (1986).

§ 18.21 —Collective Entity and Act of Production Doctrines

The collective entity doctrine prohibits an individual from invoking the privilege against self-incrimination with respect to records of an organization or collective entity, even though the records might be personally incriminating.[148] Corporations which are essentially one-person operations cannot invoke the Fifth Amendment to protect the content of corporate records which incriminate the sole shareholder.[149] A law firm prior to its incorporation has been considered as a collective entity rather than as a solo practice.[150]

Although the contents of the requested records are unprivileged, the act of producing them may be sufficiently testimonial to be privileged. In *United States v. Doe,*[151] the Supreme Court held that a sole proprietor could not be compelled to produce records when the act of production would have involved compelled admissions that the documents existed, were in the proprietor's possession, and were authentic.[152] In other words, a subpoena for unprivileged records of a sole proprietorship cannot be enforced if the production would be incriminatory.[153] Similarly, the refusal of a lawyer in sole practice to produce personal business records in her possession was considered a proper invocation of the privilege when the documents could have constituted incriminatory testimonial acts.[154] However, a subpoena directed to the bookkeeper of a sole proprietor has been upheld.[155] Several circuits have held that no Fifth Amendment protection exists for producing required records.[156]

Whether the collective entity doctrine survives if the act of production is incriminating is an open issue.[157] The Third Circuit permitted a sole stockholder

---

[148] Bellis v. United States, 417 U.S. 85, 88–89 (1974) (law partnership); Curcio v. United States, 354 U.S. 118, 122 (1957) (labor union); Wilson v. United States, 221 U.S. 361, 374–76 (1911) (corporate records).

[149] *In re* Grand Jury Matter (Brown), 768 F.2d 525, 529 (3d Cir. 1985) (en banc); *In re* Two Grand Jury Subpoenae Duces Tecum, 769 F.2d 52, 57 (2d Cir. 1985); *In re* Grand Jury Proceedings (Manges), 745 F.2d 1250, 1251 (9th Cir. 1984).

[150] *In re* Two Grand Jury Subpoenae Duces Tecum Dated August 21, 1985, 793 F.2d 69, 72 (2d Cir. 1986).

[151] 465 U.S. 605 (1984).

[152] *Id.* at 612–13, 617.

[153] *Id.*

[154] *In re* Kave, 760 F.2d 343, 358 (1st Cir. 1985).

[155] *In re* Grand Jury Proceedings (Manges), 745 F.2d 1250, 1252 (9th Cir. 1984).

[156] *In re* Grand Jury Proceedings, 801 F.2d 1164, 1169 (9th Cir. 1986); *In re* Two Grand Jury Subpoenae Duces Tecum Dated August 21, 1985, 793 F.2d 69, 73 (2d Cir. 1986); *In re* Grand Jury Subpoena Duces Tecum (Underhill), 781 F.2d 64, 69–70 (6th Cir.), *cert denied,* ____ U.S. ____, 107 S. Ct. 64 (1986).

[157] *See generally* Webb & Ferguson, *United States v. Doe: The Supreme Court and the Fifth Amendment and Production of Documents After United States v. Doe,* 66 Boston U.L. Rev. 95

of a professional corporation to assert the privilege when faced with a subpoena requiring him to authenticate the corporation's records.[158] On the other hand, most circuits have upheld production of partnership and corporate records, including records of sole shareholders, on the theory that the custodian is acting only in a representational capacity and that, therefore, the act of production is not testimonial.[159] A few circuits have attempted to find a middle ground in which unusual circumstances may permit a corporate custodian to assert the privilege because the individual compelled to produce and authenticate the records would incriminate himself by such disclosure.[160]

If the act of production is considered testimonial, the government can obtain the production by granting use immunity[161] to the individual producing the documents.[162] The court cannot prohibit the production of records produced under a grant of immunity on the theory that the act of production would convey information not already known to the government, because the scope of immunity is a question for subsequent suppression hearings.[163] While a private litigant cannot force an individual to authenticate the records in violation of the privilege, a corporation may be required to designate a person to produce the documents who will not invoke the privilege, even if this involves going outside the corporate structure to appoint a special agent to perform that task.[164]

(1986); Comment, *Fifth Amendment Privilege and Compelled Production of Corporate Papers After Fisher and Doe,* 54 Fordham L. Rev. 935 (1986); Note, *Fifth Amendment Privilege For Producing Corporate Documents,* 84 Mich. L. Rev. 1544 (1986); Note, *Organizational Papers and the Privilege Against Self-Incrimination,* 99 Harv. L. Rev. 640 (1986); Comment, *United States v. Doe and Its Progeny: A Reevaluation of the Fifth Amendment's Application to Custodians of Corporate Records,* 40 U. Miami L. Rev. 793 (1985).

[158] *In re* Grand Jury Matter (Brown), 768 F.2d 525, 529 (3d Cir. 1985) (en banc); *see* Comment, *Corporation Law: The Fifth Amendment Privilege and the Corporate Custodian: In Re Grand Jury Matter (Brown),* 11 J. Corp. Law 295 (1986).

[159] *In re* Grand Jury Subpoena Duces Tecum, 795 F.2d 904, 907 (11th Cir. 1986); *In re* Grand Jury Subpoena, 784 F.2d 857, 861–62 (8th Cir. 1986); *In re* Grand Jury Proceedings (Morganstern), 771 F.2d 143, 148 (6th Cir.) (en banc), *cert. denied,* ____ U.S. ____, 106 S. Ct. 594 (1985); *In re* Grand Jury Subpoena (Lincoln), 767 F.2d 1130, 1131 (5th Cir. 1985); United States v. Malis, 737 F.2d 1511, 1512 (9th Cir. 1984); *In re* Grand Jury Proceedings (Vargas), 727 F.2d 941, 946 (10th Cir.), *cert. denied,* 469 U.S. 819 (1984).

[160] United States v. Lang, 792 F.2d 1235, 1240–42 (4th Cir. 1986), *cert. denied,* ____ U.S. ____, 107 S. Ct. 574 (1986); *In re* Two Grand Jury Subpoenae Duces Tecum, 769 F.2d 52, 57 (2d Cir. 1985).

[161] 18 U.S.C. §§ 6002, 6003 (1982).

[162] United States v. Doe, 465 U.S. 605, 614–15 (1984).

[163] *In re* Sealed Case, 791 F.2d 179, 181 (D.C. Cir. 1986). *But see* United States v. Porter, 711 F.2d 1397, 1404 (7th Cir. 1983).

[164] United States v. Sancetta, 788 F.2d 67, 74 (2d Cir. 1986).

§ 18.22 Other Federal Privileges

Some courts have recognized a qualified privilege for self-critical analyses.[165] The existence of this privilege may become an issue when peer reviews or affirmative action plans are involved in the litigation. It is often invoked in Title VII litigation when the basis for an adverse tenure decision is alleged to be discrimination.[166] The circuits are split as to whether to recognize a qualified academic freedom privilege.[167] Where recognized, discovery of tenure votes and discussions is usually permitted only in the absence of a contemporary statement of reasons for the committee's actions or upon a showing of particularized need.[168]

The government has several privileges which apply in civil as well as criminal cases, including a privilege to suppress classified information,[169] a qualified informer's privilege, which protects the identity of people who aid law enforcement officers,[170] and a qualified official information privilege, which includes intragovernmental memoranda containing policymaking recommendations[171] as well as law enforcement investigatory files.[172] Congress has also enacted laws prohibiting the disclosure of various records, including certain types of accident reports[173] and information provided to governmental agencies.[174]

---

[165] *See, e.g.,* Coates v. Johnson & Johnson, 756 F.2d 524, 551 (7th Cir. 1985); *see generally* Flanagan, *Rejecting a General Privilege for Self-Critical Analyses,* 51 Geo. Wash. L. Rev. 551 (1983); Note, *The Privilege of Self-Critical Analysis,* 96 Harv. L. Rev. 1083 (1983).

[166] *See, e.g.,* Note, *The Self-Critical Analysis Privilege and Discovery of Affirmative Action Plans in Title VII Suits,* 83 Mich. L. Rev. 405 (1984).

[167] *Compare* EEOC v. University of Notre Dame Du Lac, 715 F.2d 331, 337–38 (7th Cir. 1983) (qualified privilege) *and* Gray v. Board of Higher Educ., 692 F.2d 901, 904–05 (2d Cir. 1982) (balancing test) *with* EEOC v. Franklin & Marshall College, 775 F.2d 110, 113–17 (3d Cir. 1985), *cert. denied,* ____ U.S. ____, 106 S. Ct. 2288 (1986) *and In re* Dinnan, 661 F.2d 426, 427 (5th Cir. 1981), *cert. denied,* 457 U.S. 1106 (1982) (rejecting privilege).

[168] *See* EEOC v. University of Norte Dame Du Lac, 715 F.2d 331, 337–38 (7th Cir. 1983); Gray v. Board of Higher Educ., 692 F.2d 901, 904–05 (2d Cir. 1982); Lynn v. Regents of Univ. of Cal., 656 F.2d 1337, 1347–49 (9th Cir. 1981), *cert. denied,* 459 U.S. 823 (1982).

[169] Classified Information Procedures Act, 18 U.S.C. App. (1982); United States v. Reynolds, 345 U.S. 1, 7–8 (1953); *see* Fitzgerald v. Penthouse Int'l, Ltd., 776 F.2d 1236, 1239–43 (4th Cir. 1985) (case dismissed when privileged materials were vital to suit); Northrop Corp. v. McDonnell Douglas Corp., 751 F.2d 395, 399 (D.C. Cir. 1984) (case remanded for proceedings without privileged matter).

[170] Roviaro v. United States, 353 U.S. 53, 59–60 (1957); *see* Brock v. On Shore Quality Control Specialists, Inc., 811 F.2d 282, 283 (5th Cir. 1987) (*Roviaro* applies in civil cases).

[171] Association for Reduction of Violence v. Hall, 734 F.2d 63, 66 (1st Cir. 1984); *see* United States v. Morgan, 313 U.S. 409, 422 (1941); *see generally* Note, *Discovery of Government Documents and the Official Information Privilege,* 76 Colum. L. Rev. 142 (1976).

[172] Association for Reduction of Violence v. Hall, 734 F.2d 63, 65–66 (1st Cir. 1984).

[173] *See, e.g.,* 45 U.S.C. § 41 (1982) (railroad).

[174] *See, e.g.,* 35 U.S.C. § 122 (1982) (patent applications).

The marital privileges which enable one spouse to refuse to testify against the other spouse[175] and both spouses to prohibit disclosure of confidential communications made during the marriage[176] are more significant in criminal than civil cases in federal court. A qualified news reporting privilege[177] as well as a qualified tax return privilege[178] have been recognized by several circuits. Because no doctor-patient or psychiatrist-patient privilege existed at common law, most courts have concluded that none exists in federal law.[179] The Noerr-Pennington doctrine, which provides an affirmative defense exempting any petitioning activity designed to influence legislative bodies or governmental agencies from antitrust liability, does not provide any privilege which bars discovery of such evidence.[180] Similarly, no privilege from discovery exists for documents which are otherwise protected by the Privacy Act, although a protective order may be appropriate concerning such information in a given case.[181]

---

[175] Trammel v. United States, 445 U.S. 40, 53 (1980).

[176] *See, e.g.,* Pereira v. United States, 347 U.S. 1, 6 (1954); *In re* Witness Before Grand Jury, 791 F.2d 234, 237–39 (2d Cir. 1986); United States v. Koehler, 790 F.2d 1256, 1258 (5th Cir. 1986); *In re* Grand Jury Investigation, 603 F.2d 786 (9th Cir. 1979).

[177] *See, e.g., In re* Selcraig, 705 F.2d 789, 792 (5th Cir. 1983).

[178] *See generally* Note, *Discovery of Federal Income Tax Returns and the New "Qualified" Privileges,* 1984 Duke L.J. 938.

[179] *In re* Doe, 711 F.2d 1187, 1193 (2d Cir. 1983) and cases cited therein. *But see In re* Zuniga, 714 F.2d 632, 639 (6th Cir.), *cert. denied,* 464 U.S. 983 (1983) (recognizing psychotherapist-patient privilege); *see generally* Note, *The Case for A Federal Psychotherapist-Patient Privilege That Protects Patient Identity,* 1985 Duke L.J. 1217; Recent Decisions, *Evidence Law-The Psychotherapist-Patient Privilege in Federal Courts,* 59 Notre Dame L. Rev. 791 (1984).

[180] North Carolina Elec. Membership Corp. v. Carolina Power & Light Co., 666 F.2d 50, 52–53 (4th Cir. 1981).

[181] Laxalt v. McClatchy, 809 F.2d 885, 888–90 (D.C. Cir. 1987); Weahkee v. Norton, 621 F.2d 1080, 1082 (10th Cir. 1980); *see* Perry v. State Farm Fire & Casualty Co., 734 F.2d 1441, 1447 (11th Cir. 1984), *cert. denied,* 469 U.S. 1108 (1985).

CHAPTER 19

PROTECTIVE ORDERS AND OTHER LIMITATIONS ON DISCOVERY

§ 19.1 Other Limitations on Discovery

Besides privilege, other limitations on discovery can prevent the disclosure of relevant information. Although boundaries of permissible discovery are hard to define, they do exist. The federal rules have several provisions which provide relief from excessive, unwarranted, or unduly embarrassing discovery. Protective orders are probably the best known and most employed method for obtaining discovery relief. A Rule 26(c) protective order is designed to shield a party or deponent from annoyance, embarrassment, oppression, or undue burden or expense. However, it is not the only provision controlling discovery. For example, Rules 16, 26(b)(1), and 26(f) should not be overlooked when counsel wishes to restrict discovery.

Rule 26(b)(1) provides that the frequency or extent of use of discovery shall be limited in the following circumstances: (1) if the discovery is unreasonably cumulative or duplicative or is obtainable from some other source that is more convenient, less burdensome, or less expensive; (2) if the party has already had ample opportunity to obtain the information by discovery in the action; or (3) the discovery is unduly burdensome or expensive, taking into account the needs of the case, the amount in controversy, limitations on the parties' resources, and the importance of the issues at stake in the litigation. The court can impose such discovery limitations on its own initiative after reasonable notice or pursuant to a motion for a protective order under Rule 26(c).

Rule 16 mandates that the court shall enter a scheduling order within 120 days after filing the complaint, which limits the time for joinder, motions, and completing discovery.[1] Although this order can be changed upon a showing of good cause, it requires counsel to analyze the case quite early to determine the realistic extent of discovery. Often, local rules require early meetings between counsel to formulate a joint timetable. If so, this opportunity should be used to incorporate counsel's own discovery plan[2] in a court-approved order.

In addition, Rule 26(f) provides for a discovery conference on the court's own direction or upon a noticed motion. This rule initially adopted in 1980 is not often used. First, the 1983 changes to Rule 16 essentially provide the same relief by requiring that a schedule order concerning all phases of the action including discovery be entered as a matter of course. Second, the requirements are fairly demanding, and the rule allows relief to be deferred until the pretrial conference authorized by Rule 16. A party who moves for a Rule 26(f) discovery conference must include: (1) a statement of the issues, (2) a proposed plan and schedule of discovery, (3) any proposed limitations to discovery, (4) any other proposed discovery orders, and (5) a statement showing that the attorney has made a reasonable effort to reach agreement with opposing attorneys as to the indicated matters. Responses are due within 10 days after service of the motion.

The parties and their attorneys have a duty to participate in drafting a Rule 26(f) discovery plan in good faith. If a party or attorney fails to participate in good faith in framing the plan, the court may, after a hearing, require such party or attorney to pay to any other party the reasonable expenses, including attorneys' fees, caused by the failure.[3] After the discovery conference, the court enters an order identifying the issues for discovery, establishing a plan and schedule for discovery, setting any limitations on discovery and determining any additional matters necessary for the proper management of discovery including allocation of expenses. The order may be changed whenever justice so requires.

§ 19.2 Use of Protective Orders

Whenever litigation could result in the disclosure of information which is sensitive or embarrassing, counsel should consider obtaining a protective order to limit inappropriate discovery and ensure that information which is divulged will not be misused. Whether or not the protective order can be negotiated with the adverse party or must meet the requirements of Rule 26(c) depends on the

---

[1] See § **16.2**.

[2] See § **17.2**.

[3] Fed. R. Civ. P. 37(g).

nature of the litigation. For example, protective orders are usually sought by corporations which fear that sensitive information will be disclosed to competitors. In business litigation, when both sides have something to lose, such orders are routinely negotiated. However, protective orders normally serve no useful purpose to individual plaintiffs who are suing large corporations for personal injuries based on negligence, strict liability, or fraud. In fact, restrictions on the exchange of such discovery with other federal or state plaintiffs in related litigation matters are viewed as a hindrance to the appropriate dispositions of these cases,[4] since they interfere with the formation of attorneys' information exchange groups to share discovery.[5] Therefore, in mass disaster cases, products liability cases, and security frauds litigation, it is likely that the party opposing open access to discovery materials will have to move for a protective order.

Similarly, a motion for protective order may be sought by the defendant in diversity actions which allege punitive damages. Although such a prayer technically entitles the plaintiff to information concerning the wealth of the individual or corporate defendant, the court has the power to delay that discovery until after motions going to the merits of the claim as well as to issue a protective order either limiting discovery until some requisite showing is made as to the appropriateness of punitive damages or limiting the persons to whom such information can be divulged.[6] Indeed, if the applicable state law limits discovery of punitive damage information,[7] it can be argued that such restrictions are substantive rather than procedural and therefore govern the action.

§ 19.3 Requirements for Obtaining a Protective Order

Rule 26(c) provides that a party or other person from whom discovery is sought can obtain a protective order if good cause is shown that the discovery will result in annoyance, embarrassment, oppression, or undue burden or expense. Nonparties as well as parties can obtain protective orders.[8] The motion is presented to the court in which the action is pending or, alternatively, on matters relating to a deposition, the court in the district where the deposition is to be taken.

---

[4] *See, e.g.*, Cohen, *Protective Orders: Manufacturers Hide Behind Them,* 22 Trial 34 (Aug. 1986); Durst, *Confidentiality Agreements—Plaintiffs' Counsel Should Resist Them,* 20 Trial 46 (Sept. 1984); *see generally* Note, *Mass Products Liability Litigation: A Proposal for Dissemination of Discovered Material Covered by a Protective Order,* 60 N.Y.U. L. Rev. 1137 (1985).

[5] *See, e.g.*, Marcus, *Myth and Reality in Protective Order Litigation,* 69 Cornell L. Rev. 1, 42 (1983). The Association of Trial Lawyers of America sponsors many such exchanges.

[6] *See generally* Woodbury, *Limiting Discovery of a Defendant's Wealth When Punitive Damages Are Alleged,* 23 Duquesne L. Rev. 349 (1985).

[7] *See, e.g.*, Cal. Civ. Code § 3295 (West Supp. 1987).

[8] Fed. R. Civ. P. 26(c), 45(b); *see, e.g., In re* Coordinated Pretrial Proceedings in Petroleum Prods. Antitrust Litig., 669 F.2d 620, 623–24 (10th Cir. 1982).

The burden is on the party seeking a protective order to show good cause.[9] Although good cause has no precise definition, courts often balance the interests alleged when determining the appropriateness of a protective order.[10] Broad allegations of harm or conclusory statements do not provide the specific demonstration of fact necessary to support a finding of good cause.[11] Therefore, a business must show with specificity that any embarrassment resulting from dissemination of the discovery would cause a significant harm to its competitive and financial position.[12] Excessive cost has supplied good cause when computerized information was indexed in such a way that the requested material could only be retrieved by hand, was not vital to the case, and an adequate substitute for the requested discovery existed.[13] On the other hand, good cause is not shown by arguing that the disclosure of information will be detrimental to the party's position in parallel lawsuits, because cooperation between state and federal parties promotes the speedy and inexpensive determination of the actions.[14]

Ordinarily a protective order must be obtained before the requested discovery is due.[15] Therefore, a party cannot contest the imposition of sanctions based on the objectional nature of the discovery without previously objecting or moving for a protective order.[16] It may be prudent to seek a protective order concerning the scope of discovery whenever a question about interpretation of a court order is present.[17]

§ 19.4 First Amendment and Privacy Concerns

In *Seattle Times Co. v. Rhinehart,*[18] the Supreme Court found that the First Amendment does not provide the right of public access to discovery materials not used at trial.[19] Most courts have interpreted *Seattle Times* as holding that

---

[9] Cipollone v. Liggett Group, Inc., 785 F.2d 1108, 1121 (3d Cir. 1986); Penthouse Int'l, Ltd. v. Playboy Enters., Inc., 663 F.2d 371, 391 (2d Cir. 1981); General Dynamics Corp. v. Selb Mfg. Co., 481 F.2d 1204, 1212 (8th Cir. 1973), *cert. denied,* 414 U.S. 1162 (1974).

[10] Farnsworth v. Procter & Gamble Co., 758 F.2d 1545, 1547 (11th Cir. 1985); Dow Chem. Co. v. Allen, 672 F.2d 1262, 1268–70 (7th Cir. 1982).

[11] Cipollone v. Liggett Group, Inc., 785 F.2d 1108, 1121 (3d Cir. 1986); United States v. Garrett, 571 F.2d 1323, 1326 n.3 (5th Cir. 1978).

[12] Cipollone v. Liggett Group, Inc., 785 F.2d 1108, 1121 (3d Cir. 1986).

[13] *See, e.g.,* Munoz-Santana v. INS, 742 F.2d 561, 563 (9th Cir. 1984).

[14] United States v. Hooker Chem. & Plastics Corp., 90 F.R.D. 421, 426 (W.D.N.Y. 1981).

[15] *See, e.g.,* United States v. IBM Corp., 79 F.R.D. 412, 414 (S.D.N.Y. 1978).

[16] Fed. R. Civ. P. 37(d); 8 C. Wright & A. Miller, Federal Practice and Procedure § 2291 (1970) [hereinafter Federal Practice and Procedure].

[17] *See, e.g.,* Fjelstad v. American Honda Motor Co., 762 F.2d 1334, 1343 (9th Cir. 1985).

[18] 467 U.S. 20 (1984).

[19] *Id.* at 31 (1984).

protective orders in civil discovery require no first amendment analysis.[20] Similarly, no public right of access exists to obtain materials filed in connection with discovery proceedings[21] or summary judgment motions which have been denied.[22] However, access has been granted when the pretrial motion in question was dispositive of the litigation.[23] The Third Circuit considers that a presumption of access exists concerning settlement agreements.[24]

Courts sometimes provide limited discovery such as ordering files redacted to remove names of individuals to protect their privacy interests[25] or restricting disclosure of confidential material to an impartial third party or expert, paid by the party seeking discovery. If records have been sealed at a litigant's request, the use of such information in a business context justifies the trial court's modification of its sealing order.[26]

§ 19.5 Types of Discovery Limitations

Rule 26(c) provides the court with a variety of options in granting the motion for a protective order. It can (1) prohibit the discovery, (2) limit it to specified terms and conditions, including designated time or place, (3) provide an alternate method of discovery, (4) limit the matters subject to discovery, (5) limit the persons present at the discovery, (6) require that a deposition be sealed, (7) provide that a trade secret or other confidential information not be disclosed or disclosed in a designated way, or (8) require that the parties simultaneously file sealed documents or information.

---

[20] Cipollone v. Liggett Group, Inc., 785 F.2d 1108, 1119 (3d Cir. 1986); Worrell Newspapers of Ind., Inc. v. Westhafer, 739 F.2d 1219, 1223–34 n.4 (7th Cir. 1984), *aff'd on other grounds,* 469 U.S. 1200 (1985); Tavoulareas v. Washington Post Co., 737 F.2d 1170, 1172–73 (D.C. Cir. 1984) (en banc); *cf.* Anderson v. Cryovac, Inc., 805 F.2d 1, 7 (1st Cir. 1986) (first amendment test is good cause inquiry). *But see* Note, *Access to Pretrial Documents Under the First Amendment,* 84 Colum. L. Rev. 1813 (1984); Note, *Protective Order and Commercial Information—Is Good Cause Good Enough?,* 59 St. John's L. Rev. 103 (1984).

[21] Anderson v. Cryovac, Inc., 805 F.2d 1, 10–13 (1st Cir. 1986); *see generally*, Recent Development, *Public Access to Civil Court Records: A Common Law Approach,* 39 Vand. L. Rev. 1465 (1986).

[22] *In re* Reporters Comm. for Freedom of the Press, 773 F.2d 1325, 1338 (D.C. Cir. 1985) (summary judgment denial). *But see* Zenith Radio Corp. v. Matsushita Elec. Indus. Co., 529 F. Supp. 866, 905–15 (E.D. Pa. 1981) (access granted re successful summary judgment motion decided pre-*Rhinehart*).

[23] *See In re* Continental Ill. Secs. Litig., 732 F.2d 1302, 1308–10 (7th Cir. 1984); Joy v. North, 692 F.2d 880, 893 (2d Cir. 1982), *cert. denied,* 460 U.S. 1051 (1983).

[24] Bank of Am. Nat'l Trust & Sav. Ass'n v. Hotel Rittenhouse Assocs., 800 F.2d 339, 346 (3d Cir. 1986).

[25] *See, e.g.,* Farnsworth v. Procter & Gamble Co., 758 F.2d 1545, 1547 (11th Cir. 1985); EEOC v. University of Notre Dame Du Lac, 715 F.2d 331, 337–38 (7th Cir. 1983); Krause v. Rhodes, 671 F.2d 212, 216–19 (6th Cir.), *cert. denied,* 459 U.S. 823 (1982).

[26] *See* Federal Sav. & Loan Ins. Corp. v. Blain, 808 F.2d 395, 400 (5th Cir. 1987) (injunction).

Protective orders can be issued in a multitude of situations. A protective order can require that a nonparty be reimbursed for the costs of producing documents.[27] However, if a subpoena is directed at a party in the same or related proceedings, courts usually decline to shift costs.[28] Obtaining a protective order is the only way to exclude a party or an expert associated with a party from attending a deposition.[29] Protective orders are commonly granted to permit defendants to be deposed at their principal place of business rather than at the location noticed by the plaintiff.[30] Such requests are usually denied only if the defendant has brought a permissive counterclaim.[31] Protective orders can be requested to stay discovery pending the outcome of transfer motions,[32] forum non conveniens motions,[33] or motions which would be depositive.[34] In class actions, discovery is often initially limited to class certification issues, but in appropriate cases, it can be restricted to individual claims.[35] Similarly, discovery of sensitive information can be delayed until after the production of nonsensitive items or until it has been reviewed in camera by the court and redacted.[36] As a practical matter, courts rarely grant orders entirely prohibiting the requested discovery[37] but frequently place conditions upon its disclosure.

Protective orders can be sought to prevent the deposition of counsel, although the more common approach is to attend the deposition and invoke attorney-client privilege or work product immunity when relevant to individual questions. However, since depositions of opposing counsel have become increasingly popular as an abusive discovery tactic, the Eighth Circuit has severely limited their use.[38] A protective order would be appropriate under the Eight Circuit standard unless the party seeking to take the deposition shows that (1) no other means exist to obtain the information than to depose opposing counsel, (2) the information sought is relevant and nonprivileged, and (3) the information is

---

[27] Fed. R. Civ. P. 45(b); *see, e.g., In re* Coordinated Pretrial Proceedings in Petroleum Prods. Antitrust Litig., 669 F.2d 620, 623–24 (10th Cir. 1982).

[28] *See, e.g.,* Oppenheimer Fund, Inc. v. Sanders, 437 U.S. 340, 358 (1978).

[29] *See, e.g.,* Galella v. Onassis, 487 F.2d 986, 997 (2d Cir. 1973).

[30] *See* 8 Federal Practice and Procedure § 2112; 4 J. Moore *et al.,* Moore's Federal Practice ¶ 26.70[1–3] (2d ed. 1984).

[31] *See* Zuckert v. Berkliff Corp., 96 F.R.D. 161, 162–63 (N.D. Ill. E.D. 1982).

[32] *See, e.g.,* McDonnell Douglas Corp. v. Polin, 429 F.2d 30, 30–31 (3d Cir. 1970).

[33] *See, e.g.,* Transunion Corp. v. Pepsico, Inc., 811 F.2d 127, 130 (2d Cir. 1987).

[34] *See, e.g.,* Harlow v. Fitzgerald, 457 U.S. 800 (1982) (no discovery until immunity question is resolved).

[35] *See* Ardrey v. United Parcel Serv., 798 F.2d 679, 684–85 (4th Cir. 1986).

[36] *See, e.g.,* Marrese v. American Academy of Orthopedic Surgeons, 726 F.2d 1150, 1160–61 (7th Cir. 1984) (en banc), *rev'd on other grounds,* 470 U.S. 373 (1985); *cf. In re* Iowa Freedom of Information Council, 724 F.2d 658, 660 (8th Cir. 1984) (procedure for in camera review re potential disclosure of trade secrets at hearing).

[37] *See, e.g.,* Salter v. Upjohn Co., 593 F.2d 649, 651 (5th Cir. 1979) (deposition).

[38] Shelton v. American Motors Corp., 805 F.2d 1323, 1327 (8th Cir. 1986).

crucial to the preparation of the case.[39] Undoubtedly, counsel in other circuits will attempt to obtain the same protection.

A significant amount of protective order litigation concerns trade secrets. Trade secrets and similar confidential business information do not have any absolute privilege from discovery.[40] If the movant shows that the information is a trade secret the disclosure of which would be harmful, the burden shifts to the party seeking discovery to show that such discovery is relevant and necessary.[41] If the burden is met, the discovery will be granted under an appropriate protective order. Courts applying a strict view of trade secrets consider the following factors in determining whether to restrict discovery: (1) the extent to which the information is known outside the business, (2) the extent to which it is known by employees and others involved in the business, (3) the extent of measures taken to guard the secrecy of the information, (4) the value of the information to the business or its competitors, (5) the amount of effort or money expended in developing the information, and (6) the ease or difficulty of duplicating or properly acquiring the information.[42] Customer lists and marketing plans can be protected as trade secrets.

Although umbrella protective orders which cover all information produced in discovery are viewed with distrust because the movant must demonstrate its right to protection, they have been approved in complex litigation.[43] In such cases, all documents designated in good faith as confidential are protected until the opposing party objects to individual documents. At that point, the burden is on the movant to show that the documents are confidential.[44] Protective orders are frowned upon when they unnecessarily limit discovery in Title VII cases.[45] However, the district court has discretion to restrict the E.E.O.C.'s use of discovery to the private litigation in which it has intervened.[46] Protective orders which forbid counsel to reveal information to clients or otherwise intrude on the attorney-client relationship are also disfavored.[47]

---

[39] *Id.*

[40] Federal Open Market Comm. of the Fed. Reserve Sys. v. Merrill, 443 U.S. 340, 362 (1979) (trade secrets); Penthouse Int'l, Ltd. v. Playboy Enters., Inc., 663 F.2d 371, 391 (2d Cir. 1981) (confidential business records).

[41] Centurion Indus., Inc. v. Warren Steurer & Assocs, 665 F.2d 323, 325 (10th Cir. 1981); 8 C. Wright & A. Miller, Federal Practice and Procedure § 2043 (1970).

[42] Restatement of Torts § 757 Comment b (1939).

[43] *See, e.g.*, Cipollone v. Liggett Group, Inc., 785 F.2d 1108, 1122 (3d Cir. 1986); Manual for Complex Litigation Second § 21.431, at 53 & § 41.36, at 379–83 (2d ed. 1985).

[44] Cipollone v. Liggett Group, Inc., 785 F.2d 1108, 1122 (3d Cir. 1986).

[45] Trevino v. Celanese Corp., 701 F.2d 397, 405–06 (5th Cir. 1983).

[46] Harris v. Amoco Prod. Co., 768 F.2d 669, 685–86 (5th Cir. 1985), *cert. denied*, ____ U.S. ____, 106 S. Ct. 1186 (1986).

[47] *See* Gulf Oil Co. v. Bernard, 452 U.S. 89, 101–04 (1981) (order limiting communication between named plaintiffs and their lawyers and members of plaintiff class invalidated); U.S.

§ 19.6 Contents of Protective Orders

Although the nature of the case determines the exact provisions of the protective order, counsel should consider the following items when drafting an order:

1. Include a definition section which indicates the documents or information to be protected and the persons who are entitled to review the protected information. Often the people qualified to review the documents should be limited to exclude employees who could make direct competitive use of the information.
2. Indicate a method to identify and inventory the protected documents.
3. Provide for a procedure to resolve disagreements as to whether a document is protected, which includes notice before the dispute information is revealed.
4. Provide for nonparties to be shown protected information if they agree in writing to be bound by the protective order. Both outside experts employed by the parties as well as nonparty deponents should be included in this provision.
5. Specify how protected information shall be used in motions and at trial without losing its confidentiality. Usually any protected documents or motions including protected information are filed under protective order and depositions are sealed.
6. Arrange for the disposition of protected materials after trial or settlement.

Since it is often difficult to prove a violation of a protective order, it is also wise to include a provision shifting the burden to the party who has received protected information to show that such documents were not the source of any apparent competitive use of any apparently disclosed information. In an administrative context, counsel may also wish to negotiate how the government will respond to document requests from other agencies or under the Freedom of Information Act.[48] Several published cases contain copies of protective orders which can be useful as models.[49]

Steel Corp. v. United States, 730 F.2d 1465, 1467–69 (Fed. Cir. 1984) (in-house counsel); Doe v. D.C., 697 F.2d 1115, 1120–21 (D.C. Cir. 1983) (attorney-client).

[48] *See, e.g.*, Benkin, *More Ado About Prehearing Discovery at FERC*, 6 Energy L.J. 1, 27–30 (1985).

[49] *E.g.*, Cipollone v. Liggett Group, Inc., 785 F.2d 1108, 1112 n.4 (3d Cir. 1986); Tavoulareas v. Washington Post Co., 724 F.2d 1010, 1013 n.6 (D.C. Cir. 1984); Koster v. Chase Manhattan Bank, 93 F.R.D. 471, 473 (S.D.N.Y. 1982); Tavoulareas v. Piro, 93 F.R.D. 24, 33–34 (D.D.C. 1981); United States v. Hooker Chem. & Plastics Corp., 90 F.R.D. 421, 423–24 (W.D.N.Y. 1981); *see* sample form in Manual for Complex Litigation § 41.36 (2d ed. 1985).

§ 19.7 Modifications of Protective Orders

When obtaining a protective order, counsel should be aware that at some later time, the government or a party in related litigation may attempt to modify the order.[50] The government can also enforce a civil investigation demand or empanel a special grand jury to obtain the information wholly apart from obtaining a modification. While these possibilities must be considered when deciding whether to fight the initial discovery request in lieu of obtaining a protective order, the risk of modification is usually slight, unless the case is of public interest or involves a mass injury resulting in numerous lawsuits.

There is no uniform standard which courts apply to modifying a protective order,[51] although some type of extraordinary circumstances or compelling need appears necessary.[52] A modification was granted which permitted the government to obtain documents selected by private litigants in a substantially similar antitrust action so that the government could avoid reviewing several million unselected documents.[53] Access to protected depositions has also been permitted through modification.[54]

When criminal penalties can result from the release of protected information, counsel must be particularly careful about originally divulging the protected materials, rather than asserting the Fifth Amendment privilege against self-incrimination.[55] Although a modification can be denied when such documents could be used to bring a criminal action and no showing of need is made, this result is not assured.[56] A litigant should not rely on informal agreements to protect confidential information in lieu of asserting a Fifth Amendment privilege.[57] However, it may not be wise to assume that even a formal protective order will suffice to protect information for which the Fifth Amendment privilege could have been invoked.[58]

---

[50] *See generally* Marcus, *Myth and Reality in Protective Order Litigation,* 69 Cornell L. Rev. 1, 41–46 (1983).

[51] *See generally* Note, *Modification of Protective Orders: Balancing Practical Considerations and Addressing Constitutional Rights,* XIV Suffolk U. L. Rev. 1013 (1980).

[52] *See, e.g.,* Martindell v. IT&T Corp., 594 F.2d 291, 296 (2d Cir. 1979).

[53] United States v. AT&T Co., 461 F. Supp. 1314, 1338–39 (D.D.C. 1978).

[54] AT&T Co. v. Grady, 594 F.2d 594, 597 (7th Cir. 1978), *cert. denied,* 440 U.S. 971 (1979).

[55] See §§ **18.19–18.21**.

[56] *See* United States v. GAF Corp., 596 F.2d 10, 15–16, 18–19 (2d Cir. 1979).

[57] *See* United States v. Davis, 702 F.2d 418, 422–23 (2d Cir.), *cert. denied,* 463 U.S. 1215 (1983).

[58] *Compare* Martindell v. IT&T Corp., 594 F.2d 291, 295–96 (2d Cir. 1979) *with* United States v. Davis, 702 F.2d 418, 422–23 (2d Cir.), *cert. denied,* 463 U.S. 1215 (1983); *cf.* Garner v. United States, 424 U.S. 648, 653–56 (1976) (discussing waiver by failure to claim Fifth Amendment). *But see* Note, *Modification of Protective Orders: Balancing Practical Considerations and Addressing Constitutional Rights,* XIV Suffolk U.L. Rev. 1011, 1055–56 (1980).

§ 19.8 Enforcement of Protective Orders

Violation of a protective order can be punished by criminal or civil contempt. Counsel should be aware that some judges will not enforce negotiated protective orders unless they meet the Rule 26(c) requirement of showing good cause.[59] A person need not be expressly named in the protective order to be held in contempt if the person has actual knowledge of the order and abets or is legally identified with a party.[60] Therefore, an expert or an employee can be held in contempt, even if never served with the order. If a party violates the order, sanctions affecting the merits of the action can be imposed under Rule 37.[61] In an appropriate case, a default can result from refusals to permit discovery under a protective order.[62]

§ 19.9 Reviewing Protective Orders

A protective order is an interlocutory order. In rare instances, the order will be certified for immediate appeal under 28 U.S.C. § 1292(b), is considered within the collateral order doctrine, or is subject to mandamus. Otherwise, it cannot be reviewed before the appeal of the entire case.[63] Counsel should be careful to petition for mandamus rather than appeal. Although most courts consider an improvident appeal as a petition for mandamus,[64] a few courts are more formal in their requirements.[65] If a party is willing to be held in contempt for violating the order, the order can be reviewed by appealing from the contempt.[66] However, the party must raise the grounds for denying the protective order at the time the

[59] *See* Orliac v. Berthe, 765 F.2d 30, 31 (2d Cir. 1985) (denying confidentiality order for unidentified papers filed on appeal).

[60] Quinter v. Volkswagen of Am., 676 F.2d 969, 972 (3d Cir. 1982).

[61] See **ch. 29**.

[62] *See* TIF Instruments, Inc. v. Colette, 713 F.2d 197, 200–01 (6th Cir. 1983).

[63] *Compare* H.L. Hayden Co. v. Siemens Med. Sys., Inc., 797 F.2d 85, 89–90 (2d Cir. 1986) *and* New York v. United States Metals Ref. Co., 771 F.2d 796, 799–802 (3d Cir. 1985) (protective order not appealable as a collateral final order or interlocutory injunction, and mandamus denied) *with* Cipollone v. Liggett Group, Inc., 785 F.2d 1108, 1111 (3d Cir. 1986) (protective order not a collateral order, but mandamus jurisdiction existed) *and In re* Reporters Comm. for Freedom of the Press, 773 F.2d 1325, 1330 (D.C. Cir. 1985) (protective order reviewed as collateral order); *see generally* 4 Moore's Federal Practice ¶ 26.79[2].

[64] *See* 9 Moore's Federal Practice ¶ 110.28, at 315–16.

[65] Bridge C.A.T. Scan Assoc. v. Technicare Corp., 710 F.2d 940, 944 (2d Cir. 1983).

[66] Marrese v. American Academy of Orthopaedic Surgeons, 726 F.2d 1150, 1157–58 (7th Cir. 1984), *rev'd on other grounds,* 470 U.S. 373 (1985); *see* United States v. Ryan, 402 U.S. 530, 532–33 (1971); 13 Federal Practice and Procedure § 3537, at 340–41.

order is considered, since no review is proper if the issue is raised for the first time in the contempt proceeding.[67] A protective order will be reversed only if the court has abused its discretion.[68]

---

[67] *See* United States v. Rylander, 460 U.S. 752, 757 (1983).

[68] Doe v. D.C., 697 F.2d 1115, 1119 (D.C. Cir. 1983); Centurion Indus., Inc. v. Warren Steurer & Assocs., 665 F.2d 323, 326 (10th Cir. 1981); Galella v. Onassis, 487 F.2d 986, 997 (2d Cir. 1973).

CHAPTER 20

DISCOVERY REGARDING EXPERTS

§ 20.1 Introduction

Although most lawyers assume that expert information is protected by work product immunity, Rule 26(b)(4), which regulates discovery from experts, adopts unfairness as the basis of restrictions on such discovery and rejects the concept of work product for an expert's opinion.[1] In practice, the distinction is relevant only in that counsel must follow the requisites of the rule rather than cite more general work product concepts when arguing for or against expert discovery.

Expert discovery in federal court is fairly restrictive compared to some state courts, which permit depositions and exchange of reports as a matter of right.[2]

[1] Advisory Committee Notes to Fed. R. Civ. P. 26(b)(4), 48 F.R.D. 505 (1970).

[2] *See, e.g.*, Cal. Code Civ. P. §§ 2034(g) & (i) (West Supp. 1987).

However, counsel generally appear to ignore federal limitations and stipulate to greater discovery than required by Rule 26(b)(4).[3] Four categories of experts have been identified who are subject to different obligations under the rule: (1) experts who are expected to be trial witnesses, (2) experts retained or specially employed in anticipation of litigation or preparation of trial who are not expected to be called at trial, (3) experts who are informally consulted, and (4) experts whose information was not acquired in preparation for trial.[4]

§ 20.2 Experts Who Will Testify

Rule 26(b)(4) permits the most discovery of experts who are identified as trial witnesses. For these experts, discovery proceeds in two steps: (1) interrogatories and (2) upon motion, further discovery such as depositions or document production. Expert interrogatories require a party to identify each person expected to be called as an expert witness, state the substance of the facts and opinions to which the expert is expected to testify, and provide a summary of the grounds for each opinion.[5] Although the rule is silent concerning any other matters which can be requested, it is common to request a statement of the expert's qualifications, as well as any information concerning impeachment. In other words, interrogatories should seek information concerning the expert's compensation, prior cases in which the expert has testified, and even information concerning disciplinary proceedings or prior convictions.

§ 20.3 Interrogatories to Experts

Although interrogatories to experts can be broadly drafted, usually some specificity is desirable. For example, besides educational and professional background, questions should be asked about whether the expert is licensed by any governmental authority and, if so, whether the expert has ever been investigated by the licensing body or had a license revoked or suspended. Identification of any publications or talks which the expert has given related to the issue at trial should be requested. The expert's analysis of any similar problems and identification of cases in which the expert testified or otherwise provided information to the court should be obtained. The interrogatories should also request a description of any tests, examinations, or analyses performed by the expert in the current case, including identification of any documents or

---

[3] *See* Day, *Expert Discovery Under Federal Rule 26(b)(4); An Empirical Study in South Dakota,* 31 S.D.L. Rev. 40, 50 (1985); Graham, *Discovery of Experts Under Rule 26(b)(4) of the Federal Rules of Civil Procedure: Part Two, An Empirical Study and A Proposal,* 1977 U. Ill. L.F. 169, 200.

[4] *See* 8 C. Wright & A. Miller, Federal Practice and Procedure § 2029, at 250 (1970) [hereinafter Federal Practice and Procedure].

[5] Fed. R. Civ. P. 26(b)(4)(A)(i).

tangible items reviewed and any reports submitted by the expert. Counsel can request that such reports be attached to the responses if there is no objection to their production. The names and positions of any person who was consulted by or assisted the expert should also be specifically requested. The heart of the interrogatories requests each fact to which the expert will testify or on which an opinion will be based, the source of each such fact, the substance of each opinion, and the grounds for each opinion.[6]

Counsel responding to such interrogatories must decide the level of detail which will be provided. If a deposition will be given, the answers are often fairly general. If any deposition will be resisted, counsel must evaluate whether giving expansive answers to the interrogatories will make it more likely that the judge will refuse to order further discovery or that such answers will merely provide additional information for the adverse party's preparation of a court-ordered deposition. Because Rule 26(b)(4) has no contemporaneous exchange provision, the fact that opposing counsel has not yet designated any experts is not grounds to object to answering such interrogatories concerning one's own experts.[7]

Formerly, many lawyers had no qualms about incorrectly stating that they had not selected a trial expert, because courts were generally unwilling to exclude the testimony of previously obtained experts when they were later designated. The certification requirement of Rule 26(g)[8] now provides for monetary as well as other appropriate sanctions for false certifications. Because courts appear quite comfortable awarding attorneys' fees for breaches of the certification requirement, this type of sharp practice is likely to decline. If counsel is unclear which of several experts will actually be used at trial, one alternative is to list each expert who is being actively considered. This has the disadvantage of disclosing the names of some nontestifying consultants whose identity might not otherwise be discoverable. On the other hand, their identities may also be disclosed if they appear at depositions or assist in the preparation of answers to Rule 33 interrogatories, because it is common to ask for the names of all individuals who were so consulted. If a party decides to call an additional expert after answering the interrogatories, Rule 26(e) imposes a duty to supplement the earlier response.[9]

§ 20.4 Obtaining Further Information

There is widespread agreement that interrogatories are incapable of producing enough information to cross-examine an expert witness effectively[10] because of

[6] *Id.*

[7] 4 J. Moore *et al.*, Moore's Federal Practice ¶ 26.66[3] (2d ed. 1984) [hereinafter Moore's Federal Practice].

[8] *See* §§ **17.3, 28.2**.

[9] See §§ **17.14–17.15**.

[10] *See, e.g.*, Graham, *Discovery of Experts Under Rule 26(b)(4) of the Federal Rules of Civil Procedure: Part Two, An Empirical Study and a Proposal*, 1977 U. Ill. L.F. 169, 172–74.

the liberalization of the Federal Rules of Evidence concerning expert testimony at trial.[11] Experts are permitted to testify as to their opinion concerning ultimate issues in the case without prior disclosure of the underlying facts, based on information which is made known to them before the hearing.[12] Such information need not be admissible in evidence as long as it is of a type reasonably relied upon by experts in the particular field.[13] Therefore, unless testifying experts can be required to produce their underlying data before trial and be subjected to rigorous questioning concerning their assumptions, cross-examination at trial is likely to become a farce, since it is too dangerous to ask questions to which counsel does not know the answer. Although the court has discretion to require experts to reveal the bases of their opinions on direct examination,[14] this provides little assistance to counsel who may require significant time and the talent of a friendly expert to meaningfully analyze the data. Moreover, the interrogatories are worthless for impeachment, because they are drafted by counsel rather than by the expert and attempt to give only enough information to avoid the imposition of sanctions. The temptation to provide vague answers has been encouraged by the knowledge that courts have considered answers sufficient even though they reveal very little substantive information.[15] As a result, the deposition of an expert should be viewed as a necessity rather than a luxury. However, some judges require a motion to compel further interrogatory answers as a prerequisite to ordering a contested deposition.

Fortunately, in most cases in which expert testimony is offered, both sides call an expert. Each counsel faces the same problem of how to obtain enough information about the opposing expert's opinions and underlying assumptions to impeach the witness at trial, and it is common to agree to an expert deposition without any court order. Refusal to permit a deposition tends to occur when only one party will present expert testimony or when the resisting counsel is confident that the other side's expert can be destroyed at trial without the need for additional discovery. In such cases, counsel cannot simply schedule the deposition of the opponent's expert and assume that sanctions will be imposed if the expert fails to attend. Instead, a motion must be made for the deposition[16] to avoid Rule 11 sanctions.[17]

Since Rule 26(b)(4) provides no criteria for determining whether or not to grant a deposition, practice varies widely depending on the court's views of such discovery.[18] Although many judges will be annoyed at the party refusing the

---

[11] *See* Fed. R. Evid. 702–705.

[12] Fed. R. Evid. 703–705.

[13] Fed. R. Evid. 703.

[14] Fed. R. Evid. 705.

[15] *See* Graham, *Discovery of Experts Under Rule 26(b)(4) of Federal Rules of Civil Procedure: Part One, An Analytical Study,* 1976 U. Ill. L. Forum 895, 918–21.

[16] *See* Shackelford v. Vermeer Mfg. Co., 93 F.R.D. 512, 513–14 (W.D. Tex. 1982).

[17] See **ch. 28**.

[18] *See generally* Graham, *Discovery of Experts Under Rule 26(b)(4) of the Federal Rules of Civil Procedure: Part One, An Analytical Study,* 1976 U. Ill. L. Forum 895, 923–25.

deposition, others are generally disenchanted with expert testimony.[19] Such disenchantment stems from several sources, including a low regard for the value of an opinion which has been bought, a belief that the war of experts at trial is a waste of time because the experts will cancel each other out, or the view that such depositions are significant impositions upon trial preparation. Therefore, a judge may refuse to order an expert's deposition or permit only depositions on written questions as a way of discouraging the use of experts at trial.

§ 20.5 Experts Hired in Anticipation of Trial

Experts retained in anticipation of litigation who are not trial witnesses can be subjected to discovery only upon a showing of exceptional circumstances or as provided in Rule 35,[20] which permits a party who has been subjected to a mental or physical examination to obtain a report of the examination in exchange for producing any of its own reports on the condition at issue.[21] To demonstrate exceptional circumstances, it must be shown that it is impracticable for the party seeking discovery to obtain facts or opinions on the same subject by other means.[22] Therefore, to obtain this discovery, it is not sufficient to show that the expert's opinion is not otherwise available, if opinions on the underlying subject can be obtained.[23] Exceptional circumstances were found when the only available expert was hired by the opposing counsel, changed circumstances prohibited a reconstruction of the tests performed by the experts, and the testifying expert relied on a computer model whose documentation and programming he could not fully explain.[24]

One issue which arises with some frequency is what standard must be shown to obtain the identity of such experts. Courts reach varying results on this question,[25] with some requiring the identity to be disclosed only upon exceptional circumstances[26] and others ordering the identity to be revealed if it is relevant under Rule 26(b)(1).[27]

---

[19] *See, e.g.*, Weinstein, *Improving Expert Testimony,* 20 U. Rich. L. Rev. 473 (1986).

[20] See § **25.13**.

[21] Fed. R. Civ. P. 26(b)(4)(B).

[22] *Id.*

[23] Marine Petroleum Co. v. Champlin Petroleum Co., 641 F.2d 984, 994–96 (D.C. Cir. 1980).

[24] Pearl Brewing Co. v. Jos. Schlitz Brewing Co., 415 F. Supp. 1122, 1138–40 (S.D. Tex. 1976).

[25] *See generally* Note, *Discovery of Retained Nontestifying Expert's Identities Under the Federal Rules of Civil Procedure,* 80 Mich. L. Rev. 514 (1982).

[26] *See, e.g.*, Ager v. Jane C. Stormont Hosp. & Training School for Nurses, 662 F.2d 496, 502–03 (10th Cir. 1980).

[27] *See, e.g.*, Baki v. B.F. Diamond Constr. Co., 71 F.R.D. 179, 181–82 (D. Md. 1976).

§ 20.6 Informally Consulted Experts

No discovery is permitted concerning an expert who is informally consulted in anticipation of trial but not retained or specifically employed.[28] This bars disclosure of the witness's identity as well as opinions. The most complete analysis of the factors involved in determining whether an expert was *informally consulted* as opposed to consulted in anticipation of litigation is found in *Ager v. Jane C. Stormont Hospital & Training School for Nurses.*[29] *Ager* viewed this issue as a question of fact for the judge to decide based on (1) the manner in which the consultation was initiated, (2) the nature, type and extent of information or material provided to, or determined by, the expert in connection with his review, (3) the duration and intensity of the consultative relationship, and (4) the terms of the consultation, if any (e.g., payment, confidentiality of test data, or opinion). For example, discovery of a letter in which an expert discussed his evaluation of "what went wrong" was denied when the expert indicated he was unwilling to become involved in the dispute and received no compensation for his services.[30] It apparently makes no difference that the existence of the informally consulted expert is discovered by happenstance rather than by stealth in preventing the opposing counsel from presenting the testimony of the informally consulted expert at trial.[31]

§ 20.7 Experts Whose Information Is Not Acquired for Litigation

Experts whose information is not acquired in preparation for trial are freely discoverable as any ordinary witness.[32] Regular employees of the parties, as well as experts who were actors or viewers of the occurrences at issue, fall within this category.[33] Difficulties arise when an expert is employed for a dual purpose. This may occur when an existing employee or consultant becomes involved in litigation support[34] or when an outside expert is hired both to assist in trial

---

[28] Marine Petroleum Co. v. Champlin Petroleum Co., 641 F.2d 984, 990 (D.C. Cir. 1980); USM Corp. v. American Aerosols, Inc., 631 F.2d 420, 424–25 (6th Cir. 1980); Ager v. Jane C. Stormont Hosp. & Training School for Nurses, 622 F.2d 496, 501 (10th Cir. 1980); *see* 8 Federal Practice and Procedure § 2033; 4 Moore's Federal Practice ¶ 26.66[4], at 26–422.

[29] 622 F.2d 496, 500–01 (10th Cir. 1980).

[30] USM Corp. v. American Aerosols, Inc., 631 F.2d 420, 425 (6th Cir. 1980).

[31] *See* Healy v. Counts, 100 F.R.D. 493, 496–97 (D. Colo. 1984).

[32] 8 Federal Practice and Procedure § 2029, at 250–51; 4 Moore's Federal Practice ¶ 26.66[2]; Ager v. Jane C. Stormont Hosp. & Training School for Nurses, 622 F.2d 496, 501 (10th Cir. 1980); *see generally,* Day, *The Ordinary Witness Doctrine: Discovery of the Pre-Retention Knowledge of a Nonwitness Expert Under Federal Rule 26(b)(4)(B),* 38 Ark. L. Rev. 763 (1985).

[33] 8 Federal Practice and Procedure § 2029, at 250–51.

[34] *See* Pielemeier, *Discovery of Non-Testifying "In-House Experts Under Federal Rule of Civil Procedure 26,* 58 Indiana L.J. 597 (1983).

preparation and also to give advice concerning product improvement. At least one court has held that, if the information was intended to prepare for litigation, the fact that a double use can be made of the expert's consultation does not deny a nontestifying expert protection from discovery.[35] However, experts who acquire information while working in non-litigation capacity can be questioned about such topics when they later switch to litigation support.[36] Similarly, when an expert's opinions were formed prior to employment, the court may permit a deposition concerning such information.[37]

When selecting an expert, counsel must carefully assess whether the person possesses discoverable information as well as information which is not subject to disclosure. The expert with two hats is bound to be questioned about both in deposition, and it is often difficult to separate where the nondiscoverable information ends and the freely discoverable information begins.[38] Similarly, if an expert is hired to look at several areas but only testifies concerning one topic, counsel must be careful to limit the deposition to the discoverable issue. The court looks to the interrelation of the two subjects in determining discoverability. This is also true when the testifying witness relies upon information which is put together by other members of the expert's firm.

§ 20.8 Protecting the Expert's Documents

Many attorneys assume that once an expert is designated, counsel is entitled to the witness's reports as well as opinion. However, some courts question whether work product protection afforded to documents under Rule 26(b)(3) is automatically waived by designation pursuant to Rule 26(b)(4)(A).[39] Thus, documents sent to the expert which are not protected by work product immunity should be distinguished from correspondence between the attorney and the expert. For example, documents transmitted to the expert for review were not considered protected by Rule 26(b)(4)(A).[40] Although a designated expert's report is not technically work product, some courts do not consider such documents within a

---

[35] Hermsdorfer v. American Motors Corp., 96 F.R.D. 13, 15 (W.D.N.Y. 1982).

[36] *See* Marine Petroleum Co. v. Champlin Petroleum Co., 641 F.2d 984, 992–94 (D.C. Cir. 1980).

[37] *See, e.g.*, Barkwell v. Sturm Ruger Co., 79 F.R.D. 444, 446–47 (D. Alaska 1978); Grinnell Corp. v. Hackett, 70 F.R.D. 326, 331–32 (D.R.I. 1976); Day, *The Ordinary Witness Doctrine: Discovery of the Pre-Retention Knowledge of a Nonwitness Expert Under Federal Rule 26(b)(4)(B),* 38 Ark. L. Rev. 763 (1985).

[38] *See generally* Comment, *Discovery of Expert Information Under the Federal Rules,* 10 U. Rich. L. Rev. 706 (1976).

[39] *See, e.g.*, Baise v. Alewel's, Inc., 99 F.R.D. 95, 97 (W.D. Mo. 1983); *see generally* Connors, *A New Look at an Old Concern—Protecting Expert Information from Discovery Under the Federal Rules,* 18 Duquesne L. Rev. 271 (1980). *But see* Wilson v. Johns-Manville Sales Corp., 810 F.2d 1358, 1362–63 (5th Cir. 1987) (expert excluded when he refused to produce written correspondence between himself and any asbestos litigation defendants, plaintiffs, litigation groups, or governmental agencies).

[40] United States v. I.B.M., 72 F.R.D. 78, 81–82 (S.D.N.Y. 1976).

Rule 34 request but rather view such information as subject to Rule 26(b)(4), which requires a court order for production.[41] In fact, some courts may refuse to order such documents produced not only if they dislike expert testimony, but also if they believe that the party can obtain the necessary discovery by deposing the expert. Conversely, local rules should also be consulted, because some districts provide for the automatic exchange of expert reports.[42]

In highly complex or technical cases, courts are more likely to permit liberal discovery of information prepared by experts. Cases in which the expert has created computer models and simulations which form the basis of the witness's opinions are particularly susceptible to a showing of need for discovery of the underlying programs, data, and assumptions,[43] but even in this area the Second Circuit has permitted expert testimony when counsel was denied the programs underlying the expert's opinion.[44] When both litigants desire the expert's prior writings and statements, it is not unusual to split the costs of such production or, if the experts are equally prolific, for each side to bear its own costs.[45]

In an effort to frustrate discovery, counsel sometimes direct experts not to prepare a report. If this procedure is contrary to the expert's normal practice, it may show evidence of a pattern of discovery abuse supporting the imposition of sanctions in any later discovery dispute. It may also result in a broader deposition of the expert than would have occurred if opposing counsel knew the nature of the expected testimony. As a general matter, many counsel are leery of having experts write draft reports, because they are usually written hurriedly and without the thorough analysis that is required for testimony at trial. Otherwise sterling experts can become useless if their final reports and conclusions are discredited by their earlier works. On the other hand, this concern can be met by deferring the timing of any written report until counsel is comfortable that it embodies the expert's final opinions.

§ 20.9 Expert Deposition Fees

Experts must be paid a reasonable fee by the party seeking discovery for the time spent responding to court-ordered depositions.[46] Similarly, the court may require or in the case of a nontestifying expert, shall require, the party seeking discovery to pay a fair portion of the fees and expenses reasonably incurred by the other party in obtaining facts and opinions from the expert.[47] If the court

---

[41] *See, e.g.*, Baise v. Alewel's, Inc., 99 F.R.D. 95, 98 (W.D. Mo. 1983).

[42] *See, e.g.*, C.D. Cal. Local R. 9.4.6.

[43] *See generally* Comment, *The Discovery and Use of Computerized Information: An Examination of Current Approaches*, 13 Pepperdine L. Rev. 405, 410–12 (1986).

[44] Perma Research & Dev. Co. v. Singer Co., 542 F.2d 111, 115 (2d Cir.), *cert. denied*, 429 U.S. 987 (1976).

[45] *See* Daniels, *Protecting Your Expert During Discovery*, 71 A.B.A. J. 50, 52 (1985).

[46] Fed. R. Civ. P. 26(b)(4)(C).

[47] *Id.*

finds that manifest injustice would result, it can dispense with any compensation for the party or the expert.[48] In expert depositions which are taken upon stipulation, the examining party usually pays the expert an agreed-upon hourly rate, although sometimes the parties agree to bear their own costs. However, the court cannot order the parties to pay their own experts without a finding of manifest injustice.[49]

Payment of the expert can be a significant portion of unrecoverable litigation expenses, because experts cannot be paid a contingent fee[50] and their compensation, other than for standard witness attendance fees, is normally not taxable as costs at the end of the case.[51] Only fees paid to court-appointed experts can be taxed as costs,[52] unless the compensation is awarded pursuant to a specific statutory grant[53] or as a sanction.[54] There is some dispute as to whether a statute which authorizes attorneys' fees includes experts as part of an attorney's reasonable and necessary expenses.[55] However, Rule 54(d) does not provide a separate source of authority to assess expert fees.[56] Although technically an occurrence witness such as a treating physician is considered an ordinary witness for purposes of subpoena and witness fees, usually the party calling such an expert offers to pay a reasonable fee for the time spent testifying on the theory than an unhappy expert is a terrible witness.

§ 20.10 Compelling Testimony of Experts Who Are Strangers to the Litigation

Occasionally an expert who has published articles or studies relevant to a case may be served with a Rule 45 subpoena duces tecum to appear at a deposition, even though that person is not a retained expert in the current litigation.[57] These

---

[48] *Id.*

[49] United States v. City of Twin Falls, 806 F.2d 862, 878–79 (9th Cir. 1986).

[50] Model Rules of Professional Conduct Rule 3.4 comment (1983).

[51] 28 U.S.C. §§ 1920 and 1821 (1982); *see* Crawford Fitting Co. v. J.T. Gibbons, Inc.,_____ U.S. _____, 107 S. Ct. 2494, 2499, 55 U.S.L.W. 4820, 4821 (June 15, 1987).

[52] 28 U.S.C. § 1920(6) (1982).

[53] See listing of 28 federal statutes providing for recovery of expert's fees in International Woodworkers v. Champion Int'l, 790 F.2d 1174, 1179 n.7 (5th Cir. 1986) (en banc), *aff'd sub nom.* Crawford Fitting Co. v. J.T. Gibbons, Inc., _____ U.S. _____, 107 S. Ct. 2494, 2499, 55 U.S.L.W. 4820, (June 15, 1987).

[54] *Id.* at 1177–79.

[55] *Id.* at 1184–88 (extensive discussion of cases) (Rubin, J., concurring and dissenting opinion); *cf.* Barber & Ross Co. v. Lifetime Doors, Inc., 810 F.2d 1276, 1282 (4th Cir. 1987) (§ 4 of Clayton Act which permits costs and attorneys' fees includes expert expenses only in exceptional circumstances).

[56] Crawford Fitting Co. v. J.T. Gibbons, Inc., _____ U.S. _____, 107 S. Ct. 2494, 2499, 55 U.S.L.W. 4820, 4821 (June 15, 1987).

[57] *See* Maurer, *Compelling the Expert Witness: Fairness and Utility Under the Federal Rules of Civil Procedure,* 19 Ga. L. Rev. 71, 94–104 (1984); Note, *Discovery and Testimony of*

individuals are not protected from discovery under Rule 26(b)(4) but fall within the ambit of Rule 45(b), which permits the subpoena to be conditioned on advancement of reasonable cost of producing the designated information. However, most courts are reluctant to require such experts to testify. The judge has discretion entirely to quash a burdensome subpoena duces tecum directed at an expert who is a stranger to the action.[58] It can also place conditions on obtaining the expert's opinion. In one case, the court ruled that the subpoenaed expert was entitled to reasonable compensation for testifying, which included not only a professional fee, the cost of supplying documents, and remuneration for the inconvenience, but also a portion of the expenses of the original research underlying his study.[59] Confidential information which has been obtained from third parties can also be ordered to be produced under a protective order fashioned to avoid needless harm to the expert and his sources of information.[60]

Factors which the court can consider in exercising its discretion include (1) the degree to which the expert is called because of knowledge of facts relevant to the case rather than to give an opinion, (2) the difference between testifying to a previously formed opinion and forming a new one, (3) the possibility that the witness is a unique expert, (4) the extent to which it is unlikely that any comparable witness will willingly testify, and (5) the degree to which the witness is being oppressed by having continually to testify.[61] Because of the discretionary approach, the cases are not consistent, as is demonstrated by the fact that the same expert had a subpoena quashed by one court, while another court ordered that he be paid for his testimony and research.[62]

§ 20.11 Deposing the Expert

An expert deposition may not be desirable in every case.[63] For example, it may be better not to take a deposition if counsel believes the case will settle before trial, the expert's testimony is not considered prejudicial, the deposition may educate the expert and result in a better prepared witness at trial, or the expert's deposition will be admitted at trial if the witness is unavailable. The cost of the deposition can also be a significant factor in determining its desirability. However, in most cases which will be tried, failure to take an expert deposition

---

Unretained Experts: Creating a Clear and Equitable Standard to Govern Compliance with Subpoenas, 1987 Duke L.J. 140.

[58] Buchanan v. American Motors Corp., 697 F.2d 151, 152 (6th Cir. 1983); *see* Kaufman v. Edelstein, 539 F.2d 811, 822 (2d Cir. 1976).

[59] Wright v. Jeep Corp., 547 F. Supp. 871, 877 (E.D. Mich. S.D. 1982).

[60] *See* Deitchman v. E.R. Squibb & Sons, Inc., 740 F.2d 556, 564 (7th Cir. 1984).

[61] Kaufman v. Edelstein, 539 F.2d 811, 822 (2d Cir. 1976).

[62] *Compare* Buchanan v. American Motors Corp., 697 F.2d 151, 152 (6th Cir. 1983) *with* Wright v. Jeep Corp., 547 F. Supp. 871, 874–77 (E.D. Mich. 1982).

[63] *See generally* Graham, *Discovery of Experts Under Rule 26(b)(4) of the Federal Rules of Civil Procedure: Part Two, An Empirical Study and a Proposal,* 1977 U. Ill. L.F. 169, 184–86.

can border on malpractice when the expert will testify about issues which are determinative of the outcome.

The deposition of an expert is often crucial in evaluating the merits of the action. If the expert is strong and the bases for the witness's opinions appear generally unassailable, it may be time to settle the case. Conversely, if the expert cannot weather deposition questioning, opposing counsel may be faced with the dilemma of either replacing the expert close to trial or settling the action. The deposition testimony can also be used to defeat or obtain summary judgment. For example, summary judgment was upheld when the plaintiff's expert opined in deposition that the probability that the defendant had caused the injury was greater than 20 percent but less than 80 percent.[64]

When the expert will testify on any theory which might be considered novel, counsel should determine whether the expert can meet the *Frye* test[65] which requires that the scientific theory be both reliable and accepted in the scientific community. Although many circuits still require both prongs to be met before admitting the expert testimony, a few circuits require only that such testimony be relevant and helpful to the jury[66] or balance reliability against prejudice.[67]

The deposition is the time to learn the bases for the opinions which will be offered at trial by the expert, as well as the expert's methodology and underlying data. If the deposition is not thorough, it may be difficult to create an effective plan to impeach the testimony at trial. In most cases, it is advisable to have a friendly expert at the deposition who can give advice about follow-up questions and explain the witness's arcane answers. At a minimum, the mere presence of the opposing party's expert will ensure that the deponent cannot get away with giving unresponsive, technical answers which are unintelligible to a lay person and when later translated yield no information.

There is a vast difference in quality among experts. Some experts think nothing of changing their testimony between deposition and trial on major issues. If so, the deposition becomes a way to demonstrate the expert's untrustworthiness. In fact, if an expert is hired in litigation involving multiple trials, a deposition in one case can be key to impeaching the expert's credibility in another action. One litigant was granted a new trial because the expert's testimony in that case was contradicted by his deposition in another suit in a manner which the court considered perjurious.[68]

At the deposition, if the expert claims not to have completed all of the pertinent tests or reviewed all of the relevant documents, counsel has several options: (1) complete as much of the deposition as is possible and require a further deposition when the expert is ready; (2) require production of any reports or test results written after the deposition; (3) move to be reimbursed for any

---

[64] Chaney v. Smithkline Beckman Corp., 764 F.2d 527, 529–30 (8th Cir. 1985).

[65] Frye v. United States, 293 F.2d 1013, 1014 (D.C. Cir. 1923); *see generally* 3 J. Weinstein & M. Berger, Weinstein's Evidence ¶ 702[03] (1985).

[66] *See* 3 J. Weinstein & M. Berger, Weinstein's Evidence ¶ 702[03] (1985).

[67] *See* United States v. Downing, 753 F.2d 1224, 1237 (3d Cir. 1985).

[68] Harre v. A.H. Robins Co., 750 F.2d 1501, 1505 (11th Cir. 1985).

costs associated with the discovery failure; or (4) move to exclude the expert's testimony at trial. Although the extent of sanctions depends in large measure on the trial judge's disposition, at least the record is protected if the expert's testimony at trial is a surprise.

From the perspective of the defending counsel, the deposition is the true test of how the expert will appear at trial. Experts are often extremely difficult to prepare for deposition[69] when they are overconfident of their opinions. One way to tone down a brilliant but arrogant expert is to play devil's disciple during deposition preparation by asking the nastiest, most difficult questions possible. Similarly, although not all volunteering on the part of an expert during deposition is necessarily bad, it is important for the expert to understand what, if any, types of questions should be answered narrowly. Preparing written answers to the questions that the expert will be asked, whether for deposition or at trial, should be avoided, because the discoverability of such "scripts" can be hotly disputed or even a matter of trial impeachment.

§ 20.12 Rule 612 and Expert Testimony

The impact of Federal Rule of Evidence 612 upon expert testimony is often an issue at the expert's deposition.[70] Rule 612 provides that the court has discretion to order the production of materials which are reviewed before the hearing to refresh a witness's recollection. Therefore, when work product, such as binders containing the lawyer's choice of the best and worst documents in the case, are reviewed by an expert prior to testifying, the question of discoverability becomes key. Similarly, if the attorney's work product is revealed to the expert and is incorporated into the expert's opinions, must the analysis be revealed to permit effective cross-examination of the expert? There is no uniformity regarding these issues. Only one appellate court has discussed both of these problems, and its conclusion is contrary to decisions reached by most district courts.[71] The Third Circuit has held that opinion work product is not waived by sending it to an expert,[72] because comprehensive examination of the expert's opinion can be obtained without inquiring into the lawyer's role in assisting with the formulation of the theory. Similarly, it has held that adverse counsel is not entitled to a general identification of work product shown to a witness, because Rule 612 requires disclosure of a documents only if the examiner learns from

[69] See § **23.17** generally concerning deposition preparation.

[70] See § **18.17**.

[71] *Compare* Bogosian v. Gulf Oil Corp., 738 F.2d 587, 593 (3d Cir. 1984) *with* James Julian, Inc. v. Raytheon Co., 93 F.R.D. 138, 144–46 (D. Del. 1982); Wheeling-Pittsburgh Steel Corp. v. Underwriters Laboratories, Inc., 81 F.R.D. 8, 9–11 (N.D. Ill. 1978); Berkey Photo, Inc. v. Eastman Kodak Co., 74 F.R.D. 613, 615–17 (S.D.N.Y. 1977).

[72] Bogosian v. Gulf Oil Corp., 738 F.2d 587, 593 (3d Cir. 1984).

questioning that a particular document was reviewed and refreshed the witness's recollection.[73]

At a minimum, it is risky to assume that materials submitted to an expert will never be discoverable. Certainly, nonprivileged materials can be ordered produced if they refresh recollection or if the court otherwise deems such discovery appropriate. Moreover, until other circuits consider whether work product immunity or other privileges are waived if they refresh the expert's recollection, counsel must act cautiously in submitting such materials to experts. This presents an acute preparation problem concerning experts, who unlike other witnesses, are likely to review massive amounts of documents and categorize them by their relative importance, often with the assistance of counsel. Discussion about critical documents may be a poor substitute for classification methods, even if the sorting results in the opponent's learning the identity of the documents which counsel considers critical.

§ 20.13 Use of the Expert Deposition at Trial

Although an expert's deposition is necessary to ensure effective cross-examination at trial, it has the risk of preserving testimony which would otherwise be unavailable.[74] Evidentiary uses of expert depositions at trial are governed by the same rules applicable to admitting other depositions.[75] Except in cases in which nationwide subpoena power exists, such as in antitrust litigation brought by the United States,[76] experts located more than 100 miles from court are unavailable if the party cannot otherwise reasonably obtain their attendance. Although a court may view expert unavailability more skeptically than it does absence of percipient witnesses,[77] especially if the party noticing the deposition or videotaping it is the proponent of the testimony at trial, such evidence is often admitted because scheduling problems result in an expert's being unable or refusing to testify when needed at trial.[78] Therefore, what was intended as a discovery deposition may metamorphosize into trial testimony.[79] Counsel should also be aware that an expert in a multiparty case may be permitted to

---

[73] Sporck v. Peil, 759 F.2d 312, 318 (3d Cir.), *cert. denied,* ____ U.S. ____, 106 S. Ct. 232 (1985).

[74] *See* Note, *Twisting the Purposes of Discovery: Expert Witnesses and the Deposition Dilemma,* 36 Vand. L. Rev. 1615 (1983).

[75] *See* Fed. R. Evid. 804(b)(1) and Fed. R. Civ. P. 32(a); §§ **23.23–23.30**.

[76] 15 U.S.C. § 23 (1982).

[77] *See* Carter-Wallace, Inc. v. Otte, 474 F.2d 529, 536 (2d Cir. 1972), *cert. denied,* 412 U.S. 929 (1973).

[78] *See* Williams v. Hughes Helicopters, Inc., 806 F.2d 1387, 1392–93 (9th Cir. 1986) (videotaped deposition admitted when expert was in Australia until after trial ended).

[79] *See, e.g.,* United States v. I.B.M., 90 F.R.D. 377, 381 (S.D.N.Y. 1981).

testify at trial against a party who was unable to attend the expert's deposition, as long as another similarly situated party examined the deponent.[80]

§ 20.14 Protecting Experts

It has been suggested that the following precautions should be taken to ensure the most confidentiality obtainable for expert information:

1. If possible, hire outside experts and give in-house experts specific litigation assignments
2. Counsel, rather than the party, should retain the expert
3. Work should be done in response to specific questions posed by counsel
4. The expert should maintain separate, confidential files for information submitted by counsel, and
5. Expert reports should be marked confidential and sent directly to counsel.[81]

Counsel should always draft a consulting agreement which specifies how the expert will be compensated, and any conditions for terminating the agreement and that all work will be performed at the direction of counsel, subject to a confidentiality agreement. The confidentiality agreement is often quite extensive. After describing the nature of the consulting work, it should require:

1. That the material reviewed be treated confidentially and only for purposes of the litigation
2. That only authorized individuals, as described in the agreement, can be shown such materials
3. That all such individuals agree to be bound by and, if necessary, will sign any protective order entered in the action
4. That the expert will immediately notify counsel if he receives any legal notice concerning disclosure of such information and withhold such production until counsel can challenge the production
5. That the expert consents to being represented by counsel for the purpose of any such challenge, which will be of no cost to the expert
6. That the expert will be available on reasonable notice to testify in any deposition or trial
7. That the results of the consultation are the property of counsel

---

[80] Mayo v. Tri-Bell Indus., Inc., 787 F.2d 1007, 1012 (5th Cir. 1986).

[81] Connors, *A New Look at an Old Concern—Protecting Expert Information from Discovery Under Federal Rules,* 18 Duquesne L. Rev. 271, 287 (1980).

8. That the expert consents to an injunction being entered against him by the court in which the underlying litigation is pending in the event of a threatened or actual violation of the agreement, and
9. That the agreement shall not cover any information which is or becomes generally known in the field.

§ 20.15 Enforcing Expert Discovery

There are several reasons why experts can be excluded from testifying at trial as a sanction for pretrial conduct, including failure to identify the expert or to adequately describe the nature of expert's opinion in answer to Rule 26 interrogatories[82] or as required in a Rule 16 pretrial statement[83] and failure to supplement answers to expert interrogatories or deposition testimony as required by Rule 26(e).[84] Caselaw is not entirely consistent about when exclusion is proper, because the trial court's ruling will only be reversed when an abuse of discretion has occurred.[85] For example, exclusion of expert testimony given by a party to the action was upheld because he was not identified in answer to expert interrogatories and the pretrial statement failed to indicate the substance of his opinion.[86] On the other hand, when an accounting expert was also a lay witness, it was error entirely to exclude his opinion of how lost profits could be calculated based on his personal knowledge of his employer's records, even though he was not identified as an expert.[87] Moreover, appellate review may be foreclosed if the proponent of the excluded testimony fails to proffer the evidence that the expert would have presented.[88]

Basically, courts first determine whether a witness is unidentified as opposed to inadequately identified. If the witness was not identified or was identified late in violation of a pretrial order, courts often cite the following four-criteria test enunciated in *Meyers v. Pennypack Woods Home Ownership Association*[89] in deciding whether to exclude the expert at trial:[90]

---

[82] *See, e.g.,* Grogan v. Garner, 806 F.2d 829, 837–38 (8th Cir. 1986).

[83] *See, e.g.,* Adalman v. Baker, Watts & Co., 807 F.2d 359, 369–70 (4th Cir. 1986); §§ **16.5, 30.10**.

[84] See §§ **17.14–17.15**.

[85] *E.g.,* Young v. City of New Orleans, 751 F.2d 794, 797 (5th Cir. 1985); Stich v. United States, 730 F.2d 115, 117–18 (3d Cir.), *cert. denied,* 469 U.S. 917 (1984); Rosemount, Inc. v. Beckman Instruments, Inc., 727 F.2d 1540, 1550 (Fed. Cir. 1984).

[86] Jenkins v. Whittaker Corp., 785 F.2d 720, 728 (9th Cir.), *cert. denied,* ____ U.S. ____, 107 S. Ct. 324 (1986).

[87] Teen-Ed, Inc. v. Kimball Int'l, Inc., 620 F.2d 399, 401–02 (3d Cir. 1980).

[88] Young v. City of New Orleans, 751 F.2d 794, 797 (5th Cir. 1985).

[89] 559 F.2d 894, 904–05 (3d Cir. 1977).

[90] *See, e.g.,* Kickapoo Oil Co. v. Clark Oil & Ref. Corp., 788 F.2d 11, 17–18 (Temp. Emer. Ct. App. 1985); Smith v. Ford Motor Co., 626 F.2d 784, 797 (10th Cir. 1980), *cert. denied,* 450

1. The prejudice or surprise in fact of the party against whom the excluded witnesses would have testified;
2. The ability of that party to cure the prejudice;
3. The extent to which waiver of the rule against calling unlisted witnesses would disrupt the orderly and efficient trial of the case or of other cases in the court; and
4. Bad faith or willfulness in failing to comply with the court's order.

Other courts weigh essentially the same factors and consider the reasons why the witness was not named, the importance of the witness's testimony, the time needed to prepare for the testimony, and whether a continuance would be useful.[91] One court presumed that failure to give notice of an expert's testimony until immediately before trial was clearly prejudicial, when earlier disclosure was required by the local rules and no justification for noncompliance was offered.[92]

When a witness is inadequately identified, either because the person was listed as a percipient rather than an expert witness or because a subject upon which the expert offers an opinion at trial was not previously disclosed, the judge is usually faced with an objection based on either Rule 26(e), which requires supplementation of discovery responses, or of court-imposed disclosure requirements mandated by a Rule 16 pretrial statement. Courts balance whether or not to admit testimony based on the conduct of the trial, the importance of the evidence to its proponent, and the ability of the opponent to formulate a response.[93] One court has noted that, in those cases in which testimony was held properly excluded, some evasion or concealment, whether or not intentional, existed on the part of the litigant offering the evidence.[94] On the other hand, when an expert was revealed approximately 10 days prior to trial in a case that was pending almost seven years, the trial court did not abuse its discretion in excluding the expert, even though it resulted in a directed verdict.[95] The issues of prejudice and surprise are carefully considered. If no prejudice exists and the testimony is essential, some courts have held that it is error to exclude expert testimony despite Rule 26(e) failure.[96]

U.S. 918 (1981); *see also* Adalman v. Baker, Watts & Co., 807 F.2d 359, 369 (4th Cir. 1986); United States v. Koziy, 728 F.2d 1314, 1320–21 (11th Cir. 1984), *cert. denied,* 469 U.S. 835 (1984).

[91] Patterson v. F.W. Woolworth Co., 786 F.2d 874, 879 (8th Cir. 1986); Murphy v. Magnolia Elec. Power Ass'n, 639 F.2d 232, 235 (5th Cir. 1981); 8 Federal Practice and Procedure § 2050, at 327.

[92] Sealy, Inc. v. Easy Living, Inc., 743 F.2d 1378, 1382–83 (9th Cir. 1984).

[93] Johnson v. H.K. Webster, Inc., 775 F.2d 1, 8 (1st Cir. 1985); DeMarines v. KLM Royal Dutch Airlines, 580 F.2d 1193, 1201–02 (3d Cir. 1978).

[94] Johnson v. H.K. Webster, Inc., 775 F.2d 1, 8 (1st Cir. 1985).

[95] Kickapoo Oil Co. v. Clark Oil & Ref. Corp., 788 F.2d 11, 19 (Temp. Emer. Ct. App. 1985).

[96] *E.g.,* Murphy v. Magnolia Elec. Power Ass'n, 639 F.2d 232, 234–35 (5th Cir. 1981).

A few circuits appear to require the surprised party to take the initiative by requesting continuance or recess rather than immediately calling for the evidence to be excluded.[97] The failure to request a continuance is considered as vitiating any claim of prejudice or surprise.[98] For example, the Seventh Circuit has specifically stated that surprise is a poor reason to exclude expert testimony or to recess a trial, because Rule 26(b)(4) makes it "so easy" to get pretrial discovery of an expert witness, and such measures break the jury's concentration and throw the trial judge's docket out of gear.[99] The court went even further and lambasted counsel for not retaining his own medical expert to testify or assist in cross-examination of the opposing expert, claiming that the lawyer had only himself to blame for his surprise, especially when counsel had not sought a commitment to be provided with any tests taken after the expert's deposition.[100] This approach appears to shift the burden to the injured party to show why it failed to acquire the information rather than evaluating the reasons why the opposing party failed to provide the discovery and any resulting prejudice from that failure.

Other types of discovery violations can also result in exclusion of experts. For example, when counsel called a designated expert of the opposing party who had been withdrawn, requested a copy of the report he had prepared, and attempted to call the expert at trial, the expert's testimony was properly excluded.[101] Not only may experts be excluded at trial for improprieties when they have switched allegiance between parties, but, in one case, the attorney who had obtained information from the turncoat expert was disqualified, even though the expert had misrepresented his previous association with the case to counsel.[102] This decision effectively terminated counsel's association with the case; his disqualification order was not immediately appealable.[103] Therefore, counsel must be extremely careful in obtaining information from sources which are not completely identified.

Although as a practical matter, until recently it appeared to be more difficult to sustain an exclusion of expert testimony on appeal than an allegedly improper admission of such evidence, considerations of fairness have resulted in reversals

---

[97] *See id.;* Stich v. United States, 730 F.2d 115, 118 (3d Cir.), *cert. denied,* 469 U.S. 917 (1984); Phil Crowley Steel Corp. v. Macomber, Inc., 601 F.2d 342, 344 (8th Cir. 1979).

[98] Patterson v. F.W. Woolworth Co., 786 F.2d 874, 879–80 (8th Cir. 1986); *see* Greenwood v. McDonough Power Equip., Inc., 731 F.2d 690, 697 (10th Cir. 1984).

[99] Abernathy v. Superior Hardwoods, Inc., 704 F.2d 963, 969 (7th Cir. 1983).

[100] *Id.* at 969.

[101] Durflinger v. Artiles, 727 F.2d 888, 891 (10th Cir. 1984).

[102] American Protection Ins. Co. v. MGM Grand Hotel-Las Vegas, Inc., Nos. CV-LV-82-26 HEC, CV-LV-82-96 HEC, slip op. at 6 (D. Nev. Dec. 9, 1983) *discussed in* Note, *Discovery of the Nontestifying Expert Witness' Identity Under the Federal Rules of Civil Procedure; You Can't Tell the Players Without a Program,* 37 Hastings L.J. 201, 215–18 (1985).

[103] American Protection Ins. Co. v. MGM Grand Hotel-Las Vegas, Inc., 765 F.2d 925 (9th Cir. 1985) (dismissing appeal on jurisdictional grounds); *see* Richardson-Merrell, Inc v. Koller, ____ U.S. ____, 105 S. Ct. 2757, 2762–63 (1985).

when the proponent of the evidence admitted at trial originally misled the adverse party concerning the nature of the proffered expert testimony.[104]

Playing games to delay revealing experts or the substance of their testimony can be dangerous as well as unethical. The tactic of answering expert interrogatories by stating that trial witnesses have not yet been determined can lead not only to a Rule 26(e) violation for failure to supplement discovery, but also to the imposition of monetary sanctions for violation of Rule 26(g)'s objective certification requirements.[105] Monetary sanctions have even been assessed when an expert's incorrect designation resulted in a partner rather than an associate taking the deposition.[106] Depositions of experts who are not fully prepared can also result in sanctions including the exclusion of any expert testimony on the topic in question at trial.[107] Moreover, assuming that state practice will be accepted in federal court is folly, as counsel discovered when unsuccessfully arguing that in state court the treating physician would be allowed to testify as to the causation of injuries although the witness was identified only on the issues of describing the plaintiff's injuries and prognosis.[108] Sharp tactics such as presenting documents to an expert only after deposition can also backfire, since the court can exclude any expert testimony concerning such documents.[109] Similarly, when medical reports of experts were produced on the eve of trial, although they were requested at least one year earlier, it was proper to exclude the experts at trial.[110] Tests performed by experts shortly before trial have also been excluded when local court rules required earlier disclosure, despite the argument that such tests were rebuttal and therefore not subject to the rules.[111] Moreover, an expert's deposition was denied and the witness's testimony excluded when counsel consulted the opposing expert ex parte.[112] In general, counsel should assume that federal judges will impose sanctions as a means of modifying attorney behavior concerning the perceived abuses surrounding expert testimony.

---

[104] *See* Smith v. Ford Motor Co., 626 F.2d 784, 797 (10th Cir. 1980), *cert. denied,* 450 U.S. 918 (1981); Holiday Inns, Inc. v. Robertshaw Controls Co., 560 F.2d 856, 858 (7th Cir. 1977).

[105] See § **28.2**.

[106] Basch v. Westinghouse Elec. Corp., 777 F.2d 165, 174 (4th Cir. 1985), *cert. denied,* _____ U.S. _____, 106 S. Ct. 1957 (1986).

[107] *See, e.g.,* Rosemount, Inc. v. Beckman Instruments, Inc., 727 F.2d 1540, 1549–50 (Fed Cir. 1984).

[108] *See* Smith v. Ford Motor Co., 626 F.2d 784, 797 (10th Cir. 1980), *cert. denied,* 450 U.S. 918 (1981).

[109] Gorby v. Schneider Tank Lines, Inc., 741 F.2d 1015, 1018–19 (7th Cir. 1984).

[110] Young v. City of New Orleans, 751 F.2d 794, 797 (5th Cir. 1985).

[111] *See, e.g.,* Emerick v. U.S. Suzuki Motor Corp., 750 F.2d 19, 21–22 (3d Cir. 1984).

[112] Campbell Indus. v. M/V Gemini, 619 F.2d 24, 27 (9th Cir. 1980).

CHAPTER 21

NONPARTY DISCOVERY

§ 21.1 Introduction

Although most discovery proceeds between the parties, information in the hands of nonparties can be important. Individuals who have witnessed events in a personal injury action as well as corporations which have had dealings with any of the parties in an antitrust case are likely candidates for such discovery. Although the full range of discovery procedures is not available, nonparties can be subpoenaed pursuant to Rule 45 to attend an oral or written deposition at which they can be directed to produce designated books, papers, documents, or tangible things for inspection and copying. The broad relevance standard found in Rule 26(b)(1) applies to nonparty as well as party discovery.[1] Rule 34(c)'s reference to independent actions which can be instituted to obtain production of documents and things as well as permission to enter upon land might be considered as another method to obtain nonparty discovery, but the jurisdictional requirements of such suits appear insurmountable.[2]

Since discovery from nonparties is perceived as an imposition, courts are generally receptive to cost shifting, which requires the subpoenaing party to pay the expenses associated with any production request.[3] Moreover, a nonparty

[1] *See* Fed. R. Civ. P. 45(d)(1).

[2] *See* Welling, *Discovery of Nonparties' Tangible Things Under the Federal Rules of Civil Procedure,* 59 Notre Dame L. Rev. 110 (1983).

[3] *See* Fed. R. Civ. P. 45(b).

cannot be required to compile information,[4] answer Rule 33 interrogatories, permit entry on land pursuant to Rule 34,[5] appear for a Rule 35 examination unless under the control of a party, or respond to Rule 36 requests for admissions.

Unlike parties who face sanctions if they do not appear at a noticed deposition, the only way to compel nonparty attendance and production of specifically identified documents is to issue a subpoena duces tecum. The procedure for obtaining such subpoenas is quite simple, and out-of-state depositions can be obtained as easily as local depositions. In fact, this is one benefit of litigating in federal court when witnesses are scattered, because obtaining such discovery is much more complicated in state practice. However, no federal procedure exists whereby a party can subpoena nonparty documents without providing for a deposition or hearing. Although many third parties will allow inspection of documents prior to the deposition, if this request is refused, counsel must either call a recess or continue the deposition to review the documents. Only if the parties agree that no deposition is necessary can the examining party avoid the expense of having a deposition officer present.

Counsel should always attempt to obtain document inspection informally from third parties prior to issuing a subpoena. First, the nonparty may have bad as well as good documents in its possession. Therefore, the overall desirability of such production must be assessed, because opposing counsel will no doubt also inspect the records. Second, even if a later deposition is necessary to authenticate records, the subpoena duces tecum can be limited to the items which counsel has previously selected.

§ 21.2 Obtaining the Subpoena

Before obtaining a subpoena, counsel must serve notice of the deposition on all parties.[6] If a subpoena duces tecum is employed, which commands the deponent to produce books, papers, documents, or tangible things designated therein for inspection and copying at the deposition, the deposition notice must attach the relevant document request.[7] The affidavit which composes the proof of service of the deposition notice is sufficient authorization for the clerk of the district court where the deposition will be taken to issue the subpoena.[8] The proof of service must be certified by the person who made service and must state the date, manner of service, and the names of the persons served.[9] The details of the

[4] 5A J. Moore & J. Lucas, Moore's Federal Practice ¶ 45.05[2] (2d ed. 1986) [hereinafter Moore's Federal Practice].

[5] Pollitt v. Mobay Chem. Corp., 95 F.R.D. 101, 106 (S.D. Ohio W.D. 1982).

[6] *See generally* Hecht, *How to Prepare a Notice of Deposition in Federal Practice (with Forms),* 32 Prac. Law. 13 (Mar. 1986).

[7] Fed. R. Civ. P. 45(d)(1).

[8] *Id.*

[9] *Id.*

subpoena are filled in by the party obtaining it. The subpoena must be personally served by a person over 18 who is not a party.[10] A subpoena issued on behalf of anyone other than the United States or its agencies is invalid unless witness fees for one day's attendance and mileage are tendered at the time of service.[11] The current amounts are found in 28 U.S. C. § 1821.

A nonparty witness can be required to attend a deposition only within 100 miles from the place where that person is served, resides, is employed, or personally transacts business.[12] Subpoenas requesting documents located in a district other than that in which a corporation was served have been quashed.[13]

§ 21.3 Procedures for Challenging Nonparty Discovery

Nonparties who are subpoenaed to give deposition testimony can only ignore the subpoena if service is improper; otherwise they must appear unless they have made a successful motion to quash.[14] Even if a deponent believes the subpoena is defective, it is safer to move to quash rather than face a contempt citation if the court upholds the subpoena.

Nonparties have several alternatives for objecting to a facially valid subpoena duces tecum but cannot simply refuse to obey it.[15] First, they can move to quash the subpoena.[16] Second, they can move to modify the subpoena if it is unreasonable and oppressive.[17] These types of motions are typically made for improper service, inability to appear, lack of possession of the designated material, failure to identify documents adequately, and recovery of the expense of complying with the subpoena.[18] Third, they can move to condition denial of the motion upon the payment of the reasonable cost of producing the materials by the subpoenaing party.[19] Fourth, they can move for a protective order under Rule 26(c)[20] and, if successful, can be awarded the costs of bringing the motion.[21]

---

[10] Fed. R. Civ. P. 45(c).

[11] CF&I Steel Corp. v. Mitsui & Co. (U.S.A.), 713 F.2d 494, 496 (9th Cir. 1983); *see* Fed. R. Civ. P. 45(c); *see generally* 5A Moore's Federal Practice ¶ 45.06[1] (2d ed. 1986); Annot., 77 A.L.R. Fed. 863 (1986).

[12] Fed. R. Civ. P. 45(d)(2).

[13] Ariel v. Jones, 693 F.2d 1058, 1060–61 (11th Cir. 1982); Cates v. LTV Aerospace Corp., 480 F.2d 620, 622–24 (5th Cir. 1973).

[14] *See* King v. Fidelity Nat'l Bank of Baton Rouge, 712 F.2d 188, 191 (5th Cir. 1983), *cert. denied,* 465 U.S. 1029 (1984).

[15] 5A Moore's Federal Practice ¶ 45.03[6].

[16]. Fed. R. Civ. P. 45(b).

[17] *Id.*

[18] 2A Moore's Federal Practice ¶ 45.05[3].

[19] Fed. R. Civ. P. 45(b).

[20] Fed. R. Civ. P. 45(d)(1).

[21] Fed. R. Civ. P. 26(c).

Each of these motions must be made promptly, at or before the time specified for compliance of the subpoena.

Nonparties can also serve written objections to producing material on the attorney designated in the subpoena.[22] Such objections are due within 10 days after being served with the subpoena, or if compliance is required earlier, on or before the time specified in the subpoena.[23] Unlike Rule 34, there is no requirement that the reasons for the objections be stated. Once objection is made, the subpoenaing party can obtain the materials only pursuant to an order of the court from which the subpoena was issued.[24] Rule 45(d)(1) provides that the subpoenaing party can move for such an order at any time before or during the deposition, but a motion to compel made after the deposition has been permitted.[25]

Serving written objections is the least expensive method that a nonparty can employ to challenge the subpoena. It also ensures that any litigation concerning enforcement will be located in the district in which the deposition will take place, rather than the district in which the action is pending. In contrast, nonparty motions for a protective order in the district where the deposition is held have been transferred to the district in which the underlying action is being litigated.[26]

§ 21.4 Grounds for Challenging Nonparty Discovery

Because document production can be extremely costly, it is not unusual for even large organizations to challenge subpoenas.[27] The burden of proving that a subpoena is oppressive is on the person challenging it.[28] In determining whether a subpoena is unreasonable, courts have balanced the relevance of the discovery sought, the requesting party's need, and the potential hardship of the nonparty

---

[22] Fed. R. Civ. P. 45(d)(1).

[23] *Id.*

[24] *Id.*

[25] Kendrick v. Heckler, 778 F.2d 253, 258 (5th Cir. 1985).

[26] *See, e.g.*, Socialist Workers Party v. Attorney Gen., 73 F.R.D. 699, 700–01 (D. Md. 1977).

[27] *See, e.g., In re* Coordinated Pretrial Proceedings In Petroleum Prods. Antitrust Litig., 669 F.2d 620, 623 (10th Cir. 1982) (discovery conditioned on payment of $8,000); Pollitt v. Mobay Chem. Corp., 95 F.R.D. 101, 105 (S.D. Ohio W.D. 1982) (protective order concerning production which would cost over $300,000 treated as motion to quash or modify); *see also* United States v. C.B.S., 666 F.2d 364, 367–68 (9th Cir.), *cert. denied,* 457 U.S. 1118 (1982) (motion for more than $2 million timely, although discovery nearly completed, when issue previously reserved).

[28] Heat & Control, Inc. v. Hester Indus., Inc., 785 F.2d 1017, 1025 (Fed. Cir. 1986); Northrop Corp. v. McDonnell Douglas Corp., 751 F.2d 395, 403 (D.C. Cir. 1984).

subject to the subpoena.[29] Courts often attempt to formulate a protective order[30] or require the subpoenaed party's expenses to be paid, rather than deny all discovery. For example, if confidentiality is an issue, a court can order disclosure of confidential material to an impartial third party or an expert paid by the party seeking discovery or require that only non-identifying information be provided.[31] Besides confidentiality, privilege is often given as a reason to withhold nonparty information from discovery. The law concerning privilege is applied equally to parties and nonparties.[32]

§ 21.5 Enforcing the Subpoena

If the nonparty fails to appear at a deposition, this can be treated as contempt of court.[33] However, although a party can be reimbursed for the expense of obtaining a motion to compel discovery under Rules 37(a)(4), and 37(d), there is no provision for obtaining costs from a nonparty for failure to attend a deposition. Therefore, an award of expenses for a motion to compel nonparty discovery can be made only if the nonparty demonstrated bad faith.[34] Conversely, the nonparty cannot obtain an award of expenses for an aborted deposition without a showing of the subpoenaing party's bad faith.[35] If counsel does not subpoena a supposedly friendly nonparty who then fails to appear at the deposition, the expenses of any other party attending the deposition can be assessed against the noticing party.[36] When a nonparty fails to obey a court order to attend or answer questions, an award of expenses is permitted under Rule 37(a)(4).

Deponents who appear but refuse to answer cannot be held in contempt without a court order directing them to respond.[37] The district court must provide an opportunity for the nonparty to show an adequate excuse for any noncompliance.[38] Employees of a party who are officers, directors, or managing agents are considered as parties for purposes of imposing sanctions and need not be subpoenaed to require their attendance.[39]

---

[29] Heat & Control, Inc. v. Hester Indus., Inc., 785 F.2d 1017, 1024 (Fed. Cir. 1986); Deitchman v. E.R. Squibb & Sons, Inc., 740 F.2d 556, 566 (7th Cir. 1984); *see* United States v. C.B.S., 666 F.2d 364, 371 n.9 (9th Cir.), *cert. denied,* 457 U.S. 1118 (1982).

[30] See **ch. 19**.

[31] Deitchman v. E.R. Squibb & Sons, Inc., 740 F.2d 556, 564–65 (7th Cir. 1984).

[32] See **ch. 18**.

[33] Fed. R. Civ. P. 45(f).

[34] Pennwalt Corp. v. Durand-Wayland, Inc., 708 F.2d 492, 494–95 (9th Cir. 1983).

[35] Westmoreland v. CBS, Inc., 770 F.2d 1168, 1178 (D.C. Cir. 1985).

[36] Fed. R. Civ. P. 30(g)(2).

[37] Fremont Energy Corp. v. Seattle Post Intelligencer, 688 F.2d 1285, 1287 (9th Cir. 1982).

[38] *Id.*

[39] Fed. R. Civ. P. 37(d).

§ 21.6 Reviewability of Orders Affecting Nonparties

The review of discovery orders and sanctions has generated inconsistent approaches among the circuits.[40] Generally, an order granting a nonparty's motion to quash is not appealable if it is issued by the court in which the litigation is pending, because it is not considered final.[41] However, if the district court which grants the motion is in a different district from the court hearing the merits, the order will be immediately reviewed[42] for abuse of discretion.[43] In multidistrict litigation, where the transferee judge issued the contempt over the telephone to a deponent in a different district, jurisdiction was appropriate in the district where the deposition was being taken.[44]

Some courts permit nonparties to obtain immediate review of an order upholding a subpoena which is issued by a different district from that hearing the underlying action.[45] The law is settled that a person who is held in criminal contempt for violating a subpoena can also immediately appeal the validity of the subpoena as long as the grounds for challenging the subpoena were raised in the district court.[46] Unlike parties, who cannot appeal from a civil contempt order prior to judgment, a nonparty can immediately appeal from a finding of civil contempt.[47] Some circuits review third party subpoenas when enforcement would violate a privilege held by a person other than the individual subpoenaed even though the third party has not been held in contempt.[48]

---

[40] See §§ **17.17–17.20**.

[41] *See generally* 9 Moore's Federal Practice ¶ 110.13[2].

[42] Heat & Control, Inc. v. Hester Indus., Inc., 785 F.2d 1017, 1021 (Fed. Cir. 1986); CF&I Steel Corp. v. Mitsui & Co. (U.S.A.), 713 F.2d 494, 496 (9th Cir. 1983); Ariel v. Jones, 693 F.2d 1058, 1059 (11th Cir. 1982); *see generally* 8 C. Wright & A. Miller, Federal Practice and Procedure § 2006 (1970).

[43] Heat & Control, Inc. v. Hester Indus., Inc., 785 F.2d 1017, 1022 (Fed. Cir. 1986); Ohio-Sealy Mattress Mfg. Co. v. Duncan, 749 F.2d 1560, 1561 (11th Cir. 1985); Deitchman v. E.R. Squibb & Sons, Inc., 740 F.2d 556, 563 (7th Cir. 1984); Dart Indus. Co. v. Westwood Chem. Co., 649 F.2d 646, 648 (9th Cir. 1980).

[44] *In re* Corrugated Container Anti-trust Litig., 662 F.2d 875, 879. 881–82 (D.C. Cir. 1981) and cases cited therein.

[45] Westmoreland v. CBS, Inc., 770 F.2d 1168, 1172 (D.C. Cir. 1985); National Life Ins. Co. v. Hartford Accident & Indem. Co., 615 F.2d 595, 597 & n.2 (3d Cir. 1980). *But see* Alexander v. United States, 201 U.S. 117, 121 (1906).

[46] *See* United States v. Rylander, 460 U.S. 752, 760–61 (1983).

[47] Alexander v. United States, 201 U.S. 117, 121 (1906); *see In re* Corrugated Container Anti-trust Litig., 662 F.2d 875, 877 (D.C. Cir. 1981).

[48] *E.g., In re* Grand Jury Subpoena Duces Tecum January 2, 1985, 767 F.2d 26, 29 (2d Cir. 1985); Wm. T. Thompson Co. v. General Nutrition Corp., 671 F.2d 100, 103 (3d Cir. 1982); *see* Perlman v. United States 247 U.S. 7, 13 (1918).

§ 21.7 Custodian of Records Depositions

Subpoenas duces tecum are commonly used to obtain custodian of records depositions. Often, documents in the possession of third parties may be relevant to the litigation. Although some of these documents are also found in the files of the parties, it still can be beneficial to take a custodian of records deposition. First, if the party sent the original of a document and kept a copy, the original will be signed, and its existence verifies that it was sent. Second, nonparty documents can be admitted into evidence only if the appropriate business record foundation has been established, unless their foundation has been admitted pursuant to a Rule 36 request. A party's mere production of such documents from its files does not make them admissible. Third, if counsel suspects that the opposing party has altered some documents, such discovery can confirm whether spoliation did occur.

The custodian should always be asked whether he has been designated as custodian for purposes of the deposition and has produced all documents subject to the subpoena. The custodian's position should be ascertained as well as a description of how and by whom the documents were selected, why any documents or categories were not produced, and whether they will be produced. Details concerning the entity's method of keeping records must be obtained, including the location of the records selected. Any produced documents which were not generated by the subpoenaed nonparty should be identified to the extent possible, including how they came to be in the organization's files.

After these preliminary matters have been determined, the remainder of the deposition focuses on establishing a business records foundation for each of the selected documents. Federal Rule of Evidence 803 (6) provides a hearsay exception[49] for any memorandum, report, record, or data compilation, in any form, of acts, events, conditions, opinion, or diagnosis which was (1) made at or near the time, (2) by or from information transmitted by a person with knowledge, (3) if kept in the course of a regularly conducted business activity, (4) if it was the regular practice of that business activity to make the record, (5) unless the source of information or the method or circumstances of preparation indicate lack of trustworthiness. Counsel must be careful to authenticate computer data as well under this rule.[50] The custodian is not required to have personal knowledge of the document, and it is sufficient that the person who authored the document is identified as an employee proceeding in the regular course of business. If reports are authenticated, counsel should inquire whether the company relied upon facts from sources which were not within the personal

---

[49] *See generally* 4 Weinstein & M. Berger, Weinstein's Evidence ¶ 803(6)[01]–[08] (1985).

[50] *See generally* Peritz, *Computer Data and Reliability: A Call for Authentication of Business Records Under the Federal Rules of Evidence,* 80 Nw. U.L. Rev. 956 (1986).

knowledge of individuals within the organization, and if so, their source should be identified.

Although the business record foundation is easily established, failure to inquire about any element will make a document inadmissible if objected to at trial.[51] Technically, if the nonparty who has produced the documents is within subpoena range, live testimony is required at trial to admit them, but most parties will stipulate to the use of a custodian deposition. Moreover, after the deposition, a party can propound requests for admissions that the relevant documents are authentic and meet the business record foundation. The pretrial order can also obviate the need to produce foundational testimony concerning such documents at trial.

Subpoenas duces tecum as well as Freedom of Information Act requests[52] can be utilized to obtain public records and reports. These materials can be admitted at trial pursuant to Federal Rule of Evidence 803(8), which also provides admission for factual findings resulting from an investigation made pursuant to authority granted by law, unless the sources of information or other circumstances indicate lack of trustworthiness.[53] Certified copies of public records are admissible at trial without authentication by a custodian.[54]

§ 21.8 Administrative Subpoenas

Administrative subpoenas are governed by the particular statutes governing the agency. To the extent that Rule 45 does not conflict with any such authority, it will be applied.[55] The granting of discovery in subpoena enforcement cases to obtain grounds to prevent enforcement is within the discretion of the district court,[56] but some circuits allow discovery only when exceptional circumstances indicate the agency has engaged in an abuse of process.[57] Targets of administrative investigations are not required to be given notice when a subpoena is issued

---

[51] *See generally* E. Imwinkelried, Evidentiary Foundations (1986) for foundational questions concerning all types of evidence.

[52] See §§ **17.6–17.7**.

[53] *See generally* 4 J. Weinstein & M. Berger, Weinstein's Evidence ¶ 803(8)[01]–[05] (1985).

[54] *See* Fed. R. Evid. P. 803(8), 902(1), (2), and 1005.

[55] 5A Moore's Federal Practice ¶ 45.02[2].

[56] *E.g.*, Chen Chi Wang v. United States, 757 F.2d 1000, 1004 (9th Cir. 1985); United States v. Merit Petroleum, Inc., 731 F.2d 901, 905 (Temp. Emer. Ct. App. 1984).

[57] *See, e.g.*, EEOC v. St. Regis Paper Co., 717 F.2d 1302, 1304 (9th Cir. 1983); *In re* EEOC, 709 F.2d 392, 400 (5th Cir. 1983).

to a third party to obtain information concerning them.[58] Similarly, when the I.R.S. serves a summons on a known taxpayer with the dual purpose of investigating that person as well as unnamed parties' tax liabilities, it need not comply with the more elaborate John Doe summons procedures.[59]

---

[58] SEC v. Jerry T. O'Brien, Inc., 467 U.S. 735, 745 (1984).

[59] Tiffany Fine Arts, Inc. v. United States, 469 U.S. 310, 324 (1985).

CHAPTER 22

INTERNATIONAL DISCOVERY

§ 22.1 Introduction

Although travel is a standard part of modern litigation practice, few attorneys are lucky enough to have depositions scheduled in such places as Bermuda. However, given the large number of transnational corporations, discovery involving foreign nationals is becoming commonplace, even if the ensuing document production or deposition takes place in the United States. International discovery can be extremely frustrating. Generalities about foreign practice are difficult, because each country has its idiosyncrasies. About all that can safely be said is that other countries are much more hostile to discovery than the United States.

§ 22.2 The Hague Convention's Impact on Federal Rule Discovery

Despite the natural assumption of attorneys that parties must respond to discovery under the federal rules whether they are located in the United States or abroad, this result is not guaranteed. Furthermore, discovery from nonparties who do not voluntarily comply with requests for production or depositions is subject to the territorial limitations of federal jurisdiction.

International discovery usually proceeds under the Federal Rules of Evidence or under the Hague Evidence Convention.[1] The convention, which has been

[1] The Hague Convention on the Taking of Evidence Abroad in Civil or Commercial Matters, opened for signature Mar. 18, 1970, 23 U.S.T. 2555, T.I.A.S. No. 7444, 847 U.N.T.S. 231,

signed by 17 countries, including the United States, Great Britain, and most of Europe, provides a means to obtain pretrial civil discovery within the signatory nations.

Federal courts have been grappling with the issue of the relationship between discovery under the convention and under the federal rules. The Supreme Court has recently rejected the extreme position that, because the United States is a signatory to the convention, the convention provides the exclusive means of discovery in transnational litigation.[2] The Court also refused to require that the litigants must first resort to convention procedures before initiating discovery under the federal rules.[3] Instead, a case-by-case inquiry was adopted as the preferred method by which district court judges determine whether to resort to convention procedures rather than federal rules discovery.[4] The Court refused to articulate specific rules to guide this delicate task of adjudication, other than to caution judges to supervise pretrial proceedings closely to prevent abusive discovery and to consider the demands of comity as well as the likelihood that resort to the convention would prove effective in a given case.[5]

In light of this policy, it is fair to infer that many district court judges will tend to favor application of the federal rules over unfamiliar, complicated, and time-consuming convention procedures.[6] However, counsel involved in litigation concerning foreign parties or foreign discovery must be prepared to argue whether the convention should be applied in a given case. Moreover, it is unlikely that the district court's decision as to which procedures to apply can be effectively reviewed, because it would be an interlocutory ruling which would not be immediately appealable and would rarely generate reversible error on any ultimate appeal of the merits of the action.[7]

Although the Supreme Court stated that the existence of a foreign blocking statute which makes compliance with a United States discovery request illegal does not require automatic resort to convention procedures,[8] it did note that the degree of friction created by the discovery requests may suggest that some efforts should be made to moderate them.[9] Litigants often argue that protective orders prohibiting discovery should be ordered and sanctions not imposed for

---

codified at 28 U.S.C. § 1781 (*reprinted in* 8 Martindale-Hubbell Law Directory pt. 7, at 12 (1987) (Hague Convention).

[2] Societe Nationale Industrielle Aerospatiale v. United States Dist. Court for S. Dist. of Iowa, ____ U.S. ____, 107 S. Ct. 2542, 2548, 55 U.S.L.W. 4842, 4844 (June 15, 1987).

[3] 107 S. Ct. at 2555.

[4] *Id.* at

[5] *Id.* at 2556-57.

[6] *See id.* at 2558 (Blackmun, Brennan, Marshall and O'Connor, JJ., concurring in part and dissenting in part).

[7] *See* §§ **17.17–17.20**.

[8] Societe Nationale Industrielle Aerospatiate v. United States Dist. Court for S. Dist. of Iowa, ____ U.S. ____, 107 S. Ct. 2542, 2556 n.29.

[9] *Id.*, quoting American Law Institute, Restatement of Foreign Relations Law of the United States (Revised) § 437, Reporter's Note 5 at 41, 42 (Tent. Draft No. 7, 1986) (approved May 14, 1986).

discovery failures caused by blocking statutes.[10] It is likely that, in determining whether to compel such discovery or sanction disobedience of such discovery orders, the federal court will employ one of the two following approaches:

1. It will adopt the comity analysis suggested by the Restatement of Foreign Relations Law of the United States (Revised) § 437(1)(c),[11] which lists the following factors:
   a. The importance to the litigation of the documents or other information requested
   b. The degree of specificity of the request
   c. Whether the information originated in the United States
   d. The availability of alternative means of securing the information, and
   e. The extent to which noncompliance with the request would undermine important interests of the United States or compliance with the request would undermine important interests of the state where the information is located.
2. It will adopt a three-factor balancing test based on *Societe Internationale v. Rogers,*[12] which views the importance of congressional policy, the importance of the requested information, and the degree of flexibility in the enforcement of the foreign country's law.[13]

An analysis of the particular facts of the case as well as sovereign interests is required in formulating counsel's argument under either of these tests.[14]

§ 22.3 Obtaining Foreign Discovery under the Rules

International discovery takes place pursuant to the federal rules when the court decides that provisions of the Hague Convention should not be followed or do not apply because the foreign country is not a signatory and no other multinational convention or bilateral treaty exists which affects pretrial discovery.[15] Of course, the parties or nonparty witnesses can agree voluntarily to comply with

---

[10] *See, e.g., In re* Westinghouse Elec. Corp. Uranium Contracts Litig., 563 F.2d 992, 996 (10th Cir. 1977).

[11] Tent. Draft No. 7, 1986 (approved May 14, 1986), *cited with approval in* Societe Nationale Industrielle Aerospatiale v. United States Dist. Court for S. Dist. of Iowa, ____ U.S. ____, 107 S. Ct. 2542, 2555, 55 U.S.L.W. 4842, 4848 n.28 (June 15, 1987).

[12] 357 U.S. 197, 205–06 (1958).

[13] *In re* Uranium Antitrust Litig., 480 F.2d 1138, 1144, 1146–48 (N.D. Ill. 1979).

[14] *See, e.g.*, Societe Nationale Industrielle Aerospatiale v. United States Dist. Court for S. Dist. of Iowa, ____ U.S. ____, 107 S. Ct. 2542, 2555-57, 55 U.S.L.W. 4842, 4848 (June 15, 1987).

[15] *See generally* Lane & Herman, *Discovery of Evidence Located in Foreign Countries—Part 1,* 8 CEB Civ. Lit. Rptr. 1, 8 (1986).

discovery abroad. However, if any doubt exists as to a witness's compliance, following the federal rules procedures as well as any local requirements is desirable, because some countries prohibit even voluntary depositions.[16] The Citizens Consular Services of the Department of State should be consulted for information concerning foreign evidentiary requirements as well as for the names of local counsel in most countries. Otherwise, simply taking the deposition can be a risky venture. For example, an attorney was arrested in Switzerland for taking a deposition, after the party being deposed called the authorities because he was upset by the questioning. Although the individual being deposed was a party to an action pending in federal court and acted against the advice of his own American counsel, the attorneys were detained nearly nine hours. Monetary sanctions were imposed by the judge in the underlying federal action and the deposition was rescheduled in the United States.[17]

Rule 28 provides that depositions can be taken in foreign countries on notice before a person authorized to administer oaths. Depositions can also be taken by a person commissioned by the court,[18] or pursuant to a letter rogatory.[19] Obtaining discovery from parties abroad is procedurally the same as in the United States. If a party does not appear for a noticed deposition, answer interrogatories, or respond to a document request, Rule 37 sanctions can be imposed.[20] Notice to a nonparty is useful only if the person is willing to appear voluntarily. Usually voluntary depositions are taken before a consular officer if this is not prohibited by local law.

It should be understood that commissions and letters rogatory are not a direct equivalent of the subpoena duces tecum for production of documents at a deposition. Not only are the procedures for obtaining such discovery different, but the commissioner has no power to compel attendance, and the host country may decline to execute the letter rogatory to require the discovery. Moreover, in some countries, a compelled oral deposition will be taken by the judge on written questions supplied by counsel.[21] Since obtaining discovery through letters rogatory is often a long and complex process, they should be used only when notice or a commission is not feasible. If discovery will take place in a country which is a party to the Hague Convention, a letter of request[22] rather than a letter rogatory should be used.

Procedurally, Rule 28 provides that a commission or letter rogatory shall be issued on application and notice on terms that are just and appropriate. No

---

[16] *See* White, *Obtaining Evidence in Europe,* 21 Trial 55, 57 n.1 (August, 1985); *see also* Lane & Herman, *Discovery of Evidence Located in Foreign Countries—Part 2,* 8 CEB Civ. Lit. Rep. 41, 42 (1986) (listing countries prohibiting voluntary depositions).

[17] *Swiss Detention of Lawyer Costly to Fraud Defendant,* Nat'l L.J., Jan. 18, 1982, at 9, col. 1.

[18] Fed. R. Civ. P. 28(b)(2).

[19] Fed. R. Civ. P. 28(b)(3).

[20] *See* Fed. R. Civ. P. 37(d); 8 Federal Practice and Procedure § 2083, at 350.

[21] *See* Shemanski, *Obtaining Evidence in the Federal Republic of Germany: Impact of the Hague Evidence Convention on German-American Judicial Cooperation,* 17 Int'l Law. 465 (1983).

[22] See § **22.5**.

criteria are listed, other than that the taking of the deposition in any other manner need not be impractical or inconvenient for such methods to be used. The refusal to issue a commission or letters rogatory is reviewed for abuse of discretion.[23] Although the judge is not required to list a reason for denying an application, abuse has been found when no reason was stated and the denial resulted in a failure to obtain evidence on critical issues.[24]

A notice or commission should designate the person before whom the deposition is to be taken either by name or descriptive title. Letters rogatory are addressed to the appropriate authority in the host country and can be issued by any federal court.[25] The request should include a translation and any necessary fees[26] as well as a description of the case, the exact relief requested, information concerning the whereabouts of the individual from whom the evidence will be taken, and any specific instructions concerning the return of the evidence. Since many countries are hostile to discovery, counsel should not mention that term. For example, a letter rogatory should simply request that a witness be compelled to appear to give evidence rather than for a deposition. The documents to be transmitted include the letter rogatory, a judicial order, and whatever certification the court uses confirming the authorization of the letter. Either the court can directly submit the letter rogatory to the appropriate foreign authority or send it to the State Department for transmittal. Evidentiary rules for depositions obtained through letters rogatory are more liberal than for domestic depositions, in that irregularities such as lack of a verbatim transcript or failure to place the deponent under oath do not necessarily require exclusion of the transcript.[27]

§ 22.4 Discovery of American Nationals Pursuant to Statute

Foreign discovery can also be obtained through 28 U.S.C. § 1783, which permits a national or resident of the United States who is in a foreign country to be subpoenaed for deposition and production of documents or tangible things. Such subpoenas are difficult to obtain because they can only be issued if the court finds that the discovery is necessary in the interest of justice and (1) it is not possible to obtain the testimony in admissible form without the witness's personal appearance or (2) the document production cannot be obtained in any other manner.[28] Therefore, the person must fail to appear before a commissioner before counsel can resort to this procedure, and then the court must be convinced that the subpoena is necessary.

---

[23] *See, e.g.*, Complaint of Bankers Trust Co., 752 F.2d 874, 889 (3d Cir. 1984).

[24] *Id.* at 890.

[25] *See* 28 U.S.C. § 1781 (1982).

[26] *See* 22 CFR § 92.66(b) (1986).

[27] Fed. R. Civ. P. 28(b).

[28] 28 U.S.C. § 1783(a) (1982).

§ 22.5 Discovery under the Hague Convention

The Hague Convention permits evidence to be obtained by using letters of request, consular officers, and commissioners. Counsel may be required to obtain evidence through the convention either as a prerequisite to obtaining federal rules discovery or as the exclusive means of obtaining discovery.[29]

A letter of request can be sent by the court directly to the proper authority to obtain testimony, documents, and the inspection of real or personal property.[30] Arguably, interrogatories are also appropriate,[31] because a request made for any special method or procedure will be followed unless it is incompatible with the laws of the country of execution.[32] Requests should be narrowly drawn and specifically identify any documents desired. Most parties to the convention have reserved their right not to execute letters of requests for the purpose of obtaining pretrial discovery of documents.[33] Therefore, a request is more likely to be granted if the documents are admissible in a judicial proceeding than merely lead to admissible evidence.

Article 3 lists all of the information which should be specified in the request including:

1. The identification of the case, the parties, and the authority requesting execution
2. The nature of the proceedings for which the evidence is required
3. A detailed description of the evidence to be obtained or other judicial act to be performed
4. Whether the evidence must be given under oath or affirmation, and
5. Any other special procedures.

If the request is not in the language of the foreign country, it should be accompanied by a translation both to avoid misunderstandings and to comply with the requirements of such countries as France and Germany which will not

---

[29] For procedures under the Hague Convention, *see generally* R. Haydock & D. Herr, Discovery Practice ch. 11 (1982); B. Ristau, International Judicial Assistance (Civil and Commercial) (1984); *Extraterritorial Discovery in International Litigation,* Seidel Chair, PLI No. 248, at 149–92 (1984); *see also* Lane & Herman, *Discovery of Evidence Located in Foreign Countries* (parts 1 and 2), 8 CEB Civ. Lit. Rep. 1, 41 (1986); Oxman, *The Choice Between Direct Discovery and Other Means of Obtaining Evidence Abroad: The Impact of the Hague Evidence Convention,* 37 U. Miami L. Rev. 733 (1983); Platto, *Taking Evidence Abroad For Use in Civil Cases in the United States—A Practical Guide,* 16 Int'l Law. 575 (1982); Radvan *The Hague Convention on Taking of Evidence Abroad in Civil or Commercial Matter: Several Notes Concerning its Scope, Methods and Compulsion,* 16 N.Y.U. J. Int'l L. & Pol. 1031 (1984); White, *Obtaining Evidence In Europe,* Trial 55 (Aug. 1985); *Cf.* Ristau, *Service of Process in Foreign Countries Under the Hague Service Convention,* 8 CEB Civ. Lit. Rep. 85 (1986).

[30] Hague Convention art. 3(e)–(g).

[31] *See id.* art. 3(e).

[32] *Id.* art. 9.

[33] *See id.* art. 23 and notifications printed following the convention.

accept a request in English.[34] A letter can request that the parties be notified where and when the request will be executed so that they can be present.[35] A model for a letter of request which can be used as a drafting guide, is printed at the end of the Hague Convention.

Once issued, the letter of request has the advantage that it can be enforced by compulsory process.[36] The person responding to the request can invoke any privilege available in either the United States or the foreign country.[37] The request should specifically set forth any relevant United States privileges which can be invoked, or such privileges will have to be confirmed.[38] Foreign privileges can be difficult to ascertain without advice of local counsel and often effectively block discovery.[39]

Counsel should also be aware that in many countries the questioning is done by a court official of the host country rather than by the parties. In such cases, written questions are submitted with the request. While the examiner has discretion to permit additional questions to be asked at the deposition, counsel should assume that such a request probably will not be granted in civil law countries.

Alternatively, the Hague Convention permits diplomatic officers and consular agents or commissioners appointed by federal courts to take evidence without compulsion.[40] Some signatories require permission for such deposition, regardless of whether the deponent is a United States or foreign national.

§ 22.6 Practical Concerns

Because of the expense and complexities involved in obtaining discovery outside the United States, counsel should attempt whenever possible to acquire such information by alternative means. For example, foreign public documents can be obtained through consular offices, and the United States has simplified authentication problems by treaty and statute.[41] It also may be feasible to have a foreign deponent travel to the United States if the witness's travel expenses are paid. If not, the Citizens Consular Service should be consulted concerning local laws, which should then be researched to ensure that appropriate local procedures are

---

[34] *See id.* art. 4 and notifications printed following the convention.

[35] *Id.* art. 9.

[36] *Id.* art. 10.

[37] *Id.* art. 11.

[38] *Id.* art. 11(b).

[39] *See* Lane & Herman, *Discovery of Evidence Located in Foreign Countries—Part 1,* 8 CEB Civ. Lit. Rep. 1, 6 (1986); Platto, *Taking Evidence Abroad for Use in Civil Cases in the United States—A Practical Guide,* 16 Int'l Law. 575 (1982).

[40] Hague Convention arts. 15, 16.

[41] *See, e.g.*, Convention Abolishing the Requirement of Legalislation of Foreign Public Documents, opened for signature Oct. 5 1961, T.I.A.S. 10072, 527 U.N.T.S. 189; 18 U.S.C. §§ 3491–3494 (1982).

followed.[42] It is often desirable to employ local counsel who is familiar with arranging foreign depositions.

The deposition must be scheduled well in advance before the appropriate commissioner or consular officer in an embassy or consulate, unless another location is permitted. The rules concerning consular depositions are equivalent to those governing depositions in the United States.[43] Counsel must hire a local interpreter and court reporter, have deposition exhibits translated, pay any required fees, and obtain any special visas. Particularly in cases involving multiple depositions in specialized areas, the examining party should consider bringing a court reporter who is familiar with the case to the deposition, although this is expensive.

Even under the best of circumstances, acquiring discovery from nationals of other countries is often slow and tedious. Most of the advantages associated with oral depositions are lost if counsel is not permitted to question the witness directly. If counsel is permitted to take the deposition, a good deal of spontaneity is still forfeited because of time constraints inherent in translating the questions and answers, which inevitably slow the pace of the questioning. Usually each side brings someone who understands the language, since differences often arise during the deposition about the accuracy of translated documents, questions, and answers. In addition, documents and interrogatory answers obtained in response to letters rogatory or letters of request as well as deposition transcripts may have to be translated into English once the evidence is returned to the issuing court.

§ 22.7 Obtaining Discovery in the United States for Litigation Abroad

Federal courts can be used to obtain discovery for litigation outside the United States. Such discovery can be secured under the Hague Convention as well as through an action initiated to obtain judicial assistance of foreign tribunals.[44] One issue which has arisen in this context is whether foreign litigants can obtain discovery of United States residents which is unavailable to them in the location where the action is pending. At least one circuit has permitted discovery without considering the availability of reciprocal procedures or the admissibility of the evidence in the foreign court.[45]

---

[42] *See, e.g.*, Lane & Herman, *Discovery of Evidence Located in Foreign Countries—Part 2*, 8 CEB Civ. Lit. Rep. 41, 48–49 (1986) (chart of discovery requirements for Hague Evidence Convention Signators).

[43] *See* 22 C.F.R. §§ 92.49 *et seq*. (1986).

[44] 28 U.S.C. § 1782 (1982).

[45] John Deere Ltd. v. Sperry Corp., 754 F.2d 132, 133 (3d Cir. 1985).

CHAPTER 23

DEPOSITIONS

§ 23.1 Strategic Overview of Deposition Practice

Depositions are the most commonly used discovery method because of their many advantages. Unlike most other discovery, which must be directed to parties in the action, any person who has information relevant to the subject matter of the litigation can be deposed. In addition, the spontaneity of an oral deposition is not available through any other means of discovery. In an oral deposition, answers to questions can be immediately followed up, and the responses come directly from the deponent without the artful editing of counsel. A deponent's demeanor and responsiveness to questions can be evaluated to determine how effective the deponent will be at trial, which may be vital in deciding whether and on what terms to settle the action. The entire range of a deponent's knowledge can be explored, including information based on hearsay which may provide valuable leads for further discovery. Admissions and impeachment materials can be developed at the deposition, and deponents can be locked into their trial testimony. The deposition may also be used to support a summary judgment motion or to preserve testimony of witnesses who will be unavailable for trial.

The major disadvantages associated with depositions relate to their cost and logistics. Transcripts are quite expensive, even if counsel does not request expedited service. Often witnesses are located far from the lawyer's home base, and counsel's time and travel expenses must be factored into any decision concerning the desirability of taking a deposition. The defending party also must bear the cost of attending the deposition. Moreover, the cost of the taking and transcribing of a deposition is taxable to the losing party if it is used at trial or in some circuits if the deposition was reasonably necessary when taken.[1] Indigent litigants face additional difficulties in obtaining depositions, because authorization to advance payment of deposition costs is discretionary with the court.[2]

Even if cost is not a significant factor, the deposition of a distant or potentially unavailable deponent can be a disaster if it results in the admissibility of damaging evidence which would not otherwise exist. Therefore, evidentiary considerations should never be overlooked when evaluating whether to take a deposition.

[1] *See* 28 U.S.C. § 1920(2) (1982); Fed. R. Civ. P. 54(d); Syntex Ophthalmics, Inc. v. Novicky, 795 F.2d 983, 986 (Fed. Cir. 1986); Hernandez v. George, 793 F.2d 264, 268–69 (10th Cir. 1986); Templeman v. Chris Craft Corp., 770 F.2d 245, 249 (1st Cir.), *cert. denied,*_____ U.S. _____, 106 S. Ct. 571 (1985); 6 J. Moore *et al.,* Moore's Federal Practice ¶ 54.77[4] (2d ed. 1986) [hereinafter Moore's Federal Practice].

[2] *See* 28 U.S.C. §1915 (1982).

§ 23.2 Alternative Methods of Taking Depositions

Less expensive methods of taking depositions are available but have some drawbacks. A deposition can be taken by written questions,[3] which does not require the examiner's presence. Such discovery has several disadvantages. First, it is little better than propounding interrogatories, because such questions can be learned by the deponent in advance and be discussed with counsel. Second, there is no opportunity for immediate followup. Third, both cross and redirect questions must be served prior to the deposition before counsel knows the witness's response.[4]

In lieu of participating in an oral examination, parties can also serve written questions which are read at the deposition.[5] Although there is no possibility for followup by the party examining by means of such written questions, this method can be useful in litigation concerning multiple parties. If several parties have similar interests, the depositions can be divided among them and the absent parties can serve written questions relating to any matters about which they wish specific responses. Although such questioning is economical, counsel must be confident that the oral questioner will in fact adequately pursue any of the answers to the written questions which are propounded, because the deposition can later be introduced against absent parties as if they were present.[6]

Telephone depositions provide a low-cost method to obtain most of the advantages of oral depositions, but they can be taken only upon written stipulation or court order.[7] They cannot be used to assess a deponent's demeanor. A speaker phone is a necessity for such depositions, and the record can be difficult to follow unless each person talking is properly identified. Even then, it is more difficult to question concerning documents in telephone than oral depositions.[8]

§ 23.3 Analyzing the Purpose of Depositions

Although deposition strategy depends on the nature of the individual action being litigated, a successful deposition is usually the result of detailed preparation.[9] Careful case analysis is a prerequisite to any deposition. Unless counsel's

---

[3] Fed. R. Civ. P. 31.

[4] Fed. R. Civ. P. 31(a).

[5] Fed. R. Civ. P. 30(c).

[6] *See* Fed. R. Civ. P. 32(a); §§ **23.29–23.30**.

[7] Fed. R. Civ. P. 30(b)(7).

[8] *See* 4A Moore's Federal Practice ¶ 30.57[15].

[9] *See generally* Deposition Strategy, Law and Forms (1986) (multiple volumes and authors); D. Danner, Pattern Deposition Checklists (2d ed. 1984); R. Haydock & D. Herr, Discovery

theories of liability or defense have been generally developed, the deposition will leave more questions unresolved than answered when it is consulted during trial preparation. This does not mean that depositions must wait until the end of discovery—only that early depositions should be preceded by both factual and legal research to determine how the deponent's testimony is expected to be helpful to the case.[10]

Identifying the purpose of the deposition is also important in determining strategy. Several different types of depositions exist which can be categorized generally as *discovery depositions, dump depositions,* and *preservation depositions.* Discovery depositions are broad, often rambling affairs whose goal is to learn all the information in the possession of the deponent, including the identification of documents and persons for future discovery. Dump depositions focus on the adverse party's key witnesses and elicit everything damaging so that counsel can prepare for the worst scenario at trial and develop ammunition for cross examination. Preservation depositions are taken to present testimony at trial of witnesses who are anticipated to be unavailable.

Obviously, the type of deposition determines the tactics and manner of questioning that counsel employs. For example, at a preservation deposition, documents must be carefully identified, authenticated, and when appropriate, a business records foundation[11] must be established in order to ensure their admissibility at trial. Similarly, counsel's questions must be framed so they do not elicit hearsay responses. In other words, counsel should assume that the questions and answers are being given at trial, subject to all pertinent trial objections. If this formula is not followed, it will be too late to try to correct any deficiencies at trial, and relevant testimony or documents may be excluded.

Custodian of records depositions are often taken as preservation depositions. However, substantive testimony of any person who may be absent from the trial should be treated as a preservation deposition, because either party can introduce such testimony at trial if the witness is unavailable.[12] As a result, counsel should be cautious to establish carefully a proper foundation for important exhibits and avoid unnecessary evidentiary problems in all depositions.

In a dump deposition, counsel must decide whether to save the best impeachment for trial or produce it during deposition questioning. Although the element of surprise will be forever lost if revealed at the deposition, the impeachment could result in a more favorable settlement. Similarly, if an expert is destroyed in

---

Practice ch. 3 (1982); J. Kelner, 1 & 1A Personal Injury Successful Litigation Techniques (1986); Blumenkopf, *Deposition Strategy and Tactics,* 5 Am. J. Trial Advoc. 231 (1981); Daniels, *Defending Depositions,* 71 A.B.A. J. 53 (Oct. 1985); Gilden, *A Practical Guide to Taking and Defending Depositions,* 88 Dick. L. Rev. 247 (1984); Johnson, *The 10 Deadly Deposition Sins,* 70 A.B.A. J. 62 (Sept. 1984); McNamara & Sorensen, *Deposition Traps and Tactics,* 12 Litigation 48 (Fall 1985).

[10] See §§ **13.1, 17.2**.

[11] *See* Fed. R. Evid. 803(6); § **21.7**.

[12] Fed. R. Evid. 804(b)(1); Fed. R. Civ. P. 32(a).

deposition, opposing counsel may decide to withdraw the witness and locate a hasty replacement. Dump depositions can be risky if the opponent has the option of introducing the deposition rather than the witness at trial, because the deponent is beyond subpoena range. However, some judges require a party to appear or produce key employees at trial even though technically unavailable because they are beyond subpoena range.

Even discovery depositions can backfire if they appear to be part of a pattern of harassment and delay because the judge can restrict further discovery or impose sanctions. In addition, such depositions may also lead the opponent to new information favorable to its position or produce damaging testimony which is introduced at trial because of the deponent's unavailability. Therefore, especially with out-of-state nonparties, informal discovery should precede the deposition. As a practical matter, nonparties may require a subpoena to appear even for a custodian of records deposition[13] to preserve their neutrality between the parties.

§ 23.4 Deposition Preparation

When preparing to take a deposition, many methods of organization can be used. Most counsel follow a direct chronological approach either solely by date or by reference to specific topics. Questions concerning the pleadings are often asked but rarely produce anything other than discomfort for a deponent who is unaware of the specific allegations therein. An indirect questioning method suited to foiling a lying or evasive witness at trial does not achieve maximum discovery at a deposition. Whether counsel adopts a sympathetic or controlled style depends on the ultimate goals of the particular deposition. If discovery is desired, questions should be worded broadly to require not only the deponent's personal knowledge, but also information based on hearsay. Although documents provide a natural source for questions, they should not be treated as ends in themselves but as reflective of the larger issues in the cases.

Because of the importance of pursuing leads provided by the deponent's answers, it is counterproductive to be wedded to a "script" while questioning. However, it is useful to have either an outline or index cards to guide the presentation of questions and ensure that important questions or topics are not forgotten. If possible, a paralegal or client representative should take notes during the deposition. This provides an ongoing digest of the deposition which can be reviewed during breaks to determine if any additional questions on particular subjects should be posed. However, if counsel is alone, it is probably better not to take notes while questioning, because this distraction can interfere with framing followup questions and maintaining rapport with the deponent.

---

[13] See § **21.7**.

§ 23.5 Deposition Procedures

Depositions are taken before an officer authorized to administer oaths and take testimony.[14] A certified court reporter has this power, but the parties can also provide that depositions be taken before any person, at any time or place, upon any notice, in any manner, and when so taken may be used like other depositions.[15] Defendants have a timing advantage in taking depositions, because they can immediately notice a deposition. A plaintiff must wait 30 days before taking a deposition without leave of court after serving the complaint unless the defendant institutes discovery within that time or special notice is given that the person to be examined is about to become unavailable.[16] The special notice procedure is a remnant from admiralty proceedings. It has limited utility, because such depositions cannot be used against a party who is unable after exercising diligence to obtain counsel at the deposition.[17] Any special notice must be signed by the plaintiff's attorney and must set forth facts supporting the deponent's unavailability.[18] The signed notice is a certification that the statement and supporting facts are true to the best the attorney's knowledge, information, and belief. Rule 11 sanctions are applicable to such certifications.[19] Neither party can depose persons confined in prison without leave of court.[20]

§ 23.6 Notice

Depositions of parties can be taken by giving reasonable notice in writing to every other party to the action. Such notice should indicate the time and place of the deposition. It must include the names and addresses of each person to be examined or a general description sufficient to identify the person or particular class or group to which the person belongs. The subject matter of the testimony is not required and should not be stated, because this could act as a limitation on the deponent's testimony. A notice can designate one or more deponents. The notice and attached document request and a proof of service must be served on the attorney for each party.[21] Local rules should be consulted to determine whether the notice and proof of service should be filed with the court. If a nonparty witness is being subpoenaed for deposition, the notice and proof of service must

---

[14] Fed. R. Civ. P. 28(a).

[15] Fed. R. Civ. P. 29.

[16] Fed. R. Civ. P. 30(a)(1).

[17] Fed. R. Civ. P. 30(b)(2).

[18] *Id.*

[19] *Id.*; see **ch. 28**.

[20] Fed. R. Civ. P. 30(a).

[21] *See generally* Hecht, *How to Prepare a Notice of Deposition or Subpoena in Federal Practice (with Forms),* 32 Prac. Law. 13 (Mar. 1986).

be filed with the court which is requested to issue the subpoena, and any documents requested must be included in the notice.[22]

Reasonable notice depends on the circumstances, but unless unexpected events require an immediate deposition, at least one week's notice should be given. The court can enlarge or shorten the time for taking the deposition.[23] Depositions should only be scheduled during business hours on weekdays unless otherwise stipulated.[24] Scheduling multiple simultaneous depositions is common in complex litigation but may be grounds for a Rule 26(c) protective order in other cases.[25] Similarly, a protective order may be sought to bar a deposition completely. Such orders are rarely granted but may be appropriate to derail the deposition of counsel to one of the litigants. For example, the Eighth Circuit has limited depositions of opposing counsel to those cases in which no other means exist to obtain the information and the information sought is relevant, nonprivileged, and crucial to the preparation of the case.[26] It is likely that counsel in other circuits will request similar restrictions via protective orders.

Often the initial notice lists all of the intended deponents and states that the depositions will take place at a time and place to be later determined. Professional courtesy as well as practicality dictate that depositions should not be scheduled without previously discussing the timing with opposing counsel. Moreover, local rules may require that the parties meet to exchange preliminary discovery schedules quite early in the litigation.[27] Only if a deponent's constant rescheduling indicates an evasion of the deposition process should notice be sent which states a specific date which has not been agreed upon. If the noticing party refuses to change the date, the deponent must obtain a protective order to avoid sanctions for failure to appear. This tactic should not be used hastily, because it will exacerbate any hostility the deponent has toward the examining party. Moreover, if the court decides that the deponent is not at fault, it may require the examining party and/or attorney to pay the deponent's expenses associated with bringing the motion.[28] A nonparty witness should be subpoenaed without warning if counsel anticipates that person will evade service of a subpoena if given advance notice, because the timing of the deposition can later be changed. All parties must be given notice of any scheduling changes to ensure that the deposition can be used against each of them and to avoid being required to pay the expenses of parties who appeared at the previously noticed time.[29]

---

[22] Fed. R. Civ. P. 45(d)(1), 30(b)(1).

[23] Fed. R. Civ. P. 30 (b)(3).

[24] 8 C. Wright & A. Miller, Federal Practice and Procedure § 2111 (1970) [hereinafter Federal Practice and Procedure].

[25] See **ch. 19**.

[26] *See* Shelton v. American Motors Corp., 805 F.2d 1323, 1327 (8th Cir. 1986).

[27] *See, e.g.*, C.D. Cal. Rule 6.1.2.

[28] *See* Fed. R. Civ. P. 26(c), 37(a)(4).

[29] *See* Fed. R. Civ. P. 30(g).

Although written notice is sufficient to subject a party to sanctions for failure to attend a deposition, a Rule 45 subpoena is necessary to compel the attendance of a nonparty who is not a director, officer or managing agent of a party.[30] Therefore, other employees of a party and former employees including those who were officers, directors, or managing agents must be subpoenaed if they will not appear voluntarily. If a subpoena duces tecum is served on the person being examined, the designation of material to be produced must be attached to or included in the notice to other parties.[31] The time for producing documents cannot be shortened by serving a subpoena duces tecum on a party deponent rather than a deposition notice accompanied by a Rule 34 request.[32] Any accompanying Rule 34 request should be made well in advance of a party's deposition, because a written response is not due for 30 days,[33] and that response is not necessarily the immediate production of the documents. Nonparties have only 10 days to object to documents which are designated in the subpoena duces tecum, unless the deposition is set earlier, in which case they must object before the date specified for compliance.[34] Usually when the subpoena requires production of voluminous documents by a nonparty, arrangements should be made to screen the documents in advance of the deposition, but this can only be done with the agreement of the subpoenaed deponent.[35]

§ 23.7 Failure to Attend

If an emergency arises which requires rescheduling a deposition, the examining party should contact all other parties who are likely to appear for the deposition. Similarly, even though the primary parties agree to reschedule depositions, other parties should be sent a revised schedule. A party who notices a deposition and fails to attend may be ordered to pay other parties who do attend the reasonable expenses incurred by them, including reasonable attorneys' fees.[36]

It is always advisable for the examining party to subpoena nonparty deponents. Even the friendliest nonparties may find excuses to avoid the deposition unless subpoenaed. Moreover, the failure of an unsubpoenaed witness to appear at the deposition can result in the noticing party's being ordered to pay the expenses of any other party attending the deposition.[37] Reimbursement has been

---

[30] *See* Fed. R. Civ. P. 30(a), 37(d); 8 Federal Practice and Procedure §§ 2103, 2107; see **ch. 21**.

[31] Fed. R. Civ. P. 30(b)(1).

[32] Fed. R. Civ. P. 29, 30(b)(5); 8 Federal Practice and Procedure § 2108, at 394–95.

[33] Fed. R. Civ. P. 34(b); see § **25.3**.

[34] Fed. R. Civ. P. 45(d)(1); see § **21.3**.

[35] See § **21.1**.

[36] Fed. R. Civ. P. 30(g)(1).

[37] Fed. R. Civ. P. 30(g)(2).

ordered when a witness was physicially present but unwilling to testify.[38] No particular procedures exist for a hearing as to the appropriateness of such awards, and the trial court has discretion to refuse a hearing when it has permitted an opportunity to be heard by such methods as a conference call with the court and the submission of a brief opposing the motion.[39]

§ 23.8 Selecting the Deposition Site

The deposition of a party may be set at any location chosen by the examiner. However, the general rule is that a defendant corporation's officers should be deposed at its principal place of business, unless that party has filed a permissive counterclaim.[40] Therefore, counsel should be prepared to face a request by opposing counsel for the expenses of bringing a motion to obtain a protective order if the location of the deposition is set elsewhere.[41] It is proper to set the deposition of a plaintiff in the district where the action was filed, even if that is not the plaintiff's home, although the court can assess any claim of financial hardship in evaluating the plaintiff's request for a protective order.[42] The travel costs and attorneys' fees associated with the deposition are borne by the parties incurring them and are rarely assessed as costs to the winning party at the end of the trial, unless attorneys' fees are otherwise recoverable in the action.[43] In some circumstances, counsel will decide to seek a protective order to prevent costly depositions due to the limited financial circumstances of a client.[44] Although a local rule may require the examining party to pay travel expenses for depositions taken at distant locations, it is rare that courts engage in cost shifting concerning parties.[45] The court can also make a conditional order that an examining party must pay the other side's travel costs unless the deposition is taken at a location which does not cause the expense.[46]

Even when deposing a witness in another city, the deposition site should be under the control of examining counsel. Depositions should be scheduled at the client's office, at a law firm, or even in a hotel meeting room, rather than at a location suggested by the deponent. First, this ensures access to appropriate

---

[38] Greenwood v. Dittmer, 776 F.2d 785, 790–91 (8th Cir. 1985).

[39] *Id.* at 791.

[40] Zuckert v. Berkliff Corp., 96 F.R.D. 161, 162 (N.D. Ill. 1982).

[41] *See* Fed. R. Civ. P. 26(g).

[42] 8 Federal Practice and Procedure § 2112.

[43] *See* 6 Moore's Federal Practice ¶ 54.77[4].

[44] *See, e.g.*, Schmertz, *Oral Depositions: The Low Income Litigant and the Federal Rules*, 54 Va. L. Rev. 391 (1968).

[45] *See generally* 8 Federal Practice and Procedure § 2112.

[46] *Id.*

copying facilities and provides a secure place to leave deposition materials. Second, friendly territory gives the deponent a psychological advantage, and, regardless of contrary orders, interruptions to take urgent calls or deal with emergency matters will be more prevalent at the deponent's office. However, deposing busy executives may require some adjustments, including scheduling depositions at nights or on weekends or at the deponent's office if this permits the examination to be taken more expeditiously. The deposition should be arranged well enough in advance to obviate any travel difficulties. Even a court reporter or microfilming equipment can be scarce in some locations, especially if the deposition is being taken outside the United States.

§ 23.9 Tape Recorded and Videotaped Depositions

Rule 30(b)(4) permits the recording of testimony at a deposition by other than stenographic means. This rule is important to both affluent and impecunious parties, because it covers both tape recording and videotaping of depositions. However, such depositions can be taken only if the parties stipulate or the court grants a motion ordering such a recording. Stipulations must be entered before the taping to be valid.[47] The rule does not mention what criteria the judge should use when deciding to grant such a deposition over the objection of a party. The D.C. Circuit limits the trial judge's discretion to deny the motion unless serious questions of accuracy exist.[48] Most courts do not permit a judge's denial of the request to be immediately reviewed by mandamus, because Rule 30(b)(4) provides no absolute right to a nonstenographic deposition.[49] A party is entitled to arrange for a stenographic transcription to be made at its own expense in addition to any other type of recording.[50] It is arguable that if the deposition is stenographically transcribed, it can also be videotaped without any stipulation or order, as long as notice is provided.[51] But unless local court rules so provide, the deponent can refuse to be videotaped, and eventually the cost of any motion may be assessed against the examining party.[52] Similarly, a deponent has no obligation to seek a protective order concerning the taping unless a stipulation or motion for an order to videotape had been filed.[53]

---

[47] *See* Westmoreland v. CBS, Inc., 770 F.2d 1168, 1176 (D.C. Cir. 1985).

[48] *See* Colonial Times, Inc. v. Gasch, 509 F.2d 517, 522 (D.C. Cir. 1975).

[49] *See In re* Sessions, 672 F.2d 564, 567 (5th Cir. 1982); *see also* International Union, UAW v. National Caucus of Labor Comms., 525 F.2d 323, 326 (2d Cir. 1975).

[50] *See* Rule 30(b)(4).

[51] G. Joseph, Modern Visual Evidence § 2.03[1] (1985).

[52] *See* Westmoreland v. CBS, Inc., 770 F.2d 1168, 1176–77 (D.C. Cir. 1985).

[53] *Id.* at 1177.

Tape recording is much less expensive than having a court reporter, but it can produce a garbled transcript. Sophisticated videotaping methods can be quite expensive, although competition among videotaping services has been cited as improving the economics,[54] and the person who operates the equipment may be able to serve as the deposition officer.[55] Undeniably, videotaping a deposition has advantages which far outweigh its expense.[56] Videotaping enables the jury to see the demeanor of witnesses who are unavailable for trial and alleviates the boredom of hearing lengthy deposition transcripts. Any potentially unavailable witness, including an expert whose testimony is peppered with references to exhibits, is a prime candidate for videotaping,[57] as is an ill or disabled plaintiff.[58] Videotaping a reenactment of relevant incidents has also been permitted.[59] Videotaping may provide a more effective impeachment tool than reading the witness's inconsistent deposition testimony. It also has a chilling effect on abusive deposition tactics, because opposing counsel realizes that any outrageous behavior will be much more obvious to the judge.[60] Objections concerning the videotaped deposition can be raised prior to trial and the tape appropriately edited before it is presented to the jury.

The stipulation or order permitting the nonstenographic deposition must designate the person before whom the deposition will be taken and the manner of recording, preserving, and filing the deposition and can include other provisions to assure that the recorded testimony will be accurate and trustworthy.[61] Any objections to the examination, changes made by the witness, signatures to the deposition and certification of the deposition must be set forth in a writing which accompanies the deposition record.[62] The Federal Judicial Center has promulgated guidelines for the actual conduct of videotaped depositions,[63] which include the type of introductory identifications and concluding statements which should be recorded, as well as indexing requirements for readily identifying relevant testimony.

---

[54] Kolczynski, *How to Take Effective Videotape Depositions,* 15 Brief 35 (Fall 1985).

[55] *See* Fed. R. Civ. P. 28(c); 4A Moore's Federal Practice ¶ 30.57[14.-4].

[56] *See generally* G. Joseph, Modern Visual Evidence chs. 2, 3 (1985); Kolczynski, *How to Take Effective Videotape Depositions,* 15 Brief 35 (Fall 1985); *see also* Underwood, *The Videotape Deposition: Using Modern Technology for Effective Discovery* (pts. 1 & 2), 31 Prac. Law. 61 (Apr. 1985), 31 Prac. Law 65 (June 1985).

[57] *See, e.g.,* Williams v. Hughes Helicopters, Inc., 806 F.2d 1387, 1392–93 (9th Cir. 1986).

[58] *See, e.g., In re* "Agent Orange" Prod. Liability Litig., 96 F.R.D. 587, 588–90 (E.D.N.Y. 1983).

[59] *See* Roberts v. Homelite Div. of Texatron, Inc., 109 F.R.D. 664, 667–68 (N.D. Ind. 1986).

[60] *See* Kolczynski, *How to Take Effective Videotape Depositions,* 15 Brief 35, 36 (Fall 1985).

[61] Fed. R. Civ. P. 30(b)(4).

[62] *Id.*

[63] Federal Judicial Center, Pub. No. 76-3, Guidelines for Pre-Recording Testimony on Videotape Prior to Trial (2d ed. 1976); *see* Uniform Audio-Visual Deposition Act, 12 U.L.A. 12 (1986 Supp.); *see generally* G. Joseph, Modern Visual Evidence §§ 2.04, 2.05 (1985).

§ 23.10 Depositions upon Written Questions

Although depositions upon written questions are rarely desirable, they may sometimes be employed as a stipulated or court-ordered compromise[64] to depose a busy executive or public official who is not a party to the action. Besides the usual notice and subpoena requirements, Rule 31 provides that, 30 days after the notice and written questions are served, a party may serve cross questions upon all other parties. Within 10 days after being served with cross questions, a party may serve redirect questions. Recross questions may be served within 10 days after service of redirect questions. Unless the court shortens the time for the deposition, this procedure requires at least 50 days' advance notice. Although the testimony is taken orally by the deposition officer, the rule does not prohibit counsel for a party who is friendly to the interests of the deponent from revealing the questions to the witness prior to the deposition. The court reporter is not permitted to record any statements as to the demeanor of the witness or remarks made by the deponent other than in answering the questions.[65] The same evidentiary and procedural rules apply to both written and oral depositions.[66]

§ 23.11 Corporate Depositions

In addition to designating specific corporate employees to be deposed, a party may, by notice or subpoena, name a public or private entity as a deponent and describe with reasonable particularity the matters on which examination is requested.[67] Such depositions are either oral or upon written questions.[68] Nonparties must be advised by subpoena of their duty to make a designation.[69]

Organizations can designate one or more persons to testify and set forth the matters about which each person designated will testify. The rule provides that such individuals be officers, directors, managing agents, or other persons who consent to testify on its behalf. Some courts define managing agents broadly as the most knowledgeable person, regardless of that person's status in the corporation.[70] Unlike other depositions which do not identify the matters upon which the deponent will be examined and can cover any relevant information in the possession of the witness, the corporate deposition is limited in scope to the subject of the notice.[71] If it appears that the organization has not designated the

---

[64] Fed. R. Civ. P. 26(c).

[65] 8 Federal Practice and Procedure § 2133.

[66] *See* Fed. R. Civ. P. 31(b), which applies Rule 30(c), (e), and (f) to written depositions.

[67] Fed. R. Civ. P. 30(b)(6).

[68] *Id.;* Fed. R. Civ. P. 31(a).

[69] Fed. R. Civ. P. 30(b)(6).

[70] *See generally* Massey, *Depositions of Corporations: Problems and Solutions—Fed. R. Civ. P. 30(b)(6),* 1986 Ariz. St. St. L.J. 81, 89–91.

[71] Paparelli v. Prudential Ins. Co. of Am., 108 F.R.D. 727, 729–30 (D. Mass. 1985).

appropriate person, whether through negligence or design, the examining counsel should request expenses pursuant to Rules 26(g) and 37(a)(4). If a corporate party fails to make a designation under Rule 30(b)(6) or 31(a), the examining party can move for an order to compel designation and is entitled to the expenses of bringing the motion, unless the failure was substantially justified.[72] Failure of a person who is designated by a corporate party to appear at the deposition after being served with proper notice subjects the party to all sanctions available pursuant to Rule 37(d), as well as to paying the reasonable expenses caused by the failure.

The most persuasive reasons for noticing corporate depositions are to obtain preliminary discovery about the organization of the corporation including its recordkeeping and computer operations and to learn the identity and duties of corporate employees. Individuals and categories of documents disclosed at the corporate deposition can become the focus of future discovery. A corporate deposition should not be considered as replacing individual depositions, because the organization rather than the examining party designates the person who will testify on its behalf. The corporate deposition has the advantage that the person designated must testify to matters known or reasonably available to the organization and that testimony can be used as admissions of a corporate party. The disadvantage is that the person designated usually gives vague testimony and may have limited personal knowledge as to some areas of questioning.

§ 23.12 People Present at the Deposition

It is not uncommon for the adverse party or expert to attend the deposition in addition to the deponent. Although this may be disconcerting, if the parties do not agree about who should attend in addition to the deponent, the only way to prevent such appearances is to obtain a protective order.[73] Unless there is evidence of harassment[74] or active collusion at the deposition, a protective order is likely to be denied, because the court will see little difference between counsel's showing these individuals the deposition transcript and their listening to the actual testimony. More than one counsel for a party can attend the deposition, and it is not per se abuse to have two attorneys rather than one question the deponent.[75] Counsel taking the deposition can also bring along a representative of the party or an expert to assist during the breaks or to pass notes concerning followup questions. Although depositions historically have been closed to the public,[76] there is statutory authority permitting the public to be

[72] Fed. R. Civ. P. 37(a)(2), (a)(4).

[73] *See* Greene, *The Folklore of Depositions,* 58 Fla. B.J. 658 (1984).

[74] *E.g.*, Galella v. Onassis, 487 F.2d 986, 997 (2d Cir. 1973).

[75] Rockwell Int'l, Inc. v. Pos-A-Traction Indus., Inc., 712 F.2d 1324, 1325 (9th Cir. 1983).

[76] *See In re* Reporters Comm. for Freedom of the Press, 773 F.2d 1325, 1337–38 (D.C. Cir. 1985).

present in antitrust cases.[77] As a practical matter, nonparties will not have notice of depositions unless informed by counsel. After the deposition, the press may want to obtain access to a deposition transcript,[78] or federal and state litigants in related cases may wish to share transcripts. Collaboration on related cases is a problem only when prohibited by a protective order, in which event the order must be modified to permit disclosure.[79]

§ 23.13 Deposition Stipulations

Before the deposition begins, any stipulations between the parties should be explained to the court reporter. Often the parties will agree to the standard stipulations. This is usually meaningless unless the exact nature of the stipulations are understood by counsel, and some perceive such a ritual to be risky if a dispute later arises.[80] Moreover, Rule 30 adequately explains deposition procedures so that there is no benefit to any stipulation which does not change the rules.

In litigation involving multiple depositions, the parties should have uniform instructions for the reporters which cover such topics as exhibit numbering and indexing, special filing instructions, and how to treat off-the-record comments in the transcript as well as provide a glossary of specialized terminology. A party should specify to the court reporter whether to edit the transcript to make the participants sound more articulate or grammatically correct; if this is done, transcripts often come back reading much better than they originally sounded. In general, treating a reporter courteously rather than as a piece of functional furniture results in a more readable transcript being prepared in a timely manner.

§ 23.14 Deposition Conduct

The examination should always begin with a description of the deposition process. Counsel should ascertain that the deponent understands the testimony is given under oath and that, unless clarification of a question is requested, anyone reading the deposition or hearing it at trial is entitled to assume that the question was understood. Any mental or physical problems which might prevent the deponent from fully testifying should also be explored to foreclose a later attempt to blunt the impeachment value of deposition answers.

---

[77] Publicity in Taking Evidence Act, 15 U.S.C. § 30 (1982).

[78] *See In re* Reporters Comm. for Freedom of the Press, 773 F.2d 1325, 1330–39 (D.C. Cir. 1985) (denying access); § **19.4**.

[79] *See* **ch. 19**.

[80] Dombroff, *Effective Discovery Techniques and Tactics under the Federal Rules of Civil Procedure,* 18 Trial 31, 34 (Winter 1982); Blumenkopf, *Deposition Strategy and Tactics,* 5 Am. J. Trial Advoc. 231, 238–239 (1981).

Every deponent should be asked to identify all documents reviewed to refresh recollection prior to testifying. Some counsel will reveal such information without a motion, while others will resist under Federal Rule of Evidence 612, which gives the court discretion as to whether to disclose documents which refreshed the witness's recollection.[81] Such documents may provide insight into what the adverse party considers significant in the litigation. If new documents are identified during the deposition, counsel should request their production. Although the opposing attorney may demand that a Rule 34 request be made, often such materials will be voluntarily produced. Even if the deposition is not intended to preserve testimony, all documents used as exhibits should be marked for identification and the appropriate foundation established. In this way, not only will the exhibits be readily usable for impeachment at trial, but they can be admitted in evidence if the authenticating witness unexpectedly becomes unavailable. Counsel should also request that the exhibits be annexed to the deposition. Copies can be substituted for the originals, as long as the originals are available for verification.[82]

If notes are passed to the deponent who is testifying, whether by counsel or an expert, this should be noted on the record, and an immediate demand for production should be made. Claims of work product and attorney-client privilege are questionable considering Federal Rule of Evidence 612, which entitles the adverse party to inspect and cross examine the witness concerning any writing which is used to refresh memory while testifying. Other evidence of coaching or excessive requests for breaks should also be indicated for the record. The examiner should assume that there will be one morning and one afternoon break as well as a recess for lunch unless the parties have agreed to other arrangements.

§ 23.15 Ending the Deposition

The concluding question at every deposition should be broadly worded to include any additional information which the deponent believes to be relevant which has not been previously requested. One litigator ended a deposition by asking, "Is there any question which you are relieved that I didn't ask you?" Although such questions may be objected to as overboard or ambiguous, they sometimes reveal helpful information. Often, whether through happenstance or design, it will be quite late in the day when the last questions are asked. Whether it is better to obtain answers when the witness is tired or to attempt to come back another day with additional questions after reviewing the transcript depends on the deponent's importance and the ease with which additional time can be rescheduled.

---

[81] See § **18.17**.

[82] Fed. R. Civ. P. 30(f); *see generally* 8 Federal Practice and Procedure § 2114.

§ 23.16 Defending Depositions

The major focus in defending a deponent is to avoid disasters. Most litigators believe that cases are rarely won in deposition but easily lost there. Every seasoned attorney has a standard liturgy of advice which is unfailingly given to deponents.[83] Invariably, it includes the following common sense maxims:

1. Be truthful. The deponent must understand that the testimony is given under oath, subject to perjury, regardless of the apparent informality of the proceedings.
2. Listen carefully to the question and ask for clarification if necessary before answering, but do not suggest new questions to the examiner.
3. Do not answer a question to which an objection is interposed until told to answer. An objection should signal that the question may be misleading. Never answer a question after counsel issues an instruction not to answer. When relevant, the deponent should be advised about the nature of the Fifth Amendment privilege. If a deponent does not take the Fifth Amendment, the deposition can be admitted in any related criminal case in which the deponent is a party.[84]
4. Think carefully before answering questions, and do not answer a question concerning an exhibit before reading it.
5. Don't volunteer any information which is not directly requested. Answer questions based solely on personal knowledge unless a question is more broadly worded.
6. Do not speculate. Don't reconstruct events about which you have no recollection or personal knowledge.
7. There is a difference between "I don't know" and "I don't remember." Answering "I don't know" assumes the deponent never had the information, and any change at trial will be suspect. "I do not remember" signals that the deponent once had knowledge which may be capable of being refreshed. The deponent should be warned that testifying to a lack of memory is the equivalent of lying if the witness does have present recollection. Moreover, convincing testimony at trial can be effectively impeached by the examiner reading a string of "I don't recalls" given at the deposition, even if the witness indicates the miraculous revival of memory was caused by reviewing relevant documents. A judge may also decide that exclusive failure of memory is actually an evasive failure to answer which justifies the imposition of sanctions.

---

[83] *See, e.g.*, D. Danner, Pattern Deposition Checklists § 6:9 (2d ed. 1984); Cook, *Preparing Your Client for Deposition*, Trial 45 (Summer 1983); *Rules for Witnesses*, in CEB, Litigation Organization and Management: Effective Tactics and Techniques app. E, at 111 (Oct. 1986).

[84] *See* United States v. Jenkins, 785 F.2d 1387, 1392–93 (9th Cir.), *cert. denied*, ____ U.S. ____, 107 S. Ct. 192 (1986); United States v. Handley, 763 F.2d 1401, 1405 (11th Cir.), *cert. denied*, ____ U.S. ____, 106 S. Ct. 318 (1985).

8. Regardless of how hostile or friendly the examiner appears, the goal of opposing counsel is to obtain material helpful to the examiner's case. Understanding that intimidation is used to force timid parties to settle and that the friendly questioner's goal is often to lure the deponent into agreeing with misleading statements will make the witness better able to handle the vagaries of the deposition process.
9. Never use irony, exaggeration, or jokes when answering questions. What sounds humorous at the deposition often appears as a serious statement in the cold transcript.
10. No remark made to the examining counsel is off the record. The examiner can question about any casual statement which the deponent utters.
11. Erroneous testimony should be corrected as soon as possible. The deponent should understand that possible discrepancies in testimony will be discussed during breaks and that the witness should not become flustered by any mistakes. If the examiner does not permit the testimony to be reopened, the deponent should be aware that the matter will be clarified at the end of the deposition when defending counsel is given an opportunity to question the witness.
12. It is not uncommon for the examiner to attempt to rattle a deponent by asking if the witness discussed the case with counsel and was told what to say. It is perfectly appropriate to talk to counsel. The usual response to such questions is that counsel told the deponent to tell the truth.

§ 23.17 Preparation and Strategy for Defending Depositions

Defending counsel's ultimate goal is to have the deponent testify truthfully and in the manner best suited to presenting the party's evidence in the most favorable light. Ethical considerations require that the witness not be told what to answer. However, an attorney would be remiss not to prepare a deponent about how to respond to questions. In preparing for the deposition, the witness should be required to answer questions which are likely to be asked by opposing counsel. This deposition simulation will enable counsel to discuss any difficulties the witness has in responding to questions as well as to point out misleading or inartful language. Difficult questions should be asked, because it is better to learn the exact response before the deposition than to be surprised by an unnecessarily bad answer during questioning. Words of art which may be misunderstood outside the context of the question should be discussed with the deponent. For example, market should not be lightly mentioned in an antitrust case. It may be important to grill deponents to toughen them for testifying. If so, it is preferable that another attorney in the office do the questioning to avoid damaging counsel's rapport with the witness. Although deponents know that counsel is playing devil's disciple, they often react personally when facing hostile or difficult questioning. Although it has become almost commonplace to videotape mock deposition sessions of important witnesses in order for deponents to appreciate how they will appear when testifying, there have been occasions when the existence of a videotape or an expert's "script" has become the focus of a discovery battle.

§ 23.18 Deposition Conduct

At the deposition itself, the witness should be protected from misleading and otherwise objectionable questions, as well as from any harassing tactics used by the examining counsel. Counsel should note when the deponent's attention begins to wane so that a break can be requested. If the deponent makes an obvious misstatement, counsel should consider immediate intervention to request clarification unless the topic is complicated and better handled during a recess. If necessary, counsel should examine the witness at the conclusion of the deposition[85] to clarify any misleading or ambiguous testimony given by the deponent and correct any wrong answers. If there is any possibility that the witness will be unavailable at trial, the deponent should also be questioned to develop favorable testimony. In this regard, the defending counsel has the right to question on any relevant topic, not only on subjects raised by the examiner.[86] Indeed, attorneys cannot exclude an otherwise admissible deposition at trial because of their failure to examine the deponent.[87]

§ 23.19 Objections, Instructions, and Harassment by Counsel

Although counsel should expect that the deposition will be held in a courteous manner, it is wise to consider in advance how to respond to disruptive conduct by opposing counsel or the deponent. Often the reaction to such behavior depends on counsel's overall case strategy. Options range from noting such outbursts on the record, to obtaining telephone access to the judge or magistrate, or, in extreme cases, to adjourning the deposition to obtain a protective order. It can also be effective to go off the record at the first indication of difficulty to indicate that all abusive tactics will be noted on the record to support a motion for protective order or appropriate sanctions. This often quiets an opposing counsel who is merely bluffing or seeing whether intimidation is an effective strategy; few attorneys are willing to test the court's patience with patently disruptive discovery conduct.

---

[85] *See* Fed. R. Civ. P. 30(c).

[86] 8 Federal Practice and Procedure § 2113.

[87] *See, e.g.*, General Business Sys. v. North Am. Phillips Corp., 699 F.2d 965, 979 (9th Cir. 1983).

Examination and cross examination of deposition witnesses proceed in the same manner as trial testimony, and evidence is taken subject to objections.[88] One annoying diversion practiced by counsel defending deponents is constantly to object and restate questions. Counsel who objects to hearsay should be referred to Rule 32(b), which preserves such objections for trial. Since objections as to the form of questions or answers are proper, an examiner must consider the advisability of adopting any of the opponent's restated questions. Often, the focus and the language of the new question vary from the original. Counsel should not be intimated by objections to leading questions, because these objections are appropriate only if counsel is examining its own party or a nonparty who is identified with the party. A hostile witness, an adverse party, or a witness identified with an adverse party can be asked leading questions.[89] Counsel should also remember that, although a leading question may not be objectional, it is ill designed to provide information for purposes of discovery.

A defending counsel can instruct the deponent not to answer only if the answer would reveal privileged information.[90] Even here, questions are proper if they concern background information necessary to determine if the privilege exists. Therefore, in order to establish an appropriate record to challenge a claim of privilege, inquiry should always be made about the date of the meeting or conversation and the identity of all persons present or party to the conversation, as well as any later discussions or distribution of the allegedly privileged material. There is some dispute whether an instruction not to answer based on relevance is ever proper.[91] It is unlikely that sanctions will be assessed for such an instruction if the questions are clearly improper and concern sensitive topics. The extent to which a relevance objection can be interposed by a nonparty is also unclear; decisions range from questioning its invocation to shifting the burden to the party to show relevance.[92]

An attorney who does not represent a deponent, such as a former employee or a third party, can only advise the witness not to answer questions which would otherwise be subject to an instruction, unless the person is considered a client for purposes of the attorney-client privilege,[93] in which case an instruction is appropriate. Examining counsel often ask about conversations between the

---

[88] Fed. R. Civ. P. 30(c).

[89] Fed. R. Evid. 611 (c).

[90] Eggleston v. Chicago Journeymen Plumbers' Local Union No. 130, 657 F.2d 890, 903 (7th Cir. 1981), *cert. denied,* 455 U.S. 1017 (1982); 4A Moore's Federal Practce ¶ 37.02[2]; 8 Federal Practice and Procedure § 2113, at 419.

[91] *Compare* Eggleston v. Chicago Journeymen Plumbers' Local Union No. 130, 657 F.2d 890, 902–03 (7th Cir. 1981), *cert. denied,* 455 U.S. 1017 (1982) (refusal to testify concerning irrelevant sensitive areas can be justified) *with* Ralston Purina Co. v. McFarland, 550 F.2d 967, 973–74 (4th Cir. 1977) (instruction concerning irrelevant areas is not proper).

[92] *Compare* Ghandi v. Police Dep't of Detroit, 74 F.R.D. 115, 123 (E.D. Mich. S.D. 1977) (relevance not applicable to nonparty) *with* Dart Indus. Co. v. Westwood Chem. Co., 649 F.2d 646, 649 (9th Cir. 1980) (restricting nonparty discovery).

[93] *See* Upjohn v. United States, 449 U.S. 383, 394–95 (1981).

deponent and an opposing counsel who does not represent that person. Although such conversations may be considered work product if the witness is identified in interest with the party represented by opposing counsel,[94] it is arguable that conversations are not protected if the deponent is merely neutral.[95]

§ 23.20 Noncooperative Witnesses

Hostile witnesses can prolong depositions and make the transcript virtually unusable for impeachment at trial. Although the tactic of feigning lack of memory at the deposition may backfire on a witness whose total recall at trial is impeached by the earlier vague testimony, it is dangerous to assume that such witnesses will be effectively destroyed at trial unless the deposition is extremely thorough. Persistent questioning may also convince the deponent to answer immediately rather than resist, because it is clear that this tactic will not result in the early termination of the deposition. If the witness takes five minutes before answering any question, this should be noted on the record. When the deponent requests that even the simplest of terms be defined, ask how he would define it or quote it from the dictionary while making clear that a motion to compel answers will be forthcoming. This is a potent threat if opposing counsel believes that the motion will be brought, since the costs of such a motion are awarded to the successful party unless the opposition is justified or the award would be unjust.[96] Disruptive or evasive behavior by a party, or officer, director, or managing agency of a party may result in sanctions which affect the merits of the case if the actions are perceived as part of a pattern of discovery abuse or persist after the court compels the deponent to answer.[97] Misbehavior by a nonparty is treated as a contempt of court.[98]

§ 23.21 Terminating or Limiting the Examination

At any time during the deposition, a party or the deponent can move for a protective order terminating or limiting the deposition by showing that the examination is being conducted in bad faith or in such a manner as unreasonably to annoy, embarrass, or oppress the deponent or party.[99] The motion can be brought in the court in which the action is pending or the court in the district

---

[94] *See* Ford v. Philips Elecs. Instruments Co., 82 F.R.D. 359, 360–61 (E.D. Pa. 1979) (mental impressions of attorney protected, no discussion of status of third party).

[95] See §§ **18.13–18.15**.

[96] Fed. R. Civ. P. 37(a)(4).

[97] *See* Fed. R. Civ. P. 37(b).

[98] *Id.*

[99] Fed. R. Civ. P. 30(d); *see* Fed. R. Civ. P. 26(c).

where the deposition is being taken.[100] If a deposition is ordered terminated, it will be resumed only if the court in which the action is pending orders its continuation.[101] The deposition is suspended during the time necessary to make a motion. Local rules should be consulted concerning any additional requirements for such motions. The successful party is entitled to the expenses of bringing the motion, including attorneys' fees, unless the circumstances make an award unjust.[102]

As a practical matter, examining counsel usually notes objections to the conduct of the deposition on the record, completes whatever questioning is feasible, and then indicates that a motion will be filed.[103] The defending counsel often responds to harassment by instructing the witness not to answer rather than suspending the deposition. This shifts the cost of obtaining relief to the examiner, who must then decide whether a motion to compel deposition answers is viable. Such a motion is proper whenever a deponent fails to answer a question or gives an evasive or incomplete answer.[104] As with other discovery motions, the winning party is entitled to the expenses of bringing the motion unless the opposition is justified.[105] Although instructions are technically permitted only to protect privileged matters, it is unlikely that the court will assess costs against the instructing party if the examiner was abusive.[106] Moreover, a district court can deny a motion to compel further answers if it concludes that the questions were irrelevant.[107]

§ 23.22 Deposition Sanctions

Only if a party deponent fails to attend the deposition or refuses to answer questions after being ordered can sanctions which affect the merits of the case be imposed.[108] Absence of an officer, director, or managing agent of a party is sufficient to impose even the most severe sanctions.[109] Cases have been terminated for repeated failures to attend a deposition.[110] Failure of a party to attend a properly noticed deposition also results in an award of expenses, including

---

[100] Fed. R. Civ. P. 30(d).

[101] *Id.*

[102] *Id.;* Fed. R. Civ. P. 37(a)(4).

[103] *See* Fed. R. Civ. P. 37(a)(2).

[104] *Id.;* Fed. R. Civ. P. 37(a)(3).

[105] Fed. R. Civ. P. 37(a)(4).

[106] *See, e.g., In re* Folding Carton Antitrust Litig., 83 F.R.D. 132, 135–36 (N.D. Ill. E.D. 1979).

[107] Commercial Union Ins. Co. v. Westrope, 730 F.2d 729, 732 (11th Cir. 1984).

[108] Fed. R. Civ. P. 37(b)(2) & 37(d).

[109] *See* Founding Church of Scientology v. Webster, 802 F.2d 1448, 1451–59 (D.C. Cir. 1986).

[110] *See, e.g., id.* at 1449; Bell & Beckwith v. IRS, 766 F.2d 910, 912 (6th Cir. 1985); Kabbe v. Rotan Mosle, Inc., 752 F.2d 1083, 1084–85 (5th Cir. 1985).

attorneys' fees associated with the noncompliance, if no adequate justification exists.[111] For example, failure to appear because local counsel could not be obtained has been considered an insufficient excuse when the examining counsel was not notified the party would not attend.[112]

The primary sanction available against a nonparty deponent is contempt.[113] Although a nonparty can be required to pay the expenses incurred by the examining party in obtaining an order to compel deposition answers,[114] there is no equivalent provision concerning expenses to compel a nonparty deponent to attend the deposition. Therefore, unless local rules provide for such awards, the court is likely to restrict expenses to cases in which the nonparty has demonstrated bad faith which justifies the court to invoke such sanctions under its inherent powers.[115] Conversely, since Rule 30(g) permits only parties to recover costs, if the examiner fails to attend and proceed, a nonparty usually cannot be reimbursed for such a failure.[116]

If deposition problems are anticipated, judges or magistrates often are willing to be accessible by telephone to resolve disputes. In extreme cases, depositions can even be conducted in the court library to avoid the necessity of an adjournment.[117]

§ 23.23 Signing the Transcript

When the testimony is fully transcribed, the deposition is submitted to the witness for examination and should be read by the deponent and signed. Any changes in form or substance which the witness desires to make are entered upon the deposition by the officer with a statement of reasons given by the witness for making them. It is imperative that the deponent read the deposition carefully, because mistranscribed questions and answers can be disastrous when introduced at trial. Similarly, an answer which the witness recognizes is misleading or incorrect should be immediately supplemented if it concerns an important issue. Although the changes can be commented upon by the examiner at trial, it is better to modify answers as soon as possible rather than explain why the deponent waited until trial to correct the testimony.

If the witness is ill, cannot be found, refuses to sign, or has waived procedural requirements, the deposition officer signs the transcript within 30 days of its submission and states on the record the reason the deponent did not sign it. The

---

[111] Fed. R. Civ. P. 37(d).

[112] Lew v. Kona Hosp., 754 F.2d 1420, 1426 (9th Cir. 1985).

[113] Fed. R. Civ. P. 37(b)(1), 45(f).

[114] Fed. R. Civ. P. 37(a)(4).

[115] *Cf.* Westmoreland v. CBS, Inc., 770 F.2d 1168, 1178 (D.C. Cir. 1985); see § **21.5**.

[116] Westmoreland v. CBS, Inc., 770 F.2d 1168, 1172–73, 1178 (D.C. Cir. 1985).

[117] *See, e.g.*, Wright v. Firestone Tire & Rubber Co., 93 F.R.D. 491, 493 (W.D. Ky. 1982).

deposition may then be used as fully as though signed, unless a motion to suppress the deposition is made[118] and the court rules that the deposition must be rejected in whole or part.[119] Although the examination, reading, and signing of the deposition can be waived, nothing is gained by such stipulations, because the deposition can be used even if it is not signed.[120] Moreover, at trial, a witness who has not reviewed the transcript may attempt to evade impeachment by claiming errors in transcription.

§ 23.24 Filing the Transcript

The deposition officer certifies the deposition and files it with the court in which the action is pending unless otherwise ordered by the court.[121] Although the officer is responsible for such procedures, counsel taking the deposition should make sure that the court reporter knows whether local rules or stipulations between the parties exist which alter filing requirements. In many districts, the local rules specifically provide that the attorney noticing the deposition should be sent the original transcript, and filing is delayed until the outset of trial or until the deposition becomes relevant to a pending motion. If depositions taken subject to a protective order are required to be filed, counsel should make sure that they are filed under seal to avoid any breach of confidentiality. Whenever a deposition is filed, the party taking it must promptly give notice to all other parties.[122]

§ 23.25 Transcript Costs

Questions sometimes arise as to who bears the costs of obtaining a copy of the deposition transcript. The rule provides that the testimony shall be transcribed if requested by one of the parties[123] and that the officer shall furnish a copy of the deposition to any party or to the deponent for a reasonable charge.[124] This has been interpreted to require that the party ordering the copy pays for its cost.[125] However, the rule is silent as to who pays the original transcription expenses if the examining party does not request a transcript. This issue may become

---

[118] Fed. R. Civ. P. 30(e), 32(d)(4).

[119] Fed. R. Civ. P. 30(e).

[120] *Id.*

[121] Fed. R. Civ. P. 30(f).

[122] Fed. R. Civ. P. 30(f)(3), 31(c).

[123] Fed. R. Civ. P. 30(c).

[124] Fed. R. Civ. P. 30(f)(2).

[125] *See* 8 Federal Practice and Procedure § 2117.

relevant, because the original transcription is significantly more expensive than subsequent copies. The court has discretion to determine whether the instigating party must pay the original cost. Financial disparity or the impecuniosity of the instigating party are factors mitigating against payment but are not dispositive.[126] An examining party can also be required to file the original with the court so that it can be read by opposing counsel.[127]

§ 23.26 Errors and Irregularities in Deposition Procedures

All errors and irregularities in the notice for taking a deposition are waived unless written objection is promptly served upon the party giving notice.[128] All objections made at the time of the examination to the qualifications of the officer taking the deposition, the manner of taking it, the evidence presented, or the conduct of any party, and any other objections to the proceedings, are noted by the officer.[129] Objections to the qualifications of the deposition officer are waived unless made before the deposition or as soon thereafter as the disqualification becomes known or could be discovered with reasonable diligence.[130] Such objections include situations in which the person taking the deposition is a relative, employee, or attorney of a party or a relative or employee of the attorney or has a financial interest in the action.[131] Objections to the form of written questions submitted under Rule 31 are waived unless served in writing upon the party propounding them within the time allowed for serving the succeeding questions and within five days after service of the last questions authorized. Errors in the manner in which the testimony is transcribed or the deposition is prepared, signed, certified, sealed, endorsed, transmitted, filed, or otherwise treated by the deposition officer are waived unless a motion to suppress the deposition in whole or part is made with reasonable promptness after the defect is or with due diligence might have been ascertained.[132]

An irregularity in deposition procedure usually does not result in the exclusion of deposition testimony unless it affects a substantive rather than a technical issue. For example, dismissal of an action for failure to take a particular deposition oath was reversed when the party's refusal was due to his religious

---

[126] *See* Melton v. McCormick, 94 F.R.D. 344, 346 (W.D.N.Y. 1982); Caldwell v. Wheeler, 89 F.R.D. 145, 148 (D. Utah 1981).

[127] *See* C.P.C. Partnership Bardot Plastics, Inc. v. P.T.R., Inc., 96 F.R.D. 184, 185–86 (E.D. Pa. 1982).

[128] Fed. R. Civ. P. 32(d)(2).

[129] Fed. R. Civ. P. 32(d).

[130] Fed. R. Civ. P. 32(d)(2).

[131] Fed. R. Civ. P. 28(c).

[132] Fed. R. Civ. P. 32(d)(4).

beliefs and the district judge did not explore less restrictive means of assuring a truthful deposition.[133] A witness who has been impeached with deposition testimony can testify on redirect concerning the circumstances of the deposition to explain why the deponent may have been confused, although no previous objection was raised.[134] On the other hand, a court may prohibit the use of a deposition which was taken on such notice that a party could not attend.[135] Similarly, when a deposition was not transcribed until shortly before trial, the adverse party was not bound by the waiver provision of Rule 32(d)(4), and the deposition was properly excluded.[136]

§ 23.27 Objections to Admissibility of Depositions

Whether the deposition is intended for use in preparing the case, during motion practice, or at trial, counsel should ensure that it is in admissible form if needed in evidence. Objections to deposition testimony are typically made at in limine hearings prior to the trial. Although Rule 32 provides for objections to be made at the trial or hearing, most local rules and judges prefer to have deposition materials designated and filed prior to trial so that evidentiary problems can be resolved out of the presence of the jury.[137] Each side designates the testimony to be offered and indicates objections to the opponent's designations. Usually, counsel chooses to designate only the significant testimony in the deposition to make the best use of jurors' limited attention span for listening to deposition transcripts. A court may dispense with an oral hearing on such evidentiary rulings and review the designations in camera, noting which objections are sustained on the transcripts.[138] Even though an advance ruling concerning the deposition is obtained, the deposition must be offered in evidence to be considered at trial.[139] The court's rulings as to admissibility of deposition testimony usually are not overturned except for abuse of discretion.[140]

Objections are permitted for any reason which would require the exclusion of the evidence if the witness were then present and testifying.[141] The only objections which must be made at the deposition itself are those which relate to the form of questions or answers, the oath and the conduct of the parties and

---

133 Gordon v. Idaho, 778 F.2d 1397, 1400–01 (9th Cir. 1985).

134 Wilmington v. J.I. Case Co., 793 F.2d 909, 921 (8th Cir. 1986).

135 Bobb v. Modern Prods., Inc., 648 F.2d 1051, 1055 (5th Cir. 1981).

136 Bunch v. Bullard, 795 F.2d 384, 391 (5th Cir. 1986).

137 *See, e.g.*, C.D. Cal. R. 9.4.9.

138 *See* Sealy, Inc. v. Easy Living, Inc., 743 F.2d 1378, 1383 (9th Cir. 1984).

139 *See, e.g.*, Lovett v. Shuster, 633 F.2d 98, 102–03 (8th Cir. 1980); *see generally* 8 Federal Practice and Procedure § 2142.

140 Bobb v. Modern Prods., Inc., 648 F.2d 1051, 1055 (5th Cir. 1981).

141 Fed. R. Civ. P. 32(b).

those which might be obviated, removed, or cured if promptly presented.[142] Objections to the competency of a witness or to the competence, relevance, or materiality of testimony are not waived by failure to make them before or during the taking of the deposition, unless the objection might have been obviated or removed if presented at that time.[143] However, since witness competence issues are decided by reference to state law in diversity cases,[144] counsel must ascertain whether any protections afforded by a dead man's act will be waived by taking a deposition.[145] Except for a few aberrational cases which suggest that objections to relevance or hearsay must be made at the deposition because in the particular case they could be cured at that time,[146] generally only objections as to privilege and the form of questions and answers are raised at the deposition. All other objections are saved until the appropriate time for designation. Objections and instructions not to answer based on relevance are made only if the questioning concerns sensitive areas or if it appears that the questions are asked to harass the deponent. Since the form of answers as well as questions must be raised at the deposition, nonresponsive answers must be objected to at the deposition.[147]

§ 23.28 Admissibility of Deposition Testimony

Rule 32(a) provides that deposition testimony can be used so far as admissible under the rules of evidence applied as though the witness were then present and testifying, against any party who was present or represented at the deposition, or who had reasonable notice in the following circumstances:

1. A party can use any deposition to contradict or impeach the testimony of a deponent who testifies as a witness or for any other purpose permitted by the Federal Rules of Evidence.[148]
2. A party can use the deposition of an adverse party for any purpose.[149]
3. A party can use a deposition of a witness for any purpose if the court finds that the witness
   - **(a)** is dead;
   - **(b)** is located more than 100 miles from the trial, or outside the United States, unless the absence of the witness was procured by the party offering the deposition;

---

[142] Fed. R. Civ. P. 32(d)(3)(B).

[143] Fed. R. Civ. P. 32(d)(3)(A).

[144] Fed. R. Evid. 601.

[145] *See* 8 Federal Practice and Procedure § 2152.

[146] *See, e.g.*, Kirschner v. Broadhead, 671 F.2d 1034, 1038–39 (7th Cir. 1982).

[147] *Id.*

[148] Fed. R. Civ. P. 32(a)(1).

[149] *Id.*

(c) is ill or imprisoned;

(d) cannot be subpoenaed, or

(e) if exceptional circumstances exist which make it desirable in the interest of justice to admit the deposition.[150]

4. An adverse party can require the party introducing only part of a deposition to introduce any other part which ought in fairness to be considered with the portion introduced, and any party may introduce any other parts.[151]

§ 23.29 Common Admissibility Issues

All provisions of Rule 32(a) apply to depositions between the same parties or their representatives, or successors in interest in other actions involving the same subject matter.[152] The most commonly used provision of the Federal Rules of Evidence to permit substantive use of depositions is Rule 804(b)(1),[153] which refers to former testimony of unavailable witnesses. Unavailability can occur for a variety of reasons, including, death, illness, lack of memory, privilege, refusal to testify, or being outside the court's subpoena range and not obtainable by other reasonable means.[154] A discovery deposition of an expert as well as of a percipient witness is admissible if the witness is unavailable at trial.[155] Mere failure to cross examine at such a deposition is considered a strategic choice which does not preclude the opponent's use of the deposition at a subsequent proceeding.[156] Circuits vary as to whether depositions taken in foreign countries, such as the Soviet Union, should be considered untrustworthy.[157]

Although depositions usually are taken in the case being litigated, deposition testimony taken in other proceedings is admissible if the party or a predecessor in interest of the party against whom the testimony is offered had an opportunity and similar motive to develop the testimony by direct, cross, or redirect examination.[158] Therefore, in multiple litigation arising out of the same

---

[150] Fed. R. Civ. P. 32(a)(3).

[151] Fed. R. Civ. P. 32(a)(4).

[152] Fed. R. Civ. P. 32(a).

[153] *See generally* 4 J. Weinstein & M. Berger, Weinstein's Evidence ¶ 804(b)(1)[01]–[04] (1985).

[154] Fed. R. Evid. 804(a); *see generally* 4 J. Weinstein & M. Berger, Weinstein's Evidence ¶ 804(a)[01] (1985).

[155] Gill v. Westinghouse Elec. Corp., 714 F.2d 1105, 1107 (11th Cir. 1983); Savoie v. Lafourche Boat Rentals, Inc., 627 F.2d 722, 724 (5th Cir. 1980).

[156] Hendrix v. Raybestos-Manhattan, Inc., 776 F.2d 1492, 1506 (11th Cir. 1985); *see generally* 4 J. Weinstein & M. Berger, Weinstein's Evidence ¶ 804(b)(1)[02] (1985).

[157] *See, e.g.,* United States v. Kungys, 793 F.2d 516, 520 n.2 (3d Cir. 1986), *cert. granted,* ____ U.S. ____, 107 S. Ct. 431 (1986); Laipenieks v. United States I.N.S., 750 F.2d 1427, 1432–33 (9th Cir. 1985).

[158] Fed. R. Evid. 804(b)(1).

incident, a deposition in one case may be admissible in subsequent actions if the deponent becomes unavailable. Moreover, some circuits eliminate the predecessor in interest requirement, as long as the former party had an opportunity and similar motive to cross examine as the present party.[159] Even when used, the predecessor in interest requirement is not limited to a legal relationship.

Other hearsay exceptions may permit the substantive use of specific portions of testimony. For example, prior inconsistent statements which are taken under oath can be admitted substantively as well as for impeachment.[160] Similarly, deposition testimony can be introduced for a nonhearsay purpose, such as to demonstrate that an individual had notice of a particular problem.[161] Deposition testimony can also be used to refresh the recollection of a witness.[162] Even if a deposition is otherwise admissible, the trial court still retains discretion to reject repetitious deposition testimony[163] or to exclude prejudicial testimony.[164]

Rule 32(a)(3) permits a party to introduce a deposition upon application and notice if exceptional circumstances exist to make it desirable, in the interest of justice and with due regard to the importance of presenting the testimony of witnesses orally in open court, to allow the deposition to be used. Although most of the requirements of Rule 32(a)(3) are identical to the former testimony hearsay exception provided in Federal Rule of Evidence 804(b)(1), Rule 32's reference to exceptional circumstances provides a means for admitting depositions which do not otherwise fit within any other rule[165] and appears broader than the catchall hearsay exception provided by Federal Rule of Evidence 804(b)(5).

Rule 32(a)(4) adopts the doctrine of completeness, which permits an adverse party to introduce deposition testimony which should in fairness be considered. This provision allows the introduction of otherwise inadmissible deposition testimony.[166] In addition, counsel can argue that such testimony must be integrated with opponent's designations rather than being read separately at the conclusion of the opponent's deposition readings.[167]

---

[159] *See* Dykes v. Raymark Indus., Inc., 801 F.2d 810, 815–16 (6th Cir. 1986); Lloyd v. American Export Lines, Inc., 580 F.2d 1179, 1185 (3d Cir.), *cert. denied,* 439 U.S. 969 (1978).

[160] Fed. R. Evid. 801(d)(1); *see* Alexander v. Conveyors & Dumpers,Inc., 731 F.2d 1221, 1231 (5th Cir. 1984).

[161] *See, e.g.,* Benford v. Richards Medical Co., 792 F.2d 1537, 1540 (11th Cir. 1986).

[162] *See* Fed. R. Evid. 612.

[163] Gauthier v. Crosby Marine Serv., Inc., 752 F.2d 1085, 1089 (5th Cir. 1985).

[164] Fed. R. Evid. 403; Murphy v. Owens-Illinois, Inc., 779 F.2d 340, 343–44 (6th Cir. 1985).

[165] *See generally,* Note, *Admissibility of Prior-Action Depositions and Former Testimony Under Fed. R. Civ. P. 32(a)(4) and Fed. R. Evid. 804(b)(1): Courts' Differing Interpretations,* 41 Wash. & Lee L. Rev. 155 (1984).

[166] *See* Fed. R. Evid. 106; United States v. Sutton, 801 F.2d 1346, 1368–69 (D.C. Cir. 1986) (fairness required inadmissible portion of statement to be introduced).

[167] *See* 8 Federal Practice and Procedure § 2148.

§ 23.30 Depositions of Parties

Since depositions of adverse parties can be used both substantively and for impeachment, it is important to know which individuals are considered parties when one of the litigants is an entity. The deposition of any officer, director, or managing agent of the party when the deposition was taken and persons designated to testify on behalf of a party under Rule 30(b)(6) or 31(a) can be used as party depositions, regardless of whether those individuals are personally sued.[168] Parties are not permitted to introduce their own self-serving deposition testimony substantively under Rule 32(a)(2); that provision authorizes introduction only by the adverse party. There is also some dispute concerning the propriety of parties introducing their own depositions if they reside more than 100 miles from trial.[169] Although at least one circuit has reversed a case in which the deposition of such a plaintiff was excluded,[170] some trial judges threaten not to admit the depositions of key corporate employees who reside outside subpoena range because the corporation can afford to secure their presence. When faced with such a choice, the party usually produces the witness rather than suffer the exclusion of the testimony, because the likelihood of obtaining interlocutory review is not great.[171]

---

[168] *Id.*

[169] *See generally* 8 Federal Practice and Procedure § 2147; 4A Moore's Federal Practice ¶ 32.05.

[170] Richmond v. Brooks, 227 F.2d 490, 492–93 (2d Cir. 1955).

[171] See §§ **17.17–17.20**.

CHAPTER 24

INTERROGATORIES

§ 24.1 Overview of Interrogatory Practice

Interrogatories are the most controversial of the discovery methods provided by the federal rules. Although envisioned as the least expensive discovery device, abusive interrogatory tactics have turned Rule 33 practice into a battleground where lawyers request opponents to prepare their cases and judges question even the most legitimate requests. Apparently, lawyers are more dissatisfied with interrogatories than any other discovery method.[1] Although an attempt to modify Rule 33 to limit the number of interrogatories was aborted,[2] local rules in many districts permit only a specified number of interrogatories without leave of court. Other local rules sharply curtail the types of information which can be obtained by interrogatories.[3] Regardless of whether such rules are invalid because they are inconsistent with Rule 33,[4] they are rarely challenged, and, as a result, the use of interrogatories is being curtailed by many district judges.

---

[1] *See, e.g.*, Brazil, *Civil Discovery: Lawyers' Views of Its Effectiveness, Its Principal Problems and Abuses,* 1980 A.B.F. Res. J. 789, 829–30.

[2] 8 C. Wright & A. Miller, Federal Practice and Procedure § 2168 (Supp. 1986) [hereinafter Federal Practice and Procedure].

[3] *See* S.D.N.Y. R. 46.

[4] *Id.* (such local rules are invalid). *But see* Local 472, United Ass'n. of Journeymen v. Georgia Power Co., 684 F.2d 721, 724 (11th Cir. 1982) (no abuse of discretion to limit parties to 20 interrogatories, including subparts).

In practice, interpretative interrogatories rarely provide the information sought. They are usually answered only after a fight, and, even then, the answers are drafted by attorneys who read each question narrowly and resist disclosing helpful information unless absolutely required to do so. Unlike depositions, which offer an opportunity to ask new questions immediately and to clarify the deponent's answers, obtaining supplemental information suggested by the answers to interrogatories may require extended negotiations concerning the sufficiency of the answers provided or service of additional interrogatories. Interrogatories are also much more difficult to use for impeachment of a witness at trial than deposition testimony.

Contention interrogatories, which explore the theories and supporting facts and information underlying the opposing party's legal claims or defenses, are often an exercise in futility, although they can sometimes be helpful when used in connection with Rule 36 requests for admissions. Although such interrogatories can encourage settlement by requiring the responding counsel to analyze the case carefully, they can also result in the opposing party being better prepared for trial.

It is generally agreed that the best and least expensive use of interrogatories is to obtain the names and addresses of percipient witnesses, to disclose the existence, identity, and source of documents or other tangible items, and to pinpoint the dates and substance of transactions and conversations.[5] Such interrogatories should be propounded early in the litigation, because the answers may require followup by way of document production requests or depositions.

§ 24.2 Scope of Interrogatories

Interrogatories can relate to any matter within the scope of Rule 26(b). Therefore, privilege, work product, and irrelevance are valid objections to interrogatories.[6] Requesting information beyond the personal knowledge of a party is not objectionable, because the party has an obligation to respond with such information as is available to it.[7]

Probably the most common objections to interrogatories are that they are vague or burdensome. Ambiguity can be caused either by poor drafting or by opposing counsel's strained interpretation of the interrogatories. Burdensomeness must now be analyzed in conjunction with the court's power under Rule

[5] *See generally* M. Dombroff, Discovery ch. 4 (1986); 8 Federal Practice and Procedure § 2163 (1970); Charfoos & Christensen, *Interrogatories—How to Use Them Effectively in Personal Injury Cases,* 22 Trial 56 (June 1986); Dombroff, *Effective Discovery Techniques and Tactics under the Federal Rules of Civil Procedure,* 18 Trial 31 (Winter, 1982); Schoone & Miner, *The Effective Use of Written Interrogatories,* 60 Marq. L. Rev. 29 (1976).

[6] See **ch. 18**.

[7] Fed. R. Civ. P. 33(a).

26(b)(1) to limit discovery which is unreasonably cumulative or duplicative or obtainable from some other source that is more convenient, less burdensome, or less expensive. Before Rule 26 was modified in 1983, mere burdensomeness was not objectionable, since responding to interrogatories is always burdensome. Only unduly burdensome interrogatories provided a basis to obtain a protective order under Rule 26(c). The change to Rule 26 appears to broaden the judge's ability to limit burdensome discovery, because this provision exists independently of the court's power to restrict discovery which is unduly burdensome or expensive.[8] Rule 26(b)(1) also permits discovery to be limited if the party has had ample opportunity to obtain the information sought by discovery.

Opinions or contentions that relate to fact or the application of law to fact are not objectionable on that ground. However, contention interrogatories will not always prevent discovery of potentially irrelevant issues since the court can delay the answers until after discovery or even later.[9] Interrogatories which request legal opinions unrelated to any relevant facts are objectionable.[10]

§ 24.3 Procedural Requirements

Interrogatories can be served only upon other parties to the action, and some dispute exists as to the conditions under which absent class members may be served.[11] Interrogatories can be served upon the plaintiff after commencement of the action and upon any other party with or after service of the complaint. Service must be made upon the attorney or pro se party pursuant to Rule 5. Each interrogatory must be answered separately and fully in writing under oath by the party or, in the case of collective entities, by any officer or agent. A corporation must designate someone who can verify the interrogatories without invoking the Fifth Amendment privilege of self-incrimination.[12] An attorney can verify the answers of a corporation as its agent,[13] but this should be avoided, because it places the attorney in an awkward posture if the answer is later used as evidence. The reasons for each objection must be set forth in writing and can be signed by the responding party's attorney.

Interrogatories must be responded to within 30 days after service, except that a defendant may respond within 45 days after being served with the complaint. The court can allow a shorter or longer time to answer, and any stipulation

---

[8] *Compare* Fed. R. Civ. P. 26(b)(1)(a)(i) *with* Fed. R. Civ. P. 26(b)(1)(a)(iii).

[9] Fed. R. Civ. P. 33(b).

[10] 4A J. Moore *et al.*, Moore's Federal Practice ¶ 33.17[2] (2d ed. 1984).

[11] *See* Cox v. American Cast Iron Pipe Co., 784 F.2d 1546, 1556 (11th Cir.), *cert. denied*, ___ U.S. ___, 107 S. Ct. 274 (1986); 4A Moore's Federal Practice ¶ 33.06; 8 Federal Practice and Procedure § 2171 (Supp. 1985); § **10.11**.

[12] See § **18.21**.

[13] 8 Federal Practice and Procedure § 2172.

extending time to respond must be approved,[14] although, as a practical matter, unapproved stipulations may not come to the judge's attention if the local rules prohibit filing discovery documents unless they relate to a pending motion. If filing is required, an affidavit of service should be included.[15] When no response is served in the requisite time, the responding party waives objections to the interrogatories and is subject to sanctions, unless a timely motion for protective order has been filed.[16] The party objecting to the discovery has the burden of specifically demonstrating that the interrogatories are improper.[17]

§ 24.4 Option to Produce Business Records

When an interrogatory requests information such as a compilation, abstract, or summary which can be derived from an examination, audit, or inspection of the party's business records, Rule 33(c) may provide relief to the responding party. If the burden of ascertaining the answer is substantially the same for the party serving the interrogatory as for the party served, it is sufficient to answer by specifying the records providing the answer and affording the requesting party a reasonable opportunity to examine, audit, or inspect the records and make copies, compilations, abstracts, or summaries of them. The specification must be in sufficient detail for the requesting party to locate and identify the records. Merely reciting that the answers can be found in partnership books of accounts, banking accounts, record, computer printouts, ledgers, and other documents is an insufficient Rule 33(c) response.[18]

There are several difficulties inherent in relying on a Rule 33(c) answer. First, it is always risky to open the party's files to perusal by opposing counsel, and all of the files produced should be reviewed for privileged information. Second, previously produced documents which were ignored or discounted may become significant to the requesting party. Similarly, documents which were never requested may be responsive to the Rule 33(c) answer and provide additional ammunition for the adverse party. In addition, if the information requested is indexed or computerized, the requesting party may argue that the responding party's familiarity with the system defeats any claim that the burden of compiling the information is substantially the same for both parties.[19] Although such familiarity is not dispositive, it will be factored into the court's Rule 33(c) determination.

---

[14] Fed. R. Civ. P. 29.

[15] *See* Fed. R. Civ. P. 5(d); 4A Moore's Federal Practice ¶ 33.24.

[16] 8 Federal Practice and Procedure § 2173.

[17] Josephs v. Harris Corp., 677 F.2d 985, 992 (3d Cir. 1982).

[18] Rainbow Pioneer v. Hawaii-Nevada Inv. Corp., 711 F.2d 902, 906 (9th Cir. 1983).

[19] *See* Sherman & Kinnard, *Federal Court Discovery in the 80's—Making the Rules Work,* 95 F.R.D. 245, 252–55 (1983); *See generally* 4A Moore's Federal Practice ¶ 33.25[5].

§ 24.5 Amending and Supplementing Answers

Supplementation of answers to interrogatories is required only if the information falls within Rule 26(e).[20] However, interrogatories answered by a plaintiff before individual defendants were dropped or dismissed from the action should always be reviewed to see whether their deletion affected the validity of previous answers. Similarly, if the plaintiff's initial theory of the case has altered, the answers should be analyzed and, if necessary, supplemented or amended to avoid a dispositive motion based in part on answers which have become unfavorable. Although technically there is no provision for amending answers, the judge has discretion to permit amendment.[21] The only way the requesting party can obtain supplementation of responses not required by Rule 26(e) is to propound a set of interrogatories at the end of discovery which requests updating of information previously disclosed. This may not be feasible if the district court permits only a limited number of interrogatories without leave of court. It is also likely to result in the responding party's attempting to have the discovery restricted under Rule 26(b)(1) or 26(c), unless the opponent also desires the same type of supplementation.

§ 24.6 Drafting Suggestions

Careful drafting is essential to obtaining useful answers to interrogatories. The cases are replete with inartfully drafted questions. For example, how many fanciful answers can be constructed to respond to the question "[i]n what way could you have avoided the collision?"[22] We will never know, because the likelihood of a judge's ordering the responding party to answer with useful information is, at best, slight. After the interrogatories are drafted, they should be reviewed to determine how the responding party might misinterpret or evade meaningfully answering the questions.

Each set should be preceded by instructions and definitions of commonly used terms.[23] Although it is not uncommon to see extensive instructions, because the provisions of the federal rules are applicable regardless of whether they are cited, a relatively short set of instructions should be crafted. The instructions should include:

---

[20] See §§ **17.14–7.15**.

[21] 4A Moore's Federal Practice ¶ 33.25[2] (2d ed. 1984); 8 Federal Practice and Procedure § 2181.

[22] Pressley v. Boehlke, 33 F.R.D. 316, 317 (W.D.N.C. 1963), *noted in* Schoone & Miner, *The Effective Use of Written Interrogatories,* 60 Marq. L. Rev. 29, 32 n.8 (1976).

[23] *See generally* Schoone & Miner, *The Effective Use of Written Interrogatories,* 60 Marq. L. Rev. 29 (1976); *see also* Seitz, *Get More Information and Less Indigestion Out of Your Interrogatories,* 71 A.B.A. J. 74 (Mar. 1985).

1. The duty of the party to make a reasonable investigation to obtain the information requested
2. The necessity to answer to the fullest extent possible, even if complete information is unavailable
3. The obligation to answer interrogatories to the extent that they are not objectionable
4. The requirement that the basis of any claim of privilege must be set forth, and
5. A general reference to the Rule 26(e) duty to supplement interrogatories.

The time frame to which the interrogatories apply should also be indicated. Often an interrogatory can force the disclosure of an expert witness at an early stage of litigation by requesting the identification of all individuals other than clerical or wordprocessing personnel who were consulted in formulating the answers.

Words such as *discusss, identify,* or *describe* which are used in the interrogatories should be defined. *Document* or *writing* should be defined broadly in the language of Rule 34(a) and Federal Rule of Evidence 1001. The individuals or entities referred to in the interrogatories should also be defined as well as any specialized terms. Contention interrogatories which ask for facts, documents, witnesses, and oral communications "supporting" the contention usually produce more helpful responses than those requesting information which relate to the contention.

Although a party cannot require that a document be produced in answer to an interrogatory, instructions requesting that the responding party append any documents identified which it does not object to producing without a separate Rule 34 request may shorten production time. A clearly permissible alternative is to serve a document production request concurrently with the interrogatories, asking for any documents identified in the answers.

§ 24.7 Restrictions on Interrogatory Practice

Care must be taken to consult the local rules to determine whether there are any restrictions on the number of interrogatories which can be propounded. In some districts, interrogatories are limited to 25 or 30 without leave of the court. It must also be determined whether subparts count as separate interrogatories for purposes of the local rule. Such limitations require counsel to save interrogatories for information which cannot otherwise be obtained. If more than one set of interrogatories is served, each set should be numbered sequentially. Some local rules also require that all interrogatories be numbered sequentially even if more than one set is used, in part for easy reference, as well as to inform the court whether Interrogatory No. 1 of the Third Set of Interrogatories is really the 30th, 300th or 3000th interrogatory requested.

Shotgun and boilerplate interrogatories rarely produce usable answers and can result in discovery motions to sanction the requesting party. Although pattern interrogatories can be a great timesaver, and reams of relevant questions may already be programmed into counsel's word processor, each question must be reviewed for its applicability to the case at hand. Airplane interrogatories are bound to be inappropriate when turned into automobile interrogatories unless significant revisions are made.

When faced with a set of voluminous boilerplate interrogatories, some counsel will respond with blanket objections claiming the interrogatories are not applicable. Although technically, specific objections must be given for each interrogatory or a protective order sought, the blanket response is much less expensive, and it is rare that the requesting party will be brash enough to bring an abusive set of interrogatories to the attention of an unsympathetic federal judge or magistrate. Indeed, some local rules specifically prohibit the use of boilerplate interrogatories. Because the net result of serving such a set is likely to be hostile negotiations ending in an agreement to modify the questions to fit the action, no strategic advantage is gained by their use. Judges have been known to strike sets of questions and answers when they appeared to have no attorney input but were produced by some word processing machine's memory of prior litigation.[24]

§ 24.8 Drafting Suggestions for Responses

Counsel should discuss the interrogatories with the client to determine the best method of obtaining the relevant information and who should draft the initial response. Usually, the client provides the requested information, and a paralegal or attorney produces the initial draft. Such answers must be carefully reviewed with the person verifying them to ascertain their factual accuracy. Conversely, if the client drafts the initial answers, the attorney must determine whether they contain inappropriate or privileged information.

An extension normally should be sought to respond to the interrogatories. Even if the set is relatively straightforward, communications with the client concerning the answers and the requirement that the answers be signed under oath will make it unlikely that 30 days is sufficient. Parties routinely stipulate to such extensions. The amount of time needed to respond should be carefully estimated, because extensions must be approved by the court,[25] which means that a second or third extension requires some justification, regardless of whether the adverse party has no objection.

---

[24] *See* Blank v. Ronson Corp., 97 F.R.D. 744, 745 (S.D.N.Y. 1983).

[25] Fed. R. Civ. P. 29.

Although blanket objections are not sufficient, it is common to include the introductory section in which all of the objections are set forth in detail. The specific response then refers to the type of objection which has been previously defined. When faced with overboard interrogatories, many counsel qualify their answers before responding; a complete refusal to respond is usually unwarranted and may subject the responding party to sanctions. However, extensive rewriting of the interrogatories by qualifying answers can be considered abusive if the interrogatories are not found to be objectionable. Evasive answers raise ethical considerations and can result in sanctions to the party and/or attorney, but effective advocacy assumes that answers are stated most favorably to the party's position.

§ 24.9 Enforcing Rule 33 Discovery

Complete failure to respond to interrogatories subjects the party to immediate sanctions under Rule 37(d), including dismissal or default.[26] Insufficient responses can be challenged under Rule 37(a) by bringing a motion to compel discovery.[27] Answers which are evasive or incomplete can be treated as a failure to answer which subjects the party to Rule 37(d) sanctions, regardless of whether an order to answer has been obtained.[28] The expenses of bringing or defending a successful motion, including reasonable attorneys' fees, are recoverable unless the court finds the losing party's position was substantially justified or other circumstances make an award of expenses unjust.[29]

The federal rules impose no time limitation for bringing motions to enforce discovery responses; however, the longer the delay, the more difficult it will be to claim that the information requested is significant. Local rules must be consulted as to any timing or other requirements which must be met before a motion can be brought. The most common requirement is that the parties must attempt to resolve the dispute in good faith before a motion is proper. Such communication is desirable even if not required, in order to determine the reason for the default or inadequate response and whether answers are forthcoming. Moreover, district court judges do not want to hear discovery disputes which have not been discussed between the parties. A joint statement concerning the dispute may also be required. It is usually necessary to include affidavits of counsel as support for the motion, and a paper trail documenting conversations with opposing counsel is usually begun at the slightest indication that a motion is forthcoming.

---

[26] See **ch. 29**.

[27] Fed. R. Civ. P. 33(a).

[28] Fed. R. Civ. P. 37(a)(3); Basch v. Westinghouse Elec. Corp., 777 F.2d 165, 174 & n.20 (4th Cir. 1985), *cert. denied*, _____ U.S. _____, 106 S. Ct. 1957 (1986); Airtex Corp. v. Shelley Radiant Ceiling Co., 536 F.2d 145, 155 (7th Cir. 1976).

[29] Fed. R. Civ. P. 37(a)(4).

In deciding what, if any, sanctions to apply, the court may consider a variety of factors, including:

1. The time which has elapsed since interrogatories were served
2. Whether the party served was previously given a voluntary extension of time
3. The numbers of interrogatories propounded
4. Whether the unanswered questions sought information which was difficult to obtain
5. Whether the answers supplied were evasive and incomplete
6. The number of questions which remained unanswered
7. Whether the questions which remain unanswered are material to a particular claim or defense
8. Whether the answering party has acted in good faith and with reasonable diligence
9. The existence of prior orders compelling discovery and the answering party's previous responses
10. Whether the party was unable to comply with the previous order of the court
11. Whether an order allowing more time to answer would enable the answering party to supply the necessary information and
12. Whether a sanction short of dismissal or default would be appropriate.[30]

Judges will often issue a conditional order imposing sanctions if the answers are not received within a set time.

Parties and attorneys may also be required to pay expenses and attorneys' fees for violations of Rule 11 or Rule 26(g) in interrogatory practice.[31] These rules provide that all papers, including discovery requests, responses, objections, and motions must be certified that, after reasonable inquiry, they are (1) consistent with the rules and warranted by existing law or good faith argument for the extension, modification, or reversal of existing law, (2) not interposed for any improper purpose, such as to harass or to cause unnecessary delay or needless increase in the cost of litigation, and (3) not unreasonable or unduly burdensome or expensive, given the needs of the case, the discovery already had in the case, the amount in controversy, and the importance of the issues at stake in the litigation. Therefore, it is likely that interrogatories will decline in popularity as a tactic to force settlement on less affluent plaintiffs whose contingency lawyers cannot afford to frolic in a sea of paper.

[30] Deyo v. Kilbourne, 84 Cal. App. 3d 771, 796–97, 149 Cal. Rptr. 499, 518 (1978) (California sanctions patterned after Rule 37).

[31] *See, e.g.*, Basch v. Westinghouse Elec. Corp., 777 F.2d 165, 174 (4th Cir. 1985), *cert. denied*, ____ U.S. ____, 106 S. Ct. 1957 (1986) (Rule 11 sanction imposed for evasive answer).

§ 24.10 Use of Interrogatories as Evidence

Interrogatory answers may be used to the extent permitted by the rules of evidence. They can be used to support summary judgment motions[32] as well as other motions which look outside the pleadings. In this context, a Rule 33(c) answer which specifies documents adopts the contents of those documents.[33] Answers to contention interrogatories can be incorporated into a Rule 16 pretrial statement, thereby becoming subject to modification only to prevent manifest injustice.[34]

In practice, regardless of the extent of hostilities engendered by pretrial interrogatory practice or the number of interrogatories actually answered, it is rare to see such answers used at trial. First, unlike Rule 36 admissions, interrogatory answers can be contradicted. Although the court has discretion to refuse to let a party contradict an answer on which the adverse party relied,[35] such power is rarely exercised. Second, the answers are written by attorneys and usually are not stated as a direct admission.[36] Third, even if used as a prior inconsistent statement of the person who signed them, the usual explanation is that the individual has no personal knowledge of the information or signed them without understanding the significance of the answers. Moreover, interrogatories which were obtained in other litigation involving the party must be authenticated to be admissible, even if they contain admissions.[37] In addition, a party's own interrogatories rarely are admissible over a hearsay objection.[38]

---

[32] Fed. R. Civ. P. 56(c).

[33] *In re* Japanese Elec. Prods., 723 F.2d 238, 301 (3d Cir. 1983), *rev'd on other grounds sub nom.* Matsushita Elec. Indus. Co. v. Zenith Radio, ____ U.S. ____, 106 S. Ct. 1348 (1986).

[34] Fed. R. Civ. P. 16(e); § **16.4**.

[35] *See, e.g.*, Wilder Enters. v. Allied Artists Pictures, 632 F.2d 1135, 1144 (4th Cir. 1980).

[36] *See* Fed. R. Evid. 801(d)(2).

[37] *See* Simmons v. Hoegh Lines, 784 F.2d 1234, 1237–38 (5th Cir. 1986) (introduction to unverified interrogatories warranted reversal).

[38] *See* Walton v. United Consumers Club, Inc., 786 F.2d 303, 313 (7th Cir. 1986).

CHAPTER 25

PRODUCTION OF DOCUMENTS AND TANGIBLE ITEMS AND ORDERS FOR MEDICAL EXAMINATIONS

RULE 34

§ 25.1 Rule 34 Overview

Rule 34 applies only to parties and provides for the discovery of documents and things and the entry upon land for inspection. Document discovery from nonparties is governed by Rule 45 subpoena duces tecum procedures.[1] The importance of Rule 34 discovery depends upon the nature of the action and is often significant in business or products liability litigation in which massive amounts of documents have been generated over a long period. In such cases, production requests usually precede other discovery, because deposition preparation may be dependent upon what the documents reveal. Document production is not a substitute for interrogatories, because Rule 34 cannot be used to require the adverse party to prepare noncomputerized materials which do not already exist. Therefore, lists or tabulations are generally requested in interrogatories, because these items are within Rule 34 only if they were previously prepared other than as work product.

Rule 34 requests can be used successfully in conjunction with interrogatories.[2] For example, an interrogatory can call for the identification of documents relevant to a contention, and an accompanying Rule 34 request can ask for production of items identified in the interrogatory answers. Indeed, some counsel try to shortcut the Rule 34 procedure entirely by requesting that documents referred to in answer to interrogatories be attached to the answers, if the adverse party has no objection to such production.

Document production can be quite expensive to all concerned. The party requesting production bears the costs of inspecting and copying whatever documents are chosen. The responding party must select the documents which are subject to the request, check that privileged documents are identified and separated from those being produced and either copy or identify the documents selected by the requestor. Although the court has power under Rule 26(c) to shift a cost of production to the opposing party,[3] such a remedy is extraordinary. Cost shifting is most likely when the responding party is asked to manipulate computerized information in ways requiring new programming.

§ 25.2 Scope of Rule 34

A party can inspect and copy any relevant documents which are described with reasonable particularity. No showing of good cause is necessary to obtain documents or to enforce a document request.[4] The definition of *documents* in the rule is broadly drafted to include writings, drawings, graphs, charts, photographs, phono-records, and other data compilations from which information can be obtained, translated, if necessary, by the respondent through detection

---

[1] See **ch. 21**.

[2] See **ch. 24**.

[3] See **ch. 19**.

[4] *See generally* 4A J. Moore's *et al.*, Moore's Federal Practice ¶ 34.05[3] (2d ed. 1984).

devices into reasonably usable form.[5] Computer data, including printouts and programs, fall within the rule. Potential problems concerning access, accuracy and admissability of computerized evidence should be analyzed early as part of counsel's overall discovery plan.[6] However, certain types of computerized information may be subject to claims of work product or attorney-client privilege.[7] Responding counsel should always consider the desirability of negotiating or moving for a protective order concerning disclosure of documents which are considered confidential.[8]

Rule 34 also permits a party to inspect and copy, test, or sample any tangible things which constitute or contain relevant matters and which are in the possession, custody, or control of the party upon whom the request is served.[9] A party can also request entry upon designated land or other property in the possession or control of the party upon whom the request is served for the purpose of inspection and measuring, surveying, photographing, testing, or sampling the property or any designated object or operation relevant to the action.[10] Although the decision to test an item is a strategic choice dependent in part on counsel's evaluation of the likely results, discovery which alters or destroys a tangible thing is objectionable.[11] If production of a tangible object is requested, counsel should determine whether it will be tested by an expert and, if so, whether the object will be returned unaltered. If the court permits such discovery, counsel should stipulate to the testing procedures or move for a Rule 26(c) protective order, which may require that the process be filmed, the expert of the producing party be present at the time of the testing, and the results of the testing be made available to all parties.[12] Reasonable conditions should be set by stipulation or protection order concerning a party's inspection of a business, because Rule 34 does not permit disruption.[13] Counsel should also be aware that statements made by employees during an inspection can form the basis for adverse expert testimony.[14]

---

[5] Fed. R. Civ. P. 34(a).

[6] Manual for Complex Litigation, § 21.446 (2d ed. 1985); see § **17.2**.

[7] *See, e.g.*, Poirier, Robb, & Mosher, *Computer-Based Litigation Support Systems: The Discoverability Issue,* 54 UMKC L. Rev. 440 (1986); Note, *Computer Discovery in Federal Litigation: Playing by the Rules,* 69 Georgetown L.J. 1465 (1981); **ch. 18**.

[8] See **ch. 19**.

[9] Fed. R. Civ. P. 34(a).

[10] *Id.*

[11] *See, e.g.*, Dabney v. Montgomery Ward & Co., 761 F.2d 494, 497–98 (8th Cir.), *cert. denied,* ____ U.S. ____, 106 S. Ct. 233 (1985); Haydock & Herr, *Production of Results Under Rule 34,* 5 Am. J. Trial Advoc. 253, 268–70 (1981).

[12] Haydock & Herr, *Production of Results Under Rule 34,* 5 Am. J. Trial Advoc. 253, 270–72 (1981).

[13] Belcher v. Bassett Furniture Indus., Inc., 588 F.2d 904, 908–11 (4th Cir. 1978).

[14] *See* New York State Ass'n for Retarded Children, Inc. v. Carey, 706 F.2d 956, 961 (2d Cir.), *cert. denied,* 464 U.S. 915 (1983).

§ 25.3 Procedural Requirements

A Rule 34 request is served without leave of court upon the plaintiff after the commencement of the action and upon any other party with or after service of the summons and complaint upon that party. The request can state that the time and place of the production will be mutually agreed upon if no agreement is reached prior to service. The items to be inspected must be specified either individually or by category, with each item and category being described with reasonable particularity. For example, a request for all business records relevant to the action would be considered too broad.

The party upon whom the request is served has 30 days in which to serve a written response, except that a defendant can respond within 45 days after being served with the complaint. Serving a subpoena duces tecum on the opposing party does not shortcut Rule 34 timing.[15] The court may allow a longer or shorter time for response. Technically, any agreement to extend the time provided in Rule 34 can be made only with the approval of the court.[16] However, when opposing counsel agrees to the extension, the question of timing often does not come to the attention of the judge, because many local rules provide that discovery materials shall not be filed unless relevant to a pending motion. Since the response rather than the production is due within 30 or 45 days, counsel should propound document requests early in the litigation, especially if the documents are needed for deposition preparation. Otherwise, counsel is likely to be confronted with a Rule 26(c) motion for a protective order to prohibit a second deposition which is sought after the documents are obtained.

In 1980, Rule 34(b) was amended to require that the documents be produced as they are kept in the usual course of business or be organized and labelled to correspond with the categories in the request.[17] There is some question whether the requesting party can dictate which of these alternative methods of production must be followed, because the section was enacted to prevent the responding party from mixing critical documents with others to obscure their significance, not to disadvantage the requesting party.[18] Therefore, it is unlikely that a court will permit discovery to be frustrated by the responding party's use of an inadequate filing system which does not produce the documents in usable fashion.[19]

If no timely response is filed, a party is subject to sanctions under Rule 37(d) and is deemed to have waived any objections to the production unless the party

---

[15] *See* Fed. R. Civ. P. 30(b)(5).

[16] Fed. R. Civ. P. 29.

[17] Fed. R. Civ. P. 34(b).

[18] *See* 8 C. Wright, A. Miller, *et al.*, Federal Practice and Procedure § 2213 (Supp. 1986).

[19] *See generally* Sherman & Kinnard, *Federal Court Discovery in the 80's—Making the Rules Work,* 95 F.R.D. 245, 255–58 (1983); *cf.* Kozlowski v. Sears, Roebuck & Co., 73 F.R.D. 73, 75–76 (D. Mass. 1976) (pre-amendment).

timely applied for a protective order.[20] Therefore, failure to respond can result in a dismissal or default in a flagrant case.[21] The response must state, with respect to each item or category, that inspection and related activities will be permitted as requested, unless the request is objected to, in which event the reasons for the objection must be stated. If the objection concerns only a portion of an individual request, that part must be specified. General objections are not sufficient and can be treated as a total failure to respond for purpose of sanctions under Rule 37(d).[22] In addition, even if the court considers untimely supplemental objections, it can impose a penalty, such as ruling against the responding party when doubt exists whether the request should be permitted.[23] The requesting party can move for an order to compel production with respect to any objection to or other failure to respond to the request or any part of it, or any failure to permit inspection as requested.[24] The party opposing discovery has the burden to show that production is improper.[25]

§ 25.4 Drafting Suggestions for Requests

Effective Rule 34 requests are broad enough to include unknown materials which are relevant and specific enough to require production of known documents. If computerized materials are requested, documentation relating to the use of the data processing system should also be requested.

Every request should include definitions and instructions.[26] Some lawyers define documents or writings in a lengthy manner which includes every conceivable form of human recording known. However, a simple reference to the Rule 34(a) definition of documents and the Federal Rule of Evidence's definitions of writings and recordings, and photographs found in Rule 1001 is sufficient to cover every possibility. It is standard to include definitions of the following terms: the persons involved in the action; possession and control of documents; discuss, describe or identify documents; and any terminology which is significant to the requests.

It is not uncommon for counsel to repeat the instructions in Rule 34 as a preface to the requests and include detailed admonitions about sanctions and

---

[20] *See* Charter House Ins. Brokers, Ltd. v. New Hampshire Ins. Co., 667 F.2d 600, 603–05 (7th Cir. 1981); 8 Federal Practice and Procedure § 2213.

[21] See **ch. 29**.

[22] *Cf. In re* Folding Carton Antitrust Litig., 83 F.R.D. 260, 264 (N.D. Ill. E.D. 1979) (interrogatories).

[23] *Id.*

[24] Fed. R. Civ. P. 34(b).

[25] 4A Moore's Federal Practice ¶ 34.05[3].

[26] *See generally* Haydock & Herr, *Production of Results Under Rule 34,* 5 Am. J. Trial Advoc. 258 (1981).

supplementation of responses. Such detail is unnecessary, because the requirements of the federal rules apply regardless of whether the language is included. Therefore, the instructions should be fairly short unless counsel expects resistance to discovery and wants to give notice that such behavior will not be tolerated. Instructions should include a request to describe the efforts which were undertaken to locate records which were not found and to identify who has control of documents not possessed by the party.

§ 25.5 Drafting Suggestions for Responses

Although blanket objections to a Rule 34 request are not sufficient, it is common to begin the written response with general objections which detail the nature of the complaint and then individually refer to such definitions in objection to the specific request. For example, an explanation of why attorney-client privilege applies to a variety of categories or that no specific time frame has been included for the production of business records is placed at the beginning of the response, and objections to individual requests refer to attorney-client privilege or lack of time frame. If the requests are overbroad, it is better policy to indicate the extent of production that the responding party believes relevant, rather than to appear before the court with a complete refusal to produce relevant as well as irrelevant documents. Similarly, the response can indicate that no objection exists to the production itself but to its time, place, or manner.

§ 25.6 Objections to Production

Typical objections to Rule 34 requests include privilege, work product, lack of particularity of the category requested, irrelevance, and nonexistence or lack of possession of the designated items. Even if a document is not in the possession of the party, the court can order the party to request release of its records to comply with discovery obligations.[27] However, a party cannot have its case terminated if it lacks control of the requested documents and is unable to obtain them.[28] Rule 26(b) now permits the court to limit requests for production which are unreasonably cumulative or duplicative or obtainable from some other source that is more convenient, less burdensome, or less expensive, or which are unduly burdensome or expensive. Such objections are also appropriate as the basis of a motion for a protective order, but it may be less costly to cite them in a Rule 34(b) response and work out a mutually agreeable production schedule than to move for a protective order. A timely written response containing the specified

---

[27] United States *ex rel.* Woodard v. Tynan, 776 F.2d 250, 252 (10th Cir. 1985).

[28] *See* Searock v. Stripling, 736 F.2d 650, 654–55 (11th Cir. 1984).

objections must be served in order to form a basis of any later motion for protective order.

§ 25.7 Enforcing Rule 34 Requests

Failure to respond to a request for production can result in the immediate imposition of Rule 37(d) sanctions.[29] Usually the dispute revolves around the adequacy of the production. In such cases, a motion must be made to compel production before any sanction other than attorneys' fees for the costs of the motion is imposed. Many local rules require that the parties meet in person to resolve their discovery disputes before a motion can be filed. A few districts even require the filing of a joint statement describing the discovery dispute and setting forth each party's position.[30] It is common for attorney affidavits to be submitted concerning discovery disputes, and a careful record should be kept of relevant conversations with opposing counsel. Document requests or responses and motions to compel discovery or their oppositions which are interposed for improper reasons or lacking in factual or legal foundation also subject a party or attorney to sanctions pursuant to Rules 11 and 26(g).[31]

§ 25.8 Destruction of Documents

Many businesses have internal policies which call for the destruction of routine documents on a periodic basis.[32] There is some question whether anticipation of litigation or the filing of a lawsuit should automatically result in the suspension of these policies concerning any documents relevant to litigation.[33] For example, the A.B.A.'s Model Rules of Professional Conduct provide that an attorney shall not unlawfully destroy material having potential evidentiary value or counsel or assist another person to do any such act.[34] If voluminous document production is anticipated, counsel should consider obtaining a stipulation or an order to

---

[29] See **ch. 29**.

[30] *E.g.*, Cal. C.D. Rule 7.15.2.

[31] See **ch. 28**.

[32] *See, e.g.*, Borow & Baskin, *The Internal Corporate Investigation: Destruction of Documents and Routine Record Retention Programs*, The Internal Corporate Investigation, PLI Handbook No. 333, at 209, 212–13 (1980); Fedders & Guttenplan, *Document Retention and Destruction: Practical, Legal and Ethical Considerations*, 56 Notre Dame Law. 5 (1980); Oesterle, *A Private Litigant's Remedies for an Opponent's Inappropriate Destruction of Relevant Documents*, 61 Tex. L. Rev. 1185 (1983).

[33] *See* Oesterle, *A Private Litigant's Remedies for an Opponent's Inappropriate Destruction of Relevant Documents*, 61 Tex. L. Rev. 1185, 1222–25 (1983) (discussing cases).

[34] Model Rules of Professional Conduct Rule 3.4(a) (1983).

preserve all relevant documents early in the litigation to avoid destruction of materials before an appropriate request has been served.[35] Moreover, since computerized databases and programs are subject to rapid change, the order should encompass not only printouts but also relevant programs. Local rules affecting the exchange of documents may also impose a duty to preserve documents on litigants.[36] Once a request has been served, it takes precedence over a routine destruction policy, even if all of the documents destroyed are considered to be duplicates. Therefore, it is counsel's obligation to determine what, if any, document destruction policy the client has instituted and ensure that the client instructs all appropriate employees that they cannot destroy relevant documents.

If documents are destroyed, sanctions are likely to be imposed under Rule 37, even in the absence of a previous order compelling production.[37] In determining whether to assess sanctions, the court will evaluate if the party destroyed material in bad faith, thereby supporting the inference that the evidence would be unfavorable to that party if introduced in court.[38] Similarly, falsification of existing documents can result in sanctions, including the termination of the action.[39] In egregious cases, such conduct subjects the attorney as well as the client to criminal sanctions for contempt or obstruction of justice.[40] In addition, an attorney can be referred for state bar disciplinary action. A few states also allow civil actions for destruction of documents.[41]

§ 25.9 Independent Actions

Rule 34 does not preclude an independent action against a nonparty for production of documents and things and permission to enter upon land.[42] Usually, documents and tangible things are obtained pursuant to a Rule 45 subpoena duces tecum. However, there is no provision which entitles a party to obtain permission to enter upon land of a nonparty, and it is unclear what

---

[35] *See* Oesterle, *A Private Litigant's Remedies for an Opponent's Inappropriate Destruction of Relevant Documents,* 61 Tex. L. Rev. 1185, 1222–25 (1983) (discussing cases).

[36] *See, e.g.,* Cal. C.D. Rule 6.1.1.

[37] *See* Oesterle, *A Private Litigant's Remedies for an Opponent's Inappropriate Destruction of Relevant Documents,* 61 Tex. L. Rev. 1185, 1222–25 (1983) (discussing cases).

[38] Eaton Corp. v. Appliance Valves Corp., 790 F.2d 874, 878 (Fed. Civ. 1986); S.C. Johnson & Sons, Inc. v. Louisville & Nashville R.R., 695 F.2d 253, 258–59 (7th Cir. 1982).

[39] *See* Professional Seminar Consultants, Inc. v. Sino Am. Tech. Exch. Council, Inc., 727 F.2d 1470, 1472–74 (9th Cir. 1984).

[40] Oesterle, *A Private Litigant's Remedies for an Opponent's Inappropriate Destruction of Relevant Documents,* 61 Tex. L. Rev. 1185, 1200, 1191–1207 (1983).

[41] *See generally,* Comment, *Spoliation: Civil Liability for Destruction of Evidence,* 20 U. Rich. L. Rev. 191 (1985).

[42] Fed. R. Civ. P. 34(c).

jurisdictional requirements must be met in order to institute an independent action to obtain such permission.[43]

§ 25.10 Use of Documents as Evidence

Documents obtained from discovery can be used at trial, as well as to support any motion or opposition which permits evidence outside of the pleadings to be considered. However, such documents are inadmissible for these purposes unless a proper foundation has been established. First, the documents must be authenticated. The mere production of documents by a party does not necessarily authenticate them, because third party documents are often found in the party's files and produced in answer to requests. On the other hand, the fact that the party's own documents were produced pursuant to a discovery request may be sufficient to authenticate those items produced from a source where the requested documents were likely to be found.[44] Even so, when those documents are used in conjunction with a motion, an affidavit should be submitted which states that they were produced by the adverse party in discovery.

In addition, documents produced in response to a Rule 34 request are only admissible if they fit within appropriate hearsay exceptions such as for admissions or business records, unless they are introduced for nonhearsay purposes. A business record foundation[45] can be established through Rule 36 requests for admissions, agreements embodied in Rule 16 pretrial statements, or through depositions or live testimony. If a proper foundation is not established, counsel may find that the smoking gun produces only ashes at trial.

RULE 35

§ 25.11 Scope of Rule 35

Rule 35 provides for mental and physical examinations. If the mental or physical condition of a party or of a person in the custody or under the legal control of a party is in controversy, the court in which the action is pending can order the

---

[43] *See generally* 8 Federal Practice and Procedure § 2209 (1970); Welling, *Discovery of Nonparties' Tangible Things Under The Federal Rules Of Civil Procedure,* 59 Notre Dame L. Rev. 110 (1983).

[44] *In re* Japanese Elec. Prods., 723 F.2d 238, 286 (3d Cir. 1983), *rev'd on other grounds sub nom.* Matsushita Elec. Indus. Co. v. Zenith Radio, _____ U.S. _____, 106 S. Ct. 1348 (1986); *see* Burgess v. Premier Corp., 727 F.2d 826, 841 (9th Cir. 1984) (sanctions appropriate for failure to admit authenticity of documents which were produced from party's own files).

[45] See § **21.7**.

party to submit to a physical or mental examination by a physician or to produce a person in the custody or legal control of the party for examination. Rule 35 does not apply to nonparty witnesses who are not in the custody or under control of a party, and there appears to be no authority to support such examinations.[46]

Unlike Rule 34 which is initiated by a request for relevant information, a party attempting to obtain a Rule 35 examination must bring a motion establishing good cause for the examination, unless the other side stipulates to the examination. The court has discretion to refuse to order the examination and will consider how painful or dangerous it will be when evaluating the necessity for the order.[47] Blood tests, X-rays, and other standard procedures are more likely to be ordered than more painful or less widely used procedures.[48] Similarly, a second examination of an individual is rarely granted. The movant must show that the condition is in controversy. This is easily satisfied when a plaintiff claims personal injury or a defendant raises an affirmative defense concerning the subject matter of the examination. However, when the opposing party raises the issue, courts more carefully scrutinize whether the condition is actually in controversy.[49]

§ 25.12 Rule 35 Order

The order must specify the time, place, manner, conditions, and scope of the examination as well as identify who will conduct the examination. The court usually accepts the physician chosen by the examining party.[50] Rule 35 requires that the examination be conducted by a physician. Therefore, mental examinations by a psychologist or clinical sociologist are not permitted, regardless of whether the individual is licensed. One issue which has arisen is whether the doctor or lawyer of the person being examined may be present at the examination. Federal practice generally permits the individual's doctor, but not the lawyer, to watch the examination.[51]

§ 25.13 Report to Examining Physician

The party being examined can obtain a detailed copy of the written report of the examining physician, including findings, results of all tests, diagnoses, and

---

[46] 8 Federal Practice and Procedure § 2233 (1970); Belcuore, *When the Witness gets a Note from His Doctor: Third-Party Witnesses, Medical Excuses, and Compelled Examinations,* 32 Fed. Bar News & J. 187, 188 (1985).

[47] *See generally* 4A Moore's Federal Practice ¶ 35.04.

[48] *See generally* 8 Federal Practice and Procedure § 2235.

[49] *See* Schlagenhauf v. Holder, 379 U.S. 104, 18–21 (1964).

[50] 8 Federal Practice and Procedure § 2234.

[51] *See generally id.* § 2236.

conclusions, together with like reports of all earlier examinations of the same condition.[52] However, the delivery of the report triggers a requirement of mutuality on the part of the requesting party. Specifically, the examining party becomes entitled to a like report of any examination previously or thereafter made of the same condition, except for any earlier report of a nonparty's examination which the party cannot obtain. Moreover, by obtaining a report or deposing the physician, the examined party waives any privilege regarding the testimony of every other person who has examined or may thereafter examine the party concerning the same mental or physical condition.[53] Some counsel believe that such a waiver is meaningless if the physician is a trial witness, because all relevant materials become subject to discovery. However, this provision also requires disclosure of physicians consulted who will not testify at trial, for whom discovery is usually unavailable.[54] Rule 35(b) also applies to examinations made by agreement of the parties, unless the stipulation expressly provides otherwise.[55]

At trial, the court can exclude the testimony of a physician who fails or refuses to make a report. This is only a remedy if the examining physician will be called as a trial witness. The rule is silent about penalties for a physician who refuses to issue a report but will not be called as a witness, which usually happens when the report is unfavorable to the examining party. Any collusion between the attorney and the witness to evade the requirements of the rule can result in penalties being invoked under Rule 37. In the absence of evidence of collusion, the court has power to order the party to have the report prepared at the expense of the party who requests it.[56]

§ 25.14 Sanctions for Failure to Submit to an Examination

If a party refuses to submit to an examination order pursuant to Rule 35 or to produce a person under the control of the party, all Rule 37 sanctions are applicable except for contempt.[57] A dismissal without prejudice was affirmed when a child's mother refused to permit her to be examined concerning alleged sexual abuse by the father unless the mother was present.[58] However, a dismissal was unwarranted when, despite the uncooperative behavior of the party, the

---

[52] Fed. R. Civ. P. 35(b).

[53] Fed. R. Civ. P. 35(b)(1).

[54] *See* Fed. R. Civ. P. 26(b)(4).

[55] Fed. R. Civ. P. 35(b)(3).

[56] *See* Salvatore v. American Cyanamid Co., 94 F.R.D. 156, 158 (D.R.I. 1982).

[57] Fed. R. Civ. P. 37(b)(2).

[58] Schempp v. Reniker, 809 F.2d 541, 542–44 (8th Cir. 1987).

physician was able to reach conclusions about the party's condition.[59] Any additional examinations caused by the party's actions can be conducted at that individual's expense.[60] If a party is unable to produce another person for examination, sanctions are also improper.[61]

---

[59] *See* DeCrescenzo v. Maersk Container Serv. Co., 741 F.2d 17, 21 (2d Cir. 1984).

[60] *Id.*

[61] Fed. R. Civ. P. 37(b)(2)(E).

CHAPTER 26

NARROWING THE ACTION BY REQUESTS FOR ADMISSIONS

§ 26.1 Rule 36 Overview

Requests for admissions (RFAs) are listed as an appropriate discovery method in Rule 26(a), but as a practical matter, Rule 36 requests follow discovery and are designed to eliminate the need to try uncontested issues.[1] RFAs are often used in conjunction with a Rule 16 pretrial order. They can also eliminate the need for trial by providing support for a summary judgment motion.[2]

Rule 36 requests are used most effectively in connection with interrogatories. It is common for an interrogatory to ask the responding party to state the facts supporting the denial of an accompanying RFA and to identify individuals, documents, and oral communications upon which the denial is based. The federal rules do not limit the number of RFAs that a party can propound, but local rules may permit only a designated number without leave of court.

Any Rule 36 request must be considered seriously, because failure to timely respond results in the matter's being admitted, unless the court relieves counsel of the default. Rule 36 admissions are deadly, because, unlike other discovery responses, they are conclusive.[3] This means that the defaulting party is not

[1] *See generally* 8 C. Wright & A. Miller, Federal Practice and Procedure § 2253 (1970); [hereinafter Federal Practice and Procedure]; 4A J. Moore *et al.*, Moore's Federal Practice ¶ 36.04[6] (2d ed. 1984) [hereinafter Moore's Federal Practice].

[2] Donovan v. Carls Drug Co., 703 F.2d 650, 651 (2d Cir. 1983) (admissions may be used for summary judgment).

[3] Fed. R. Civ. P. 36(b).

permitted to contradict the admission, although admissions made by a coparty are not conclusively binding on a party who has actually responded.[4] It is not uncommon for requests going to the heart of the case to be asked in the hope that the judge will uphold any admissions obtained through the default of the opposing party, thereby resulting in summary judgment. A surprising number of cases are won because of such admissions by default; federal judges, unlike some state judges, are quite restrictive in permitting withdrawal of such admissions. The importance of responding in a timely manner to RFAs or obtaining extensions cannot be overstated. Sloppy practice culminating in a grant of summary judgment may result in a malpractice action against an attorney.

§ 26.2 The Request for Admission

A written request for admission can be served upon any party for purposes of the pending action only. It cannot be used in any other proceeding or for any other purpose.[5] The party can be requested to admit the truth of any relevant matter that relates to statements or opinions of fact or the application of law to fact, including the genuineness of any documents described in the request. Copies of documents must be served with the request unless they have been or are otherwise furnished or made available for inspection and copying. Rule 36 does not limit the number of requests which may be propounded, but overuse of RFAs can be controlled through the court's power to regulate discovery pursuant to Rule 26(b)(1), (c), and (g). For example, submission of 2,028 RFAs was considered an abuse of discovery and an improper attempt to circumvent a local rule limiting parties to 30 interrogatories.[6]

§ 26.3 Procedural Requirements

Rule 36(a) sets forth the procedural requirements concerning requests. A plaintiff may be served without leave of court at any time after commencement of the action, and other parties can be served with or after service of the complaint. Service should be made on a pro se party or a represented party's attorney pursuant to Rule 5. Each factual request must be separately set forth. Unlike other discovery rules, Rule 36 is self-executing. If no response is submitted within 30 days after service of request, the matter is deemed admitted. However, a defendant is not required to serve answers or objections within 45 days after service of the complaint. The court may shorten or lengthen the time for response, and all extensions are subject to court approval.[7] Rule 36 procedure

---

[4] Riberglass, Inc. v. Techni-Glass Indus., Inc., 811 F.2d 565, 566 (11th Cir. 1987).

[5] Fed. R. Civ. P. 36(a).

[6] Misco, Inc. v. United States Steel Corp., 784 F.2d 198, 206 (6th Cir. 1986).

[7] Fed. R. Civ. P. 29.

must be followed in order to obtain the benefits of an admission. For example, negotiated responses to RFAs agreed upon as part of settlement which were never filed could not be used to authenticate documents at trial.[8]

§ 26.4 Responses

The responding party must state the reasons for any objection.[9] Privilege can be asserted to a Rule 36 request as well as to other forms of discovery.[10] The answer must specifically deny the matter or detail the reasons why the party cannot truthfully admit or deny the matter. If only part of the answer is subject to denial, the party has a good faith obligation to qualify the answer, admitting the true portion and denying the remainder. Counsel usually shy away from qualified admissions, fearing that they will be deemed to be full admissions. Lack of information or knowledge is not a valid reason to fail to admit or deny unless the party states that a reasonable inquiry has been made and the information known or readily obtainable is insufficient to enable the party to admit or deny.

The fact that an admission relates to a genuine issue for trial is not grounds to object to the request. The party must either deny the matter or set forth reasons why it cannot admit or deny it. The extent to which a party can be required to obtain information from third persons in order to respond to an RFA is somewhat unclear, because Rule 36(a) mentions reasonable inquiry. Some courts do not require an employer to obtain information from employees who have an adverse interest in the litigation.[11] The court has discretion to delay the final disposition of the request to the pretrial conference or another designated time before trial.[12]

§ 26.5 Drafting Suggestions

The key to drafting RFAs is brevity. Including more than one piece of factual information in a request or stating opinions works only if the opposing party does not respond and the RFAs are deemed admitted. Otherwise, each fact or opinion should be separately stated, so that counsel will not deny a request which is only partially true. Besides authenticating documents, RFAs are frequently used to establish the foundation for business records.

Responses to RFAs which do not admit or deny the requests must be carefully worded to avoid their being considered evasive, justifying their consideration as a full admission because they are not in compliance with the literal requirements of Rule 36(a). Similarly, the reasons for any objection must be specifically

---

[8] Mayer v. Angelica, 790 F.2d 1315, 1327, 1339–40 (7th Cir. 1986).

[9] *See generally* 8 Federal Practice and Procedure § 2259.

[10] *See id.* § 2262.

[11] *See, e.g.*, Al-Jundi v. Rockefeller, 91 F.R.D. 590, 593–94 (W.D.N.Y. 1981).

[12] Fed. R. Civ. P. 36(a).

stated. Avoid the commonly used buzzwords that "after reasonable inquiry the available information is insufficient to admit or deny the request," unless that is truly the case and a good reason exists for not denying the request.

§ 26.6 Sanctions for Rule 36 Violations

If the responses to RFAs are considered insufficient, the requesting party may move to have an answer or amended answer served or for the matter to be deemed admitted. As with other discovery disputes, counsel must follow any procedures required by the local rules before bringing the appropriate motion. The cost of the motion, including reasonable attorneys' fees, must be awarded to the successful party, unless the motion or opposition was substantially justified or other circumstances make an award of expenses unjust.

Rule 37(c) provides that if a party fails to admit the genuineness of any document or the truth of any matter as requested under Rule 36, which is proved at trial, the party which requested the admission can move for an order requiring the other party to pay the reasonable expenses incurred in proving the request, including reasonable attorneys' fees. This provision is mandatory, and the court must assess such costs unless it finds that (1) the request was objectionable; (2) the admission was of no substantial importance; (3) the responding party had reasonable ground to believe it might prevail on the matter; or (4) there was other good reason for the failure to admit. In practice, such motions are quite rare, since it is unusual for a party not to have some appropriate reason to deny a disputed matter which is important to the outcome of the case. On the other hand, the court can decide that the profferred reason is nothing more than an attempt to obstruct the speedy resolution of the case.[13] Such motions are usually filed post-trial, and the district court apparently has jurisdiction to hear the motion while an appeal is pending.[14]

It is much safer to deny an RFA, even with the possibility of paying for the proof, than to answer that the party is continuing its investigation and cannot admit or deny the matter. Although the court will ordinarily order an amended answer if it finds that such a response is not made in good faith, such matters are within the discretion of the district judge.[15] Therefore, sanctions under Rule 37, including deeming the requests admitted, have been ordered in addition to or in lieu of awarding costs.[16] Similarly, if the inquiry made by the responding party is not considered reasonable, the matter can be deemed admitted.[17] Sanctions

---

[13] *See, e.g.*, Burgess v. Premier Corp., 727 F.2d 826, 841–42 (9th Cir. 1984).

[14] *See* Chemical Eng'g Corp. v. Essef Indus., Inc., 795 F.2d 1565, 1574 (Fed. Cir. 1986) (applying 7th Cir. law).

[15] Asea, Inc. v. Southern Pac. Transp. Co., 669 F.2d 1242, 1247 (9th Cir. 1982); Brown v. Arlen Mgmt. Corp., 663 F.2d 575, 580 (5th Cir. 1981).

[16] *See* Asea, Inc. v. Southern Pac. Transp. Co., 669 F.2d 1242, 1246–47 (9th Cir. 1982).

[17] Brown v. Arlen Mgmt. Corp., 663 F.2d 575, 580 (5th Cir. 1981).

pursuant to Rule 11 or 26(g), including awards of attorneys' fees may also be applicable in a given case.[18]

§ 26.7 Amending or Withdrawing an Admission

A Rule 36 admission is conclusive unless the court grants a party's motion to amend or withdraw the admission. The court may permit withdrawal or amendment when the merits of the action will be aided and no prejudice to the party obtaining the admission will result.[19] Because the defaulting party has no absolute right to amend or withdraw an admission,[20] the court can deny the motion even if these criteria are met,[21] and many district courts are cautious about granting such motions.[22] However, there are some limits on the court's discretion. For example, denial of the motion merely because the parties informally agreed to an extension which was not filed with the court was an abuse of discretion when the court did not consider the criteria set forth in the rule.[23] The prejudice required by the rule related to the difficulty a party may face in proving its case because of the sudden need to obtain evidence required to prove the matter that had been admitted.[24] A party is not prejudiced under the rule because it must prove matter which is difficult or costly to demonstrate.[25]

Once trial has commenced or a final Rule 16 pretrial order has been issued, the moving party must show that manifest injustice will occur if a withdrawal is not permitted.[26] At trial, evidence which contradicts the admission is objectionable.[27] Therefore, the court must give binding effect to an admission, even if evidence presented at trial contradicts it, unless no rational factfinder could believe the facts established by the admission to be true.[28] A party obtaining an admission by default does not waive the right to rely thereon by presenting evidence at trial which overlaps the matter controlled by the admission.[29]

---

[18] See **ch. 28**.

[19] Fed. R. Civ. P. 36(b).

[20] Asea, Inc. v. Southern Pac. Transp. Co., 669 F.2d 1242, 1247–48 (9th Cir. 1982).

[21] Donovan v. Carls Drug Co., 703 F.2d 650, 651–52 (2d Cir. 1983).

[22] *See* 999 v. C.I.T. Corp., 776 F.2d 866, 869 (9th Cir. 1985); 8 Federal Practice and Procedure § 2264, at 745.

[23] *See* Gutting v. Falstaff Brewing Corp., 710 F.2d 1309, 1313–14 (8th Cir. 1983).

[24] *Id.* at 1314; Brook Village N. Assocs. v. G.E. Co., 686 F.2d 66, 70 (1st Cir. 1982).

[25] Brook Village N. Assocs. v. G.E. Co., 686 F.2d 66, 70 (1st Cir. 1982).

[26] 999 v. C.I.T. Corp., 776 F.2d 866, 869 (9th Cir. 1985) (trial); Brook Village N. Assocs. v. G.E. Co., 686 F.2d 66, 71–73 (1st Cir. 1982) (pretrial order).

[27] 999 v. C.I.T. Corp., 776 F.2d 866, 869 (9th Cir. 1985).

[28] Brook Village N. Assocs. v. G.E. Co., 686 F.2d 66, 73 (1st Cir. 1982); *see* Rainbolt v. Johnson, 669 F.2d 767, 769 (D.C. Cir. 1981). *But see* Warren v. International Bhd. of Teamsters, 544 F.2d 334, 338–40 (8th Cir. 1976).

[29] Brook Village N. Assocs. v. G.E. Co., 686 F.2d 66, 72 (1st Cir. 1982).

When no response is served, counsel is always faced with a strategic dilemma. No action need be taken to confirm the admissions. However, it is risky to rely on the admissions and forgo discovery or appropriate preparation on the admitted matters, because the defaulting party can move to withdraw the admissions. On the other hand, drawing attention to the admissions is likely to result in the defaulting party's asking for an extension or immediately moving to withdraw them. A judge is more likely to allow the withdrawal of admissions before the final pretrial order is entered, unless the defaulting counsel has been completely dilatory over a significant period of time or has otherwise engaged in discovery abuse. At a minimum, shortly after the default, opposing counsel should be notified to determine the reason for the failure to respond and the status of the answers.

When inadequate answers are filed, the party requesting the admission can move to determine the sufficiency of the answer, to compel a proper response or to have the matter ordered admitted.[30] Local rules should be consulted as to any requirements for resolving the issue before a motion can be filed.

---

[30] Asea, Inc. v. Southern Pac. Transp. Co., 669 F.2d 1242, 1247 (9th Cir. 1981).

PART V

SANCTIONS FOR PRETRIAL ABUSES

CHAPTER 27

SANCTIONS PRACTICE

§ 27.1 Discovery Abuse

At present, the public has a fairly low regard for lawyers and the civil litigation system. Plaintiffs have been accused of bringing meritless actions, which defendants settle for nuisance value rather than subject themselves to extensive costly and possibly embarrassing discovery.[1] Defendants with greater economic resources are viewed as drowning less affluent plaintiffs in a sea of paper.[2] Courts are sensitive to complaints that the public has lost respect for the judicial system, because those with limited means cannot afford to litigate just claims or fight unjust actions.[3] As the Seventh Circuit recently noted: "Mounting federal caseloads and growing public dissatisfaction with the costs and delays of litigation have made it imperative that the federal courts impose sanctions on persons and firms that abuse their right of access to these courts."[4] Therefore,

[1] *See, e.g.*, Blue Chip Stamps v. Manor Drug Stores, 421 U.S. 723, 740 (1975); Amendments to the Federal Rules of Civil Procedure, 85 F.R.D. 521 (1979) (Powell, Stewart and Rehnquist, JJ., dissenting).

[2] Amendments to the Federal Rules of Civil Procedure, 85 F.R.D. 521 (1979) (Powell, Stewart and Rehnquist, JJ., dissenting).

[3] *Id.*

[4] Dreis & Krump Mfg. v. International Ass'n of Machinists, 802 F.2d 247, 255 (7th Cir. 1986).

judges are now receptive to imposing sanctions for a variety of practices, some of which were previously considered within the range of zealous advocacy. In fact, if the number of cases being decided on sanctions issues is any indication, judges are being flooded with requests to impose sanctions, including many Rule 11 motions which attempt to recoup attorneys' fees.

Although the actual extent of discovery abuse is disputed,[5] it is not surprising that the tension between a self-executing discovery policy and the adversary system has resulted in attorneys testing the limits of zealous advocacy within the bounds of law.[6] Optimistically establishing a policy that litigants willingly exchange relevant information conflicted with the role of the attorney as an advocate who resolves all disputes in the client's favor.[7] Moreover, some of the reasons why counsel engage in extensive discovery or employ dilatory practices are endemic to our system of litigation.[8] For example, the nominal costs of bringing an action and the general ban on requiring the loser to pay the winner's attorneys' fees fosters litigation and expensive discovery requests. The inability to obtain prejudgment interest in many cases and low pre- and postjudgment interest rates encourages defendants to use extensive discovery as a means of delaying the proceedings. In addition, courts are now being used as forums for complex political and social issues which by their nature generate vast amounts of discovery, often on sensitive issues. The willingness of courts to expand theories of liability also provides plaintiffs with an incentive to test the bounds of relevance. Moreover, the difficulty of obtaining summary judgment results in weak cases going to trial unless a defendant is willing to settle for nuisance value. In general, because most civil cases settle, pretrial practice has become big business for lawyers who generate much of their billings from discovery and motions and who are also concerned that limiting discovery or acquiescing without a fight to discovery requests may result in a malpractice action if the case is lost.[9]

Until recently these systemic pressures went unchecked by judges, who were reluctant to become involved in discovery because they felt that taking sides in

---

[5] *Compare* Renfrew, *Discovery Sanctions: A Judicial Perspective,* 67 Cal. L. Rev. 264 (1979) (widespread) *with* Federal Judicial Center, *Controls and the Civil Litigative Process: Discovery,* 24 (P. Connally, E. Holleman, & M. Kuhlman eds. 1978) (sanctions requested for less than 1% of discovery requests studied).

[6] *See, e.g.,* Ebersole, *Discovery Problems: Is Help on the Way,* 66 A.B.A. J. 50 (1980); Brazil, *The Adversary Character of Civil Discovery: A Critique and Proposals for Change,* 31 Vand. L. Rev. 1295 (1978).

[7] *See* Cohn, *Federal Discovery: A Survey of Local Rules and Practices in View of Proposed Changes to the Federal Rules,* 63 Minn. L. Rev. 253, 256 n.25 (1979).

[8] *See generally,* Sofaer, *Sanctioning Attorneys for Discovery Abuse Under the New Federal Rules: On the Limited Utility of Punishment,* 57 St. John's L. Rev. 684, 720–29 (1983); *see also* Edelstein, *The Ethics of Dilatory Motion Practice: Time for Change,* 44 Fordham L. Rev. 1069, 1076 (1976).

[9] *See* Rosenberg & King, *Curbing Discovery Abuse in Civil Litigation: Enough is Enough,* 1981 B.Y.U. L. Rev. 579, 582.

discovery disputes is unseemly, interferes with their role as impartial fact-finders, exacerbates personal conflict between the attorneys, discourages the loser from later litigating legitimate discovery disputes, and wastes the court's time because the case is likely to settle regardless of the outcome of the dispute.[10] Many attorneys as well as the public became disappointed with the failure of judges to impose sanctions for discovery abuse,[11] because there appeared no other way to set the adversarial limits of discovery practice. Without appropriate checks, discovery abuse had become simply another tactical weapon of the adversary system. Some even felt that the negative side of discovery, which is manifested by both overdiscovery and resistance to discovery, outweighed its positive values.

§ 27.2 Rule Changes Which Have Encouraged the Imposition of Sanctions

In this atmosphere, the 1983 revisions to the federal rules focused on the judge's power and responsibility to control litigation and for the first time explicitly provided relief for the problems associated with overdiscovery.[12] Changes to Rules 11, 16, and 26 were adopted to force litigators and judges to reassess previous practices. Rule 26(g) requires the person signing a discovery request, response, or objection to certify its reasonableness. Rule 11 applies this standard to every pleading, motion, and other legal paper filed in an action. A violation of Rules 11 or 26(g) can result in the striking of an unsigned document and the imposition of appropriate sanctions, including attorneys' fees, for improper certifications. Violations of Rule 26(g) reach overdiscovery as well as resistance to proper discovery. Ethical responsibilities in discovery were also clarified by prohibiting lawyers from making a frivolous discovery request and requiring them to make a reasonably diligent effort to comply with legally proper discovery requests of the opposing party.[13]

In addition, federal judges were explicitly encouraged to become case managers by the revisions to Rule 16,[14] which lists among the objectives of pretrial conferences (1) establishing early and continuing control so that the case will not be protracted because of lack of management and (2) discouraging wasteful

[10] *See, e.g.*, Cavanagh, *The August 1, 1983 Amendmends to the Federal Rules of Civil Procedure: A Critical Evaluation and A Proposal for More Effective Discovery Through Local Rules,* 30 Villanova L. Rev. 767, 795–97 (1985); Berger, *Sanctions Under Rule 37: The Growing Irritation with Discovery Abuses,* N.Y.S.B.J. 106, 108 (Feb. 1979).

[11] *E.g.*, Brazil, *Views from the Front Lines: Observations by Chicago Lawyers About the System of Civil Discovery,* 1980 A.B.F. Res. J. 217, 245.

[12] *See* Schwarzer, *Sanctions Under the New Federal Rule 11—A Closer Look,* 104 F.R.D. 181, 183 (1985).

[13] Model Rules of Professional Responsibility Rule 3.4(d).

[14] *See generally* Resnik, *Managerial Judges,* 96 Harv. L. Rev. 374 (1982); §§ **16.1–16.3**.

pretrial activities. Rule 16(b) mandates that the court must enter a scheduling order which limits the time to file and hear motions and complete discovery. Rule 26(f) permits the court or a party to enter a formal discovery plan setting limitations on discovery if the attorneys have not been able to reach agreement after reasonable effort. Failure to participate in good faith in framing the plan subjects the party or its attorney to pay the reasonable expenses, including attorneys' fees, caused by the failure. Parties and their attorneys can also be sanctioned under Rule 16(f) for failure to obey a scheduling or pretrial order, not appearing at such conferences, being substantially unprepared to participate in the conference, or not participating in good faith. Sanctions for such Rule 16 violations include preclusion orders, striking pleadings, staying the proceedings, entering a dismissal or default, and contempt, as well as paying the reasonable expenses, including attorneys' fees, incurred because of the noncompliance.

Rule 26(b)(1) was adopted specifically to correct problems associated with overdiscovery. It provides that the court shall limit the frequency or extent of use of discovery if:

1. The discovery sought is unreasonably cumulative or duplicative or is obtainable from some other source that is more convenient, less burdensome, or less expensive
2. The party seeking discovery has had ample opportunity by discovery in the action to obtain the information sought, or
3. The discovery is unduly burdensome or expensive, taking into account the needs of the case, the amount in controversy, limitations on the parties' resources, and the importance of the issues at stake in the litigation.

§ 27.3 Effect of the Changed Rules

Each sanction has its own requirements, which are separately discussed in this part of this book. It is clear, however, that federal discovery must now be viewed fairly cautiously. Excessive use of interrogatories, boilerplate interrogatories, overly long depositions, numerous inconsequential depositions, and excessive requests for production of documents should be regarded as suspect. A significant number of cases have been terminated for discovery and pretrial abuses. As the Seventh Circuit has noted, a dismissal caused by an attorney's misconduct may result in a successful malpractice action against the plaintiff's attorney.[15] Costs and attorneys' fees are now routinely levied against practitioners as well as their clients.[16] In fact, many judges are more comfortable sanctioning attorneys

[15] Tolliver v. Northrop Corp., 786 F.2d 316, 318 (7th Cir. 1986).

[16] *See, e.g.*, Burger, *Abuses of Discovery, Judges Are Correcting the Problem,* 20 Trial 18, 19–20 (Sept. 1984).

than imposing sanctions which will affect the merits of the action. Therefore, the certification requirements mandated by Rules 7, 11, and 26(g), as well as the trial court's explicit power to curtail discovery under Rule 26(b)(1) and to manage the litigation process under Rule 16, must be considered when counsel evaluates discovery strategy.

Whether the changed attitude toward the proper bounds of discovery and the judge's role as case manager have resulted in real differences in practice or more cost-effective use of discovery remains to be seen. The requirements of federal pretrial practice are considered by many to be more costly to litigants than equivalent state practice. It is unlikely that any changes in discovery practice will affect that result. Moreover, the frequency of sanction motions in federal court has clearly increased in the last few years, adding to the costs of litigation[17] and potentially delaying the resolution of the underlying action. Similarly, the changes to Rule 16 have resulted in what many litigators believe to be overly expensive and complex requirements aptly described as "pretrial by ordeal."[18] Because not all judges have wholeheartedly embraced the role of case managers, and not all attorneys are willing to request sanctions, the likelihood of obtaining relief for abusive pretrial tactics varies significantly. There are also real differences in how the circuits approach discovery sanctions on appeal.[19] For example, the Third Circuit appears to be the most hostile to the imposition of severe sanctions, while the First and Second Circuits consistently affirm sanctions with terminate cases.[20]

Although litigants and courts should not tolerate unethical or sharp practices, attorneys should not be deterred from aggressive lawyering on their client's behalf because of the modification of the rules. However, some uncertainty exists whether requiring attorneys to certify their reasonableness has fundamentally changed counsel's role as an advocate. For example, requiring aggressive litigators to unconditionally certify that a motion or discovery request or response is not interposed solely for improper reasons should not result in hindering discovery. On the other hand, if tactical considerations are not considered proper reasons, how many litigators can truly certify that their requests and motions are not interposed for any improper purpose, as Rules 11 and 26(g) require? Unless the lawyers handling large cases who responded in one survey that tactical considerations affected how they conducted or responded to

---

[17] *See, e.g.*, Cavanagh, *The August 1, 1983 Amendments to the Federal Rules of Civil Procedure: A Critical Evaluation and a Proposal for More Effective Discovery Through Local Rules*, 30 Villanova L. Rev. 767, 794 (1985).

[18] Comment, *Recent Changes in the Federal Rules of Civil Procedure: Prescription to Ease the Pain?*, 15 Texas Tech. L. Rev. 887, 904–08 (1984).

[19] *See, e.g.*, Epstein, Corcoran, Krieger, & Carr, *An Up-Date on Rule 37 Sanctions After National Hockey League v. Metropolitan Hockey Clubs, Inc.*, 84 F.R.D. 145 (1979).

[20] See **chs. 29** and **30**.

discovery in 99 percent of their cases[21] have changed their behavior, certifications signify only that some proper purpose supports the position taken, not that no improper purpose exists.

Litigators should be aware that the modifications to the rules may also result in the deemphasis of previously important goals such as ease of access to courts, procedural simplicity, and self-executing discovery, due to the shift to more complex rules overseen by the judge as case manager.[22] Uniformity of practice in federal courts also appears to be disappearing with the enactment of some 3,000 local rules by district courts and individual judges, whose violation may result in the imposition of sanctions.[23]

§ 27.4 Overview of Existing Sanctions

Rules, statutes, and the inherent power of courts to manage their dockets provide the basic authority which judges rely upon for imposing sanctions. The requirements for any particular sanction vary with the authority cited. On appeal, sanctions usually are reviewed under the following standards: factual inquiries are reviewed under the clearly erroneous standard, legal conclusions are reviewed de novo, and the appropriateness of the sanction is reviewed for abuse of discretion.[24]

§ 27.5 Primary Sources for Obtaining Attorneys' Fees

Attorneys' fees can be awarded pursuant to a number of rules and statutes as well as by reference to the court's inherent powers. The following authorities are most frequently cited for imposition of attorneys' fees:

1. Rules 11 and 26(g)[25] permit an appropriate sanction to be invoked for improperly certifying that the attorney or party has made a reasonable inquiry into the factual and legal basis of any pleading, motion, or paper

---

[21] Brazil, *Civil Discovery: Lawyers' Views of Its Effectiveness, Its Principal Problems and Abuses,* 1980 A.B.F. Res. J. 787, 871; Brazil, *Civil Discovery: How Bad Are The Problems?,* 67 A.B.A. J. 450, 451 (1981).

[22] *See* Comment, *Recent Changes in the Federal Rules of Civil Procedure: Prescriptions to Ease the Pain?,* 15 Texas Tech. L. Rev. 887, 890 (1984).

[23] *See* Roberts, *The Myth of Uniformity in Federal Civil Procedure: Federal Civil Rule 83 and District Court Local Rulemaking Powers,* 8 U. Puget Sound L. Rev. 537, 538 (1985).

[24] *See, e.g.,* United States v. National Medical Enters., Inc., 792 F.2d 906, 910–11 (9th Cir. 1986) (Rule 37); *In re* Itel Secs. Litig., 791 F.2d 672, 674 (9th Cir. 1986) (1927 and Rule 11), *cert. denied,* _____ U.S. _____, 107 S. Ct. 880 (1987); Eastway Constr. Corp. v. City of New York, 762 F.2d 243, 254 n.7 (2d Cir. 1985) (Rule 11); Eastway Gen. Hosp., Ltd. v. Eastway Women's Clinic, Inc., 737 F.2d 503, 505 (5th Cir. 1984), *cert. denied,* 470 U.S. 1052 (1985) (Rule 37).

[25] See **ch. 28**.

submitted to court and any discovery request, response, or objection. Monetary sanctions can be awarded against the attorney or party without any showing of bad faith.

2. 28 U.S.C. § 1927[26] provides that any attorney who multiplies the proceedings in any case unreasonably and vexatiously may be required personally to satisfy the excess costs, expenses, and attorneys' fees reasonably incurred because of such conduct. Bad faith is a prerequisite,[27] although a few circuits appear to permit such sanctions for reckless behavior.[28]
3. A variety of rules, such as Rule 37(a)(4), provide for attorneys' fees for bringing motions or defending against them when the opposition is not justified.

§ 27.6 Primary Sources for Sanctions Affecting the Merits of the Action

Some of the same rules can be used to obtain sanctions affecting the merits of the action as well as attorneys' fees, but there is not a complete overlap. The following authorities support imposition of outcome determinative sanctions:

1. Rule 37[29] remains the main weapon in the arsenal against abuse caused by total or partial resistance to valid discovery requests. It applies to all parties and their attorneys as well as nonparty deponents. Unlike the modifications to the rules which focus on imposing monetary sanctions on lawyers and parties to discourage abuse, Rule 37 is directed primarily at sanctions which affect the merits of the actions. Judges appear to apply Rule 37 more frequently, because the rules have been changed to encourage sanctions and case management. Sanctions for a party who disobeys a court order concerning discovery or for total discovery failures under Rule 37(d) range from issue preclusion, establishment of designated facts, and contempt to dismissal and default. In addition, Rule 37 explicitly permits the imposition of any order which is just in regard to the failure. Willfulness is usually thought necessary before a court will terminate an action under this rule, although some circuits permit dismissals for gross negligence. Lesser sanctions may be applied for all types of conduct which results in failure to comply with court

---

[26] *Id.*

[27] Kamen v. AT&T Co., 791 F.2d 1006, 1010 (2d Cir. 1986); Dreiling v. Peugeot Motors of Am., Inc., 768 F.2d 1159, 1164–65 (10th Cir. 1985); Baker Indus., Inc. v. Cerberus Ltd., 764 F.2d 204, 209 (3d Cir. 1985).

[28] Estate of Blas through Chargualaf v. Winkler, 792 F.2d 858, 860 (9th Cir. 1986); United States v. Ross, 535 F.2d 346, 349–50 (6th Cir. 1976).

[29] See **ch. 29**.

orders. Monetary sanctions can be imposed against the attorney and the party under this rule as well as an award of expenses, which includes reasonable attorneys' fees, for successfully bringing or defeating a discovery motion.[30]

2. Rule 41(b)[31] permits the defendant to obtain the dismissal of an action for the plaintiff's failure to prosecute or obey the rules or any court order. Although courts vary as to the length of time a case must be inactive before dismissal, federal courts are generally much stricter than state courts in meting out such dismissals. This rule mentions only dismissals, but less severe sanctions can be imposed. Sanctions under Rules 41(b) and 37 often overlap when aimed at abusive tactics of a plaintiff.
3. Courts have inherent power to manage their own affairs to achieve the orderly and expeditious disposition of cases.[32] Judges can terminate cases or impose other sanctions, including assessments of attorneys' fees, to control their own dockets. The court can sua sponte initiate sanctions to ensure that cases are prosecuted and court orders obeyed, similar to Rule 41(b) sanctions. The court's inherent powers also include its ability to hold an individual in criminal or civil contempt. In addition, some courts fine litigants and attorneys for behavior not reaching contempt. Inherent powers are strictly construed and require bad faith of the individual being sanctioned.[33]
4. Rule 16(f)[34] provides that most of the sanctions available under Rule 37 can be imposed for failure to obey a scheduling or pretrial order, failure to appear at a scheduling or pretrial conference, or failure to prepare or participate in good faith at the conference. This rule is rarely cited as the sole justification for severe sanctions and is treated as codifying some of the court's inherent powers for failure to prosecute and obey court orders.

§ 27.7 Other Sanctions

Sanctions such as fines and contempt can also be imposed for civil pretrial abuses. The authority for such sanctions is as follows:

1. Local rules may expand the obligations of counsel and provide sanctions for their violation.[35]

---

[30] Rule 37(a)(4), (b), (d).

[31] See **ch. 30**.

[32] *See* Link v. Wabash R.R., 370 U.S. 626, 630–31 (1962); **ch. 30**.

[33] Roadway Express, Inc. v. Piper, 447 U.S. 752, 766 (1980).

[34] See §§ **16.5** and **30.10**.

[35] See § **31.11** and passim.

2. Criminal contempt is authorized by statute[36] as well as under Rule 37 and the court's inherent powers.
3. Civil contempt is also available as a sanction, although its use is strictly construed.[37]

§ 27.8 Citing Appropriate Authority for Specific Sanctions

A quick review of the alternatives indicates that the same behavior may justify imposition of a sanction under one rule which is prohibited under another. For example, conduct which is not in bad faith cannot result in attorneys' fees under 28 U.S.C. § 1927 or the court's inherent powers, but such relief may be available under Rules 11 or 37. Therefore, the basis for any sanction motion must be carefully set forth to ensure that the conduct falls within the rule counsel has cited for support. If the wrong rule is cited by counsel, the judge can deny the sanction. Conversely, when defending against a sanctions motion, counsel should be careful to ascertain whether the cited authority supports the particular sanction requested. If any sanction is awarded incorrectly, the appellate court may remand the case for findings under the appropriate rule rather than affirming the award under the correct standard.[38]

§ 27.9 Review of Sanction Orders

Most orders compelling discovery or imposing sanctions are not immediately appealable.[39] For example, the majority of circuits do not permit interlocutory appeals of an order requiring a party to pay monetary sanctions for a routine discovery failure,[40] and such orders are not usually a proper subject for mandamus. Even important discovery issues raised by the sanctions order may not result in an immediate appeal.[41] Similarly, the judge's certification of a

---

[36] 18 U.S.C. § 401 (1982); Fed. R. Crim. P. 42; see **ch. 31**.

[37] See **ch. 31**.

[38] *See, e.g.*, Roadway Express, Inc. v. Piper, 447 U.S. 752, 767–68 (1980); *see also In re* Yagman, 796 F.2d 1165, 1184–87, *modified on other grounds*, 803 F.2d 1085 (9th Cir. 1986).

[39] *See, e.g.*, Robinson v. Tanner, 798 F.2d 1378, 1380–81 (11th Cir. 1986) (extensive citations).

[40] Coleman v. Sherwood Med. Indus., 746 F.2d 445, 447 (8th Cir. 1984); *see* D & H Marketers, Inc. v. Freedom Oil & Gas, Inc., 744 F.2d 1443, 1444–46 (10th Cir. 1984); Mulay Plastics, Inc. v. Grand Truck Western R.R., 742 F.2d 369, 370–71 (7th Cir. 1984), *cert. denied*, 470 U.S. 1037 (1985); Meche v. Dan-Tex Int'l, Inc., 681 F.2d 264, 265 (5th Cir. 1982); Johnny Pflocks, Inc. v. Firestone Tire & Rubber Co., 634 F.2d 1215, 1217 (9th Cir. 1980).

[41] *Compare* Boreri v. Fiat S.P.A., 763 F.2d 17, 21–22 (1st Cir. 1985) (denying review of order rejecting primacy of Hague Convention in discovery of foreign parties) *with* Ohio v. Arthur Andersen & Co., 570 F.2d 1370, 1372 (10th Cir. 1978), *cert. denied*, 439 U.S. 833 (1979) (permitting review when compliance with discovery order could have resulted in violation of foreign law).

monetary award for immediate appeal under Rule 54(b) was ineffective to permit appeal because the order did not affect a substantial claim.[42] In some circuits, if the award of attorneys' fees is part of a sanction, the amount of the award must be determined before review is appropriate, even if the action has been dismissed with prejudice.[43]

If a party is held in contempt[44] or the sanction results in dismissal, an immediate appeal is appropriate.[45] A sanction which affects the granting or denial of an injunction can also be appealed when imposed.[46] An order imposing a sanction upon counsel or other nonparties in the underlying action is often considered final and appealable as a collateral order when the sanction is imposed,[47] but even here, not all circuits agree.[48]

§ 27.10 Sanctions Checklist

Conduct Warranting Sanctions

1. Was there a total failure of discovery warranting an immediate motion for sanctions?

2. Is a motion to compel necessary before sanctions other than recovery of the costs of obtaining the order can be requested?

3. Has the plaintiff failed to prosecute the action?

4. Has any party failed to obey a court order?

5. Has any party violated a local rule?

6. Is the pleading, motion, or other paper

- **a.** Well grounded in fact?
- **b.** Warranted by existing law or by a good faith argument for its modification?
- **c.** Not interposed for any improper purpose, such as to harass or to cause unnecessary delay or needless increase in the cost of litigation?

---

[42] Mulay Plastics, Inc. v. Grand Trunk Western R.R., 742 F.2d 369, 371 (7th Cir. 1984), *cert. denied,* 470 U.S. 1037 (1985).

[43] *See* Jaffe v. Sundowner Properties, Inc., 808 F.2d 1425, 1427 (11th Cir. 1987); *cf.* Phelps v. Washburn Univ., 807 F.2d 153, 154–55 (10th Cir. 1986) (1988 action surveying general case law).

[44] United States v. Ryan, 402 U.S. 530, 532–33 (1971).

[45] *See, e.g.*, Robinson v. Tanner, 798 F.2d 1378, 1380–81 (11th Cir. 1986) (extensive citations).

[46] Aurora Bancshares Corp. v. Weston, 777 F.2d 385, 386 (7th Cir. 1985).

[47] *See* Estate of Blas through Chargualaf v. Winkler, 792 F.2d 858, 860 n.2 (9th Cir. 1986); Knorr Brake Corp. v. Harbil, Inc., 738 F.2d 223, 226 (7th Cir. 1984); Cheng v. GAF Corp., 713 F.2d 886, 888–89 (2d Cir. 1983).

[48] *See In re* Licht & Semonoff, 796 F.2d 564, 569–73 (1st Cir. 1986) (surveying case law).

7. Is the discovery request, response or objection
   a. Warranted by existing law or a good faith argument for its modification?
   b. Not interposed for any improper purpose, such as to harass or to cause unnecessary delay or needless increase in the cost of litigation?
   c. Not unreasonable or unduly burdensome or expensive, given the needs of the case, the discovery already had in the case, the amount in controversy, and the importance of the issues at stake in the litigation?
8. Does the adversary's misconduct warrant recovery of attorneys' fees?
9. Does the adversary's misconduct warrant sanctions regarding the merits of action?
10. Does the adversary's misconduct warrant dismissal or default of the action?
    a. Does the conduct involve bad faith, willfulness, or fault?
    b. What is the extent of the party's personal responsibility?
    c. What prejudice has been caused by the misconduct?
    d. Is there a history of dilatoriness?
    e. Will sanctions other than dismissal be effective?

Procedural Requirements for Motions to Compel and for Sanctions Motions

1. Is there a requirement to meet and confer before the motion can be brought?
2. Is a joint statement required
   a. Concerning factual matters?
   b. Concerning legal questions?
3. Is a supporting memorandum of law required?
4. Have affidavits, declarations or any other evidentiary support concerning factual disputes been submitted with the motion?
5. Has a request been included for the expenses associated with the motion, including attorneys' fees?
6. Have the appropriate sanctions been specified in detail?
7. Is any reply to the adversary's opposition permitted?

Oppositions to Motions to Compel and Sanctions Motions

1. Is a written opposition required
   a. Concerning factual matters?

- **b.** Concerning legal questions?
- **c.** As part of a joint statement?
  - **(1)** Is any reply to the joint statement permitted by either party?

2. Is a request for a protective order appropriate?

- **a.** Was a timely objection made to the discovery in dispute?

3. Should a Rule 26(f) discovery conference be requested?

4. Have affidavits, declarations, or any other evidentiary support concerning factual disputes been submitted with the motion?

5. Has a request been included for the expenses associated with successfully defending the motion, including attorneys' fees?

Commonly Cited Authority for Granting Sanctions

1. Rule 11 permits any appropriate sanction, including attorneys' fees, to be assessed for improperly certifying that any paper is

- **a.** Well grounded in fact
- **b.** Warranted by existing law or by a good faith argument for its modification
- **c.** Not interposed for any improper purpose, such as to harass or to cause unnecessary delay or needless increase in the cost of litigation.

2. Rule 16(f) permits Rule 37(b)(2)(B), (C) and (D) sanctions (including case terminating and evidentiary sanctions), as well as expenses (including attorneys' fees caused by the noncompliance) to be assessed if a party or attorney

- **a.** Fails to obey a scheduling or pretrial order
- **b.** Is absent from a pretrial conference
- **c.** Is unprepared or fails to participate in good faith at a pretrial conference.

3. Rule 26(g) permits any appropriate sanction, including attorneys' fees, to be assessed for improperly certifying that a discovery request, response, or objection is:

- **a.** Warranted by existing law or a good faith argument for its modification
- **b.** Not interposed for any improper purpose, such as to harass or to cause unnecessary delay or needless increase in the cost of litigation
- **c.** Not unreasonable or unduly burdensome or expensive, given the needs of the case, the discovery already had in the case, the amount in controversy, and the importance of the issues at stake in the litigation.

4. Rule 37 permits a full range of sanctions to be assessed against parties for discovery abuse as well as an award of expenses to be imposed against any offending party or attorney as well as reasonable expenses including attorneys' fees to be assessed for successfully bringing or defending against the motion. (See Rule 37 checklist in § **29.11**).

5. Rule 41(b) permits a case to be dismissed or lesser sanctions assessed for failure of the plaintiff to

  a. Prosecute the action

  b. Comply with the rules

  c. Comply with any order of court.

6. 28 U.S.C. § 1927 permits an attorney to be assessed any excess costs, expenses, and attorneys' fees caused by conduct which unreasonably and vexatiously multiplies the proceedings.

7. Local rules may permit a full range of sanctions to be imposed for violations of any of their requirements.

8. Criminal and civil contempt are authorized by statute, rules, and the court's inherent powers

  a. For failure to obey court orders

  b. For other contemptuous misbehavior by attorneys or parties.

9. Fines are authorized by local rules, the court's inherent powers, Rule 11, and as sanction for contempt by attorneys or parties.

10. Inherent power of the court authorizes a full range of sanctions to be assessed for misconduct by attorneys or parties.

CHAPTER 28

RECOVERING ATTORNEYS' FEES

§ 28.1 Attorneys' Fees as a Sanction

Attorneys' fees are usually the most expensive, unrecoverable cost of litigation. Therefore, the possibility of recovering such fees as a pretrial sanction is particularly appealing. When such recovery was limited to situations in which the opposing side demonstrated bad faith, not much litigation ensued. However, since Rules 11 and 37(a)(4) have increased the realistic chances of recovering such fees, litigation concerning attorneys' fees has significantly increased.

RULES 11 AND 26(g)

§ 28.2 Sanctions Under Rules 11 and 26(g)

Rules 11 and 26(g) adopt objective certification requirements concerning the reasonableness of every pleading, motion, or other paper filed with the court, as well as the reasonableness of discovery requests, responses, and objections. The signature of the attorney or party constitutes a certification that the individual has read the document and that, to the best of that person's knowledge, information, and belief formed after reasonable inquiry, the pleading, motion, or other paper

1. Is well grounded in fact, or the discovery request, response, or objection is consistent with the rules
2. Is warranted by existing law or a good faith argument for the extension, modification, or reversal of existing law, and
3. Is not interposed for any improper purpose, such as to harass or to cause unnecessary delay or needless increase in the cost of litigation.

Discovery papers also must not be unreasonable or unduly burdensome or expensive, given the needs of the case, the discovery already had in the case, the amount in controversy, and the importance of the issues at stake in the litigation.[1] Both rules require the striking of any unsigned paper, unless it is promptly signed after this omission is pointed out. In addition, they require the imposition of an appropriate sanction for an improper certification on the party or attorney who signed the paper, or both, including an order to pay the amount of the reasonable expenses and attorneys' fees incurred because of the violation. The court may impose these sanctions upon its own initiative as well as upon motion.

§ 28.3 Frequency of Rule 11 Motions

Rule 11 is becoming the most frequently cited provision for assessing attorneys' fees against lawyers as well as parties. Although the rule permits appropriate sanctions, which can even include dismissal and default, it is generally not being used as a substitute for Rule 37.[2] Instead, courts are attempting to persuade

---

[1] Fed. R. Civ. P. 26(g)(3).

[2] *See generally* A.B.A. Section of Litigation, Sanctions: Rule 11 and Other Powers (1986); Note, *The 1983 Amendments of Rule 11: Answering the Critics' Concern With Judicial Self-Restraint,* 61 Notre Dame L. Rev. 798 (1986).

lawyers to curtail sharp practices and clean up sloppy factual and legal investigations preceding the filing of complaints by hitting them with monetary sanctions which are often nonrecoverable from the client.[3] In practice, even if the court order does not prohibit reimbursement, if it is specifically directed at the attorney rather than the client, it may be difficult to bill the client for the sanction. The size of such awards vary significantly and range from several hundred to several hundred thousand dollars depending on the judge and the egregiousness of the behavior. Attorneys' fees have also been awarded for the prosecution of an appeal from an order denying Rule 11 sanctions in the district court,[4] as well as for papers filed in the appellate courts which violated Rule 11 standards.[5] Even petitioning the district court for reconsideration of Rule 11 sanctions, can result in the imposition of additional fees when the motion unsuccessfully attempts to document the underlying claim rather than focus on reasons for the attorney's conduct.[6] Several circuits permit attorneys and pro se litigants to be fined by the court under Rule 11, but appear to require criminal contempt procedures to be utilized before such fines can be imposed.[7] The Fifth Circuit has limited Rule 11's applicability to those attorneys who sign a document (not the firm or other attorneys who appear in the suit).[8] Because Rule 11 became effective in August 1983, pleadings filed before that time are not subject to the new rule.[9] However, the Seventh Circuit has applied Rule 11 to any filings after that date in a pending case.[10]

Although the rule provides for sanctions, not fee shifting,[11] the frequency with which Rule 11 is being applied to actions which are terminated by dismissal or summary judgment requires counsel to be fairly cautious about invoking federal jurisdiction. Sanctions can be imposed even if the district court lacked jurisdiction to consider the merits of the case.[12] Therefore, if subject matter jurisdiction is clearly lacking for any reason, including an absence of complete diversity, sanctions will be imposed. In other words, the mandatory language of

---

[3] *See generally* Note, *The Dynamics of Rule 11: Preventing Frivolous Litigation by Demanding Professional Responsibility,* 61 N.Y.U. L. Rev. 300 (1986); Note, *Litigant Responsibility: Federal Rule of Civil Procedure 11 and Its Application,* 27 B.U. L. Rev. 385 (1986).

[4] Westmoreland v. CBS, Inc., 770 F.2d 1168, 1179–80 (D.C. Cir. 1985).

[5] *In re* Kelley, 808 F.2d 549, 552 (7th Cir. 1986).

[6] *See* Brown v. National Bd. of Medical Examiners, 800 F.2d 168, 173 (7th Cir. 1986); *see also* EBI, Inc. v. Gator Indus., Inc., 807 F.2d 1, 6 (1st Cir. 1986).

[7] *See* Cotner v. Hopkins, 795 F.2d 900, 903 (10th Cir. 1986).

[8] Robinson v. National Cash Register Co., 808 F.2d 1119, 1130 (5th Cir. 1987).

[9] Pantry Queen Foods, Inc. v. Lifschultz Fast Freight, Inc., 809 F.2d 451, 454 (7th Cir. 1987); Glaser v. Cincinnati Milacron, Inc., 808 F.2d 285, 288 (3d Cir. 1986).

[10] Pantry Queen Foods, Inc. v. Lifschultz Fast Freight, Inc., 809 F.2d 451, 454 (7th Cir. 1987).

[11] Schwarzer, *Sanctions Under the New Federal Rule 11—A Closer Look,* 104 F.R.D. 181, 185 (1985).

[12] Orange Prod. Credit v. Frontline Ventures Ltd., 792 F.2d 797, 801 (9th Cir. 1986).

Rule 11 requires that, once the behavior is found to fall within the rule's prohibition, sanctions must be applied.

There are some limitations on the scope of Rule 11. For example, the Ninth Circuit has reversed Rule 11 sanctions based on a law firm's failure to indicate that its position called for an extension of existing law and to cite arguably contrary authority.[13] Such requirements were viewed as interfering with counsel's zealous representation of clients as well as imposing unwarranted burdens on both counsel and the court.[14] However, the Eleventh Circuit has upheld a Rule 11 sanction for counsel's lack of factual candor in his original motion and brief.[15]

Because Rule 11 encompasses every piece of paper which is filed in court, judges refer to Rule 11 sanctions even when the pretrial failure is more appropriately a discovery violation which falls within Rule 26(g). In fact, the Ninth Circuit has cautioned that Rule 26(g) or 56(g) violations should not be brought as Rule 11 motions.[16]

§ 28.4 Objective Certification

The most important change wrought Rules 11 and 26(g) is the elimination of subjective bad faith as a requirement for its invocation.[17] Courts generally agree that an objective good faith standard of reasonable inquiry governs the imposition of Rule 11 and 26(g) sanctions.[18] Moreover, the rule reaches pleadings and papers which are not necessarily frivolous but which are brought for an improper purpose.

The reasonable person against which the conduct is tested is a competent attorney admitted to practice before the district court.[19] The Advisory Committee Notes to Rule 11 indicate that reasonableness under the circumstances is what is sought and list the following factors in determining reasonable inquiry: (1) the amount of time for investigation available to the signer; (2) whether the signer had to rely on a client for any factual information underlying the pleading, motion or other paper; (3) whether the position taken was based on a plausible

[13] Golden Eagle Distrib. Corp. v. Burroughs Corp., 801 F.2d 1531, 1542 (9th Cir. 1986).

[14] *Id.* at 1541–42.

[15] Blackwell v. Department of Offender Rehabilitation, 807 F.2d 914, 915–16 (11th Cir. 1987) (per curiam).

[16] Zaldivar v. City of Los Angeles, 780 F.2d 823, 830 (9th Cir. 1986).

[17] *See, e.g., id.* at 829.

[18] *See, e.g.*, Brown v. National Bd. of Medical Examiners, 800 F.2d 168, 171 (7th Cir. 1986); Kamen v. AT&T Co., 791 F.2d 1006, 1010 (2d Cir. 1986); Stevens v. Lawyers Mut. Liability Ins. Co., 789 F.2d 1056, 1060 (4th Cir. 1986); Hale v. Harney, 786 F.2d 688, 692 (5th Cir. 1986); Eavenson, Auchmuty & Greenwald v. Holtzman, 775 F.2d 535, 540 (3d Cir. 1985).

[19] Zaldivar v. City of Los Angeles, 780 F.2d 823, 830 (9th Cir. 1986); *see* Eastway Constr. Corp. v. City of New York, 762 F.2d 243, 254 (2d Cir. 1985).

view of the law; and (4) whether the signer depended on forwarding counsel or another member of the bar. It is unclear how local counsel will fare under the rule, because many times papers are filed which were written by the out-of-state attorney actually responsible for the litigation.[20] However, the first indication is that an attorney cannot simply delegate to forwarding cocounsel his duty of reasonable inquiry.[21]

Some courts require the paper to be frivolous, legally unreasonable, or without factual foundation[22] before finding a Rule 11 violation, applying the same standard that is applicable for the award of fees to prevailing defendants in litigation under the civil rights acts.[23] An action which claimed that an insurer failed to "settle fast enough" and misrepresented the outcome of the underlying litigation was considered frivolous when it was controverted by the record.[24] However, if a motion is not frivolous, the fact that one of the arguments supporting it has no merit will not support the imposition of sanctions.[25]

In general, counsel can assume that sanctions will be imposed for failure to undertake reasonable prefiling inquiries.[26] A statement from the client may not be sufficient for counsel to rely on for certification, unless the client has supplied facts which support the claim. Mere conclusory opinions of the client are insufficient without any factual investigation which supports the claim.[27] For example, the Fifth Circuit has stated that blind reliance on the client is seldom a sufficient inquiry.[28] Sanctions can also be awarded for the inclusion of improper parties even if the complaint is otherwise valid.[29] Therefore, attorneys cannot merely amend the complaint to drop a party and assume that they are insulated from penalties.[30] A split exists as to whether Rule 11 imposes a continuing obligation to reevaluate the case as the litigation develops.[31]

---

[20] *See* Schwarzer, *Sanctions Under the New Federal Rule 11—A Closer Look,* 104 F.R.D. 181, 186 (1985).

[21] *See* Unioil, Inc. v. E.F. Hutton & Co., 809 F.2d 548, 557–59 (9th Cir. 1986) (affirming Rule 11 sanction).

[22] *E.g.*, Zaldivar v. City of Los Angeles, 780 F.2d 823, 831 (9th Cir. 1986).

[23] *See* Christiansburg Garment Co. v. EEOC, 434 U.S. 412, 421–22 (1978).

[24] Brown v. Nationwide Mut. Ins. Co., 805 F.2d 1242, 1244 (5th Cir. 1986).

[25] Golden Eagle Distrib. Corp. v. Burroughs Corp., 801 F.2d 1531, 1540–41 (9th Cir. 1986).

[26] *See, e.g.*, Cabell v. Petty, 810 F.2d 463, 466 (4th Cir. 1987); Schwarzer, *Sanctions Under the New Federal Rule 11—A Closer Look,* 104 F.R.D. 181, 188 (1985); *See generally* A.B.A. Section of Litigation, Sanctions, Rule 11 and Other Powers (1986).

[27] *See* Schwarzer, *Sanctions Under the New Federal Rule 11—A Closer Look,* 104 F.R.D. 181, 187 (1985).

[28] Southern Leasing Partners, Ltd. v. McMullan, 801 F.2d 783, 788 (5th Cir. 1986).

[29] *See* Albright v. Upjohn Co., 788 F.2d 1217, 1219–21 (6th Cir. 1986).

[30] *See, e.g., id.*

[31] *See* Southern Leasing Partners, Ltd. v. McMullan, 801 F.2d 783, 788 (5th Cir. 1986). *But see* Oliveri v. Thompson, 803 F.2d 1265, 1274–76 (2d Cir. 1986) (Rule 11 does not impose any continuing obligation on attorney).

Few cases deal with filings for improper purpose. The Ninth Circuit has stated that Rule 11 focuses upon the improper purpose of the signer, objectively tested, rather than the consequences of the signer's act subjectively viewed by the signer's opponent.[32] On the other hand, the Third Circuit has noted that a pleader may not escape liability because he or she did not intend to bring about additional delay or expense, if reasonable preparatory steps would have avoided those consequences.[33] Therefore, filing a motion which the movant intended to withdraw if it was opposed resulted in sanctions even though there was a legal basis for the motion.[34] In such cases, the court cautioned that opposing counsel should be informally contacted to determine whether they will object, rather than requiring them to answer the motion.[35] However, sanctions were denied when a plaintiff did not oppose a grant of summary judgment to two defendants who had been voluntarily dismissed by other plaintiffs, because it was not considered unreasonable to join the defendants to determine their responsibility.[36] Moreover, the Fifth Circuit has stated that plaintiffs are not required by Rule 11 to voluntarily dismiss their claims once they decide to pursue them, as long as they do not oppose the defendant's efforts to secure summary dismissal.[37] It is an open question whether a paper which is well grounded in fact and law may result in sanctions because it is filed for an improper purpose. The Ninth Circuit has held that a complaint which initiates the action cannot be subject to sanctions for harassment.[38]

Judge Schwarzer has commented that in assessing the cause of the reasonableness of the conduct, experience and past performance of the lawyer and the lawyer's firm should be considered as well as the general standard of conduct of the bar appearing before the court.[39] Therefore, the fact that counsel is experienced may be used to infer that the action was brought for an improper purpose, because such attorneys are assumed to know whether a cause of action or jurisdiction exists.[40]

---

[32] Zaldivar v. City of Los Angeles, 780 F.2d 823, 832 (1986).

[33] Lieb v. Topstone Indus., Inc., 788 F.2d 151, 157 (3d Cir. 1986).

[34] Cohen v. Virginia Elec. & Power Co., 788 F.2d 247, 249 (4th Cir. 1986).

[35] *Id.* at 249.

[36] *See* Jackson Marine Corp. v. Harvey Barge Repair, Inc., 794 F.2d 989, 992 (5th Cir. 1986).

[37] *Id.*

[38] Zaldivar v. City of Los Angeles, 780 F.2d 823, 832 (9th Cir. 1986).

[39] Schwarzer, *Sanctions Under the New Federal Rule 11—A Closer Look,* 104 F.R.D. 181, 201 (1985).

[40] Huettig & Schromm, Inc. v. Landscape Contractors Council, 790 F.2d 1421, 1426–27 (9th Cir. 1986).

§ 28.5 Assessment of Sanctions

Due to the mandatory language of Rule 11, the court's discretion is now directed more to the nature and extent of sanctions than to their initial imposition.[41] Once a court finds that a paper is factually or legally unwarranted or dilatory, sanctions of some sort must be applied.[42] In fact, appellate courts are ordering district judges to impose sanctions that were denied.[43] Although a subjective test is not used in deciding initially whether sanctions should be imposed, it may be relevant in determining the form and amount of sanctions assessed.[44] The conduct of an experienced lawyer or bad faith of a lawyer is more apt to invite a substantial penalty than that of a less experienced or merely negligent lawyer.[45] Sanctions may include a reprimand, reference to a bar association grievance committee, the imposition of part or all of the adversary's expenses[46] or even a fine.[47] Such sanctions can be imposed for punitive and deterrent reasons as well as to compensate the movant.

Judge Weinstein has catalogued the factors considered in assessing sanctions, starting with the numbers of hours reasonably expended in responding to the frivolous paper, multiplied by a reasonable hourly fee based on the prevailing market rate, which may be adjusted upward as a reward for exceptional work.[48] After this figure is reached, mitigating factors must be considered, including absence of willfulness and whether this is a first offense. Deterrence should be dependent on the sanctioned party's ability to pay. Judge Weinstein regarded fee awards for the full market value of services as reserved for extremely frivolous cases, while more moderate awards should be given for other filings so as not to chill advocacy. When the movant also bears some fault, sanctions can be

---

[41] Lieb v. Topstone Indus., Inc., 788 F.2d 151, 157 (3d Cir. 1986); Westmoreland v. CBS, Inc., 770 F.2d 1168, 1174 (D.C. Cir. 1985); Eastway Constr. Corp. v. City of New York, 762 F.2d 243 (2d Cir. 1985); 2A J. Moore *et al.*, Moore's Federal Practice ¶ 11.02[2] (2d ed. 1985) [hereinafter Moore's Federal Practice].

[42] Robinson v. National Cash Register Co., 808 F.2d 1119, 1126 n.12, 1130–31 (5th Cir. 1987); *see* Nelken, *Sanctions Under Amended Federal Rule 11—Some "Chilling" Problems in the Struggle Between Compensation and Punishment,* 74 Geo. L.J. 1313, 1321 (1986).

[43] *See, e.g.*, Albright v. Upjohn Co., 788 F.2d 1217, 1221–22 (6th Cir. 1986); Eastway Constr. Corp. v. City of New York, 762 F.2d 243, 254 (2d Cir. 1985).

[44] Lieb v. Topstone Indus., Inc., 788 F.2d 151, 158 (3d Cir. 1986).

[45] *Id.*

[46] *Id.*

[47] *Id.*

[48] Eastway Constr. Corp. v. City of New York, 637 F. Supp. 558, 571–76 (E.D.N.Y. 1986), *aff'd in part,* 821 F.2d 121, 123 (2d Cir.), 56 U.S.L.W. 2001 (July 7, 1987) (the Second Circuit noted it did not necessarily endorse the pertinence of each factor but agreed the district court had discretion to award a sanction substantially less than the lodestar calculation of attorneys' fees, although it increased the award from $1,000 to $10,000).

apportioned to delete that portion of attorneys' fees provoked by the moving attorney's misconduct.[49]

§ 28.6 Hearings and Review

Most Rule 11 sanctions are imposed early in the action. However, the judge has authority to wait until the end of trial to impose sanctions, although notice should be provided that such sanctions will be imposed if appropriate.[50] Counsel facing a Rule 11 motion should attempt to obtain a hearing and disclose information to the court, in camera if necessary, concerning the underlying basis of the certification. However, the Advisory Committee Notes indicate that in many situations the judge's participation in the proceedings may provide the requisite information. A few circuits do not require a hearing concerning Rule 11 violations when the determination is not based on bad faith but on counsel's incompetence in handling the matter by making frivolous or worthless claims without a proper inquiry into the relevant law and facts.[51] If bad faith is involved, a hearing will be allowed.[52] Conversely, counsel bringing a Rule 11 motion can request discovery related to its claim, but such decisions are discretionary and may be unfavorably viewed as costly satellite litigation.[53]

Although sanctions which do not terminate the action are normally not immediately reviewable,[54] Rule 11 sanctions have been reviewed in several circuits when they are applied solely against an attorney.[55] Often the sanction is imposed at the termination of the action by dismissal or summary judgment. Similarly, if the sanction results in the attorney's withdrawing from the case[56] or relates to a deposition of a nonparty in a court not adjudicating the merits,[57] it may be treated as a collateral order which is immediately appealable. District

---

[49] Mossman v. Roadway Express, Inc., 789 F.2d 804, 806 (9th Cir. 1986).

[50] *See In re* Yagman, 796 F.2d 1165, 1183–84, *modified on other grounds*, 803 F.2d 1085 (9th Cir. 1986).

[51] *See* McLaughlin v. Bradlee, 803 F.2d 1197, 1205 (D.C. Cir. 1986); Rodgers v. Lincoln Towing Serv., Inc., 771 F.2d 194, 205–06 (7th Cir. 1985). *But see* Eavenson, Auchmuty & Greenwald v. Holtzman, 775 F.2d 535, 540 (3d Cir. 1985) (imposition of attorneys' fees requires fair notice and an opportunity for a hearing on the record).

[52] Rodgers v. Lincoln Towing Serv., Inc., 771 F.2d 194, 206 (7th Cir. 1985); Eavenson, Auchmuty & Greenwald v. Holtzman, 775 F.2d 535, 540–41 (3d Cir. 1985)

[53] *See* Indianapolis Colts v. Mayor of Baltimore, 775 F.2d 177, 182–83 (7th Cir. 1985).

[54] See § **27.9**.

[55] *See* Unioil, Inc. v. E.F. Hutton & Co., Inc., 809 F.2d 548, 556 (9th Cir. 1986); Frazier v. Cast, 771 F.2d 259, 262 (7th Cir. 1985); *But see In re* Licht & Semonoff, 796 F.2d 564, 568–73 (1st Cir. 1986).

[56] Eavenson, Auchmuty & Greenwald v. Holtzman, 775 F.2d 535, 539 (3d Cir. 1985); *see* Knorr Brake Corp. v. Harbil, Inc., 738 F.2d 223, 225–26 (7th Cir. 1984).

[57] Westmoreland v. CBS, Inc., 770 F.2d 1168, 1172 (D.C. Cir. 1985).

courts often wait to impose Rule 11 sanctions based on the complaint until the end of the litigation. The standard of review depends on the aspect of the order being considered, with findings of fact reviewed as clearly erroneous, legal conclusions as de novo, and the amount and type of sanction imposed reviewed under the abuse of discretion standard.[58]

INHERENT POWERS AND § 1927

§ 28.7 Recovery of Attorneys' Fees for Bad Faith Conduct

The American Rule concerning attorneys' fees is that parties to litigation must bear their own fees.[59] This avoids unjustly discouraging the poor from instituting actions to vindicate their rights or penalizing litigants for merely defending or prosecuting lawsuits.[60] However, federal courts invoke their inherent powers as well as 28 U.S.C. § 1927 to permit attorneys' fees in limited circumstances.

§ 28.8 Inherent Powers and § 1927

Federal courts have created an exception to the American Rule in order to assess attorneys' fees against parties and counsel who willfully abuse judicial process or otherwise conduct ligation in bad faith.[61] The Supreme Court expressly upheld this use of inherent powers in *Roadway Express, Inc. v. Piper.*[62] Bad faith can justify the withholding of statutory attorneys' fees as well as the award of attorneys' fees.[63]

The bad faith exception for attorney conduct[64] has been codified in 28 U.S.C. § 1927. Because of its penal nature, § 1927 is strictly construed.[65] Similarly,

---

[58] Robinson v. National Cash Register Co., 808 F.2d 1119, 1125–26 (5th Cir. 1987); *see* Zaldivar v. City of Los Angeles, 780 F.2d 823, 828 (9th Cir. 1986).

[59] *See* Alyeska Pipeline Serv. Co. v. Wilderness Soc'y, 421 U.S. 240, 247, 257–59 (1975).

[60] F.D. Rich Co. v. United States, 417 U.S. 116, 129 (1974).

[61] *See* Roadway Express, Inc. v. Piper, 447 U.S. 752, 764–66 (1980).

[62] *Id.*

[63] *See* Litton Sys., Inc. v. AT&T Co., 700 F.2d 785, 827 (2d Cir. 1983), *cert. denied,* 464 U.S. 1073 (1984).

[64] *See generally* 6 Moore's Federal Practice ¶ 54.77[2]; Mallor, *Punitive Attorneys' Fees for Abuses of the Judicial System,* 61 N.C. L. Rev. 613 (1983); Note, *Attorneys' Fees—Nemeroff v. Abelson and the Bad Faith Exception to the American Rule,* 58 Tulane L. Rev. 1519 (1984); *see also* Axelberg, *Sanctions Available for Attorney Misconduct: A Glimpse at the "Other" Remedies,* 47 Mont. L. Rev. 87 (1986).

[65] Indianapolis Colts v. Mayor of Baltimore, 775 F.2d 177, 182 (7th Cir. 1985).

because inherent powers are shielded from direct democratic controls, they must be exercised with restraint and discretion.[66] Although a party will not be penalized for maintaining an aggressive litigation posture, advocacy simply for the sake of burdening an opponent can result in an award of attorneys' fees.[67] Such fees are not limited by Rule 37(d)'s requirement that they must be caused by the failure to comply with the discovery order but can encompass all fees caused by an attorney's misconduct.[68] However, because § 1927 applies to excess fees, a blanket award of all fees is not justified.[69] Often § 1927 and inherent powers are jointly invoked to ensure that fees can be assessed against the adverse party as well as the attorney. Such sanctions apply to diversity cases as well as other actions.[70]

Most circuits appear to refer to the bad faith exception and § 1927 interchangeably when dealing with attorney misconduct,[71] applying identical standards and procedures. The only variation that has emerged is whether bad faith is a prerequisite to § 1927 actions[72] or whether some different and lower standard applies because the statute refers solely to conduct which unreasonably and vexatiously multiplies the proceedings. Some circuits find that reckless behavior as well as bad faith satisfies § 1927.[73] A few apply a less stringent standard which mirrors Rule 11, assessing sanctions when an attorney who is not guilty of conscious impropriety intentionally pursues a claim that lacks a plausible legal or factual basis or uses tactics which needlessly obstruct the litigation of a nonfrivolous claim.[74] Except in those circuits permitting an award of attorneys' fees for conduct not reaching bad faith, it is usually easier to recover attorneys' fees under Rules 11 or 37 than § 1927 or the court's inherent power.[75] Moreover, § 1927 is specifically limited to attorney misconduct and cannot be used against parties.[76] Therefore, counsel should not invoke § 1927 or the court's inherent

---

[66] Roadway Express, Inc. v. Piper, 447 U.S. 752, 764 (1980).

[67] *See* Batson v. Neal Spelce Assocs., Inc., 805 F.2d 546, 550–51 (5th Cir. 1986); Lipsig v. National Student Marketing Corp., 663 F.2d 178, 181 (D.C. Cir. 1980).

[68] Batson v. Neal Spelce Assocs., Inc., 805 F.2d 546, 551 (5th Cir. 1986).

[69] *In re* Yagman, 796 F.2d 1165, 1184, *modified on other grounds,* 803 F.2d 1085 (9th Cir. 1986).

[70] Sterling Energy, Ltd. v. Friendly Nat'l Bank, 744 F.2d 1433, 1435 n.2 (10th Cir. 1984).

[71] *See, e.g.,* Ford v. Temple Hosp., 790 F.2d 342, 346–47 (3d Cir. 1986).

[72] Kamen v. AT&T Co., 791 F.2d 1006, 1010 (2d Cir. 1986); Dreiling v. Peugeot Motors of Am., Inc., 768 F.2d 1159, 1164–65 (10th Cir. 1985); Baker Indus., Inc. v. Cerberus Ltd., 764 F.2d 204, 209 (3d Cir. 1985).

[73] United States v. Associated Convalescent Enters., Inc., 766 F.2d 1342, 1346 (9th Cir. 1985); United States v. Ross, 535 F.2d 346, 349 (6th Cir. 1976).

[74] Jones v. Continental Corp., 789 F.2d 1225, 1230 (6th Cir. 1986); Knorr Brake Corp. v. Harbil, Inc., 738 F.2d 223, 226–27 (7th Cir. 1984).

[75] *See* Zaldivar v. City of Los Angeles, 780 F.2d 823, 831 (9th Cir. 1986) (Rule 11).

[76] *See* F.T.C. v. Alaska Leasing Inc., 799 F.2d 507, 510 (9th Cir. 1986).

power unless the offending conduct does not violate any rule which permits recovery on a lesser standard than bad faith.

§ 28.9 Defining Bad Faith

Bad faith generally falls within one of three categories:

1. Bad faith during the course of the litigation
2. Bad faith in bringing or causing an action to be brought, and
3. Bad faith in the acts giving rise to the substantive claim.

The bad faith in filing an action or maintaining a defense must be distinguished from the bad faith in the acts giving rise to the claim, because one circuit has refused to award attorneys' fees based on bad faith in the act underlying the substantive claim.[77] Other circuits find § 1927 inapplicable to initial pleadings, because it addresses only the multiplication of proceedings.[78] Several circuits have held that a party acts in bad faith in bringing the action only when the claim brought is entirely without color and has been asserted wantonly for purposes of harassment or delay or other improper reasons.[79]

The fact that the litigation had a factual and legal basis is not dispositive, because bad faith may be found not only in bringing the litigation but in its conduct.[80] For example, the filing of an untimely complaint did not demonstrate bad faith, because the statute of limitations is an affirmative defense which may be waived or subject to estoppel, but when it became evident that a valid defense was asserted, fees could be assessed for continued litigation.[81] Bad faith in the conduct of the litigation has also been found when counsel brought a meritless disqualification motion for tactical reasons[82] and when counsel breached their stipulation not to appeal the decision of a referree.[83] Bad faith can even be demonstrated by deliberately misquoting precedent.[84]

---

[77] Shimman v. International Union of Operating Eng'rs, 744 F.2d 1226, 1231 (6th Cir. 1984) (en banc), *cert. denied,* 469 U.S. 1215 (1985). *But see* Richardson v. Communications Workers, 530 F.2d 126, 133 (8th Cir.), *cert. denied,* 429 U.S. 824 (1976).

[78] *See, e.g., In re* Yagman, 796 F.2d 1165, 1187, *modified on other grounds,* 803 F.2d 1085 (9th Cir. 1986).

[79] Sterling Energy, Ltd. v. Friendly Nat'l Bank, 744 F.2d 1433, 1435 (10th Cir. 1984); Browning Debenture Holders' Committee v. DASA Corp., 560 F.2d 1078, 1088 (2d Cir. 1977).

[80] Roadway Express, Inc. v. Piper, 447 U.S. 752, 766 (1980); Lipsig v. National Student Marketing Corp., 663 F.2d 178, 182 (D.C. Cir. 1980).

[81] *See* Ford v. Temple Hosp., 790 F.2d 342, 347–50 (3d Cir. 1986).

[82] Optyl Eyewear Fashion Int'l Corp. v. Style Cos., 760 F.2d 1045, 1050–51 (9th Cir. 1985).

[83] Baker Indus., Inc. v. Cerberus Ltd., 764 F.2d 204, 211 (3d Cir. 1985).

[84] *See* McCandless v. Great Atl. & Pac. Tea Co., 697 F.2d 198, 202 (7th Cir. 1983); Lipsig v. National Student Marketing Corp., 663 F.2d 178, 181 (D.C. Cir. 1980).

§ 28.10 Awarding Attorneys' Fees

Unlike Rule 11 which requires a sanction to be imposed, once a finding of bad faith or its equivalent under § 1927 has been made, the appropriateness of assessing fees is a matter for the court's discretion. Therefore, a district court may refuse to award fees even if it finds bad faith, if in balancing the equities it determines that an award would not serve the interests of justice.[85] If neither party litigated in good faith or the guilty party had financial difficulties, an award can be denied or reduced.[86] The party or attorney who has acted in bad faith has the burden of proving any mitigating factors.[87]

Courts vary as to what, if any, factors must be set forth in determining the amount of an award. For example, the actual attorneys' fees balanced against the possible chilling effect of the award on future representation by counsel has been considered sufficient.[88] The Seventh Circuit has even permitted the reasonable fee to be determined without reference to the amount of fees actually incurred by the wronged party when in-house counsel was used, although recognizing that actual fees could serve as a rational starting point for determining the size of the award.[89] The First Circuit permitted a lodestar fee calculated by multiplying a reasonable hourly rate by the number of hours reasonably expended on the lawsuit, adjusted to reflect factors such as the quality of legal representation.[90] The Ninth Circuit is not consistent as to whether the 12-factor test[91] it applies to other attorneys' fee awards must be considered.[92]

§ 28.11 Hearings and Review of § 1927 Awards

Fair notice and an opportunity for a hearing on the record appear to be mandated before attorneys' fees can be assessed under § 1927 or the court's inherent

---

85 *See* Ford v. Temple Hosp., 790 F.2d 342, 347–50 (3d Cir. 1986).

86 *Id.*

87 *Id.*

88 *See* McCandless v. Great Atl. & Pac. Tea Co., 697 F.2d 198, 202 (7th Cir. 1983); Lipsig v. National Student Marketing Corp., 663 F.2d 178, 181 (D.C. Cir. 1980).

89 Textor v. Board of Regents of N. Ill. Univ., 711 F.2d 1387, 1396 (7th Cir. 1983).

90 United States v. Nesglo, Inc., 744 F.2d 887, 892 (1st Cir. 1984).

91 Kerr v. Screen Extras Guild, Inc., 526 F.2d 67, 70 (9th Cir. 1975), *cert. denied,* 425 U.S. 951 (1976).

92 *Compare* General Signal Corp. v. Donallco, Inc., 787 F.2d 1376, 1380 (9th Cir. 1986) *and* Beaudry Motor Co. v. Abko Properties, Inc., 780 F.2d 751, 757 (9th Cir.) (citing *Kerr* standard), *cert. denied,* ____ U.S. ____, 107 S. Ct. 100 (1986) *with In re* Yagman, 796 F.2d 1165, 1185, *modified on other grounds,* 803 F.2d 1085 (9th Cir. 1986), *and* Toombs v. Leone, 777 F.2d 465, 471 (9th Cir. 1985) *and* Masalosalo v. Stonewall Ins. Co., 718 F.2d 955, 957 (9th Cir. 1983) (detailed review of *Kerr* standard not necessary).

powers.[93] Notice can be either actual or constructive.[94] However, such hearings prior to awarding attorneys' fees, although desirable, are not invariably required. For example, when the court had no reason to believe the motion was opposed,[95] or when the court had extensive familiarity with the case,[96] hearings were not necessary.

On review, factual inquiries, including the finding of bad faith, are reviewed under the clearly erroneous standard; legal conclusions are reviewed de novo, and the appropriateness of the sanction is reviewed under an abuse of discretion standard.[97] If no express finding of bad faith is made, an appellate court can remand for finding of facts[98] or reverse the sanction[99] unless bad faith is evident from the record.[100] For example, there is no basis to assume that counsel acted in bad faith from the fact that a suit was unsuccessful, so a hearing is necessary to impose attorneys' fees under § 1927 when counsel's conduct is as indicative of incompetence as it is of bad faith.[101] On the other hand, Rule 11 sanctions may be appropriate without a hearing if the claim which was dismissed was legally or factually frivolous.

OTHER AWARDS OF ATTORNEYS' FEES

§ 28.12 Reimbursement for Expenses Associated with Discovery Motions

Rule 37(a)(4) mandates the court to require the party, deponent, or attorney who unsuccessfully brings or defends a discovery motion to pay the winning party's reasonable expenses, including attorneys' fees. This rule has obviated the need to show bad faith to obtain attorneys' fees for conduct falling within its ambit and shifts the burden to the losing party to demonstrate that its conduct was substantially justified or other circumstances make an award of expenses

---

93 *See* Roadway Express, Inc. v. Piper, 447 U.S. 752, 767 (1980); T.W. Elec. Serv. v. Pacific Elec. Contractors Ass'n, 809 F.2d 626, 638 (9th Cir. 1987).

94 F.T.C. v. Alaska Land Leasing, Inc., 799 F.2d 507, 510 (9th Cir. 1986).

95 United States v. Nesglo, Inc., 744 F.2d 887, 891 (1st Cir. 1984).

96 *Id.; cf.* Copeland v. Marshall, 641 F.2d 880, 905 (D.C. Cir. 1980) (Civil rights action).

97 *In re* Itel Secs. Litig., 791 F.2d 672, 674 (9th Cir. 1986), *cert. denied,* _____ U.S. _____, 107 S. Ct. 880 (1987); Dreiling v. Peugeot Motors of Am., Inc., 768 F.2d 1159, 1165 (10th Cir. 1985).

98 *See* Barnd v. City of Tacoma, 664 F.2d 1339, 1342–43 (9th Cir. 1982).

99 *See* Estate of Blas through Chargualaf v. Winkler, 792 F.2d 858, 860–61 (9th Cir. 1986).

100 *See* Optyl Eyewear Fashion Int'l v. Style Cos., 760 F.2d 1045, 1051 (9th Cir. 1985).

101 *See* Textor v. Board of Regents of N. Ill. Univ., 711 F.2d 1387, 1395 (7th Cir. 1983).

unjust.[102] Substantial justification exists if reasonable people could differ as to whether the position taken is appropriate.[103] When the expenses are levied against the parties, an appellate court will not permit them to shift the blame to their attorneys for the failures when nothing in the record indicates that the attorneys were acting outside the scope of their authority.[104]

The court may apportion reasonable expenses incurred in a just manner if the motion is partially granted. The provisions of Rule 37(a)(4) also apply to an award of expenses for protective orders.[105] Similarly, noncompliance with Rule 16 procedures results in the imposition of reasonable expenses including attorneys' fees, under the Rule 37(a)(4) standard, regardless of other sanctions imposed.[106] Rule 37(g) also provides for an award of expenses, including attorneys' fees, for failure to participate in good faith in framing a Rule 26(f) discovery plan. These rules provide that an opportunity for hearing must be afforded before monetary compensation is awarded.

§ 28.13 Other Sources for Awards of Attorneys' Fees as Sanctions

In patent cases, 35 U.S.C. § 285 permits the award of reasonable fees for "exceptional" cases. Such awards are reserved for willful misconduct or bad faith,[107] and fees are recoverable for the entire lawsuit rather than just for expenses arising out of abusive conduct.[108] The Ninth Circuit requires a finding of bad faith or frivolity for an award of attorneys' fees under § 17 U.S.C. 505 in copyright actions.[109] In civil rights actions, a prevailing defendant may be awarded counsel fees if the plaintiff's claim is frivolous, unreasonable, or without foundation.[110] An explicit finding may be required to uphold such a decision.[111]

---

[102] *See* Merritt v. International Bhd. of Boilermakers, 649 F.2d 1013, 1019 (5th Cir. 1981).

[103] Reygo Pac. Corp. v. Johnston Pump Co., 680 F.2d 647, 649 (9th Cir. 1982); 8 C. Wright & A. Miller, Federal Practice and Procedure § 2288 (Supp. 1985).

[104] Merritt v. International Bhd. of Boilermakers, 649 F.2d 1013, 1019 (5th Cir. 1981).

[105] Fed. R. Civ. P. 26(c).

[106] Fed. R. Civ. P. 16(f).

[107] *See, e.g.*, Loctite Corp. v. Fel-Pro, Inc., 667 F.2d 577, 584–85 (7th Cir. 1981).

[108] *Id.* at 585.

[109] Cooling Sys. & Flexibles, Inc. v. Stuart Radiator, Inc., 777 F.2d 485, 493 (9th Cir. 1985).

[110] Christiansburg Garment Co. v. EEOC, 434 U.S. 412, 422 (1978).

[111] *See* Batson v. Neal Spelce Assocs., Inc., 765 F.2d 511, 517 (5th Cir. 1985).

CHAPTER 29

RULE 37 SANCTIONS FOR DISCOVERY ABUSES

§ 29.1 Sanctions Affecting the Merits of an Action

The federal rules are designed to ensure litigants their day in court. However, abuse of those rules can result in the imposition of sanctions which terminate the action. Rule 37 is the primary weapon in the war against abusive discovery. Because it applies only to the discovery process,[1] a litigant may decide to cite Rule 37 in conjunction with Rules 11 or 41(b), 28 U.S.C. § 1927, or the court's inherent power to obtain sanctions in cases when other conduct is also implicated. However, unlike Rule 11's mandatory approach, the award of sanctions under Rule 37 is more permissive.[2] Sanctions against nonparty deponents are limited to contempt of court[3] and an award of expenses, including attorneys' fees, incurred in obtaining an order to compel the deponent to answer a question.[4] Because Rule 37 only provides for recovery of costs for obtaining or

[1] *See, e.g.*, Loctite Corp. v. Fel-Pro, Inc., 667 F.2d 577, 585 (7th Cir. 1981).

[2] *See, e.g.*, Westmoreland v. CBS, Inc., 770 F.2d 1168, 1174 n.8 (D.C. Cir. 1985).

[3] Fed. R. Civ. P. 37(b)(1).

[4] Fed. R. Civ. P. 37(a)(4).

opposing orders compelling discovery from nonparties, it cannot be used to obtain relief from other orders such as a frivolous petition to hold the deponent in contempt.[5]

Rule 37 sanctions which affect the merits of the action apply to parties and persons who are officers, directors, or managing agents of a party or designated by the party to testify on its behalf.[6] It can also be used to sanction the United States as well as private litigants.[7] The rule provides for whatever sanctions are just in the circumstances and specifically mentions:

1. An order which designated matters or facts for the purposes of the action[8]
2. An order refusing to allow the disobedient party to support or oppose designated claims or defenses or prohibiting the introduction of designated matters in evidence[9]
3. An order striking out pleadings or parts thereof, staying further proceedings until the order is obeyed, dismissing the action in whole or part, or rendering a default against the disobedient party[10]
4. An order treating the failure to obey an order as a contempt of court, except for an order to submit to a physical or mental examination
5. Payment of reasonable expenses, including attorneys' fees, for any failure which was not substantially justified, unless other circumstances make an award of expenses unjust.[11]

Rule 37 also provides that all sanctions other than contempt are available if a party fails to comply with an order under Rule 35(a) which requires the production of another individual for examination, unless the party is unable to produce the individual.[12] Expenses for wrongfully failing to admit the genuineness of any document or the truth of any matter as requested under Rule 36 are also provided in Rule 37(c).[13]

---

[5] Westmoreland v. CBS, Inc., 770 F.2d 1168, 1173 (D.C. Cir. 1985) (applying Rule 11 when petition was groundless).

[6] Fed. R. Civ. P. 37(b)(2); *see, e.g.*, Founding Church of Scientology v. Webster, 802 F.2d 1448, 1451–59 (D.C. Cir. 1986) (affirming termination for repeated failure of managing agent to attend deposition).

[7] *See* 28 U.S.C. § 2412(b) (Supp. III 1985); Potlatch Corp. v. United States, 679 F.2d 153, 159 n.1 (9th Cir. 1982).

[8] Fed. R. Civ. P. 37(b)(2)(A).

[9] Fed. R. Civ. P. 37(b)(2)(B).

[10] Fed. R. Civ. P. 37(b)(2)(C).

[11] Fed. R. Civ. P. 37(b)(2).

[12] Fed. R. Civ. P. 37(b)(2)(E).

[13] See § **26.6**.

§ 29.2 Procedures

There are two methods to obtain relief under Rule 37, depending upon whether there is a partial or complete failure of discovery. First, if there has been a complete failure of discovery, such as failure of a party to attend a deposition, answer interrogatories, or provide a written response to a Rule 34 request, counsel can move immediately for sanctions under Rule 37(d) without any previous order to compel discovery.[14] Second, if there is a partial discovery failure, the party must invoke two steps before sanctions can be awarded. First, the party may move to compel the requested discovery under Rule 37(a) and may be awarded expenses for obtaining the court order. Second, only if the order compelling discovery is violated can the party move for sanctions affecting the outcome of the case to be assessed pursuant to Rule 37(b).

The two-step process is mandated whenever (1) a party or deponent fails to answer a deposition question, (2) a corporation fails to designate a person to speak on its behalf, (3) a party fails to answer an interrogatory, or (4) a party fails to permit Rule 34 productions or responds that it will not permit production as requested. A party need not formally move to compel if the court has issued an oral or written order.[15] The order need not refer to the specific discovery in dispute as long as it is clear. Therefore, an order to provide complete answers to interrogatories is sufficient, without reference to individual interrogatories.[16] A party's failure to object to the production of the disputed material[17] and an attorney's promise in open court to produce documents[18] have been treated as the equivalent of an order for Rule 37(b) purposes. However, if no order is violated, the court must rely on its inherent power to impose sanctions.[19]

Although the rule itself does not specify any timing requirements, local rules may mandate that discovery motions be brought within a given time after the noncompliance to avoid waiver. The Second Circuit has indicated that a motion will be deemed waived if it is not made prior to judgment, unless the issue is expressly reserved in the judgment, and that generally a motion should be brought prior to trial to avoid waiver, unless a later motion is made within a reasonable time after the noncompliance.[20]

---

[14] Charter House Ins. Brokers, Ltd. v. New Hampshire Ins. Co., 667 F.2d 600, 604 (7th Cir. 1981); Guidry v. Continental Oil Co., 640 F.2d 523, 533 (5th Cir.), *cert. denied,* 454 U.S. 818 (1981); 8 C. Wright & A. Miller, Federal Practice and Procedure § 2291 (1970) [hereinafter Federal Practice and Procedure].

[15] *See* Tamari v. Bache & Co. (Lebanon) S.A.L., 729 F.2d 469, 473 (7th Cir. 1984); Professional Seminar Consultants, Inc. v. Sino Am. Tech. Exch. Council, Inc., 727 F.2d 1470, 1474 (9th Cir. 1984); Properties Int'l Ltd. v. Turner, 706 F.2d 308, 310 (11th Cir. 1983).

[16] *See* Fjelstad v. American Honda Motor Co., 762 F.2d 1334, 1339 (9th Cir. 1985).

[17] Penthouse Int'l, Ltd. v. Playboy Enters., Inc., 663 F.2d 371, 389–90 (2d Cir. 1981).

[18] Charter House Ins. Brokers, Ltd. v. New Hampshire Ins. Co., 667 F.2d 600, 604 (7th Cir. 1981).

[19] Penthouse Int'l, Ltd. v. Playboy Enters., Inc., 663 F.2d 371, 389–90 (2d Cir. 1981).

[20] Mercy v. County of Suffolk, 748 F.2d 52, 55–56 (2d Cir. 1984); *see* Airtex Corp. v. Shelley Radiant Ceiling Co., 536 F.2d 145, 155 (7th Cir. 1976).

Many local rules also provide that before a motion can be made counsel must meet and confer regarding the disputed discovery and certify that they are unable after reasonable effort to resolve the dispute,[21] although such conferences may be limited to partial rather than total discovery failures. Delegation of this obligation to someone other than an attorney has been considered insufficient compliance.[22] In some courts, a joint motion is required, which often has the practical effect of deterring parties from requesting sanctions based on minor differences due to the increased cost of such motions to both parties as well as the inevitable delay in bringing them. Parties who cannot agree on discovery matters often cannot even agree about whose word processor will be used to create the final document.

§ 29.3 The Rule 37 Standard

In *National Hockey League v. Metropolitan Hockey Club,*[23] the Supreme Court approved a standard for terminating an action for discovery abuse which requires a minimum of willfulness, bad faith, or fault.[24] A dismissal cannot be granted when the failure to comply is solely due to inability.[25] Therefore, a pro se plaintiff who informs the court he is unable to pay a monetary sanction cannot be dismissed without a showing that he had the ability to pay.[26] Inability is often an issue when the discovery materials are located in a country which has a statute blocking its production.[27] Some circuits hold that fault can justify a dismissal or default in the absence of willfulness or bad faith,[28] permitting terminations for gross negligence[29] or recklessness.[30]

National Hockey League also adopted deterrence as a legitimate goal in meting out sanctions in order to deter other parties who are tempted to such conduct.[31] Therefore, even if the noncompliant party appears repentant and

---

[21] *See* Crown, Cork & Seal Co. v. Chemed Corp., 101 F.R.D. 105, 106 n.1 (E.D. Pa. 1984) (listing all courts with such rules).

[22] *Id.* at 107.

[23] 427 U.S. (1976).

[24] National Hockey League v. Metropolitan Hockey Club, 427 U.S. 639, 643 (1976).

[25] Societe Internationale v. Rogers, 357 U.S. 197, 212 (1958).

[26] Thomas v. Gerber Prods., 703 F.2d 353, 356–57 (9th Cir. 1983).

[27] *See* Societe Internationale v. Rogers, 357 U.S. 197, 212 (1958); General Atomic Co. v. Exxon Nuclear Co., 90 F.R.D. 290, 291 (S.D. Cal. 1981); § **22.1**.

[28] United Artists Corp. v. La Cage Aux Folles, Inc., 771 F.2d 1265, 1270 (9th Cir. 1985).

[29] *See, e.g.,* Rabb v. Amatex Corp., 769 F.2d 996, 1000 (4th Cir. 1985); Weisburg v. Webster, 749 F.2d 864, 871 (D.C. Cir. 1984); Penthouse Int'l, Ltd. v. Playboy Enters. Inc., 663 F.2d 371, 388 (2d Cir. 1981); Affanato v. Merrill Bros., 547 F.2d 138, 141 (1st Cir. 1977).

[30] Hritz v. Woma Corp., 732 F.2d 1178, 1183 (3d Cir. 1984).

[31] 427 U.S. at 643; *see generally* Note, *the Emerging Deterrence Orientation in the Imposition of Discovery Sanctions,* 91 Harv. L. Rev. 1033 (1978).

tenders the disputed materials after the dismissal motion is filed, the trial judge can still dismiss the action.[32] The deterrence rationale has even been used to affirm dismissal of an entire case, although the discovery dispute focused on a single claim.[33]

When applying sanctions, courts are guided by the Supreme Court's decision in *Insurance Corp. of Ireland v. Compagnie Des Bauxites De Guinee,*[34] which limited the district court's discretion in assigning sanctions to Rule 37(b)(2)'s by requiring that (1) sanctions must be just and (2) the sanction must be specifically related to the particular claim which was at issue in the order to provide discovery.[35] Due process is satisfied as long as the conduct supports an inference that the refusal to provide the requested information is an admission of the lack of merit of the claim or defense.[36] If the behavior does not support this presumption, due process is violated.[37] Therefore, a case cannot be terminated merely to punish a litigant who fails to comply with an order to deposit money in the court's registry.[38] Similarly, refusal to pay a monetary sanction is not sufficient, by itself, to support a default.[39] A partial default has also been reversed because the failure to supplement a response concerning potential witnesses did not give rise to a presumption that the denials in its answer to the complaint were untrue or that its defenses were meritless.[40]

§ 29.4 Reviewing Discovery Sanctions

National Hockey League limited the appellate court's review of discovery sanctions to whether the district court abused its discretion.[41] This reduces the possibility of a reversal on appeal because the appellate court believes the sanction is too harsh in the circumstances, as long as the behavior supports a dismissal or default.[42] Similarly, it is rare that an appellate court will reverse a trial court's decision not to impose a Rule 37 sanction, because Rule 37, unlike

---

[32] *See, e.g.,* Wyle v. R.J. Reynolds Indus., Inc., 709 F.2d 585, 591 (9th Cir. 1983); G-K Properties v. Redevelopment Agency, 577 F.2d 645, 647–48 (9th Cir. 1978).

[33] *See* Weisburg v. Webster, 749 F.2d 864, 872 (D.C. Cir. 1984).

[34] 456 U.S. 694 (1982).

[35] *Id.* at 707.

[36] *Id.* at 705–06; *see* Hammond Packing Co. v. Arkansas, 212 U.S. 322, 350–51 (1909).

[37] Insurance Corp. of Ireland, Ltd. v. Compagnie Des Bauxites de Guinee, 456 U.S. at 706.

[38] Hovey v. Elliott, 167 U.S. 409, 413–14 (1897).

[39] SEC v. Seaboard Corp., 666 F.2d 414, 416–17 (9th Cir. 1982).

[40] Fjelstad v. American Honda Motor Co., 762 F.2d 1334, 1342 (9th Cir. 1985).

[41] National Hockey League v. Metropolitan Hockey Club, 427 U.S. 639, 642 (1976) (per curiam).

[42] *Id.* at 642–43; Aruba Bonaire Curacao Trust Co. v. Commissioner, 777 F.2d 38, 44 (D.C. Cir. 1985), *cert. denied,* _____ U.S. _____, 106 S. Ct. 1469 (1986).

Rule 11, is permissive as to the imposition of any sanction as well as the nature of any sanction imposed.[43]

Although the appropriateness of the sanction is reviewed under an abuse of discretion standard, factual inquiries under Rule 37 are reviewed under the clearly erroneous standard, and any legal conclusions are reviewed de novo.[44] When reviewing the propriety of sanctions for failure to cooperate in discovery, the court also reviews the propriety of the underlying discovery order.[45] If the order disobeyed was invalid, any sanctions must necessarily fall.[46] Therefore, if no reasonable notice of the order was given[47] or the disputed discovery was not relevant to the action or was privileged, a dismissal cannot be sustained.[48] However, the reason for the invalid order must be raised before the trial judge, or it will not be heard on appeal.[49]

§ 29.5 Factors Considered by the Circuits When Reviewing Sanctions Which Terminate the Action

The circuits vary in their approach to Rule 37 sanctions. At one end of the spectrum, some circuits affirm dismissals and default even if the judge did not consider lesser sanctions, because Rule 37 does not state or suggest this requirement.[50] Similarly, the First Circuit noted that the claim of abuse of discretion does not receive its sympathetic ear, as shown by its affirmance of all dismissals but one from 1964 to 1983.[51] On the other hand, most of the circuits

[43] *Compare* Dellums v. Powell, 566 F.2d 231, 236 (D.C. Cir. 1977) (sanction required) *with* Augustine v. United States, 810 F.2d 991, 996 (10th Cir. 1987) *and* Hazen v. Pasley, 768 F.2d 226, 229 (8th Cir. 1985) *and* Forro Precision Inc. v. I.B.M. Corp., 673 F.2d 1045, 1053 (9th Cir. 1982) (sanction not required).

[44] United States v. National Medical Enters., Inc., 792 F.2d 906, 910–11 (9th Cir. 1986); Eastway Gen. Hosp., Ltd. v. Eastway Women's Clinic, Inc., 737 F.2d 503, 505 (5th Cir. 1984), *cert. denied,* 470 U.S. 1052 (1985).

[45] Patton v. Aerojet Ordnance Co., 765 F.2d 604, 608 (6th Cir. 1985); Hastings v. North E. Indep. School Dist., 615 F.2d 628, 631 (5th Cir. 1980).

[46] Donovan v. Mosher Steel Co., 791 F.2d 1535, 1537 (11th Cir. 1986), *cert. denied,*_____ U.S. _____, 107 S. Ct. 874 (1987); Holcomb v. Allis-Chalmers Corp., 774 F.2d 398, 400–01 (10th Cir. 1985); Hastings v. North E. Indep. School Dist., 615 F.2d 628, 631 (5th Cir. 1980).

[47] Holcomb v. Allis-Chalmers Corp., 774 F.2d 398, 400–01 (10th Cir. 1985).

[48] *See, e.g.,* Fonseca v. Regan, 734 F.2d 944, 948 (2d Cir.), *cert. denied,* 469 U.S. 882 (1984); Savola v. Webster, 644 F.2d 743, 747 (8th Cir. 1981); Dunbar v. United States, 502 F.2d 506, 509–10 (5th Cir. 1974).

[49] *See* United States v. Rylander, 460 U.S. 752, 755–57 (1983); Rainbow Pioneer v. Hawaii-Nevada Inv. Corp., 711 F.2d 902, 905 (9th Cir. 1983).

[50] Damiani v. Rhode Island Hosp., 704 F.2d 12, 15 (1st Cir. 1983).

[51] *Id.* at 17.

view dismissals and defaults as a draconian remedy or a sanction of last resort.[52] These circuits require that the judge consider less drastic sanctions which would be equally effective before terminating the action[53] and explicitly articulate the resolution of the factual, legal, and discretionary issues presented.[54] The use of an ultimate sanction is upheld without explicit balancing only if the conduct clearly justifies dismissal.[55] Even if the transgression is willful, some circuits require the punishment to fit the crime rather than generally approving sanctions which terminate the action.[56] Although a showing of prejudice or irreparable harm may not be required, it is a relevant factor that courts consider before terminating an action.[57]

Probably the most stringent review of severe sanctions occurs in the Third Circuit, which has established a strong presumption against sanctions that decide the issues of a case.[58] The trial judge must consider the following factors before terminating an action as sanction: (1) the extent of the party's personal responsibility; (2) the prejudice to the adversary caused by the failure to meet scheduling orders and respond to discovery; (3) a history of dilatoriness; (4) whether the conduct of the party or the attorney was willful or in bad faith; (5) the effectiveness of sanctions other than dismissal, which entails an analysis of alternative sanctions; and (6) the meritoriousness of the claim or defense.[59] Most of these criteria also are required by the Fourth Circuit,[60] and the Ninth Circuit also applies several of these factors as well as evaluating whether notice and warning have been given to the recalcitrant party before dismissal.[61] These criteria are useful as guidelines in bringing or defending against sanctions motions even in circuits not requiring that the entire standard be applied.

---

[52] Patton v. Aerojet Ordnance Co., 765 F.2d 604, 607 (6th Cir. 1985); Batson v. Neal Spelce Assocs., Inc., 765 F.2d 511, 515 (5th Cir. 1985); Searock v. Stripling, 736 F.2d 650, 653 (11th Cir. 1984).

[53] *E.g.*, Batson v. Neal Spelce Assocs., Inc., 765 F.2d 511, 516 (5th Cir. 1985); United Artists Corp. v. La Cage Aux Folles, Inc., 771 F.2d 1265, 1270 (9th Cir. 1985); Searock v. Stripling, 736 F.2d 650, 653 (11th Cir. 1984); Hritz v. Woma Corp., 732 F.2d 1178, 1182 (3d Cir. 1984).

[54] Patton v. Aerojet Ordnance Co., 765 F.2d 604, 608 (6th Cir. 1985); Quality Prefabrication, Inc. v. Daniel J. Keating Co., 675 F.2d 77, 81 (3d Cir. 1982).

[55] *See* Batson v. Neal Spelce Assocs., Inc., 765 F.2d 511, 516 n.2 (5th Cir. 1985).

[56] *See* Givens v. A.H. Robins Co., 751 F.2d 261, 263 (8th Cir. 1984) (dismissal for willful failure to comply with discovery deadline reversed).

[57] United States v. National Medical Enters., Inc., 792 F.2d 906, 913 (9th Cir. 1986); Searock v. Stripling, 736 F.2d 650, 653 (11th Cir. 1984); Marshall v. Segona, 621 F.2d 763, 768 (5th Cir. 1980).

[58] Ali v. Sims, 788 F.2d 954, 958 (3d Cir. 1986).

[59] Poulis v. State Farm Fire & Casualty Co., 747 F.2d 863, 868–70 (3d Cir. 1984), *followed in* Ennis v. New Jersey Bell Tel. Co., 782 F.2d 396, 397 (3d Cir. 1985), *cert. denied*, ____ U.S. ____, 106 S. Ct. 1461 (1986).

[60] Chandler Leasing Corp. v. Lopez, 669 F.2d 919, 920 (4th Cir. 1982).

[61] *See In re* Rubin, 769 F.2d 611, 616 (9th Cir. 1985).

It is a common practice for trial courts to issue warnings or make dismissal or default orders conditional on a party's continued noncompliance with an outstanding order to compel.[62] The district court can also order discovery to determine whether the original discovery violation was willful and assess the costs of such discovery against the noncomplying party.[63] As a practical matter, the district court usually looks to a pattern of discovery abuse before terminating a case.[64] Therefore, although the violation which brings the motion to the court's attention may be minor, dismissal can be ordered if it is part of a continuing saga of dilatory or obstructive conduct.[65]

§ 29.6 Terminations for Attorney Misconduct

If the fault lies with the attorney rather than the party, some circuits consider dismissal too severe a sanction,[66] while others cite the Supreme Court's admonition in *Link v. Wabash Railroad Co.*[67] that the party "voluntarily chose this attorney as his representative in the action, and he cannot now avoid the consequences of the acts or omissions of this freely selected agent."[68] Usually the deciding factor is whether counsel was guilty of repeated abuse of the judicial process and indifference to court orders.[69]

§ 29.7 Lesser Sanctions Affecting the Merits

Lesser sanctions than those terminating the action are employed for mere failures to respond to discovery[70] or other negligent behavior.[71] Therefore, a

---

[62] *See id.*

[63] *See, e.g.*, Tamari v. Bache & Co. (Lebanon) S.A.L., 729 F.2d 469, 471–72 (7th Cir. 1984).

[64] *See, e.g.*, United States Freight Co. v. Penn Cent. Transp. Co., 716 F.2d 954, 954–55 (2d Cir. 1983).

[65] *See id.* at 955; Penthouse Int'l, Ltd. v. Playboy Enters., Inc., 663 F.2d 371, 388–90 (2d Cir. 1981).

[66] *See, e.g.*, D.G. Shelter Prods. Co. v. Forest Prods. Co., 769 F.2d 644, 645 (10th Cir. 1985); *In re* MacMeekin, 722 F.2d 32, 35 (3d Cir. 1983).

[67] 370 U.S. 626, 633–34 (1962).

[68] *Id.* at 633–34; *see* United Artists Corp. v. La Cage Aux Folles, Inc., 771 F.2d 1265, 1271 (9th Cir. 1985); Damiani v. Rhode Island Hosp., 704 F.2d 12, 16 (1st Cir. 1983).

[69] *See, e.g.*, Vela v. Western Elec. Co., 709 F.2d 375, 376–77 (5th Cir. 1983).

[70] Weisberg v. Webster, 749 F.2d 864, 871 (D.C. Cir. 1984); *see* Societe International v. Rogers, 357 U.S. 197, 212–13 (1958).

[71] Fjelstad v. American Honda Motor Co., 762 F.2d 1334, 1343 (9th Cir. 1985); Tamari v. Bache & Co. (Lebanon) S.A.L., 729 F.2d 469, 474 (7th Cir. 1984).

preclusion order which does not result in a dismissal need not be based on willfulness.[72] Lesser sanctions such as striking a defense or a preclusion order which is tantamount to dismissal are usually treated under the *National Hockey League* standard.[73] In *Insurance Corp. of Ireland v. Compagnie Des Bauxites,*[74] the Supreme Court permitted personal jurisdiction to be presumed as a discovery sanction. The Court noted that the sanction was just because the defendants had been warned that the judge would presume personal jurisdiction unless the requested materials were produced, they had repeatedly promised compliance and then defaulted, the claim that personal jurisdiction existed was not frivolous, and they were allowed to present evidence contradicting the presumption.[75] Subject matter jurisdiction cannot be presumed as a sanction,[76] although sanctions can be invoked against parties whose misfeasance involves procedures connected with the court's determination of whether it has subject matter jurisdiction.[77]

Rule 37 sanctions can be invoked even if the disputed information is not admitted at trial. For example, the Second Circuit has affirmed a Rule 37 sanction denying a victorious antitrust plaintiff attorneys' fees amounting to $10 million for its intentional concealment of evidence which was ultimately ruled inadmissible.[78] Other sanctions not specifically mentioned in Rule 37 which have been applied include presuming exhibits admissible when authentication and hearsay problems were caused by the adverse party's misconduct[79] and assessing attorneys' fees and office expenses for a second deposition required because of an expert's lack of preparation.[80]

A compensatory award under Rule 37 is limited to the actual losses sustained as a result of contumacy.[81] Sanctions cannot be assessed against one party because of the failure of another party to comply with discovery, absent a showing that the sanctioned party controlled the actions of the noncomplying

---

[72] *See* Cope v. McPherson, 781 F.2d 207, 209 (D.C. Cir. 1985).

[73] *See* Rabb v. Amatex Corp., 769 F.2d 996, 1000 (4th Cir. 1985) (applying gross negligence standard); Parrott v. Wilson, 707 F.2d 1262, 1273 n.26 (11th Cir.), *cert. denied,* 464 U.S. 936 (1983).

[74] 456 U.S. 694 (1982).

[75] *Id.* at 707–08.

[76] *See id.* at 701–02.

[77] Davis v. Cluet, Peabody & Co., 667 F.2d 1371, 1374 n.8 (11th Cir. 1982).

[78] Litton Sys., Inc. v. AT&T Co., 700 F.2d 785, 827 (2d Cir. 1983), *cert. denied,* 464 U.S. 1073 (1984).

[79] General Atomic Co. v. Exxon Nuclear Co., 90 F.R.D. 290, 309 (S.D. Cal. 1981).

[80] Admiral Theatre Corp. v. Douglas Theatre Co., 585 F.2d 877, 899 (8th Cir. 1978).

[81] *See* United States v. National Medical Enters., Inc., 792 F.2d 906, 910 (9th Cir. 1986).

party.[82] A pattern of dilatory conduct may also be used to support a judge's refusal to grant a continuance for trial.[83]

§ 29.8 Expenses for Rule 37 Violations

The plain language of Rule 37(b)(2)(E) provides that only those expenses, including attorneys' fees, caused by the failure to comply may be assessed against the noncomplying party. Therefore, attorneys' fees for discovery matters not related to failure to comply with discovery orders are not recoverable under Rule 37,[84] although in a given case another rule or statute or the court's inherent power may justify such awards. A reviewing court may view an extraordinarily large award of Rule 37 attorneys' fees as unreasonable on its face if not supported by documentation.[85] Because an appellate court can remand an action for the trial judge to articulate reasons for its assessment of fees,[86] counsel obtaining a fee award should always ensure that the record is sufficient on this issue. Specific findings may also be required to determine the allocation of expenses between the noncomplying party and attorney.[87] Some circuits are strict about the type of documentation necessary to recover attorneys' fees,[88] requiring contemporaneous, complete, standardized time records which accurately reflect the work done by each attorney.[89] Attorneys' fees on appeal have also been awarded based on the rationale that such costs were caused by the discovery failure.[90]

---

[82] Letelier v. Republic of Chile, 748 F.2d 790, 795 n.2 (2d Cir. 1984), *cert. denied,* 471 U.S. 1125 (1985); 4A J. Moore *et al.,* Moore's Federal Practice ¶ 37.05 (2d ed. 1984) [hereinafter Moore's Federal Practice].

[83] *See, e.g.,* Watson v. Miears, 772 F.2d 433, 437–38 (8th Cir. 1985).

[84] Batson v. Neal Spelce Assocs., Inc., 765 F.2d 511, 516 (5th Cir. 1985).

[85] *Id.; In re* Yagman, 796 F.2d 1165, 1180–81, *modified on other grounds,* 803 F.2d 1085 (9th Cir. 1986).

[86] Batson v. Neal Spelce Assocs., Inc., 765 F.2d 511, 517 (5th Cir. 1985).

[87] *See* Weisberg v. Webster, 749 F.2d 864, 873–74 (D.C. Cir. 1984).

[88] *See, e.g.,* Day v. Allstate Ins. Co., 788 F.2d 1110, 1113 (5th Cir. 1986) (following Johnson v. Georgia Highway Express, Inc., 488 F.2d 714, 717–19 (5th Cir. 1974)).

[89] *See* Weisberg v. Webster, 749 F.2d 864, 872–73 (D.C. Cir. 1984) (following National Ass'n of Concerned Veterans v. Secretary of Defense, 675 F.2d 1319, 1327 (D.C. Cir. 1982) (per curiam)).

[90] Mickwee v. Hsu, 753 F.2d 770, 770 (9th Cir. 1985) (per curiam); Tamari v. Bache & Co. (Lebanon) S.A.L., 729 F.2d 469, 475 (7th Cir. 1984).

§ 29.9 Hearings

There is no right to a jury trial in Rule 37 proceedings,[91] even though termination of the action is equivalent to an adjudication of the merits.[92] *Roadway Express Inc. v. Piper*[93] specifically states that "[l]ike other sanctions, attorney's fees certainly should not be assessed lightly or without fair notice and an opportunity for a hearing on the record."[94] However, a hearing, though desirable, is not considered necessary in all circumstances, even if the sanction terminates the action.[95] Factors considered in determining the necessity of holding a hearing include the judge's familiarity with the disruptive behavior, the type of notice given the noncomplying party that sanctions would be imposed, the vagueness or specificity of the discovery order, and the opportunity of the noncomplying party to respond. Similarly, Rule 55(b)(2) concerning defaults,[96] which provides that the court can conduct a hearing if necessary to determine the amount of damages, does not mandate hearings in all cases,[97] although a few circuits require a hearing unless the amount of damages claimed is a liquidated sum or one capable of mathematical calculation.[98] However, if a hearing is mandated, the rule provides that the court must afford a right to a jury trial when and as required by any statute of the United States.[99] Because such a statute would have to require a jury for damages, it is extremely rare for a case to indicate that a jury trial on damages has been granted for a default entered as a discovery sanction.[100] If the defaulting party appeared in the action, Rule 55(b)(2) requires that three days' notice of the default hearing be given, although it is unclear whether this is engrafted on to Rule 37 procedures.[101] At the damage

---

[91] Wyle v. R.J. Reynolds Indus., Inc., 709 F.2d 585, 592 (9th Cir. 1983).

[92] *Id.; see* Woods v. Tsuchiya, 754 F.2d 1571, 1582 (Fed. Cir.), *cert. denied,* _____ U.S. _____, 106 S. Ct. 81 (1985).

[93] 447 U.S. 752 (1980).

[94] *Id.* at 767.

[95] *See id.*; Professional Seminar Consultants, Inc. v. Sino Am. Tech. Exch. Council, Inc., 727 F.2d 1470, 1473 (9th Cir. 1984); Vela v. Western Elec. Co., 709 F.2d 375, 377 (5th Cir. 1983).

[96] See **ch. 12**.

[97] *See* Brockton Sav. Bank v. Peat, Marwick, Mitchell & Co., 771 F.2d 5, 12–13 (1st Cir. 1985), *cert. denied,* _____ U.S. _____, 106 S. Ct. 1204 (1986); United States v. DeFrantz, 708 F.2d 310, 312–13 (7th Cir. 1983).

[98] *See* Adolph Coors Co. v. Movement Against Racism, 777 F.2d 1538, 1543–44 (11th Cir. 1985); United Artist Corp. v. Freeman, 605 F.2d 854, 857 (5th Cir. 1979) (per curiam).

[99] *See* Fed. R. Civ. P. 55(b); 6 Moore's Federal Practice ¶ 55.09.

[100] *See, e.g.,* Griffin v. Swim-Tech Corp., 722 F.2d 677, 679 (11th Cir. 1984).

[101] *See* Au Bon Pain Corp. v. Artect, Inc., 653 F.2d 61, 65 (2d Cir. 1981) (default entered for discovery failure required Rule 55 procedures).

inquest, the court accepts as true all of the factual allegations of the complaint except those relating to damages.[102]

Rule 37(a)(4) specifically mentions opportunity for a hearing, but the judge's perusal of transcripts of disputed deposition testimony and memoranda justifying counsel's position has been held sufficient.[103] Counsel should request a hearing after the imposition of sanctions, if one has not previously been afforded.

§ 29.10 Setting Aside Defaults and Dismissals

A Rule 55(c) motion is appropriate to set aside an entry of default before judgment has been entered, while a Rule 60(b) motion requesting relief from judgment based on mistake, inadvertence, surprise, or excusable neglect should be addressed to the trial court if sanctions result in termination of the action.[104] Even if the judge does not grant the motion, its presence may be a factor considered by the appellate court. At a minimum, it enables the noncomplying party to proffer whatever reasons it has for excusable neglect, because an appellate court will not consider any affidavits concerning justification which were not presented below.[105] Counsel must be careful to appeal both the judgment of dismissal and the denial of the Rule 60(b) motion, because Rule 60(b) denials are reviewed more narrowly in scope than dismissals so as not to vitiate the requirements of a timely appeal.[106] Filing a Rule 60(b) motion does not toll the time in which an appeal can be taken from judgment.[107] Denials of Rule 60(b) motions are reviewed for abuse of discretion.[108]

Motions to set aside the default under either Rule 55(c) or Rule 60(b) must be filed within a reasonable time and require an acceptable reason for the default as well as the existence of a meritorious defense.[109] The culpability of the defendant's conduct and the prejudice to the plaintiff if the default is lifted also are considered.[110] A court can order conditions on reopening a default, such as waiver of the statute of limitations, to avoid hurting the adverse party.[111] It is

---

[102] *Id.*

[103] Hayden Stone, Inc. v. Brode, 508 F.2d 895, 897 (7th Cir. 1974).

[104] *See* 7 Moore's Federal Practice ¶ 60.09–.30; §§ **12.3** and **14.70**.

[105] Rainbow Pioneer v. Hawaii-Nevada Inv. Corp., 711 F.2d 902, 906 (9th Cir. 1983).

[106] Vela v. Western Elec. Co., 709 F.2d 375, 376 (5th Cir. 1983).

[107] Barta v. Long, 670 F.2d 907, 909 (10th Cir. 1982); 11 Federal Practice and Procedure § 2871.

[108] *Id.*

[109] Barta v. Long, 670 F.2d 907, 909 (10th Cir. 1982).

[110] Hritz v. Woma Corp., 732 F.2d 1178, 1181 (3d Cir. 1984).

[111] *Id.* at 1182 & n.3.

also common to require that the defaulting party cure all previous discovery violations.[112] A Rule 60 movant should always tender any outstanding discovery with the motion to ensure that the reviewing court does not consider its absence as justifying a denial of relief.[113]

§ 29.11 Rule 37 Checklist

Total Failure of Discovery

1. No motion to compel is necessary before Rule 37(d) sanctions can be assessed for failure of a party or officer, director, or managing agent of a party or a person designated as a deponent under Rule 30(b)(6) or 31(a) to

- **a.** Appear for deposition after proper notice
- **b.** Serve answers or objections to properly served interrogatories
- **c.** Serve a written response to a properly served Rule 34 request.

Partial Failure of Discovery

1. A motion to compel is necessary to obtain discovery pursuant to Rule 37(a) for

- **a.** Failure to answer an oral or written deposition question
- **b.** Failure to make a Rule 30(b)(6) or 31(a) deponent designation
- **c.** Failure to answer or making an evasive or incomplete answer to a Rule 33 interrogatory
- **d.** Failure to respond that a Rule 34 inspection will be permitted as requested
- **e.** Failure to permit a Rule 34 inspection as requested.

Obtaining an Award of Expenses Concerning a Rule 37 Motion

1. Expenses are available for any motion granted under Rule 37(a), (b), (d), or (g).

---

[112] *See* Tolliver v. Northrop Corp., 786 F.2d 316, 319 (7th Cir. 1986).

[113] *See id.*

2. A party or deponent and/or an attorney is liable for the reasonable expenses incurred in successfully bringing or defending against a motion
   a. To obtain a Rule 37(a) order
   b. Caused by the failure to comply with a Rule 37(a) order
   c. Caused by a Rule 37(d) failure
   d. Caused by a failure to participate in good faith in framing a Rule 26(f) discovery plan.
   e. Deponents and/or their attorneys are liablefor expenses under 2a or 2b.
3. Reasonable expenses include attorneys' fees.
4. The court must make the expense award unless the motion or opposition was substantially justified, unless other circumstances make an award of expenses unjust.

Other Rule 37 Sanctions

1. Sanctions are available for a Rule 37(d) failure or a Rule 37(b) failure by a party or an officer, director, or managing agent of a party or a person designated as a deponent under Rule 30(b)(6) or 31(a) to obey an order issued under Rule 37(a), 35(a) or 26(f).
2. Any order which is just in regard to the aforementioned discovery failures can be assessed including
   a. Designating facts as established for the purposes of the action
   b. Refusing to allow the disobedient party to support or oppose designated claims or defenses
   c. Prohibiting the disobedient party from introducing designated matters in evidence
   d. Striking pleadings or parts thereof
   e. Staying proceedings until the order is obeyed
   f. Dismissing the action, or any part thereof
   g. Rendering a default judgment against the disobedient party
   h. Citing the disobedient party for contempt of court.
3. A party's failure to produce another for examination under Rule 35(a) can result in the imposition of any sanction except contempt, unless party shows inability to produce the required person for examination.
4. A deponent who fails to be sworn or to answer a question after being ordered can be held in contempt.

Failure to Admit a Rule 36 Request

1. Failure to admit the genuineness of any document or the truth of any matter requested which is proved at trial permits the following sanctions to be assessed pursuant to Rule 37(c)
   a. Reasonable expenses incurred in making the proof
   b. Reasonable attorneys' fees incurred in making the proof.
2. The court must make the expense award unless
   a. The request was objectionable under Rule 36(a)
   b. The admission was of no substantial importance
   c. The party failing to admit had reasonable ground to believe that it might prevail on the matter
   d. Other good reason existed for the failure to admit.
3. An improper refusal to admit or deny may also fall within Rule 37(b) permitting the party to be sanctioned by deeming the requests admitted.

Where to Bring the Motion

1. If the motion concerns a deposition
   a. Of a party may it bring it in the district where the action is pending or in the district where the deposition is being taken
   b. Of a nonparty may it bring it in the district where the deposition is being taken.
2. Other matters must be brought in the district in which the action is pending.

CHAPTER 30

SANCTIONS FOR FAILURE TO PROSECUTE OR OBEY COURT ORDERS

§ 30.1 Introduction

Because Rule 37 applies only to discovery abuses, courts have used their inherent powers as well as Rules 41 and 16 to impose sanctions for failure to prosecute and otherwise obey court orders. Although Rule 41 is primarily directed at plaintiffs, inherent powers and Rule 16 permit sanctions against all litigants.

§ 30.2 Rule 41(b) Overview

Rule 41(b) provides that a defendant can move for dismissal of an action or claim for failure of the plaintiff to prosecute or to comply with the federal rules or any order of the court. Unless otherwise specified, such dismissals operate as an adjudication upon the merits.[1] Unlike Rule 37, which can be invoked by both

[1] Fed. R. Civ. P. 41(b). *But see* Combined Network v. Equitable Life Assurance Soc'y, 805 F.2d 1292, 1298 (7th Cir. 1986).

parties, Rule 41 provides sanctions solely against claimants. Therefore, a defendant's conduct can only be reached through Rule 41(b) as to any counterclaim, cross-claim or third party action which it has brought. A dismissal under Rule 41(b) or the court's inherent power is reviewed for abuse of discretion.[2] Dismissals without prejudice are reviewed under the same standard as dismissals with prejudice when they result in time barring of a claim.[3]

Practitioners who are used to state systems in which it is usual for cases to drag on for several years with no activity are often unprepared for the swiftness with which federal judges dismiss actions for failure to prosecute. Because federal rules rather than state procedures govern such dismissals in diversity actions,[4] counsel must be prepared to proceed quickly, although a plaintiff will not be penalized for any diliatory conduct in state court prior to removal.[5] In some district courts, the goal is to try cases within 12 to 18 months of filing, and the local rules are written accordingly to prod lawyers into action at the risk of sanctions ranging from fines to dismissals.[6] A significant number of such dismissals are ordered sua sponte by the court without any notice or hearing; therefore, counsel cannot rely on the defendant's acquiescense to dilatory conduct. If a plaintiff's counsel is experiencing difficulty in obtaining discovery or witnesses, the court should be notified of any reasons causing the delay to avoid a sua sponte dismissal.[7]

§ 30.3 Rule 41(b) Standard

Most circuits have adopted basically identical standards for evaluating sanctions imposed under Rules 41(b) and 37.[8] Often it is difficult to tell which of these rules is being invoked to authorize a given sanction.[9] Although the Supreme Court has distinguished them on the basis that Rule 37 applies to discovery failures, whereas Rule 41 is concerned with trials,[10] it is often appropriate to cite

---

[2] Link v. Wabash R.R., 370 U.S. 626, 633 (1962).

[3] McGowan v. Faulkner Concrete Pipe Co., 659 F.2d 554, 556 (5th Cir. 1981).

[4] *See* Olympic Sports Prods., Inc. v. Universal Athletic Sales Co., 760 F.2d 910, 916 (9th Cir. 1985), *cert. denied,* ____ U.S. ____, 106 S. Ct. 804 (1986) (California five-year rule does not apply in federal court).

[5] Nealey v. Transportacion Maritima Mexicana, S.A., 662 F.2d 1275, 1279 (9th Cir. 1980).

[6] *See, e.g.,* Cal. C.D. Rules 6 and 9.

[7] *See* Sturgeon v. Airborne Freight Corp., 778 F.2d 1154, 1160–61 (5th Cir. 1985).

[8] *See, e.g.,* Scarborough v. Eubanks, 747 F.2d 871, 874–78 (3d Cir. 1984).

[9] *See, e.g.,* Fletcher v. Southern Farm Bureau Life Ins. Co., 757 F.2d 953, 956 (8th Cir. 1985); Corchado v. Puerto Rico Marine Mgmt., Inc., 665 F.2d 410, 413 (1st Cir. 1981), *cert. denied,* 459 U.S. 826 (1982).

[10] Societe Internationale v. Rogers, 357 U.S. 197, 206–07 (1958).

both rules when the plaintiff is guilty of both dilatory discovery conduct and violating court orders. Courts appear to treat failures to prosecute interchangeably with failures to comply with court orders.[11]

Although Rule 41(b) provides only for dismissal, courts can and do invoke lesser sanctions, including fines, costs, damages, attorney disciplinary measures, formal reprimands, placing the case at the bottom of the calendar, the temporary suspension of culpable counsel from practice before the court, preclusion of claims or defenses, dismissal unless new counsel is secured, and dismissal without prejudice.[12] In fact, most circuits require the judge to consider or make express findings that less drastic sanctions would not be effective before permitting a Rule 41(b) dismissal.[13] Rule 41(b) dismissals are usually reserved for those cases in which there is a clear record of delay or contumacious conduct.[14] Simple negligence is not thought to warrant dismissal.[15] In general, when deciding Rule 41(b) motions, the district court weighs the court's need to manage its docket, the public interest in expeditious resolution of litigation, and the risk of prejudice to the defendants against the policy favoring disposition of cases on their merits.[16]

Several circuits view the following specific factors as relevant to determining whether a dismissal with prejudice is appropriate:

1. The degree of the plaintiff's personal responsibility for the delay
2. Prejudice to the defendant occasioned by the delay
3. Any history that the plaintiff proceeded in a dilatory manner, and
4. The effectiveness of sanctions other than dismissal.[17]

---

[11] *See* 5 J. Moore *et al.*, Moore's Federal Practice ¶ 41.12, at 41–152 (2d ed. 1986) [hereinafter Moore's Federal Practice].

[12] *See, e.g.*, Sturgeon v. Airborne Freight Corp., 778 F.2d 1154, 1159 (5th Cir. 1985); Titus v. Mercedes Benz of N. Am., 695 F.2d 746, 749 n.6 (3d Cir. 1982); Zavala Santiago v. Gonzalez Rivera, 553 F.2d 710, 712 n.1 (1st Cir. 1977).

[13] *See* Shea v. Donohoe Constr. Co., 795 F.2d 1071, 1072 (D.C. Cir. 1986); Webber v. Eye Corp., 721 F.2d 1067, 1070 (7th Cir. 1983); Harding v. Federal Reserve Bank of New York, 707 F.2d 46, 50 (2d Cir. 1983); Titus v. Mercedes Benz of N. Am., 695 F.2d 746, 747–48 (3d Cir. 1982); Raiford v. Pounds, 640 F.2d 944, 945 (9th Cir. 1981) (per curiam).

[14] *See, e.g.*, Jackson v. Schoemehl, 788 F.2d 1296, 1299 (8th Cir. 1986); Judkins v. Beech Aircraft Corp., 723 F.2d 818, 819–20 (11th Cir. 1984); Webber v. Eye Corp., 721 F.2d 1067, 1069 (7th Cir. 1983); Madesky v. Campbell, 705 F.2d 703, 704 (3d Cir. 1983); Gonzales v. Firestone Tire & Rubber Co., 610 F.2d 241, 247 (5th Cir. 1980).

[15] McKelvey v. AT&T Technologies, Inc., 789 F.2d 1518, 1520 (11th Cir. 1986).

[16] Mir v. Fosburg, 706 F.2d 916, 918 (9th Cir. 1983); *see* Lyell Theatre Corp. v. Loews Corp., 682 F.2d 37, 43 (2d Cir. 1982).

[17] Donnelly v. Johns-Mansville Sales Corp., 677 F.2d 339, 342 (3d Cir. 1982); Morris v. Ocean Sys., Inc., 730 F.2d 248, 252 (5th Cir. 1984); Davis v. Williams, 588 F.2d 69, 70 (4th Cir. 1978); *see* Romandette v. Weetabix Co., 807 F.2d 309, 312 (2d Cir. 1986); Ash v. Cvetkov, 739 F.2d 493, 496 (9th Cir. 1984), *cert. denied,* 470 U.S. 1007 (1985).

A court may also consider whether the plaintiff had received notice that further delays would result in dismissal.[18] Irreparable harm to the adverse party is probably the most important factor considered.[19] These criteria should be kept in mind when structuring motions and responses even in those circuits not requiring their mandatory consideration. Counsel should be aware that Rule 41(b) motions which are brought well after the offending conduct are not likely to be granted.[20] It is also rare that the court's refusal to dismiss an action for failure to prosecute will be an abuse of discretion.[21]

§ 30.4 Evaluating Delay

A single failure to attend a pretrial hearing or otherwise prosecute or comply with the court's order is usually not considered sufficient to warrant a dismissal.[22] However, a court can rely on all circumstances in the case, including earlier delays, in justifying its dismissal.[23] Therefore, a pattern of intentional delay is sufficiently egregious conduct to support a dismissal.[24] Although there is no magic age beyond which dismissal is justified, the younger the case, the more likely an appellate court will reverse a dismissal.[25] However, even an action which is pending only for one year can warrant dismissal when it has been neglected by counsel and court orders are ignored.[26] The length of delay may be an indication that prejudice has occurred, but it is not clear whether delay alone justifies dismissal.[27] In a few circuits, prejudice cannot be presumed or

---

18 *See* Hamilton v. Neptune Orient Lines, Ltd., 811 F.2d 498, 500 (9th Cir. 1987); Cohen v. Carnival Cruise Lines, Inc., 782 F.2d 923, 925–26 (11th Cir. 1986); Harding v. Federal Reserve Bank of New York, 707 F.2d 46, 50 (2d Cir. 1983).

19 *See, e.g.,* Raiford v. Pounds, 640 F.2d 944, 945 (9th Cir. 1981) (per curiam).

20 *See, e.g.,* Stock Pot Restaurant, Inc. v. Stockpot, Inc., 737 F.2d 1576, 1581 (Fed. Cir. 1984).

21 *See, e.g.,* United States v. Berney, 713 F.2d 568, 571 (10th Cir. 1983).

22 Trakas v. Quality Brands, Inc., 759 F.2d 185, 188 (D.C. Cir. 1985); *see* Pardee v. Stock, 712 F.2d 1290, 1292 (8th Cir. 1983).

23 Link v. Wabash R.R., 370 U.S. 626, 634–35 (1962); Jones v. Graham, 709 F.2d 1457, 1462 (11th Cir. 1983); Harding v. Federal Reserve Bank of New York, 707 F.2d 46, 50 (2d Cir. 1983); *see* Stevens v. Greyhound Lines, Inc., 710 F.2d 1224, 1230 (7th Cir. 1983).

24 Garrison v. International Paper Co., 714 F.2d 757, 760 (8th Cir. 1983); *see* Link v. Wabash R.R., 370 U.S. 626, 633 (1962); Lyell Theatre Corp. v. Loews Corp., 682 F.2d 37, 43 (2d Cir. 1982).

25 *See* Shea v. Donohoe Constr. Co., 795 F.2d 1071, 1072 (D.C. Cir. 1986); Batson v. Neal Spelce Assocs., Inc., 765 F.2d 511, 516 n.2 (5th Cir. 1985); Webber v. Eye Corp., 721 F.2d 1067, 1070 (7th Cir. 1983); Harding v. Federal Reserve Bank of New York, 707 F.2d 46, 50 (2d Cir. 1983); Titus v. Mercedes Benz of N. Am., 695 F.2d 746, 749 (3d Cir. 1982); Raiford v. Pounds, 640 F.2d 944, 945 (9th Cir. 1981) (per curiam).

26 *See* Chira v. Lockheed Aircraft Corp., 634 F.2d 664, 665–66 (2d Cir. 1980).

27 *See* Mir v. Fosburg, 706 F.2d 916, 919 n.2 (9th Cir. 1983).

established by conclusory allegations,[28] while in other circuits, unreasonable delay spanning several years appears to entitle a court to presume prejudice.[29] If a plaintiff comes forth with a nonfrivolous excuse for the delay, the burden of production shifts to the defendant to show at least some actual prejudice.[30] The plaintiff must then persuade the court that such prejudice is either illusory or relatively insignificant when compared to the reason for the delay.[31]

Local rules should always be consulted, because it is common for such rules to obligate plaintiffs to take affirmative action to bring the case to trial and authorize dismissal for inactivity. Often such rules can reverse the normal presumption that a dismissal is with prejudice and authorize dismissals without prejudice in the absence of a court directive to the contrary. In the absence of local rules, a plaintiff is not obligated to notify the court of its readiness or procure a trial date after the completion of discovery.[32] When faced with delay in the absence of a local rule, defense counsel can request or the judge can sua sponte impose a discovery and trial schedule, the violation of which can result in dismissal.[33]

§ 30.5 Rule 41(b) Oddities

Unlike Rule 37, which does not permit a dismissal for failure to pay monetary sanctions unrelated to the merits, a dismissal for failure to prosecute or comply with court orders may be upheld when a plaintiff who was able to pay court-ordered sanctions failed to do so.[34] Similarly, a dismissal without prejudice may be turned into a dismissal with prejudice if a party fails to follow a court's directive. For example, when a dismissal is granted without prejudice to filing an amended complaint, the court can dismiss with prejudice under Rule 41(b) if no amendment is served.[35] The Ninth Circuit has cautioned that a plaintiff who takes a dismissal with prejudice under Rule 41(b) to challenge the denial of a

---

[28] *See, e.g.*, Tamini v. M/V Jewon, 808 F.2d 1978, 981 (2d Cir. 1987).

[29] Shea v. Donohoe Constr. Co., 795 F.2d 1071, 1075–77 (D.C. Cir. 1986); 9 C. Wright & A. Miller, Federal Practice and Procedure § 2370, at 216 (1971) [hereinafter Federal Practice and Procedure]; *see* Washington v. Walker, 734 F.2d 1237, 1240 (7th Cir. 1984); Garrison v. International Paper Co., 714 F.2d 757, 760 (8th Cir. 1983).

[30] Nealey v. Transportacion Maritima Mexicana, S.A., 662 F.2d 1275, 1281 (9th Cir. 1980).

[31] *Id.*

[32] *See* Ace Novelty Co. v. Gooding Amusement Co., 664 F.2d 761, 763 (9th Cir. 1981).

[33] *See* Rules 16(b) and 26(f); *see also* Mir v. Fosburg, 706 F.2d 916, 919 (9th Cir. 1983).

[34] *See* Hornbuckle v. Arco Oil & Gas Co., 770 F.2d 1321, 1322 (5th Cir. 1985), *cert. denied,* ____ U.S. ____, 106 S. Ct. 1198 (1986); Gibbs v. Maxwell House, 738 F.2d 1153, 1154–55 (11th Cir. 1984).

[35] *See* Toyota Landscape Co. v. Building Material & Dump Truck Drivers Local 420, 726 F.2d 525, 528 (9th Cir.), *cert. denied,* 469 U.S. 825 (1984).

dismissal without prejudice under Rule 41(a)(2) proceeds at its peril.[36] Failure to comply with Rule 8 to set forth a short, clear, concise statement of a claim can also support a Rule 41(b) dismissal.[37]

Although the complaints of pro se litigants can be dismissed for failure to prosecute,[38] dismissals of pro se litigants who are incarcerated for failure to appear have been reversed.[39] Similarly, a delay in paying a filing fee after being denied in forma pauperis status did not justify dismissal.[40] However, the Sixth Circuit has permitted dismissal of an indigent plaintiff's complaint when the failure to produce witnesses resulted from lack of funds to pay attendance fees.[41] In some circuits the failure of the district judge to warn a pro se litigant of the consequences of neglect may result in a reversal of a dismissal for failure to prosecute.[42]

§ 30.6 Misconduct of Counsel

Many dismissals for failure to prosecute turn on the conduct of counsel. In *Link v. Wabash Railroad Co.*,[43] the Supreme Court made clear that a plaintiff cannot avoid dismissal by disclaiming counsel's unexcused conduct, because the party voluntarily chose counsel and cannot avoid the consequences of counsel's acts or omissions.[44] Most circuits temper this language by requiring that the client knew of or participated in the attorney's failure to prosecute as a prerequisite to dismissal,[45] unless no other sanction would cure the harm caused to the defendant.[46] For example, the D.C. Circuit has held that an attorney's failure to

---

[36] Kern Oil & Ref. Co. v. Tenneco Oil Co., 792 F.2d 1380, 1389 (9th Cir. 1986).

[37] Nevijel v. North Coast Life Ins. Co., 651 F.2d 671, 673 (9th Cir. 1981).

[38] *See, e.g.*, Bomate v. Ford Motor Co., 761 F.2d 713, 714 (D.C. Cir. 1985) (with prejudice) Stevens v. Greyhound Lines, Inc., 710 F.2d 1224, 1230 (7th Cir. 1983) (with prejudice); Schooley v. Kennedy, 712 F.2d 372, 373–74 (11th Cir. 1983) (without prejudice).

[39] Reynolds v. Foree, 771 F.2d 1179, 1181 (8th Cir. 1985); Sisk v. United States, 756 F.2d 497, 499–500 (7th Cir. 1985); Holt v. Pitts, 619 F.2d 558, 562 (6th Cir. 1980); *cf.* Romandette v. Weetabix Co., 807 F.2d 309, 312 (2d Cir. 1986) (41(b) dismissal reversed when failure of incarcerated plaintiff to serve complaint was because of delay by marshal).

[40] Rodgers v. Bowen, 790 F.2d 1550, 1553 (11th Cir. 1986).

[41] Johnson v. Hubbard, 698 F.2d 286, 291 (6th Cir.), *cert. denied,* 464 U.S. 917 (1983).

[42] *See, e.g.*, Schilling v. Walworth County Parks & Planning Comm'n, 805 F.2d 272, 277–78 (7th Cir. 1986).

[43] 370 U.S. 626 (1962).

[44] *Id.* at 633–34.

[45] *See, e.g.*, Carter v. Albert Einstein Medical Center, 804 F.2d 805, 807 (3d Cir. 1986); Shea v. Donohoe Constr. Co., 795 F.2d 1071, 1077–78 (D.C. Cir. 1986); Taylor v. Combustion Eng'g, Inc., 782 F.2d 525, 528 (5th Cir. 1986). *But see* Corchado v. Puerto Rico Marine Mgmt., Inc., 665 F.2d 410, 413 (1st Cir. 1981), *cert. denied,* 459 U.S. 826 (1982).

[46] Goforth v. Owens, 766 F.2d 1533, 1535 (11th Cir. 1985); *see* Shea v. Donohoe Constr. Co., 795 F.2d 1071, 1077–78 (D.C. Cir. 1986).

attend three separate status calls was not sufficient to justify dismissal, but only a sanction directed against the attorney, unless the plaintiff had been previously notified that any recurrence of the attorney's misconduct would result in dismissal.[47] Similarly, when the plaintiff was blameless, dismissals have been reversed, even though counsel's efforts were wholly insufficient.[48] Courts have suggested that the offending attorney be required to pay costs and expenses or face attorney disciplinary proceedings in lieu of dismissing a plaintiff who lacked culpability.[49] On the other hand, it was not an abuse of discretion to refuse to reinstate the action of an initially blameless plaintiff who waited several months after learning of the dismissal to request reconsideration.[50]

§ 30.7 Opportunity to Respond to a Rule 41(b) Dismissal

The Supreme Court specifically held that the absence of notice and an adversary hearing did not render a Rule 41(b) dismissal void,[51] because a party's knowledge of the circumstances surrounding the dilatory conduct may be taken to show notice of the consequences of the party's misconduct. Therefore, counsel cannot be assured of obtaining notice and a hearing prior to dismissal.[52]

If it is unclear whether the dismissal was with prejudice, a motion for clarification or in the alternate to vacate judgment should be brought.[53] If the action is dismissed with prejudice or after the statute of limitations has run, the plaintiff should always bring a Rule 60(b) motion to reopen the case in order to establish whatever justification exists for the dilatory or contumacious conduct. Failure to do so is often considered as a factor weighing against reversal, because the court can assume that the offending behavior was deliberate rather than negligent in the absence of adequate explanations given in a Rule 60(b) motion.[54] Because the Rule 60(b) motion does not extend the time to appeal, counsel must be careful to appeal from the underlying dismissal as well as the denial to reopen, as a Rule 60(b) motion does not permit the review of the

---

47 Shea v. Donohoe Constr. Co., 795 F.2d 1071, 1078–79 (D.C. Cir. 1986).

48 *See* Haley v. Kansas City Star, 761 F.2d 489, 491 (8th Cir. 1985); Carter v. City of Memphis, 636 F.2d 159, 161 (6th Cir. 1980).

49 *See* Shea v. Donohoe Constr. Co., 795 F.2d 1071, 1077–78 (D.C. Cir. 1986); Hollis v. United States, 744 F.2d 1430, 1433 (10th Cir. 1984); Webber v. Eye Corp., 721 F.2d 1067, 1069 n.2 (7th Cir. 1983).

50 Kagan v. Caterpillar Tractor Co., 795 F.2d 601, 611–12 (7th Cir. 1986).

51 Link v. Wabash R.R., 370 U.S. 626, 632 (1962).

52 *See, e.g.*, Price v. McGlathery, 792 F.2d 472, 475 (5th Cir. 1986) (per curiam); Colokathis v. Wentworth-Douglass Hosp., 693 F.2d 7, 10 (1st Cir. 1982), *cert. denied*, 461 U.S. 915 (1983).

53 *See, e.g.*, *In re* Jee, 799 F.2d 532, 534 (9th Cir. 1986).

54 *See, e.g.*, Link v. Wabash R.R., 370 U.S. 626, 632, 635–36 (1962); Price v. McGlathery, 792 F.2d 472, 476 (5th Cir. 1986) (per curiam).

underlying judgment, even if it was erroneous.[55] If a timely appeal was not filed, counsel should request the appellate court to treat a Rule 60(b) motion made within 10 days of judgment as a Rule 59(e) motion to alter judgment, because the denial of that motion would permit an otherwise untimely appeal of the underlying dismissal.[56]

§ 30.8 Sanctions Pursuant to the Court's Inherent Powers

Inherent powers are those which are necessary to the exercise of all others.[57] Since they are shielded from direct democratic controls, inherent powers are required to be exercised with restraint and discretion.[58] Although the court has inherent power to enter appropriate orders to facilitate the deposition of court business,[59] the entry of such orders must comport with due process.[60] The court has inherent power to sanction attorneys as well as parties. As discussed in **Chapter 23,** attorneys' fees can be awarded under the court's inherent power on a finding of bad faith,[61] even if the litigation had a factual and legal basis, because bad faith may be found not only in bringing the litigation but in its conduct.[62] An attorney's failure to file answers by the date ordered by the court can also result in monetary sanctions under the court's inherent power.[63]

§ 30.9 Terminations Pursuant to the Court's Inherent Powers

Courts can terminate cases under their inherent powers. Although Rule 41(b) provides for dismissal only upon motion of a defendant, the court has inherent power to dismiss an action sua sponte for the plaintiff's failure to prosecute or obey court orders[64] and frequently uses this power. This authority is vested in courts so that judges can manage their own affairs to achieve the orderly and

[55] Carter by Carter v. United States, 780 F.2d 925, 927–28 (11th Cir. 1986); *see* Kagan v. Caterpillar Tractor Co., 795 F.2d 601, 606–07 (7th Cir. 1986).

[56] *See, e.g.*, Jackson v. Schoemehl, 788 F.2d 1296, 1297–99 (8th Cir. 1986); Lyell Theatre Corp. v. Loews Corp., 682 F.2d 37, 41 (2d Cir. 1982).

[57] Roadway Express, Inc. v. Piper, 447 U.S. 752, 764 (1980).

[58] *Id.*

[59] Holcomb v. Allis-Chalmers Corp., 774 F.2d 398, 401–02 (10th Cir. 1985).

[60] *Id.* at 402.

[61] *See* Roadway Express, Inc. v. Piper, 447 U.S. 752, 766–67 (1980); §§ 28.7–28.11.

[62] *Id.*; Hall v. Cole, 412 U.S. 1, 15 (1973); Lipsig v. National Student Marketing Corp., 663 F.2d 178, 182 (D.C. Cir. 1980).

[63] *In re* Howe, 800 F.2d 1251, 1252–53 (4th Cir. 1986).

[64] Link v. Wabash R.R., 370 U.S. 626, 630–31 (1962).

expeditious disposition of cases.[65] Such power is considered necessary in order to prevent undue delays in the disposition of pending cases and to avoid congestion in the court's calendar.[66] The same standards apply to Rule 41(b) motions and dismissals under the court's inherent powers for failure to prosecute or comply with court orders.[67] The 1983 revisions to the federal rules codified some of the court's inherent authority in Rule 16(f).[68]

The court also has inherent power to dismiss an action if a party has willfully deceived the court and engaged in conduct utterly inconsistent with the orderly administration of justice.[69] Such dismissals are imposed only in extreme circumstances in which the deceptive conduct is willful or in bad faith or relates to the matters in controversy in such a way as to interfere with the rightful decision of the case.[70] Similarly, a default was proper to vindicate the integrity of court proceedings when the defendants purposely misled the judge, even though the conduct leading to the default was not technically within Rule 37.[71] On the other hand, a partial default imposed pursuant to the court's inherent powers was reversed when the party's failure to provide information occurred before it was joined as a defendant.[72] When the deceit related to a peripheral matter, a default was also improper.[73]

§ 30.10 Rule 16(f) Sanctions

Rule 16(f) provides that if a party or party's attorney fails to obey a scheduling or pretrial order, fails to appear at a conference, or is unprepared for or does not participate in good faith at a pretrial conference, the judge can apply sanctions as provided in Rule 37(b)(2)(B), (C), and (D) as well as impose attorneys' fees incurred by the noncompliance. Therefore, a full range of discovery sanctions, including dismissal, default, preclusion orders, contempt, and awards of expenses are available for breaches of pretrial practice.[74] Although this rule has not been frequently cited, it has been considered as an alternative reason to justify a

---

65 *Id.*

66 *Id.* at 629–30.

67 *See id.* at 630.

68 See §§ **16.5** and **30.10**.

69 Fjelstad v. American Honda Motor Co., 762 F.2d 1334, 1338 (9th Cir. 1985).

70 United States v. National Medical Enters., Inc., 792 F.2d 906, 912 (9th Cir. 1986).

71 Brockton Sav. Bank v. Peat, Marwick, Mitchell & Co., 771 F.2d 5, 11–12 (1st Cir. 1985), *cert. denied,* ____ U.S. ____, 106 S. Ct. 1204 (1986).

72 Fjelstad v. American Honda Motor Co., 762 F.2d 1334, 1338 (9th Cir. 1985).

73 Phoceene Sous-Marine, S.A. v. U.S. Phosmarine, Inc., 682 F.2d 802, 806 (9th Cir. 1982).

74 Rabb v. Amatex Corp., 769 F.2d 996, 999 (4th Cir. 1985); *see generally* 3 Moore's Federal Practice ¶ 16.22 (2d ed. 1985).

dismissal for failure to prosecute or obey a court order.[75] The rule is intended to encourage forceful judicial management, but the Second Circuit has noted that it "did not loose a strange and capricious new beast."[76] Rule 16(f) is designed to punish lawyers and parties for conduct which unreasonably delays or otherwise interferes with the expeditious management of trial preparation.[77] Therefore, when the misconduct is caused by counsel, sanctions should be directed against that individual rather than the party.[78]

Common pretrial failings which are subject to sanctions under either Rule 41(b) or 16(f) include ignoring discovery deadlines or requirements for disclosure of expert witnesses, not filing or failing to amend pretrial statements, and unexcused absences from pretrial conferences. Rule 16(f) has also been cited as authority to assess a fine on attorneys who have not been held in contempt.[79] The Fifth Circuit has noted that the same criteria developed for evaluating Rule 41(b) dismissals apply to Rule 16(f),[80] while the Second and Fourth Circuits have considered such sanctions as more appropriately falling within Rule 37.[81] As a practical matter, most circuits apply virtually identical criteria to Rule 37 and 41 sanctions.[82] The Ninth Circuit has required notice and an opportunity to be heard before the imposition of Rule 16(f) sanctions,[83] but not all circuits can be expected to follow this procedure.

There appears to be some disagreement as to whether Rule 16(f) sanctions are appropriate if there has been no violation of an explicit order.[84] Rule 16(f) sanctions were not considered appropriate as a means for clubbing the parties into an involuntary settlement by assessing attorneys' fees against a defendant who failed to settle a case prior to trial.[85] The validity of a Rule 16(f) dismissal for failure to file a timely pretrial order depends upon the circumstances of the case and whether the failure is willful as opposed to merely negligent.[86] As with

---

[75] Sherman v. United States, 801 F.2d 1133, 1134–35 (9th Cir. 1986); Goforth v. Owens, 766 F.2d 1533, 1535 (11th Cir. 1985).

[76] Salahuddin v. Harris, 782 F.2d 1127, 1133 (2d Cir. 1986).

[77] *In re* Baker, 744 F.2d 1438, 1441 (10th Cir. 1984) (en banc), *cert. denied,* 471 U.S. 1014 (1985).

[78] Seismic Int'l Research Corp. v. South Ranch Oil Co., 793 F.2d 227, 230 (10th Cir. 1986).

[79] Smith v. Rowe, 761 F.2d 360, 366 (7th Cir. 1985); *In re* Baker, 744 F.2d 1438, 1440 (10th Cir. 1984) (en banc), *cert. denied,* 471 U.S. 1014 (1985).

[80] Price v. McGlathery, 792 F.2d 472, 474 (5th Cir. 1986) (per curiam).

[81] *See* Salahuddin v. Harris, 782 F.2d 1127, 1133 (2d Cir. 1986); Rabb v. Amatex Corp., 769 F.2d 996, 999 (4th Cir. 1985).

[82] See §§ **29.3, 29.5** and **30.3**.

[83] Ford v. Alfaro, 785 F.2d 835, 840 (9th Cir. 1986).

[84] *Compare* Salahuddin v. Harris, 782 F.2d 1127, 1133 (2d Cir. 1986) (no sanctions if order implicit) *with In re* Baker, 744 F.2d 1438, 1440 (10th Cir. 1984) (en banc), *cert. denied,* 471 U.S. 1014 (1985) (not necessary to violate court order).

[85] Kothe v. Smith, 771 F.2d 667, 669 (2d Cir. 1985).

[86] *See* Woodmore v. Git-N-Go, 790 F.2d 1497, 1498–99 (10th Cir. 1986); Ford v.Fogarty Van Lines, Inc., 780 F.2d 1582, 1583 (11th Cir. 1986) (dismissals reversed).

other dismissals, a Rule 60(b) motion should be made to proffer the reasons for the specific pretrial violation.[87]

Often Rule 16(f) is not mentioned at all when dealing with pretrial violations. For example, whether or not to exclude testimony or exhibits proffered in violation of the pretrial order is a frequently litigated issue.[88] Courts established standards to resolve this problem well before the advent of Rule 16(f) and continue to refer to previous case law rather than to Rule 16(f). The most commonly cited test[89] was enunciated in *Meyers v. Pennypack Woods Home Ownership Association,*[90] which considers (1) the prejudice or surprise in fact of the party against whom the excluded witnesses would have testified, (2) the ability of that party to cure the prejudice, (3) the extent to which waiver of the rule against calling unlisted witnesses would disrupt the orderly and efficient trial of the case or of other cases in the court, and (4) bad faith or willfulness in failing to comply with the court's order. These criteria have also been applied in determining whether documents were properly excluded.[91] Other courts weigh essentially the same factors and consider the reasons why the witness was not named, the importance of the witness's testimony, the time needed to prepare for the testimony, and whether a continuance would be useful.[92] The Ninth Circuit presumed that failure to give notice of an expert's testimony until immediately before trial was clearly prejudicial when earlier disclosure was required by the local rules and no justification for noncompliance was offered.[93] As with other discovery rulings, such orders are reviewed for abuse of discretion.[94]

---

[87] Price v. McGlathery, 792 F.2d 472, 476 (5th Cir. 1986) (per curiam); *see* §§ **14.70** and **29.10**.

[88] See §§ **16.4, 20.15**.

[89] *See, e.g.*, Kickapoo Oil Co. Co. v. Clark Oil & Ref. Corp., 788 F.2d 11, 17–18 (Temp. Emer. Ct. App. 1985); United States v. Koziy, 728 F.2d 1314, 1320–21 (11th Cir.), *cert. denied,* 469 U.S. 835 (1984); Smith v. Ford Motor Co., 626 F.2d 784, 797 (10th Cir. 1980), *cert. denied,* 450 U.S. 918 (1981).

[90] 559 F.2d 894, 904–05 (3d Cir. 1977).

[91] Smith v. Rowe, 761 F.2d 360, 365 (7th Cir. 1985).

[92] *See* Patterson v. F.W. Woolworth Co., 786 F.2d 874, 879 (8th Cir. 1986); Murphy v. Magnolia Elec. Power Ass'n, 639 F.2d 232, 235 (5th Cir. 1981); 8 Federal Practice and Procedure § 2050, at 327.

[93] Sealy, Inc. v. Easy Living, Inc., 743 F.2d 1378, 1382–83 (9th Cir. 1984).

[94] *See, e.g.*, Perry v. Winspur, 782 F.2d 893, 895 (10th Cir. 1986); Young v. City of New Orleans, 751 F.2d 794, 797 (5th Cir. 1985).

CHAPTER 31

CONTEMPT AND OTHER SANCTIONS

§ 31.1 Introduction

In addition to the frequently imposed sanctions under Rules 37 and 41, courts have the power to adjudicate litigants in contempt for abusive pretrial practices as well as to issue fines for violations of local rules.

§ 31.2 Distinguishing Civil and Criminal Contempt

There are several sources for applying contempt as a sanction, including the court's inherent power, 18 U.S.C. § 401, Federal Rules of Civil Procedure 37 and 41, and Federal Rule of Criminal Procedure 42. As a practical matter, many courts appear to require that criminal contempts brought as sanctions for abuse of discovery or pretrial orders follow the requirements established under 18 U.S.C. § 401 and Federal Rule of Criminal Procedure 42. For example, the Ninth Circuit has noted that there is nothing to indicate that Rule 37 has changed the law relative to civil and criminal contempt or traditional concepts of the due process limitations on the exercise of contempt power.[1]

It is important to distinguish civil and criminal contempt, because the procedural requirements and standards vary depending upon the type of contempt involved. However, it is often difficult to determine whether a contempt proceeding is criminal or civil in nature, because the same facts can give rise to both types of contempt.[2] For example, when an attorney was ordered to pay a remedial fine for failing to appear and misrepresenting his whereabouts to the court, the contempt was considered civil rather than criminal.[3] The focus in determining the nature of the contempt is not the fact of the punishment but rather its character and purpose.[4]

Criminal contempt vindicates the authority of the court and places great reliance upon the discretion of the trial judge.[5] Civil contempt attempts to coerce the defendant into compliance with the court's order and compensates the complainant for its losses.[6] Therefore, some courts view the discretion of the trial judge as more limited in civil contempt, because the rights of the complainant, not the authority of the court are at stake.[7] Imprisonment and monetary fines are available in both types of contempt proceedings.[8] However, if a money fine is not compensatory or conditioned on the occurrence of future violation of court orders, it raises a presumption that the fine is punitive in nature.[9] Usually a criminal fine is paid to the court, while a civil fine can be paid to the aggrieved party.

When a judgment contains a mixture of criminal and civil elements, the criminal aspect of the order fixes its character for purposes of procedures on review.[10] The imposition of civil contempt does not preclude later criminal contempt sanctions based on the same conduct under either the double jeopardy clause[11] or the res judicata doctrine.[12] Similarly, collateral estoppel does not bar the second action if the defendant did not prevail on the relevant issues in the first prosecution.[13]

---

[1] Falstaff Brewing Corp. v. Miller Brewing Co., 702 F.2d 770, 783 (9th Cir. 1983).

[2] *See* United States v. United Mine Workers of Am., 330 U.S. 258, 298–99 (1947).

[3] *In re* Jaques, 761 F.2d 302, 304–06 (6th Cir. 1985).

[4] Shillitani v. United States, 384 U.S. 364, 369 (1966).

[5] United States v. United Mine Workers of Am., 330 U.S. 258, 302–03 (1947).

[6] *Id.* at 303–04.

[7] *See* Thompson v. Cleland, 782 F.2d 719, 721 (7th Cir. 1986).

[8] *In re* Kave, 760 F.2d 343, 351 (1st Cir. 1985).

[9] *Id.; see* McDonald's Corp. v. Victory Invs., 727 F.2d 82, 87 (3d Cir. 1984).

[10] Falstaff Brewing Corp. v. Miller Brewing Co., 702 F.2d 770, 778 (9th Cir. 1983).

[11] *See* Yates v. United States, 355 U.S. 66, 74 (1957); United States v. Monteleone, 804 F.2d 1004, 1008–09 (7th Cir. 1986).

[12] United States v. Ryan, 810 F.2d 650, 654 (7th Cir. 1987).

[13] *Id.* at 654–55.

§ 31.3 Civil Contempt

Civil contempt occurs when a party fails to comply with a court order.[14] Sanctions for civil contempt are considered wholly remedial and aimed at coercing compliance with a court order or compensating the injured party for the results of the contemptuous behavior or both.[15] Civil contempt issues usually concern refusals to testify, disobedience of injunctions, and refusals to produce documents to the grand jury or in IRS enforcement actions. Failure to obey a protective order can also result in a civil contempt citation. In a discovery setting, any refusal to produce existing documents can be treated as civil contempt, but courts usually do not use this procedure, favoring Rule 37 sanctions which affect the merits of the action. Similarly, although the only remedy against nonparties for noncompliance of subpoenas duces tecum is contempt, judges usually resort to criminal rather than civil proceedings.

§ 31.4 Procedures for Invoking Civil Contempt

Civil contempt is a civil action governed by the Federal Rules of Civil Procedure,[16] including the pleading requirements of Rule 8.[17] Therefore, if a defendant in a civil contempt proceeding fails to file a responsive pleading admitting or denying the accusation, a district court could ordinarily deem the opponent's averments as admitted.[18] A court can also require that affidavits on file be controverted by counteraffidavits and treat uncontroverted affidavits as containing true facts.[19] If the defendant responds by invoking the Fifth Amendment privilege, this is considered the equivalent of a specific denial which requires the plaintiff to provide proof of its claims.[20] Privilege should be raised in a formal answer or response to ensure that the court will not find a technical waiver.[21] If a Fifth Amendment claim is denied, the defendant is given an opportunity to reconsider its response before being penalized for a refusal to

---

[14] General Signal Corp. v. Donallco, Inc., 787 F.2d 1376, 1379 (9th Cir. 1986).

[15] United States v. United Mine Workers of Am., 330 U.S. 258, 303–04 (1947); *see generally* 11 C. Wright & A. Miller, Federal Practice and Procedure § 2960 (1973) [hereinafter Federal Practice and Procedure].

[16] Rogers v. Webster, 776 F.2d 607, 610 (6th Cir. 1985); 3 Federal Practice and Procedure § 705.

[17] Rogers v. Webster, 776, F.2d 607, 610 (6th Cir. 1985); Shakman v. Democratic Org. of Cook County, 533 F.2d 344, 352 (7th Cir.), *cert. denied,* 429 U.S. 858 (1976).

[18] Rogers v. Webster, 776 F.2d 607, 611 (6th Cir. 1985).

[19] *Id.;* Hoffman v. Beer Drivers & Salesmen's Local Union No. 888, 536 F.2d 1268, 1277 (9th Cir. 1976).

[20] Rogers v. Webster, 776 F.2d 607, 611 (6th Cir. 1985); *see* National Acceptance Co. of Am. v. Bathalter, 705 F.2d 924, 926, 932 (7th Cir. 1983); see §§ **7.6** and **18.19.**

[21] *See* Rogers v. Webster, 776 F.2d 607, 611 n.4 (6th Cir. 1985).

answer.[22] Therefore, refusing to accept the defendant's affidavits as untimely and prohibiting him from testifying because of his earlier invocation of the Fifth Amendment privilege was reversible error, even though the defendant admitted the alleged misconduct,[23] because the defendant was entitled to offer matter in explanation of his conduct or in mitigation of any coercive punishment.[24]

It is unclear whether willfulness is an element of civil contempt.[25] However, the contemnor's state of mind, such as good faith or reliance on the advice of counsel, is always considered relevant to mitigation of any penalty. Compensatory awards are limited to actual losses sustained as a result of the contumacy.[26] If the fine is coercive, it will be paid to the court rather than the opposing party.[27] Coercive sanctions consider the character and magnitude of the harm threatened by the continued contumacy and the probable effectiveness of any suggested sanction.[28]

In civil contempt proceedings, the plaintiff has the burden of establishing that the defendant disobeyed the orders of the district court. If compensation is sought, similar to tort action, the complainant must prove that the defendant's actions in violation of the court order caused the injury.[29] Clear and convincing evidence, rather than proof beyond a reasonable doubt, is required for such violations.[30] No right to a jury exists in civil contempt cases.[31] However, a trend exists to afford the same or similar procedural safeguards to persons charged with civil contempt as to those charged with criminal contempt.[32] The extent of any required hearing varies with the nature of the contempt.[33]

---

[22] Garner v. United States, 424 U.S. 648, 663 (1976).

[23] Rogers v. Webster, 776 F.2d 607, 612 (6th Cir. 1985).

[24] *Id.; cf.* Groppi v. Leslie, 404 U.S. 496, 502–03 (1972).

[25] *Compare* SEC v. Ormont Drug & Chem. Co., 739 F.2d 654, 656 (D.C. Cir. 1984), Shuffler v. Heritage Bank, 720 F.2d 1141, 1146 (9th Cir. 1983) (willful) *with* Rogers v. Webster, 776 F.2d 607, 612 (6th Cir. 1985) *and* 3 Federal Practice and Procedure § 705 (willfulness not necessary).

[26] Shuffler v. Heritage Bank, 720 F.2d 1141, 1148 (9th Cir. 1983); *see* United States v. United Mine Workers of Am., 330 U.S. 258, 304 (1947).

[27] General Signal Corp. v. Donallco, Inc., 787 F.2d 1376, 1380 (9th Cir. 1986); *In re* Winner Corp., 511 F.2d 1010, 1015 (6th Cir. 1975).

[28] United States v. United Mine Workers of Am., 330 U.S. 258, 304 (1947).

[29] Thompson v. Cleland, 782 F.2d 719, 722 (7th Cir. 1986); Vuitton et Fils, S.A. v. Carousel Handbags, 592 F.2d 126, 130 (2d Cir. 1979).

[30] Hayden v. Oak Terrace Apartments, 808 F.2d 1269, 1270 (7th Cir. 1987); Neely v. City of Grenada, 799 F.2d 203, 207 (5th Cir. 1986); *In re* Kitchen, 706 F.2d 1266, 1271 (2d Cir. 1983); *see* Rogers v. Webster, 776 F.2d 607, 612 n.6 (6th Cir. 1985); 3 Federal Practice and Procedure § 705.

[31] *In re* Kitchen, 706 F.2d 1266, 1271 (2d Cir. 1983).

[32] *In re* Rosahn, 671 F.2d 690, 697 (2d Cir. 1982); *see In re* Grand Jury Proceedings, 795 F.2d 226, 234 (1st Cir. 1986), *cert. denied,* ____ U.S. ____, 107 S. Ct. 950 (1987).

[33] *See In re* Grand Jury Proceedings, 795 F.2d 226, 234 (1st Cir. 1986), *cert. denied,* ____ U.S. ____, 107 S. Ct. 950 (1987).

§ 31.5 Defense to Civil Contempt

Present inability to comply is a complete defense to civil contempt.[34] Substantial compliance is also a defense if the violating party has taken all reasonable steps to comply with the court order.[35] The defendant has the burden to produce evidence supporting such defenses.[36] For example, if the defendant shows that the documents do not exist or are not in that person's custody or control, contempt is unavailable. Similarly, financial inability to comply with an order is a complete defense to civil contempt.[37] The mere existence of a foreign law blocking access to documents located in another country is usually not sufficient to excuse noncompliance with a court order.[38]

A previous finding of ability to comply is not res judicata, because only present inability is required to avoid civil contempt.[39] However, if a court finds that a defendant could have previously complied with a court order it presumes a present ability to comply which imposes a burden of producing contrary evidence on the defendant.[40] Once this burden of production is met, the burden of persuasion shifts back to the party seeking contempt.[41] The defendant's invocation of the Fifth Amendment is not a substitute for relevant evidence meeting the defendant's burden of producing evidence in support of a defense.[42]

When the underlying order is held invalid, such as the imposition of fees on attorneys whose conduct did not fall within Rule 37 or 18 U.S.C. § 1927, the civil contempt adjudication must fail.[43] However, a party cannot raise defenses to the underlying order in the contempt proceeding if they were not previously raised to challenge the validity of the original order.[44]

---

[34] *See* United States v. Rylander, 460 U.S. 752, 757 (1983); Shillitani v. United States, 384 U.S. 364, 371 (1966); Maggio v. Zeitz, 333 U.S. 56, 59, 69 (1948).

[35] General Signal Corp. v. Donallco, Inc., 787 F.2d 1376, 1379 (9th Cir. 1986).

[36] United States v. Rylander, 460 U.S. 752, 757 (1983).

[37] Badgley v. Santa Croce, 800 F.2d 33, 37 (2d Cir. 1986); SEC v. Ormont Drug & Chem. Co., 739 F.2d 654, 657 (D.C. Cir. 1984).

[38] *See, e.g., In re* Grand Jury Proceedings Bank of Nova Scotia, 740 F.2d 817, 832 (11th Cir. 1984), *cert. denied,* 469 U.S. 1106 (1985); *In re* Marc Rich & Co., 736 F.2d 864, 866 (2d Cir. 1984); § **22.2**.

[39] United States v. Rylander, 460 U.S. 752, 757 (1983).

[40] *Id.;* United States *ex rel.* Thom v. Jenkins, 760 F.2d 736, 739–40 (7th Cir. 1985).

[41] United States *ex rel.* Thom v. Jenkins, 760 F.2d 736, 740 (7th Cir. 1985).

[42] United States v. Rylander, 460 U.S. 752, 761 (1983).

[43] *In re* Air Crash Disaster Near Saigon, 671 F.2d 564, 568 (D.C. Cir. 1982); *see* United States v. United Mine Workers of Am., 330 U.S. 258, 294–95 (1947).

[44] United States v. Rylander, 460 U.S. 752, 757 (1983).

§ 31.6 Review of Civil Contempt Orders

Both the determination of contempt and the sanctions imposed are reviewed for abuse of discretion,[45] although factual decisions are reviewed on a clearly erroneous standard.[46] Counsel should always request clarification of the ruling if its basis is not apparent, because several circuits will remand for an entry of a statement of the purpose and basis of the sanction to aid appellate review.[47]

An order adjudging a party in civil contempt is not an appealable final order.[48] However, in many cases, appeal is proper, because the civil contempt proceeding is the sole action before the court.[49] Even if the contempt is appealable, some circuits prohibit review until sanctions have been imposed.[50] For example, if a party can purge the contempt by complying with the order it is considered interlocutory, whereas if the fine or penalty cannot be avoided the order is immediately appealable.[51] A judgment of civil contempt entered against a nonparty is appealable as a final judgment.[52] Paying an ordered fine ends the civil contempt aspect of a case or controversy for appeal,[53] unless the court has permitted a motion for refund to be entertained.[54]

§ 31.7 Criminal Contempt

Criminal contempt is punitive and is imposed for conduct which affronts the honor and dignity of the court. Criminal contempt citations for discovery and pretrial abuses are uncommon, because of the formalities surrounding their

---

[45] Gifford v. Heckler, 741 F.2d 263, 266 (9th Cir. 1984).

[46] Anderson v. City of Bessemer City, 470 U.S. 564, 573 (1985); United States v. Seetapun, 750 F.2d 601, 604 n.4 (7th Cir. 1984).

[47] *See, e.g.*, Shuffler v. Heritage Bank, 720 F.2d 1141, 1147 (9th Cir. 1983); Perfect Fit Indus., Inc. v. Acme Quilting Co., 646 F.2d 800, 810 (2d Cir. 1981), *cert. denied,* 459 U.S. 832 (1982).

[48] Fox v. Capital Co., 299 U.S. 105, 107 (1936). *But see* N.Y. State Urban Dev. Corp. v. VSL Corp., 738 F.2d 61, 64–65 (2d Cir. 1984) (finding limited exception to rule).

[49] *See, e.g.*, Shuffler v. Heritage Bank, 720 F.2d 1141, 1145 (9th Cir. 1983).

[50] Motorola, Inc. v. Computer Displays Int'l, Inc., 739 F.2d 1149, 1154 (7th Cir. 1984); Donovan v. Mazzola, 761 F.2d 1411, 1417 (9th Cir. 1985); *see* United States Steel Corp. v. Fraternal Ass'n of Steel Haulers, 601 F.2d 1269, 1273 (3d Cir. 1979).

[51] Combs v. Ryan's Coal Co., 785 F.2d 970, 976 (11th Cir.), *cert. denied,* ____ U.S. ____, 107 S. Ct. 187 (1986).

[52] New York Times Co. v. Jascalevich, 439 U.S. 1317, 1319 (1978) (White, J., in chambers); Lamb v. Cramer, 285 U.S. 217, 221 (1932); United States v. Johnson, 736 F.2d 358, 359 n.1 (6th Cir. 1984).

[53] McDonald's Corp. v. Victory Invs., 727 F.2d 82, 85–86 (3d Cir. 1984); *In re* Cordova Gonzalez, 726 F.2d 16, 21 (1st Cir.), *cert. denied,* 466 U.S. 951 (1984); *In re* Campbell, 628 F.2d 1260, 1261 (9th Cir. 1980).

[54] *See* Falstaff Brewing Corp. v. Miller Brewing Co., 702 F.2d 770, 777 (9th Cir. 1983).

imposition and the reluctance of judges to hold attorneys in contempt. Moreover, some courts will not impose a contempt sanction for conduct not punishable under the judge's inherent powers.[55]

Criminal contempt can occur in a variety of pretrial situations, because any willful violation of a court order can be considered contemptuous. For example, a lawyer was held in criminal contempt under 18 U.S.C. § 401(3) for failure to comply with an order directing her to submit a written narrative witness statement prior to trial.[56] Dilatory tactics by lawyers who have "sold out to the client" have also been treated as contempt.[57]

§ 31.8 Procedures For Invoking Criminal Contempt

Summary disposition of contempt charges is reserved for exceptional circumstances such as acts threatening the judge, disrupting a hearing, or obstructing court proceedings.[58] Conduct outside the actual presence of the court must follow normal procedures established in Federal Rule of Criminal Procedure 42(b).[59] Summary contempt usually occurs during jury trials when attorneys are questioning witnesses and become embroiled in disputes with the judge,[60] not in pretrial proceedings. Rule 42(a) which provides for summary adjudication, cannot be used to punish an attorney for statements made in a written paper.[61] Similarly, summary adjudication ordinarily cannot be used when an attorney fails to attend a scheduled court appearance.[62] However, when counsel had previously informed the court of the reasons for an intended absence, summary contempt was upheld.[63] A pro se litigant's refusal to proceed with trial also warranted summary contempt.[64]

---

[55] *See* United States v. Stoneberger, 805 F.2d 1391, 1394 (9th Cir. 1986).

[56] Chapman v. Pacific Tel. & Tel. Co., 613 F.2d 193, 194 (9th Cir. 1979).

[57] *E.g.*, Pesaplastic, C.A. v. Cincinnati Milacron Co., 799 F.2d 1510, 1522 (11th Cir. 1986).

[58] Harris v. United States, 382 U.S. 162, 164 (1965).

[59] *Id.* at 164–65.

[60] *See, e.g.*, United States v. Lowery, 733 F.2d 441, 442–44 (7th Cir.), *cert. denied*, 469 U.S. 932 (1984).

[61] *See In re* Jafree, 741 F.2d 133, 136 (7th Cir. 1984); United States v. Lee, 720 F.2d 1049, 1052 (9th Cir. 1983).

[62] United States v. Nunez, 801 F.2d 1260, 1264 (11th Cir. 1986); United States v. Onu, 730 F.2d 253, 255–56 (5th Cir.), *cert. denied*, 469 U.S. 856 (1984); *In re* Allis, 531 F.2d 1391, 1392 (9th Cir.), *cert. denied*, 429 U.S. 900 (1976). *But see In re* Niblack, 476 F.2d 930, 933 (D.C. Cir.), *cert. denied*, 414 U.S. 909 (1973).

[63] United States v. Baldwin, 770 F.2d 1550, 1555–56 (11th Cir. 1985), *cert. denied*, ____ U.S ____, 106 S. Ct. 1636 (1986).

[64] United States v. Brown, 791 F.2d 577, 578 (7th Cir. 1986).

Rule 42(b) provides for notice which allows a reasonable time for the preparation of the defense and states the essential facts constituting the charge as well as the time and place of the hearing. The contemnor is protected by a presumption of innocence[65] and can be convicted only by proof beyond a reasonable doubt.[66] No right exists for a jury trial in a criminal contempt proceeding unless the judge imposes a prison sentence exceeding six months.[67] When the contempt involves disrespect or criticism of a judge so that he becomes personally embroiled in the controversy or when there is likelihood of bias or the appearance of bias, recusal is required.[68] Although a private attorney can be appointed as prosecutor in the contempt action, the Supreme Court recently prohibited counsel for a party that is the beneficiary of a court to prosecute the contempt.[69]

Willfulness is an essential element of criminal contempt[70] and implies a deliberate or intended violation, as distinguished from an accidental, inadvertent, or negligent violation of an order.[71] Conduct which is merely disrespectful is not contemptuous.[72] A good faith belief that the party is complying with the order may also prevent a finding of willfulness.[73] It is unclear whether good faith reliance on the advice of counsel to disobey a court order is a defense to criminal contempt.[74]

18 U.S.C. § 401 authorizes either a fine or imprisonment for criminal contempt, but not both.[75] However, 18 U.S.C. § 3013 provides for specific fines in criminal cases which can be imposed in addition to any other punishment. In determining what sentence to impose in a criminal contempt case, the court

---

[65] *In re* Kave, 760 F.2d 343, 351 (1st Cir. 1985).

[66] Gompers v. Bucks Stove & Range Co., 221 U.S. 418, 444 (1911); Falstaff Brewing Corp. v. Miller Brewing Co., 702 F.2d 770, 778 (9th Cir. 1983).

[67] Bloom v. Illinois, 391 U.S. 194, 210–11 (1968).

[68] Fed. R. Crim. P. 42(b); Taylor v. Hayes, 418 U.S. 488, 501 (1974); Mayberry v. Pennsylvania, 400 U.S. 455, 464–65 (1971).

[69] *See* Young v. United States *ex. rel* Vuitton et Fils S.A., _____ U.S. _____, 107 S. Ct. 2124, 2128, 2130 (1987).

[70] United States v. McCargo, 783 F.2d 507, 510 (5th Cir. 1986); United States v. Armstrong, 781 F.2d 700, 706 (9th Cir. 1986).

[71] Falstaff Brewing Corp. v. Miller Brewing Co., 702 F.2d 770, 782 (9th Cir. 1983), *quoted in* United States v. Baldwin, 770 F.2d 1550, 1558 (11th Cir. 1985), *cert. denied,* _____ U.S. _____, 106 S. Ct. 1636 (1986); *accord* Hubbard v. Fleet Mortgage Co., 810 F.2d 778, 781 (8th Cir. 1987).

[72] Tyler v. City of Milwaukee, 740 F.2d 580, 582 (7th Cir. 1984); *see In re* Little, 404 U.S. 553, 555 (1972) (per curiam).

[73] United States v. Armstrong, 781 F.2d 700, 706 (9th Cir. 1986).

[74] *Compare* United States v. Armstrong, 781 F.2d 700, 706 (9th Cir. 1986) (not a defense) *with* Williamson v. United States, 207 U.S. 425, 453 (1908) (court cited instruction approving the defense).

[75] 18 U.S.C. § 401 (1982); United States v. McCargo, 783 F.2d 507, 510 (5th Cir. 1986).

considers the extent of the willful and deliberate defiance of the court's order, the seriousness of the consequences of the contumacious behavior, the necessity of effectively terminating the defendant's defiance as required by the public interest, and the importance of deterring such acts in the future.[76]

§ 31.9 Reviewing Criminal Contempt Orders

A party can usually appeal a criminal contempt ruling,[77] but an appeal does not necessarily permit review of the validity of the order whose violation led to the contempt.[78] If the underlying order is not appealable and compliance will bring irreparable harm, the individual disobeying the order can raise its invalidity as a defense in a subsequent contempt proceeding.[79] In such cases, if the underlying order is invalidated, the contempt judgment falls with it.[80] However, if the order is appealable, some circuits do not permit its invalidity to be raised as a defense to a contempt proceeding if review of the order was not sought.[81] Similarly, when compliance with the disputed order posed no irreparable harm, its invalidity was not permitted to be raised as a defense to a contempt charge.[82] Usually issues of privilege are considered as resulting in irreparable harm.[83] There is a split among the circuits as to when clients can appeal orders for their attorneys to produce documents which are allegedly privileged. The Supreme Court permitted such an appeal in *Perlman v. United States*.[84] *Perlman* has been interpreted by most circuits as always permitting clients to appeal as soon as their attorneys are required to produce documents, while a minority permit an appeal in advance of a citation for contempt only when contempt is unlikely as a practical matter.[85]

---

[76] United States v. United Mine Workers of Am., 330 U.S. 258, 303 (1947).

[77] *See* United States v. Ryan, 402 U.S. 530, 532–33 (1971).

[78] *See, e.g.*, Walker v. City of Birmingham, 388 U.S. 307, 317–21 (1967).

[79] Maness v. Meyers, 419 U.S. 449, 460 (1975); United States v. Ryan, 402 U.S. 530, 532–33 (1971).

[80] United States v. Ryan, 402 U.S. 530, 533 (1971).

[81] *See* Marrese v. American Academy of Orthopaedic Surgeons, 726 F.2d 1150, 1157 (7th Cir. 1984) (en banc), *rev'd on other grounds,* 470 U.S. 373 (1985); Halderman v. Pennhurst State School & Hospital, 673 F.2d 628, 636–37 (3d Cir. 1982) (en banc), *cert. denied,* 465 U.S. 1038 (1984).

[82] Pennsylvania v. Local Union 542, Int'l Union of Operating Eng'rs, 552 F.2d 498, 505–06 (3d Cir. 1977), *cert. denied,* 434 U.S. 822 (1977).

[83] *See, e.g.*, Maness v. Meyers, 419 U.S. 449, 460 (1975); United States v. Pearce, 792 F.2d 397, 401 n.5 (3d Cir. 1986); *In re* Grand Jury Proceedings, 601 F.2d 162, 169 (5th Cir. 1979).

[84] 247 U.S. 7, 12–13 (1918).

[85] *In re* Klein, 776 F.2d 628, 630 (7th Cir. 1985) (extensive citations); *see* Comment, *The Perlman Exception: Limitations Required by the Final Decision Rule,* 49 U. Chi. L. Rev. 798 (1982).

Contempt orders against nonparties, such as attorneys, are appealable.[86] Criminal contempt sanctions are reviewed for abuse of discretion.[87]

§ 31.10 Fines

Most circuits permit fines to be imposed against attorneys and litigants absent a finding of contempt.[88] Often such fines arise out of violations of local rules, but they can also be imposed to punish counsel for Rule 37 violations or failures to prosecute or obey court orders under Rules 16(f) or 41(b) or the court's inherent powers. Fines have also been imposed for Rule 11 violations.[89] However, it appears that notice, an opportunity to respond, and a hearing are required before a fine can be invoked.[90] As a practical matter, courts resort to such fines as a way of sanctioning attorneys without having to worry about the consequences that a finding of contempt may have upon an attorney's reputation or practice.

§ 31.11 Sanctions for Violations of Local Rules

Often local rules specifically authorize sanctions which can be invoked for noncomplying conduct. A district court's authority to adopt local rules stems from its inherent power, 28 U.S.C. § 2071, and Federal Rule of Civil Procedure 83.[91] The only requirement for such rules is that they be consistent with the federal statutes and rules of practice.[92] One common rule enables the court to consider a motion unopposed when no opposition or an untimely response is made. Another permits the court to impose monetary sanctions for failure to

---

[86] Combs v. Ryan's Coal Co., 785 F.2d 970, 977 (11th Cir. 1986), *cert. denied,* ____ U.S. ____, 107 S. Ct. 187 (1986); *see* 9 J. Moore, *et al.,* Moore's Federal Practice ¶ 110.14[1], at 198 (2d ed. 1976) [hereinafter Moore's Federal Practice].

[87] United States v. McCargo, 783 F.2d 507, 510 (5th Cir. 1986).

[88] *See, e.g.,* Eash v. Riggins Trucking Inc., 757 F.2d 557, 568 (3d Cir. 1985) (en banc); Miranda v. Southern Pac. Transp. Co., 710 F.2d 516, 521–22 (9th Cir. 1983); Martinez v. Thrifty Drug & Discount Co., 593 F.2d 992, 993–94 (10th Cir. 1979); *In re* Sutter, 543 F.2d 1030, 1036–38 (2d Cir. 1987); Flaska v. Little River Marine Constr. Co., 389 F.2d 885, 888 & n.10 (5th Cir.), *cert. denied,* 392 U.S. 928 (1968); J. M. Cleminshaw Co. v. City of Norwich, 93 F.R.D. 338, 358–60 (D. Conn. 1981); *see also* Cotner v. Hopkins, 795 F.2d 900, 903 (10th Cir. 1986); White v. Raymark Indus., Inc., 783 F.2d 1175, 1177 (4th Cir. 1986) (litigants as well as attorneys can be fined).

[89] Cotner v. Hopkins, 795 F.2d 900, 903 (10th Cir. 1986).

[90] *See* Eash v. Riggins Trucking Inc., 757 F.2d 557, 570–71 (3d Cir. 1985) (en banc); Miranda v. Southern Pac. Transp. Co., 710 F.2d 516, 522–23 (9th Cir. 1983).

[91] White v. Raymark Indus., 783 F.2d 1175, 1176–77 (4th Cir. 1986); Transamerica Corp. v. Transamerica Bancgrowth Corp., 627 F.2d 963, 965 (9th Cir. 1980).

[92] White v. Raymark Indus., 783 F.2d 1175, 1176–77 (4th Cir. 1986).

follow local rules. It is rare that such rules are challenged,[93] in part because such sanctions cannot usually be immediately appealed. However, when local rules conflict with the federal rules, they will be overturned.[94] Therefore, local rules which provide for sanctions which terminate a case are judged by the same standard as other sanctions resulting in dismissals and defaults.[95] For example, dismissals of actions for failure to file a memorandum of points and authorities have been reversed when there was no other evidence of dilatoriness.[96] Similarly, a dismissal for failure to notify the clerk of the name, address, and telephone number of defendant's counsel was reversed as being too severe.[97] Several circuits have held that summary judgment cannot be granted for violation of a local rule when it would not otherwise be appropriate,[98] although a few circuits uphold dismissals for failure to file an opposition.[99]

Local rules are narrowly construed. When suspension from the district court bar was not specifically mentioned as a sanction for an attorney's tardiness, the appellate court refused to interpret a local rule governing conduct unbecoming a member of the bar to include a late appearance.[100] Sanctions for violating a judge's unwritten rules were also overturned when the party was not given fair warning.[101] On the other hand, excluding an expert witness from testifying because the expert's designation was untimely under a local rule[102] or refusing to permit discovery beyond the period provided by a local rule[103] were not abuses of discretion.

§ 31.12 Sanctions in Actions under Specialized Rules

Although Tax Court is not governed by the Federal Rules of Civil Procedure,[104] it can impose a variety of sanctions when a party fails to obey a discovery order,

---

[93] *See generally* Cohn, *Federal discovery: A Survey of Local Rules and Practices in View of Proposed Changes to the Federal Rules,* 63 Minn. L. Rev. 253 (1979); Roberts, *The Myth of Uniformity in Federal Civil Procedure: Federal Civil Rule 83 and District Court Local Rulemaking Powers,* 8 Univ. Puget Sound L. Rev. 537 (1985).

[94] *Cf.* Miner v. Atlass, 363 U.S. 641, 647 (1960) (Admiralty Rules).

[95] *See* Hall v. Commissioner, 805 F.2d 1511, 1514–15 (11th Cir. 1986).

[96] *See, e.g.*, Witt v. United States, 681 F.2d 1144, 1149 (9th Cir. 1982).

[97] Farmers Plant Food, Inc. v. Fisher, 746 F.2d 451, 452 (8th Cir. 1984).

[98] Dixie Stevedores, Inc. v. Marinic Maritime, Ltd., 778 F.2d 670, 672–73 (11th Cir. 1985); John v. Louisana, 757 F.2d 698, 707–09 (5th Cir. 1985).

[99] *See, e.g.*, Lepkowski v. United States Dep't of Treasury, 804 F.2d 1310, 1312–13 (D.C. Cir. 1986).

[100] *See* United States v. Stoneberger, 805 F.2d 1391, 1393–94 (9th Cir. 1986).

[101] *In re* Richardson, 793 F.2d 37, 41 (1st Cir. 1986).

[102] Sturgeon v. Airborne Freight Corp., 778 F.2d 1154, 1159 (5th Cir. 1985).

[103] Public Loan Co. v. FDIC, 803 F.2d 82, 86 (3d Cir. 1986).

[104] 7, pt. 2 Moore's Federal Practice ¶ 81.03[3].

including dismissal of a case.[105] The imposition of such sanctions appear to be guided by Rule 37.[106] Tax Court sanctions are reviewed for abuse of discretion and appear to require willfull or bad faith conduct.[107] In addition, a total failure to respond to the discovery requested may be a prerequisite to dismissal.[108] Rule 37 applies to bankruptcy procedure,[109] and the Commodity Futures Trading Commission (CFTC) has promulgated regulations prescribing sanctions for a party's failure to comply with discovery[110] which have been reviewed under the same standard as used in Rule 37(b).[111] Although many administrative agencies have adopted the federal rules, including Rule 37 sanctions, the imposition of sanctions terminating cases is not uniformly accepted among the circuits.[112] Tax Court and Court of Claims rules also permit a dismissal for failure to prosecute or comply with court orders[113] which has been analogized to a Rule 41 dismissal.[114]

---

[105] Tax Ct. R. 104(c); Hart v. Commissioner, 730 F.2d 1206, 1208 (8th Cir. 1984).

[106] Aruba Bonaire Curacao Trust Co. v. Commissioner, 777 F.2d 38, 44 (D.C. Cir. 1985), *cert. denied,* ____ U.S. ____, 106 S. Ct. 1469 (1986).

[107] Hart v. Commissioner, 730 F.2d 1206, 1208 (8th Cir. 1984); Fox v. Commissioner, 718 F.2d 251, 254 (7th Cir. 1983).

[108] *See* Fox v. Commissioner, 718 F.2d 251, 254 (7th Cir. 1983); Laclede Gas Co. v. G.W. Warnecke Corp., 604 F.2d 561, 565 (8th Cir. 1979).

[109] Bankr. R. 7037; King v. Fidelity Nat'l Bank of Baton Rouge, 712 F.2d 188, 191 (5th Cir. 1983), *cert. denied,* 465 U.S. 1029 (1984).

[110] 17 C.F.R. § 12.35 (1986).

[111] Chapman v. U.S. Commodity Futures Trading Comm'n, 788 F.2d 408, 410–11 & n.1 (7th Cir. 1986) (per curiam).

[112] *See generally* Note, *The Use of Discovery Sanctions in Administrative Agency Adjudication,* 59 Ind. L.J. 113 (1983).

[113] Tax Ct. R. 123(b); Ct. Cl. R. 41(b).

[114] Ducommun v. Commissioner, 732 F.2d 752, 754 (10th Cir.), *cert. denied,* 464 U.S. 939 (1983); Watson v. Commissioner, 690 F.2d 429, 431 (5th Cir. 1982) (Tax Court); Kadin Corp. v. United States, 782 F.2d 175, 176–77 (Fed. Cir.), *cert. denied,* ____ U.S. ____, 106 S. Ct. 2895 (1986) (Court of Claims).

TABLE OF CASES

Case	*Book §*
"Agent Orange" Prod. Liability Litig., *In re,* 800 F.2d 14 (2d Cir. 1986)	§ 16.9
"Agent Orange" Prod. Liability Litig., *In re,* 787 F.2d 822 (2d Cir. 1986)	§ 14.39
"Agent Orange" Prod. Liability Litig., *In re,* 100 F.R.D. 718 (E.D.N.Y. 1983), *mandamus denied,* 725 F.2d 858 (2d Cir.), *cert. denied,* 465 U.S. 1067 (1984)	§ 10.7
"Agent Orange" Prod. Liability Litig., *In re,* 96 F.R.D. 587 (E.D.N.Y. 1983)	§ 23.9
"Agent Orange" Prod. Liability Litig., *In re,* 94 F.R.D. 173 (E.D.N.Y. 1982)	§ 16.16
Ager v. Jane C. Stormont Hosp. & Training School for Nurses, 622 F.2d 496 (10th Cir. 1980)	§§ 20.5, 20.6, 20.7
Aguilar v. Los Angeles County, 751 F.2d 1089 (9th Cir.), *cert. denied,* 471 U.S. 1125 (1985)	§ 9.3
A.H. Robins Co. v. Piccinin, 788 F.2d 994 (4th Cir.), *cert. denied,* ___ U.S. ___, 107 S. Ct. 251 (1986)	§ 6.4
Aircraft Co. v. Reyno, 454 U.S. 235 (1981)	§ 6.16
Air Crash Disaster Near Saigon, *In re,* 671 F.2d 564 (D.C. Cir. 1982)	§ 31.5
Airtex Corp. v. Shelley Radiant Ceiling Co., 536 F.2d 145 (7th Cir. 1976)	§§ 24.9, 29.2
Akerman v. Oryx Communications, Inc., 810 F.2d 336 (2d Cir. 1987)	§§ 15.10, 15.14
Alabama v. Pugh, 438 U.S. 781 (1978)	§ 2.6
Alaniz v. California Processors, Inc., 690 F.2d 717 (9th Cir. 1982)	§ 16.13
Alaniz v. Tillie Lewis Foods, 572 F.2d 657 (9th Cir.), *cert. denied,* 439 U.S. 837 (1978)	§ 10.16
Albright v. Upjohn Co., 788 F.2d 1217 (6th Cir. 1986)	§§ 28.4, 28.5
Alcaraz v. Block, 746 F.2d 593 (9th Cir. 1984)	§ 15.28
Aldabe v. Aldabe, 616 F.2d 1089 (9th Cir. 1980)	§§ 14.46, 14.54
Aldinger v. Howard, 427 U.S. 1 (1976)	§§ 2.25, 2.28, 2.30
Alexander v. Conveyors & Dumpers, Inc., 731 F.2d 1221 (5th Cir. 1984)	§ 23.29
Alexander v. Cox, 348 F.2d 894 (5th Cir. 1986)	§ 3.15
Alexander v. Unification Church, 634 F.2d 673 (2d Cir. 1980)	§ 14.39
Alexander v. United States, 201 U.S. 117 (1906)	§§ 17.17, 17.19, 21.6
Ali v. Offshore Co., 753 F.2d 1327 (5th Cir. 1985)	§ 6.18
Ali v. Sims, 788 F.2d 954 (3d Cir. 1986)	§ 29.5
Al-Jundi v. Rockefeller, 91 F.R.D. 590 (W.D.N.Y. 1981)	§ 26.4
Allen v. C.I.A., 636 F.2d 1287 (D.C. Cir. 1980), *overruled sub nom.* Founding Church of Scientology v. Smith, 721 F.2d 828 (D.C. Cir. 1983)	§ 17.8
Allen v. Ferguson, 791 F.2d 611 (7th Cir. 1986)	§§ 3.3, 3.19, 3.21, 14.24
Allen v. Wright, 468 U.S. 737 (1984)	§ 2.3
Allied Chem. Corp. v. Daiflon, Inc., 449 U.S. 33 (1980)	§§ 14.68, 17.18
Allis, *In re,* 531 F.2d 1391 (9th Cir.), *cert. denied,* 429 U.S. 900 (1976)	§ 31.8

Case	*Book §*
Amusement Equip., Inc. v. Mordilt, 779 F.2d 264 (5th Cir. 1985)	§ 4.9
Analytica, Inc. v. NPD Research, Inc., 708 F.2d 1263 (7th Cir. 1983)	§ 16.9
Anchor Motor Freight v. International Bhd. of Teamsters, 700 F.2d 1067 (6th Cir.), *cert. denied,* 464 U.S. 819 (1983)	§ 15.24
Anderson v. Allstate Ins. Co., 630 F.2d 677 (9th Cir. 1980)	§ 8.16
Anderson v. City of Bessemer City, 470 U.S. 564 (1985)	§§ 11.7, 14.11, 31.6
Anderson v. Coughlin, 700 F.2d 37 (2d Cir. 1983)	§ 14.7
Anderson v. Cramlet, 789 F.2d 840 (10th Cir. 1986)	§ 15.20
Anderson v. Cryovac, Inc., 805 F.2d 1 (1st Cir. 1986)	§ 19.4
Anderson v. Liberty Lobby, Inc., ____ U.S. ____, 106 S. Ct. 2505 (1986)	§§ 15.6, 15.9, 15.14, 15.28, 15.30
Anderson v. Marathon Petroleum Co., 801 F.2d 936 (7th Cir. 1986)	§ 1.11
Andes v. Versant Corp., 788 F.2d 1033 (4th Cir. 1986)	§ 12.6
Andrews v. Bechtel Power Corp., 780 F.2d 124 (1st Cir. 1985), *cert. denied,* ____ U.S. ____, 106 S. Ct. 2896 (1986)	§ 8.3
Andrews v. Heinold Commodities, Inc., 771 F.2d 184 (7th Cir. 1985)	§ 14.30
Anger v. Revco Drug Co., 791 F.2d 956 (D.C. Cir. 1986)	§ 14.7
Ansam Assoc., Inc. v. Cola Petroleum Ltd., 760 F.2d 442 (2d Cir. 1985)	§ 15.29
Anthuis v. Colt Indus. Operating Corp., 789 F.2d 207 (3d Cir. 1986)	§§ 15.3, 15.28
Antitrust Grand Jury, *In re,* 805 F.2d 155 (6th Cir. 1986)	§§ 17.12, 18.12, 18.18
Applegate v. Top Assocs., Inc., 425 F.2d 92 (2d Cir. 1970)	§§ 15.11, 15.17
Appleyard v. Wallace, 754 F.2d 955 (11th Cir. 1985)	§ 10.6
Archambault v. United Computing Sys., Inc., 786 F.2d 1507 (11th Cir. 1986)	§ 16.16
Archie v. Christian, 808 F.2d 1132 (5th Cir. 1987) (en banc)	§ 16.13
Ardoin v. J. Ray McDermott & Co., 641 F.2d 277 (5th Cir. 1981)	§ 15.28
Ardrey v. United Parcel Serv., 798 F.2d 679 (4th Cir. 1986)	§ 19.5
Ariel v. Jones, 693 F.2d 1058 (11th Cir. 1982)	§§ 21.2, 21.6
Arizona v. Manypenny, 451 U.S. 232 (1981)	§ 3.5
Arkla Exploration Co. v. Texas Oil & Cas Corp., 734 F.2d 347 (8th Cir. 1984)	§ 6.8
Armco, Inc., *In re,* 770 F.2d 103 (8th Cir. 1985)	§ 16.16
Armco, Inc. v. Penrod-Stauffer Bldg. Sys., 733 F.2d 1087 (4th Cir. 1984)	§§ 5.9, 14.40
Armstrong v. McAlpin, 699 F.2d 79 (2d Cir. 1983)	§ 8.5
Armstrong v. McAlpin, 625 F.2d 433 (2d Cir. 1980) (en banc), *vacated,* 449 U.S. 1106 (1981)	§ 16.9
Army Times Pub. Co. v. Watts, 730 F.2d 1398 (11th Cir. 1984)	§ 14.29
Arrowsmith v. United Press Int'l, 320 F.2d 219 (2d Cir. 1963)	§ 5.7
Arthur Guinness & Sons, PLC v. Sterling Publishing Co., 732 F.2d 1095 (2d Cir. 1984)	§ 11.4
Arthur Treacher's Franchisee Litig., *In re,* 92 F.R.D. 398 (E.D. Pa. 1981)	§§ 14.26, 14.27

Case	*Book §*
Badgley v. SantaCroce, 800 F.2d 33 (2d Cir. 1986)	§ 31.5
Baer v. R & F Coal Co., 782 F.2d 600 (6th Cir. 1986)	§ 2.29
Bailey v. Carnival Cruise Lines, Inc., 774 F.2d 1577 (11th Cir. 1985)	§ 7.8
Bailey v. V & O Press Co., 770 F.2d 601 (6th Cir. 1985)	§ 1.11
Baird v. Koerner, 279 F.2d 623 (9th Cir. 1960)	§ 18.2
Baise v. Alewel's, Inc., 99 F.R.D. 95 (W.D. Mo. 1983)	§ 20.8
Baker, *In re,* 744 F.2d 1438 (10th Cir. 1984) (en banc), *cert. denied,* 471 U.S. 1014 (1985)	§ 30.10
Baker v. Carr, 369 U.S. 186 (1962)	§ 2.2
Baker v. Chicago Fire & Burglary Detection, Inc., 489 F.2d 953 (7th Cir. 1973)	§ 15.3
Baker v. Gold Seal Liquors, Inc., 417 U.S. 467 (1974)	§§ 7.9, 7.10
Baker Indus., Inc. v. Cerberus Ltd., 764 F.2d 204 (3d Cir. 1985)	§§ 27.5, 28.8, 28.9
Baki v. B.F. Diamond Constr. Co., 71 F.R.D. 179 (D. Md. 1976)	§ 20.5
Bakia v. County of Los Angeles, 687 F.2d 299 (9th Cir. 1982)	§§ 9.4, 14.53
Baldwin-United Corp., *In re,* 770 F.2d 328 (2d Cir. 1985)	§ 10.5
Bally Export Corp. v. Balicar, Ltd., 804 F.2d 398 (7th Cir. 1986)	§ 12.3
Baltimore Orioles v. Major League Baseball Players, 805 F.2d 663 (7th Cir. 1986)	§ 15.28
Bangert v. Harris, 553 F. Supp. 235 (M.D. Pa. 1982)	§ 14.50
Bankers Life & Casualty Co. v. Holland, 346 U.S. 379 (1953)	§ 6.5
Bankers Trust Co., Complaint of, 752 F.2d 874 (3d Cir. 1984)	§ 22.3
Bank of Am. Nat'l Trust & Sav. Ass'n v. Hotel Rittenhouse Assocs., 800 F.2d 339 (3d Cir. 1986)	§ 19.4
Bank of Am. Nat'l Trust & Sav. Ass'n v. Summerland County Water Dist., 767 F.2d 544 (9th Cir. 1985)	§ 2.6
Bank of Cal. v. Opie, 663 F.2d 977 (9th Cir. 1981)	§ 15.6
Baptiste v. Sennet & Krumholz, 788 F.2d 910 (2d Cir. 1986)	§ 15.28
Barbar & Ross Co. v. Lifetime Doors, Inc., 810 F.2d 1276 (4th Cir. 1987)	§ 20.9
Barber v. Motor Vessel "Blue Cat," 372 F.2d 626 (5th Cir. 1967)	§ 14.41
BarclaysAmerican Corp. v. Kane, 746 F.2d 653 (10th Cir. 1984)	§§ 17.17, 17.18, 18.2
Barkwell v. Sturm Ruger Co., 79 F.R.D. 444 (D. Alaska 1978)	§ 20.7
Barnd v. City of Tacoma, 664 F.2d 1339 (9th Cir. 1982)	§ 28.11
Barnes v. Arden Mayfair, Inc., 759 F.2d 676 (9th Cir. 1985)	§ 15.6
Barr v. Abrams, 810 F.2d 358 (2d Cir. 1987)	§ 7.3
Barrows v. Forest Laboratories, Inc., 742 F.2d 54 (2d Cir. 1984)	§ 8.3
Barta v. Long, 670 F.2d 907 (10th Cir. 1982)	§ 29.10
Barwick v. Celotex Corp., 736 F.2d 946 (4th Cir. 1984)	§§ 15.18, 15.30
Basch v. Westinghouse Elec. Corp., 777 F.2d 165 (4th Cir. 1985), *cert. denied,* _____ U.S. _____, 106 S. Ct. 1957 (1986)	§§ 20.15, 24.9
Basso v. Utah Power & Light Co., 495 F.2d 906 (10th Cir. 1974)	§ 14.8
Batson v. Neal Spelce Assocs., Inc., 805 F.2d 546 (5th Cir. 1986)	§ 28.8
Baston v. Neal Spelce Assocs., Inc., 765 F.2d 511 (5th Cir. 1985)	§§ 28.13, 29.5, 29.8, 30.4
Batterton v. Texas Gen. Land Office, 783 F.2d 1220 (5th Cir.), *cert. denied,* _____ U.S. _____, 107 S. Ct. 316 (1986)	§ 15.28
Baxter v. Palmigiano, 425 U.S. 308 (1976)	§ 18.19

Case	*Book §*
Bayron v. Trudeau, 702 F.2d 43 (2d Cir. 1983)	§ 14.7
Bayou Steel Corp. v. M/V Amstelvoorn, 809 F.2d 1147 (5th Cir. 1987)	§ 14.27
Beacon Enters., Inc. v. Menzies, 715 F.2d 757 (2d Cir. 1983)	§§ 14.19, 15.25
Beal v. Missouri Pac. R.R., 312 U.S. 45 (1941)	§ 14.55
Beary v. West Publishing Co., 763 F.2d 66 (2d Cir.), *cert. denied,* ___ U.S. ___, 106 S. Ct. 232 (1985)	§§ 14.3, 14.61
Beaudett v. City of Hampton, 775 F.2d 1274 (4th Cir. 1985), *cert. denied,* ___ U.S. ___, 106 S. Ct. 1475 (1986)	§ 14.42
Beaudry Motor Co. v. Abko Properties, Inc., 780 F.2d 751 (9th Cir.), *cert. denied,* ___ U.S. ___, 107 S. Ct. 100 (1986)	§ 28.10
Bechtel v. Liberty Nat'l Bank, 534 F.2d 1335 (9th Cir. 1976)	§§ 14.3, 14.62
Beckman v. Safeco Ins. Co., 691 F.2d 898 (9th Cir. 1982)	§ 2.22
Beech-Nut, Inc. v. Warner Lambert Co., 480 F.2d 801 (2d Cir. 1973)	§ 3.19
Beef Indus. Antitrust Litig., *In re,* 607 F.2d 167 (5th Cir. 1979), *cert. denied,* 452 U.S 905 (1981)	§§ 10.12, 10.13
Beef Indus. Antitrust Litig., *In re,* 600 F.2d 1148 (5th Cir. 1979)	§ 14.60
Beef Nebraska, Inc. v. United States, 807 F.2d 712 (8th Cir. 1986)	§ 17.4
Behagen v. Amateur Basketball Ass'n of U.S.A., 744 F.2d 731 (10th Cir. 1984), *cert. denied,* 471 U.S. 1010 (1985)	§§ 14.19, 14.20
Behring Int'l, Inc. v. Imperial Iranian Air Force, 712 F.2d 45 (3d Cir. 1983)	§ 15.29
Belcher v. Bassett Furniture Indus., Inc., 588 F.2d 904 (4th Cir. 1978)	§ 25.2
Bell v. Cameron Meadows Land Co., 669 F.2d 1278 (9th Cir. 1982)	§ 7.15
Bell v. Hood, 327 U.S. 678 (1946)	§§ 14.12, 14.13
Bell & Beckwith v. IRS, 766 F.2d 910 (6th Cir. 1985)	§§ 2.9, 23.22
Bellis v. United States, 417 U.S. 85 (1974)	§ 18.21
Bellmore v. Mobil Oil Corp., 783 F.2d 300 (2d Cir. 1986)	§ 7.17
Bencivenga v. Western Pa. Teamsters, 763 F.2d 574 (3d Cir. 1985)	§ 15.13
Bender v. Williamsport Area School Dist., ___ U.S. ___, 106 S. Ct. 1326 (1986)	§ 2.3
Beneficial Life Ins. Co. v. Knobelauch, 653 F.2d 393 (9th Cir. 1981)	§ 14.47
Benford v. Richards Medical Co., 792 F.2d 1537 (11th Cir. 1986)	§ 23.29
Bennerson v. Joseph, 583 F.2d 633 (3d Cir. 1978)	§ 16.12
Bennet v. Behring Corp., 737 F.2d 982 (11th Cir. 1984)	§ 10.13
Bennett v. Berg, 685 F.2d 1053 (8th Cir. 1982), *cert. denied,* 464 U.S. 1008 (1983)	§ 14.42
Benny v. Pipes, 799 F.2d 489 (9th Cir. 1986)	§§ 14.26, 14.39, 14.40
Bergquist v. County of Cochise, 806 F.2d 1364 (9th Cir. 1986)	§ 7.3
Berkey Photo, Inc. v. Eastman Kodak Co., 74 F.R.D. 613 (S.D.N.Y. 1977)	§§ 18.17, 20.12
Berkley & Co., *In re,* 629 F.2d 548 (8th Cir. 1980)	18.12
Berndt v. Tennessee, 796 F.2d 879 (6th Cir. 1986)	§ 8.7
Bernstein v. Lind-Waldock & Co., 738 F.2d 179 (7th Cir. 1984)	§ 3.15
Berroyer v. Hertz, 672 F.2d 334 (3d Cir. 1982)	§ 17.15

Case	*Book §*
Berry v. Bean, 796 F.2d 713 (4th Cir. 1986)	§ 11.3
Besig v. Dolphin Boating & Swimming Club, 683 F.2d 1271 (9th Cir. 1982)	§ 8.15
Best Canvas Prods. & Supplies, Inc. v. Ploof Truck Lines, Inc., 713 F.2d 618 (11th Cir. 1983)	§ 8.3
Betar v. DeHavilland Aircraft of Canada, Ltd., 603 F.2d 30 (7th Cir. 1979), *cert. denied,* 444 U.S. 1098 (1980)	§ 2.17
Bethlehem Contracting Co. v. Lehrer/McGovern, Inc., 800 F.2d 325 (2d Cir. 1986)	§ 2.6
Bettin v. Nelson, 744 F.2d 53 (8th Cir, 1984)	§ 15.23
Bevill, Bresler & Schulman Asset Mgmt. Corp., *In re,* 805 F.2d 120 (3d Cir. 1986)	§§ 18.8, 18.19
Beyah v. Coughlin, 789 F.2d 986 (2d Cir. 1986)	§ 15.16
Bianca v. Parke-Davis Pharmaceutical Div., 723 F.2d 392 (5th Cir. 1984)	§ 2.17
Bieganek v. Taylor, 801 F.2d 879 (7th Cir. 1986)	§ 12.3
Biesenbach v. Guenther, 588 F.2d 400 (3d Cir. 1978)	§§ 14.50, 14.71
Birmingham Fire Ins. v. Winegardner & Hammons, 714 F.2d 548 (5th Cir. 1983)	§ 2.25
Bishop v. Hendricks, 495 F.2d 289 (4th Cir.), *cert. denied,* 419 U.S. 1056 (1976)	§ 2.17
Bishop, Baldwin, Rewald, Dillingham & Wong, Inc., *In re,* 779 F.2d 471 (9th Cir. 1985)	§ 15.24
Black v. Acme Markets, Inc., 564 F.2d 681 (5th Cir. 1977)	§ 14.20
Black Panther Party v. Smith, 661 F.2d 1243 (D.C. Cir. 1981), *vacated as moot sub nom.* Moore v. Black Panther Party, 458 U.S. 1118 (1982)	§ 18.19
Blackwell v. Department of Offender Rehabilitation, 807 F.2d 914 (11th Cir. 1987)	§ 28.3
Blaha v. A.H. Robbins & Co., 708 F.2d 238 (6th Cir. 1983)	§ 5.4
Blair Foods, Inc. v. Ranchers Cotton Oil, 610 F.2d 665 (9th Cir. 1980)	§ 15.17
Blakemore v. Missouri Pac. R.R., 789 F.2d 616 (8th Cir. 1986)	§§ 2.13, 14.11
Blakesley v. Wolford, 789 F.2d 236 (3d Cir. 1986)	§ 1.11
Blank v. Ronson Corp., 97 F.R.D. 744 (S.D.N.Y. 1983)	§ 24.7
Blau v. Del Monte Corp., 748 F.2d 1348 (9th Cir. 1984)	§ 7.17
Bloom v. Illinois, 391 U.S. 194 (1968)	§ 31.8
Blue Chip Stamps v. Manor Drug Stores, 421 U.S. 723 (1975)	§ 27.1
Blue Ridge Bank v. Veribanc, Inc., 755 F.2d 371 (4th Cir. 1985)	§ 4.12
Board of Educ. v. Nyquist, 590 F.2d 1241 (2d Cir. 1979)	§ 16.9
Bobb v. Modern Prods., Inc., 648 F.2d 1051 (5th Cir. 1981)	§§ 23.26, 23.27
Boda v. United States, 698 F.2d 1174 (11th Cir. 1983)	§ 14.14
Boelens v. Redman Homes, Inc., 759 F.2d 504 (5th Cir. 1985)	§ 2.12
Bogosian v. Gulf Oil Corp., 738 F.2d 587 (3d Cir. 1984)	§§ 18.17, 20.12
Boileau v. Bethlehem Steel Corp., 730 F.2d 929 (3d Cir.), *cert. denied,* 469 U.S. 871 (1984)	§ 8.3
Bomate v. Ford Motor Co., 761 F.2d 713 (D.C. Cir. 1985)	§ 30.5
Bond Leather Co. v. Q.T. Shoe Mfg. Co., 764 F.2d 928 (1st Cir. 1985)	§ 4.4
Bonilla v. Oakland Scavenger Co., 697 F.2d 1297 (9th Cir. 1982), *cert. denied,* 467 U.S. 1251 (1984)	§ 14.47

Case	*Book §*
Bonner v. City of Prichard, 661 F.2d 1206 (11th Cir. 1981)	§ 13.5
Booth v. Mary Carter Paint Co., 202 So. 2d 8 (Fla. 1967)	§ 16.6
Boreri v. Fiat S.P.A., 763 F.2d 17 (1st Cir. 1985)	§ 27.9
Borg-Warner Acceptance Corp. v. Lovett & Tharpe, Inc., 786 F.2d 1055 (11th Cir. 1986)	§§ 4.5, 4.6
Boruski v. United States, 803 F.2d 1421 (7th Cir. 1986)	§ 15.14
Borzeka v. Herkler, 739 F.2d 444 (9th Cir. 1984)	§ 5.8
Boston Five Cents Sav. Bank v. Department of Housing & Urban Dev., 768 F.2d 5 (1st Cir. 1985)	§ 15.13
Bottaro v. Hatton Assocs., 680 F.2d 895 (2d Cir. 1982)	§ 16.9
Bouchet v. National Urban League, Inc., 730 F.2d 799 (D.C. Cir. 1984)	§ 2.28
Bourjaily v. United States, ____ U.S. ____, 107 S. Ct. 2775 (1987)	§ 15.21
Bowers v. DeVito, 686 F.2d 616 (7th Cir. 1982)	§ 15.10
Boyce v. Alizaduh, 595 F.2d 948 (4th Cir. 1979)	§ 14.7
Brackin Tie, Lumber & Chip Co. v. McLarty Farms, Inc., 704 F.2d 585 (11th Cir. 1983)	§ 8.3
Bradford v. Sears, Roebuck & Co., 673 F.2d 792 (5th Cir. 1982)	§ 10.10
Bradford Trust Co. v. Merrill Lynch, Pierce, Fenner & Smith, Inc., 805 F.2d 49 (2d Cir. 1986)	§ 16.4
Bradshaw v. G.M. Corp., 805 F.2d 110 (3d Cir. 1986)	§ 14.67
Brand v. Menlove Dodge, 796 F.2d 1070 (9th Cir. 1986)	§§ 4.5, 4.11
Brandon v. D.C. Bd. of Parole, 734 F.2d 56 (D.C. Cir. 1984), *cert. denied,* 469 U.S. 1127 (1985)	§ 14.7
Brastex Corp. v. Allen Int'l Inc., 702 F.2d 326 (2d Cir. 1983)	§ 11.8
Bratt v. I.B.M., 785 F.2d 352 (1st Cir. 1986)	§ 15.27
Brennan v. Midwestern Life Ins. Co., 450 F.2d 999 (7th Cir. 1971), *cert. denied,* 405 U.S. 921 (1972)	§ 10.11
Bridge C.A.T. Scan Assoc. v. Technicare Corp., 710 F.2d 940 (2d Cir. 1983)	§ 19.9
Brillhart v. Mutual Med. Ins., Inc., 768 F.2d 196 (7th Cir. 1985)	§ 14.42
Brink's Inc. v. City of New York, 717 F.2d 700 (2d Cir. 1983)	§§ 17.12, 18.19
Bristol Indus. Corp., *In re,* 690 F.2d 26 (2d Cir. 1982)	§ 15.25
British Airways Bd. v. Boeing Co., 585 F.2d 946 (9th Cir. 1978), *cert. denied,* 440 U.S. 981 (1979)	§ 15.6
Britt v. Simi Valley Unified School Dist., 708 F.2d 452 (5th Cir. 1983)	§ 16.12
Britton v. Howard Sav. Bank, 727 F.2d 315 (3d Cir. 1984)	§ 11.8
Broadcast Music, Inc. v. M.T.S. Enters., Inc., 811 F.2d 278 (5th Cir. 1987)	§§ 12.1, 14.26
Brobst v. Columbus Servs., Int'l, 761 F.2d 148 (3d Cir. 1985)	§ 15.5
Brock v. On Shore Quality Control Specialists, Inc., 811 F.2d 282 (5th Cir. 1987)	§ 18.22
Brock v. Unique Racquetball & Health Clubs, Inc., 786 F.2d 61 (2d Cir. 1986)	§ 12.1
Brockton Sav. Bank v. Peat, Marwick, Mitchell & Co., 771 F.2d 5 (1st Cir. 1985), *cert. denied,* ____ U.S. ____, 106 S. Ct. 1204 (1986)	§§ 29.9, 30.9
Brohan *ex rel.* Brohan v. Volkswagen Mfg. Corp., 97 F.R.D. 46 (E.D.N.Y. 1983)	§§ 14.60, 14.64

Case	*Book §*
Brook Village N. Assocs. v. G.E. Co., 686 F.2d 66 (1st Cir. 1982)	§ 26.7
Brotherhood of R.R. Trainmen v. Baltimore & O. R.R., 331 U.S. 519 (1947)	§ 9.9
Browder v. Director, Ill. Dep't of Corrections, 434 U.S. 257 (1978)	§§ 12.3, 14.70
Brown v. Arlen Mgmt. Corp., 663 F.2d 575 (5th Cir. 1981)	§ 26.6
Brown v. Capitol Air, Inc., 797 F.2d 106 (2d Cir. 1986)	§ 3.23
Brown v. Chote, 411 U.S. 452 (1973)	§ 11.4
Brown v. Demco, Inc., 792 F.2d 478 (5th Cir. 1986)	§ 3.15
Brown v. Flowers Indus., Inc., 688 F.2d 328 (5th Cir. 1982), *cert. denied,* 460 U.S. 1023 (1983)	§ 14.20
Brown v. Kerr-McGee Chem. Corp., 767 F.2d 1234 (7th Cir. 1985), *cert. denied,* ____ U.S. ____ , 106 S. Ct. 882 (1986)	§ 15.28
Brown v. Mine Safety Appliances Co., 753 F.2d 393 (5th Cir. 1985)	§ 2.16
Brown v. National Bd. of Medical Examiners, 800 F.2d 168 (7th Cir. 1986)	§§ 28.3, 28.4
Brown v. Webster, 156 U.S. 328 (1895)	§ 2.12
Brown v. Wesley's Quaker Maid, Inc., 771 F.2d 952 (6th Cir. 1985)	§§ 16.13, 16.16
Brown-Bey v. United States, 720 F.2d 467 (7th Cir. 1983)	§§ 17.16, 17.17
Browning v. Navarro, 743 F.2d 1069 (5th Cir. 1984)	§ 3.19
Browning Debenture Holders' Committee v. DASA Corp., 560 F.2d 1078 (2d Cir. 1977)	§ 28.9
Bruce v. United States, 759 F.2d 755 (9th Cir. 1985)	§ 2.3
Brunken v. Lance, 807 F.2d 1325 (7th Cir. 1986)	§ 2.6
Brunswick Corp. v. Jones, 784 F.2d 271 (7th Cir. 1986)	§ 11.4
Brunswick Corp. v. Pueblo Bowl-O-Mat, Inc., 429 U.S. 477 (1977)	§ 2.3
Bryant v. Ford Motor Co., 794 F.2d 450 (9th Cir. 1986)	§ 3.11
Bryson v. Brand Insulations, Inc., 621 F.2d 556 (3d Cir. 1980)	§ 14.6
Bryson v. Royal Business Group, 763 F.2d 491 (1st Cir. 1985)	§ 15.10
Buchanan v. American Motors Corp., 697 F.2d 151 (6th Cir. 1983)	§ 20.10
Buchanan v. Stanships, Inc., 744 F.2d 1070 (5th Cir. 1984)	§§ 15.17, 15.22
Buder v. Merrill Lynch, Pierce, Fenner & Smith, 644 F.2d 690 (8th Cir. 1981)	§ 8.3
Buffalo Valley Gas Auth. Litig., *In re,* 429 F. Supp. 1029 (J.P.M.L. 1977)	§ 6.12
Bulthuis v. Rexall Corp., 789 F.2d 1315 (9th Cir. 1986)	§ 15.10
Bunch v. Bullard, 795 F.2d 384 (5th Cir. 1986)	§ 23.26
Bunch v. United States, 680 F.2d 1271 (9th Cir. 1982)	§ 17.15
Burford v. Sun Oil Co., 319 U.S. 315 (1943)	§§ 2.6, 2.32
Burger King Corp. v. Rudzewicz, 471 U.S. 462 (1985)	§§ 4.3, 4.4, 4.5, 4.8, 4.11, 14.19
Burgess v. Premier Corp., 727 F.2d 826 (9th Cir. 1984)	§§ 25.10, 26.6
Burgoyne v. Frank B. Hall & Co. of Hawaii, Inc., 781 F.2d 1418 (9th Cir. 1986)	§ 2.22
Burgs v. Sissel, 745 F.2d 526 (8th Cir. 1984)	§ 16.5
Burlington Coat Factory Warehouse v. Espirt de Corps, 769 F.2d 919 (2d Cir. 1985)	§§ 15.17, 15.24

Case	*Book §*
Cargill, Inc. v. Sabine Trading & Shipping Co., 756 F.2d 224 (2d Cir. 1985)	§ 14.27
Carl Heck Eng'rs v. Lafourche Parish Police Jury, 622 F.2d 133 (5th Cir. 1980)	§ 3.4
Carlsberg Resources Corp. v. Cambria Sav. & Loan Ass'n, 554 F.2d 1254 (3d Cir. 1977)	§ 2.21
Carlson Cos., Inc. v. Sperry & Hutchinson Co., 374 F. Supp. 1080 (D. Minn. 1974)	§ 17.5
Carlyle v. United States, 674 F.2d 554 (6th Cir. 1982)	§ 16.4
Carpenters S. Cal. Admin. v. D & L Camp Constr., 738 F.2d 999 (9th Cir. 1984)	§ 2.30
Carr v. Veterans Admin., 522 F.2d 1355 (5th Cir. 1975)	§§ 5.5, 8.14
Carson v. American Brands, Inc., 450 U.S. 79 (1981)	§§ 11.7, 15.28
Carter v. Albert Einstein Medical Center, 804 F.2d 805 (3d Cir. 1986)	§ 30.6
Carter v. City of Memphis, 636 F.2d 159 (6th Cir. 1980)	§ 30.6
Carter v. Norfolk Community Hosp. Ass'n, 761 F.2d 970 (4th Cir. 1985)	§§ 14.14, 14.49
Carter v. Stanton, 405 U.S. 669 (1972)	§§ 14.47, 15.25, 15.28
Carter v. Washington Metropolitan Area Transit Auth., 764 F.2d 854 (D.C. Cir. 1985)	§ 7.8
Carter by Carter v. United States, 780 F.2d 925 (11th Cir. 1986)	§ 30.7
Carter-Wallace, Inc. v. Otte, 474 F.2d 529 (2d Cir. 1972), *cert. denied,* 412 U.S. 929 (1973)	§ 20.13
Cascone v. Ortho Pharmaceutical Corp., 702 F.2d 389 (2d Cir. 1983)	§ 3.22
Cassidy, Inc. v. Hantz, 717 F.2d 1233 (8th Cir. 1983)	§ 15.24
Castle v. Sangamo Weston, Inc., 744 F.2d 1464 (11th Cir. 1984)	§§ 17.20, 18.14, 18.15
Carter v. Hutto, 781 F.2d 1028 (4th Cir. 1986)	§ 16.5
Cates v. LTV Aerospace Corp., 480 F.2d 620 (5th Cir. 1973)	§ 21.2
Catlin v. United States, 324 U.S. 229 (1945)	§ 14.69
Catts Co. v. Gulf Ins. Co., 723 F.2d 1494 (10th Cir. 1983)	§ 15.30
Cay v. Estelle, 789 F.2d 318 (5th Cir. 1986)	§ 14.7
Celotex Corp. v. Catrett, ____ U.S. ____, 106 S. Ct. 2548 (1986)	§§ 15.1, 15.5, 15.7, 15.9, 15.15, 15.17
Cenco Inc. v. Seidman & Seidman, 686 F.2d 449 (7th Cir. 1982)	§ 2.27
Centurion Indus., Inc. v. Warren Steurer & Assocs., 665 F.2d 323 (10th Cir. 1981)	§§ 19.5, 19.9
CF&I Steel Corp. v. Mitsui & Co. (U.S.A.), 713 F.2d 494 (9th Cir. 1983)	§§ 21.2, 21.6
Chagnon v. Bell, 642 F.2d 1248 (D.C. Cir. 1980), *cert. denied,* 643 U.S. 911 (1981)	§ 15.24
Chambers v. McLean Trucking Co., 550 F. Supp. 1335 (M.D.N.C. 1981)	§ 15.13
Chandler Leasing Corp. v. Lopez, 669 F.2d 919 (4th Cir. 1982)	§ 29.5
Chandler Supply Co. v. G.A.F. Corp., 650 F.2d 983 (9th Cir. 1980)	§ 3.22

Case	*Book §*
Chrylser Corp. v. Brown, 441 U.S. 281 (1979)	§ 17.10
Chrylser Corp. v. Fedders Corp., 643 F.2d 1229 (6th Cir.), *cert. denied,* 454 U.S. 893 (1981)	§ 4.14
Chrysler Credit Corp. v. Macino, 710 F.2d 363 (7th Cir. 1983)	§§ 12.1, 12.3
Chung v. Nana Dev. Corp., 783 F.2d 1124 (4th Cir.), *cert. denied,* ____ U.S. ____, 107 S. Ct. 431, (1986)	§ 4.5
Church of Scientology v. I.R.S., 792 F.2d 153 (D.C. Cir. 1986) (en banc), *cert. granted,* ____ U.S. ____, 107 S. Ct. 947 (1987)	§ 17.9
Church of Scientology v. I.R.S., 792 F.2d 146 (D.C. Cir. 1986)	§ 17.9
Church of Scientology of Cal. v. Flynn, 744 F.2d 694 (9th Cir. 1984)	§§ 14.42, 14.51
CIA Petrolera Caribe, Inc. v. Arco Caribbean, Inc., 754 F.2d 404 (1st Cir. 1985)	§§ 15.3, 15.27
Cinema 5, Ltd. v. Cinerama, Inc., 528 F.2d 1384 (2d Cir. 1976)	§ 16.9
Cipollone v. Liggett Group, Inc., 785 F.2d 1108 (3d Cir. 1986)	§§ 17.17, 17.19, 19.3, 19.5, 19.6, 19.9
C.I.T. Corp v. Duncan Grading & Constr., Inc., 739 F.2d 359 (8th Cir. 1984)	§ 16.13
C.K.S. Eng'rs, Inc. v. White Mountain Gypsum Co., 726 F.2d 1202 (7th Cir. 1984)	§ 12.3
Clarence E. Morris, Inc. v. Vitek, 412 F.2d 1174 (9th Cir. 1969)	§ 3.10
Clark v. Amoco Prod. Co., 794 F.2d 967 (5th Cir. 1986)	§ 14.41
Clark v. Tarrant County, Tex., 798 F.2d 736 (5th Cir. 1986)	§§ 2.6, 14.13, 15.5
Clark v. United States, 289 U.S. 1 (1933)	§ 18.12
Clark Equip. Co. v. International Union, Allied Indus. Workers, 803 F.2d 878 (6th Cir. 1986)	§ 10.13
Claus v. Gyorkey, 674 F.2d 427 (5th Cir. 1982)	§ 15.24
Clay v. Equifax, Inc., 762 F.2d 952 (11th Cir. 1985)	§ 15.28
Cleburne Living Center v. City of Cleburne, 726 F.2d 191 (5th Cir. 1984), *aff'd,* ____ U.S. ____, 105 S. Ct. 3249 (1985)	§ 2.3
C & L Farms, Inc. v. Federal Crop Ins. Corp., 771 F.2d 407 (8th Cir. 1985)	§ 5.8
Clinton, City of v. Moffitt, 812 F.2d 341 (7th Cir. 1987)	§ 2.21
Clipper Express v. Rocky Mountain Motor Tariff Bureau, Inc., 690 F.2d 1240 (9th Cir. 1982), *cert. denied,* 459 U.S. 1227 (1983)	§ 8.12
Clorox Co. v. United States Dist. Ct., 779 F.2d 517 (9th Cir. 1985)	§ 3.19
Cloverleaf Standardbred Owners Ass'n, Inc. v. National Bank, 699 F.2d 1274 (D.C. Cir. 1983)	§§ 9.4, 14.53
Coastal Steel v. Tilghman Wheelabrator Ltd., 709 F.2d 190 (3d Cir.), *cert. denied,* 464 U.S. 938 (1983)	§ 6.21
Coates v. Johnson & Johnson, 756 F.2d 524 (7th Cir. 1985)	§ 18.22
Coates & Clark, Inc. v. Gay, 755 F.2d 1506 (11th Cir.), *cert. denied,* ____ U.S. ____, 106 S. Ct. 231 (1985)	§ 15.10
Cobbledick v. United States, 309 U.S. 323 (1940)	§ 17.20
Coca-Cola Co. v. Tropicana Prods., Inc., 690 F.2d 312 (2d Cir. 1982)	§ 11.7
Cochran v. Birkel, 651 F.2d 1219 (6th Cir. 1981), *cert. denied,* 454 U.S. 1152 (1982)	§ 7.16

Case	*Book §*
Cook v. Weber, 698 F.2d 907 (7th Cir. 1983)	§§ 3.18, 3.19
Cookish v. Cunningham, 787 F.2d 1 (1st Cir. 1986)	§ 14.7
Cool Fuel, Inc. v. Connett, 685 F.2d 309 (9th Cir. 1982)	§§ 15.3, 15.4
Cooling Sys. & Flexibles, Inc. v. Stuart Radiator, Inc., 777 F.2d 485 (9th Cir. 1985)	§ 28.13
Cooper v. Federal Reserve Bank, 467 U.S. 867 (1984)	§ 10.5
Cooper v. Shumway, 780 F.2d 27 (10th Cir. 1985)	§ 8.8
Coopers & Lybrand v. Livesay, 437 U.S. 463 (1978)	§§ 10.17, 17.19
Coordinated Pretrial Proceedings In Petroleum Prods. Antitrust Litig., *In re,* 669 F.2d 620 (10th Cir. 1982)	§§ 19.3, 19.5, 21.3
Coordinated Pretrial Proceedings in Petroleum Prods. Antitrust Litig., *In re,* 658 F.2d 1355 (9th Cir. 1981)	§ 18.4
Cope v. McPherson, 781 F.2d 207 (D.C. Cir. 1985)	§ 29.6
Copeland v. Marshall, 641 F.2d 880 (D.C. Cir. 1980)	§ 28.11
Corchado v. Puerto Rico Marine Mgmt., Inc., 665 F.3d 410 (1st Cir. 1981), *cert, denied,* 459 U.S. 826 (1982)	§§ 30.3, 30.6
Cordis Corp., *In re,* 769 F.2d 733 (Fed. Cir. 1985)	§ 14.37
Cordova Gonzalez, *In re,* 726 F.2d 16 (1st Cir.), *cert. denied,* 466 U.S. 951 (1984)	§ 31.6
Corey v. Mast Road Grain & Bldg. Materials Co., 738 F.2d 11 (1st Cir. 1984)	§ 14.70
Corn Derivatives Antitrust Litig., *In re,* 748 F.2d 157 (3d Cir. 1984), *cert. denied,* ____ U.S. ____, 105 S. Ct. 2702 (1985)	§ 16.9
Cornwall v. United States Constr. Mfg., Inc., 800 F.2d 250 (Fed. Cir. 1986)	§ 8.7
Corporacion Venezolana de Fomento v. Vintero Sales Corp., 629 F.2d 786 (2d Cir. 1980), *cert. denied,* 449 U.S. 1080 (1981)	§ 2.13
Corrugated Container Anti-trust Litig., *In re,* 756 F.2d 411 (5th Cir. 1985)	§ 18.19
Corrugated Container Anti-trust Litig., *In re,* 694 F.2d 1041 (5th Cir. 1983)	§ 15.28
Corrugated Container Anti-trust Litig., *In re,* 687 F.2d 52 (5th Cir. 1982)	§ 17.12
Corrugated Container Anti-trust Litig., *In re,* 662 F.2d 875 (D.C. Cir. 1981)	§§ 6.13, 21.6
Corrugated Container Anti-trust Litig., *In re,* 620 F.2d 1086 (5th Cir. 1980)	§ 6.10
Cosme Nieves v. Deshler, 786 F.2d 445 (1st Cir. 1986)	§ 3.8
Costlow v. Weeks, 790 F.2d 1486 (9th Cir. 1986)	§§ 14.34, 14.36
Cote v. Wadel, 796 F.2d 981 (7th Cir. 1986)	§§ 2.20, 14.30
Cotner v. Hopkins, 795 F.2d 900 (10th Cir. 1986)	§§ 14.7, 28.3, 31.10
Couch v. United States, 409 U.S. 322 (1973)	§ 18.10
Coulter v. Tennessee, 805 F.2d 146 (6th Cir. 1986)	§ 10.14
County Sanitation Dist. No. 2 v. Inland Container Corp., 803 F.2d 1074 (9th Cir. 1986)	§ 9.4
Cowen v. J.C. Penney Co., 790 F.2d 1529 (11th Cir. 1986)	§ 15.24
Cowgill v. Raymark Indus., Inc., 780 F.2d 324 (3d Cir. 1985)	§§ 15.3, 15.27
Cowin v. Bresler, 741 F.2d 410 (D.C. Cir. 1984)	§ 14.42

Case	*Book §*
Dart Indus., Inc. v. Plunkett Co. of Okla., 704 F.2d 496 (10th Cir. 1983)	§ 8.3
Dart Indus. Co. v. Westwood Chem. Co., 649 F.2d 646 (9th Cir. 1980)	§§ 21.6, 23.19
Data Disc., Inc. v. Systems Technology Assocs., Inc., 557 F.2d 1280 (9th Cir. 1977)	§§ 4.11, 4.12, 6.4, 14.18, 14.20, 14.21, 17.16
Dataphase Sys., Inc. v. C L Sys., Inc., 640 F.2d 109 (8th Cir. 1981) (en banc)	§ 11.4
Daves v. Payless Cashways, Inc., 661 F.2d 1022 (5th Cir. 1981)	§ 8.3
Davidson v. Keenan, 740 F.2d 129 (2d Cir. 1984)	§ 15.3
Davis v. A & J Elecs., 792 F.2d 74 (7th Cir. 1986)	§ 4.14
Davis v. Ball Memorial Hosp. Ass'n, Inc., 753 F.2d 1410 (7th Cir. 1985)	§ 10.5
Davis v. Bryan, 810 F.2d 42 (2d Cir. 1987)	§ 7.7
Davis v. CIA, 711 F.2d 858 (8th Cir. 1983), *cert. denied,* 465 U.S. 1035 (1984)	§ 15.20
Davis v. Cluet, Peabody, & Co., 667 F.2d 1371 (11th Cir. 1982)	§ 29.7
Davis v. Howard, 561 F.2d 565 (5th Cir. 1977)	§ 15.25
Davis v. Musler, 713 F.2d 907 (2d Cir. 1983)	§ 12.3
Davis v. Veslan Enters., 765 F.2d 494 (5th Cir. 1985)	§§ 3.10, 3.23
Davis v. Williams, 588 F.2d 69 (4th Cir. 1978)	§ 30.3
Davis v. Zahradnick, 600 F.2d 458 (4th Cir. 1979)	§§ 14.55, 15.3, 15.25
Day v. Allstate Ins. Co., 788 F.2d 1110 (5th Cir. 1986)	§ 29.8
Dayco Corp v. Goodyear Tire & Rubber Co., 523 F.2d 389 (6th Cir. 1975)	§ 15.25
Dean Witter Reynolds Inc. v. Byrd, 470 U.S. 213 (1985)	§ 1.12
DeBry v. Transamerica Corp., 601 F.2d 480 (10th Cir. 1979)	§ 8.5
D.E.C. v. Emulex Corp., 805 F.2d 380 (Fed. Cir. 1986)	§ 11.5
Decker v. Massey-Ferguson, Ltd., 681 F.2d 111 (2d Cir. 1982)	§§ 14.41, 14.49
Decker Coal Co. v. Commonwealth Edison Co., 805 F.2d 834 (9th Cir. 1986)	§§ 4.5, 6.3, 6.4, 6.7, 6.9
DeCrescenzo v. Maersk Container Serv. Co., 741 F.2d 17 (2d Cir. 1984)	§ 25.14
DeGioia v. United States Lines Co., 304 F.2d 421 (2d Cir. 1962)	§ 7.18
Deitchman v. E.R. Squibb & Sons, Inc., 740 F.2d 556 (7th Cir. 1984)	§§ 20.10, 21.4, 21.6
DeJames v. Magnificence Carriers, Inc., 654 F.2d 280 (3d Cir.), *cert. denied,* 454 U.S. 1085 (1981)	§ 4.13
De La Fuente v. Stokely-Van Camp, Inc., 713 F.2d 225 (7th Cir. 1983)	§ 10.6
Delgado v. Bowen, 782 F.2d 79 (7th Cir. 1986)	§ 16.12
Dellums v. Powell, 566 F.2d 231 (D.C. Cir. 1977)	§§ 10.11, 29.4
Delta Air Lines, Inc. v. August, 450 U.S. 346 (1981)	§ 16.6
Delta S.S. Lines, Inc. v. Albano, 768 F.2d 728 (5th Cir. 1985)	§§ 5.1, 5.9

Case	*Book §*
Doe v. District of Columbia, 697 F.2d 1115 (D.C. Cir. 1983)	§§ 19.5, 19.9
Doe v. N.Y.U., 666 F.2d 761 (2d Cir. 1981)	§§ 15.20, 15.30
Doe v. Stegall, 653 F.2d 180 (5th Cir. 1981)	§ 2.10
Doe v. United States Dep't of Justice, 753 F.2d 1092 (D.C. Cir. 1985)	§§ 14.41, 14.49
Dollar Sav. Bank v. First Sec. Bank of Utah, 746 F.2d 208 (3d Cir. 1984)	§§ 4.11, 14.30
Domingo v. New England Fish Co., 727 F.2d 1429 (9th Cir. 1984), *modified,* 742 F.2d 520 (9th Cir. 1984)	§ 10.10
Donaldson v. Clark, 786 F.2d 1570 (11th Cir. 1986)	§ 15.27
Donaldson v. United States, 400 U.S. 517 (1971)	§ 17.4
Donnelly v. Johns-Mansville Sales Corp., 677 F.2d 339 (3d Cir. 1982)	§ 30.3
Donovan v. Carls Drug Co., 703 F.2d 650 (2d Cir. 1983)	§§ 15.19, 26.1, 26.7
Donovan v. F.B.I., 806 F.2d 55 (2d Cir. 1986)	§ 17.8
Donovan v. Mazzola, 761 F.2d 1411 (9th Cir. 1985)	§ 31.6
Donovan v. Mosher Steel Co., 791 F.2d 1535 (11th Cir. 1986), *cert. denied,* _____ U.S. _____, 107 S. Ct. 874 (1987)	§ 29.4
Doran v. Salem Inn, Inc., 422 U.S. 922 (1975)	§ 11.7
Douglas Oil Co. v. Petrol Stops Nw., 441 U.S. 211 (1979)	§ 17.12
Dow Chem. Co. v. Allen, 672 F.2d 1262 (7th Cir. 1982)	§ 19.3
Dowling v. Richardson-Merrell, Inc., 727 F.2d 608 (6th Cir. 1984)	§ 6.17
Downes v. Beach, 587 F.2d 469 (10th Cir. 1978)	§ 15.11
Drake v. Raymark Indus., 772 F.2d 1007 (1st Cir. 1985), *cert. denied,* _____ U.S. _____, 106 S. Ct. 1994 (1986)	§ 2.24
Dredge Corp. v. Penny, 338 F.2d 456 (9th Cir. 1964)	§ 15.27
Dreiling v. Peugeot Motors of Am., Inc., 768 F.2d 1159 (10th Cir. 1985)	§§ 27.5, 28.8, 28.11
Dreis & Krump Mfg. v. International Ass'n of Machinists, 802 F.2d 247 (7th Cir. 1986)	§ 27.1
Drexel v. Union Prescription Centers, Inc., 582 F.2d 781 (3d Cir. 1978)	§ 15.28
Dubin v. United States, 380 F.2d 813 (5th Cir. 1967)	§§ 6.6, 6.9, 14.34
Ducommun v. Commissioner, 732 F.2d 752 (10th Cir.), *cert. denied,* 464 U.S. 939 (1983)	§ 31.12
Dudley v. South Jersey Metal, Inc., 555 F.2d 96 (3d Cir. 1977)	§ 17.14
Dudo v. Schaffer, 91 F.R.D. 128 (E.D. Pa. 1981)	§ 15.18
Duke Power Co. v. Carolina Envtl. Study Group, Inc., 438 U.S. 59 (1978)	§ 14.12
Dukes v. South Carolina Ins. Co., 770 F.2d 545 (5th Cir. 1985)	§§ 3.15, 3.17
Dunbar v. United States, 502 F.2d 506 (5th Cir. 1974)	§§ 9.6, 29.4
Duncan v. Leeds, 742 F.2d 989 (6th Cir. 1984)	§ 14.48
Dunton v. County of Suffolk, 729 F.2d 903 (2d Cir. 1984)	§ 2.29
Durflinger v. Artiles, 727 F.2d 888 (10th Cir. 1984)	§ 20.15
Durham v. Kelly, 810 F.2d 1500 (9th Cir. 1987)	§ 2.29
Durkin v. Taylor, 444 F. Supp. 879 (E. D. Va. 1977)	§ 15.28
Durns v. Bureau of Prisons, 804 F.2d 701 (D.C. Cir. 1986)	§ 17.9
Dussouy v. Gulf Coast Inv. Corp., 660 F.2d 594 (5th Cir. 1981)	§ 8.9

Case	*Book §*
Eggleston v. Chicago Journeymen Plumbers' Local Union No. 130, 657 F.2d 890 (7th Cir. 1981), *cert. denied,* 455 U.S. 1017 (1982)	§§ 17.5, 23.19
Eguia v. Tompkins, 756 F.2d 1130 (5th Cir. 1985)	§ 15.16
Eisen v. Carlisle & Jacquelin, 417 U.S. 156 (1974)	§§ 10.10, 10.12, 10.17, 17.5
Eisenberg, *In re,* 654 F.2d 1107 (5th Cir. 1981)	§ 17.13
Eitel v. Holland, 787 F.2d 995 (5th Cir. 1986)	§ 2.6
Eitmann v. New Orleans Pub. Serv., Inc., 730 F.2d 359 (5th Cir.), *cert. denied,* 419 U.S. 1018 (1984)	§ 3.2
Electrical Constr. & Maint. Co. v. Maeda Pac. Corp., 764 F.2d 619 (9th Cir. 1985)	§ 14.43
Elfenbein v. Gulf & W. Indus., Inc., 590 F.2d 445 (2d Cir. 1978)	§§ 8.8, 8.9
Eli Lilly & Co. v. Generix Drug Sales, Inc., 460 F.2d 1096 (5th Cir. 1972)	§ 11.3
Eli Lilly & Co. v. Home Ins. Co., 794 F.2d 710 (D.C. Cir. 1986)	§§ 4.14, 6.3
Ellis v. Brotherhood of Ry., Airline, & S.S. Clerks, 685 F.2d 1065 (9th Cir. 1982), *rev'd,* 446 U.S. 435 (1984)	§§ 2.4, 17.16
Ellis v. Great Sw. Corp., 646 F.2d 1099 (5th Cir. 1981)	§§ 6.8, 6.9
Ellis v. United States Postal Serv., 784 F.2d 835 (7th Cir. 1986)	§ 8.3
Elston Inv., Ltd. v. David Altman Leasing Corp., 731 F.2d 436 (7th Cir. 1984)	§ 2.21
Emerick v. U.S. Suzuki Motor Corp., 750 F.2d 19 (3d Cir. 1984)	§ 20.15
Emmons v. Southern Pac. Transp. Co., 701 F.2d 1112 (5th Cir. 1983)	§ 16.4
Employees Sav. Plan of Mobil Oil Corp. v. Vickery, 99 F.R.D. 138 (S.D.N.Y. 1983)	§ 8.11
Encoder Communications, Inc. v. Telegen, Inc., 654 F.2d 198 (2d Cir. 1981)	§ 3.19
Ennis v. New Jersey Bell Tel. Co., 782 F.2d 396 (3d Cir. 1985), *cert. denied,* ___ U.S. ___, 106 S. Ct. 1461 (1986)	§ 29.5
Enquip, Inc. v. Smith-McDonald Corp., 655 F.2d 115 (7th Cir. 1981)	§§ 15.16, 15.20
Enterprise Int'l v. Corporacion Estatal Petrolere, 762 F.2d 464 (5th Cir. 1985)	§ 14.21
Envirotech Corp. v. Bethlehem Steel Corp., 729 F.2d 70 (2d Cir. 1984)	§ 9.3
Erff v. Markhon Indus., Inc., 781 F.2d 613 (7th Cir. 1986)	§ 16.4
Erie R.R. v. Tompkins, 304 U.S. 64 (1938)	§§ 1.11, 2.23, 4.12
Estate of Bailey by Oare v. County of York, 768 F.2d 503 (3d Cir. 1985)	§ 14.42
Estate of Blas through Chargualaf v. Winkler, 792 F.2d 858 (9th Cir. 1986)	§§ 27.5, 27.9, 28.11
Estate of Domingo v. Republic of Philippines, 808 F.2d 1349 (9th Cir. 1987)	§ 17.19
Estate of Smith v. Tarrant County Hosp. Dist., 691 F.2d 207 (5th Cir. 1982)	§ 14.47
Eureka Inv. Corp. v. Chicago Title Ins. Co., 743 F.2d 932 (D.C. Cir. 1984)	§ 18.8

Case	*Book §*
Feist v. Jefferson County Comm'rs Court, 778 F.2d 250 (5th Cir. 1985)	§ 5.1
Feller v. Brock, 802 F.2d 722 (4th Cir. 1986)	§ 11.7
Fellman v. Fireman's Fund Ins. Co., 735 F.2d 55 (2d Cir. 1984)	§ 16.13
Fern v. Turman, 736 F.2d 1367 (9th Cir. 1984), *cert. denied,* 469 U.S. 1210 (1985)	§ 2.6
Fernhoff v. Tahoe Regional Planning Agency, 803 F.2d 979 (9th Cir. 1986)	§ 15.27
Fidelity & Deposit Co. v. City of Sheboygan Falls, 713 F.2d 1261 (7th Cir. 1983)	§ 2.16
Fiedler v. First City Nat'l Bank, 807 F.2d 315 (2d Cir. 1986)	§ 4.5
Field v. Volkswagenwerk AG, 626 F.2d 293 (3d Cir. 1980)	§§ 2.13, 14.10
Fielding v. Brebbia, 399 F.2d 1003 (D.C. Cir. 1968)	§ 14.41
Fields v. Sedgwick Associated Risks, Ltd., 796 F.2d 299 (9th Cir. 1986)	§§ 4.8, 14.26
Filco v. Amana Refrigeration, Inc., 709 F.2d 1257 (9th Cir.), *cert. dismissed,* 464 U.S. 956 (1983)	§ 15.20
Fine Paper Antitrust Litig., *In re,* 695 F.2d 494 (3d Cir. 1982)	§ 10.16
Fine Paper Antitrust Litig., *In re,* 685 F.2d 810 (3d Cir. 1982)	§§ 6.7, 6.14
Finkle v. Gulf & W. Mfg. Co., 744 F.2d 1015 (3d Cir. 1984)	§ 2.26
Finn v. Consol Rail Corp., 782 F.2d 13 (1st Cir. 1986)	§ 15.17
Finn v. Gunter, 722 F.2d 711 (11th Cir. 1984)	§§ 15.3, 15.26, 15.30
Firefighters Local Union No. 1784 v. Stotts, 467 U.S. 561 (1984)	§ 2.4
Fireman's Ins. Co. v. Dufresne, 676 F.2d 965 (3d Cir. 1982)	§§ 15.6, 15.10
Firestone Tire & Rubber Co. v. Risjord, 449 U.S. 368 (1981)	§§ 15.28, 16.9
First Brands Corp. v. Fred Meyer, Inc., 809 F.2d 1378 (9th Cir. 1987)	§ 11.4
First Nat'l Bank Co. v. Ins. Co. of N. Am., 606 F.2d 760 (7th Cir. 1979)	§ 15.6
First Nat'l Bank v. Cities Serv. Co., 391 U.S. 253 (1968)	§ 15.14, 15.24
Fischel, *In re,* 557 F.2d 209 (9th Cir. 1977)	§ 18.2
Fisher v. Agios Nicolaos V, 628 F.2d 308 (5th Cir. 1980), *cert. denied,* 454 U.S. 816 (1981)	§ 6.18
Fisher v. United States, 425 U.S. 391 (1976)	§§ 18.9, 18.20
Fitzgerald v. Penthouse Int'l, Ltd., 776 F.2d 1236 (4th Cir. 1985)	§ 18.22
Fitzgerald v. Penthouse Int'l, Ltd., 639 F.2d 1076 (4th Cir. 1981), *cert. denied,* 460 U.S. 1024 (1983)	§§ 15.6, 15.17
Fitzgerald v. Seaboard Sys. R.R., Inc., 760 F.2d 1249 (11th Cir. 1985)	§§ 2.7, 2.20, 2.31, 14.8
Fitzpatrick v. Bitzer, 427 U.S. 445 (1976)	§ 2.6
Fjelstad v. American Honda Motor Co., 762 F.2d 1334 (9th Cir. 1985)	§§ 19.3, 29.2, 29.3, 29.7, 30.9
Flaherty v. Coughlin, 713 F.2d 10 (2d Cir. 1983)	§§ 15.20, 15.22
Flaminio v. Honda Motor Co., 733 F.2d 463 (7th Cir. 1984)	§ 16.3
Flaska v. Little River Marine Constr. Co., 389 F.2d 885 (5th Cir.), *cert. denied,* 392 U.S. 928 (1968)	§ 31.10
Flast v. Cohen, 392 U.S. 83 (1968)	§ 2.3

Case	*Book §*
Franchise Tax Bd. v. Construction Laborer's Vacation Trust, 463 U.S. 1 (1983)	§§ 2.8, 2.9, 3.2
Franchise Tax Bd. v. U.S. Postal Serv., 467 U.S. 512 (1984)	§ 3.5
Francis v. INA Life Ins. Co., 809 F.2d 183 (2d Cir. 1987)	§ 1.11
Frank Briscoe Co. v. Morrison-Knudsen Co., 776 F.2d 1414 (9th Cir. 1985)	§ 15.29
Franklin v. Murphy, 745 F.2d 1221 (9th Cir. 1984)	§§ 14.6, 14.7
Franklin v. Oregon State Welfare Div., 662 F.2d 1337 (9th Cir. 1981)	§ 14.6
Franklin Nat'l Bank Secs. Litig., 574 F.2d 662, *modified,* 599 F.2d 1109 (2d Cir. 1978)	§ 10.12
Franks v. Bowman Transp. Co., 424 U.S. 747 (1976)	§ 10.10
Franks v. Kroger Co., 649 F.2d 1216 (6th Cir. 1981)	§ 10.13
Franks v. Nimmo, 796 F.2d 1230 (10th Cir. 1986)	§§ 15.18, 16.8
Frazier v. Cast, 771 F.2d 259 (7th Cir. 1985)	§§ 15.1, 28.6
Frederic P. Wiedersum Assocs. v. National Homes Constr. Corp., 540 F.2d 62 (2d Cir. 1976)	§ 7.5
Fredieu v. Rowan Cos., 738 F.2d 651 (5th Cir. 1984)	§§ 7.15, 7.17
Freeman v. Continental Gin Co., 381 F.2d 459 (5th Cir. 1967)	§ 8.3
Freeman v. Michigan Dept. of State, 808 F.2d 1174 (6th Cir. 1987)	§ 2.6
Freeman v. Northwest Acceptance Corp., 754 F.2d 553 (5th Cir. 1985)	§§ 2.14, 2.15, 9.3, 14.8, 14.15, 14.61
Fremont Energy Corp. v. Seattle Post Intelligencer, 688 F.2d 1285 (9th Cir. 1982)	§ 21.5
Friedlander v. Nims, 755 F.2d 810 (11th Cir. 1985)	§ 14.49
Friends for All Children v. Lockheed Aircraft Corp., 717 F.2d 602 (D.C. Cir. 1983)	§ 6.16
Frito-Lay of Puerto Rico v. Canas, 92 F.R.D. 384 (D.P.R. 1981)	§§ 15.10, 15.28
Fritz v. American Home Shield Corp., 751 F.2d 1152 (11th Cir. 1985)	§§ 2.15, 2.20
Frye v. United States, 293 F. 1013 (D.C. Cir. 1923)	§ 20.11
F.T.C. v. Alaska Leasing Inc., 799 F.2d 507 (9th Cir. 1986)	§§ 28.8, 28.11
F.T.C. v. Compagnie de Saint-Gobain-Pont-A-Mousson, 636 F.2d 1300 (D.C. Cir. 1980)	§§ 5.1, 14.39
F.T.C. v. Grolier, 462 U.S. 19 (1983)	§§ 17.9, 18.3
F.T.C. v. Jim Walter Corp., 651 F.2d 251 (5th Cir. 1981)	§§ 4.13, 4.14
Fuller v. Marx, 724 F.2d 717 (8th Cir. 1984)	§ 8.12
Fullman v. Graddick, 739 F.2d 553 (11th Cir. 1984)	§§ 14.43, 14.44, 15.11
Fund of Funds, Ltd. v. Arthur Andersen & Co., 567 F.2d 225 (2d Cir. 1977)	§ 16.9
GAB Business Servs., Inc. v. Syndicate 627, 809 F.2d 755 (11th Cir. 1987)	§ 18.8
GAC Corp., *In re,* 681 F.2d 1295 (11th Cir. 1982)	§ 10.2
GAF Corp v. Transamerica Ins. Co., 665 F.2d 364 (D.C. Cir. 1981)	§ 12.6
Gairola v. Virginia Dep't of General Servs., 753 F.2d 1281 (4th Cir. 1985)	§ 16.13

Case	*Book §*
Georgia S. & Fl. Ry. v. Atlantic Coast Line R.R., 373 F.2d 493 (5th Cir.), *cert. denied,* 389 U.S. 851 (1967)	§ 15.25
Ghandi v. Police Dep't of Detroit, 74 F.R.D. 115 (E.D. Mich. S.D. 1977)	§ 23.19
Giampaoli v. Califano, 628 F.2d 1190 (9th Cir. 1980)	§ 12.1
Giannakos v. M/V Bravo Trader, 762 F.2d 1295 (5th Cir. 1985)	§ 2.13
Gibbs v. Maxwell House, 738 F.2d 1153 (11th Cir. 1984)	§ 30.5
Gieringer v. Silverman, 731 F.2d 1272 (7th Cir. 1984)	§§ 15.14, 15.24
Gifford v. Heckler, 741 F.2d 263 (9th Cir. 1984)	§ 31.6
Gilbert v. David, 235 U.S. 561 (1915)	§ 14.15
Gilboe, *In re,* 699 F.2d 71 (2d Cir. 1983)	§ 18.19
Gill v. Westinghouse Elec. Corp., 714 F.2d 1105 (11th Cir. 1983)	§ 23.29
Gillespie v. Civiletti, 629 F.2d 637 (9th Cir. 1980)	§ 2.10
Gillespie v. United States Steel, 379 U.S. 148 (1964)	§ 15.28
Gillis v. United States Dep't of Health & Human Servs., 759 F.2d 565 (6th Cir. 1985)	§ 14.68
Giotis v. Apollo of the Ozarks, Inc., 800 F.2d 660 (7th Cir. 1986)	§§ 4.5, 4.12, 14.26, 14.63
Givens v. A.H. Robins Co., 751 F.2d 261 (8th Cir. 1984)	§ 29.5
G-K Properties v. Redevelopment Agency, 577 F.2d 645 (9th Cir. 1978)	§ 29.3
Glaser v. Cincinnati Milacron, Inc., 808 F.2d 285 (3d Cir. 1986)	§ 28.3
Glasser v. Amalgamated Workers Union Local 88, 806 F.2d 1539 (11th Cir. 1986)	§ 3.19
Glasstech, Inc. v. AB Kyro Oy, 769 F.2d 1574 (Fed. Cir. 1985)	§ 6.14
Glater v. Eli Lilly & Co., 712 F.2d 735 (1st Cir. 1983)	§ 14.64
Glazer v. J.C. Bradford & Co., 616 F.2d 167 (5th Cir. 1980)	§ 16.7
Glen Eden Hosp. v. Blue Cross & Blue Shield, 740 F.2d 423 (6th Cir. 1984)	§ 15.23
Glick v. Koenig, 766 F.2d 265 (7th Cir. 1985)	§ 8.5
Glidden v. Chromalloy Am. Corp., 808 F.2d 621 (7th Cir. 1986)	§§ 10.15, 10.17
Glovatorium, Inc. v. NCR Corp., 684 F.2d 658 (9th Cir. 1982)	§ 18.12
Goar v. Compania Peruana de Vapores, 688 F.2d 417 (5th Cir. 1982)	§ 2.20
Goble v. Marsh, 684 F.2d 12 (D.C. Cir. 1982)	§§ 6.10, 14.10
Goforth v. Owens, 766 F.2d 1533 (11th Cir. 1985)	§§ 30.6, 30.10
Goins v. Goins 777 F.2d 1059 (5th Cir. 1985)	§ 2.6
Golden v. Cox Furniture Mfg. Co., 683 F.2d 115 (5th Cir. 1982)	§ 14.26
Golden v. Zwickler, 394 U.S. 103 (1969)	§ 2.4
Golden Eagle Distrib. Corp. v. Burroughs Corp., 801 F.2d 1531 (9th Cir. 1986)	§§ 28.3, 28.4
Goldlawr, Inc. v. Heiman, 369 U.S. 463 (1962)	§§ 4.1, 6.9, 14.30
Goldman v. Belden, 754 F.2d 1059 (2d Cir. 1985)	§§ 14.47, 15.25
Golman v. Tesoro Drilling Corp., 700 F.2d 249 (5th Cir. 1983)	§ 15.26
Gompers v. Bucks Stove & Range Co., 221 U.S. 418 (1911)	§ 31.8
Goney v. Clark, 749 F.2d 5 (3d Cir. 1984)	§ 16.12
Gonsalves v. Amoco Shipping Co., 733 F.2d 1020 (2d Cir. 1984)	§§ 3.8, 3.20
Gonzalez v. Firestone Tire & Rubber Co., 610 F.2d 241 (5th Cir. 1980)	§ 30.3

Case	*Book §*
Grand Jury Subpoena Duces Tecum Tecum, *In re,* 795 F.2d 904 (11th Cir. 1986)	§ 18.21
Grand Jury Subpoena Duces Dated January 2, 1985, *In re,* 767 F.2d (2d Cir. 1985)	§ 21.6
Grand Jury Subpoena Duces Tecum Dated September 15, 1983, *In re,* 731 F.2d 1032 (2d Cir. 1984)	§§ 18.6, 18.10, 18.12
Grand Jury Subpoena Duces Tecum Dated September 15, 1983 (Marc Rich & Co.), *In re,* 731 F.2d 1032 (2d Cir. 1984)	§ 17.20
Grand Jury Subpoena Duces Tecum (Underhill), *In re,* 781 F.2d 64 (6th Cir.), *cert. denied,* ____ U.S. ____ , 107 S. Ct. 64 (1986)	§ 18.21
Grand Jury Subpoena (Lincoln), *In re,* 767 F.2d 1130 (5th Cir. 1985)	§ 18.21
Grand Jury Subpoena of Flanagan, *In re,* 691 F.2d 116 (2d Cir. 1982)	§ 18.19
Grand Jury Subpoenas Duces Tecum, *In re,* 798 F.2d 32 (2d Cir. 1986)	§ 18.12
Grand Jury Subpoena Served Upon Doe, *In re,* 759 F.2d 968 (2d Cir. 1985), *cert. denied,* ____ U.S. ____ , 106 S. Ct. 1515 (1986)	§ 17.20
Grand Union Co. v. Cord Meyer Dev. Corp., 735 F.2d 714 (2d Cir. 1984)	§ 15.28
Granny Goose Foods, Inc. v. Brotherhood of Teamsters & Auto Truck Drivers, 415 U.S. 423 (1974)	§§ 3.15, 11.2
Gravitt v. Southwestern Bell Tel. Co., 430 U.S. 723 (1977)	§ 3.19
Gray v. Board of Higher Educ., 692 F.2d 901 (2d Cir. 1982)	§ 18.22
Gray v. O'Brien, 777 F.2d 864 (1st Cir. 1985)	§ 4.12
Gray v. Udevitz, 656 F.2d 588 (10th Cir. 1981)	§ 15.24
Great N. Life Ins. Co. v. Read, 322 U.S. 47 (1944)	§ 2.6
Great S. Fire Proof Hotel Co. v. Jones, 177 U.S. 449 (1900)	§ 2.21
Green v. Amerada Hess Corp., 707 F.2d 201 (5th Cir. 1983), *cert. denied,* 464 U.S. 1039 (1984)	§ 3.11
Green v. Department of Commerce, 618 F.2d 836 (D.C. Cir. 1980)	§ 17.10
Green v. Lindsey, 456 U.S. 444 (1982)	§ 5.4
Green v. McKaskle, 788 F.2d 1116 (5th Cir. 1986)	§ 14.7
Green v. Occidental Petroleum Corp., 541 F.2d 1335 (9th Cir. 1976)	§ 10.7
Greenberg v. F.D.A., 803 F.2d 1213 (D.C. Cir. 1986)	§§ 15.12, 17.9
Greene v. Union Mut. Life Ins. Co. of Am., 764 F.2d 19 (1st Cir. 1985)	§§ 14.2, 14.50, 14.70
Greenhaw v. Lubbock County Beverage Ass'n, 721 F.2d 1019 (5th Cir. 1983), *overruled by* International Woodworkers v. Champion Int'l Corp., 790 F.2d 1174 (5th Cir.), *aff'd sub nom.* Crawford Fitting Co. v. J.T. Gibbons, Inc., ____ U.S. ____ , ____ S. Ct. ____ , 55 U.S.L.W. 4820 (June 15, 1987)	§ 10.9
Greenwood v. Dittmer, 776 F.2d 785 (8th Cir. 1985)	§ 23.6

Case	*Book §*
Greenwood v. McDonough Power Equip., Inc., 731 F.2d 690 (10th Cir. 1984)	§ 20.15
Greenwood, City of, v. Peacock, 384 U.S. 808 (1966)	§ 3.6
Griffin v. Sandy Howard Prods., 800 F.2d 612 (6th Cir. 1986)	§ 2.22
Griffin v. Swim-Tech Corp., 722 F.2d 677 (11th Cir. 1984)	§ 29.9
Griggs v. Provident Consumer Discount Co., 459 U.S. 56 (1982)	§ 15.29
Grigoleit Co. v. United Rubber, Local No. 270, 769 F.2d 434 (7th Cir. 1985)	§§ 15.3, 15.27
Grigsby v. CMI Corp., 765 F.2d 1369 (9th Cir. 1985)	§ 14.19
Grinnell Corp. v. Hackett, 70 F.R.D. 326 (D.R.I. 1976)	§ 20.7
Grogan v. Garner, 806 F.2d 829 (8th Cir. 1986)	§ 20.15
Groppi v. Leslie, 404 U.S. 496 (1972)	§ 31.4
Gross v. Hougland, 712 F.2d 1034 (6th Cir. 1983), *cert. denied,* 465 U.S. 1025 (1984)	§§ 2.17, 2.21, 14.8
Grosso v. United States, 390 U.S. 62 (1986)	§ 18.20
Grosvenor v. Brienen, 801 F.2d 944 (7th Cir. 1986)	§ 16.6
Ground Saucer Watch, Inc. v. CIA, 692 F.2d 770 (D.C. Cir. 1981)	§ 15.6
Group Health Inc. v. Blue Cross Ass'n, 793 F.2d 491 (2d Cir. 1986)	§ 15.28
Grove v. Mead School Dist. No. 354, 753 F.2d 1528 (9th Cir.), *cert. denied,* ____ U.S. ____, 106 S. Ct. 85 (1985)	§ 15.25
Growden v. Ed Bowlin & Assocs., Inc., 733 F.2d 1149 (5th Cir. 1984)	§ 14.29
Grubbs v. General Elec. Credit Corp., 405 U.S. 699 (1972)	§§ 3.17, 3.20
G.T.E. Sylvania, Inc. v. Consumer's Union, Inc., 445 U.S. 375 (1980)	§ 17.9
Guam Inv. Co. v. Central Bldg., Inc., 288 F.2d 19 (9th Cir. 1961)	§ 14.48
Guaranty Trust Co. v. York, 326 U.S. 99 (1945)	§§ 2.23, 5.4, 7.8
Guidry v. Continental Oil Co., 640 F.2d 523 (5th Cir.), *cert. denied,* 454 U.S. 818 (1981)	§ 29.2
Gulf Oil Co. v. Bernard, 452 U.S. 89 (1981)	§§ 10.10, 19.5
Gulf Oil Corp. v. Gilbert, 330 U.S. 501 (1947)	§ 6.16
Gully v. First Nat'l Bank in Meridian, 299 U.S. 109 (1936)	§§ 2.8, 3.9
Guthrie v. J.C. Penney Co., 803 F.2d 202 (5th Cir. 1986)	§ 8.3
Gutting v. Falstaff Brewing Corp., 710 F.2d 1309 (8th Cir. 1983)	§ 16.9, 26.7
Gutwein v. Roche Laboratories, 739 F.2d 93 (2d Cir. 1984)	§ 15.3
Haase v. Webster, 807 F.2d 208 (D.C. Cir. 1986)	§ 15.14
Hackney v. Newman Memorial Hosp., Inc., 621 F.2d 1069 (10th Cir. 1980)	§ 2.17
Hagans v. Lavine, 415 U.S. 528 (1973)	§§ 2.28, 14.12
Haines v. Kerner, 404 U.S. 519 (1972)	§§ 14.7, 14.10, 14.42
Haisten v. Grass Valley Medical Reimbursement, 784 F.2d 1392 (9th Cir. 1986)	§ 4.11
Haitian Refugee Center v. Gracey, 809 F.2d 794 (D.C. Cir. 1987)	2.3
Hale v. Firestone Tire & Rubber Co., 756 F.2d 1332 (8th Cir. 1985)	§ 16.4
Hale v. Harney, 786 F.2d 688 (5th Cir. 1986)	§ 28.4

Case	*Book §*
Haley v. Kansas City Star, 761 F.2d 489 (8th Cir. 1985)	§ 30.6
Hall v. City of Santa Barbara, 797 F.2d 1493 (9th Cir. 1986)	§ 8.8
Hall v. Cole, 412 U.S. 1 (1973)	§ 30.8
Hall v. Commissioner, 805 F.2d 1511 (11th Cir. 1986)	§ 31.11
Hall v. Hawaii, 791 F.2d 759 (9th Cir. 1986)	§ 15.23
Halliburton & Assocs. v. Henderson, Few & Co., 774 F.2d 441 (11th Cir. 1985)	§§ 8.5, 8.7
Hallmark Builders, Inc. v. Gaylord Broadcasting Co., 733 F.2d 1461 (11th Cir. 1984)	§ 15.6
Halphen v. Johns-Mansville Sales Corp., 737 F.2d 462 (5th Cir. 1984)	§ 17.15
Hamilton v. Keystone Tankship Corp., 539 F.2d 684 (9th Cir. 1976)	§ 15.9
Hamilton v. Neptune Orient Lines, Ltd., 811 F.2d 498 (9th Cir. 1987)	§ 30.3
Hamman v. Southwestern Gas Pipeline, Inc., 721 F.2d 140 (5th Cir. 183)	§ 15.27
Hammond Packing Co. v. Arkansas, 212 U.S. 322 (1909)	§ 29.3
Handley v. Indiana & Mich. Elec. Co., 732 F.2d 1265 (6th Cir. 1984)	§§ 4.13, 14.21, 14.30
Handschu v. Special Servs. Div., 787 F.2d 828 (2d Cir. 1986)	§ 10.13
Hanna v. Plumer, 380 U.S. 460 (1965)	§ 5.4
Hans v. Louisiana, 134 U.S. 1 (1890)	§ 2.6
Hansberry v. Lee, 311 U.S. 32 (1940)	§ 10.6
Hansen v. Prentice-Hall Inc., 788 F.2d 892 (2d Cir.), *cert. denied,* ____ U.S. ____, 107 S. Ct. 178 (1986)	§ 15.10
Hanson v. Denckla, 357 U.S. 235 (1958)	§ 4.4
Hanson v. Polk County Land, Inc., 608 F.2d 129 (5th Cir. 1979)	§ 15.3
Harding v. Federal Reserve Bank of New York, 707 F.2d 46 (2d Cir. 1983)	§§ 30.3, 30.4
Hardy v. Johns-Mansville Sales Corp., 681 F.2d 334 (5th Cir. 1982)	§ 16.4
Hargrave v. Fibreboard Corp., 710 F.2d 1154 (5th Cir. 1983)	§ 15.28
Harlow v. Fitzgerald, 457 U.S. 800 (1982)	§ 19.5
Haroco v. American Nat'l Bank & Trust Co., 747 F.2d 384 (7th Cir. 1984), *aff'd,* ____ U.S. ____, 105 S. Ct. 3291 (1985)	§ 7.3
Harper & Row Publishers, Inc. v. Decker, 423 F.2d 487 (7th Cir. 1970), *aff'd,* 400 U.S. 348 (1971)	§ 18.4
Harre v. A.H. Robins Co., 750 F.2d 1501 (11th Cir. 1985)	§ 20.11
Harris v. Amoco Prod. Co., 768 F.2d 669 (5th Cir. 1985), *cert. denied,* ____ U.S. ____, 106 S. Ct. 1186 (1986)	§§ 9.7, 9.8, 19.5
Harris v. Cuyler, 664 F.2d 388 (3d Cir. 1981)	§ 14.7
Harris v. Edward Hyman Co., 664 F.2d 943 (5th Cir. 1981)	§ 3.17
Harris v. Johnson, 784 F.2d 222 (6th Cir. 1986)	§ 14.7
Harris v. United States, 382 U.S. 162 (1965)	§ 31.8
Harris Corp. v. National Iranian Radio & Television, 691 F.2d 1344 (11th Cir. 1982)	§§ 6.1, 14.26, 14.31, 14.36, 14.38, 14.62

Case	*Book §*
Hart v. Commissioner, 730 F.2d 1206 (8th Cir. 1984)	§ 31.12
Harville v. Johns-Mansville Prods. Corp., 731 F.2d 775 (11th Cir. 1984)	§ 2.24
Hasse v. American Photograph Corp., 299 F.2d 666 (10th Cir. 1962)	§ 14.27
Hastings v. North E. Indep. School Dist., 615 F.2d 628 (5th Cir. 1980)	§ 29.4
Havenfield Corp. v. H. & R. Block, Inc., 509 F.2d 1263 (8th Cir.), *cert. denied,* 421 U.S. 999 (1975)	§ 17.14
Havens Realty Corp. v. Coleman, 455 U.S. 363 (1982)	§ 2.3, 14.57
Hawaii Hous. Auth. v. Midkiff, 467 U.S. 229 (1984)	§ 2.6
Hayden v. McDonald, 719 F.2d 266 (8th Cir. 1983)	§ 15.29
Hayden v. Oak Terrace Apartments, 808 F.2d 1269 (7th Cir. 1987)	§ 31.4
Hayden Stone, Inc. v. Brode, 508 F.2d 895 (7th Cir. 1974)	§ 29.9
Hayduk v. Lanna, 775 F.2d 441 (1st Cir. 1985), *cert. denied,* ___ U.S. ___ , 106 S. Ct. 1790 (1986)	§§ 7.3, 8.5
Hazen v. Pasley, 768 F.2d 226 (8th Cir. 1985)	§ 29.4
H.D. Corp. of Puerto Rico v. Ford Motor Co., 791 F.2d 987 (1st Cir. 1986)	§ 9.3
Healy v. Counts, 100 F.R.D. 493 (D. Colo. 1984)	§ 20.6
Heartfield v. Heartfield, 749 F.2d 1138 (5th Cir. 1985)	§ 2.6
Heat & Control, Inc. v. Hester Indus., Inc., 785 F.2d 1017 (Fed. Cir. 1986)	§§ 17.19, 21.4, 21.6
Hefner v. Alexander, 779 F.2d 277 (5th Cir. 1985)	§ 2.29
Helicopteros Nacionales de Colombia, S.A. v. Hall, 466 U.S. 408 (1984)	§§ 4.2, 4.4
Helmich v. Kennedy, 796 F.2d 1441 (11th Cir. 1986)	§ 15.10
Helvering v. Gowran, 302 U.S. 238 (1937)	§ 15.28
Helzberg's Diamond Shops v. Valley West Des Moines Shopping Center, Inc., 564 F.2d 816 (8th Cir. 1977)	§ 14.69
Hendrix v. Raybestos-Manhattan, Inc., 776 F.2d 1492 (11th Cir. 1985)	§§ 16.3, 23.29
Heniford v. American Motors Sales Corp., 471 F. Supp. 328 (D.S.C. 1979), *appeal dismissed,* 622 F.2d 584 (4th Cir. 1980)	§ 3.10
Henz v. Superior Trucking Co., 96 F.R.D. 219 (M.D. Pa. 1982)	§ 14.50
Herbert v. Wicklund, 744 F.2d 218 (1st Cir. 1984)	§ 15.24
Hermsdorfer v. American Motors Corp., 96 F.R.D. 13 (W.D.N.Y. 1982)	§ 20.7
Hernandez v. George, 793 F.2d 264 (10th Cir. 1986)	§ 23.1
Hervey v. City of Little Rock, 787 F.2d 1223 (8th Cir. 1986)	§ 10.6
Hewitt v. City of Stanton, 798 F.2d 1230 (9th Cir. 1986)	§ 3.23
H.F. Livermore Corp. v. Aktiengesellschaft Gebruder Loepfe, 432 F.2d 689 (D.C. Cir. 1970)	§ 12.2
Hibernia Nat'l Bank v. Administracion Central Sociedad Anonima, 776 F.2d 1277 (5th Cir. 1985)	§ 15.28
Hickey v. Baxter, 800 F.2d 430 (4th Cir. 1986)	§ 2.6
Hickman v. Taylor, 329 U.S. 495 (1947)	§ 18.13
Hifai v. Shell Oil Co., 704 F.2d 1425 (9th Cir. 1983)	§ 7.7

Case	Book §
Higgenbotham v. Ochsner Found. Hosp., 607 F.2d 653 (5th Cir. 1979)	§ 15.12
Hiley v. United States, 807 F.2d 623 (7th Cir. 1986)	§ 18.19
Hilgeman v. National Ins. Co. of America, 547 F.2d 298 (5th Cir. 1977)	§ 6.5
Hill v. Western Elec. Co., 672 F.2d 381 (4th Cir.), *cert. denied,* 459 U.S. 981 (1982)	§ 10.16
Hirsch v. Blue Cross, Blue Shield of Kansas City, 800 F.2d 1474 (9th Cir. 1986)	§ 4.14
Hispanic Society v. New York City Police Dep't, 806 F.2d 1147 (2d Cir. 1986)	§ 9.9
Hixon v. Sherwin-Williams Co., 671 F.2d 1005 (7th Cir. 1982)	§ 2.30
H.L. Hayden Co. v. Siemens Med. Sys., Inc., 797 F.2d 85 (2d Cir. 1986)	§ 19.9
Hobbs & Co. v. American Investors Mgmt., Inc., 576 F.2d 29 (3d Cir. 1978)	§ 16.7
Hobson v. Wilson, 737 F.2d 1 (D.C. Cir. 1984), *cert. denied,* 470 U.S. 1084 (1985)	§§ 7.3, 14.44
Hodge v. Police Officers, 802 F.2d 58 (2d Cir. 1986)	§ 14.7
Hodges v. United States, 597 F.2d 1014 (5th Cir. 1979)	§ 16.2
Hodges, Grant & Kaufmann v. United States, 768 F.2d 719 (5th Cir. 1985)	§§ 18.2, 18.8, 18.14
Hodson v. A.H. Robins Co., 715 F.2d 142 (4th Cir. 1983)	§ 6.21
Hoffman v. Beer Drivers & Salesmen's Local Union No. 888, 536 F.2d 1268 (9th Cir. 1976)	§ 31.4
Hoffman v. Blaski, 363 U.S. 335 (1960)	§§ 6.7, 14.36
Hoffman v. United States, 341 U.S. 479 (1951)	§ 18.19
Hoffritz for Cutlery, Inc. v. Amajac, Ltd., 763 F.2d 55 (2d Cir. 1985)	§§ 14.12, 14.19, 14.20
Hogan v. Midland County Comm'rs Court, 680 F.2d 1101 (5th Cir. 1982)	§ 14.7
Hogan v. Overman, 767 F.2d 1093 (4th Cir. 1985)	§ 2.24
Holcolm v. Aetna Life Ins. Co., 255 F.2d 577 (10th Cir.), *cert. denied,* 358 U.S. 879 (1958)	§ 15.5
Holcomb v. Allis-Chalmers Corp., 774 F.2d 398 (10th Cir. 1985)	§§ 29.4, 30.8
Holiday Inns, Inc. v. Robertshaw Controls Co., 560 F.2d 856 (7th Cir. 1977)	§ 20.15
Holland v. Sterling Enters., Inc., 777 F.2d 1288 (7th Cir. 1985)	§ 9.8
Hollis v. United States, 744 F.2d 1430 (10th Cir. 1984)	§ 30.6
Holmes v. Continental Can Co., 706 F.2d 1144 (11th Cir. 1983)	§§ 10.8, 10.13
Holt v. Pitts, 619 F.2d 558 (6th Cir. 1980)	§ 30.5
Holt Oil & Gas Corp. v. Harvey, 801 F.2d 773 (5th Cir. 1986)	§ 4.2
Holzsager v. Valley Hosp., 646 F.2d 792 (2d Cir. 1981)	§§ 14.26, 14.64
Hooks v. Hooks, 771 F.2d 935 (6th Cir. 1985)	§§ 15.3, 15.16
Hoopes v. Equifax, Inc., 611 F.2d 134 (6th Cir. 1979)	§ 15.3
Hoover v. Switlik Parachute Co., 663 F.2d 964 (9th Cir. 1981)	§ 15.18
Hornbuckle v. Arco Oil & Gas Co., 770 F.2d 1321 (5th Cir. 1985), *cert. denied,* ____ U.S. ____, 106 S. Ct. 1198 (1986)	§ 30.5

Case	*Book §*
Illinois v. City of Milwaukee, 406 U.S. 91 (1972)	§ 2.8
Illinois Brick Co. v. Illinois, 431 U.S. 720 (1977)	§ 2.3
Illinois Cent. Gulf R.R. v. Pargas, Inc., 706 F.2d 633 (5th Cir. 1983)	§§ 2.18, 2.20, 14.10
Illinois Employers Ins. v. Mihalcik, 801 F.2d 949 (7th Cir. 1986)	§ 9.6
Illinois Tool Works, Inc. v. Sweetheart Plastics, Inc., 436 F.2d 1180 (7th Cir. 1971)	§ 6.10
IMFC Professional v. Latin Am. Home Health, 676 F.2d 152 (5th Cir. 1982)	§ 3.3
Imperial Enters., Inc. v. Fireman's Fund Ins. Co., 535 F.2d 287 (5th Cir. 1976)	§ 7.10
Indianapolis Colts v. Mayor of Baltimore, 741 F.2d 954 (7th Cir. 1984), *cert. denied,* 470 U.S. 1052 (1985)	§ 9.6
Indianapolis Colts v. Mayor of Baltimore, 775 F.2d 177 (7th Cir. 1985)	§§ 28.6, 28.8
Indiana Port Comm'n v. Bethlehem Steel Corp., 702 F.2d 107 (7th Cir. 1983)	§ 15.3
Indium Corp. of Am. v. Semi-Alloys, Inc., 781 F.2d 879 (Fed. Cir. 1985), *cert. denied,* ____ U.S. ____, 107 S. Ct. 84 (1986)	§ 14.15
Industrial Elec. Corp. v. Cline, 330 F.2d 480 (3d Cir. 1964)	§ 14.11
Ingraham v. United States, 808 F.2d 1075 (5th Cir. 1987)	§ 7.7
Ingram v. Kumar, 585 F.2d 566 (2d Cir. 1978), *cert. denied,* 440 U.S. 940 (1979)	§ 8.13
Inland Rubber Corp. v. Triple A Tire Serv., Inc., 220 F. Supp. 490 (S.D.N.Y. 1963)	§ 2.20
Inryco, Inc. v. Metropolitan Eng'g Co., 708 F.2d 1225 (7th Cir.), *cert. denied,* 464 U.S. 937 (1983)	§ 12.3
Institutional Food Marketing Assocs. v. Golden State Strawberries, Inc., 747 F.2d 488 (8th Cir. 1984)	§§ 4.11, 14.19
Insurance Co. of N. Am. (I.N.A.) v. Marina Salina Cruz, 649 F.2d 1266 (9th Cir. 1981)	§ 4.11
Insurance Corp. of Ireland, Ltd. v. Compagnie des Bauxites de Guinee, 456 U.S. 694 (1982)	§§ 5.11, 14.23, 14.25, 14.26, 29.3, 29.7
Intermedics Infusaid, Inc. v. Regents of Univ. of Minn., 804 F.2d 129 (Fed. Cir. 1986)	§ 14.67
International Ass'n of Machinists v. Northwest Airlines, Inc., 673 F.2d 700 (3d Cir. 1982)	§§ 14.11, 14.13
International Ass'n of Machinists v. United Technologies Corp., 704 F.2d 569 (11th Cir. 1983)	§ 15.25
International Bhd. of Teamsters v. Western Pa. Motor Carriers Ass'n, 660 F.2d 76 (3d Cir. 1981)	§ 11.4
International Shoe Co. v. Washington, 326 U.S. 310 (1945)	§§ 4.3, 4.8, 4.9
International Soc'y for Krishna Consciousness, Inc. v. Air Canada, 727 F.2d 253 (2d Cir. 1984)	§ 14.68
International Sys. & Controls Corp. Secs. Litig., *In re,* 693 F.2d 1235 (5th Cir. 1982)	§§ 18.14, 18.18
International Union of Bricklayers v. Meese, 761 F.2d 798 (D.C Cir. 1985)	§ 2.4

Case	*Book §*
International Union, UAW v. Brock, _____ U.S. _____, 106 S. Ct. 2523 (1986)	§ 2.3
International Union, UAW v. National Caucus of Labor Comms., 525 F.2d 323 (2d Cir. 1975)	§ 23.9
International Woodworkers v. Champion Int'l, 790 F.2d 1174 (5th Cir. 1986) (en banc), *aff'd sub nom.* Crawford Fitting Co. v. J.T. Gibbons, Inc., _____ U.S. _____, 107 S. Ct. 2494, 55 U.S.L.W. 4820 (June 15, 1987)	§§ 10.9, 20.9
Iowa Beef Processors, Inc. v. Bagley, 601 F.2d 949 (8th Cir. 1979)	§ 17.18
Iowa Freedom of Information Council, *In re,* 724 F.2d 658 (8th Cir. 1984)	§ 19.5
Iowa Mfg. Co. of Cedar Rapids, *In re,* 747 F.2d 462 (8th Cir. 1984)	§ 3.10
Iowa Mut. Ins. Co. v. La Plante, _____ U.S. _____, 107 S. Ct. 971 (187)	§ 2.22
Irish Nat'l Ins. Co., Ltd. v. Aer Lingus Teoranta, 739 F.2d 90 (2d Cir. 1984)	§ 6.21
Irvin v. Griffin Corp., 808 F.2d 802 (11th Cir. 1987)	§§ 15.1, 16.6
Isaac v. Harvard Univ., 769 F.2d 817 (1st Cir. 1985)	§ 8.3
Isra Fruit Ltd. v. Agrexco Agr. Export Co., 804 F.2d 24 (2d Cir. 1986)	§ 14.69
I-T-E Circuit Breaker Co. v. Becker, 343 F.2d 361 (8th Cir. 1965)	§ 6.8
Itel Secs. Litig., *In re,* 791 F.2d 672 (9th Cir. 1986), *cert. denied,* _____ U.S. _____, 107 S. Ct. 880 (1987)	§§ 27.4, 28.11
Jackson v. American Bar Ass'n, 538 F.2d 829 (9th Cir. 1976)	§ 8.9
Jackson v. Consolidated Rail Corp., 717 F.2d 1045 (7th Cir. 1983)	§ 2.7
Jackson v. Dallas Police Dep't, 811 F.2d 260 (5th Cir. 1986)	§ 14.7
Jackson v. Procunier, 789 F.2d 307 (5th Cir. 1986)	§ 14.47
Jackson v. Schoemehl, 788 F.2d 1296 (8th Cir. 1986)	§§ 30.3, 30.7
Jackson v. Seaboard Coastline R.R., 678 F.2d 992 (11th Cir. 1982)	§ 7.7
Jackson Marine Corp. v. Harvey Barge Repair, Inc., 794 F.2d 989 (5th Cir. 1986)	§ 28.4
Jack Walters & Sons Corp. v. Morton Bldg., Inc., 737 F.2d 698 (7th Cir.), *cert. denied,* 469 U.S. 1018 (1984)	§§ 15.29, 16.16
Jacobsen v. Filler, 790 F.2d 1362 (9th Cir. 1986)	§§ 14.2, 14.50, 15.3, 15.12, 15.25
Jafree, *In re,* 741 F.2d 133 (7th Cir. 1984)	§ 31.8
Jafree v. Barber, 689 F.2d 640 (7th Cir. 1982)	§ 8.8
James v. Bellotti, 733 F.2d 989 (1st Cir. 1984)	§ 3.19
James Julian, Inc. v. Raytheon Co., 93 F.R.D. 138 (D. Del. 1982)	§§ 18.7, 18.17, 20.12
Jamieson v. Shaw, 772 F.2d 1205 (5th Cir. 1985)	§ 8.5
Japanese Elec. Prods., *In re,* 723 F.2d 238 (3d Cir. 1983), *rev'd sub nom.* Matsushita Elec. Indus. Co. v. Zenith Radio, _____ U.S. _____, 106 S. Ct. 1348 (1986)	§§ 15.5, 15.7, 15.19, 15.20, 15.28, 24.10, 25.10
Japan Petroleum Co. (Nigeria) v. Ashland Oil, Inc., 456 F. Supp. 831 (D. Del. 1978)	§ 14.53
Jaques, *In re,* 761 F.2d 302 (6th Cir. 1985)	§ 31.2

Case	*Book §*
Jason's Foods Inc. v. Peter Eckrich & Sons, Inc., 768 F.2d 189 (7th Cir. 1985)	§§ 2.20, 14.10
Jee, *In re,* 799 F.2d 532 (9th Cir. 1986)	§ 30.7
Jenkins v. Raymark Indus., 782 F.2d 468 (5th Cir. 1986)	§ 10.7
Jenkins v. Whittaker Corp., 785 F.2d 720 (9th Cir.), *cert. denied,* _____ U.S. _____, 107 S. Ct. 324 (1986)	§§ 4.12, 4.29, 20.15
Jerguson v. Blue Dot Inv., Inc., 659 F.2d 31 (5th Cir. 1981)	§ 2.20
Jim Fox Enters. Inc. v. Air France, 705 F.2d 738 (5th Cir. 1983)	§ 5.7
J. M. Cleminshaw Co. v. City of Norwich, 93 F.R.D. 338 (D. Conn. 1981)	§ 31.10
JM Mechanical Corp. v. United States, 716 F.2d 190 (3d Cir. 1983)	§ 14.14
Johansen v. E.I. DuPont de Nemours & Co., 810 F.2d 1377 (5th Cir. 1987)	§ 8.16
John v. Louisiana, 757 F.2d 698 (5th Cir. 1985)	§§ 14.2, 14.25, 15.11, 15.13, 31.11
John Cooper Produce v. Paxton Nat'l Ins. Co., 774 F.2d 433 (11th Cir. 1985)	§ 2.22
John Deere Ltd. v. Sperry Corp., 754 F.2d 132 (3d Cir. 1985)	§ 22.7
John Doe Corp., *In re,* 675 F.2d 482 (2d Cir. 1982)	§§ 18.8, 18.12, 18.18
Johnny Pflocks, Inc. v. Firestone Tire and Rubber Co., 634 F.2d 1215 (9th Cir. 1980)	§ 27.9
Johnson v. Ashby, 808 F.2d 676 (8th Cir. 1987)	§ 16.3
Johnson v. Bechtel Assocs. Prof. Corp., 717 F.2d 574 (D.C. Cir. 1983), *cert. denied,* 464 U.S. 1070 (1984)	§ 8.12
Johnson v. Georgia Highway Express, Inc., 488 F.2d 714 (5th Cir. 1974)	§ 29.8
Johnson v. H.K. Webster, Inc., 775 F.2d 1 (1st Cir. 1985)	§§ 17.15, 20.15
Johnson v. Hubbard, 698 F.2d 286 (6th Cir.), *cert. denied,* 464 U.S. 917 (1983)	§ 30.5
Johnson v. Hussmann Corp., 805 F.2d 795 (8th Cir. 1986)	§ 3.2
Johnson v. Levy Org. Dev. Co., 789 F.2d 601 (7th Cir. 1986)	§ 8.8
Johnson v. Trueblood, 629 F.2d 287 (3d Cir. 1980), *cert. denied,* 450 U.S. 999 (1981)	§ 16.8
Johnson Creative Arts, Inc. v. Wool Masters, 743 F.2d 947 (1st Cir. 1984)	§§ 4.14, 6.3
Johnsrud v. Carter, 620 F.2d 29 (3d Cir. 1980)	§ 14.49
Johnston v. Penrod Drilling Co., 803 F.2d 867 (5th Cir 1986)	§ 16.6
Jones v. Caddo Parish School Bd., 704 F.2d 206 (5th Cir. 1983)	§§ 10.10, 10.16
Jones v. Continental Corp., 789 F.2d 1225 (6th Cir. 1986)	§ 28.8
Jones v. Graham, 709 F.2d 1457 (11th Cir. 1983)	§ 30.4
Jones v. Intermountain Power Project, 794 F.2d 546 (10th Cir. 1986)	§§ 2.25, 2.28
Jones v. Miles, 656 F.2d 103 (5th Cir. 1981)	§ 14.63
Jones v. Louisiana, 764 F.2d 1183 (5th Cir. 1985)	§ 8.1
Jones v. Morris, 777 F.2d 1277 (7th Cir. 1985)	§ 14.7
Jones v. Newton, 775 F.2d 1316 (5th Cir. 1985)	§§ 3.15, 3.17, 3.18
Jones v. Nuclear Regulatory Comm'n, 654 F. Supp. 130 (D.D.C.1987)	§ 17.8
Jones v. Wike, 654 F.2d 1129 (5th Cir. 1981)	§ 15.10

Case	*Book §*
Keniston v. Roberts, 717 F.2d 1295 (9th Cir. 1983)	§ 8.5
Kennedy v. City of Cleveland, 797 F.2d 297 (6th Cir. 1986)	§§ 15.1, 17.16
Kenneth Leventhal & Co. v. Joyner Wholesale Co., 736 F.2d 29 (2d Cir. 1984)	§ 7.13
Kennett-Murray Corp. v. Bone, 622 F.2d 887 (5th Cir. 1980)	§ 15.18
Kentucky v. Graham, 473 U.S. 159, 167–69 (1985)	§ 2.6
Kentucky W. Va. Gas Co. v. Pennsylvania Pub. Util. Comm'n, 791 F.2d 1111 (3d Cir. 1986)	§ 2.6
Kern v. TXO Prod. Corp., 738 F.2d 968 (8th Cir. 1984)	§ 12.6
Kern Oil & Ref. Co. v. Tenneco Oil Co., 792 F.2d 1380 (9th Cir. 1986)	§§ 12.7, 30.5
Kerr v. Screen Extras Guild, Inc., 526 F.2d 67 (9th Cir. 1975), *cert. denied,* 425 U.S. 951 (1976)	§ 28.10
Kerr v. United States Dist. Court, 426 U.S. 394 (1976)	§ 17.18
Kershner v. Mazurkiewicz, 670 F.2d 440 (3d Cir. 1982)	§ 10.17
Kickapoo Oil Co. v. Clark Oil & Ref. Corp., 788 F.2d 11 (Temp. Emer. Ct. App. 1985)	§§ 20.15, 30.10
Kifer v. Liberty Mut. Ins. Co., 777 F.2d 1325 (8th Cir. 1985)	§ 1.11
Kilkenny v. Arco Marine Inc., 800 F.2d 853 (9th Cir. 1986)	§ 8.13
King v. Fidelity Nat'l Bank of Baton Rouge, 712 F.2d 188 (5th Cir. 1983), *cert. denied,* 465 U.S. 1029 (1984)	§§ 21.3, 31.12
King v. Wells, 94 F.R.D. 675 (E.D. Mich. 1982)	§ 15.4
Kirby v. United States Gov't, 745 F.2d 204 (3d Cir. 1984)	§ 2.4
Kirk v. Cronvich, 629 F.2d 404 (5th Cir. 1980)	§ 8.13
Kirkland v. New York State Dep't of Correctional Servs., 711 F.2d 1117 (2d Cir. 1983), *cert. denied,* 465 U.S. 1005 (1984)	§ 9.7
Kirschner v. Broadhead, 671 F.2d 1034 (7th Cir. 1982)	§ 23.27
Kissinger v. Reporters Comm. for Freedom of the Press, 445 U.S. 136 (1980)	§ 17.10
Kitchen, *In re,* 706 F.2d 1266 (2d Cir. 1983)	§ 31.4
Kittitas Reclamation Dist. v. Sunnyside Valley Irrigation Dist., 763 F.2d 1032 (9th Cir. 1985)	§ 2.2
Klaxon Co. v. Stentor Elec. Mfg. Co., 313 U.S. 487 (1941)	§ 1.11
Klein, *In re,* 776 F.2d 628 (7th Cir. 1985)	§§ 17.20, 31.9
Kleiner v. First Nat'l Bank of Atlanta, 751 F.2d 1193 (11th Cir. 1985)	§§ 10.3, 10.16
Kline v. Wolf, 702 F.2d 400 (2d Cir. 1983)	§§ 10.6, 10.13
K.M.C. Co. v. Irving Trust Co., 757 F.2d 752 (6th Cir. 1985)	§§ 16.13, 17.15
Kneeland v. National Collegiate Athletic Ass'n, 806 F.2d 1285 (5th Cir. 1987)	§ 9.7
Knorr Brake Corp. v. Harbil, Inc., 738 F.2d 223 (7th Cir. 1984)	§§ 27.9, 28.6, 28.8
Koke v. Phillips Petroleum Co., 730 F.2d 211 (5th Cir. 1984)	§ 6.21
Koke v. Stifel, Nicolaus & Co., 620 F.2d 1340 (8th Cir. 1980)	§ 2.29
Konisberg v. Shute, 435 F.2d 551 (3d Cir. 1970)	§ 14.64
Kontoulas v. A.H. Robins Co., 745 F.2d 312 (4th Cir. 1984)	§§ 6.7, 6.15, 6.21
Korf v. Ball State Univ., 726 F.2d 1222 (7th Cir. 1984)	§ 15.23
Korn v. Royal Caribbean Cruise Line, Inc., 724 F.2d 1397 (9th Cir. 1984)	§§ 8.11, 8.12, 8.13
Koster v. Chase Manhattan Bank, 93 F.R.D. 471 (S.D.N.Y. 1982)	§ 19.6
Kothe v. Smith, 771 F.2d 667 (2d Cir. 1985)	§§ 16.5, 30.10
Kozlowski v. Sears, Roebuck & Co., 73 F.R.D. 73 (D. Mass. 1976)	§ 25.3

Case	*Book §*
Kramer v. Caribbean Mills, Inc., 394 U.S. 823 (1969)	§ 2.17
Krasnov v. Dinan, 465 F.2d 1298 (3d Cir. 1972)	§ 14.11
Krause v. Rhodes, 671 F.2d 212 (6th Cir.), *cert. denied,* 459 U.S. 823 (1982)	§ 19.4
Kremer v. Chemical Constr. Corp., 456 U.S. 461 (1982)	§ 2.6
Kryvicky v. Scandinavian Airlines Sys., 807 F.2d 514 (6th Cir. 1986)	§ 14.24
Labadie Coal Co. v. Black, 672 F.2d 92 (D.C. Cir. 1982)	§ 17.15
LaBatt v. Twomey, 513 F.2d 641 (7th Cir. 1975)	§ 8.8
La Buy v. Howes Leather, 352 U.S. 249 (1957)	§ 16.16
Lac Courte Oreilles Band v. Voigt, 700 F.2d 341 (7th Cir.), *cert. denied,* 464 U.S. 805 (1983)	§ 15.13
La Chemise Lacoste v. Alligator Co., 506 F.2d 339 (3d Cir. 1974), *cert. denied,* 421 U.S. 937 (1975)	§§ 3.2, 3.19
Laclede Gas Co. v. G.W. Warnecke Corp., 604 F.2d 561 (8th Cir. 1979)	§ 31.12
L.A. Draper & Son v. Wheelabrator-Frye, Inc., 735 F.2d 414 (11th Cir. 1984)	§ 2.29
LaDuke v. Nelson, 762 F.2d 1318 (9th Cir. 1985)	§ 2.3
Laipenieks v. United States I.N.S., 750 F.2d 1427 (9th Cir. 1985)	§ 23.29
Lake Invs. Dev. Group v. Egidi Dev. Group, Inc., 715 F.2d 1256 (7th Cir. 1983)	§ 9.9
Lakeside Bridge & Steel Co. v. Mountain State Constr. Co., 597 F.2d 596 (7th Cir. 1979), *cert. denied,* 445 U.S. 907 (1980)	§§ 4.5, 4.12
Lamb v. Cramer, 285 U.S. 217 (1932)	§ 31.6
Lampliter Dinner Theater, Inc. v. Liberty Mut. Ins. Co., 792 F.2d 1036 (11th Cir. 1986)	§ 9.5
Land v. Dollar, 330 U.S. 731 (1947)	§§ 14.8, 14.14
Landis v. North Am. Co., 299 U.S. 248 (1936)	§ 16.3
Landmark Dev. Corp. v. Chambers Corp., 752 F.2d 369 (9th Cir. 1985)	§ 15.24
Lane v. Celotex Corp., 782 F.2d 1526 (11th Cir. 1986)	§ 15.18
LaPorte Constr. Co. v. Bayshore Nat'l Bank, 805 F.2d 1254 (5th Cir. 1986)	§ 2.29
La Seguridad v. Transytur Line, 707 F.2d 1304 (11th Cir. 1983)	§§ 6.16, 6.17, 6.18, 6.20, 6.21
Las Vegas, City of, v. Clark County, 755 F.2d 697 (9th Cir. 1985)	§ 14.9
Lau v. Glendora Unified School Dist., 792 F.2d 929 (9th Cir. 1986)	§§ 12.6, 12.7
Law Enforcement Ins. Co. v. Corcoran, 807 F.2d 38 (2d Cir. 1986)	§ 2.6
Lawson Prods., Inc. v. Avnet, Inc., 782 F.2d 1429 (7th Cir. 1986)	§§ 11.4, 11.7
Laxalt v. McClatchy, 809 F.2d 885 (D.C. Cir. 1987)	§ 18.22
Lay v. Justices-Middle Dist. Court, 811 F.2d 285 (5th Cir. 1987)	§ 14.7
Leachman v. Beech Aircraft Corp., 694 F.2d 1301 (D.C. Cir. 1982)	§ 8.15
Lead Indus. Ass'n v. Occupational Safety & Health Admin., 610 F.2d 70 (2d Cir. 1979)	§ 6.8
LeaseAmerica Corp. v. Eckel, 710 F.2d 1470 (10th Cir. 1983)	§ 8.2
LeBeau v. Spirito, 703 F.2d 639 (1st Cir. 1983)	§ 11.4
Ledwith v. Douglas, 568 F.2d 117 (8th Cir. 1978)	§ 15.7
LeFevre v. Spacecom, 771 F.2d 421 (10th Cir. 1985)	§ 15.14

Case	*Book §*
LeGrand v. Evan, 702 F.2d 415 (2d Cir. 1983)	§§ 2.10, 8.8, 14.7
Leif Hoegh & Co. v. Alpha Moto Ways, Inc., 534 F. Supp. 624 (S.D.N.Y. 1982)	§ 14.66
Lelsz v. Kavanagh, 710 F.2d 1040 (5th Cir. 1983)	§ 10.16
Lemelson v. TRW, 760 F.2d 1254 (Fed. Cir. 1985)	§ 15.14
Leninger v. Leninger, 705 F.2d 727 (5th Cir. 1983)	§ 3.14
Leonhard v. United States, 633 F.2d 599 (2d Cir. 1980), *cert. denied,* 451 U.S. 908 (1981)	§§ 14.6, 14.67
Lepkowski v. United States Dep't of Treasury, 804 F.2d 1310 (D.C. Cir. 1986)	§ 31.11
Leroy v. Great W. United Corp., 443 U.S. 173 (1978)	§§ 6.1, 6.4, 14.24, 14.31, 14.35, 14.36
Lesher v. Lavrich, 784 F.2d 193 (6th Cir. 1986)	§ 7.7
Letelier v. Republic of Chile, 748 F.2d 790 (2d Cir. 1984), *cert. denied,* 471 U.S. 1125 (1985)	§ 29.7
Levitch v. C.B.S., Inc., 94 F.R.D. 292 (S.D.N.Y. 1982), *aff'd,* 697 F.2d 495 (2d Cir. 1983)	§ 14.47
Levoy v. Mills, 788 F.2d 1437 (10th Cir. 1986)	§ 14.7
Lew v. Kona Hosp., 754 F.2d 1420 (9th Cir. 1985)	§§ 15.16, 23.22
Lew v. Moss, 797 F.2d 747 (9th Cir. 1986)	§§ 2.14, 14.10, 14.11
Lewis v. Faulkner, 689 F.2d 100 (7th Cir. 1982)	§§ 14.55, 15.3, 15.25
Lewis v. Knutson, 699 F.2d 230 (5th Cir. 1983)	§§ 8.2, 14.8, 14.13, 14.14
Lewis v. Thigpen, 767 F.2d 252 (5th Cir. 1985)	§ 7.17
LFC Lessors, Inc. v. Pacific Sewer Maintenance Corp., 739 F.2d 4 (1st Cir. 1984)	§ 14.15
Liaw Su Teng v. Skaarup Shipping Corp., 743 F.2d 1140 (5th Cir. 1984)	§§ 6.9, 6.15, 14.26
Liberty Mut. Ins. Co. v. EEOC, 691 F.2d 438 (9th Cir. 1982)	§ 16.6
Liberty Mut. Ins. Co. v. Wetzel, 424 U.S. 737 (1976)	§§ 2.7, 3.16
Licht & Semonoff, *In re,* 796 F.2d 564 (1st Cir. 1986)	§§ 17.19, 27.9, 28.6
Liddy v. Urbanek, 707 F.2d 1222 (11th Cir. 1983)	§§ 9.3, 10.18
Lieb v. Topstone Indus., Inc., 788 F.2d 151 (3d Cir. 1986)	§§ 28.4, 28.5
Liew v. Breen, 640 F.2d 1046 (9th Cir. 1981)	§ 18.2
Lindley v. General Elec. Co., 780 F.2d 797 (9th Cir.), *cert. denied,* _____ U.S. _____, 106 S. Ct. 2926 (1986)	§§ 3.11, 8.16
Lindy Bros. Builders, Inc. v. American Radiator & Standard Sanitary Corp., 487 F.2d 161 (3d Cir. 1973)	§ 10.14
Linhart v. Glatfelter, 771 F.2d 1004 (7th Cir. 1985)	§ 15.6
Link v. Wabash R.R., 370 U.S. 626 (1962)	§§ 27.6, 29.6, 30.2, 30.4, 30.6, 30.7, 30.9
Lipsig v. National Student Marketing Corp., 663 F.2d 178 (D.C. Cir. 1980)	§§ 28.8, 28.9, 28.10, 30.8
Lirette v. N.L. Sperry Sun, Inc., 810 F.2d 533 (5th Cir. 1987)	§ 3.17
Little, *In re*, 404 U.S. 553 (1972)	§ 31.8

Case	*Book §*
Littlefield v. Fort Dodge Messenger, 614 F.2d 581 (8th Cir. 1980)	§ 7.17
Littlejohn v. Shell Oil Co., 483 F.2d 1140 (5th Cir.) (en banc), *cert. denied,* 414 U.S. 1116 (1973)	§ 15.24
Litton Sys., Inc. v. AT&T Co., 700 F.2d 785 (2d Cir. 1983), *cert. denied,* 464 U.S. 1073 (1984)	§§ 28.8, 29.7
Lloyd v. American Export Lines, Inc., 580 F.2d 1179 (3d Cir.), *cert. denied,* 439 U.S. 969 (1978)	§ 23.29
Lloyd v. Loeffler, 694 F.2d 489 (7th Cir. 1982)	§ 2.6
Local 472 of Plumbing & Pipefitting Indus. v. Georgia Power Co., 684 F.2d 721 (11th Cir. 1982)	§ 8.3
Local 472, United Ass'n of Journeymen v. Georgia Power Co., 684 F.2d 721 (11th Cir. 1982)	§ 24.1
Local P-171 v. Thompson Farms Co., 642 F.2d 1065 (7th Cir. 1981)	§ 15.29
Lockett v. General Fin. Loan Co., 623 F.2d 1128 (5th Cir. 1980)	§ 14.62
Loctite Corp. v. Fel-Pro, Inc., 667 F.2d 577 (7th Cir. 1981)	§§ 28.13, 29.1
Loehr v. Ventura County Community College Dist., 743 F.2d 1310 (9th Cir. 1984)	§§ 8.3, 8.7
Loftin v. Rush, 767 F.2d 800 (11th Cir. 1985)	§§ 3.5, 3.17, 3.19
Lombard's Inc. v. Prince Mfg., Inc., 753 F.2d 974 (11th Cir. 1985), *cert. denied,* ___ U.S. ___, 106 S. Ct. 851 (1986)	§§ 14.43, 14.45
Londrigan v. F.B.I., 670 F.2d 1164 (D.C. Cir. 1981)	§§ 15.16, 15.24
Lopez v. General Motors Corp., 697 F.2d 1328 (9th Cir. 1983)	§ 3.11
Lopez v. Heckler, 713 F.2d 1432 (9th Cir. 1983)	§ 11.7
Lorber Indus. v. Los Angeles Printworks, 803 F.2d 523 (9th Cir. 1986)	§ 1.12
Los Angeles, City of, v. Lyons, 461 U.S. 95 (1983)	§§ 2.3, 2.4
Los Angeles, County of, v. Davis, 440 U.S. 625 (1979)	§ 2.4
Louisiana v. Mississippi, 466 U.S. 92 (1984)	§ 16.15
Louisville & N.R.R. v. Mottley, 211 U.S. 149 (1908)	§ 2.7
Loveridge v. Pendleton Woolen Mills, Inc., 788 F.2d 914 (2d Cir. 1986)	§ 11.4
Lovett v. Shuster, 633 F.2d 98 (8th Cir. 1980)	§ 23.27
Lowe v. Ingalls Shipbuilding, 723 F.2d 1173 (5th Cir. 1984)	§ 2.24
LTV Secs. Litig., *In re*, 89 F.R.D. 595 (N.D. Tex. 1981)	§ 18.8
Lucas v. Bolivar County, 756 F.2d 1230 (5th Cir. 1985)	§ 11.7
Lucas v. United States, 807 F.2d 414 (5th Cir. 1986)	§ 7.7
Luce v. Edelstein, 802 F.2d 49 (2d Cir. 1986)	§ 7.3
Lucha, Inc. v. Goeglein, 575 F. Supp. 785 (E.D. Mo. 1983)	§§ 14.1, 14.2
Luick v. Graybar Elec. Co., 473 F.2d 1360 (8th Cir. 1973)	§ 15.19
Luis C. Forteza e Hijos, Inc. v. Mills, 534 F.2d 415 (1st Cir. 1976)	§ 16.7
Lumbermens Mut. Cas. Co. v. Connecticut Bank & Trust Co., 806 F.2d 411 (2d Cir. 1986)	§ 2.6
Lumen Constr., Inc. v. Brant Constr. Co., 780 F.2d 691 (7th Cir. 1986)	§ 2.6
Lundsford v. United States, 570 F.2d 221 (8th Cir. 1977)	§ 14.60
Lusardi v. Xerox Corp., 747 F.2d 174 (3d Cir. 1984)	§ 10.17
Lyell Theatre Corp. v. Loews Corp., 682 F.2d 37 (2d Cir. 1982)	§§ 30.3, 30.4, 30.7
Lykins v. Pointer Inc., 725 F.2d 645 (11th Cir. 1984)	§ 2.30

Case	*Book §*
Lynk v. LaPorte Super. Ct. No. 2, 789 F.2d 554 (7th Cir. 1986)	§ 2.6
Lynn v. Regents of Univ. of Cal., 656 F.2d 1337 (9th Cir. 1981), *cert. denied,* 459 U.S. 823 (1982)	§ 18.22
Macedo v. Boeing Co., 693 F.2d 683 (7th Cir. 1982)	§§ 6.16, 6.19
Mack v. South Bay Beer Distribs., Inc., 798 F.2d 1279 (9th Cir. 1986)	§ 14.47
Macklin v. Butler, 553 F.2d 525 (7th Cir. 1977)	§ 15.20
MacMeekin, *In re,* 722 F.2d 32 (3d Cir. 1983)	§ 29.6
MacNeil v. Whittemore, 254 F.2d 820 (2d Cir. 1958)	§ 14.62
Madesky v. Campbell, 705 F.2d 703 (3d Cir. 1983)	§ 30.3
Maggette v. Dalsheim, 709 F.2d 800 (2d Cir. 1983)	§§ 14.2, 14.46, 14.50, 14.54, 14.55
Maggio v. Zeitz, 333 U.S. 56 (1948)	§ 31.5
Magnetic Eng'g & Mfg. Co. v. Dings, 178 F.2d 866 (2d Cir. 1950)	§§ 6.10, 6.13
Maher v. Zapata Corp., 714 F.2d 436 (5th Cir. 1983)	§ 10.18
Majd-Pour v. Georgiana Community Hosp., 724 F.2d 901 (11th Cir. 1984)	§§ 11.7, 14.11, 14.16
Majerus v. Walk, 275 F. Supp. 952 (D. Minn. 1967)	§ 14.46
Malak v. Associated Physicians, Inc., 784 F.2d 277 (7th Cir. 1986)	§§ 14.15, 15.5
Malchman v. Davis, 761 F.2d 893 (2d Cir. 1985), *cert. denied,* _____ U.S. _____, 106 S. Ct. 1798 (1986)	§ 10.14
Malchman v. Davis, 706 F.2d 426 (2d Cir. 1983)	§§ 10.12, 10.13
Maldonado v. Ramirez, 757 F.2d 48 (3d Cir. 1985)	§ 15.16
Malone v. Colyer, 710 F.2d 258 (6th Cir. 1983)	§ 14.7
Mandujano v. Basic Vegetable Prods., Inc., 541 F.2d 832 (9th Cir. 1976)	§ 10.13
Maness v. Meyers, 419 U.S. 449 (1975)	§ 31.9
Mangual v. General Battery Corp., 710 F.2d 15 (1st Cir. 1983)	§ 14.25
Manley v. Engram, 755 F.2d 1463 (11th Cir. 1985)	§§ 6.8, 6.9, 14.36
Mann v. City of Tucson, Dep't of Police, 782 F.2d 790 (9th Cir. 1986)	§§ 2.13, 14.10
Mann v. Smith, 796 F.2d 79 (5th Cir. 1986)	§ 7.6
Manu Int'l, S.A. v. Avon Prods., Inc., 641 F.2d 62 (2d Cir. 1981)	§ 6.16
Marane Inc. v. McDonald's Corp., 755 F.2d 106 (7th Cir. 1985)	§ 15.29
Marathon Oil Co. v. United States, 807 F.2d 759 (9th Cir. 1986)	§ 2.9
Marcial Ucin, S.A. v. SS Galicia, 723 F.2d 994 (1st Cir. 1983)	§ 14.26
Marc Rich & Co., *In re,* 736 F.2d 864 (2d Cir. 1984)	§ 31.5
Marek v. Chesny, _____ U.S. _____, 105 S. Ct. 3012 (1985)	§ 16.6
Mariash v. Morrill, 496 F.2d 1138 (2d Cir. 1974)	§ 4.14
Marine Coatings of Ala., Inc. v. United States, 792 F.2d 1565 (11th Cir. 1986)	§§ 14.12, 14.14
Marine Midland Bank, N.A. v. Miller, 664 F.2d 889 (2d Cir. 1981)	§§ 4.6, 4.20, 4.21
Marine Overseas Servs. v. Crossocean Shipping, 791 F.2d 1227 (5th Cir. 1986)	§ 7.7
Marine Petroleum Co. v. Champlin Petroleum Co., 641 F.2d 984 (D.C. Cir. 1980)	§§ 20.5, 20.6, 20.7

Case	*Book §*
Marrese v. American Academy of Orthopaedic Surgeons, 726 F.2d 1150 (7th Cir. 1984) (en banc), *rev'd,* 470 U.S. 373 (1985)	§§ 19.5, 19.19, 31.9
Marshall v. City of Cape Coral, 797 F.2d 1555 (11th Cir. 1986)	§ 15.3
Marshall v. Holiday Magic, Inc., 550 F.2d 1173 (9th Cir. 1977)	§ 10.12
Marshall v. Mulrenin, 508 F.2d 39 (1st Cir. 1974)	§ 8.16
Marshall v. Segona, 621 F.2d 763 (5th Cir. 1980)	§ 29.5
Martin v. Gibson, 723 F.2d 989 (D.C. Cir. 1983)	§ 2.12
Martin v. Mogan Drive Away, Inc., 665 F.2d 598 (5th Cir.), *cert. denied,* 458 U.S. 1122 (1982)	§ 14.51
Martin v. Reynolds Metals Corp., 297 F.2d 49 (9th Cir. 1961)	§ 17.13
Martindell v. IT&T Corp., 594 F.2d 291 (2d Cir. 1979)	§ 19.6
Martinez v. Thrifty Drug & Discount Co., 593 F.2d 992 (10th Cir. 1979)	§ 31.10
Martinez v. United States Olympic Comm., 802 F.2d 1275 (10th Cir. 1986)	§ 2.17
Martinez v. Winner, 771 F.2d 424 (10th Cir. 1985), *vacated,* _____ U.S. _____, 106 S. Ct. 1787 (1986)	§ 2.10
Martin Ice Cream Co. v. Chipwich, Inc., 554 F. Supp. 933 (S.D.N.Y. 1983)	§ 15.22
Martin-Trigona v. Stewart, 691 F.2d 856 (8th Cir. 1982)	§§ 14.6, 14.7
Martz v. Union Labor Life Ins. Co., 757 F.2d 135 (7th Cir. 1985)	§ 15.17
Maryland Casualty Co. v. Pacific Coal & Oil Co., 312 U.S. 270 (1941)	§ 2.2
Marziliano v. Heckler, 728 F.2d 151 (2d Cir. 1984)	§ 12.1
Masalosalo v. Stonewall Ins. Co., 718 F.2d 955 (9th Cir. 1983)	§ 28.10
Mason v. United States, 244 U.S. 362 (1917)	§ 18.19
Massa v. Eaton Corp., 109 F.R.D. 312 (W.D. Mich. S.D. 1985)	§ 18.4
Massachusetts v. Russell Stover Candies, 541 F. Supp. 143 (D. Mass. 1982)	§ 14.60
Massop v. Coughlin, 770 F.2d 299 (2d Cir. 1985)	§ 14.7
Matsumoto v. Republic Ins. Co., 792 F.2d 869 (9th Cir. 1986)	§ 8.3
Matsushita Elec. Indus. Co. v. Zenith Radio, _____ U.S. _____, 106 S. Ct. 1348 (1986)	§§ 15.6, 15.10, 15.14, 15.30
Matthews v. Ashland Chem., Inc., 770 F.2d 1303 (5th Cir. 1985)	§ 15.30
Max Daetwyler Corp. v. Meyer, 762 F.2d 290 (3d Cir.), *cert. denied,* _____ U.S. _____, 106 S. Ct. 383 (1985)	§ 4.14
May v. Transworld Drilling Co., 786 F.2d 1261 (5th Cir. 1986)	§ 2.24
Mayacamas v. Gulfstream Aerospace Corp., 806 F.2d 928 (9th Cir. 1986)	§ 2.6
Mayberry v. Pennsylvania, 400 U.S. 455 (1971)	§ 31.8
Mayer v. Angelica, 790 F.2d 1315 (7th Cir. 1986)	§§ 18.19, 26.3
Mayo v. Tri-Bell Indus., Inc., 787 F.2d 1007 (5th Cir. 1986)	§ 20.13
McCabe v. General Foods Corp., 811 F.2d 1336 (9th Cir. 1987)	§§ 3.11, 3.23
McCaffrey v. Rex Motor Transp., Inc., 672 F.2d 246 (1st Cir. 1982)	§ 7.9
McCandless v. Great Atl. & Pac. Tea Co., 697 F.2d 198 (7th Cir. 1983)	§§ 28.9, 28.10

Case	*Book §*
McCargo v. Hedrick, 545 F.2d 393 (4th Cir. 1976)	§ 16.4
McCarney v. Ford Motor Co., 657 F.2d 230 (8th Cir. 1981)	§§ 2.2, 14.15
McCarthy v. Andstein, 266 U.S. 34 (1924)	§ 18.19
McCarthy v. Kleindienst, 741 F.2d 1406 (D.C. Cir. 1984)	§§ 10.10, 10.16
McClelland Eng'rs, Inc., *In re,* 742 F.2d 837 (5th Cir. 1984)	§ 6.21
McCloud River R.R. v. Sabine River Forest Prods., Inc., 735 F.2d 879 (5th Cir. 1984)	§ 15.17
McCone v. Holiday Inn Convention Center, 797 F.2d 853 (10th Cir. 1986)	§ 14.7
McCoy v. Richards, 771 F.2d 1108 (7th Cir. 1985)	§ 1.11
McCrary v. Poythress, 638 F.2d 1308 (5th Cir.), *cert. denied,* 454 U.S. 865 (1981)	§§ 14.46, 14.71
McDonald v. Oliver, 642 F.2d 169 (5th Cir. 1981)	§ 7.11
McDonald v. Smith, 472 U.S. 479 (1985)	§ 14.69
McDonald v. Union Carbide Corp., 734 F.2d 182 (5th Cir. 1984)	§ 7.13
McDonald's Corp. v. Victory Invs., 727 F.2d 82 (3d Cir. 1984)	§§ 31.2, 31.6
McDonnell Douglas Corp. v. Polin, 429 F.2d 30 (3d Cir. 1970)	§ 19.5
McDougald v. Jensen, 786 F.2d 1465 (11th Cir. 1986)	§ 2.6
McFadden v. Sanchez, 710 F.2d 907 (2d Cir.), *cert. denied,* 464 U.S. 961 (1983)	§ 16.4
McGee v. Hester, 724 F.2d 89 (8th Cir. 1983)	§ 15.14
McGowan v. Faulkner Concrete Pipe Co., 659 F.2d 554 (5th Cir. 1981)	§§ 10.6, 30.2
MCI Communications v. AT&T Co., 708 F.2d 1081 (7th Cir.), *cert. denied,* 464 U.S. 891 (1983)	§ 16.4
McIntyre v. McIntyre, 771 F.2d 1316 (9th Cir. 1985)	§ 2.6
McKay v. Boyd Constr. Co., 769 F.2d 1084 (5th Cir. 1985)	§§ 3.1, 3.3, 3.4, 3.17
McKelvey v. AT&T Technologies, Inc., 789 F.2d 1518 (11th Cir. 1986)	§ 30.3
McKenzie v. Sawyer, 684 F.2d 62 (D.C. Cir. 1982)	§ 15.14
McKinney v. Dole, 765 F.2d 1129 (D.C. Cir. 1985)	§ 15.28
McKinney v. U.S. Dep't of Treasury, 799 F.2d 1544 (Fed. Cir. 1986)	§ 2.3
McLain v. Real Estate Bd. of New Orleans, Inc., 444 U.S. 232 (1980)	§ 14.42
McLaughlin v. Bradlee, 803 F.2d 1197 (D.C. Cir. 1986)	§ 28.6
McMillan v. City of Rockmart, 653 F.2d 907 (5th Cir. 1981)	§ 15.27
McNutt v. General Motors Acceptance Corp., 298 U.S. 178 (1936)	§§ 2.14, 14.10, 14.15, 14.19
McSparran v. Weist, 402 F.2d 867 (3d Cir. 1968), (en banc), *cert. denied,* 395 U.S. 903 (1969)	§ 2.17
McWhirter Distrib. Co. v. Texaco, Inc., 668 F.2d 511 (Temp. Emer. Ct. App. 1981)	§ 15.9
Meadows v. Bicrodyne Corp., 785 F.2d 670 (9th Cir. 1986)	§ 3.17
Mechanical Appliance Co. v. Castleman, 215 U.S. 437 (1910)	§ 14.39.
Meche v. Dan-Tex Int'l, Inc., 681 F.2d 264 (5th Cir. 1982)	§ 27.9
Mechmetals Corp. v. Telex Computer Prods., Inc., 709 F.2d 1287 (9th Cir. 1983)	§ 16.4

Case	*Book §*
(3d Cir. 1983), *cert. denied,* 467 U.S. 1215 (1984)	§ 15.24
Mid-South Towing Co. v. Har-Win, Inc., 733 F.2d 386 (5th Cir. 1984)	§ 16.7
Miera v. First See, Bank of Utah, N.A., 776 F.2d 902 (10th Cir. 1985)	§ 15.5
Milburn v. United States, 734 F.2d 762 (11th Cir. 1984)	§§ 15.3, 15.25, 15.27
Milene Music Inc. v. Gotauco, 551 F. Supp. 1288 (D.R.I. 1982)	§ 15.19
Miles v. M/V Mississippi Queen, 753 F.2d 1349 (5th Cir. 1985)	§ 18.16
Military Audit Project v. Casey, 656 F.2d 724 (D.C. Cir. 1981)	§ 15.24
Miller v. A.H. Robbins Co., 766 F.2d 1102 (7th Cir. 1985)	§ 15.18
Miller v. Grgurich, 763 F.2d 372 (9th Cir. 1985)	§ 3.3
Miller v. Honda Motor Co., Ltd., 779 F.2d 769 (1st Cir. 1985)	§ 4.6
Miller v. Los Angeles County Bd. of Educ., 799 F.2d 486 (9th Cir. 1986)	§ 16.3
Miller v. Mackey Int'l, Inc., 452 F.2d 424 (5th Cir. 1971)	§ 14.48
Miller v. New York State Serv. Comm'n, 807 F.2d 28 (2d Cir. 1986)	§ 2.22
Miller v. Solem, 728 F.2d 1020 (8th Cir.), *cert. denied,* 469 U.S. 841 (1984)	§§ 15.3, 15.16
Milwaukee Typographical Union No. 23 v. Newspaper, Inc., 639 F.2d 386 (7th Cir.), *cert. denied,* 454 U.S. 838 (1981)	§ 15.25
Miner v. Atlass, 363 U.S. 641 (1960)	§ 31.11
Mineral Indus. & Heavy Constr. Group v. OSHRC, 639 F.2d 1289 (5th Cir. 1981)	§ 8.2
Minority Police Officers Ass'n v. City of South Bend, 721 F.2d 197 (11th Cir. 1983)	§ 10.17
Mir v. Fosburg, 706 F.2d 916 (9th Cir. 1983)	§§ 30.3, 30.4
Miranda v. Southern Pac. Transp. Co., 710 F.2d 516 (9th Cir. 1983)	§ 31.10
Miree v. DeKalb County, 433 U.S. 25 (1977)	§ 14.42
Misco, Inc. v. United States Steel Corp., 784 F.2d 198 (6th Cir. 1986)	§§ 7.17, 26.2
Miskow v. Boeing Co., 664 F.2d 205 (9th Cir. 1981)	§§ 6.19, 6.20
Mississippi Power & Light v. United Gas Pipe Line, 760 F.2d 618 (5th Cir. 1985)	§ 11.4
Mitchell v. Forsyth, ____ U.S. ____, 105 S. Ct. 2806 (1985)	§§ 14.68, 14.69, 15.28
Mobil Oil Corp. v. City of Long Beach, 772 F.2d 534 (9th Cir. 1985)	§ 2.6
Moffatt Enters., Inc. v. Borden Inc., 807 F.2d 1169 (3d Cir. 1986)	§ 8.5
Monaghan v. Deakins, 798 F.2d 632 (3d Cir. 1986)	§ 2.6
Moncrief v. Lexington Herald-Leader Co., 807 F.2d 217 (D.C. Cir. 1986)	§ 4.10
Montalbano v. Easco Hand Tools, 766 F.2d 737 (2d Cir. 1985)	§§ 4.5, 5.11, 14.39
Montana v. United States, 440 U.S. 147 (1979)	§ 14.49
Montelongo v. Meese, 803 F.2d 1341 (5th Cir. 1986)	§ 10.10
Moody v. I.R.S., 654 F.2d 795 (D.C. Cir. 1981)	§ 18.18
Moody v. Town of Weymouth, 805 F.2d 30 (1st Cir. 1986)	§ 15.25

Case	*Book §*
Myers v. American Dental Ass'n, 695 F.2d 716 (3d Cir. 1982), *cert. denied,* 462 U.S. 1106 (1983)	§§ 14.26, 14.31, 14.32, 14.62
NAACP v. New York, 413 U.S. 345 (1973)	§ 9.8
Naartex Consulting Corp. v. Watt, 722 F.2d 779 (D.C. Cir. 1983), *cert. denied,* 467 U.S. 1210 (1984)	§§ 9.3, 14.16, 17.5, 17.16
Nadler v. American Motors Sales Corp., 764 F.2d 409 (5th Cir. 1985)	§ 14.10
Nagle v. Lee, 807 F.2d 435 (5th Cir. 1987)	§ 7.7
Nalls v. Rolls-Royce Ltd., 702 F.2d 255 (D.C. Cir.), *cert. denied,* 461 U.S. 970 (1983)	§ 6.21
Nash v. Black, 781 F.2d 665 (8th Cir. 1986)	§ 16.12
Nasuti v. Scannell, 792 F.2d 264 (1st Cir. 1986)	§ 3.19
National Acceptance Co. of Am. v. Bathalter, 705 F.2d 924 (7th Cir. 1983)	§§ 18.19, 31.4
National Ass'n of Concerned Veterans v. Secretary of Defense, 675 F.2d 1319 (D.C. Cir. 1982)	§ 29.8
National City Bank v. Coopers & Lybrand, 802 F.2d 990 (8th Cir. 1986)	§ 3.19
National Developers, Inc., *In re,* 803 F.2d 616 (11th Cir. 1986)	§ 3.19
National Hockey League v. Metropolitan Hockey Club, 427 U.S. 639 (1976)	§§ 29.3, 29.4, 29.7
National Indus., Inc. v. Republic Nat'l Life Ins. Co., 677 F.2d 1258 (9th Cir. 1982)	§ 15.30
National Life Ins. Co. v. Hartford Accident & Indem. Co., 615 F.2d 595 (3d Cir. 1980)	§ 21.6
National R.R. Passenger Corp. v. Koch Indus., Inc., 701 F.2d 108 (10th Cir. 1983)	§ 16.16
National Union Fire Ins. Co. v. Argonaut Ins. Co., 701 F.2d 95 (9th Cir. 1983)	§ 15.14
National Wildlife Fed'n v. Coston, 773 F.2d 1513 (9th Cir. 1985)	§ 11.4
Nationwide Investors v. Miller, 793 F.2d 1044 (9th Cir. 1986)	§ 3.5
Nationwide Mut. Fire Ins. v. T & D Cottage Auto Parts & Serv., Inc., 705 F.2d 685 (3d Cir. 1983)	§ 7.9
Naulty v. Fuinch, 686 F.2d 190 (3d Cir. 1982)	§ 14.20
Navarro Sav. & Loan Ass'n v. Lee, 446 U.S. 458 (1980)	§ 2.21
Nealy v. Transportacion Maritima Mexicana, S.A., 662 F.2d 1275 (9th Cir. 1980)	§§ 30.2, 30.4
Nebenzahl v. Credit Suisse, 705 F.2d 1139 (9th Cir. 1983)	§ 6.20
Needham v. Phillips Petroleum Co. of Norway, 719 F.2d 1481 (10th Cir. 1983)	§ 6.18
Neely v. City of Grenada, 799 F.2d 203 (5th Cir. 1986)	§ 31.4
Nehemiah v. Athletics Congress of U.S.A., 765 F.2d 42 (3d Cir. 1985)	§§ 4.9, 14.23
Neifeld v. Steinberg, 438 F.2d 423 (3d Cir. 1971)	§ 14.27
Neiman v. Rudolf Wolff & Co., 619 F.2d 1189 (7th Cir.), *cert. denied,* 449 U.S. 920 (1980)	§ 14.20

Case	*Book §*
Northrop Corp. v. McDonnell Douglas Corp., 751 F.2d 395 (D.C. Cir. 1984)	§§ 18.22, 21.4
Northrop Corp. v. McDonnell Douglas Corp., 705 F.2d 1030 (9th Cir.), *cert. denied,* 464 U.S. 849 (1983)	§ 15.14
Norwood v. Kirkpatrick, 349 U.S. 29 (1955)	§ 6.7
Novak v. World Bank, 703 F.2d 1305 (D.C. Cir. 1983)	§ 14.39
Novinger v. E.I. DuPont de Nemours & Co., 809 F.2d 212 (3d Cir. 1987)	§ 2.26
Noxell Corp. v. Firehouse No. 1 Bar-B-Que Restaurant, 760 F.2d 312 (D.C. Cir. 1985)	§§ 6.4, 6.6, 14.34, 14.69
NRM Corp. v. Hercules Inc., 758 F.2d 676 (D.C. Cir. 1985)	§ 15.12
N.Y. State Urban Dev. Corp. v. VSL Corp., 738 F.2d 61 (2d Cir. 1984)	§ 31.6
Oakland, County of, v. City of Berkeley, 742 F.2d 289 (6th Cir. 1984)	§ 2.25
Oakland Tribune, Inc. v. Chronicle Publishing Co., 762 F.2d 1374 (9th Cir. 1985)	§ 11.7
O'Brien v. Avco Corp., 425 F.2d 1030 (2d Cir. 1969)	§ 2.17
Ocean Drilling & Exploration Co. v. Mont Boat Rental Servs., Inc., 799 F.2d 213 (5th Cir. 1986)	§ 12.5
O'Donnell v. Georgia Osteopathic Hosp., Inc., 748 F.2d 1543 (11th Cir. 1984)	§§ 17.14, 17.15
Office of Personnel Mgmt. v. American Fed'n of Gov't Employees, ___ U.S. ___, 105 S. Ct. 3467 (1985)	§ 11.7
Officers for Justice v. Civil Serv. Comm'n, 688 F.2d 615 (9th Cir. 1932), *cert. denied,* 459 U.S. 1217 (1983)	§ 10.13
Ohio v. Arthur Andersen & Co., 570 F.2d 1370 (10th Cir. 1978), *cert. denied,* 439 U.S. 833 (1979)	§ 27.9
Ohio-Sealy Mattress Mfg. Co. v. Duncan, 749 F.2d 1560 (11th Cir. 1985)	§ 21.6
Okeson v. Tolley School Dist. No. 25, 760 F.2d 864, *rev'd,* 766 F.2d 378 (8th Cir. 1985)	§ 14.63
Olberding v. Illinois Cent. Ry., 346 U.S. 338 (1953)	§ 14.36
Oliveri v. Thompson, 803 F.2d 1265 (2d Cir. 1986)	§ 28.4
Olsen By Sheldon v. Government of Mexico, 729 F.2d 641 (9th Cir.), *cert. denied,* 469 U.S. 917 (1984)	§§ 4.2, 4.11
Olympic Sports Prods., Inc. v. Universal Athletic Sales Co., 760 F.2d 910 (9th Cir. 1985), *cert. denied,* ___ U.S. ___, 106 S. Ct. 804 (1986)	§ 30.2
Oman v. Johns-Mansville Corp., 764 F.2d 224 (4th Cir.) (en banc), *cert. denied,* ___ U.S. ___, 106 S. Ct. 351 (1985)	§ 2.24
Omawale v. WBZ, 610 F.2d 20 (1st Cir. 1979)	§ 7.16
Ondis v. Barrows, 538 F.2d 904 (1st Cir. 1976)	§ 8.9
Oppenheimer Fund, Inc. v. Sanders, 437 U.S. 340 (1978)	§§ 10.12, 10.17, 14.16, 17.5, 19.5
Optyl Eyewear Fashion Int'l Corp. v. Style Corp., 760 F.2d 1045 (9th Cir. 1985)	§§ 28.9, 28.11
O'Quinn v. Manuel, 773 F.2d 605 (5th Cir. 1985)	§ 8.8

Case	*Book §*
Pan American Petroleum Corp. v. Superior Ct., 366 U.S. 656 (1961)	§ 2.8
Panhandle E. Pipe Line Co. v. Federal Power Comm'n, 324 U.S. 635 (1945)	§§ 6.1, 14.31
Panola Land Buyers Ass'n v. Shuman, 762 F.2d 1550 (11th Cir. 1985)	§ 17.17
Pantry Queen Foods, Inc. v. Lifschultz Fast Freight, Inc., 809 F.2d 451 (7th Cir. 1987)	§ 28.3
Paparelli v. Prudential Ins. Co. of Am., 108 F.R.D. 727 (D. Mass. 1985)	§ 23.11
Papilsky v. Berndt, 466 F.2d 251 (2d Cir.), *cert. denied,* 409 U.S. 1077 (1972)	§ 10.18
Pardee v. Stock, 712 F.2d 1290 (8th Cir. 1983)	§ 30.4
Paris v. United States Dep't of Housing & Urban Dev., 713 F.2d 1341 (7th Cir. 1983)	§ 11.3
Parish v. Howard, 459 F.2d 616 (8th Cir. 1972)	§ 15.27
Parker v. Anderson, 667 F.2d 1204 (5th Cir.), *cert. denied,* 459 U.S. 828 (1982)	§ 10.13
Parker v. FNMA, 741 F.2d 975 (7th Cir. 1984)	§ 15.14
Parks v. Collins, 736 F.2d 313 (5th Cir. 1984)	§ 16.13
Parks v. Pavkovic, 753 F.2d 1397 (7th Cir.), *cert. denied,* ___ U.S. ___, 106 S. Ct. 246 (1985)	§ 15.28
Parrish v. Board of Comm'rs, 533 F.2d 942 (5th Cir. 1973)	§ 15.24
Parrott v. Wilson, 707 F.2d 1262 (11th Cir.), *cert. denied,* 464 U.S. 936 (1983)	§§ 7.7, 18.18, 29.7
Parsons Steel, Inc. v. First Alabama Bank, ___ U.S. ___, 106 S. Ct. 768 (1986)	§ 2.6
Passarella v. Hilton Int'l Co., 810 F.2d 674 (7th Cir. 1987)	§ 12.1
Pasternak v. Lear Petroleum Exploration, Inc., 790 F.2d 828 (10th Cir. 1986)	§§ 15.23, 15.24
Patchick v. Kensington Pub. Corp., 743 F.2d 675 (9th Cir. 1984)	§ 14.67
Patrick v. LeFevre, 745 F.2d 153 (2d Cir. 1984)	§§ 15.1, 15.14
Patterson v. Dietze, Inc., 764 F.2d 1145 (5th Cir. 1985)	§ 14.23
Patterson v. F.W. Woolworth Co., 786 F.2d 874 (8th Cir. 1986)	§§ 20.15, 30.10
Patton v. Aerojet Ordnance Co., 765 F.2d 604 (6th Cir. 1985)	§§ 29.4, 29.5
Paul Kadair, Inc. v. Sony Corp. of Am., 694 F.2d 1017 (5th Cir. 1983)	§ 15.24
Paxton v. Union Nat'l Bank, 688 F.2d 552 (8th Cir. 1982), *cert. denied,* 460 U.S. 1083 (1983)	§ 10.10
Peake v. First Nat'l Bank and Trust Co., 717 F.2d 1016 (6th Cir. 1983)	§ 15.29
Pearl Brewing Co. v. Jos. Schlitz Brewing Co., 415 F. Supp. 1122 (S.D. Tex 1976)	§ 20.5
Peat, Marwick, Mitchell & Co. v. West, 748 F.2d 540 (10th Cir. 1984), *cert. denied,* 469 U.S. 1199 (1985)	§ 18.2
Pecherski v. General Motors Corp., 636 F.2d 1156 (8th Cir. 1981)	§§ 3.1, 3.11
Pelleport Investors, Inc. v. Budco Quality Theatres, Inc., 741 F.2d 273 (9th Cir. 1984)	§§ 3.11, 3.19
Pelphrey v. United States, 674 F.2d 243 (4th Cir. 1982)	§ 15.14
Pennhurst State School & Hosp. v. Halderman, 465 U.S. 89 (1984)	§§ 2.6, 3.3

Case	*Book §*
Pennsylvania v. General Pub. Utils. Corp., 710 F.2d 117 (3d Cir. 1983)	§ 15.24
Pennsylvania v. Local Union 542, Int'l Union of Operating Eng'rs, 552 F.2d 498 (3d Cir.), *cert. denied,* 434 U.S. 822 (1977)	§ 31.9
Pennwalt Corp. v. Plough, Inc., 676 F.2d 77 (3d Cir. 1982)	§§ 16.7, 21.5
Pennzoil Co. v. Texaco, Inc., ____ U.S. ____, 107 S. Ct. 1519, 55 U.S.L.W. 4457 (Apr. 6, 1987)	§ 2.6
Penson v. Terminal Transport Co., 634 F.2d 989 (5th Cir. 1981)	§ 10.8
Penthouse Int'l, Ltd. v. Playboy Enters., Inc., 663 F.2d 371 (2d Cir. 1981)	§§ 19.3, 19.5, 29.2, 29.3, 29.5
Peoples Bank of Polk County v. Roberts, 779 F.2d 1544 (11th Cir. 1986)	§ 1.11
Pepsico, Inc. v. McMillen, 764 F.2d 458 (7th Cir. 1985)	§ 16.8
Pereira v. United States, 347 U.S. 1 (1954)	§ 18.22
Pereira v. Utah Transport, Inc., 764 F.2d 686 (9th Cir. 1985), *cert. denied,* ____ U.S. ____, 106 S. Ct. 1253 (1986)	§ 6.18
Perfect Fit Indus., Inc. v. Acme Quilting Co., 646 F.2d 800 (2d Cir. 1981), *cert. denied,* 459 U.S. 832 (1982)	§ 31.6
Perington Wholesale, Inc. v. Burger King Corp., 631 F.2d 1369 (10th Cir. 1979)	§ 14.43
Perkins v. Benguet Consolidated Mining Co., 342 U.S. 437 (1952)	§ 4.2
Perlman v. United States, 247 U.S. 7 (1918)	§§ 17.20, 21.6, 31.9
Perma Research & Dev. Co. v. Singer Co., 542 F.2d 111 (2d Cir.), *cert. denied,* 429 U.S. 987 (1976)	§ 20.8
Perma Research & Dev. Co. v. Singer Co., 410 F.2d 572 (2d Cir. 1969)	§ 15.18
Permian Corp. v. United States, 665 F.2d 1214 (D.C. Cir. 1981)	§ 18.8
Perpetual Am. Bank v. Terrestrial Sys., Inc., 811 F.2d 504 (9th Cir. 1987)	§ 11.8
Perrignon v. Bergen Brunswig Corp., 77 F.R.D. 455 (N.D. Cal. 1978)	§ 18.1
Perry v. State Farm Fire & Casualty Co., 734 F.2d 1441 (11th Cir. 1984), *cert. denied,* 469 U.S. 1108 (1985)	§ 18.22
Perry v. Winspur. 782 F.2d 893 (10th Cir. 1986)	§ 30.10
Pesaplastic, C.A. v. Cincinnati Milacron Co., 799 F.2d 1510 (11th Cir. 1986)	§ 31.7
Peterson v. Lehigh Valley Dist. Council, 676 F.2d 81 (3d Cir. 1982)	§ 15.11
Pfeil v. Rogers, 757 F.2d 850 (7th Cir. 1985), *cert. denied,* ____ U.S. ____, 106 S. Ct. 1513 (1986)	§§ 15.3, 15.16, 15.17, 15.24
P.G.&E. Co. v. F.E.R.C., 746 F.2d 1383 (9th Cir. 1983)	§ 17.4
Phelps v. Washburn Univ., 807 F.2d 153 (10th Cir. 1986)	§ 27.9
Philbrook v. Glodgett, 421 U.S. 707 (1975)	§ 14.8
Phil Crowley Steel Corp. v. Macomber, Inc., 601 F.2d 342 (8th Cir. 1979)	§ 20.15
Philippine Packing Corp. v. Maritime Co., 519 F.2d 811 (9th Cir. 1975)	§ 6.20

Case	***Book §***
Phillips v. Kaplus, 764 F.2d 807 (11th Cir. 1985), *cert. denied,* ____ U.S. ____, 106 S. Ct. 802 (1986)	§ 7.16
Phillips v. Mashburn, 746 F.2d 782 (11th Cir. 1984)	§ 14.7
Phillips v. Smalley Maintenance Servs., Inc., 711 F.2d 1524 (11th Cir. 1983)	§ 2.28
Phillips Petroleum Co. v. Pickens, 105 F.R.D. 545 (N.D. Tex. 1985)	§ 17.10
Phillips Petroleum Co. v. Shutts, 472 U.S. 797 (1985)	§§ 2.3, 4.10, 10.5
Phillips Petroleum Co. v. Texaco, Inc., 415 U.S. 125 (1974)	§ 2.9
Phoceene Sous-Marine, S.A. v. U.S. Phosmarine, Inc., 682 F.2d 802 (9th Cir. 1982)	§ 30.9
Photolab Corp. v. Simplex Specialty Co., 806 F.2d 807 (8th Cir. 1986)	§§ 8.13, 14.39
Piambino v. Bailey, 757 F.2d 1112 (11th Cir. 1985), *cert. denied,* ____ U.S. ____, 106 S. Ct. 2889 (1986)	§§ 9.9, 10.2, 10.15
Pickle v. International Oilfield Divers, Inc., 791 F.2d 1237 (5th Cir. 1986), *cert. denied,* ____ U.S. ____ 107 S. Ct. 939 (1987)	§§ 9.4, 14.53
Pierson v. Dean, Witter, Reynolds, Inc., 551 F. Supp. 497 (C.D. Ill. 1982)	§ 14.60
Pila v. G.R. Leasing & Rental Corp., 551 F.2d 941 (1st Cir. 1977)	§ 14.62
Pillsbury Co. v. Conboy, 459 U.S. 248 (1983)	§ 18.19
Pinemont Bank v. Belk, 722 F.2d 232 (5th Cir. 1984)	§§ 7.16, 7.17
Pink Supply Corp. v. Hiebert, Inc., 788 F.2d 1313 (8th Cir. 1986)	§ 15.17
Piper Acceptance Corp. v. Roudybush, 748 F.2d 471 (8th Cir. 1984)	§ 4.11
Piper Aircraft Co. v. Reyno, 454 U.S. 235 (1981)	§§ 6.7, 6.15–6.17, 6.19–6.21, 14.30
Placid Oil Co., *In re,* 802 F.2d 783 (5th Cir. 1986)	§ 16.8
Plains Cotton Co-op v. Goodpasture Computer Serv., 807 F.2d 1256 (5th Cir. 1987)	§ 11.7
Plant v. Blazer Financial Servs., Inc., 598 F.2d 1357 (5th Cir. 1979)	§ 7.10
Point Landing, Inc. v. Omni Capital Int'l, Ltd., 795 F.2d 415 (5th Cir. 1986) (en banc), *cert. granted,* ____ U.S. ____, 107 S. Ct. 946 (1987)	§ 4.14
Poller v. CBS, Inc., 368 U.S. 464 (1962)	§ 15.14
Poller v. Columbia Broadcasting Sys., Inc., 368 U.S. 464 (1962)	§ 15.14
Pollitt v. Mobay Chem. Corp., 95 F.R.D. 101 (S.D. Ohio W.D. 1982)	§§ 21.1, 21.3
Polyplastics, Inc. v. Transconex, Inc., 713 F.2d 875 (1st Cir. 1983)	§§ 3.11, 3.19
Portsmouth Square, Inc. v. Shareholders Protective Comm., 770 F.2d 866 (9th Cir. 1985)	§§ 15.3, 15.5, 16.3
Posey v. Skyline Corp., 702 F.2d 102 (7th Cir.), *cert. denied,* 464 U.S. 960 (1983)	§ 15.10
Potlatch Corp. v. United States, 679 F.2d 153 (9th Cir. 1982)	§ 29.1
Poulis v. State Farm Fire & Casualty Co., 747 F.2d 863 (3d Cir. 1984)	§ 29.5
Powe v. City of Chicago, 664 F.2d 639 (7th Cir. 1981)	§ 14.47
Powers v. Chesapeake & Ohio Ry., 169 U.S. 92 (1898)	§ 3.10

Case	*Book §*
Powers v. McGuigan, 769 F.2d 72 (2d Cir. 1985)	§ 15.24
Pradier v. Elespuru, 641 F.2d 808 (9th Cir. 1981)	§ 7.16
Prakash v. American Univ., 727 F.2d 1174 (D.C. Cir. 1984)	§§ 2.13, 14.9, 14.11, 14.15
Prandini v. National Tea Co., 557 F.2d 1015 (3d Cir. 1977)	§ 10.14
Prater v. United Mine Workers of Am., 793 F.2d 1201 (11th Cir. 1986)	§ 2.29
Pravic v. U.S. Indus.—Clearing, 109 F.R.D. 620 (E.D. Mich. 1986)	§ 3.23
Preaseau v. Prudential Ins. Co. of Am., 591 F.2d 74 (9th Cir. 1979)	§§ 3.10, 3.14
Precision Constr. Co. v. J.A. Slattery Co., 765 F.2d 114 (8th Cir. 1985)	§§ 4.5, 4.11
Presinzano v. Hoffman-LaRoche, Inc., 726 F.2d 105 (3d Cir. 1984)	§ 15.28
Pressley v. Boehlke, 33 F.R.D. 316 (W.D.N.C. 1963)	§ 24.6
Price v. McGlathery, 792 F.2d 472 (5th Cir. 1986)	§§ 30.7, 30.10
Prinzi v. Keydrel Co., 738 F.2d 707 (5th Cir. 1984)	§ 15.14
Pritchard-Keang Nam Corp. v. Jaworski, 751 F.2d 277 (8th Cir. 1984), *cert. dismissed,* ____ U.S. ____, 105 S. Ct. 3491 (1985)	§ 18.12
Proceedings Before the Aug. 6, 1984 Grand Jury, *In re,* 767 F.2d 39 (2d Cir. 1985)	§ 18.20
Procup v. Strickland, 792 F.2d 1069 (11th Cir. 1986)	§ 14.7
Professional Asset Mgmt., Inc. v. Penn Square Bank, 566 F. Supp. 134 (W.D. Okla. 1983)	§ 14.60
Professional Mgrs. v. Fawer, Brian, Hardy & Zatzkis, 799 F.2d 218 (5th Cir. 1986)	§§ 15.1, 15.6, 15.30
Professional Seminar Consultants, Inc. v. Sino Am. Tech. Exch. Council, Inc., 727 F.2d 1470 (9th Cir. 1984)	§§ 25.8, 29.2, 29.9
Proimos v. Fair Automotive Repair, Inc., 808 F.2d 1273 (7th Cir. 1987)	§ 11.3
Project Release v. Prevost, 722 F.2d 960 (2d CIr. 1983)	§ 15.4
Properties Int'l Ltd. v. Turner, 706 F.2d 308 (11th Cir. 1983)	§ 29.2
Property Mgmt. & Invs., Inc. v. Lewis, 752 F.2d 599 (11th Cir. 1985)	§ 15.25
Prospero Assoc. v. Burroughs Corp., 714 F.2d 1022 (10th Cir. 1983)	§ 15.25
Protective Comm. for Indep. Stockholders of TMT Trailer Ferry, Inc. v. Anderson, 390 U.S. 414 (1968)	§ 10.13
Provident Bank & Trust Co. v. Patterson, 390 U.S. 102 (1968)	§ 2.15
Provident Tradesmens Bank & Trust Co. v. Patterson, 390 U.S. 102 (1968)	§§ 9.3, 9.4, 14.6, 14.53
Province v. Cleveland Press Pub. Co., 787 F.2d 1047 (6th Cir. 1986)	§§ 2.3, 2.29
Prow v. Medtronic, Inc., 770 F.2d 117 (8th Cir. 1985)	§ 17.17
Prudential Ins. Co. of Am. v. Sipula, 776 F.2d 157 (7th Cir. 1985)	§ 14.42
Public Citizen Health Research Group v. F.D.A., 704 F.2d 1280 (D.C. Cir. 1983)	§ 17.10

Case	*Book §*
Public Loan Co. v. FDIC, 803 F.2d 82 (3d Cir. 1986)	§ 31.11
Pueblo of Santa Ana v. Mountain States Tel. & Tel. Co., 734 F.2d 1402 (10th Cir. 1984), *rev'd,* ___ U.S. ___, 105 S. Ct. 2587 (1985)	§ 15.4
Puerto Rico Elec. Power Auth., *In re,* 687 F.2d 501 (1st Cir. 1982)	§ 15.28
Pullman Co. v. Jenkins, 305 U.S. 534 (1939)	§§ 2.32, 3.3
Quality Foods v. Latin Am. Agribusiness Dev. Corp., 711 F.2d 989 (11th Cir. 1983)	§§ 14.42–14.45, 14.57
Quality Prefabrication, Inc. v. Daniel J. Keating Co., 675 F.2d 77 (3d Cir. 1982)	§ 29.5
Quern v. Jordan, 440 U.S. 332 (1979)	§ 2.6
Quiller v. Barclays American/Credit, Inc., 727 F.2d 1067 (11th Cir. 1984), *cert. denied,* ___ U.S. ___, 106 S. Ct. 1992 (1986)	§ 14.48
Quinones v. Pennsylvania Gen. Ins. Co., 804 F.2d 1167 (10th Cir. 1986)	§ 5.2
Quinter v. Volkswagen of Am., 676 F.2d 969 (3d Cir. 1982)	§ 19.8
Rabb v. Amatex Corp., 769 F.2d 996 (4th Cir. 1985)	§§ 16.2, 29.3, 29.7, 30.10
Rachal v. Ingram Corp., 795 F.2d 1210 (5th Cir. 1986)	§ 8.3
Radobenko v. Automated Equip. Corp., 520 F.2d 540 (9th Cir. 1975)	§ 15.18
RAD Servs., Inc. v. Aetna Casualty & Sur. Co., 808 F.2d 271 (3d Cir. 1986)	§§ 17.12, 18.19
Raiford v. Pounds, 640 F.2d 944 (9th Cir. 1981)	§§ 30.3, 30.4
Railroad Comm'n of Tex. v. Pullman Co., 312 U.S. 496 (1941)	§ 2.6
Rainbolt v. Johnson, 669 F.2d 767 (D.C. Cir. 1981)	§ 26.7
Rainbow Pioneer v. Hawaii-Nevada Inv. Corp., 711 F.2d 902 (9th Cir. 1983)	§§ 24.4, 29.4, 29.10
Raines v. Block, 798 F.2d 377 (10th Cir. 1986)	§ 6.10
Ralston Oil & Gas Co. v. Gensco, Inc., 706 F.2d 685 (5th Cir. 1983)	§ 7.7
Ralston Purina Co. v. McFarland, 550 F.2d 967 (4th Cir. 1977)	§ 23.19
Rann v. McInnis, 789 F.2d 374 (6th Cir. 1986)	§ 4.12
Ratner v. Sioux Natural Gas Corp., 770 F.2d 512 (5th Cir. 1985)	§ 2.4
Rauch v. Day & Night Mfg. Corp., 576 F.2d 697 (6th Cir. 1978)	§§ 2.7, 14.61, 14.62
Raynor Bros. v. American Cyanamid Co., 695 F.2d 382 (9th Cir. 1982)	§ 8.15
Redding v. Essex Crane Rental Corp. of Ala., 752 F.2d 1077 (5th Cir. 1985)	§§ 5.12, 14.39
Rees v. Mosaic Tech., Inc., 742 F.2d 765 (3d Cir. 1984)	§ 4.6
Refrigeration Sales Co. v. Mitchell-Jackson, Inc., 770 F.2d 98 (7th Cir. 1985)	§ 15.28
Regional Rail Act Cases, 419 U.S. 102 (1974)	§ 2.25
Reid v. Sears Roebuck & Co., 790 F.2d 453 (6th Cir. 1986)	§§ 15.6, 15.18

Case	*Book §*
Rodgers v. Bowen, 790 F.2d 1550 (11th Cir. 1986)	§ 30.5
Rodgers v. Lincoln Towing Serv., Inc., 771 F.2d 194 (7th Cir. 1985)	§§ 8.9, 28.6
Rodriguez v. Banco Central, 790 F.2d 172 (1st Cir. 1986)	§ 10.17
Roe v. New York, 49 F.R.D. 279 (S.D.N.Y 1970)	§ 2.10
Rogers v. Platt, 814 F.2d 683 (D.C. Cir. 1987)	§ 2.6
Rogers v. Stratton Indus., Inc., 798 F.2d 913 (6th Cir. 1986)	§§ 14.11, 14.15
Rogers v. Webster, 776 F.2d 607 (6th Cir. 1985)	§§ 18.19, 31.4
Rohrer, Hibler & Replogle, Inc. v. Perkins, 728 F.2d 860 (7th Cir. 1984)	§ 3.19
Rollins Envtl. Servs., Inc. v. Parish of St. James, 775 F.2d 627 (5th Cir. 1985)	§ 14.14
Romandette v. Weetabix Co., 807 F.2d 309 (2d Cir. 1986)	§§ 5.12, 30.3, 30.5
Romero v. International Terminal Operating Co., 358 U.S. 354 (1959)	§§ 2.16, 15.28
Romulus Community Schools, *In re,* 729 F.2d 431 (6th Cir. 1984)	§ 3.16
Roofing & Sheet Metal Servs., Inc. v. La Quinta Motor Inns, Inc., 689 F.2d 982 (11th Cir. 1982)	§ 6.10
Rosa v. Cantrell, 705 F.2d 1208 (10th Cir. 1982), *cert denied,* 464 U.S. 821 (1983)	§ 5.4
Rosado v. Wyman, 397 U.S. 397 (1970)	§§ 2.29, 3.3
Rosahn, *In re,* 671 F.2d 690 (2d Cir. 1982)	§ 31.4
Rosales v. Honda Motor Co., 726 F.2d 259 (5th Cir. 1984)	§ 16.3
Rosebud Sioux Tribe v. A&P Steel Inc., 733 F.2ed 509 (8th Cir.), *cert. denied,* 469 U.S. 1072 (1984)	§§ 17.12, 18.19
Rosemount, Inc. v. Beckman Instruments, Inc., 727 F.2d 1540 (Fed. Cir. 1984)	§ 20.15
Rosenberg v. Martin, 478 F.2d 520 (2d Cir.), *cert. denied,* 414 U.S. 872 (1973)	§ 8.12
Rosenfeld v. S.F.C. Corp., 702 F.2d 282 (1st Cir. 1983)	§ 6.4
Rosenstein v. Merrell Dow Pharmaceuticals, Inc., 769 F.2d 352 (6th Cir. 1985)	§ 6.21
Ross v. Bernhard, 396 U.S. 531 (1970)	§§ 9.3, 10.18
Ross v. Communications Satellite Corp., 759 F.2d 355 (4th Cir. 1985)	§ 15.14
Rossini v. Oglivy & Mather, Inc., 798 F.2d 590 (2d Cir. 1986)	§ 10.4
Roviaro v. United States, 353 U.S. 53 (1957)	§ 18.22
Rowley v. McMillan, 502 F.2d 1326 (4th Cir. 1974)	§ 14.64
Royal Idem. Co. v. Petrozzino, 598 F.2d 816 (3d Cir. 1979)	§ 8.16
Rozier v. Ford Motor Co., 573 F.2d 1332 (5th Cir. 1978)	§ 17.14
Rubaii v. Lakewood Pipe of Tex., Inc., 695 F.2d 541 (11th Cir. 1983)	§ 14.19
Rubin, *In re,* 769 F.2d 611 (9th Cir. 1985)	§ 29.5
Rubin v. Buckman, 727 F.2d 71 (3d Cir. 1984)	§§ 2.7, 2.13, 2.23, 2.31
Ruby v. Secretary of United States Navy, 365 F.2d 385 (9th Cir. 1966)	§ 8.9
Ruckelshaus v. Monsanto Co., 467 U.S. 986 (1984)	§ 17.10
Rucker v. Higher Educ. Aids Bd., 669 F.2d 1179 (7th Cir. 1982)	§ 2.6
Rudd Constr. Equip. Co. v. Home Ins. Co., 711 F.2d 54 (6th Cir. 1983)	§ 15.29

Case	*Book §*
Ruiz v. Estelle, 666 F.2d 854 (5th Cir. 1982)	§ 11.7
Rutherford v. United States, 702 F.2d 580 (5th Cir. 1983)	§ 15.28
Ryder Energy Distrib. Corp. v. Merrill Lynch Commodities, Inc., 748 F.2d 774 (2d Cir. 1984)	§ 14.47, 14.55
Saez Rivera v. Nissan Mfg. Co., 788 F.2d 819 (1st Cir. 1986)	§ 14.39
Saladin v. City of Milledgeville, 812 F.2d 687 (11th Cir. 1987)	§ 2.3
Salahuddin v. Harris, 782 F.2d 1127 (2d Cir. 1986)	§§ 16.5, 30.10
Salibra v. Supreme Court of Ohio, 730 F.2d 1059 (6th Cir.), *cert. denied,* 469 U.S. 917 (1984)	§§ 14.6, 14.7
Salinas v. Roadway Express, Inc. 802 F.2d 787 (5th Cir. 1986)	§ 10.13
Sally Beauty v. Nexxus Prods., Co., 801 F.2d 1001 (7th Cir. 1986)	§ 15.28
Salter v. Upjohn Co., 593 F.2d 649 (5th Cir. 1979)	§ 19.5
Salvatore v. American Cyanamid Co., 94 F.R.D. 156 (D.R.I. 1982)	§ 25.13
Salveson v. Western States Bankcard Ass'n, 731 F.2d 1423 (9th Cir. 1984)	§§ 3.3, 3.15
Samaha v. Presbyterian Hosp., 757 F.2d 529 (2d Cir. 1985)	§ 2.15
Samayoa v. Chicago Bd. of Educ., 783 F.2d 102 (7th Cir. 1986)	§ 11.7
Sames v. Gable, 732 F.2d 49 (3d Cir. 1984)	§§ 15.22, 15.24
Sample v. Johnson, 771 F.2d 1335 (9th Cir. 1985), *cert. denied,* _____ U.S. _____, 106 S. Ct. 1206 (1986)	§ 2.4
Sampson v. Murray, 415 U.S. 61 (1974)	§§ 11.1, 11.4
Sanchez-Mariana v. Ellingwood, 691 F.2d 592 (1st Cir. 1982)	§ 5.8
Sandidge v. Salem Offshore Drilling Co., 764 F.2d 252 (5th Cir. 1985)	§ 14.68
Sanguine, Ltd. v. United States Dep't of Interior, 736 F.2d 1416 (10th Cir. 1984)	§ 9.7
Sarnoff v. American Home Prods. Corp., 798 F.2d 1075 (7th Cir. 1986)	§ 2.30
Sartor v. Arkansas Natural Gas Corp., 321 U.S. 620 (1944)	§ 15.14
Satterwhite v. City of Greenville, 634 F.2d 231 (5th Cir. 1981) (en banc), *vacated,* 445 U.S. 940 (1980)	§ 10.6
Savidge v. Fincannon, 768 F.2d 639 (5th Cir. 1985), *modified,* 784 F.2d 186 (5th Cir. 1986)	§ 6.84
Savings & Profit Sharing Fund of Sears Employees v. Gago, 717 F.2d 1038 (7th Cir. 1983)	§ 7.7
Savoie v. Lafourche Boat Rentals, Inc., 627 F.2d 722 (5th Cir. 1980)	§ 23.29
Savola v. Webster, 644 F.2d 743 (8th Cir. 1981)	§ 29.4
Sax v. World Wide Press, Inc., 809 F.2d 610 (9th Cir. 1987)	§ 10.18
Saxe, Bacon & Bolan, P.C. v. Martindale-Hubbell, Inc., 710 F.2d 87 (2d Cir. 1983)	§ 2.20
Scam Instrument Corp. v. C.D.C., 458 F.2d 885 (7th Cir. 1972)	§ 12.5
Scarborough v. Eubanks, 747 F.2d 871 (3d Cir. 1984)	§ 30.3
Schempp v. Reniker, 809 F.2d 541 (8th Cir. 1987)	§ 25.14
Schering Corp. v. Home Ins. Co., 712 F.2d 4 (2d Cir. 1983)	§ 15.24
Scheuer v. Rhodes, 416 U.S. 232 (1974)	§§ 2.6, 14.9, 14.12, 14.42
Schiavone v. Fortune, _____ U.S. _____, 106 S. Ct. 2379 (1986)	§§ 5.4, 8.11, 8.13
Schilling v. Walworth County Parks & Planning Comm'n, 805 F.2d 272 (7th Cir. 1986)	§ 30.5

Case	*Book §*
Schlagenhauf v. Holder, 379 U.S. 104 (1964)	§ 25.11
School Asbestos Litig., *In re,* 789 F.2d 996 (3d Cir.), *cert. denied,* ____ U.S. ____, 107 S. Ct. 318 (1986)	§§ 10.5, 10.7
Schooley v. Kennedy, 712 F.2d 372 (11th Cir. 1983)	§ 30.5
Schreiber Distrib. v. Serv-Well Furniture Co., 806 F.2d 1393 (9th Cir. 1986)	§§ 7.2, 7.3, 14.49
Schroeder v. Trans World Airlines, Inc., 702 F.2d 189 (9th Cir. 1983)	§ 3.3
Schultz v. Frisby, 807 F.2d 1339 (7th Cir. 1986)	§ 11.4
Schwabenbauer v. Board of Educ., 667 F.2d 305 (2d Cir. 1981)	§ 15.13
S.C. Johnson & Son, Inc. v. Louisville & Nashville R.R., 695 F.2d 253 (7th Cir. 1982)	§ 25.8
Scott, *In re,* 709 F.2d 717 (D.C. Cir. 1983)	§§ 6.8, 6.10
Scott & Fetzer Co. v. Dile, 643 F.2d 670 (9th Cir. 1981)	§ 17.14
Scot Typewriter Co. v. Underwood Corp., 170 F. Supp. 862 (S.D.N.Y. 1959)	§ 2.20
Scullin Steel v. National Ry. Utilization Corp., 676 F.2d 309 (8th Cir. 1982)	§ 4.12
Scutieri v. Paige, 808 F.2d 785 (11th Cir. 1987)	§ 16.4
Sea-Land Serv., Inc. v. R.V. D'Alfonso Co., 727 F.2d 1 (1st Cir. 1984)	§ 14.4
Sealed Case, *In re,* 801 F.2d 1379 (D.C. Cir. 1986)	§ 17.12
Sealed Case, *In re,* 791 F.2d 179 (D.C. Cir. 1986)	§ 18.21
Sealed Case, *In re,* 754 F.2d 395 (D.C. Cir. 1985)	§ 18.12
Sealed Case, *In re,* 737 F.2d 94 (D.C. Cir. 1984)	§§ 17.20, 18.2, 18.4, 18.6
Sealed Case, *In re,* 676 F.2d 793 (D.C. Cir. 1982)	§§ 18.8, 18.18
Sealed Case, *In re,* 655 F.2d 1298 (D.C. Cir. 1981)	§ 17.20
Sea Lift, Inc. v. Refinadora Costarricense, 792 F.2d 989 (11th Cir. 1986)	§§ 4.4, 4.5
Sealy, Inc. v. Easy Living, Inc., 743 F.2d 1378 (9th Cir. 1984)	§§ 20.15, 23.27, 30.10
Searock v. Stripling, 736 F.2d 650 (11th Cir. 1984)	§§ 25.6, 29.5
Season-All Indus., Inc. v. Turkiye Sise Ve Cam Fabrikalari, A.S., 425 F.2d 34 (3d Cir. 1970)	§ 15.27
Seattle Times Co. v. Rhinehart, 467 U.S. 20 (1984)	§ 19.4
SEC v. Dresser Indus., Inc., 628 F.2d 1368 (D.C. Cir.) (en banc), *cert. denied,* 449 U.S. 993 (1980)	§ 17.11
SEC v. Frank, 388 F.2d 486 (2d Cir. 1968)	§ 11.5
SEC v. Hardy, 803 F.2d 1034 (9th Cir. 1986)	§ 11.9
SEC v. Jerry T. O'Brien, Inc., 467 U.S. 735 (1984)	§ 21.8
SEC v. Medical Comm. for Human Rights, 404 U.S. 403 (1972)	§ 2.2
SEC v. Ormont Drug & Chem. Co., 739 F.2d 654 (D.C. Cir. 1984)	§§ 31.4, 31.5
SEC v. Research Automation Corp., 585 F.2d 31 (2d Cir. 1978)	§ 15.12
SEC v. Safety Finance Serv., Inc., 674 F.2d 368 (5th Cir. 1982)	§ 11.9
SEC v. Seaboard Corp., 677 F.2d 1315 (9th Cir. 1982)	§§ 14.44, 14.45, 15.28
SEC v. Seaboard Corp., 666 F.2d 414 (9th Cir. 1982)	§ 29.3
SEC v. Spence & Green Chem. Co., 612 F.2d 896 (5th Cir. 1980), *cert. denied,* 449 U.S. 1082 (1981)	§ 15.23

Case	*Book §*
Secretary of Labor v. Fitzsimmons, 805 F.2d 682 (7th Cir. 1986)	§§ 9.7, 10.6, 10.10
Securities Investors Protection Corp. v. Vigman, 764 F.2d 1309 (9th Cir. 1985)	§§ 4.14, 5.2, 6.5
Security Nat'l Bank v. Belleville Livestock Comm'n Co., 619 F.2d 840 (10th Cir. 1980)	§ 15.9
Sedco Int'l, S.A. v. Cory, 683 F.2d 1201 (8th Cir.), *cert. denied,* 459 U.S. 1017 (1982)	§§ 18.2, 18.8
Sedima, S.P.R.L. v. Imrex Co., 473 U.S. 479 (1985)	§§ 2.3, 7.3
Segal v. Gordon, 467 F.2d 602 (2d Cir. 1972)	§ 7.3
Seglin v. Esau, 769 F.2d 1274 (7th Cir. 1985)	§§ 14.11, 14.42
Seismic Int'l Research Corp. v. South Ranch Oil Co., 793 F.2d 227 (10th Cir. 1986)	§ 30.10
Selcraig, *In re,* 705 F.2d 789 (5th Cir. 1983)	§ 18.22
Self v. General Motors Corp., 588 F.2d 655 (9th Cir. 1978)	§ 3.10
Sellers v. Baisier, 792 F.2d 690 (7th Cir. 1986)	§ 16.3
Sellers v. O'Connell, 701 F.2d 575 (6th Cir. 1983)	§ 2.12
Sellers v. United States, 709 F.2d 1469 (11th Cir. 1983)	§ 9.9
Selva & Sons, Inc. v. Nina Footwear, Inc., 705 F.2d 1316 (Fed. Cir. 1983)	§ 15.25
Semegen v. Weidner, 780 F.2d 727 (9th Cir. 1985)	§ 7.3
Senior Loiza Corp. v. Vento Dev. Corp., 760 F.2d 20 (1st Cir. 1985)	§ 5.4
Sentry Life Ins. Co. v. Borad, 759 F.2d 695 (9th Cir. 1985)	§ 11.7
Senza-Gel Corp. v. Seiffhart, 803 F.2d 661 (Fed. Cir. 1986)	§ 8.2
Serrano v. Torres, 764 F.2d 47 (1st Cir. 1985)	§§ 8.12, 14.44, 14.63
Serrano Medina v. United States, 709 F.2d 104 (1st Cir. 1983)	§ 8.3
Sessions, *In re,* 672 F.2d 564 (5th Cir. 1982)	§ 23.9
Shackelford v. Vermeer Mfg. Co., 93 F.R.D. 512 (W.D. Tex. 1982)	§ 20.4
Shaffer v. Heitner, 433 U.S. 186 (1977)	§§ 4.3, 4.4, 4.6, 4.9
Shaklee Corp. v. Gunnell, 748 F.2d 548 (10th Cir. 1984)	§ 17.17
Shakman v. Democratic Org. of Cook County, 533 F.2d 344 (7th Cir.), *cert. denied,* 429 U.S. 858 (1976)	§ 31.4
Shamrock Oil & Gas Corp. v. Sheets, 313 U.S. 100 (1941)	§§ 2.11, 3.3
Shanks v. City of Dallas, 752 F.2d 1092 (5th Cir. 1985)	§ 10.17
Shapiro v. United States, 335 U.S. 1 (1948)	§ 18.20
Shargel, *In re,* 742 F.2d 61 (2d Cir. 1984)	§ 18.2
Shawmut Boston Int'l Banking Corp. v. Duque-Pena, 767 F.2d 1504 (11th Cir. 1985)	§ 14.26
Shawnee Int'l, N.V. v. Hondo Drilling Co., 742 F.2d 234 (5th Cir. 1984)	§ 14.6
Shea v. Donohoe Constr. Co., 795 F.2d 1071 (D.C. Cir. 1986)	§§ 30.3, 30.4, 30.6
Shearer v. Homestake Mining Co., 557 F. Supp. 549 (D.S.D. 1983), *aff'd,* 727 F.2d 707 (8th Cir. 1984)	§§ 15.18, 15.22, 15.27
Shearson/American Express, Inc. v. McMahon, _____ U.S. _____, 107 S. Ct. 2332, 55 U.S.L.W. 4757 (June 8, 1987)	§ 1.2
Sheet Metal Workers Int'l Ass'n v. Seay, 693 F.2d 1000 (10th Cir. 1982)	§ 3.19

Case	*Book §*
Shell Oil Co. v. M/T Gilda, 790 F.2d 1209 (5th Cir. 1986)	§ 16.3
Shelter Mut. Ins. Co. v. Public Water Supply Dist. No. 7, 747 F.2d 1195 (8th Cir. 1984)	§§ 14.47, 14.49
Shelton v. American Motors Corp., 805 F.2d 1323 (8th Cir. 1986)	§§ 18.2, 18.13, 19.5, 23.6
Sherman v. Hallbauer, 455 F.2d 1236 (5th Cir. 1972)	§ 8.7
Sherman v. United States, 801 F.2d 1133 (9th Cir. 1986)	§ 30.10
Shevlin v. Schewe, 809 F.2d 447 (7th Cir. 1987)	§ 9.9
Shillitani v. United States, 384 U.S. 364 (1966)	§§ 31.2, 31.5
Shimman v. International Union of Operating Eng'rs, 744 F.2d 1226 (6th Cir. 1984) (en banc), *cert. denied,* 469 U.S. 1215 (1985)	§ 28.9
Shook v. United States, 713 F.2d 662 (11th Cir. 1983)	§§ 15.8, 15.13
Shore v. Acands, Inc., 644 F.2d 386 (5th Cir. 1981)	§ 17.13
Shouse v. Ljunggren, 792 F.2d 902 (9th Cir. 1986)	§ 15.30
Shuffler v. Heritage Bank, 720 F.2d 1141 (9th Cir. 1983)	§§ 31.4, 31.6
Shuford v. Anderson, 352 F.2d 755 (10th Cir. 1965), *cert. denied,* 383 U.S. 935 (1966)	§ 14.62
Sibaja v. Dow Chem. Co., 757 F.2d 1215 (11th Cir.), *cert. denied,* ___ U.S. ___, 106 S. Ct. 347 (1985)	§ 6.20
Sidney-Vinstein v. A.H. Robins Co., 697 F.2d 880 (9th Cir. 1983)	§ 14.60
Siegel v. Converters Transp., Inc., 714 F.2d 213 (2d Cir. 1983)	§ 8.12
Sierra Club v. Leathers, 754 F.2d 952 (11th Cir. 1985)	§§ 9.3, 14.53
Sigalas v. Lido Maritime, Inc., 776 F.2d 1512 (11th Cir. 1985)	§ 6.21
Sills v. Bureau of Prisons, 761 F.2d 792 (D.C. Cir. 1985)	§ 14.7
Silver v. Baggiano, 804 F.2d 1211 (11th Cir. 1986)	§ 2.6
Silverman v. Commodity Futures Trading Comm'n, 549 F.2d 28 (7th Cir. 1977)	§ 17.4
Simmons v. Hoegh Lines, 784 F.2d 1234 (5th Cir. 1986)	§ 24.10
Simon v. Eastern Kentucky Welfare Rights Org., 426 U.S. 26 1976)	§ 2.3
Sims v. National Transp. Safety Bd., 662 F.2d 668 (10th Cir. 1981)	§ 17.4
Sinclair v. Kleindienst, 711 F.2d 291 (D.C. Cir. 1983)	§ 6.9
Singleton v. Wulff, 428 U.S. 106 (1976)	§ 15.28
Sinking of M/V Ukola, *In re,* 806 F.2d 1 (1st Cir. 1986)	§ 9.6
Sinwell v. Shapp, 536 F.2d 15 (3d Cir. 1976)	§§ 14.7, 14.36
Sirota v. Solitron Devices, Inc., 673 F.2d 566 (2d Cir.), *cert. denied,* 459 U.S. 838 (1982)	§ 10.11
Sisk v. United States, 756 F.2d 497 (7th Cir. 1985)	§ 30.5
Sitts v. United States, 811 F.2d 736 (2d Cir. 1987)	§§ 15.10, 15.16
Skelly Oil Co. v. Phillips Petroleum Co., 339 U.S. 667 (1950)	§§ 2.9, 3.2
Slaughter v. Allstate Ins. Co., 803 F.2d 857 (5th Cir. 1986)	§ 15.14
Smiga v. Dean Witter Reynolds, Inc., 766 F.2d 698 (2d Cir. 1985), *cert. denied,* ___ U.S. ___, 106 S. Ct. 1381 (1986)	§ 6.4
Smith, *In re,* 735 F.2d 459 (11th Cir. 1984)	§ 15.28
Smith v. City of Pittsburgh, 764 F.2d 188 (3d Cir.), *cert. denied,* ___ U.S. ___, 106 S. Ct. 349 (1985)	§ 15.14
Smith v. Danyo, 585 F.2d 83 (3d Cir. 1978)	§ 16.8
Smith v. Ford Motor Co., 626 F.2d 784 (10th Cir. 1980), *cert. denied,* 450 U.S. 918 (1981)	§§ 16.4, 20.15, 30.10

Case	*Book §*
U.S. 896 (1976)	§ 15.3
Spiegel v. Continental Ill. Nat'l Bank, 790 F.2d 638 (7th Cir.), *cert. denied,* _____ U.S. _____, 107 S. Ct. 579 (1986)	§§ 14.9, 15.30
Spiess v. C. Itoh & Co., 725 F.2d 970 (5th Cir.), *cert. denied,* 469 U.S. 812 (1984)	§ 14.69
Sporck v. Peil, 759 F.2d 312 (3d Cir.), *cert. denied,* _____ U.S. _____, 106 S. Ct. 232 (1985)	§§ 18.13, 18.17, 20.12
Sprague v. Director, Office of Workers' Comp. Programs, 688 F.2d 862 (1st Cir. 1982)	§ 18.13
Springfield, City of v. Washington Pub. Power Supply Sys., 752 F.2d 1423 (9th Cir. 1985), *cert. denied,* _____ U.S. _____, 106 S. Ct. 792 (1986)	§ 15.24
Sprow v. Hartford Ins. Co., 594 F.2d 412 (5th Cir. 1979)	§ 5.2
Spruytte v. Walters, 753 F.2d 498 (6th Cir. 1985), *cert. denied,* _____ U.S. _____, 106 S. Ct. 788 (1986)	§ 14.7
Square D. Co. v. Niagara Frontier Tariff Bureau, Inc., 760 F.2d 1347 (2d Cir. 1985), *aff'd,* _____ U.S. _____, 106 S. Ct. 1922 (1986)	§ 14.6
SRI Int'l v. Matsushita Elec. Corp. of Am., 775 F.2d 1107 (Fed. Cir. 1985)	§ 15.14
Stallworth v. Monsanto Co., 558 F.2d 257 (5th Cir. 1977)	§ 9.8
St. Amant v. Benoit, 806 F.2d 1294 (5th Cir. 1987)	§ 15.6
Stamford Bd. of Educ. v. Stamford Educ. Ass'n, 697 F.2d 70 (2d Cir. 1982)	§ 2.27
Staren v. American Nat'l Bank & Trust Co., 529 F.2d 1257 (7th Cir. 1976)	§ 8.15
Starnes v. McGuire, 512 F.2d 918 (D.C. Cir. 1974)	§ 6.10
Starsky v. Williams, 512 F.2d 109 (9th Cir. 1975)	§ 15.13
Stebbins v. Nationwide Mut. Ins. Co., 757 F.2d 364 (D.C. Cir. 1985)	§ 17.8
Steele, *In re,* 799 F.2d 461 (9th Cir. 1986)	§ 17.10
Steel Valley Auth. v. Union Switch & Signal Div., 809 F.2d 1006 (3d Cir. 1987)	§§ 3.3, 9.4
Steinbrecher v. Commissioner, 712 F.2d 195 (5th Cir. 1983)	§ 18.19
Steinle v. Warren, 765 F.2d 95 (7th Cir. 1985)	§ 15.16
Stephanischen v. Merchants Despatch Transp. Corp., 722 F.2d 922 (1st Cir. 1983)	§§ 8.3, 15.12
Stephens v. Portal Boat Co., 781 F.2d 481 (5th Cir. 1986)	§ 3.15
Sterling Energy, Ltd. v. Friendly Nat'l Bank, 744 F.2d 1433 (10th Cir. 1984)	§§ 28.8, 28.9
Stevens v. Gay, 792 F.2d 1000 (11th Cir. 1986)	§ 8.2
Stevens v. Greyhound Lines, Inc., 710 F.2d 1224 (7th Cir. 1983)	§§ 30.4, 30.5
Stevens v. Lawyers Mut. Liability Ins. Co., 789 F.2d 1056 (4th Cir. 1986)	§ 28.4
Stewart v. Credit Bureau, Inc., 734 F.2d 47 (D.C. Cir. 1984)	§ 15.5
Stewart v. General Motors Corp., 756 F.2d 1285 (7th Cir. 1985)	§ 11.4
Stewart v. RCA Corp., 790 F.2d 624 (7th Cir. 1986)	§ 15.14
Stewart v. United States, 655 F.2d 741 (7th Cir. 1981)	§ 5.5
Stewart v. Winter, 669 F.2d 328 (5th Cir. 1982)	§§ 10.10, 10.11
Stich v. United States, 730 F.2d 115 (3d Cir.), *cert. denied,* 469 U.S. 917 (1984)	§ 20.15

Case	*Book §*
Tavoulareas v. Washington Post Co., 737 F.2d 1170 (D.C. Cir. 1984) (en banc)	§ 19.4
Tavoulareas v. Washington Post Co., 724 F.2d 1010 (D.C. Cir. 1984)	§ 19.6
Taylor v. Combustion Eng'g, Inc., 782 F.2d 525 (5th Cir. 1986)	§ 30.6
Taylor v. Gibson, 529 F.2d 709 (5th Cir. 1976)	§ 14.7
Taylor v. Hayes, 418 U.S. 488 (1974)	§ 31.8
Teen-Ed, Inc. v. Kimball Int'l, Inc., 620 F.2d 399 (3d Cir. 1980)	§ 20.15
Tefft v. Seward, 689 F.2d 637 (6th Cir. 1982)	§ 8.7
Telecommunications Research & Action Center v. Allnet Communication Servs., Inc., 806 F.2d 1093 (D.C. Cir. 1986)	§ 2.3
Tele-Radio Sys., Ltd. v. De Forest Elecs., Inc., 92 F.R.D. 371 (D.N.J. 1981)	§ 15.7
Templeman v. Chris Craft Corp., 770 F.2d 245 (1st Cir), *cert. denied,* ____ U.S. ____, 106 S. Ct. 571 (1985)	§ 23.1
Ten Mile Indus. Park v. Western Plains Serv. Corp., 810 F.2d 1518 (10th Cir. 1987)	§ 4.6
Terre Du Lac Ass'n, Inc. v. Terre Du Lac, Inc., 772 F.2d 467 (8th Cir. 1985), *cert. denied,* ____ U.S. ____, 106 S. Ct. 1460 (1986)	§ 2.3
Terrell v. United States, 783 F.2d 1562 (11th Cir. 1986)	§ 2.6
Terry v. Raymond Int'l, Inc., 658 F.2d 398 (5th Cir. 1981), *cert. denied,* 456 U.S. 928 (1982)	§ 14.38
Texaco, Inc. v. Cottage Hill Operating Co., 709 F.2d 452 (7th Cir. 1983)	§ 14.69
Textor v. Board of Regents of N. Ill. Univ., 711 F.2d 1387 (7th Cir. 1983)	§§ 8.8, 28.10, 28.11
Thermtron Prods., Inc. v. Hermansdorfer, 423 U.S. 336 (1976)	§§ 3.16, 3.19
Thoen v. United States, 765 F.2d 1110 (Fed. Cir. 1985)	§ 15.25
Thomas v. Arn, ____ U.S. ____, 106 S. Ct. 466 (1985)	§ 16.12
Thomas v. Board of Trustees, 195 U.S. 207 (1904)	§ 2.18
Thomas v. Brock, 810 F.2d 448 (4th Cir. 1987)	§ 11.5
Thomas v. Farmville Mfg. Co., 705 F.2d 1307 (11th Cir. 1983)	§ 8.8
Thomas v. Gerber Prods., 703 F.2d 353 (9th Cir. 1983)	§ 29.3
Thomas v. Shelton, 740 F.2d 478 (7th Cir. 1984)	§ 3.4
Thompkins v. Stuttgart School Dist. No. 22, 787 F.2d 439 (8th Cir. 1986)	§ 2.28
Thompson v. Betts, 754 F.2d 1243 (5th Cir. 1985)	§§ 14.68, 14.69
Thompson v. Board of Educ., 709 F.2d 1200 (6th Cir. 1983)	§ 10.8
Thompson v. Chrysler Motors Corp., 755 F.2d 1162 (5th Cir. 1985)	§§ 4.11, 4.12, 14.18, 14.19, 14.30
Thompson v. Cleland, 782 F.2d 719 (7th Cir. 1986)	§§ 31.2, 31.4
Thompson v. Johns-Manville Sales Corp., 714 F.2d 581 (5th Cir. 1983), *cert. denied,* 465 U.S. 1102 (1984)	§ 15.9
Thompson v. Thompson, 798 F.2d 1547 (9th Cir. 1986), *cert. granted,* ____ U.S. ____, 107 S. Ct. 946 (1987)	§ 2.6
Thornbrough v. Columbus & Greenville R. Co., 760 F.2d 633 (5th Cir. 1986)	§ 15.7
Thornbill Pub. Co. v. G.T.&E. Corp., 594 F.2d 730 (9th Cir. 1979)	§§ 14.11, 14.13, 14.14

Case	*Book §*
Thornton v. Evans, 692 F.2d 1064 (7th Cir. 1982)	§§ 15.9, 15.15
Thor Power Tool Co. v. Weintraub, 791 F.2d 579 (7th Cir. 1986)	§ 9.2
Thrasher v. State Farm Fire & Casualty Co., 734 F.2d 637 (11th Cir. 1984)	§§ 15.6, 15.28
T.I.A.A. v. Shamrock Broadcasting Co., 521 F. Supp. 638 (S.D.N.Y. 1981)	§ 18.8
Tick v. Cohen, 787 F.2d 1490 (11th Cir. 1986)	§ 9.4
Tiernan v. Blyth, Eastman, Dillon & Co., 719 F.2d 1 (1st Cir 1983)	§ 8.3
Tiffany Fine Arts, Inc. v. United States, 469 U.S. 310 (1985)	§ 21.8
TIF Instruments, Inc. v. Colette, 713 F.2d 197 (6th Cir. 1983)	§ 19.8
Timberlane Lumber Co. v. Bank of Am., 749 F.2d 1378 (9th Cir. 1984), *cert. denied,* _____ U.S. _____, 105 S. Ct. 3514 (1985)	§ 14.13
Time Share Vacation Club v. Atlantic Resorts, Ltd., 735 F.2d 61 (3d Cir. 1984)	§§ 14.19, 14.20
Titus v. Mercedes Benz of N. Am., 695 F.2d 746 (3d Cir. 1982)	§§ 30.3, 30.4
TNT Marketing, Inc. v. Agresti, 796 F.2d 276 (9th Cir. 1986)	§ 16.7
Tokio Marine & Fire Ins. Co. v. Employers Ins. of Wausau, 786 F.2d 101 (2d Cir. 1986)	§ 8.6
Tolliver v. Northrop Corp., 786 F.2d 316 (7th Cir. 1986)	§§ 27.3, 29.10
Toombs v. Leone, 777 F.2d 465 (9th Cir. 1985)	§ 28.10
Townsend v. Columbia Operations, 667 F.2d 844 (9th Cir. 1982)	§ 15.25
Toyota Landscape Co. v. Building Material & Dump Truck Drivers Local 420, 726 F.2d 525 (9th Cir.), *cert. denied,* 469 U.S. 825 (1984)	§ 30.5
Traguth v. Zuck, 710 F.2d 90 (2d Cir. 1983)	§ 12.3
Trakas v. Quality Brands, Inc., 759 F.2d 185 (D.C. Cir. 1985)	§ 30.4
Trammel v. United States, 445 U.S. 40 (1980)	§ 18.22
TrampOil & Marine Ltd. v. M/V Mermaid I, 743 F.2d 48 (1st Cir. 1984)	§ 6.16
Transamerica Computer Co. v. I.B.M. Corp., 573 F.2d 646 (9th Cir. 1978)	§ 18.9
Transamerica Corp. v. Transamerica Bancgrowth Corp., 627 F.2d 963 (9th Cir. 1980)	§ 31.11
Transamerica Occidental Life Ins. Co. v. Digregorio, 811 F.2d 1249 (9th Cir. 1987)	§ 2.6
Trans-Asiatic Oil Ltd. S.A. v. Apex Oil Co., 743 F.2d 956 (1st Cir. 1984)	§§ 4.13, 14.26
Transunion Corp. v. Pepsico, Inc., 811 F.2d 127 (2d Cir. 1987)	§ 19.5
Transure, Inc. v. Marsh & McLennan, Inc., 766 F.2d 1297 (9th Cir. 1985)	§§ 2.20, 3.7, 4.6, 6.1
Travelers Indem. Co. v. Calvert Fire Ins. Co., 798 F.2d 826 (5th Cir. 1986)	§ 14.20
Travelers Ins. Co. v. First Nat'l Bank, 675 F.2d 633 (5th Cir. 1982)	§ 2.26
Trevino v. Celanese Corp., 701 F.2d 397 (5th Cir. 1983)	§§ 15.14, 19.5
Tri-Hawaii, Inc. v. First Commerce Fin. Corp., 627 F.2d 991 (9th Cir. 1980)	§ 15.24
Trinity Carton Co. v. Falstaff Brewing Corp., 767 F.2d 184 (5th Cir. 1985), *cert. denied,* _____ U.S. _____, 106 S. Ct. 1202 (1986)	§§ 7.7, 8.9, 16.4

Case	*Book §*
Triplett v. LeFlore County, 712 F.2d 444 (10th Cir. 1983)	§§ 8.7, 8.8
Trone v. Smith, 621 F.2d 994 (9th Cir. 1980)	§ 16.9
Troxler v. Owens-Illinois, Inc., 717 F.2d 530 (11th Cir. 1983)	§ 7.7
Trust Corp. of Mont. v. Piper Aircraft Corp., 701 F.2d 85 (9th Cir. 1983)	§ 16.9
Trustees of Sabine Area Carpenters' Health & Welfare Fund v. Don Lightfoot Home Builder, Inc., 704 F.2d 822 (5th Cir. 1983)	§ 15.3
TSC Indus., Inc. v. Northway, Inc., 426 U.S. 438 (1976)	§ 15.6
T.W. Elec. Serv., Inc. v. Pacific Elec. Contractors Ass'n, 809 F.2d 626 (9th Cir. 1987)	§§ 15.14, 28.11
20th Century Wear, Inc. v. Sanmark-Stardust Inc., 747 F.2d 81 (2d Cir. 1984), *cert. denied,* 470 U.S. 1052 (1985)	§ 18.18
Two Grand Jury Subpoenae Duces Tecum, *In re,* 769 F.2d 52 (2d Cir. 1985)	§ 18.21
Two Grand Jury Subpoenae Duces Tecum Dated August 21, 1985, *In re,* 793 F.2d 69 (2d Cir. 1986)	§§ 18.2, 18.21
Twohy v. First Nat'l Bank of Chicago, 758 F.2d 1185 (7th Cir. 1985)	§§ 8.7, 8.9, 14.71
Tyler v. City of Milwaukee, 740 F.2d 580 (7th Cir. 1984)	§ 31.8
Underwriters at Lloyd's, *In re*, 666 F.2d 55 (4th Cir. 1981)	§ 17.17
Underwriters Nat'l Assurance Co. v. North Carolina Life & Accident & Health Ins. Guaranty Ass'n., 455 U.S. 691 (1982)	§ 14.19
Unioil, Inc. v. E.F. Hutton & Co., 809 F.2d 548 (9th Cir. 1986)	§§ 12.7, 28.4, 28.6
Union Carbide Corp. v. U.S. Cutting Serv., Inc., 782 F.2d 710 (7th Cir. 1986)	§§ 17.17, 17.20
Union Carbide Corp. Gas Plant Disaster, *In re,* 809 F.2d 195 (2d Cir. 1987)	§§ 6.17, 12.7
Union Planters Nat'l Leasing, Inc. v. Woods, 687 F.2d 117 (5th Cir. 1982)	§§ 8.3, 15.6, 15.17
United Airlines, Inc. v. McDonald, 432 U.S. 385 (1977)	§§ 9.8, 10.16
United Artists Corp. v. Freeman, 605 F.2d 854 (5th Cir. 1979)	§ 29.9
United Artists Corp. v. La Cage Aux Folles, Inc., 771 F.2d 1265 (9th Cir. 1985)	§§ 29.3, 29.5, 29.6
United Beverage Co. v. Indiana Alcoholic Beverage Comm'n, 760 F.2d 155 (7th Cir. 1985)	§ 2.29
United Coin Meter Co. v. Seaboard Coastline R.R., 705 F.2d 839 (6th Cir. 1983)	§ 12.3
United Food & Commercial Workers Union v. Alpha Beta Co., 736 F.2d 1371 (9th Cir. 1984)	§§ 5.1, 14.39
United Jersey Banks v. Parell, 783 F.2d 360 (3d Cir. 1986), *cert. denied,* _____ U.S. _____, 106 S. Ct. 2892 (1986)	§ 3.2
United Mine Workers of Am. v. Gibbs, 383 U.S. 715 (1966)	§§ 2.16, 2.25, 2.27–2.29, 3.3
United Presbyterian Church in the U.S.A. v. Reagan, 738 F.2d 1375 (D.C. Cir. 1984)	§§ 14.16, 17.5, 17.17
United States v. Amerada Hess Corp., 619 F.2d 980 (3d Cir. 1980)	§ 18.2
United States v. American Cyanamid Co., 719 F.2d 558 (2d Cir. 1983), *cert. denied,* 465 U.S. 1101 (1984)	§ 9.7
United States v. Aquavella, 615 F.2d 12 (2d Cir. 1979)	§ 7.10

Case	*Book §*
Cir. 1984)	§ 9.7
United States v. Hooker Chem. & Plastics Corp., 90 F.R.D. 421 (W.D.N.Y. 1981)	§§ 19.3, 19.6
United States v. Horton, 622 F.2d 144 (5th Cir. 1980)	§ 15.26
United States v. Hougham, 364 U.S. 310 (1960)	§ 16.4
United States v. Huckaby, 776 F.2d 564 (5th Cir.), *cert. denied,* ___ U.S. ___, 106 S. Ct. 1468 (1986)	§ 18.19
United States v. I.B.M., 90 F.R.D. 377 (S.D.N.Y. 1981)	§ 20.13
United States v. I.B.M., 72 F.R.D. 78 (S.D.N.Y. 1976)	§ 20.8
United States v. Jefferson County, 720 F.2d 1511 (11th Cir. 1983)	§ 9.8
United States v. Jenkins, 785 F.2d 1387 (9th Cir.), *cert. denied,* ___ U.S. ___, 107 S. Ct. 192 (1986)	§ 23.16
United States v. John Doe, Inc. I, ___ U.S. ___, 107 S. Ct. 1656 (1987)	§ 17.12
United States v. Johnson, 736 F.2d 358 (6th Cir. 1984)	§ 31.6
United States v. Jones, 703 F.2d 473 (10th Cir. 1983)	§ 18.19
United States v. Jones, 696 F.2d 1069 (4th Cir. 1982)	§§ 17.20, 18.6, 18.8
United States v. Joudis, 800 F.2d 159 (7th Cir. 1986)	§ 18.19
United States v. Kemper Money Market Fund, Inc., 704 F.2d 389 (7th Cir. 1983)	§ 9.8
United States v. Keplinger, 776 F.2d 678 (7th Cir. 1985), *cert. denied,* ___ U.S. ___, 106 S. Ct. 2919 (1986)	§§ 18.2, 18.5, 18.8
United States v. Koehler, 790 F.2d 1256 (5th Cir. 1986)	§ 18.22
United States v. Kordel, 397 U.S. 1 (1970)	§ 18.19
United States v. Koziy, 728 F.2d 1314 (11th Cir.), *cert. denied,* 469 U.S. 835 (1984)	§§ 20.15, 30.10
United States v. Kungys, 793 F.2d 516 (3d Cir. 1986), *cert. granted,* ___ U.S. ___, 107 S. Ct. 431 (1986)	§ 23.29
United States v. Lang, 792 F.2d 1235 (4th Cir.), *cert. denied,* ___ U.S. ___, 107 S. Ct. 574 (1986)	§ 18.21
United States v. Lask, 703 F.2d 293 (8th Cir.), *cert. denied,* 464 U.S. 829 (1983)	§ 17.4
United States v. Lawless, 709 F.2d 485 (7th Cir. 1983)	§ 18.10
United States v. Lee, 720 F.2d 1049 (9th Cir. 1983)	§ 31.8
United States v. Lopez, 777 F.2d 543 (10th Cir. 1985)	§ 18.8
United States v. Lowery, 733 F.2d 441 (7th Cir.), *cert. denied,* 469 U.S. 932 (1984)	§ 31.8
United States v. LTV Corp., 746 F.2d 51 (D.C. Cir. 1984)	§ 9.9
United States v. Malis, 737 F.2d 1511 (9th Cir. 1984)	§ 18.21
United States v. Marshall, 609 F.2d 152 (5th Cir. 1980)	§ 16.12
United States v. Mayton, 335 F.2d 153 (5th Cir. 1964)	§ 8.9
United States v. McCargo, 783 F.2d 507 (5th Cir. 1986)	§§ 31.8, 31.9
United States v. McConney, 728 F.2d 1195 (9th Cir.) (en banc), *cert. denied,* 469 U.S. 824 (1984)	§ 11.7
United States v. Merit Petroleum, Inc., 731 F.2d 901 (Temp. Emer. Ct. App. 1984)	§ 21.8
United States v. Monteleone, 804 F.2d 1004 (7th Cir. 1986)	§ 31.2
United States v. Morgan, 313 U.S. 409 (1941)	§ 18.22
United States v. National Medical Enters., Inc., 792 F.2d 906 (9th Cir. 1986)	§§ 27.4, 29.4, 29.5, 29.7, 30.9

Case	*Book §*
United States v. Nesglo, Inc., 744 F.2d 887 (1st Cir. 1984)	§§ 28.10, 28.11
United States v. Nunez, 801 F.2d 1260 (11th Cir. 1986)	§ 31.8
United States v. $129,374 in U.S. Currency, 769 F.2d 583 (9th Cir. 1985), *cert. denied,* ____ U.S. ____, 106 S. Ct. 863 (1986)	§§ 9.8, 9.9
United States v. One 1977 Mercedes Benz, 708 F.2d 444 (9th Cir. 1983), *cert. denied,* 464 U.S. 1071 (1984)	§ 7.13
United States v. One Piper Navajo PA-31 Aircraft, 748 F.2d 316 (5th Cir. 1984)	§ 12.3
United States v. 1966 Beechcraft Aircraft Model King Air, 777 F.2d 947 (4th Cir. 1985)	§ 7.18
United States v. One Tintoretto Painting, 691 F.2d 603 (2d Cir. 1982)	§§ 15.6, 15.14
United States v. Onu, 730 F.2d 253 (5th Cir.), *cert. denied,* 469 U.S. 856 (1984)	§ 31.8
United States v. Outboard Marine Corp., 789 F.2d 497 (7th Cir.), *cert. denied,* ____ U.S. ____, 107 S. Ct. 457 (1986)	§§ 12.6, 12.7
United States v. Pearce, 792 F.2d 397 (3d Cir. 1986)	§ 31.9
United States v. Price, 688 F.2d 204 (3d Cir. 1982)	§§ 11.4, 11.7
United States v. Porter, 711 F.2d 1397 (7th Cir. 1983)	§ 18.21
United States v. Probst, 792 F.2d 111 (8th Cir. 1986)	§ 16.8
United States v. Raddatz, 447 U.S. 667 (1980)	§ 16.12
United States v. Reynolds, 345 U.S. 1 (1953)	§ 18.22
United States v. Ross, 535 F.2d 346 (6th Cir. 1976)	§§ 27.5, 28.8
United States v. Ryan, 810 F.2d 650 (7th Cir. 1987)	§ 31.2
United States v. Ryan, 402 U.S. 530 (1971)	§§ 17.20, 19.9, 27.9, 31.9
United States v. Rylander, 460 U.S. 752 (1983)	§§ 18.19, 19.9, 21.6, 29.4, 31.5
United States v. Sancetta, 788 F.2d 67 (2d Cir. 1986)	§ 18.21
United States v. Seetapun, 750 F.2d 601 (7th Cir. 1984)	§ 31.6
United States v. Sells Eng'g, Inc., 463 U.S. 418 (1983)	§ 17.12
United States v. Snider, 779 F.2d 1151 (6th Cir. 1985)	§ 7.10
United States v. Stoneberger, 805 F.2d 1391 (9th Cir. 1986)	§§ 31.7, 31.11
United States v. Stribling Flying Serv., 734 F.2d 221 (5th Cir. 1984)	§ 15.16
United States v. Stringfellow, 783 F.2d 821 (9th Cir. 1986), *vacated,* ____ U.S. ____, 107 S. Ct. 1177 (1987)	§ 9.7
United States v. Sutton, 801 F.2d 1346 (D.C. Cir. 1986)	§ 23.29
United States v. 30.64 Acres of Land, 795 F.2d 796 (9th Cir. 1986)	§ 14.7
United States v. (Under Seal), 794 F.2d 920 (4th Cir.), *stay of contempt granted sub nom.* Arantea v. United States, ____ U.S. ____, 107 S. Ct. 1, *cert. denied,* ____ U.S. ____, 107 S. Ct. 331 (1986)	§ 18.19
United States v. (Under Seal), 745 F.2d 834 (4th Cir. 1984), *vacated*, 471 U.S. 1001 (1985)	§ 18.20
United States v. (Under Seal), 748 F.2d 871 (4th Cir. 1984)	§§ 18.2, 18.10
United States v. Union Gas Co., 792 F.2d 372 (3d Cir. 1986)	§ 2.6
United States v. United Mine Workers of Am., 330 U.S. 258 (1947)	§§ 31.2, 31.3, 31.4, 31.5, 31.8
United States v. United Shoe Mach. Corp., 391 U.S. 244 (1968)	§ 11.4

Case	*Book §*
United States v. U.S. Gypsum, 340 U.S. 76 (1950)	§ 15.13
United States v. Valencia-Copete, 792 F.2d 4 (1st Cir. 1986)	§ 16.12
United States v. Walters, 638 F.2d 947 (6th Cir. 1981)	§ 16.12
United States v. Ward Baking Co., 376 U.S. 327 (1964)	§ 16.7
United States v. Webb, 655 F.2d 977 (9th Cir. 1981)	§ 8.3
United States v. Weber Aircraft Corp., 465 U.S. 792 (1984)	§ 17.9
United States v. Whittington, 786 F.2d 644 (5th Cir. 1986)	§ 18.19
United States v. Will, 671 F.2d 963 (6th Cir. 1982)	§ 17.4
United States v. Wilson, 798 F.2d 509 (1st Cir. 1986)	§ 18.1
United States v. Windfelder, 790 F.2d 576 (7th Cir. 986)	§ 18.10
United States v. Zima, 766 F.2d 1153 (7th Cir. 1985)	§ 2.27
United States v. Zolin, 908 F.2d 1411 (9th Cir. 1987)	§ 18.12
United States *ex rel.* DeLoss v. Kenner Gen. Contractors, Inc., 764 F.2d 707 (9th Cir. 1985)	§ 5.12
United States *ex rel.* Thom v. Jenkins, 760 F.2d 736 (7th Cir. 1985)	§ 31.5
United States *ex rel.* Woodard v. Tynan, 776 F.2d 250 (10th Cir. 1985)	§ 25.6
United States Freight Co. v. Penn Cent. Transp. Co., 716 F.2d 954 (2d Cir. 1983)	§ 29.5
United States Gen., Inc. v. Albert, 792 F.2d 678 (7th Cir. 1986)	§ 15.29
United States Parole Comm'n v. Geraghty, 445 U.S. 388 (1980)	§ 10.5
United States Steel Corp. v. Fraternal Ass'n of Steel Haulers, 601 F.2d 1269 (3d Cir. 1979)	§ 31.6
United Steelworkers v. American Int'l Alum. Corp., 334 F.2d 147 (5th Cir. 1964)	§ 8.8
United Steelworkers v. R.H. Bouligny, Inc., 382 U.S. 145 (1965)	§ 2.21
University of Tex. v. Camenisch, 451 U.S. 390 (1981)	§ 11.3
Upjohn v. United States, 449 U.S. 383 (1981)	§§ 18.2, 18.4, 18.5, 23.19
Uranium Antitrust Litig., *In re,* 480 F. Supp. 1138 (N.D. Ill. 1979)	§ 22.2
Urban v. United Nations, 768 F.2d 1497 (D.C. Cir. 1985)	§ 14.7
Usatorres v. Marina Mercante Nicaraguenses, S.A., 768 F.2d 1285 (11th Cir. 1985)	§§ 3.15, 3.21
U.S. Dominator, Inc. v. Factory Ship Robert E. Resoff, 768 F.2d 1099 (9th Cir. 1985)	§§ 16.2, 16.11
USM Corp. v. American Aerosols, Inc., 631 F.2d 420 (6th Cir. 1980)	§ 20.6
U.S. Steel Corp. v. United States, 730 F.2d 1465 (Fed. Cir. 1984)	§ 19.5
Utley v. Varian Assocs., Inc., 811 F.2d 1279 (9th Cir. 1987)	§ 2.8
Valedon Martinez v. Hosp. Presbiteriano de la Comunidad, Inc., 806 F.2d 1128 (1st Cir. 1986)	§§ 2.13, 2.14
Valley Forge Christian College v. Americans United for Separation of Church & State, Inc., 454 U.S. 464 (1982)	§ 2.3
Vanderbilt v. Geo-Energy Ltd., 725 F.2d 204 (3d Cir. 1983)	§ 10.18
Van Dusen v. Barrack, 376 U.S. 612 (1964)	§§ 4.1, 6.6, 6.7, 6.8, 14.32
Van T. Jinkins & Assoc. v. U.S. Indus., 736 F.2d 656 (11th Cir. 1984)	§ 15.18

Case	*Book §*
Walderman v. Pennhurst State School & Hospital, 673 F.2d 628 (3d Cir. 1982) (en banc), *cert. denied,* 465 U.S. 1038 (1984)	§ 31.9
Walker v. Armco Steel Corp., 446 U.S. 740 (1980)	§§ 2.23, 5.4, 7.8
Walker v. City of Birmingham, 388 U.S. 307 (1967)	§ 31.9
Walker v. Pritzker, 705 F.2d 942 (7th Cir. 1983)	§ 9.6
Wall v. National R.R. Passenger Corp., 718 F.2d 906 (9th Cir. 1983)	§§ 3.22, 7.16
Wallace v. Brownell Pontiac-GMC Co., 703 F.2d 525 (11th Cir. 1983)	§§ 15.23, 15.24
Wallace v. Herron, 778 F.2d 391 (7th Cir. 1985), *cert. denied,* ____ U.S. ____, 106 S. Ct. 1642 (1986)	§ 4.7
Walsh v. Centeio, 692 F.2d 1239 (9th Cir. 1982)	§§ 9.4, 14.53
Walsh v. Ford Motor Co., 807 F.2d 1000 (D.C. Cir. 1986)	§§ 10.4, 10.17
Walsh v. Great Atl. & Pac. Tea Co., 726 F.2d 956 (3d Cir. 1983)	§ 10.13
Walton v. Eaton Corp., 563 F.2d 66 (3d Cir. 1977) (en banc)	§ 7.15
Walton v. United Consumers Club, Inc., 786 F.2d 303 (7th Cir. 1986)	§ 24.10
Ware v. Associated Milk Producers, Inc., 614 F.2d 413 (5th Cir. 1980)	§ 15.25
Warren v. International Bhd. of Teamsters, 544 F.2d 334 (8th Cir. 1976)	§ 26.7
Warrensburg, City of, v. RCA Corp., 550 F. Supp. 1364 (W.D. Mo. 1982)	§ 15.11
Warrior Tombigbee Transp. Co. v. M/V Nan Fung, 695 F.2d 1294 (11th Cir. 1983)	§ 15.14
Warth v. Seldin, 422 U.S. 490 (1975)	§§ 2.3, 7.3, 14.57
Washington v. New York City Bd. of Estimate, 709 F.2d 792 (2d Cir.), *cert. denied,* 464 U.S. 1013 (1983)	§§ 7.17, 8.3, 8.8
Washington v. Walker, 734 F.2d 1237 (7th Cir. 1984)	§ 30.4
Waste Sys., Inc. v. Clean Air Water Corp., 683 F.2d 927 (5th Cir. 1982)	§ 2.27
Water West, Inc. v. Entek Corp., 788 F.2d 627 (9th Cir. 1986)	§ 6.4
Watson v. Commissioner, 690 F.2d 429 (5th Cir. 1982)	§ 31.12
Watson v. Fort Worth Bank & Trust, 798 F.2d 791 (5th Cir. 1986)	§ 10.10
Watson v. Merrell Dow Pharmaceuticals, Inc., 769 F.2d 354 (6th Cir. 1985)	§ 6.17
Watson v. Miears, 772 F.2d 433 (8th Cir. 1985)	§ 29.7
Watson v. Unipress, Inc., 733 F.2d 1386 (10th Cir. 1984)	§§ 8.13, 8.16
Weahkee v. Norton, 621 F.2d 1080 (10th Cir. 1980)	§ 18.22
Weaver, *In re,* 610 F.2d 335 (5th Cir. 1980)	§ 3.19
Webb v. Tom Brown, Inc., 807 F.2d 783 (9th Cir. 1987)	§ 2.22
Webber v. Eye Corp., 721 F.2d 1067 (7th Cir. 1983)	§§ 30.3, 30.4, 30.6
Wechsler v. Steinberg, 733 F.2d 1054 (2d Cir. 1984)	§ 15.14
Wehling v. C.B.S., 608 F.2d 1084 (5th Cir. 1979)	§ 18.19
Wei v. Hawaii, 763 F.2d 370 (9th Cir. 1985)	§ 5.12
Weil v. Investment/Indicators, Research & Mgmt. Inc., 647 F.2d 18 (9th Cir. 1981)	§ 18.8
Weinberger v. Kendrick, 698 F.2d 61 (2d Cir. 1982), *cert. denied,* 464 U.S. 818 (1983)	§§ 2.30, 10.12, 10.13

Case	*Book §*
Weinstein v. Bradford, 423 U.S. 147 (1975)	§ 2.4
Weisberg v. United States Dep't of Justice, 627 F.2d 365 (D.C. Cir. 1980)	§ 17.4
Weisburg v. Webster, 749 F.2d 864 (D.C. Cir. 1984)	§§ 17.8, 29.3, 29.7, 29.8
Weisgal v. Smith, 774 F.2d 1277 (4th Cir. 1985)	§ 8.14
Weiss v. Duberstein, 445 F.2d 1297 (2d Cir. 1971)	§ 15.28
Welch v. Heckler, 808 F.2d 264 (3d Cir. 1986)	§ 16.12
Weller v. Cromwell Oil Co., 504 F.2d 927 (6th Cir. 1974)	§ 14.20
Wells v. Rockefeller, 728 F.2d 209 (3d Cir. 1984), *cert. denied,* 471 U.S. 1107 (1985)	§ 12.3
Wells v. South Main Bank, 532 F.2d 1005 (5th Cir. 1976)	§ 8.9
Wells Fargo Co. v. Wells Fargo Express Co., 556 F.2d 406 (9th Cir. 1977)	§ 4.14
Welsh v. Gibbs, 631 F.2d 436 (6th Cir. 1980), *cert. denied,* 450 U.S. 981 (1981)	§ 14.18
Wesley-Jessen Div. v. Bausch & Lomb Inc., 698 F.2d 862 (7th Cir. 1983)	§ 11.4
West v. Conrail, ____ U.S. ____, ____ S. Ct. ____, 55 U.S.L.W. 4466 (Apr. 7, 1987)	§§ 5.5, 5.11
West Am. Corp. v. Vaughan-Bassett Furniture Co., 765 F.2d 932 (9th Cir. 1985)	§ 3.11
Western Fire Ins. Co. v. Copeland, 786 F.2d 649 (5th Cir. 1986)	§ 15.3
Western Transp. Co. v. Wilson & Co., 682 F.2d 1227 (7th Cir. 1982)	§ 15.20
Westinghouse Elec. Corp. Uranium Contracts Litig., *In re,* 563 F.2d 992 (10th Cir. 1977)	§ 22.2
Westlake v. Lucas, 537 F.2d 857 (6th Cir. 1976)	§ 14.7
Westmoreland v. CBS, Inc., 770 F.2d 1168 (D.C. Cir. 1985)	§§ 17.19, 21.5, 21.6, 23.9, 23.22, 28.3, 28.5, 28.6, 29.1
Wetzel v. Liberty Mut. Ins. Co., 508 F.2d 239 (3d Cir.), *cert. denied,* 421 U.S. 1011 (1975)	§ 10.8
Whale v. United States, 792 F.2d 951 (9th Cir. 1986)	§ 5.8
Wheeler Mach. Co. v. Mountain States Mineral Enters., Inc., 696 F.2d 787 (10th Cir. 1983)	§ 15.29
Wheeling-Pittsburgh Steel Corp. v. Underwriters Laboratories, Inc., 81 F.R.D. 8 (N.D. Ill. 1978)	§§ 18.17, 20.12
Whitaker v. Carney, 778 F.2d 216 (5th Cir. 1985), *cert. denied,* ____ U.S. ____, 107 S. Ct. 64 (1986)	§ 3.19
White v. Arco/Polymers, Inc., 720 F.2d 1391 (5th Cir. 1983)	§ 7.5
White v. Raymark Indus., Inc., 783 F.2d 1175 (4th Cir. 1986)	§ 31.10
White Farm Equip. Co. v. Kupcho, 792 F.2d 526 (5th Cir. 1986)	§ 16.7
Whittaker Corp v. Execuair Corp., 736 F.2d 1341 (9th Cir. 1984)	§ 17.16
Whittington v. Whittington, 733 F.2d 620 (9th Cir. 1984)	§ 14.67
Wickland Oil Terminals v. Asarco, Inc., 792 F.2d 887 (9th Cir. 1986)	§ 12.7
Wiggins v. New Mexico State Supreme Court Clerk, 664 F.2d 812 (10th Cir. 1981), *cert. denied,* 459 U.S.840 (1982)	§ 14.7

Case	*Book §*
Wilborn v. Escalderon, 789 F.2d 1328 (9th Cir. 1986)	§ 8.7
Wilder Enters. v. Allied Artists Pictures, 632 F.2d 1135 (4th Cir. 1980)	§ 24.10
Wilfing v. G.M. Corp., 685 F.2d 1049 (8th Cir. 1982)	§ 17.16
Wilger v. Department of Pensions & Sec., 593 F.2d 12 (5th Cir. 1979)	§ 8.7
Will v. Calvert Fire Ins. Co., 437 U.S. 655 (1978)	§ 14.68
Will v. United States, 389 U.S. 90 (1967)	§ 17.18
William Inglis & Sons Baking Co. v. ITT Continental Baking Co., 668 F.2d 1014 (9th Cir. 1981), *cert. denied,* 459 U.S. 825 (1982)	§ 8.17
Williams v. Caterpillar Tractor Co., 786 F.2d 928 (9th Cir. 1986), *aff'd,* ___ U.S. ___, 107 S. Ct. 2425 (1987)	§§ 3.2, 3.3, 3.9
Williams v. City of Atlanta, 794 F.2d 624 (11th Cir. 1986)	§ 3.16
Williams v. City of St. Louis, 783 F.2d 114 (8th Cir. 1986)	§ 15.5
Williams v. Georgia Dep't of Human Resources, 789 F.2d 881 (11th Cir. 1986)	§ 15.5
Williams v. Hughes Helicopters, Inc., 806 F.2d 1387 (9th Cir. 1986)	§§ 20.13, 23.9
Williams v. New Orleans Pub. Serv., Inc., 728 F.2d 730 (5th Cir. 1984)	§ 12.3
Williams v. Owens-Illinois, Inc., 665 F.2d 918 (9th Cir.), *cert. denied,* 459 U.S. 971 (1982)	§ 17.5
Williams v. United States, 711 F.2d 893 (9th Cir. 1983)	§ 8.14
Williams v. United States, 405 F.2d 234 (5th Cir. 1968)	§ 8.15
Williamsburg Wax Museum v. Historic Figures, Inc., 810 F.2d 243 (D.C. Cir. 1987)	§ 8.3
Williamson v. Tucker, 645 F.2d 404 (5th Cir.), *cert. denied,* 454 U.S. 897 (1981)	§§ 14.8, 14.11
Williamson v. United States, 207 U.S. 425 (1908)	§ 31.8
Willingham v. Morgan, 395 U.S. 402 (1969)	§ 3.5
Willmar Poultry Co. v. Morton-Norwich Prods., Inc., 520 F.2d 289 (8th Cir. 1975)	§ 15.23
Wilmington v. J.I. Case Co., 793 F.2d 909 (8th Cir. 1986)	§ 23.26
Wilsey v. Eddingfield, 780 F.2d 614 (7th Cir. 1985), *cert. denied,* ___ U.S. ___, 106 S. Ct. 1660 (1986)	§ 2.17
Wilson v. Beebe, 770 F.2d 578 (6th Cir. 1985)	§ 2.6
Wilson v. Johns-Manville Sales Corp., 810 F.2d 1358 (5th Cir. 1987)	§ 20.8
Wilson v. Republic Iron & Steel Co., 257 U.S. 92 (1921)	§ 3.3
Wilson v. Retail Credit Co., 474 F.2d 1260 (5th Cir. 1973)	§ 15.30
Wilson v. United States, 221 U.S. 361 (1911)	§ 18.21
Winbourne v. Eastern Airlines, Inc., 632 F.2d 219 (2d Cir. 1980)	§ 15.3
Winfrey v. Brewer, 570 F.2d 761 (8th Cir. 1978)	§ 15.25
Winner Corp., *In re,* 511 F.2d 1010 (6th Cir. 1975)	§ 31.4
Winterland Concessions Co. v. Trela, 735 F.2d 257 (7th Cir. 1984)	§ 11.4
Winters v. Teledyne Movible Offshore, Inc., 776 F.2d 1304 (5th Cir. 1985)	§ 5.12
Wisconsin Knife Works v. National Metal Crafters, 781 F.2d 1280 (7th Cir. 1986)	§ 2.20

Case	*Book §*
774 F.2d 1008 (10th Cir. 1985)	§ 8.2
Yagman, *In re,* 796 F.2d 1165, *modified,* 803 F.2d 1085 (9th Cir. 1986)	§§ 27.8, 28.6, 28.8, 28.9, 28.10, 29.8
Yarber v. Allstate Ins. Co., 674 F.2d 232 (4th Cir. 1982)	§ 14.48
Yarn Processing Patent Validity Litig., *In re,* 530 F.2d 83 (5th Cir. 1976)	§ 16.9
Yashon v. Gregory, 737 F.2d 547 (6th Cir. 1984)	§ 15.5
Yates v.United States, 355 U.S. 66 (1957)	§ 31.2
Yoder v. Orthomolecular Nutrition Inst., Inc., 751 F.2d 555 (2d Cir. 1985)	§ 14.43
Yorger v. Pittsburgh Corning Corp., 733 F.2d 1215 (7th Cir. 1984)	§§ 15.9, 15.11, 15.16, 15.28
Young v. City of New Orleans, 751 F.2d 794 (5th Cir. 1985)	§§ 7.10, 20.15, 30.10
Young v. Colgate-Palmolive Co., 790 F.2d 567 (7th Cir. 1986)	§§ 4.6, 4.12
Young v. United States *ex rel.* Vuitton et Fils S.A.,_____ U.S. _____, 107 S. Ct. 2124 (1987)	§ 31.8
Younger v. Harris, 401 U.S. 37 (1971)	§§ 2.6, 2.32
Zacharia v. Harbor Island Spa, Inc., 684 F.2d 199 (2d Cir. 1982)	§ 2.12
Zahn v. International Paper Co., 414 U.S. 291 (1973)	§§ 2.12, 2.30, 4.10, 10.4
Zaidi v. Ehrlich, 732 F.2d 1218 (5th Cir. 1984)	§§ 8.7, 8.8, 13.7
Zaldivar v. City of Los Angeles, 780 F.2d 823 (9th Cir. 1986)	§§ 28.3, 28.4, 28.6, 28.8
Zanghi v. Incorporated Village of Old Brookville, 752 F.2d 42 (2d Cir. 1985)	§ 15.10
Zardui-Quintana v. Richard, 768 F.2d 1213 (11th Cir. 1985)	§ 11.4
Zavala Santiago v. Gonzalez Rivera, 553 F.2d 710 (1st Cir. 1977)	§ 30.3
Zell v.InterCapital Income Secs., Inc., 675 F.2d 1041 (9th Cir. 1982)	§ 15.22
Zenith Radio Corp. v. Hazeltine Research, Inc., 401 U.S. 321 (1971)	§§ 2.15, 8.9
Zenith Radio Corp. v. Hazeltine Research, Inc., 395 U.S. 100 (1969)	§ 11.5
Zenith Radio Corp. v. Matsushita Elec. Indus. Co., 529 F. Supp. 866 (E.D. Pa. 1981)	§ 19.4
Zenith Radio Corp. v. Matsushita Elec. Indus. Co., 478 F. Supp. 889 (E.D. Pa. 1979)	§§ 15.3, 16.4
Zenith Radio Corp. v. United States, 764 F.2d 1577 (Fed. Cir. 1985)	§ 18.8
Zepeda v. United States I.N.S., 753 F.2d 719 (9th Cir. 1983)	§ 11.7
Zerilli v. Smith, 656 F.2d 705 (D.C. Cir. 1981)	§ 15.24
Zerman v. Ball, 735 F.2d 15 (2d Cir. 1984)	§ 14.44
Zeviar v. Local No. 2747, Airline Employees, 733 F.2d 556 (8th Cir. 1984)	§ 5.1
Zicarelli v. New Jersey State Comm'n of Investigation, 406 U.S. 472 (1972)	§ 18.19

TABLE OF STATUTES

United States Code	Book §
	15.28
28 U.S.C. § 1651(a)	§§ 14.37, 14.68, 17.18
28 U.S.C. § 1653	§§ 2.19, 2.20, 14.10
28 U.S.C. § 1738A	§ 2.6
28 U.S.C. § 1746	§ 15.16
28 U.S.C. § 1781	§§ 22.1, 22.3
28 U.S.C. § 1782	§ 22.6
28 U.S.C. § 1783	§§ 17.21, 22.4
28 U.S.C. § 1783(a)	§ 22.4
28 U.S.C. § 1821	§§ 20.9, 21.2
28 U.S.C. § 1915	§ 14.7
28 U.S.C. § 1915(d)	§ 14.7
28 U.S.C. § 1920	§ 20.9
28 U.S.C. § 1920(2)	§ 23.1
28 U.S.C. § 1920(6)	§ 20.9
28 U.S.C. § 1927	§§ 13.9, 27.4, 27.5, 27.8, 27.10, 28.7, 28.8, 28.9, 28.10, 28.11, 29.1
28 U.S.C. § 1963	§ 1.9
28 U.S.C. § 2071	§ 31.11
28 U.S.C. § 2283	§§ 2.6, 10.5
28 U.S.C. § 2284	§ 11.1
28 U.S.C. § 2361	§ 11.1
28 U.S.C. § 2401(b)	§ 5.5
28 U.S.C. § 2412(b)	§ 29.1
29 U.S.C. § 160(b)	§ 5.11
29 U.S.C. § 185	§ 5.11
Labor Management Relations Act, 29 U.S.C. § 185(a)	§ 3.2
29 U.S.C. § 216(b)	§ 3.8
35 U.S.C. § 122	§ 18.22
35 U.S.C. § 285	§ 28.13
42 U.S.C. § 1981	§ 2.6
42 U.S.C. § 1983	§§ 2.6, 14.44
42 U.S.C. § 1985	§ 2.6
42 U.S.C. § 2000e-5(f)(5)	§ 16.13
45 U.S.C. § 41	§ 18.22
45 U.S.C. §§ 51–60	§ 3.17
Jones Act, 46 U.S.C. § 688	§ 2.16
50 U.S.C. App. § 501 *et seq.*	§ 12.1

TABLE OF FEDERAL RULES

Federal Rules of Civil Procedure	*Book §*
Fed. R. Civ. P. 3	§§ 5.4, 5.5, 7.8
Fed. R. Civ. P. 4	§§ 3.21, 5.1, 5.2, 5.3, 5.9, 5.10, 5.11, 5.12, 7.14, 9.6, 9.11, 14.39
Fed. R. Civ. P. 4(c)(2)(A)	§ 5.6
Fed. R. Civ. P. 4(c)(2)(B)	§ 5.6
Fed. R. Civ. P. 4(c)(2)(C)(i)	§ 5.3
Fed. R. Civ. P. 4(c)(2)(C)(ii)	§§ 5.3, 5.9
Fed. R. Civ. P. 4(c)(2)(D)	§ 5.9
Fed. R. Civ. P. 4(d)	§§ 5.3, 5.6, 5.8, 7.13
Fed. R. Civ. P. 4(d)(3)	§§ 5.7, 5.8
Fed. R. Civ. P. 4(d)(4)	§ 5.8
Fed. R. Civ. P. 4(d)(5)	§ 5.8
Fed. R. Civ. P. 4(e)	§§ 4.12, 5.2, 11.8, 14.3
Fed. R. Civ. P. 4(f)	§§ 5.2, 11.8
Fed. R. Civ. P. 4(h)	§ 14.39
Fed. R. Civ. P. 4(i)	§ 5.11
Fed. R. Civ. P. 4(i)(1)	§ 5.14
Fed. R. Civ. P. 4(j)	§§ 5.11, 5.12, 5.14, 13.9, 14.39, 14.72
Fed. R. Civ. P. 5	§§ 7.12, 7.14, 9.9, 13.2, 24.3, 26.3
Fed. R. Civ. P. 5(a)	§ 13.2
Fed. R. Civ. P. 5(b)	§ 13.3
Fed. R. Civ. P. 5(d)	§ 24.3

Federal Rules of Civil Procedure	*Book §*
Fed. R. Civ. P. 6	§ 13.2
Fed. R. Civ. P. 6(a)	§ 13.4
Fed. R. Civ. P. 6(b)	§ 13.9
Fed. R. Civ. P. 6(b)(1)	§§ 5.12, 13.4
Fed. R. Civ. P. 6(b)(2)	§§ 5.12, 13.4, 15.3
Fed. R. Civ. P. 6(d)	§§ 13.4, 15.3
Fed. R. Civ. P. 6(e)	§§ 9.10, 13.2, 13.3
Fed. R. Civ. P. 7	§§ 7.10, 13.2, 27.3
Fed. R. Civ. P. 7(a)	§§ 7.6, 7.10
Fed. R. Civ. P. 7(b)(1)	§§ 13.1, 13.2
Fed. R. Civ. P. 8	§§ 7.2, 30.5, 31.4
Fed. R. Civ. P. 8(a)(1)	§ 14.10
Fed. R. Civ. P. 8(a)(2)	§§ 7.2, 14.43
Fed. R. Civ. P. 8(c)	§§ 7.7, 14.48, 14.63
Fed. R. Civ. P. 8(d)	§ 7.6
Fed. R. Civ. P. 8(e)(2)	§ 7.5
Fed. R. Civ. P. 8(f)	§§ 8.1, 14.43
Fed. R. Civ. P. 9	§§ 7.3, 13.9, 14.43, 14.44, 14.72
Fed. R. Civ. P. 9(a)	§ 7.7
Fed. R. Civ. P. 9(b)	§§ 7.3, 7.19, 14.57
Fed. R. Civ. P. 10(a)	§ 2.10
Fed. R. Civ. P. 10(b)	§§ 1.12, 7.5
Fed. R. Civ. P. 10(c)	§ 14.47

Federal Rules of Civil Procedure	*Book §*
	15.31, 16.1, 16.2, 16.3, 16.4, 16.6, 17.3, 17.15, 19.1, 20.15, 24.10, 26.1, 26.7, 27.2, 27.3, 28.12, 30.1
Fed. R. Civ. P. 16(a)	§ 16.1
Fed. R. Civ. P. 16(b)	§§ 16.2, 17.2, 27.2, 30.4
Fed. R. Civ. P. 16(c)	§§ 15.19, 16.3
Fed. R. Civ. P. 16(d)	§ 16.3
Fed. R. Civ. P. 16(e)	§§ 15.19, 16.2, 16.4, 24.10
Fed. R. Civ. P. 16(f)	§§ 13.9, 16.5, 27.2, 27.6, 27.10, 28.12, 30.9, 30.10, 31.10
Fed. R. Civ. P. 17	§ 9.2
Fed. R. Civ. P. 17(a)	§§ 9.2, 9.11
Fed. R. Civ. P. 17(b)	§ 9.2
Fed. R. Civ. P. 17(c)	§ 9.2
Fed. R. Civ. P. 18	§ 2.12
Fed. R. Civ. P. 19	§§ 2.15, 2.26, 7.12, 9.3, 9.4, 10.7, 14.53, 14.61
Fed. R. Civ. P. 19(a)	§ 9.3
Fed. R. Civ. P. 19(b)	§§ 9.3, 9.4, 14.53
Fed. R. Civ. P. 19(c)	§ 9.4
Fed. R. Civ. P. 19(d)	§ 9.4
Fed. R. Civ. P. 20	§§ 2.26, 7.12, 9.5
Fed. R. Civ. P. 20(a)	§ 9.5
Fed. R. Civ. P. 20(b)	§ 9.5
Fed. R. Civ. P. 21	§§ 9.1, 9.2, 9.5, 12.4, 13.9
Fed. R. Civ. P. 22	§§ 2.9, 2.13, 2.26, 9.6, 9.11, 13.9
Fed. R. Civ. P. 22(1)	§ 9.6
Fed. R. Civ. P. 23	§§ 10.1, 10.6, 10.10, 10.11, 13.9, 14.48,
Fed. R. Civ. P. 23(a)	§ 10.4
Fed. R. Civ. P. 23(b)	§ 10.6
Fed. R. Civ. P. 23(b)(1)	§ 10.7
Fed. R. Civ. P. 23(b)(2)	§ 10.8
Fed. R. Civ. P. 23(b)(3)	§§ 10.9, 10.12, 18.16
Fed. R. Civ. P. 23(c)(2)	§ 10.12
Fed. R. Civ. P. 23(c)(4)	§ 10.10
Fed. R. Civ. P. 23(d)	§ 10.10
Fed. R. Civ. P. 23(d)(2)	§ 10.12
Fed. R. Civ. P. 23(e)	§§ 10.10, 10.13, 10.15, 10.18
Fed. R. Civ. P. 23.1	§§ 2.22, 7.5, 10.18, 13.9
Fed. R. Civ. P. 23.2	§ 10.18
Fed. R. Civ. P. 24	§§ 9.7, 9.8, 10.16, 13.9
Fed. R. Civ. P. 24(a)	§§ 2.26, 9.9
Fed. R. Civ. P. 24(a)(2)	§ 9.7
Fed. R. Civ. P. 24(b)	§§ 2.26, 9.7
Fed. R. Civ. P. 24(c)	§ 10.16
Fed. R. Civ. P. 25	§§ 9.10, 9.11, 13.9
Fed. R. Civ. P. 25(c)	§ 9.10
Fed. R. Civ. P. 25(d)	§ 9.10
Fed. R. Civ. P. 26	§§ 17.3, 17.4, 17.21,

Federal Rules of Civil Procedure	*Book §*
Fed. R. Civ. P. 30(b)(6)	§§ 23.11, 23.30, 29.11
Fed. R. Civ. P. 30(b)(7)	§ 23.2
Fed. R. Civ. P. 30(c)	§§ 23.2, 23.10, 23.18, 23.19, 23.25
Fed. R. Civ. P. 30(d)	§ 23.21
Fed. R. Civ. P. 30(e)	§§ 23.10, 23.23
Fed. R. Civ. P. 30(f)	§§ 23.10, 23.14, 23.24
Fed. R. Civ. P. 30(f)(2)	§ 23.25
Fed. R. Civ. P. 30(f)(3)	§ 23.24
Fed. R. Civ. P. 30(g)	§§ 23.6, 23.22
Fed. R. Civ. P. 30(g)(1)	§ 23.7
Fed. R. Civ. P. 30(g)(2)	§§ 21.5, 23.7
Fed. R. Civ. P. 31	§§ 23.2, 23.10, 23.26
Fed. R. Civ. P. 31(a)	§§ 23.2, 23.11, 23.30, 29.11
Fed. R. Civ. P. 31(b)	§ 23.10
Fed. R. Civ. P. 31(c)	§ 23.24
Fed. R. Civ. P. 32	§ 23.27
Fed. R. Civ. P. 32(a)	§§ 20.13, 23.2, 23.28, 23.29
Fed. R. Civ. P. 32(a)(1)	§ 23.28
Fed. R. Civ. P. 32(a)(2)	§ 23.30
Fed. R. Civ. P. 32(a)(3)	§§ 23.28, 23.29
Fed. R. Civ. P. 32(a)(4)	§§ 23.28, 23.29
Fed. R. Civ. P. 32(b)	§§ 23.3, 23.19, 23.27
Fed. R. Civ. P. 32(d)	§ 23.26
Fed. R. Civ. P. 32(d)(2)	§ 23.26
Fed. R. Civ. P. 32(d)(3)(A)	§ 23.27
Fed. R. Civ. P. 32(d)(3)(B)	§ 23.27
Fed. R. Civ. P. 32(d)(4)	§§ 23.23, 23.26
Fed. R. Civ. P. 33	§§ 20.3, 21.1, 24.1, 24.9, 29.11
Fed. R. Civ. P. 33(a)	§§ 24.2, 24.9
Fed. R. Civ. P. 33(b)	§ 24.2
Fed. R. Civ. P. 33(c)	§§ 17.22, 24.4, 24.10
Fed. R. Civ. P. 34	§§ 13.9, 17.10, 17.13, 18.2, 21.1, 23.6, 23.14, 24.6, 25.1, 25.2, 25.3, 25.4, 25.5, 25.6, 25.7, 25.9, 25.11, 29.2, 29.11
Fed. R. Civ. P. 34(a)	§§ 24.6, 25.2, 25.4
Fed. R. Civ. P. 34(b)	§§ 23.6, 25.3, 25.6
Fed. R. Civ. P. 34(c)	§§ 21.1, 25.9
Fed. R. Civ. P. 35	§§ 17.13, 20.5, 21.1, 25.11, 25.12, 25.14
Fed. R. Civ. P. 35(a)	§§ 13.9, 29.1, 29.2, 29.11
Fed. R. Civ. P. 35(b)	§ 25.13
Fed. R. Civ. P. 35(b)(1)	§ 25.13
Fed. R. Civ. P. 35(b)(3)	§ 25.13
Fed. R. Civ. P. 36	§§ 13.9, 15.19, 15.31, 21.1, 21.7, 24.1, 24.10, 25.10, 26.1, 26.2, 26.3, 26.4, 26.6, 26.7,

INDEX